Solution Key

Algebra

and Trigonometry

Structure and Method **Book 2**

Richard G. Brown
Mary P. Dolciani
Robert H. Sorgenfrey
Robert B. Kane

McDougal Littell/Houghton Mifflin
Evanston, Illinois
Boston Dallas Phoenix

Printed in U.S.A.

ISBN-13: 978-0-395-67765-0 ISBN-10: 0-395-67765-3

11 2241 12

4500396442

Contents

CHAPTER 1 • Basic Concepts of Algebra

Pages 4–5 • WRITTEN EXERCISES

A **1.** -6 **2.** 5 **3.** 0 **4.** -1 **5.** -1 **6.** $-\frac{7}{2}$ **7.** -4 **8.** -1 **9.** $-\frac{1}{2}$

10. 0 **11.** $0 > -6$ **12.** $-2 < 2$ **13.** $-3 < -1$ **14.** $1 > -10$ **15.** $6 > -5$

16. $-6 < -\frac{5}{8}$

17. $-5 \quad -4 \quad -3 \quad -2 \quad -1 \quad 0 \quad 1$ $\quad 0 > -4$

18. $-4 \quad -2 \quad 0 \quad 2 \quad 4$ $\quad 3 > -3$

19. $-2 \quad -1 \quad 0 \quad 1$ $\quad \frac{1}{2} > -\frac{3}{2}$

20. $-2 \quad -1 \quad 0$ $\quad -\frac{5}{4} < -\frac{3}{4}$

21. $-2 \quad -1 \quad 0 \quad 1$ $\quad 0.5 > -1.5$

22. $-3 \quad -2 \quad -1 \quad 0$ $\quad -2.5 < -0.75$

23. $-|-5| = -5$ **24.** $2 \cdot |-5| = 2 \cdot 5 = 10$ **25.** $|5| - |-2| = 5 - 2 = 3$

26. $|-5| - |2| = 5 - 2 = 3$

B **27.** $-5, -1, 0, 2, 4$ **28.** $-5, -3, -1, 1, 3$ **29.** $-2, -\frac{3}{2}, -\frac{1}{2}, 2, \frac{5}{2}$

30. $-\frac{3}{4}, -\frac{1}{2}, -\frac{1}{4}, \frac{1}{2}, \frac{3}{4}$ **31.** $-2.6, -1.8, -1.6, -0.6$ **32.** $-2.4, -2.0, -1.9, -1.7$

33. $1 - 2 = -1; -1$ **34.** $-5 + 3 = -2; -2$ **35.** $-5 + 1.4 = -3.6; -3.6$

36. $1 - 2.6 = -1.6; -1.6$ **37.** $-5 + 5\frac{1}{3} = \frac{1}{3}; 1 - \frac{2}{3} = \frac{1}{3}; \frac{1}{3}$

38. $-5 + 4\frac{1}{2} = -\frac{1}{2}; 1 - 1\frac{1}{2} = -\frac{1}{2}; -\frac{1}{2}$

C **39.** The points are to the right of A. Let $x =$ the coordinate. If the point lies between A and B, then $x - (-5) = 2(1 - x)$; $x + 5 = 2 - 2x$; $x = -1$. If the point is to the right of B, then $x - (-5) = 2(x - 1)$; $x + 5 = 2x - 2$; $x = 7$. -1 or 7.

40. The points are to the left of B. Let $x =$ the coordinate. If the point is to the left of A, $-5 - x = \frac{1}{2}(1 - x)$; $-5 - x = \frac{1}{2} - \frac{1}{2}x$; $-\frac{11}{2} = \frac{1}{2}x$; $x = -11$. If the point is between A and B, $x - (-5) = \frac{1}{2}(1 - x)$; $x + 5 = \frac{1}{2} - \frac{1}{2}x$; $\frac{3}{2}x = -\frac{9}{2}$; $x = -3$. -11 or -3.

Page 5 • MIXED REVIEW EXERCISES

1. $\frac{1}{2} + \frac{2}{3} = \frac{3}{6} + \frac{4}{6} = \frac{7}{6}; \frac{7}{6} \neq \frac{3}{5}$; false **2.** $3\frac{2}{5} - 2\frac{3}{10} = 3\frac{4}{10} - 2\frac{3}{10} = 1\frac{1}{10}; 1\frac{1}{10} > 1$; false

3. $\frac{4}{7} \times \frac{4}{7} = \frac{16}{49}; \frac{4}{7} = \frac{28}{49}; \frac{16}{49} < \frac{28}{49}$; false

4. $6\frac{3}{8} \div 2\frac{1}{4} = \frac{51}{8} \div \frac{9}{4} = \frac{51}{8} \times \frac{4}{9} = \frac{17}{2} \times \frac{1}{3} = \frac{17}{6} = 2\frac{5}{6}$; true

5. $5.31 + 24.7 = 30.01; 30.01 \neq 29.01$; false **6.** $0.1 - 0.09 = 0.01; 0.01 > 0.001$; false

7. $1.3 \times 0.1 = 0.13$; true **8.** $1 \div 0.99 = 1 \div \frac{99}{100} = 1 \times \frac{100}{99} = \frac{100}{99}; \frac{100}{99} > 1$; true

9. $|-6| = 6; 6 > -6$; true **10.** $|-1| = 1; -(-1) = 1$; true **11.** true

12. $|-3| = 3; 3 \not< 0$; false

Page 5 • COMPUTER EXERCISES

1. Answers may vary. A sample program is given.

```
10 INPUT "ENTER TWO NUMBERS: "; A, B
20 IF A > B THEN PRINT A; ">"; B
30 IF A = B THEN PRINT A; "="; B
40 IF A < B THEN PRINT A; "<"; B
50 END
```

2. a. $-8 < -7$ **b.** $0.1 > 0.01$ **c.** $0 = 0$ **d.** $3.65 > 3.56$ **e.** $4 > -4$ **f.** $800 < 8000$

3. Answers may vary. A sample program is given.

```
10 INPUT "ENTER TWO COORDINATES: "; A, B
20 LET M = (A + B)/2
30 PRINT "MIDPOINT IS "; M
40 END
```

4. a. 5.5 **b.** 0 **c.** 1.565 **d.** −5.16 **e.** 9.055 **f.** 1

Pages 10–12 • WRITTEN EXERCISES

A **1.** $5 \cdot 1 = 5; 5 \div 1 = 5; 5 = 5$; = **2.** $1 \cdot 5 = 5; 1 \div 5 = \frac{1}{5}; 5 > \frac{1}{5}$; >

3. $\frac{3+2}{3-2} = \frac{5}{1} = 5; \frac{4+2}{4-2} = \frac{6}{2} = 3; 5 > 3$; >

4. $\frac{3+2}{3-2} = \frac{5}{1} = 5; \frac{6+4}{6-4} = \frac{10}{2} = 5; 5 = 5$; =

5. $3^2 \cdot 4^2 = 9 \cdot 16 = 144; (3 \cdot 4)^2 = 12^2 = 144; 144 = 144$; =

6. $3^2 + 4^2 = 9 + 16 = 25; (3 + 4)^2 = 7^2 = 49; 25 < 49$; <

7. $(9 - 3) - 2 = 6 - 2 = 4; 9 - (3 - 2) = 9 - 1 = 8; 4 < 8$; <

8. $(9 + 3) + 2 = 12 + 2 = 14; 9 + (3 + 2) = 9 + 5 = 14; 14 = 14$; =

9. $(9 \cdot 3) \cdot 2 = 27 \cdot 2 = 54; 9 \cdot (3 \cdot 2) = 9 \cdot 6 = 54; 54 = 54$; =

10. $(12 \div 6) \div 2 = 2 \div 2 = 1; 12 \div (6 \div 2) = 12 \div 3 = 4; 1 < 4$; <

11. **a.** $11 - 3 + 5 - 2 = 8 + 5 - 2 = 13 - 2 = 11$

b. $11 - (3 + 5) - 2 = 11 - 8 - 2 = 3 - 2 = 1$

c. $11 - (3 + 5 - 2) = 11 - (8 - 2) = 11 - 6 = 5$

12. **a.** $12 - 5 - 2 + 3 = 7 - 2 + 3 = 5 + 3 = 8$

b. $12 - (5 - 2) + 3 = 12 - 3 + 3 = 9 + 3 = 12$

c. $12 - (5 - 2 + 3) = 12 - (3 + 3) = 12 - 6 = 6$

13. **a.** $3 \cdot 8 + 4 \cdot 5 = 24 + 20 = 44$ **b.** $3 \cdot (8 + 4) \cdot 5 = 3 \cdot 12 \cdot 5 = 36 \cdot 5 = 180$

c. $3 \cdot (8 + 4 \cdot 5) = 3 \cdot (8 + 20) = 3 \cdot 28 = 84$

14. **a.** $4^2 - 6 \div 2 + 3 = 16 - 6 \div 2 + 3 = 16 - 3 + 3 = 13 + 3 = 16$

b. $(4^2 - 6) \div 2 + 3 = (16 - 6) \div 2 + 3 = 10 \div 2 + 3 = 5 + 3 = 8$

c. $(4^2 - 6) \div (2 + 3) = (16 - 6) \div (2 + 3) = 10 \div 5 = 2$

15. $6 - [7 - (5 - 2)] = 6 - [7 - 3] = 6 - 4 = 2$

16. $14 - 2[9 - 2(5 - 3)] = 14 - 2[9 - 2(2)] = 14 - 2[9 - 4] = 14 - 2[5] = 14 - 10 = 4$

17. $\dfrac{2^3 + 1}{2^2 - 1} = \dfrac{8 + 1}{4 - 1} = \dfrac{9}{3} = 3$ **18.** $\dfrac{3^2}{5 - (3 - 1)} = \dfrac{9}{5 - 2} = \dfrac{9}{3} = 3$

19. $\dfrac{1}{3}\left|\dfrac{1 + 7^2}{5^2}\right| = \dfrac{1}{3}\left|\dfrac{1 + 49}{25}\right| = \dfrac{1}{3}\left|\dfrac{50}{25}\right| = \dfrac{1}{3}(2) = \dfrac{2}{3}$

20. $\dfrac{2^2(3^2 + 4^2)}{10^2} = \dfrac{2^2(9 + 16)}{10^2} = \dfrac{4(25)}{100} = 1$

21. $64 \div 4^2 + 3(3^2 - 1) = 64 \div 16 + 3(9 - 1) = 64 \div 16 + 3(8) = 4 + 3(8) = 4 + 24 = 28$

22. $2^2 \cdot 3^2 - (5^2 - 4^2) = 4 \cdot 9 - (25 - 16) = 4 \cdot 9 - (9) = 36 - 9 = 27$

23. $[3^3 - (2^3 + 2^2)] \div 5 = [27 - (8 + 4)] \div 5 = [27 - 12] \div 5 = 15 \div 5 = 3$

24. $\dfrac{1}{10}[2(3 + 4) - 3^2] = \dfrac{1}{10}[2(7) - 9] = \dfrac{1}{10}[14 - 9] = \dfrac{5}{10} = \dfrac{1}{2}$

25. $2(3^2) + 3 - 2 = 2(9) + 3 - 2 = 18 + 3 - 2 = 19$

26. $3(2^2) - 2 - 5 = 3(4) - 2 - 5 = 12 - 2 - 5 = 5$

27. $[2(5) - 3]^3 = (10 - 3)^3 = 7^3 = 343$ **28.** $[3(5) - 5(2)]^3 = (15 - 10)^3 = 5^3 = 125$

29. $\dfrac{4(5^3)}{3^2 - 2^2} = \dfrac{4(125)}{9 - 4} = \dfrac{500}{5} = 100$ **30.** $\dfrac{4(3)(2)(5)}{5^2 - 3^2} = \dfrac{120}{25 - 9} = \dfrac{120}{16} = \dfrac{15}{2}$

31. $\dfrac{3 + 5}{2} - \dfrac{3 + 2}{2(5)} = \dfrac{8}{2} - \dfrac{5}{10} = \dfrac{8}{2} - \dfrac{1}{2} = \dfrac{7}{2}$ **32.** $\dfrac{5^2}{3 + 2} - \dfrac{2^2}{5 - 3} = \dfrac{25}{5} - \dfrac{4}{2} = 5 - 2 = 3$

33. $\left(\dfrac{3(2)(5)}{3 - 2 + 5}\right)^4 = \left(\dfrac{30}{6}\right)^4 = 5^4 = 625$

34. $\left(\dfrac{5^2 - 2^2 - 3^2}{3(2)}\right)^5 = \left(\dfrac{25 - 4 - 9}{6}\right)^5 = \left(\dfrac{12}{6}\right)^5 = 2^5 = 32$

35. $\dfrac{5^2 - (3^2 - 2^2)}{3(2^2)(5)} = \dfrac{25 - (9 - 4)}{3(4)(5)} = \dfrac{25 - 5}{60} = \dfrac{20}{60} = \dfrac{1}{3}$

36. $\dfrac{5^2 - 2^2}{3(5) - 2(2)(5 - 3)} = \dfrac{25 - 4}{15 - 2(2)(2)} = \dfrac{21}{15 - 8} = \dfrac{21}{7} = 3$

37. $2|6| + |-2| = 2(6) + 2 = 12 + 2 = 14$

38. $|6| - 3|-2| = 6 - 3(2) = 6 - 6 = 0$

39. $|6|^2 - |-2|^2 = 6^2 - 2^2 = 36 - 4 = 32$ **40.** $|6^2 - (-2)^2| = |36 - 4| = |32| = 32$

B **41.** $\frac{3(4)^2 - 2(5-3)^2}{2(4^2-1) - 5^2} = \frac{3(16) - 2(2^2)}{2(16-1) - 25} = \frac{48 - 2(4)}{2(15) - 25} = \frac{48-8}{30-25} = \frac{40}{5} = 8$

42. $\frac{3(7^2 - 3^2) + 5(7-3)^2}{(7+3)^2} = \frac{3(49-9) + 5(4^2)}{10^2} = \frac{3(40) + 5(16)}{100} = \frac{120 + 80}{100} = \frac{200}{100} = 2$

43. $\frac{[2(3^2) + 8^2][13(3) - 3(8)]^2}{5(3)^2 + 4(3)(8) + 8^2} = \frac{[2(9) + 64][39 - 3(8)]^2}{5(9) + 96 + 64} = \frac{(18 + 64)(39 - 24)^2}{45 + 96 + 64} = \frac{82(15)^2}{205} =$

$\frac{82(225)}{205} = \frac{18{,}450}{205} = 90$

44. $\frac{(6^2 + 8^2)(6^2 - 8)^2}{(6+8)^2[3(8^2) - 2(6)(8) - 6^2]} = \frac{(36 + 64)(36 - 8)^2}{(14^2)[3(64) - 96 - 36]} = \frac{100(28^2)}{196(192 - 96 - 36)} =$

$\frac{100(784)}{196(96 - 36)} = \frac{78{,}400}{196(60)} = \frac{78{,}400}{11{,}760} = \frac{20}{3}$

45. $18 \div 2 - 3(2 + 1) = 0$ **46.** $(7 - 2) \cdot (5 - 3) + 2 = 12$ **47.** $[6 - (5 - 3)] \cdot 2 = 8$

48. $[24 \div (3 + 1 - 2)] \cdot (2 + 3) = 60$ **49.** $(3^2 - 2)^2 - 4 \cdot (3 + 3) = 25$

50. $[(6 + 5) \cdot 2 - 7] \div (2 \cdot 2 + 1) = 3$

51. a. $n = 2, \frac{1}{4}(2^2)(2 + 1)^2 = \frac{1}{4}(4)(3^2) = \frac{1}{4}(4)(9) = 9; n = 3, \frac{1}{4}(3^2)(3 + 1)^2 = \frac{1}{4}(9)(16) =$

$36; n = 4, \frac{1}{4}(4^2)(4 + 1)^2 = \frac{1}{4}(16)(25) = 100; n = 5, \frac{1}{4}(5^2)(5 + 1)^2 = \frac{1}{4}(25)(36) = 225$

b. $1^3 + 2^3 = 1 + 8 = 9; 1^3 + 2^3 + 3^3 = 9 + 27 = 36; 1^3 + 2^3 + 3^3 + 4^3 =$
$36 + 64 = 100; 1^3 + 2^3 + 3^3 + 4^3 + 5^3 = 100 + 125 = 225$

C For Exercises 52–54, answers may vary. Examples are given.

52. $2 + 2 + 2 + \frac{2}{2} = 7$ **53.** $3 \cdot 3 + \frac{3 + 3}{3} = 11$

54. $(2 + 2) - (2 + 2) = 0; \frac{2 + 2}{2 + 2} = 1; \frac{2}{2} + \frac{2}{2} = 2; 2 + 2 - \frac{2}{2} = 3; 2 + 2 + 2 - 2 = 4;$

$2 + 2 + \frac{2}{2} = 5; 2\left(2 + \frac{2}{2}\right) = 6$

Page 12 • CALCULATOR KEY-IN

1. 45 **2.** 24 **3.** 15 **4.** 50 **5.** 4.25 **6.** 23.5 **7.** 3.965517 **8.** 55
9. 0.7777778 **10.** 1.1849275 **11.** 22.7375 **12.** 0.55798449

Pages 17–19 • WRITTEN EXERCISES

A **1.** $96 + 13 + 4 + 37 = (96 + 4) + (13 + 37) = 100 + 50 = 150$

2. $-6 + x + 6 = (-6 + 6) + x = 0 + x = x$

3. $\frac{1}{3}(1 \cdot 3) + (-1) = \frac{1}{3}(3 \cdot 1) + (-1) = \left(\frac{1}{3} \cdot 3\right)1 + (-1) = 1 \cdot 1 + (-1) = 1 + (-1) = 0$

4. $\frac{1}{3}(1 \cdot 3) + (-3 + 3) = \left(\frac{1}{3} \cdot 3\right) \cdot 1 + 0 = 1 \cdot 1 + 0 = 1 + 0 = 1$

5. $4\left(z + \frac{1}{4}\right) = 4z + 4\left(\frac{1}{4}\right) = 4z + 1$ **6.** $\frac{1}{4}(z + 4) = \frac{1}{4}z + \frac{1}{4}(4) = \frac{1}{4}z + 1$

7. $1 \cdot (-t + t) = 1 \cdot 0 = 0$ **8.** $\left(\frac{2}{3}a\right)\left(\frac{3}{2}b\right) = \left(\frac{2}{3} \cdot \frac{3}{2}\right)(ab) = 1(ab) = ab$

9. $2(a + 4) + (-8) = 2a + 2(4) + (-8) = 2a + (8 + (-8)) = 2a + 0 = 2a$

10. $\left(\frac{1}{3} \cdot 3\right)[p + (-1)] + 1 = 1[p + (-1)] + 1 = p + [(-1) + 1] = p + 0 = p$

11. $(-x + 6) + (-6 + x) = (-x + x) + (6 + (-6)) = 0 + 0 = 0$; true

12. $2(x + 3) + (-3) = 2x + 2(3) + (-3) = 2x + 6 + (-3) = 2x + 3$; false

13. $\frac{1}{2}(2t + 2) + (-2) = \frac{1}{2}(2t) + \frac{1}{2}(2) + (-2) = \left(\frac{1}{2}(2)\right)t + 1 + (-2) = t + 1 + (-2) =$ $t - 1$; false

14. $(7p)\frac{1}{7} + (-p) = \left[7\left(\frac{1}{7}\right)\right]p + (-p) = 1p + (-p) = 0$; true

15. $5(2n + 1) + (-5) = 5(2n) + 5(1) + (-5) = (5 \cdot 2)n + [5 + (-5)] = 10n + 0 = 10n$; true

16. $(5x)(5y) = (5 \cdot 5)(xy) = 25xy$; false

17. **a.** Dist. prop. **b.** Assoc. prop. of mult. **c.** Prop. of recip. **d.** Ident. prop. of mult.

18. **a.** Comm. prop. of add. **b.** Assoc. prop. of add. **c.** Prop. of opp. **d.** Ident. prop. of add.

19. **a.** Comm. prop. of add. **b.** Assoc. prop. of add. **c.** Prop. of opp. **d.** Ident. prop. of add. **e.** Prop. of recip.

20. **a.** Dist. prop. **b.** Ident. prop. of mult. **c.** Comm. prop. of add. **d.** Assoc. prop. of add.

21. **a.** Assoc. prop. of add. **b.** Ident. prop. of mult. **c.** Dist. prop. **d.** Ident. prop. of mult. **e.** Dist. prop.

22. **a.** Comm. prop. of mult. **b.** Dist. prop. **c.** Assoc. prop. of add. **d.** Prop. of opp. **e.** Ident. prop. of add.

B **23.** **a.** Add. prop. of equal. **b.** Assoc. prop. of add. **c.** Prop. of opp. **d.** Ident. prop. of add. **e.** Mult. prop. of equal. **f.** Assoc. prop. of mult. **g.** Prop. of recip. **h.** Ident. prop. of mult.

24. $\frac{1}{2}x + (-3) = 0$ (Given); $\left[\frac{1}{2}x + (-3)\right] + 3 = 0 + 3$ (Add. prop. of equal.); $\frac{1}{2}x + [(-3) + 3] = 0 + 3$ (Assoc. prop. of add.); $\frac{1}{2}x + 0 = 0 + 3$ (Prop. of opp.); $\frac{1}{2}x = 3$ (Ident. prop. of add.); $2\left(\frac{1}{2}x\right) = 2(3)$ (Mult. prop. of equal.); $\left(2 \cdot \frac{1}{2}\right)x = 2(3)$ (Assoc. prop. of mult.); $1 \cdot x = 2(3)$ (Prop. of recip.); $x = 2(3)$ (Ident. prop. of mult.); $x = 6$ (Substitution)

25. **a.** Closed under addition **b.** Closed under multiplication

26. **a.** Not closed under addition; $1 + 1 = 2$ **b.** Closed under multiplication

27. **a.** Closed under addition **b.** Closed under multiplication

28. **a.** Not closed under addition; $1 + 3 = 4$ **b.** Closed under multiplication

29. **a.** Closed under addition **b.** Closed under multiplication

30. **a.** Not closed under addition; $1 + \frac{1}{2} = \frac{3}{2}$ **b.** Closed under multiplication

31. **a.** Closed under addition **b.** Closed under multiplication

32. **a.** Not closed under addition; $\sqrt{2} + (-\sqrt{2}) = 0$, and 0 is rational
b. Not closed under multiplication; $(\sqrt{2})(\sqrt{2}) = 2$, and 2 is rational

33. **a.** Not closed under addition; $0.75 + 0.5 = 1.25$ **b.** Closed under multiplication

C **34.** Not a field; since 0 is not a natural number, the ident. prop. of add. does not hold.

35. Not a field; since integers other than 1 and -1 do not have integral reciprocals, the prop. of recip. does not hold.

36. Field

37. Not a field; since 0 is not a negative rational number, the ident. prop. of add. does not hold.

Page 20 • MIXED REVIEW EXERCISES

1. $>$ **2.** $3(8 - 5) = 3(3) = 9;\ 3 \cdot 8 - 5 = 24 - 5 = 19;\ 9 < 19;\ <$
3. $17 - (8 + 5) = 17 - 13 = 4;\ 17 - 8 + 5 = 14;\ 4 < 14;\ <$
4. $(3 + 4)^2 = 7^2 = 49;\ 3^2 + 2 \cdot 3 \cdot 4 + 4^2 = 9 + 24 + 16 = 49;\ =$
5. $\frac{7 + 5}{8 - 2} = \frac{12}{6} = 2;\ \frac{8 + 2}{7 - 5} = \frac{10}{2} = 5;\ 2 < 5;\ <$ **6.** $\frac{1 + 1}{2 + 2} = \frac{2}{4} = \frac{1}{2};\ \frac{1}{2} + \frac{1}{2} = 1;\ \frac{1}{2} < 1;\ <$

Page 20 • EXTRA

1. $\forall_x\ 2x = x + x$ **2.** $\exists_y\ y^2 = 17$ **3.** $\forall_x \forall_y\ x + y = y + x$ **4.** $\forall_r \exists !_x\ r + x = 0$
5. False; for example, let $a = -1$. **6.** True **7.** True
8. False; for example, let $a = 0$, $b = 2$, $c = 2$.

Pages 24–25 • WRITTEN EXERCISES

A **1.** -21 **2.** -58 **3.** 34 **4.** 43 **5.** 25 **6.** -34 **7.** 7.4 **8.** -11.1 **9.** -23
10. 52.4 **11.** 30.7 **12.** 4.3 **13.** -2 **14.** -25 **15.** 8 **16.** -32
17. $5 - (-7) - (-7) = 5 + 7 + 7 = 19$
18. $-16 - (2 + 61) - (-4) = -16 - 63 + 4 = -75$
19. $(-7) - (-6 + 8) = -7 - 2 = -9$ **20.** $-12 - (8 - 4 + 7) = -12 - 11 = -23$
21. $|-7| - |28| = 7 - 28 = -21$ **22.** $|-55| - |9| = 55 - 9 = 46$
23. $4(p - 2q) = 4p - 4(2q) = 4p - 8q$ **24.** $5(3y - 2x) = 5(3y) - 5(2x) = 15y - 10x$
25. $\frac{1}{2}(2a - 4b + 6) = \frac{1}{2}(2a) - \frac{1}{2}(4b) + \frac{1}{2}(6) = a - 2b + 3$
26. $\frac{2}{3}(6r - 9s - 27) = \frac{2}{3}(6r) - \frac{2}{3}(9s) - \frac{2}{3}(27) = 4r - 6s - 18$
27. $8c + 2(c + 3) = 8c + 2c + 6 = (8 + 2)c + 6 = 10c + 6$
28. $5(d + 2) - 3d = 5d + 10 - 3d = (5 - 3)d + 10 = 2d + 10$
29. $7(x + 2) + 4(x - 4) = 7x + 14 + 4x - 16 = (7 + 4)x + (14 - 16) = 11x - 2$
30. $4(3 - y) + 2(1 - y) = 12 - 4y + 2 - 2y = (12 + 2) - (4 + 2)y = 14 - 6y$
31. $7p - 4q + 3q - 10p = (7 - 10)p + (3 - 4)q = -3p - q$

32. $6m - 4n + (-7)m - (-5)n = [6 + (-7)]m - [4 + (-5)]n = -1m - (-1)n =$
$-1m + 1n = n - m$

33. $(-2r + s + 5) + 2(r - 3s + 2) = -2r + s + 5 + 2r - 6s + 4 =$
$(-2 + 2)r + (1 - 6)s + (5 + 4) = 0r + (-5)s + 9 = -5s + 9$

34. $(6x - 5y + 4) + 2(-2x + 3y - 2) = 6x - 5y + 4 - 4x + 6y - 4 =$
$(6 - 4)x + (6 - 5)y + (4 - 4) = 2x + 1y + 0 = 2x + y$

B **35.** 9 **36.** 5 **37.** −3 **38.** −5 **39.** 4 **40.** −9 **41.** 10.1 **42.** 9.3

43. $30.5 - (-122.2) = 152.7$; 152.7°C **44.** $20{,}320 - (-282) = 20{,}602$; 20,602 ft

45. $1493 - 5315 = -3822$; 3822 ft below sea level.

46. $103 + (15 - 9) + (27 - 13) + (8 - 53) = 103 + 6 + 14 - 45 = 78$; 78 passengers

47. $72\frac{3}{4} + 1\frac{7}{8} = 72\frac{6}{8} + 1\frac{7}{8} = 73\frac{13}{8} = 74\frac{5}{8}$; the opening price was $74\frac{5}{8}$

48. The countdown resumed 37 seconds after 7:38:16, that is, at 7:38:53;
7:38:53 + 14:42 = 7:53:35; the rocket took off at 7:53:35 A.M.

For Ex. 49 and 50, answers may vary. Examples are given.

49. $5 - 2 = 3$; $2 - 5 = -3$; $3 \neq -3$

50. $15 - (10 - 2) = 15 - 8 = 7$; $(15 - 10) - 2 = 5 - 2 = 3$; $7 \neq 3$

C **51.** Not closed; $0 - 1 = -1$ **52.** Not closed; $-1 - 1 = -2$

53. Not closed; $2 - 5 = -3$ **54.** Not closed; $-3 - (-5) = 2$ **55.** Closed

56. Not closed; $\sqrt{2} - \sqrt{2} = 0$

Page 26 • READING ALGEBRA

1. To solve certain equations in one variable.
2. open sentence, solution, root, satisfy, solution set, equivalent equations, solve, empty set, null set, identity, formula, constants
3. An equation or inequality containing a variable; equations having the same solution set over a given domain.
4. Simplifying either side; adding the same number or expression to each side; multiplying each side by the same nonzero number.
5. $3(4x - 9) = 5x - 6$; $12x - 27 = 5x - 6$; $12x - 27 + 27 = 5x - 6 + 27$; $12x = 5x + 21$;

   $12x - 5x = 5x + 21 - 5x$; $7x = 21$; $\frac{7x}{7} = \frac{21}{7}$; $x = 3$; $\{3\}$
6. The glossary or index; page 38 **7.** Table 7, page 831

Pages 30–31 • WRITTEN EXERCISES

A **1.** −210 **2.** 84 **3.** 12 **4.** 12 **5.** −2.4 **6.** −1.8 **7.** $2(-5)(-6)(xy) = 60xy$

8. $(-3)(-1)(-7)(uv) = -21uv$ **9.** $(-1)(-2)(-3)(abc) = -6abc$

10. $\left(-\frac{1}{2}\right)(4)(-rs) = 2rs$ **11.** $(-10)(-1) = 10$

12. $17(-13 + (-7)) = 17(-20) = -340$ **13.** $12(-1)(-8) = 96$

14. $\left(-\frac{1}{5}\right)^2(-5)^2(-5) = \frac{1}{25}(25)(-5) = -5$ **15.** $(-1)^3(-4)(-6)(-4) = 96$

16. $(-9)^2(0)(-5) = 0$ **17.** $(-2)(1) - 2(-2)x - 2(-3)x^2 = -2 + 4x + 6x^2$

18. $-3(2a) - 3\left(-\frac{2}{3}\right) = -6a + 2$ **19.** $-\frac{1}{2}(6z^2) - \frac{1}{2}(-4z) - \frac{1}{2}(2) = -3z^2 + 2z - 1$

20. $(-1)[-t^3 - 1] = t^3 + 1$ **21.** $-3(xy) + (2)(-3)(xy) = (-3 - 6)xy = -9xy$

22. $ab - 6ab = (1 - 6)ab = -5ab$ **23.** $7k - 12k - 24 = (7 - 12)k - 24 = -5k - 24$

24. $-3p + 15 - 7p = (-3 - 7)p + 15 = -10p + 15$

25. $(5 - 3)(x - y) = 2(x - y) = 2x - 2y$

26. $(-4 + 2)(a - b) = -2(a - b) = -2a + 2b$

27. $-15a^3 - 10 - 6 - 3a^3 = (-15 - 3)a^3 - 10 - 6 = -18a^3 - 16$

28. $8y^2 - 12 - 8 - 2y^2 = (8 - 2)y^2 - 12 - 8 = 6y^2 - 20$

29. $2tw - 9t - 4t - 14 = 2tw - (9 + 4)t - 14 = 2tw - 13t - 14$

30. $-cd - 5c + 12 - 6cd = (-1 - 6)cd - 5c + 12 = -7cd - 5c + 12$

B **31.** **a.** $1(1 - 2)(1 - 4) = 1(-1)(-3) = 3$ **b.** $3(3 - 2)(3 - 4) = 3(1)(-1) = -3$

c. $2(2 - 2)(2 - 4) = 2(0)(-2) = 0$

32. **a.** $2(2 + 1)(2 - 3) = 2(3)(-1) = -6$ **b.** $(-1)(-1 + 1)(-1 - 3) = -1(0)(-4) = 0$

c. $1(1 + 1)(1 - 3) = 1(2)(-2) = -4$

33. **a.** $2^3 - 3(2^2) + 4 = 8 - 3(4) + 4 = 8 - 12 + 4 = 0$

b. $(-1)^3 - 3(-1)^2 + 4 = -1 - 3(1) + 4 = 0$ **c.** $3^3 - 3(3^2) + 4 = 4$

34. **a.** $2(2^3) + 3(2^2) - 2 + 3 = 2(8) + 3(4) - 2 + 3 = 29$

b. $2(-2)^3 + 3(-2)^2 - (-2) + 3 = 2(-8) + 3(4) + 2 + 3 = -16 + 12 + 5 = 1$

c. $2(0^3) + 3(0^2) - 0 + 3 = 3$

35. (1) Ident. prop. of mult. (2) Prop. of opp. of a prod. (3) Comm. prop. of mult.

(4) Trans. prop. of equal. (5) Sym. prop. of equal.

C **36.** **a.** 0 **b.** The possible answers are: 1, 3, and 6 **c.** 8 **d.** -2 **e.** $3\frac{1}{2}$

Page 31 • MIXED REVIEW EXERCISES

1. $3 + (-2) - 1 = 0$ **2.** $|3| - |-2| = 3 - 2 = 1$ **3.** $3^2 + (-2) = 9 - 2 = 7$

4. $-|3 + (-2)| = -|1| = -1$ **5.** $-2 - (3 - 1) = -2 - 2 = -4$

6. $4(3) - (-2) = 12 + 2 = 14$ **7.** Comm. prop. of add. **8.** Ident. prop. of add.

9. Sym. prop. of equal. **10.** Prop. of recip. **11.** Assoc. prop. of mult. **12.** Dist. prop.

Page 32 • COMPUTER EXERCISES

1. Answers may vary. A sample program is given.

```
10 INPUT "ENTER X: "; X
20 LET V = 5 * X ^ 3 - 7 * X ^ 2 + 3 * X + 2
30 PRINT "VALUE OF EXPRESSION = "; V
40 END
```

2. **a.** 3 **b.** 380.585 **c.** -127.375 **d.** -212.28352

3. Answers may vary. For example, add line 5 and change line 20 as follows:

```
5  INPUT "ENTER CONSTANTS A, B, C, D: "; A, B, C, D
20 LET V = A * X ^ 3 + B * X ^ 2 + C * X + D
```

4. a. 5.897 **b.** −186.542125 **c.** 29.921848 **d.** 392.66634

Page 35 • WRITTEN EXERCISES

A **1.** 3 **2.** $\frac{1}{3}$ **3.** $(-16) \div (-2) = 8$ **4.** $64 \div 2 = 32$

5. $\left[(-6)\left(-\frac{3}{1}\right)\right] \div (-1) = 18 \div (-1) = -18$ **6.** $\left[-\frac{1}{2} \cdot \frac{4}{1}\right] \div (-4) = -2 \div (-4) = \frac{1}{2}$

7. $\frac{-144}{-36} = 4$ **8.** -2 **9.** $(-12)(-4) = 48$ **10.** $-54 \div 81 = -\frac{2}{3}$

11. $\frac{-48 \div 2}{16} = \frac{-24}{16} = -\frac{3}{2}$ **12.** $\frac{-8}{-20 \div 2} = \frac{-8}{-10} = \frac{4}{5}$ **13.** $\frac{9 - 25}{-2} = \frac{-16}{-2} = 8$

14. $\frac{16 - 25}{-9} = \frac{-9}{-9} = 1$ **15.** $\frac{-6}{-10 \cdot \left(-\frac{3}{2}\right)} = \frac{-6}{15} = -\frac{2}{5}$

16. $\frac{(-12)\left(-\frac{5}{4}\right)}{\frac{5}{9} \cdot \left(-\frac{1}{10}\right)} = \frac{15}{-\frac{1}{18}} = 15 \cdot \left(-\frac{18}{1}\right) = -270$ **17.** $\frac{-24\left[-18 \cdot \left(-\frac{3}{2}\right)\right]}{(-18)\left(-\frac{2}{3}\right)} = \frac{-24(27)}{12} = -54$

18. $\frac{\left(\frac{6}{9}\right)\left(\frac{4}{3}\right)^2}{\frac{5}{9} \cdot \left(-\frac{3}{10}\right)} = \frac{\left(\frac{2}{3}\right)\left(\frac{16}{9}\right)}{\left(-\frac{1}{6}\right)} = \left[\left(\frac{2}{3}\right)\left(\frac{16}{9}\right)\right]\left(-\frac{6}{1}\right) = -\frac{64}{9}$ **19.** $\frac{9x^2}{-3} + \frac{27}{-3} = -3x^2 - 9$

20. $\frac{24}{2} - \frac{6t^2}{2} = 12 - 3t^2$ **21.** $\frac{1}{-1} - \frac{n^2}{-1} = -1 + n^2 = n^2 - 1$

22. $\frac{2n^2}{-2} - \frac{4}{-2} = -1n^2 + 2 = -n^2 + 2 = 2 - n^2$ **23.** $\frac{36c^2}{6} - \frac{24c}{6} - \frac{6}{6} = 6c^2 - 4c - 1$

24. $\frac{-15r^3}{-5} - \frac{5r}{-5} - \frac{5}{-5} = 3r^2 + r + 1$

B **25. a.** $\frac{1(1 - 3)}{1 - 2} = \frac{1(-2)}{-1} = 2$ **b.** $\frac{4(4 - 3)}{4 - 2} = \frac{4(1)}{2} = 2$ **c.** $\frac{3(3 - 3)}{3 - 2} = \frac{3(0)}{1} = 0$

26. a. $\frac{(1^2 - 4)(1 - 3)}{1 + 1} = \frac{(-3)(-2)}{2} = 3$ **b.** $\frac{(2^2 - 4)(2 - 3)}{2 + 1} = \frac{(4 - 4)(-1)}{3} = 0$

c. $\frac{[(-2)^2 - 4](-2 - 3)}{(-2 + 1)} = \frac{(4 - 4)(-5)}{(-1)} = 0$

27. a. $\frac{(2 - 1)(2 + 1)(2 - 3)}{\frac{1}{2}(2) + 2} = \frac{1(3)(-1)}{3} = -1$

b. $\frac{(0 - 1)(0 + 1)(0 - 3)}{\frac{1}{2}(0) + 2} = \frac{(-1)(1)(-3)}{2} = \frac{3}{2}$

c. $\frac{(-2 - 1)(-2 + 1)(-2 - 3)}{\frac{1}{2}(-2) + 2} = \frac{(-3)(-1)(-5)}{-1 + 2} = \frac{-15}{1} = -15$

28. a. $\dfrac{\left(\frac{1}{2}-3\right)\left(\frac{1}{2}\right)\left(\frac{1}{2}+3\right)}{\left(\frac{1}{2}-2\right)\left(\frac{1}{2}+2\right)} = \dfrac{\left(-\frac{5}{2}\right)\left(\frac{1}{2}\right)\left(\frac{7}{2}\right)}{\left(-\frac{3}{2}\right)\left(\frac{5}{2}\right)} = \dfrac{-\frac{7}{4}}{-\frac{3}{2}} = \dfrac{7}{6}$

b. $\dfrac{(-1-3)(-1)(-1+3)}{(-1-2)(-1+2)} = \dfrac{(-4)(-1)(2)}{(-3)(1)} = \dfrac{8}{-3} = -\dfrac{8}{3}$ **c.** $\dfrac{(0-3)(0)(0+3)}{(0-2)(0+2)} = 0$

29. Answers may vary. For example, $4 \div 2 = 2$; $2 \div 4 = \frac{1}{2}$; $2 \neq \frac{1}{2}$

30. Answers may vary. For example, $8 \div (4 \div 2) = 8 \div 2 = 4$; $(8 \div 4) \div 2 = 2 \div 2 = 1$; $4 \neq 1$

C **31.** Closed **32.** Not closed; $\frac{1}{0}$ does not exist **33.** Closed **34.** Closed

35. Closed **36.** Not closed; $\sqrt{2} \div \sqrt{2} = 1$

Pages 40–42 • WRITTEN EXERCISES

A **1.** $3x - 4 = 5$; $3x = 9$; $x = 3$; $\{3\}$ **2.** $4z + 11 = 3$; $4z = -8$; $z = -2$; $\{-2\}$

3. $\frac{2}{3}t - 8 = 0$; $\frac{2}{3}t = 8$; $t = 12$; $\{12\}$ **4.** $15 - \frac{1}{8}d = -1$; $-\frac{1}{8}d = -16$; $d = 128$; $\{128\}$

5. $5r = 18 + 2r$; $3r = 18$; $r = 6$; $\{6\}$ **6.** $24 - 2y = 6y$; $24 = 8y$; $3 = y$; $\{3\}$

7. $3(t-1) = -(t-5)$; $3t - 3 = -t + 5$; $4t - 3 = 5$; $4t = 8$; $t = 2$; $\{2\}$

8. $2(x-3) = x + 3$; $2x - 6 = x + 3$; $x - 6 = 3$; $x = 9$; $\{9\}$

9. $2k - 1 = k - 5 + 3k$; $2k - 1 = 4k - 5$; $-2k - 1 = -5$; $-2k = -4$; $k = 2$; $\{2\}$

10. $3(2z-1) = 6z + 5$; $6z - 3 = 6z + 5$; $-3 = 5$; $\emptyset$

11. $-(5-x) = x + 3$; $-5 + x = x + 3$; $-5 = 3$; $\emptyset$

12. $\frac{1}{3}(s-2) = s + 4$; $s - 2 = 3s + 12$; $-2s - 2 = 12$; $-2s = 14$; $s = -7$; $\{-7\}$

13. $1.5(u+2) = 7.5$; $1.5u + 3 = 7.5$; $1.5u = 4.5$; $u = 3$; $\{3\}$

14. $1.6(2t-1) = 14.4$; $2t - 1 = 9$; $2t = 10$; $t = 5$; $\{5\}$

15. $0.2(x-5) = x + 5$; $0.2x - 1 = x + 5$; $-0.8x - 1 = 5$; $-0.8x = 6$; $x = -7.5$; $\{-7.5\}$

16. $0.3(2r-3) = 0.2r + 0.9$; $0.6r - 0.9 = 0.2r + 0.9$; $0.4r - 0.9 = 0.9$; $0.4r = 1.8$; $r = 4.5$; $\{4.5\}$

17. $3(x-2) - x = 2(2x+1)$; $3x - 6 - x = 4x + 2$; $2x - 6 = 4x + 2$; $-6 = 2x + 2$, $-8 = 2x$; $x = -4$; $\{-4\}$

18. $\frac{2}{5}(x-2) = x + 4$; $2(x-2) = 5(x+4)$; $2x - 4 = 5x + 20$; $-4 = 3x + 20$; $-24 = 3x$; $x = -8$; $\{-8\}$

19. $2z - (1-z) = 11 - z$; $2z - 1 + z = 11 - z$; $3z - 1 = 11 - z$; $4z - 1 = 11$; $4z = 12$; $z = 3$; $\{3\}$

20. $3(1-t) + 5 = 3(1+t) - 7$; $3 - 3t + 5 = 3 + 3t - 7$; $8 - 3t = 3t - 4$; $8 = 6t - 4$; $12 = 6t$; $2 = t$; $\{2\}$

21. $2(5t-3) - t = 3(3t-2)$; $10t - 6 - t = 9t - 6$; $9t - 6 = 9t - 6$, identity; {real numbers}

22. $3(5z-1) + 5(3z+2) = 7$; $15z - 3 + 15z + 10 = 7$; $30z + 7 = 7$; $30z = 0$; $z = 0$; $\{0\}$

23. $\frac{6x - 2(x - 4)}{3} = 8; 6x - 2(x - 4) = 24; 6x - 2x + 8 = 24; 4x + 8 = 24; 4x = 16;$ $x = 4; \{4\}$

24. $\frac{3y - 2(y - 1)}{6} = -1; 3y - 2(y - 1) = -6; 3y - 2y + 2 = -6; y + 2 = -6; y = -8;$ $\{-8\}$

25. $(-2)(-2 - 3)(-2 + 2) = 0$, yes; $(-3)(-3 - 3)(-3 + 2) = -18$, no

26. $0(0 + 1)(0 - 2) = 0$, yes; $(-1)(-1 + 1)(-1 - 2) = 0$, yes

27. $2^3 - 4(2^2) + 2 + 6 = 8 - 16 + 2 + 6 = 0$, yes; $3^3 - 4(3^2) + 3 + 6 = 27 - 36 + 3 + 6 = 0$, yes

28. $1^3 - 7(1) - 6 = 1 - 13 = -12$, no; $(-2)^3 - 7(-2) - 6 = -8 + 14 - 6 = 0$, yes

29. $\frac{-2 + 12}{-2 - 4} = -\frac{5}{3}, -2 - 3 = -5$, no; $\frac{0 + 12}{0 - 4} = -3, 0 - 3 = -3$, yes

30. $\frac{2(0)}{2(0) - 1} = 0, \frac{0 + 2}{0 + 1} = 2$, no; $\frac{2(2)}{2(2) - 1} = \frac{4}{3}, \frac{2 + 2}{2 + 1} = \frac{4}{3}$, yes

31. $2x - 5y = 10; 2x = 5y + 10; x = \frac{5}{2}y + 5$ **32.** $A = \frac{1}{2}bh; 2A = bh; \frac{2A}{b} = h$

33. $I = prt; \frac{I}{rt} = p$ **34.** $C = 2\pi r; \frac{C}{2\pi} = r$ **35.** $y = mx + b; y - b = mx; \frac{y - b}{m} = x$

36. $ax + by = c; by = c - ax; y = \frac{c - ax}{b}$

37. $P = 2l + 2w; P - 2l = 2w; \frac{1}{2}P - l = w$

38. $P = 2(l + w); \frac{1}{2}P = l + w; \frac{1}{2}P - w = l$

B **39.** $a(x - b) = c + ab; ax - ab = c + ab; ax = c + 2ab; x = \frac{c}{a} + 2b$

40. $5cy - d = 4d - cy; 6cy - d = 4d; 6cy = 5d; y = \frac{5d}{6c}$

41. $S = -\frac{1}{2}gt^2 + vt; S + \frac{1}{2}gt^2 = vt, \frac{S}{t} + \frac{1}{2}gt = v$

42. $C = \frac{5}{9}(F - 32); \frac{9}{5}C = F - 32; \frac{9}{5}C + 32 = F$

43. $128 = \pi(8^2)h; 128 = 64\pi h; h = \frac{128}{64\pi} = \frac{2}{\pi}$

44. $48 = \frac{1}{3}\pi(4^2)h; 48 = \frac{16}{3}\pi h; h = \frac{3}{16\pi} \cdot 48 = \frac{9}{\pi}$

45. $168 = 150(1 + 0.08t); 168 = 150 + 12t; 18 = 12t; t = \frac{18}{12} = 1.5$

46. $1000 = \frac{140^2}{2g}; 2000g = 140^2; g = \frac{140^2}{2000} = 9.8$

47. $100 = \frac{5}{2}(b_1 + 12); 40 = b_1 + 12; b_1 = 28$

48. $80\pi = 2\pi(5)(5 + h); 80\pi = 10\pi(5 + h); 8 = 5 + h; h = 3$

49. $100\pi = \pi(5)(s + 5)$; $20 = s + 5$; $s = 15$

50. $80 = \frac{a(1 - 3^4)}{1 - 3}$; $80 = \frac{a(1 - 81)}{-2}$; $80 = 40a$; $a = 2$

C **51.** $A = 2\pi r(r + h)$; $\frac{A}{2\pi r} = r + h$; $h = \frac{A}{2\pi r} - r$

52. $A = \pi r(s + r)$; $\frac{A}{\pi r} = s + r$; $s = \frac{A}{\pi r} - r$

53. $S = \frac{a(1 - r^n)}{1 - r}$; $S(1 - r) = a(1 - r^n)$; $\frac{S(1 - r)}{1 - r^n} = a$

Page 42 • MIXED REVIEW EXERCISES

1. $7 - (-1) = 8$ **2.** $-2(3) = -6$ **3.** $(-5)^2 = 25$ **4.** $|-4| = 4$ **5.** -12 **6.** $\frac{8}{-4} = -2$

7. $3x - 2x - 8 = x - 8$ **8.** $-20ab + 24ab = 4ab$ **9.** $x^2(-y^3) = -x^2y^3$

10. $2c - 6d + 10d - 5c = -3c + 4d$ **11.** $-3 + 3 - 5x + 5x = 0$ **12.** $-1 + m$

Pages 46–48 • WRITTEN EXERCISES

A **1.** Let l = the garden's length; $2l + 2w = 120$; $l + w = 60$; $l = 60 - w$; $(60 - w)$ ft

2. Let s = the length of each leg; $2s + b = 300$; $2s = 300 - b$; $s = \frac{300 - b}{2}$; $\left(\frac{300 - b}{2}\right)$ cm

3. The team's scores are x and $\frac{1}{2}x - 2$; difference in scores $= x - \left(\frac{1}{2}x - 2\right) =$ $x - \frac{1}{2}x + 2 = \frac{1}{2}x + 2$; $\left(\frac{1}{2}x + 2\right)$ points

4. Let b = number of tapes that brother has; $y + 15 = \frac{1}{2}b$; $2y + 30 = b$; $(2y + 30)$ tapes

5. The rectangle's width is $(l - 2)$ cm. **a.** $l(l - 2)$ cm^2
b. perimeter $= 2l + 2(l - 2) = 2l + 2l - 4 = 4l - 4$; $(4l - 4)$ cm

6. The other dimensions are $k - 1$ and $k - 2$; $V = k(k - 1)(k - 2)$ cm^3

7. The southbound jet's speed is $2r$ mi/h; distance apart $= 3r + 3(2r) = 3r + 6r = 9r$; $9r$ mi

8. The slower speed is $(r - 10)$ mi/h; distance traveled $= 2r + 1(r - 10) = 3r - 10$; $(3r - 10)$ mi

9. The sum of the other three measures is $(360 - a)°$; average $= \frac{360 - a}{3} = 120 - \frac{a}{3}$; $\left(120 - \frac{a}{3}\right)^\circ$

10. The complement measures $(90 - x)°$; the supplement measures $(180 - x)°$; average $= \frac{(90 - x) + (180 - x)}{2} = \frac{270 - 2x}{2} = 135 - x$; $(135 - x)°$

11. Each edge of the base measures $(2x - 3)$ cm; the area of the base is $(2x - 3)^2$; $V = \frac{1}{3}x(2x - 3)^2 \text{ cm}^3$

12. The length, width, and height are x, $x - 2$, and $x - 4$; $V = \frac{1}{3}x(x - 2)(x - 4)$

13. The club sold $t - 100$ adult tickets; money collected $= 1.50t + 2.50(t - 100) = 1.50t + 2.50t - 250 = 4t - 250$; $(4t - 250)$ dollars

14. He bought $3s$ 25-cent stamps; money spent $= 0.40s + 0.25(3s) = 0.40s + 0.75s = 1.15s$; $1.15s$ dollars

15. There are $18 - q$ dimes; value $= 0.25q + 0.10(18 - q)$; $0.25q + 1.80 - 0.10q = 0.15q + 1.80$; $(0.15q + 1.80)$ dollars

16. The field's length is $(w + 45)$ ft; total fencing $= 2(w + 45) + 3w = 2w + 90 + 3w = 5w + 90$; $(5w + 90)$ ft

17. Let x = the length of the shortest side; $x + (x + 2) + (x + 4) + (x + 6) = 60$

18. Let d = the denominator; $\frac{d - 6}{d} = \frac{3}{5}$

B **19.** Let x = the regular price; $x + 2(x - 2) = 41$

20. Let m = the number of laps Mary swims; $[(m - 2) + 7] + (m + 7) = 3m$

21. Let g = the amount of money that Greg has; $g + (g + 12) + 2(g + 12) = 124$

22. Let q = the number of quarters Paula has; $0.25q + 0.10(2q) + 0.05(2q - 3) = 3.15$

23. Let c = the car's speed; $2c + 2\left(\frac{2}{3}c\right) = 140$

24. Let r = Tom's speed; $2.5r + 2.5(r + 4) = 50$

25. Let b = the measure of $\angle B$; $(b + 20) + b + 2b + 4b = 360$

26. Let s = the length of one side; $s = \frac{1}{3}s + 20$

27. Let c = the number of kilograms of cashews; $7c + 9(20 - c) = 7.80(20)$

28. Let a = the cost of an adult ticket; $\frac{2a + 3(a - 1.50)}{5} = 3.35$

C **29.** Let r = Kevin's speed going; $\frac{320}{r} + \frac{1}{3} = \frac{320}{r - 4}$

Page 48 • CHALLENGE

Answers may vary. For example, $23 = 2^3 + 2^3 + 1^3 + 1^3 + 1^3 + 1^3 + 1^3 + 1^3 + 1^3$

Pages 52–54 • PROBLEMS

A **1.** Let m = the amount of money Maria has; $m - 8$ = the amount Amy has; $m + (m - 8) = 30$; $2m - 8 = 30$; $2m = 38$; $m = 19$; Maria has \$19 and Amy has \$11.

2. Let a = Alicia's pay; $\frac{2}{3}a$ = Jim's pay; $a + \frac{2}{3}a = 600$; $\frac{5}{3}a = 600$; $a = 360$; Alicia earns \$360 and Jim earns \$240.

3. Let r = the number of records sold; $r - 60$ = the number of tapes; $7r + 7.50(r - 60) = 2160$; $7r + 7.5r - 450 = 2160$; $14.5r - 450 = 2160$; $14.5r = 2610$; $r = 180$; 180 records were sold.

4. Let p = the number of pizza slices sold; $p - 40$ = the number of hamburgers sold; $0.75p + 1.35(p - 40) = 292.50$; $0.75p + 1.35p - 54 = 292.50$; $2.1p = 346.50$; $p = 165$; they sold 165 slices of pizza.

5. Let w = the width of the court in ft; $w + 35$ = the length; $2w + 2(w + 35) = 266$; $2w + 2w + 70 = 266$; $4w = 196$; $w = 49$; the court is 49 ft by 84 ft.

6. Let s = the length of the square in cm; the dimensions of the rectangle are $(s + 8)$ cm by $(s - 2)$ cm; $2(s + 8) + 2(s - 2) = 40$; $2s + 16 + 2s - 4 = 40$; $4s + 12 = 40$; $4s = 28$; $s = 7$; each side of the square is 7 cm.

7. Let a = the measure of the angle in degrees; the supplement measures $180 - a$, and the complement measures $90 - a$; $180 - a = 3(90 - a) + 12$; $180 - a = 270 - 3a + 12$; $180 + 2a = 282$; $2a = 102$; $a = 51$; the angle measures 51°

8. Let the measures of the angles be x, $x + 2$, $x + 4$, $x + 6$, and $x + 8$; $x + (x + 2) + (x + 4) + (x + 6) + (x + 8) = 540$; $5x + 20 = 540$; $5x = 520$; $x = 104$; $x + 8 = 112$; the largest angle is 112°.

9. Let t = the planes' flying time; $560t + 640t = 2100$; $1200t = 2100$; $t = 1.75$; they will be 2100 km apart after $1\frac{3}{4}$ h, at 12:15 P.M.

10. Let d = Elisa's walking distance; $2d$ = her jogging distance; $\frac{d}{5} + \frac{2d}{8} = 2\frac{1}{4}$; $\frac{9d}{20} = \frac{9}{4}$; $d = 5$; $2d = 10$; the walkathon was 15 mi long.

11. Let d = the number of dimes; $40 - d$ = the number of quarters; $0.10d + 0.25(40 - d) = 4.90$; $0.10d + 10 - 0.25d = 4.90$; $10 - 0.15d = 4.90$; $-0.15d = -5.10$; $d = 34$; there are 34 dimes and 6 quarters.

12. Let x = the amount invested at 5%; $3000 - x$ = the amount invested at 8%; $0.05x + 0.08(3000 - x) = 213$; $0.05x + 240 - 0.08x = 213$; $-0.03x + 240 = 213$; $-0.03x = -27$; $x = 900$; he invested \$900 at 5% and 2100 at 8%.

13. There is not enough information to solve this problem.

14. Let n = the number of nickels; $2n$ = the number of dimes; $30 - 3n$ = the number of quarters; $0.05n + 0.10(2n) + 0.25(30 - 3n) = 5.50$; $0.05n + 0.20n + 7.5 - 0.75n = 5.50$; $-0.50n + 7.5 = 5.50$; $-0.50n = -2$; $n = 4$; $30 - 3n = 18$; there are 18 quarters.

15. Let d = the distance traveled at 80 km/h; $260 - d$ = the distance traveled at 100 km/h; $\frac{d}{80} + \frac{260 - d}{100} = 2.5$; $10d + 8(260 - d) = 2.5(800)$; $10d + 2080 - 8d = 2000$; $2d + 2080 = 2000$; $2d = -80$; $d = -40$; since a negative distance is impossible, the problem has no solution

16. Let the lengths of the sides, in cm, be x, $x + 2$, and $x + 4$; $x + (x + 2) + (x + 4) = 29$; $3x + 6 = 29$; $3x = 23$; $x = \frac{23}{3} = 7\frac{2}{3}$; since this is not an integer, the problem has no solution.

B 17. Let r = the interest rate for the \$1200 investment; $r + 0.03$ = the interest rate for the \$2200 investment; $1200r + 2200(r + 0.03) = 253$; $1200r + 2200r + 66 = 253$; $3400r = 187$; $r = 0.055$; the interest rates were $5\frac{1}{2}$% and $8\frac{1}{2}$%. The fact that the larger investment earned \$121 more was not used.

18. There is not enough information to solve this problem.

19. Let t = the time that eastbound train traveled at 90 mi/h; $t - \frac{1}{4}$ = the time that westbound train traveled at 100 mi/h; $90t + 100\left(t - \frac{1}{4}\right) = 450$; $90t + 100t - 25 = 450$; $190t = 475$; $t = 2.5$; the trains passed each other at 2:30 P.M.

20. Let t = the time that Lionel travels at 17 km/h; $t + \frac{1}{4}$ = the time that Robert travels at 14 km/h; $17t = 14\left(t + \frac{1}{4}\right) + \frac{1}{2}$; $17t = 14t + \frac{7}{2} + \frac{1}{2}$; $3t = 4$; $t = \frac{4}{3}$; Lionel needs $1\frac{1}{3}$ h to overtake Robert.

21. Let x = the rate of emission, in ppm per hour, of pollutant in the exhaust originally; $3x = 10(x - 56)$; $3x = 10x - 560$; $7x = 560$; $x = 80$; the car originally emitted pollutants at the rate of 80 ppm/h.

22. Let x = the number of pounds of peanuts at \$4.80/lb; $20 - x$ = the number of pounds of cashews at \$8/lb; $4.8x + 8(20 - x) = 124$; $4.8x + 160 - 8x = 124$; $-3.2x = -36$; $x = 11.25$; she should mix 11.25 lb of peanuts with 8.75 lb of cashews.

C **23.** Let x = the number of votes received by the winner; $(1401 - x)$ = the number of votes received by the loser; $(x - 30) + 5 = (1401 - x) + 30$; $x - 25 = 1431 - x$; $2x = 1456$; $x = 728$; the winner received 728 votes, and the loser received 673 votes.

Page 54 • MIXED REVIEW EXERCISES

1. $3x + 2 = -4$; $3x = -6$; $x = -2$; $\{-2\}$

2. $4(2 - y) = y - 7$; $8 - 4y = y - 7$; $-5y = -15$; $y = 3$; $\{3\}$

3. $1 - 5t = t + 7$; $-6t = 6$, $t = -1$; $\{-1\}$ **4.** $(-4)^2 - 6^2 = 16 - 36 = -20$

5. $(-4 - 6)^2 = (-10)^2 = 100$ **6.** $|2(-4) - 3(6)| = |-8 - 18| = |-26| = 26$

7. $\frac{-4 + 6}{-2} = \frac{2}{-2} = -1$ **8.** $\frac{(-4)(6)}{8} = \frac{-24}{8} = -3$ **9.** $\frac{6 - (-4)}{5} = \frac{10}{5} = 2$

Pages 55–56 • CHAPTER REVIEW

1. c; $\frac{-3 + 7}{2} = 2$ **2.** b; $|-5| - |5| = 5 - 5 = 0$ **3.** d; $\frac{2(25) + 1}{2(9) - 1} = \frac{50 + 1}{18 - 1} = \frac{51}{17} = 3$

4. a; $4(3 - 1)^2 = 4(2^2) = 4(4) = 16$ **5.** a; $\frac{1}{2}(2a) + \frac{1}{2}(1) = a + \frac{1}{2}$ **6.** d

7. c; $-6 - (-7) = 1$ **8.** b; $(8 - 1)m + (-6 + 2)n = 7m - 4n$

9. d; $6x - 3y - 4x + 8y = 2x + 5y$ **10.** d

11. c; $6(-4) \div (-8) \div (-1) = -24 \div (-8) \div (-1) = 3 \div -1 = -3$

12. a; $\frac{24}{-4} + \frac{-20x}{-4} = -6 + 5x = 5x - 6$

13. b; $2(3 - x) = 3x + 1$; $6 - 2x = 3x + 1$; $6 = 5x + 1$; $5 = 5x$; $x = 1$

14. d; $A = 2\pi r(r + h)$; $\frac{A}{2\pi r} = r + h$; $\frac{A}{2\pi r} - r = h$ **15.** c; $x + (x - 2) + (x - 4) = 3x - 6$

16. a; let w = rectangle's width; $2y + 2w = 24$; $y + w = 12$; $w = 12 - y$

17. a; let x = the number of pens sold; $0.20x + 0.05(x + 8) = 8.90$; $0.25x + 0.40 = 8.90$; $0.25x = 8.50$; $x = 34$; $x + 8 = 42$; 42 pencils were sold.

18. c; let t = time spent traveling at 50 mi/h; $3.5 - t$ = time spent traveling at 55 mi/h; $50t + 55(3.5 - t) = 185$; $50t + 192.5 - 55t = 185$; $-5t = -7.5$; $t = 1.5$; $50t = 75$; she traveled 75 mi at 50 mi/h.

Page 57 • CHAPTER TEST

1. The distance from A to B is 9; $\frac{2}{3}(9) = 6$; $-4 + 6 = 2$ **2.** $-1, -0.8, -0.2, 0.6, 1.4$

3. $5 \cdot 9 - 2(10) = 45 - 20 = 25$ **4.** $\frac{(2 + 4)^2}{2^2 + 4^2} = \frac{6^2}{4 + 16} = \frac{36}{20} = \frac{9}{5}$

5. **a.** Dist. prop. **b.** Assoc. prop. of mult. **c.** Prop. of recip. **d.** Ident. prop. of mult.

6. $|-5| - |-3| = 5 - 3 = 2$ **7.** $-1m + 3 = -m + 3$ **8.** $-(-1)(4) = 4$

9. $15x - 10y - 24y + 4x = 19x - 34y$ **10.** $(-3)(4 - (-3))(-3 + 1) = (-3)(7)(-2) = 42$

11. $7 - 2(-3) - (-3)^2 = 7 + 6 - 9 = 4$ **12.** $\left|\frac{36 + 12}{-6}\right| = \left|\frac{48}{-6}\right| = |-8| = 8$

13. $-3 + 4x^2 = 4x^2 - 3$ **14.** $\frac{3}{2}x - 7 = 2x + 3$; $-\frac{1}{2}x - 7 = 3$; $-\frac{1}{2}x = 10$; $x = -20$; $\{-20\}$

15. $6(5x - 4) = 7(4x + 5) - 19$; $30x - 24 = 28x + 35 - 19$; $30x - 24 = 28x + 16$; $2x - 24 = 16$; $2x = 40$; $x = 20$; $\{20\}$

16. $x - \frac{3}{4}x + 10 = \frac{1}{4}x + 10$; $\left(\frac{1}{4}x + 10\right)$ gallons

17. Let x = amount invested at 5%; $6000 - x$ = amount invested at 7%; $0.05x + 0.07(6000 - x) = 372$; $0.05x + 420 - 0.07x = 372$; $-0.02x = -48$; $x = 2400$; he invested \$2400 at 5% and \$3600 at 7%.

Pages 62–63 • WRITTEN EXERCISES

A 1. $x - 7 > -5$; $x > 2$; $\{x : x > 2\}$

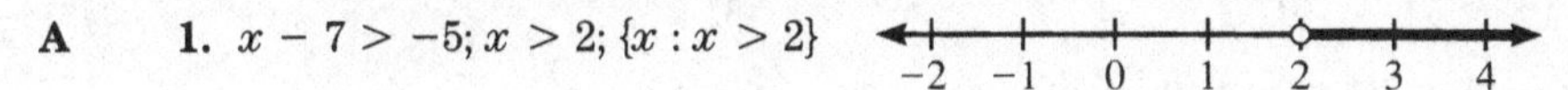

2. $y + 4 < 3$; $y < -1$; $\{y : y < -1\}$

3. $2t < 6$; $t < 3$; $\{t : t < 3\}$

4. $3u > -6$; $u > -2$; $\{u : u > -2\}$

5. $-5x < 10$; $x > -2$; $\{x : x > -2\}$

6. $-12 > -4y$; $3 < y$; $\{y : y > 3\}$

7. $-\frac{t}{2} > \frac{3}{2}$; $t < -3$; $\{t : t < -3\}$

8. $-\frac{3}{4}k < -6$; $k > 8$; $\{k : k > 8\}$

9. $3s - 1 > -4$; $3s > -3$; $s > -1$; $\{s : s > -1\}$

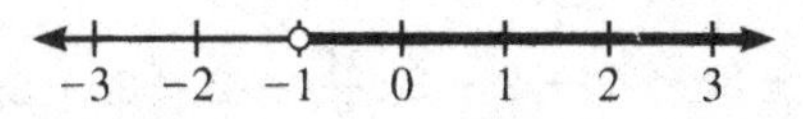

10. $2r + 5 < -1$; $2r < -6$; $r < -3$; $\{r : r < -3\}$

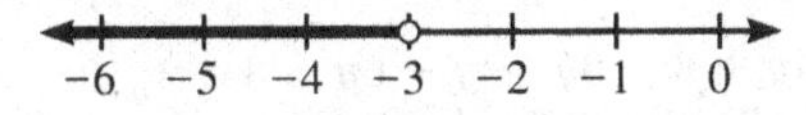

11. $y < 7y - 24$; $-6y < -24$; $y > 4$; $\{y : y > 4\}$

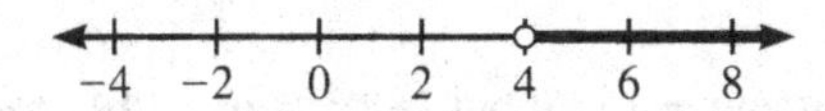

12. $3t > 6t + 12$; $-3t > 12$; $t < -4$; $\{t : t < -4\}$

13. $2 - h < 4 + h$; $-2h < 2$; $h > -1$; $\{h : h > -1\}$

14. $1 + 2x < 2(x - 1)$; $1 + 2x < 2x - 2$; $1 < -2$; false; $\emptyset$

15. $5(2u + 3) > 2(u - 3) + u$; $10u + 15 > 2u - 6 + u$; $7u > -21$; $u > -3$; $\{u : u > -3\}$

16. $3(x-2)-2<x-5$; $3x-6-2<x-5$, $2x<3$; $x<\frac{3}{2}$;

$\left\{x : x<\frac{3}{2}\right\}$ 0 1 2 3

17. $5(x-7)+2(1-x)>3(x-11)$; $5x-35+2-2x>3x-33$;
$3x-33>3x-33$; false; $\emptyset$

18. $4s+3(2-3s)<5(2-s)$; $4s+6-9s<10-5s$; $-5s+6<10-5s$; $6<10$;
true for all values of s; {real numbers}

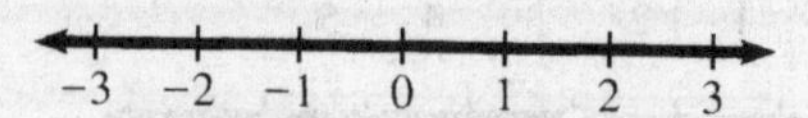

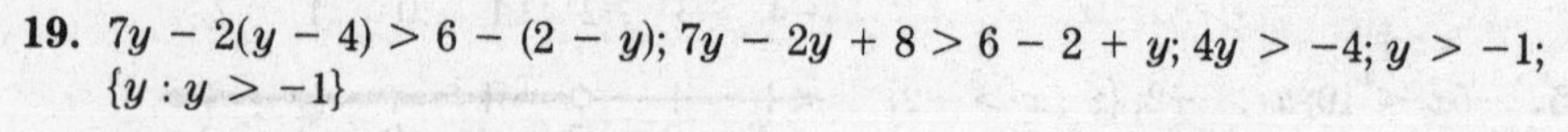

19. $7y-2(y-4)>6-(2-y)$; $7y-2y+8>6-2+y$; $4y>-4$; $y>-1$;
$\{y : y>-1\}$

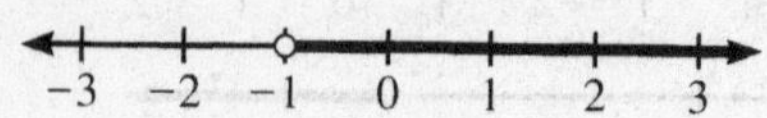

20. $4(2-x)-3(1+x)<5(1-x)$; $8-4x-3-3x<5-5x$; $-7x+5<5-5x$;
$-2x<0$; $x>0$; $\{x : x>0\}$

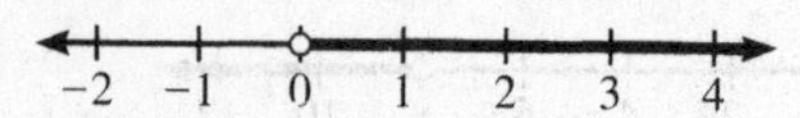

B **21.** $k-3(2-4k)<7-(8k-9+k)$; $k-6+12k<7-9k+9$;
$13k-6<-9k+16$; $22k<22$; $k<1$; $\{k : k<1\}$

22. $\frac{2}{3}t-(2-3t)<5t+2(1-t)$; $\frac{2}{3}t-2+3t<5t+2-2t$; $\frac{11}{3}t-2<3t+2$;

$\frac{2}{3}t<4$; $t<6$; $\{t : t<6\}$

23. $4(y+2)-9y>y-3(2y+1)-1$; $4y+8-9y>y-6y-3-1$;
$-5y+8>-5y-4$, $8>-4$; true for all values of y; {real numbers}

24. $4[5x-(3x-7)]<2(4x-5)$; $4[2x+7]<8x-10$; $8x+28<8x-10$; $28<-10$;
false; $\emptyset$

25. True **26.** True **27.** False; for example, $-1<0$ but $(-1)^2>0^2$. **28.** True

29. True **30.** False; for example, $3<4$ and $0<2$, but $(3-0)>(4-2)$.

C **31.** True **32.** True

33. If you multiply any number between 0 and 1 by itself, the result is smaller than the original number.

Page 63 • MIXED REVIEW EXERCISES

1. $(8t-5)-(5-8t)=16t-10$ **2.** $(-4)(5)(-1)(-3)=-60$ **3.** $(-2)^4(-p)^3=-16p^3$

4. $\frac{5^2-7^2}{5-7}=\frac{-24}{-2}=12$ **5.** $\frac{8cd-6}{-2}=-4cd+3$ **6.** $\frac{6(2+3)}{6\cdot 2+3}=\frac{6(5)}{12+3}=\frac{30}{15}=2$

7. $|3(-4)-2|=|-12-2|=|-14|=14$ **8.** $-2(5-8)^3=-2(-3)^3=-2(-27)=54$

9. $2a^2-5a-(a^2-7)=2a^2-5a-a^2+7=a^2-5a+7$

10. $6x-y+2x-4y=8x-5y$ **11.** $|-4|-|-9|=4-9=-5$

12. $4(3-m)-(2m+1)=12-4m-2m-1=11-6m$

Page 64 • COMPUTER EXERCISES

1.
```
10 INPUT "ENTER SMALLEST AND LARGEST INTEGERS IN DOMAIN:";M,N
20 INPUT "ENTER VALUES OF A,B,C IN AX + B < C:";A,B,C
30 FOR X = M TO N
40 IF A * X + B > = C THEN 60
50 PRINT X; "IS A SOLUTION."
60 NEXT X
70 END
```

2. **a.** {1, 2, 3, 4, 5, 6} **b.** {5, 6, 7} **c.** ∅

3. Add these lines.
```
5  LET K = 0
55 LET K = K + 1
65 IF K > 0 THEN 70
66 PRINT "THERE ARE NO SOLUTIONS."
```

4. **a.** No solutions **b.** {−10, −9, −8, −7, −6, −5, −4, −3, −2, −1, 0, 1} **c.** {1}

Pages 67–68 • WRITTEN EXERCISES

A 1. $3 \le x < 5$; $\{x : 3 \le x < 5\}$

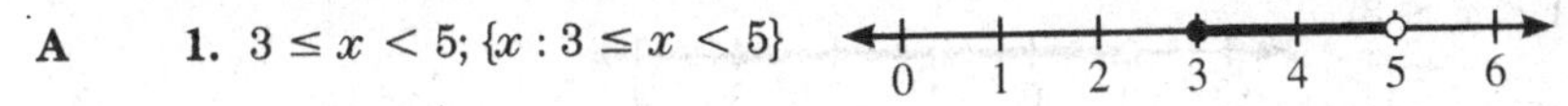

2. $z > -1$ and $z < 3$; $\{z : -1 < z < 3\}$

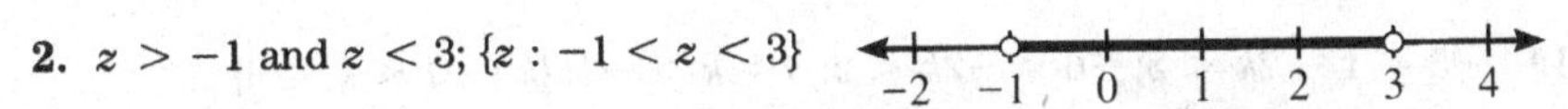

3. $t < 1$ or $t \ge 3$; $\{t : t < 1 \text{ or } t \ge 3\}$

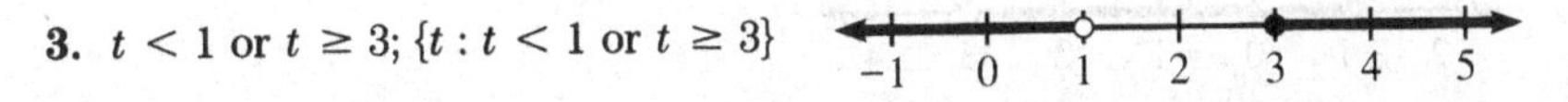

4. $p > 1$ or $p < 1$; $\{p : p \ne 1\}$

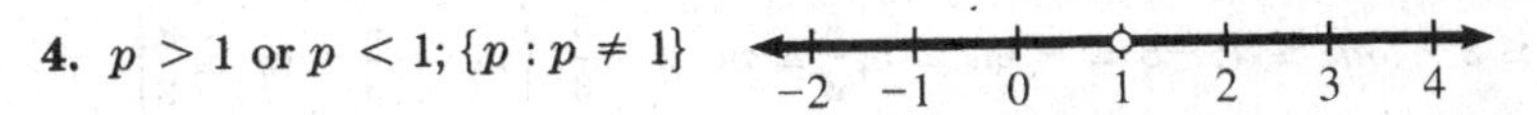

5. $y \ge -1$ and $y \ge 3$; $\{y : y \ge 3\}$

6. $y \ge -1$ or $y \ge 3$; $\{y : y \ge -1\}$

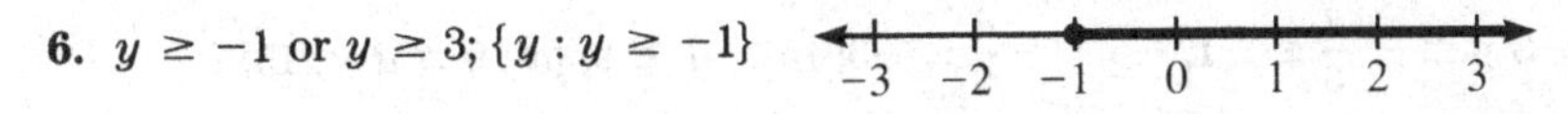

7. $t > 0$ or $t < 2$; {real numbers}

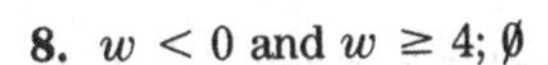

8. $w < 0$ and $w \ge 4$; ∅

9. $0 \le x - 2 < 3$; $2 \le x < 5$; $\{x : 2 \le x < 5\}$

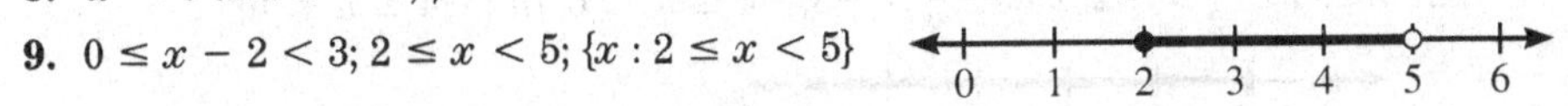

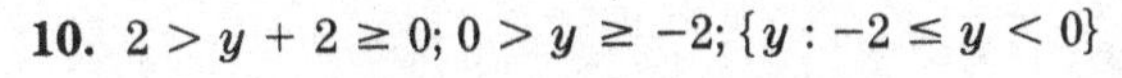

10. $2 > y + 2 \ge 0$; $0 > y \ge -2$; $\{y : -2 \le y < 0\}$

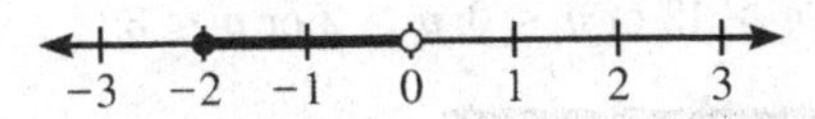

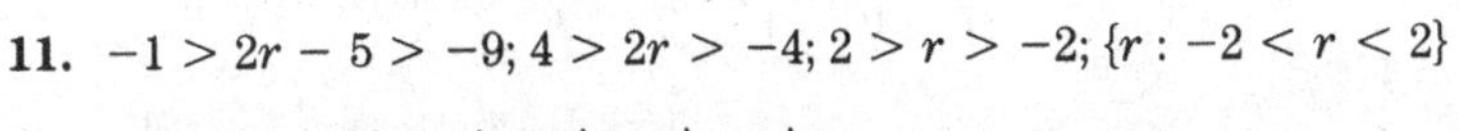

11. $-1 > 2r - 5 > -9$; $4 > 2r > -4$; $2 > r > -2$; $\{r : -2 < r < 2\}$

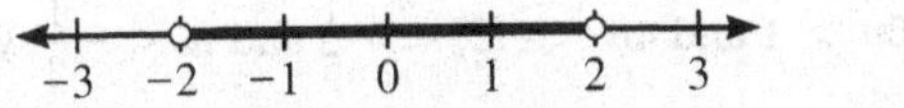

12. $-1 \le 3z + 2 \le 8$; $-3 \le 3z \le 6$; $-1 \le z \le 2$; $\{z : -1 \le z \le 2\}$

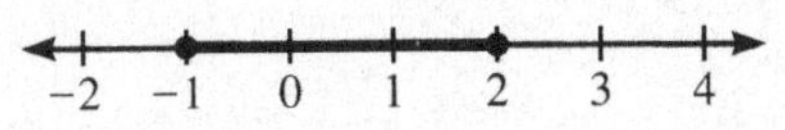

13. $2z - 1 \le 5$ or $3z - 5 > 10$; $2z \le 6$ or $3z > 15$; $z \le 3$ or $z > 5$; $\{z : z \le 3 \text{ or } z > 5\}$

14. $3k + 7 < 1$ or $2k - 3 > 1$; $3k < -6$ or $2k > 4$; $k < -2$ or $k > 2$; $\{k : k < -2 \text{ or } k > 2\}$

15. $2t + 7 \ge 13$ or $5t - 4 < 6$; $2t \ge 6$ or $5t < 10$; $t \ge 3$ or $t < 2$; $\{t : t \ge 3 \text{ or } t < 2\}$

16. $2x + 3 > 1$ or $5x - 9 \le 6$; $2x > -2$ or $5x \le 15$; $x > -1$ or $x \le 3$; {real numbers}

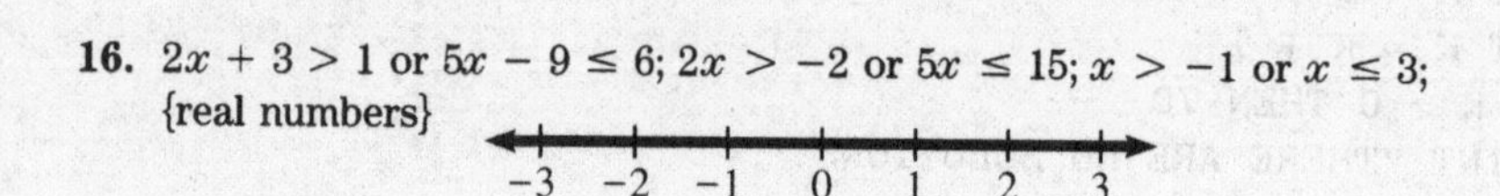

17. $2t + 7 \ge 13$ and $5t - 4 < 6$; $2t \ge 6$ and $5t < 10$; $t \ge 3$ and $t < 2$; $\emptyset$

18. $2x + 3 > 1$ and $5x - 9 \le 6$; $2x > -2$ and $5x \le 15$; $x > -1$ and $x \le 3$; $\{x : -1 < x \le 3\}$

19. $-5 < 1 - 2k < 3$; $-6 < -2k < 2$; $3 > k > -1$; $\{k : -1 < k < 3\}$

20. $-6 \le 2 - 3m \le 7$; $-8 \le -3m \le 5$; $\frac{8}{3} \ge m \ge -\frac{5}{3}$; $\left\{m : -\frac{5}{3} \le m \le \frac{8}{3}\right\}$

21. $-3 < 2 - \frac{d}{3} \le -1$; $-5 < -\frac{d}{3} \le -3$; $15 > d \ge 9$; $\{d : 9 \le d < 15\}$

22. $3 \ge 1 - \frac{n}{2} > -2$; $2 \ge -\frac{n}{2} > -3$; $-4 \le n < 6$; $\{n : -4 \le n < 6\}$

B **23.** $7q - 1 > q + 11$ or $-11q > -33$; $6q > 12$ or $q < 3$; $q > 2$ or $q < 3$; {real numbers}

24. $5n - 1 > 0$ and $4n + 2 < 0$; $5n > 1$ and $4n < -2$; $n > \frac{1}{5}$ and $n < -\frac{1}{2}$; $\emptyset$

25. $x - 7 < 3x - 5 < x + 11$; $x - 7 < 3x - 5$ and $3x - 5 < x + 11$; $-2 < 2x$ and $2x < 16$; $-1 < x$ and $x < 8$; $\{x : -1 < x < 8\}$

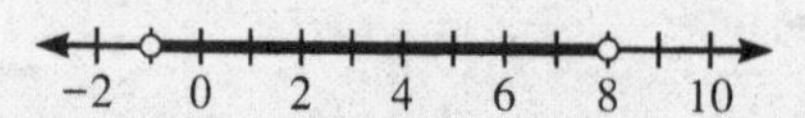

26. $3y + 5 \ge 2y + 1 > y - 1$; $3y + 5 \ge 2y + 1$ and $2y + 1 > y - 1$; $y \ge -4$ and $y > -2$; $\{y : y > -2\}$

−3 −2 −1 0 1 2 3

27. $-\frac{3}{4}m \ge m - 1$ or $-\frac{3}{4}m < m + 1$; $-\frac{7}{4}m \ge -1$ or $-\frac{7}{4}m < 1$; $m \le \frac{4}{7}$ or $m > -\frac{4}{7}$; {real numbers}

−3 −2 −1 0 1 2 3

28. $3z + 7 \le 4z$ and $3z + 7 > -4z$; $7 \le z$ and $7 > -7z$; $7 \le z$ and $-1 < z$; $\{z : z \ge 7\}$

0 2 4 6 8 10 12

29. $-3 \le -2(t - 3) < 6$; $\frac{3}{2} \ge t - 3 > -3$; $\frac{9}{2} \ge t > 0$; $\left\{t : 0 < t \le \frac{9}{2}\right\}$

30. $-5 < 2(2 - s) + 1 \le 9$; $-6 < 2(2 - s) \le 8$; $-3 < 2 - s \le 4$; $-5 < -s \le 2$; $5 > s \ge -2$; $\{s : -2 \le s < 5\}$

31. $\frac{t}{4} + 2 < t + 3$ and $t - 3 > \frac{t}{2} - 4$; $-\frac{3t}{4} < 1$ and $\frac{t}{2} > -1$; $t > -\frac{4}{3}$ and $t > -2$; $\left\{t : t > -\frac{4}{3}\right\}$

32. $\frac{r - 3}{6} \le r - 1$ or $\frac{r - 6}{3} \le r + 4$; $r - 3 \le 6(r - 1)$ or $r - 6 \le 3(r + 4)$; $r - 3 \le 6r - 6$ or $r - 6 \le 3r + 12$; $3 \le 5r$ or $-18 \le 2r$; $\frac{3}{5} \le r$ or $-9 \le r$; $\{r : r \ge -9\}$

C **33.** $0 < 1 - x \le 3$ or $-1 \le 2x - 3 \le 5$; $-1 < -x \le 2$ or $2 \le 2x \le 8$; $1 > x \ge -2$ or $1 \le x \le 4$; $\{x : -2 \le x \le 4\}$

34. $1 < -(2s + 1) < 5$ or $1 < 2s - 1 < 5$; $-1 > 2s + 1 > -5$ or $2 < 2s < 6$; $-2 > 2s > -6$ or $1 < s < 3$; $-1 > s > -3$ or $1 < s < 3$; $\{s : -3 < s < -1 \text{ or } 1 < s < 3\}$

35. $2 < \frac{y + 6}{2} < 5$ and $(4 - y > 5$ or $4 + y > 7)$; $4 < y + 6 < 10$ and $(-y > 1$ or $y > 3)$; $-2 < y < 4$ and $(y < -1$ or $y > 3)$; $\{y : -2 < y < -1 \text{ or } 3 < y < 4\}$

36. $\left(x \le \frac{x + 4}{3} + 2 \text{ or } x \ge 2x - 1\right)$ and $1 \le \frac{x - 1}{2} \le 3$; $(3x \le x + 4 + 6$ or $1 \ge x)$ and $2 \le x - 1 \le 6$; $(2x \le 10$ or $1 \ge x)$ and $3 \le x \le 7$; $(x \le 5$ or $x \le 1)$ and $3 \le x \le 7$; $x \le 5$ and $3 \le x \le 7$; $\{x : 3 \le x \le 5\}$

Pages 71–72 • PROBLEMS

A **1.** Let x = the number of games attended. Then $9x$ = the cost of the separate tickets. $9x \le 580$; $x \le \frac{580}{9}$; $x \le 64\frac{4}{9}$. The number of games is at most 64.

2. Let x = the number of trips through the tunnel. Without a sticker, the trips cost $0.50x$. With a sticker, the trips cost $5.50 + 0.35x$. $5.50 + 0.35x < 0.50x$; $5.50 < 0.15x$; $x > \frac{5.50}{0.15}$; $x > 36\frac{2}{3}$. At least 37 trips are needed.

3. Let w = the width of the rectangle. Then $2w + 5$ = the length. $2w + 2(2w + 5) \le 64$; $2w + 4w + 10 \le 64$; $6w \le 54$; $w \le 9$. The largest possible width is 9 cm.

4. Let x = the length of a leg. Then $\frac{1}{2}x$ = the length of the base. $6 < x + x + \frac{1}{2}x < 16$; $6 < \frac{5}{2}x < 16$; $\frac{12}{5} < x < \frac{32}{5}$; $2\frac{2}{5} < x < 6\frac{2}{5}$. Since the lengths of the legs are integers, the possibilities are 3, 4, 5, or 6 units.

5. Let the consecutive odd integers be x, $x + 2$, and $x + 4$. $20 < x + (x + 2) + (x + 4) < 30$; $20 < 3x + 6 < 30$; $14 < 3x < 24$; $\frac{14}{3} < x < 8$; $4\frac{2}{3} < x < 8$. Since x is an odd integer, $x = 5$ or $x = 7$. The possible sets are {5, 7, 9} and {7, 9, 11}.

6. Let the consecutive even integers be x, $x + 2$, and $x + 4$. Then $25 < x + (x + 2) + (x + 4) < 45$; $25 < 3x + 6 < 45$; $19 < 3x < 39$; $\frac{19}{3} < x < 13$; $6\frac{1}{3} < x < 13$. Since x is an even integer, $x = 8$, $x = 10$, or $x = 12$. The sets are {8, 10, 12}, {10, 12, 14}, and {12, 14, 16}.

7. Let x = her score on her next test. $\frac{1}{5}(80 + 65 + 87 + 75 + x) \ge 80$; $307 + x \ge 400$; $x \ge 93$. Her score will have to be at least 93.

8. Let x = Jim's first score. Then $x + 8$ = his second score. His average was $\frac{1}{3}(x + x + 8 + 88)$. $80 \le \frac{1}{3}(x + x + 8 + 88) \le 89$; $240 \le 2x + 96 \le 267$; $144 \le 2x \le 171$; $72 \le x \le 85.5$. Jim's first score was between 72 and 85.5, inclusive.

9. Let x = the length of a side of the square. Then $x + 6$ and $x + 10$ are the length and width of the rectangle. $4x$ = the perimeter of the square, and $2(x + 6) + 2(x + 10)$ = the perimeter of the rectangle. $2(x + 6) + 2(x + 10) \ge 2(4x)$; $4x + 32 \ge 8x$; $32 \ge 4x$; $8 \ge x$. The side of the square is at most 8 cm.

10. Let x = the length of a side of the original triangle. Then $x + 20$, $x + 30$, and $x + 40$ are the lengths of the sides of the new triangle. $2(3x) < (x + 20) + (x + 30) + (x + 40) < 3(3x)$; $6x < 3x + 90 < 9x$; $6x < 3x + 90$ and $3x + 90 < 9x$; $3x < 90$ and $90 < 6x$; $x < 30$ and $15 < x$; $15 < x < 30$. The sides of the original triangle are between 15 cm and 30 cm long.

B 11. Let x = the minutes of telephone use each month. Then $6.50 + 0.10(x - 40)$ = the cost of calls using Plan B. $18.50 < 6.50 + 0.10(x - 40)$; $12 < 0.10(x - 40)$; $120 < x - 40$; $160 < x$. Plan A is better if more than 160 min of calls are made.

12. Let r = Roger's average speed during the final 30 mi. Since time = $\frac{\text{distance}}{\text{rate}}$, $\frac{20}{16} + \frac{30}{r} < 2.5$; $\frac{30}{r} < 1.25$; $30 < 1.25r$; $24 < r$. He must average more than 24 mi/h.

13. Let t = the length in min of each stop. Since 36 km/h = 0.6 km/min, $\frac{21}{20 + 6t} \ge 0.6$; $21 \ge 0.6(20 + 6t)$; $21 \ge 12 + 3.6t$; $9 \ge 3.6t$; $2.5 \ge t$. Each stop can last at most 2.5 or $2\frac{1}{2}$ min.

14. Let w = the width, in cm, of the original rectangle. Then $2w$ = the length. After trimming, the width and length are $w - 2$ and $2w - 2$. Since 1 m = 100 cm, $2(w - 2) + 2(2w - 2) \leq 100$; $6w - 8 \leq 100$; $w \leq 18$. The largest possible dimensions of the trimmed sheet are 16 cm by 34 cm.

C **15.** Let x = the width, in m, of the pool. Then the other dimensions are as shown. $(x + 4)(x + 9) \geq x(x + 5) + 140$; $x^2 + 13x + 36 \geq x^2 + 5x + 140$; $8x \geq 104$; $x \geq 13$. The pool is at least 13 m by 18 m.

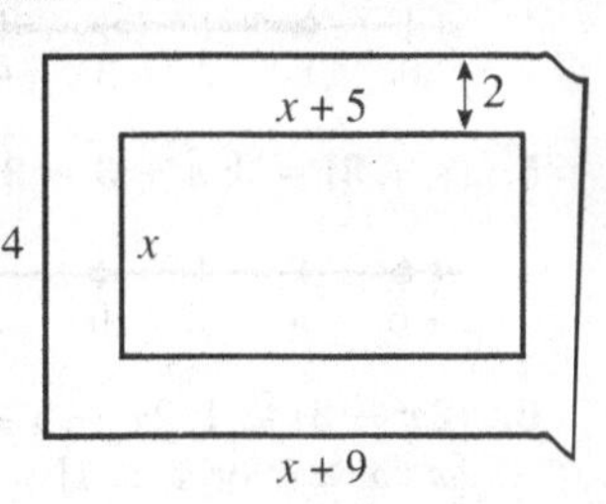

16. Let the consecutive integers be x, $x + 1$, and $x + 2$. $11(x + 2) \geq x(x + 1) + 46$; $11x + 22 \geq x^2 + x + 46$; $0 \geq x^2 - 10x + 24$; $0 \geq (x - 6)(x - 4)$; $x - 6 \leq 0$ and $x - 4 \geq 0$; $x \leq 6$ and $x \geq 4$. The triples are {4, 5, 6}, {5, 6, 7}, and {6, 7, 8}.

Page 72 • MIXED REVIEW EXERCISES

1. $3x - 2 \geq -8$; $3x \geq -6$; $x \geq -2$; $\{x : x \geq -2\}$

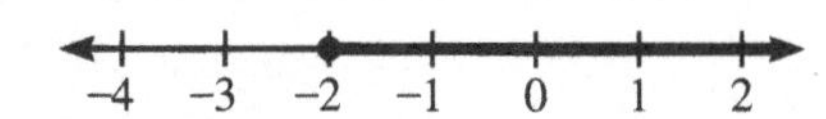

2. $\frac{1}{2}t \leq -2$ or $t - 4 \geq -3$; $t \leq -4$ or $t \geq 1$; $\{t : t \leq -4 \text{ or } t \geq 1\}$

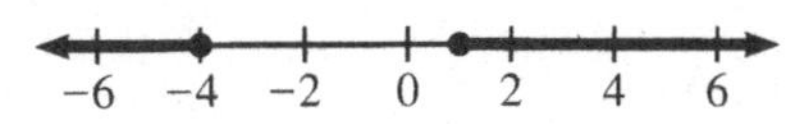

3. $2(m - 2) > 4 - 3(1 - m)$; $2m - 4 > 4 - 3 + 3m$; $-1m > 5$; $m < -5$; $\{m : m <$ -

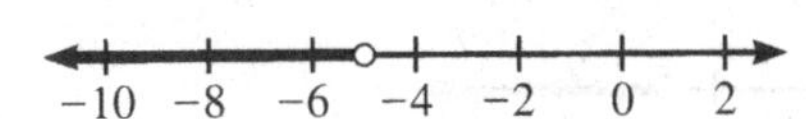

4. $-2y < -6$ and $y + 3 \leq 1$; $y > 3$ and $y \leq -2$; $\emptyset$

5. $7 - 4d < 3$; $-4d < -4$; $d > 1$; $\{d : d > 1\}$

−2 −1 0 1 2 3 4

6. $-1 < 5 - 2p < 5$; $-6 < -2p < 0$; $3 > p > 0$; $\{p : 0 < p < 3\}$

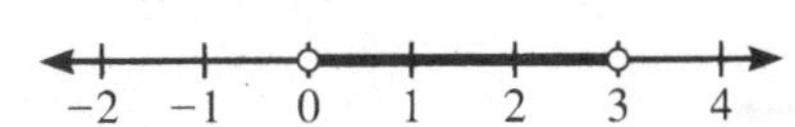

7. $|x + y| = |-7 + 3| = |-4| = 4$ **8.** $|x| + |y| = |-7| + |3| = 7 + 3 = 10$

9. $|xy| = |(-7)(3)| = |-21| = 21$ **10.** $|x| \cdot |y| = |-7| \cdot |3| = 7 \cdot 3 = 21$

Page 75 • WRITTEN EXERCISES

A **1.** $|x| \leq 3$; $\{x : -3 \leq x \leq 3\}$

−6 −4 −2 0 2 4 6

2. $|t| = 2$; $\{2, -2\}$

−3 −2 −1 0 1 2 3

3. $|z| > 0$; $\{z : z \neq 0\}$

4. $|y - 3| \leq 2$; $y - 3 \leq 2$ and $y - 3 \geq -2$; $y \leq 5$ and $y \geq 1$; $\{y : 1 \leq y \leq 5\}$

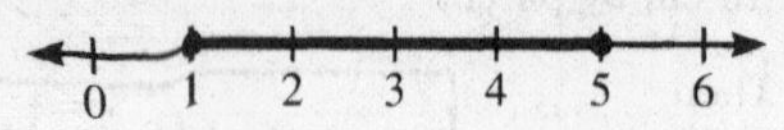

5. $|s + 3| = 3$; $s + 3 = 3$ or $s + 3 = -3$; $s = 0$ or $s = -6$; $\{0, -6\}$

6. $|2x - 3| \geq 1$; $2x - 3 \geq 1$ or $2x - 3 \leq -1$; $2x \geq 4$ or $2x \leq 2$; $x \geq 2$ or $x \leq 1$; $\{x : x \geq 2 \text{ or } x \leq 1\}$

7. $|3t - 1| \leq 2$; $-2 \leq 3t - 1 \leq 2$; $-1 \leq 3t \leq 3$; $-\frac{1}{3} \leq t \leq 1$; $\left\{t : -\frac{1}{3} \leq t \leq 1\right\}$

8. $|5 - 2z| < 3$; $-3 < 5 - 2z < 3$; $-8 < -2z < -2$; $4 > z > 1$; $\{z : 1 < z < 4\}$

9. $|2t + 5| < 3$; $-3 < 2t + 5 < 3$; $-8 < 2t < -2$; $-4 < t < -1$; $\{t : -4 < t < -1\}$

10. $|3x + 2| > 4$; $3x + 2 > 4$ or $3x + 2 < -4$; $3x > 2$ or $3x < -6$; $x > \frac{2}{3}$ or $x < -2$; $\left\{x : x < -2 \text{ or } x > \frac{2}{3}\right\}$

11. $|2u - 5| = 0$; $2u - 5 = 0$; $2u = 5$; $u = \frac{5}{2}$; $\left\{\frac{5}{2}\right\}$

12. $8 = |5y + 2|$; $5y + 2 = 8$ or $5y + 2 = -8$; $5y = 6$ or $5y = -10$; $y = \frac{6}{5}$ or $y = -2$; $\left\{-2, \frac{6}{5}\right\}$

13. $\left|1 - \frac{x}{3}\right| \geq \frac{2}{3}$; $1 - \frac{x}{3} \geq \frac{2}{3}$ or $1 - \frac{x}{3} \leq -\frac{2}{3}$; $-\frac{x}{3} \geq -\frac{1}{3}$ or $-\frac{x}{3} \leq -\frac{5}{3}$; $x \leq 1$ or $x \geq 5$; $\{x : x \leq 1 \text{ or } x \geq 5\}$

14. $\left|1 - \frac{p}{2}\right| \leq 2$; $-2 \leq 1 - \frac{p}{2} \leq 2$; $-3 \leq -\frac{p}{2} \leq 1$; $6 \geq p \geq -2$; $\{p : -2 \leq p \leq 6\}$

15. $0 \le |4u - 7|$; {real numbers}

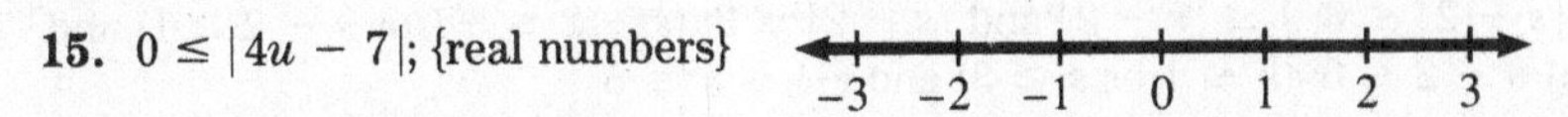

16. $|3r - 12| > 0$; $3r - 12 \ne 0$; $r \ne 4$; $\{r : r \ne 4\}$

0 1 2 3 4 5 6

17. $\left|\frac{t-2}{4}\right| \le \frac{1}{2}$; $-\frac{1}{2} \le \frac{t-2}{4} \le \frac{1}{2}$; $-2 \le t - 2 \le 2$; $0 \le t \le 4$; $\{t : 0 \le t \le 4\}$

-1 0 1 2 3 4 5

18. $1 > |2 - 0.8n|$; $-1 < 2 - 0.8n < 1$; $-3 < -0.8n < -1$; $\frac{15}{4} > n > \frac{5}{4}$;

$\left\{n : \frac{5}{4} < n < \frac{15}{4}\right\}$

1 2 3 4

B

19. $|x + 5| - 3 = 1$; $|x + 5| = 4$; $x + 5 = 4$ or $x + 5 = -4$; $x = -1$ or $x = -9$; $\{-1, -9\}$

20. $|2t - 3| + 2 = 5$; $|2t - 3| = 3$; $2t - 3 = 3$ or $2t - 3 = -3$; $2t = 6$ or $2t = 0$; $t = 3$ or $t = 0$; $\{0, 3\}$

21. $|2u - 1| + 3 \le 6$; $|2u - 1| \le 3$; $-3 \le 2u - 1 \le 3$; $-2 \le 2u \le 4$; $-1 \le u \le 2$; $\{u : -1 \le u \le 2\}$

22. $4 - |3k + 1| < 2$; $-|3k + 1| < -2$; $|3k + 1| > 2$; $3k + 1 > 2$ or $3k + 1 < -2$;

$3k > 1$ or $3k < -3$; $k > \frac{1}{3}$ or $k < -1$; $\left\{k : k < -1 \text{ or } k > \frac{1}{3}\right\}$

23. $7 - 3|4d - 7| \ge 4$; $-3|4d - 7| \ge -3$; $|4d - 7| \le 1$; $-1 \le 4d - 7 \le 1$;

$6 \le 4d \le 8$; $\frac{3}{2} \le d \le 2$; $\left\{d : \frac{3}{2} \le d \le 2\right\}$

24. $6 + 5|2r - 3| \ge 4$; $5|2r - 3| \ge -2$; $|2r - 3| \ge -\frac{2}{5}$; {real numbers}

25. $4 + 2\left|\frac{3t-5}{2}\right| > 5$; $2\left|\frac{3t-5}{2}\right| > 1$; $\left|\frac{3t-5}{2}\right| > \frac{1}{2}$; $\frac{3t-5}{2} > \frac{1}{2}$ or $\frac{3t-5}{2} < -\frac{1}{2}$;

$3t - 5 > 1$ or $3t - 5 < -1$; $3t > 6$ or $3t < 4$; $t > 2$ or $t < \frac{4}{3}$; $\left\{t : t < \frac{4}{3} \text{ or } t > 2\right\}$

26. $2\left|\frac{2t-5}{3}\right| - 3 \ge 5$; $2\left|\frac{2t-5}{3}\right| \ge 8$; $\left|\frac{2t-5}{3}\right| \ge 4$; $\frac{2t-5}{3} \ge 4$ or $\frac{2t-5}{3} \le -4$;

$2t - 5 \ge 12$ or $2t - 5 \le -12$; $t \ge \frac{17}{2}$ or $t \le -\frac{7}{2}$; $\left\{t : t \le -\frac{7}{2} \text{ or } t \ge \frac{17}{2}\right\}$

27. $7 + 5|c| \le 1 - 3|c|$; $8|c| \le -6$; $|c| \le -\frac{3}{4}$; $\emptyset$

28. $\frac{1}{2}|d| + 5 \ge 2|d| - 13$; $18 \ge \frac{3}{2}|d|$; $12 \ge |d|$; $-12 \le d \le 12$; $\{d : -12 \le d \le 12\}$

C

29. $2 < |w| < 4$; $2 < |w|$ and $|w| < 4$; ($w < -2$ or $w > 2$) and $-4 < w < 4$

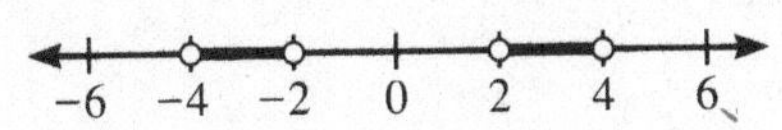

30. $1 \le |s - 2| \le 3$; $1 \le |s - 2|$ and $|s - 2| \le 3$; $(s - 2 \le -1$ or $s - 2 \ge 1)$ and $-3 \le s - 2 \le 3$; $(s \le 1$ or $s \ge 3)$ and $-1 \le s \le 5$

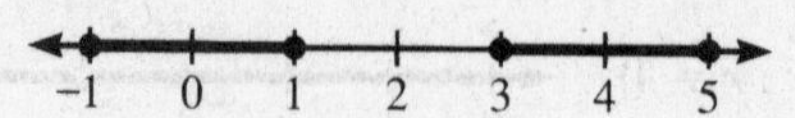

31. $1 \le |2x + 1| < 3$; $1 \le |2x + 1|$ and $|2x + 1| < 3$; $(2x + 1 \ge 1$ or $2x + 1 \le -1)$ and $-3 < 2x + 1 < 3$; $(x \ge 0$ or $x \le -1)$ and $-2 < x < 1$

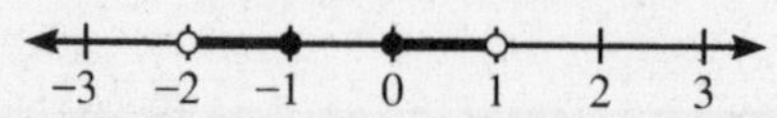

32. $0 < |2 - r| \le 2$; $0 < |2 - r|$ and $|2 - r| \le 2$; $r \ne 2$ and $-2 \le 2 - r \le 2$; $r \ne 2$ and $-4 \le -r \le 0$; $r \ne 2$ and $4 \ge r \ge 0$

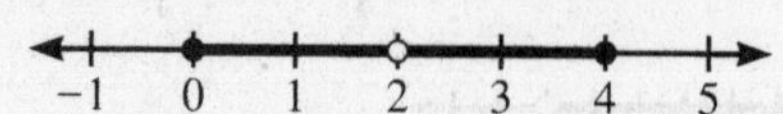

33. $|2x| \le |x - 3|$; $x - 3 \ge |2x|$ or $x - 3 \le -|2x|$; $[-(x - 3) \le 2x \le x - 3]$ or $-(x - 3) \ge |2x|$; $[-x + 3 \le 2x \le x - 3]$ or $[(x - 3) \le 2x \le -(x - 3)]$; $[x \ge 1$ and $x \le -3]$ or $[x \ge -3$ and $x \le 1]$; $\{x : -3 \le x \le 1\}$

34. $|t| > |2t - 6|$; $t > |2t - 6|$ or $t < -|2t - 6|$; $(-t < 2t - 6 < t)$ or $(t < 2t - 6 < -t)$; $(t > 2$ and $t < 6)$ or $(t > 6$ and $t < 2)$; $\{t : 2 < t < 6\}$

Page 75 • COMPUTER EXERCISES

1.
```
10 LET K = 0
20 INPUT "ENTER VALUES OF A, B, C, D:"; A, B, C, D
30 FOR X = -50 TO 50
40 IF A > = ABS (C * X + D) THEN 80
50 IF ABS (C * X + D) > = B THEN 80
60 PRINT X; "IS A SOLUTION."
70 LET K = K + 1
80 NEXT X
90 IF K > 0 THEN 110
100 PRINT "THERE ARE NO SOLUTIONS."
110 END
```

2. a. $\{-3, -2, -1, 0, 1, 2, 15, 16, 17, 18, 19\}$

b. $\{-12, -11, -10, -9, -8, -7, -6, -5, -4, -3, -2\}$

Pages 78–79 • WRITTEN EXERCISES

A **1.** $\{-4, 4\}$

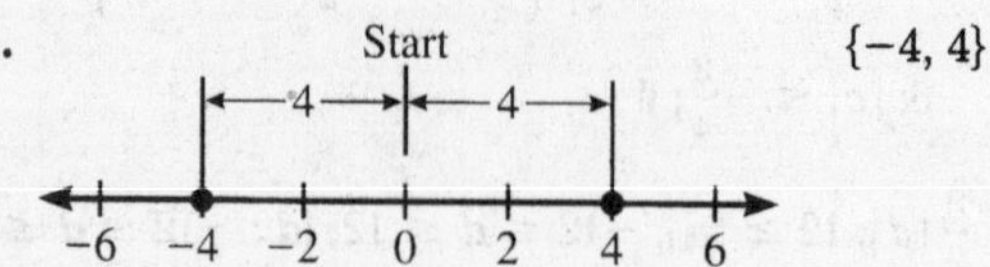

2. $\{1, 5\}$

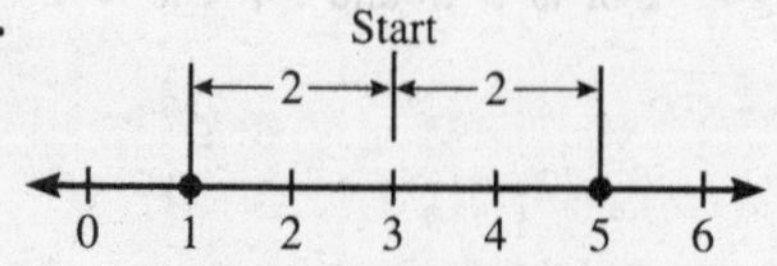

3.

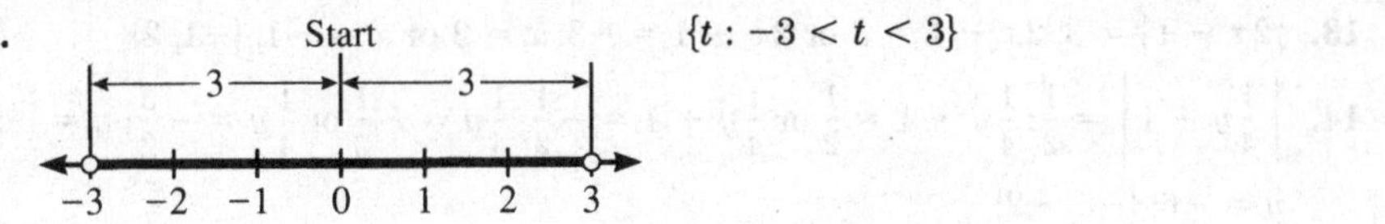

$\{t : -3 < t < 3\}$

4.

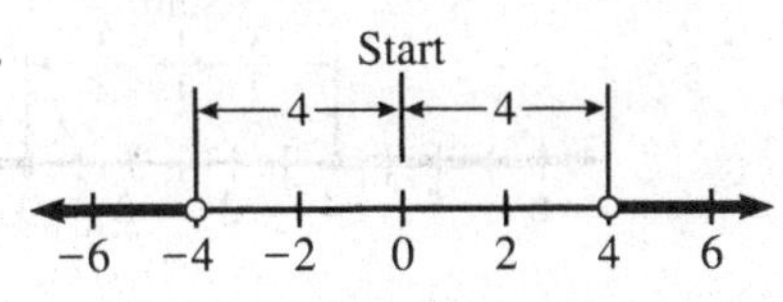

$\{y : y < -4 \text{ or } y > 4\}$

5.

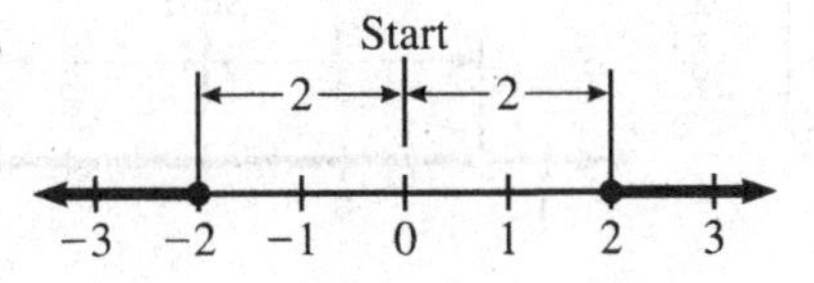

$\{u : u \leq -2 \text{ or } u \geq 2\}$

6.

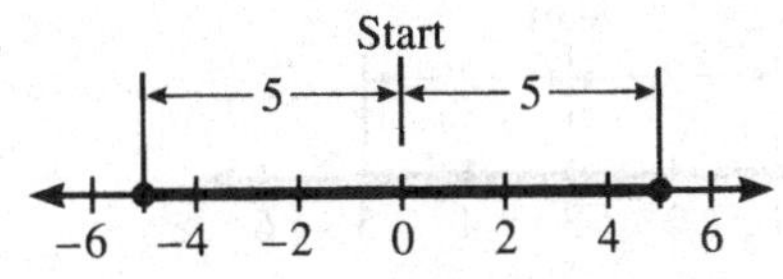

$\{p : -5 \leq p \leq 5\}$

7.

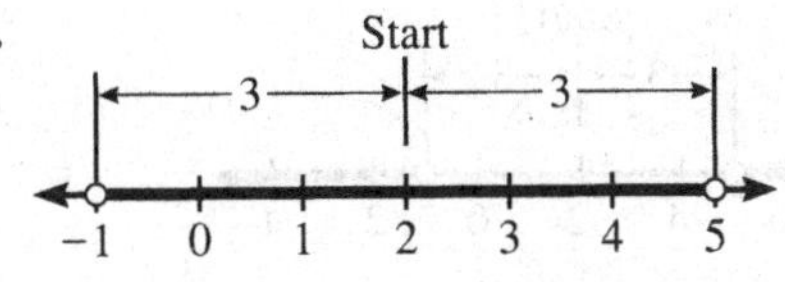

$\{y : -1 < y < 5\}$

8.

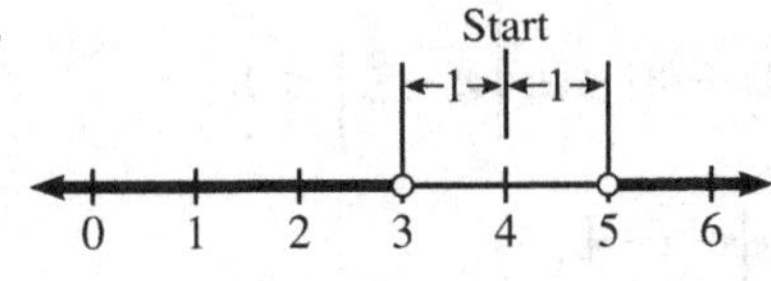

$\{k : k < 3 \text{ or } k > 5\}$

9.

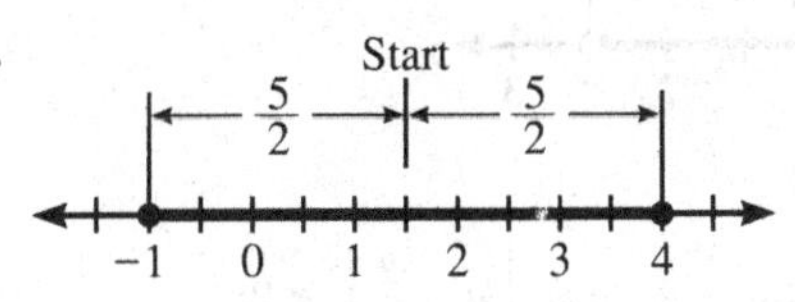

$\{t : -1 \leq t \leq 4\}$

10.

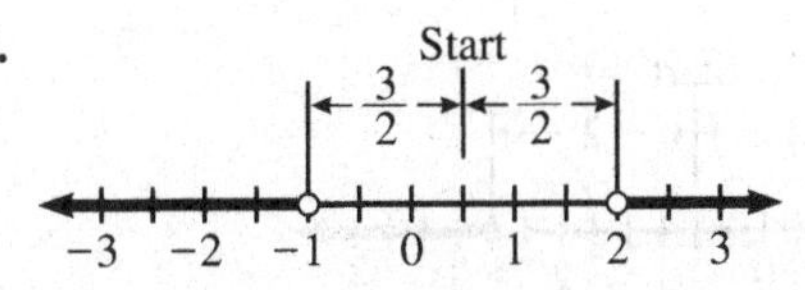

$\{x : x < -1 \text{ or } x > 2\}$

11.

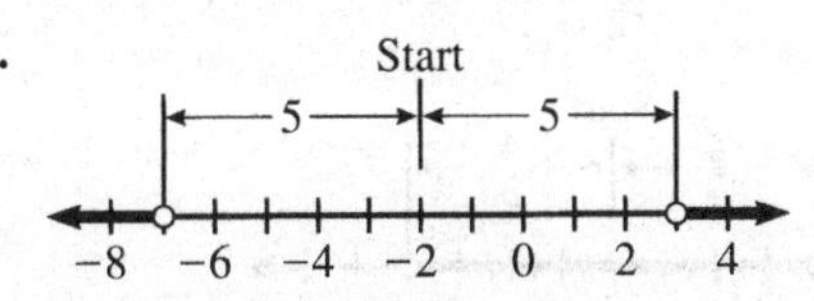

$\{r : r < -7 \text{ or } r > 3\}$

12.

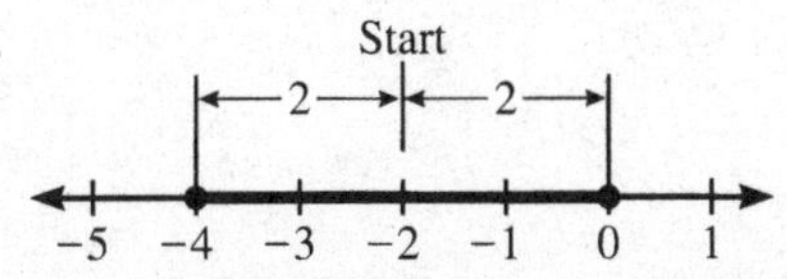

$\{w : -4 \leq w \leq 0\}$

B

13. $|2x - 1| = 3$; $2x - 1 = 3$ or $2x - 1 = -3$; $x = 2$ or $x = -1$; $\{-1, 2\}$

14. $\left|\frac{1}{4}y + 1\right| = \frac{1}{2}$; $\frac{1}{4}y + 1 = \frac{1}{2}$ or $\frac{1}{4}y + 1 = -\frac{1}{2}$; $\frac{1}{4}y = -\frac{1}{2}$ or $\frac{1}{4}y = -\frac{3}{2}$; $y = -2$ or $y = -6$; $\{-6, -2\}$

15. $|2p + 5| \geq 3$; $2\left|p + \frac{5}{2}\right| \geq 3$; $\left|p + \frac{5}{2}\right| \geq \frac{3}{2}$;

$\{p : p \leq -4 \text{ or } p \geq -1\}$

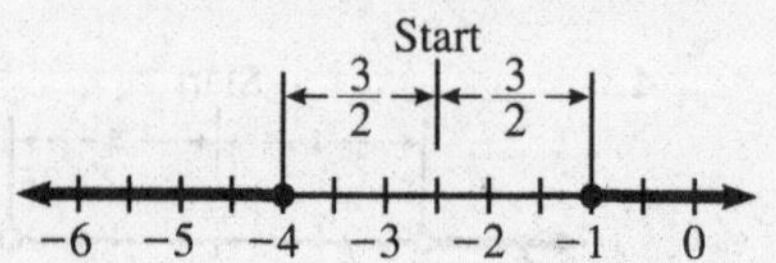

16. $|3k - 2| < 4$; $3\left|k - \frac{2}{3}\right| < 4$; $\left|k - \frac{2}{3}\right| < \frac{4}{3}$;

$\left\{k : -\frac{2}{3} < k < 2\right\}$

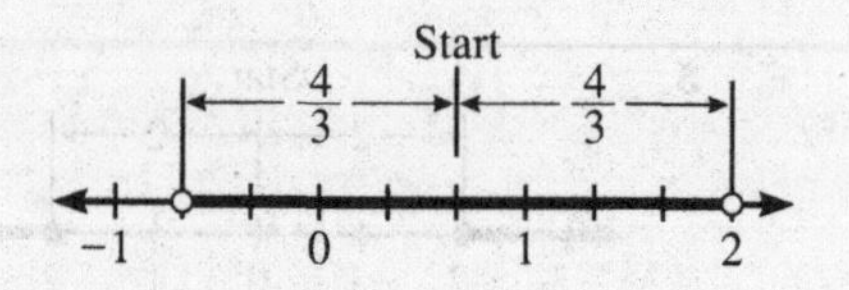

17. $\left|\frac{1}{3}t - 1\right| \leq \frac{2}{3}$; $|t - 3| \leq 2$;

$\{t : 1 \leq t \leq 5\}$

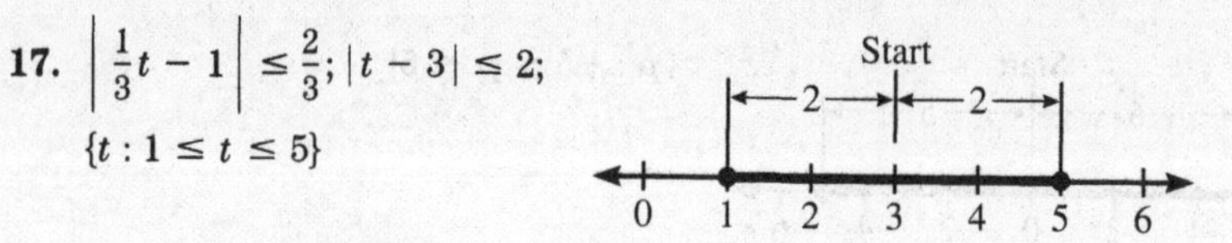

18. $\left|\frac{y}{4} + \frac{1}{2}\right| > \frac{3}{4}$; $|y + 2| > 3$;

$\{y : y < -5 \text{ or } y > 1\}$

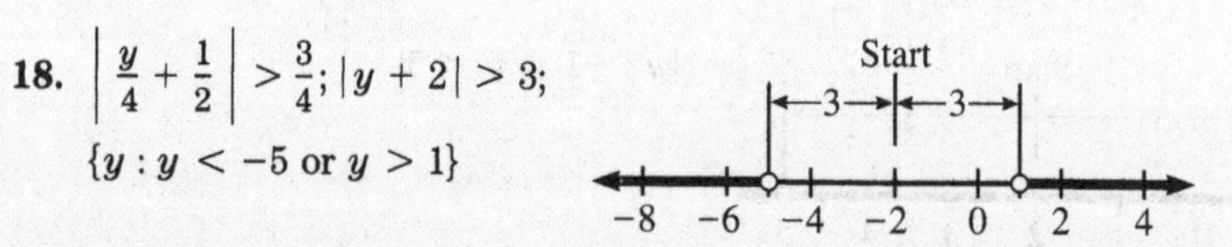

19. $3 - |2x - 3| > 1$; $-|2x - 3| > -2$; $|2x - 3| < 2$; $\left|x - \frac{3}{2}\right| < 1$;

$\left\{x : \frac{1}{2} < x < \frac{5}{2}\right\}$

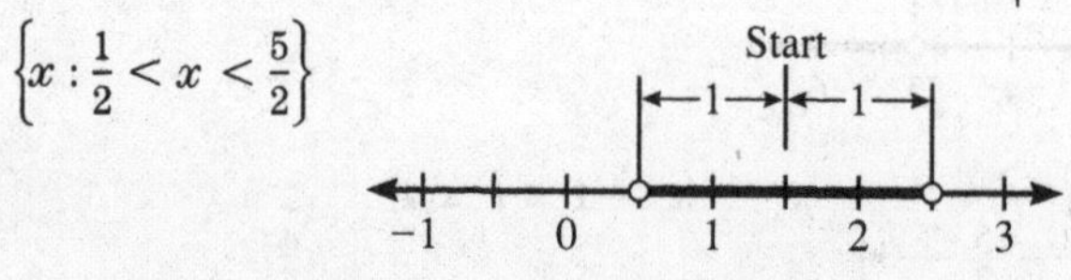

20. $7 - |3y - 2| \leq 1$; $-|3y - 2| \leq -6$; $|3y - 2| \geq 6$; $\left|y - \frac{2}{3}\right| \geq 2$;

$\left\{y : y \leq -\frac{4}{3} \text{ or } y \geq \frac{8}{3}\right\}$

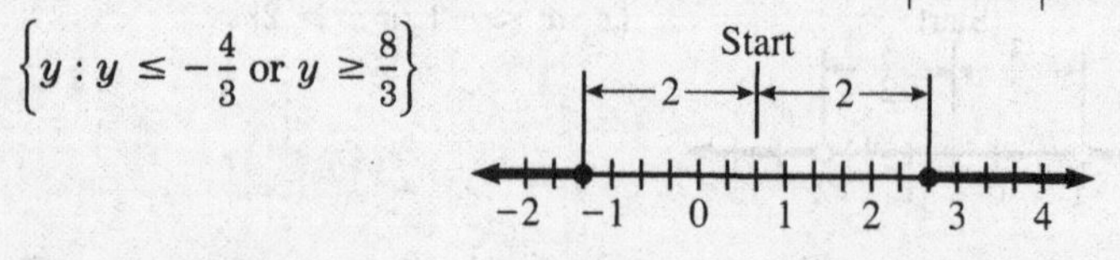

21. $|9 + 3f| < 4$; $|3 + f| < \frac{4}{3}$;

$\left\{f : -\frac{13}{3} < f < -\frac{5}{3}\right\}$

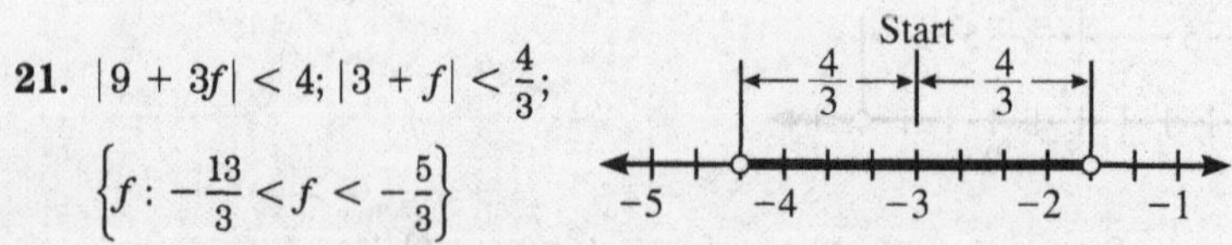
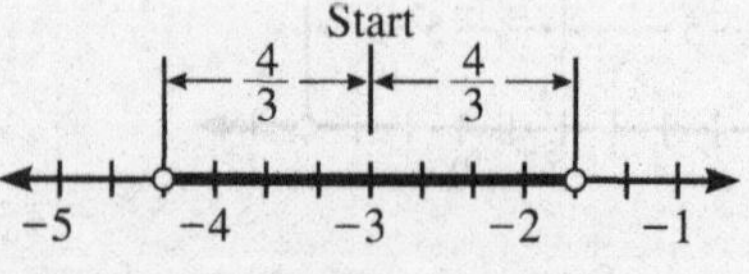

22. $|4 + 2y| \geq 3$; $|2 + y| \geq \frac{3}{2}$;

$\left\{y : y \leq -\frac{7}{2} \text{ or } y \geq -\frac{1}{2}\right\}$

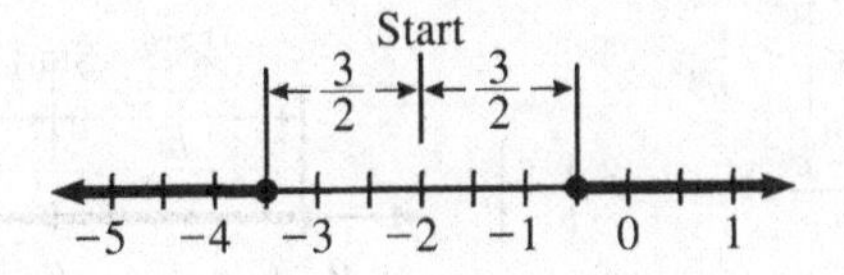

23. $|1.2 + 0.4t| < 2$; $|3 + t| < 5$;
$\{t : -8 < t < 2\}$

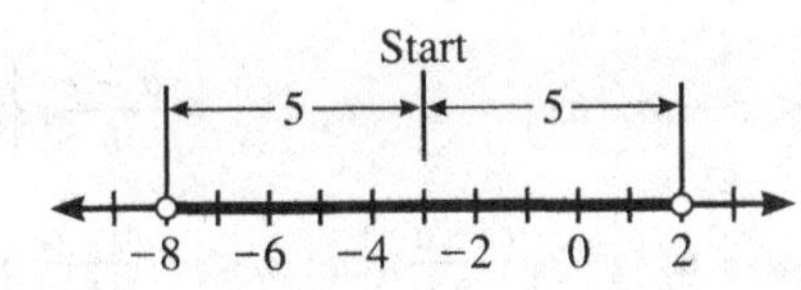

24. $|1 - 0.3x| \geq 1.5$; $\left|\frac{10}{3} - x\right| \geq 5$; $\left|x - \frac{10}{3}\right| \geq 5$;

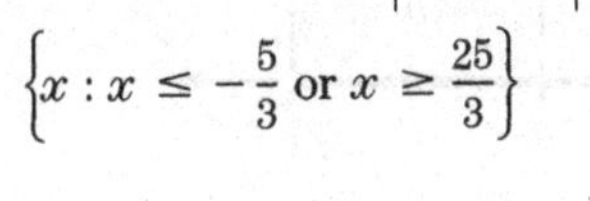
$\left\{x : x \leq -\frac{5}{3} \text{ or } x \geq \frac{25}{3}\right\}$

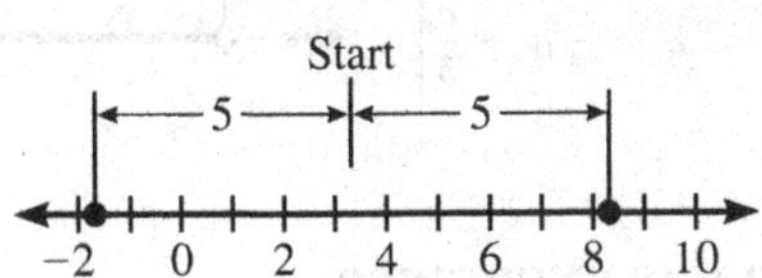

C **25.** $\{x : x \leq a - c \text{ or } x \geq a + c\}$

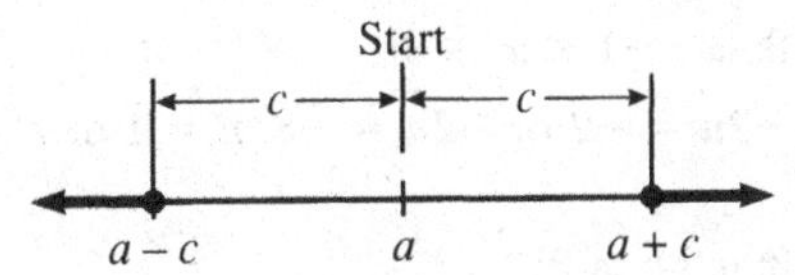

26. $\{x : -a - c \leq x \leq -a + c\}$

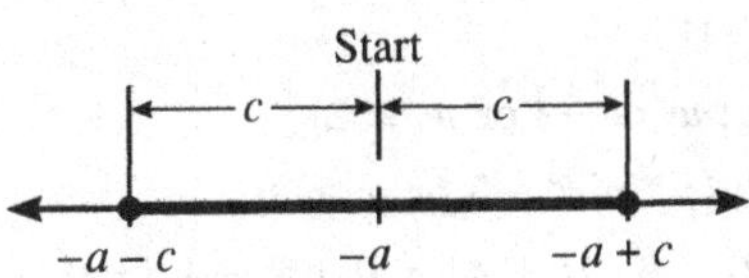

27. $\{x : 0 < x < 2c\}$

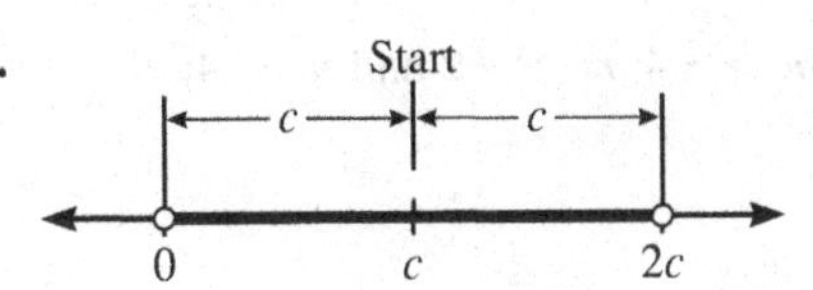

28. $\{x : x < -2c \text{ or } x > 0\}$

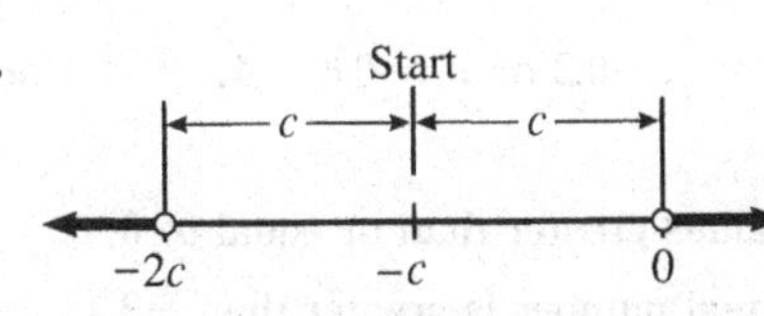

29. $\left|\frac{a}{b} + x\right| \geq \frac{c}{b}$;

$\left\{x : x \leq \frac{-a - c}{b} \text{ or } x \geq \frac{-a + c}{b}\right\}$

Start: $\frac{c}{b}$, $\frac{c}{b}$; $\frac{-a-c}{b}$, $\frac{-a}{b}$, $\frac{-a+c}{b}$

30. $\left|\frac{a}{b} - x\right| \le \frac{c}{b}$; $\left\{x : \frac{a-c}{b} \le x \le \frac{a+c}{b}\right\}$

Start; $\frac{c}{b}$; $\frac{c}{b}$; $\frac{a-c}{b}$; $\frac{a}{b}$; $\frac{a+c}{b}$

31. $-|bx| < c - a$; $|bx| > a - c$; $|x| > \frac{a-c}{b}$; $\left\{x : x < -\frac{a-c}{b} \text{ or } x > \frac{a-c}{b}\right\}$

32. $|bx| > c - a$; $|x| > \frac{c-a}{b}$; $\left\{x : x < -\frac{c-a}{b} \text{ or } x > \frac{c-a}{b}\right\}$

33. $|x + a| < \frac{c}{b}$; $\left\{x : -a - \frac{c}{b} < x < -a + \frac{c}{b}\right\}$

Start; $\frac{c}{b}$; $\frac{c}{b}$; $-a - \frac{c}{b}$; $-a$; $-a + \frac{c}{b}$

Page 79 • MIXED REVIEW EXERCISES

1. $1 \le 3x + 4 \le 13$; $-3 \le 3x \le 9$; $-1 \le x \le 3$; $\{x : -1 \le x \le 3\}$

2. $|5 - 2n| = 3$; $5 - 2n = 3$ or $5 - 2n = -3$; $-2n = -2$ or $-2n = -8$; $n = 1$ or $n = 4$; $\{1, 4\}$

3. $4(2c - 3) > 7c - 9$; $8c - 12 > 7c - 9$; $c > 3$; $\{c : c > 3\}$

4. $|6y + 6| > 0$; $6y + 6 \ne 0$; $y \ne -1$; $\{y : y \ne -1\}$

5. $|w| + 4 \ge 6$; $|w| \ge 2$; $w \ge 2$ or $w \le -2$; $\{w : w \le -2 \text{ or } w \ge 2\}$

6. $p + 2 < -1$ or $-4p \le -8$; $p < -3$ or $p \ge 2$; $\{p : p < -3 \text{ or } p \ge 2\}$

7. $5z + 11 \le 1$; $5z \le -10$; $z \le -2$; $\{z : z \le -2\}$ **8.** $|t + 4| = 0$; $t = -4$; $\{-4\}$

9. $\frac{1}{2}m > -1$ and $5 - m > 1$; $m > -2$ and $-m > -4$; $m > -2$ and $m < 4$; $\{m : -2 < m < 4\}$

Page 80 • COMPUTER KEY-IN

1. $-1.5 < x < 4$ **2.** $x < -5$ or $x > -4$ **3.** $x < -0.2$ or $x > 0.6$ **4.** $x < 1$ or $x > 9$

5. $-8 < x < 5$ **6.** $-1 < x < 3$

7. No solution; all real numbers have absolute values greater than or equal to 0.

8. Any real number; the absolute value of every real number is greater than -3.

Pages 85–87 • WRITTEN EXERCISES

A In Exercises 1–4, answers may vary.

1. $(-1)^2 = 1^2$ but $-1 \ne 1$ **2.** $1 < 2$ but $2 - 1 \not< 0$ **3.** $|0 - 1| \ne |0| - |1|$

4. $|-(-1)| \not< 0$

5. (1) Comm. prop. of mult.; (2) Proved in Example 4; (3) Comm. prop. of mult.

6. (1) Prop. of opp. of a prod.; (2) Prop. of opp. of a prod.; (3) Proved in Example 3

7. (1) Def. of subtr.; (2) Assoc. prop. of add.; (3) Prop. of opp.; (4) Ident. prop. of add.

8. (1) Given; (2) Add. prop. of eq.; (3) Assoc. prop. of add.; (4) Prop. of opp.; (5) Ident. prop. of add.

9. (1) Given; (2) Def. of u^2; (3) Prop. of recip.; (4) Mult. prop. of eq.; (5) Assoc. prop. of mult.; (6) Prop. of recip.; (7) Ident. prop. of mult.

10. (1) Given; (2) Prop. of recip.; (3) Mult. prop. of eq.; (4) Assoc. prop. of mult.; (5) Prop. of recip.; (6) Ident. prop. of mult.

11. (1) Given; (2) Prop. of recip.; (3) Mult. prop. of eq.; (4) Mult. prop. of 0; (5) Assoc. prop. of mult.; (6) Prop. of recip.; (7) Ident. prop. of mult.; (8) Steps 2–7

12. (1) Def. of subtr.; (2) Dist. prop.; (3) prop. of opp. of a prod.; (4) Def. of subtr.

13. (1) Given; prop. of recip.; (2) Def. of div.; (3) Distr. prop. of mult. with respect to subtr.; (4) Def. of div.

14. (1) Given; (2) Prop. of recip.; (3) Mult. prop. of eq.; (4) Assoc. prop. of mult.; (5) Prop. of recip.; (6) Ident. prop. of mult.

B **15.** (1) $a \neq 0$ (Given); (2) $\frac{1}{a} \cdot a = 1$ (Prop. of recip.); (3) $\frac{1}{a} \cdot \frac{1}{\frac{1}{a}} = 1$ (Prop. of recip.); (4) $\therefore a = \frac{1}{\frac{1}{a}}$ (Steps 2 and 3 and prop. of recip. (uniqueness))

16. (1) $b \neq 0$ (Given); (2) $\frac{-a}{b} = (-a) \cdot \left(\frac{1}{b}\right)$ (Def. of div.); (3) $\frac{-a}{b} = -\left(a \cdot \frac{1}{b}\right)$ (Prop. of opp. of a prod.); (4) $\therefore \frac{-a}{b} = -\frac{a}{b}$ (Def. of div.)

17. (1) $b \neq 0$ (Given); (2) $(-b)\left(-\frac{1}{b}\right) = b \cdot \frac{1}{b}$ (prod. of opp. (Ex. 6)); (3) $(-b)\left(-\frac{1}{b}\right) = 1$ (Prop. of recip.); (4) $\therefore -\frac{1}{b} = \frac{1}{-b}$ (Prop. of recip. (uniqueness of recip. of $-b$))

18. (1) $b \neq 0$ (Given); (2) $\frac{a}{-b} = a\left(\frac{1}{-b}\right)$ (Def. of div.); (3) $\frac{a}{-b} = a\left(-\frac{1}{b}\right)$ (Proved in Ex. 17); (4) $\frac{a}{-b} = -\left(a \cdot \frac{1}{b}\right)$ (Prop. of opp. of a prod. (Ex. 5)); (5) $\therefore \frac{a}{-b} = -\frac{a}{b}$ (Def. of div.)

19. (1) $b \neq 0$ (Given); (2) $\frac{-a}{-b} = (-a)\left(\frac{1}{-b}\right)$ (Def. of div.); (3) $\frac{-a}{-b} = (-a)\left(-\frac{1}{b}\right)$ (Proved in Ex. 17); (4) $\frac{-a}{-b} = a \cdot \frac{1}{b}$ (Prop. of prod. of opp. (Ex. 6)); (5) $\therefore \frac{-a}{-b} = \frac{a}{b}$ (Def. of div.)

20. (1) $a \neq 0, b \neq 0$ (Given); (2) $(ab)\left(\frac{1}{a} \cdot \frac{1}{b}\right) = \left(a \cdot \frac{1}{a}\right)\left(b \cdot \frac{1}{b}\right)$ (Assoc. and comm. prop. of mult.); (3) $(ab)\left(\frac{1}{a} \cdot \frac{1}{b}\right) = 1 \cdot 1$ (Prop of recip.); (4) $(ab)\left(\frac{1}{a} \cdot \frac{1}{b}\right) = 1$ (Ident. prop. of mult.); (5) $\therefore \frac{1}{a} \cdot \frac{1}{b} = \frac{1}{ab}$ (Prop. of recip. (uniqueness of recip. of ab))

21. (1) $b \neq 0, d \neq 0$ (Given); (2) $\frac{a}{b} \cdot \frac{c}{d} = \left(a \cdot \frac{1}{b}\right)\left(c \cdot \frac{1}{d}\right)$ (Def. of div.);

(3) $\frac{a}{b} \cdot \frac{c}{d} = (ac)\left(\frac{1}{b} \cdot \frac{1}{d}\right)$ (Assoc. and comm. prop. of mult.); (4) $\frac{a}{b} \cdot \frac{c}{d} = (ac)\left(\frac{1}{bd}\right)$

(Proved in Ex. 20); (5) $\therefore \frac{a}{b} \cdot \frac{c}{d} = \frac{ac}{bd}$ (Def. of div.)

C **22.** (1) $c \neq 0, d \neq 0$ (Given); (2) $\frac{c}{d} \cdot \frac{d}{c} = \frac{cd}{dc}$ (Proved in Ex. 21); (3) $\frac{c}{d} \cdot \frac{d}{c} = (cd)\left(\frac{1}{cd}\right)$

(Comm. prop. of mult.; def. of div.); (4) $\frac{c}{d} \cdot \frac{d}{c} = 1$ (Prop. of recip.); (5) $\therefore \frac{1}{\frac{c}{d}} = \frac{d}{c}$ (Prop.

of recip. (uniqueness of recip.))

23. (1) $c \neq 0, d \neq 0$ (Given); (2) $\frac{a}{b} \div \frac{c}{d} = \frac{a}{b} \cdot \frac{1}{\frac{c}{d}}$ (Def. of div.); (3) $\frac{a}{b} \div \frac{c}{d} = \frac{a}{b} \cdot \frac{d}{c}$ (Proved in

Ex. 22); (4) $\therefore \frac{a}{b} \div \frac{c}{d} = \frac{ad}{bc}$ (Proved in Ex. 21)

24. If $a = 0$ and a has a reciprocal (call it b), then $ab = 1$. But by the zero-product property, $ab = 0$ if $a = 0$.

25. Call the numbers a and b. If $ab = 0$, then at least one of a and b must be 0 by the zero-product property. But both a and b are given to be nonzero.

Pages 90–91 • WRITTEN EXERCISES

A **1.** (1) Given; (2) Second Mult. prop. of order; (3) Mult. prop. of -1

2. (1) Given; (2) Add. prop. of order; (3) Def. of subtr.

3. (1) Given; (2) Add. prop. of order; (3) Given; (4) Add. prop. of order; (5) Trans. prop. of order (Steps 2 and 4)

4. (1) Given; (2) First mult. prop. of order; (3) First mult. prop. of order; (4) Trans. prop. of order (Steps 2 and 3); (5) Def. of a^2 and b^2

5. (1) Given; (2) Second mult. prop. of order; (3) Given; (4) Second mult. prop. of order; (5) Trans. prop. of order (Steps 2 and 4); (6) Def. a^2 and b^2

6. (1) Given; (2) First Mult. prop. of order; (3) Given; (4) First Mult. prop. of order; (5) Trans. prop. of order (Steps 2 and 4);

7. (1) $a > 0$ (Given); (2) $a + (-a) > 0 + (-a)$ (Add. prop. of order); (3) $0 > 0 + (-a)$ (Prop. of opp.); (4) $\therefore 0 > -a$, or $-a < 0$ (Ident. prop. of add.)

8. (1) $a < 1$ and $a > 0$ (Given); (2) $a \cdot a < a \cdot 1$ (First mult. prop. of order); (3) $a \cdot a < a$ (Ident. prop. of mult.); (4) $\therefore a^2 < a$ (Def. of a^2)

9. (1) $a > 0$ and $b > 0$ (Given); (2) $ab > 0 \cdot b$ (First mult. prop. of order); (3) $\therefore ab > 0$ (Mult. prop. of 0)

10. (1) $a > 0$ and $b > 0$ (Given); (2) $ab > 0$ (Proved in example 9); (3) $|ab| = ab$ (Def. of abs. value); (4) $|a| = a, |b| = b$. (Def. of abs. value); (5) $|a| \cdot |b| = ab$ (Mult. prop. of eq.); (6) $\therefore |ab| = |a| \cdot |b|$ (Subst. prin. (Steps 3 and 5))

B **11.** (1) $a > 0$ and $b > 0$ (Given); (2) $a \cdot \frac{1}{b} > 0 \cdot \frac{1}{b}$ $\left(\text{First mult. prop. of order } \left(\text{assuming } \frac{1}{b} > 0\right)\right)$; (3) $a \cdot \frac{1}{b} > 0$ (Mult. prop. of 0); (4) $\therefore \frac{a}{b} > 0$ (Def. of div.)

12. (1) $a < 0$ and $b < 0$ (Given); (2) $a \cdot \frac{1}{b} > 0 \cdot \frac{1}{b}$ $\left(\text{Second mult. prop. of order } \left(\text{assuming } \frac{1}{b} < 0\right)\right)$; (3) $a \cdot \frac{1}{b} > 0$ (Mult. prop. of 0); (4) $\therefore \frac{a}{b} > 0$ (Def. of div.)

13. (1) $a > 0$ and $b < 0$ (Given); (2) $a \cdot \frac{1}{b} < 0 \cdot \frac{1}{b}$ $\left(\text{Second mult. prop. of order } \left(\text{assuming } \frac{1}{b} < 0\right)\right)$; (3) $a \cdot \frac{1}{b} < 0$ (Mult. prop. of 0); (4) $\therefore \frac{a}{b} < 0$ (Def. of div.)

14. (1) $a < 0$ and $b > 0$ (Given); (2) $a \cdot \frac{1}{b} < 0 \cdot \frac{1}{b}$ $\left(\text{First mult. prop. of order } \left(\text{assuming } \frac{1}{b} > 0\right)\right)$; (3) $a \cdot \frac{1}{b} < 0$ (Mult. prop. of 0); (4) $\therefore \frac{a}{b} < 0$ (Def. of div.)

15. (1) $a > 0$, $b > 0$, and $\frac{1}{a} > \frac{1}{b}$ (Given); (2) $ab > 0$ (Proved in Example 9); (3) $(ab) \cdot \frac{1}{a} > (ab) \cdot \frac{1}{b}$ (First mult. prop. of order); (4) $\left(a \cdot \frac{1}{a}\right) \cdot b > a \cdot \left(b \cdot \frac{1}{b}\right)$ (Assoc. and comm. prop. of mult.); (5) $1 \cdot b > a \cdot 1$ (Prop. of recip.); (6) $\therefore b > a$, or $a < b$ (Ident. prop. of mult.)

16. (1) $a > 0$, $b > 0$, and $a < b$ (Given); (2) $ab > 0$ (Proved in Example 9); (3) $\frac{1}{ab} \cdot a < \frac{1}{ab} \cdot b$ $\left(\text{First mult. prop. of order } \left(\text{assuming } \frac{1}{ab} > 0\right)\right)$; (4) $\left(\frac{1}{a} \cdot \frac{1}{b}\right) \cdot a < \left(\frac{1}{a} \cdot \frac{1}{b}\right) \cdot b$ (Ex. 20, page 87); (5) $\left(\frac{1}{a} \cdot a\right) \cdot \frac{1}{b} < \frac{1}{a} \cdot \left(\frac{1}{b} \cdot b\right)$ (Assoc. and comm. prop. of mult.); (6) $1 \cdot \frac{1}{b} < \frac{1}{a} \cdot 1$ (Prop. of recip.); (7) $\therefore \frac{1}{b} < \frac{1}{a}$, or $\frac{1}{a} > \frac{1}{b}$ (Ident. prop. of mult.)

C **17.** (1) $a < b$ (Given); (2) $a + a < a + b$ and $a + b < b + b$ (Add. prop. of order); (3) $2a < a + b$ and $a + b < 2b$ (Simplification); (4) $\therefore a < \frac{a+b}{2}$ and $\frac{a+b}{2} < b$, or $a < \frac{a+b}{2} < b$ $\left(\text{First mult. prop. of order } \left(\text{using the fact } \frac{1}{2} > 0\right)\right)$

18. Part 1: (1) $a > 0$ and $a > \frac{1}{a}$ (Given); (2) Assume $a = 1$ (Assumption for indirect proof); (3) $\frac{1}{a} \cdot a = \frac{1}{a} \cdot 1$ (Mult. prop. of eq.); (4) $1 = \frac{1}{a}$ (Prop. of recip.; ident. prop. of mult.); (5) $\therefore a = \frac{1}{a}$ (Trans. prop. of eq. (Steps 2 and 4)). But $a = \frac{1}{a}$ contradicts the given, $a > \frac{1}{a}$. So $a \neq 1$. Part 2: (1) $a > 0$ and $a > \frac{1}{a}$ (Given); (2) Assume $a < 1$ (Assumption for indirect proof); (3) $\frac{1}{a} \cdot a < \frac{1}{a} \cdot 1$ $\left(\text{First mult. prop. of order } \left(\text{assuming } \frac{1}{a} > 0\right)\right)$; (4) $1 < \frac{1}{a}$ (Prop. of recip.; ident. prop. of mult.); (5) $\therefore a < \frac{1}{a}$ (Trans. prop. of order (Steps 2 and 4)). But $a < \frac{1}{a}$ contradicts the given, $a > \frac{1}{a}$. So $a \nless 1$. Since $a \neq 1$ (Part 1) and $a \nless 1$ (Part 2), $a > 1$ by the comparison property of order.

Page 91 • MIXED REVIEW EXERCISES

1. True **2.** True **3.** True

4. $|x - 3| = 1$; $x - 3 = 1$ or $x - 3 = -1$; $x = 4$ or $x = 2$; $\{2, 4\}$

−1 0 1 2 3 4 5

5. $4d + 5 \geq 1$; $4d \geq -4$; $d \geq -1$; $\{d : d \geq -1\}$

−3 −2 −1 0 1 2 3

6. $-1 < 2 - y < 3$; $-3 < -y < 1$; $3 > y > -1$; $\{y : -1 < y < 3\}$

−2 −1 0 1 2 3 4

7. $6r + 13 = 25$; $6r = 12$; $r = 2$; $\{2\}$

−3 −2 −1 0 1 2 3

8. $|n| + 7 < 5$; $|n| < -2$; $\emptyset$

9. $-2k > 8$ or $k - 4 \geq 0$; $k < -4$ or $k \geq 4$; $\{k : k < -4 \text{ or } k \geq 4\}$

−6 −4 −2 0 2 4 6

Pages 93–94 • CHAPTER REVIEW

1. b; $-\frac{m}{2} < -2$; $-2\left(-\frac{m}{2}\right) > (-2)(-2)$; $m > 4$

2. d; $3(n - 1) > 5n + 7$; $3n - 3 > 5n + 7$; $-10 > 2n$; $-5 > n$

3. a; $-3 < 4c + 5 \leq 1$; $-8 < 4c \leq -4$; $-2 < c \leq -1$

4. d; $4 - w \leq 3$ or $w + 5 < 3$; $-w \leq -1$ or $w < -2$; $w \geq 1$ or $w < -2$

5. b; let x = the number of tapes rented. Then $1.5x$ = the cost of the rentals. $1.5x \leq 20$; $x \leq 13\frac{1}{3}$

6. a; $\left|5 - \frac{x}{3}\right| = 7$; $5 - \frac{x}{3} = 7$ or $5 - \frac{x}{3} = -7$; $-\frac{x}{3} = 2$ or $-\frac{x}{3} = -12$; $x = -6$ or $x = 36$

7. c; $|2y + 9| < 13$; $-13 < 2y + 9 < 13$; $-22 < 2y < 4$; $-11 < y < 2$

8. a; $|4 - h| \geq 5$; $4 - h \geq 5$ or $4 - h \leq -5$; $-1 \geq h$ or $9 \leq h$

9. b **10.** b **11.** d **12.** c **13.** c

Page 94 • CHAPTER TEST

1. $5x - 9 > 6x$; $-9 > x$; $\{x : x < -9\}$

2. $3(2y + 1) < 2(y - 3) + 1$; $6y + 3 < 2y - 5$; $4y < -8$; $y < -2$; $\{y : y < -2\}$

3. $-3 < 4 - m < 6$; $-7 < -m < 2$; $7 > m > -2$; $\{m : -2 < m < 7\}$

4. $-2n \geq 8$ or $n + 3 < 7$; $n \leq -4$ or $n < 4$; $\{n : n < 4\}$

5. Let w and $w + 2$ be the width and length of the rectangle. Then the perimeter is $2w + 2(w + 2)$. $2w + 2(w + 2) \geq 35$; $4w + 4 \geq 35$; $4w \geq 31$; $w \geq 7\frac{3}{4}$. Since w is an odd integer, $w \geq 9$. The smallest rectangle is 9 cm by 11 cm.

6. $|9 - 2k| = 5$; $9 - 2k = 5$ or $9 - 2k = -5$; $-2k = -4$ or $-2k = -14$; $k = 2$ or $k = 7$; $\{2,7\}$

7. $\left|\frac{c}{3} + 1\right| > 2$; $\frac{c}{3} + 1 > 2$ or $\frac{c}{3} + 1 < -2$; $\frac{c}{3} > 1$ or $\frac{c}{3} < -3$; $c > 3$ or $c < -9$; $\{c : c < -9 \text{ or } c > 3\}$

8. $|4f + 3| \leq 5$; $-5 \leq 4f + 3 \leq 5$; $-8 \leq 4f \leq 2$; $-2 \leq f \leq \frac{1}{2}$; $\left\{f : -2 \leq f \leq \frac{1}{2}\right\}$

9. $\{w : w \leq 3 \text{ or } w \geq 5\}$

10. $\{h : -5 < h < 1\}$

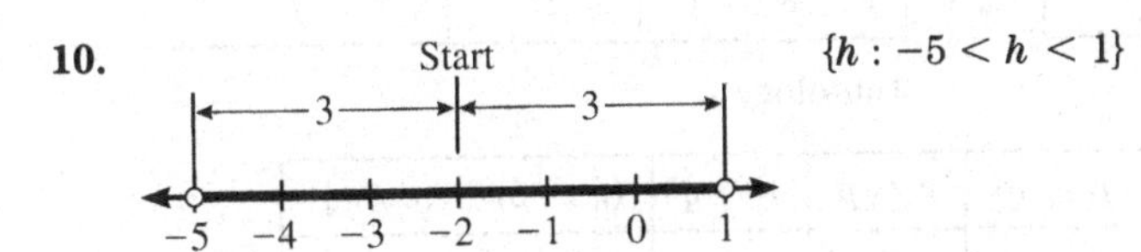

11. If $x^2 > x$, then $x > 1$. False.

12. (1) (Given); (2) Prop. of recip.; (3) Mult. prop. of eq.; (4) Assoc. prop. of mult.; (5) Prop. of recip.; (6) Ident. prop. of mult.

13. False; for example, $1 > -2$, but $|1| \not> |-2|$.

14. False; for example, $-1 < 2$ and $-2 > -3$ but $(-1)(-3) \not< (2)(-2)$.

15. False; for example, $-2 < 3$ and $-1 < 0$, but $(-2)(-1) \not< (3)(-1)$.

16. False; for example, $-2 < -1 < 0$, but $(-2)^2 \not< (-1)^2$.

Page 97 • EXTRA

1. Since q is false, $q \rightarrow r$ is true. **2.** Since r is true, $\sim r$ is false; $\sim r \wedge p$ is false.

3. Since p is true, $p \vee \sim q$ is true.

4. Since p is true; $p \vee q$ is true; r is true; $r \wedge (p \vee q)$ is true.

5. Since p is true, $p \vee (q \wedge r)$ is true.

6. Since p is true, $p \vee r$ is true; q is false; $(p \vee r) \rightarrow q$ is false.

7. Since p is true, $\sim p$ is false; $\sim p \rightarrow (q \vee \sim r)$ is true.

8. Since q is false, $q \rightarrow r$ is true; r is true, $r \rightarrow (q \rightarrow r)$ is true.

9. Since p is true, $p \vee q$ is true; r is true; $r \wedge (p \vee q)$ is true; r and p are true, so $(r \wedge p)$ is true and $(r \wedge p) \vee (r \wedge q)$ is true; $[r \wedge (p \vee q)] \rightarrow [(r \wedge p) \vee (r \wedge q)]$ is true.

10–12. $p \rightarrow q$ is false only when p is true and q is false.

10. q is false; p is true; $q \rightarrow p$ is true. **11.** p is true; $\sim q$ is true; $p \wedge \sim q$ is true.

12. p is true; q is false; $p \vee q$ is true; $(p \vee q) \wedge p$ is true.

13.

p	q	$p \vee q$	$q \vee p$
T	T	T	T
T	F	T	T
F	T	T	T
F	F	F	F

Logically equivalent

14.

q	$\sim q$	$q \vee \sim q$
T	F	T
F	T	T

Not logically equivalent

15.

p	q	$p \vee q$	$(p \vee q) \rightarrow p$
T	T	T	T
T	F	T	T
F	T	T	F
F	F	F	T

Not a tautology

16.

p	q	$\sim q$	$q \wedge \sim q$	$(q \wedge \sim q) \rightarrow p$
T	T	F	F	T
T	F	T	F	T
F	T	F	F	T
F	F	T	F	T

Tautology

17.

p	q	r	$p \vee q$	$r \wedge (p \vee q)$	$r \wedge p$	$r \wedge q$	$(r \wedge p) \vee (r \wedge q)$
T	T	T	T	T	T	T	T
T	T	F	T	F	F	F	F
T	F	T	T	T	T	F	T
T	F	F	T	F	F	F	F
F	T	T	T	T	F	T	T
F	T	F	T	F	F	F	F
F	F	T	F	F	F	F	F
F	F	F	F	F	F	F	F

Recall that $p \leftrightarrow q$ is true whenever p and q have the same truth value. Since columns 5 and 8 are identical, $r \wedge (p \vee q)$ and $(r \wedge p) \vee (r \wedge q)$ always have the same truth value; then $r \wedge (p \vee q) \leftrightarrow (r \wedge p) \vee (r \wedge q)$ is always true; tautology.

18.

p	q	r	$p \to q$	$q \to r$	$(p \to q) \land (q \to r)$	$p \to r$	$[(p \to q) \land (q \to r)] \to (p \to r)$
T	T	T	T	T	T	T	T
T	T	F	T	F	F	F	T
T	F	T	F	T	F	T	T
T	F	F	F	T	F	F	T
F	T	T	T	T	T	T	T
F	T	F	T	F	F	T	T
F	F	T	T	T	T	T	T
F	F	F	T	T	T	T	T

Tautology

Page 98 • MIXED PROBLEM SOLVING

A

1. Let q = the number of quarters. Then $40 - q$ = the number of dimes. The value of the coins is $0.25q + 0.10(40 - q)$. $0.25q + 0.10(40 - q) > 6.00$; $0.15q + 4.00 > 6.00$; $q > \frac{2.00}{0.15}$; $q > 13\frac{1}{3}$. There are at least 14 quarters.
2. The length is $w + 2$, and the perimeter is $2w + 2(w + 2) = 4w + 4$
3. Let h = the number of hours Percy works. Then Selena works $h - 8$ hours. Percy's pay is $6h$, and Selena's is $(6 + 2)(h - 8)$. $6h = 8(h - 8)$; $6h = 8h - 64$; $2h = 64$; $h = 32$. Percy works 32 h per week.
4. $17 - (-16) = 33$; 33°C
5. Let x = amount invested at 5%. Then $4000 - x$ = amount invested at 8%. The total interest earned by these investments is $0.05x + 0.08(4000 - x)$. $0.05x + 0.08(4000 - x) = 272$; $0.05x + 320 - 0.08x = 272$; $-0.03x = -48$; $x = 1600$. Marcus invested \$1600 at 5% and \$2400 at 8%.
6. Let x = number of erasers. Then $4x$ = number of pencils. The total cost of the purchase is $0.19x + 0.04(4x)$. $0.19x + 0.16x = 2.10$; $0.35x = 2.10$, $x = 6$. Megan bought $4 \cdot 6 = 24$ pencils.
7. The cost of one ball is $\frac{d}{4}$ dollars. So for \$8, you can buy $8 \div \frac{d}{4} = \frac{32}{d}$ balls.
8. Let x = Drew's first score. Then $\frac{1}{2}[x + (x + 6)] < 80$; $\frac{1}{2}(2x + 6) < 80$; $x + 3 < 80$; $x < 77$. His first score was less than 77.
9. Let x = the measure of the angle. Then the supplement and complement measure $180 - x$ and $90 - x$, respectively. $180 - x = 4(90 - x)$; $180 - x = 360 - 4x$; $3x = 180$; $x = 60$. The angle measures 60°.
10. Let x = the amount Helen has in her savings account. Then she has $57 + x$ dollars in checking. $x + (57 + x) = 239$; $2x = 182$, $x = 91$. She has \$91 in savings.

B **11.**

	Amount × (lb)	rate (dollars/lb)	= cost (dollars)
apple	x	1.80	$1.80x$
banana	$5 - x$	2.10	$2.10(5 - x)$
mixture	5	1.92	1.92(5)

$1.80x + 2.10(5 - x) = 1.92(5)$; $-0.30x + 10.50 = 9.60$; $-0.30x = -0.90$; $x = 3$. There are 3 lb of apple slices.

12. Let d = the distance from the Petersons' to their friend's house. Then their times in hours on the trip are $\frac{d}{80}$ and $\frac{d}{80 - 10}$; $\frac{d}{80} + \frac{d}{70} = 3$; $\frac{15d}{560} = 3$; $d = 112$. The total distance was $2(112) = 224$ km.

13. Let l = the length of the rectangle. Then the width is $\frac{1}{2}l + 1$. The dimensions of the new rectangle are $l + 1$ and $\frac{1}{2}l + 2$. $l\left(\frac{1}{2}l + 1\right) + 20 = (l + 1)\left(\frac{1}{2}l + 2\right)$; $\frac{1}{2}l^2 + l + 20 = \frac{1}{2}l^2 + \frac{5}{2}l + 2$; $18 = \frac{3}{2}l$; $l = 12$. The original rectangle was 7 cm by 12 cm.

14.

	Rate × (km/h)	Time = (h)	Distance (km)
Sue	6	$x + \frac{1}{4}$	$6\left(x + \frac{1}{4}\right)$
Sandy	8	x	$8x$

$8x + 6\left(x + \frac{1}{4}\right) = 5$; $14x + \frac{3}{2} = 5$; $14x = \frac{7}{2}$; $x = \frac{1}{4}$. Sandy left at 1:15 P.M. and walked for $\frac{1}{4}$ h. They met at 1:30 P.M. Sue walked $6\left(\frac{1}{4} + \frac{1}{4}\right) = 3$ km, while Sandy walked 2 km. Sue walked farther.

Page 99 • PREPARING FOR COLLEGE ENTRANCE EXAMS

1. C **2.** D **3.** C **4.** D **5.** D **6.** D **7.** A

CHAPTER 3 • Linear Equations and Functions

Pages 104–105 • WRITTEN EXERCISES

A

1. $2x + 3y = 7$; $3y = -2x + 7$; $y = -\frac{2}{3}x + \frac{7}{3}$; $y = -\frac{2}{3}(-1) + \frac{7}{3} = 3$;

$y = -\frac{2}{3}(0) + \frac{7}{3} = \frac{7}{3}$; $y = -\frac{2}{3}(2) + \frac{7}{3} = 1$; $\left\{(-1, 3), \left(0, \frac{7}{3}\right), (2, 1)\right\}$

2. $3x + 6y = 9$; $6y = -3x + 9$; $y = -\frac{1}{2}x + \frac{3}{2}$; $y = -\frac{1}{2}(-1) + \frac{3}{2} = 2$;

$y = -\frac{1}{2}(0) + \frac{3}{2} = \frac{3}{2}$; $y = -\frac{1}{2}(2) + \frac{3}{2} = \frac{1}{2}$; $\left\{(-1, 2), \left(0, \frac{3}{2}\right), \left(2, \frac{1}{2}\right)\right\}$

3. $-x - 2y = 0$; $-2y = x$; $y = -\frac{1}{2}x$; $y = -\frac{1}{2}(-1) = \frac{1}{2}$; $y = -\frac{1}{2}(0) = 0$;

$y = -\frac{1}{2}(2) = -1$; $\left\{\left(-1, \frac{1}{2}\right), (0, 0), (2, -1)\right\}$

4. $-2x + y = -3$; $y = 2x - 3$; $y = 2(-1) - 3 = -5$; $y = 2(0) - 3 = -3$;
$y = 2(2) - 3 = 1$; $\{(-1, -5), (0, -3), (2, 1)\}$

5. $4x - 9y = 5$; $-9y = -4x + 5$; $y = \frac{4}{9}x - \frac{5}{9}$; $y = \frac{4}{9}(-1) - \frac{5}{9} = -1$;

$y = \frac{4}{9}(0) - \frac{5}{9} = -\frac{5}{9}$; $y = \frac{4}{9}(2) - \frac{5}{9} = \frac{1}{3}$; $\left\{(-1, -1), \left(0, -\frac{5}{9}\right), \left(2, \frac{1}{3}\right)\right\}$

6. $6x - \frac{1}{2}y = 3$; $-\frac{1}{2}y = -6x + 3$; $y = 12x - 6$; $y = 12(-1)-6 = -18$;

$y = 12(0) - 6 = -6$; $y = 12(2) - 6 = 18$; $\{(-1, -18), (0, -6), (2, 18)\}$

7. $2x + 3y = 7$; $3y = -2x + 7$; $y = -\frac{2}{3}x + \frac{7}{3}$; $y = -\frac{2}{3}(-2) + \frac{7}{3} = \frac{11}{3}$;

$y = -\frac{2}{3}(1) + \frac{7}{3} = \frac{5}{3}$; $y = -\frac{2}{3}(3) + \frac{7}{3} = \frac{1}{3}$; $\left\{\left(-2, \frac{11}{3}\right), \left(1, \frac{5}{3}\right), \left(3, \frac{1}{3}\right)\right\}$

8. $3x + 6y = 9$; $6y = -3x + 9$; $y = -\frac{1}{2}x + \frac{3}{2}$; $y = -\frac{1}{2}(-2) + \frac{3}{2} = \frac{5}{2}$;

$y = -\frac{1}{2}(1) + \frac{3}{2} = 1$; $y = -\frac{1}{2}(3) + \frac{3}{2} = 0$; $\left\{\left(-2, \frac{5}{2}\right), (1, 1), (3, 0)\right\}$

9. $-x - 2y = 0$; $2y = -x$; $y = -\frac{1}{2}x$; $y = -\frac{1}{2}(-2) = 1$; $y = -\frac{1}{2}(1) = -\frac{1}{2}$;

$y = -\frac{1}{2}(3) = -\frac{3}{2}$; $\left\{(-2, 1), \left(1, -\frac{1}{2}\right), \left(3, -\frac{3}{2}\right)\right\}$

10. $-2x + y = -3$; $y = 2x - 3$; $y = 2(-2) - 3 = -7$; $y = 2(1) - 3 = -1$;
$y = 2(3) - 3 = 3$; $\{(-2, -7), (1, -1), (3, 3)\}$

11. $4x - 9y = 5$; $-9y = -4x + 5$; $y = \frac{4}{9}x - \frac{5}{9}$; $y = \frac{4}{9}(-2) - \frac{5}{9} = -\frac{13}{9}$;

$y = \frac{4}{9}(1) - \frac{5}{9} = -\frac{1}{9}$; $y = \frac{4}{9}(3) - \frac{5}{9} = \frac{7}{9}$; $\left\{\left(-2, -\frac{13}{9}\right), \left(1, -\frac{1}{9}\right), \left(3, \frac{7}{9}\right)\right\}$

12. $6x - \frac{1}{2}y = 3; -\frac{1}{2}y = -6x + 3; y = 12x - 6; y = 12(-2) - 6 = -30;$

$y = 12(1) - 6 = 6; y = 12(3) - 6 = 30; \{(-2, -30), (1, 6), (3, 30)\}$

13. $3x + 2y = 12; 3(0) + 2y = 12$, so $y = 6; 3x + 2(0) = 12$, so $x = 4; 3(2) + 2y = 12$, so $y = 3; (0, 6), (4, 0), (2, 3)$

14. $4x + 3y = 8; 4(0) + 3y = 8$, so $y = \frac{8}{3}; 4x + 3(0) = 8$, so $x = 2; 4(5) + 3y = 8$, so

$y = -4; \left(0, \frac{8}{3}\right), (2, 0), (5, -4)$

15. $5x - 2y = 7; 5(0) - 2y = 7$, so $y = -\frac{7}{2}; 5x - 2(0) = 7$, so $x = \frac{7}{5}; 5(-3) - 2y = 7$,

so $y = -11; \left(0, -\frac{7}{2}\right), \left(\frac{7}{5}, 0\right), (-3, -11)$

16. $x + 6y = -9; 0 + 6y = -9$, so $y = -\frac{3}{2}; x + 6(0) = -9$, so $x = -9; -3 + 6y =$

-9, so $y = -1; \left(0, -\frac{3}{2}\right), (-9, 0), (-3, -1)$

17. $2x - 2y = 3; 2(1) - 2y = 3$, so $y = -\frac{1}{2}; 2\left(\frac{1}{2}\right) - 2y = 3$, so $y = -1;$

$2x - 2\left(\frac{1}{2}\right) = 3$, so $x = 2; \left(1, -\frac{1}{2}\right), \left(\frac{1}{2}, -1\right), \left(2, \frac{1}{2}\right)$

18. $3x + 5y = 3; 3(1) + 5y = 3$, so $y = 0; 3\left(-\frac{2}{3}\right) + 5y = 3$, so $y = 1; 3x + 5\left(\frac{7}{5}\right) = 3$,

so $x = -\frac{4}{3}; (1, 0), \left(-\frac{2}{3}, 1\right), \left(-\frac{4}{3}, \frac{7}{5}\right)$

19. $\frac{1}{2}x - 2y = 1; \frac{1}{2}(1) - 2y = 1$, so $y = -\frac{1}{4}; \frac{1}{2}(6) - 2y = 1$, so $y = 1; \frac{1}{2}x - 2(0) = 1$,

so $x = 2; \left(1, -\frac{1}{4}\right), (6, 1), (2, 0)$

20. $x + \frac{1}{3}y = 2; 1 + \frac{1}{3}y = 2$, so $y = 3; x + \frac{1}{3}(6) = 2$, so $x = 0; \frac{1}{3} + \frac{1}{3}y = 2$, so $y = 5;$

$(1, 3), (0, 6), \left(\frac{1}{3}, 5\right)$

21. $2x + y = k; 2(2) + 1 = k; k = 5$ **22.** $3x - y = k; 3(1) - (-3) = k; k = 6$

23. $3x - ky = 4; 3(2) - k(-1) = 4; 6 + k = 4; k = -2$

24. $kx + 3y = 7; k(-1) + 3(3) = 7; -k + 9 = 7; k = 2$

25. $kx + 2y = k; k(3) + 2(3) = k; 3k + 6 = k; 2k = -6; k = -3$

26. $6x - ky = k; 6(2) - k(2) = k; 12 - 2k = k; 12 = 3k; k = 4$

B **27.**

x	$y = -x + 4$
0	4
1	3
2	2
3	1
4	0

If $x > 4$, then $y < 0$;
$\{(0, 4), (1, 3), (2, 2), (3, 1), (4, 0)\}$

28.

x	$y = -2x + 6$
0	6
1	4
2	2
3	0

If $x > 3$, then $y < 0$;
$\{(0, 6), (1, 4), (2, 2), (3, 0)\}$

29.

x	$y = -4x + 15$
0	15
1	11
2	7
3	3

If $x \geq 4$, then $y \leq 0$;
$\{(0, 15), (1, 11), (2, 7), (3, 3)\}$

30.

y	$x = -5x + 24$
0	24
1	19
2	14
3	9
4	4

If $y \geq 5$, then $x \leq 0$;
$\{(4, 4), (9, 3), (14, 2), (19, 1), (24, 0)\}$

31.

x	$y = \frac{18 - 2x}{3}$
0	6
3	4
6	2
9	0

If $x > 9$, then $y < 0$;
$\{(0, 6), (3, 4), (6, 2), (9, 0)\}$

32.

x	$y = \frac{30 - 5x}{2}$
0	15
2	10
4	5
6	0

If $x > 6$, then $y < 0$;
$\{(0, 15), (2, 10), (4, 5), (6, 0)\}$

33. $y < -x + 5$;

x	$-x + 5$	y
1	4	1, 2, 3
2	3	1, 2
3	2	1

If $x > 3$, $y \leq 0$; $\{(1, 1), (1, 2), (1, 3), (2, 1), (2, 2), (3, 1)\}$

34. $y < -2x + 6$;

x	$-2x + 6$	y
1	4	1, 2, 3
2	2	1

If $x > 2$, $y \leq 0$; $\{(1, 1), (1, 2), (1, 3), (2, 1)\}$

35. $y \le \frac{-2x + 12}{3}$;

x	$\frac{-2x+12}{3}$	y
1	$\frac{10}{3}$	1, 2, 3
2	$\frac{8}{3}$	1, 2
3	2	1, 2
4	$\frac{4}{3}$	1

If $x > 4$, then $y < 1$; {(1, 1), (1, 2), (1, 3), (2, 1), (2, 2), (3, 1), (3, 2), (4, 1)}

36. $y \le \frac{-3x + 19}{5}$;

x	$\frac{-3x+19}{5}$	y
1	$\frac{16}{5}$	1, 2, 3
2	$\frac{13}{5}$	1, 2
3	2	1, 2
4	$\frac{7}{5}$	1

If $x > 4$, $y \le 0$; {(1, 1), (1, 2), (1, 3), (2, 1), (2, 2), (3, 1), (3, 2), (4, 1)}

37.

y	$x = 10 - y^2$
1	9
2	6
3	1

If $y > 3$, then $x < 0$;
{(1, 3), (6, 2), (9, 1)}

38. $y < \frac{-x^2 + 11}{2}$;

x	$\frac{-x^2+11}{2}$	y
1	5	1, 2, 3, 4
2	$\frac{7}{2}$	1, 2, 3

If $x > 2$, then $y \le 0$;
{(1, 1), (1, 2), (1, 3), (1, 4), (2, 1), (2, 2), (2, 3)}

C In Exercises 39 and 40, let t = the tens' digit of N and u = the units' digit of N; then $N = 10t + u$, and $K = 10u + t$.

39. $N - K = (10t + u) - (10u + t) = 9t - 9u = 9(t - u)$; since $(t - u)$ is an integer, $9(t - u) = N - K$ is an integral multiple of 9.

40. $N + K = (10t + u) + (10u + t) = 11t + 11u = 11(t + u)$; since $(t + u)$ is an integer, $11(t + u) = N + K$ is an integral multiple of 11.

Pages 105–106 • PROBLEMS

A **1. a.** Let f = number of \$5 bills; t = number of \$20 bills **b.** $5f + 20t = 75$

c. $5f = -20t + 75$; $f = -4t + 15$; if $t = 0, f = 15$; if $t = 1, f = 11$; if $t = 2, f = 7$; if $t = 3, f = 3$; if $t > 3, f < 0$; combinations of \$5 bills and \$20 bills, respectively, are 15 and 0, 11 and 1, 7 and 2, and 3 and 3.

2. a. Let w = number of washers and r = number of refrigerators

b. $50w + 100r = 500$

c. $50w = -100r + 500$; $w = -2r + 10$; if $r = 0$, $w = 10$; if $r = 1$, $w = 8$; if $r = 2$, $w = 6$; if $r = 3$, $w = 4$; if $r = 4$, $w = 2$; if $r = 5$, $w = 0$; if $r > 5$, $w < 0$; possible combinations of washers and refrigerators, respectively, are 10 and 0, 8 and 1, 6 and 2, 4 and 3, 2 and 4, and 0 and 5.

3. a. Let d = numbers of dimes; q = number of quarters **b.** $10d + 25q = 95$

c. $10d = -25q + 95$; $d = \frac{-5q + 19}{2}$; since d is an integer, q is odd; if $q = 1$, $d = 7$; if $q = 3$, $d = 2$; if $q > 3$, $d < 0$; he could have either 1 quarter and 7 dimes or 3 quarters and 2 dimes.

4. a. Let d = number of dimes; q = number of quarters **b.** $10d + 25q = 195$

c. $10d = -25q + 195$; $d = \frac{-5q + 39}{2}$; since d is an integer, q is odd; if $q = 1$, $d = 17$; if $q = 3$, $d = 12$; if $q = 5$, $d = 7$; if $q = 7$, $d = 2$; if $q > 7$, $d < 0$; possible combinations of (dimes, quarters) are (17, 1), (12, 3), (7, 5), (2, 7).

5. a. Let x = length, in centimeters, of each of the three equal sides; y = length, in centimeters, of the fourth side.

b. $3x + y = 19$ and $3x > y$

c. $y = -3x + 19$; $3x > -3x + 19$; $6x > 19$; $x > \frac{19}{6}$; if $x = 4$, $y = 7$; if $x = 5$, $y = 4$; if $x = 6$, $y = 1$; if $x > 6$, $y < 0$; the sides could be 4 cm, 4 cm, 4 cm, and 7 cm; 5 cm, 5 cm, 5 cm, and 4 cm; or 6 cm, 6 cm, 6 cm, and 1 cm.

6. a. Let x = length, in meters, of the equal sides; y = length, in meters, of the third side.

b. $2x + y = 15$ and $2x > y$

c. $y = -2x + 15$, so $2x > -2x + 15$; $4x > 15$; $x > \frac{15}{4}$; if $x = 4$, $y = 7$; if $x = 5$, $y = 5$; if $x = 6$, $y = 3$; if $x = 7$, $y = 1$; if $x > 7$, $y < 0$; the lengths are 4 m, 4 m, and 7 m; 5 m, 5 m, and 5 m; 6 m, 6 m, and 3 m; or 7 m, 7 m, and 1 m.

B

7. a. Let n = number of nickels; q = number of quarters; $d = q + 3$ = number of dimes.

b. $5n + 25q + 10(q + 3) = 200$

c. $5n + 35q = 170$; $n = -7q + 34$; if $q = 0$, $n = 34$ and $d = 3$; if $q = 1$, $n = 27$ and $d = 4$; if $q = 2$, $n = 20$ and $d = 5$; if $q = 3$, $n = 13$ and $d = 6$; if $q = 4$, $n = 6$, and $d = 7$; if $q > 4$, $n < 0$; the possibilities for the numbers of nickels, dimes, and quarters, respectively, are: 34, 3, and 0; 27, 4, and 1; 20, 5, and 2; 13, 6, and 3; and 6, 7, and 4.

8. a. Let n = number of nickels; q = number of quarters; $p = 2n$ = number of pennies; $d = q + 4$ = number of dimes.

b. $5n + 25q + 2n + 10(q + 4) = 201$

c. $7n + 35q = 161$; $n = -5q + 23$; if $q = 0$, $n = 23$, $p = 46$, and $d = 4$; if $q = 1$, $n = 18$, $p = 36$, and $d = 5$; if $q = 2$, $n = 13$, $p = 26$, and $d = 6$; if $q = 3$, $n = 8$, $p = 16$, and $d = 7$; if $q = 4$, $n = 3$, $p = 6$, and $d = 8$; if $q > 4$, $n < 0$; the possibilities for the numbers of pennies, nickels, dimes, and quarters, respectively, are: 46, 23, 4, and 0; 36, 18, 5, and 1; 26, 13, 6, and 2; 16, 8, 7, and 3; and 6, 3, 8, and 4.

In Problems 9–12, let t = the tens' digit of N and u = the units' digit of N. Then $N = 10t + u$ and $K = 10u + t$.

9. Since N is odd, $u = 1, 3, 5, 7$, or 9; $N > K + 18$; $10t + u > 10u + t + 18$; $9t > 9u + 18$; $t > u + 2$; if $u = 1$, $t = 4, 5, 6, 7, 8$, or 9; if $u = 3$, $t = 6, 7, 8$, or 9; if $u = 5$, $t = 8$ or 9; if $u \geq 7$, $t > 9$; N = 41, 51, 61, 63, 71, 73, 81, 83, 85, 91, 93, or 95.

10. $\frac{N + K + 35}{3} = 30$; $\frac{10t + u + 10u + t + 35}{3} = 30$; $\frac{11t + 11u + 35}{3} = 30$; $11t + 11u = 55$; $t + u = 5$; $u = -t + 5$; if $t = 1$, $u = 4$; if $t = 2$, $u = 3$, if $t = 3$, $u = 2$; if $t = 4$, $u = 1$; if $t = 5$, $u = 0$; if $t > 5$, $u < 0$; N = 14, 23, 32, 41, or 50.

C **11.** $K + 2N < 60$; $10u + t + 2(10t + u) < 60$; $12u + 21t < 60$; $12u < -21t + 60$; $u < \frac{-7t + 20}{4}$; if $t = 1$, $u < \frac{13}{4}$, so $u = 0, 1, 2$, or 3; if $t = 2$, $u < \frac{3}{2}$, so $u = 0$ or 1; if $t > 2$, $u < 0$; N = 10, 11, 12, 13, 20, or 21.

12. Since N is even, $u = 0, 2, 4, 6$, or 8; $N > K + 50$; $10t + u > 10u + t + 50$; $9t > 9u + 50$; $t > \frac{9u + 50}{9}$; if $u = 0$, $t > \frac{50}{9}$, so $t = 6, 7, 8$, or 9; if $u = 2$, $t > \frac{68}{9}$, so $t = 8$ or 9; if $u > 2$, $t > 9$; N = 60, 70, 80, 82, 90, or 92.

13. Let x = number attending the first meeting; y = number attending the second; then $2x$ = number attending the third meeting; $9 = \frac{x + y + 2x}{3}$; $27 = 3x + y$; $y = -3x + 27$; since the committee has 15 members, $y \leq 15$ and $2x \leq 15$; $x \leq 7.5$; if $x < 4$, $y > 15$; if $x = 4$, $y = 15$; if $x = 5$, $y = 12$; if $x = 6$, $y = 9$; if $x = 7$, $y = 6$; the possibilities for attendance at the first, second, and third meetings, respectively, are: 4, 15, and 8; 5, 12, and 10; 6, 9, and 12; and 7, 6, and 14.

14. Let x = the length, in cm, of the shortest piece; y = the length, in cm, of the second piece; then the longest piece measures $24 - (x + y)$ cm; $x < y$ and $y < 24 - (x + y)$; $2y < 24 - x$; $x < y < \frac{24 - x}{2}$; if $x = 2$, $2 < y < 11$, so $y = 4, 6, 8$, or 10; if $x = 4$, $4 < y < 10$, so $y = 6$ or 8; if $x = 6$, $6 < y < 9$, so $y = 8$; the possible lengths are: 2 cm, 4 cm, and 18 cm; 2 cm, 6 cm, and 16 cm; 2 cm, 8 cm, and 14 cm; 2 cm, 10 cm, and 12 cm; 4 cm, 6 cm, and 14 cm; 4 cm, 8 cm, and 12 cm; and 6 cm, 8 cm, and 10 cm.

Page 106 • MIXED REVIEW EXERCISES

1. $2x - 5y = 2(-3) - (5)(4) = -26$ **2.** $-x^2y = -(-3)^2(4) = -36$

3. $|x - y| = |(-3) - 4| = |-7| = 7$

4. $(x - 2)(y + 1) = [(-3) - 2](4 + 1) = (-5)(5) = -25$

5. $\frac{3x + 1}{y} = \frac{3(-3) + 1}{4} = \frac{-9 + 1}{4} = -2$ **6.** $|xy| = |(-3)4| = |-12| = 12$

7. $x + 3y = -3 + 3(4) = -3 + 12 = 9$ **8.** $\dfrac{x - y}{x + y} = \dfrac{-3 - 4}{-3 + 4} = \dfrac{-7}{1} = -7$

9. $-7 < 2y - 5 \le 3$; $-2 < 2y \le 8$; $-1 < y \le 4$; $\{y : -1 < y \le 4\}$;

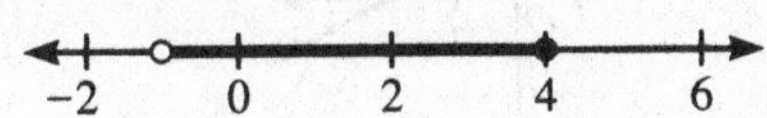

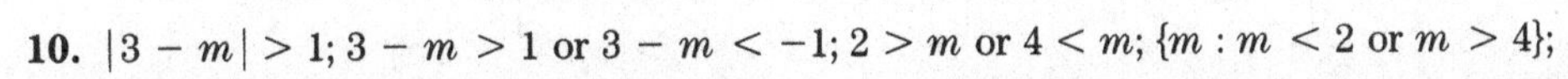

10. $|3 - m| > 1$; $3 - m > 1$ or $3 - m < -1$; $2 > m$ or $4 < m$; $\{m : m < 2$ or $m > 4\}$;

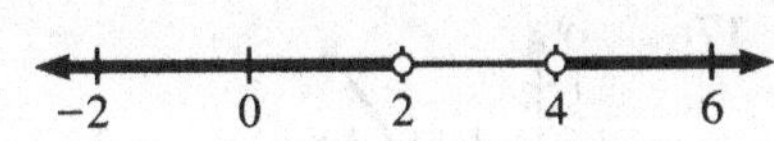

11. $3n + 7 \le 8n - 13$; $20 \le 5n$; $4 \le n$; $\{n : n \ge 4\}$;

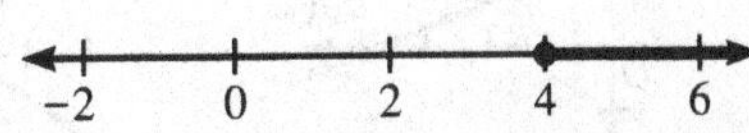

Page 111 · WRITTEN EXERCISES

A **1.**

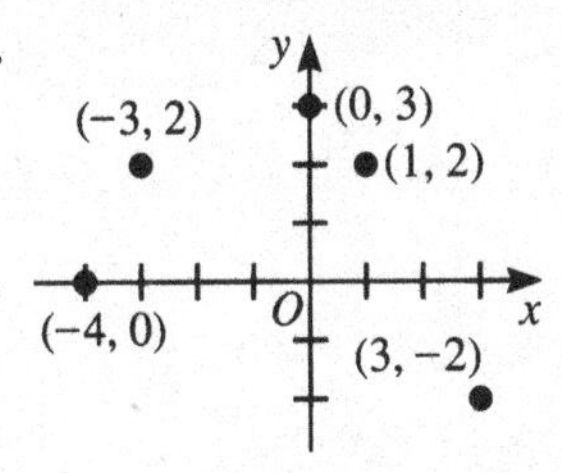

2.

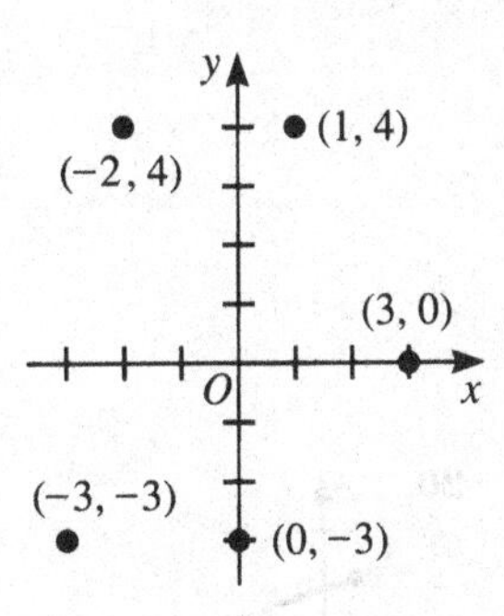

3.

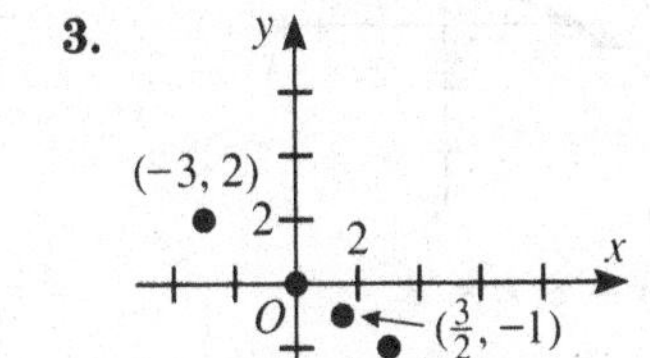

4.

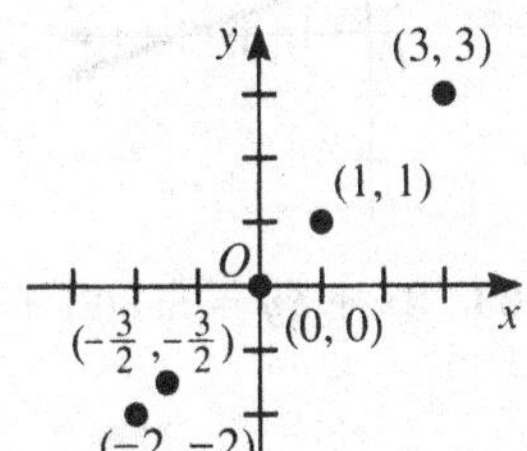

5.

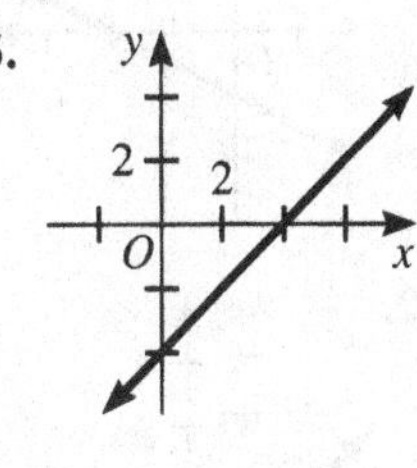

6.

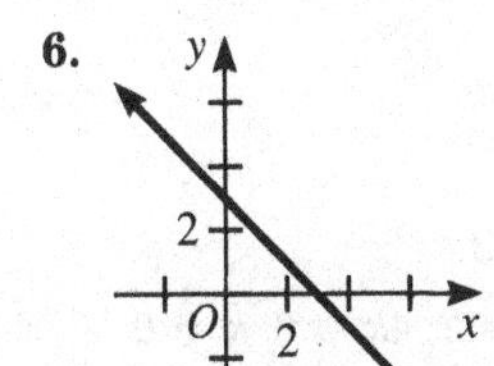

7.

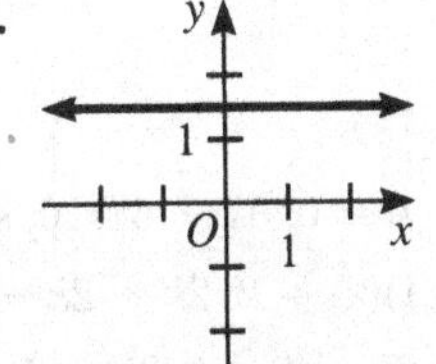

8.

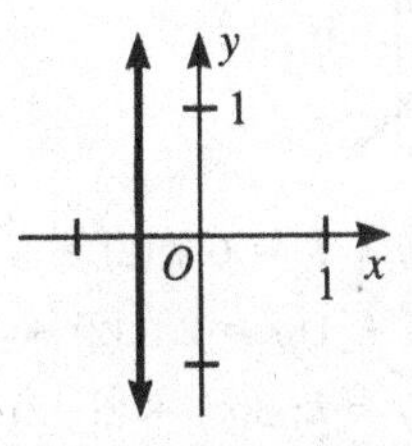

9.

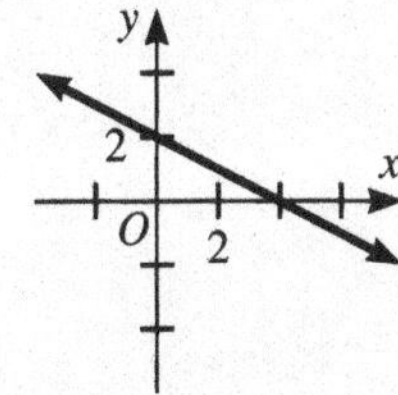

10.

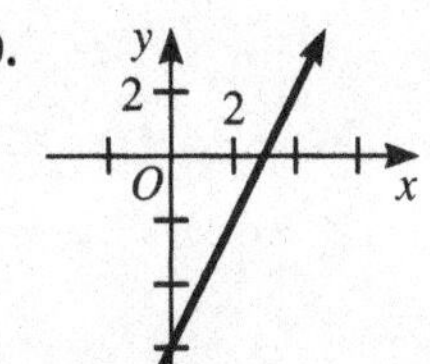

11.

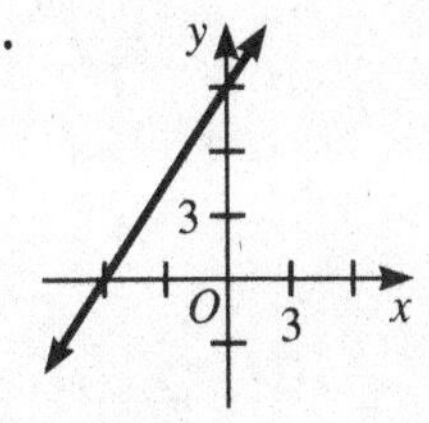

12.

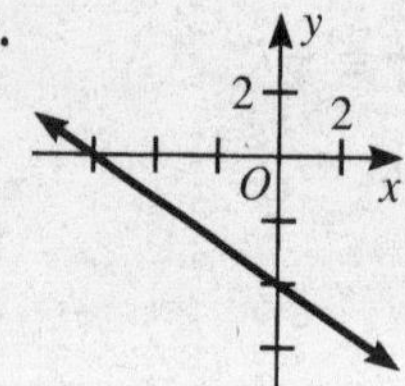

13.

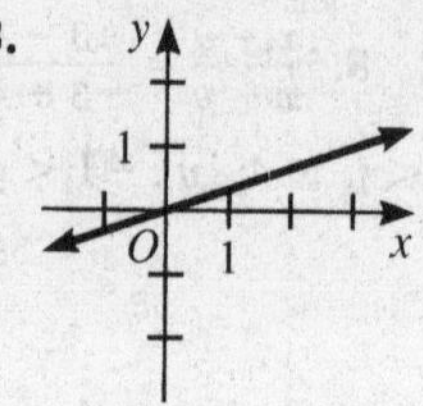

14.

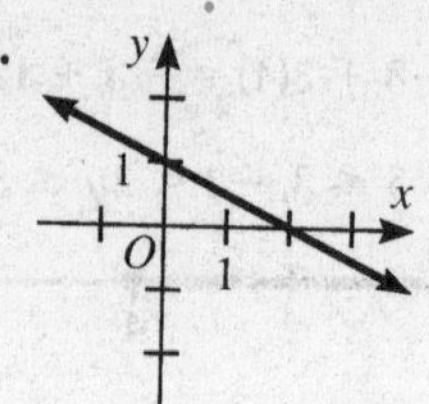

15.

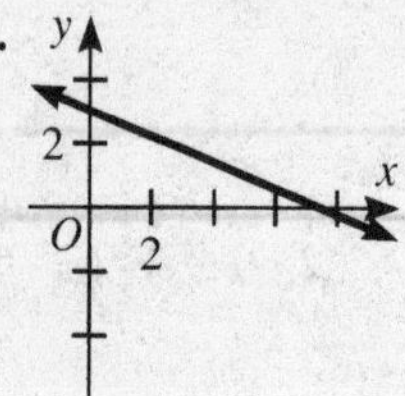

16.

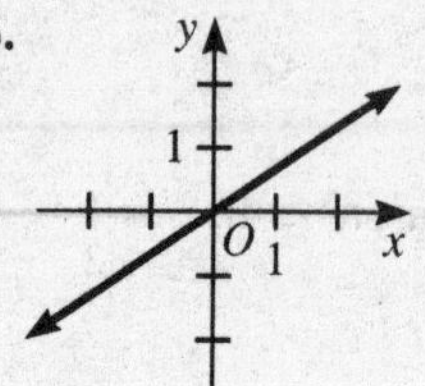

17.

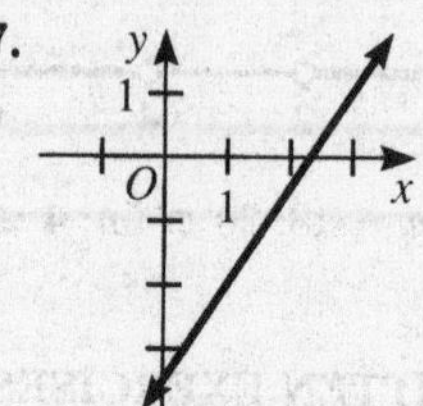

18.

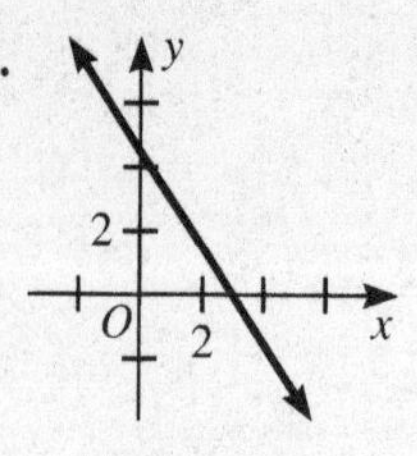

B **19.**

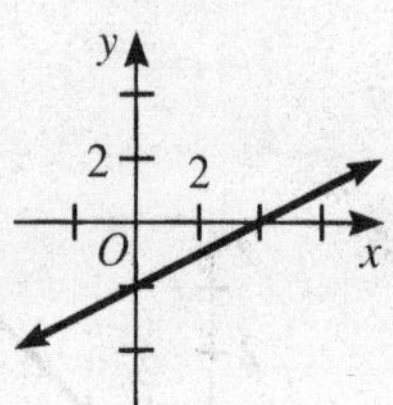

20.

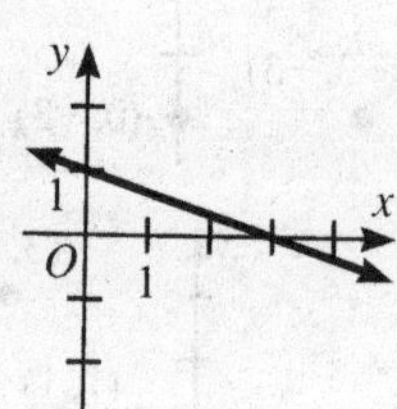

21.

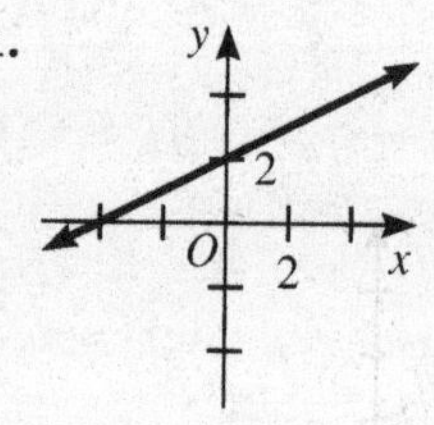

22.

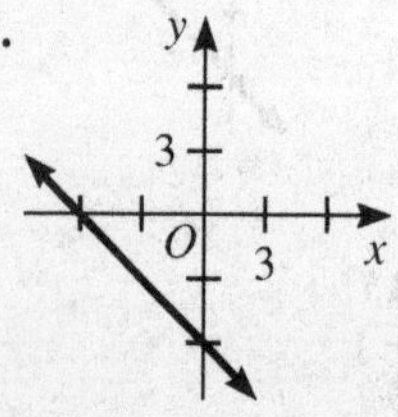

23. $3x + ky = 8; 3(2) + k(1) = 8; k = 2$

24. $kx - 2y + k = 0; k(2) - 2(3) + k = 0; 3k - 6 = 0; k = 2$

25. $kx + (k + 1)y = 2; k(2) + (k + 1)(2) = 2; 2k + 2k + 2 = 2; 4k = 0; k = 0$

26. $3x + 2y = k; 3(k) + 2(-2) = k; 3k - 4 = k; 2k = 4; k = 2$

27.

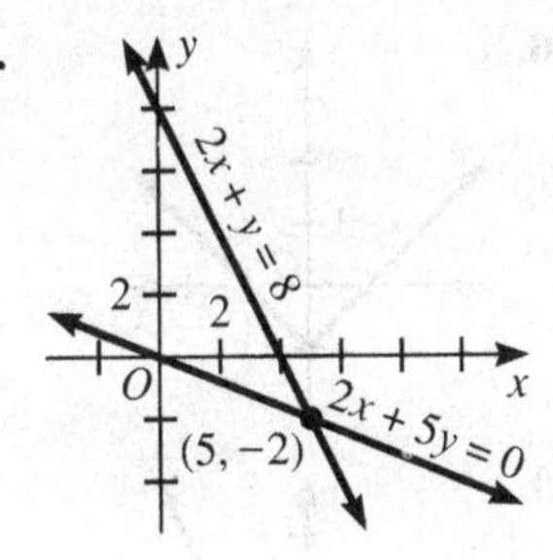

Graphs intersect at (5, −2);
2(5) + 5(−2) = 0; 2(5) + (−2) = 8

28.

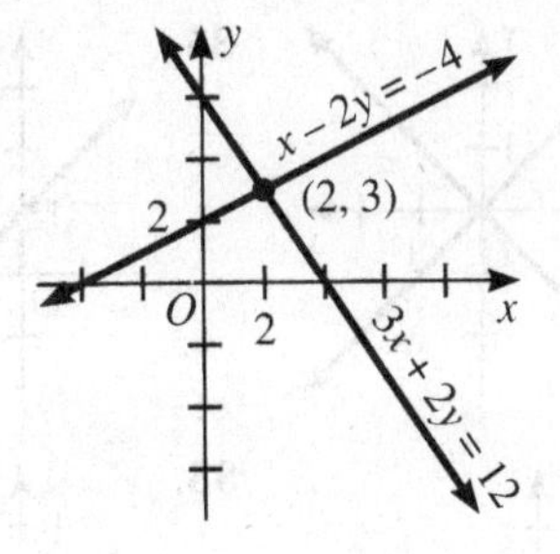

Graphs intersect at (2, 3);
2 − 2(3) = −4; 3(2) + 2(3) = 12

29.

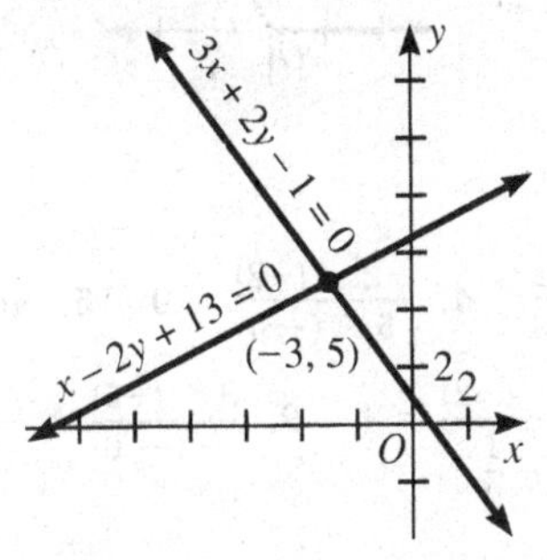

Graphs intersect at (−3, 5); 3(−3) + 2(5) − 1 = 0; −3 − 2(5) + 13 = 0

30.

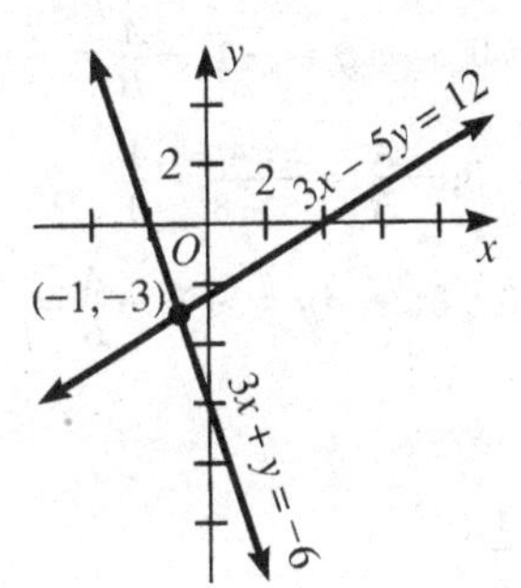

Graphs intersect at (−1, −3); 3(−1) − 5(−3) = 12; 3(−1) + (−3) = −6

31.

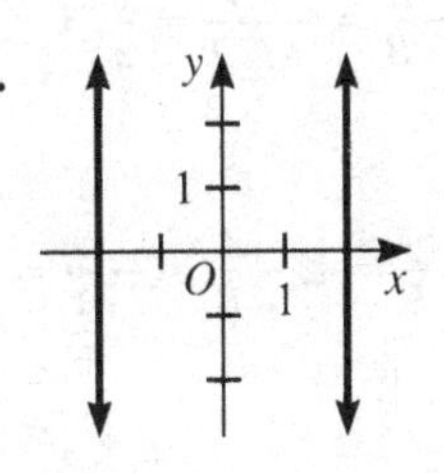

32.

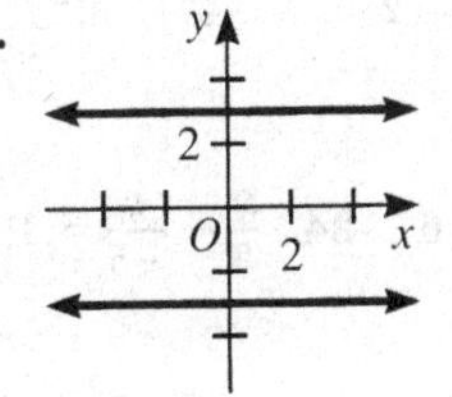

33.

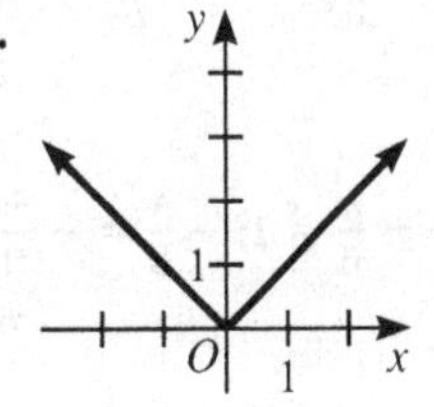

C **34.** 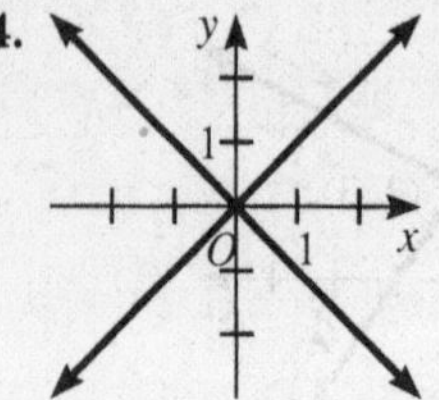

35. 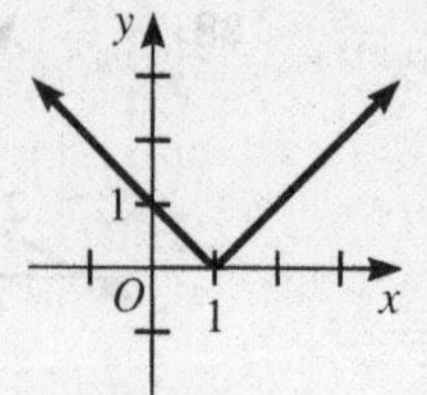

36. 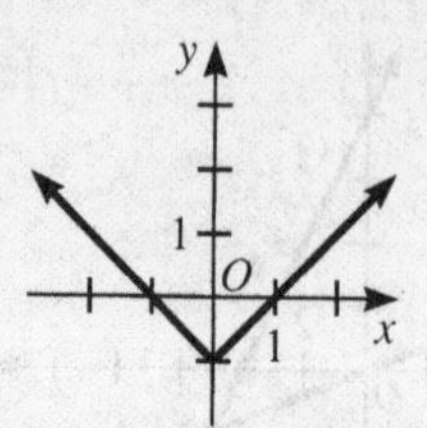

37. 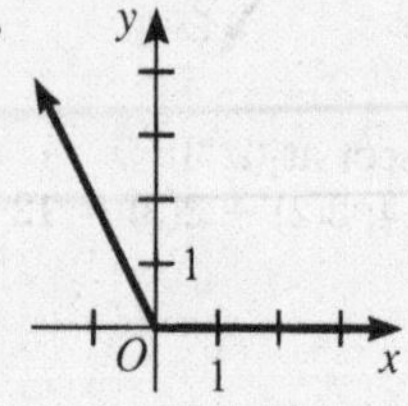

38. 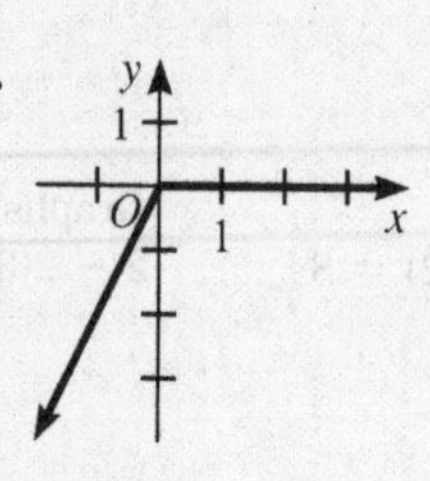

39. 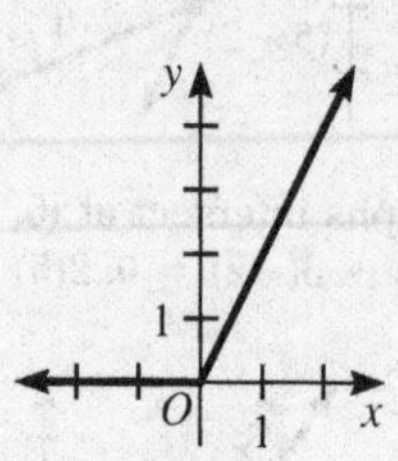

Pages 116–117 • WRITTEN EXERCISES

A **1.** $\frac{5-1}{5-3} = 2$ **2.** $\frac{3-1}{4-0} = \frac{1}{2}$ **3.** $\frac{3-(-1)}{-2-4} = -\frac{2}{3}$ **4.** $\frac{-2-(-2)}{5-(-5)} = 0$ **5.** vertical

6. $\frac{1-(-1)}{-3-3} = -\frac{1}{3}$ **7.** $\frac{-7-(-3)}{\frac{1}{2}-\frac{3}{2}} = 4$ **8.** $\frac{-4-(-2)}{0-\frac{1}{2}} = 4$ **9.** $\frac{3-(-5)}{-4-6} = -\frac{4}{5}$

10. $\frac{-1.6-2.4}{1.5-0.5} = -4$ **11.** $\frac{a-b}{b-a} = -1$ **12.** $\frac{-a-b}{-b-a} = 1$

13. $x + y = 7; -\frac{A}{B} = -\frac{1}{1} = -1$ **14.** $x - y + 1 = 0; x - y = -1; -\frac{A}{B} = -\frac{1}{-1} = 1$

15. $2x + 4y = 5; -\frac{A}{B} = -\frac{2}{4} = -\frac{1}{2}$ **16.** $4x - 3y = 3; -\frac{A}{B} = -\frac{4}{-3} = \frac{4}{3}$

17. $3x - 3y = 5; -\frac{A}{B} = -\frac{3}{-3} = 1$ **18.** $4y - 5 = 6x; 6x - 4y = -5; -\frac{A}{B} = -\frac{6}{-4} = \frac{3}{2}$

19. $x = 3y + 2; x - 3y = 2; -\frac{A}{B} = -\frac{1}{-3} = \frac{1}{3}$

20. $2(1 - y) = x; 2 - 2y = x; x + 2y = 2; -\frac{A}{B} = -\frac{1}{2}$

21. $\frac{1}{2}x + \frac{1}{3}y = 1; -\frac{A}{B} = -\frac{\frac{1}{2}}{\frac{1}{3}} = -\frac{3}{2}$ **22.** $\frac{1}{4}x - \frac{1}{2}y = 1; -\frac{A}{B} = -\frac{\frac{1}{4}}{-\frac{1}{2}} = \frac{1}{2}$

23. $\frac{x}{-1} + \frac{y}{6} = 1; -\frac{A}{B} = -\frac{-1}{\frac{1}{6}} = 6$ **24.** $\frac{x}{3} - \frac{y}{-5} = 1; \frac{x}{3} + \frac{y}{5} = 1; -\frac{A}{B} = -\frac{\frac{1}{3}}{\frac{1}{5}} = -\frac{5}{3}$

Exercises 25–36. Points chosen may vary. Examples are given.

25.

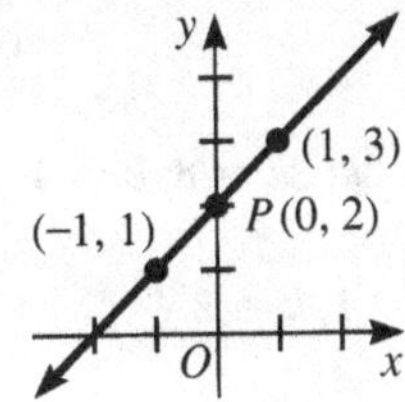

26.

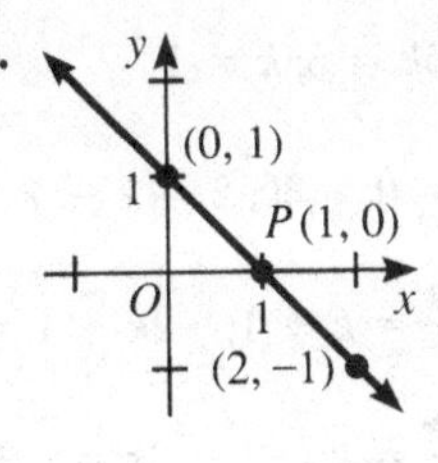

27.

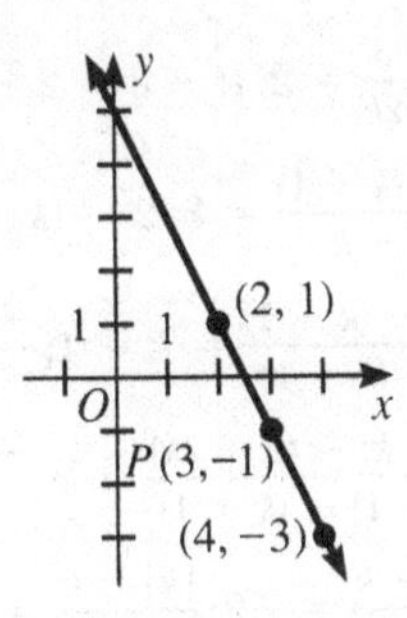

28.

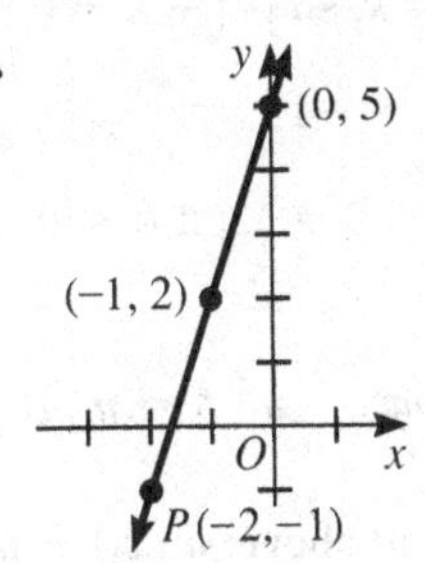

29.

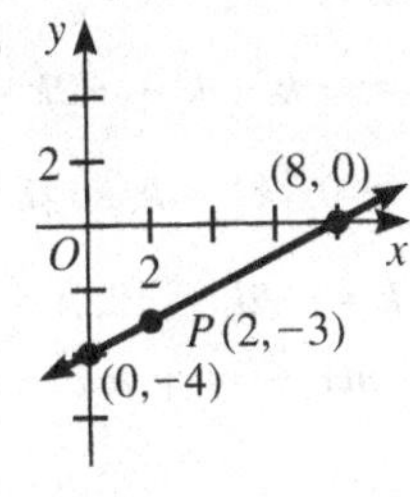

30.

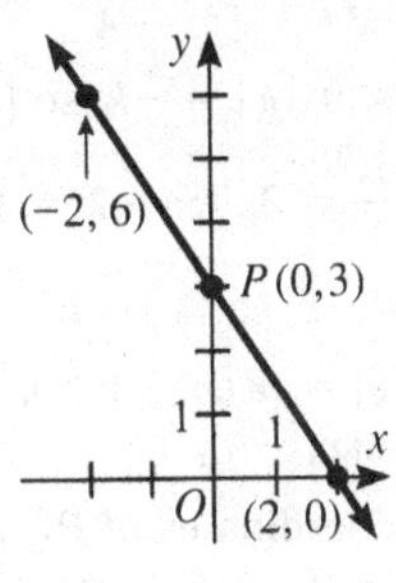

B **31.**

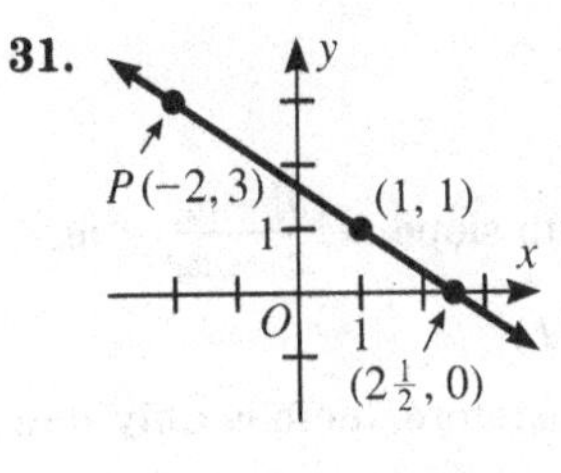

32.

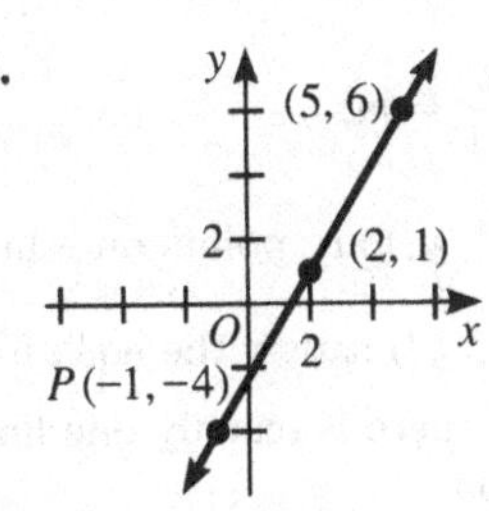

33.

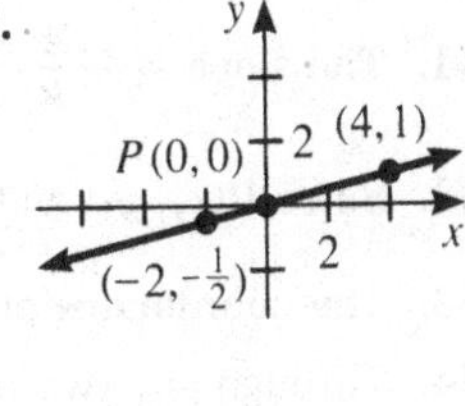

34.

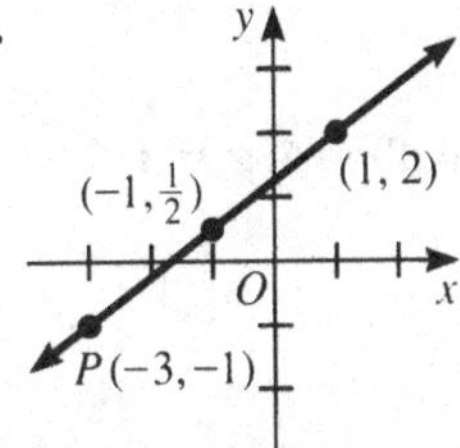

35.

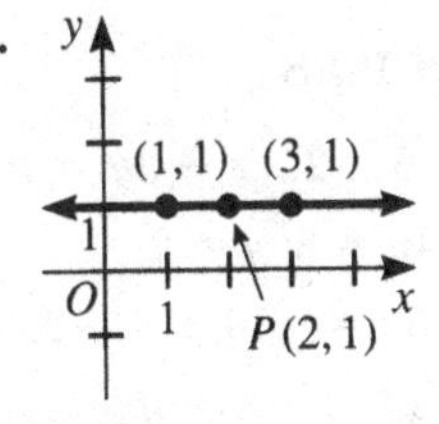

36.

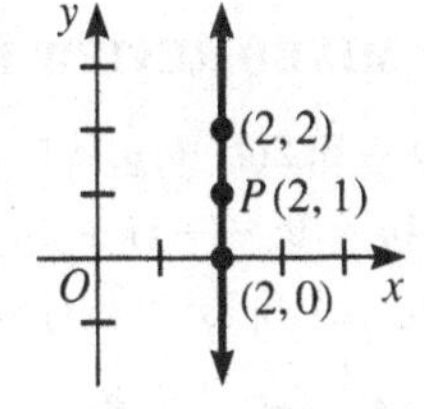

37. Let x = the length, in feet, of the base of the ramp; $m = 0.05 = \frac{3}{x}$; $0.05x = 3$; $x = 60$; the ramp should have a 60-foot base.

38. Let y = the altitude gained, in miles; $m = 0.25 = \frac{y}{5}$; $y = 1.25$; the jet gained an altitude of 1.25 mi.

39. $kx - 3y = 7$; $-\frac{A}{B} = -\frac{k}{-3} = 2$; $k = 6$

40. $6x + ky = 10$; $-\frac{A}{B} = -\frac{6}{k} = -2$; $-6 = -2k$; $k = 3$

41. $(k + 3)x - 3y = 1$; $-\frac{A}{B} = -\frac{(k + 3)}{-3} = k$; $3k = k + 3$; $2k = 3$; $k = \frac{3}{2}$

42. $(k + 1)x + 2y = 6; -\frac{A}{B} = -\frac{(k + 1)}{2} = k - 2; k + 1 = -2k + 4; 3k = 3; k = 1$

43. $\frac{k - 3}{1 - 2k} = 2; k - 3 = 2 - 4k; 5k = 5; k = 1$

44. $\frac{2 - (k + 1)}{3 - k} = 3; 2 - (k + 1) = 9 - 3k; 2 - k - 1 = 9 - 3k; 2k = 8; k = 4$

45. $\frac{-k - (k - 1)}{k - (k + 1)} = k + 1; \frac{-2k + 1}{-1} = k + 1; -2k + 1 = -k - 1; k = 2$

46. $\frac{(1 - k) - (3 + 2k)}{(k - 1) - (k + 1)} = k; \frac{-2 - 3k}{-2} = k; -2 - 3k = -2k; k = -2$

C **47.** $\frac{|k| - k}{-1 - 3} = -2; \frac{|k| - k}{-4} = -2; |k| - k = 8$; if $k \geq 0, |k| = k$, so $|k| - k = 0 \neq 8$; if $k < 0, |k| = -k$, so $|k| - k = -k - k = -2k = 8; k = -4$

48. $\frac{|k| - k}{5 - 1} = 3; |k| - k = 12$; if $k \geq 0, |k| = k$, so $|k| - k = 0 \neq 12$; if $k < 0$, $|k| = -k$, so $|k| - k = -k - k = -2k = 12; k = -6$

49. $y - y_1 = m(x - x_1); y - y_1 = mx - mx_1; mx - y = mx_1 - y_1; A = m, B = -1, C = mx_1 - y_1$

50. The coordinates of $P(x_1, y_1)$ satisfy the equation in Ex. 49 above: $m(x_1) - y_1 = mx_1 - y_1$

51. The slope $= -\frac{A}{B} = -\frac{m}{-1} = m$.

52. Since $P(x_1, y_1)$ and $Q(x', y')$ are points on a line with slope m, $\frac{y' - y_1}{x' - x_1} = m$.

53. The coordinates of $Q(x', y')$ satisfy the equation of L.

54. Through any two points there is exactly one line. Therefore, there is **only one** line through P having slope m.

Page 117 • MIXED REVIEW EXERCISES

1. $2x + y = 5; 2(4) + y = 5; y = -3$ **2.** $x - 3y = 7; x - 3(-2) = 7; x = 1$

3. $-x + 4y = 9; -(-1) + 4y = 9; 4y = 8; y = 2$

4. $5x + 2y = -8; 5x + 2(1) = -8; 5x = -10; x = -2$

5.

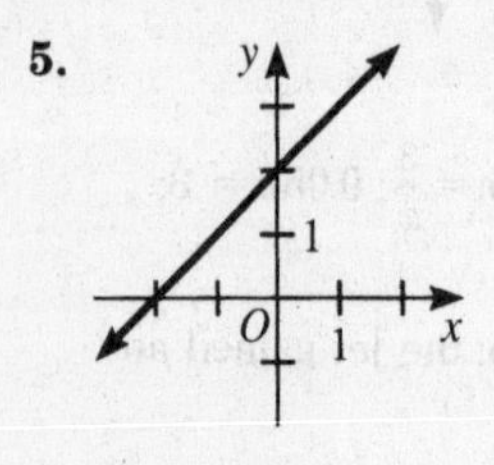

6.

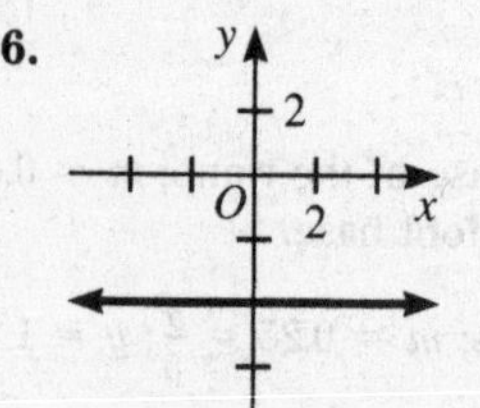

7.

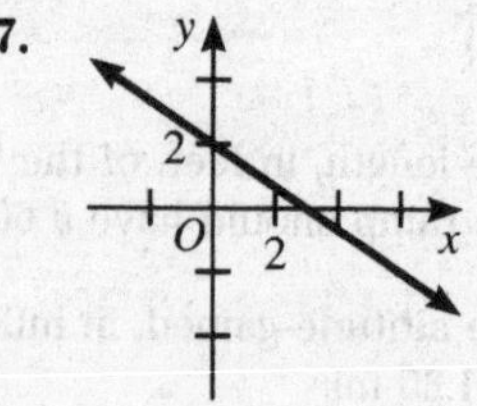

8.

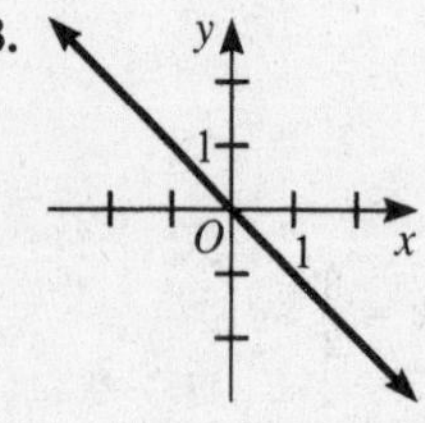

9.

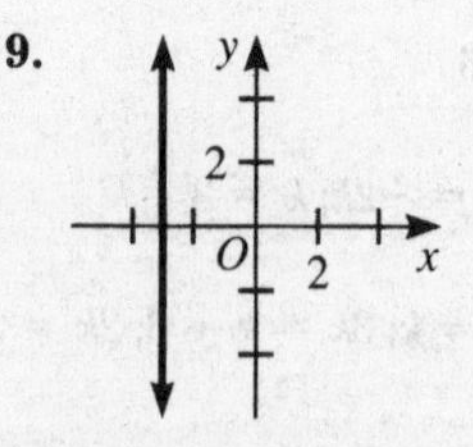

10.

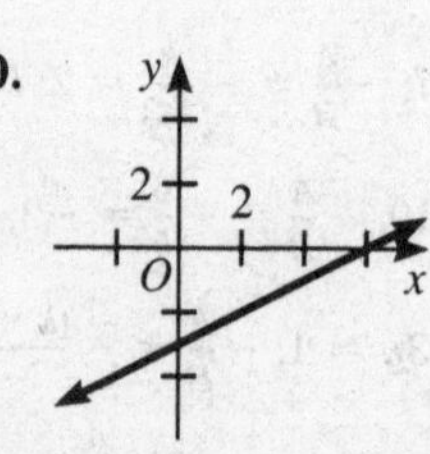

Pages 121–122 • WRITTEN EXERCISES

A

1. $y - 3 = 1(x - 2); y - 3 = x - 2; x - y = -1$

2. $y - 1 = -1(x - 2); y - 1 = -x + 2; x + y = 3$

3. $y - 0 = -2(x - 5); y = -2x + 10; 2x + y = 10$ **4.** $y = 4$

5. $y - (-2) = \frac{1}{2}[x - (-3)]; y + 2 = \frac{1}{2}x + \frac{3}{2}; 2y + 4 = x + 3; x - 2y = 1$

6. $y - 1 = \frac{2}{3}(x - 2); 3y - 3 = 2x - 4; 2x - 3y = 1$

7. $y - (-3) = \frac{1}{5}(x - 4); 5y + 15 = x - 4; x - 5y = 19$

8. $y = -\frac{3}{2}x + 6; 2y = -3x + 12; 3x + 2y = 12$ **9.** $y = -1$

10. $y - 3 = -\frac{4}{3}[x - (-3)]; 3y - 9 = -4x - 12; 4x + 3y = -3$

11. $y - 4 = 0.4[x - (-2)]; y - 4 = \frac{2}{5}(x + 2); 5y - 20 = 2x + 4; 2x - 5y = -24$

12. $y - 0 = -0.6(x - 4); y = -\frac{3}{5}(x - 4); 5y = -3x + 12; 3x + 5y = 12$

13. $y = -1(x) + 2; x + y = 2$ **14.** $y = 1x - 3; x - y = 3$

15. $y = \frac{1}{2}x + \frac{3}{2}; 2y = x + 3; x - 2y = -3$

16. $y = -\frac{3}{4}x - \frac{5}{4}; 4y = -3x - 5; 3x + 4y = -5$

17. $y = 1.2x - 0.6; y = \frac{6}{5}x - \frac{3}{5}; 5y = 6x - 3; 6x - 5y = 3$

18. $y = -0.8x + 1.4; y = -\frac{4}{5}x + \frac{7}{5}; 5y = -4x + 7; 4x + 5y = 7$

19. $m = \frac{-2 - 0}{5 - 0} = -\frac{2}{5}; b = 0; y = -\frac{2}{5}x + 0; 5y = -2x; 2x + 5y = 0$

20. $m = \frac{1 - 0}{-3 - 0} = -\frac{1}{3}; b = 0; y = -\frac{1}{3}x + 0; 3y = -x; x + 3y = 0$

21. $m = \frac{3 - (-2)}{-2 - 3} = \frac{5}{-5} = -1; y - (-2) = -1(x - 3); y + 2 = -x + 3; x + y = 1$

22. $m = \frac{-3 - (-2)}{2 - 3} = \frac{-1}{-1} = 1; y - (-2) = 1(x - 3); y + 2 = x - 3; x - y = 5$

23. $m = \frac{2 - (-2)}{-3 - 3} = \frac{4}{-6} = -\frac{2}{3}; y - (-2) = -\frac{2}{3}(x - 3); 3y + 6 = -2x + 6;$

$2x + 3y = 0$

24. $m = \frac{-2 - (-2)}{-3 - 3} = 0; y = -2$ **25.** There is no slope; $x = -2$

26. $m = \frac{-4 - (-5)}{1 - 4} = -\frac{1}{3}; y - (-5) = -\frac{1}{3}(x - 4); 3y + 15 = -x + 4; x + 3y = -11$

27. $m = \frac{\frac{1}{2} - \frac{1}{2}}{3 - (-3)} = 0; y = \frac{1}{2}$

28. $m = \dfrac{\frac{5}{2} - \left(-\frac{1}{2}\right)}{-\frac{1}{2} - \frac{3}{2}} = -\frac{3}{2}$; $y - \left(-\frac{1}{2}\right) = -\frac{3}{2}\left(x - \frac{3}{2}\right)$; $4y + 2 = -6x + 9$; $6x + 4y = 7$

29. $m = \dfrac{-1 - \left(-\frac{1}{2}\right)}{\frac{1}{6} - \frac{2}{3}} = 1$; $y - (-1) = 1\left(x - \frac{1}{6}\right)$; $6y + 6 = 6x - 1$; $6x - 6y = 7$

30. $m = \dfrac{\frac{1}{2} - \frac{5}{4}}{-\frac{1}{4} - \frac{3}{4}} = \frac{3}{4}$; $y - \frac{1}{2} = \frac{3}{4}\left[x - \left(-\frac{1}{4}\right)\right]$; $16y - 8 = 12x + 3$; $12x - 16y = -11$

31. The slope of L is -1. **a.** $m = -1$; $b = 3$; $y = -1x + 3$; $x + y = 3$
b. $m = 1$; $b = 3$; $y = 1x + 3$; $x - y = -3$

32. The slope of L is 1. **a.** $m = 1$; $b = -2$; $y = 1x + (-2)$; $x - y = 2$
b. $m = -1$; $b = -2$; $y = -1x - 2$; $x + y = -2$

33. The slope of L is $\frac{1}{2}$. **a.** $m = \frac{1}{2}$; $b = -4$; $y = \frac{1}{2}x - 4$; $2y = x - 8$; $x - 2y = 8$
b. $m = -2$; $b = -4$; $y = -2x - 4$; $2x + y = -4$

34. The slope of L is $-\frac{3}{2}$.
a. $m = -\frac{3}{2}$; $b = 1$; $y = -\frac{3}{2}x + 1$; $2y = -3x + 2$; $3x + 2y = 2$
b. $m = \frac{2}{3}$; $b = 1$; $y = \frac{2}{3}x + 1$; $3y = 2x + 3$; $2x - 3y = -3$

35. The slope of L is $-\frac{1}{2}$. **a.** $m = -\frac{1}{2}$; $y - 0 = -\frac{1}{2}(x - 2)$; $2y = -x + 2$; $x + 2y = 2$
b. $m = 2$; $y - 0 = 2(x - 2)$; $y = 2x - 4$; $2x - y = 4$

36. The slope of L is $\frac{1}{3}$. **a.** $m = \frac{1}{3}$; $y - 2 = \frac{1}{3}(x + 1)$; $3y - 6 = x + 1$; $x - 3y = -7$
b. $m = -3$; $y - 2 = -3(x + 1)$; $y - 2 = -3x - 3$; $3x + y = -1$

37. The slope of L is 0. **a.** $m = 0$; $y = 1$ **b.** The line is vertical; $x = -4$

38. L has no slope. **a.** The line is vertical; $x = -1$ **b.** The line is horizontal; $y = -2$

B **39.** $m = \dfrac{4 - 4}{-3 - 1} = 0$; $y = 4$ **40.** The line is vertical; $x = -2$ **41.** $x = 0$

42. $y = 0$ **43.** The line is horizontal; $y = 6$ **44.** The line is vertical; $x = -4$

45. The line passes through (4, 0) and (0, 3); $m = \dfrac{3 - 0}{0 - 4} = -\frac{3}{4}$; $b = 3$; $y = -\frac{3}{4}x + 3$; $4y = -3x + 12$; $3x + 4y = 12$

46. The line passes through $(-3, 0)$ and $(0, -1)$; $m = \dfrac{-1 - 0}{0 - (-3)} = -\frac{1}{3}$; $b = -1$;
$y = -\frac{1}{3}x - 1$; $3y = -x - 3$; $x + 3y = -3$

47. The slope of the line through (1, 4) and (2, 3) is $\dfrac{3 - 4}{2 - 1} = -1$; $m = -1$;
$y - 1 = -1[x - (-2)]$; $y - 1 = -x - 2$; $x + y = -1$

48. The slope of the line through (2, 3) and (1, −2) is $\frac{-2-3}{1-2} = \frac{-5}{-1} = 5$; $m = 5$;

$y - 2 = 5[x - (-3)]$; $y - 2 = 5x + 15$; $5x - y = -17$

49. Slope of $\overleftrightarrow{AB} = \frac{2-0}{-2-2} = -\frac{1}{2}$; slope of $\overleftrightarrow{CD} = \frac{6-8}{6-2} = -\frac{1}{2}$; $\overleftrightarrow{AB} \parallel \overleftrightarrow{CD}$; slope of

$\overleftrightarrow{BC} = \frac{8-2}{2-(-2)} = \frac{3}{2}$; slope of $\overleftrightarrow{DA} = \frac{6-0}{6-2} = \frac{3}{2}$; $\overleftrightarrow{BC} \parallel \overleftrightarrow{DA}$; ∴ *ABCD* is a parallelogram.

Since $\left(-\frac{1}{2}\right)\left(\frac{3}{2}\right) \neq -1$, *ABCD* is not a rectangle.

50. The slope of $\overleftrightarrow{AB} = \frac{4-3}{1-(-2)} = \frac{1}{3}$; the slope of $\overleftrightarrow{CD} = \frac{-2-(-1)}{0-3} = \frac{1}{3}$; $\overleftrightarrow{AB} \parallel \overleftrightarrow{CD}$; slope

of $\overleftrightarrow{BC} = \frac{-1-4}{3-1} = -\frac{5}{2}$; slope of $\overleftrightarrow{DA} = \frac{-2-3}{0-(-2)} = -\frac{5}{2}$; $\overleftrightarrow{BC} \parallel \overleftrightarrow{DA}$; ∴ *ABCD* is a

parallelogram. Since $\frac{1}{3}\left(-\frac{5}{2}\right) \neq -1$, *ABCD* is not a rectangle.

51. Slope of $\overleftrightarrow{AB} = \frac{0-(-2)}{6-0} = \frac{1}{3}$; slope of $\overleftrightarrow{CD} = \frac{1-3}{-1-5} = \frac{1}{3}$; $\overleftrightarrow{AB} \parallel \overleftrightarrow{CD}$. Slope of $\overleftrightarrow{BC}$ =

$\frac{3-0}{5-6} = -3$; slope of $\overleftrightarrow{AD} = \frac{1-(-2)}{-1-0} = -3$; $\overleftrightarrow{BC} \parallel \overleftrightarrow{AD}$; ∴ *ABCD* is a parallelogram.

Since $\left(\frac{1}{3}\right)(-3) = -1$, adjacent sides are perpendicular and *ABCD* is a rectangle.

52. Slope of $\overleftrightarrow{AB} = \frac{1-(-2)}{5-4} = 3$; slope of $\overleftrightarrow{CD} = \frac{0-3}{-2-0} = -\frac{3}{2}$; $\overleftrightarrow{AB} \nparallel \overleftrightarrow{CD}$; ∴ *ABCD* is not

a parallelogram.

53. Slope of $\overleftrightarrow{BC} = \frac{-1-4}{-2-1} = \frac{5}{3}$; slope of $\overleftrightarrow{AD} = \frac{-5-1}{6-7} = 6$; $\overleftrightarrow{AD} \nparallel \overleftrightarrow{BC}$; ∴ *ABCD* is not a

parallelogram.

54. Slope of $\overleftrightarrow{AB} = \frac{5-1}{-1-5} = -\frac{2}{3}$; slope of $\overleftrightarrow{CD} = \frac{-2-2}{3-(-3)} = -\frac{2}{3}$; $\overleftrightarrow{AB} \parallel \overleftrightarrow{CD}$; slope of

$\overleftrightarrow{BC} = \frac{2-5}{-3-(-1)} = \frac{3}{2}$; slope of $\overleftrightarrow{AD} = \frac{-2-1}{3-5} = \frac{3}{2}$; $\overleftrightarrow{AD} \parallel \overleftrightarrow{BC}$; ∴ *ABCD* is a

parallelogram. Since $-\frac{2}{3}\left(\frac{3}{2}\right) = -1$, adjacent sides are perpendicular and *ABCD* is a

rectangle.

C **55.** The slope of $L_1 = -\frac{A_1}{B_1}$; the slope of $L_2 = -\frac{A_2}{B_2}$.

a. The lines are parallel if and only if $-\frac{A_1}{B_1} = -\frac{A_2}{B_2}$; $-A_1B_2 = -A_2B_1$; $A_1B_2 = A_2B_1$

b. The lines are perpendicular if and only if $\left(-\frac{A_1}{B_1}\right)\left(-\frac{A_2}{B_2}\right) = -1$; $A_1A_2 = -B_1B_2$;

$A_1A_2 + B_1B_2 = 0$

56. The slope is $\frac{y_2 - y_1}{x_2 - x_1} = m$. Substitution into the point-slope form $y - y_1 = m(x - x_1)$

gives $y - y_1 = \frac{y_2 - y_1}{x_2 - x_1}(x - x_1)$.

57. The line passes through $(a, 0)$ and $(0, b)$. Assume $a \neq 0$ and $b \neq 0$. The slope is $\frac{b-0}{0-a} = -\frac{b}{a}$. Using the slope-intercept form, $y = -\frac{b}{a}x + b$. Dividing by b yields $\frac{y}{b} = -\frac{x}{a} + 1$; $\frac{x}{a} + \frac{y}{b} = 1$. (If $a = 0$ or $b = 0$, this form cannot be used.)

Pages 122–123 • COMPUTER EXERCISES

1.
```
10 INPUT "ENTER X1, Y1: "; X1, Y1
20 INPUT "ENTER X2, Y2: "; X2, Y2
30 IF X1 = X2 THEN PRINT "THE LINE IS VERTICAL."
40 IF X1 < > X2 THEN PRINT "SLOPE = "; (Y2 - Y1)/(X2 - X1)
50 END
```

2. **a.** 4.5 **b.** −2.28571429 **c.** vertical

3.
```
10 INPUT "ENTER THE SLOPE: "; M
20 INPUT "ENTER THE COORDINATES OF A POINT: "; X, Y
30 LET B = Y - M * X
40 PRINT "Y = "; M; "X + "; B
50 END
```

4. $y = 1.72x + 17.2$

5.
```
10 INPUT "ENTER X1, Y1: "; X1, Y1
20 INPUT "ENTER X2, Y2: "; X2, Y2
30 IF X1 = X2 THEN 80
40 LET M = (Y2 - Y1)/(X2 - X1)
50 LET B = Y1 - M * X1
60 PRINT "Y = "; M; "X + "; B
70 GOTO 90
80 PRINT "X = "; X1
90 END
```

6. **a.** $y = 4.5x - 14.5$ **b.** $y = -2.28571429x - 4.42857143$ **c.** $x = 7$

Pages 129–130 • WRITTEN EXERCISES

A

1. $\begin{array}{l} 2x + y = 1 \\ 2x + 3y = 7 \end{array}$; $y = 1 - 2x$; $2x + 3(1 - 2x) = 7$; $2x + 3 - 6x = 7$; $-4x = 4$; $x = -1$; $y = 1 - 2(-1)$; $y = 3$; $(-1, 3)$

2. $\begin{array}{l} 2x - 3y = 7 \\ 3x + y = 5 \end{array}$; $y = 5 - 3x$; $2x - 3(5 - 3x) = 7$; $2x - 15 + 9x = 7$; $11x = 22$; $x = 2$; $y = 5 - 3(2) = -1$; $(2, -1)$

3. $\begin{array}{l} 5x - 6y = 9 \\ 2x - 3y = 3 \end{array}$, $\begin{array}{l} 5x - 6y = 9 \\ -4x + 6y = -6 \end{array}$; $x = 3$; $5(3) - 6y = 9$; $-6y = -6$; $y = 1$; $(3, 1)$

4. $\begin{array}{l} 4x - 3y = 6 \\ 2x - 5y = -4 \end{array}$, $\begin{array}{l} 4x - 3y = 6 \\ -4x + 10y = 8 \end{array}$; $7y = 14$; $y = 2$; $4x - 3(2) = 6$; $4x = 12$; $x = 3$; $(3, 2)$

5. $\begin{array}{l} 2x - 3y = 3 \\ 5x + 2y = 17 \end{array}$, $\begin{array}{l} -10x + 15y = -15 \\ 10x + 4y = 34 \end{array}$; $19y = 19$; $y = 1$; $2x - 3(1) = 3$; $2x = 6$; $x = 3$; $(3, 1)$

6. $\begin{array}{l}4x + 5y = 3\\ 3x + 2y = 4\end{array};\ \begin{array}{l}-12x - 15y = -9\\ 12x + 8y = 16\end{array};\ -7y = 7;\ y = -1;\ 4x + 5(-1) = 3;\ 4x = 8;\ x = 2;\ (2, -1)$

7. $\begin{array}{l}2x - 7y = 10\\ 5x - 6y = 2\end{array};\ \begin{array}{l}10x - 35y = 50\\ -10x + 12y = -4\end{array};\ -23y = 46;\ y = -2;\ 2x - 7(-2) = 10;\ 2x + 14 = 10;\ x = -2;\ (-2, -2)$

8. $\begin{array}{l}5x + 6y + 8 = 0\\ 3x - 2y + 16 = 0\end{array};\ \begin{array}{l}5x + 6y = -8\\ 3x - 2y = -16\end{array};\ \begin{array}{l}5x + 6y = -8\\ 9x - 6y = -48\end{array};\ 14x = -56;\ x = -4;$

$5(-4) + 6y = -8;\ -20 + 6y = -8;\ 6y = 12;\ y = 2;\ (-4, 2)$

9. $\begin{array}{l}3x - 2y + 2 = 0\\ x + 3y = 14\end{array};\ \begin{array}{l}3x - 2y = -2\\ x + 3y = 14\end{array};\ \begin{array}{l}3x - 2y = -2\\ -3x - 9y = -42\end{array};\ -11y = -44;\ y = 4;$

$x + 3(4) = 14;\ x + 12 = 14;\ x = 2;\ (2, 4)$

10. $\begin{array}{l}8x - 3y = 3\\ 3x - 2y + 5 = 0\end{array};\ \begin{array}{l}8x - 3y = 3\\ 3x - 2y = -5\end{array};\ \begin{array}{l}16x - 6y = 6\\ -9x + 6y = 15\end{array};\ 7x = 21;\ x = 3;\ 8(3) - 3y = 3;$

$24 - 3y = 3;\ -3y = -21;\ y = 7;\ (3, 7)$

11. $\begin{array}{l}6u + 5v = -2\\ 2u + 3v = 6\end{array};\ \begin{array}{l}6u + 5v = -2\\ -6u - 9v = -18\end{array};\ -4v = -20;\ v = 5;\ 2u + 3(5) = 6;\ 2u + 15 = 6;$

$2u = -9;\ u = -\frac{9}{2};\ \left(-\frac{9}{2}, 5\right)$

12. $\begin{array}{l}3p + 2q = -2\\ 9p - q = -6\end{array};\ \begin{array}{l}3p + 2q = -2\\ 18p - 2q = -12\end{array};\ 21p = -14;\ p = -\frac{2}{3};\ 3\left(-\frac{2}{3}\right) + 2q = -2;$

$-2 + 2q = -2;\ 2q = 0;\ q = 0;\ \left(-\frac{2}{3}, 0\right)$

13.

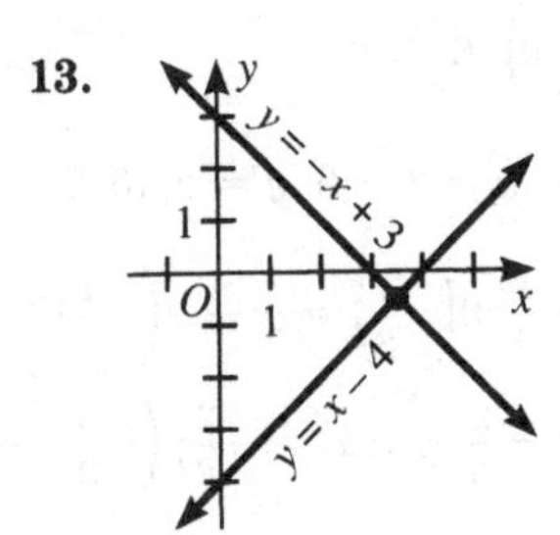

The graphs intersect at (3.5, −0.5).

14.

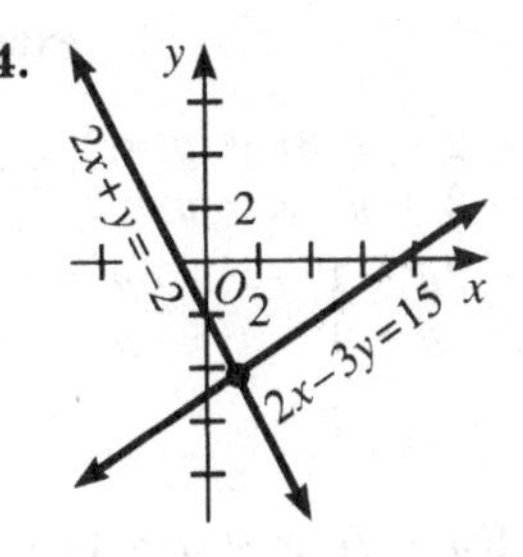

The graphs intersect at approximately (1, −4).

15.

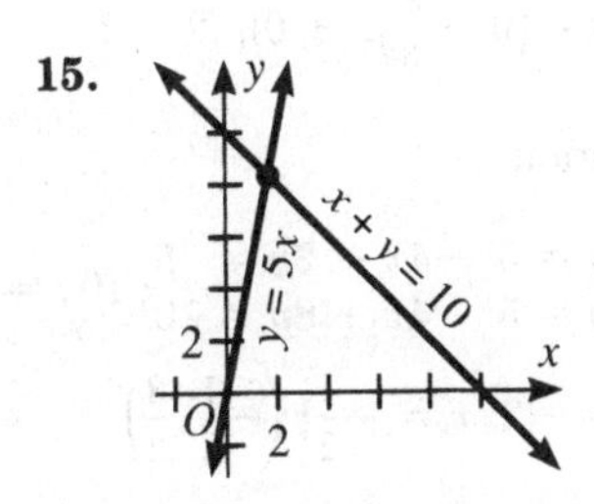

The graphs intersect at approximately (2, 8).

16.

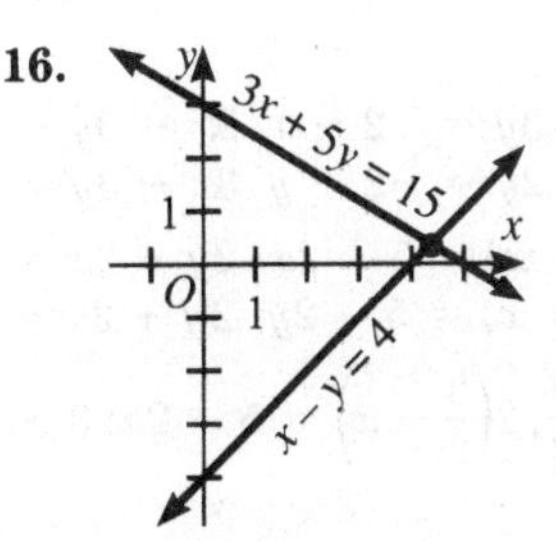

The graphs intersect at approximately (4.5, 0.5).

17. $\begin{array}{l} 3x+3y=6 \\ 5x-6y=15 \end{array}$; $\begin{array}{l} 6x+6y=12 \\ 5x-6y=15 \end{array}$; $11x=27$; $x=\frac{27}{11}$; $3\left(\frac{27}{11}\right)+3y=6$; $3y=-\frac{15}{11}$; $y=-\frac{5}{11}$; $\left(\frac{27}{11}, -\frac{5}{11}\right)$

18. $\begin{array}{l} 3x-2y=6 \\ 5x+3y+9=0 \end{array}$; $\begin{array}{l} 3x-2y=6 \\ 5x+3y=-9 \end{array}$; $\begin{array}{l} 9x-6y=18 \\ 10x+6y=-18 \end{array}$; $19x=0$; $x=0$; $3(0)-2y=6$; $y=-3$; $(0, -3)$

19. $\begin{array}{l} x-y=2x-2 \\ x+y=2y-2 \end{array}$; $\begin{array}{l} -x-y=-2 \\ x-y=-2 \end{array}$; $-2y=-4$; $y=2$; $x+2=2(2)-2$; $x+2=2$; $x=0$; $(0, 2)$

20. $\begin{array}{l} 6x=4y+5 \\ 6y=9x-5 \end{array}$; $\begin{array}{l} 6x-4y=5 \\ -9x+6y=-5 \end{array}$; $\begin{array}{l} 3x-2y=\frac{5}{2} \\ -3x+2y=-\frac{5}{3} \end{array}$; $0=\frac{5}{6}$; no solution

21. $\begin{array}{l} 2p-5q=14 \\ p+\frac{3}{2}q=5 \end{array}$; $\begin{array}{l} 2p-5q=14 \\ -2p-3q=-10 \end{array}$; $-8q=4$; $q=-\frac{1}{2}$; $2p-5\left(-\frac{1}{2}\right)=14$; $2p+\frac{5}{2}=14$; $2p=\frac{23}{2}$; $p=\frac{23}{4}$; $\left(\frac{23}{4}, -\frac{1}{2}\right)$

22. $\begin{array}{l} d=2-6c \\ \frac{1}{2}d-c=1 \end{array}$; $\frac{1}{2}(2-6c)-c=1$; $1-3c-c=1$; $-4c=0$; $c=0$; $d=2-6(0)$; $d=2$; $(0, 2)$

23. $\begin{array}{l} x+y=3x-1 \\ x-y=1-x \end{array}$; $\begin{array}{l} -2x+y=-1 \\ 2x-y=1 \end{array}$; $0=0$; $\{(x, y)\colon 2x-y=1\}$; examples: $(0, -1)$, $\left(\frac{1}{2}, 0\right)$, $(2, 3)$

24. $\begin{array}{l} 2x+y=2-x \\ x+2y=2+y \end{array}$; $\begin{array}{l} 3x+y=2 \\ x+y=2 \end{array}$; $2x=0$; $x=0$; $2(0)+y=2-0$; $y=2$; $(0, 2)$

25. $\begin{array}{l} 3y=x-2y-1 \\ 3x=2x-y-1 \end{array}$; $\begin{array}{l} -x+5y=-1 \\ x+y=-1 \end{array}$; $6y=-2$; $y=-\frac{1}{3}$; $3\left(-\frac{1}{3}\right)=x-2\left(-\frac{1}{3}\right)-1$; $-1=x+\frac{2}{3}-1$; $x=-\frac{2}{3}$; $\left(-\frac{2}{3}, -\frac{1}{3}\right)$

26. $\begin{array}{l} x+y=4(y+2) \\ x-y=2(y+4) \end{array}$; $\begin{array}{l} x+y=4y+8 \\ x-y=2y+8 \end{array}$; $\begin{array}{l} x-3y=8 \\ x-3y=8 \end{array}$; $0=0$; $\{(x, y)\colon x-3y=8\}$; examples: $\left(0, -\frac{8}{3}\right)$, $(8, 0)$, $(2, -2)$

27. $\begin{array}{l} 2x-3y=2-x \\ 3x-2y=-2+y \end{array}$; $\begin{array}{l} 3x-3y=2 \\ 3x-3y=-2 \end{array}$; $0=4$; no solution

28. $\begin{array}{l} 2(y-x)=5+2x \\ 2(y+x)=5-2y \end{array}$; $\begin{array}{l} 2y-2x=5+2x \\ 2y+2x=5-2y \end{array}$; $\begin{array}{l} -4x+2y=5 \\ 2x+4y=5 \end{array}$; $\begin{array}{l} -4x+2y=5 \\ 4x+8y=10 \end{array}$; $10y=15$; $y=\frac{3}{2}$; $2\left(\frac{3}{2}-x\right)=5+2x$; $3-2x=5+2x$; $4x=-2$; $x=-\frac{1}{2}$; $\left(-\frac{1}{2}, \frac{3}{2}\right)$

B

29. $\begin{matrix} 3x = 4y - 4 \\ 4y = 3x - 3 \end{matrix}$; $\begin{matrix} 4y = 3x + 4 \\ 4y = 3x - 3 \end{matrix}$; $\begin{matrix} y = \frac{3}{4}x + 1 \\ y = \frac{3}{4}x - \frac{3}{4} \end{matrix}$; inconsistent

30. $\begin{matrix} 3x = 4y + 8 \\ 3y = 4x + 8 \end{matrix}$; $\begin{matrix} 4y = 3x - 8 \\ 3y = 4x + 8 \end{matrix}$; $\begin{matrix} y = \frac{3}{4}x - 2 \\ y = \frac{4}{3}x + \frac{8}{3} \end{matrix}$; consistent

31. $\begin{matrix} 3x - 4y = 12 \\ 4x - 3y = 12 \end{matrix}$; $\begin{matrix} 4y = 3x - 12 \\ 3y = 4x - 12 \end{matrix}$; $\begin{matrix} y = \frac{3}{4}x - 3 \\ y = \frac{4}{3}x - 4 \end{matrix}$; consistent

32. $\begin{matrix} 3x - 6y = 9 \\ 4x - 3y = 12 \end{matrix}$; $\begin{matrix} 6y = 3x - 9 \\ 3y = 4x - 12 \end{matrix}$; $\begin{matrix} y = \frac{1}{2}x - \frac{3}{2} \\ y = \frac{4}{3}x - 4 \end{matrix}$; consistent

In Exercises 33–38, let $x = \frac{1}{u}$ and $y = \frac{1}{v}$.

33. $\begin{matrix} \frac{6}{u} + \frac{3}{v} = 2 \\ \frac{2}{u} - \frac{9}{v} = 4 \end{matrix}$; $\begin{matrix} 6x + 3y = 2 \\ 2x - 9y = 4 \end{matrix}$; $\begin{matrix} 18x + 9y = 6 \\ 2x - 9y = 4 \end{matrix}$; $20x = 10$; $x = \frac{1}{2}$; $u = 2$; $6\left(\frac{1}{2}\right) + 3y = 2$; $3y = -1$; $y = -\frac{1}{3}$; $v = -3$; $(2, -3)$

34. $\begin{matrix} \frac{6}{u} + \frac{5}{v} = 1 \\ \frac{3}{u} - \frac{10}{v} = 3 \end{matrix}$; $\begin{matrix} 6x + 5y = 1 \\ 3x - 10y = 3 \end{matrix}$; $\begin{matrix} 12x + 10y = 2 \\ 3x - 10y = 3 \end{matrix}$; $15x = 5$; $x = \frac{1}{3}$; $u = 3$; $6\left(\frac{1}{3}\right) + 5y = 1$; $5y = -1$; $y = -\frac{1}{5}$; $v = -5$; $(3, -5)$

35. $\begin{matrix} \frac{2}{u} - \frac{3}{v} + 2 = 0 \\ \frac{4}{u} + \frac{3}{v} + 1 = 0 \end{matrix}$; $\begin{matrix} 2x - 3y = -2 \\ 4x + 3y = -1 \end{matrix}$; $6x = -3$; $x = -\frac{1}{2}$; $u = -2$; $2\left(-\frac{1}{2}\right) - 3y = -2$; $-3y = -1$; $y = \frac{1}{3}$; $v = 3$; $(-2, 3)$

36. $\begin{matrix} \frac{3}{u} + \frac{4}{v} = 1 \\ \frac{6}{u} - \frac{2}{v} = 1 \end{matrix}$; $\begin{matrix} 3x + 4y = 1 \\ 6x - 2y = 1 \end{matrix}$; $\begin{matrix} 3x + 4y = 1 \\ 12x - 4y = 2 \end{matrix}$; $15x = 3$; $x = \frac{1}{5}$; $u = 5$; $3\left(\frac{1}{5}\right) + 4y = 1$; $4y = \frac{2}{5}$; $y = \frac{1}{10}$; $v = 10$; $(5, 10)$

37. $\begin{array}{l}\frac{3}{u} - \frac{4}{v} = 4 \\ \frac{5}{u} - \frac{6}{v} = 7\end{array}$; $\begin{array}{l}3x - 4y = 4 \\ 5x - 6y = 7\end{array}$; $\begin{array}{l}-15x + 20y = -20 \\ 15x - 18y = 21\end{array}$; $2y = 1$; $y = \frac{1}{2}$; $v = 2$;

$3x - 4\left(\frac{1}{2}\right) = 4$; $3x = 6$; $x = 2$; $u = \frac{1}{2}$; $\left(\frac{1}{2}, 2\right)$

38. $\begin{array}{l}\frac{4}{u} + \frac{3}{v} = 3 \\ \frac{6}{u} + \frac{5}{v} = 4\end{array}$; $\begin{array}{l}4x + 3y = 3 \\ 6x + 5y = 4\end{array}$; $\begin{array}{l}12x + 9y = 9 \\ -12x - 10y = -8\end{array}$; $-y = 1$; $y = -1$; $v = -1$;

$4x + 3(-1) = 3$; $4x = 6$; $x = \frac{3}{2}$; $u = \frac{2}{3}$; $\left(\frac{2}{3}, -1\right)$

C **39.** $\begin{array}{l}ax + y = b \\ bx + y = a\end{array}$; $ax - bx = b - a$; $x(a - b) = -1(a - b)$; if $a \neq b$, $x = -1$;

$a(-1) + y = b$; $y = a + b$; if $a \neq b$, the system has the unique solution $(-1, a + b)$

40. $\begin{array}{l}ax - by = c \\ bx + ay = d\end{array}$; eliminating y: $\begin{array}{l}a^2x - aby = ac \\ b^2x + aby = bd\end{array}$; $a^2x + b^2x = ac + bd$;

$x(a^2 + b^2) = ac + bd$; if a and b are not both zero, $x = \frac{ac + bd}{a^2 + b^2}$;

eliminating x: $\begin{array}{l}abx - b^2y = bc \\ abx + a^2y = ad\end{array}$; $a^2y + b^2y = ad - bc$; $y(a^2 + b^2) = ad - bc$;

if a and b are not both zero, $y = \frac{ad - bc}{a^2 + b^2}$; if a and b are not both zero, the system has the unique solution $\left(\frac{ac + bd}{a^2 + b^2}, \frac{ad - bc}{a^2 + b^2}\right)$

41. $\begin{array}{l}ax + by = e \\ cx + dy = f\end{array}$; eliminating x: $\begin{array}{l}acx + bcy = ce \\ acx + ady = af\end{array}$; $ady - bcy = af - ce$;

$y(ad - bc) = af - ce$; if $ad \neq bc$, $y = \frac{af - ce}{ad - bc}$; eliminating y: $\begin{array}{l}adx + bdy = de \\ bcx + bdy = bf\end{array}$;

$adx - bcx = de - bf$; $x(ad - bc) = de - bf$; if $ad \neq bc$, $x = \frac{de - bf}{ad - bc}$; if $ad \neq bc$, the system has the unique solution $\left(\frac{de - bf}{ad - bc}, \frac{af - ce}{ad - bc}\right)$

42. Suppose the equations have a common solution; substitution for y yields $mx + b_1 = mx + b_2$, or $b_1 = b_2$; but this contradicts the assumption that $b_1 \neq b_2$; so the equations have no common solution.

43. $y = m_1x + b_1$ and $y = m_2x + b_2$; eliminating y: $0 = x(m_1 - m_2) + b_1 - b_2$, $x = \frac{b_2 - b_1}{m_1 - m_2}$. Since $m_1 \neq m_2$, $x \in R$. $y = m_1\left(\frac{b_2 - b_1}{m_1 - m_2}\right) + b_1 =$

$\frac{m_1b_2 - m_1b_1 + b_1m_1 - b_1m_2}{m_1 - m_2} = \frac{m_1b_2 - m_2b_1}{m_1 - m_2}$, $y \in R$. Solution: $\left(\frac{b_2 - b_1}{m_1 - m_2}, \frac{m_1b_2 - m_2b_1}{m_1 - m_2}\right)$

Page 130 • MIXED REVIEW EXERCISES

1. a. $m = \frac{1 - 0}{0 - (-2)} = \frac{1}{2}$ **b.** $b = 1$; $y = \frac{1}{2}x + 1$; $x - 2y = -2$

2. a. $m = \frac{4 - (-2)}{3 - 1} = 3$ **b.** $y - 4 = 3(x - 3)$; $3x - y = 5$

3. a. $m = \frac{2-(-4)}{3-(-6)} = \frac{2}{3}$ **b.** $y - 2 = \frac{2}{3}(x - 3); 3y - 6 = 2x - 6; 2x - 3y = 0$

4. a. $m = \frac{-1-(-1)}{5-1} = 0$ **b.** $y = -1$

5. a. $m = \frac{-2-2}{1-(-3)} = -1$ **b.** $y - (-2) = -1(x - 1); x + y = -1$

6. a. $m = \frac{4-0}{-3-0} = -\frac{4}{3}$ **b.** $b = 0; y = -\frac{4}{3}x + 0; 4x + 3y = 0$

7. $x - y = 4; y = x - 4; m = 1; b = -4$

8. $5x + 3y = 6; 3y = -5x + 6; y = -\frac{5}{3}x + 2; m = -\frac{5}{3}; b = 2$

9. $-2x + y = 1; y = 2x + 1; m = 2; b = 1$ **10.** $y - 5 = 0; y = 5; m = 0; b = 5$

11. $y = 3x + 2; m = 3; b = 2$

12. $x = 4 - 6y; 6y = -x + 4; y = -\frac{1}{6}x + \frac{2}{3}; m = -\frac{1}{6}; b = \frac{2}{3}$

Pages 132–134 • PROBLEMS

A **1.** Let t = the number of \$20 bills; let f = number of \$50 bills; $\begin{matrix} 20t + 50f = 390 \\ t + f = 15 \end{matrix}$;

$t = 15 - f; 20(15 - f) + 50f = 390; 300 - 20f + 50f = 390; 30f = 90; f = 3;$
$t = 15 - 3 = 12$; she received 12 \$20 bills and 3 \$50 bills

2. Let s = number of single's tickets; let c = number of couple's tickets;

$\begin{matrix} s + 2c = 128 \\ 20s + 35c = 2280 \end{matrix}; s = 128 - 2c; 20(128 - 2c) + 35c = 2280;$

$2560 - 40c + 35c = 2280; -280 = -5c; c = 56; s = 128 - 2(56) = 16$; 16 single's tickets and 56 couple's tickets were sold

3. Let v = degree measure of the vertex angle; let b = degree measure of each base angle; $\begin{matrix} v + 2b = 180 \\ v = 2b - 40 \end{matrix}; 2b - 40 + 2b = 180; 4b = 220; b = 55; v = 2(55) - 40 = 70;$

the angles measure 55°, 55°, and 70°

4. Let b = the length, in cm, of each base; let x = the length, in cm, of the shorter legs; then $2x$ = length of longer legs; $\begin{matrix} b + x + x = 23 \\ b + 2x + 2x = 41 \end{matrix}, \begin{matrix} b + 2x = 23 \\ b + 4x = 41 \end{matrix}; 2x = 18,$

$x = 9; b + 2(9) = 23, b = 5$; the sides of the smaller triangle are 5 cm, 9 cm, and 9 cm; the sides of the larger are 5 cm, 18 cm, and 18 cm.

5. Let j = number of pairs of jeans sold each day; let s = number of shirts sold;

$\begin{matrix} 25j + 18s = 441 \\ 20j + 20s = 420 \end{matrix}, \begin{matrix} 25j + 18s = 441 \\ 25j + 25s = 525 \end{matrix}; 7s = 84; s = 12; 25j + 18(12) = 441; 25j = 225;$

$j = 9$; they sold 9 pairs of jeans and 12 shirts each day

6. Let x = number of 20-ton bins; let y = number of 15-ton bins; $\begin{matrix} x + y = 30 \\ 20x + 15y = 510 \end{matrix}$;

$y = 30 - x; 20x + 15(30 - x) = 510; 20x + 450 - 15x = 510; 5x = 60; x = 12;$
$y = 30 - 12 = 18$; there are 12 20-ton bins and 18 15-ton bins

7. Let h = air speed in mi/h; let w = wind speed in mi/h;

$\begin{matrix} \frac{5}{3}(h + w) = 300 \\ 2(h - w) = 300 \end{matrix}$; $\begin{matrix} h + w = 180 \\ h - w = 150 \end{matrix}$; $2h = 330$; $h = 165$; $165 + w = 180$;
$w = 15$; the air speed was 165 mi/h; the wind speed was 15 mi/h

8. Let p = plane's air speed in mi/h; let w = wind speed in mi/h;

$\begin{matrix} 4(p - w) = 1000 \\ \frac{10}{3}(p + w) = 1000 \end{matrix}$; $\begin{matrix} p - w = 250 \\ p + w = 300 \end{matrix}$; $2p = 550$; $p = 275$; $275 - w = 250$; $w = 25$;

the plane's air speed is 275 mi/h; the wind speed is 25 mi/h.

9. Let f = cost, in dollars, of the first minute; let a = cost, in dollars, of each additional minute; $\begin{matrix} f + 6a = 10 \\ f + 3a = 6.40 \end{matrix}$; $3a = 3.60$; $a = 1.20$; $f + 3(1.20) = 6.40$; $f = 2.8$;

the first minute costs \$2.80; each additional minute costs \$1.20

10. Let f = the fixed cost, in dollars, per party; let g = cost per guest, in dollars;

$\begin{matrix} f + 25g = 300 \\ f + 40g = 420 \end{matrix}$; $15g = 120$; $g = 8$; $f + 25(8) = 300$; $f = 100$; the fixed cost is \$100;
the additional cost per guest is \$8

11. Let x = amount, in dollars, invested at 15%; let y = amount, in dollars, invested at 6%; $\begin{matrix} x + y = 8000 \\ 0.15x + 0.06y = 930 \end{matrix}$; $y = 8000 - x$; $0.15x + 0.06(8000 - x) = 930$;

$0.15x + 480 - 0.06x = 930$; $0.09x = 450$; $x = 5000$; $y = 8000 - 5000 = 3000$; the financial planner should invest \$5000 at 15% and \$3000 at 6%

12. Let p = number of hours the plumber worked; let a = number of hours the apprentice worked; $\begin{matrix} p = a + 3 \\ 28p + 15a = 213 \end{matrix}$; $28(a + 3) + 15a = 213$; $28a + 84 + 15a =$

213; $43a = 129$; $a = 3$; $p = 6$; the plumber earned $6 \times 28 = \$168$; the apprentice earned $3 \times 15 = \$45$

B **13.** Let p = the plane's air speed in km/h; let d = the distance, in km;

$\begin{matrix} \frac{7}{3}(p - 15) = d \\ \frac{7}{5}(p + 15) = d \end{matrix}$; $\frac{7}{3}(p - 15) = \frac{7}{5}(p + 15)$; $5p - 75 = 3p + 45$; $2p = 120$; $p = 60$;

$d = \frac{7}{3}(60 - 15) = 105$; the plane's air speed was 60 km/h;

the distance to the town was 105 km

14. Let w = wind speed in mi/h; let d = distance, in mi, from Abbot to Blair;

$\begin{matrix} 2(150 + w) = d \\ 2(150 - w) = d - 60 \end{matrix}$; $\begin{matrix} 300 + 2w = d \\ 300 - 2w = d - 60 \end{matrix}$; $600 = 2d - 60$; $2d = 660$; $d = 330$;

$2(150 + w) = 330$; $150 + w = 165$; $w = 15$; the distance was 330 mi; the wind speed was 15 mi/h

15. $v = v_0 + at$; $\begin{matrix} 28 = v_0 + a(4) \\ 43 = v_0 + a(7) \end{matrix}$; $15 = 3a$; $a = 5$; $28 = v_0 + 5(4)$; $v_0 = 8$; $a = 5$ m/s^2 and $v_0 = 8$ m/s

16. Let s = Kevin's swimming rate in km/h; let r = his running rate in km/h;

$\begin{matrix} \frac{45}{60}s + \frac{20}{60}r = 9 \\ \frac{30}{60}s + \frac{40}{60}r = 14 \end{matrix}$; $\begin{matrix} \frac{3}{4}s + \frac{1}{3}r = 9 \\ \frac{1}{2}s + \frac{2}{3}r = 14 \end{matrix}$; $\begin{matrix} \frac{3}{2}s + \frac{2}{3}r = 18 \\ \frac{1}{2}s + \frac{2}{3}r = 14 \end{matrix}$; $s = 4$; $\frac{3}{4}(4) + \frac{1}{3}r = 9$; $\frac{1}{3}r = 6$; $r = 18$; he swam at 4 km/h and ran at 18 km/h.

17. Let f = price, in dollars, of a week's rental; let m = price, in dollars, of a mile driven; $\begin{matrix} f + 520m = 250 \\ 2f + 800m = 440 \end{matrix}$; $\begin{matrix} 2f + 1040m = 500 \\ 2f + 800m = 440 \end{matrix}$; $240m = 60$; $m = 0.25$; $f + 520(0.25) = 250$; $f = 120$; the weekly charge is \$120; the cost per mile is \$.25

18. a.

b. $R = C$; $0.5x = 0.3x + 3.5$; $0.2x = 3.5$; $x = 17.5$; break-even point is 17.5 tons

c. $R - C$ measures profit

19. a.

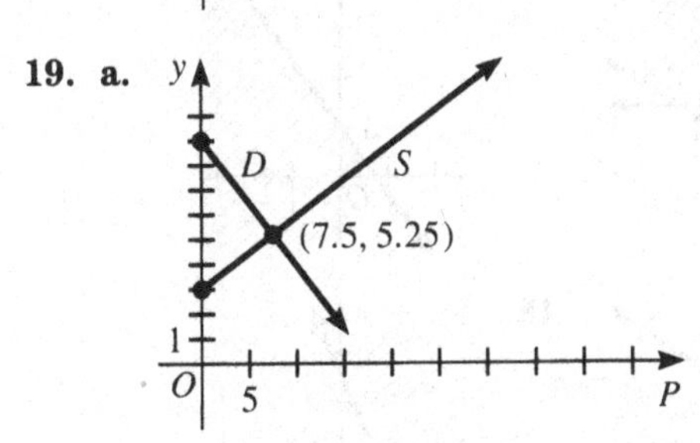

b. $S = D$; $0.3p + 3 = -0.5p + 9$; $0.8p = 6$; $p = 7.5$; equilibrium price is \$7.50

c. If price is more than \$7.50, supply will be greater than demand

C **20.** Let c = speed of current in mi/h; let r = canoeist's speed, in mi/h, in still water; let t = time, in h, it takes the log to travel 2 mi; $2 + 1(r - c) = (r + c)(t - 1)$; $2 + r - c = rt + ct - r - c$; $2r - rt - ct = -2$; since $ct = 2$, $2r - rt = 0$; $r(2 - t) = 0$; $2 - t = 0$; $t = 2$; $c(2) = 2$; $c = 1$; the current's speed is 1 mi/h

Pages 138–139 • WRITTEN EXERCISES

A **1.**

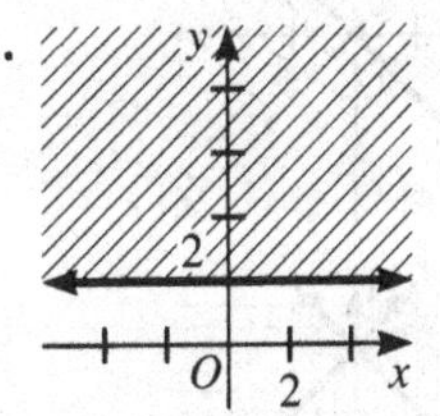

2.

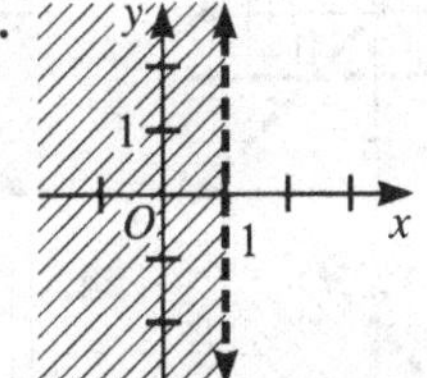

3.

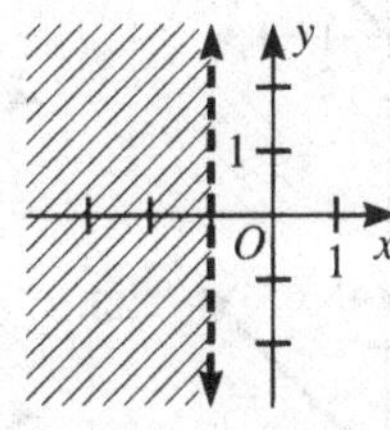

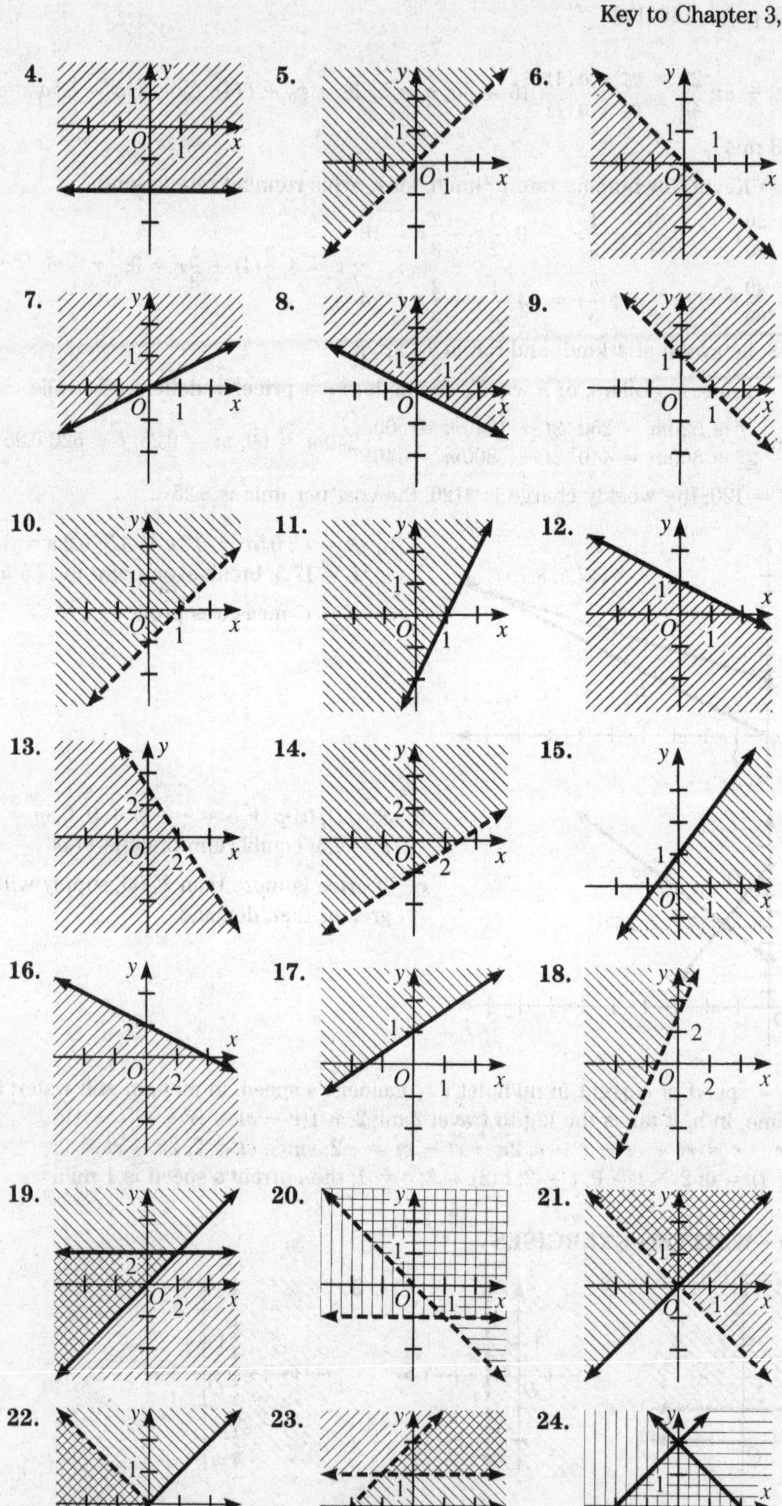
4.
5.
6.
7.
8.
9.
10.
11.
12.
13.
14.
15.
16.
17.
18.
19.
20.
21.
22.
23.
24.

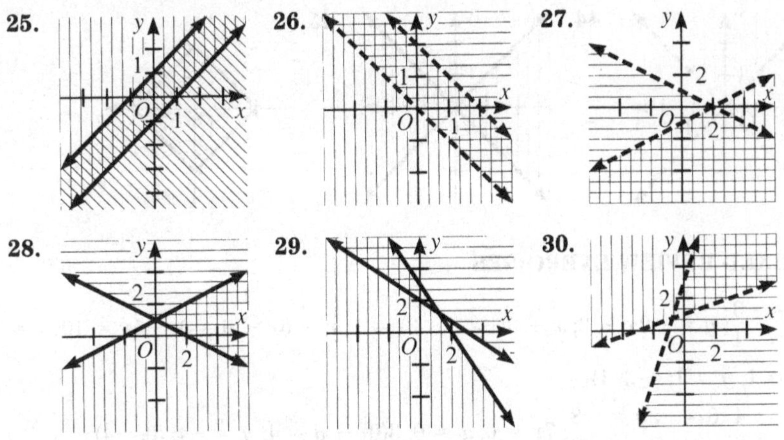

Exercises 31–45. Note: Only the graph of the system is shaded.

B

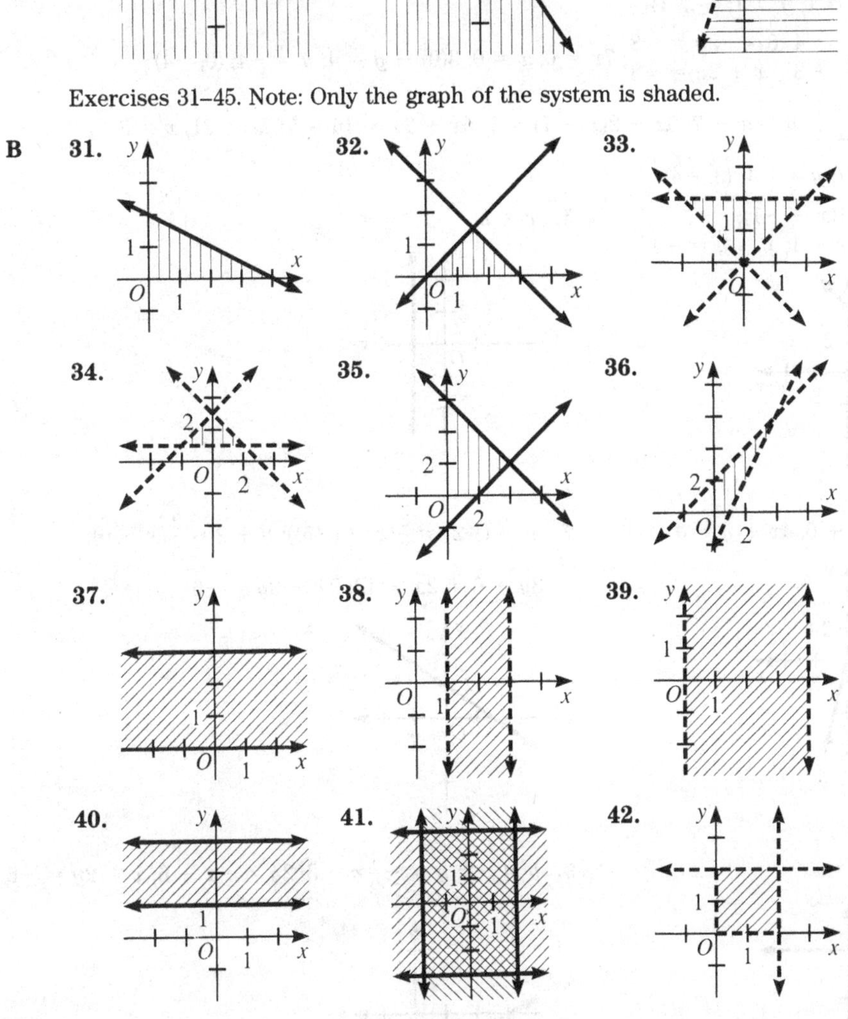

C **43.** 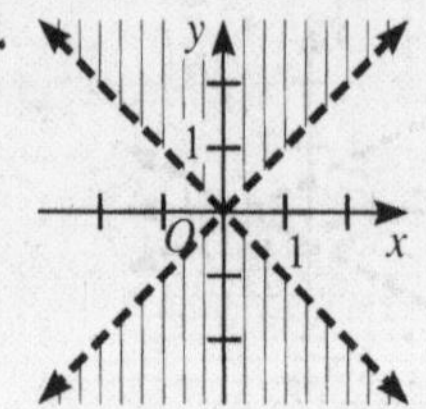 **44.** 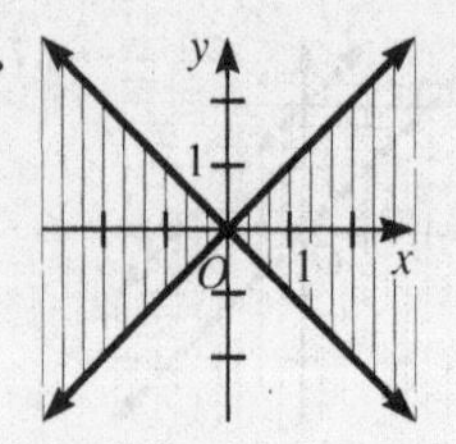 **45.** 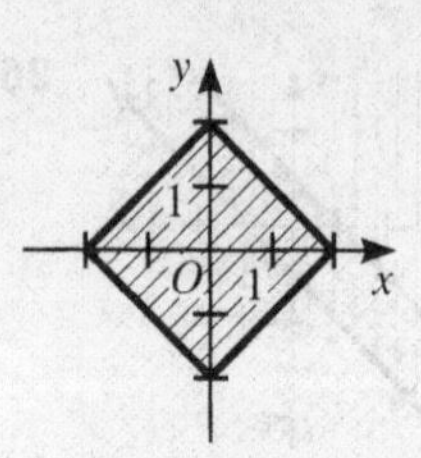

Page 139 • MIXED REVIEW EXERCISES

1. $\begin{array}{l} 2x + y = -3 \\ x + 3y = 1 \end{array}$; $y = -2x - 3$; $x + 3(-2x - 3) = 1$; $x - 6x - 9 = 1$; $-5x = 10$; $x = -2$; $-2 + 3y = 1$; $y = 1$; $(-2, 1)$

2. $\begin{array}{l} 3x - y = 4 \\ x + 2y = -8 \end{array}$; $\begin{array}{l} 6x - 2y = 8 \\ x + 2y = -8 \end{array}$; $7x = 0$; $x = 0$; $3(0) - y = 4$; $y = -4$; $(0, -4)$

3. $\begin{array}{l} 5x + 2y = 7 \\ x - y = 7 \end{array}$; $y = x - 7$; $5x + 2(x - 7) = 7$; $5x + 2x - 14 = 7$; $7x = 21$; $x = 3$; $3 - y = 7$; $y = -4$; $(3, -4)$

4. $y - 3 = 1(x - -1)$; $y - 3 = x + 1$; $x - y = -4$

5. $x = 2$

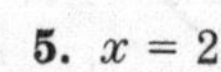

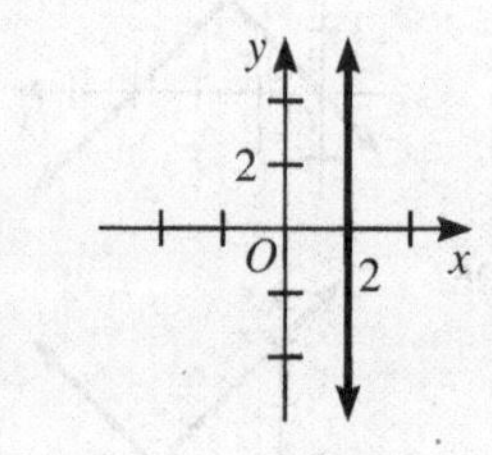

6. $y = -4x + 0$; $4x + y = 0$

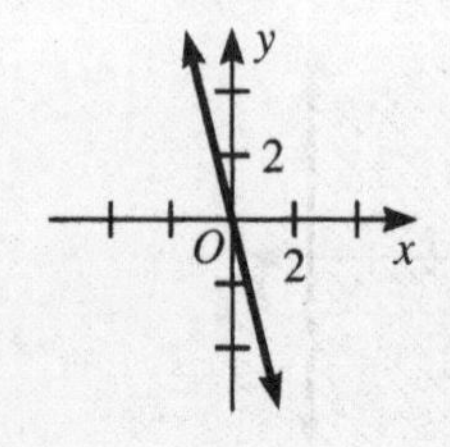

7. $y - (-2) = \frac{2}{3}(x - (-6))$; $y + 2 = \frac{2}{3}(x + 6)$; $3y + 6 = 2x + 12$; $2x - 3y = -6$

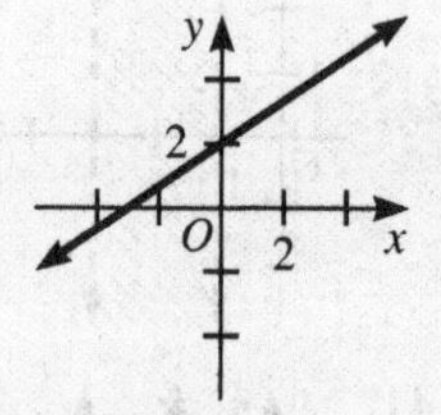

8. $y = 7$

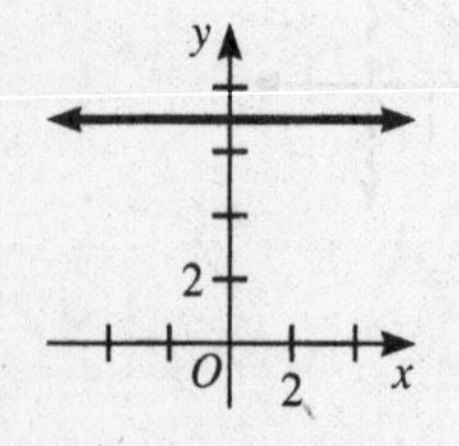

9. $b = -3$; $y = -\frac{1}{2}x - 3$; $2y = -x - 6$; $x + 2y = -6$

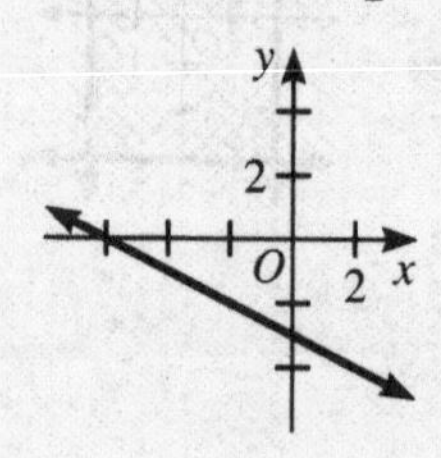

Page 140 • CHALLENGE

Let A, B, C, and D represent the people's ages, and let $A < B$? represent the question "Beth, are you older than Alicia?". First ask the following two questions: $A < B$? $C < D$? Then compare the two older people in each pair. For example, if $A < B$ and $C < D$, ask $B < D$? From the answer to this question, you know who the oldest person is. Now compare the younger person in the pair that contains the oldest person with each of the people in the other pair. For example, if $B < D$, ask $C < B$? $C < A$? The answers to these two questions determine the order of the ages. Thus 5 questions suffice.

Pages 144–145 • WRITTEN EXERCISES

A

1. $f(0) = 3 - 2(0) = 3; f(1) = 3 - 2(1) = 1; f(2) = 3 - 2(2) = -1; f(3) = 3 - 2(3) = -3; R = \{-3, -1, 1, 3\}$
2. $\phi(0) = 3(0) - 5 = -5;\ \phi(1) = 3(1) - 5 = -2;\ \phi(2) = 3(2) - 5 = 1;\ \phi(3) = 3(3) - 5 = 4;\ R = \{-5, -2, 1, 4\}$
3. $g(-2) = (-2)^2 - 2 = 2; g(0) = 0^2 - 2 = -2; g(2) = 2^2 - 2 = 2; R = \{-2, 2\}$
4. $f(-1) = 1 - (-1)^2 = 0; f(0) = 1 - 0^2 = 1; f(1) = 1 - 1^2 = 0; R = \{0, 1\}$
5. $f(-1) = (-1)^2 - 3(-1) = 1 + 3 = 4; f(0) = 0^2 - 3(0) = 0; f(1) = 1^2 - 3(1) = -2; f(2) = 2^2 - 3(2) = -2; f(3) = 3^2 - 3(3) = 0; R = \{-2, 0, 4\}$
6. $h(-1) = 4(-1) - (-1)^2 = -4 - 1 = -5; h(-2) = 4(-2) - (-2)^2 = -8 - 4 = -12; h(0) = 4(0) - 0^2 = 0; R = \{-12, -5, 0\}$
7. $G(0) = 0^2 - 4(0) + 4 = 4; G(1) = 1^2 - 4(1) + 4 = 1; G(2) = 2^2 - 4(2) + 4 = 4 - 8 + 4 = 0; G(3) = 3^2 - 4(3) + 4 = 9 - 12 + 4 = 1; R = \{0, 1, 4\}$
8. $k(-2) = (-2)^2 + (-2) - 2 = 0; k(-1) = (-1)^2 + (-1) - 2 = -2; k(0) = 0^2 + 0 - 2 = -2; k(1) = 1^2 + 1 - 2 = 0; R = \{-2, 0\}$
9. $g(-2) = (-2)^4 - (-2)^2 = 16 - 4 = 12; g(0) = 0^4 - 0^2 = 0; g(2) = 2^4 - 2^2 = 16 - 4 = 12; R = \{0, 12\}$
10. $H(-1) = (-1)^2 - (-1)^3 = 1 - (-1) = 2; H(0) = 0^2 - 0^3 = 0; H(1) = 1^2 - 1^3 = 0; H(2) = 2^2 - 2^3 = 4 - 8 = -4; R = \{-4, 0, 2\}$
11. $m(-2) = 1 - |-2| = 1 - 2 = -1; m(-1) = 1 - |-1| = 1 - 1 = 0; m(0) = 1 - |0| = 1 - 0 = 1; m(2) = 1 - |2| = 1 - 2 = -1; R = \{-1, 0, 1\}$
12. $r(-2) = |1 - (-2)| = |1 + 2| = 3; r(-1) = |1 - (-1)| = |1 + 1| = 2; r(0) = |1 - 0| = 1; r(1) = |1 - 1| = 0; r(2) = |1 - 2| = |-1| = 1; R = \{0, 1, 2, 3\}$

13. 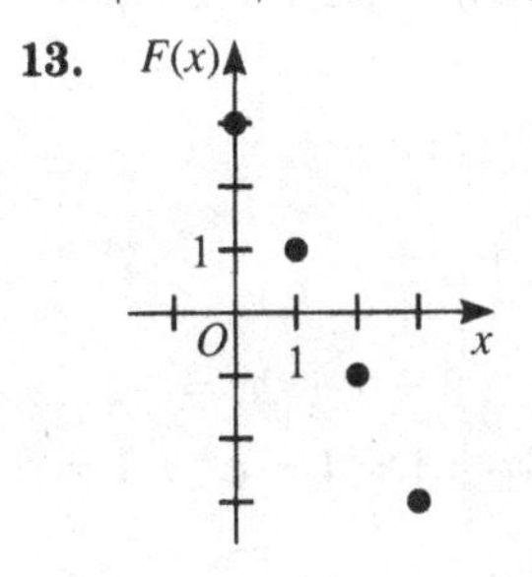

14. 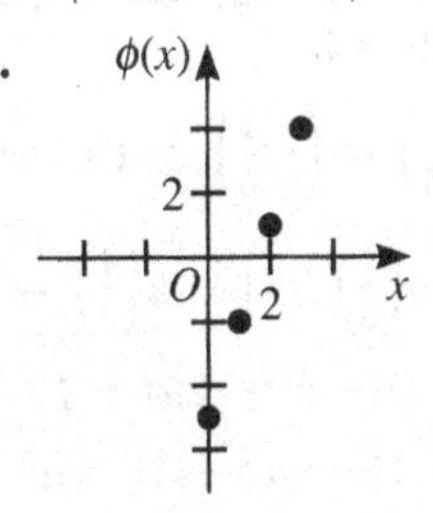

15. 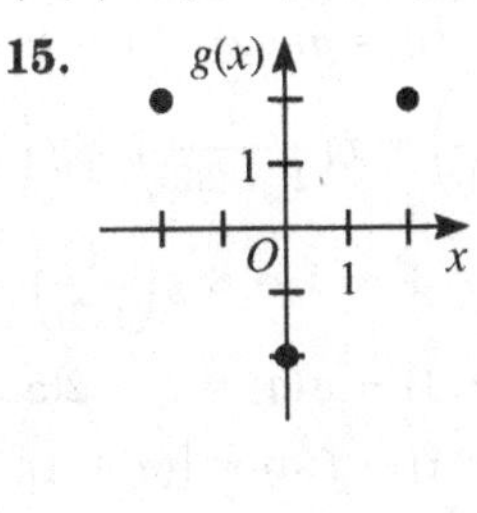

16. 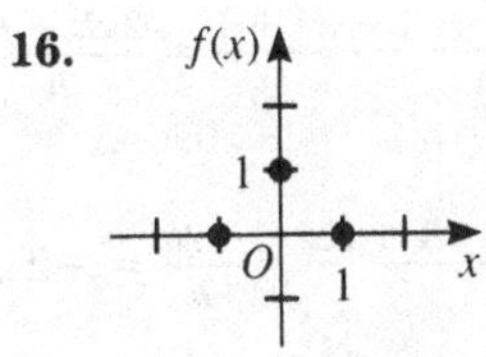

17. 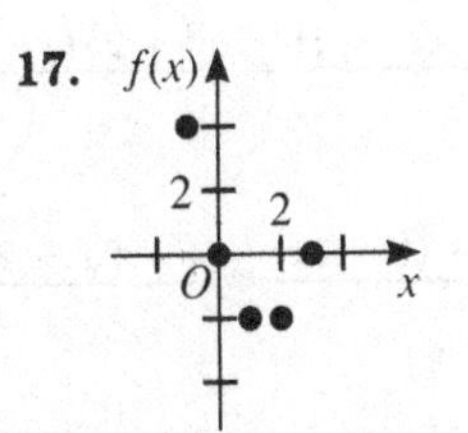

18. 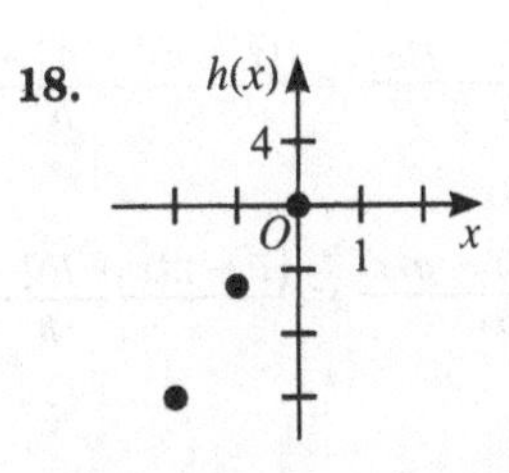

19. 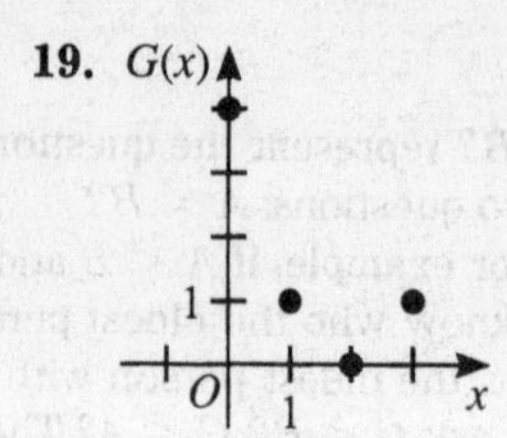

20. 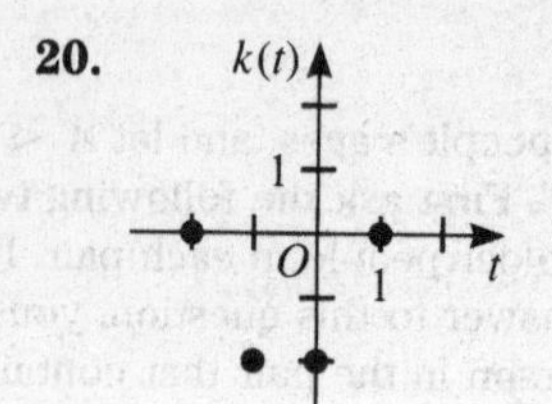

21. 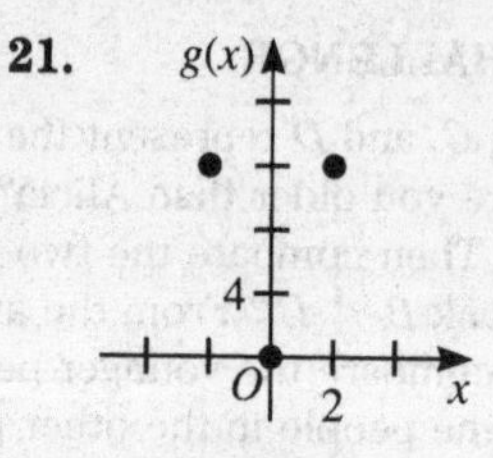

22. 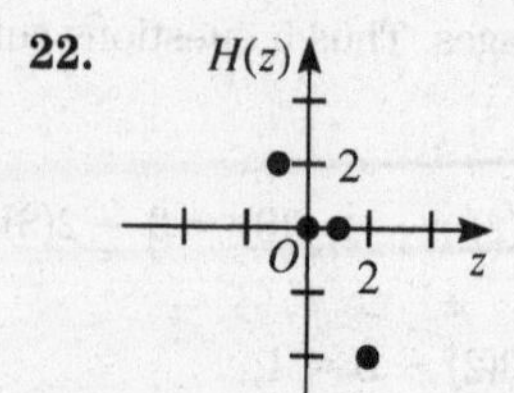

23. 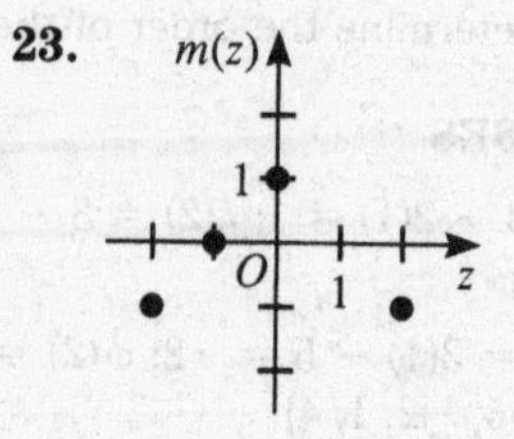

24. 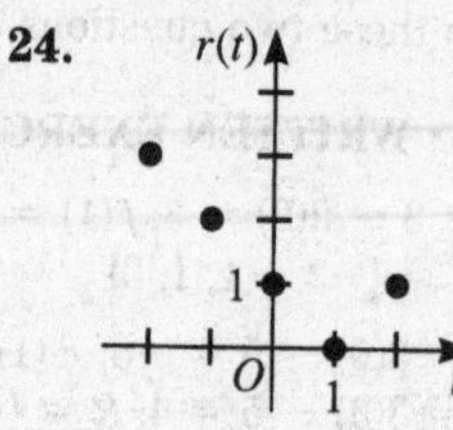

B **25.** $f(x) = 2x + 1$ **26.** $g(x) = x \cdot x = x^2$ **27.** $h(x) = 2x$ **28.** $F(x) = -2x + 5$

29. $D = \{\text{real numbers}\}$ **30.** $D = \{x : x \neq -3\}$ **31.** $D = \{\text{real numbers}\}$

32. F is not defined when $2x - 1 < 0$; $x < \frac{1}{2}$; $\therefore D = \left\{x : x \geq \frac{1}{2}\right\}$

33. f is not defined when $x^2 + 5x + 6 = 0$; $(x + 2)(x + 3) = 0$; $x = -2$ or $x = -3$; $\therefore D = \{x : x \neq -2 \text{ and } x \neq -3\}$

34. $D = \{x : x \neq 1 \text{ and } x \neq -2\}$

35. $f(g(1)) = f(1 - 2(1)) = f(-1) = (-1)^2 - 1 = 0$; $g(f(1)) = g(1^2 - 1) = g(0) = 1 - 2(0) = 1$

36. $f(g(-1)) = f(1 - 2(-1)) = f(3) = 3^2 - 1 = 8$; $g(f(-1)) = g((-1)^2 - 1) = g(0) = 1 - 2(0) = 1$

37. $f(g(2)) = f(1 - 2(2)) = f(-3) = (-3)^2 - 1 = 8$; $g(f(2)) = g(2^2 - 1) = g(3) = 1 - 2(3) = -5$

38. $f(g(-2)) = f(1 - 2(-2)) = f(5) = 5^2 - 1 = 24$; $g(f(-2)) = g((-2)^2 - 1) = g(3) = 1 - 2(3) = -5$

39. $f(f(2)) = f(2^2 - 1) = f(3) = 3^2 - 1 = 8$; $f(2f(1)) = f(2(1^2 - 1)) = f(2(0)) = f(0) = 0^2 - 1 = -1$

40. $g(g(2)) = g(1 - 2(2)) = g(-3) = 1 - 2(-3) = 7$; $g(2g(1)) = g(2[1 - 2(1)]) = g(2(-1)) = g(-2) = 1 - 2(-2) = 5$

C **41.** $f\left(\frac{1}{g(3)}\right) = f\left(\frac{1}{1 - 2(3)}\right) = f\left(-\frac{1}{5}\right) = \left(-\frac{1}{5}\right)^2 - 1 = -\frac{24}{25}$

42. $f(3) = 3^2 - 1 = 8$; $g\left(\frac{1}{f(3)}\right) = g\left(\frac{1}{8}\right) = 1 - 2\left(\frac{1}{8}\right) = 1 - \frac{1}{4} = \frac{3}{4}$

43. $g(a + 1) - g(a) = 1 - 2(a + 1) - (1 - 2a) = 1 - 2a - 2 - 1 + 2a = -2$

44. $f(a + 1) - f(a) = [(a + 1)^2 - 1] - (a^2 - 1) = a^2 + 2a + 1 - 1 - a^2 + 1 = 2a + 1$

45. $\frac{f(x + h) - f(x)}{h} = \frac{[(x + h)^2 - 1] - (x^2 - 1)}{h} = \frac{x^2 + 2xh + h^2 - 1 - x^2 + 1}{h} = \frac{2xh + h^2}{h} = 2x + h$

46. $\frac{g(x + h) - g(x)}{h} = \frac{[1 - 2(x + h)] - (1 - 2x)}{h} = \frac{1 - 2x - 2h - 1 + 2x}{h} = \frac{-2h}{h} = -2$

47. **a.** $f(0) = f(0 + 0) = f(0) + f(0)$. Since $f(0) = f(0) + f(0)$, $f(0)$ is additive identity, i.e., $f(0) = 0$.

b. $f(2a) = f(a + a) = f(a) + f(a) = 2f(a)$

c. $f(a + (-a)) = f(a) + f(-a)$; $f(0) = f(a) + f(-a)$; from part **(a)**, $f(0) = 0$; $0 = f(a) + f(-a)$; $f(-a) = -f(a)$

48.

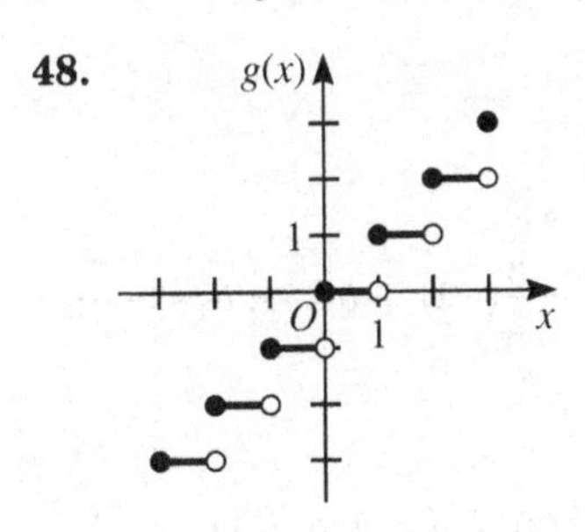

49.

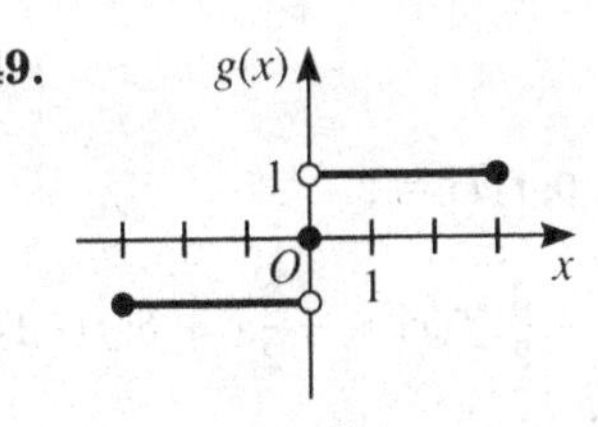

$f(x) = \frac{x}{|x|}$ is not defined for $x = 0$

Pages 149–150 • WRITTEN EXERCISES

A

1. $f(x) = 2x + 3$ **2.** $f(x) = -x + \frac{1}{2}$

3. $f(x) = 3x + b; f(0) = 3(0) + b = 1; b = 1; f(x) = 3x + 1$

4. $f(x) = -\frac{3}{2}x + b; b = -\frac{1}{2}; f(x) = -\frac{3}{2}x - \frac{1}{2}$ **5.** $b = -2, m = \frac{1}{2}; f(x) = \frac{1}{2}x - 2$

6. $b = 1; m = -1; f(x) = -x + 1$ **7.** $b = 1; m = \frac{6}{3} = 2; f(x) = 2x + 1$

8. $b = -1; m = \frac{-3}{1} = -3; f(x) = -3x - 1$

9. $f(x) = 2x + b; f(1) = 2(1) + b = 5; b = 3; f(x) = 2x + 3$

10. $f(x) = -1x + b; f(2) = -1(2) + b = 3; b = 5; f(x) = -x + 5$

11. $f(x) = -\frac{3}{2}x + b; f(4) = -\frac{3}{2}(4) + b = -1; -6 + b = -1; b = 5; f(x) = -\frac{3}{2}x + 5$

12. $f(x) = \frac{2}{3}x + b; f(6) = \frac{2}{3}(6) + b = -2; 4 + b = -2; b = -6; f(x) = \frac{2}{3}x - 6$

13. $b = 1; m = \frac{7 - 1}{3 - 0} = \frac{6}{3} = 2; f(x) = 2x + 1$

14. $b = -2; m = \frac{4 - (-2)}{2 - 0} = \frac{6}{2} = 3; f(x) = 3x - 2$

15. $b = -3; m = \frac{-3 - (-3)}{3 - 0} = 0; f(x) = 0x - 3; f(x) = -3$

16. $b = 0; m = \frac{4 - 0}{-2 - 0} = -2; f(x) = -2x$

17. $m = \frac{5 - 2}{2 - 1} = 3; f(x) = 3x + b; f(1) = 3(1) + b = 2; b = -1; f(x) = 3x - 1$

18. $m = \frac{0-6}{4-2} = -\frac{6}{2} = -3; f(x) = -3x + b; f(2) = -3(2) + b = 6; b = 12;$

$f(x) = -3x + 12$

19. $m = \frac{-3-3}{2-(-2)} = \frac{-6}{4} = -\frac{3}{2}; f(x) = -\frac{3}{2}x + b; f(-2) = -\frac{3}{2}(-2) + b = 3; b = 0;$

$f(x) = -\frac{3}{2}x$

20. $m = \frac{2-2}{2-(-1)} = 0; f(x) = 2$

21. $m = \frac{-2-1}{1-(-1)} = -\frac{3}{2}; f(x) = -\frac{3}{2}x + b; f(-1) = -\frac{3}{2}(-1) + b = 1; b = -\frac{1}{2};$

$f(x) = -\frac{3}{2}x - \frac{1}{2}$

22. $m = \frac{-3-4}{6-3} = -\frac{7}{3}; f(x) = -\frac{7}{3}x + b; f(3) = -\frac{7}{3}(3) + b = 4; b = 11;$

$f(x) = -\frac{7}{3}x + 11$

B Exercises 23–26: Answers are circled.

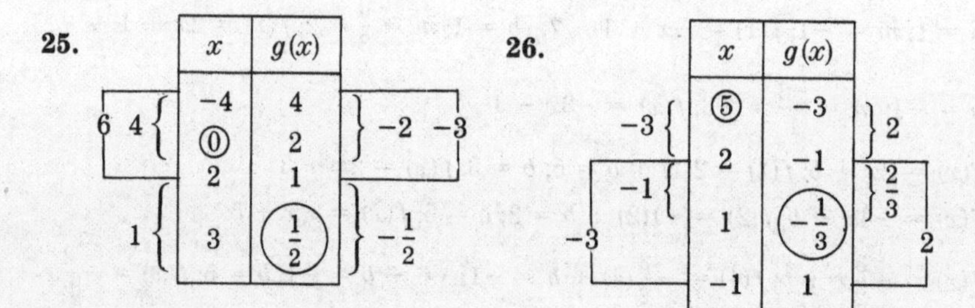

27. $f(x) = mx + b; \begin{matrix} f(6) = m(6) + b = 7 \\ f(3) = m(3) + b = 2 \end{matrix}; 3m = 5; m = \frac{5}{3}; f(6) = \frac{5}{3}(6) + b = 7;$

$10 + b = 7; b = -3; f(x) = \frac{5}{3}x - 3; f(-3) = \frac{5}{3}(-3) - 3 = -8;$

$f(10) = \frac{5}{3}(10) - 3 = \frac{41}{3}$

28. $f(x) = mx + b; \begin{matrix} f(2) = m(2) + b = 10 \\ f(10) = m(10) + b = -2 \end{matrix}; 8m = -12; m = -\frac{3}{2};$

$f(2) = -\frac{3}{2}(2) + b = 10; -3 + b = 10; b = 13; f(x) = -\frac{3}{2}x + 13;$

$f(-10) = -\frac{3}{2}(-10) + 13 = 28; f(100) = -\frac{3}{2}(100) + 13 = -137$

29. $f(x) = mx + b;\ \begin{matrix} f(1) = m(1) + b = 2 \\ f(7) = m(7) + b = -6 \end{matrix};\ 6m = -8;\ m = -\frac{4}{3};\ f(1) = -\frac{4}{3}(1) + b = 2;$

$b = \frac{10}{3};\ f(x) = -\frac{4}{3}x + \frac{10}{3};\ f(10) = -\frac{4}{3}(10) + \frac{10}{3} = -10;\ f(20) = -\frac{4}{3}(20) + \frac{10}{3} =$

$-\frac{70}{3}$

30. $f(x) = mx + b;\ \begin{matrix} f(5) = m(5) + b = -5 \\ f(-25) = m(-25) + b = -25 \end{matrix};\ 30m = 20;\ m = \frac{2}{3};$

$f(5) = \frac{2}{3}(5) + b = -5;\ b = -\frac{25}{3};\ f(x) = \frac{2}{3}x - \frac{25}{3};\ f(2) = \frac{2}{3}(2) - \frac{25}{3} = -7;$

$f(50) = \frac{2}{3}(50) - \frac{25}{3} = 25$

C **31.** $\frac{f(x + k) - f(x)}{k} = \frac{m(x + k) + b - (mx + b)}{k} = \frac{mx + mk + b - mx - b}{k} = \frac{mk}{k} = m$

32. $\frac{f(x_2) - f(x_1)}{x_2 - x_1} = \frac{mx_2 + b - (mx_1 + b)}{x_2 - x_1} = \frac{mx_2 - mx_1}{x_2 - x_1} = \frac{m(x_2 - x_1)}{(x_2 - x_1)} = m$

33. a. If $m > 0$, then $m = \frac{f(x_2) - f(x_1)}{x_2 - x_1} > 0$; if $x_2 > x_1$, then $x_2 - x_1 > 0$ and

$f(x_2) - f(x_1) > 0$; so $f(x_2) > f(x_1)$, and f is increasing

b. If $m < 0$, then $m = \frac{f(x_2) - f(x_1)}{x_2 - x_1} < 0$; if $x_2 > x_1$, then $x_2 - x_1 > 0$ and

$f(x_2) - f(x_1) < 0$; so $f(x_2) < f(x_1)$, and f is decreasing

Pages 150–152 • PROBLEMS

A **1.** Let $v(t)$ = value of the machine, in dollars, after t years; $v(t) = -900t + 4500$

a. $t = 1.5$; $v(1.5) = -900(1.5) + 4500 = 3150$; the machine will be worth $3150 after 18 months

b. $v(t) = 1200$; $1200 = -900t + 4500$; $-900t = -3300$; $t = 3\frac{2}{3}$; the machine will be worth $1200 in 3 years, 8 months

2. Let $c(m)$ = rental cost for m mi driven; $c(m) = 24 + 0.15m$

a. $c(85) = 24 + 0.15(85) = 36.75$; the rental cost is $36.75

b. $c(m) = 42$; $24 + 0.15m = 42$; $0.15m = 18$; $m = 120$; she drove 120 mi

3. Let $p(h)$ = plumber's charge, in dollars, for an h-hour job; $p(h) = mh + b$;

$\begin{matrix} p(3) = m(3) + b = 110 \\ p(5) = m(5) + b = 160 \end{matrix};\ 2m = 50;\ m = 25;\ p(3) = 25(3) + b = 110;\ b = 35;\ p(h) =$

$25h + 35$; $p(8) = 25(8) + 35 = 235$; he would charge $235 for an eight-hour job

4. Let $c(x)$ = cost, in dollars, to manufacture x VCRs; $c(x) = mx + b$;

$\begin{matrix} c(10) = m(10) + b = 1900 \\ c(16) = m(16) + b = 2200 \end{matrix};\ 6m = 300;\ m = 50;\ c(10) = 50(10) + b = 1900;\ b =$

1400; $c(x) = 50x + 1400$; $c(25) = 50(25) + 1400 = 2650$; it would cost $2650 to make 25 VCRs

5. Let $c(x)$ = cost, in dollars, of a ticket to fly x miles; $c(x) = mx + b$;

$\begin{matrix} c(260) = m(260) + b = 90 \\ c(500) = m(500) + b = 150 \end{matrix}$; $240m = 60$; $m = 0.25$; $c(260) = 0.25(260) + b = 90$;

$65 + b = 90$; $b = 25$; $c(x) = 0.25x + 25$; $c(1000) = 0.25(1000) + 25 = 275$; the ticket would cost $275

6. Let $l(x)$ = the length, in cm, of the spring with an x-kg weight attached;

$l(x) = mx + b$; $\begin{matrix} l(8) = m(8) + b = 76 \\ l(14) = m(14) + b = 85 \end{matrix}$; $6m = 9$; $m = \frac{3}{2}$; $l(8) = \frac{3}{2}(8) + b = 76$;

$b = 64$; $l(x) = \frac{3}{2}x + 64$; $l(0) = 64$; the spring is 64 cm long

7. Let $w(x)$ = Alan's weight, in lb, after dieting x days; $w(x) = mx + b$;

$\begin{matrix} w(15) = m(15) + b = 176 \\ w(45) = m(45) + b = 170 \end{matrix}$; $30m = -6$, $m = -\frac{1}{5}$; $w(15) = -\frac{1}{5}(15) + b = 176$;

$b = 179$; $w(x) = -\frac{1}{5}x + 179$ **a.** $w(0) = 179$; he began at 179 lb

b. $w(x) = 165$; $-\frac{1}{5}x + 179 = 165$; $-\frac{1}{5}x = -14$; $x = 70$; he will weigh 165 lb in 70 days

8. Let $h(t)$ = height, in m, of the climber after t hours; $h(t) = mt + b$; $m = 240$; $h(t) = 240t + b$; $h(3) = 240(3) + b = 6500$; $b = 5780$

a. $h(0) = 5780$; the base camp is at 5780 m

b. $h(t) = 7400$; $240t + 5780 = 7400$; $1620 = 240t$; $t = 6.75$; the summit is reached after 6.75 h, at 11:45 A.M.

B

9. a. Let $c(f)$ = Celsius temperature equivalent to $f°$ Fahrenheit; $c(f) = mf + b$;

$\begin{matrix} c(32) = m(32) + b = 0 \\ c(212) = m(212) + b = 100 \end{matrix}$; $180m = 100$; $m = \frac{5}{9}$; $\frac{5}{9}(32) + b = 0$; $b = -\frac{160}{9}$;

$c(f) = \frac{5}{9}f - \frac{160}{9}$

b. $c(98.6) = \frac{5}{9}(98.6) - \frac{160}{9} = 37$; $98.6°F = 37°C$

c. $c(f) = f$; $\frac{5}{9}f - \frac{160}{9} = f$, $\frac{4}{9}f = -\frac{160}{9}$, $f = -40$; $-40°F = -40°C$

10. a. Answering all 50 questions correctly yields the best score; $(50)(3) = 150$; 150 points

b. Answering all 50 incorrectly gives the worst score; $(50)(-1) = -50$; -50 points

c. Let $f(x)$ = the conversion of a raw score of x points; $f(x) = mx + b$;

$\begin{matrix} f(-50) = m(-50) + b = 0 \\ f(150) = m(150) + b = 100 \end{matrix}$; $200m = 100$; $m = \frac{1}{2}$; $\frac{1}{2}(-50) + b = 0$; $b = 25$;

$f(x) = \frac{1}{2}x + 25$

d. $38(3) + 4(-1) + 8(0) = 110$; $f(110) = \frac{1}{2}(110) + 25 = 80$; 80 points

C

11. a. For $0 \le n \le 800$, $C(n) = 4.5 + 0.062n$

b. $C(800) = 4.5 + 0.062(800) = 54.1$; for $n > 800$, $C(n) = 54.1 + 0.055(n - 800) = 10.1 + 0.055n$

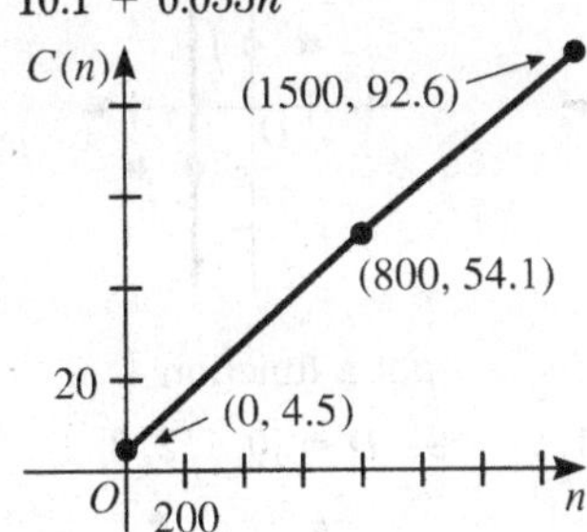

Page 152 • MIXED REVIEW EXERCISES

1. 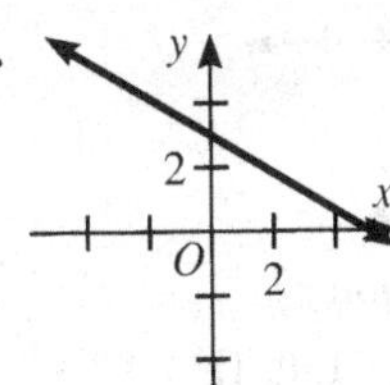

2. 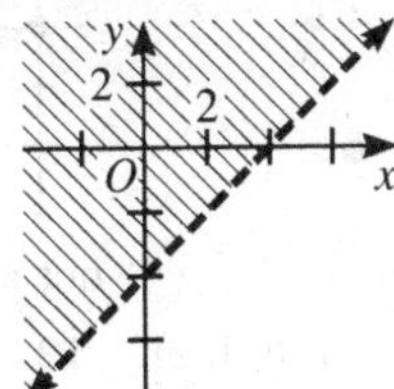

3. 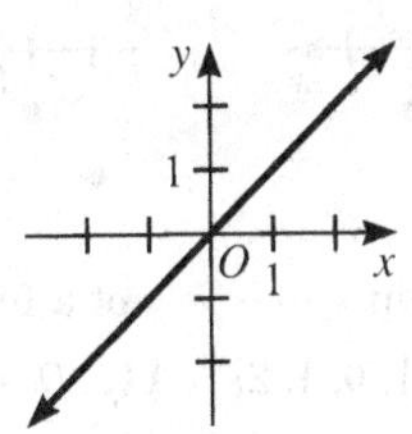

4. 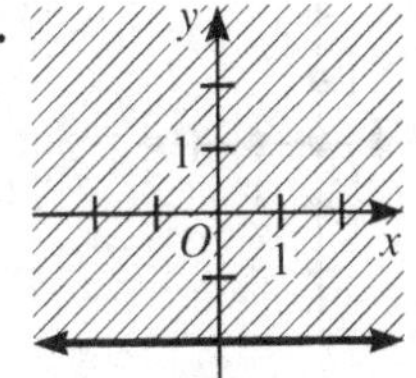

5. 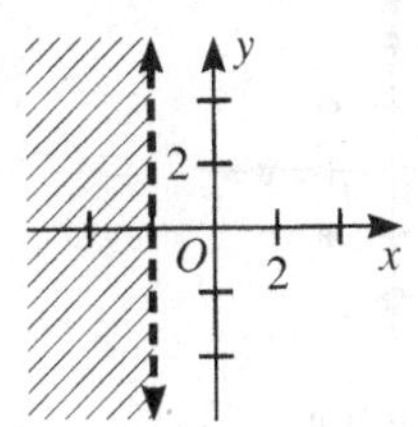

6. 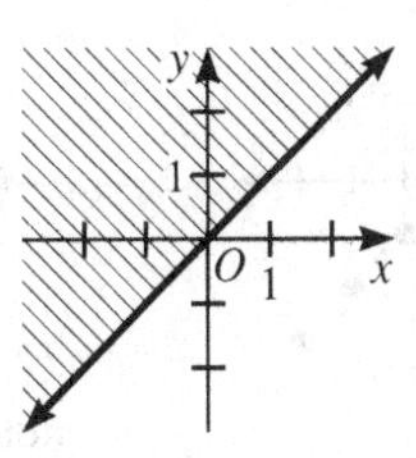

7. 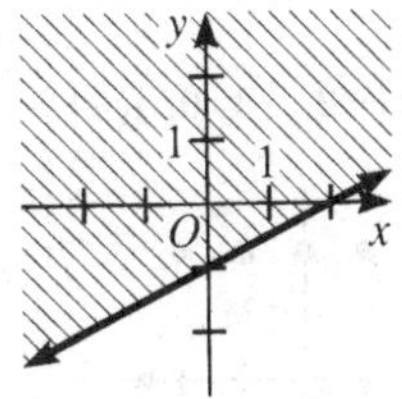

8. 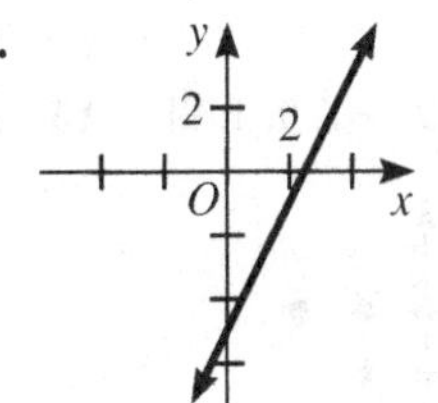

9. 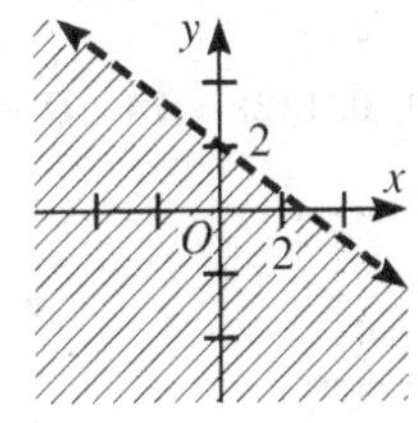

10. $f(-2) = 3(-2) + 2 = -4; f(-1) = 3(-1) + 2 = -1; f(0) = 3(0) + 2 = 2; R = \{-4, -1, 2\}$

11. $g(-1) = 1 - (-1)^2 = 0; g(0) = 1 - 0^2 = 1; g(1) = 1 - 1^2 = 0; R = \{0, 1\}$

12. $F(-3) = |-3 - 4| = |-7| = 7; F(-2) = |-2 - 4| = |-6| = 6; F(-1) = |-1 - 4| = |-5| = 5; R = \{5, 6, 7\}$

13. $G(1) = 8 - 5(1) = 3; G(2) = 8 - 5(2) = -2; G(3) = 8 - 5(3) = -7; R = \{-7, -2, 3\}$

Pages 156–157 • WRITTEN EXERCISES

A **1.** 
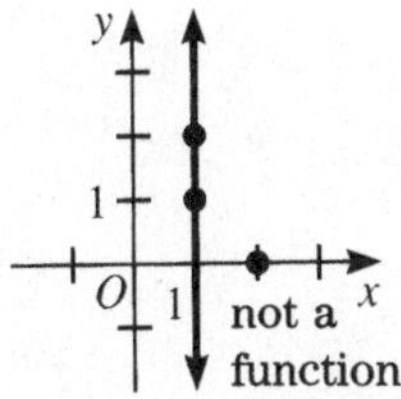

2. 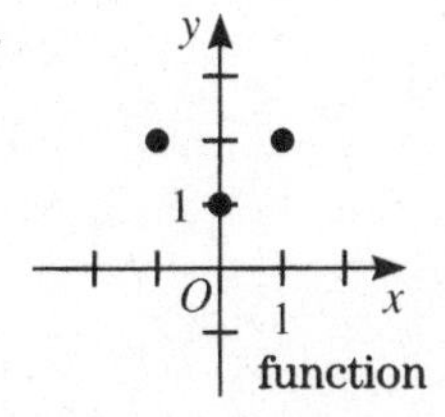

3. 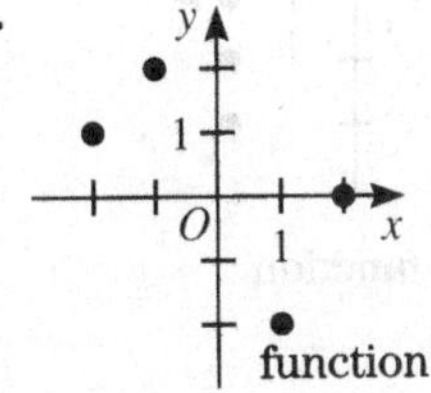

4.

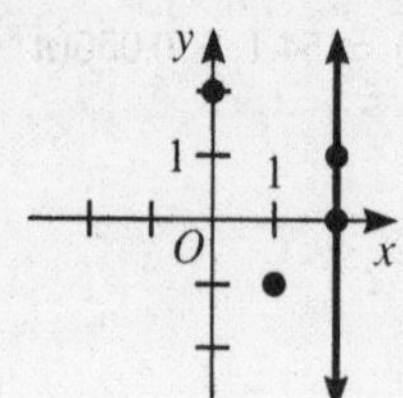

not a function

5.

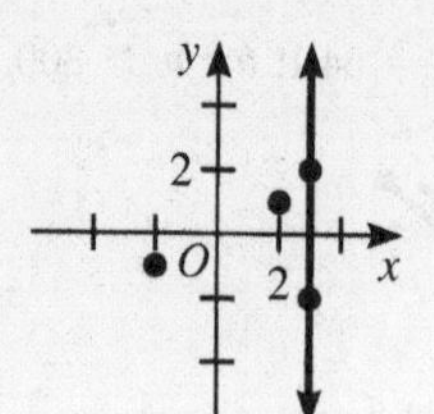

not a function

6.

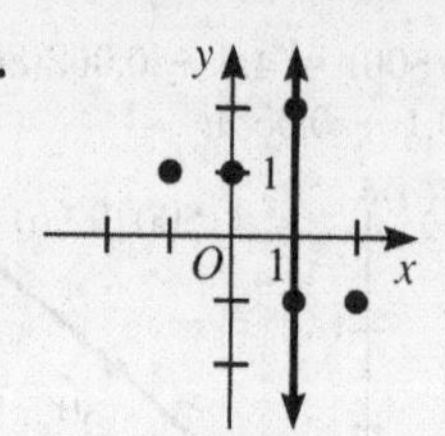

not a function

7. $D = \{-1, 0, 1\}$

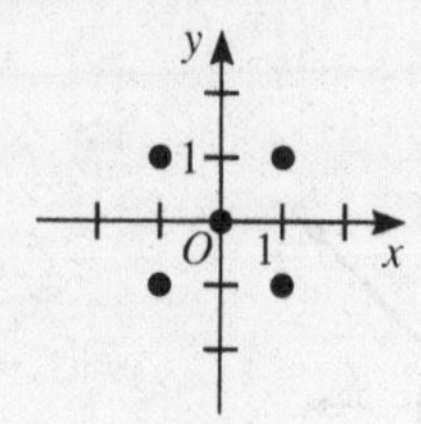

not a function

8. $D = \{-2, -1, 0, 1, 2\}$

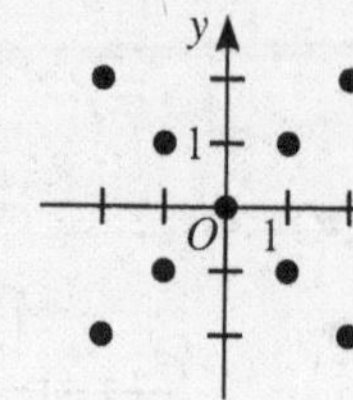

not a function

9. $D = \{0, 1, 2, 3\}$

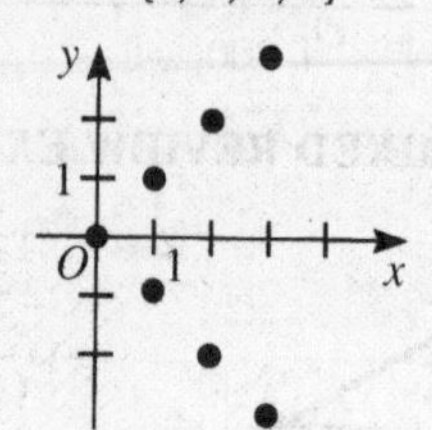

not a function

10. $D = \{-2, -1, 0, 1, 2\}$

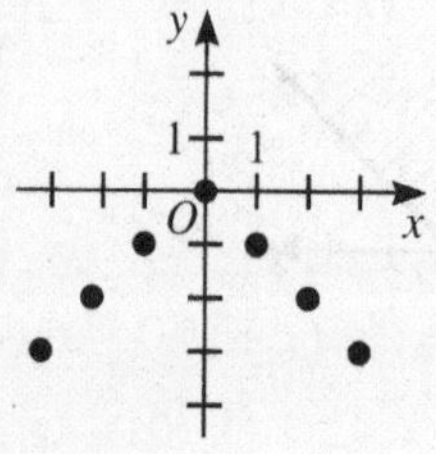

function

11. $D = \{-2, -1, 0, 1, 2\}$

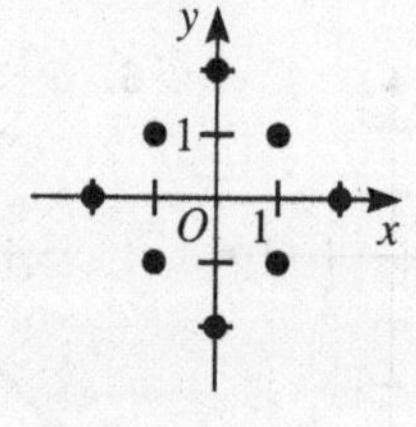

not a function

12. $D = \{-1, 0, 1\}$

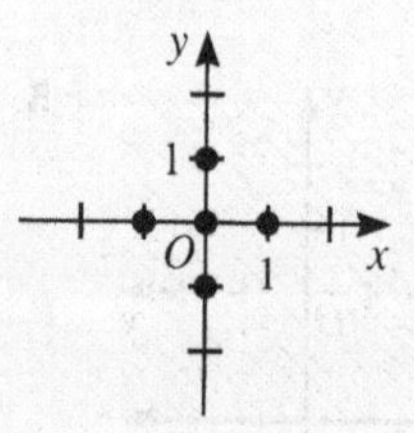

not a function

13. $D = \{-2, -1, 0, 1, 2\}$

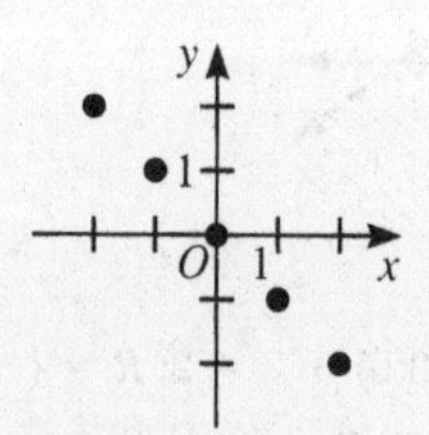

function

14. $D = \{-2, -1, 0, 1, 2\}$

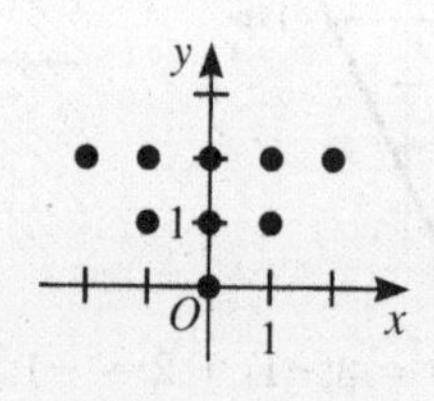

not a function

15. $D = \{-2, -1, 0, 1, 2\}$

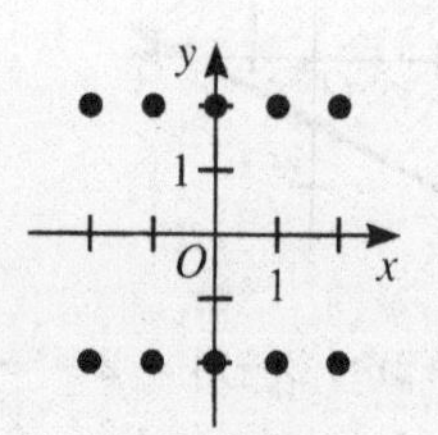

not a function

16. $D = \{-2, 2\}$

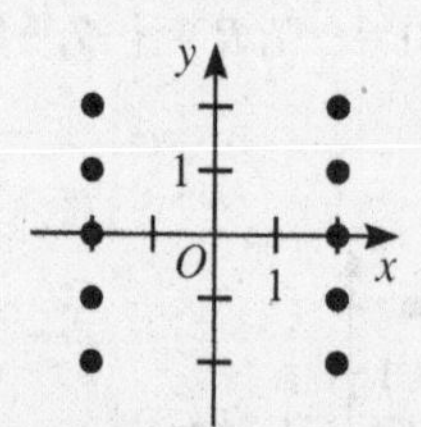

not a function

B **17.** $D = \{-2, -1, 1, 2\}$

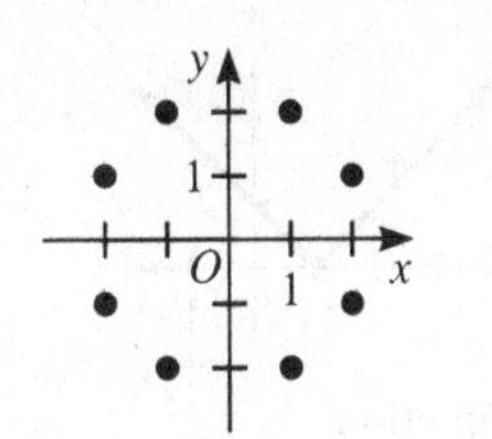

not a function

18. $D = \{1, 2\}$

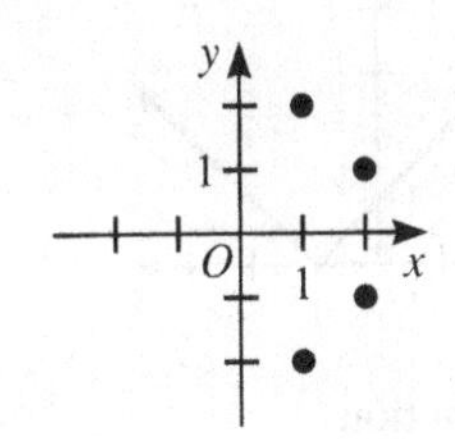

not a function

19. $D = \{-2, -1, 1, 2\}$

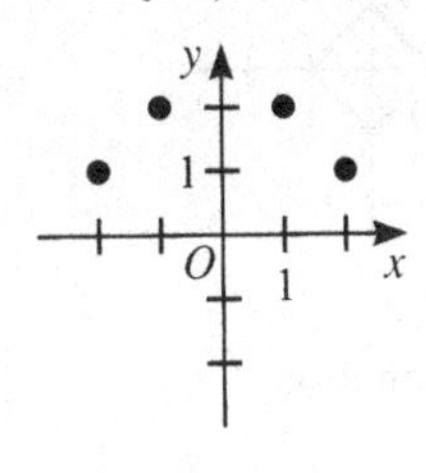

function

20. $D = \{\text{integers}\}$

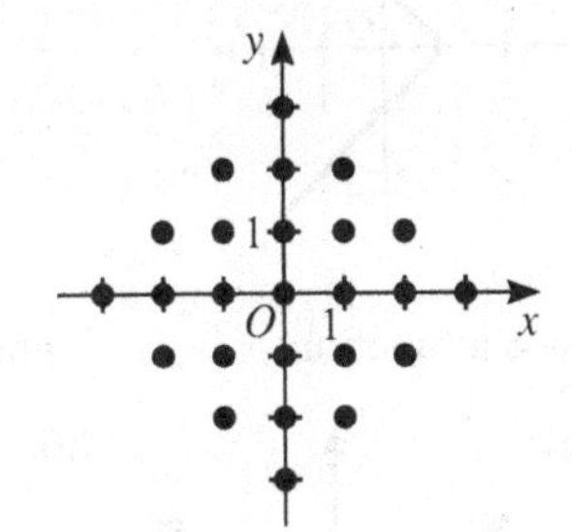

not a function

21.

x	-1	0	1	2	3
$f(x)$	-1	1	3	5	7
$g(x)$	7	5	3	1	-1

; $f \neq g$

22. If $x \geq -1$, $x + 1 = |1 + x|$ and $g(x) = x|1 + x| = x(x + 1) = x^2 + x = f(x)$; $f = g$

23.

x	-2	-1	1	2
$f(x)$	0	3	3	0
$g(x)$	0	3	3	0

; $f = g$

24.

x	-2	-1	0	1	2
$f(x)$	-2	-1	0	3	6
$g(x)$	6	3	0	-1	-2

; $f \neq g$

25.

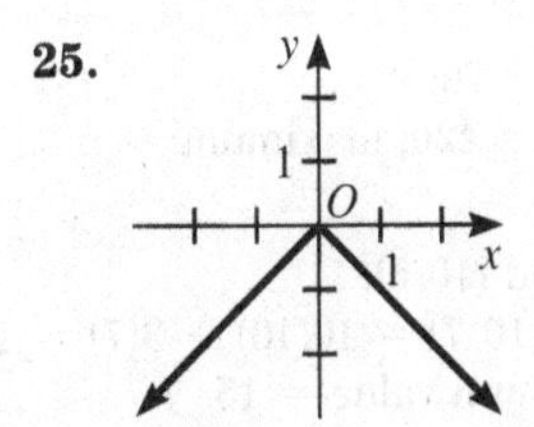

function

26.

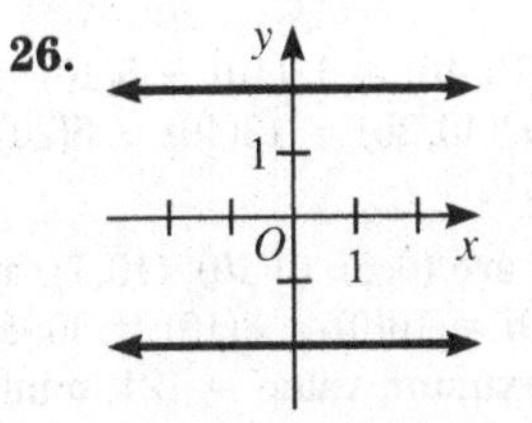

not a function

27.

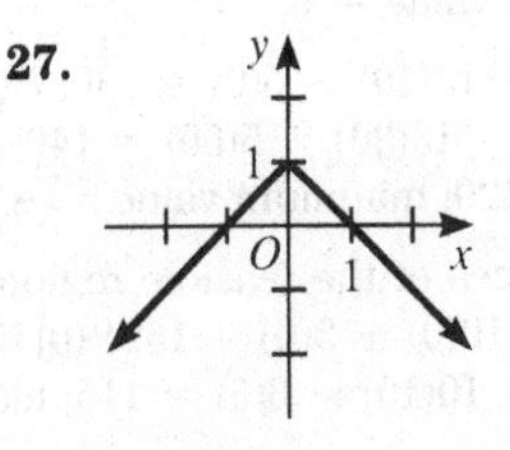

function

28.

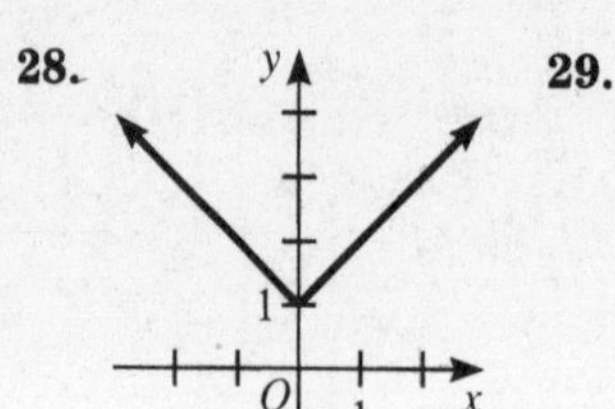

function

29.

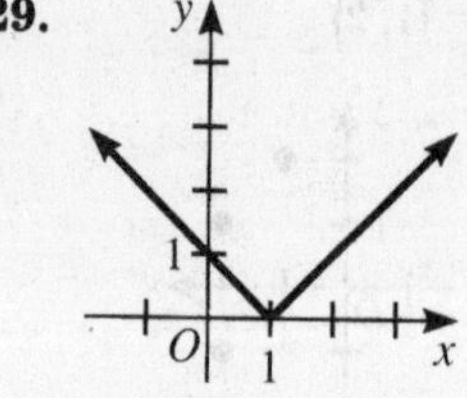

function

30.

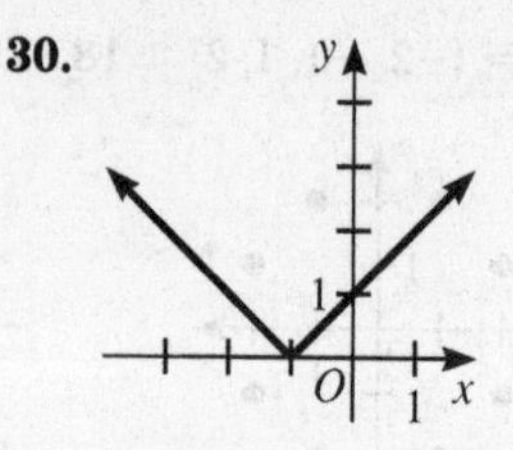

function

C **31.**

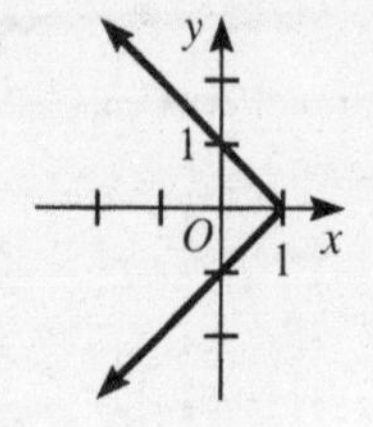

not a function

32.

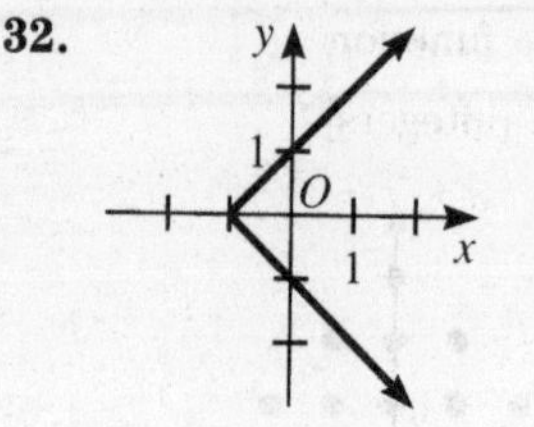

not a function

33.

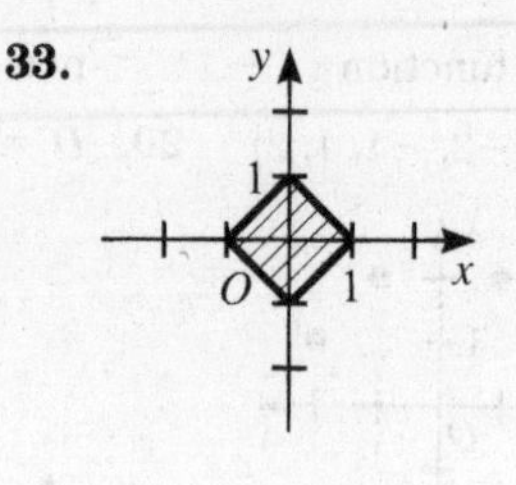

not a function

34.

not a function

35.

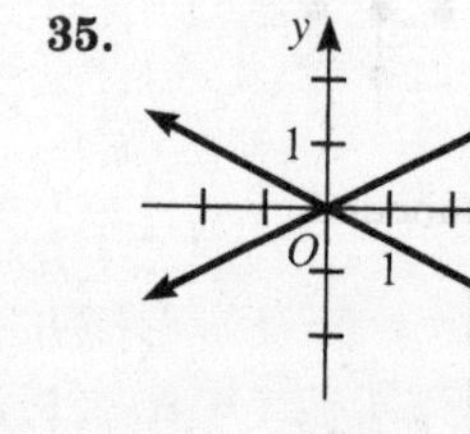

not a function

36.

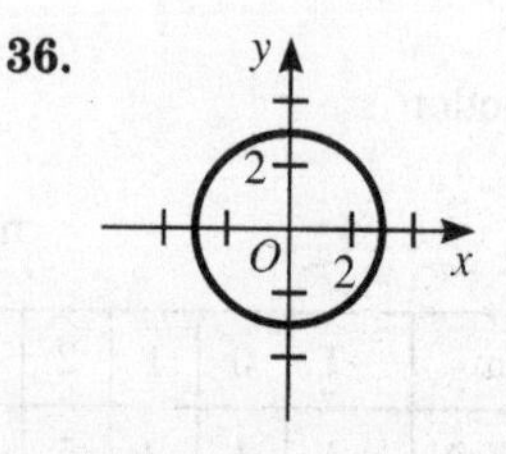

not a function

37. **a.** $(5, 3) = \{\{5, 3\}, 5\} = \{5, \{5, 3\}\} = \{5, \{3, 5\}\}$

b. $(4, 1)$ **c.** $(a, b, c) = \{a, \{\{a, b\}, \{a, b, c\}\}\}$

Page 158 • CHALLENGE

1 g, 3 g, and 9 g; in the following let the numbers on either side of the equal sign represent the weights on either side of the balance; the underlined number represents the weight of the object;

$\underline{1} = 1$; $1, \underline{2} = 3$; $\underline{3} = 3$; $\underline{4} = 1, 3$; $1, 3, \underline{5} = 9$; $3, \underline{6} = 9$; $3, \underline{7} = 1, 9$; $1, \underline{8} = 9$; $\underline{9} = 9$; $\underline{10} = 1, 9$; $1, \underline{11} = 3, 9$; $\underline{12} = 3, 9$; $\underline{13} = 1, 3, 9$

Page 161 • APPLICATION

1. $P(0,0) = 3(0) + 4(0) = 0$; $P(0,90) = 3(0) + 4(90) = 360$; $P(50,80) = 3(50) + 4(80) = 470$; $P(70,20) = 3(70) + 4(20) = 290$; $P(70,0) = 3(70) + 4(0) = 210$; maximum value $= 470$; minimum value $= 0$.
2. $P(10,0) = 13(10) - 5(0) = 130$; $P(10,40) = 13(10) - 5(40) = -70$; $P(30,50) = 13(30) - 5(50) = 140$; $P(40,20) = 13(40) - 5(20) = 420$; maximum value $= 420$; minimum value $= -70$.
3. The vertices of the feasible region are $(0,5)$, $(0,10)$, $(10,7)$, and $(10,5)$; $S(0,5) = 10(0) + 3(5) = 15$; $S(0,10) = 10(0) + 3(10) = 30$; $S(10,7) = 10(10) + 3(7) = 121$; $S(10,5) = 10(10) + 3(5) = 115$; maximum value $= 121$; minimum value $= 15$.

4. The vertices of the feasible region are $(2,0)$, $(-3,10)$, $(1,10)$, and $(6,0)$; $S(2,0) = 6(2) - 2(0) = 12$; $S(-3,10) = 6(-3) - 2(10) = -38$; $S(1,10) = 6(1) - 2(10) = -14$; $S(6,0) = 6(6) - 2(0) = 36$; maximum value $= 36$; minimum value $= -38$.

5. Let x = number of packages of Trailblazer mix, y = number of packages of Frontier Mix; the center must maximize $I = 9.75x + 9.50y$ subject to $x \geq 0$, $y \geq 0$, $4x + 3y \leq 120$, and $x + 2y \leq 60$; the vertices of the feasible region are $(0,0)$, $(0,30)$, $(12,24)$, and $(30,0)$; $I(0,0) = 9.75(0) + 9.50(0) = 0$; $I(0,30) = 9.75(0) + 9.50(30) = 285$; $I(12,24) = 9.75(12) + 9.50(24) = 117 + 228 = 345$; $I(30,0) = 9.75(30) + 9.50(0) = 292.5$; maximum occurs at $(12,24)$; the center should sell 12 packages of Trailblazer mix and 24 packages of Frontier mix.

Pages 162–163 • CHAPTER REVIEW

1. c

2. c; let d = number of dimes; let q = number of quarters; $10d + 25q = 185$; $d = \frac{185 - 25q}{10}$; solutions for (d,q) are: $(16,1)$, $(11,3)$, $(6,5)$, and $(1,7)$

3. d; $2x - y = 1$; $y = 2x - 1$; $m = 2$; $b = -1$

4. c; $3x + ky = 7$; $3(-3) + k(-2) = 7$; $-9 - 2k = 7$; $-2k = 16$; $k = -8$

5. b; $m = \frac{-5 - 3}{2 - (-4)} = \frac{-8}{6} = -\frac{4}{3}$ **6.** c; $2x - 5y = 8$; $m = -\frac{A}{B} = \frac{-2}{-5} = \frac{2}{5}$

7. a; $y - 2 = -\frac{3}{4}(x - (-1))$; $4y - 8 = -3x - 3$; $3x + 4y = 5$

8. b; $m = -\frac{4}{-1} = 4$; $y - (-2) = 4(x - 3)$; $y + 2 = 4x - 12$; $4x - y = 14$

9. c; $m = \frac{1}{3}$; $y - 1 = \frac{1}{3}(x - 4)$; $3y - 3 = x - 4$; $x - 3y = 1$

10. c; $\begin{array}{r} 4x + 3y = 7 \\ -2x + y = 9 \end{array}$; $y = 2x + 9$; $4x + 3(2x + 9) = 7$; $4x + 6x + 27 = 7$; $10x = -20$; $x = -2$; $4(-2) + 3y = 7$; $3y = 15$; $y = 5$; $(-2, 5)$

11. d; $y = ax^2 + b$; $1 = a(-1)^2 + b$; $1 = a + b$; $7 = a(2)^2 + b$; $7 = 4a + b$; $6 = 3a$; $a = 2$; $1 = 2 + b$; $b = -1$; $(a, b) = (2, -1)$; $y = 2x^2 - 1$

12. d; let x = cost of a shirt and y = cost of a tie; $\begin{array}{r} 2x + y = 42 \\ x + 2y = 39 \end{array}$; $\begin{array}{r} 2x + y = 42 \\ -2x - 4y = -78 \end{array}$; $-3y = -36$; $y = 12$; $2x + 12 = 42$; $2x = 30$; $x = 15$; a shirt costs \$15

13. b; substitution of $x = 1$ and $y = 1$ into the second inequality gives $1 - 3(1) > 4$; $-2 \not> 4$

14. a; $f(g(1)) = f(1 + 2) = f(3) = 3 - 3^2 = -6$

15. d;

x	−2	−1	0	1	2
$g(x)$	0	0	0	2	4

; $R = \{0, 2, 4\}$

16. a; $f(x) = mx + b$; $\begin{array}{r} f(2) = 2m + b = 2 \\ f(-6) = -6m + b = 6 \end{array}$; $8m = -4$; $m = -\frac{1}{2}$; $2\left(-\frac{1}{2}\right) + b = 2$; $b = 3$; $f(x) = -\frac{1}{2}x + 3$; $f(6) = -\frac{1}{2}(6) + 3 = 0$

17. c; let $f(x)$ = the conversion of the raw score x; $f(x) = mx + b$;
$\begin{matrix} f(200) = m(200) + b = 0 \\ f(800) = m(800) + b = 100 \end{matrix}$; $600m = 100$; $m = \frac{1}{6}$; $\frac{1}{6}(200) + b = 0$; $b = -\frac{100}{3}$;

$f(x) = \frac{1}{6}x - \frac{100}{3}$; $f(684) = \frac{1}{6}(684) - \frac{100}{3} = \frac{242}{3} = 80\frac{2}{3}$

18. d; this graph passes the vertical line test

Page 164 • CHAPTER TEST

1. $k(-2) + 6(1) = k$; $-2k + 6 = k$; $3k = 6$; $k = 2$

2. $3x + 2y = 12$; $y = \frac{12 - 3x}{2}$; x is even; if $x = 2$, $y = 3$; if $x \geq 4$, $y \leq 0$; $\{(2, 3)\}$

3. a.

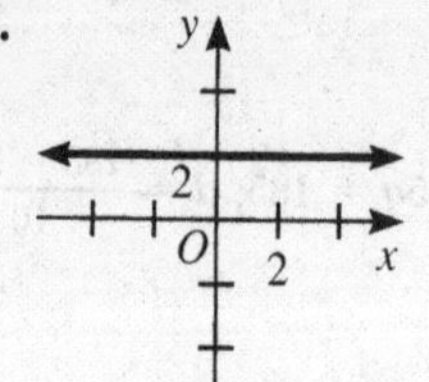

b.

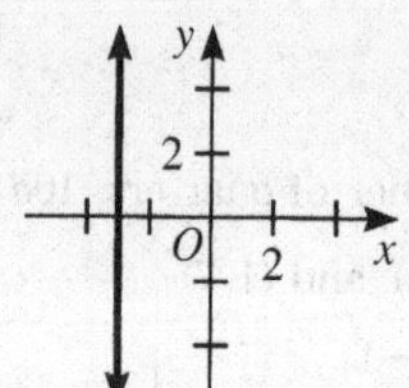

c.

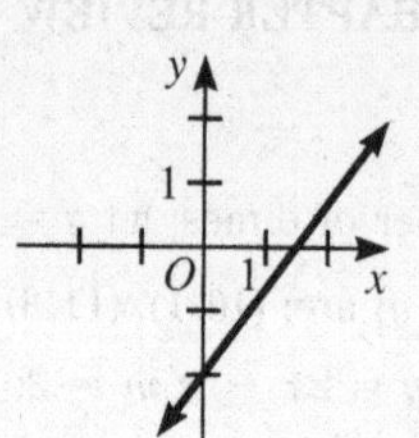

d.

4. 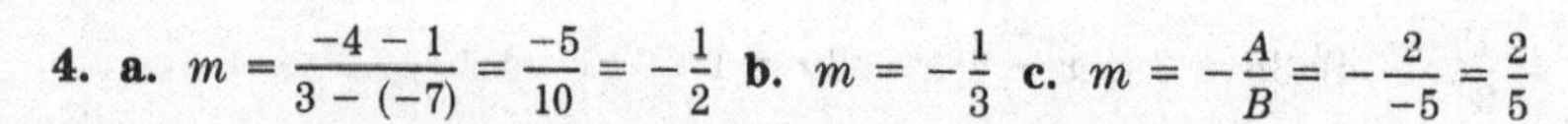
a. $m = \frac{-4 - 1}{3 - (-7)} = \frac{-5}{10} = -\frac{1}{2}$ **b.** $m = -\frac{1}{3}$ **c.** $m = -\frac{A}{B} = -\frac{2}{-5} = \frac{2}{5}$

5. $m = -\frac{A}{B} = -\frac{k + 2}{-3} = 2$; $k + 2 = 6$; $k = 4$

6. a. $y - 4 = -3(x - (-2))$; $y - 4 = -3x - 6$; $3x + y = -2$

b. $m = \frac{3 - (-1)}{3 - (-5)} = \frac{4}{8} = \frac{1}{2}$; $y - 3 = \frac{1}{2}(x - 3)$; $2y - 6 = x - 3$; $x - 2y = -3$

c. $b = -6$; $y = mx - 6$; $0 = m(4) - 6$; $m = \frac{3}{2}$; $y = \frac{3}{2}x - 6$; $2y = 3x - 12$; $3x - 2y = 12$

7. a. $m = -\frac{A}{B} = -\frac{4}{-3} = \frac{4}{3}$; $y - (-1) = \frac{4}{3}(x - 3)$; $3y + 3 = 4x - 12$; $4x - 3y = 15$

b. $m = -\frac{3}{4}$; $y - (-1) = -\frac{3}{4}(x - 3)$; $4y + 4 = -3x + 9$; $3x + 4y = 5$

8. $\begin{matrix} 5x - 4y = 13 \\ 2x + 3y = -4 \end{matrix}$, $\begin{matrix} -10x + 8y = -26 \\ 10x + 15y = -20 \end{matrix}$; $23y = -46$; $y = -2$; $5x - 4(-2) = 13$; $5x = 5$; $x = 1$; $(1, -2)$

9. Let x = weight, in lb, of a cement block; y = weight, in lb, of a brick; $\begin{matrix} 2x + 3y = 102 \\ x + 10y = 102 \end{matrix}$,

$\begin{matrix} 2x + 3y = 102 \\ -2x - 20y = -204 \end{matrix}$; $-17y = -102$; $y = 6$; a brick weighs 6 lb

10.

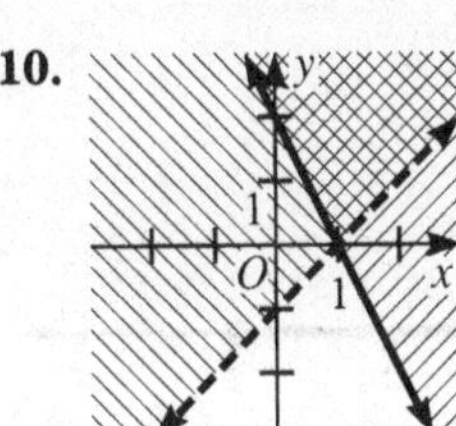

11. $f(0) = (0 - 2)^2 = 4; f(1) = (1 - 2)^2 = 1; f(2) = (2 - 2)^2 = 0;$
$f(3) = (3 - 2)^2 = 1; f(4) = (4 - 2)^2 = 4; R = \{0, 1, 4\}$

12. $f(g(1)) = f(1 - 4) = f(-3) = |2(-3) + 1| = |-6 + 1| = |-5| = 5; g(f(1)) =$
$g(|2(1) + 1|) = g(|3|) = g(3) = 3 - 4 = -1$

13. $m = \frac{8 - (-1)}{4 - 1} = \frac{9}{3} = 3; y - (-1) = 3(x - 1); y + 1 = 3x - 3; y = 3x - 4; f(x) = 3x - 4$

14. Let x = repairman's hourly rate; y = fixed charge for a service call; $\begin{matrix} 2x + y = 50 \\ 4x + y = 74 \end{matrix}$;

$\begin{matrix} -2x - y = -50 \\ 4x + y = 74 \end{matrix}$; $2x = 24$; $x = 12$; the repairman charges \$12 for each hour of work

15.

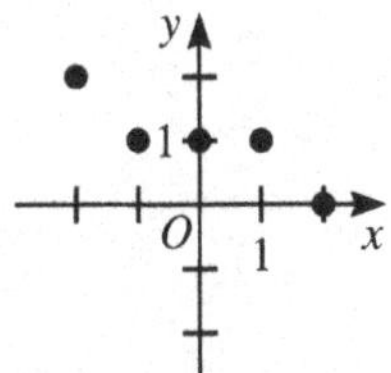

function

16.

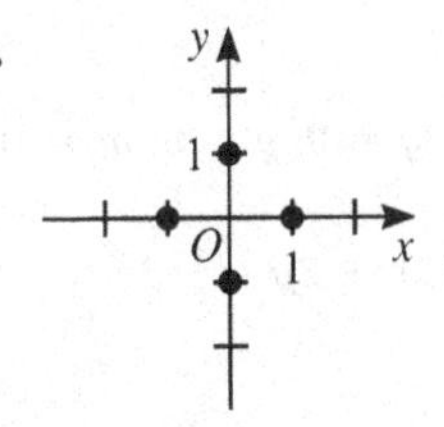

not a function

Page 165 • CUMULATIVE REVIEW

1. $-1(4 - 7)^2 + 6 = -1(-3)^2 + 6 = -1(9) + 6 = -9 + 6 = -3$
2. $2 - |(-3)(4) + (-1)^2| = 2 - |-12 + 1| = 2 - |-11| = 2 - 11 = -9$
3. $2(x + y) - 3(y - x) = 2x + 2y - 3y + 3x = 5x - y$
4. $\frac{|a| + |b|}{|a + b|} = \frac{|-6| + |2|}{|-6 + 2|} = \frac{6 + 2}{|-4|} = \frac{8}{4} = 2$
5. Let x = time, in hours, driving 55 mi/h; $5 - x$ = time, in hours, driving 30 mi/h; $30(5 - x) + 55x = 250$; $150 - 30x + 55x = 250$; $25x = 100$; $x = 4$; he spent 4 h at 55 mi/h
6. $3(2x - 1) = 4x + 7$; $6x - 3 = 4x + 7$; $2x = 10$; $x = 5$; $\{5\}$

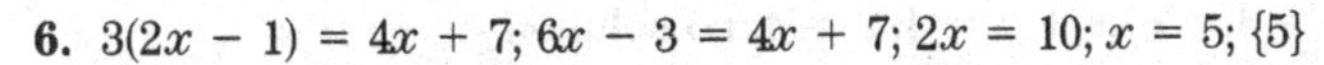

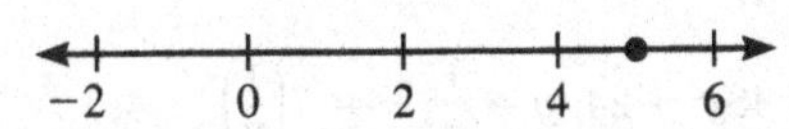

7. $13 - 7y \geq 34$; $-7y \geq 21$; $y \leq -3$; $\{y : y \leq -3\}$

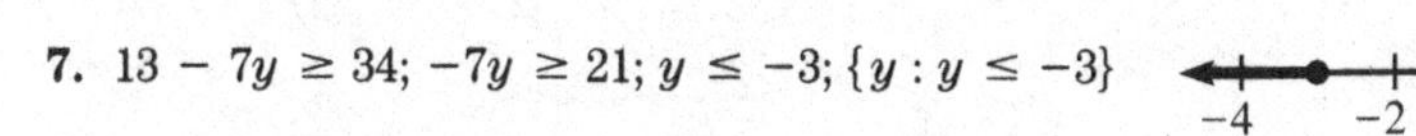

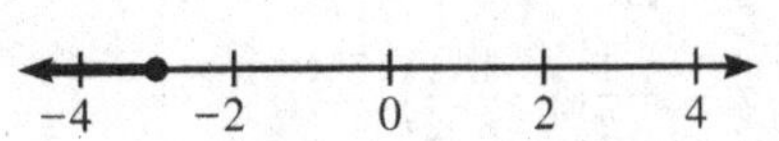

8. $5 < 3w + 8 < 14$; $-3 < 3w < 6$; $-1 < w < 2$; $\{w : -1 < w < 2\}$

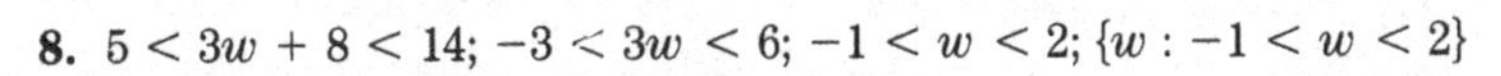

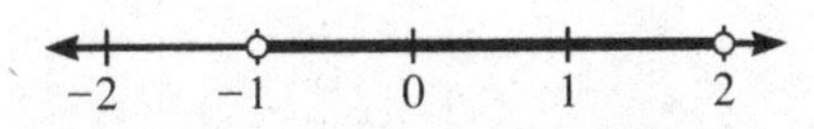

9. $|2m + 3| = 5$; $2m + 3 = 5$ or $2m + 3 = -5$; $2m = 2$ or $2m = -8$; $m = 1$ or $m = -4$; $\{-4, 1\}$

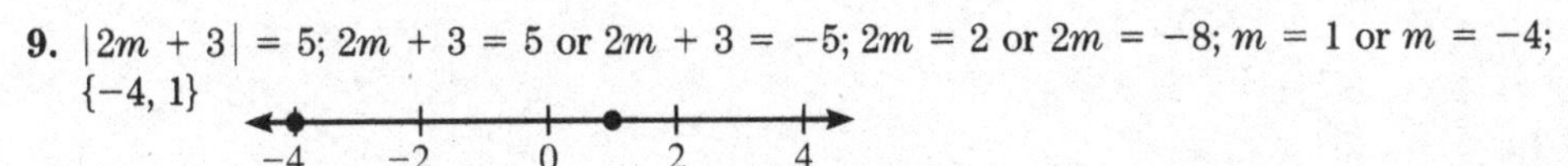

10. $\left|\frac{c-3}{2}\right| < 1$; $|c-3| < 2$; $-2 < c-3 < 2$; $1 < c < 5$; $\{c : 1 < c < 5\}$

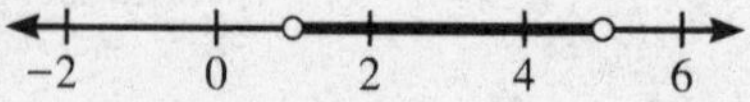

11. $6 - |n| \ge 4$; $2 \ge |n|$; $-2 \le n \le 2$; $\{n : -2 \le n \le 2\}$

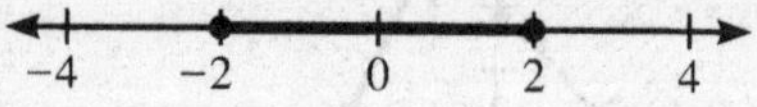

12. (1) $a + (b - a) = a + (b + (-a))$ (Def. of subtr.);
(2) $a + (b - a) = a + ((-a) + b)$ (Comm. prop. of add.);
(3) $a + (b - a) = (a + (-a)) + b$ (Assoc. prop. of add.);
(4) $a + (b - a) = 0 + b$ (Prop. of opposites);
(5) $a + (b - a) = b$ (Ident. prop. of add.)

13. $3x - 2y = 1$; $y = \frac{3x-1}{2}$; $y = \frac{3(-1)-1}{2} = -2$; $y = \frac{3(0)-1}{2} = -\frac{1}{2}$; $y = \frac{3(1)-1}{2} = 1$;
$\left\{(-1, -2), \left(0, -\frac{1}{2}\right), (1, 1)\right\}$

14. $m = -\frac{A}{B} = -\frac{8}{-6} = \frac{4}{3}$ **15.** $3y - 9 = 0$; $3y = 9$; $y = 3$; $m = 0$

16. $y - (-3) = -\frac{1}{2}(x - 4)$; $2y + 6 = -x + 4$; $x + 2y = -2$

17. $m = \frac{\frac{1}{2} - 4}{-3 - (-2)} = \frac{-\frac{7}{2}}{-1} = \frac{7}{2}$; $y - 4 = \frac{7}{2}(x - (-2))$; $2y - 8 = 7x + 14$; $7x - 2y = -22$

18. $b = 4$; $y = mx + 4$; $0 = m(6) + 4$; $m = -\frac{2}{3}$; $y = -\frac{2}{3}x + 4$; $3y = -2x + 12$;
$2x + 3y = 12$

19. $m = -\frac{A}{B} = -\frac{5}{-4} = \frac{5}{4}$; $y - (-2) = \frac{5}{4}(x - (-1))$; $4y + 8 = 5x + 5$; $5x - 4y = 3$

20. The slope of the line $2x + y = 5$ is -2; $m = \frac{1}{2}$; $y - 2 = \frac{1}{2}(x - 3)$; $2y - 4 = x - 3$;
$x - 2y = -1$

21. $\begin{matrix} 3x - 4y = 10 \\ 2x + 3y = 1 \end{matrix}$; $\begin{matrix} 6x - 8y = 20 \\ 6x + 9y = 3 \end{matrix}$; $-17y = 17$; $y = -1$; $3x - 4(-1) = 10$; $3x = 6$; $x = 2$;
$(2, -1)$

22. $\begin{matrix} y = \frac{1}{2}x - 1 \\ x - 2y = 4 \end{matrix}$; $x - 2\left(\frac{1}{2}x - 1\right) = 4$; $x - x + 2 = 4$; $2 = 4$; no solution

23. $\begin{matrix} x = 7y - 4 \\ y = 7x + 4 \end{matrix}$; $y = 7(7y - 4) + 4$; $y = 49y - 28 + 4$; $48y = 24$; $y = \frac{1}{2}$; $x = 7\left(\frac{1}{2}\right) - 4$;
$x = -\frac{1}{2}$; $\left(-\frac{1}{2}, \frac{1}{2}\right)$

24.

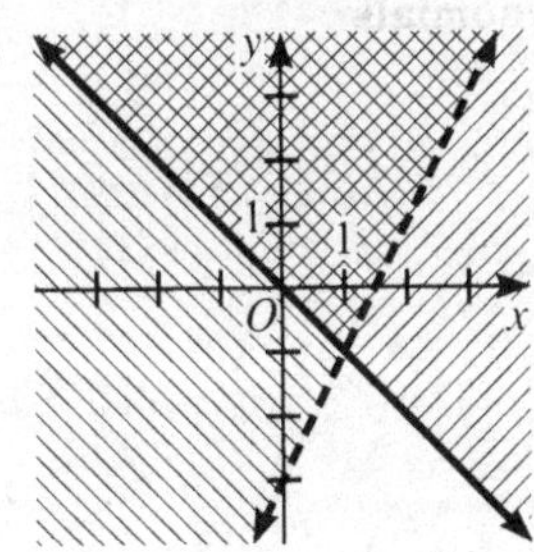

25. Let a = cost, in dollars, of an adult ticket, c = cost, in dollars, of a child's ticket;

$\begin{aligned} 2a + c &= 20 \\ a + 2c &= 16 \end{aligned}$; $c = 20 - 2a$; $a + 2(20 - 2a) = 16$; $a + 40 - 4a = 16$; $-3a = -24$; $a = 8$;

an adult's ticket costs \$8

26. $f(g(2)) = f(|2(2) - 7|) = f(|-3|) = f(3) = 4 - (3)^2 = 4 - 9 = -5$;
$g(f(2)) = g(4 - (2)^2) = g(4 - 4) = g(0) = |2(0) - 7| = |-7| = 7$

27. $m = \frac{-4 - 2}{1 - (-3)} = \frac{-6}{4} = -\frac{3}{2}$; $h(x) = -\frac{3}{2}x + b$; $h(1) = -\frac{3}{2}(1) + b = -4$; $b = -\frac{5}{2}$;

$h(x) = -\frac{3}{2}x - \frac{5}{2}$; $h(7) = -\frac{3}{2}(7) - \frac{5}{2} = -\frac{26}{2} = -13$

28.

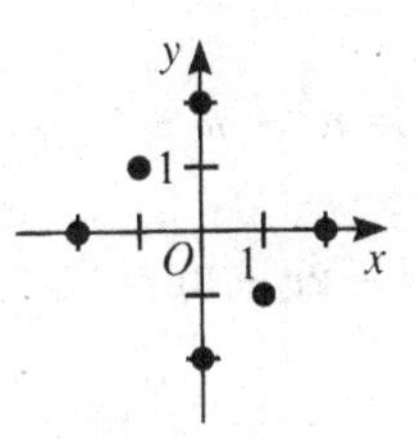

not a function

CHAPTER 4 • Products and Factors of Polynomials

Page 170 • WRITTEN EXERCISES

A

1. $2 - x^2 + 3x + 2x^2 - 5x = x^2 - 2x + 2; 2$

2. $x^3 - 4x + 7x^2 + 3 + 2x = x^3 + 7x^2 - 2x + 3; 3$

3. $-x^2 + 3x^3 - 3x + x^2 + 2x = 3x^3 - x; 3$

4. $2x^3 - 7 + 5x^2 - x^3 + 3x - x^3 = 5x^2 + 3x - 7; 2$

5. $x^2y^2 - x^2 + 8x^2y^2 + 5xy^2 - 2x^2 = 9x^2y^2 - 3x^2 + 5xy^2; 4$

6. $4x^2y^3 - xy^2 + 2x^3y - 2xy^2 = 2x^3y + 4x^2y^3 - 3xy^2; 5$

7. $4x^2yz^3 - xyz + 2x^2yz^3 + 5x^3y^2z^2 = 5x^3y^2z^2 + 6x^2yz^3 - xyz; 7$

8. $7xy^2z^3 - 4xy^2z^3 + 2x^2yz^2 - 3xy^2z^3 = 2x^2yz^2; 5$

9. **a.** $(5m - 4) + (2m + 3) = 7m - 1$

b. $(5m - 4) - (2m + 3) = (5m - 4) + (-2m - 3) = 3m - 7$

10. **a.** $(3u + 7) + (u - 8) = 4u - 1$

b. $(3u + 7) - (u - 8) = (3u + 7) + (-u + 8) = 2u + 15$

11. **a.** $(t^2 - 8t - 7) + (t^2 + 5t - 6) = 2t^2 - 3t - 13$

b. $(t^2 - 8t - 7) - (t^2 + 5t - 6) = (t^2 - 8t - 7) + (-t^2 - 5t + 6) = -13t - 1$

12. **a.** $(2n^2 - n + 5) + (n^2 + 1) = 3n^2 - n + 6$

b. $(2n^2 - n + 5) - (n^2 + 1) = (2n^2 - n + 5) + (-n^2 - 1) = n^2 - n + 4$

13. **a.** $(5v^3 - 2v + 1) + (v^2 + 2v - 2) = 5v^3 + v^2 - 1$

b. $(5v^3 - 2v + 1) - (v^2 + 2v - 2) = (5v^3 - 2v + 1) + (-v^2 - 2v + 2) =$
$5v^3 - v^2 - 4v + 3$

14. **a.** $(w^3 - w^2 + w - 1) + (1 - w - w^2 - w^3) = -2w^2$

b. $(w^3 - w^2 + w - 1) - (1 - w - w^2 - w^3) = (w^3 - w^2 + w - 1) +$
$(-1 + w + w^2 + w^3) = 2w^3 + 2w - 2$

15. **a.** $(3x^2 - 2xy + 4y^2) + (2x^2 + 3y^2) = 5x^2 - 2xy + 7y^2$

b. $(3x^2 - 2xy + 4y^2) - (2x^2 + 3y^2) = (3x^2 - 2xy + 4y^2) + (-2x^2 - 3y^2) =$
$x^2 - 2xy + y^2$

16. **a.** $(4a^2 + 3ab - b^2) + (b^2 - 2ab) = 4a^2 + ab$

b. $(4a^2 + 3ab - b^2) - (b^2 - 2ab) = (4a^2 + 3ab - b^2) + (-b^2 + 2ab) =$
$4a^2 + 5ab - 2b^2$

B

17. $3(x^2 - 2x + 4) + 2(5x^2 - 7) = 3x^2 - 6x + 12 + 10x^2 - 14 = 13x^2 - 6x - 2$

18. $4(3y^2 - 2y) + 3(y^2 + 5y - 1) = 12y^2 - 8y + 3y^2 + 15y - 3 = 15y^2 + 7y - 3$

19. $2(4m^2 + 3) - 7(m^2 - 2) + 1 = 8m^2 + 6 - 7m^2 + 14 + 1 = m^2 + 21$

20. $5(2n^2 - 3) - 2(5n^2 + 2) - 6 = 10n^2 - 15 - 10n^2 - 4 - 6 = -25$

21. $4a(x - y) + 3a(x + y) + ay = 4ax - 4ay + 3ax + 3ay + ay = 7ax$

22. $2d(3m + n) - 5d(m - 4n) - 10dm = 6dm + 2dn - 5dm + 20dn - 10dm =$
$-9dm + 22dn$

23. $3[2p^2 - q(3p + 4q)] - 2[4q^2 - 3p(p - 2q)] = 3(2p^2 - 3pq - 4q^2) - 2(4q^2 - 3p^2 + 6pq) = 6p^2 - 9pq - 12q^2 - 8q^2 + 6p^2 - 12pq = 12p^2 - 21pq - 20q^2$

24. $4[2a(3a - b) + 3ab] + 5[3b(a + 2b) - 4ab)] = 4(6a^2 - 2ab + 3ab) + 5(3ab + 6b^2 - 4ab) = 4(6a^2 + ab) + 5(6b^2 - ab) = 24a^2 + 4ab + 30b^2 - 5ab = 24a^2 - ab + 30b^2$

C **25.** $(4t^3 - at^2 - 2bt + 5) - (ct^3 + 2t^2 - 6t + 3) = t^3 - 2t + d$; $(4 - c)t^3 + (-a - 2)t^2 + (-2b + 6)t + 2 = t^3 - 2t + d$; $4 - c = 1$, $-a - 2 = 0$, $-2b + 6 = -2$, and $2 = d$; $a = -2$, $b = 4$, $c = 3$, $d = 2$

26. $(ax^3 - 3x^2 + 2bx - 2) - (2x^3 - cx^2 - 5x - 4d) = x^2 + x - 6$; $(a - 2)x^3 + (-3 + c)x^2 + (2b + 5)x + (-2 + 4d) = x^2 + x - 6$; $a - 2 = 0$, $-3 + c = 1$, $2b + 5 = 1$, and $-2 + 4d = -6$; $a = 2$, $b = -2$, $c = 4$, $d = -1$

27. $(x^2 + ax + 2b) + (x^2 - 2bx + 3a) = cx^2 - 7x + 3$; $2x^2 + (a - 2b)x + (2b + 3a) = cx^2 - 7x + 3$; $2 = c$; $a - 2b = -7$, and $2b + 3a = 3$; $a = 2b - 7$, $2b + 3(2b - 7) = 3$, $2b + 6b - 21 = 3$, $8b = 24$, $b = 3$, $a = -1$; $a = -1$, $b = 3$, $c = 2$

Page 170 • MIXED REVIEW EXERCISES

1. $f(x) = -2x + b; f(4) = -6; -6 = -2(4) + b, -6 = -8 + b, b = 2; f(x) = -2x + 2$

2. $f(0) = 5; 5 = 0x + b; b = 5; f(x) = mx + 5; f(2) = 7; 7 = m(2) + 5, 2m = 2, m = 1;$ $f(x) = x + 5$

3. $f(-1) = 3; 3 = m(-1) + b; f(3) = 1; 1 = m(3) + b; \begin{matrix} -m + b = 3 \\ 3m + b = 1 \end{matrix}; 4m = -2, m = -\frac{1}{2};$ $-\left(-\frac{1}{2}\right) + b = 3, b = \frac{5}{2}; f(x) = -\frac{1}{2}x + \frac{5}{2}$

4. a. $m = \frac{0 - 4}{4 - 0} = -1$ **b.** $b = 4; y = -x + 4; x + y = 4$

5. a. $m = \frac{3 - 1}{5 - (-3)} = \frac{2}{8} = \frac{1}{4}$

b. $y - 3 = \frac{1}{4}(x - 5); 4(y - 3) = x - 5, 4y - 12 = x - 5, x - 4y = -7$

6. a. $m = \frac{2 - 0}{-3 - 0} = -\frac{2}{3}$ **b.** $b = 0; y = -\frac{2}{3}x + 0; 2x + 3y = 0$

7. a. $m = \frac{1 - (-5)}{-2 - 6} = \frac{6}{-8} = -\frac{3}{4}$

b. $y - 1 = -\frac{3}{4}(x - (-2)); 4(y - 1) = -3(x + 2); 4y - 4 = -3x - 6; 3x + 4y = -2$

8. a. $m = \frac{9 - 7}{1 - (-4)} = \frac{2}{5}$

b. $y - 9 = \frac{2}{5}(x - 1); 5(y - 9) = 2(x - 1); 5y - 45 = 2x - 2; 2x - 5y = -43$

9. a. $m = \frac{5 - 5}{3 - (-2)} = 0$ **b.** $y - 5 = 0(x - 3); y - 5 = 0; y = 5$

Page 173 • WRITTEN EXERCISES

A

1. $3z^2 \cdot 2z^3 = 6 \cdot z^{2+3} = 6z^5$ **2.** $5r^2 \cdot r^4 = 5 \cdot r^{2+4} = 5r^6$

3. $(-t^4)^3 = (-1)^3(t^4)^3 = -1 \cdot t^{4 \cdot 3} = -t^{12}$ **4.** $(-t^3)^4 = (-1)^4(t^3)^4 = 1 \cdot t^{3 \cdot 4} = t^{12}$

5. $(3x^2y)(xy^2) = 3 \cdot x^{2+1} \cdot y^{1+2} = 3x^3y^3$ **6.** $(4p^2q)(p^2q^3) = 4 \cdot p^{2+2} \cdot q^{1+3} = 4p^4q^4$

7. $(-2u^2)(uv^3)(-u^2v^2) = (-2)(-1) \cdot u^{2+1+2} \cdot v^{3+2} = 2u^5v^5$

8. $(r^2s)(-3rs^3)(2rs) = (-3)(2) \cdot r^{2+1+1} \cdot s^{1+3+1} = -6r^4s^5$

9. $(4a^3b^2)^2 = 4^2 \cdot (a^3)^2 \cdot (b^2)^2 = 16a^6b^4$

10. $(2c^2d^3)^3 = 2^3 \cdot (c^2)^3 \cdot (d^3)^3 = 8c^{2 \cdot 3}d^{3 \cdot 3} = 8c^6d^9$

11. $(-3pq^4r^2)^3 = (-3)^3 \cdot p^3 \cdot (q^4)^3 \cdot (r^2)^3 = -27p^3q^{12}r^6$

12. $(-x^2yz^3)^4 = (-1)^4 \cdot (x^2)^4 \cdot y^4 \cdot (z^3)^4 = x^8y^4z^{12}$

13. $(-z^3)(-z)^3 = (-1)(z^3)(-1)^3(z^3) = (-1)(-1)(z^{3+3}) = z^6$

14. $(-c)^2(-c^4) = (-1)^2(c^2)(-1)(c^4) = (1)(-1)(c^{2+4}) = -1 \cdot c^6 = -c^6$

15. $(s^2t)^3(st^3)^2 = (s^2)^3(t^3)(s^2)(t^3)^2 = (s^{2 \cdot 3})(t^3)(s^2)(t^{3 \cdot 2}) = (s^6)(t^3)(s^2)(t^6) = (s^{6+2})(t^{3+6}) = s^8t^9$

16. $(2x^2y^3)^3(3x^3y)^2 = (2^3)(x^2)^3(y^3)^3(3^2)(x^3)^2(y^2) = (8)(x^{2 \cdot 3})(y^{3 \cdot 3})(9)(x^{3 \cdot 2})(y^2) = (8)(x^6)(y^9)(9)(x^6)(y^2) = (8)(9)(x^{6+6})(y^{9+2}) = 72x^{12}y^{11}$

17. $3y(y^3 - 2y^2 + 3) = 3y(y^3) + 3y(-2y^2) + 3y(3) = 3y^{1+3} - 6y^{1+2} + 9y = 3y^4 - 6y^3 + 9y$

18. $x^2(x - 2x^2 + 3x^3) = x^2(x) + x^2(-2x^2) + x^2(3x^3) = x^{2+1} - 2x^{2+2} + 3x^{2+3} = x^3 - 2x^4 + 3x^5$

19. $rs^2(r^2 - 2rs - s^2) = rs^2(r^2) + rs^2(-2rs) + rs^2(-s^2) = (r^{1+2})(s^2) - 2(r^{1+1})(s^{2+1}) - r(s^{2+2}) = r^3s^2 - 2r^2s^3 - rs^4$

20. $p^2q^3(p^2 - 4q) = p^2q^3(p^2) + p^2q^3(-4q) = (p^{2+2})(q^3) - 4(p^2)(q^{3+1}) = p^4q^3 - 4p^2q^4$

21. $z^{n-2} \cdot z^{n+2} = z^{[(n-2)+(n+2)]} = z^{2n}$ **22.** $t^4 \cdot t^{k-4} = t^{[4+(k-4)]} = t^k$

23. $x^{m-1} \cdot x \cdot x^m = x^{[(m-1)+1+m]} = x^{2m}$ **24.** $y^{p+2} \cdot y^p \cdot y^{p-2} = y^{[(p+2)+p+(p-2)]} = y^{3p}$

25. $r^{h-2}(r^{h+1})^2 = r^{h-2} \cdot r^{2(h+1)} = r^{h-2}r^{(2h+2)} = r^{[(h-2)+(2h+2)]} = r^{3h}$

26. $s^3(s^{2k-1})^3 = s^3 \cdot s^{3(2k-1)} = s^3s^{6k-3} = s^{[3+(6k-3)]} = s^{6k}$

B

27. $t(t^{n-1} + t^n + t^{n+1}) = t(t^{n-1}) + t(t^n) + t(t^{n+1}) = t^{1+(n-1)} + t^{1+n} + t^{1+(n+1)} = t^n + t^{n+1} + t^{n+2}$

28. $x^2(x^k - x^{k-1} + x^{k-2}) = x^2(x^k) - x^2(x^{k-1}) + x^2(x^{k-2}) = x^{2+k} - x^{2+(k-1)} + x^{2+(k-2)} = x^{k+2} - x^{k+1} + x^k$

29. $p^n(p^{m-n+1}) + p^{m-n} = p^n(p^{m-n+1}) + p^n(p^{m-n}) = p^{[n+(m-n+1)]} + p^{[n+(m-n)]} = p^{m+1} + p^m$

30. $s^{2n}(s^{2m-n} - s^{m-2n}) = s^{2n}(s^{2m-n}) - s^{2n}(s^{m-2n}) = s^{2n+(2m-n)} - s^{2n+(m-2n)} = s^{2m+n} - s^m$

31. $z^{m-n}(z^{n+m} - z^{n-m} + z^n) = z^{m-n}(z^{n+m}) - z^{m-n}(z^{n-m}) + z^{m-n}(z^n) = z^{(m-n)+(n+m)} - z^{(m-n)+(n-m)} + z^{(m-n)+n} = z^{2m} - z^0 + z^m = z^{2m} + z^m - 1$

32. $x^{h+k}(x^{2h-k} - x^{h-2k} + x^k) = x^{h+k}(x^{2h-k}) - x^{h+k}(x^{h-2k}) + x^{h+k}(x^k) = x^{(h+k)+(2h-k)} - x^{(h+k)+(h-2k)} + x^{(h+k)+k} = x^{3h} - x^{2h-k} + x^{h+2k}$

33. $(t^m)^n(t^n)^{n-m} = (t^{mn})(t^{n^2-nm}) = t^{mn+(n^2-nm)} = t^{n^2}$

34. $(y^{h-k})^h(y^{h+k})^k = y^{(h^2-hk)}y^{(hk+k^2)} = y^{(h^2-hk)+(hk+k^2)} = y^{h^2+k^2}$

35. $3^{5n} = 3^5(3^{2n})^2$; $3^{5n} = 3^5 3^{4n}$; $3^{5n} = 3^{4n+5}$; $5n = 4n + 5, n = 5$; {5}

36. $(2^{3n})^2 = (2^n)^3 \cdot 2^{n+6}$; $2^{6n} = 2^{3n} \cdot 2^{n+6}$; $2^{6n} = 2^{4n+6}$; $6n = 4n + 6$; $2n = 6$; $n = 3$; {3}

37. $3 \cdot 9^{2n} = (3^{n+1})^3$; $3 \cdot (3^2)^{2n} = 3^{3n+3}$; $3 \cdot 3^{4n} = 3^{3n+3}$; $3^{4n+1} = 3^{3n+3}$; $4n + 1 = 3n + 3$; $n = 2$; {2}

38. $4^{n+3} \cdot 16^n = 8^{3n}$; $(2^2)^{n+3} \cdot (2^4)^n = (2^3)^{3n}$; $2^{2n+6} \cdot 2^{4n} = 2^{9n}$; $2^{6n+6} = 2^{9n}$; $6n + 6 = 9n$; $3n = 6$; $n = 2$; {2}

C **39.** **1.** $a^m \cdot a^n = \underbrace{(a \cdot a \cdot \ldots \cdot a)}_{m \text{ factors}}\underbrace{(a \cdot a \cdot \ldots \cdot a)}_{n \text{ factors}}$ (Def. of a power)

2. $\underbrace{(a \cdot a \cdot \ldots \cdot a)}_{m \text{ factors}}\underbrace{(a \cdot a \cdot \ldots \cdot a)}_{n \text{ factors}} = \underbrace{a \cdot a \cdot \ldots \cdot a}_{m + n \text{ factors}}$ (Assoc. prop. for mult.)

3. $\underbrace{a \cdot a \cdot \ldots \cdot a}_{m + n \text{ factors}} = a^{m+n}$ (Def. of a power)

4. $a^m \cdot a^n = a^{m+n}$ (Trans. prop. of equal.)

40. **1.** $(a^m)^n = \underbrace{a^m \cdot a^m \cdot \ldots \cdot a^m}_{n \text{ factors}}$ (Def. of a power)

2. $\underbrace{a^m \cdot a^m \cdot \ldots \cdot a^m}_{n \text{ factors}} = a^{\overbrace{m+m+\ldots+m}^{n \text{ addends}}}$ (First law of exp.)

3. $a^{\overbrace{m+m+\ldots+m}^{n \text{ addends}}} = a^{mn}$ (Def. of mult.) **4.** $(a^m)^n = a^{mn}$ (Trans. prop. of equal.)

41. **1.** $((a^m)^n)^r = (a^{mn})^r$ (Third law of exp.) **2.** $(a^{mn})^r = a^{(mn)r}$ (Third law of exp.)

3. $a^{(mn)r} = a^{mnr}$ (Assoc. prop. for mult.)

4. $((a^m)^n)^r = a^{mnr}$ (Trans. prop. of equal.)

42. **1.** $(a^m)^n = a^{mn}$ (Third law of exp.) **2.** $mn = nm$ (Comm. prop. for mult.)

3. $a^{mn} = a^{nm}$ (Subst.) **4.** $a^{nm} = (a^n)^m$ (Third law of exp.)

5. $(a^m)^n = (a^n)^m$ (Trans. prop.)

Pages 175–176 • WRITTEN EXERCISES

A **1.** $(3v + 1)(2v - 5) = 6v^2 - 15v + 2v - 5 = 6v^2 - 13v - 5$

2. $(2x - 3)(3x + 2) = 6x^2 + 4x - 9x - 6 = 6x^2 - 5x - 6$

3. $(4z + 3)(3z - 4) = 12z^2 - 16z + 9z - 12 = 12z^2 - 7z - 12$

4. $(r - 4)(3r - 2) = 3r^2 - 2r - 12r + 8 = 3r^2 - 14r + 8$

5. $(3x + 10)^2 = (3x)^2 + 2(3x)(10) + 10^2 = 9x^2 + 60x + 100$

6. $(4k - 5)^2 = (4k)^2 - 2(4k)(5) + 5^2 = 16k^2 - 40k + 25$

7. $(5y - 2)(5y + 2) = (5y)^2 - (2)^2 = 25y^2 - 4$

8. $(2s + 7)(2s - 7) = (2s)^2 - 7^2 = 4s^2 - 49$

9. $(7t + 2)(2t - 1) = 14t^2 - 7t + 4t - 2 = 14t^2 - 3t - 2$

10. $(5z + 6)(6z - 5) = 30z^2 - 25z + 36z - 30 = 30z^2 + 11z - 30$

11. $(9t + 1)(1 - 9t) = (1 + 9t)(1 - 9t) = 1^2 - (9t)^2 = 1 - 81t^2$

12. $(9 - 5t)(5t - 9) = -(5t - 9)^2 = -[(5t)^2 - 2(5t)(9) + 9^2] = -(25t^2 - 90t + 81) = -25t^2 + 90t - 81$

13. $(x - 2y)(3x + 4y) = 3x^2 + 4xy - 6xy - 8y^2 = 3x^2 - 2xy - 8y^2$

14. $(5h - 3k)(h - 2k) = 5h^2 - 10hk - 3hk + 6k^2 = 5h^2 - 13hk + 6k^2$

15. $(2p + 3q)(3p - 2q) = 6p^2 - 4pq + 9pq - 6q^2 = 6p^2 + 5pq - 6q^2$

16. $(10r - 3s)(r + 2s) = 10r^2 + 20rs - 3rs - 6s^2 = 10r^2 + 17rs - 6s^2$

17. $(x^2 - 3)(x^2 + 3) = (x^2)^2 - 3^2 = x^4 - 9$

18. $(p^2 - 2q^2)(p^2 + 2q^2) = (p^2)^2 - (2q^2)^2 = p^4 - 4q^4$

19. $(s^3 + t^3)^2 = (s^3)^2 + 2(s^3)(t^3) + (t^3)^2 = s^6 + 2s^3t^3 + t^6$

20. $(2z^2 - 5)^2 = (2z^2)^2 - 2(2z^2)(5) + 5^2 = 4z^4 - 20z^2 + 25$

21. $t(t - 2)(t + 1) = t(t^2 + t - 2t - 2) = t(t^2 - t - 2) = t^3 - t^2 - 2t$

22. $x^2(x - 3)(x + 3) = x^2[(x^2) - (3)^2] = x^2(x^2 - 9) = x^4 - 9x^2$

23. $xy(x - y)^2 = xy(x^2 - 2xy + y^2) = x^3y - 2x^2y^2 + xy^3$

24. $mn(m - n)(m - 2n) = mn(m^2 - 2mn - mn + 2n^2) = mn(m^2 - 3mn + 2n^2) =$ $m^3n - 3m^2n^2 + 2mn^3$

25. $(2c + 1)(c^2 - 3c + 2) = 2c(c^2 - 3c + 2) + 1(c^2 - 3c + 2) = 2c^3 - 6c^2 + 4c +$ $c^2 - 3c + 2 = 2c^3 - 5c^2 + c + 2$

26. $(t - 3)(2t^2 - t + 2) = t(2t^2 - t + 2) - 3(2t^2 - t + 2) = 2t^3 - t^2 + 2t - 6t^2 +$ $3t - 6 = 2t^3 - 7t^2 + 5t - 6$

27. $(x^2 + 3x - 5)(x + 2) = (x^2 + 3x - 5)x + (x^2 + 3x - 5)(2) = x^3 + 3x^2 - 5x +$ $2x^2 + 6x - 10 = x^3 + 5x^2 + x - 10$

28. $(z^2 - 2z + 4)(z + 3) = (z^2 - 2z + 4)(z) + (z^2 - 2z + 4)(3) = z^3 - 2z^2 + 4z +$ $3z^2 - 6z + 12 = z^3 + z^2 - 2z + 12$

29. $(y^4 - 3y^2 + 1)(y^2 - 2) = (y^4 - 3y^2 + 1)(y^2) + (y^4 - 3y^2 + 1)(-2) = y^6 - 3y^4 +$ $y^2 - 2y^4 + 6y^2 - 2 = y^6 - 5y^4 + 7y^2 - 2$

30. $(3 - k^2)(2 - k^2 - k^4) = 3(2 - k^2 - k^4) - k^2(2 - k^2 - k^4) = 6 - 3k^2 - 3k^4 -$ $2k^2 + k^4 + k^6 = 6 - 5k^2 - 2k^4 + k^6 = k^6 - 2k^4 - 5k^2 + 6$

B 31. $(x^2 - x + 2)(x^2 + x - 1) = x^2(x^2 + x - 1) - x(x^2 + x - 1) + 2(x^2 + x - 1) =$ $x^4 + x^3 - x^2 - x^3 - x^2 + x + 2x^2 + 2x - 2 = x^4 + 3x - 2$

32. $(y^2 - 2y + 1)(y^2 + y + 1) = y^2(y^2 + y + 1) - 2y(y^2 + y + 1) +$ $1(y^2 + y + 1) = y^4 + y^3 + y^2 - 2y^3 - 2y^2 - 2y + y^2 + y + 1 =$ $y^4 - y^3 - y + 1$

33. $(a + 2b)(a^3 - 2a^2b - b^3) = a(a^3 - 2a^2b - b^3) + 2b(a^3 - 2a^2b - b^3) =$ $a^4 - 2a^3b - ab^3 + 2a^3b - 4a^2b^2 - 2b^4 = a^4 - 4a^2b^2 - ab^3 - 2b^4$

34. $(3s + 2t)(s^3 - 3st^2 + 2t^3) = 3s(s^3 - 3st^2 + 2t^3) + 2t(s^3 - 3st^2 + 2t^3) =$ $3s^4 - 9s^2t^2 + 6st^3 + 2s^3t - 6st^3 + 4t^4 = 3s^4 + 2s^3t - 9s^2t^2 + 4t^4$

35. $(p^n - 1)^2 = (p^n)^2 - 2(1)(p^n) + 1^2 = p^{2n} - 2p^n + 1$

36. $(x^{2n} - y^n)^2 = (x^{2n})^2 - 2(x^{2n})(y^n) + (y^n)^2 = x^{4n} - 2x^{2n}y^n + y^{2n}$

37. $(r^n - s^n)(r^n + 2s^n) = r^nr^n + 2r^ns^n - r^ns^n - (s^n)(2s^n) = r^{2n} + r^ns^n - 2s^{2n}$

38. $(x^n + 1)(x^n - 1) = (x^n)^2 - 1^2 = x^{2n} - 1$

39. $(a - b)^3 = (a - b)(a - b)^2 = (a - b)(a^2 - 2ab + b^2) = a(a^2 - 2ab + b^2) -$ $b(a^2 - 2ab + b^2) = a^3 - 2a^2b + ab^2 - a^2b + 2ab^2 - b^3 = a^3 - 3a^2b +$ $3ab^2 - b^3$

40. $(a + b)^3 = (a + b)(a + b)^2 = (a + b)(a^2 + 2ab + b^2) = a(a^2 + 2ab + b^2) +$ $b(a^2 + 2ab + b^2) = a^3 + 2a^2b + ab^2 + a^2b + 2ab^2 + b^3 =$ $a^3 + 3a^2b + 3ab^2 + b^3$

41. $(a + b)(a^2 - ab + b^2) = a(a^2 - ab + b^2) + b(a^2 - ab + b^2) = a^3 - a^2b + ab^2 +$ $a^2b - ab^2 + b^3 = a^3 + b^3$

42. $(a - b)(a^2 + ab + b^2) = a(a^2 + ab + b^2) - b(a^2 + ab + b^2) = a^3 + a^2b + ab^2 - a^2b - ab^2 - b^3 = a^3 - b^3$

43. $(a - b)(a^3 + a^2b + ab^2 + b^3) = a(a^3 + a^2b + ab^2 + b^3) - b(a^3 + a^2b + ab^2 + b^3) = a^4 + a^3b + a^2b^2 + ab^3 - a^3b - a^2b^2 - ab^3 - b^4 = a^4 - b^4$

44. $(a + b)(a^3 - a^2b + ab^2 - b^3) = a(a^3 - a^2b + ab^2 - b^3) + b(a^3 - a^2b + ab^2 - b^3) = a^4 - a^3b + a^2b^2 - ab^3 + a^3b - a^2b^2 + ab^3 - b^4 = a^4 - b^4$

45. $(x - y)(x + y)(x^2 + y^2) = (x^2 - y^2)(x^2 + y^2) = (x^2)^2 - (y^2)^2 = x^4 - y^4$

46. $(x + y)^2(x - y)^2 = [(x + y)(x - y)]^2 = (x^2 - y^2)^2 = (x^2)^2 - 2(x^2)(y^2) + (y^2)^2 = x^4 - 2x^2y^2 + y^4$

47. $(x^2 + 2x + 2)(x^2 - 2x + 2) = x^2(x^2 - 2x + 2) + 2x(x^2 - 2x + 2) + 2(x^2 - 2x + 2) = x^4 - 2x^3 + 2x^2 + 2x^3 - 4x^2 + 4x + 2x^2 - 4x + 4 = x^4 + 4$

48. $(x^2 - 4x + 8)(x^2 + 4x + 8) = x^2(x^2 + 4x + 8) - 4x(x^2 + 4x + 8) + 8(x^2 + 4x + 8) = x^4 + 4x^3 + 8x^2 - 4x^3 - 16x^2 - 32x + 8x^2 + 32x + 64 = x^4 + 64$

C **49.** 4 terms **50.** 9 terms **51.** 4 terms **52.** 4 terms

53. $(x + 2k)(x - 3k) = x^2 - 3kx + 2kx - 6k^2 = x^2 - kx - 6k^2; x^2 - kx - 6k^2 = x^2 + 2x - 24; k = -2$

54. $(2x + k)(x - 2k) = 2x^2 - 4kx + kx - 2k^2 = 2x^2 - 3kx - 2k^2; 2x^2 - 3kx - 2k^2 = 2x^2 + 9x - 18; k = -3$

55. $(2x - k)(3x + 2k) = 6x^2 + 4kx - 3kx - 2k^2 = 6x^2 + kx - 2k^2;$ $6x^2 + kx - 2k^2 = 6x^2 + kx - 32; -2k^2 = -32, k^2 = 16, k = 4$ or $k = -4$

56. $(3kx + 2)^2 = (3kx)^2 + 2(3kx)(2) + 2^2 = 9k^2x^2 + 12kx + 4; 9k^2x^2 + 12kx + 4 = 81x^2 + 12kx + 4; 9k^2 = 81; k^2 = 9; k = 3$ or $k = -3$

Page 176 • MIXED REVIEW EXERCISES

1. $(3x^2 - 7x + 9) - (x^2 + 4x - 1) = (3x^2 - 7x + 9) + (-x^2 - 4x + 1) = 2x^2 - 11x + 10$
2. $(a^2b^3)^3 = (a^2)^3(b^3)^3 = a^{2\cdot3}b^{3\cdot3} = a^6b^9$
3. $(4m^2n)(-3mn^3) = 4(-3)m^{2+1}n^{1+3} = -12m^3n^4$
4. $5(2y - 1) - 3(y + 2) = 10y - 5 - 3y - 6 = 7y - 11$
5. $2c(d - 3) + 3d(c + 4) = 2cd - 6c + 3cd + 12d = 5cd - 6c + 12d$
6. $4p(2p^2 - p + 5) = 8p^3 - 4p^2 + 20p$
7. $(-u^2)^4(-u^3) = [(-1)^4(u^2)^4][-u^3] = (u^8)(-u^3) = -u^{11}$
8. $(9z^3 - 4z) + (5z^2 - 8) = 9z^3 + 5z^2 - 4z - 8$
9. $(y^2 - 5y + 9) - (9 + 5y + y^2) = (y^2 - 5y + 9) + (-9 - 5y - y^2) = -10y$
10. $\left(-\frac{1}{2}x^2\right)(-4x^4) = -\frac{1}{2}(-4)(x^2)(x^4) = 2x^{2+4} = 2x^6$

Page 178 • READING ALGEBRA

1. **a.** Two divides eight; true **b.** Four divides four; true **c.** Two divides one; false
   d. Two divides zero; true **e.** Zero divides three; false
2. does not equal (or is not equal to); does not divide

3. a. true **b.** true **c.** false **4.** yes **5.** no **6.** $17 \equiv 2 (\text{mod } 5)$ **7.** $5 | (19 - 4)$

8. yes

9. a. One hundred is congruent to twenty-five (mod five); true

b. Negative three is congruent to three (mod five); false

c. Six is congruent to one (mod five); true

d. Zero is congruent to five (mod five); true

10. even integers **11.** odd integers

12. Answers may vary. Examples: **a.** $n = 2$ **b.** $n = 2$

Pages 181–182 • WRITTEN EXERCISES

A **1.** $140 = 2^2 \cdot 5 \cdot 7$ **2.** $198 = 2 \cdot 3^2 \cdot 11$ **3.** 89 is prime **4.** $756 = 2^2 \cdot 3^3 \cdot 7$

5. $441 = 3^2 \cdot 7^2$ **6.** $203 = 7 \cdot 29$ **7.** $2548 = 2^2 \cdot 7^2 \cdot 13$ **8.** $3861 = 3^3 \cdot 11 \cdot 13$

9. $20 = 2^2 \cdot 5$; $35 = 5 \cdot 7$ **a.** 5 **b.** $2^2 \cdot 5 \cdot 7 = 140$

10. $45 = 3^2 \cdot 5$; $75 = 3 \cdot 5^2$ **a.** 15 **b.** $3^2 \cdot 5^2 = 225$

11. $-48 = -2^4 \cdot 3$; $108 = 2^2 \cdot 3^3$ **a.** $2^2 \cdot 3 = 12$ **b.** $2^4 \cdot 3^3 = 432$

12. $315 = 3^2 \cdot 5 \cdot 7$; $-525 = -3 \cdot 5^2 \cdot 7$ **a.** $3 \cdot 5 \cdot 7 = 105$ **b.** $3^2 \cdot 5^2 \cdot 7 = 1575$

13. $84 = 2^2 \cdot 3 \cdot 7$; $-56 = -2^3 \cdot 7$; $140 = 2^2 \cdot 5 \cdot 7$ **a.** $2^2 \cdot 7 = 28$ **b.** $2^3 \cdot 3 \cdot 5 \cdot 7 = 840$

14. $168 = 2^3 \cdot 3 \cdot 7$; $280 = 2^3 \cdot 5 \cdot 7$; $196 = 2^2 \cdot 7^2$ **a.** $2^2 \cdot 7 = 28$

b. $2^3 \cdot 3 \cdot 5 \cdot 7^2 = 5880$

15. a. 1 **b.** $5 \cdot 7 \cdot 9 = 315$

16. $30 = 2 \cdot 3 \cdot 5$; $35 = 5 \cdot 7$; $36 = 2^2 \cdot 3^2$; $42 = 2 \cdot 3 \cdot 7$ **a.** 1 **b.** $2^2 \cdot 3^2 \cdot 5 \cdot 7 = 1260$

17. $9p^3q = 3^2p^3q$; $15p^2 = 3 \cdot 5p^2$ **a.** $3p^2$ **b.** $3^2 \cdot 5 \cdot p^3q = 45p^3q$

18. $49x^3 = 7^2x^3$; $35x^2y = 5 \cdot 7 \cdot x^2y$ **a.** $7x^2$ **b.** $5 \cdot 7^2 \cdot x^3 \cdot y = 245x^3y$

19. $68xy^2z = 2^2 \cdot 17xy^2z$; $51y^2z^2 = 3 \cdot 17 \cdot y^2z^2$ **a.** $17y^2z$

b. $2^2 \cdot 3 \cdot 17 \cdot x \cdot y^2 \cdot z^2 = 204xy^2z^2$

20. $52r^2s = 2^2 \cdot 13r^2s$; $78rs^2t = 2 \cdot 3 \cdot 13rs^2t$ **a.** $2 \cdot 13rs = 26rs$

b. $2^2 \cdot 3 \cdot 13 \cdot r^2 \cdot s^2t = 156r^2s^2t$

21. $110h^3k^2r = 2 \cdot 5 \cdot 11 \cdot h^3k^2r$; $-88h^2k^2r^2 = -2^3 \cdot 11 \cdot h^2k^2r^2$

a. $2 \cdot 11 \cdot h^2k^2r = 22h^2k^2r$ **b.** $2^3 \cdot 5 \cdot 11 \cdot h^3 \cdot k^2 \cdot r^2 = 440h^3k^2r^2$

22. $98a^2b^2c = 2 \cdot 7^2a^2b^2c$; $-70abc^2 = -2 \cdot 5 \cdot 7abc^2$ **a.** $2 \cdot 7 \cdot a \cdot b \cdot c = 14abc$

b. $2 \cdot 5 \cdot 7^2 \cdot a^2 \cdot b^2 \cdot c^2 = 490a^2b^2c^2$

23. $14ab = 2 \cdot 7 \cdot ab$; $14bc = 2 \cdot 7 \cdot bc$; $21ac = 3 \cdot 7 \cdot ac$ **a.** 7

b. $2 \cdot 3 \cdot 7 \cdot a \cdot b \cdot c = 42abc$

24. $22xy^2z^2 = 2 \cdot 11 \cdot xy^2z^2$; $33x^2yz^2 = 3 \cdot 11x^2yz^2$; $44x^2yz = 2^2 \cdot 11x^2yz$ **a.** $11xyz$

b. $2^2 \cdot 3 \cdot 11 \cdot x^2y^2z^2 = 132x^2y^2z^2$

25. $26p^3q^2r^2 = 2 \cdot 13p^3q^2r^2$; $39p^2q^3r^2 = 3 \cdot 13p^2q^3r^2$; $78p^2q^2r^3 = 2 \cdot 3 \cdot 13p^2q^2r^3$

a. $13p^2q^2r^2$ **b.** $2 \cdot 3 \cdot 13 \cdot p^3 \cdot q^3 \cdot r^3 = 78p^3q^3r^3$

26. $200a^3b^2c = 2^3 \cdot 5^2 \cdot a^3b^2c$; $300a^2bc^3 = 2^2 \cdot 3 \cdot 5^2 \cdot a^2bc^3$; $400ab^3c^2 = 2^4 \cdot 5^2 \cdot ab^3c^2$

a. $2^2 \cdot 5^2 \cdot a \cdot b \cdot c = 100abc$ b. $2^4 \cdot 3 \cdot 5^2 \cdot a^3 \cdot b^3 \cdot c^3 = 1200a^3b^3c^3$

B 27. $84 = 2^2 \cdot 3 \cdot 7$; let the other number be n; since the GCF $= 42 = 2 \cdot 3 \cdot 7$, n has exactly one factor of 2 and at least one factor of each of 3 and 7; since the LCM $= 252 = 2^2 \cdot 3^2 \cdot 7$, n has exactly 2 factors of 3 and one factor of 7; thus, $n = 2 \cdot 3^2 \cdot 7 = 126$

28. $12x^2y^3 = 2^2 \cdot 3x^2y^3$; let the other monomial be n; since the GCF $= 6xy^3 = 2 \cdot 3 \cdot xy^3$, n has exactly one factor of 2, at least one factor of 3, exactly one factor of x, and at least 3 factors of y; since the LCM $= 36x^2y^4 = 2^2 \cdot 3^2 \cdot x^2y^4$, n has exactly 2 factors of 3 and 4 factors of y; thus, $n = 2 \cdot 3^2 \cdot x \cdot y^4 = 18xy^4$

29. The positive factors of 496 are 1, 2, 4, 8, 16, 31, 62, 124, 248, and 496. $1 + 2 + 4 + 8 + 16 + 31 + 62 + 124 + 248 = 496$

30. $6 = 1 + 2 + 3$; $28 = 1 + 2 + 4 + 7 + 14$; 6 and 28

31. a. $1, p, q, pq$ b. $1, p, q, p^2, q^2, pq, p^2q, pq^2, p^2q^2$

c. $1, p, q, p^2, q^2, pq, p^3, p^2q, pq^2, q^3, p^3q, p^2q^2, pq^3, p^3q^2, p^2q^3, p^3q^3$

32. Each factor of p^mq^m is of the form p^kq^j, where $k = 0, 1, 2, \ldots, m$ and $j = 0, 1, 2, 3, \ldots, m$. There are $(m + 1)(m + 1) = (m + 1)^2$ factors

33. The LCM of two numbers is the product of the greatest power of each prime factor of both numbers. If the numbers are relatively prime, they have no factors in common and the LCM is the product of the prime factors.

34. If the integers are divided by their GCF, the resulting quotients have no common factors other than 1 and are relatively prime.

C 35. False; 2 and 3 are relatively prime, as are 3 and 4, but 2 and 4 are not relatively prime since their GCF is 2.

36. Let h, k, m, and n be integers such that $hm - kn = 1$ and suppose m and n are not relatively prime. Then there is an integer $x > 1$ and integers y and z such that $m = xy$ and $n = xz$. Then $hxy - kxz = 1$ or $x(hy - kz) = 1$ and $hy - kz$ is the reciprocal of x. Since h, y, k, and z are integers, so is $hy - kz$. There are only two integers whose reciprocals are integers, -1 and 1. This contradicts the fact that $x > 1$. It follows that m and n are relatively prime.

Pages 185–186 • WRITTEN EXERCISES

A 1. $16x^2(x - 4)$ 2. $2x^2y(3y + 4x)$ 3. $(t + 9)^2$ 4. $(z - 6)^2$

5. $(4k - 1)(4k + 1)$ 6. $(11x - 1)(11x + 1)$ 7. $(2y + 5)^2$ 8. $(3s - 4)^2$

9. $(4x - 5)(4x + 5)$ 10. $(2h - 9)(2h + 9)$ 11. $(11s - 3t)^2$ 12. $(4x + 5y)^2$

13. $(6p - 7q)(6p + 7q)$ 14. $(3x^2 - 4z)(3x^2 + 4z)$ 15. $s(t^2 - 1) = s(t - 1)(t + 1)$

16. $pq(p^2 - 1) = pq(p - 1)(p + 1)$ 17. $(t - 3)(t^2 + 3t + 9)$

18. $(2p + 1)(4p^2 - 2p + 1)$ 19. $2rs(8r^3 + s^3) = 2rs(2r + s)(4r^2 - 2rs + s^2)$

20. $3x^2y(y^3 - 27) = 3x^2y(y - 3)(y^2 + 3y + 9)$ 21. $(x + 2)(y - 3)$

22. $(u - 2)(v - 1)$ 23. $x(y - 3) - 2(y - 3) = (x - 2)(y - 3)$

24. $u(v - 1) + 2(v - 1) = (u + 2)(v - 1)$

25. $q(p - 2) + 2(p - 2) = (q + 2)(p - 2)$

26. $y(x - 2) - 1(x - 2) = (y - 1)(x - 2)$

27. $ab + a - (2b + 2) = a(b + 1) - 2(b + 1) = (a - 2)(b + 1)$

28. $4ab - 2a - (2b - 1) = 2a(2b - 1) - 1(2b - 1) = (2a - 1)(2b - 1)$

29. $(x^2 - 6x + 9) - 4y^2 = (x - 3)^2 - 4y^2 = (x - 3 - 2y)(x - 3 + 2y)$

30. $(z^2 + 2z + 1) - w^2 = (z + 1)^2 - w^2 = (z + 1 - w)(z + 1 + w)$

31. $u^2 - (v^2 - 2v + 1) = u^2 - (v - 1)^2 = [u - (v - 1)][u + (v - 1)] =$
$(u - v + 1)(u + v - 1)$

32. $x^2 - (y^2 + 4y + 4) = x^2 - (y + 2)^2 = [x - (y + 2)][x + (y + 2)] =$
$(x - y - 2)(x + y + 2)$

B **33.** $(x^2 - y)^2$ **34.** $(2u^2v + 1)^2$ **35.** $(a^2 + b)(a^4 - a^2b + b^2)$

36. $2x^2(125 - x^3) = 2x^2(5 - x)(25 + 5x + x^2)$

37. $(4s^2 - 9)(4s^2 + 9) = (2s - 3)(2s + 3)(4s^2 + 9)$

38. $(p^2 - q^2)(p^2 + q^2) = (p - q)(p + q)(p^2 + q^2)$

39. $(x^3 - y^3)(x^3 + y^3) = (x - y)(x^2 + xy + y^2)(x + y)(x^2 - xy + y^2)$

40. $(8 - z^3)(8 + z^3) = (2 - z)(4 + 2z + z^2)(2 + z)(4 - 2z + z^2)$

41. $(u - v)(u + v) - 2(u + v) = (u + v)(u - v - 2)$

42. $(a - b)(a + b) + 1(a - b) = (a - b)(a + b + 1)$

43. $[(p + q) - (p - q)][(p + q)^2 + (p + q)(p - q) + (p - q)^2] =$
$(2q)(p^2 + 2pq + q^2 + p^2 - q^2 + p^2 - 2pq + q^2) = 2q(3p^2 + q^2)$

44. $[(x + y) + (x - y)][(x + y)^2 - (x + y)(x - y) + (x - y)^2] =$
$(2x)(x^2 + 2xy + y^2 - x^2 + y^2 + x^2 - 2xy + y^2) = 2x(x^2 + 3y^2)$

45. $(s^3 + s^2t) + (t^3 + st^2) = s^2(s + t) + t^2(t + s) = (s + t)(s^2 + t^2)$

46. $(u^3 - u^2v) + (uv^2 - v^3) = u^2(u - v) + v^2(u - v) = (u - v)(u^2 + v^2)$

C **47.** $[(a + b)^3 - (a - b)^3][(a + b)^3 + (a - b)^3] =$
$[(a + b) - (a - b)][(a + b)^2 + (a + b)(a - b) + (a - b)^2][(a + b) +$
$(a - b)][(a + b)^2 - (a + b)(a - b) + (a - b)^2] =$
$(2b)(a^2 + 2ab + b^2 + a^2 - b^2 + a^2 - 2ab + b^2)(2a)$
$(a^2 + 2ab + b^2 - a^2 + b^2 + a^2 - 2ab + b^2) = (2b)(3a^2 + b^2)(2a)(a^2 + 3b^2) =$
$4ab(3a^2 + b^2)(a^2 + 3b^2)$

48. $[(a + b)^2 - (a - b)^2][(a + b)^2 + (a - b)^2] =$
$[(a + b) - (a - b)][(a + b) + (a - b)][(a^2 + 2ab + b^2) + (a^2 - 2ab + b^2)] =$
$(2b)(2a)(2a^2 + 2b^2) = (2b)(2a)(2)(a^2 + b^2) = 8ab(a^2 + b^2)$

49. $(x^n - 1)(x^n + 1)$ **50.** $(x^n - 1)^2$ **51.** $(x^n + y^n)^2$

52. $(x^n + y^n)(x^{2n} - x^ny^n + y^{2n})$ **53.** $x^{2n}(x^{2n} - y^{2n}) = x^{2n}(x^n - y^n)(x^n + y^n)$

54. $x^{2n}(x^{2n} - 2x^ny^n + y^{2n}) = x^{2n}(x^n - y^n)^2$

55. $x^4 + 2x^2 + 1 - x^2 = (x^2 + 1)^2 - x^2 = (x^2 + 1 - x)(x^2 + 1 + x) =$
$(x^2 - x + 1)(x^2 + x + 1)$

56. $x^4 + 4x^2 + 4 - 4x^2 = (x^2 + 2)^2 - 4x^2 = (x^2 + 2 - 2x)(x^2 + 2 + 2x) =$
$(x^2 - 2x + 2)(x^2 + 2x + 2)$

57. $x^4 + 2x^2y^2 + y^4 - x^2y^2 = (x^2 + y^2)^2 - x^2y^2 = (x^2 + y^2 - xy)(x^2 + y^2 + xy)$

58. $x^4 + 4x^2y^2 + 4y^4 - 4x^2y^2 = (x^2 + 2y^2)^2 - 4x^2y^2 =$
$(x^2 + 2y^2 - 2xy)(x^2 + 2y^2 + 2xy)$

59. **a.** $x^4 - y^4 = (x^2 - y^2)(x^2 + y^2) = (x - y)(x + y)(x^2 + y^2)$

b. $x^8 - y^8 = (x^4 - y^4)(x^4 + y^4) = (x^2 - y^2)(x^2 + y^2)(x^4 + y^4) =$
$(x - y)(x + y)(x^2 + y^2)(x^4 + y^4)$

c. $x^n - y^n = (x - y)(x + y)(x^2 + y^2)(x^4 + y^4) \ldots (x^{n/2} + y^{n/2})$

Page 187 • MIXED REVIEW EXERCISES

1. $(x - 3)^2 = x^2 - 6x + 9$ **2.** $(2y + 3)(y - 4) = 2y^2 - 8y + 3y - 12 = 2y^2 - 5y - 12$

3. $m^2n(2m - 3n) = 2m^3n - 3m^2n^2$ **4.** $(3c - 4) - (5 - c) = 3c - 4 - 5 + c = 4c - 9$

5. $(a^2 + 2)(a - 6) = a^3 - 6a^2 + 2a - 12$ **6.** $(-w)^2(2w)^3 = w^2(8w^3) = 8w^5$

7. $18x = 2 \cdot 3^2 \cdot x$; $24x^3 = 2^3 \cdot 3 \cdot x^3$ **a.** $6x$ **b.** $72x^3$

8. $30a^2b^4 = 2 \cdot 3 \cdot 5 \cdot a^2b^4$; $75a^3b^3 = 3 \cdot 5^2 \cdot a^3b^3$ **a.** $15a^2b^3$ **b.** $150a^3b^4$

9. $63mp^2 = 3^2 \cdot 7 \cdot mp^2$; $42mp^3 = 2 \cdot 3 \cdot 7 \cdot mp^3$ **a.** $21mp^2$ **b.** $126mp^3$

Page 187 • COMPUTER EXERCISES

1. Answers may vary. A sample program is given.

```
10 INPUT "ENTER COEFFICIENTS A1, B, C: "; A1, B, C
20 LET RA = 0
30 FOR I = 1 TO A1
40 IF I * I = A1 THEN LET RA = I
50 NEXT I
60 LET RC = 0
70 FOR J = 1 TO C
80 IF J * J = C THEN LET RC = J
90 NEXT J
100 LET FLAG = 0
110 IF RA > 0 AND RC > 0 AND B = 2 * RA * RC THEN LET FLAG = 1
120 IF RA > 0 AND RC > 0 AND B = -2 * RA * RC THEN LET FLAG = 2
130 IF FLAG = 0 THEN PRINT A; "X↑2 + "; B; "XY + "; C; "Y↑2 IS NOT
    A PERFECT SQUARE."
140 IF FLAG = 1 THEN PRINT "("; RA; "X + "; RC; "Y)("; RA; "X + ";
    RC; "Y)"
150 IF FLAG = 2 THEN PRINT "("; RA; "X - "; RC; "Y)("; RA; "X - ";
    RC; "Y)"
160 END
```

2. **a.** `(1X - 28Y)(1X - 28Y)` **b.** `(3X + 24Y)(3X + 24Y)`

c. `64X↑2 + 56XY + 49Y↑2 IS NOT A PERFECT SQUARE.`

d. `(25X - 21Y)(25X - 21Y)`

3. Answers may vary. For example, add lines 65, 66, 125, and 155, and change lines 70, 80, and 110–130, as follows:

```
65 LET NC = C
66 IF NC < 0 THEN LET NC = -NC
70 FOR J = 1 TO NC
80 IF J * J = NC THEN LET RC = J
```

Continued on next page

```
110 IF C > 0 AND RA > 0 AND RC > 0 AND B = 2 * RA * RC THEN LET
    FLAG = 1
120 IF C > 0 AND RA > 0 AND RC > 0 AND B = -2 * RA * RC THEN LET
    FLAG = 2
125 IF C < 0 AND RA > 0 AND RC > 0 AND B = 0 THEN LET FLAG = 3
130 IF FLAG = 0 THEN PRINT A; "X↑2 + "; B; "XY + "; C; "Y↑2 IS
    NOT A PERFECT SQUARE OR DIFFERENCE OF SQUARES."
155 IF FLAG = 3 THEN PRINT "("; RA; "X + "; RC; "Y)("; RA; "X - ";
    RC; "Y)"
```

4. a. `(12X - 2Y)(12X - 2Y)` **b.** `(12X + 2Y)(12X - 2Y)`
c. `(12X + 2Y)(12X + 2Y)` **d.** `144X↑2 + 0XY + 4Y↑2` IS NOT A PERFECT SQUARE OR A DIFFERENCE OF SQUARES.

Pages 191–192 • WRITTEN EXERCISES

A **1.** $(x - 8)(x - 1)$ **2.** $(t + 7)(t + 2)$ **3.** $(z - 9)(z - 2)$ **4.** $(u - 9)(u - 1)$
5. $(r + 2)(r + 10)$ **6.** $(y - 3)(y - 2)$ **7.** prime **8.** $(h - 4)(h - 6)$
9. $(s - 2)(s - 18)$ **10.** prime **11.** $(x + 4)(x - 3)$ **12.** $(t + 5)(t - 3)$
13. $(t - 7)(t + 5)$ **14.** $(s + 3)(s - 9)$ **15.** $(3z + 1)(z + 1)$ **16.** $(5v - 1)(v + 1)$
17. $-s^2 + 2s + 8 = -(s^2 - 2s - 8) = -(s - 4)(s + 2)$
18. $-x^2 - 4x + 21 = -(x^2 + 4x - 21) = -(x + 7)(x - 3)$ **19.** $(x - 6y)(x + 5y)$
20. $(p + 6q)(p - 4q)$ **21.** prime **22.** prime **23.** $(2t - 1)(t + 3)$
24. $(3x - 5)(x - 1)$ **25.** $(p - 3)(3p + 2)$ **26.** $(2r + 1)(2r + 3)$
27. $(2x - 3y)(3x + y)$ **28.** $(s + t)(6s - 5t)$ **29.** $(2h - 3k)(h + 5k)$
30. $(2u + 7v)(u - 3v)$

B **31.** $(6x - 5)(x + 2)$ **32.** $(y - 3)(4y - 5)$ **33.** prime **34.** $(5u - 2)^2$
35. prime **36.** $2(2r^2 + 8rs - 5s^2)$
37. $x(4x^2 + 8xy - 5y^2) = x(2x - y)(2x + 5y)$ **38.** prime
39. $4pq(q^3 - 8) = 4pq(q - 2)(q^2 + 2q + 4)$
40. $3u(27v^3 + u^3) = 3u(3v + u)(9v^2 + 3uv + u^2)$
41. $(r^2 - 4s^2)(r^2 + 4s^2) = (r - 2s)(r + 2s)(r^2 + 4s^2)$
42. $(x^3 - 8y^3)(x^3 + 8y^3) = (x - 2y)(x^2 + 2xy + 4y^2)(x + 2y)(x^2 - 2xy + 4y^2)$
43. $(x^2 - 4)(x^2 + 1) = (x - 2)(x + 2)(x^2 + 1)$
44. $(z^2 - 9)(z^2 - 1) = (z - 3)(z + 3)(z - 1)(z + 1)$
45. $x^2 - 3x + 2 = (x - 2)(x - 1)$; $x^2 - 4x + 4 = (x - 2)^2$ **a.** $x - 2$
b. $(x - 1)(x - 2)^2$
46. $x^2 - 16 = (x - 4)(x + 4)$; $x^2 + 2x - 8 = (x + 4)(x - 2)$ **a.** $x + 4$
b. $(x - 4)(x + 4)(x - 2)$
47. $t^3 - 2t^2 - 3t = t(t^2 - 2t - 3) = t(t - 3)(t + 1)$; $t^3 + 5t^2 + 4t = t(t^2 + 5t + 4) = t(t + 4)(t + 1)$ **a.** $t(t + 1)$ **b.** $t(t + 1)(t - 3)(t + 4)$
48. $y^3 - 4y = y(y^2 - 4) = y(y - 2)(y + 2)$; $y^4 - 8y = y(y^3 - 8) = y(y - 2)(y^2 + 2y + 4)$ **a.** $y(y - 2)$ **b.** $y(y - 2)(y + 2)(y^2 + 2y + 4)$
49. $p^3 - q^3 = (p - q)(p^2 + pq + q^2)$ **a.** $p - q$ **b.** $(p - q)(p^2 + pq + q^2)$
50. $x^3 + y^3 = (x + y)(x^2 - xy + y^2)$; **a.** 1 **b.** $(x + y)(x^2 - xy + y^2)(x^2 + y^2)$

C **51.** Suppose $x^2 + x + k$ is not prime. Then there are nonzero integers r and s such that $rs = k$ and $r + s = 1$. Since k is positive r and s are both negative or both positive. The sum of two negative numbers is negative so r and s must both be positive. But the sum of two positive integers is greater than or equal to 2. Thus there can be no such integers r and s and $x^2 + x + k$ is prime.

52. $x^2 + (k + 1)x + k = (x + k)(x + 1)$ for all positive integers k.

53. $(a^{2n} - b^{2n})(a^{2n} + b^{2n}) = (a^n - b^n)(a^n + b^n)(a^{2n} + b^{2n})$

54. $(a^{3n} - b^{3n})(a^{3n} + b^{3n}) = (a^n - b^n)(a^{2n} + a^n b^n + b^{2n})(a^n + b^n)(a^{2n} - a^n b^n + b^{2n})$

55. $(x^{2n} - 4)(x^{2n} - 1) = (x^n - 2)(x^n + 2)(x^n - 1)(x^n + 1)$

56. $(x^{4n} - 1)^2 = [(x^{2n} - 1)(x^{2n} + 1)]^2 = [(x^n - 1)(x^n + 1)(x^{2n} + 1)]^2 =$
$(x^n - 1)^2(x^n + 1)^2(x^{2n} + 1)^2$

57. $[(x^2 - 2x + 3) - (x^2 - 4x - 1)][(x^2 - 2x + 3) + (x^2 - 4x - 1)] =$
$(2x + 4)(2x^2 - 6x + 2) = [2(x + 2)][2(x^2 - 3x + 1)] = 4(x + 2)(x^2 - 3x + 1)$

58. $[(x^2 + 2x - 4) - (x^2 - 2x - 4)][(x^2 + 2x - 4) + (x^2 - 2x - 4)] =$
$(4x)(2x^2 - 8) = (4x)[2(x^2 - 4)] = 8x(x - 2)(x + 2)$

59. $x^3 - 3x^2 + 3x - 2 = x^3 - 2x^2 - x^2 + 2x + x - 2 = x^2(x - 2) - x(x - 2) +$
$1(x - 2) = (x - 2)(x^2 - x + 1)$; $x^2 - x + 1$

Page 193 • COMPUTER KEY-IN

1. `(3 * X + 8) * (4 * X + -15)` **2.** `(3 * X + -8) * (-5 * X + -6)`

3. `(1 * X + -8) * (6 * X + -7)` **4.** `1X↑2 + 5 * X + -4 IS IRREDUCIBLE.`

5. `(1 * X + -1) * (2 * X + 10)` **6.** `(2 * X + 5) * (2 * X + -5)`

Pages 196–197 • WRITTEN EXERCISES

A **1.** $(x - 1)(x - 4) = 0$; $x - 1 = 0$ or $x - 4 = 0$; $x = 1$ or $x = 4$; $\{1, 4\}$

2. $(t + 2)(t - 5) = 0$; $t + 2 = 0$ or $t - 5 = 0$; $t = -2$ or $t = 5$; $\{-2, 5\}$

3. $t(t + 1)(t - 2) = 0$; $t = 0$ or $t + 1 = 0$ or $t - 2 = 0$; $t = 0$ or $t = -1$ or $t = 2$; $\{0, -1, 2\}$

4. $z^2(2z - 1) = 0$; $z^2 = 0$ or $2z - 1 = 0$; $z = 0$ (double root) or $z = \frac{1}{2}$; $\left\{0, \frac{1}{2}\right\}$

5. $(s - 1)^2(s - 3)^2 = 0$; $(s - 1)^2 = 0$ or $(s - 3)^2 = 0$; $s = 1$ (double root) or $s = 3$ (double root); $\{1, 3\}$

6. $y(y + 1)^2(y - 2) = 0$; $y = 0$ or $(y + 1)^2 = 0$ or $y - 2 = 0$; $y = 0$ or $y = -1$ (double root) or $y = 2$; $\{0, -1, 2\}$

7. $z^2 + 3 = 4z$; $z^2 - 4z + 3 = 0$; $(z - 3)(z - 1) = 0$; $z - 3 = 0$ or $z - 1 = 0$; $z = 3$ or $z = 1$; $\{1, 3\}$

8. $x^2 - 12 = 4x$; $x^2 - 4x - 12 = 0$; $(x - 6)(x + 2) = 0$; $x - 6 = 0$ or $x + 2 = 0$; $x = 6$ or $x = -2$; $\{-2, 6\}$

9. $t^3 - t = 0$; $t(t^2 - 1) = 0$; $t(t - 1)(t + 1) = 0$; $t = 0$ or $t - 1 = 0$ or $t + 1 = 0$; $t = 0$, $t = 1$, or $t = -1$; $\{-1, 0, 1\}$

10. $s^3 - s^2 = 0$; $s^2(s - 1) = 0$; $s^2 = 0$ or $s - 1 = 0$; $s = 0$ (double root) or $s = 1$; $\{0, 1\}$

11. $x^3 + 4x = 4x^2$; $x^3 - 4x^2 + 4x = 0$; $x(x^2 - 4x + 4) = 0$; $x(x - 2)^2 = 0$; $x = 0$ or $(x - 2)^2 = 0$; $x = 0$ or $x = 2$ (double root); $\{0, 2\}$

12. $y^3 + 6y^2 = 27y$; $y^3 + 6y^2 - 27y = 0$; $y(y^2 + 6y - 27) = 0$; $y(y + 9)(y - 3) = 0$; $y = 0$ or $y + 9 = 0$ or $y - 3 = 0$; $y = 0$, $y = -9$, or $y = 3$; $\{-9, 0, 3\}$

13. $3r^2 = 4r - 1$; $3r^2 - 4r + 1 = 0$; $(3r - 1)(r - 1) = 0$; $3r - 1 = 0$ or $r - 1 = 0$; $r = \frac{1}{3}$ or $r = 1$; $\left\{\frac{1}{3}, 1\right\}$

14. $6x^2 = 1 - x$; $6x^2 + x - 1 = 0$, $(3x - 1)(2x + 1) = 0$; $3x - 1 = 0$ or $2x + 1 = 0$; $x = \frac{1}{3}$ or $x = -\frac{1}{2}$; $\left\{-\frac{1}{2}, \frac{1}{3}\right\}$

15. $2y^2 + y = 6$; $2y^2 + y - 6 = 0$; $(2y - 3)(y + 2) = 0$; $2y - 3 = 0$ or $y + 2 = 0$; $y = \frac{3}{2}$ or $y = -2$; $\left\{-2, \frac{3}{2}\right\}$

16. $10t^2 - 9t = 1$; $10t^2 - 9t - 1 = 0$; $(10t + 1)(t - 1) = 0$; $10t + 1 = 0$ or $t - 1 = 0$; $t = -\frac{1}{10}$ or $t = 1$; $\left\{-\frac{1}{10}, 1\right\}$

17. $6 - 7u = 3u^2$; $3u^2 + 7u - 6 = 0$; $(3u - 2)(u + 3) = 0$; $3u - 2 = 0$ or $u + 3 = 0$; $u = \frac{2}{3}$ or $u = -3$; $\left\{-3, \frac{2}{3}\right\}$

18. $5s - 1 = 6s^2$; $6s^2 - 5s + 1 = 0$; $(2s - 1)(3s - 1) = 0$; $2s - 1 = 0$ or $3s - 1 = 0$; $s = \frac{1}{2}$ or $s = \frac{1}{3}$; $\left\{\frac{1}{3}, \frac{1}{2}\right\}$

19. $6(x + 12) = x^2$; $6x + 72 = x^2$; $x^2 - 6x - 72 = 0$; $(x - 12)(x + 6) = 0$; $x - 12 = 0$ or $x + 6 = 0$; $x = 12$ or $x = -6$; $\{-6, 12\}$

20. $(u + 3)(u - 3) = 8u$; $u^2 - 9 = 8u$; $u^2 - 8u - 9 = 0$; $(u - 9)(u + 1) = 0$; $u - 9 = 0$ or $u + 1 = 0$; $u = 9$ or $u = -1$; $\{-1, 9\}$

21. $(y - 4)^2 = 2y$; $y^2 - 8y + 16 = 2y$; $y^2 - 10y + 16 = 0$; $(y - 8)(y - 2) = 0$; $y - 8 = 0$ or $y - 2 = 0$; $y = 8$ or $y = 2$; $\{2, 8\}$

22. $x = (x - 6)^2$; $x = x^2 - 12x + 36$; $x^2 - 13x + 36 = 0$; $(x - 9)(x - 4) = 0$; $x - 9 = 0$ or $x - 4 = 0$; $x = 9$ or $x = 4$; $\{4, 9\}$

23. $3t(t + 1) = 4(t + 1)$; $3t^2 + 3t = 4t + 4$; $3t^2 - t - 4 = 0$; $(3t - 4)(t + 1) = 0$; $3t - 4 = 0$ or $t + 1 = 0$; $t = \frac{4}{3}$ or $t = -1$; $\left\{-1, \frac{4}{3}\right\}$

24. $2(r^2 + 1) = 5r$; $2r^2 + 2 = 5r$; $2r^2 - 5r + 2 = 0$; $(2r - 1)(r - 2) = 0$; $2r - 1 = 0$ or $r - 2 = 0$; $r = \frac{1}{2}$ or $r = 2$; $\left\{\frac{1}{2}, 2\right\}$

25. $(x - 1)(x^2 + x - 2) = 0$; $(x - 1)(x - 1)(x + 2) = 0$; $(x - 1)^2 = 0$ or $x + 2 = 0$; $x = 1$ (double root) or $x = -2$; $\{-2, 1\}$

26. $(x + 2)(x^2 - 4) = 0$; $(x + 2)(x + 2)(x - 2) = 0$; $(x + 2)^2 = 0$ or $x - 2 = 0$; $x = -2$ (double root) or $x = 2$; $\{-2, 2\}$

27. $y^2(y - 3)(y^2 - 9) = 0$; $y^2(y - 3)(y - 3)(y + 3) = 0$; $y^2 = 0$ or $(y - 3)^2 = 0$ or $y + 3 = 0$; $y = 0$ (double root) or $y = 3$ (double root) or $y = -3$; $\{-3, 0, 3\}$

28. $(x^2 - 1)(x^2 + 3x + 2) = 0$; $(x - 1)(x + 1)(x + 2)(x + 1) = 0$; $x - 1 = 0$ or $(x + 1)^2 = 0$ or $x + 2 = 0$; $x = -1$ (double root), $x = 1$, or $x = -2$; $\{-2, -1, 1\}$

B

29. $x^4 - 2x^2 + 1 = 0$; $(x^2 - 1)^2 = 0$; $[(x - 1)(x + 1)]^2 = 0$; $(x - 1)^2(x + 1)^2 = 0$; $(x - 1)^2 = 0$ or $(x + 1)^2 = 0$; $x = 1$ (double root) or $x = -1$ (double root); $\{-1, 1\}$

30. $y^4 - 5y^2 + 4 = 0$; $(y^2 - 1)(y^2 - 4) = 0$; $(y - 1)(y + 1)(y - 2)(y + 2) = 0$; $y - 1 = 0, y + 1 = 0, y - 2 = 0$, or $y + 2 = 0$; $y = 1, y = -1, y = 2$, or $y = -2$; $\{-2, -1, 1, 2\}$

31. $t^6 + 9t^2 = 10t^4$; $t^6 - 10t^4 + 9t^2 = 0$; $t^2(t^4 - 10t^2 + 9) = 0$; $t^2(t^2 - 9)(t^2 - 1) = 0$, $t^2(t - 3)(t + 3)(t - 1)(t + 1) = 0$; $t^2 = 0, t - 3 = 0, t + 3 = 0, t - 1 = 0$, or $t + 1 = 0$; $t = 0$ (double root), $t = 3, t = -3, t = 1$, or $t = -1$; $\{-3, -1, 0, 1, 3\}$

32. $x^2(x^4 + 16) = 8x^4$; $x^2(x^4 + 16) - 8x^4 = 0$; $x^2(x^4 + 16 - 8x^2) = 0$; $x^2(x^4 - 8x^2 + 16) = 0$; $x^2(x^2 - 4)^2 = 0$; $x^2(x - 2)^2(x + 2)^2 = 0$; $x^2 = 0$, $(x - 2)^2 = 0$, or $(x + 2)^2 = 0$; $x = 0$ (double root), $x = 2$ (double root), or $x = -2$ (double root); $\{-2, 0, 2\}$

33. $(u - 2)^3 - 3u + 8 = 0$; $u^3 - 6u^2 + 12u - 8 - 3u + 8 = 0$; $u^3 - 6u^2 + 9u = 0$; $u(u^2 - 6u + 9) = 0$; $u(u - 3)^2 = 0$; $u = 0$ or $(u - 3)^2 = 0$; $u = 0$ or $u = 3$ (double root); $\{0, 3\}$

34. $(s - 6)^3 = 27(s - 8)$; $s^3 - 18s^2 + 108s - 216 = 27s - 216$; $s^3 - 18s^2 + 81s = 0$; $s(s^2 - 18s + 81) = 0$; $s(s - 9)^2 = 0$; $s = 0$ or $(s - 9)^2 = 0$; $s = 0$ or $s = 9$ (double root); $\{0, 9\}$

35. $0.3x^2 + 0.2x - 0.1 = 0$; $3x^2 + 2x - 1 = 0$; $(3x - 1)(x + 1) = 0$; $3x - 1 = 0$ or $x + 1 = 0$; $x = \frac{1}{3}$ or $x = -1$; $\left\{-1, \frac{1}{3}\right\}$

36. $0.2x^2 - 1.1x + 0.5 = 0$; $2x^2 - 11x + 5 = 0$; $(2x - 1)(x - 5) = 0$; $2x - 1 = 0$ or $x - 5 = 0$; $x = \frac{1}{2}$ or $x = 5$; $\left\{\frac{1}{2}, 5\right\}$

37. $\frac{1}{6}x^2 + \frac{1}{2}x - \frac{2}{3} = 0$; $x^2 + 3x - 4 = 0$; $(x + 4)(x - 1) = 0$; $x + 4 = 0$ or $x - 1 = 0$; $x = -4$ or $x = 1$; $\{-4, 1\}$

38. $\frac{1}{3}x^2 - \frac{1}{2}x - \frac{1}{3} = 0$; $2x^2 - 3x - 2 = 0$; $(2x + 1)(x - 2) = 0$; $2x + 1 = 0$ or $x - 2 = 0$; $x = -\frac{1}{2}$ or $x = 2$; $\left\{-\frac{1}{2}, 2\right\}$

39. $(x - 1)^3 - (x - 1)^2 = 0$; $(x - 1)^2[(x - 1) - 1] = 0$; $(x - 1)^2(x - 2) = 0$; $(x - 1)^2 = 0$ or $x - 2 = 0$; $x = 1$ (double root) or $x = 2$; $\{1, 2\}$

40. $(t - 2)^3 - (t - 2) = 0$; $(t - 2)[(t - 2)^2 - 1] = 0$, $(t - 2)[(t - 2) - 1][(t - 2) + 1] = 0$; $(t - 2)(t - 3)(t - 1) = 0$; $t - 2 = 0$ or $t - 3 = 0$ or $t - 1 = 0$; $t = 2, t = 3$, or $t = 1$; $\{1, 2, 3\}$

41. $(x^2 - 4)^3 = 0$; $[(x - 2)(x + 2)]^3 = 0$; $(x - 2)^3(x + 2)^3 = 0$; $(x - 2)^3 = 0$ or $(x + 2)^3 = 0$; $x = 2$ (triple root) or $x = -2$ (triple root); $\{-2, 2\}$

42. $(x^2 - 3x + 2)^3 = 0$; $[(x - 2)(x - 1)]^3 = 0$; $(x - 2)^3(x - 1)^3 = 0$; $(x - 2)^3 = 0$ or $(x - 1)^3 = 0$; $x = 2$ (triple root) or $x = 1$ (triple root); $\{1, 2\}$

43. $(x^2 + 1)^2 - 4(x^2 + 1) + 4 = 0$; $[(x^2 + 1) - 2]^2 = 0$, $(x^2 - 1)^2 = 0$; $[(x - 1)(x + 1)]^2 = 0$; $(x - 1)^2(x + 1)^2 = 0$; $(x - 1)^2 = 0$ or $(x + 1)^2 = 0$; $x = 1$ (double root) or $x = -1$ (double root); $\{1, -1\}$

44. $(x^2 - 3)^2 + (x^2 - 3) - 2 = 0$, $[(x^2 - 3) + 2][(x^2 - 3) - 1] = 0$; $(x^2 - 1)(x^2 - 4) = 0$; $(x - 1)(x + 1)(x - 2)(x + 2) = 0$; $x - 1 = 0, x + 1 = 0$, $x - 2 = 0$, or $x + 2 = 0$; $x = 1, x = -1, x = 2$, or $x = -2$; $\{-2, -1, 1, 2\}$

45. $(x - 4)^3 - 4(x - 4) = 0$; $(x - 4)[(x - 4)^2 - 4] = 0$; $(x - 4)[(x - 4) - 2][(x - 4) + 2] = 0$; $(x - 4)(x - 6)(x - 2) = 0$; $x - 4 = 0$, $x - 6 = 0$, or $x - 2 = 0$; $x = 4, x = 6$, or $x = 2$; 2, 4, and 6

46. $(t-2)^3 - (t-2) = 0$; $(t-2)[(t-2)^2 - 1] = 0$; $(t-2)[(t-2) - 1][(t-2) + 1] = 0$; $(t-2)(t-3)(t-1) = 0$; $t - 2 = 0$, $t - 3 = 0$, or $t - 1 = 0$; $t = 2$, $t = 3$, or $t = 1$; 1, 2, and 3

47. $9z^4 - 12z^3 + 4z^2 = 0$; $z^2(9z^2 - 12z + 4) = 0$; $z^2(3z-2)^2 = 0$; $z^2 = 0$ or $(3z-2)^2 = 0$; $z = 0$ (double zero) or $z = \frac{2}{3}$ (double zero); 0 and $\frac{2}{3}$

48. $4s^4 - 17s^2 + 4 = 0$; $(s^2 - 4)(4s^2 - 1) = 0$; $(s-2)(s+2)(2s-1)(2s+1) = 0$; $s - 2 = 0$, $s + 2 = 0$, $2s - 1 = 0$, or $2s + 1 = 0$; $s = 2$, $s = -2$, $s = \frac{1}{2}$, or $s = -\frac{1}{2}$; $-\frac{1}{2}, \frac{1}{2}$, -2, and 2

49. $(x-1)^4 - 4(x-1)^3 = 0$; $(x-1)^3[(x-1) - 4] = 0$; $(x-1)^3(x-5) = 0$; $(x-1)^3 = 0$ or $x - 5 = 0$; $x = 1$ (triple zero) or $x = 5$; 1 and 5

50. $(y^2 - 9)^3 = 0$; $[(y-3)(y+3)]^3 = 0$; $(y-3)^3(y+3)^3 = 0$; $(y-3)^3 = 0$ or $(y+3)^3 = 0$; $y = 3$ (triple zero) and $y = -3$ (triple zero); -3 and 3

C **51.** $a^2x^2 - b^2 = 0$; $(ax - b)(ax + b) = 0$; $ax - b = 0$ or $ax + b = 0$; $x = \frac{b}{a}$ or $x = -\frac{b}{a}$; $\left\{-\frac{b}{a}, \frac{b}{a}\right\}$

52. $x^2 + ax - bx - ab = 0$; $(x^2 - bx) + (ax - ab) = 0$; $x(x-b) + a(x-b) = 0$; $(x+a)(x-b) = 0$; $x + a = 0$ or $x - b = 0$; $x = -a$ or $x = b$; $\{-a, b\}$

53. $x^3 + ax^2 = x + a$; $x^3 + ax^2 - x - a = 0$; $x^2(x+a) - 1(x+a) = 0$; $(x+a)(x^2-1) = 0$; $(x+a)(x-1)(x+1) = 0$; $x + a = 0$, $x - 1 = 0$, or $x + 1 = 0$; $x = -a$, $x = 1$, or $x = -1$; $\{-a, 1, -1\}$

54. $x^3 - bx^2 - 4x + 4b = 0$; $x^2(x-b) - 4(x-b) = 0$; $(x^2-4)(x-b) = 0$; $(x-2)(x+2)(x-b) = 0$; $x - 2 = 0$, $x + 2 = 0$, or $x - b = 0$; $x = 2$, $x = -2$, or $x = b$; $\{-2, 2, b\}$

55. $(x+y)^2 = x^2 + 2xy + y^2$; $x^2 + 2xy + y^2 = x^2 + y^2$ only if $2xy = 0$; $x = 0$ or $y = 0$

56. $(x+y)^3 = x^3 + 3x^2y + 3xy^2 + y^3$; $x^3 + 3x^2y + 3xy^2 + y^3 = x^3 + y^3$ only if $3x^2y + 3xy^2 = 0$; $3xy(x+y) = 0$; $x = 0$, $y = 0$, or $x = -y$

Page 197 • MIXED REVIEW EXERCISES

1. $(x-3)^2$ **2.** prime **3.** $2n(4m-5) + 3(4m-5) = (2n+3)(4m-5)$
4. $(4a-5b)(4a+5b)$
5. $24x^3 - 34x^2 + 12x = 2x(12x^2 - 17x + 6) = 2x(4x-3)(3x-2)$
6. $(2u+1)(4u^2 - 2u + 1)$ **7.** $z^3 - z^2$ **8.** $16a^2 + 40a + 25$
9. $3m - 7 + 2m + 8 = 5m + 1$ **10.** $p^4 - 3p^2 + 2p^2 - 6 = p^4 - p^2 - 6$
11. $x - x - 1 = -1$ **12.** $(-3)^3(c^2)^3d^3 = -27c^6d^3$

Pages 199–201 • PROBLEMS

A **1.** Let x = the number; $x^2 + x = 72$, $x^2 + x - 72 = 0$, $(x+9)(x-8) = 0$, $x = 8$ or $x = -9$; -9 or 8

2. Let x = the number; $x^2 - x = 56$, $x^2 - x - 56 = 0$, $(x-8)(x+7) = 0$, $x = 8$ or $x = -7$; -7 or 8

3. Let the integers be n and $n + 2$; $n(n + 2) = 143$, $n^2 + 2n - 143 = 0$, $(n + 13)(n - 11) = 0$, $n = 11$ or $n = -13$; if $n = 11$, $n + 2 = 13$; if $n = -13$, $n + 2 = -11$; -13 and -11 or 11 and 13

4. Let the integers be n and $n + 2$; $n^2 + (n + 2)^2 = 130$, $n^2 + n^2 + 4n + 4 = 130$, $2n^2 + 4n - 126 = 0$, $n^2 + 2n - 63 = 0$, $(n + 9)(n - 7) = 0$, $n = 7$ or $n = -9$; if $n = 7$, $n + 2 = 9$; if $n = -9$, $n + 2 = -7$; -9 and -7 or 7 and 9

5. Let w and $(w + 4)$ be the width and length, respectively, in cm; $w(w + 4) = 117$, $w^2 + 4w - 117 = 0$, $(w + 13)(w - 9) = 0$, $w = 9$ or $w = -13$ (reject); if $w = 9$, $w + 4 = 13$; 9 cm by 13 cm

6. Let l and w be the length and width, in ft; $2(l + w) = 66$ and $lw = 216$; $l + w = 33$, $w = 33 - l$; $l(33 - l) = 216$; $33l - l^2 = 216$, $l^2 - 33l + 216 = 0$, $(l - 9)(l - 24) = 0$, $l = 9$ or $l = 24$; if $l = 9$, $w = 33 - 9 = 24$; if $l = 24$, $w = 33 - 24 = 9$; 9 ft by 24 ft

7. Let x and $x + 3$ be the length in m of the legs; $\frac{1}{2}x(x + 3) = 44$, $x(x + 3) = 88$, $x^2 + 3x - 88 = 0$, $(x + 11)(x - 8) = 0$, $x = -11$ (reject) or $x = 8$; if $x = 8$, $x + 3 = 11$; 8 m and 11 m

8. Let x = distance in mi of the southbound ship from port; then $x + 7$ = distance in mi of the eastbound ship from port; $x^2 + (x + 7)^2 = 17^2$, $x^2 + x^2 + 14x + 49 = 289$, $2x^2 + 14x - 240 = 0$, $x^2 + 7x - 120 = 0$, $(x + 15)(x - 8) = 0$, $x = -15$ (reject) or $x = 8$; if $x = 8$, $x + 7 = 15$; 8 mi and 15 mi

9. Let x = distance in feet that the foot of the ladder is from the bottom of the wall; $x^2 + (x + 3)^2 = 15^2$, $x^2 + x^2 + 6x + 9 = 225$, $2x^2 + 6x - 216 = 0$, $x^2 + 3x - 108 = 0$, $(x + 12)(x - 9) = 0$, $x = -12$ (reject) or $x = 9$; 9 ft

10. Let x and $x + 7$ be the base and height respectively of the triangle in cm; $\frac{1}{2}x(x + 7) = 15$, $x(x + 7) = 30$, $x^2 + 7x - 30 = 0$, $(x - 3)(x + 10) = 0$, $x = 3$ or $x = -10$ (reject); if $x = 3$, $x + 7 = 10$; 10 cm

11. Let x and $2x - 10$ be the lengths in meters of the legs of the triangle; $x^2 + (2x - 10)^2 = 25^2$, $x^2 + 4x^2 - 40x + 100 = 625$, $5x^2 - 40x - 525 = 0$, $x^2 - 8x - 105 = 0$, $(x - 15)(x + 7) = 0$, $x = 15$ or $x = -7$ (reject); if $x = 15$, $2x - 10 = 20$; 15 m and 20 m

12. Let x and $2x - 6$ be the height and base, respectively, of the triangle in ft; $\frac{1}{2}(x)(2x - 6) = 54$, $x(x - 3) = 54$, $x^2 - 3x - 54 = 0$, $(x - 9)(x + 6) = 0$, $x = 9$ or $x = -6$ (reject); if $x = 9$, $2x - 6 = 12$; 9 ft high and 12 ft long

13. Let x = amount of decrease in cm; $15 \cdot 18 - 116 = 154$; $(15 - x)(18 - x) = 154$, $270 - 33x + x^2 = 154$, $x^2 - 33x + 116 = 0$, $(x - 29)(x - 4) = 0$, $x = 29$ (reject since $x < 15$) or $x = 4$; if $x = 4$, $15 - x = 11$ and $18 - x = 14$; 11 cm by 14 cm

14. Let w and $2w$ be the width and length respectively in cm; $(2w + 4)(w - 3) = 100$, $2w^2 - 2w - 12 = 100$, $2w^2 - 2w - 112 = 0$, $w^2 - w - 56 = 0$, $(w - 8)(w + 7) = 0$, $w = 8$ or $w = -7$ (reject); if $w = 8$, $2w = 16$; 8 cm by 16 cm

15. $h = vt - 4.9t^2$; $h = 98t - 4.9t^2$; $98t - 4.9t^2 = 0$, $980t - 49t^2 = 0$, $49t(20 - t) = 0$, $t = 0$ or $t = 20$; if $t = \frac{20}{2} = 10$, $h = 98(10) - 4.9(10)^2 = 490$; 490 m; after 20 s

16. $h = vt - 16t^2$; $h = 80t - 16t^2$; $80t - 16t^2 = 0$, $16t(5 - t) = 0$, $t = 0$ or $t = 5$; if $t = \frac{5}{2}$, $h = 80\left(\frac{5}{2}\right) - 16\left(\frac{5}{2}\right)^2 = 100$; 100 ft; after 5 s.

B **17.** $h = 294t - 4.9t^2$; $2450 = 294t - 4.9t^2$, $4.9t^2 - 294t + 2450 = 0$, $t^2 - 60t + 500 = 0$, $(t - 50)(t - 10) = 0$, $t = 10$ or $t = 50$; the balloonist sees the flare pass up at 10 s and down at 50 s; 40 s

18. $h = 56t - 16t^2$; $40 = 56t - 16t^2$, $16t^2 - 56t + 40 = 0$, $2t^2 - 7t + 5 = 0$, $(2t - 5)(t - 1) = 0$, $t = \frac{5}{2}$ or $t = 1$; the apple passes up at $t = 1$ s and down at $t = 2.5$ s; 2.5 s

19. $h = 245t - 4.9t^2$, $0 = 245t - 4.9t^2$, $4.9t(50 - t) = 0$, $t = 0$ or $t = 50$; if $t = \frac{50}{2} = 25$, $h = 245(25) - 4.9(25)^2 = 3062.5$; 3062.5 m

20. $h = 39.2t - 4.9t^2$; $-98 = 39.2t - 4.9t^2$, $4.9t^2 - 39.2t - 98 = 0$, $t^2 - 8t - 20 = 0$, $(t - 10)(t + 2) = 0$, $t = 10$ or $t = -2$ (reject); 10 s

21. $240 = 0.05r^2 + r$, $0.05r^2 + r - 240 = 0$, $r^2 + 20r - 4800 = 0$, $(r - 60)(r + 80) = 0$, $r = 60$ or $r = -80$ (reject); $60 > 55$; No

22. $5200 = n(20 - 0.01n) + 100$, $5200 = 20n - 0.01n^2 + 100$, $0.01n^2 - 20n + 5100 = 0$, $n^2 - 2000n + 510{,}000 = 0$, $(n - 1700)(n - 300) = 0$, $n = 1700$ (reject since $n \le 500$) or $n = 300$; 300 calculators

23. Let x = length in cm of each edge of the original cube; $x^3 - 169 = (x - 1)^3$, $x^3 - 169 = x^3 - 3x^2 + 3x - 1$, $3x^2 - 3x - 168 = 0$, $x^2 - x - 56 = 0$, $(x - 8)(x + 7) = 0$, $x = -7$ (reject) or $x = 8$; $8^3 - 169 = 343$; 343 cm^3

24. Let x = length in m of each side perpendicular to the existing wall; then $21 - 2x$ = the length of the third side; $x(21 - 2x) = 55$, $21x - 2x^2 = 55$, $2x^2 - 21x + 55 = 0$, $(2x - 11)(x - 5) = 0$, $x = 5.5$ or $x = 5$; if $x = 5.5$, $21 - 2x = 10$; if $x = 5$, $21 - 2x = 11$; 5 m by 11 m or 5.5 m by 10 m

25. Let n, $n + 2$ and $n + 4$ be the width, length, and diagonal respectively of the rectangle; $n^2 + (n + 2)^2 = (n + 4)^2$, $n^2 + n^2 + 4n + 4 = n^2 + 8n + 16$, $n^2 - 4n - 12 = 0$, $(n - 6)(n + 2) = 0$, $n = 6$ or $n = -2$ (reject); if $n = 6$, $n + 2 = 8$ and $n + 4 = 10$; 6, 8, 10

26. If the width, length, and diagonal of a rectangle are consecutive odd integers, they could be represented by n, $n + 2$, and $n + 4$ respectively. By the Pythagorean Theorem, the resulting equation would be the same as in Ex. 25 with solution $n = 6$. Therefore, the width, length, and diagonal of a rectangle cannot be consecutive odd integers.

27. Let w and $2w$ be the width and length respectively in meters of the original lot; $(w - 2)(2w - 2) = 684$, $2w^2 - 6w + 4 = 684$, $w^2 - 3w - 340 = 0$, $(w - 20)(w + 17) = 0$, $w = 20$ or $w = -17$ (reject); if $w = 20$, $w - 2 = 18$ and $2w - 2 = 38$; 18 m by 38 m

28. Let x be the width, in meters, of the margin around the rug; $(9 - 2x)(12 - 2x) = \frac{1}{2}(9 \cdot 12)$, $108 - 42x + 4x^2 = 54$, $4x^2 - 42x + 54 = 0$, $2x^2 - 21x + 27 = 0$, $(2x - 3)(x - 9) = 0$, $x = \frac{3}{2}$ or $x = 9$ (reject, since $x < 9$); if $x = \frac{3}{2}$, $9 - 2x = 6$ and $12 - 2x = 9$; 6 m by 9 m

29. Let x = width in m of the border; $(5 + x)(15 + 2x) = 2(5 \cdot 15)$, $75 + 25x + 2x^2 = 150$, $2x^2 + 25x - 75 = 0$, $(2x - 5)(x + 15) = 0$, $x = \frac{5}{2}$ or $x = -15$ (reject); 2.5 m

30. Let x = length in yd of the shorter sides; then $\frac{1}{2}(160 - 3x)$ is the length in yd of the longer sides; $x\left[\frac{1}{2}(160 - 3x)\right] = 1000$, $80x - \frac{3}{2}x^2 = 1000$, $\frac{3}{2}x^2 - 80x + 1000 = 0$, $3x^2 - 160x + 2000 = 0$, $(3x - 100)(x - 20) = 0$, $x = \frac{100}{3}$ or $x = 20$; if $x = \frac{100}{3}$, then the "longer side" is $\frac{1}{2}\left(160 - 3\left(\frac{100}{3}\right)\right) = 30$ (reject); if $x = 20$, then $\frac{1}{2}(160 - 3x) = 50$; 20 yd by 50 yd

C **31.** $h = vt - \frac{1}{2}gt^2$; $0 = vt - \frac{1}{2}gt^2$, $t\left(v - \frac{g}{2}t\right) = 0$, $t = 0$ or $v - \frac{g}{2}t = 0$, $t = 0$ or $t = \frac{2v}{g}$; maximum height is reached at $t = \frac{\frac{2v}{g}}{2} = \frac{v}{g}$; $h = v\left(\frac{v}{g}\right) - \frac{1}{2}g\left(\frac{v}{g}\right)^2 = \frac{v^2}{g} - \frac{1}{2}\frac{v^2}{g} = \frac{v^2}{2g}$

Pages 204–205 • WRITTEN EXERCISES

A **1.** $(x - 2)(x - 5) < 0$; $x - 2 < 0$ and $x - 5 > 0$, or $x - 2 > 0$ and $x - 5 < 0$; $x < 2$ and $x > 5$, or $x > 2$ and $x < 5$; $\{x : 2 < x < 5\}$

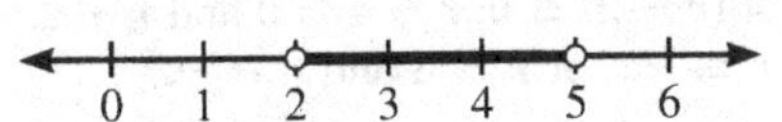

2. $(t + 1)(t - 2) > 0$; $t + 1 > 0$ and $t - 2 > 0$, or $t + 1 < 0$ and $t - 2 < 0$; $t > -1$ and $t > 2$, or $t < -1$ and $t < 2$; $t > 2$ or $t < -1$; $\{t : t > 2 \text{ or } t < -1\}$

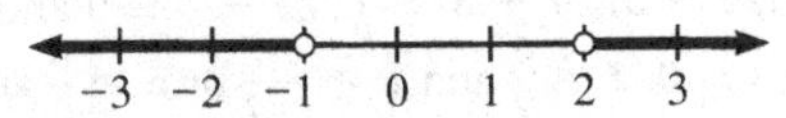

3. $x^2 - 4 \le 0$; $(x - 2)(x + 2) \le 0$; $x - 2 \le 0$ and $x + 2 \ge 0$, or $x - 2 \ge 0$ and $x + 2 \le 0$; $x \le 2$ and $x \ge -2$, or $x \ge 2$ and $x \le -2$; $\{x : -2 \le x \le 2\}$

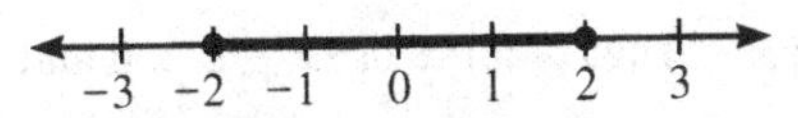

4. $x^2 \le 9$; $x^2 - 9 \le 0$, $(x - 3)(x + 3) \le 0$; $x - 3 \ge 0$ and $x + 3 \le 0$, or $x - 3 \le 0$ and $x + 3 \ge 0$; $x \ge 3$ and $x \le -3$, or $x \le 3$ and $x \ge -3$; $\{x : -3 \le x \le 3\}$

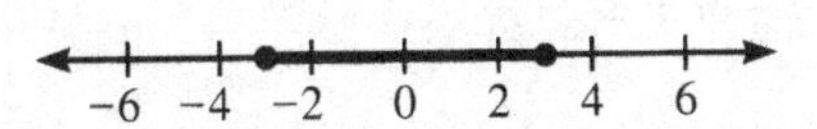

5. $z^2 - 4z > 0$, $z(z - 4) > 0$; $z > 0$ and $z - 4 > 0$, or $z < 0$ and $z - 4 < 0$; $z > 0$ and $z > 4$, or $z < 0$ and $z < 4$; $z > 4$ or $z < 0$; $\{z : z < 0 \text{ or } z > 4\}$

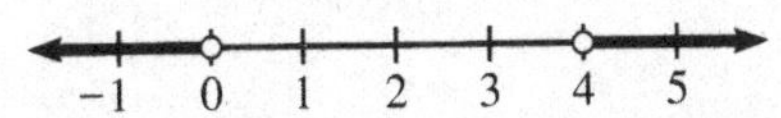

6. $x^2 + 2x \ge 0$; $x(x + 2) \ge 0$; $x \ge 0$ and $x + 2 \ge 0$, or $x \le 0$ and $x + 2 \le 0$; $x \ge 0$ and $x \ge -2$, or $x \le 0$ and $x \le -2$; $x \ge 0$ or $x \le -2$; $\{x : x \le -2 \text{ or } x \ge 0\}$

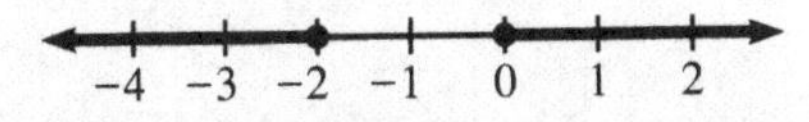

7. $4y^2 \geq 36$, $4y^2 - 36 \geq 0$, $y^2 - 9 \geq 0$, $(y - 3)(y + 3) \geq 0$; $y - 3 \geq 0$ and $y + 3 \geq 0$, or $y - 3 \leq 0$ and $y + 3 \leq 0$; $y \geq 3$ and $y \geq -3$, or $y \leq 3$ and $y \leq -3$; $y \geq 3$ or $y \leq -3$; $\{y : y \leq -3 \text{ or } y \geq 3\}$

−6 −4 −2 0 2 4 6

8. $3s^2 < 48$, $s^2 < 16$, $s^2 - 16 < 0$, $(s - 4)(s + 4) < 0$; $s - 4 > 0$ and $s + 4 < 0$, or $s - 4 < 0$ and $s + 4 > 0$; $s > 4$ and $s < -4$, or $s < 4$ and $s > -4$; $\{s : -4 < s < 4\}$

−6 −4 −2 0 2 4 6

9. $x^2 - 5x + 4 < 0$, $(x - 4)(x - 1) < 0$; $x - 4 < 0$ and $x - 1 > 0$, or $x - 4 > 0$ and $x - 1 < 0$; $x < 4$ and $x > 1$, or $x > 4$ and $x < 1$; $\{x : 1 < x < 4\}$

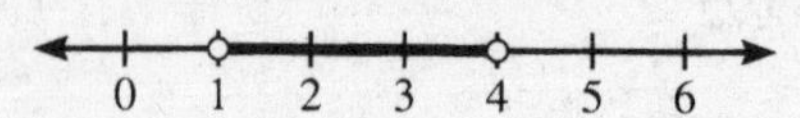

10. $z^2 - z - 6 > 0$, $(z - 3)(z + 2) > 0$; $z - 3 > 0$ and $z + 2 > 0$, or $z - 3 < 0$ and $z + 2 < 0$; $z > 3$ and $z > -2$, or $z < 3$ and $z < -2$; $z > 3$ or $z < -2$; $\{z : z < -2 \text{ or } z > 3\}$

−6 −4 −2 0 2 4 6

11. $t^2 > 9(t - 2)$, $t^2 - 9t + 18 > 0$, $(t - 6)(t - 3) > 0$; $t - 6 > 0$ and $t - 3 > 0$, or $t - 6 < 0$ and $t - 3 < 0$; $t > 6$ and $t > 3$, or $t < 6$ and $t < 3$; $t > 6$ or $t < 3$; $\{t : t < 3 \text{ or } t > 6\}$

1 2 3 4 5 6 7

12. $r^2 \leq 2(r + 4)$, $r^2 - 2r - 8 \leq 0$, $(r - 4)(r + 2) \leq 0$; $r - 4 \geq 0$ and $r + 2 \leq 0$, or $r - 4 \leq 0$ and $r + 2 \geq 0$; $r \geq 4$ and $r \leq -2$, or $r \leq 4$ and $r \geq -2$; $\{r : -2 \leq r \leq 4\}$

−6 −4 −2 0 2 4 6

13. $4z(z - 1) \leq 15$, $4z^2 - 4z - 15 \leq 0$, $(2z - 5)(2z + 3) \leq 0$; $2z - 5 \leq 0$ and $2z + 3 \geq 0$, or $2z - 5 \geq 0$ and $2z + 3 \leq 0$; $z \leq \frac{5}{2}$ and $z \geq -\frac{3}{2}$ or $z \geq \frac{5}{2}$ and $z \leq -\frac{3}{2}$; $\left\{z : -\frac{3}{2} \leq z \leq \frac{5}{2}\right\}$

−3 −2 −1 0 1 2 3

14. $4x(x + 1) \geq 3$, $4x^2 + 4x - 3 \geq 0$, $(2x - 1)(2x + 3) \geq 0$; $2x - 1 \geq 0$ and $2x + 3 \geq 0$, or $2x - 1 \leq 0$ and $2x + 3 \leq 0$; $x \geq \frac{1}{2}$ and $x \geq -\frac{3}{2}$, or $x \leq \frac{1}{2}$ and $x \leq -\frac{3}{2}$; $x \geq \frac{1}{2}$ or $x \leq -\frac{3}{2}$; $\left\{x : x \geq \frac{1}{2} \text{ or } x \leq -\frac{3}{2}\right\}$

−2 −1 0 1

15. $t^2 + 16 \geq 8t$, $t^2 - 8t + 16 \geq 0$; $(t - 4)^2 \geq 0$; {real numbers}

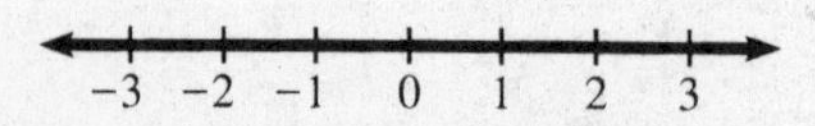

16. $x^2 + 9 \le 6x$, $x^2 - 6x + 9 \le 0$, $(x - 3)^2 \le 0$; $x - 3 = 0$; $x = 3$; $\{3\}$

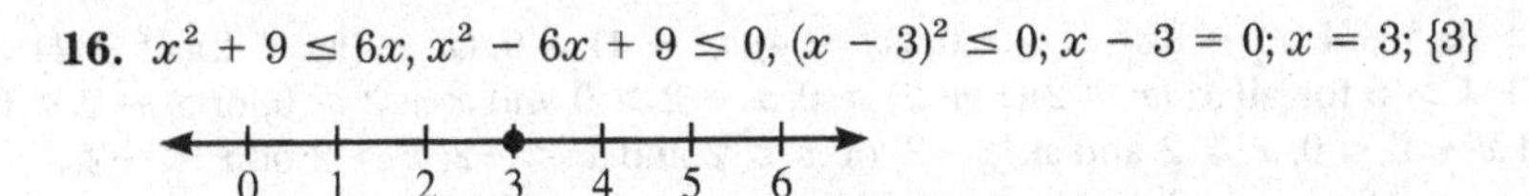

17. $12 + s - s^2 \ge 0$, $s^2 - s - 12 \le 0$, $(s - 4)(s + 3) \le 0$; $s - 4 \le 0$ and $s + 3 \ge 0$, or $s - 4 \ge 0$ and $s + 3 \le 0$; $s \le 4$ and $s \ge -3$, or $s \ge 4$ and $s \le -3$;
$\{s : -3 \le s \le 4\}$

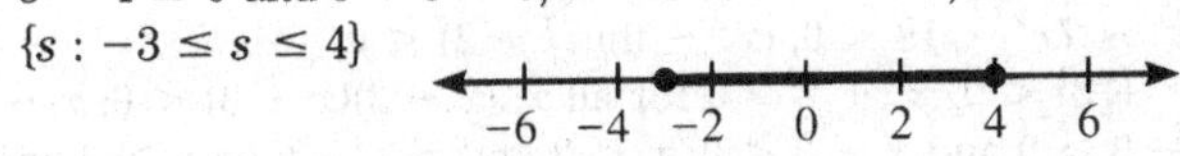

18. $9 - 3t - 2t^2 > 0$, $2t^2 + 3t - 9 < 0$, $(2t - 3)(t + 3) < 0$; $2t - 3 < 0$ and $t + 3 > 0$, or $2t - 3 > 0$ and $t + 3 < 0$, $t < \frac{3}{2}$ and $t > -3$, or $t > \frac{3}{2}$ and $t < -3$;

$\left\{t : -3 < t < \frac{3}{2}\right\}$;

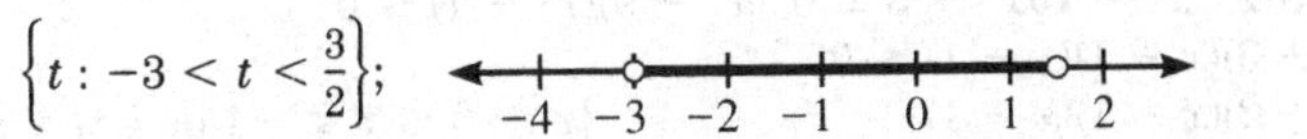

B **19.** $x^3 - 16x > 0$, $x(x^2 - 16) > 0$, $x(x - 4)(x + 4) > 0$
$x(x - 4)(x + 4)$ $\{x : -4 < x < 0 \text{ or } x > 4\}$

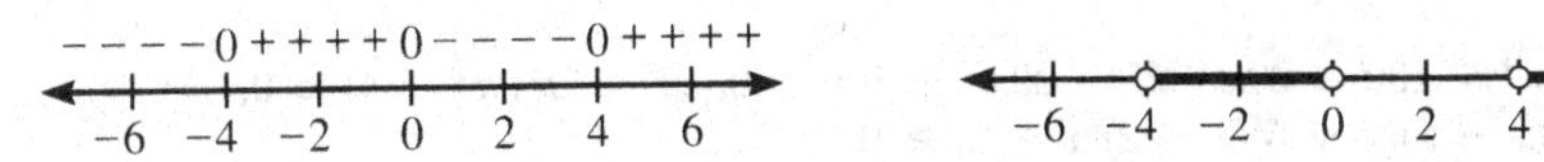

20. $t^3 < 9t^2$, $t^3 - 9t^2 < 0$, $t^2(t - 9) < 0$; $t^2 > 0$ for all $t \ne 0$; $t \ne 0$ and $t - 9 < 0$; $t \ne 0$ and $t < 9$; $\{t : t \ne 0 \text{ and } t < 9\}$

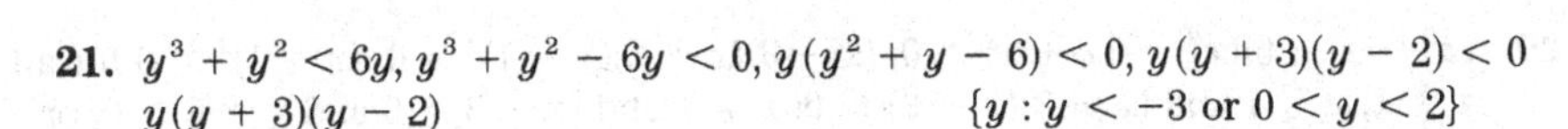

21. $y^3 + y^2 < 6y$, $y^3 + y^2 - 6y < 0$, $y(y^2 + y - 6) < 0$, $y(y + 3)(y - 2) < 0$
$y(y + 3)(y - 2)$ $\{y : y < -3 \text{ or } 0 < y < 2\}$

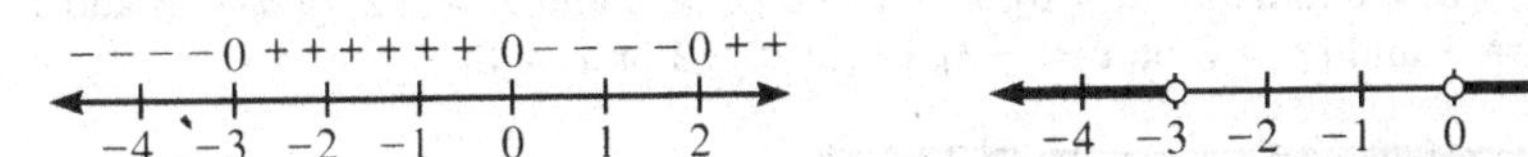

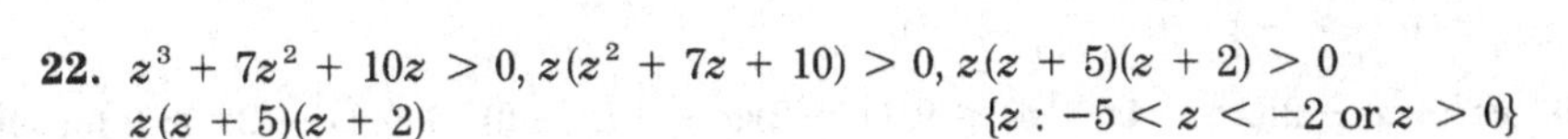

22. $z^3 + 7z^2 + 10z > 0$, $z(z^2 + 7z + 10) > 0$, $z(z + 5)(z + 2) > 0$
$z(z + 5)(z + 2)$ $\{z : -5 < z < -2 \text{ or } z > 0\}$

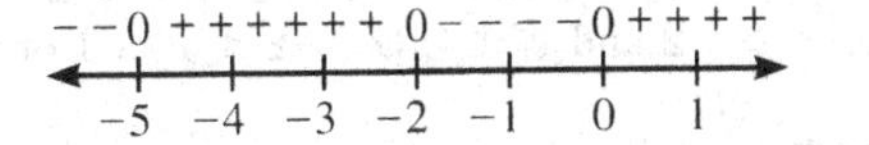

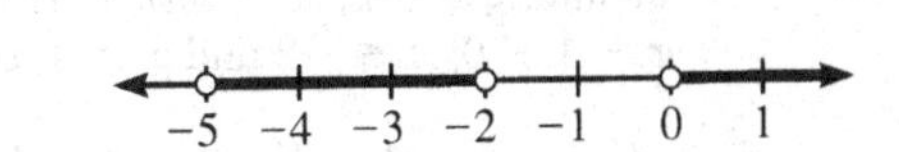

23. $(x^2 - 4x)(x^2 - 4) < 0$, $x(x - 4)(x - 2)(x + 2) < 0$
$x(x - 4)(x - 2)(x + 2)$ $\{x : -2 < x < 0 \text{ or } 2 < x < 4\}$

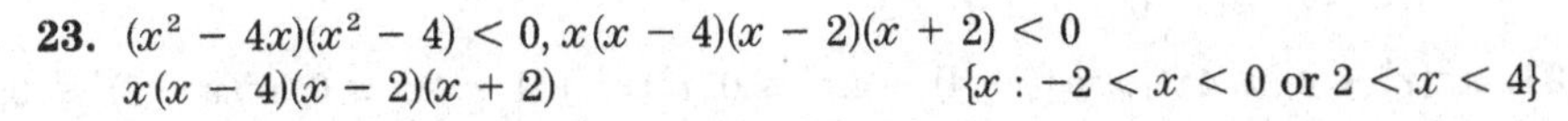

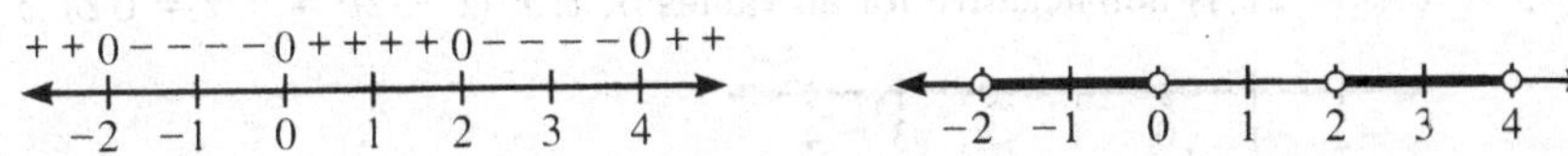

24. $(x^2 + 4)(x^2 + 4x) > 0$; $(x^2 + 4)(x)(x + 4) > 0$; $x^2 + 4 > 0$ for all x; $x(x + 4) > 0$; $x > 0$ and $x + 4 > 0$, or $x < 0$ and $x + 4 < 0$; $x > 0$ and $x > -4$, or $x < 0$ and $x < -4$; $x > 0$ or $x < -4$; $\{x : x < -4 \text{ or } x > 0\}$

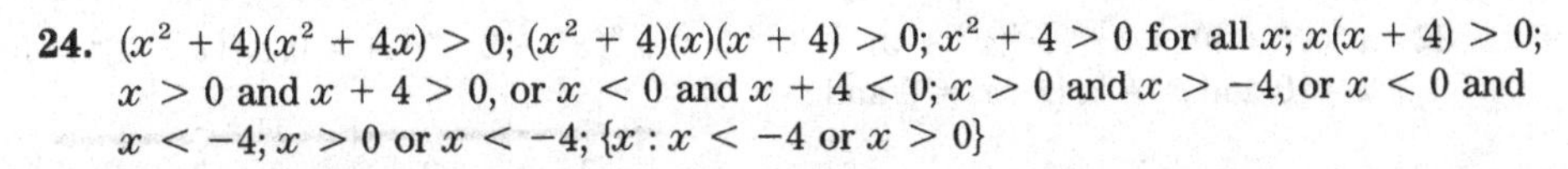

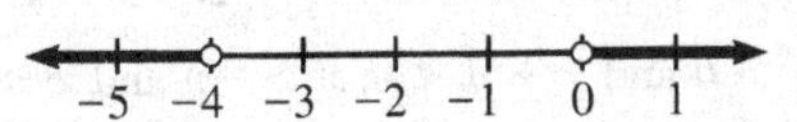

25. $x^4 > 3x^2 + 4$, $x^4 - 3x^2 - 4 > 0$, $(x^2 - 4)(x^2 + 1) > 0$, $(x - 2)(x + 2)(x^2 + 1) > 0$; $x^2 + 1 > 0$ for all x; $(x - 2)(x + 2) > 0$; $x - 2 > 0$ and $x + 2 > 0$, or $x - 2 < 0$ and $x + 2 < 0$; $x > 2$ and $x > -2$, or $x < 2$ and $x < -2$; $x > 2$ or $x < -2$; $\{x : x < -2 \text{ or } x > 2\}$

26. $x^4 - 18 < 7x^2$, $x^4 - 7x^2 - 18 < 0$, $(x^2 - 9)(x^2 + 2) < 0$, $(x - 3)(x + 3)(x^2 + 2) < 0$; $x^2 + 2 > 0$ for all x; $(x - 3)(x + 3) < 0$; $x - 3 < 0$ and $x + 3 > 0$, or $x - 3 > 0$ and $x + 3 < 0$; $x < 3$ and $x > -3$, or $x > 3$ and $x < -3$; $\{x : -3 < x < 3\}$

C **27.** $x^4 + 9 \leq 10x^2$, $x^4 - 10x^2 + 9 \leq 0$, $(x^2 - 9)(x^2 - 1) \leq 0$
$(x - 3)(x + 3)(x - 1)(x + 1) \leq 0$
$(x - 3)(x + 3)(x - 1)(x + 1)$ $\{x : -3 \leq x \leq -1 \text{ or } 1 \leq x \leq 3\}$

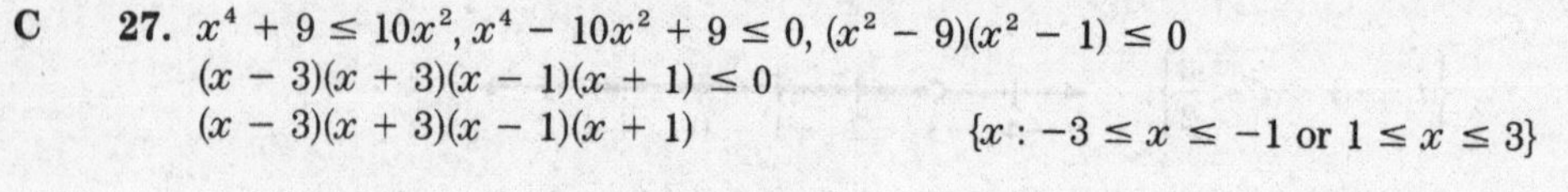

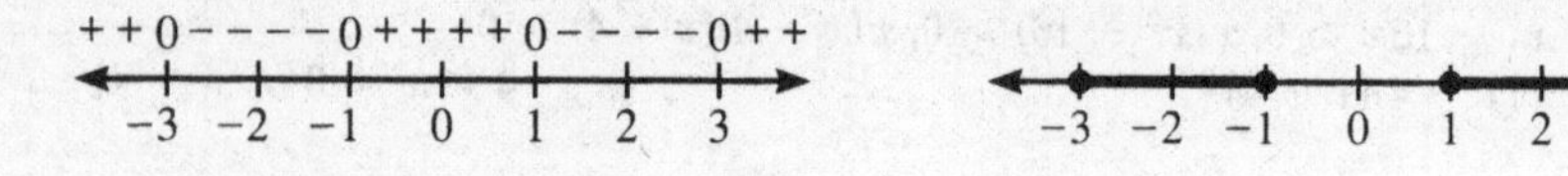

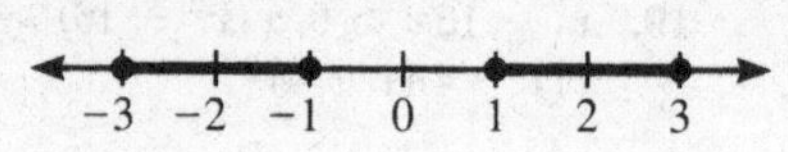

28. $x^4 + 100 \geq 29x^2$, $x^4 - 29x^2 + 100 \geq 0$, $(x^2 - 25)(x^2 - 4) \geq 0$,
$(x - 5)(x + 5)(x - 2)(x + 2) \geq 0$
$(x - 5)(x + 5)(x - 2)(x + 2)$ $\{x : x \leq -5 \text{ or } -2 \leq x \leq 2 \text{ or } x \geq 5\}$

+++0−−−0++++0−−−0+++

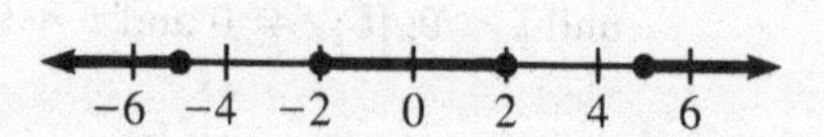

29. $(x^2 - x - 6)(x^2 - 2x + 1) > 0$, $(x - 3)(x + 2)(x - 1)^2 > 0$; $(x - 1)^2 > 0$ for all $x \neq 1$; $x \neq 1$ and $(x - 3)(x + 2) > 0$; $x \neq 1$ and $[x - 3 > 0$ and $x + 2 > 0$, or $x - 3 < 0$ and $x + 2 < 0]$; $x \neq 1$ and $[x > 3$ and $x > -2$, or $x < 3$ and $x < -2]$; $x \neq 1$ and $[x > 3$ or $x < -2]$; $\{x : x < -2 \text{ or } x > 3\}$

30. $(x^2 + x - 2)(x^2 - 4x + 4) \leq 0$, $(x + 2)(x - 1)(x - 2)^2 \leq 0$; $(x - 2)^2 \geq 0$ for all x including $x = 2$; $(x + 2)(x - 1) \leq 0$, $x + 2 \leq 0$ and $x - 1 \geq 0$, or $x + 2 \geq 0$ and $x - 1 \leq 0$; $x \leq -2$ and $x \geq 1$, or $x \geq -2$ and $x \leq 1$; $\{x : -2 \leq x \leq 1 \text{ or } x = 2\}$

31. $x^2(x^2 + 4) \leq 4x^3$, $x^2(x^2 + 4) - 4x^3 \leq 0$, $x^2(x^2 + 4 - 4x) \leq 0$, $x^2(x - 2)^2 \leq 0$; $x^2(x - 2)^2$ is non-negative for all values of x; $x^2(x - 2)^2 = 0$, $x = 0$ or $x = 2$; $\{0, 2\}$;

32. $x^2(x^2 + 9) > 6x^3$, $x^2(x^2 + 9) - 6x^3 > 0$, $x^2(x^2 + 9 - 6x) > 0$, $x^2(x - 3)^2 > 0$; $x \neq 0$ and $x \neq 3$; $\{x : x \neq 0 \text{ and } x \neq 3\}$

33. $x + p > 0$ and $x + q > 0$, or $x + q > 0$ and $x + p < 0$; $x > -p$ and $x < -q$, or $x > -q$ and $x < -p$; solutions exist if $-p < -q$ or if $-q < -p$, that is if $p > q$ or $q > p$. Then $(x + p)(x + q) < 0$ has a solution for all real numbers p and q such that $p \neq q$.

Page 205 • MIXED REVIEW EXERCISES

1. $(2x + 3)(x - 1) = 0$; $2x + 3 = 0$ or $x - 1 = 0$, $x = -\frac{3}{2}$ or $x = 1$; $\left\{-\frac{3}{2}, 1\right\}$

2. $3p - 7 = 8$, $3p = 15$, $p = 5$; $\{5\}$ **3.** $5 - |b| = 1$, $|b| = 4$, $b = 4$ or $b = -4$; $\{-4, 4\}$

4. $z(z - 1) = z(z + 1)$, $z^2 - z = z^2 + z$, $-z = z$, $2z = 0$, $z = 0$; $\{0\}$

5. $|2u - 5| = 3$; $2u - 5 = 3$ or $2u - 5 = -3$; $2u = 8$ or $2u = 2$; $u = 4$ or $u = 1$; $\{1, 4\}$

6. $2a^2 = 7a + 4$, $2a^2 - 7a - 4 = 0$, $(2a + 1)(a - 4) = 0$; $2a + 1 = 0$ or $a - 4 = 0$, $a = -\frac{1}{2}$ or $a = 4$; $\left\{-\frac{1}{2}, 4\right\}$

7. $|8 - t| = 0$, $8 - t = 0$, $t = 8$; $\{8\}$

8. $(n - 1)^2 = 1$; $n - 1 = 1$ or $n - 1 = -1$, $n = 2$ or $n = 0$; $\{0, 2\}$

9. $(3c + 1)^2 = 0$, $3c + 1 = 0$, $c = -\frac{1}{3}$; $\left\{-\frac{1}{3}\right\}$

10. $m^2 = m$, $m^2 - m = 0$, $m(m - 1) = 0$; $m = 0$ or $m - 1 = 0$, $m = 0$ or $m = 1$; $\{0, 1\}$

11. $y^2(4 - y) = 0$; $y^2 = 0$ or $4 - y = 0$, $y = 0$ or $y = 4$; $\{0, 4\}$

12. $4(3d - 5) = 2(5d + 1)$, $12d - 20 = 10d + 2$, $2d = 22$, $d = 11$; $\{11\}$

Pages 207–208 • CHAPTER REVIEW

1. c; $(x^3 - 3x^2 - 2x + 5) - (x^2 - 2x + 2) = (x^3 - 3x^2 - 2x + 5) + (-x^2 + 2x - 2) = x^3 - 4x^2 + 3$

2. b; $p(p - 2q) + 3(pq - q^2) = p^2 - 2pq + 3pq - 3q^2 = p^2 + pq - 3q^2$

3. d; $(-x^3)^2x^4 = (-1)^2(x^3)^2x^4 = x^6 \cdot x^4 = x^{10}$

4. c; $xy^2(x + y) - x^2y(y - x) = x^2y^2 + xy^3 - x^2y^2 + x^3y = xy^3 + x^3y$

5. a; $(3t - 4)(2t + 3) = 6t^2 + 9t - 8t - 12 = 6t^2 + t - 12$

6. c; $ax(x - a)(x + a) = ax(x^2 - a^2) = ax^3 - a^3x$ **7.** c

8. a; $54s^2t^3 = 2 \cdot 3^3 \cdot s^2t^3$; $90s^3t^2 = 2 \cdot 3^2 \cdot 5 \cdot s^3t^2$; $108s^4t = 2^2 \cdot 3^3 \cdot s^4t$; GCF $= 2 \cdot 3^2s^2t = 18s^2t$

9. d; $9a^2b^2c = 3^2a^2b^2c$, $15a^2b^3 = 3 \cdot 5a^2b^3$, $6a^3b^2 = 2 \cdot 3a^3b^2$; LCM $= 2 \cdot 3^2 \cdot 5a^3b^3c = 90a^3b^3c$

10. c **11.** b; $3x^3 - 27x = 3x(x^2 - 9) = 3x(x - 3)(x + 3)$

12. a; $x^2 - x - a - a^2 = (x^2 - a^2) - (x + a) = (x + a)(x - a) - (x + a) = (x + a)(x - a - 1)$

13. b **14.** c; $x^4 - 3x^2 - 4 = (x^2 - 4)(x^2 + 1) = (x - 2)(x + 2)(x^2 + 1)$

15. c; $6x^2 = 5x - 1$; $6x^2 - 5x + 1 = 0$; $(3x - 1)(2x - 1) = 0$; $3x - 1 = 0$ or $2x - 1 = 0$; $x = \frac{1}{3}$ or $x = \frac{1}{2}$

16. c; $x^3 - 4x = 0$; $x(x^2 - 4) = 0$; $x(x - 2)(x + 2) = 0$; $x = 0$ or $x - 2 = 0$ or $x + 2 = 0$; $x = 0$, $x = 2$, or $x = -2$

17. a; Let x = length of longer side; $x \cdot \left[\frac{1}{2}(25 - x)\right] = 63$; $25x - x^2 = 126$; $x^2 - 25x + 126 = 0$; $(x - 18)(x - 7) = 0$; $x - 7 = 0$ or $x - 18 = 0$; $x = 7$ and $\frac{1}{2}(25 - x) = 9$ (reject), or $x = 18$ and $\frac{1}{2}(25 - x) = 3.5$; 18 m by 3.5 m

18. b; $x^2 + 2x - 8 > 0$; $(x + 4)(x - 2) > 0$; $x + 4 > 0$ and $x - 2 > 0$, or $x + 4 < 0$ and $x - 2 < 0$; $x > -4$ and $x > 2$, or $x < -4$ and $x < 2$; $x > 2$ or $x < -4$; $\{x : x < -4$ or $x > 2\}$

19. a; $x^3 + x^2 < 2x$; $x^3 + x^2 - 2x < 0$, $x(x^2 + x - 2) < 0$, $x(x + 2)(x - 1) < 0$;
$x(x + 2)(x - 1)$ − − − − 0 + + + + 0 − − − − 0 + + + + $\{x < -2$ or $0 < x < 1\}$

−3 −2 −1 0 1 2 3

Page 208 • CHAPTER TEST

1. $-3(x^2 - 2) + 2(3 - 2x^2) = -3x^2 + 6 + 6 - 4x^2 = -7x^2 + 12$

2. $(2xy^2 + 2x^3 - x^2y) - (-2x^2y + 2xy^2 - y^3) = 2xy^2 + 2x^3 - x^2y + 2x^2y - 2xy^2 + y^3 = 2x^3 + x^2y + y^3$

3. $(-2p^2q^3)^2(-p^2q)^3 = (4p^4q^6)(-p^6q^3) = -4p^{10}q^9$ **4.** $3xy^2(x^2 - 2xy) = 3x^3y^2 - 6x^2y^3$

5. $(2x - 3a)(x + 2a) = 2x^2 + 4ax - 3ax - 6a^2 = 2x^2 + ax - 6a^2$

6. $rs(r + 2s)(2s - r) = rs(2rs - r^2 + 4s^2 - 2rs) = rs(4s^2 - r^2) = 4rs^3 - r^3s$

7. $315 = 3^2 \cdot 5 \cdot 7$, $882 = 2 \cdot 3^2 \cdot 7^2$ **a.** GCF $= 3^2 \cdot 7 = 63$ **b.** LCM $= 2 \cdot 3^2 \cdot 5 \cdot 7^2 = 4410$

8. $12a^2b^2 = 2^2 \cdot 3 \cdot a^2b^2$; $8ab^3 = 2^3ab^3$; $16b^4 = 2^4b^4$ **a.** GCF $= 2^2b^2 = 4b^2$
b. LCM $= 2^4 \cdot 3 \cdot a^2 \cdot b^4 = 48a^2b^4$

9. $x^4 - 8x^2 + 16 = (x^2 - 4)^2 = [(x - 2)(x + 2)]^2 = (x - 2)^2(x + 2)^2$

10. $xy + 2 - 2x - y = (xy - 2x) - 1(y - 2) = x(y - 2) - 1(y - 2) = (x - 1)(y - 2)$

11. $(5s - 6)(s - 2)$ **12.** $a(6a^2 - 7ab - 2b^2)$

13. $3t^2 - 10t + 3 = 0$, $(3t - 1)(t - 3) = 0$; $3t - 1 = 0$ or $t - 3 = 0$, $t = \frac{1}{3}$ or $t = 3$; $\left\{\frac{1}{3}, 3\right\}$

14. $x^4 = 8(x^2 - 2)$, $x^4 = 8x^2 - 16$, $x^4 - 8x^2 + 16 = 0$, $(x^2 - 4)^2 = 0$, $[(x - 2)(x + 2)]^2 = 0$, $(x - 2)^2(x + 2)^2 = 0$; $(x - 2)^2 = 0$ or $(x + 2)^2 = 0$, $x = 2$ (double root) or $x = -2$ (double root); $\{-2, 2\}$

15. Let x and $x + 3$ be the lengths in cm of the hour and minute hands respectively. $x^2 + (x + 3)^2 = 15^2$, $x^2 + x^2 + 6x + 9 = 225$, $2x^2 + 6x - 216 = 0$, $x^2 + 3x - 108 = 0$, $(x - 9)(x + 12) = 0$, $x = 9$ or $x = -12$ (reject); $9 + 3 = 12$; 12 cm

16. $x^2 \le x + 12$, $x^2 - x - 12 \le 0$, $(x - 4)(x + 3) \le 0$; $x - 4 \le 0$ and $x + 3 \ge 0$, or $x - 4 \ge 0$ or $x + 3 \le 0$; $x \le 4$ and $x \ge -3$, or $x \ge 4$ or $x \le -3$; $x \le 4$ and $x \ge -3$; $\{x : -3 \le x \le 4\}$

−6 −4 −2 0 2 4 6

17. $x^3 > 4x$, $x^3 - 4x > 0$, $x(x - 2)(x + 2) > 0$

$x(x - 2)(x + 2)$ $\{x : -2 < x < 0 \text{ or } x > 2\}$

- - - - 0 + + + + 0 - - 0 + + + + + +

−3 −2 −1 0 1 2 3

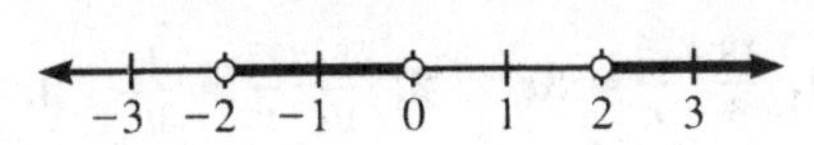

Page 209 • PREPARING FOR COLLEGE ENTRANCE EXAMS

1. B; Let the lengths of the sides be n, $n + 3$, and $n + 6$. $n^2 + (n + 3)^2 = (n + 6)^2$, $n^2 + n^2 + 6n + 9 = n^2 + 12n + 36$, $n^2 - 6n - 27 = 0$, $(n - 9)(n + 3) = 0$, $n = 9$ or $n = -3$ (reject); $A = \frac{1}{2}n(n + 3) = \frac{1}{2}(9)(12) = 54$

2. C; $m = \frac{2 - (-7)}{-4 - 2} = -\frac{9}{6} = -\frac{3}{2}$; the slope of $3x - 2y = 6$ is $\frac{3}{2}$; thus, the lines are not parallel because their slopes are not equal

3. C; $\begin{matrix} 2(x + y) = 3(x - 1) \\ x - 3y = 3 - y \end{matrix}$; $\begin{matrix} 2x + 2y = 3x - 3 \\ x - 3y = 3 - y \end{matrix}$; $\begin{matrix} x - 2y = 3 \\ x - 2y = 3 \end{matrix}$; the equations represent the same line.

4. B; Let c = the speed of the current in km/h and r = the speed in km/h of the boat in still water; $\begin{matrix} r - c = \frac{18}{3.75} = 4.8 \\ r + c = \frac{18}{2.5} = 7.2 \end{matrix}$, $2r = 12$, $r = 6$; $c = 7.2 - r$; $c = 7.2 - 6$; $c = 1.2$; 1.2 km/h

5. A; $x^{n+5} \cdot x^{n-5} = x^{(n+5)+(n-5)} = x^{2n}$ **6.** D

7. D; $9u^2 + 49 < 42u$; $9u^2 - 42u + 49 < 0$; $(3u - 7)^2 < 0$; all squares are non-negative

CHAPTER 5 • Rational Expressions

Pages 213–214 • WRITTEN EXERCISES

A **1.** $\frac{18}{6} \cdot \frac{x^3}{x} = 3x^2$ **2.** $\frac{5}{15} \cdot \frac{t^3}{t^5} = \frac{1}{3t^2}$ **3.** $\frac{-12}{4} \cdot \frac{p^3}{p^2} \cdot \frac{q}{q^2} = -\frac{3p}{q}$ **4.** $\frac{30}{-6} \cdot \frac{x^2}{x^3} \cdot \frac{y^3}{y^2} = -\frac{5y}{x}$

5. $\frac{-15}{-25} \cdot \frac{u^5}{u^4} \cdot \frac{v^3}{v^2} = \frac{3uv}{5}$ **6.** $\frac{48}{32} \cdot \frac{x^5}{x^4} \cdot \frac{y^5}{y^6} = \frac{3x}{2y}$ **7.** $\frac{(3r)^3}{(s^2)^3} = \frac{27r^3}{s^6}$ **8.** $\frac{(2x^2)^4}{(-y)^4} = \frac{16x^8}{y^4}$

9. $\frac{3s^3}{t^3}$ **10.** $\frac{3u^2 \cdot 2}{v^4 \cdot 2} = \frac{3u^2}{v^4}$ **11.** $\frac{3x \cdot 3xy}{2y \cdot 3xy} = \frac{3x}{2y}$ **12.** $\frac{3x^2 \cdot 2y^2}{2y^2} = 3x^2$

13. $\frac{t^2 \cdot rs^2t}{r^2 \cdot rs^2t} = \frac{t^2}{r^2}$ **14.** $\frac{b^2 \cdot a^2bc}{ac \cdot a^2bc} = \frac{b^2}{ac}$ **15.** $\frac{u^2 \cdot 9v^2}{v \cdot u^4} = \frac{9v \cdot vu^2}{u^2 \cdot vu^2} = \frac{9v}{u^2}$

16. $\frac{2x^2}{y^3} \cdot \frac{y^6}{4x^4} = \frac{y^3 \cdot 2x^2y^3}{2x^2 \cdot 2x^2y^3} = \frac{y^3}{2x^2}$ **17.** $\frac{16r^4s^4}{16r^4s^2} = s^2$ **18.** $\frac{8h^3k^9}{h^4k^4} = \frac{8k^5}{h}$

19. $\frac{x^2y^2z^4}{x^4y^2z^2} = \frac{z^2}{x^2}$ **20.** $\frac{p^3q^6r^9}{p^6q^2r^4} = \frac{q^4r^5}{p^3}$

B **21.** $\frac{4y^4}{9} \cdot \frac{3x}{y^4} = \frac{4x \cdot 3y^4}{3 \cdot 3y^4} = \frac{4x}{3}$ **22.** $\frac{4x^2}{yz^2} \cdot \frac{z^3}{8x^3} = \frac{z \cdot 4x^2z^2}{2xy \cdot 4x^2z^2} = \frac{z}{2xy}$

23. $\frac{c^6}{d^8} \cdot \frac{-c^3d^3}{h^3} = -\frac{c^9}{d^5h^3}$ **24.** $\frac{16a^4}{9b^2} \cdot \frac{-b^3}{8a^3} = -\frac{2ab}{9}$

25. $\frac{a^{2m}b^{2m+1}}{a^{2m}b^{2m}} = \frac{a^{2m}}{a^{2m}} \cdot \frac{b^{2m+1}}{b^{2m}} = 1 \cdot b^1 = b$ **26.** $\frac{x^{n+1}}{x^n} \cdot \frac{y^n}{y^{n-1}} = x^1 \cdot y^{n-(n-1)} = x^1y^1 = xy$

27. $\frac{(pq)^n}{pq^n} = \frac{p^nq^n}{pq^n} = p^{n-1}$ **28.** $\frac{z^{3n}}{z^nz^3} = \frac{z^{3n}}{z^{n+3}} = z^{3n-(n+3)} = z^{2n-3}$

29. $\frac{t^{n+1}t^{n-1}}{t^n} = \frac{t^{2n}}{t^n} = t^{2n-n} = t^n$ **30.** $\frac{a^{n-1}b^{2n}}{a^{n+1}b^{2n-2}} = \frac{b^{2n-(2n-2)}}{a^{(n+1)-(n-1)}} = \frac{b^2}{a^2}$

31. The statement $(p - q) + (r - s) = (p + r) - (q + s)$ is true.

32. **a.** $(p \cdot r) \div (q \cdot r) = p \div q$ **b.** The statement $(p + r) - (q + r) = p - q$ is true

33. (1) Def. of division; (2) Comm. and assoc. prop. of mult.; (3) Prop. of recip. of a product; (4) Def. of division

34. (1) Def. of exponent; (2) Mult. rule for fractions

C **35.** (1) $m > n$ or $m - n > 0$ (Given); (2) $a^{m-n} \cdot a^n = a^{m-n+n} = a^m$ (Law 1 of exp.); (3) $a^{m-n} = \frac{a^m}{a^n}$ (Div. prop. of equality)

36. For law 2: $m(a + b) = ma + mb$; true. For law 3: $n(ma) = mn(a)$; true. For law 4: $ma - na = (m - n)a$; true. For law 5: $m(a - b) = ma - mb$; true.

Page 215 • MIXED REVIEW EXERCISES

1. $x^2 + 2x - 8 > 0$; $(x + 4)(x - 2) > 0$; $x < -4$ or $x > 2$; $\{x : x < -4 \text{ or } x > 2\}$

2. $4y + 9 \le 1$; $4y \le -8$; $y \le -2$; $\{y : y \le -2\}$

3. $w^2 < 4$; $w^2 - 4 < 0$; $(w - 2)(w + 2) < 0$; $-2 < w < 2$; $\{w : -2 < w < 2\}$

4. $5 - 3p > -7$; $-3p > -12$; $p < 4$; $\{p : p < 4\}$

5. $|2t + 5| \le 3$; $-3 \le 2t + 5 \le 3$; $-8 \le 2t \le -2$; $-4 \le t \le -1$; $\{t : -4 \le t \le -1\}$

6. $2a^2 < a + 3; 2a^2 - a - 3 < 0; (2a - 3)(a + 1) < 0; a > -1 \text{ and } a < \frac{3}{2};$
$\left\{a : -1 < a < \frac{3}{2}\right\}$

7. $-3 < 2c - 1 < 5; -2 < 2c < 6, -1 < c < 3; \{c : -1 < c < 3\}$

8. $m(m - 1) \geq 2; m^2 - m - 2 \geq 0; (m - 2)(m + 1) \geq 0; m \geq 2 \text{ or } m \leq -1;$
$\{m : m \leq -1 \text{ or } m \geq 2\}$

9. $|d + 2| > 1; d + 2 > 1 \text{ or } d + 2 < -1; d > -1 \text{ or } d < -3; \{d : d < -3 \text{ or } d > -1\}$

10. $g \leq g^2; g - g^2 \leq 0; g(1 - g) \leq 0; g(g - 1) \geq 0; g \leq 0 \text{ or } g \geq 1; \{g : g \leq 0 \text{ or } g \geq 1\}$

11. $n^2 + 2 \leq 3n; n^2 - 3n + 2 \leq 0; (n - 2)(n - 1) \leq 0; n \leq 2 \text{ and } n \geq 1;$
$\{n : 1 \leq n \leq 2\}$

12. $-2u < -6 \text{ or } u - 1 \leq 1; u > 3 \text{ or } u \leq 2; \{u : u \leq 2 \text{ or } u > 3\}$

Page 215 • COMPUTER KEY-IN

1. a. 48 **b.** 2 **c.** 37 **d.** 6

2. a. GCF = 87; $\frac{1}{19}$ **b.** GCF = 512; $\frac{23}{31}$ **c.** GCF = 396; $\frac{7}{15}$ **d.** GCF = 1; $\frac{2048}{40{,}387}$

Pages 218–220 • WRITTEN EXERCISES

A

1. $3 \cdot \frac{1}{5} = \frac{3}{5}$ **2.** $\frac{1}{3 \cdot 5} = \frac{1}{15}$ **3.** $\left(-\frac{1}{3}\right)^{-2} = (-3)^2 = 9$ **4.** $\left(-\frac{1}{4}\right)^{-1} = -4$

5. $(2^{-2})^{-1} \cdot (3^{-1})^{-1} \cdot (5^0)^{-1} = 2^2 \cdot 3^1 \cdot 5^0 = 4 \cdot 3 \cdot 1 = 12$ **6.** $5^{-1} \cdot 1 = \frac{1}{5}$

7. $2\left(\frac{5^2}{2^2}\right) = \frac{2 \cdot 25}{2^2} = \frac{25}{2}$ **8.** $\frac{4}{3}\left(\frac{3^2}{4^2}\right) = \frac{3}{4}$ **9.** $\frac{7}{10^4} = 7 \times 10^{-4}$ **10.** $\frac{3}{10^3} = 3 \times 10^{-3}$

11. $6x^2y^{-3}$ **12.** $x^2y^{-1}z^{-4}$ **13.** $596 \times \frac{1}{10^2} = \frac{596}{100} = 5.96$

14. $238 \times \frac{1}{10^3} = \frac{238}{1000} = 0.238$ **15.** $7.2 \times \frac{1}{10^3} = \frac{7.2}{1000} = 0.0072$

16. $1.45 \times \frac{1}{10^2} = \frac{1.45}{100} = 0.0145$ **17.** $\left(-\frac{3}{5}\right)^3 = -\frac{3^3}{5^3} = -\frac{27}{125} = -0.216$

18. $\left(-\frac{5}{2}\right)^2 = \frac{5^2}{2^2} = \frac{25}{4} = 6.25$ **19.** $(3^{-1})^{-2} \cdot (2^2)^{-2} = 3^2 \cdot 2^{-4} = \frac{3^2}{2^4} = \frac{9}{16} = 0.5625$

20. $\left(-\frac{1}{5}\right)^2 \cdot (2^{-2})^2 = \frac{1}{25} \cdot \frac{1}{2^4} = \frac{1}{25} \cdot \frac{1}{16} = \frac{1}{400} = 0.0025$ **21.** $\frac{3y}{x^2}$ **22.** $\frac{p^3}{p^1q^2} = \frac{p^2}{q^2}$

23. $s^{-2+1} \cdot t^{-3-0} = s^{-1} \cdot t^{-3} = \frac{1}{st^3}$ **24.** $\frac{6}{-2} \cdot x^{1-(-2)}y^{-1-(-1)} = -3x^3y^0 = -3x^3$

25. $\frac{(u^{-2})^{-1}}{v^{-1}} = \frac{u^2}{v^{-1}} = u^2v$ **26.** $\frac{2^{-2}}{h^{-4}k^6} = \frac{h^4}{2^2k^6} = \frac{h^4}{4k^6}$

27. $2^{-2} \cdot (x^{-2})^{-2}(y^2)^{-2} = \frac{1}{2^2} \cdot x^4 \cdot y^{-4} = \frac{x^4}{4y^4}$ **28.** $\frac{3^{-1}x^2y^{-1}}{1} = \frac{1}{3} \cdot x^2 \cdot \frac{1}{y} = \frac{x^2}{3y}$

29. $3x^2 \cdot 3^{-2} \cdot x^{-2}(y^{-1})^{-2} = 3^{1-2}x^{2-2}y^2 = 3^{-1}x^0y^2 = \frac{y^2}{3}$

30. $5t(s^{-1})^{-2}(t^{-2})^{-2} = 5ts^2t^4 = 5s^2t^{1+4} = 5s^2t^5$ **31.** $\frac{2^{-2}(x^{-1})^{-2}}{2y^2} = \frac{x^2}{2^{1-(-2)}y^2} = \frac{x^2}{2^3y^2} = \frac{x^2}{8y^2}$

32. $\frac{4q^2}{2pq^{-1}} = \frac{2q^3}{p}$ **33.** $\frac{y^2}{x} \cdot \frac{x^{-4}}{y^2} = \frac{1}{x^5}$ **34.** $\frac{t^2}{3} \cdot \frac{3^2}{t^2} = 3$

35. $\frac{p^{-1}q^{-2}}{p^{-2}q^{-1}} = p^{-1-(-2)}q^{-2-(-1)} = p^1q^{-1} = \frac{p}{q}$ **36.** $\frac{a^{-1}x^{-2}}{a^{-2}x^{-2}} = a^{-1-(-2)}x^{-2-(-2)} = a^1x^0 = a$

37. $\frac{x^{-4}}{y^2} \cdot \frac{y^4}{x^{-2}} = \frac{y^2}{x^2}$ **38.** $\frac{r^{-2}}{s^2} \cdot (rs)^2 = \frac{r^{-2}r^2s^2}{s^2} = r^0s^0 = 1$

39. $1 \cdot \frac{u^{-2}}{v^4} \cdot u^{-1}v^{-2} = u^{-2-1}v^{-2-4} = u^{-3}v^{-6} = \frac{1}{u^3v^6}$ **40.** $\frac{1}{b^{-2}} \cdot \frac{a^{-2}}{b^4} = \frac{a^{-2}}{b^2} = \frac{1}{a^2b^2}$

41. $4x^3y^{-6} + x^3y^{-6} = 5x^3y^{-6} = \frac{5x^3}{y^6}$ **42.** $\frac{u^4}{v^2} + (-1)^{-2}(u^4v^{-2}) = \frac{u^4}{v^2} + \frac{u^4}{v^2} = \frac{2u^4}{v^2}$

Exercises 43–46. Answers may vary. Examples are given.

B **43.** Let $x = 1$ and $y = 2$; $(x + y)^{-1} = (1 + 2)^{-1} = 3^{-1} = \frac{1}{3}$; $x^{-1} + y^{-1} = 1 + \frac{1}{2} = \frac{3}{2}$; $\frac{1}{3} \neq \frac{3}{2}$

44. Let $x = 2$ and $y = 3$; $(xy)^{-1} = (2 \cdot 3)^{-1} = 6^{-1} = \frac{1}{6}$; $\frac{x}{y} = \frac{2}{3}$; $\frac{1}{6} \neq \frac{2}{3}$

45. Let $x = 2$ and $y = 3$; $xy^{-1} = 2 \cdot 3^{-1} = \frac{2}{3}$; $\frac{1}{xy} = \frac{1}{2 \cdot 3} = \frac{1}{6}$; $\frac{2}{3} \neq \frac{1}{6}$

46. Let $x = -1$; $(1 - x)^{-2} = \frac{1}{(1 - x)^2} = \frac{1}{(1 - (-1))^2} = \frac{1}{2^2} = \frac{1}{4}$; $1 - x^{-2} = 1 - \frac{1}{x^2} = 1 - \frac{1}{(-1)^2} = 1 - 1 = 0$; $\frac{1}{4} \neq 0$

47. $x^{-3}(x^2 - 4x + 2)$ **48.** $x^{-2}(2 + x - 3x^2)$ **49.** $x^{-2}(4x^2 - 5x + 1)$

50. $x^{-3}(x^2 - 9)$

C **51.** $(x - 1)^{-2}[x^2 - 4(x - 1)] = (x - 1)^{-2}(x^2 - 4x + 4)$

52. $(x^2 + 4)^{-2}[(x^2 + 4) - 5] = (x^2 + 4)^{-2}(x^2 - 1)$

53. (1) m and n are positive integers; $m > n$ (Given)

(2) $a^m \cdot a^{-n} = a^m \cdot \frac{1}{a^n}$ (Def. of neg. exp.)

(3) $= \frac{a^m}{a^n}$ (Def. of div.)

(4) $= a^{m-n}$ (Law 4a of pos. exp.)

(5) $= a^{m+(-n)}$ (Def. of subtr.)

(6) $\therefore a^m \cdot a^{-n} = a^{m+(-n)}$ (Trans. prop. of equality)

54. (1) $(a^m)^{-n} = \frac{1}{(a^m)^n}$ (Def. of neg. exp.)

(2) $= \frac{1}{a^{mn}}$ (Subst.; Law 3 of pos. exp.)

(3) $= a^{-(mn)}$ (Def. of neg. exp.)

(4) $= a^{m(-n)}$ (The opp. of a prod. is the prod. of the opp. of one factor and the other factors.)

(5) $\therefore (a^m)^{-n} = a^{m(-n)}$ (Trans. prop. of equality)

55. (1) m and n are positive integers; $m > n$ (Given)

(2) $a^{-m}a^n = \frac{1}{a^m} \cdot a^n$ (Def. of neg. exp.)

(3) $= \frac{a^n}{a^m}$ (Def. of div.)

(4) $= \frac{1}{a^{m-n}}$ (Law 4b of pos. exp.)

(5) $= a^{-(m-n)}$ (Def. of neg. exp.)

(6) $= a^{-(m+(-n))}$ (Def. of subtr.)

(7) $= a^{(-m) + [-(-n)]}$ (Prop. of the opp. of a sum)

(8) $= a^{(-m)+n}$ (For every real number x, $-(-x) = x$.)

(9) $\therefore a^{-m}a^n = a^{(-m)+n}$ (Trans. prop. of equality)

56. (1) $\frac{a^{-m}}{a^n} = a^{-m} \cdot \frac{1}{a^n}$ (Def. of div.)

(2) $= \frac{1}{a^m} \cdot \frac{1}{a^n}$ (Def. of neg. exp.)

(3) $= \frac{1}{a^m \cdot a^n}$ (Rule for mult. fractions)

(4) $= \frac{1}{a^{m+n}}$ (Law 1 of pos. exp.)

(5) $= a^{-(m+n)}$ (Def. of neg. exp.)

(6) $= a^{(-m)+(-n)}$ (Prop. of the opp. of a sum)

(7) $= a^{(-m)-n}$ (Def. of subtr.)

(8) $\therefore \frac{a^{-m}}{a^n} = a^{(-m)-n}$ (Trans. prop. of equality)

57. (1) $\frac{a^m}{a^{-n}} = a^m \div \frac{1}{a^n}$ (Def. of neg. exp.)

(2) $= a^m \cdot \frac{1}{\frac{1}{a^n}}$ (Def. of div.)

(3) $= a^m \cdot a^n$ (For every nonzero real number x, $\frac{1}{\frac{1}{x}} = x$.)

(4) $= a^{m+n}$ (Law 1 of pos. exp.)

(5) $= a^{m+[-(-n)]}$ (For every real number x, $-(-x) = x$.)

(6) $= a^{m-(-n)}$ (Def. of subtr.)

(7) $\therefore \frac{a^m}{a^{-n}} = a^{m-(-n)}$ (Trans. prop. of equality)

58. (1) $\frac{a^{-m}}{a^{-n}} = a^{-m} \cdot \frac{1}{a^{-n}}$ (Def. of div.)

(2) $= \frac{1}{a^m} \cdot a^n$ (Def. of neg. exp.)

(3) $= \frac{a^n}{a^m}$ (Def. of div.)

(4) $= \frac{1}{a^{m-n}}$ (Law 4b of pos. exp.)

(5) $= a^{-(m-n)}$ (Def. of neg. exp.)

(6) $= a^{-[m+(-n)]}$ (Def. of subtr.)

(7) $= a^{(-m)+[-(-n)]}$ (Prop. of the opp. of a sum)

(8) $= a^{(-m)-(-n)}$ (Def. of subtr.)

(9) $\therefore \frac{a^{-m}}{a^{-n}} = a^{(-m)-(-n)}$ (Trans. prop. of equality)

Page 223 • WRITTEN EXERCISES

A **1.** 7.5×10^3 **2.** 1.06×10^5 **3.** 6.08×10^{-1} **4.** 3.8×10^{-3} **5.** 1.005×10^1
6. 7.6220×10^2 **7.** 3.20×10^{-2} **8.** 4.60×10^{-5}
9. $(6.55 \times 10^2) \times 10^3 = 6.55 \times 10^5$ **10.** $(2.5 \times 10^{-2}) \times 10^{-2} = 2.5 \times 10^{-4}$
11. $(5.60 \times 10^{-1}) \times 10^{-3} = 5.60 \times 10^{-4}$ **12.** $(4.775 \times 10^3) \times 10^{-2} = 4.775 \times 10^1$
13. 5000 **14.** 0.0001 **15.** 0.0043 **16.** 10,000,000 **17.** 67,500 **18.** 0.0620
19. 0.00750 **20.** 400.0 **21.** $(2 \times 10^3)^2 = 4 \times 10^6$; $4 \times 10^6 > 5 \times 10^5$; $>$
22. $(1.2 \times 10^9)^2 = 1.44 \times 10^{18}$; $1.6 \times 10^{18} > 1.44 \times 10^{18}$; $>$
23. $(0.005)^3 = (5 \times 10^{-3})^3 = 125 \times 10^{-9} = 1.25 \times 10^{-7}$; $1.25 \times 10^{-7} > 2 \times 10^{-8}$; $>$
24. $(2 \times 10^3)^{-2} = 0.25 \times 10^{-6} = 2.5 \times 10^{-7}$; $(2 \times 10^{-3})^2 = 4 \times 10^{-6}$;
$2.5 \times 10^{-7} < 4 \times 10^{-6}$; $<$

B **25.** $\frac{4.78 \times 10^2 \times 2.30 \times 10^{-1}}{2.81 \times 10^{-2} \times 3.24 \times 10^1} \approx \frac{5 \times 2}{3 \times 3} \times 10^{2+(-1)-(-2)-1} \approx 1.11 \times 10^2 \approx 1 \times 10^2$, or 100

26. $\frac{5.25 \times 10^{-1} \times 7.82 \times 10^3}{2.25 \times 10^1 \times 4.75 \times 10^{-3}} \approx \frac{5 \times 8}{2 \times 5} \times 10^{-1+3-1-(-3)} = 4 \times 10^4$, or 40,000

27. $\frac{7.31 \times 10^1 \times (4.93 \times 10^{-1})^2}{6.20 \times 10^{-1} \times (3.26 \times 10^1)^2} \approx \frac{7 \times (5^2)}{6 \times (3^2)} \times 10^{1+2(-1)-(-1)-2(1)} \approx 3 \times 10^{-2}$, or 0.03

28. $\frac{2.12 \times 10^{-4} \times (5.88 \times 10^2)^2}{5.77 \times 10^1 \times (6.20 \times 10^{-2})^2} \approx \frac{2 \times (6^2)}{6 \times (6^2)} \times 10^{-4+2(2)-1-2(-2)} \approx 0.3 \times 10^3 = 3 \times 10^2$, or 300

29. $\frac{8 \times 2}{4} \times 10^{6+(-2)-2} = 4 \times 10^2$ **30.** $\frac{7.5 \times 5.0}{1.5} \times 10^{6+(-1)-8} = 25 \times 10^{-3} = 2.5 \times 10^{-2}$

31. $\frac{8.4 \times 1.5}{4.0 \times 1.2} \times 10^{15+(-5)-4-3} = 2.625 \times 10^3 \approx 2.6 \times 10^3$

Pages 224–225 • PROBLEMS

A **1.**

	1987 Pop.	Land Area (km^2)
USA	244,000,000	9,360,000
China	1,060,000,000	9,600,000
Italy	57,400,000	301,000
World	5,030,000,000	149,000,000

2. a. $\frac{9.36 \times 10^6}{1.49 \times 10^8} = \frac{9.36}{1.49} \times 10^{-2} \approx 6.28 \times 10^{-2} = 6.28\%$

b. $\frac{9.60 \times 10^6}{1.49 \times 10^8} = \frac{9.60}{1.49} \times 10^{-2} \approx 6.44 \times 10^{-2} = 6.44\%$

c. $\frac{3.01 \times 10^5}{1.49 \times 10^8} = \frac{3.01}{1.49} \times 10^{-3} \approx 2.02 \times 10^{-3} = 0.202 \times 10^{-2} = 0.202\%$

3. a. $\frac{2.44 \times 10^8}{5.03 \times 10^9} = \frac{2.44}{5.03} \times 10^{8-9} \approx 0.485 \times 10^{-1} = 0.0485 = 4.85\%$

b. $\frac{1.06 \times 10^9}{5.03 \times 10^9} = \frac{1.06}{5.03} \times 10^{9-9} \approx 0.211 = 21.1\%$

c. $\frac{5.74 \times 10^7}{5.03 \times 10^9} = \frac{5.74}{5.03} \times 10^{7-9} \approx 1.14 \times 10^{-2} = 1.14\%$

4. a. $\frac{2.44 \times 10^8}{9.36 \times 10^6} \approx 0.261 \times 10^2$; 26.1 persons per km^2

b. $\frac{1.06 \times 10^9}{9.60 \times 10^6} \approx 1.10 \times 10^2$; 110 persons per km^2

c. $\frac{5.74 \times 10^7}{3.01 \times 10^5} \approx 1.91 \times 10^2$; 191 persons per km^2

d. $\frac{5.03 \times 10^9}{1.49 \times 10^8} \approx 3.38 \times 10^1$; 33.8 persons per km^2

5. $\frac{2.50 \times 10^{12}}{2.44 \times 10^8} \approx 1.02 \times 10^4$; \$10,200.

6. Let t = time; $\frac{60}{2.4 \times 10^{10}} = t$; $\frac{6 \times 10^1}{2.4 \times 10^{10}} = t$; $t = 2.5 \times 10^{-9}$; 2.5 nanoseconds

7. Let d = distance between components; $\frac{d}{2.4 \times 10^{10}} \le 4.0 \times 10^{-9}$; $d \le 2.4 \times 10^{10} \times 4.0 \times 10^{-9} = 9.6 \times 10^1 = 96$; components should be no more than 96 cm apart

8. $\frac{1.67 \times 10^{-24}}{9.11 \times 10^{-28}} \approx 0.183 \times 10^{-24+28} = 0.183 \times 10^4 = 1830$; 1830 to 1

B **9.**

	AU	parsec	lt.-yr.
1 AU	1	4.85×10^{-6}	1.58×10^{-5}
1 parsec	2.06×10^5	1	3.26
1 lt.-yr.	6.33×10^4	0.307	1

10. 1 AU $\approx 1.58 \times 10^{-5}$ light-years $\approx (1.58 \times 10^{-5} \times 9.46 \times 10^{12})$ km $\approx 14.9 \times 10^{7}$ or 1.49×10^{8} km; 1 parsec $\approx$ 3.26 light-years $\approx (3.26 \times 9.46 \times 10^{12})$ km $\approx 30.8 \times 10^{12}$ or 3.08×10^{13} km

11. Since 1 AU $\approx 1.49 \times 10^{8}$ km, the distance from the sun to Mercury is approximately $\frac{5.79 \times 10^{7}}{1.49 \times 10^{8}} \approx 3.89 \times 10^{-1}$ AU or 0.389 AU; the distance to Neptune is approximately $\frac{4.51 \times 10^{9}}{1.49 \times 10^{8}} \approx 3.03 \times 10^{1}$ AU or 30.3 AU

12. $1.12 \times 10^{-3} \times 60 \times 60 \times 12.0 = 48{,}384 \times 10^{-3} \approx 48.4$ g

13. $\frac{100 \text{ watts}}{115 \text{ volts}} \approx 0.870$ amperes; $0.870 \times 6.2 \times 10^{18} \approx 5.4 \times 10^{18}$ electrons/sec; $5.4 \times 10^{18} \times 60 \times 60 = 19{,}440 \times 10^{18} \approx 1.9 \times 10^{22}$ electrons

14. On day n, you receive 2^{n-1} cents. For $n = 31$, $2^{n-1} = 2^{30} = (2^{10})^3 \approx (10^3)^3 = 10^9$; 10^9 cents $= 10^7$ dollars; approximately $10,000,000.

C **15.** Volume of sun $= \frac{4}{3}\pi(7.0 \times 10^8)^3 = \frac{4}{3}\pi(343 \times 10^{24})$; density of sun $= \frac{2.0 \times 10^{30}}{\frac{4}{3}\pi(3.43 \times 10^{26})}$; volume of Earth $= \frac{4}{3}\pi(6.4 \times 10^6)^3 \approx \frac{4}{3}\pi(262 \times 10^{18}) = \frac{4}{3}\pi(2.62 \times 10^{20})$; density of Earth $\approx \frac{6.0 \times 10^{24}}{\frac{4}{3}\pi(2.62 \times 10^{20})}$; $\frac{\text{density of Earth}}{\text{density of sun}} \approx$

$$\frac{6.0 \times 10^{24}}{\frac{4}{3}\pi(2.62 \times 10^{20})} \div \frac{2.0 \times 10^{30}}{\frac{4}{3}\pi(3.43 \times 10^{26})} = \frac{6.0 \times 10^{24}}{\frac{4}{3}\pi(2.62 \times 10^{20})} \cdot \frac{\frac{4}{3}\pi(3.43 \times 10^{26})}{2.0 \times 10^{30}} =$$

$$\frac{6.0 \times 3.43}{2.62 \times 2.0} \times 10^{24+26-(20+30)} \approx 3.9 \times 10^{0} \approx 4$$

Page 225 • MIXED REVIEW EXERCISES

1. $\frac{2x \cdot 9x^2y}{3y^3 \cdot 9x^2y} = \frac{2x}{3y^3}$ **2.** $\frac{9a^2}{4b^2}$ **3.** $\frac{4m^3}{5n^2}$ **4.** $\frac{c^6d^3}{c^3d^6} = \frac{c^3}{d^3}$ **5.** $\frac{2p^2q^3}{2p^3q} = \frac{q^2}{p}$

6. $\frac{w^2}{-w^2} = -1$ **7.** $\frac{7}{5}$ **8.** $\frac{u^4v^4}{vu^6} = \frac{v^3}{u^2}$ **9.** $x^3y^{-2} = \frac{x^3}{y^2}$ **10.** $\frac{c^2}{d^{-2}} = c^2d^2$

11. $6m^2\left(\frac{1}{4m^2}\right) = \frac{3}{2}$ **12.** $a^{-4-2}b^{1-(-3)} = a^{-6}b^4 = \frac{b^4}{a^6}$

Page 226 • CALCULATOR KEY-IN

Answers may vary.

1. 1,000,000,000 or 1×10^9 **2.** 1.4655×10^{11} **3.** 1×10^{-10} **4.** 4.246×10^{18}

5. 1.081×10^{-4} **6.** 5.194×10^{-6} **7.** 9.517×10^{0}

8. **a.** 0.66666666 or 0.66666667

b. If the last digit is 6, the calculator truncates. If the last digit is 7, the calculator rounds.

Pages 228–229 • WRITTEN EXERCISES

A

1. $\frac{5x^2 - 15x}{10x^2} = \frac{5x(x-3)}{5x(2x)} = \frac{x-3}{2x}$ 2. $\frac{3t^4 - 9t^3}{6t^2} = \frac{3t^3(t-3)}{6t^2} = \frac{t(t-3)}{2}$

3. $\frac{u^2 - u - 2}{u^2 + u} = \frac{(u-2)(u+1)}{u(u+1)} = \frac{u-2}{u}$

4. $\frac{z^3 - 4z}{z^2 - 4z + 4} = \frac{z(z^2-4)}{(z-2)^2} = \frac{z(z-2)(z+2)}{(z-2)^2} = \frac{z(z+2)}{z-2}$ 5. $\frac{(p-q)}{(q-p)} = -1$

6. $\frac{r^2 - rs}{r^2 - s^2} = \frac{r(r-s)}{(r+s)(r-s)} = \frac{r}{r+s}$ 7. $\frac{s^2 - t^2}{(t-s)^2} = \frac{(s-t)(s+t)}{(s-t)^2} = \frac{s+t}{s-t}$

8. $\frac{(a-x)^2}{x^2 - a^2} = \frac{(a-x)^2}{(x-a)(x+a)} = -\frac{a-x}{x+a} = \frac{x-a}{x+a}$

9. $\frac{x^2 - 5x + 6}{x^2 - 7x + 12} = \frac{(x-3)(x-2)}{(x-3)(x-4)} = \frac{x-2}{x-4}$ 10. $\frac{2t^2 + 5t - 3}{2t^2 + 7t + 3} = \frac{(2t-1)(t+3)}{(2t+1)(t+3)} = \frac{2t-1}{2t+1}$

11. $\frac{6y^2 - 5y + 1}{1 - y - 6y^2} = \frac{(3y-1)(2y-1)}{(1-3y)(1+2y)} = -\frac{2y-1}{1+2y} = \frac{1-2y}{1+2y}$

12. $\frac{9 - 4z^2}{6z^2 - 5z - 6} = \frac{(3-2z)(3+2z)}{(3z+2)(2z-3)} = -\frac{3+2z}{3z+2}$ 13. $\frac{r^2 - 5r + 4}{(r-4)^2} = \frac{(r-4)(r-1)}{(r-4)^2} = \frac{r-1}{r-4}$

14. $\frac{p^2 + 4p - 5}{(p-1)^2} = \frac{(p-1)(p+5)}{(p-1)^2} = \frac{p+5}{p-1}$ 15. $\frac{x^2 + 2x - 8}{(2-x)(4+x)} = \frac{(x+4)(x-2)}{(2-x)(4+x)} = -1$

16. $\frac{(t+1)(t^2-1)}{(t-1)(t+1)^2} = \frac{(t+1)(t+1)(t-1)}{(t-1)(t+1)^2} = 1$ 17. $\frac{z^4 - 1}{z^4 - z^2} = \frac{(z^2-1)(z^2+1)}{z^2(z^2-1)} = \frac{z^2+1}{z^2}$

18. $\frac{1 - r^3}{(1-r)^3} = \frac{(1-r)(1+r+r^2)}{(1-r)^3} = \frac{1+r+r^2}{(1-r)^2}$

19. $\frac{(x^2 - a^2)^2}{(x-a)^2} = \frac{[(x-a)(x+a)]^2}{(x-a)^2} = (x+a)^2$

20. $\frac{t^4 - c^4}{(t+c)^2(t^2+c^2)} = \frac{(t^2+c^2)(t^2-c^2)}{(t+c)^2(t^2+c^2)} = \frac{(t+c)(t-c)}{(t+c)^2} = \frac{t-c}{t+c}$

21. $f(t) = \frac{(t-3)(t+3)}{t(t-9)}$ **a.** reals except 0 and 9 **b.** 3 and -3

22. $g(x) = \frac{x(x^2+2)}{(x+2)(x-2)}$ **a.** reals except 2 and -2 **b.** 0

23. $F(x) = \frac{(x^2+4)(x+2)(x-2)}{(x-1)(x^2+x+1)}$ **a.** reals except 1 **b.** 2 and -2

24. $h(y) = \frac{(y-2)(y^2+2y+4)}{(y+2)^3}$ **a.** reals except -2 **b.** 2

25. $g(t) = \frac{(2t-3)(t+3)}{t(t-2)(t+2)}$ **a.** reals except -2, 0, and 2 **b.** -3 and $\frac{3}{2}$

26. $G(s) = \frac{(4s-1)(s+4)}{(2s-1)^2}$ **a.** reals except $\frac{1}{2}$ **b.** $\frac{1}{4}$ and -4

B

27. $f(x) = \frac{x^2(x-2) + (x-2)}{(x^2-1)(x^2+2)} = \frac{(x^2+1)(x-2)}{(x+1)(x-1)(x^2+2)}$ **a.** reals except 1 and -1 **b.** 2

28. $h(t) = \frac{t^2(t+4) - (t+4)}{t^2(t-1) + (t-1)} = \frac{(t^2-1)(t+4)}{(t^2+1)(t-1)} = \frac{(t-1)(t+1)(t+4)}{(t^2+1)(t-1)}$ **a.** reals except 1 **b.** -1 and -4

29. $\frac{x^3 + x^2 - x - 1}{x^3 - x^2 - x + 1} = \frac{x^2(x+1) - (x+1)}{x^2(x-1) - (x-1)} = \frac{(x^2-1)(x+1)}{(x^2-1)(x-1)} = \frac{x+1}{x-1}$

30. $\frac{t^4 - 1}{t^3 + t^2 + t + 1} = \frac{(t^2 + 1)(t^2 - 1)}{t^2(t + 1) + (t + 1)} = \frac{(t^2 + 1)(t + 1)(t - 1)}{(t^2 + 1)(t + 1)} = t - 1$

31. $\frac{x^3 - x^2y + xy^2 - y^3}{x^4 - y^4} = \frac{x^2(x - y) + y^2(x - y)}{(x^2 - y^2)(x^2 + y^2)} = \frac{(x^2 + y^2)(x - y)}{(x^2 + y^2)(x - y)(x + y)} = \frac{1}{x + y}$

32. $\frac{x^4 - 2x^2y^2 + y^4}{x^4 - x^3y - xy^3 + y^4} = \frac{(x^2 - y^2)^2}{x^3(x - y) - y^3(x - y)} = \frac{(x - y)^2(x + y)^2}{(x - y)(x^3 - y^3)} =$
$\frac{(x - y)(x + y)^2}{(x - y)(x^2 + xy + y^2)} = \frac{(x + y)^2}{x^2 + xy + y^2}$

33. $\frac{s^4 - t^4}{s^4 - 2s^2t^2 + t^4} = \frac{(s^2 + t^2)(s^2 - t^2)}{(s^2 - t^2)^2} = \frac{s^2 + t^2}{s^2 - t^2} = \frac{s^2 + t^2}{(s - t)(s + t)}$

34. $\frac{u^4 - v^4}{u^4 + 2u^2v^2 + v^4} = \frac{(u^2 - v^2)(u^2 + v^2)}{(u^2 + v^2)^2} = \frac{(u - v)(u + v)}{u^2 + v^2}$

35. $\frac{x^4 + x^3y - xy^3 - y^4}{x^4 - y^4} = \frac{x^3(x + y) - y^3(x + y)}{(x^2 + y^2)(x^2 - y^2)} = \frac{(x^3 - y^3)(x + y)}{(x - y)(x + y)(x^2 + y^2)} =$
$\frac{(x - y)(x^2 + xy + y^2)}{(x - y)(x^2 + y^2)} = \frac{x^2 + xy + y^2}{x^2 + y^2}$

36. $\frac{x^2 - y^2 - 4x + 4y}{x^2 - y^2 + 4x - 4y} = \frac{(x - y)(x + y) - 4(x - y)}{(x - y)(x + y) + 4(x - y)} = \frac{(x - y)(x + y - 4)}{(x - y)(x + y + 4)} = \frac{x + y - 4}{x + y + 4}$

37. $\frac{x^2 - y^2 - 4y - 4}{x^2 - y^2 - 4x + 4} = \frac{x^2 - (y + 2)^2}{(x - 2)^2 - y^2} = \frac{(x - (y + 2))(x + (y + 2))}{(x - 2 - y)(x - 2 + y)} =$
$\frac{(x - y - 2)(x + y + 2)}{(x - y - 2)(x + y - 2)} = \frac{x + y + 2}{x + y - 2}$

38. $\frac{ax + by - bx - ay}{ax - by + bx - ay} = \frac{x(a - b) - y(a - b)}{x(a + b) - y(a + b)} = \frac{(x - y)(a - b)}{(x - y)(a + b)} = \frac{a - b}{a + b}$

C 39. $\frac{x^2 - y^2 - z^2 - 2yz}{x^2 - y^2 + z^2 - 2xz} = \frac{x^2 - (y^2 + 2yz + z^2)}{(x^2 - 2xz + z^2) - y^2} = \frac{x^2 - (y + z)^2}{(x - z)^2 - y^2} =$
$\frac{[x - (y + z)][x + (y + z)]}{[(x - z) - y][(x - z) + y]} = \frac{(x - y - z)(x + y + z)}{(x - y - z)(x + y - z)} = \frac{x + y + z}{x + y - z}$

40. $\frac{x^2 + y^2 - z^2 - 2xy}{x^2 - y^2 + z^2 - 2xz} = \frac{(x^2 - 2xy + y^2) - z^2}{(x^2 - 2xz + z^2) - y^2} = \frac{(x - y)^2 - z^2}{(x - z)^2 - y^2} = \frac{(x - y - z)(x - y + z)}{(x - z - y)(x - z + y)} =$
$\frac{x - y + z}{x + y - z}$

41. $\frac{x^4 + x^2y^2 + y^4}{x^3 + y^3} = \frac{x^4 + 2x^2y^2 + y^4 - x^2y^2}{(x + y)(x^2 - xy + y^2)} = \frac{(x^2 + y^2)^2 - (xy)^2}{(x + y)(x^2 - xy + y^2)} =$
$\frac{(x^2 + y^2 - xy)(x^2 + y^2 + xy)}{(x + y)(x^2 - xy + y^2)} = \frac{x^2 + xy + y^2}{x + y}$

42. $\frac{x^{2n} + 2x^ny^n - 3y^{2n}}{x^{2n} + 5x^ny^n + 6y^{2n}} = \frac{(x^n - y^n)(x^n + 3y^n)}{(x^n + 2y^n)(x^n + 3y^n)} = \frac{x^n - y^n}{x^n + 2y^n}$

43. $\frac{x^{2n} - 2x^ny^n + y^{2n}}{x^{2n} + 3x^ny^n - 4y^{2n}} = \frac{(x^n - y^n)^2}{(x^n - y^n)(x^n + 4y^n)} = \frac{x^n - y^n}{x^n + 4y^n}$

Page 231 • EXTRA

A 1.
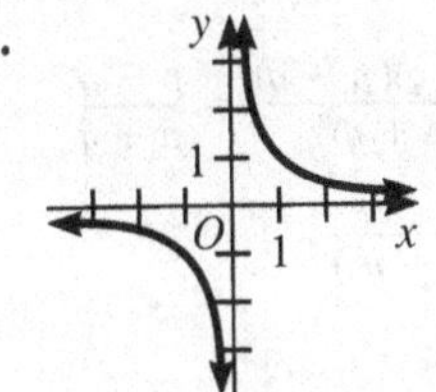

2.
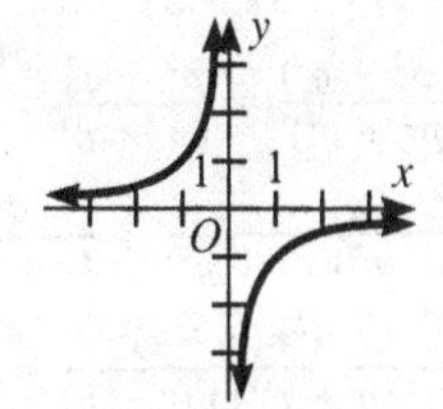

3.
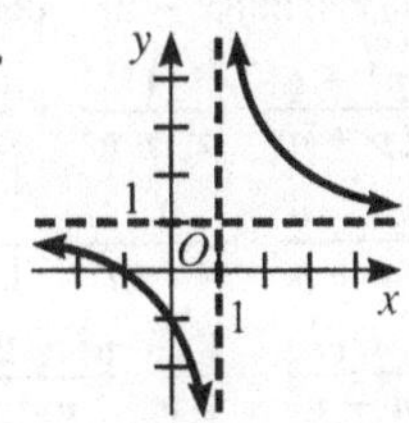

4.
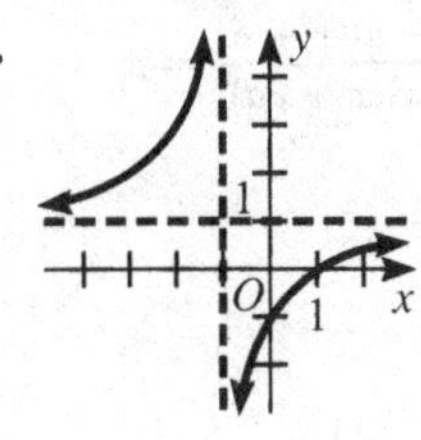

5.
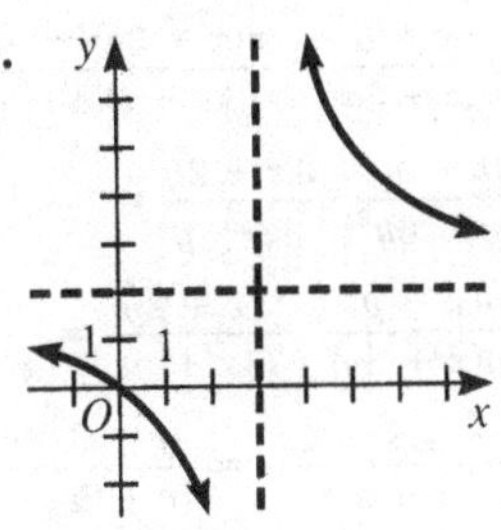

6.
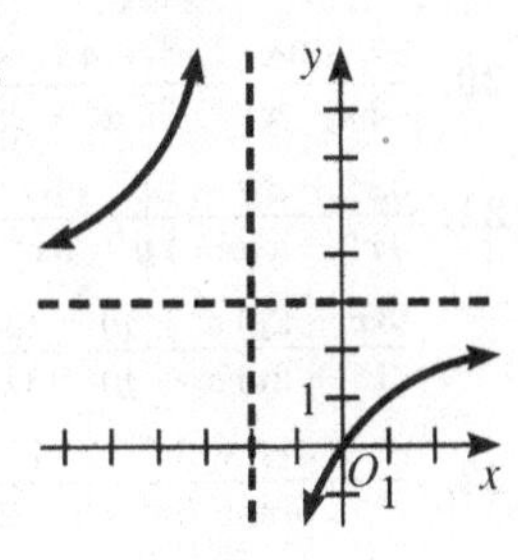

B 7.
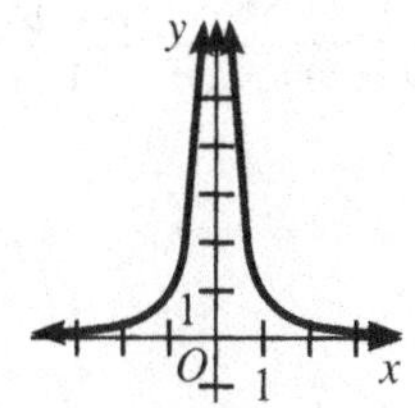

8.
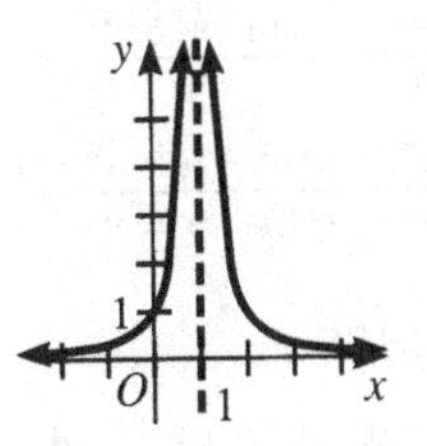

9.
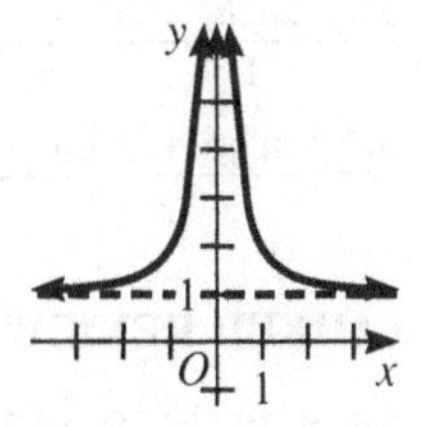

10.
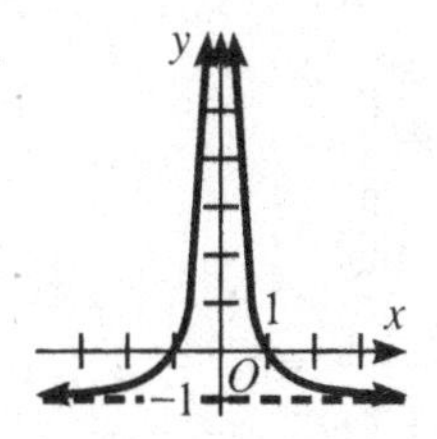

11.
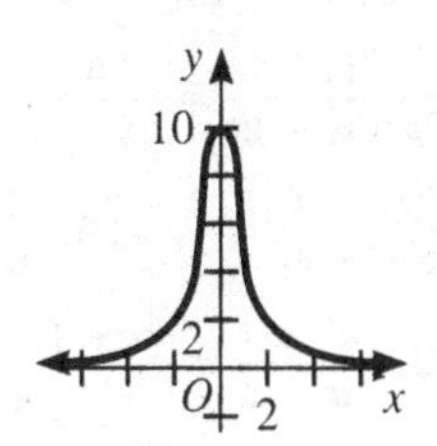

12.
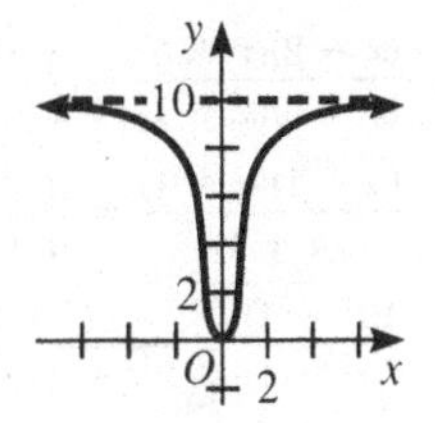

Page 234 • WRITTEN EXERCISES

A 1. $\frac{-10}{21} \cdot \frac{28}{15} = -\frac{8}{9}$ 2. $-\frac{26}{25} \cdot \frac{20}{39} = -\frac{8}{15}$ 3. $\frac{5x^3}{-3} \cdot \frac{-6}{10x^2} = \frac{5(-6)x^3}{(-3)10x^2} = x$

4. $\frac{22(-5)z^2}{15(11)z^3} = -\frac{2}{3z}$ 5. $\frac{8t^2}{3} \cdot \frac{9}{2t} = \frac{8 \cdot 9 \cdot t^2}{2 \cdot 3t} = 12t$ 6. $\frac{28x}{25} \cdot \frac{15}{21x^3} = \frac{28 \cdot 15 \cdot x}{21 \cdot 25 \cdot x^3} = \frac{4}{5x^2}$

7. $\frac{x^2}{4} \cdot \frac{6}{xy} \cdot \frac{2y^2}{x} = \frac{2 \cdot 6 \cdot x^2 \cdot y^2}{4 \cdot x^2 \cdot y} = 3y$ 8. $2uv \cdot \frac{v}{2u^2} \cdot \frac{u}{2v^2} = \frac{1}{2}$

9. $\frac{4rs^2}{45} \cdot \frac{27r}{8s} \cdot \frac{10}{9rs} = \frac{4 \cdot 27 \cdot 10 \cdot r^2s^2}{8 \cdot 9 \cdot 45rs^2} = \frac{r}{3}$ 10. $\frac{7x^2}{9y} \cdot \frac{15y^2}{4x} \cdot \frac{6xy}{35} = \frac{7 \cdot 15 \cdot 6 \cdot x^3y^3}{35 \cdot 9 \cdot 4 \cdot xy} = \frac{x^2y^2}{2}$

11. $\frac{x(x-1)}{(x-2)^2} \cdot \frac{x-2}{(x-1)^2} = \frac{x}{(x-2)(x-1)}$ 12. $\frac{t-2}{t+3} \cdot \frac{(t-1)(t+3)}{(t-2)(t+1)} = \frac{t-1}{t+1}$

13. $\frac{(2u-1)(2u+1)}{(u-2)(u+2)} \cdot \frac{u-2}{2u-1} = \frac{2u+1}{u+2}$ 14. $\frac{x^2}{x-1} \cdot \frac{x+1}{x+2} \cdot \frac{(x-1)(x+2)}{x} = x(x+1)$

15. $\frac{(x-2)(x+2)}{(2x-1)(x-2)} \cdot \frac{(2x+1)(2x-1)}{(2x+1)(x-2)} = \frac{x+2}{x-2}$

16. $\frac{(3x-2)(x-2)}{(3x+2)(3x-2)} \cdot \frac{(3x+1)(3x-2)}{(3x+1)(x-2)} = \frac{3x-2}{3x+2}$

B 17. $\frac{p^4-q^4}{(p+q)^2} \cdot \frac{1}{p^2+q^2} = \frac{(p^2+q^2)(p^2-q^2)}{(p+q)^2(p^2+q^2)} = \frac{p^2-q^2}{(p+q)^2} = \frac{(p+q)(p-q)}{(p+q)^2} = \frac{p-q}{p+q}$

18. $\frac{x^2-y^2}{x+y} \cdot \frac{1}{x^4-y^4} = \frac{x^2-y^2}{(x+y)(x^2-y^2)(x^2+y^2)} = \frac{1}{(x+y)(x^2+y^2)}$

19. $\frac{u^2v}{u+v} \cdot \frac{1}{u+v} \cdot \frac{u^2+2uv+v^2}{uv^2-u^2v} = \frac{u^2v(u+v)^2}{(u+v)^2uv(v-u)} = \frac{u}{v-u}$

20. $\frac{x^2+3ax}{3a-x} \cdot \frac{x^2-4ax+3a^2}{a^2-x^2} \cdot \frac{x+a}{x+3a} = \frac{x(x+3a)(x-3a)(x-a)(x+a)}{(3a-x)(a-x)(a+x)(x+3a)} = x$

21. $\frac{3x^2+xy-2y^2}{3x^2-xy-2y^2} \cdot \frac{3x^2-2xy-y^2}{3x^2+7xy-6y^2} \cdot \frac{3x+2y}{3x+y} =$

$\frac{(3x-2y)(x+y)}{(3x+2y)(x-y)} \cdot \frac{(3x+y)(x-y)}{(3x-2y)(x+3y)} \cdot \frac{(3x+2y)}{(3x+y)} = \frac{x+y}{x+3y}$

22. $\frac{r^2+4rs+3s^2}{r^2+5rs+6s^2} \cdot \frac{1}{r+2s} \cdot \frac{r^2+4rs+4s^2}{r+s} = \frac{(r+3s)(r+s)}{(r+2s)(r+3s)} \cdot \frac{1}{(r+2s)} \cdot \frac{(r+2s)^2}{(r+s)} = 1$

23. $\frac{a^4+2a^2b^2+b^4}{1} \cdot \frac{1}{a^4-b^4} \cdot \frac{(a-b)}{1} = \frac{(a^2+b^2)^2}{1} \cdot \frac{1}{(a^2+b^2)(a-b)(a+b)} \cdot \frac{a-b}{1} = \frac{a^2+b^2}{a+b}$

C 24. $\frac{(u^4+u^2v^2+v^4)(u^2-v^2)}{u^6-v^6} = \frac{(u^4+u^2v^2+v^4)(u^2-v^2)}{(u^2-v^2)(u^4+u^2v^2+v^4)} = 1$

Page 234 • MIXED REVIEW EXERCISES

1. 5.4×10^{-4} 2. 6.34×10^7 3. 1×10^{-1} 4. 3.281×10^3

5. $\frac{(x-2)(x+3)}{(x-2)(x+1)} = \frac{x+3}{x+1}$ 6. $\frac{15y^2}{5y^2(3y-2)} = \frac{3}{3y-2}$ 7. $\frac{2c^2}{3d^3}$

8. $\frac{(a-1)(a+1)}{(a+1)^2} = \frac{a-1}{a+1}$ 9. $\frac{3(m+4)}{2(m+4)} = \frac{3}{2}$ 10. $\frac{36z^4}{64z^9} = \frac{9}{16z^5}$

11. $\frac{4(t^2+1)}{8(t^2-1)} = \frac{t^2+1}{2(t+1)(t-1)}$ 12. $\frac{u^3+1}{u+1} = \frac{(u+1)(u^2-u+1)}{u+1} = u^2-u+1$

Page 237 • WRITTEN EXERCISES

A 1. $\frac{5}{16} - \frac{12}{16} + \frac{3}{16} = \frac{-4}{16} = -\frac{1}{4}$ 2. $\frac{7}{10} + \frac{11}{20} - \frac{9}{20} = \frac{14+11-9}{20} = \frac{16}{20} = \frac{4}{5}$

3. $\frac{1}{2} - \frac{3}{7} + \frac{5}{14} = \frac{7}{14} - \frac{6}{14} + \frac{5}{14} = \frac{6}{14} = \frac{3}{7}$ 4. $\frac{2}{3} - \frac{3}{5} + \frac{4}{15} = \frac{10}{15} - \frac{9}{15} + \frac{4}{15} = \frac{5}{15} = \frac{1}{3}$

5. $\frac{5}{12} + \frac{5}{18} - \frac{5}{36} = \frac{15}{36} + \frac{10}{36} - \frac{5}{36} = \frac{20}{36} = \frac{5}{9}$

6. $\frac{7}{12} - 1 + \frac{19}{20} = \frac{35}{60} - \frac{60}{60} + \frac{57}{60} = \frac{32}{60} = \frac{8}{15}$

7. $\frac{t+2}{3} + \frac{t-4}{6} = \frac{2(t+2)}{6} + \frac{t-4}{6} = \frac{2t+4+t-4}{6} = \frac{3t}{6} = \frac{t}{2}$

8. $\frac{x+3}{5} - \frac{2x+1}{10} = \frac{2(x+3)}{10} - \frac{2x+1}{10} = \frac{2x+6-2x-1}{10} = \frac{5}{10} = \frac{1}{2}$

9. $\frac{z-1}{z} + \frac{z+1}{z^2} = \frac{z(z-1)}{z^2} + \frac{z+1}{z^2} = \frac{z^2-z+z+1}{z^2} = \frac{z^2+1}{z^2}$

10. $\frac{x+2}{x^2} + \frac{x-2}{2x} = \frac{2(x+2)}{2x^2} + \frac{x(x-2)}{2x^2} = \frac{2x+4+x^2-2x}{2x^2} = \frac{x^2+4}{2x^2}$

11. $\frac{t-4}{2t} - \frac{t-6}{3t} = \frac{3(t-4)}{6t} - \frac{2(t-6)}{6t} = \frac{3t-12-2t+12}{6t} = \frac{t}{6t} = \frac{1}{6}$

12. $\frac{2x+5}{4x^2} + \frac{2x-5}{10x} = \frac{5(2x+5)}{20x^2} + \frac{2x(2x-5)}{20x^2} = \frac{10x+25+4x^2-10x}{20x^2} = \frac{4x^2+25}{20x^2}$

13. $\frac{1}{2pq^4} + \frac{2}{p^3q^2} = \frac{p^2}{2p^3q^4} + \frac{2(2q^2)}{2p^3q^4} = \frac{p^2+4q^2}{2p^3q^4}$

14. $\frac{1}{xy^3} - \frac{1}{x^3y} = \frac{x^2}{x^3y^3} - \frac{y^2}{x^3y^3} = \frac{x^2-y^2}{x^3y^3} = \frac{(x+y)(x-y)}{x^3y^3}$

15. $\frac{a}{b} - \frac{b}{a} = \frac{a^2}{ab} - \frac{b^2}{ab} = \frac{a^2-b^2}{ab} = \frac{(a+b)(a-b)}{ab}$

16. $\frac{4}{s^2} - \frac{1}{(4t)^2} = \frac{4}{s^2} - \frac{1}{16t^2} = \frac{(16t^2)4}{16s^2t^2} - \frac{s^2}{16s^2t^2} = \frac{64t^2-s^2}{16s^2t^2} = \frac{(8t+s)(8t-s)}{16s^2t^2}$

17. $\frac{a}{bc} + \frac{b}{ac} + \frac{c}{ab} = \frac{a^2}{abc} + \frac{b^2}{abc} + \frac{c^2}{abc} = \frac{a^2+b^2+c^2}{abc}$

18. $\frac{1}{yz} + \frac{1}{zx} + \frac{1}{xy} = \frac{x}{xyz} + \frac{y}{xyz} + \frac{z}{xyz} = \frac{x+y+z}{xyz}$

19. $\frac{y-z}{yz} - \frac{z-x}{zx} - \frac{x-y}{xy} = \frac{x(y-z)}{xyz} - \frac{y(z-x)}{xyz} - \frac{z(x-y)}{xyz} =$

$\frac{xy-xz-yz+xy-xz+yz}{xyz} = \frac{2xy-2xz}{xyz} = \frac{2x(y-z)}{xyz} = \frac{2(y-z)}{yz}$

20. $\frac{1}{x^2} + \frac{1}{xy} + \frac{1}{4y^2} = \frac{4y^2}{4x^2y^2} + \frac{4xy}{4x^2y^2} + \frac{x^2}{4x^2y^2} = \frac{x^2+4xy+4y^2}{4x^2y^2} = \frac{(x+2y)^2}{4x^2y^2}$

21. $\frac{1}{z-4} - \frac{1}{z+4} = \frac{z+4}{(z-4)(z+4)} - \frac{z-4}{(z-4)(z+4)} = \frac{8}{(z-4)(z+4)}$

22. $\frac{x}{x-1} - \frac{1}{x+1} = \frac{x(x+1)}{(x-1)(x+1)} - \frac{x-1}{(x-1)(x+1)} = \frac{x^2+x-x+1}{(x-1)(x+1)} = \frac{x^2+1}{(x-1)(x+1)}$

23. $\frac{1}{t^2+t} + \frac{1}{t^2-t} = \frac{1}{t(t+1)} + \frac{1}{t(t-1)} = \frac{(t-1)+(t+1)}{t(t-1)(t+1)} = \frac{2t}{t(t-1)(t+1)} = \frac{2}{(t-1)(t+1)}$

24. $\frac{1}{u^2-2u} - \frac{1}{u^2-4} = \frac{1}{u(u-2)} - \frac{1}{(u-2)(u+2)} = \frac{(u+2)-u}{u(u-2)(u+2)} = \frac{2}{u(u-2)(u+2)}$

25. $\frac{1}{x^2-1} - \frac{1}{(x-1)^2} = \frac{1}{(x-1)(x+1)} - \frac{1}{(x-1)^2} = \frac{(x-1)-(x+1)}{(x-1)^2(x+1)} = -\frac{2}{(x-1)^2(x+1)}$

26. $\frac{1}{y^2-y-2} + \frac{1}{y^2+y} = \frac{1}{(y-2)(y+1)} + \frac{1}{y(y+1)} = \frac{y+(y-2)}{y(y+1)(y-2)} =$

$\frac{2y-2}{y(y+1)(y-2)} = \frac{2(y-1)}{y(y+1)(y-2)}$

27. $\frac{1}{s^2+2s+1} - \frac{1}{s^2-1} = \frac{1}{(s+1)^2} - \frac{1}{(s+1)(s-1)} = \frac{(s-1)-(s+1)}{(s+1)^2(s-1)} = -\frac{2}{(s+1)^2(s-1)}$

28. $\frac{1}{p^2-2p+1} - \frac{1}{p^2+p-2} = \frac{1}{(p-1)^2} - \frac{1}{(p-1)(p+2)} = \frac{(p+2)-(p-1)}{(p-1)^2(p+2)} =$

$\frac{3}{(p-1)^2(p+2)}$

B

29. $\frac{a+b}{a-b}+\frac{a-b}{a+b}+\frac{b-a}{a-b}+\frac{b-a}{a+b}=\frac{(a+b)+(b-a)}{a-b}+\frac{(a-b)+(b-a)}{a+b}=\frac{2b}{a-b}+0=\frac{2b}{a-b}$

30. $\frac{a+b}{a-b}+\frac{a-b}{a+b}-\frac{b-a}{a-b}+\frac{b-a}{a+b}=\frac{(a+b)-(b-a)}{a-b}+\frac{(a-b)+(b-a)}{a+b}=\frac{2a}{a-b}+0=\frac{2a}{a-b}$

31. $\frac{1}{x-y}-\frac{1}{x+y}=\frac{(x+y)-(x-y)}{(x-y)(x+y)}=\frac{2y}{(x-y)(x+y)}$

32. $\frac{1}{(x-y)^2}-\frac{1}{(x+y)^2}=\frac{(x+y)^2-(x-y)^2}{(x-y)^2(x+y)^2}=\frac{[(x+y)-(x-y)][(x+y)+(x-y)]}{(x-y)^2(x+y)^2}=\frac{(2y)(2x)}{(x-y)^2(x+y)^2}=\frac{4xy}{(x-y)^2(x+y)^2}$

33. $\frac{3}{x^2-5x+6}+\frac{2}{x^2-4}=\frac{3}{(x-3)(x-2)}+\frac{2}{(x+2)(x-2)}=\frac{3(x+2)+2(x-3)}{(x-3)(x+2)(x-2)}=\frac{3x+6+2x-6}{(x-3)(x+2)(x-2)}=\frac{5x}{(x-3)(x+2)(x-2)}$

34. $\frac{1}{4t^2-4t+1}+\frac{1}{4t^2-1}=\frac{1}{(2t-1)^2}+\frac{1}{(2t-1)(2t+1)}=\frac{(2t+1)+(2t-1)}{(2t-1)^2(2t+1)}=\frac{4t}{(2t-1)^2(2t+1)}$

35. $\frac{1}{2u^2-3uv+v^2}+\frac{1}{4u^2-v^2}=\frac{1}{(2u-v)(u-v)}+\frac{1}{(2u+v)(2u-v)}=\frac{(2u+v)+(u-v)}{(2u-v)(u-v)(2u+v)}=\frac{3u}{(2u-v)(2u+v)(u-v)}$

36. $\frac{3}{4x^2-12xy+9y^2}+\frac{1}{2xy-3y^2}=\frac{3}{(2x-3y)^2}+\frac{1}{y(2x-3y)}=\frac{3y+(2x-3y)}{y(2x-3y)^2}=\frac{2x}{y(2x-3y)^2}$

37. $\frac{x}{x-a}-\frac{x^2+a^2}{x^2-a^2}+\frac{a}{x+a}=\frac{x(x+a)}{(x-a)(x+a)}-\frac{x^2+a^2}{(x-a)(x+a)}+\frac{a(x-a)}{(x-a)(x+a)}=\frac{x^2+ax-x^2-a^2+ax-a^2}{(x-a)(x+a)}=\frac{2ax-2a^2}{(x-a)(x+a)}=\frac{2a(x-a)}{(x-a)(x+a)}=\frac{2a}{x+a}$

38. $\frac{3u}{2u-v}-\frac{2u}{2u+v}+\frac{2v^2}{4u^2-v^2}=\frac{3u(2u+v)-2u(2u-v)+2v^2}{(2u+v)(2u-v)}=\frac{6u^2+3uv-4u^2+2uv+2v^2}{(2u+v)(2u-v)}=\frac{2u^2+5uv+2v^2}{(2u+v)(2u-v)}=\frac{(2u+v)(u+2v)}{(2u+v)(2u-v)}=\frac{u+2v}{2u-v}$

39. a.

(1) $\frac{a}{c}+\frac{b}{c}=a\cdot\frac{1}{c}+b\cdot\frac{1}{c}$ (Def. of division)

(2) $=(a+b)\frac{1}{c}$ (Dist. prop.)

(3) $=\frac{a+b}{c}$ (Def. of division)

(4) $\therefore \frac{a}{c}+\frac{b}{c}=\frac{a+b}{c}$ (Trans. prop.)

b. (1) $\frac{a}{c} - \frac{b}{c} = a \cdot \frac{1}{c} - b \cdot \frac{1}{c}$ (Def. of division)

(2) $= (a - b)\frac{1}{c}$ (Dist. prop.)

(3) $= \frac{a - b}{c}$ (Def. of division)

(4) $\therefore \frac{a}{c} - \frac{b}{c} = \frac{a - b}{c}$ (Trans. prop.)

C **40.** $\frac{2x - 9}{x^2 - x - 6} = \frac{2x - 9}{(x - 3)(x + 2)} = \frac{A}{(x - 3)} + \frac{B}{(x + 2)} = \frac{A(x + 2) + B(x - 3)}{(x - 3)(x + 2)} =$

$\frac{Ax + 2A + Bx - 3B}{(x - 3)(x + 2)} = \frac{(A + B)x + 2A - 3B}{(x - 3)(x + 2)}$. $\therefore (A + B)x + 2A - 3B = 2x - 9;$

$\begin{matrix} A + B = 2 \\ 2A - 3B = -9 \end{matrix}; \begin{matrix} 3A + 3B = 6 \\ 2A - 3B = -9 \end{matrix}; 5A = -3; A = -\frac{3}{5}, B = \frac{13}{5}.$

41. $\frac{x - 7}{x^2 + x - 6} = \frac{x - 7}{(x + 3)(x - 2)} = \frac{A}{x + 3} + \frac{B}{x - 2} = \frac{A(x - 2) + B(x + 3)}{(x + 3)(x - 2)} =$

$\frac{Ax - 2A + Bx + 3B}{(x + 3)(x - 2)} = \frac{(A + B)x - 2A + 3B}{(x + 3)(x - 2)}$. $\therefore (A + B)x - 2A + 3B = x - 7;$

$\begin{matrix} A + B = 1 \\ -2A + 3B = -7 \end{matrix}; \begin{matrix} 2A + 2B = 2 \\ -2A + 3B = -7 \end{matrix}; 5B = -5; B = -1, A = 2.$

Pages 239–241 • WRITTEN EXERCISES

A **1.** $\frac{\left(1 - \frac{1}{3}\right) \cdot 6}{\left(\frac{1}{2} - \frac{1}{6}\right) \cdot 6} = \frac{6 - 2}{3 - 1} = \frac{4}{2} = 2$

2. $\frac{\left(\frac{1}{2} + \frac{1}{3}\right) \cdot 6}{\left(1 - \frac{1}{6}\right) \cdot 6} = \frac{3 + 2}{6 - 1} = \frac{5}{5} = 1$

3. $\frac{\left(1 - \frac{4}{5}\right) \cdot 20}{\left(\frac{1}{4} - \frac{1}{5}\right) \cdot 20} = \frac{20 - 16}{5 - 4} = \frac{4}{1} = 4$

4. $\frac{\frac{2}{3} - \frac{5}{6}}{\frac{1}{3} + \frac{2}{9}} = \frac{\frac{4 - 5}{6}}{\frac{3 + 2}{9}} = \frac{-\frac{1}{6}}{\frac{5}{9}} = -\frac{1}{6} \cdot \frac{9}{5} = -\frac{3}{10}$

5. $\frac{x + 1}{1 + \frac{1}{x}} = \frac{x + 1}{\frac{x + 1}{x}} = \frac{x + 1}{1} \cdot \frac{x}{x + 1} = x$

6. $\frac{\left(z - \frac{1}{z}\right) \cdot z}{\left(1 - \frac{1}{z}\right) \cdot z} = \frac{z^2 - 1}{z - 1} = \frac{(z - 1)(z + 1)}{(z - 1)} = z + 1$

7. $\frac{a - b}{\frac{1}{a} - \frac{1}{b}} = \frac{a - b}{\frac{b - a}{ab}} = \frac{a - b}{1} \cdot \frac{ab}{b - a} = -ab$

8. $\frac{1 - \frac{x}{y}}{\frac{1}{x} - \frac{1}{y}} = \frac{\frac{y - x}{y}}{\frac{y - x}{xy}} = \frac{y - x}{y} \cdot \frac{xy}{y - x} = x$

9. $$\frac{\left(\frac{1}{u^2}-\frac{1}{v^2}\right)\cdot u^2v^2}{\left(\frac{1}{u}-\frac{1}{v}\right)\cdot u^2v^2} = \frac{v^2-u^2}{uv^2-u^2v} = \frac{(v-u)(v+u)}{uv(v-u)} = \frac{v+u}{uv}$$

10. $$\frac{\left(\frac{1}{a^2}-\frac{1}{b^2}\right)a^2b^2}{\left(\frac{1}{a}+\frac{1}{b}\right)a^2b^2} = \frac{b^2-a^2}{ab^2+a^2b} = \frac{(b-a)(b+a)}{ab(a+b)} = \frac{b-a}{ab}$$

11. $$\frac{\left(\frac{1}{x^2}-\frac{1}{y^2}\right)x^2y^2}{\left(\frac{1}{x^2}+\frac{2}{xy}+\frac{1}{y^2}\right)x^2y^2} = \frac{y^2-x^2}{y^2+2xy+x^2} = \frac{(y-x)(y+x)}{(y+x)^2} = \frac{y-x}{y+x}$$

12. $$\frac{\left(\frac{1}{p^2}-\frac{1}{q^2}\right)\cdot p^2q^2}{\left(\frac{2}{p^2}-\frac{1}{pq}-\frac{1}{q^2}\right)p^2q^2} = \frac{q^2-p^2}{2q^2-pq-p^2} = \frac{(q-p)(q+p)}{(2q+p)(q-p)} = \frac{q+p}{2q+p}$$

13. $$\frac{h+\frac{1}{h^2}}{1+\frac{1}{h}} = \frac{\frac{h^3+1}{h^2}}{\frac{h+1}{h}} = \frac{h^3+1}{h^2}\cdot\frac{h}{h+1} = \frac{(h+1)(h^2-h+1)}{h(h+1)} = \frac{h^2-h+1}{h}$$

14. $$\frac{\left(\frac{1}{x^2}-x^2\right)x^2}{\left(\frac{1}{x}-x\right)x^2} = \frac{1-x^4}{x-x^3} = \frac{(1-x)(1+x)(1+x^2)}{x(1-x)(1+x)} = \frac{1+x^2}{x}$$

15. $$\frac{\left(s^2-\frac{1}{t^2}\right)t^2}{\left(s-\frac{1}{t}\right)t^2} = \frac{s^2t^2-1}{st^2-t} = \frac{(st-1)(st+1)}{t(st-1)} = \frac{st+1}{t}$$

16. $$\frac{\left(\frac{1}{x}-\frac{1}{y}\right)xy}{\left(\frac{y}{x}-\frac{x}{y}\right)xy} = \frac{y-x}{y^2-x^2} = \frac{y-x}{(y-x)(y+x)} = \frac{1}{y+x}$$

17. $$\frac{\left(\frac{2}{y+2}-1\right)(y+2)}{\left(\frac{1}{y+2}+1\right)(y+2)} = \frac{2-(y+2)}{1+y+2} = -\frac{y}{y+3}$$

18. $$\frac{1+\frac{1}{t-1}}{1-\frac{1}{t+1}} = \frac{\frac{t-1+1}{t-1}}{\frac{t+1-1}{t+1}} = \frac{t}{t-1}\cdot\frac{t+1}{t} = \frac{t+1}{t-1}$$

B 19. $$\frac{\left(\frac{1}{a+1}+\frac{1}{a-1}\right)(a+1)(a-1)}{\left(\frac{1}{a+1}-\frac{1}{a-1}\right)(a+1)(a-1)} = \frac{a-1+a+1}{a-1-(a+1)} = \frac{2a}{-2} = -a$$

20. $$\frac{\left(\frac{1}{x}+\frac{1}{x+1}\right)x(x+1)}{\left(\frac{1}{x}-\frac{1}{x+1}\right)x(x+1)} = \frac{x+1+x}{x+1-x} = 2x+1$$

21. $$\frac{1+\frac{1}{x-1}}{1+\frac{1}{x^2-1}} = \frac{\frac{x-1+1}{x-1}}{\frac{x^2-1+1}{x^2-1}} = \frac{x}{x-1}\cdot\frac{x^2-1}{x^2} = \frac{(x-1)(x+1)}{(x-1)x} = \frac{x+1}{x}$$

22. $$\frac{\frac{1}{1-t}-\frac{1}{t}}{\frac{1}{1+t}-\frac{1}{t}} = \frac{\frac{t-(1-t)}{(1-t)t}}{\frac{t-(1+t)}{(1+t)t}} = \frac{\frac{2t-1}{(1-t)t}}{\frac{-1}{t(1+t)}} = \frac{2t-1}{(1-t)t}\cdot\frac{t(1+t)}{-1} = \frac{(2t-1)(1+t)}{-(1-t)} =$$
$$\frac{(2t-1)(t+1)}{t-1}$$

23. $$\frac{\frac{a}{b}-\frac{a-b}{a+b}}{\frac{a}{b}+\frac{a+b}{a-b}} = \frac{\frac{a(a+b)-b(a-b)}{b(a+b)}}{\frac{a(a-b)+b(a+b)}{b(a-b)}} = \frac{a^2+ab-ab+b^2}{b(a+b)}\cdot\frac{b(a-b)}{a^2-ab+ab+b^2} =$$
$$\frac{a^2+b^2}{a+b}\cdot\frac{a-b}{a^2+b^2} = \frac{a-b}{a+b}$$

24. $$\frac{\left(\frac{u+v}{u-v}-\frac{u-v}{u+v}\right)\cdot(u+v)(u-v)}{\left(\frac{u+v}{u-v}+\frac{u-v}{u+v}\right)\cdot(u+v)(u-v)} = \frac{(u+v)^2-(u-v)^2}{(u+v)^2+(u-v)^2} =$$
$$\frac{u^2+2uv+v^2-u^2+2uv-v^2}{u^2+2uv+v^2+u^2-2uv+v^2} = \frac{4uv}{2u^2+2v^2} = \frac{2uv}{u^2+v^2}$$

25. $$\frac{1-\frac{2-\frac{1}{x}}{x}}{1-\frac{1}{x}} = \frac{1-\frac{2x-1}{x^2}}{1-\frac{1}{x}} = \frac{\frac{x^2-2x+1}{x^2}}{\frac{x-1}{x}} = \frac{(x-1)^2}{x^2}\cdot\frac{x}{x-1} = \frac{x-1}{x}$$

26. $$\frac{u+\frac{1}{1+\frac{1}{u}}}{\frac{1}{u+1}} = \frac{u+\frac{1}{\frac{u+1}{u}}}{\frac{1}{u+1}} = \left(u+\frac{u}{u+1}\right)\cdot\frac{u+1}{1} = u(u+1)+u = u^2+2u$$

27. **a.** $1+\frac{1}{2} = 1.500$

b. $1+\dfrac{1}{2+\frac{1}{2}} = 1+\dfrac{1\cdot 2}{\left(2+\frac{1}{2}\right)2} = 1+\dfrac{2}{4+1} = 1+\dfrac{2}{5} = 1.400$

c. $1+\dfrac{1}{2+\dfrac{1}{2+\frac{1}{2}}} = 1+\dfrac{1}{2+\dfrac{1\cdot 2}{\left(2+\frac{1}{2}\right)2}} = 1+\dfrac{1}{2+\frac{2}{5}} =$

$1+\dfrac{1\cdot 5}{\left(2+\frac{2}{5}\right)5} = 1+\dfrac{5}{10+2} = 1+\dfrac{5}{12} = \dfrac{17}{12} \approx 1.417$

(Continued)

d. $$1 + \cfrac{1}{2 + \cfrac{1}{2 + \cfrac{1 \cdot 2}{\left(2 + \frac{1}{2}\right)2}}} = 1 + \cfrac{1}{2 + \cfrac{1}{2 + \frac{2}{4 + 1}}} =$$

$$1 + \cfrac{1}{2 + \cfrac{1 \cdot 5}{\left(2 + \frac{2}{5}\right)5}} = 1 + \cfrac{1}{2 + \frac{5}{10 + 2}} = 1 + \cfrac{1 \cdot 12}{\left(2 + \frac{5}{12}\right)12} = 1 + \frac{12}{24 + 5} =$$

$$1 + \frac{12}{29} = \frac{41}{29} \approx 1.414$$

C

28. $$\frac{f(x + h) - f(x)}{h} = \frac{\frac{1}{x + h} - \frac{1}{x}}{h} = \frac{\frac{x}{x(x + h)} - \frac{x + h}{x(x + h)}}{h} = \frac{x - (x + h)}{hx(x + h)} = \frac{-h}{hx(x + h)} = -\frac{1}{x(x + h)}$$

29. $$\frac{f(x + h) - f(x)}{h} = \frac{\frac{1}{x + h + 1} - \frac{1}{x + 1}}{h} = \frac{\frac{x + 1}{(x + 1)(x + h + 1)} - \frac{x + h + 1}{(x + 1)(x + h + 1)}}{h} =$$
$$\frac{x + 1 - (x + h + 1)}{h(x + 1)(x + h + 1)} = \frac{-h}{h(x + 1)(x + h + 1)} = -\frac{1}{(x + 1)(x + h + 1)}$$

30. $$\frac{f(x + h) - f(x)}{h} = \frac{\frac{1 - (x + h)}{x + h} - \frac{1 - x}{x}}{h} = \frac{\frac{x[1 - (x + h)]}{x(x + h)} - \frac{(x + h)(1 - x)}{x(x + h)}}{h} =$$
$$\frac{x - x^2 - xh + x^2 + xh - x - h}{hx(x + h)} = \frac{-h}{hx(x + h)} = -\frac{1}{x(x + h)}$$

31. $$\frac{f(x + h) - f(x)}{h} = \frac{\frac{1}{(x + h)^2} - \frac{1}{x^2}}{h} = \frac{\frac{x^2}{x^2(x + h)^2} - \frac{(x + h)^2}{x^2(x + h)^2}}{h} = \frac{x^2 - x^2 - 2hx - h^2}{hx^2(x + h)^2} =$$
$$\frac{-h(2x + h)}{hx^2(x + h)^2} = -\frac{2x + h}{x^2(x + h)^2}$$

32. $$f(f(x)) = f\left(\frac{1}{x + 1}\right) = \frac{1}{\frac{1}{x + 1} + 1} = \frac{1(x + 1)}{\left(\frac{1}{x + 1} + 1\right)(x + 1)} = \frac{x + 1}{1 + x + 1} = \frac{x + 1}{x + 2}$$

33. $$f(f(x)) = f\left(\frac{x}{x + 1}\right) = \frac{\frac{x}{x + 1}}{\frac{x}{x + 1} + 1} = \frac{\left(\frac{x}{x + 1}\right)(x + 1)}{\left(\frac{x}{x + 1} + 1\right)(x + 1)} = \frac{x}{x + x + 1} = \frac{x}{2x + 1}$$

34. $$f(f(x)) = f\left(\frac{1 + x}{1 - x}\right) = \frac{1 + \frac{1 + x}{1 - x}}{1 - \frac{1 + x}{1 - x}} = \frac{\left(1 + \frac{1 + x}{1 - x}\right)(1 - x)}{\left(1 - \frac{1 + x}{1 - x}\right)(1 - x)} = \frac{1 - x + 1 + x}{1 - x - 1 - x} = -\frac{1}{x}$$

35. $$f(f(x)) = f((1 - x)^{-1}) = [1 - (1 - x)^{-1}]^{-1} = \frac{1}{1 - \frac{1}{1 - x}} = \frac{1(1 - x)}{\left(1 - \frac{1}{1 - x}\right)(1 - x)} =$$
$$\frac{1 - x}{1 - x - 1} = \frac{-(x - 1)}{-x} = \frac{x - 1}{x}$$

Page 241 • MIXED REVIEW EXERCISES

1. $\frac{1}{x^2y} + \frac{1}{xy^2} = \frac{y + x}{x^2y^2}$ 2. $\frac{8}{a^2 - 3a} \cdot \frac{a^2 - 9}{6a} = \frac{8}{a(a - 3)} \cdot \frac{(a - 3)(a + 3)}{6a} = \frac{4(a + 3)}{3a^2}$

3. $\frac{36u^2}{25v} \cdot \frac{10v^3}{27u^4} = \frac{8v^2}{15u^2}$

4. $\frac{t}{t - 2} - \frac{1}{t + 2} = \frac{t(t + 2) - (t - 2)}{(t - 2)(t + 2)} = \frac{t^2 + 2t - t + 2}{(t - 2)(t + 2)} = \frac{t^2 + t + 2}{(t - 2)(t + 2)}$

5. $-\frac{8a^2b^3}{16a^3b^2} = -\frac{b}{2a}$ 6. $\frac{x}{2y} + \frac{y}{2x} = \frac{x^2}{2xy} + \frac{y^2}{2xy} = \frac{x^2 + y^2}{2xy}$

7. $\frac{x - 2}{4} - \frac{2 - x}{8} = \frac{2x - 4 - 2 + x}{8} = \frac{3x - 6}{8}$ 8. $\frac{2y - x}{x - 2y} = -1$

9. $\frac{(a - 2)^2}{b^2} \div \frac{6a - 12}{4b} = \frac{(a - 2)^2}{b^2} \cdot \frac{4b}{6(a - 2)} = \frac{2(a - 2)}{3b}$

10. $\begin{array}{l} 4x - y = 14 \\ 5x + 3y = 9 \end{array}$; $\begin{array}{l} 12x - 3y = 42 \\ 5x + 3y = 9 \end{array}$; $17x = 51$; $x = 3$; $12 - y = 14$; $-y = 2$; $y = -2$; $(3, -2)$

11. $\begin{array}{l} 2x + 5y = 17 \\ x - 2y = -5 \end{array}$; $\begin{array}{l} 2x + 5y = 17 \\ -2x + 4y = 10 \end{array}$; $9y = 27$; $y = 3$; $2x + 15 = 17$; $2x = 2$; $x = 1$; $(1, 3)$

12. $\begin{array}{l} x - 4y = -4 \\ 2x + 10y = 1 \end{array}$; $\begin{array}{l} -2x + 8y = 8 \\ 2x + 10y = 1 \end{array}$; $18y = 9$; $y = \frac{1}{2}$; $x - 2 = -4$; $x = -2$; $\left(-2, \frac{1}{2}\right)$

Page 245 • WRITTEN EXERCISES

A

1. $\frac{x}{9} + \frac{1}{6} = \frac{2}{3}$; $18\left(\frac{x}{9} + \frac{1}{6}\right) = \frac{2}{3} \cdot 18$; $2x + 3 = 12$; $2x = 9$; $x = \frac{9}{2}$; $\left\{\frac{9}{2}\right\}$

2. $\frac{3u}{5} - \frac{5}{6} = \frac{u}{10}$; $30\left(\frac{3u}{5} - \frac{5}{6}\right) = 30 \cdot \frac{u}{10}$; $18u - 25 = 3u$; $15u = 25$; $u = \frac{25}{15} = \frac{5}{3}$; $\left\{\frac{5}{3}\right\}$

3. $\frac{2t - 1}{6} = \frac{t + 2}{4} + \frac{1}{3}$; $12\left(\frac{2t - 1}{6}\right) = 12\left(\frac{t + 2}{4} + \frac{1}{3}\right)$; $4t - 2 = 3t + 6 + 4$; $t = 12$; $\{12\}$

4. $\frac{s - 2}{2} - \frac{s - 1}{5} = \frac{1}{4}$; $20\left(\frac{s - 2}{2} - \frac{s - 1}{5}\right) = \frac{1}{4} \cdot 20$; $10s - 20 - 4s + 4 = 5$; $6s = 21$; $s = \frac{21}{6} = \frac{7}{2}$; $\left\{\frac{7}{2}\right\}$

5. $\frac{z}{4} - \frac{z - 1}{6} \le \frac{5}{12}$; $12\left(\frac{z}{4} - \frac{z - 1}{6}\right) \le 12 \cdot \frac{5}{12}$; $3z - 2z + 2 \le 5$; $z \le 3$; $\{z : z \le 3\}$

6. $\frac{t}{4} - \frac{t + 2}{3} + \frac{1}{6} \ge 0$; $12\left(\frac{t}{4} - \frac{t + 2}{3} + \frac{1}{6}\right) \ge 12(0)$; $3t - 4t - 8 + 2 \ge 0$; $-t - 6 \ge 0$; $t \le -6$; $\{t : t \le -6\}$

7. $\frac{r - 2}{8} < \frac{3r + 1}{6} + \frac{1}{3}$; $24 \cdot \frac{r - 2}{8} < 24\left(\frac{3r + 1}{6} + \frac{1}{3}\right)$; $3r - 6 < 12r + 4 + 8$; $-18 < 9r$; $r > -2$; $\{r : r > -2\}$

8. $\frac{x - 5}{9} \le \frac{2x}{15} - \frac{2}{5}$; $45\left(\frac{x - 5}{9}\right) \le 45\left(\frac{2x}{15} - \frac{2}{5}\right)$; $5x - 25 \le 6x - 18$; $x \ge -7$; $\{x : x \ge -7\}$

9. $\frac{y^2}{4} - \frac{3y}{2} + 2 = 0$; $4\left(\frac{y^2}{4} - \frac{3y}{2} + 2\right) = 4(0)$; $y^2 - 6y + 8 = 0$; $(y - 4)(y - 2) = 0$; $y = 4$ or $y = 2$; $\{2, 4\}$

10. $\frac{t^2}{6} - \frac{t}{2} - \frac{2}{3} = 0$; $6\left(\frac{t^2}{6} - \frac{t}{2} - \frac{2}{3}\right) = 6(0)$; $t^2 - 3t - 4 = 0$; $(t - 4)(t + 1) = 0$; $t = 4$ or $t = -1$; $\{-1, 4\}$

11. $\frac{z^2}{3} - \frac{z}{6} = 1$; $6\left(\frac{z^2}{3} - \frac{z}{6} - 1\right) = 6(0)$; $2z^2 - z - 6 = 0$; $(2z + 3)(z - 2) = 0$; $z = -\frac{3}{2}$ or $z = 2$; $\left\{-\frac{3}{2}, 2\right\}$

12. $\frac{v^2}{6} + \frac{1}{8} = \frac{v}{3}$; $24\left(\frac{v^2}{6} - \frac{v}{3} + \frac{1}{8}\right) = (0)\ 24$; $4v^2 - 8v + 3 = 0$; $(2v - 1)(2v - 3) = 0$; $v = \frac{1}{2}$ or $v = \frac{3}{2}$; $\left\{\frac{1}{2}, \frac{3}{2}\right\}$

13. $\frac{x^2}{9} + \frac{x - 1}{10} = 0$; $90\left(\frac{x^2}{9} + \frac{x - 1}{10}\right) = 90(0)$; $10x^2 + 9x - 9 = 0$; $(5x - 3)(2x + 3) = 0$; $x = \frac{3}{5}$ or $x = -\frac{3}{2}$; $\left\{-\frac{3}{2}, \frac{3}{5}\right\}$

14. $\frac{t(t - 1)}{3} = \frac{t + 1}{2}$; $6\left(\frac{t(t - 1)}{3}\right) = 6\left(\frac{t + 1}{2}\right)$; $2t^2 - 2t = 3t + 3$; $2t^2 - 5t - 3 = 0$; $(2t + 1)(t - 3) = 0$; $t = -\frac{1}{2}$ or $t = 3$; $\left\{-\frac{1}{2}, 3\right\}$

15. $\frac{y(2y - 1)}{2} = \frac{1 - y}{3}$; $6\left(\frac{y(2y - 1)}{2}\right) = 6\left(\frac{1 - y}{3}\right)$; $3y(2y - 1) = 2 - 2y$; $6y^2 - 3y = 2 - 2y$; $6y^2 - y - 2 = 0$; $(2y + 1)(3y - 2) = 0$; $y = -\frac{1}{2}$ or $y = \frac{2}{3}$; $\left\{-\frac{1}{2}, \frac{2}{3}\right\}$

16. $\frac{w(w - 1)}{3} + \frac{1}{2} = \frac{w + 1}{4}$; $12\left(\frac{w(w - 1)}{3} + \frac{1}{2}\right) = 12\left(\frac{w + 1}{4}\right)$; $4w(w - 1) + 6 = 3w + 3$; $4w^2 - 4w + 6 = 3w + 3$; $4w^2 - 7w + 3 = 0$; $(4w - 3)(w - 1) = 0$; $w = \frac{3}{4}$ or $w = 1$; $\left\{\frac{3}{4}, 1\right\}$

B 17. $\frac{x(x + 1)}{5} - \frac{x + 1}{6} = \frac{1}{3}$; $30\left(\frac{x(x + 1)}{5} - \frac{x + 1}{6}\right) = 30\left(\frac{1}{3}\right)$; $6x(x + 1) - 5(x + 1) = 10$; $6x^2 + 6x - 5x - 5 = 10$; $6x^2 + x - 15 = 0$; $(2x - 3)(3x + 5) = 0$; $x = \frac{3}{2}$ or $x = -\frac{5}{3}$; $\left\{\frac{3}{2}, -\frac{5}{3}\right\}$

18. $\frac{2t(3t + 1)}{5} - \frac{t + 1}{2} = \frac{1}{10}$; $10\left(\frac{2t(3t + 1)}{5} - \frac{t + 1}{2}\right) = 10\left(\frac{1}{10}\right)$; $4t(3t + 1) - 5(t + 1) = 1$; $12t^2 + 4t - 5t - 5 = 1$; $12t^2 - t - 6 = 0$; $(3t + 2)(4t - 3) = 0$; $t = -\frac{2}{3}$ or $t = \frac{3}{4}$; $\left\{-\frac{2}{3}, \frac{3}{4}\right\}$

19. $\frac{y(2y-1)}{4}+\frac{3}{10}=\frac{y(y+2)}{5}$; $20\left(\frac{y(2y-1)}{4}+\frac{3}{10}\right)=20\left(\frac{y(y+2)}{5}\right)$;

$5y(2y-1)+6=4y(y+2)$; $10y^2-5y+6=4y^2+8y$; $6y^2-13y+6=0$;

$(2y-3)(3y-2)=0$; $y=\frac{3}{2}$ or $y=\frac{2}{3}$; $\left\{\frac{2}{3},\frac{3}{2}\right\}$

20. $\frac{u(u-1)}{2}+\frac{1}{3}=\frac{u(2-u)}{4}$; $12\left(\frac{u(u-1)}{2}+\frac{1}{3}\right)=12\left(\frac{u(2-u)}{4}\right)$;

$6u(u-1)+4=3u(2-u)$; $6u^2-6u+4=6u-3u^2$; $9u^2-12u+4=0$;

$(3u-2)^2=0$; $u=\frac{2}{3}$; $\left\{\frac{2}{3}\right\}$

21. $\frac{y^2+4}{6}+\frac{y+1}{3}<\frac{3}{2}$; $6\left(\frac{y^2+4}{6}+\frac{y+1}{3}\right)<6\left(\frac{3}{2}\right)$; $y^2+4+2(y+1)<9$;

$y^2+2y-3<0$; $(y+3)(y-1)<0$; $-3<y<1$; $\{y:-3<y<1\}$

22. $\frac{z^2+1}{6}\geq\frac{z+2}{3}$; $6\left(\frac{z^2+1}{6}\right)\geq 6\left(\frac{z+2}{3}\right)$; $z^2+1\geq 2(z+2)$; $z^2+1\geq 2z+4$;

$z^2-2z-3\geq 0$; $(z-3)(z+1)\geq 0$; $z\geq 3$ or $z\leq -1$; $\{z:z\leq -1 \text{ or } z\geq 3\}$

23. $\frac{t^2}{6}+\frac{t-2}{4}\geq\frac{t+1}{3}$; $\left(\frac{t^2}{6}+\frac{t-2}{4}\right)12\geq\left(\frac{t+1}{3}\right)12$; $2t^2+3(t-2)\geq 4(t+1)$;

$2t^2+3t-6\geq 4t+4$; $2t^2-t-10\geq 0$; $(2t-5)(t+2)\geq 0$; $t\leq -2$ or $t\geq\frac{5}{2}$;

$\left\{t:t\leq -2 \text{ or } t\geq\frac{5}{2}\right\}$

24. $\frac{u^2}{15}\leq\frac{u+2}{6}-\frac{2}{5}$; $30\left(\frac{u^2}{15}\right)\leq 30\left(\frac{u+2}{6}-\frac{2}{5}\right)$; $2u^2\leq 5(u+2)-12$;

$2u^2\leq 5u+10-12$; $2u^2-5u+2\leq 0$; $(2u-1)(u-2)\leq 0$; $\frac{1}{2}\leq u\leq 2$;

$\left\{u:\frac{1}{2}\leq u\leq 2\right\}$

Pages 245–246 • PROBLEMS

1–4. Let n be the number.

A **1.** $\frac{5}{16}\cdot\frac{4}{5}n=15$; $\frac{20}{80}n=15$; $\frac{1}{4}n=15$; $n=60$; 60

2. $12=\frac{3}{5}\cdot\frac{10}{21}n$; $12=\frac{2}{7}n$; $84=2n$; $n=42$; 42

3. $30=0.20(0.30n)$; $30=0.06n$; $500=n$; 500

4. $0.75(0.60n)=36$; $0.45n=36$; $n=80$; 80

5. Let x = time; in hours, for both pumps to empty the ship. $\frac{x}{30}+\frac{x}{24}=1$;

$4x+5x=120$; $9x=120$; $x=\frac{40}{3}$; $13\frac{1}{3}$ h

6. Let x = time, in hours, for both belts to move the coal. $\frac{x}{21}+\frac{x}{15}=1$;

$5x+7x=105$; $12x=105$; $x=\frac{105}{12}$; $8\frac{3}{4}$ h

7. Let x = number of liters of antifreeze to be added; present solution contains $0.40(12) = 4.8$ L of antifreeze; $4.8 + x = 0.60(12 + x)$; $4.8 + x = 7.2 + 0.60x$; $0.40x = 2.4$, $x = 6$; 6 L

8. Let x = number of liters of water to be evaporated; the present solution contains $0.98(300) = 294$ L of water; $294 - x = 0.95(300 - x)$; $294 - x = 285 - 0.95x$; $9 = 0.05x$; $180 = x$; 180 L

9. Let d = distance, in km, the boat traveled upstream; $\frac{d}{12} + 2 + \frac{d}{18} = 7$; $3d + 72 + 2d = 252$; $5d = 180$; $d = 36$; 36 km

10. Let d = distance, in km, Pam jogged uphill; $\frac{d}{6} + \frac{d}{10} = \frac{4}{3}$; $5d + 3d = 40$; $8d = 40$; $d = 5$; the total distance was $2(5) = 10$ km

11. Let x = amount, in dollars, invested at 4.5%; $0.045x + 0.07(2200 - x) = 144$; $0.045x + 154 - 0.07x = 144$; $-0.025x = -10$; $x = 400$; \$400 at 4.5% and \$1800 at 7%

12. Let x = amt., in dollars, invested at 8%. $0.08x = \frac{2}{3}[0.072(24{,}000 - x)]$; $0.08x = 0.048(24{,}000 - x)$; $0.08x = 1152 - 0.048x$; $0.128x = 1152$; $x = 9000$; \$9000 at 8% and \$15,000 at 7.2%

B

13. Let x = number of liters of 7.5% solution. Then $(1.8 - x)$L of 12% solution will be used. $0.075x + 0.12(1.8 - x) = 0.10(1.8)$; $0.075x + 0.216 - 0.12x = 0.18$; $75x + 216 - 120x = 180$; $-45x = -36$; $x = 0.8$; 0.8 L of 7.5% solution and 1 L of 12% solution

14. Let x = number of mL of 18% solution to be added. $0.18x + 0.10(360) = 0.15(360 + x)$; $0.18x + 36 = 54 + 0.15x$; $0.03x = 18$; $x = 600$; 600 mL.

15. Let t = time, in h, to pave 21 km with both machines; $\frac{t}{10} + \frac{t}{18} = 21$; $9t + 5t = 1890$; $14t = 1890$; $t = 135$; 135 h

16. Let t = time, in hours, that pipe B was turned on; $\frac{t + 1.5}{8} + \frac{t}{12} = 1$; $3(t + 1.5) + 2t = 24$; $5t + 4.5 = 24$; $5t = 19.5$; $t = 3.9$; pipe B was on 3 h 54 min; the tank was full at 5:24 P.M.

17. Let d = distance, in km, she drove at 45 km/h; $\frac{d}{45} + \frac{150 - d}{75} = \frac{8}{3}$; $5d + 3(150 - d) = 600$; $5d + 450 - 3d = 600$; $2d = 150$; $d = 75$; 75 km at 45 km/h and 75 km at 75 km/h

18. Let h = height, in m, of the tower; $\frac{h}{4} + 90 + \frac{h}{5} = 270$; $\frac{h}{4} + \frac{h}{5} = 180$; $20\left(\frac{h}{4} + \frac{h}{5}\right) = 20 \cdot 180$; $9h = 3600$; $h = 400$; 400 m

C **19.** Let d = distance between the two cities, in mi; let t = time, in hours, of flight.

	Rate (mi/h)	Time (h)	Distance from San Francisco (mi)	Distance from Dallas (mi)
Commercial jet	$\frac{d}{3}$	t	$\frac{dt}{3}$	$d - \frac{dt}{3}$
Private jet	$\frac{d}{3.5}$	t	$\frac{dt}{3.5}$	$d - \frac{dt}{3.5}$

$d - \frac{dt}{3.5} = 2\left(d - \frac{dt}{3}\right)$; $d - \frac{2dt}{7} = 2d - \frac{2dt}{3}$; $1 - \frac{2t}{7} = 2 - \frac{2t}{3}$; $21 - 6t = 42 - 14t$;
$8t = 21$; $t = \frac{21}{8} = 2\frac{5}{8}$; $2\frac{5}{8}$ h

20. Let x = number of liters removed; $0.25(5 - x) + 0.75x = 0.55(5)$;
$25(5 - x) + 75x = 55(5)$; $125 - 25x + 75x = 275$; $50x = 150$; $x = 3$; 3 L

21. Let x = shorter distance, in km; $\frac{x}{60} + \frac{x + 96}{120} = \frac{2x + 96}{100}$; $10x + 5(x + 96) =$
$6(2x + 96)$; $10x + 5x + 480 = 12x + 576$; $3x = 96$; $x = 32$; $32 + 32 + 96 = 160$;
160 km

Pages 249–250 • WRITTEN EXERCISES

A **1.** $\frac{3}{t} - \frac{1}{3t} = \frac{2}{3}$; $3t\left(\frac{3}{t} - \frac{1}{3t}\right) = 3t\left(\frac{2}{3}\right)$; $9 - 1 = 2t$; $8 = 2t$; $t = 4$; $\{4\}$

2. $\frac{2}{x} + \frac{1}{4} = \frac{1}{x}$; $4x\left(\frac{2}{x} + \frac{1}{4}\right) = 4x \cdot \frac{1}{x}$; $8 + x = 4$; $x = -4$; $\{-4\}$

3. $\frac{1}{x} = \frac{2}{x - 3}$; $1(x - 3) = 2(x)$; $x - 3 = 2x$; $x = -3$; $\{-3\}$

4. $\frac{3}{u + 2} = \frac{1}{u - 2}$; $3(u - 2) = 1(u + 2)$; $3u - 6 = u + 2$; $2u = 8$; $u = 4$; $\{4\}$

5. $\frac{2}{s + 3} - \frac{1}{s - 3} = 0$; $(s + 3)(s - 3)\left(\frac{2}{s + 3} - \frac{1}{s - 3}\right) = (s + 3)(s - 3)0$;
$2(s - 3) - 1(s + 3) = 0$; $2s - 6 - s - 3 = 0$; $s - 9 = 0$; $s = 9$; $\{9\}$

6. $\frac{5}{2r + 1} - \frac{3}{2r - 1} = 0$; $5(2r - 1) - 3(2r + 1) = 0(2r + 1)(2r - 1)$;
$10r - 5 - 6r - 3 = 0$; $4r = 8$; $r = 2$; $\{2\}$

7. $\frac{t}{t - 1} = \frac{t + 2}{t}$; $t^2 = (t + 2)(t - 1)$; $t^2 = t^2 + t - 2$; $t = 2$; $\{2\}$

8. $\frac{x - 3}{x} = \frac{x - 4}{x - 2}$; $(x - 3)(x - 2) = x(x - 4)$; $x^2 - 5x + 6 = x^2 - 4x$; $6 = x$; $\{6\}$

9. $\frac{6t^2 - t - 1}{3(t^2 + 1)} = 2$; $6t^2 - t - 1 = 2[3(t^2 + 1)]$; $6t^2 - t - 1 = 6t^2 + 6$; $t = -7$; $\{-7\}$

10. $\frac{(y + 1)^2}{(y - 3)^2} = 1$; $(y + 1)^2 = 1(y - 3)^2$; $y^2 + 2y + 1 = y^2 - 6y + 9$; $8y = 8$; $y = 1$; $\{1\}$

11. $\frac{x}{x+3} + \frac{1}{x-3} = 1$; $x(x-3) + 1(x+3) = 1(x-3)(x+3)$; $x^2 - 3x + x + 3 = x^2 - 9$; $-2x = -12$; $x = 6$; $\{6\}$

12. $\frac{1}{s} + \frac{s}{s+2} = 1$; $1(s+2) + s^2 = 1(s)(s+2)$; $s + 2 + s^2 = s^2 + 2s$; $s = 2$; $\{2\}$

13. $\frac{1}{y-2} + \frac{1}{y+2} = \frac{4}{y^2-2}$; $1(y+2) + 1(y-2) = 4$; $2y = 4$; $y = 2$ (reject); no solution

14. $\frac{k}{k+1} + \frac{k}{k-2} = 2$; $k(k-2) + k(k+1) = 2(k+1)(k-2)$; $k^2 - 2k + k^2 + k = 2(k^2 - k - 2)$; $2k^2 - k = 2k^2 - 2k - 4$; $k = -4$; $\{-4\}$

15. $\frac{3}{x+1} - \frac{1}{x-2} = \frac{1}{x^2-x-2}$; $3(x-2) - 1(x+1) = 1$; $3x - 6 - x - 1 = 1$; $2x = 8$; $x = 4$; $\{4\}$

16. $\frac{1}{t-1} + \frac{1}{t+2} = \frac{3}{t^2+t-2}$; $1(t+2) + 1(t-1) = 3$; $t + 2 + t - 1 = 3$; $2t = 2$; $t = 1$ (reject); no solution

17. $\frac{6}{t} - \frac{2}{t-1} = 1$; $6(t-1) - 2(t) = 1(t)(t-1)$; $6t - 6 - 2t = t^2 - t$; $t^2 - 5t + 6 = 0$; $(t-3)(t-2) = 0$; $t = 3$ or $t = 2$; $\{2, 3\}$

18. $\frac{1}{x+1} - \frac{1}{x+2} = \frac{1}{2}$; $1(x+2) - 1(x+1) = \frac{1}{2}(x+1)(x+2)$; $x + 2 - x - 1 = \frac{1}{2}(x^2 + 3x + 2)$; $1 = \frac{1}{2}(x^2 + 3x + 2)$; $2 = x^2 + 3x + 2$; $0 = x^2 + 3x$; $x(x+3) = 0$; $x = 0$ or $x = -3$; $\{-3, 0\}$

B

19. $\frac{u}{u-2} + \frac{30}{u+2} = 9$; $(u+2)u + 30(u-2) = 9(u+2)(u-2)$; $u^2 + 2u + 30u - 60 = 9u^2 - 36$; $8u^2 - 32u + 24 = 0$; $u^2 - 4u + 3 = 0$; $(u-3)(u-1) = 0$; $u = 3$ or $u = 1$; $\{1, 3\}$

20. $\frac{1}{s+3} + \frac{1}{s-5} = \frac{1-s}{s+3}$; $\frac{1}{s-5} = \frac{1-s}{s+3} - \frac{1}{s+3}$; $\frac{1}{s-5} = \frac{-s}{s+3}$; $s + 3 = -s(s-5)$; $s + 3 = -s^2 + 5s$; $s^2 - 4s + 3 = 0$; $(s-3)(s-1) = 0$; $s = 3$ or $s = 1$; $\{1, 3\}$

21. $\frac{2}{x-1} - \frac{x}{x+3} = \frac{6}{x^2+2x-3}$; $2(x+3) - x(x-1) = 6$; $2x + 6 - x^2 + x = 6$; $x^2 - 3x = 0$; $x(x-3) = 0$; $x = 0$ or $x = 3$; $\{0, 3\}$

22. $\frac{x}{x+3} + \frac{1}{x-1} = \frac{4}{x^2+2x-3}$; $x(x-1) + 1(x+3) = 4$; $x^2 - x + x + 3 = 4$; $x^2 = 1$; $x = 1$ (reject) or $x = -1$; $\{-1\}$

23. $\frac{5}{u^2+u-6} = 2 - \frac{u-3}{u-2}$; $(u+3)(u-2) \cdot \frac{5}{(u+3)(u-2)} = \left(2 - \frac{u-3}{u-2}\right)(u+3)(u-2)$; $5 = 2(u+3)(u-2) - (u-3)(u+3)$; $5 = 2(u^2 + u - 6) - (u^2 - 9)$; $5 = 2u^2 + 2u - 12 - u^2 + 9$; $u^2 + 2u - 8 = 0$; $(u+4)(u-2) = 0$; $u = -4$ or $u = 2$ (reject); $\{-4\}$

24. $\frac{y}{y-2} - \frac{2}{y+3} = \frac{10}{y^2+y-6}$; $y(y+3) - 2(y-2) = 10$; $y^2 + 3y - 2y + 4 = 10$;
$y^2 + y - 6 = 0$; $(y+3)(y-2) = 0$; $y = -3$ (reject) or $y = 2$ (reject); no solution

25. $\frac{t}{t-1} = \frac{1}{t+2} + \frac{3}{t^2+t-2}$; $t(t+2) = t - 1 + 3$; $t^2 + 2t = t - 1 + 3$;
$t^2 + t - 2 = 0$; $(t+2)(t-1) = 0$; $t = -2$ (reject) or $t = 1$ (reject); no solution

26. $\frac{9}{t^2-2t-8} + \frac{t}{t+2} = 2$; $(t+2)(t-4)\left[\frac{9}{(t+2)(t-4)} + \frac{t}{t+2}\right] = 2(t+2)(t-4)$;
$9 + t(t-4) = 2(t^2 - 2t - 8)$; $9 + t^2 - 4t = 2t^2 - 4t - 16$; $t^2 = 25$; $t = \pm 5$; $\{5, -5\}$

27. $\left(\frac{x-3}{x+1}\right)^2 = 2 \cdot \frac{x-3}{x+1} + 3$; $(x-3)^2 = 2(x-3)(x+1) + 3(x+1)^2$; $x^2 - 6x + 9 =$
$2(x^2 - 2x - 3) + 3(x^2 + 2x + 1)$; $x^2 - 6x + 9 = 2x^2 - 4x - 6 + 3x^2 + 6x + 3$;
$4x^2 + 8x - 12 = 0$; $x^2 + 2x - 3 = 0$; $(x+3)(x-1) = 0$; $x = -3$ or $x = 1$; $\{-3, 1\}$

28. $\left(\frac{t+3}{t-1}\right)^2 = 2 + \frac{t+3}{t-1}$; $(t+3)^2 = 2(t-1)^2 + (t+3)(t-1)$; $t^2 + 6t + 9 =$
$2(t^2 - 2t + 1) + t^2 + 2t - 3$; $t^2 + 6t + 9 = 2t^2 - 4t + 2 + t^2 + 2t - 3$;
$2t^2 - 8t - 10 = 0$; $t^2 - 4t - 5 = 0$; $(t-5)(t+1) = 0$; $t = 5$ or $t = -1$; $\{-1, 5\}$

C **29.** $\frac{\frac{1}{x^2} - x^2}{\frac{1}{x} + x} = \frac{3}{2}$; $\frac{\frac{1-x^4}{x^2}}{\frac{1+x^2}{x}} = \frac{3}{2}$; $\frac{1-x^4}{x^2} \cdot \frac{x}{1+x^2} = \frac{3}{2}$; $\frac{(1-x^2)(1+x^2)}{x^2} \cdot \frac{x}{1+x^2} = \frac{3}{2}$;
$\frac{1-x^2}{x} = \frac{3}{2}$; $2(1-x^2) = 3x$; $2 - 2x^2 = 3x$; $2x^2 + 3x - 2 = 0$; $(2x-1)(x+2) = 0$;
$x = \frac{1}{2}$ or $x = -2$; $\left\{-2, \frac{1}{2}\right\}$

30. $\left(\frac{1}{x} - \frac{x}{2}\right)\left(\frac{2}{x} - x\right) = \frac{1}{2}$; $\frac{2}{x^2} - 1 - 1 + \frac{x^2}{2} = \frac{1}{2}$; $2x^2\left(\frac{2}{x^2} - 2 + \frac{x^2}{2}\right) = 2x^2\left(\frac{1}{2}\right)$;
$4 - 4x^2 + x^4 = x^2$; $x^4 - 5x^2 + 4 = 0$; $(x^2 - 4)(x^2 - 1) = 0$; $x^2 = 4$ or $x^2 = 1$;
$x = \pm 2$ or $x = \pm 1$; $\{1, -1, 2, -2\}$

Pages 250–252 • PROBLEMS

A **1.** Let x and $x + 8$ be the numbers; $\frac{1}{x} - \frac{1}{x+8} = \frac{1}{6}$; $6(x+8) - 6x = 1(x)(x+8)$;
$6x + 48 - 6x = x^2 + 8x$; $x^2 + 8x - 48 = 0$; $(x-4)(x+12) = 0$; $x = -12$ (reject) or $x = 4$; 4 and 12

2. Let x and $25 - x$ be the numbers; $\frac{1}{x} + \frac{1}{25-x} = \frac{1}{6}$; $6(25-x) + 6(x) = x(25-x)$;
$150 - 6x + 6x = 25x - x^2$; $x^2 - 25x + 150 = 0$; $(x-10)(x-15) = 0$; $x = 10$ or $x = 15$; 10 and 15

3. Let x = the number; $\frac{1}{\frac{1}{2}x} + \frac{1}{2}\left(\frac{1}{x}\right) = \frac{1}{2}$; $\frac{2}{x} + \frac{1}{2x} = \frac{1}{2}$; $4 + 1 = x$; $x = 5$; 5

4. Let x = the number; $\frac{1}{\frac{x}{3}} - \frac{1}{3}\left(\frac{1}{x}\right) = \frac{1}{3}$; $\frac{3}{x} - \frac{1}{3x} = \frac{1}{3}$; $9 - 1 = x$; $x = 8$; 8

5. Let t = time, in hours, for the new sweeper to do the job alone; $\frac{15}{60} + \frac{15}{t} = 1$; $\frac{1}{4} + \frac{15}{t} = 1$; $\frac{15}{t} = \frac{3}{4}$; $3t = 60$; $t = 20$; 20 h

6. Let t = time in hours it takes the outlet pipe to empty the tank; $\frac{t}{6} - \frac{t}{9} = 1$; $3t - 2t = 18$; $t = 18$; 18 h

7. Let x = highway mileage in mi/gal; $\frac{60}{15} + \frac{140}{x} = \frac{200}{25}$; $4 + \frac{140}{x} = 8$; $\frac{140}{x} = 4$; $4x = 140$; $x = 35$; 35 mi/gal

8.

	Rate (km/h)	Time (h)	Distance (km)
Usual trip	r	$\frac{4400}{r}$	4400
With jet stream	$1.1r$	$\frac{4400}{1.1r}$	4400

$\frac{4400}{1.1r} = \frac{4400}{r} - \frac{1}{2}$;

$\frac{4000}{r} = \frac{4400}{r} - \frac{1}{2}$; $-\frac{400}{r} = -\frac{1}{2}$;

$r = 800$; 800 km/h

9. Let c = rate, in km/h, of current;

	Rate (km/h)	Time (h)	Distance (km)
Upstream	$15 - c$	$\frac{35}{15 - c}$	35
Downstream	$15 + c$	$\frac{35}{15 + c}$	35

$\frac{35}{15 - c} + \frac{35}{15 + c} = 4.8$; $35(15 + c) + 35(15 - c) = 4.8(15 - c)(15 + c)$;

$35(15 + c + 15 - c) = 4.8(225 - c^2)$; $350(30) = 48(225 - c^2)$;

$10{,}500 = 10{,}800 - 48c^2$; $-300 = -48c^2$; $\frac{25}{4} = c^2$; $c = \pm\frac{5}{2}$; 2.5 km/h

10. Let r = rate, in km/h, of the boat in still water; $\frac{12}{r - 3} + \frac{12}{r + 3} = \frac{16}{3}$;

$3(r + 3)12 + 3(r - 3)12 = 16(r - 3)(r + 3)$; $36(r + 3) + 36(r - 3) = 16(r^2 - 9)$;
$36(r + 3 + r - 3) = 16r^2 - 144$; $36(2r) = 16r^2 - 144$; $16r^2 - 72r - 144 = 0$;

$2r^2 - 9r - 18 = 0$; $(r - 6)(2r + 3) = 0$; $r = 6$ or $r = -\frac{3}{2}$ (reject); at 6 km/h Tim could have paddled 32 km in still water.

11. Let x = number of members after 8 joined; $\frac{1200}{x - 8} - 7.5 = \frac{1200}{x}$; $\frac{12{,}000}{x - 8} - 75 = \frac{12{,}000}{x}$; $\frac{160}{x - 8} - 1 = \frac{160}{x}$; $x(160) - x(x - 8) = 160(x - 8)$; $160x - x^2 + 8x = 160x - 1280$; $x^2 - 8x - 1280 = 0$; $(x - 40)(x + 32) = 0$; $x = 40$ or $x = -32$ (reject); 40 members

12. Let x = number of people who went on the trip; $\frac{1800}{x+6} = \frac{1800}{x} - 10$;

$1800x = 1800(x+6) - 10(x)(x+6)$; $1800x = 1800x + 10{,}800 - 10x^2 - 60x$; $10x^2 + 60x - 10{,}800 = 0$; $x^2 + 6x - 1080 = 0$; $(x+36)(x-30) = 0$; $x = 30$ or $x = -36$ (reject); 30 people

13. Let r = speed, in km/h, of the jet stream; $\frac{800}{750-r} + \frac{800}{750+r} = 2.4$;

$\frac{8000}{750-r} + \frac{8000}{750+r} = 24$; $8000(750+r) + 8000(750-r) = 24(750+r)(750-r)$;
$8000(750 + r + 750 - r) = 24(562{,}500 - r^2)$; $8000(1500) = 24(562{,}500 - r^2)$;
$500{,}000 = 562{,}500 - r^2$; $r^2 = 62{,}500$; $r = \pm 250$; 250 km/h

14. Let r = speed of new planes in km/h; $\frac{2800}{r-100} - \frac{1}{2} = \frac{2800}{r}$; $2r(2800) - r(r-100) =$
$2(r-100)2800$; $5600r - r^2 + 100r = 5600r - 560{,}000$; $r^2 - 100r - 560{,}000 = 0$;
$(r+700)(r-800) = 0$; $r = -700$ (reject) or $r = 800$; 800 km/h

B **15.** Let d = distance, in mi, from Ashton to Dover; the time for the whole trip was

$\frac{\frac{d}{2}}{40} + \frac{\frac{d}{2}}{60} = \frac{d}{80} + \frac{d}{120} = \frac{3d + 2d}{240} = \frac{5d}{240} = \frac{d}{48}$ h; the average speed was

$\frac{d}{\frac{d}{48}} = 48$ mi/h

16. Let d = distance, in mi, for the whole trip; let r = average speed, in mi/h, of the

second half; $\frac{\frac{d}{2}}{36} + \frac{\frac{d}{2}}{r} = \frac{d}{45}$; $\frac{d}{72} + \frac{d}{2r} = \frac{d}{45}$; $360r\left(\frac{1}{72} + \frac{1}{2r}\right) = \frac{1}{45}\left(360r\right)$;

$5r + 180 = 8r$; $3r = 180$; $r = 60$; 60 mi/h

17. Let d = distance, in km, the train travelled; let r = rate, in km/h, of the final third;

$\frac{\frac{2d}{3}}{120} + \frac{\frac{d}{3}}{r} = \frac{d}{100}$; $\frac{d}{180} + \frac{d}{3r} = \frac{d}{100}$; $900r\left(\frac{1}{180} + \frac{1}{3r}\right) = 900r\left(\frac{1}{100}\right)$; $5r + 300 = 9r$;

$4r = 300$; $r = 75$; 75 km/h

18. Let d = distance, in km, of her trip; let r = speed, in km/h, of the final 80%;

$\frac{0.20d}{40} + \frac{0.80d}{r} = \frac{d}{75}$; $\frac{2d}{40} + \frac{8d}{r} = \frac{10d}{75}$; $\frac{1}{20} + \frac{8}{r} = \frac{2}{15}$; $3r + 480 = 8r$; $5r = 480$;

$r = 96$; 96 km/h

19. Let t = time, in h, for pipe C to drain; $\frac{3}{5} + \frac{3}{t-2} - \frac{3}{t} = 1$;

$3(t-2)t + 3(5t) - 3(5)(t-2) = 5(t)(t-2)$; $3t^2 - 6t + 15t - 15t + 30 = 5t^2 - 10t$;
$2t^2 - 4t - 30 = 0$; $t^2 - 2t - 15 = 0$; $(t-5)(t+3) = 0$; $t = 5$ or $t = -3$ (reject); 5 h

20. Let r = speed, in m/s, of the elevator going up; $\frac{240}{r} + 12 + \frac{240}{r+1} = 120$;

$\frac{20}{r} + 1 + \frac{20}{r+1} = 10$; $20(r+1) + 1(r)(r+1) + 20r = 10r(r+1)$;

$20r + 20 + r^2 + r + 20r = 10r^2 + 10r$; $9r^2 - 31r - 20 = 0$; $(r-4)(9r+5) = 0$;

$r = 4$ or $r = -\frac{5}{9}$ (reject); 4 m/s

C **21.** Let x = the number; $\frac{1}{2}\left(\frac{1}{x} + \frac{1}{5}\right) = \frac{1}{8}$; $\frac{1}{2}\left(\frac{5+x}{5x}\right) = \frac{1}{8}$; $\frac{5+x}{10x} = \frac{1}{8}$; $40 + 8x = 10x$;

$40 = 2x$; $x = 20$; 20

22. Let x and $x + 12$ be the numbers; $\frac{1}{2}\left(\frac{1}{x} + \frac{1}{x+12}\right) = \frac{1}{5}$; $\frac{1}{2}\left(\frac{x+12+x}{x(x+12)}\right) = \frac{1}{5}$;

$\frac{1}{2}\left(\frac{2x+12}{x(x+12)}\right) = \frac{1}{5}$; $\frac{x+6}{x(x+12)} = \frac{1}{5}$; $5x + 30 = x(x+12)$; $5x + 30 = x^2 + 12x$;

$x^2 + 7x - 30 = 0$; $(x+10)(x-3) = 0$; $x = -10$ (reject) or $x = 3$; 3 and 15

23. Let d = distance of trip; let s = the average speed of the trip; then the time of the first half of the trip + the time of the second half of the trip = the total time of the trip, or $\frac{\frac{1}{2}d}{u} + \frac{\frac{1}{2}d}{v} = \frac{d}{s}$; $\frac{\frac{1}{2}}{u} + \frac{\frac{1}{2}}{v} = \frac{1}{s}$; $\frac{1}{2}\left(\frac{1}{u} + \frac{1}{v}\right) = \frac{1}{s}$.

$\therefore$ s is the harmonic mean of u and v.

Page 252 • MIXED REVIEW EXERCISES

1. $\frac{x^2 - 1}{1 - x} = \frac{(x-1)(x+1)}{-(x-1)} = -(x+1) = -x - 1$

2. $\frac{8t^2 - 2}{8t + 4} = \frac{2(4t^2 - 1)}{4(2t+1)} = \frac{(2t-1)(2t+1)}{2(2t+1)} = \frac{2t-1}{2}$ **3.** $\frac{32m^5n}{24m^2n^2} = \frac{4m^3}{3n}$

4. $\frac{(4z^3)^{-2}}{(2z^4)^{-1}} = \frac{2z^4}{(4z^3)^2} = \frac{2z^4}{16z^6} = \frac{1}{8z^2}$ **5.** $\frac{\left(\frac{1}{a} + \frac{1}{b^2}\right)a^2b^2}{\left(\frac{1}{a^2} + \frac{1}{b}\right)a^2b^2} = \frac{ab^2 + a^2}{b^2 + a^2b} = \frac{a(b^2+a)}{b(b+a^2)}$

6. $\frac{c^2 - c - 12}{c^2 - 2c - 8} = \frac{(c-4)(c+3)}{(c-4)(c+2)} = \frac{c+3}{c+2}$

7. $\frac{2x-1}{3} = \frac{3x+2}{6}$; $6(2x-1) = 3(3x+2)$; $12x - 6 = 9x + 6$; $3x = 12$; $x = 4$; $\{4\}$

8. $3 - \frac{1}{2}x \le 4$; $-\frac{1}{2}x \le 1$, $x \ge -2$; $\{x : x \ge -2\}$

9. $\frac{x^2}{6} = \frac{x}{3} + \frac{5}{2}$; $x^2 = 2x + 15$; $x^2 - 2x - 15 = 0$; $(x-5)(x+3) = 0$; $x = 5$ or $x = -3$; $\{-3, 5\}$

10. $\frac{3x}{4} + 1 > \frac{x-1}{2}$; $3x + 4 > 2(x-1)$; $3x + 4 > 2x - 2$; $x > -6$; $\{x : x > -6\}$

11. $\frac{3}{2}x - 1 = 5; \frac{3}{2}x = 6; x = 6\left(\frac{2}{3}\right); x = 4; \{4\}$

12. $\frac{1}{2}x^2 + \frac{7}{3}x - 4 < 0; 3x^2 + 14x - 24 < 0; (3x - 4)(x + 6) < 0; x < \frac{4}{3}$ and $x > -6$; $\left\{x : -6 < x < \frac{4}{3}\right\}$

Page 254 • APPLICATION

1. $\frac{1}{R_c} = \frac{1}{10} + \frac{1}{15} = \frac{1}{6}; R_c = 6; R = 6 + 8 + 4 = 18; X = \frac{27}{18} = 1.5; 1.5A$

2. $\frac{1}{R} = \frac{1}{15} + \frac{1}{15} + \frac{1}{15} = \frac{3}{15} = \frac{1}{5}; R = 5; 2.5 = \frac{E}{5}; E = 12.5; 12.5V$

3. $\frac{1}{R} = \frac{1}{X} + \frac{1}{X + 5} = \frac{X + 5 + X}{X^2 + 5X}; R = \frac{X^2 + 5X}{2X + 5}; 2 = \frac{12}{\frac{X^2 + 5X}{2X + 5}}; 2\left(\frac{X^2 + 5X}{2X + 5}\right) = 12;$

$\frac{X^2 + 5X}{2X + 5} = 6; X^2 + 5X = 12X + 30; X^2 - 7X - 30 = 0; (X + 3)(X - 10) = 0;$

$X = -3$ (reject) or $X = 10$; $10\ \Omega$

4. $\frac{1}{R_c} = \frac{1}{X} + \frac{1}{X} = \frac{2}{X}; R_c = \frac{X}{2}; R = \frac{X}{2} + 5 = \frac{X + 10}{2}; 1.5 = \frac{24}{\frac{X + 10}{2}}; 1.5\left(\frac{X + 10}{2}\right) = 24;$

$\frac{X + 10}{2} = 16; X + 10 = 32; X = 22; 22\ \Omega$

Pages 255–256 • CHAPTER REVIEW

1. b; $\frac{18x^3y}{12x^2y^4} = \frac{(6x^2y)(3x)}{(6x^2y)(2y^3)} = \frac{3x}{2y^3}$ **2.** d; $\frac{(a^2bc^3)^3}{(-ab^3c^2)^2} = \frac{a^6b^3c^9}{a^2b^6c^4} = \frac{a^4c^5}{b^3}$

3. a; $\frac{(p^2q)^{-1}}{p^2q^{-1}} = \frac{q}{p^2(p^2q)} = \frac{1}{p^4}$ **4.** d; $\left(\frac{m^2}{n}\right)^{-2} \cdot \left(\frac{m^0}{n^{-1}}\right)^3 = \frac{m^{-4}}{n^{-2}} \cdot \frac{1^3}{n^{-3}} = \frac{m^{-4}}{n^{-5}} = \frac{n^5}{m^4}$

5. b **6.** b; $\frac{(6 \times 10^{-2})(2 \times 10^3)}{3 \times 10^{-1}} = 4 \times 10^2$ **7.** d; $\frac{y^2 - 4}{y^2 + y - 6} = \frac{(y - 2)(y + 2)}{(y + 3)(y - 2)} = \frac{y + 2}{y + 3}$

8. a; $f(x) = \frac{2x^2 - x - 1}{2x^2 + 3x - 2} = \frac{(2x + 1)(x - 1)}{(2x - 1)(x + 2)} = 0$ if $x = 1$ or $x = -\frac{1}{2}$

9. a; $\frac{u^2 + 3u}{u^2 + 2u - 3} \cdot \frac{u^3 - u}{u^2 - u - 2} = \frac{u(u + 3)}{(u + 3)(u - 1)} \cdot \frac{u(u^2 - 1)}{(u - 2)(u + 1)} = \frac{u^2(u - 1)(u + 1)}{(u - 1)(u - 2)(u + 1)} =$

$\frac{u^2}{u - 2}$

10. c; $\frac{m^2}{n^3} \cdot \frac{n}{m^4} \div \frac{1}{mn} = \frac{m^2}{n^3} \cdot \frac{n}{m^4} \cdot \frac{mn}{1} = \frac{m^3n^2}{n^3m^4} = \frac{1}{mn}$

11. b; $\frac{a + 2}{2a} + \frac{1 - a}{a^2} = \frac{a(a + 2) + 2(1 - a)}{2a^2} = \frac{a^2 + 2a + 2 - 2a}{2a^2} = \frac{a^2 + 2}{2a^2}$

12. c; $\frac{x - 1}{x + 1} - \frac{x^2 - x - 6}{x^2 + 4x + 3} = \frac{(x + 3)(x - 1) - (x^2 - x - 6)}{(x + 3)(x + 1)} = \frac{x^2 + 2x - 3 - (x^2 - x - 6)}{(x + 3)(x + 1)} =$

$\frac{3x + 3}{(x + 3)(x + 1)} = \frac{3(x + 1)}{(x + 3)(x + 1)} = \frac{3}{x + 3}$

13. d; $\dfrac{y - \dfrac{2}{y+1}}{1 - \dfrac{2}{y+1}} = \dfrac{y(y+1) - 2}{(y+1) - 2} = \dfrac{y^2 + y - 2}{y - 1} = \dfrac{(y+2)(y-1)}{y-1} = y + 2$

14. a; $\dfrac{x+1}{6} < x - \dfrac{3x-2}{4}$; $2(x+1) < 12x - 3(3x-2)$; $2x + 2 < 12x - 9x + 6$; $2x + 2 < 3x + 6$, $-4 < x$; $\{x : x > -4\}$

15. c; $\dfrac{x(x-2)}{6} = \dfrac{x+1}{8}$; $4(x)(x-2) = 3(x+1)$; $4x^2 - 8x = 3x + 3$; $4x^2 - 11x - 3 = 0$; $(x-3)(4x+1) = 0$; $x = 3$ or $x = -\frac{1}{4}$; $\left\{-\frac{1}{4}, 3\right\}$

16. c; let x = mL of 8% solution to be added; $0.08x + 0.03(600) = 0.05(600 + x)$; $8x + 3(600) = 5(600 + x)$; $8x + 1800 = 3000 + 5x$; $3x = 1200$; $x = 400$; 400 mL

17. b; $\dfrac{2}{x+2} + \dfrac{x^2}{(x+2)(x-2)} = \dfrac{1}{x-2}$; $2(x-2) + x^2 = 1(x+2)$; $2x - 4 + x^2 = x + 2$; $x^2 + x - 6 = 0$; $(x+3)(x-2) = 0$; $x = 2$ (reject) or $x = -3$; $\{-3\}$

18. b; let r = rate in still water; $\dfrac{30}{r-2} + \dfrac{30}{r+2} = 8$; $30(r+2) + 30(r-2) = 8(r-2)(r+2)$; $30(r + 2 + r - 2) = 8(r^2 - 4)$; $60r = 8r^2 - 32$; $8r^2 - 60r - 32 = 0$; $2r^2 - 15r - 8 = 0$; $(r-8)(2r+1) = 0$; $r = 8$ or $r = -\frac{1}{2}$ (reject); 8 km/h

Page 257 • CHAPTER TEST

1. $\dfrac{(3xy^3)^2}{6x^5y^4} = \dfrac{9x^2y^6}{6x^5y^4} = \dfrac{(3x^2y^4)(3y^2)}{(3x^2y^4)(2x^3)} = \dfrac{3y^2}{2x^3}$ **2.** $\dfrac{m^4}{4n^3}\left(\dfrac{2n}{m^3}\right)^3 = \dfrac{m^4}{4n^3}\left(\dfrac{8n^3}{m^9}\right) = \dfrac{2}{m^5}$

3. $pq^4(p^{-1}q^2)^{-2} = pq^4(p^2q^{-4}) = p^3 \cdot 1 = p^3$

4. $\left(\dfrac{u^2}{v}\right)^{-2}\left(\dfrac{v^3}{u}\right)^{-1} = \left(\dfrac{u^{-4}}{v^{-2}}\right)\left(\dfrac{v^{-3}}{u^{-1}}\right) = u^{-3}v^{-1} = \dfrac{1}{u^3v}$

5. $(2.1 \times 10^3)(1.6 \times 10^{-5}) = (2.1 \times 1.6) \times (10^3 \times 10^{-5}) = 3.36 \times 10^{-2} \approx 3.4 \times 10^{-2}$

6. $\dfrac{5.2 \times 10^2}{1.2 \times 10^{-4}} = \dfrac{5.2}{1.2} \times 10^{2-(-4)} \approx 4.3 \times 10^6$

7. $f(x) = \dfrac{3x - 2}{x^2 - x - 12} = \dfrac{3x - 2}{(x-4)(x+3)}$ **a.** reals except 4 and -3 **b.** $\dfrac{2}{3}$

8. $f(x) = \dfrac{x^2 - x - 12}{3x - 2} = \dfrac{(x-4)(x+3)}{3x - 2}$ **a.** reals except $\dfrac{2}{3}$ **b.** 4, -3

9. $\dfrac{6x^3}{y^2} \div \dfrac{3xy}{2} = \dfrac{6x^3}{y^2} \cdot \dfrac{2}{3xy} = \dfrac{12x^3}{3xy^3} = \dfrac{4x^2}{y^3}$

10. $\dfrac{u^2 - 9}{u + 2} \div \dfrac{u + 3}{u^2 - 4} = \dfrac{(u-3)(u+3)}{u+2} \cdot \dfrac{(u+2)(u-2)}{u+3} = (u-3)(u-2)$

11. $\dfrac{p-2}{2p} + \dfrac{p+3}{3p} = \dfrac{3(p-2) + 2(p+3)}{6p} = \dfrac{3p - 6 + 2p + 6}{6p} = \dfrac{5p}{6p} = \dfrac{5}{6}$

12. $\dfrac{1}{s-1} - \dfrac{2}{s^2 - 1} = \dfrac{1}{s-1} - \dfrac{2}{(s-1)(s+1)} = \dfrac{s + 1 - 2}{(s+1)(s-1)} = \dfrac{s-1}{(s+1)(s-1)} = \dfrac{1}{s+1}$

13. $\dfrac{\frac{a}{b}+1}{\frac{b}{a}+1} = \dfrac{\frac{a+b}{b}}{\frac{b+a}{a}} = \dfrac{a+b}{b} \cdot \dfrac{a}{b+a} = \dfrac{a}{b}$

14. $\dfrac{\frac{x+y}{x-y}}{\frac{y-x}{xy}} = \dfrac{x+y}{x-y} \cdot \dfrac{xy}{(y-x)} = -\dfrac{xy(x+y)}{(x-y)^2}$

15. $\dfrac{x+7}{8} - \dfrac{1}{2} \geq \dfrac{x}{4}$; $x + 7 - 4 \geq 2x$; $3 \geq x$; $\{x : x \leq 3\}$

16. $\dfrac{x^2}{9} = \dfrac{x+2}{2}$; $2x^2 = 9(x+2)$; $2x^2 = 9x + 18$; $2x^2 - 9x - 18 = 0$;

$(x - 6)(2x + 3) = 0$; $x = 6$ or $x = -\dfrac{3}{2}$; $\left\{-\dfrac{3}{2}, 6\right\}$

17. Let t = time, in days, that both crews work together; $\dfrac{t+2}{6} + \dfrac{t}{4} = 1$;

$2(t + 2) + 3t = 12$; $2t + 4 + 3t = 12$; $5t = 8$; $t = \dfrac{8}{5} = 1\dfrac{3}{5}$; $1\dfrac{3}{5}$ days

18. $\dfrac{3}{x^2 - 2x - 8} + \dfrac{1}{x+2} = \dfrac{4}{x^2 - 16}$; $\dfrac{3}{(x-4)(x+2)} + \dfrac{1}{x+2} = \dfrac{4}{(x-4)(x+4)}$;

$3(x + 4) + 1(x - 4)(x + 4) = 4(x + 2)$; $3x + 12 + x^2 - 16 = 4x + 8$;
$x^2 - x - 12 = 0$; $(x - 4)(x + 3) = 0$; $x = 4$ (reject) or $x = -3$; $\{-3\}$

19. Let n = number of members in the club after four joined; $\dfrac{400}{n-4} - 5 = \dfrac{400}{n}$;

$400n - 5(n)(n - 4) = 400(n - 4)$; $400n - 5n^2 + 20n = 400n - 1600$;
$5n^2 - 20n - 1600 = 0$; $n^2 - 4n - 320 = 0$; $(n - 20)(n + 16) = 0$; $n = 20$ or
$n = -16$ (reject); 20 members

CHAPTER 6 • Irrational and Complex Numbers

Pages 262–263 • WRITTEN EXERCISES

A **1.** **a.** 4 **b.** -4 **c.** not real **d.** 2 **2.** **a.** 8 **b.** not real **c.** 4 **d.** -4

3. **a.** 9 **b.** -9 **c.** not real **d.** 3 **4.** **a.** 12 **b.** not real **c.** -12 **d.** not real

5. **a.** 0.1 **b.** not real **c.** 0.1 **d.** -0.1 **6.** **a.** 0.2 **b.** -0.2 **c.** 0.02 **d.** not real

7. **a.** 7 **b.** 7 **c.** 7 **d.** -7 **8.** **a.** 5 **b.** not real **c.** -5 **d.** -5

9. **a.** $\frac{1}{8}$ **b.** $\frac{1}{8}$ **c.** $-\frac{1}{4}$ **d.** $-\frac{1}{4}$ **10.** **a.** $\frac{1}{4}$ **b.** $\frac{9}{4}$ **c.** $\frac{1}{2}$ **d.** $\frac{3}{2}$

11. **a.** 10 **b.** $\sqrt{10^4} = \sqrt{(10^2)^2} = 10^2$ **c.** $\sqrt{10^6} = \sqrt{(10^3)^2} = 10^3$
d. $\sqrt{10^{20}} = \sqrt{(10^{10})^2} = 10^{10}$

12. **a.** $\sqrt[3]{10^{-3}} = \sqrt[3]{(10^{-1})^3} = 10^{-1} = \frac{1}{10}$ **b.** $\sqrt[3]{10^{-6}} = \sqrt[3]{(10^{-2})^3} = 10^{-2} = \frac{1}{10^2}$
c. $\sqrt[3]{10^{-9}} = \sqrt[3]{(10^{-3})^3} = 10^{-3} = \frac{1}{10^3}$ **d.** $\sqrt[3]{10^{-30}} = \sqrt[3]{(10^{-10})^3} = 10^{-10} = \frac{1}{10^{10}}$

13. **a.** $\sqrt{a^2} = |a|$ **b.** $\sqrt{a^4} = |a^2| = a^2$ **c.** $\sqrt[3]{a^6} = a^2$ **d.** $\sqrt[6]{a^6} = |a|$

14. **a.** not real when $a \neq 0$ **b.** $\sqrt{(-a)^2} = |-a| = |a|$ **c.** $\sqrt[4]{a^4} = |a|$ **d.** $\sqrt{a^6} = |a^3|$

15. $x^2 = 144; x = \pm 12$ **16.** $y^2 = 0; y = 0$

17. $x^2 + 9 = 0; x^2 = -9$; no real roots **18.** $y^2 - 7 = 0; y^2 = 7; y = \pm\sqrt{7}$

19. $9x^2 = 4; x^2 = \frac{4}{9}; x = \pm\frac{2}{3}$ **20.** $25y^2 = -16; y^2 = -\frac{16}{25}$; no real roots.

21. $16y^2 = 25; y^2 = \frac{25}{16}; y = \pm\frac{5}{4}$ **22.** $9x^2 - 81 = 0; 9x^2 = 81; x^2 = 9; x = \pm 3$

23. $4 - 16x^2 = 0; 16x^2 = 4; x^2 = \frac{1}{4}; x = \pm\frac{1}{2}$

24. $0 = 4 + 16x^2; 16x^2 = -4; x^2 = -\frac{1}{4}$; no real roots

25. $81 - 9x^2 = 0; -9x^2 = -81; x^2 = 9; x = \pm 3$

26. $25y^2 + 16 = 17; 25y^2 = 1; y^2 = \frac{1}{25}; y = \pm\frac{1}{5}$

B **27.** $\sqrt{(x+5)^2} = x + 5$ if $x + 5 \geq 0; x \geq -5$

28. $\sqrt{(a-2)^2} = 2 - a$ if $a - 2 \leq 0; a \leq 2$

29. $\sqrt[3]{(n+1)^3} = n + 1$; true for all reals **30.** $\sqrt{y^4} = |y^2| = y^2$; true for all reals

31. $\sqrt{c^2 + 4c + 4} = \sqrt{(c+2)^2} = |c + 2|$; true for all reals

32. $\sqrt{b^2 - 2b + 1} = \sqrt{(b-1)^2} = |b - 1| = b - 1$ if $b - 1 \geq 0; b \geq 1$

33. **a.** $x \geq -1$ **b.** $x \geq 1$ **c.** all reals **d.** $x^2 - 1 \geq 0; x^2 \geq 1; |x| \geq 1; x \leq -1$ or $x \geq 1$

34. **a.** $4 - x \geq 0; x \leq 4$ **b.** $4 - x^2 \geq 0; x^2 \leq 4; -2 \leq x \leq 2$ **c.** all reals
d. $4 + x^2 \geq 0$ for all reals

C **35.** $x^3 - 9x \geq 0$; $x(x^2 - 9) \geq 0$; ($x \geq 0$ and $x^2 \geq 9$) or ($x \leq 0$ and $x^2 \leq 9$); ($x \geq 0$ and ($x \leq -3$ or $x \geq 3$)) or ($x \leq 0$ and $-3 \leq x \leq 3$); $x \geq 3$ or $-3 \leq x \leq 0$

36. $16x - x^2 \geq 0$; $x(16 - x) \geq 0$; ($x \geq 0$ and $16 \geq x$) or ($x \leq 0$ and $16 \leq x$); $0 \leq x \leq 16$

37. $\sqrt{x} - x \geq 0$; $\sqrt{x}(1 - \sqrt{x}) \geq 0$; $x \geq 0$ and $1 - \sqrt{x} \geq 0$; $x \geq 0$ and $1 \geq \sqrt{x}$; $x \geq 0$ and $x \leq 1$; $0 \leq x \leq 1$

38. $x - \sqrt{x} \geq 0$; $\sqrt{x}(\sqrt{x} - 1) \geq 0$; $x \geq 0$ and $\sqrt{x} - 1 \geq 0$; $x \geq 0$ and $\sqrt{x} \geq 1$; $x \geq 0$ and $x \geq 1$; $x \geq 1$

Page 263 • MIXED REVIEW EXERCISES

1. $\frac{x}{x-1} = \frac{2x}{x+2}$; $x(x + 2) = 2x(x - 1)$; $x^2 + 2x = 2x^2 - 2x$; $x^2 - 4x = 0$; $x(x - 4) = 0$; $x = 0$ or $x = 4$; $\{0, 4\}$

2. $-3y = y^2$; $y^2 + 3y = 0$; $y(y + 3) = 0$; $y = 0$ or $y = -3$, $\{-3, 0\}$

3. $\frac{3n-1}{4} + \frac{n+1}{2} = 4$; $3n - 1 + 2(n + 1) = 4(4)$; $3n - 1 + 2n + 2 = 16$; $5n = 15$; $n = 3$; $\{3\}$

4. $|5 - 2w| = 1$; $5 - 2w = 1$ or $5 - 2w = -1$; $2w = 4$ or $2w = 6$; $w = 2$ or $w = 3$; $\{2, 3\}$

5. $\frac{d}{d+2} + \frac{3}{d} = 2$; $d(d) + 3(d + 2) = 2(d + 2)(d)$; $d^2 + 3d + 6 = 2d^2 + 4d$; $d^2 + d - 6 = 0$; $(d - 2)(d + 3) = 0$; $d = 2$ or $d = -3$; $\{-3, 2\}$

6. $\frac{u^2}{3} = \frac{u+1}{6}$; $2u^2 = u + 1$; $2u^2 - u - 1 = 0$; $(2u + 1)(u - 1) = 0$; $u = -\frac{1}{2}$ or $u = 1$; $\left\{-\frac{1}{2}, 1\right\}$

7. $3(2m - 1) = 4m + 7$; $6m - 3 = 4m + 7$; $2m = 10$; $m = 5$; $\{5\}$

8. $2p^2 = 12 - 5p$; $2p^2 + 5p - 12 = 0$; $(2p - 3)(p + 4) = 0$; $p = \frac{3}{2}$ or $p = -4$; $\left\{-4, \frac{3}{2}\right\}$

9. $3k + 6 = 3(k + 4)$; $3k + 6 = 3k + 12$; $6 = 12$; no solution

10. $\frac{1}{f} + \frac{1}{f-1} = \frac{1}{f^2 - f}$; $f - 1 + f = 1$; $2f - 1 = 1$; $2f = 2$; $f = 1$; since $f \neq 1$, no solution

Page 263 • CALCULATOR KEY-IN

1. 105 **2.** 1005 **3.** 0.99 **4.** 0.999 **5.** $\sqrt{4 \times 10^{10}} = 2 \times 10^5$
6. $\sqrt{2.5 \times 10^{-11}} = 5 \times 10^{-6}$ **7.** Both expressions equal 0.51763809 on a calculator.

Pages 267–269 • WRITTEN EXERCISES

A **1.** $2\sqrt{13}$ **2.** $5\sqrt{5}$ **3.** $9\sqrt{2}$ **4.** $11\sqrt{3}$ **5.** 14 **6.** 18 **7.** $\frac{\sqrt{8}}{\sqrt{9}} = \frac{2\sqrt{2}}{3}$

8. $\frac{\sqrt{50}}{\sqrt{49}} = \frac{5\sqrt{2}}{7}$ **9.** $\frac{\sqrt{4}}{\sqrt{3}} = \frac{2}{\sqrt{3}} \cdot \frac{\sqrt{3}}{\sqrt{3}} = \frac{2\sqrt{3}}{3}$ **10.** $\frac{\sqrt{9}}{\sqrt{5}} = \frac{3}{\sqrt{5}} \cdot \frac{\sqrt{5}}{\sqrt{5}} = \frac{3\sqrt{5}}{5}$

11. $\frac{4}{\sqrt{2}} \cdot \frac{\sqrt{2}}{\sqrt{2}} = \frac{4\sqrt{2}}{2} = 2\sqrt{2}$ **12.** $\frac{6}{\sqrt{3}} \cdot \frac{\sqrt{3}}{\sqrt{3}} = \frac{6\sqrt{3}}{3} = 2\sqrt{3}$

13. $\sqrt{\frac{270}{6}} = \sqrt{45} = 3\sqrt{5}$ **14.** $\sqrt{\frac{96}{3}} = \sqrt{32} = 4\sqrt{2}$

15. $\sqrt{6 \cdot 5} \cdot \sqrt{6 \cdot 7} = \sqrt{6^2 \cdot 5 \cdot 7} = 6\sqrt{35}$

16. $\sqrt{7 \cdot 5} \cdot \sqrt{7 \cdot 3} = \sqrt{7^2 \cdot 5 \cdot 3} = 7\sqrt{15}$ **17.** $\sqrt{\frac{6 \cdot 2}{3}} = \sqrt{4} = 2$

18. $\sqrt{\frac{15 \cdot 3}{5}} = \sqrt{9} = 3$ **19.** $\sqrt[3]{125 \cdot 2} = 5\sqrt[3]{2}$ **20.** $\sqrt[3]{27 \cdot 5} = 3\sqrt[3]{5}$

21. $\frac{\sqrt[3]{5}}{\sqrt[3]{4}} \cdot \frac{\sqrt[3]{2}}{\sqrt[3]{2}} = \frac{\sqrt[3]{10}}{\sqrt[3]{8}} = \frac{\sqrt[3]{10}}{2}$ **22.** $\frac{\sqrt[3]{2}}{\sqrt[3]{9}} \cdot \frac{\sqrt[3]{3}}{\sqrt[3]{3}} = \frac{\sqrt[3]{6}}{3}$ **23.** $\frac{9\sqrt{2}}{3\sqrt{2}} = 3$ **24.** $\frac{4\sqrt{3}}{2\sqrt{3}} = 2$

25. $2^2(\sqrt{7})^2 = 4 \cdot 7 = 28$ **26.** $3^2(\sqrt{6})^2 = 9 \cdot 6 = 54$

27. $\sqrt[3]{9} \cdot \sqrt[3]{5} \cdot \sqrt[3]{3} \cdot \sqrt[3]{4} = \sqrt[3]{27} \cdot \sqrt[3]{20} = 3\sqrt[3]{20}$

28. $\sqrt[3]{4} \cdot \sqrt[3]{5} \cdot \sqrt[3]{2} \cdot \sqrt[3]{7} = \sqrt[3]{8} \cdot \sqrt[3]{35} = 2\sqrt[3]{35}$

29. $\sqrt[3]{\frac{60}{36}} = \sqrt[3]{\frac{5}{3}} = \frac{\sqrt[3]{5}}{\sqrt[3]{3}} \cdot \frac{\sqrt[3]{9}}{\sqrt[3]{9}} = \frac{\sqrt[3]{45}}{3}$ **30.** $\sqrt[3]{\frac{175}{50}} = \sqrt[3]{\frac{7}{2}} = \frac{\sqrt[3]{7}}{\sqrt[3]{2}} \cdot \frac{\sqrt[3]{4}}{\sqrt[3]{4}} = \frac{\sqrt[3]{28}}{2}$

31. **a.** $4\sqrt{2}$ **b.** $2\sqrt[3]{4}$ **c.** $2\sqrt[4]{2}$ **d.** 2

32. **a.** $\frac{\sqrt{3}}{2\sqrt{2}} \cdot \frac{\sqrt{2}}{\sqrt{2}} = \frac{\sqrt{6}}{4}$ **b.** $\frac{\sqrt[3]{3}}{\sqrt[3]{8}} = \frac{\sqrt[3]{3}}{2}$ **c.** $\frac{\sqrt[4]{3}}{\sqrt[4]{8}} \cdot \frac{\sqrt[4]{2}}{\sqrt[4]{2}} = \frac{\sqrt[4]{6}}{2}$ **d.** $\frac{\sqrt[5]{3}}{\sqrt[5]{8}} \cdot \frac{\sqrt[5]{4}}{\sqrt[5]{4}} = \frac{\sqrt[5]{12}}{2}$

33. 6.24 **34.** 29.50 **35.** 7.66 **36.** 19.40 **37.** 3.46 **38.** 5.48

39. $\sqrt{9 \cdot 2 \cdot x^2} = 3|x|\sqrt{2}$ **40.** $\sqrt{4 \cdot 3 \cdot x^4 \cdot x} = 2x^2\sqrt{3x}$

41. $\sqrt[3]{125 \cdot 3 \cdot a^3 \cdot a^2} = 5a\sqrt[3]{3a^2}$ **42.** $\sqrt[3]{8 \cdot 2 \cdot c^3 \cdot c} = 2c\sqrt[3]{2c}$

43. $\frac{\sqrt{x^2}}{\sqrt{y^2 \cdot y}} = \frac{|x|}{y\sqrt{y}} \cdot \frac{\sqrt{y}}{\sqrt{y}} = \frac{|x|\sqrt{y}}{y^2}$ **44.** $\frac{\sqrt{y^2}}{\sqrt{x^5}} \cdot \frac{\sqrt{x}}{\sqrt{x}} = \frac{|y|\sqrt{x}}{x^3}$

45. $\frac{3\sqrt[3]{a}}{b\sqrt[3]{4b}} \cdot \frac{\sqrt[3]{2b^2}}{\sqrt[3]{2b^2}} = \frac{3\sqrt[3]{2ab^2}}{b\sqrt[3]{8b^3}} = \frac{3\sqrt[3]{2ab^2}}{2b^2}$ **46.** $\frac{2\sqrt[3]{c}}{d\sqrt[3]{9d^2}} \cdot \frac{\sqrt[3]{3d}}{\sqrt[3]{3d}} = \frac{2\sqrt[3]{3cd}}{3d^2}$

B **47.** $\sqrt{16(a + b)} = 4\sqrt{a + b}$ **48.** $\sqrt{9(a^2 - b^2)} = 3\sqrt{a^2 - b^2}$

49. $\sqrt{2(a + 1)^2} = |a + 1|\sqrt{2}$ **50.** $\sqrt{3(x - 2)^2} = |x - 2|\sqrt{3}$

51. $\sqrt{\frac{1}{4} \cdot \frac{1}{9}} = \frac{1}{6}$ **52.** $\sqrt[3]{\frac{1}{32}} = \frac{1}{2\sqrt[3]{4}} \cdot \frac{\sqrt[3]{2}}{\sqrt[3]{2}} = \frac{\sqrt[3]{2}}{4}$ **53.** $\sqrt[3]{\frac{1}{4} + \frac{1}{8}} = \sqrt[3]{\frac{3}{8}} = \frac{\sqrt[3]{3}}{2}$

54. $\sqrt{\frac{1}{16} + \frac{1}{9}} = \sqrt{\frac{25}{144}} = \frac{5}{12}$ **55.** $\sqrt[3]{(3 - 4)^{-1}} = \sqrt[3]{(-1)^{-1}} = -1$

56. $\sqrt{(4 + 8)^{-1}} = \sqrt{\frac{1}{12}} = \frac{1}{2\sqrt{3}} \cdot \frac{\sqrt{3}}{\sqrt{3}} = \frac{\sqrt{3}}{6}$

57. $\sqrt[6]{(4 \cdot 3)^8} = 12\sqrt[6]{12^2} = 12\sqrt[3]{\sqrt[2]{12^2}} = 12\sqrt[3]{12}$

58. $\sqrt[4]{4 \cdot 3^8} = 9\sqrt[4]{4} = 9\sqrt{\sqrt{2^2}} = 9\sqrt{2}$ **59.** $\sqrt{\frac{9 \cdot 3 \cdot x^2 \cdot x}{y^2}} = \frac{3x\sqrt{3x}}{|y|}$

60. $\sqrt[3]{\frac{8 \cdot 4 \cdot b^3 \cdot b}{a^3}} = \frac{2b\sqrt[3]{4b}}{a}$ **61.** $\frac{\sqrt{3a} \cdot \sqrt{15}}{\sqrt{a^2}} = \frac{3\sqrt{5a}}{a}$ **62.** $\sqrt{\frac{2}{x^2 \cdot x}} \cdot \sqrt{6x} = \frac{2\sqrt{3}}{x}$

63. $\sqrt[3]{\frac{2 \cdot 3}{y^3 \cdot y}} \cdot \sqrt[3]{3^2 \cdot y^2} = \frac{3\sqrt[3]{2y}}{y}$ **64.** $\sqrt[3]{6c} \cdot \frac{2}{\sqrt[3]{c^5}} \cdot \frac{\sqrt[3]{c}}{\sqrt[3]{c}} = \frac{2\sqrt[3]{6c^2}}{c^2}$ **65.** $\sqrt{\frac{1}{4x^2}} = \frac{1}{2x}$

66. $\sqrt{9x^2} = 3x$

C **67.** **a.** $(\sqrt[n]{a} \cdot \sqrt[n]{b})^n = (\sqrt[n]{a})^n \cdot (\sqrt[n]{b})^n = ab$

b. If n is odd, $\sqrt[n]{a} \cdot \sqrt[n]{b}$ is the only root and therefore the principal root. If n is even, $\sqrt[n]{a}$ and $\sqrt[n]{b}$ are both nonnegative; thus $\sqrt[n]{a} \cdot \sqrt[n]{b}$ is the nonnegative nth root of ab.

68. $\left(\frac{\sqrt[n]{a}}{\sqrt[n]{b}}\right)^n = \frac{(\sqrt[n]{a})^n}{(\sqrt[n]{b})^n} = \frac{a}{b}$. Thus, $\frac{\sqrt[n]{a}}{\sqrt[n]{b}}$ is an nth root of $\frac{a}{b}$. If n is odd, $\frac{\sqrt[n]{a}}{\sqrt[n]{b}}$ is the only nth root of $\frac{a}{b}$. If n is even $\sqrt[n]{a}$ and $\sqrt[n]{b}$ are both nonnegative, and so is $\frac{\sqrt[n]{a}}{\sqrt[n]{b}}$.

69. 1. $(\sqrt[n]{\sqrt[q]{b}})^{nq} = [(\sqrt[n]{\sqrt[q]{b}})^n]^q$ (Third law of exponents, page 171);

2. $(\sqrt[n]{\sqrt[q]{b}})^{nq} = (\sqrt[q]{b})^q$ (Property 1, page 261);

3. $(\sqrt[n]{\sqrt[q]{b}})^{nq} = b$ (Property 1, page 261)

Thus $\sqrt[n]{\sqrt[q]{b}}$ is an nqth root of b. If $b < 0$, then n and q are odd and there is only one root. If $b \geq 0$, then $\sqrt[q]{b}$ is nonnegative and so is $\sqrt[n]{\sqrt[q]{b}}$.

70. 1. $[(\sqrt[n]{b})^m]^n = (\sqrt[n]{b})^{mn}$ (Third law of exponents, page 171);

2. $[(\sqrt[n]{b})^m]^n = (\sqrt[n]{b})^{nm}$ (Comm. prop. of mult.)

3. $[(\sqrt[n]{b})^m]^n = [(\sqrt[n]{b})^n]^m$ (Third law of exponents, page 171);

4. $[(\sqrt[n]{b})^m]^n = b^m$ (Property 1, page 261)

Thus $(\sqrt[n]{b})^m$ is an nth root of b^m. If n is odd, there is only one nth root of b^m. If n is even, then $\sqrt[n]{b}$ is nonnegative and so is $(\sqrt[n]{b})^m$.

Page 269 • CALCULATOR KEY-IN

1. 5.47 **2.** 4.78 **3.** 0.46 **4.** 1.14×10^{-5} **5.** No; 10 is not a power of 2
6. 13.50 **7.** 7.83 **8.** 0.90 **9.** 107.81 **10.** 1

Pages 272–273 • WRITTEN EXERCISES

A **1.** $5\sqrt{2} + 3\sqrt{2} = 8\sqrt{2}$ **2.** $3\sqrt{5} - 2\sqrt{5} = \sqrt{5}$ **3.** $6\sqrt{3} - 4\sqrt{3} = 2\sqrt{3}$
4. $3\sqrt{3} + 10\sqrt{3} = 13\sqrt{3}$ **5.** not possible to simplify **6.** not possible to simplify
7. $\sqrt{6} + 6 + 6\sqrt{6} = 6 + 7\sqrt{6}$ **8.** $\sqrt{5} + 5 + 5\sqrt{5} = 5 + 6\sqrt{5}$
9. $5\sqrt{2} + 3\sqrt{7} - 4\sqrt{2} = \sqrt{2} + 3\sqrt{7}$ **10.** $3\sqrt{2} + 2\sqrt{6} - 3\sqrt{6} = 3\sqrt{2} - \sqrt{6}$
11. $3\sqrt[3]{2} + 2\sqrt[3]{5} + 2\sqrt[3]{2} = 5\sqrt[3]{2} + 2\sqrt[3]{5}$ **12.** $2\sqrt[3]{3} - 2\sqrt[3]{7} + 3\sqrt[3]{3} = 5\sqrt[3]{3} - 2\sqrt[3]{7}$
13. $\frac{3\sqrt{3}}{\sqrt{5}} - \frac{\sqrt{3}}{\sqrt{5}} = \frac{2\sqrt{3}}{\sqrt{5}} \cdot \frac{\sqrt{5}}{\sqrt{5}} = \frac{2\sqrt{15}}{5}$ **14.** $\frac{5\sqrt{3}}{\sqrt{2}} - \frac{\sqrt{3}}{\sqrt{2}} = \frac{4\sqrt{3}}{\sqrt{2}} \cdot \frac{\sqrt{2}}{\sqrt{2}} = 2\sqrt{6}$
15. $\frac{\sqrt{2}}{\sqrt{3}} + \frac{\sqrt{3}}{\sqrt{2}} = \frac{\sqrt{6}}{3} + \frac{\sqrt{6}}{2} = \frac{2\sqrt{6}}{6} + \frac{3\sqrt{6}}{6} = \frac{5\sqrt{6}}{6}$
16. $\frac{\sqrt{10}}{2} + \frac{\sqrt{10}}{5} = \frac{5\sqrt{10}}{10} + \frac{2\sqrt{10}}{10} = \frac{7\sqrt{10}}{10}$ **17.** $\sqrt[3]{4} + \frac{\sqrt[3]{4}}{2} = \frac{3\sqrt[3]{4}}{2}$
18. $2\sqrt[3]{2} - \frac{\sqrt[3]{2}}{2} = \frac{3\sqrt[3]{2}}{2}$ **19.** $\sqrt{16} + \sqrt{20} = 4 + 2\sqrt{5}$
20. $\sqrt{36} - \sqrt{72} = 6 - 6\sqrt{2}$ **21.** $\sqrt{45} + 2\sqrt{75} = 3\sqrt{5} + 10\sqrt{3}$

22. $3\sqrt{98} - \sqrt{147} = 21\sqrt{2} - 7\sqrt{3}$ **23.** $2\sqrt{144} - 10\sqrt{36} = 24 - 60 = -36$

24. $15 + 6\sqrt{375} = 15 + 30\sqrt{15}$ **25.** $\sqrt{3} - \sqrt{12} = \sqrt{3} - 2\sqrt{3} = -\sqrt{3}$

26. $\sqrt{6} - \sqrt{2}$ **27.** $4\sqrt{25} - \sqrt{9} = 20 - 3 = 17$

28. $\sqrt{4} - \frac{2}{\sqrt{2}} = 2 - \frac{2\sqrt{2}}{2} = 2 - \sqrt{2}$ **29.** $\sqrt{\frac{2}{3}}\left(3\sqrt{\frac{3}{2}} - \frac{3}{\sqrt{2}}\right) = 3 - \frac{3}{\sqrt{3}} = 3 - \sqrt{3}$

30. $\frac{\sqrt{3}}{2\sqrt{2}}\left(\frac{\sqrt{3}}{2} + \frac{2}{\sqrt{3}}\right) = \frac{3}{4\sqrt{2}} + \frac{1}{\sqrt{2}} = \frac{3\sqrt{2}}{8} + \frac{\sqrt{2}}{2} = \frac{7\sqrt{2}}{8}$

B **31.** $\sqrt[3]{1000} - \sqrt[3]{80} = 10 - 2\sqrt[3]{10}$ **32.** $2\sqrt[3]{5}(\sqrt[3]{25} + 2\sqrt[3]{5}) = 10 + 4\sqrt[3]{25}$

33. $\sqrt[3]{6} + 3\sqrt[3]{18}$ **34.** $\frac{\sqrt[3]{64}}{2} + \frac{\sqrt[3]{250}}{2} = \frac{4}{2} + \frac{5\sqrt[3]{2}}{2} = 2 + \frac{5\sqrt[3]{2}}{2}$

35. $2x\sqrt{2x} - 3x\sqrt{2x} = -x\sqrt{2x}$ **36.** $3y^2\sqrt{5y} + 2y^2\sqrt{5y} = 5y^2\sqrt{5y}$

37. $p\sqrt{pr} + r\sqrt{pr} = (p + r)\sqrt{pr}$ **38.** $|a|b^2\sqrt{2} + 2|a|b^2\sqrt{2} = 3|a|b^2\sqrt{2}$

39. $\sqrt{10a} - \frac{\sqrt{10a}}{2} + \frac{\sqrt{10a}}{5} = \frac{7\sqrt{10a}}{10}$ **40.** $\sqrt{6x} + \frac{\sqrt{6x}}{3} - \frac{\sqrt{6x}}{2} = \frac{5\sqrt{6x}}{6}$

41. $\sqrt{18w^2} + \sqrt{12w^4} = 3w\sqrt{2} + 2w^2\sqrt{3}$ **42.** $\sqrt{20t^6} - \sqrt{50t^2} = 2t^3\sqrt{5} - 5t\sqrt{2}$

43. $x^2 = 10^2 + (\sqrt{2})^2; x^2 = 100 + 2 = 102; x = \sqrt{102}$

44. $x^2 + (3\sqrt{5})^2 = (5\sqrt{3})^2; x^2 + 45 = 75; x^2 = 30; x = \sqrt{30}$

Page 273 • MIXED REVIEW EXERCISES

1. $\sqrt{7 \cdot 4 \cdot x^2 \cdot x} = 2|x|\sqrt{7x}$ **2.** $\frac{9}{7}$ **3.** $\frac{a}{xy}$ **4.** $\frac{3\sqrt{5x}}{4y^2\sqrt{2}} \cdot \frac{\sqrt{2}}{\sqrt{2}} = \frac{3\sqrt{10x}}{8y^2}$

5. $\frac{(x-3)(x-2)}{-1(x-2)} = \frac{x-3}{-1} = 3 - x$ **6.** $\sqrt[3]{-27 \cdot 5} = -3\sqrt[3]{5}$ **7.** $9x^2 - 1$

8. $\frac{1}{\sqrt{x}} \cdot \frac{\sqrt{x}}{\sqrt{x}} = \frac{\sqrt{x}}{|x|}$ **9.** $\sqrt[3]{2^3 \cdot x^3 \cdot x \cdot (y^2)^3} = 2xy^2\sqrt[3]{x}$

Page 273 • EXTRA

1. Suppose $\sqrt{3}$ is rational. Then $\sqrt{3} = \frac{a}{b}$ for some integers a and b. Assume $\frac{a}{b}$ is in lowest terms. Then $3 = \frac{a^2}{b^2}$, and $3b^2 = a^2$. Since 3 divides $3b^2$, 3 divides a^2, and so 3 divides a. Hence $a = 3c$ for some integer c. Therefore $3b^2 = (3c)^2 = 9c^2$, and $b^2 = 3c^2$. Thus 3 divides b^2 and 3 divides b. But this is impossible since a and b have no common factor other than 1. $\therefore$ $\sqrt{3}$ is irrational.

2. Suppose $\sqrt{p}$ is rational. Then $\sqrt{p} = \frac{a}{b}$ for some integers a and b. Assume $\frac{a}{b}$ is in lowest terms. Then $p = \frac{a^2}{b^2}$ and $pb^2 = a^2$. Since p divides pb^2, p divides a^2, and (since p is prime) p divides a. Hence $a = pc$ for some integer c. Therefore $pb^2 = (pc)^2 = p^2c^2$, and $b^2 = pc^2$. Thus p divides b^2 and p divides b. But this is impossible since a and b have no common factor other than 1. $\therefore$ $\sqrt{p}$ is irrational.

Pages 275–276 • WRITTEN EXERCISES

A

1. $9 - 7 = 2$ **2.** $25 - 2 = 23$ **3.** $7 + 2\sqrt{7} + 1 = 8 + 2\sqrt{7}$

4. $5 + 4\sqrt{5} + 4 = 9 + 4\sqrt{5}$ **5.** $3 + 4\sqrt{2} + 2 = 5 + 4\sqrt{2}$

6. $24 + 2\sqrt{3} - 3 = 21 + 2\sqrt{3}$ **7.** $\frac{1}{4 - \sqrt{3}} \cdot \frac{4 + \sqrt{3}}{4 + \sqrt{3}} = \frac{4 + \sqrt{3}}{13}$

8. $\frac{1}{6 + \sqrt{3}} \cdot \frac{6 - \sqrt{3}}{6 - \sqrt{3}} = \frac{6 - \sqrt{3}}{33}$ **9.** $7 - 2\sqrt{14} + 2 = 9 - 2\sqrt{14}$

10. $99 - 6\sqrt{110} + 10 = 109 - 6\sqrt{110}$ **11.** $6 + 5\sqrt{3} - 12 = -6 + 5\sqrt{3}$

12. $15 - 13\sqrt{2} + 4 = 19 - 13\sqrt{2}$

13. $\frac{3}{\sqrt{5} + \sqrt{2}} \cdot \frac{\sqrt{5} - \sqrt{2}}{\sqrt{5} - \sqrt{2}} = \frac{3(\sqrt{5} - \sqrt{2})}{3} = \sqrt{5} - \sqrt{2}$

14. $\frac{10}{2\sqrt{3} - \sqrt{7}} \cdot \frac{2\sqrt{3} + \sqrt{7}}{2\sqrt{3} + \sqrt{7}} = \frac{10(2\sqrt{3} + \sqrt{7})}{5} = 4\sqrt{3} + 2\sqrt{7}$

15. $11 - 7 = 4$ **16.** $13 - 3 = 10$ **17.** $40 - 2\sqrt{3} - 6 = 34 - 2\sqrt{3}$

18. $12 - 7\sqrt{6} - 60 = -48 - 7\sqrt{6}$

19. $\frac{\sqrt{15}}{\sqrt{3} + \sqrt{5}} \cdot \frac{\sqrt{3} - \sqrt{5}}{\sqrt{3} - \sqrt{5}} = \frac{\sqrt{45} - \sqrt{75}}{-2} = \frac{3\sqrt{5} - 5\sqrt{3}}{-2} = \frac{5\sqrt{3} - 3\sqrt{5}}{2}$

20. $\frac{\sqrt{6}}{\sqrt{2} + \sqrt{3}} \cdot \frac{\sqrt{2} - \sqrt{3}}{\sqrt{2} - \sqrt{3}} = \frac{\sqrt{12} - \sqrt{18}}{-1} = \frac{2\sqrt{3} - 3\sqrt{2}}{-1} = 3\sqrt{2} - 2\sqrt{3}$

21. $20 + 4\sqrt{35} + 7 = 27 + 4\sqrt{35}$ **22.** $18 + 6\sqrt{12} + 6 = 24 + 12\sqrt{3}$

23. $12 - 5 = 7$ **24.** $63 - 20 = 43$ **25.** $6 - 2\sqrt{90} + 15 = 21 - 6\sqrt{10}$

26. $20 - 4\sqrt{50} + 10 = 30 - 20\sqrt{2}$ **27.** $\frac{5 - 3}{4} = \frac{1}{2}$ **28.** $\frac{28 - 1}{9} = 3$

29. $60 - 20\sqrt{18} + 6\sqrt{12} - 12\sqrt{6} = 60 - 60\sqrt{2} + 12\sqrt{3} - 12\sqrt{6}$

30. $12\sqrt{15} - 9\sqrt{75} + 8\sqrt{45} - 90 = 12\sqrt{15} - 45\sqrt{3} + 24\sqrt{5} - 90$

31. $\frac{\sqrt{5} + 1}{\sqrt{5} - 3} \cdot \frac{\sqrt{5} + 3}{\sqrt{5} + 3} = \frac{5 + 4\sqrt{5} + 3}{5 - 9} = \frac{8 + 4\sqrt{5}}{-4} = -2 - \sqrt{5}$

32. $\frac{2\sqrt{7} - \sqrt{3}}{\sqrt{7} + \sqrt{3}} \cdot \frac{\sqrt{7} - \sqrt{3}}{\sqrt{7} - \sqrt{3}} = \frac{14 - 3\sqrt{21} + 3}{7 - 3} = \frac{17 - 3\sqrt{21}}{4}$

B

33. $f(1 - \sqrt{2}) = \frac{1 - \sqrt{2}}{1 - \sqrt{2} + 1} = \frac{1 - \sqrt{2}}{2 - \sqrt{2}} \cdot \frac{2 + \sqrt{2}}{2 + \sqrt{2}} = \frac{2 - \sqrt{2} - 2}{2} = -\frac{\sqrt{2}}{2}$

34. $g(1 + \sqrt{2}) = \frac{(1 + \sqrt{2})^2}{1 + \sqrt{2} - 1} = \frac{1 + 2\sqrt{2} + 2}{\sqrt{2}} = \frac{3 + 2\sqrt{2}}{\sqrt{2}} \cdot \frac{\sqrt{2}}{\sqrt{2}} = \frac{3\sqrt{2} + 4}{2}$

35. $(3 + \sqrt{5})^2 - 6(3 + \sqrt{5}) + 4 = 9 + 6\sqrt{5} + 5 - 18 - 6\sqrt{5} + 4 = 0$; $(3 - \sqrt{5})^2 - 6(3 - \sqrt{5}) + 4 = 9 - 6\sqrt{5} + 5 - 18 + 6\sqrt{5} + 4 = 0$

36. $2\left(1+\frac{\sqrt{2}}{2}\right)^2 - 4\left(1+\frac{\sqrt{2}}{2}\right) + 1 = 2\left(1+\sqrt{2}+\frac{1}{2}\right) - 4 - 2\sqrt{2} + 1 =$

$2 + 2\sqrt{2} + 1 - 4 - 2\sqrt{2} + 1 = 0;\ 2\left(1-\frac{\sqrt{2}}{2}\right)^2 - 4\left(1-\frac{\sqrt{2}}{2}\right) +$

$1 = 2\left(1 - \sqrt{2} + \frac{1}{2}\right) - 4 + 2\sqrt{2} + 1 = 2 - 2\sqrt{2} + 1 - 4 + 2\sqrt{2} + 1 = 0$

37. a. $2\sqrt{5} + 3\sqrt{2}$ **b.** $\frac{1}{2\sqrt{5}+3\sqrt{2}} \cdot \frac{2\sqrt{5}-3\sqrt{2}}{2\sqrt{5}-3\sqrt{2}} = \frac{2\sqrt{5}-3\sqrt{2}}{2}$

c. The reciprocal is $\frac{1}{2\sqrt{5}-3\sqrt{2}} \cdot \frac{2\sqrt{5}+3\sqrt{2}}{2\sqrt{5}+3\sqrt{2}} = \frac{2\sqrt{5}+3\sqrt{2}}{2}$; the conjugate of the reciprocal is $\frac{2\sqrt{5}-3\sqrt{2}}{2}$

38. The reciprocal of $\frac{\sqrt{5}+1}{2}$ is $\frac{2}{\sqrt{5}+1} = \frac{2}{\sqrt{5}+1} \cdot \frac{\sqrt{5}-1}{\sqrt{5}-1} = \frac{2(\sqrt{5}-1)}{4} = \frac{\sqrt{5}-1}{2}$; this is the conjugate of $\frac{\sqrt{5}+1}{2}$

39. $x^2 = (4-\sqrt{2})^2 + (4+\sqrt{2})^2;\ x^2 = 16 - 8\sqrt{2} + 2 + 16 + 8\sqrt{2} + 2;\ x^2 = 36;$ $x = 6$

40. $x^2 + (4+3\sqrt{2})^2 = (6+2\sqrt{2})^2;\ x^2 + 16 + 24\sqrt{2} + 18 = 36 + 24\sqrt{2} + 8;$

$x^2 = 10;\ x = \sqrt{10}$

41. $(\sqrt{n+1} + \sqrt{n})(\sqrt{n+1} - \sqrt{n}) = n + 1 - n = 1$

42. $(b+\sqrt{b})^2 - (b-\sqrt{b})^2 = [(b+\sqrt{b}) + (b-\sqrt{b})][(b+\sqrt{b}) - (b-\sqrt{b})] =$ $2b(2\sqrt{b}) = 4b\sqrt{b}$

43. $\frac{\sqrt{w}}{\sqrt{w}+1} \cdot \frac{\sqrt{w}-1}{\sqrt{w}-1} + \frac{\sqrt{w}}{\sqrt{w}-1} \cdot \frac{\sqrt{w}+1}{\sqrt{w}+1} = \frac{w-\sqrt{w}}{w-1} + \frac{w+\sqrt{w}}{w-1} = \frac{2w}{w-1}$

44. $\sqrt{1-y^2} + \frac{y^2\sqrt{1-y^2}}{1-y^2} = \frac{(1-y^2)\sqrt{1-y^2}}{1-y^2} + \frac{y^2\sqrt{1-y^2}}{1-y^2} = \frac{\sqrt{1-y^2}(1-y^2+y^2)}{1-y^2} =$ $\frac{\sqrt{1-y^2}}{1-y^2}$

C **45.** $\frac{\sqrt{a^2-a}}{\sqrt{a-1}} = \frac{\sqrt{a(a-1)}}{\sqrt{a-1}} = \sqrt{a}$

46. $\frac{\sqrt{x}(\sqrt{x}-\sqrt{y})}{(\sqrt{x}+\sqrt{y})(\sqrt{x}-\sqrt{y})} + \frac{\sqrt{y}(\sqrt{x}+\sqrt{y})}{(\sqrt{x}-\sqrt{y})(\sqrt{x}+\sqrt{y})} = \frac{x-\sqrt{xy}}{x-y} + \frac{\sqrt{xy}+y}{x-y} = \frac{x+y}{x-y}$

47. $(a+\sqrt{b})^3 + (a-\sqrt{b})^3 = (a^3 + 3a^2\sqrt{b} + 3ab + b\sqrt{b}) +$

$(a^3 - 3a^2\sqrt{b} + 3ab - b\sqrt{b}) = 2a^3 + 6ab$, which is rational if a and b are rational.

Pages 280–281 • WRITTEN EXERCISES

A **1.** $\sqrt{4x-3} = 5;\ 4x - 3 = 25;\ 4x = 28;\ x = 7;\ \{7\}$

2. $\sqrt{3n+1} = 7;\ 3n + 1 = 49;\ 3n = 48;\ n = 16;\ \{16\}$

3. $3\sqrt{t} - 5 = 13;\ 3\sqrt{t} = 18;\ \sqrt{t} = 6;\ t = 36;\ \{36\}$

4. $7 + 4\sqrt{a} = 3$; $4\sqrt{a} = -4$; no real solution

5. $\sqrt{2x^2 - 7} = 5$; $2x^2 - 7 = 25$; $2x^2 = 32$; $x^2 = 16$; $x = \pm 4$; $\{-4, 4\}$

6. $\sqrt{5y^2 + 1} = 9$; $5y^2 + 1 = 81$; $5y^2 = 80$; $y^2 = 16$; $y = \pm 4$; $\{-4, 4\}$

7. $\sqrt[3]{3m + 1} = 4$; $3m + 1 = 64$; $3m = 63$; $m = 21$; $\{21\}$

8. $\sqrt[3]{2w - 5} = 3$; $2w - 5 = 27$; $2w = 32$; $w = 16$; $\{16\}$

9. $\sqrt[3]{2d} + 5 = 3$; $\sqrt[3]{2d} = -2$; $2d = -8$; $d = -4$; $\{-4\}$

10. $7 - \sqrt[3]{9c} = 4$; $\sqrt[3]{9c} = 3$; $9c = 27$; $c = 3$; $\{3\}$

11. $2\sqrt[3]{x} = \sqrt[3]{x^2}$; $8x = x^2$; $x^2 - 8x = 0$; $x(x - 8) = 0$; $x = 0$ or $x = 8$; $\{0, 8\}$

12. $\frac{\sqrt[3]{x}}{2} = \sqrt[3]{x - 7}$; $\frac{x}{8} = x - 7$; $\frac{7x}{8} = 7$; $x = 8$; $\{8\}$

13. $\sqrt{x + 2} = x$; $x + 2 = x^2$; $x^2 - x - 2 = 0$; $(x - 2)(x + 1) = 0$; $x = 2$ or $x = -1$ (reject); $\{2\}$

14. $\sqrt{2n + 3} = n$; $2n + 3 = n^2$; $n^2 - 2n - 3 = 0$; $(n - 3)(n + 1) = 0$; $n = 3$ or $n = -1$ (reject); $\{3\}$

15. $\sqrt{t - 2} + t = 4$; $\sqrt{t - 2} = -t + 4$; $t - 2 = t^2 - 8t + 16$; $t^2 - 9t + 18 = 0$; $(t - 6)(t - 3) = 0$; $t = 6$ (reject) or $t = 3$; $\{3\}$

16. $5 + \sqrt{a + 7} = a$; $\sqrt{a + 7} = a - 5$; $a + 7 = a^2 - 10a + 25$; $a^2 - 11a + 18 = 0$; $(a - 9)(a - 2) = 0$; $a = 9$ or $a = 2$ (reject); $\{9\}$

17. $\sqrt{2x + 5} - 1 = x$; $\sqrt{2x + 5} = x + 1$; $2x + 5 = x^2 + 2x + 1$; $x^2 = 4$; $x = 2$ or $x = -2$ (reject); $\{2\}$

18. $\sqrt{3n + 10} - 4 = n$; $\sqrt{3n + 10} = n + 4$; $3n + 10 = n^2 + 8n + 16$; $n^2 + 5n + 6 = 0$; $(n + 2)(n + 3) = 0$; $n = -2$ or $n = -3$; $\{-3, -2\}$

19. **a.** $5\sqrt{x} = 10$; $\sqrt{x} = 2$; $x = 4$; $\{4\}$ **b.** $x\sqrt{5} = 10$; $x = \frac{10}{\sqrt{5}} = \frac{10\sqrt{5}}{5} = 2\sqrt{5}$; $\{2\sqrt{5}\}$

20. **a.** $3\sqrt{x} = 12$; $\sqrt{x} = 4$; $x = 16$; $\{16\}$ **b.** $x\sqrt{3} = 12$; $x = \frac{12}{\sqrt{3}} = \frac{12\sqrt{3}}{3} = 4\sqrt{3}$; $\{4\sqrt{3}\}$

21. **a.** $5 + 2\sqrt{x} = 7$; $2\sqrt{x} = 2$; $\sqrt{x} = 1$; $x = 1$; $\{1\}$

b. $5 + x\sqrt{2} = 7$; $x\sqrt{2} = 2$; $x = \frac{2}{\sqrt{2}} = \sqrt{2}$; $\{\sqrt{2}\}$

22. **a.** $2 + 3\sqrt{x} = 8$; $3\sqrt{x} = 6$; $\sqrt{x} = 2$; $x = 4$; $\{4\}$

b. $2 + x\sqrt{3} = 8$; $x\sqrt{3} = 6$; $x = \frac{6}{\sqrt{3}} = 2\sqrt{3}$; $\{2\sqrt{3}\}$

23. **a.** $x = 3 + 2\sqrt{x}$; $2\sqrt{x} = x - 3$; $4x = x^2 - 6x + 9$; $x^2 - 10x + 9 = 0$; $(x - 9)(x - 1) = 0$; $x = 9$ or $x = 1$ (reject); $\{9\}$

b. $x = 3 + x\sqrt{2}$; $x(1 - \sqrt{2}) = 3$; $x = \frac{3}{1 - \sqrt{2}} \cdot \frac{1 + \sqrt{2}}{1 + \sqrt{2}}$, $x = \frac{3(1 + \sqrt{2})}{1 - 2} = -3 - 3\sqrt{2}$; $\{-3 - 3\sqrt{2}\}$

24. a. $3x = 7\sqrt{x} - 2$; $7\sqrt{x} = 3x + 2$; $49x = 9x^2 + 12x + 4$; $9x^2 - 37x + 4 = 0$; $(9x - 1)(x - 4) = 0$; $x = \frac{1}{9}$ or $x = 4$; $\left\{\frac{1}{9}, 4\right\}$

b. $3x = x\sqrt{7} - 2$; $x(3 - \sqrt{7}) = -2$; $x = \frac{-2}{3 - \sqrt{7}} \cdot \frac{3 + \sqrt{7}}{3 + \sqrt{7}} = \frac{-2(3 + \sqrt{7})}{2} = -3 - \sqrt{7}$; $\{-3 - \sqrt{7}\}$

B **25.** $\sqrt{y} + \sqrt{y + 5} = 5$; $\sqrt{y + 5} = 5 - \sqrt{y}$; $y + 5 = 25 - 10\sqrt{y} + y$; $-20 = -10\sqrt{y}$; $\sqrt{y} = 2$; $y = 4$; $\{4\}$

26. $\sqrt{x - 7} + \sqrt{x} = 7$; $\sqrt{x - 7} = 7 - \sqrt{x}$; $x - 7 = 49 - 14\sqrt{x} + x$; $-56 = -14\sqrt{x}$; $\sqrt{x} = 4$; $x = 16$; $\{16\}$

27. $\sqrt{2n - 5} - \sqrt{3n + 4} = 2$; $\sqrt{2n - 5} = 2 + \sqrt{3n + 4}$; $2n - 5 = 4 + 4\sqrt{3n + 4} + 3n + 4$; $-n - 13 = 4\sqrt{3n + 4}$; $n^2 + 26n + 169 = 16(3n + 4)$; $n^2 - 22n + 105 = 0$; $(n - 7)(n - 15) = 0$, $n = 7$ (reject) or $n = 15$ (reject); no real solution.

28. $\sqrt{3a - 2} - \sqrt{2a - 3} = 1$; $\sqrt{3a - 2} = 1 + \sqrt{2a - 3}$; $3a - 2 = 1 + 2\sqrt{2a - 3} + 2a - 3$; $a = 2\sqrt{2a - 3}$; $a^2 = 4(2a - 3)$; $a^2 = 8a - 12$; $a^2 - 8a + 12 = 0$; $(a - 6)(a - 2) = 0$; $a = 6$ or $a = 2$; $\{2, 6\}$

29. $\sqrt{3b - 2} - \sqrt{2b + 5} = 1$; $\sqrt{3b - 2} = 1 + \sqrt{2b + 5}$; $3b - 2 = 1 + 2\sqrt{2b + 5} + 2b + 5$; $b - 8 = 2\sqrt{2b + 5}$; $b^2 - 16b + 64 = 4(2b + 5)$; $b^2 - 24b + 44 = 0$; $(b - 2)(b - 22) = 0$; $b = 2$ (reject) or $b = 22$; $\{22\}$

30. $\sqrt{5y - 1} - \sqrt{7y + 9} = 2$; $\sqrt{5y - 1} = 2 + \sqrt{7y + 9}$; $5y - 1 = 4 + 4\sqrt{7y + 9} + 7y + 9$; $-2y - 14 = 4\sqrt{7y + 9}$; $y + 7 = -2\sqrt{7y + 9}$; $y^2 + 14y + 49 = 4(7y + 9)$; $y^2 - 14y + 13 = 0$; $(y - 13)(y - 1) = 0$; $y = 1$ (reject) or $y = 13$ (reject); no real solution

31. $\sqrt{x} + \sqrt{3} = \sqrt{x + 3}$; $x + 2\sqrt{3x} + 3 = x + 3$; $2\sqrt{3x} = 0$; $\sqrt{3x} = 0$; $x = 0$; $\{0\}$

32. $\sqrt{n + 6} - \sqrt{n} = \sqrt{6}$; $\sqrt{n + 6} = \sqrt{n} + \sqrt{6}$; $n + 6 = n + 2\sqrt{6n} + 6$; $2\sqrt{6n} = 0$; $n = 0$; $\{0\}$

33. a. $d = \sqrt{\frac{3}{2}(607)} = \sqrt{910.5} \approx 30$; 30 mi **b.** $d = \sqrt{\frac{3}{2}h}$; $d^2 = \frac{3}{2}h$; $h = \frac{2}{3}d^2$

34. a. $T \approx 2(3.14)\sqrt{\frac{20}{980}} \approx 6.28\sqrt{0.0204} \approx 0.9$; 0.9 s

b. $T = 2\pi\sqrt{\frac{l}{g}}$; $\frac{T}{2\pi} = \frac{\sqrt{l}}{\sqrt{g}}$; $\frac{T\sqrt{g}}{2\pi} = \sqrt{l}$; $\frac{gT^2}{4\pi^2} = l$

35. a. Perimeter $= x + x + x\sqrt{2} = 10$; $2x + x\sqrt{2} = 10$; $x(2 + \sqrt{2}) = 10$;

$$x = \frac{10}{2 + \sqrt{2}} \cdot \frac{2 - \sqrt{2}}{2 - \sqrt{2}} = \frac{10(2 - \sqrt{2})}{2} = 10 - 5\sqrt{2}$$

b. Area $= \frac{1}{2}x^2 = 12$; $x^2 = 24$; $x = \sqrt{24} = 2\sqrt{6}$

36. **a.** Perimeter $= x + x\sqrt{3} + 2x = 18$; $3x + x\sqrt{3} = 18$; $x(3 + \sqrt{3}) = 18$;

$$x = \frac{18}{3 + \sqrt{3}} \cdot \frac{3 - \sqrt{3}}{3 - \sqrt{3}} = \frac{18(3 - \sqrt{3})}{6} = 9 - 3\sqrt{3}$$

b. Area $= \frac{1}{2}x^2\sqrt{3} = 24$; $x^2 = \frac{48}{\sqrt{3}} = \frac{48\sqrt{3}}{3} = 16\sqrt{3}$; $x = \sqrt{16\sqrt{3}} = 4\sqrt[4]{3}$

37. **a.** $QN = NR = 5$ cm; $(PQ)^2 = (QN)^2 + (PN)^2 = 5^2 + x^2 = 25 + x^2$;

$PQ = \sqrt{25 + x^2}$; since $PQ = PR$, $PR = \sqrt{25 + x^2}$

b. Perimeter $= PQ + PR + QR = 3(PN)$; $2\sqrt{25 + x^2} + 10 = 3x$; $2\sqrt{25 + x^2} = 3x - 10$; $4(25 + x^2) = 9x^2 - 60x + 100$; $5x^2 - 60x = 0$; $5x(x - 12) = 0$; $x = 0$ (reject) or $x = 12$; $x = 12$; 12 cm

C **38.** $BD = \sqrt{(x + 1)^2 - x^2}$; $DC = \sqrt{(x + 3)^2 - x^2}$; $BD + DC = \sqrt{(x + 1)^2 - x^2} + \sqrt{(x + 3)^2 - x^2} = 14$; $\sqrt{(x + 1)^2 - x^2} = 14 - \sqrt{(x + 3)^2 - x^2}$; $\sqrt{2x + 1} = 14 - \sqrt{6x + 9}$; $2x + 1 = 196 - 28\sqrt{6x + 9} + 6x + 9$; $-4x - 204 = -28\sqrt{6x + 9}$; $x + 51 = 7\sqrt{6x + 9}$; $x^2 + 102x + 2601 = 49(6x + 9)$; $x^2 - 192x + 2160 = 0$; $(x - 12)(x - 180) = 0$; $x = 12$ or $x = 180$ (reject); $x = 12$

39. **a.** $V = \frac{1}{3}Bh = \frac{1}{3}x^2h$. Let F be the foot of the altitude; note $FC = \frac{x\sqrt{2}}{2}$ since it is half the diagonal of a square of side x. Then $(EF)^2 + (FC)^2 = (EC)^2$;

$$h^2 + \left(\frac{x\sqrt{2}}{2}\right)^2 = x^2;\ h^2 + \frac{x^2}{2} = x^2;\ h^2 = \frac{x^2}{2};\ h = \frac{x}{\sqrt{2}} = \frac{x\sqrt{2}}{2} \cdot V = \frac{1}{3}x^2\left(\frac{x\sqrt{2}}{2}\right) = \frac{x^3\sqrt{2}}{6}$$

b. $V = \frac{x^3\sqrt{2}}{6} = 9$; $x^3 = \frac{54}{\sqrt{2}} = 27\sqrt{2}$; $x = \sqrt[3]{27\sqrt{2}} = 3\sqrt[6]{2}$

Page 282 • MIXED REVIEW EXERCISES

1. $\sqrt{5} + \sqrt{2}$ **2.** $2\sqrt{18} - 3\sqrt{12} = 6\sqrt{2} - 6\sqrt{3}$

3. $\frac{(a - b)(a^2 + ab + b^2)}{a - b} = a^2 + ab + b^2$ **4.** $\frac{2}{4 - \sqrt{6}} \cdot \frac{4 + \sqrt{6}}{4 + \sqrt{6}} = \frac{2(4 + \sqrt{6})}{10} = \frac{4 + \sqrt{6}}{5}$

5. $(m^6n^3)(m^2n^6) = m^8n^9$ **6.** $5 + 2\sqrt{50} + 10 = 15 + 10\sqrt{2}$

7. $\frac{x - 1}{(1 - x)^2} = \frac{x - 1}{(x - 1)^2} = \frac{1}{x - 1}$ **8.** $5\sqrt{3} - 2\sqrt{3} + 3\sqrt{3} = 6\sqrt{3}$

9. $18 - 12\sqrt{18} + \sqrt{12} - 4\sqrt{6} = 18 - 36\sqrt{2} + 2\sqrt{3} - 4\sqrt{6}$

10. $\frac{12\sqrt{2}}{6\sqrt{3}} = \frac{2\sqrt{2}}{\sqrt{3}} \cdot \frac{\sqrt{3}}{\sqrt{3}} = \frac{2\sqrt{6}}{3}$

11. $5y^3 - 15y^2 + 20y + 2y^2 - 6y + 8 = 5y^3 - 13y^2 + 14y + 8$

12. $2\sqrt[3]{5} + 5\sqrt[3]{5} - 3\sqrt[3]{5} = 4\sqrt[3]{5}$

Pages 286–287 • WRITTEN EXERCISES

A **1.** **a.** rational **b.** irrational **2.** **a.** irrational **b.** rational

3. **a.** irrational **b.** rational

4. a. $\frac{\sqrt{2}}{2} + \frac{\sqrt{2}}{4} = \frac{3\sqrt{2}}{4}$; irrational **b.** $\sqrt{\frac{1}{16}} = \frac{1}{4}$; rational

5. a. rational **b.** rational **c.** irrational

6. a. rational **b.** rational **c.** irrational **7.** 0.625 **8.** $0.\overline{45}$ **9.** $1.\overline{857142}$

10. 3.25 **11.** $\frac{506}{100} = \frac{253}{50}$ **12.** $\frac{3004}{1000} = \frac{751}{250}$ **13.** $\frac{472}{100} = \frac{118}{25}$ **14.** $\frac{1375}{10{,}000} = \frac{11}{80}$ **15.** $\frac{4}{9}$

16. $\frac{5}{9}$ **17.** $N = 0.8\overline{3}$; $10N = 8.\overline{3}$; $9N = 7.5$; $N = \frac{7.5}{9} = \frac{75}{90} = \frac{5}{6}$

18. $N = 0.08\overline{3}$; $10N = 0.8\overline{3}$; $9N = 0.75$; $N = \frac{0.75}{9} = \frac{75}{900} = \frac{1}{12}$

19. $N = 2.\overline{36}$; $100N = 236.\overline{36}$; $99N = 234$; $N = \frac{234}{99} = \frac{26}{11}$

20. $N = 1.\overline{27}$; $100N = 127.\overline{27}$; $99N = 126$; $N = \frac{126}{99} = \frac{14}{11}$

21. $N = 3.\overline{033}$; $1000N = 3033.\overline{033}$; $999N = 3030$; $N = \frac{3030}{999} = \frac{1010}{333}$

22. $N = 1.\overline{101}$; $1000N = 1101.\overline{101}$; $999N = 1100$; $N = \frac{1100}{999}$

23–31. Answers may vary; examples are given.

23. a. 0.15 **b.** $\frac{\sqrt{2}}{10}$ **24. a.** 0.37255 **b.** 0.372515115111 . . . **25. a.** 2.5 **b.** $\sqrt{6.5}$

26. a. 3.1 **b.** $\frac{3 + \pi}{2}$ **27. a.** 3.9 **b.** $\sqrt{15.5}$

28. a. 5×10^{-9} **b.** 0.0000000101001000 . . .

29. a. $\frac{1}{2}\left(\frac{7}{8} + \frac{8}{9}\right) = \frac{127}{144}$ **b.** 0.87515115111 . . . **30. a.** $3\frac{13}{84}$ **b.** $\pi + 0.01$

31. a. 0.45 **b.** $\frac{\sqrt{5}}{5}$

B

32. a. The arithmetic mean is rational.

b. No; if the product xy is not a perfect square, $\sqrt{xy}$ is irrational.

33. Answers may vary; examples are given.

a. $x = \sqrt{2}$ and $y = -\sqrt{2}$; $\frac{\sqrt{2} - \sqrt{2}}{2} = 0$ is rational

b. $a = \sqrt{2}$ and $b = \sqrt{3}$; $\frac{\sqrt{2} + \sqrt{3}}{2}$ is irrational

34. It is possible to create an infinite sequence of rational numbers between x and y by successively finding the arithmetic mean of x and the previous mean. For example, between 2 and 4 are 3, $2\frac{1}{2}, 2\frac{1}{4}, 2\frac{1}{8}, 2\frac{1}{16}, \ldots$

35. (1) and (4)

36. a. There can be no more than 16 digits. There are only 16 possible remainders when dividing by 17 (excluding 0, which would indicate a terminating decimal).

b. $0.\overline{0588235294117647}$

37. Answers may vary. Any unit fraction of the form $\frac{1}{2^n 5^m}$, where n and m are whole numbers. For example: $\frac{1}{10}, \frac{1}{16}, \frac{1}{20}, \frac{1}{50}$.

38. Let $x = \frac{a}{b}$ and $y = \frac{c}{d}$ where a, b, c, and d are integers and $bd \neq 0$. Then $x + y = \frac{a}{b} + \frac{c}{d} = \frac{ad + bc}{bd}$. Since $ad + bc$ and bd are integers, $x + y$ is rational.

39. a. Let $x = \frac{a}{b}$ and $y = \frac{c}{d}$ where a, b, c, d are integers and $bd \neq 0$. Then $xy = \frac{ac}{bd}$, which is the ratio of two integers

b. The product may be rational ($\sqrt{2} \cdot \sqrt{2} = 2$) or irrational ($\sqrt{2} \cdot \sqrt{3} = \sqrt{6}$).

C **40.** Let $x = \frac{a}{b}$ where a and b are integers and $b \neq 0$. Assume $x + z$ is rational; that is, $x + z = \frac{c}{d}$ where c and d are integers and $d \neq 0$. Then $z = (x + z) - x = \frac{c}{d} - \frac{a}{b} = \frac{bc - ad}{bd}$. Since $bc - ad$ and bd are integers, z is rational. But since this contradicts the fact that z is irrational, $x + z$ must be irrational.

41. The product is irrational. Let z be an irrational number. Let $x = \frac{a}{b}$ where a and b are nonzero integers. Assume xz is rational; that is, $xz = \frac{c}{d}$ where c and d are integers and $d \neq 0$. Then $z = (xz) \div x = \frac{c}{d} \div \frac{a}{b} = \frac{bc}{ad}$, which is rational. But since this contradicts the fact that z is irrational, xz must be irrational.

42. a. Multiplying N by 10^p shifts the decimal point p digits to the right but does not affect the digits' pattern.

b. The repeating blocks in $N \cdot 10^p$ and N subtract to zero, yielding a terminating decimal.

c. All terminating decimals are rational; $N(10^p - 1) = N \cdot 10^p - N$

d. $\frac{N(10^p - 1)}{10^p - 1}$ is the quotient of rational numbers and is therefore rational.

Pages 290–291 • WRITTEN EXERCISES

A **1.** $9i$ **2.** $11i$ **3.** $-24i$ **4.** $-24i$ **5.** $2i\sqrt{5}$ **6.** $5i\sqrt{3}$ **7.** $6i\sqrt{2}$ **8.** $15i\sqrt{3}$ **9.** -6 **10.** -15 **11.** $7i$ **12.** $2i\sqrt{3}$ **13.** $(i\sqrt{5})(i\sqrt{10}) = -5\sqrt{2}$ **14.** $(i\sqrt{3})(i\sqrt{6}) = -3\sqrt{2}$ **15.** -49 **16.** -64 **17.** -1 **18.** -25 **19.** -2 **20.** -45 **21.** -3 **22.** -54 **23.** $\frac{-2i}{i^2} = 2i$ **24.** $\frac{8i}{3i^2} = -\frac{8i}{3}$

25. $\frac{1}{i\sqrt{5}} \cdot \frac{i\sqrt{5}}{i\sqrt{5}} = \frac{i\sqrt{5}}{-5} = -\frac{i\sqrt{5}}{5}$ **26.** $\frac{4}{2i} \cdot \frac{i}{i} = \frac{4i}{-2} = -2i$

27. $\frac{3\sqrt{2}}{2i\sqrt{6}} \cdot \frac{i\sqrt{6}}{i\sqrt{6}} = \frac{3i\sqrt{12}}{-12} = -\frac{i\sqrt{3}}{2}$ **28.** $\frac{2\sqrt{7}}{4i\sqrt{7}} = \frac{1}{2i} \cdot \frac{i}{i} = -\frac{i}{2}$

29. $\frac{2\sqrt{15}}{i\sqrt{15}} = \frac{2}{i} \cdot \frac{i}{i} = -2i$ **30.** $-\frac{2\sqrt{3}}{3i\sqrt{2}} \cdot \frac{i\sqrt{2}}{i\sqrt{2}} = -\frac{2i\sqrt{6}}{-6} = \frac{i\sqrt{6}}{3}$

31. $x^2 + 144 = 0; x^2 = -144; x = \pm\sqrt{-144} = \pm 12i; \{\pm 12i\}$

32. $y^2 + 400 = 0; y^2 = -400; y = \pm\sqrt{-400} = \pm 20i; \{\pm 20i\}$

33. $2w^2 = -98; w^2 = -49; w = \pm\sqrt{-49} = \pm 7i; \{\pm 7i\}$

34. $5t^2 = -20; t^2 = -4; t = \pm\sqrt{-4} = \pm 2i; \{\pm 2i\}$

35. $3u^2 + 40 = 4; 3u^2 = -36; u^2 = -12; u = \pm\sqrt{-12} = \pm 2i\sqrt{3}; \{\pm 2i\sqrt{3}\}$

36. $4z^2 + 39 = 7; 4z^2 = -32; z^2 = -8; z = \pm\sqrt{-8} = \pm 2i\sqrt{2}; \{\pm 2i\sqrt{2}\}$

37. **a.** $5i + 6i = 11i$ **b.** $(5i)(6i) = -30$

38. **a.** $i\sqrt{3} + 3i\sqrt{3} = 4i\sqrt{3}$ **b.** $(i\sqrt{3})(3i\sqrt{3}) = -9$

39. **a.** $3i\sqrt{2} - 5i\sqrt{2} = -2i\sqrt{2}$ **b.** $(3i\sqrt{2})(-5i\sqrt{2}) = 30$

40. **a.** $4i\sqrt{6} - 3i\sqrt{6} = i\sqrt{6}$ **b.** $(4i\sqrt{6})(-3i\sqrt{6}) = 72$

41. **a.** $3i\sqrt{2} + 2i\sqrt{2} = 5i\sqrt{2}$ **b.** $(3i\sqrt{2})(2i\sqrt{2}) = -12$

42. **a.** $-7\sqrt{2} - 7\sqrt{2} = -14\sqrt{2}$ **b.** $(-7\sqrt{2})(-7\sqrt{2}) = 98$

B **43.** $(2i\sqrt{3a})(i\sqrt{3a}) = -6a$ **44.** $(-3\sqrt{2c})(ic\sqrt{2c}) = -6c^2 i$

45. $\left(i\sqrt{\frac{r}{5}}\right)\left(2i\sqrt{\frac{5}{r}}\right) = -2$ **46.** $\left(t^2 i\sqrt{\frac{t}{2}}\right)\left(\frac{i}{t}\sqrt{\frac{2}{t}}\right) = -t$

47. $ic\sqrt{3} + 3ic\sqrt{3} - 3ic\sqrt{5} = 4ic\sqrt{3} - 3ic\sqrt{5}$

48. $t^2 i\sqrt{2t} + 2t^2 i\sqrt{2t} - 3t^2 i\sqrt{2t} = 0$ **49.** $2ri\sqrt{r} + 8ri\sqrt{r} - 16ri\sqrt{r} = -6ri\sqrt{r}$

50. $5ai\sqrt{a} - 15ai\sqrt{a} + 20ai\sqrt{a} = 10ai\sqrt{a}$

51. $x^2 i\sqrt{x} + 5x^2 i - 5x^2 i\sqrt{x} = 5x^2 i - 4x^2 i\sqrt{x}$

52. $4y^2 i^2 + 4y^2 - 3y^2 i^2 = -4y^2 + 4y^2 + 3y^2 = 3y^2$

53. $i^2 = -1; i^3 = -i; i^4 = 1; i^5 = i; i^6 = -1; i^7 = -i; i^8 = 1; i^9 = i; i^{10} = -1;$
$i^{11} = -i; i^{12} = 1$. If $n = 4k + r$ (k and r integers), then $i^n = i^r$.

54. **a.** $i^{100} = i^4 = 1$ **b.** $i^{101} = i^1 = i$ **c.** $i^{102} = i^2 = -1$ **d.** $i^{103} = i^3 = -i$

Page 291 • MIXED REVIEW EXERCISES

1. $\sqrt{2x - 3} = 5; 2x - 3 = 25; 2x = 28; x = 14; \{14\}$

2. $15 - 2n = n^2; n^2 + 2n - 15 = 0; (n - 3)(n + 5) = 0; n = 3$ or $n = -5; \{-5, 3\}$

3. $\sqrt{y^2 + 12} = 2y; y^2 + 12 = 4y^2; 3y^2 = 12; y^2 = 4; y = \pm 2$; reject -2; $\{2\}$

4. $\frac{3y - 4}{5} = \frac{y + 1}{2}; 2(3y - 4) = 5(y + 1); 6y - 8 = 5y + 5; y = 13; \{13\}$

5. $\frac{1}{n} + \frac{2}{n - 2} = \frac{4}{n(n - 2)}; n - 2 + 2n = 4; 3n = 6; n = 2$ (reject); no real solution

6. $2\sqrt[3]{x} + 9 = 5; 2\sqrt[3]{x} = -4; \sqrt[3]{x} = -2; x = -8; \{-8\}$

7. $y = \sqrt{5y - 6}; y^2 = 5y - 6; y^2 - 5y + 6 = 0; (y - 3)(y - 2) = 0; y = 3$ or $y = 2$;
$\{2, 3\}$

8. $5|n| - 7 = 3; 5|n| = 10; |n| = 2; n = \pm 2; \{-2, 2\}$

9. $x = 2 + \sqrt{x+4}$; $x - 2 = \sqrt{x+4}$; $x^2 - 4x + 4 = x + 4$; $x^2 - 5x = 0$; $x(x-5) = 0$; $x = 0$ (reject) or $x = 5$; $\{5\}$

10. rational 11. rational 12. irrational 13. irrational

Pages 295–296 • WRITTEN EXERCISES

A 1. $10 - 5i$ 2. $-2 - 6i$ 3. $-3 - 9i$ 4. $10 - 5i$

5. $-6 + 3i - 12 + 8i = -18 + 11i$ 6. $-2 + 12i - 6 - 15i = -8 - 3i$

7. $3i + 4i^2 = -4 + 3i$ 8. $15i - 18i^2 = 18 + 15i$ 9. $8i - 4i^2 = 4 + 8i$

10. $-2i + 6i^2 = -6 - 2i$ 11. 10 12. 17 13. 58

14. $-10 + 15i + 6i - 9i^2 = -1 + 21i$ 15. $-32 - 20i + 8i + 5i^2 = -37 - 12i$

16. $6 + 12i - 14i - 28i^2 = 34 - 2i$ 17. $-2 - 6i + 5i + 15i^2 = -17 - i$

18. $-6 + 9i - 8i + 12i^2 = -18 + i$ 19. 21 20. 7

21. $4 - 16i + 16i^2 = -12 - 16i$ 22. $36 - 84i + 49i^2 = -13 - 84i$

23. $1 - 2i\sqrt{3} + 3i^2 = -2 - 2i\sqrt{3}$ 24. $9 + 6i\sqrt{5} + 5i^2 = 4 + 6i\sqrt{5}$

25. $[(3+2i)(3-2i)]^2 = 13^2 = 169$ 26. $[(2-3i)(2+3i)]^2 = 13^2 = 169$

27. $(\sqrt{2} - i\sqrt{5})(\sqrt{2} + i\sqrt{5}) = 7$ 28. $(\sqrt{3} + i\sqrt{7})(\sqrt{3} - i\sqrt{7}) = 10$

29. $\frac{5}{3+4i} \cdot \frac{3-4i}{3-4i} = \frac{5(3-4i)}{25} = \frac{3}{5} - \frac{4}{5}i$ 30. $\frac{15}{2-i} \cdot \frac{2+i}{2+i} = \frac{15(2+i)}{5} = 6 + 3i$

31. $\frac{2}{3-i} \cdot \frac{3+i}{3+i} = \frac{2(3+i)}{10} = \frac{3}{5} + \frac{1}{5}i$ 32. $\frac{10}{1+7i} \cdot \frac{1-7i}{1-7i} = \frac{10(1-7i)}{50} = \frac{1}{5} - \frac{7}{5}i$

33. $\frac{-1-2i}{-1+2i} \cdot \frac{-1-2i}{-1-2i} = \frac{1+4i+4i^2}{5} = -\frac{3}{5} + \frac{4}{5}i$

34. $\frac{5+i}{5-i} \cdot \frac{5+i}{5+i} = \frac{24+10i}{26} = \frac{12}{13} + \frac{5}{13}i$

35. $\frac{6-i\sqrt{2}}{6+i\sqrt{2}} \cdot \frac{6-i\sqrt{2}}{6-i\sqrt{2}} = \frac{34-12i\sqrt{2}}{38} = \frac{17}{19} - \frac{6\sqrt{2}}{19}i$

36. $\frac{-3+i\sqrt{5}}{-3-i\sqrt{5}} \cdot \frac{-3+i\sqrt{5}}{-3+i\sqrt{5}} = \frac{4-6i\sqrt{5}}{14} = \frac{2}{7} - \frac{3\sqrt{5}}{7}i$

37. $\frac{1}{2+3i} \cdot \frac{2-3i}{2-3i} = \frac{2-3i}{13} = \frac{2}{13} - \frac{3}{13}i$ 38. $\frac{1}{1-4i} \cdot \frac{1+4i}{1+4i} = \frac{1+4i}{17} = \frac{1}{17} + \frac{4}{17}i$

39. $\frac{1}{-\sqrt{3}+i\sqrt{6}} \cdot \frac{-\sqrt{3}-i\sqrt{6}}{-\sqrt{3}-i\sqrt{6}} = \frac{-\sqrt{3}-i\sqrt{6}}{9} = \frac{-\sqrt{3}}{9} - \frac{\sqrt{6}}{9}i$

40. $\frac{1}{-\sqrt{5}-i\sqrt{2}} \cdot \frac{-\sqrt{5}+i\sqrt{2}}{-\sqrt{5}+i\sqrt{2}} = \frac{-\sqrt{5}+i\sqrt{2}}{7} = -\frac{\sqrt{5}}{7} + \frac{\sqrt{2}}{7}i$

41. $f(1+3i) = 1 + 3i + \frac{1}{1+3i} = 1 + 3i + \frac{1}{1+3i} \cdot \frac{1-3i}{1-3i} = 1 + 3i + \frac{1-3i}{10} =$
$\frac{11}{10} + \frac{27}{10}i$

42. $g(2-i) = 2 - i - \frac{1}{2-i} \cdot \frac{(2+i)}{(2+i)} = 2 - i - \frac{2+i}{5} = \frac{8}{5} - \frac{6}{5}i$

43. $g(1+i\sqrt{3}) = \frac{(1+i\sqrt{3})-1}{(1+i\sqrt{3})+1} = \frac{i\sqrt{3}}{2+i\sqrt{3}} \cdot \frac{2-i\sqrt{3}}{2-i\sqrt{3}} = \frac{2i\sqrt{3}+3}{7} = \frac{3}{7} + \frac{2\sqrt{3}}{7}i$

44. $f(1 - i) = \frac{2 + (1 - i)}{2 - (1 - i)} = \frac{3 - i}{1 + i} \cdot \frac{1 - i}{1 - i} = \frac{2 - 4i}{2} = 1 - 2i$

B **45.** $(2 + i)^2 - 4(2 + i) + 5 = 3 + 4i - 8 - 4i + 5 = 0$

46. $(1 - 3i)^2 - 2(1 - 3i) + 10 = -8 - 6i - 2 + 6i + 10 = 0$

47. a. $\left(\frac{\sqrt{2}}{2} + \frac{\sqrt{2}}{2}i\right)^2 = \frac{1}{2} + \frac{1}{2}i + \frac{1}{2}i + \frac{i^2}{2} = i$ **b.** $-\frac{\sqrt{2}}{2} - \frac{\sqrt{2}}{2}i$

48. a. $(-1 - i\sqrt{3})^3 = (-1 - i\sqrt{3})(-1 - i\sqrt{3})^2 = (-1 - i\sqrt{3})(-2 + 2i\sqrt{3}) =$
$2 - 2i\sqrt{3} + 2i\sqrt{3} - 6i^2 = 8$

b. $(-1 + i\sqrt{3})^3 = (-1 + i\sqrt{3})(-1 + i\sqrt{3})^2 = (-1 + i\sqrt{3})(-2 - 2i\sqrt{3}) =$
$2 + 2i\sqrt{3} - 2i\sqrt{3} - 6i^2 = 8$; $-1 + i\sqrt{3}$ is a cube root of 8.

49. $\left(\frac{3}{5} + \frac{4}{5}i\right)\left(\frac{3}{5} - \frac{4}{5}i\right) = \frac{9}{25} - \frac{16}{25}i^2 = 1$; since their product is 1, the numbers are reciprocals

50. $\left(\frac{1}{2} + \frac{\sqrt{3}}{2}i\right)\left(\frac{1}{2} - \frac{\sqrt{3}}{2}i\right) = \frac{1}{4} - \frac{3}{4}i^2 = 1$; since their product is 1, the numbers are reciprocals

C **51.** Answers may vary. Any complex numbers of the form $a \pm bi$ where $a^2 + b^2 = 1$.
Example: $\frac{1}{3} + \frac{2\sqrt{2}}{3}i$ and $\frac{1}{3} - \frac{2\sqrt{2}}{3}i$

52. Since the numbers are reciprocals, $(a + bi)(a - bi) = 1$; therefore $a^2 + b^2 = 1$

53–56. Let $a + bi$, $c + di$, and $e + fi$ be any three complex numbers where a, b, c, d, e, and f are real numbers.

53. (1) $[(a + bi) + (c + di)] + (e + fi) = [(a + c) + (b + d)i] + (e + fi)$ (Def. of complex add.)

(2) $= [(a + c) + e] + [(b + d) + f]i$ (Def. of complex add.)

(3) $= [a + (c + e)] + [b + (d + f)]i$ (Assoc. prop. of real add.)

(4) $= (a + bi) + [(c + e) + (d + f)i]$ (Def. of complex add.)

(5) $= (a + bi) + [(c + di) + (e + fi)]$ (Def. of complex add.)

54. (1) $(a + bi)(c + di) = (ac - bd) + (ad + bc)i$ (Def. of complex mult.)

(2) $= (ca - db) + (da + cb)i$ (Comm. prop. of real mult.)

(3) $= (c + di)(a + bi)$ (Def. of complex mult.)

55. (1) $[(a + bi)(c + di)](e + fi) = [(ac - bd) + (ad + bc)i](e + fi)$ (Def. of complex mult.)

(2) $= [(ac - bd)e - (ad + bc)f] + [(ad + bc)e + (ac - bd)f]i$ (Def. of complex mult.)

(3) $= [ace - bde - adf - bcf] + [ade + bce + acf - bdf]i$ (Dist. prop. of reals)

(Continued)

(4) $[(a + bi)(c + di)](e + fi) = [a(ce - df) - b(de + cf)] + [a(de + cf) + b(ce - df)]i$ (Dist. prop. of reals)

(5) $= (a + bi)[(ce - df) + (de + cf)i]$ (Def. of complex mult.)

(6) $= (a + bi)[(c + di)(e + fi)]$ (Def. of complex mult.)

56. (1) $(a + bi)[(c + di) + (e + fi)] = (a + bi)[(c + e) + (d + f)i]$ (Def. of complex add.)

(2) $= [a(c + e) - b(d + f)] + [a(d + f) + b(c + e)]i$ (Def. of complex mult.)

(3) $= [ac + ae - bd - bf] + [ad + af + bc + be]i$ (Dist. prop. of reals)

(4) $= [(ac - bd) + (ae - bf)] + [(ad + bc) + (af + be)]i$ (Assoc. and comm. prop. of real add.)

(5) $= [(ac - bd) + (ad + bc)i] + [(ae - bf) + (af + be)i]$ (Def. of complex add.)

(6) $= (a + bi)(c + di) + (a + bi)(e + fi)$ (Def. of complex mult.)

Page 300 • EXTRA

A **1.** $\sqrt{(-4)^2 + 3^2} = 5$ **2.** $\sqrt{12^2 + (-5)^2} = 13$ **3.** $\sqrt{2^2} = 2$ **4.** $\sqrt{(-3)^2} = 3$

5. $\sqrt{\left(\frac{\sqrt{2}}{2}\right)^2 + \left(\frac{\sqrt{2}}{2}\right)^2} = \sqrt{\frac{1}{2} + \frac{1}{2}} = 1$ **6.** $\sqrt{\left(\frac{\sqrt{3}}{2}\right)^2 + \left(-\frac{1}{2}\right)^2} = \sqrt{\frac{3}{4} + \frac{1}{4}} = 1$

7. $|z|^2 = 5^2 = 25; \overline{z} = -4 - 3i; \frac{1}{z} = -\frac{4}{25} - \frac{3}{25}i$

8. $|z|^2 = 13^2 = 169; \overline{z} = 12 + 5i; \frac{1}{z} = \frac{12}{169} + \frac{5}{169}i$

9. $|z|^2 = 2^2 = 4; \overline{z} = -2i; \frac{1}{z} = -\frac{1}{2}i$ **10.** $|z|^2 = 3^2 = 9; \overline{z} = -3; \frac{1}{z} = \frac{-3}{9} = -\frac{1}{3}$

11. $|z|^2 = 1^2 = 1; \overline{z} = \frac{\sqrt{2}}{2} - \frac{\sqrt{2}}{2}i; \frac{1}{z} = \frac{\sqrt{2}}{2} - \frac{\sqrt{2}}{2}i$

12. $|z|^2 = 1^2 = 1; \overline{z} = \frac{\sqrt{3}}{2} + \frac{1}{2}i; \frac{1}{z} = \frac{\sqrt{3}}{2} + \frac{1}{2}i$

13. Let $z = u + vi; \overline{z} = u - vi; |\overline{z}| = \sqrt{u^2 + (-v)^2} = \sqrt{u^2 + v^2}; |z| = \sqrt{u^2 + v^2}$

14. Let $z = u + vi; z + \overline{z} = (u + vi) + (u - vi) = 2u$

15. a. Let $z = u + vi; z - \overline{z} = (u + vi) - (u - vi) = 2vi; v = \frac{z - \overline{z}}{2i} \cdot \frac{i}{i} = \frac{(z - \overline{z})i}{-2} = \frac{(\overline{z} - z)i}{2}$

b. Let $z = u + vi$. If $z = \overline{z}$, then $u + vi = u - vi; v = 0$. If $v = 0$, then $z = u + 0 = u$ and $\overline{z} = u - 0 = u; z = \overline{z}$.

16–17. Let $w = u + vi$ and $z = x + yi$ be complex numbers with u, v, x, and y real.

16. $\overline{w + z} = \overline{(u + x) + (v + y)i} = (u + x) - (v + y)i; \overline{w} + \overline{z} = (u - vi) + (x - yi) = (u + x) + (-v - y)i = (u + x) - (v + y)i$

17. $\overline{w - z} = \overline{(u + vi) - (x + yi)} = \overline{(u - x) + (v - y)i} = (u - x) + (y - v)i$;
$\overline{w} - \overline{z} = (u - vi) - (x - yi) = (u - x) + (-v + y)i = (u - x) + (y - v)i$

B **18.** Let $z = u + vi$; $\overline{\left(\frac{1}{z}\right)} = \overline{\left(\frac{1}{u + vi} \cdot \frac{u - vi}{u - vi}\right)} = \overline{\left(\frac{u - vi}{u^2 + v^2}\right)} = \frac{u}{u^2 + v^2} + \frac{v}{u^2 + v^2}i$;
$\frac{1}{\overline{z}} = \frac{1}{u - vi} \cdot \frac{u + vi}{u + vi} = \frac{u + vi}{u^2 + v^2} = \frac{u}{u^2 + v^2} + \frac{v}{u^2 + v^2}i$

19. $\overline{\left(\frac{w}{z}\right)} = \overline{\left(w \cdot \frac{1}{z}\right)} = \overline{w} \cdot \overline{\left(\frac{1}{z}\right)} = \overline{w} \cdot \frac{1}{\overline{z}} = \frac{\overline{w}}{\overline{z}}$.

20. $\left|\frac{w}{z}\right|^2 = \frac{w}{z}\overline{\left(\frac{w}{z}\right)} = \frac{w}{z} \cdot \frac{\overline{w}}{\overline{z}} = \frac{|w|^2}{|z|^2}$. Since $\left|\frac{w}{z}\right|$, $|w|$, $|z| \geq 0$, taking principal square roots gives $\left|\frac{w}{z}\right| = \frac{|w|}{|z|}$.

C **21.** $w\overline{z} + \overline{w}z = w\overline{z} + \overline{w\overline{z}}$ = twice the real part of $w\overline{z}$ (see Exercise 14). Let $w\overline{z} = u + vi$; then $w\overline{z} + \overline{w}z = 2u$. $u \leq \sqrt{u^2 + v^2} = |w\overline{z}|$; $u \leq |w\overline{z}|$;
$w\overline{z} + \overline{w}z = 2u \leq 2|w\overline{z}| = 2|w|\,|\overline{z}| = 2|w||z|$

22.

$\lvert w + z\rvert^2 = (w + z)(\overline{w + z})$	(If z is a complex number, then $\lvert z\rvert^2 = z\overline{z}$.)
$= (w + z)(\overline{w} + \overline{z})$	(If w and z are complex numbers, then $\overline{w + z} = \overline{w} + \overline{z}$.)
$= w\overline{w} + w\overline{z} + \overline{w}z + z\overline{z}$	(Distributive prop.)
$\leq w\overline{w} + 2\lvert w\rvert\,\lvert z\rvert + z\overline{z}$	(Exercise 21)
$\leq \lvert w\rvert^2 + 2\lvert w\rvert\,\lvert z\rvert + \lvert z\rvert^2$	(If z is a complex number, then $\lvert z\rvert^2 = z\overline{z}$.)
$\leq (\lvert w\rvert + \lvert z\rvert)^2$	(Distributive prop.)
$\therefore \lvert w + z\rvert \leq \lvert w\rvert + \lvert z\rvert$	(If a and $b \geq 0$ and $a^2 < b^2$, then $a < b$.)

Pages 302–303 • CHAPTER REVIEW

1. c **2.** c; $2 - y^2 = 0$; $2 = y^2$; $y = \pm\sqrt{2}$ **3.** b

4. a; $\sqrt{18} \cdot \sqrt{\frac{3}{10}} = \frac{3\sqrt{2} \cdot \sqrt{3}}{\sqrt{10}} = \frac{3\sqrt{3}}{\sqrt{5}} \cdot \frac{\sqrt{5}}{\sqrt{5}} = \frac{3\sqrt{15}}{5}$

5. a; $\sqrt{6}\left(\frac{\sqrt{2}}{2} + \sqrt{3}\right) - \sqrt{8} = \frac{\sqrt{12}}{2} + \sqrt{18} - 2\sqrt{2} = \sqrt{3} + 3\sqrt{2} - 2\sqrt{2} =$
$\sqrt{3} + \sqrt{2}$

6. d; $\sqrt{72x^3} - 5x\sqrt{2x} = 6x\sqrt{2x} - 5x\sqrt{2x} = x\sqrt{2x}$

7. c; $(2\sqrt{6} - \sqrt{3})^2 = 24 - 4\sqrt{18} + 3 = 27 - 12\sqrt{2}$

8. c; $\frac{6}{3 + 2\sqrt{3}} \cdot \frac{3 - 2\sqrt{3}}{3 - 2\sqrt{3}} = \frac{6(3 - 2\sqrt{3})}{-3} = -6 + 4\sqrt{3}$

9. d; $3 - 2\sqrt{x} = 7$; $2\sqrt{x} = -4$; $\sqrt{x} = -2$; no real solution

10. a; $2 - y = \sqrt{y + 4}$; $4 - 4y + y^2 = y + 4$; $y^2 - 5y = 0$; $y(y - 5) = 0$; $y = 0$ or $y = 5$ (reject); $\{0\}$

11. b; Let $N = 0.\overline{675}$; then $1000N = 675.\overline{675}$; $999N = 675$; $N = \frac{675}{999} = \frac{25}{37}$ **12.** d

13. a; $3i\sqrt{2} \cdot \sqrt{-12} = (3i\sqrt{2})(2i\sqrt{3}) = -6\sqrt{6}$

14. c; $3x^2 + 14 = 8$; $3x^2 = -6$; $x^2 = -2$; $x = \pm\sqrt{-2} = \pm i\sqrt{2}$; $\{\pm i\sqrt{2}\}$

15. b; $(2 + 3i)(1 - i) = 2 + i + 3 = 5 + i$

16. d; $\frac{3 - 4i}{-2 + i} \cdot \frac{-2 - i}{-2 - i} = \frac{-10 + 5i}{5} = -2 + i$

Page 303 • CHAPTER TEST

1. $\sqrt[3]{(-8)^3} = -8$ **2.** $(\sqrt{49})^2 = 49$ **3.** $\sqrt[3]{-64} = -4$ **4.** $\sqrt[4]{81} = 3$

5. $16x^2 = 81; x^2 = \frac{81}{16}; x = \pm\frac{9}{4}; \left\{\pm\frac{9}{4}\right\}$

6. $2x^3 = -16; x^3 = -8; x = \sqrt[3]{-8} = -2; \{-2\}$

7. $\frac{\sqrt{15}\cdot\sqrt{42}}{\sqrt{35}} = \frac{\sqrt{5\cdot 3}\cdot\sqrt{2\cdot 3\cdot 7}}{\sqrt{5\cdot 7}} = 3\sqrt{2}$ **8.** $\sqrt{\frac{75a^6}{32b^3}} = \frac{5|a|^3\sqrt{3}}{4b\sqrt{2b}}\cdot\frac{\sqrt{2b}}{\sqrt{2b}} = \frac{5|a|^3\sqrt{6b}}{8b^2}$

9. $13\sqrt{5} - \sqrt{10}(3\sqrt{2} + 4\sqrt{5}) = 13\sqrt{5} - 3\sqrt{20} - 4\sqrt{50} =$
$13\sqrt{5} - 6\sqrt{5} - 20\sqrt{2} = 7\sqrt{5} - 20\sqrt{2}$

10. $\frac{\sqrt{5x}}{\sqrt{3}} + \sqrt{\frac{3x}{5}} = \frac{\sqrt{15x}}{3} + \frac{\sqrt{15x}}{5} = \frac{5\sqrt{15x} + 3\sqrt{15x}}{15} = \frac{8\sqrt{15x}}{15}$

11. $(5 + 2\sqrt{6})(8 - 3\sqrt{6}) = 40 + \sqrt{6} - 36 = 4 + \sqrt{6}$

12. $\frac{2}{3 - \sqrt{5}}\cdot\frac{3 + \sqrt{5}}{3 + \sqrt{5}} = \frac{2(3 + \sqrt{5})}{4} = \frac{3 + \sqrt{5}}{2}$

13. $\sqrt[3]{4x - 1} = 3; 4x - 1 = 27; 4x = 28; x = 7; \{7\}$

14. $\sqrt{3y + 4} = 2 + \sqrt{y + 2}; 3y + 4 = 4 + 4\sqrt{y + 2} + y + 2; 2y - 2 = 4\sqrt{y + 2};$
$y - 1 = 2\sqrt{y + 2}; y^2 - 2y + 1 = 4(y + 2); y^2 - 6y - 7 = 0; (y - 7)(y + 1) = 0;$
$y = 7$ or $y = -1$ (reject); $\{7\}$

15. Let $N = 0.7\overline{45}$, then $100N = 74.5\overline{45}; 99N = 73.8; N = \frac{73.8}{99} = \frac{41}{55}$

16. Answers may vary. Examples are 1.9995 and 1.99909999099999 . . .

17. $(3i\sqrt{5})(2i\sqrt{5}) = -30$ **18.** $2i\sqrt{3} - 5i\sqrt{3} = -3i\sqrt{3}$ **19.** $2 + 3i$

20. $9 - 8i$ **21.** $12 + 14i + 48 = 60 + 14i$

22. $\frac{6 + i}{3 - 2i}\cdot\frac{3 + 2i}{3 + 2i} = \frac{18 + 15i - 2}{13} = \frac{16}{13} + \frac{15}{13}i$

Page 304 • MIXED PROBLEM SOLVING

A **1.** Let x = number of lemons bought and y = number of limes. Each lemon costs 20¢ and each lime costs 25¢. $20x + 25y = 210; 25y = -20x + 210; y = \frac{-4x + 42}{5}$. Since x and y are positive integers, the possible values for (x, y) are (3, 6) and (8, 2). Either 3 lemons and 6 limes or 8 lemons and 2 limes.

2. Let d = number of dimes and q = number of quarters. $\begin{matrix} d + q = 20 \\ 10d + 25q = 315 \end{matrix};$

$\begin{matrix} 10d + 10q = 200 \\ 10d + 25q = 315 \end{matrix}; 15q = 115; q = 7\frac{2}{3}$; this is impossible since q is an integer. There is no solution.

3. Let t = number of daily tickets purchased. $1.25t \le 34.00; t \le 27.2$. At most 27 daily passes can be purchased.

4. 1 micron $= 10^{-6}$ m; 0.2 micron $= 0.2 \times 10^{-6} = 2 \times 10^{-7}$ m

5. Let x = amount, in dollars, invested at 6%. Then $7000 - x$ was invested at 10%. $0.06x + 0.10(7000 - x) - 120 = 0.06(7000 - x) + 0.10x$; $0.06x + 700 - 0.10x - 120 = 420 - 0.06x + 0.10x$; $-0.08x = -160$; $x = 2000$. \$2000 was invested at 6% and \$5000 was invested at 10%.

6. He wants at least a \$500 commission. Let x = monthly sales in dollars. $0.02x \geq 500$; $x \geq 25{,}000$. He must have at least \$25,000 in sales per month.

7. Let d = the denominator of the fraction. Then the numerator is $3 + 2d$. $\frac{3 + 2d}{d} = \frac{9}{4}$; $12 + 8d = 9d$; $d = 12$. The fraction is $\frac{27}{12}$.

B

8. The rate traveling downstream was $\frac{36}{2} = 18$ km/h; the rate upstream was $\frac{36}{3} = 12$ km/h. Let r = the rate of the boat in still water (km/h) and c = the rate of the current (km/h). $\begin{matrix} r + c = 18 \\ r - c = 12 \end{matrix}$; $2c = 6$; $c = 3$. The current is 3 km/h.

9. Let l = length in cm; w = width in cm. Then $P = 2(l + w) = 18$ and $A = lw = 18$; $w = \frac{18}{l}$; $2\left(l + \frac{18}{l}\right) = 18$; $l + \frac{18}{l} = 9$; $l^2 + 18 = 9l$; $l^2 - 9l + 18 = 0$; $(l - 6)(l - 3) = 0$; $l = 3$ or $l = 6$; The length is 6 cm and the width is 3 cm.

10. Let profit, $P(x)$, be a function of sales, x (both in dollars). $P(x) = mx + b$; $P(50{,}000) = 6000 = m(50{,}000) + b$; $P(70{,}000) = 9000 = m(70{,}000) + b$; $20{,}000m = 3000$; $m = \frac{3}{20}$; $6000 = \frac{3}{20}(50{,}000) + b$; $b = -1500$; $0 \leq P(x)$; $0 \leq \frac{3}{20}x - 1500$; $1500 \leq \frac{3}{20}x$; $x \geq 10{,}000$. There must be at least \$10,000 in sales to avoid a loss.

11. Let x = the time, in hours, Marie spent making salads. $\frac{1}{2}x + \frac{1}{3}(x - 1) = 1$; $3x + 2x - 2 = 6$; $5x = 8$; $x = \frac{8}{5}$. Marie spent 1 h 36 min. They finished at 11:36 A.M.

12. Let l = length of shorter leg; $l^2 + (l + 3)^2 = (l + 6)^2$; $l^2 + l^2 + 6l + 9 = l^2 + 12l + 36$; $l^2 - 6l - 27 = 0$; $(l - 9)(l + 3) = 0$; $l = 9$; $9 + 6 = 15$; hypotenuse is 15.

Page 305 • PREPARING FOR COLLEGE ENTRANCE EXAMS

1. B; $(y - 3)(y + 2) = 0$; $y = 3$ or -2; $\{-2, 3\}$

2. B; $(1 + x)(1 - x)\left[\frac{1}{1 - x} + \frac{1}{1 + x}\right] = 4(1 + x)(1 - x)$; $1 + x + 1 - x = 4 - 4x^2$; $4x^2 = 2$, $x^2 = \frac{1}{2}$; $x^4 = \frac{1}{4}$

3. D; $-3\sqrt[3]{2} - 5\sqrt[3]{2} + 2\sqrt[3]{4} = -8\sqrt[3]{2} + 2\sqrt[3]{4} = 2(\sqrt[3]{4} - 4\sqrt[3]{2})$

4. D; $\frac{r^4 - 13r^2 + 36}{r^3 + r^2 - 6r} = \frac{(r^2 - 9)(r^2 - 4)}{r(r^2 + r - 6)} = \frac{(r + 3)(r - 3)(r + 2)(r - 2)}{r(r + 3)(r - 2)} = \frac{(r - 3)(r + 2)}{r}$;

$\frac{(r - 3)(r + 2)}{r} = 0$ if $r = 3$ or $r = -2$

5. B; $\frac{1}{2}x + 5 = \frac{1}{4}x^2 - x + 1$; $\frac{1}{4}x^2 - \frac{3}{2}x - 4 = 0$; $x^2 - 6x - 16 = 0$;

$(x - 8)(x + 2) = 0$; $x = 8$ or $x = -2$ (reject)

6. A; $6i\left(9i - \frac{2\sqrt{2}}{3i\sqrt{2}}\right) = -54 - 4 = -58$

7. C; $\frac{3^2 - \frac{1}{-3}}{2 - \frac{1}{(-2)^2}} = \frac{9 + \frac{1}{3}}{2 - \frac{1}{4}} = \frac{\frac{28}{3}}{\frac{7}{4}} = \frac{28}{3} \cdot \frac{4}{7} = \frac{16}{3}$

8. B; $\frac{1}{\sqrt{2} + \sqrt{3} - \sqrt{5}} \cdot \frac{(\sqrt{2} + \sqrt{3} + \sqrt{5})}{(\sqrt{2} + \sqrt{3} + \sqrt{5})} = \frac{\sqrt{2} + \sqrt{3} + \sqrt{5}}{(\sqrt{2} + \sqrt{3})^2 - 5} =$

$\frac{\sqrt{2} + \sqrt{3} + \sqrt{5}}{2\sqrt{6}} \cdot \frac{\sqrt{6}}{\sqrt{6}} = \frac{\sqrt{12} + \sqrt{18} + \sqrt{30}}{12} = \frac{2\sqrt{3} + 3\sqrt{2} + \sqrt{30}}{12}$

CHAPTER 7 • Quadratic Equations and Functions

Pages 309–310 • WRITTEN EXERCISES

A

1. **a.** $x^2 = 3; x = \pm\sqrt{3}; \{\pm\sqrt{3}\}$

b. $(x - 1)^2 = 3; x - 1 = \pm\sqrt{3}; x = 1 \pm \sqrt{3}; \{1 \pm \sqrt{3}\}$

c. $(2x - 1)^2 = 3; 2x - 1 = \pm\sqrt{3}; 2x = 1 \pm \sqrt{3}; x = \frac{1 \pm \sqrt{3}}{2}; \left\{\frac{1 \pm \sqrt{3}}{2}\right\}$

2. **a.** $x^2 = 6; x = \pm\sqrt{6}; \{\pm\sqrt{6}\}$

b. $(x + 4)^2 = 6; x + 4 = \pm\sqrt{6}; x = -4 \pm \sqrt{6}; \{-4 \pm \sqrt{6}\}$

c. $(3x + 4)^2 = 6; 3x + 4 = \pm\sqrt{6}; 3x = -4 \pm \sqrt{6}; x = \frac{-4 \pm \sqrt{6}}{3}; \left\{\frac{-4 \pm \sqrt{6}}{3}\right\}$

3. **a.** $y^2 = 16; y = \pm 4; \{\pm 4\}$ **b.** $(y + 7)^2 = 16; y + 7 = \pm 4; y = -7 \pm 4; \{-3, -11\}$

c. $(3y + 7)^2 = 16; 3y + 7 = \pm 4; 3y = -7 \pm 4; y = \frac{-7 \pm 4}{3}; \left\{-1, -\frac{11}{3}\right\}$

4. **a.** $y^2 = 49; y = \pm 7; \{\pm 7\}$ **b.** $(y - 8)^2 = 49; y - 8 = \pm 7; y = 8 \pm 7; \{15, 1\}$

c. $(5y - 8)^2 = 49; 5y - 8 = \pm 7; 5y = 8 \pm 7; y = \frac{8 \pm 7}{5}; \left\{3, \frac{1}{5}\right\}$

5. **a.** $x^2 = -4; x = \pm 2i; \{\pm 2i\}$

b. $(x + 7)^2 = -4; x + 7 = \pm 2i; x = -7 \pm 2i; \{-7 \pm 2i\}$

c. $(2x + 7)^2 = -4; 2x + 7 = \pm 2i; 2x = -7 \pm 2i; x = \frac{-7 \pm 2i}{2}; \left\{-\frac{7}{2} \pm i\right\}$

6. **a.** $z^2 = -5; z = \pm i\sqrt{5}; \{\pm i\sqrt{5}\}$

b. $(z - 3)^2 = -5; z - 3 = \pm i\sqrt{5}; z = 3 \pm i\sqrt{5}; \{3 \pm i\sqrt{5}\}$

c. $(5z - 3)^2 = -5; 5z - 3 = \pm i\sqrt{5}; 5z = 3 \pm i\sqrt{5}; z = \frac{3 \pm i\sqrt{5}}{5}; \left\{\frac{3}{5} \pm \frac{\sqrt{5}}{5}i\right\}$

7. $(y - 7)^2 = 12; y - 7 = \pm\sqrt{12} = \pm 2\sqrt{3}; y = 7 \pm 2\sqrt{3}; \{7 \pm 2\sqrt{3}\}$

8. $(t - 3)^2 = 8; t - 3 = \pm\sqrt{8} = \pm 2\sqrt{2}; t = 3 \pm 2\sqrt{2}; \{3 \pm 2\sqrt{2}\}$

9. $\left(\frac{1}{3}n + 2\right)^2 = 18; \frac{1}{3}n + 2 = \pm\sqrt{18} = \pm 3\sqrt{2}; \frac{1}{3}n = -2 \pm 3\sqrt{2}; n = -6 \pm 9\sqrt{2};$

$\{-6 \pm 9\sqrt{2}\}$

10. $\left(\frac{1}{2}t - 12\right)^2 = 50; \frac{1}{2}t - 12 = \pm\sqrt{50} = \pm 5\sqrt{2}; \frac{1}{2}t = 12 \pm 5\sqrt{2}; t = 24 \pm 10\sqrt{2};$

$\{24 \pm 10\sqrt{2}\}$

11. $3(y - 7)^2 = -12; (y - 7)^2 = -4; y - 7 = \pm 2i; y = 7 \pm 2i; \{7 \pm 2i\}$

12. $\frac{(x - 5)^2}{3} = -8; (x - 5)^2 = -24; x - 5 = \pm\sqrt{-24} = \pm 2i\sqrt{6}; x = 5 \pm 2i\sqrt{6};$

$\{5 \pm 2i\sqrt{6}\}$

13. $x^2 - 2x - 5 = 0; x^2 - 2x = 5; x^2 - 2x + 1 = 6; (x - 1)^2 = 6; x - 1 = \pm\sqrt{6};$
$x = 1 \pm \sqrt{6}; \{1 \pm \sqrt{6}\}$

14. $x^2 - 4x + 2 = 0; x^2 - 4x = -2; x^2 - 4x + 4 = 2; (x - 2)^2 = 2; x - 2 = \pm\sqrt{2};$
$x = 2 \pm \sqrt{2}; \{2 \pm \sqrt{2}\}$

15. $y^2 + 6y - 2 = 0; y^2 + 6y = 2; y^2 + 6y + 9 = 11; (y + 3)^2 = 11; y + 3 = \pm\sqrt{11};$
$y = -3 \pm \sqrt{11}; \{-3 \pm \sqrt{11}\}$

16. $y^2 + 8y + 6 = 0; y^2 + 8y = -6; y^2 + 8y + 16 = 10; (y + 4)^2 = 10;$
$y + 4 = \pm\sqrt{10}; y = -4 \pm \sqrt{10}; \{-4 \pm \sqrt{10}\}$

17. $p^2 + 20p + 200 = 0; p^2 + 20p + 100 = -100; (p + 10)^2 = -100; p + 10 = \pm 10i;$
$p = -10 \pm 10i; \{-10 \pm 10i\}$

18. $k^2 - 10k + 30 = 0; k^2 - 10k + 25 = -5; (k - 5)^2 = -5; k - 5 = \pm i\sqrt{5};$
$k = 5 \pm i\sqrt{5}; \{5 \pm i\sqrt{5}\}$

19. $x^2 - 1 = 4x; x^2 - 4x = 1; x^2 - 4x + 4 = 5; (x - 2)^2 = 5; x - 2 = \pm\sqrt{5};$
$x = 2 \pm \sqrt{5}; \{2 \pm \sqrt{5}\}$

20. $t^2 + 8 = 4t; t^2 - 4t = -8; t^2 - 4t + 4 = -4; (t - 2)^2 = -4; t - 2 = \pm 2i;$
$t = 2 \pm 2i; \{2 \pm 2i\}$

21. $2t^2 + 4t + 1 = 0; 2t^2 + 4t = -1; t^2 + 2t = -\frac{1}{2}; t^2 + 2t + 1 = \frac{1}{2}; (t + 1)^2 = \frac{1}{2};$
$t + 1 = \frac{\pm\sqrt{2}}{2}; t = -1 \pm \frac{\sqrt{2}}{2}; \left\{-1 \pm \frac{\sqrt{2}}{2}\right\}$

22. $3n^2 + 12n + 1 = 0; 3n^2 + 12n = -1; n^2 + 4n = -\frac{1}{3}; n^2 + 4n + 4 = \frac{11}{3};$
$(n + 2)^2 = \frac{11}{3}; n + 2 = \pm\sqrt{\frac{11}{3}} = \pm\frac{\sqrt{33}}{3}; n = -2 \pm \frac{\sqrt{33}}{3}; \left\{-2 \pm \frac{\sqrt{33}}{3}\right\}$

23. $5n^2 + 100 = 30n; 5n^2 - 30n = -100; n^2 - 6n = -20; n^2 - 6n + 9 = -11;$
$(n - 3)^2 = -11; n - 3 = \pm i\sqrt{11}; n = 3 \pm i\sqrt{11}; \{3 \pm i\sqrt{11}\}$

24. $2n^2 - 8n - 3 = 0; 2n^2 - 8n = 3; n^2 - 4n = \frac{3}{2}; n^2 - 4n + 4 = \frac{11}{2}; (n - 2)^2 = \frac{11}{2};$
$n - 2 = \pm\sqrt{\frac{11}{2}} = \pm\frac{\sqrt{22}}{2}; n = 2 \pm \frac{\sqrt{22}}{2}; \left\{2 \pm \frac{\sqrt{22}}{2}\right\}$

25. $x^2 - x - 1 = 0; x^2 - x = 1; x^2 - x + \frac{1}{4} = \frac{5}{4}; \left(x - \frac{1}{2}\right)^2 = \frac{5}{4}; x - \frac{1}{2} = \pm\frac{\sqrt{5}}{2};$
$x = \frac{1}{2} \pm \frac{\sqrt{5}}{2}; \left\{\frac{1}{2} \pm \frac{\sqrt{5}}{2}\right\}$

26. $y^2 - 3y - 5 = 0; y^2 - 3y = 5; y^2 - 3y + \frac{9}{4} = \frac{29}{4}; \left(y - \frac{3}{2}\right)^2 = \frac{29}{4}; y - \frac{3}{2} = \pm\frac{\sqrt{29}}{2};$
$y = \frac{3}{2} \pm \frac{\sqrt{29}}{2}; \left\{\frac{3}{2} \pm \frac{\sqrt{29}}{2}\right\}$

27. $3k^2 + 5k + 2 = 0; 3k^2 + 5k = -2; k^2 + \frac{5}{3}k = -\frac{2}{3}; k^2 + \frac{5}{3}k + \frac{25}{36} = \frac{1}{36};$
$\left(k + \frac{5}{6}\right)^2 = \frac{1}{36}; k + \frac{5}{6} = \pm\frac{1}{6}; k = -\frac{5}{6} \pm \frac{1}{6}; \left\{-\frac{2}{3}, -1\right\}$

B

28. $\frac{1}{2}x^2 - 3x = 2$; $x^2 - 6x = 4$; $x^2 - 6x + 9 = 13$; $(x-3)^2 = 13$; $x - 3 = \pm\sqrt{13}$; $x = 3 \pm \sqrt{13}$; $\{3 \pm \sqrt{13}\}$

29. $\frac{y^2}{4} - \frac{y}{2} + 1 = 0$; $\frac{y^2}{4} - \frac{y}{2} = -1$; $y^2 - 2y = -4$; $y^2 - 2y + 1 = -3$; $(y-1)^2 = -3$; $y - 1 = \pm i\sqrt{3}$; $y = 1 \pm i\sqrt{3}$; $\{1 \pm i\sqrt{3}\}$

30. $0.1x^2 - 0.6x + 9 = 0$; $0.1x^2 - 0.6x = -9$; $x^2 - 6x = -90$; $x^2 - 6x + 9 = -81$; $(x-3)^2 = -81$; $x - 3 = \pm 9i$; $x = 3 \pm 9i$; $\{3 \pm 9i\}$

31. $0.6x^2 + 2 = 2.4x$; $0.6x^2 - 2.4x = -2$; $x^2 - 4x = -\frac{10}{3}$; $x^2 - 4x + 4 = \frac{2}{3}$; $(x-2)^2 = \frac{2}{3}$; $x - 2 = \pm\sqrt{\frac{2}{3}} = \pm\frac{\sqrt{6}}{3}$; $x = 2 \pm \frac{\sqrt{6}}{3}$; $\left\{2 \pm \frac{\sqrt{6}}{3}\right\}$

32. $7x(1-x) = 5(x-2)$; $7x - 7x^2 = 5x - 10$; $7x^2 - 2x = 10$; $x^2 - \frac{2}{7}x = \frac{10}{7}$; $x^2 - \frac{2}{7}x + \frac{1}{49} = \frac{71}{49}$; $\left(x - \frac{1}{7}\right)^2 = \frac{71}{49}$; $x - \frac{1}{7} = \pm\frac{\sqrt{71}}{7}$; $x = \frac{1}{7} \pm \frac{\sqrt{71}}{7}$; $\left\{\frac{1}{7} \pm \frac{\sqrt{71}}{7}\right\}$

33. $2x(x-4) = 3(1-x)$; $2x^2 - 8x = 3 - 3x$; $2x^2 - 5x = 3$; $x^2 - \frac{5}{2}x = \frac{3}{2}$; $x^2 - \frac{5}{2}x + \frac{25}{16} = \frac{49}{16}$; $\left(x - \frac{5}{4}\right)^2 = \frac{49}{16}$; $x - \frac{5}{4} = \pm\frac{7}{4}$; $x = \frac{5}{4} \pm \frac{7}{4}$; $\left\{-\frac{1}{2}, 3\right\}$

34. $\frac{1}{x+1} + \frac{1}{x-1} = 1$; $1(x-1) + 1(x+1) = 1(x+1)(x-1)$; $2x = x^2 - 1$; $x^2 - 2x = 1$; $x^2 - 2x + 1 = 2$; $(x-1)^2 = 2$; $x - 1 = \pm\sqrt{2}$; $x = 1 \pm \sqrt{2}$; $\{1 \pm \sqrt{2}\}$

35. $\frac{1}{y+2} + \frac{1}{y+6} = 1$; $y + 6 + y + 2 = (y+2)(y+6)$; $2y + 8 = y^2 + 8y + 12$; $y^2 + 6y = -4$; $y^2 + 6y + 9 = 5$; $(y+3)^2 = 5$; $y + 3 = \pm\sqrt{5}$; $y = -3 \pm \sqrt{5}$; $\{-3 \pm \sqrt{5}\}$

36. $\sqrt{x+3} = 2x$; $x + 3 = 4x^2$; $4x^2 - x = 3$; $x^2 - \frac{x}{4} = \frac{3}{4}$; $x^2 - \frac{x}{4} + \frac{1}{64} = \frac{49}{64}$; $\left(x - \frac{1}{8}\right)^2 = \frac{49}{64}$; $x - \frac{1}{8} = \pm\frac{7}{8}$; $x = \frac{1}{8} \pm \frac{7}{8}$; $x = 1$ or $x = -\frac{3}{4}$ (reject); $\{1\}$

37. $\frac{x}{x-1} - \frac{x}{x+1} = 3 + \frac{2x^2}{1-x^2}$; $x(x+1) - x(x-1) = 3(x-1)(x+1) - 2x^2$; $x^2 + x - x^2 + x = 3x^2 - 3 - 2x^2$; $x^2 - 2x = 3$; $x^2 - 2x + 1 = 4$; $(x-1)^2 = 4$; $x - 1 = \pm 2$; $x = 1 \pm 2$; $x = 3$ or $x = -1$ (reject); $\{3\}$

38. $\frac{x+2}{x-2} + \frac{x-2}{x+2} = \frac{8-4x}{x^2-4}$; $(x+2)(x+2) + (x-2)(x-2) = 8 - 4x$; $x^2 + 4x + 4 + x^2 - 4x + 4 = 8 - 4x$; $2x^2 = -4x$; $x^2 + 2x = 0$; $x^2 + 2x + 1 = 1$; $(x+1)^2 = 1$; $x + 1 = \pm 1$; $x = -1 \pm 1$; $x = 0$ or $x = -2$ (reject); $\{0\}$

39. $\sqrt{x-4} - \frac{2}{\sqrt{x-4}} = 1; x - 4 - 2 = \sqrt{x-4}; x - 6 = \sqrt{x-4};$

$x^2 - 12x + 36 = x - 4; x^2 - 13x = -40; x^2 - 13x + \frac{169}{4} = \frac{9}{4}; \left(x - \frac{13}{2}\right)^2 = \frac{9}{4};$

$x - \frac{13}{2} = \pm\frac{3}{2}; x = \frac{13}{2} \pm \frac{3}{2}; x = 8$ or $x = 5$ (reject); $\{8\}$

C **40.** $x^2 + x + c = 0; x^2 + x = -c; x^2 + x + \frac{1}{4} = \frac{1}{4} - c; \left(x + \frac{1}{2}\right)^2 = \frac{1-4c}{4};$

$x + \frac{1}{2} = \pm\frac{\sqrt{1-4c}}{2}; x = -\frac{1}{2} \pm \frac{\sqrt{1-4c}}{2}; \left\{-\frac{1}{2} \pm \frac{\sqrt{1-4c}}{2}\right\}$

41. $x^2 + bx + c = 0; x^2 + bx = -c; x^2 + bx + \frac{b^2}{4} = \frac{b^2}{4} - c; \left(x + \frac{b}{2}\right)^2 = \frac{b^2 - 4c}{4};$

$x + \frac{b}{2} = \pm\frac{\sqrt{b^2-4c}}{2}; x = -\frac{b}{2} \pm \frac{\sqrt{b^2-4c}}{2}; \left\{-\frac{b}{2} \pm \frac{\sqrt{b^2-4c}}{2}\right\}$

42. $ax^2 + bx + c = 0; ax^2 + bx = -c; x^2 + \frac{b}{a}x = -\frac{c}{a}; x^2 + \frac{b}{a}x + \frac{b^2}{4a^2} = \frac{b^2}{4a^2} - \frac{c}{a};$

$\left(x + \frac{b}{2a}\right)^2 = \frac{b^2 - 4ac}{4a^2}; x + \frac{b}{2a} = \pm\frac{\sqrt{b^2-4ac}}{2a}; x = -\frac{b}{2a} \pm \frac{\sqrt{b^2-4ac}}{2a};$

$\left\{-\frac{b}{2a} \pm \frac{\sqrt{b^2-4ac}}{2a}\right\}$

Page 310 • MIXED REVIEW EXERCISES

1. $5i\sqrt{2}$ **2.** $12 + 3i - 8i - 2i^2 = 14 - 5i$ **3.** $27(2\sqrt{2}) = 54\sqrt{2}$

4. $7\sqrt{2} - 2\sqrt{2} = 5\sqrt{2}$ **5.** $4(-1)6 = -24$ **6.** $16 - 6i - 4 + 5i = 12 - i$

7. $\frac{\sqrt{10}}{5} + \frac{\sqrt{10}}{2} = \frac{2\sqrt{10}}{10} + \frac{5\sqrt{10}}{10} = \frac{7\sqrt{10}}{10}$ **8.** $-\frac{x}{3y}$

9. $\frac{x^2 - 5x + 6}{x^2 - 9} = \frac{(x-3)(x-2)}{(x-3)(x+3)} = \frac{x-2}{x+3}$

Pages 313–314 • WRITTEN EXERCISES

A **1.** $x^2 + 6x + 4 = 0; x = \frac{-6 \pm \sqrt{6^2 - 4(1)(4)}}{2} = \frac{-6 \pm \sqrt{20}}{2} = \frac{-6 \pm 2\sqrt{5}}{2} = -3 \pm \sqrt{5};$

$\{-3 \pm \sqrt{5}\}$

2. $v^2 + 3v - 5 = 0; v = \frac{-3 \pm \sqrt{3^2 - 4(1)(-5)}}{2} = \frac{-3 \pm \sqrt{29}}{2}; \left\{\frac{-3 \pm \sqrt{29}}{2}\right\}$

3. $y^2 - 4y + 13 = 0; y = \frac{4 \pm \sqrt{(-4)^2 - 4(1)(13)}}{2} = \frac{4 \pm \sqrt{-36}}{2} = \frac{4 \pm 6i}{2} = 2 \pm 3i;$

$\{2 \pm 3i\}$

4. $t^2 + 6t + 6 = 0; t = \frac{-6 \pm \sqrt{6^2 - 4(1)(6)}}{2} = \frac{-6 \pm \sqrt{12}}{2} = \frac{-6 \pm 2\sqrt{3}}{2} = -3 \pm \sqrt{3};$

$\{-3 \pm \sqrt{3}\}$

5. $5k^2 + 3k - 2 = 0; k = \frac{-3 \pm \sqrt{3^2 - 4(-2)(5)}}{2(5)} = \frac{-3 \pm \sqrt{49}}{10} = \frac{-3 \pm 7}{10}; \left\{\frac{2}{5}, -1\right\}$

6. $2p^2 - 3p - 2 = 0; p = \frac{3 \pm \sqrt{(-3)^2 - 4(2)(-2)}}{2(2)} = \frac{3 \pm \sqrt{25}}{4} = \frac{3 \pm 5}{4}; \left\{2, -\frac{1}{2}\right\}$

7. $5r^2 + 8 = -12r; 5r^2 + 12r + 8 = 0; r = \frac{-12 \pm \sqrt{12^2 - 4(5)(8)}}{2(5)} = \frac{-12 \pm \sqrt{-16}}{10} =$

$\frac{-12 \pm 4i}{10} = \frac{-6 \pm 2i}{5}; \left\{-\frac{6}{5} \pm \frac{2}{5}i\right\}$

8. $2w^2 + 4w = -3; 2w^2 + 4w + 3 = 0; w = \frac{-4 \pm \sqrt{4^2 - 4(2)(3)}}{2(2)} = \frac{-4 \pm \sqrt{-8}}{4} =$

$\frac{-4 \pm 2i\sqrt{2}}{4} = \frac{-2 \pm i\sqrt{2}}{2}; \left\{-1 \pm \frac{\sqrt{2}}{2}i\right\}$

9. $3y^2 = 1 - y; 3y^2 + y - 1 = 0; y = \frac{-1 \pm \sqrt{1^2 - 4(3)(-1)}}{2(3)} = \frac{-1 \pm \sqrt{13}}{6};$

$\left\{\frac{-1 \pm \sqrt{13}}{6}\right\}$

10. $8x = 1 - x^2; x^2 + 8x - 1 = 0; x = \frac{-8 \pm \sqrt{8^2 - 4(1)(-1)}}{2} = \frac{-8 \pm \sqrt{68}}{2} =$

$\frac{-8 \pm 2\sqrt{17}}{2} = -4 \pm \sqrt{17}; \{-4 \pm \sqrt{17}\}$

11. $2x(x + 1) = 7; 2x^2 + 2x - 7 = 0; x = \frac{-2 \pm \sqrt{2^2 - 4(2)(-7)}}{2(2)} = \frac{-2 \pm \sqrt{60}}{4} =$

$\frac{-2 \pm 2\sqrt{15}}{4} = \frac{-1 \pm \sqrt{15}}{2}; \left\{\frac{-1 \pm \sqrt{15}}{2}\right\}$

12. $5 = 4r(2r + 3); 5 = 8r^2 + 12r; 8r^2 + 12r - 5 = 0; r = \frac{-12 \pm \sqrt{12^2 - 4(8)(-5)}}{2(8)} =$

$\frac{-12 \pm \sqrt{304}}{16} = \frac{-12 \pm 4\sqrt{19}}{16} = \frac{-3 \pm \sqrt{19}}{4}; \left\{\frac{-3 \pm \sqrt{19}}{4}\right\}$

13. $(3n - 5)(2n - 2) = 6; 6n^2 - 16n + 10 = 6; 6n^2 - 16n + 4 = 0; n =$

$\frac{16 \pm \sqrt{(-16)^2 - 4(6)(4)}}{2(6)} = \frac{16 \pm \sqrt{160}}{12} = \frac{16 \pm 4\sqrt{10}}{12} = \frac{4 \pm \sqrt{10}}{3}; \left\{\frac{4 \pm \sqrt{10}}{3}\right\}$

14. $(2x + 1)(2x - 1) = 4x; 4x^2 - 1 = 4x; 4x^2 - 4x - 1 = 0;$

$x = \frac{4 \pm \sqrt{(-4)^2 - 4(4)(-1)}}{2(4)} = \frac{4 \pm \sqrt{32}}{8} = \frac{4 \pm 4\sqrt{2}}{8} = \frac{1 \pm \sqrt{2}}{2}; \left\{\frac{1 \pm \sqrt{2}}{2}\right\}$

15. $\frac{w^2}{2} - w = \frac{3}{4}; \frac{w^2}{2} - w - \frac{3}{4} = 0; 2w^2 - 4w - 3 = 0; w = \frac{4 \pm \sqrt{(-4)^2 - 4(2)(-3)}}{2(2)} =$

$\frac{4 \pm \sqrt{40}}{4} = \frac{4 \pm 2\sqrt{10}}{4} = \frac{2 \pm \sqrt{10}}{2}; \left\{\frac{2 \pm \sqrt{10}}{2}\right\}$

16. $\frac{t^2}{2} + 1 = \frac{t}{5}$; $5t^2 - 2t + 10 = 0$; $t = \frac{2 \pm \sqrt{(-2)^2 - 4(5)(10)}}{2(5)} = \frac{2 \pm \sqrt{-196}}{10} =$

$\frac{2 \pm 14i}{10} = \frac{1 \pm 7i}{5}$; $\left\{\frac{1}{5} \pm \frac{7}{5}i\right\}$

17. $\frac{2m^2 + 16}{5} = 2m$; $2m^2 - 10m + 16 = 0$; $m^2 - 5m + 8 = 0$;

$m = \frac{5 \pm \sqrt{(-5)^2 - 4(1)(8)}}{2(1)} = \frac{5 \pm \sqrt{-7}}{2} = \frac{5 \pm i\sqrt{7}}{2}$; $\left\{\frac{5}{2} \pm \frac{\sqrt{7}}{2}i\right\}$

18. $\frac{4 - 2y^2}{7} = 2y$; $2y^2 + 14y - 4 = 0$; $y^2 + 7y - 2 = 0$; $y = \frac{-7 \pm \sqrt{7^2 - 4(1)(-2)}}{2(1)} =$

$\frac{-7 \pm \sqrt{57}}{2}$; $\left\{\frac{-7 \pm \sqrt{57}}{2}\right\}$

19. $2n^2 - 4n = 8$; $n^2 - 2n - 4 = 0$; $n = \frac{2 \pm \sqrt{(-2)^2 - 4(1)(-4)}}{2(1)} = \frac{2 \pm \sqrt{20}}{2} = 1 \pm \sqrt{5}$;

$\{-1.24, 3.24\}$

20. $2x^2 - 3x = 7$; $2x^2 - 3x - 7 = 0$; $x = \frac{3 \pm \sqrt{(-3)^2 - 4(2)(-7)}}{2(2)} = \frac{3 \pm \sqrt{65}}{4}$;

$\{-1.27, 2.77\}$

21. $3t^2 - 6t - 7 = 0$; $t = \frac{6 \pm \sqrt{(-6)^2 - 4(3)(-7)}}{2(3)} = \frac{6 \pm \sqrt{120}}{6} = \frac{3 \pm \sqrt{30}}{3}$; $\{-0.83, 2.83\}$

22. $4x(x + 1) = 2.75$; $4x^2 + 4x - 2.75 = 0$; $x = \frac{-4 \pm \sqrt{4^2 - 4(4)(-2.75)}}{2(4)} = \frac{-4 \pm \sqrt{60}}{8} =$

$\frac{-2 \pm \sqrt{15}}{4}$; $\{-1.47, 0.47\}$

23. $3x(x + 2) = -2.5$; $3x^2 + 6x + 2.5 = 0$; $x = \frac{-6 \pm \sqrt{6^2 - 4(3)(2.5)}}{2(3)} = \frac{-6 \pm \sqrt{6}}{6}$;

$\{-1.41, -0.59\}$

24. $2t(t - 4) = -3$; $2t^2 - 8t + 3 = 0$; $t = \frac{8 \pm \sqrt{(-8)^2 - 4(2)(3)}}{2(2)} = \frac{8 \pm \sqrt{40}}{4} = \frac{4 \pm \sqrt{10}}{2}$;

$\{0.42, 3.58\}$

25. a. $5x^2 - 45 = 0$; $5(x^2 - 9) = 0$; $5(x - 3)(x + 3) = 0$; $x = 3$ or -3; $\{\pm 3\}$

b. $5x^2 - 45 = 0$; $x = \frac{0 \pm \sqrt{0^2 - 4(5)(-45)}}{2(5)} = \frac{\pm\sqrt{900}}{10} = \pm\frac{30}{10} = \pm 3$; $\{\pm 3\}$

26. a. $3y^2 - 48 = 0$; $3(y^2 - 16) = 0$; $3(y - 4)(y + 4) = 0$; $y = 4$ or -4; $\{\pm 4\}$

b. $3y^2 - 48 = 0$; $y = \frac{0 \pm \sqrt{0^2 - 4(3)(-48)}}{2(3)} = \frac{\pm\sqrt{576}}{6} = \pm\frac{24}{6} = \pm 4$; $\{\pm 4\}$

27. a. $3x^2 - 6x + 3 = 0$; $3(x^2 - 2x + 1) = 0$; $3(x - 1)^2 = 0$; $x = 1$; $\{1\}$

b. $3x^2 - 6x + 3 = 0$; $x = \frac{6 \pm \sqrt{(-6)^2 - 4(3)(3)}}{2(3)} = \frac{6 \pm \sqrt{0}}{6} = 1$; $\{1\}$

28. a. $4y^2 + 4y - 15 = 0; (2y - 3)(2y + 5) = 0; y = \frac{3}{2}$ or $y = -\frac{5}{2}; \left\{\frac{3}{2}, -\frac{5}{2}\right\}$

b. $4y^2 + 4y - 15 = 0; y = \frac{-4 \pm \sqrt{(4)^2 - 4(4)(-15)}}{2(4)} = \frac{-4 \pm \sqrt{256}}{8} = \frac{-4 \pm 16}{8} = -\frac{5}{2}$ or $\frac{3}{2}; \left\{-\frac{5}{2}, \frac{3}{2}\right\}$

B **29.** $x^2 - x\sqrt{2} - 1 = 0; x = \frac{\sqrt{2} \pm \sqrt{(-\sqrt{2})^2 - 4(-1)}}{2} = \frac{\sqrt{2} \pm \sqrt{6}}{2}; \left\{\frac{\sqrt{2} \pm \sqrt{6}}{2}\right\}$

30. $x^2 - x\sqrt{5} - 1 = 0; x = \frac{\sqrt{5} \pm \sqrt{(-\sqrt{5})^2 - 4(-1)}}{2} = \frac{\sqrt{5} \pm \sqrt{9}}{2} = \frac{\sqrt{5} \pm 3}{2}; \left\{\frac{\sqrt{5} \pm 3}{2}\right\}$

31. $t^2 - 2t\sqrt{2} + 1 = 0; t = \frac{2\sqrt{2} \pm \sqrt{(-2\sqrt{2})^2 - 4(1)}}{2} = \frac{2\sqrt{2} \pm \sqrt{4}}{2} = \sqrt{2} \pm 1;$ $\{\sqrt{2} \pm 1\}$

32. $u^2 + 2u\sqrt{3} - 3 = 0; u = \frac{-2\sqrt{3} \pm \sqrt{(2\sqrt{3})^2 - 4(-3)}}{2} = \frac{-2\sqrt{3} \pm \sqrt{24}}{2} =$ $-\sqrt{3} \pm \sqrt{6}; \{-\sqrt{3} \pm \sqrt{6}\}$

33. $\sqrt{2}x^2 + 5x + 2\sqrt{2} = 0; x = \frac{-5 \pm \sqrt{5^2 - 4(\sqrt{2})(2\sqrt{2})}}{2(\sqrt{2})} = \frac{-5 \pm \sqrt{9}}{2\sqrt{2}} = \frac{-5 \pm 3}{2\sqrt{2}};$

$x = -2\sqrt{2}$ or $x = -\frac{\sqrt{2}}{2}; \left\{-2\sqrt{2}, -\frac{\sqrt{2}}{2}\right\}$

34. $\sqrt{3}x^2 - 2x + 2\sqrt{3} = 0; x = \frac{2 \pm \sqrt{(-2)^2 - 4(\sqrt{3})(2\sqrt{3})}}{2(\sqrt{3})} = \frac{2 \pm \sqrt{-20}}{2\sqrt{3}} = \frac{1 \pm i\sqrt{5}}{\sqrt{3}} =$ $\frac{\sqrt{3} \pm i\sqrt{15}}{3}; \left\{\frac{\sqrt{3}}{3} \pm \frac{\sqrt{15}}{3}i\right\}$

35. $z^2 + iz + 2 = 0; z = \frac{-i \pm \sqrt{i^2 - 4(2)}}{2} = \frac{-i \pm \sqrt{-9}}{2} = \frac{-i \pm 3i}{2}; \{-2i, i\}$

36. $z^2 + 2iz - 1 = 0; z = \frac{-2i \pm \sqrt{(2i)^2 - 4(-1)}}{2} = \frac{-2i \pm \sqrt{0}}{2} = -i; \{-i\}$

37. $z^2 - (3 + 2i)z + (1 + 3i) = 0; z = \frac{(3 + 2i) \pm \sqrt{(-(3 + 2i))^2 - 4(1 + 3i)}}{2} =$ $\frac{3 + 2i \pm \sqrt{5 + 12i - 4 - 12i}}{2} = \frac{3 + 2i \pm \sqrt{1}}{2} = \frac{4 + 2i}{2}$ or $\frac{2 + 2i}{2}; \{2 + i, 1 + i\}$

38. $iz^2 + (2 - 3i)z - (3 + i) = 0; z = \frac{-(2 - 3i) \pm \sqrt{(2 - 3i)^2 + 4(i)(3 + i)}}{2i} =$ $\frac{-2 + 3i \pm \sqrt{-5 - 12i + 12i - 4}}{2i} = \frac{-2 + 3i \pm 3i}{2i}; z = \frac{-2}{2i} = \frac{-1}{i} = i$ or

$z = \frac{-2 + 6i}{2i} = \frac{-1 + 3i}{i} = 3 + i; \{i, 3 + i\}$

39. $\frac{2w+i}{w-i} = \frac{3w+4i}{w+3i}$; $(2w+i)(w+3i) = (3w+4i)(w-i)$; $2w^2 + 7iw - 3 =$

$3w^2 + iw + 4$; $w^2 - 6iw + 7 = 0$; $w = \frac{6i \pm \sqrt{(-6i)^2 - 4(7)}}{2} = \frac{6i \pm \sqrt{-64}}{2} =$

$\frac{6i \pm 8i}{2}$; $\{-i, 7i\}$

40. $\frac{1}{2z+i} + \frac{1}{2z-i} = \frac{4}{z+2i}$; $(2z-i)(z+2i) + (2z+i)(z+2i) = 4(2z+i)(2z-i)$;

$2z^2 + 3iz + 2 + 2z^2 + 5iz - 2 = 16z^2 + 4$; $12z^2 - 8iz + 4 = 0$;

$3z^2 - 2iz + 1 = 0$; $z = \frac{2i \pm \sqrt{(-2i)^2 - 4(3)(1)}}{2(3)} = \frac{2i \pm \sqrt{-16}}{6} = \frac{i \pm 2i}{3}$; $\left\{-\frac{1}{3}i, i\right\}$

41. $3x^2 - 2x + 3 = 0$; $x = \frac{2 \pm \sqrt{(-2)^2 - 4(3)(3)}}{2(3)} = \frac{2 \pm \sqrt{-32}}{6} = \frac{1 \pm 2i\sqrt{2}}{3}$; the solutions

are $x_1 = \frac{1}{3} + \frac{2\sqrt{2}}{3}i$ and $x_2 = \frac{1}{3} - \frac{2\sqrt{2}}{3}i$; $x_1x_2 = \left(\frac{1}{3} + \frac{2\sqrt{2}}{3}i\right)\left(\frac{1}{3} - \frac{2\sqrt{2}}{3}i\right) =$

$\frac{1}{9} + \frac{8}{9} = 1$; since $x_1x_2 = 1$, they are reciprocals.

C **42.** The roots of $ax^2 + bx + c = 0$ are $x_1 = \frac{-b + \sqrt{b^2 - 4ac}}{2a}$ and $x_2 = \frac{-b - \sqrt{b^2 - 4ac}}{2a}$.

If x_1 and x_2 are reciprocals, $x_1x_2 = 1$; $\frac{(-b + \sqrt{b^2 - 4ac})(-b - \sqrt{b^2 - 4ac})}{(2a)(2a)} = 1$;

$\frac{b^2 - (b^2 - 4ac)}{4a^2} = 1$; $\frac{4ac}{4a^2} = 1$; $a = c$.

Pages 314–315 • PROBLEMS

A **1.** $(4 + x)^2 = 2(16)$; $16 + 8x + x^2 = 32$; $x^2 + 8x - 16 = 0$; $x = \frac{-8 \pm \sqrt{8^2 - 4(-16)}}{2} =$

$\frac{-8 \pm \sqrt{128}}{2} = \frac{-8 \pm 8\sqrt{2}}{2}$; $x = -4 - 4\sqrt{2}$ (reject) or $x = -4 + 4\sqrt{2}$; $x \approx 1.66$

2. $(6 + x)(5 + x) = 3(30)$; $30 + 11x + x^2 = 90$; $x^2 + 11x - 60 = 0$;

$x = \frac{-11 \pm \sqrt{11^2 - 4(-60)}}{2} = \frac{-11 \pm \sqrt{361}}{2} = \frac{-11 \pm 19}{2}$; $x = -15$ (reject) or

$x = 4$; $x = 4$

3. Let x = the number; $x = 1 + \frac{1}{x}$; $x^2 - x - 1 = 0$; $x = \frac{1 \pm \sqrt{(-1)^2 - 4(-1)}}{2} =$

$\frac{1 \pm \sqrt{5}}{2}$; $x = \frac{1 - \sqrt{5}}{2}$ (reject) or $x = \frac{1 + \sqrt{5}}{2}$; the number is approximately 1.62

4. Let x and y be the numbers; $x + y = 5$ and $xy = 5$; $y = 5 - x$; $x(5 - x) = 5$;

$x^2 - 5x + 5 = 0$; $x = \frac{5 \pm \sqrt{(-5)^2 - 4(5)}}{2} = \frac{5 \pm \sqrt{5}}{2}$; $x = \frac{5 + \sqrt{5}}{2}$ and $y = \frac{5 - \sqrt{5}}{2}$,

or $x = \frac{5 - \sqrt{5}}{2}$ and $y = \frac{5 + \sqrt{5}}{2}$; the numbers are approximately 1.38 and 3.62

5. Let x and y be the length and width, in meters, of the field; area $= xy = 5000$; perimeter $= 2(x + y) = 300$; $x + y = 150$; $y = 150 - x$; $x(150 - x) = 5000$;

$x^2 - 150x + 5000 = 0$; $x = \frac{150 \pm \sqrt{(-150)^2 - 4(5000)}}{2} = \frac{150 \pm 50}{2}$; $x = 100$ and $y = 50$, or $x = 50$ and $y = 100$; the field is 50 m by 100 m.

6. Let x = the width of the pen in meters; then the length is $(100 - 2x)$ m; area $= x(100 - 2x) = 1200$; $2x^2 - 100x + 1200 = 0$; $x^2 - 50x + 600 = 0$; $(x - 20)(x - 30) = 0$; $x = 20$ or $x = 30$; the pen is 20 m by 60 m or 30 m by 40 m.

7. Let x = the width of the walk in meters; $(10 + 2x)(8 + 2x) - 8(10) = 72$; $80 + 36x + 4x^2 - 80 = 72$; $4x^2 + 36x - 72 = 0$; $x^2 + 9x - 18 = 0$;

$x = \frac{-9 \pm \sqrt{9^2 - 4(-18)}}{2} = \frac{-9 \pm \sqrt{153}}{2} = \frac{-9 \pm 3\sqrt{17}}{2}$; $x \approx -10.68$ (reject) or $x \approx 1.68$; the walkway is approximately 1.68 m wide

8. Let x = the width of the frame in inches; $(5 + 2x)(7 + 2x) - 35 = 35$;

$35 + 24x + 4x^2 - 35 = 35$; $4x^2 + 24x - 35 = 0$; $x = \frac{-24 \pm \sqrt{24^2 - 4(4)(-35)}}{2(4)} =$

$\frac{-24 \pm \sqrt{1136}}{8} = \frac{-6 \pm \sqrt{71}}{2}$; $x \approx -7.21$ (reject) or $x \approx 1.21$; the frame is approximately 1.21 in. wide

9. Let x = the original radius of the pipe in millimeters; $\pi(x - 1)^2 = 0.80(\pi x^2)$; $x^2 - 2x + 1 = 0.8x^2$; $0.2x^2 - 2x + 1 = 0$; $x^2 - 10x + 5 = 0$;

$x = \frac{10 \pm \sqrt{(-10)^2 - 4(5)}}{2} = \frac{10 \pm \sqrt{80}}{2} = 5 \pm 2\sqrt{5}$; $x \approx 0.53$ (reject since $x > 1$) or $x \approx 9.47$; the original diameter was approximately 18.94 mm

10. $\frac{1}{2}(2x + x)(x + 6) = 90$; $3x^2 + 18x = 180$; $x^2 + 6x - 60 = 0$;

$x = \frac{-6 \pm \sqrt{6^2 - 4(-60)}}{2} = \frac{-6 \pm \sqrt{276}}{2} = -3 \pm \sqrt{69}$; $x \approx -11.31$ (reject) or $x \approx 5.31$

B **11.** $2[(x)(x + 2)] + 2[(x)(2x)] + 2[(2x)(x + 2)] = 36$; $x^2 + 2x + 2x^2 + 2x^2 + 4x = 18$;

$5x^2 + 6x - 18 = 0$; $x = \frac{-6 \pm \sqrt{6^2 - 4(5)(-18)}}{2(5)} = \frac{-6 \pm \sqrt{396}}{10} = \frac{-6 \pm 6\sqrt{11}}{10} =$

$\frac{-3 \pm 3\sqrt{11}}{5}$; $x = -2.59$ (reject) or $x \approx 1.39$

12. Let r = the golden ratio, w = width, and l = length; $r = \frac{l}{w} = \frac{l + w}{l}$; $l = wr$,

$\frac{wr + w}{wr} = r$; $wr + w = wr^2$; $r^2 - r - 1 = 0$; $r = \frac{1 \pm \sqrt{(-1)^2 - 4(-1)}}{2} = \frac{1 \pm \sqrt{5}}{2}$;

$r = \frac{1 - \sqrt{5}}{2}$ (reject) or $r = \frac{1 + \sqrt{5}}{2}$

13. Volume = (base area) × (height); $x^2(x + 5) = (x + 1)^2(x + 2)$;
$x^3 + 5x^2 = (x^2 + 2x + 1)(x + 2)$; $x^3 + 5x^2 = x^3 + 4x^2 + 5x + 2$;

$x^2 - 5x - 2 = 0$; $x = \frac{5 \pm \sqrt{(-5)^2 - 4(-2)}}{2} = \frac{5 \pm \sqrt{33}}{2}$; $x = \frac{5 - \sqrt{33}}{2}$ (reject) or

$x = \frac{5 + \sqrt{33}}{2} \approx 5.37$

14. Let x = length, in centimeters, of the base edge of the box; volume = 100 = $5x^2$;
$x^2 = 20$; $x = \pm 2\sqrt{5}$; the base edge is approximately 4.47 cm; the original piece of metal was $x + 10 \approx 14.47$ cm on a side

15. Let x = number of hours going out; $4 - x$ = number of hours returning;

$\frac{72}{x} - 15 = \frac{72}{4 - x}$; $72(4 - x) - 15x(4 - x) = 72x$; $288 - 72x - 60x + 15x^2 = 72x$;

$15x^2 - 204x + 288 = 0$, $5x^2 - 68x + 96 = 0$; $(5x - 8)(x - 12) = 0$; $x = 12$ (reject,

since $x < 4$) or $x = \frac{8}{5} = 1.6$; the average speed going out was $\frac{72}{1.6} = 45$ km/h; the

average return speed was $\frac{72}{4 - 1.6} = 30$ km/h

Pages 320–321 • WRITTEN EXERCISES

A

1. $D = 45$; two different irrational real roots

2. $D = 36$; two different rational real roots

3. $D = -16$; two conjugate imaginary roots

4. $D = 124$; two different irrational real roots

5. $D = 57$; two different irrational real roots

6. $D = -44$; two conjugate imaginary roots

7. $D = -4$; two conjugate imaginary roots **8.** $D = 0$; a double rational real root

9. $D = \frac{121}{9}$; two different rational real roots

10. $\sqrt{3}\,x^2 - 4\sqrt{3} = 0$, $x^2 - 4 = 0$; $D = 16$; two different rational real roots

11. $D = 25 - 16\sqrt{2} > 0$; two different irrational real roots

12. $D = 0$; a double irrational real root

13. $x^2 - 6x + 5 = 0$; $(x - 1)(x - 5) = 0$; $x = 1$ or $x = 5$; $\{1, 5\}$

14. $y^2 + 2y - 24 = 0$; $(y - 4)(y + 6) = 0$; $y = 4$ or $y = -6$; $\{4, -6\}$

15. $9x^2 - 12x + 4 = 0$; $(3x - 2)^2 = 0$; $3x - 2 = 0$; $x = \frac{2}{3}$; $\left\{\frac{2}{3}\right\}$

16. $4y^2 + 12y + 9 = 0$; $(2y + 3)^2 = 0$; $2y + 3 = 0$; $y = -\frac{3}{2}$; $\left\{-\frac{3}{2}\right\}$

17. $5(x + 7)^2 = 0$; $x + 7 = 0$; $x = -7$; $\{-7\}$

18. $5(x + 7)^2 = 25$; $(x + 7)^2 = 5$; $x + 7 = \pm\sqrt{5}$; $x = -7 \pm \sqrt{5}$; $\{-7 \pm \sqrt{5}\}$

19. $y^2 - 2y = 99$; $y^2 - 2y + 1 = 100$; $(y - 1)^2 = 100$; $y - 1 = \pm 10$; $y = 1 \pm 10$;
$\{-9, 11\}$

20. $10 = 6t - t^2$; $t^2 - 6t = -10$; $t^2 - 6t + 9 = -1$; $(t - 3)^2 = -1$; $t - 3 = \pm i$; $t = 3 \pm i$; $\{3 \pm i\}$

21. $3(x - 2)^2 = 18$; $(x - 2)^2 = 6$; $x - 2 = \pm\sqrt{6}$; $x = 2 \pm \sqrt{6}$; $\{2 \pm \sqrt{6}\}$

22. $x^2 + 4x - 396 = 0$; $x^2 + 4x + 4 = 400$; $(x + 2)^2 = 400$; $x + 2 = \pm 20$; $x = -2 \pm 20$; $\{-22, 18\}$

23. $(2x + 5)(x - 3) = 0$; $2x + 5 = 0$ or $x - 3 = 0$; $x = -\frac{5}{2}$ or $x = 3$; $\left\{-\frac{5}{2}, 3\right\}$

24. $(2x + 5)(x - 3) = 6$; $2x^2 - x - 15 = 6$; $2x^2 - x - 21 = 0$; $(x + 3)(2x - 7) = 0$; $x = -3$ or $x = \frac{7}{2}$; $\left\{-3, \frac{7}{2}\right\}$

B

25. $2(y - 1)^2 = y^2$; $2(y^2 - 2y + 1) = y^2$; $y^2 - 4y + 2 = 0$; $y = \frac{4 \pm \sqrt{16 - 4(2)}}{2} = \frac{4 \pm \sqrt{8}}{2} = 2 \pm \sqrt{2}$; $\{2 \pm \sqrt{2}\}$

26. $2w^2 = 3(w - 2)^2$; $2w^2 = 3(w^2 - 4w + 4)$; $w^2 - 12w + 12 = 0$;

$$w = \frac{12 \pm \sqrt{(-12)^2 - 4(12)}}{2} = \frac{12 \pm \sqrt{96}}{2} = 6 \pm 2\sqrt{6}; \{6 \pm 2\sqrt{6}\}$$

27. $\frac{x}{3} + \frac{3}{x} = 1$; $x^2 + 9 = 3x$; $x^2 - 3x + 9 = 0$; $x = \frac{3 \pm \sqrt{(-3)^2 - 4(9)}}{2} = \frac{3 \pm \sqrt{-27}}{2} = \frac{3 \pm 3i\sqrt{3}}{2}$; $\left\{\frac{3}{2} \pm \frac{3\sqrt{3}}{2}i\right\}$

28. $\frac{x + 1}{x} - \frac{x}{x + 1} = 2$; $(x + 1)^2 - x^2 = 2(x)(x + 1)$; $x^2 + 2x + 1 - x^2 = 2x^2 + 2x$;

$2x^2 = 1$; $x^2 = \frac{1}{2}$; $x = \pm\sqrt{\frac{1}{2}} = \pm\frac{\sqrt{2}}{2}$; $\left\{\pm\frac{\sqrt{2}}{2}\right\}$

29. $\frac{y + 1}{y - 1} - \frac{y}{3} = \frac{2}{y - 1}$; $\frac{y + 1}{y - 1} - \frac{2}{y - 1} = \frac{y}{3}$; $\frac{y - 1}{y - 1} = \frac{y}{3}$; $1 = \frac{y}{3}$; $y = 3$; $\{3\}$

30. $\frac{t}{t - 2} + \frac{2t}{t - 1} = 6$; $t(t - 1) + 2t(t - 2) = 6(t - 2)(t - 1)$; $t^2 - t + 2t^2 - 4t =$

$6t^2 - 18t + 12$; $3t^2 - 13t + 12 = 0$; $(t - 3)(3t - 4) = 0$; $t = 3$ or $t = \frac{4}{3}$; $\left\{3, \frac{4}{3}\right\}$

31. $D = 4^2 - 4(2)k = 16 - 8k$ **a.** $16 - 8k = 0$; $k = 2$ **b.** $16 - 8k > 0$; $k < 2$

c. $16 - 8k < 0$; $k > 2$

32. $D = (-6)^2 - 4(3)(-k) = 36 + 12k$ **a.** $36 + 12k = 0$; $k = -3$

b. $36 + 12k > 0$; $12k > -36$; $k > -3$ **c.** $36 + 12k < 0$; $12k < -36$; $k < -3$

33. $D = (-8)^2 - 4(k^2)(4) = 64 - 16k^2$ **a.** $64 - 16k^2 = 0$; $k^2 = 4$; $k = \pm 2$

b. $64 - 16k^2 > 0$; $16(4 - k^2) > 0$; $16(2 - k)(2 + k) > 0$; $-2 < k < 2$

c. $64 - 16k^2 < 0$; $16(2 - k)(2 + k) < 0$; $k < -2$ or $k > 2$

34. $D = (-6)^2 - 4(9)k^2 = 36 - 36k^2$

a. $36 - 36k^2 = 0$; $36(1 - k^2) = 0$; $36(1 - k)(1 + k) = 0$; $k = \pm 1$

b. $36 - 36k^2 > 0$; $36(1 - k)(1 + k) > 0$; $-1 < k < 1$

c. $36 - 36k^2 < 0$; $36(1 - k)(1 + k) < 0$; $k < -1$ or $k > 1$

35. $D = (-4)^2 - 4(k)(k) = 16 - 4k^2$

a. $16 - 4k^2 = 0; 4(4 - k^2) = 0; 4(2 - k)(2 + k) = 0; k = \pm 2$

b. $16 - 4k^2 > 0; 4(2 - k)(2 + k) > 0; -2 < k < 2$

c. $16 - 4k^2 < 0; 4(2 - k)(2 + k) < 0; k < -2$ or $k > 2$

36. $D = (-6k)^2 - 4(3)(12) = 36k^2 - 144$

a. $36k^2 - 144 = 0; 36(k^2 - 4) = 0; 36(k - 2)(k + 2) = 0; k = \pm 2$

b. $36k^2 - 144 > 0; 36(k - 2)(k + 2) > 0; k < -2$ or $k > 2$

c. $36k^2 - 144 < 0; 36(k - 2)(k + 2) < 0; -2 < k < 2$

37. If $16x^2 + 8x + 2k$ is a perfect square, then the equation $16x^2 + 8x + 2k = 0$ has one real double root; $D = 8^2 - 4(16)(2k) = 0; 64 - 128k = 0; k = \frac{1}{2}$

38. For $3x^2 - 6x + k$ to be factorable, $D = (-6)^2 - 4(3)k = 36 - 12k$ is a perfect square. Answers may vary. For example: $k = 0, 3$, or -9

39. a. $2x^2 - 5x + 7 = 0; x = \frac{5 \pm \sqrt{(-5)^2 - 4(2)(7)}}{2(2)} = \frac{5 \pm \sqrt{-31}}{4} = \frac{5 \pm i\sqrt{31}}{4} = \frac{5}{4} \pm \frac{\sqrt{31}}{4}i$; the sum of the roots is $\frac{5}{4} + \frac{\sqrt{31}}{4}i + \frac{5}{4} - \frac{\sqrt{31}}{4}i = \frac{10}{4} = \frac{5}{2}$; the product of the roots is $\left(\frac{5}{4} + \frac{\sqrt{31}}{4}i\right)\left(\frac{5}{4} - \frac{\sqrt{31}}{4}i\right) = \frac{25}{16} + \frac{31}{16} = \frac{56}{16} = \frac{7}{2}$

b. $2x^2 + 13x + 11 = 0; x = \frac{-13 \pm \sqrt{13^2 - 4(11)(2)}}{2(2)} = \frac{-13 \pm \sqrt{81}}{4} = \frac{-13 \pm 9}{4}$; $x = -\frac{11}{2}$ or $x = -1$; the sum of the roots is $-\frac{11}{2} + -1 = -\frac{13}{2}$; the product of the roots is $\left(-\frac{11}{2}\right)(-1) = \frac{11}{2}$

c. The roots are $\frac{-b + \sqrt{b^2 - 4ac}}{2a}$ and $\frac{-b - \sqrt{b^2 - 4ac}}{2a}$; the sum of the roots is $\frac{-b + \sqrt{b^2 - 4ac}}{2a} + \frac{-b - \sqrt{b^2 - 4ac}}{2a} = -\frac{2b}{2a} = -\frac{b}{a}$; the product of the roots is $\left(\frac{-b + \sqrt{b^2 - 4ac}}{2a}\right)\left(\frac{-b - \sqrt{b^2 - 4ac}}{2a}\right) = \frac{(-b)^2 - (\sqrt{b^2 - 4ac})^2}{4a^2} = \frac{4ac}{4a^2} = \frac{c}{a}$

40. a. $9x^2 - 6x + 2 = 0; x = \frac{6 \pm \sqrt{(-6)^2 - 4(2)(9)}}{2(9)} = \frac{6 \pm \sqrt{-36}}{18} = \frac{6 \pm 6i}{18} = \frac{1 \pm i}{3}$; $\left\{\frac{1}{3} \pm \frac{1}{3}i\right\}$

b. The sum of the roots is $\frac{1}{3} + \frac{1}{3}i + \frac{1}{3} - \frac{1}{3}i = \frac{2}{3} = \frac{6}{9}$; the product of the roots is $\left(\frac{1}{3} + \frac{1}{3}i\right)\left(\frac{1}{3} - \frac{1}{3}i\right) = \frac{1}{9} + \frac{1}{9} = \frac{2}{9}$

c. sum of the roots is $-\frac{7}{3}$; product of the roots is $\frac{8}{3}$

C **41.** $\frac{1}{x+r} = \frac{1}{x} + \frac{1}{r}$; $xr = r(x + r) + x(x + r)$; $xr = xr + r^2 + x^2 + xr$;
$x^2 + xr + r^2 = 0$; $D = r^2 - 4r^2 = -3r^2 < 0$; therefore, the roots are imaginary

42. $x^2 + kx + (k - 1) = 0$; $D = k^2 - 4(k - 1) = k^2 - 4k + 4 = (k - 2)^2$; since D is a perfect square when k is an integer, the roots are rational

43. **a.** $D = (-3)^2 - 4(i)(-2i) = 9 + 8i^2 = 9 - 8 = 1$

b. $z = \frac{3 \pm \sqrt{D}}{2i} = \frac{3 \pm 1}{2i}$; $z = \frac{4}{2i} = -2i$ or $z = \frac{2}{2i} = -i$; the roots are $-2i$ and $-i$

c. The rule applies only to quadratic equations with real coefficients.

Page 321 • MIXED REVIEW EXERCISES

1. $(x - 2)^2 = 18$; $x - 2 = \pm\sqrt{18}$; $x = 2 \pm 3\sqrt{2}$; $\{2 \pm 3\sqrt{2}\}$

2. $y^2 = 3y + 4$; $y^2 - 3y - 4 = 0$; $(y - 4)(y + 1) = 0$; $y = 4$ or $y = -1$; $\{-1, 4\}$

3. $2w(w - 3) = -1$; $2w^2 - 6w + 1 = 0$; $w = \frac{6 \pm \sqrt{(-6)^2 - 4(2)(1)}}{2(2)} = \frac{6 \pm \sqrt{28}}{4} = \frac{3 \pm \sqrt{7}}{2}$; $\left\{\frac{3 \pm \sqrt{7}}{2}\right\}$

4. $u^2 + 5 = u$; $u^2 - u + 5 = 0$; $u = \frac{1 \pm \sqrt{(-1)^2 - 4(5)}}{2} = \frac{1 \pm \sqrt{-19}}{2} = \frac{1 \pm i\sqrt{19}}{2}$; $\left\{\frac{1}{2} \pm \frac{\sqrt{19}}{2}i\right\}$

5. $6v^2 - 13v - 28 = 0$; $(3v + 4)(2v - 7) = 0$; $3v + 4 = 0$ or $2v - 7 = 0$; $v = -\frac{4}{3}$ or $v = \frac{7}{2}$; $\left\{-\frac{4}{3}, \frac{7}{2}\right\}$

6. $3t^2 = 1 - 4t$; $3t^2 + 4t - 1 = 0$; $t = \frac{-4 \pm \sqrt{4^2 - 4(3)(-1)}}{2(3)} = \frac{-4 \pm \sqrt{28}}{6} = \frac{-2 \pm \sqrt{7}}{3}$; $\left\{\frac{-2 \pm \sqrt{7}}{3}\right\}$

7. x^6 **8.** $6x\sqrt{2x}$ **9.** $x^{-2} = \frac{1}{x^2}$ **10.** x^3y^4 **11.** $\frac{1}{(\sqrt{x})^3} = \frac{1}{x\sqrt{x}} = \frac{\sqrt{x}}{x^2}$

12. $(x^{-2}y^1)(xy) = x^{-1}y^2 = \frac{y^2}{x}$ **13.** $((5x)^{1/2})^2 = 5x$ **14.** $(x^2y^{-3})^{-2} = x^{-4}y^6 = \frac{y^6}{x^4}$

Page 321 • COMPUTER EXERCISES

1.
```
10 INPUT "ENTER COEFFICIENTS A, B, C: "; A, B, C
20 LET D = B * B - 4 * A * C
30 IF D > 0 THEN GOSUB 100
40 IF D = 0 THEN PRINT "ROOT IS A DOUBLE REAL ROOT."
50 IF D < 0 THEN PRINT "ROOTS ARE IMAGINARY."
60 END
100 LET R = INT(SQR(D) + 0.5)
```

Continued on next page

```
110 IF R * R = D THEN PRINT "ROOTS ARE REAL AND RATIONAL."
120 IF R * R <> D THEN PRINT "ROOTS ARE REAL AND IRRATIONAL."
130 RETURN
```

2. a. real, irrational **b.** real, rational **c.** imaginary

3. Change line 40 to:

```
40 IF D = 0 THEN GOSUB 200
```

Then add the following lines:

```
122 LET R1 = (-B + SQR(D))/(2 * A)
124 LET R2 = (-B - SQR(D))/(2 * A)
126 PRINT "ROOTS ="; R1; ", "; R2
200 PRINT "ROOT IS A DOUBLE REAL ROOT."
210 PRINT "ROOT = "; -B/(2 * A)
220 RETURN
```

4. a. `ROOTS ARE REAL AND RATIONAL.`
`ROOTS = 5, -2.33333334`
b. `ROOTS ARE REAL AND IRRATIONAL.`
`ROOTS = 0.192582404, -5.1925824`
c. `ROOTS ARE REAL AND IRRATIONAL`
`ROOTS = 5.10977223, -4.10977223`

5. Change line 50 to:

```
50 IF D < 0 THEN GOSUB 300
```

Then add the following lines:

```
300 PRINT "ROOTS ARE IMAGINARY."
310 LET RP = -B/(2 * A)
320 LET IP = SQR (ABS(D))/(2 * A)
330 PRINT "ROOTS = "; RP; "+"; IP; "i, "; RP; "-"; IP; "i"
340 RETURN
```

6. a. `ROOTS ARE IMAGINARY.`
`ROOTS = -1 + 2.64575131i, -1 - 2.64575131i`
b. `ROOTS ARE REAL AND IRRATIONAL.`
`ROOTS = 2.39718086, -1.14718086`
c. `ROOTS ARE IMAGINARY.`
`ROOTS = 1.5 + 1.11803399i, 1.5 - 1.11803399i`

Pages 324–325 • WRITTEN EXERCISES

A

1. a. $(x + 3)^2 - 5(x + 3) + 4 = 0$; let $z = x + 3$; $z^2 - 5z + 4 = 0$; $(z - 4)(z - 1) = 0$; $z = 4$ or $z = 1$; $x = z - 3$; $x = 1$ or $x = -2$; $\{1, -2\}$

b. $(2x - 1)^2 - 5(2x - 1) + 4 = 0$; let $z = 2x - 1$; $z^2 - 5z + 4 = 0$; as in (a), $z = 1$ or $z = 4$; $x = \frac{z + 1}{2}$; $x = 1$ or $x = \frac{5}{2}$; $\left\{1, \frac{5}{2}\right\}$

c. $x^4 - 5x^2 + 4 = 0$; let $z = x^2$; $z^2 - 5z + 4 = 0$; as in (a), $z = 1$ or $z = 4$; $x = \pm\sqrt{z}$; $x = \pm 1$ or $x = \pm 2$; $\{\pm 1, \pm 2\}$

2. a. $(x-7)^2 - 13(x-7) + 36 = 0$; let $z = x - 7$; $z^2 - 13z + 36 = 0$; $(z-9)(z-4) = 0$; $z = 9$ or $z = 4$; $x = z + 7$; $x = 16$ or $x = 11$; $\{11, 16\}$

b. $(1-3x)^2 - 13(1-3x) + 36 = 0$; let $z = 1 - 3x$; $z^2 - 13z + 36 = 0$; as in (a), $z = 4$ or $z = 9$; $x = \frac{1-z}{3}$; $x = -1$ or $x = -\frac{8}{3}$; $\left\{-1, -\frac{8}{3}\right\}$

c. $x^4 - 13x^2 + 36 = 0$; let $z = x^2$; $z^2 - 13z + 36 = 0$; as in (a), $z = 4$ or $z = 9$; $x = \pm\sqrt{z}$; $x = \pm 2$ or $x = \pm 3$; $\{\pm 2, \pm 3\}$

3. a. $2\left(\frac{1}{2y}\right)^2 + 5\left(\frac{1}{2y}\right) - 3 = 0$; let $z = \frac{1}{2y}$; $2z^2 + 5z - 3 = 0$; $(2z-1)(z+3) = 0$; $z = \frac{1}{2}$ or $z = -3$; $y = \frac{1}{2z}$; $y = 1$ or $y = -\frac{1}{6}$; $\left\{-\frac{1}{6}, 1\right\}$

b. $2(y^2-4)^2 + 5(y^2-4) - 3 = 0$; let $z = y^2 - 4$; $2z^2 + 5z - 3 = 0$; as in (a), $z = \frac{1}{2}$ or $z = -3$; $y = \pm\sqrt{z+4}$; $y = \pm\sqrt{\frac{9}{2}}$ or $y = \pm\sqrt{1}$; $\left\{\pm\frac{3\sqrt{2}}{2}, \pm 1\right\}$

c. $2y^{-2} + 5y^{-1} - 3 = 0$; let $z = y^{-1}$; $2z^2 + 5z - 3 = 0$; as in (a), $z = \frac{1}{2}$ or $z = -3$; $y = \frac{1}{z}$; $y = 2$ or $y = -\frac{1}{3}$; $\left\{-\frac{1}{3}, 2\right\}$

4. a. $3\left(\frac{w}{6}\right)^2 - 8\left(\frac{w}{6}\right) + 4 = 0$; let $z = \frac{w}{6}$; $3z^2 - 8z + 4 = 0$; $(z-2)(3z-2) = 0$; $z = 2$ or $z = \frac{2}{3}$; $w = 6z$; $w = 12$ or $w = 4$; $\{4, 12\}$

b. $3(w^2-2)^2 - 8(w^2-2) + 4 = 0$; let $z = w^2 - 2$; $3z^2 - 8z + 4 = 0$; as in (a), $z = \frac{2}{3}$ or $z = 2$; $w = \pm\sqrt{z+2}$; $w = \pm\sqrt{\frac{8}{3}}$ or $w = \pm 2$; $\left\{\pm 2, \pm\frac{2\sqrt{6}}{3}\right\}$

c. $3w^{-2} - 8w^{-1} + 4 = 0$; let $z = w^{-1}$; $3z^2 - 8z + 4 = 0$; as in (a), $z = \frac{2}{3}$ or $z = 2$; $w = \frac{1}{z}$; $w = \frac{3}{2}$ or $w = \frac{1}{2}$; $\left\{\frac{1}{2}, \frac{3}{2}\right\}$

5. a. $x^4 - 3x^2 - 4 = 0$; let $z = x^2$; $z^2 - 3z - 4 = 0$; $(z-4)(z+1) = 0$; $z = 4$ or $z = -1$; $x = \pm\sqrt{z}$; $x = \pm 2$ or $x = \pm i$; $\{\pm i, \pm 2\}$

b. $x - 3\sqrt{x} - 4 = 0$; let $z = \sqrt{x}$; $z^2 - 3z - 4 = 0$; as in (a), $z = 4$ or $z = -1$; $x = z^2$; $x = 16$ or $x = 1$ (reject); $\{16\}$

6. a. $x^4 + 7x^2 - 8 = 0$; let $z = x^2$; $z^2 + 7z - 8 = 0$; $(z+8)(z-1) = 0$; $z = -8$ or $z = 1$; $x = \pm\sqrt{z}$; $x = \pm\sqrt{-8} = \pm 2i\sqrt{2}$ or $x = \pm 1$; $\{\pm 2i\sqrt{2}, \pm 1\}$

b. $x + 7\sqrt{x} - 8 = 0$; let $z = \sqrt{x}$; $z^2 + 7z - 8 = 0$; as in (a), $z = -8$ or $z = 1$; $x = z^2$; $x = 64$ (reject) or $x = 1$; $\{1\}$

7. a. $x^4 + 5x^2 - 36 = 0$; $(x^2+9)(x^2-4) = 0$; $x^2 = -9$ or $x^2 = 4$; $x = \pm 3i$ or $x = \pm 2$; $\{\pm 3i, \pm 2\}$

b. $x^{-4} + 5x^{-2} - 36 = 0$; $(x^{-2}+9)(x^{-2}-4) = 0$; $x^{-2} = -9$ or $x^{-2} = 4$; $x^2 = -\frac{1}{9}$ or $x^2 = \frac{1}{4}$; $x = \pm\frac{i}{3}$ or $x = \pm\frac{1}{2}$; $\left\{\pm\frac{1}{3}i, \pm\frac{1}{2}\right\}$

8. a. $2x^4 + 7x^2 - 4 = 0$; let $z = x^2$; $2z^2 + 7z - 4 = 0$; $(2z - 1)(z + 4) = 0$; $z = \frac{1}{2}$ or $z = -4$; $x = \pm\sqrt{z}$; $x = \pm\frac{\sqrt{2}}{2}$ or $x = \pm 2i$; $\left\{\pm 2i, \pm\frac{\sqrt{2}}{2}\right\}$

b. $2(x - 1)^4 + 7(x - 1)^2 - 4 = 0$; let $z = (x - 1)^2$; $2z^2 + 7z - 4 = 0$; as in (a), $z = \frac{1}{2}$ or $z = -4$; $x = 1 \pm \sqrt{z}$; $x = 1 \pm \frac{\sqrt{2}}{2}$ or $x = 1 \pm 2i$; $\left\{1 \pm 2i, 1 \pm \frac{\sqrt{2}}{2}\right\}$

9. $x - 11\sqrt{x} + 30 = 0$; let $z = \sqrt{x}$; $z^2 - 11z + 30 = 0$; $(z - 6)(z - 5) = 0$; $z = 6$ or $z = 5$; $x = z^2$; $x = 36$ or $x = 25$; $\{25, 36\}$

10. $x + 4\sqrt{x} - 21 = 0$; let $z = \sqrt{x}$; $z^2 + 4z - 21 = 0$; $(z + 7)(z - 3) = 0$; $z = -7$ or $z = 3$; $x = z^2$; $x = 49$ (reject) or $x = 9$; $\{9\}$

11. $(x^2 - 1)^2 - 11(x^2 - 1) + 24 = 0$; let $z = x^2 - 1$; $z^2 - 11z + 24 = 0$; $(z - 8)(z - 3) = 0$; $z = 8$ or $z = 3$; $x = \pm\sqrt{z + 1}$; $x = \pm\sqrt{9}$ or $x = \pm\sqrt{4}$; $\{\pm 2, \pm 3\}$

12. $(x^2 + 3)^2 - 6(x^2 + 3) = 7$; let $z = x^2 + 3$; $z^2 - 6z - 7 = 0$; $(z - 7)(z + 1) = 0$; $z = 7$ or $z = -1$; $x = \pm\sqrt{z - 3}$; $x = \pm\sqrt{4}$ or $x = \pm\sqrt{-4}$; $\{\pm 2i, \pm 2\}$

B

13. $\left(\frac{1 + x}{2}\right)^2 - 3\left(\frac{1 + x}{2}\right) = 18$; let $z = \frac{1 + x}{2}$; $z^2 - 3z - 18 = 0$; $(z - 6)(z + 3) = 0$; $z = 6$ or $z = -3$; $x = 2z - 1$; $x = 11$ or $x = -7$; $\{-7, 11\}$

14. $\left(\frac{1}{x - 1}\right)^2 - \left(\frac{1}{x - 1}\right) = 2$; let $z = \frac{1}{x - 1}$; $z^2 - z - 2 = 0$; $(z - 2)(z + 1) = 0$; $z = 2$ or $z = -1$; $x = 1 + \frac{1}{z}$; $x = \frac{3}{2}$ or $x = 0$; $\left\{0, \frac{3}{2}\right\}$

15. $\frac{2}{y} + \frac{1}{\sqrt{y}} = 1$; let $z = \frac{1}{\sqrt{y}}$; $2z^2 + z - 1 = 0$; $(2z - 1)(z + 1) = 0$; $z = \frac{1}{2}$ or $z = -1$; $y = \left(\frac{1}{z}\right)^2$; $y = 4$ or $y = 1$ (reject); $\{4\}$

16. $\frac{3}{n} - \frac{7}{\sqrt{n}} - 6 = 0$; let $z = \frac{1}{\sqrt{n}}$; $3z^2 - 7z - 6 = 0$; $(3z + 2)(z - 3) = 0$; $z = -\frac{2}{3}$ or $z = 3$; $-\frac{2}{3} = \frac{1}{\sqrt{n}}$ (reject) or $3 = \frac{1}{\sqrt{n}}$; $\sqrt{n} = \frac{1}{3}$; $n = \frac{1}{9}$; $\left\{\frac{1}{9}\right\}$

17. a. $x - 10 = 3\sqrt{x}$; $x^2 - 20x + 100 = 9x$; $x^2 - 29x + 100 = 0$; $(x - 4)(x - 25) = 0$; $x = 4$ (reject) or $x = 25$; $\{25\}$

b. $x - 3\sqrt{x} - 10 = 0$; $(\sqrt{x} - 5)(\sqrt{x} + 2) = 0$; $\sqrt{x} = 5$ or $\sqrt{x} = -2$; $x = 25$ or $x = 4$ (reject); $\{25\}$

18. a. $x + 3 = 4\sqrt{x}$; $x^2 + 6x + 9 = 16x$; $x^2 - 10x + 9 = 0$; $(x - 9)(x - 1) = 0$; $x = 9$ or $x = 1$; $\{1, 9\}$

b. $x - 4\sqrt{x} + 3 = 0$; $(\sqrt{x} - 3)(\sqrt{x} - 1) = 0$; $\sqrt{x} = 3$ or $\sqrt{x} = 1$; $x = 9$ or $x = 1$; $\{1, 9\}$

19. a. $2y - 2 = 3\sqrt{y}$; $4y^2 - 8y + 4 = 9y$; $4y^2 - 17y + 4 = 0$; $(4y - 1)(y - 4) = 0$;

$y = \frac{1}{4}$ (reject) or $y = 4$; $\{4\}$

b. $2y - 3\sqrt{y} - 2 = 0$; $(2\sqrt{y} + 1)(\sqrt{y} - 2) = 0$; $\sqrt{y} = -\frac{1}{2}$ (reject) or $\sqrt{y} = 2$;

$y = 4$; $\{4\}$

20. a. $2t + 3 = 5\sqrt{t}$; $4t^2 + 12t + 9 = 25t$; $4t^2 - 13t + 9 = 0$; $(4t - 9)(t - 1) = 0$;

$t = \frac{9}{4}$ or $t = 1$; $\left\{1, \frac{9}{4}\right\}$

b. $2t - 5\sqrt{t} + 3 = 0$; $(2\sqrt{t} - 3)(\sqrt{t} - 1) = 0$; $\sqrt{t} = \frac{3}{2}$ or $\sqrt{t} = 1$; $t = \frac{9}{4}$ or $t = 1$;

$\left\{1, \frac{9}{4}\right\}$

21. $3|x|^2 = 7|x| + 5$; let $z = |x|$; $3z^2 - 7z - 5 = 0$; $z = \frac{7 \pm \sqrt{109}}{6}$; $z \approx -0.57$ (reject) or $z \approx 2.91$; $x = \pm 2.91$; $\{\pm 2.91\}$

22. $|x| \cdot (|x| - 3) = 1$; $|x|^2 - 3|x| - 1 = 0$; let $z = |x|$; $z^2 - 3z - 1 = 0$;

$z = \frac{3 \pm \sqrt{13}}{2}$; $z \approx -0.30$ (reject) or $z \approx 3.30$; $x = \pm 3.30$; $\{\pm 3.30\}$

23. $3x + 6\sqrt{x} - 2 = 0$; $\sqrt{x} = \frac{-6 \pm \sqrt{60}}{6}$; $\sqrt{x} \approx -2.29$ (reject) or $\sqrt{x} \approx 0.29$;

$x = 0.08$; $\{0.08\}$

24. $\frac{2}{x} - \frac{5}{\sqrt{x}} = 1$; let $z = \frac{1}{\sqrt{x}}$; $2z^2 - 5z - 1 = 0$; $z = \frac{5 \pm \sqrt{33}}{4}$; $z \approx -0.19$ (reject) or

$z \approx 2.69$; $x = \left(\frac{1}{z}\right)^2$; $x = 0.14$; $\{0.14\}$

25. $(x^2 - 3x)^2 - 3(x^2 - 3x) = 10$; let $z = x^2 - 3x$; $z^2 - 3z - 10 = 0$;
$(z - 5)(z + 2) = 0$; $z = 5$ or $z = -2$; $x^2 - 3x = 5$ or $x^2 - 3x = -2$;

$x^2 - 3x - 5 = 0$ or $x^2 - 3x + 2 = 0$; $x = \frac{3 \pm \sqrt{29}}{2}$ or $(x - 2)(x - 1) = 0$;

$x \approx -1.19$ or $x \approx 4.19$ or $x = 2$ or $x = 1$; $\{-1.19, 1, 2, 4.19\}$

26. $(x^2 + 6x)^2 + 9(x^2 + 6x) + 20 = 0$; let $z = x^2 + 6x$; $z^2 + 9z + 20 = 0$;
$(z + 5)(z + 4) = 0$; $z = -5$ or $z = -4$; $x^2 + 6x = -5$ or $x^2 + 6x = -4$;

$x^2 + 6x + 5 = 0$ or $x^2 + 6x + 4 = 0$; $(x + 5)(x + 1) = 0$ or $x = \frac{-6 \pm \sqrt{20}}{2}$;

$x = -5$ or $x = -1$ or $x \approx -5.24$ or $x \approx -0.76$; $\{-5.24, -5, -1, -0.76\}$

27. $4x^{-4} - 73x^{-2} + 144 = 0$ has the desired roots; multiplying by x^4 gives
$144x^4 - 73x^2 + 4 = 0$

28. $4(x - 1)^4 - 55(x - 1)^2 + 39 = 0$

C **29.** $\sqrt{x+6} - 6\sqrt[4]{x+6} + 8 = 0$; let $z = \sqrt[4]{x+6}$; $z^2 - 6z + 8 = 0$; $(z-4)(z-2) = 0$; $z = 4$ or $z = 2$; $x = z^4 - 6$; $x = 250$ or $x = 10$; $\{10, 250\}$

30. Let $z = \sqrt[4]{x-2}$. Then $\sqrt{x-2} + \sqrt{\sqrt{x-2}} - 2 = z^2 + z - 2 = 0$; $(z+2)(z-1) = 0$; $z = -2$ (reject) or $z = 1$. If $\sqrt[4]{x-2} = 1$, $x - 2 = 1$; $x = 3$; $\{3\}$

31. $(s^2 - 9)(s^4 - 3s^2 - 2) - 2(s^2 - 9) = (s^2 - 9)(s^4 - 3s^2 - 2 - 2) =$ $(s^2 - 9)(s^4 - 3s^2 - 4) = 0$; $s^2 - 9 = 0$ and $s = \pm 3$ or $s^4 - 3s^2 - 4 = 0$. Let $z = s^2$; $z^2 - 3z - 4 = 0$; $(z-4)(z+1) = 0$; $z = 4$ or $z = -1$. If $s^2 = 4$, $s = \pm 2$; if $s^2 = -1$, $s = \pm i$; $\{\pm i, \pm 3, \pm 2\}$

32. $(\sqrt{y} - 3)(y - \sqrt{y} - 1) = \sqrt{y} - 3$; $(\sqrt{y} - 3)(y - \sqrt{y} - 1 - 1) = 0$; $(\sqrt{y} - 3)(y - \sqrt{y} - 2) = 0$; $(\sqrt{y} - 3)(\sqrt{y} - 2)(\sqrt{y} + 1) = 0$; $\sqrt{y} = 3$ or $\sqrt{y} = 2$ or $\sqrt{y} = -1$ (reject); $y = 9$ or $y = 4$; $\{4, 9\}$

Page 325 • CHALLENGE

If $a = 2$, $b = 3$, and $c = 6$, then $\frac{1}{a} + \frac{1}{b} + \frac{1}{c} = \frac{1}{2} + \frac{1}{3} + \frac{1}{6} = 1$

Pages 331–332 • WRITTEN EXERCISES

A **1.**

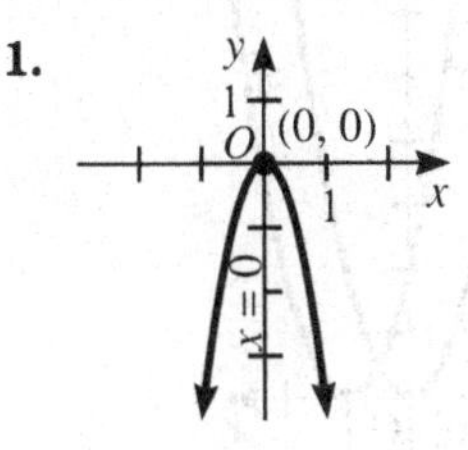

x-intercept: 0
y-intercept: 0

2.

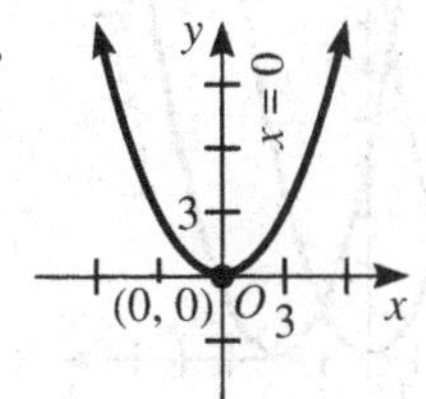

x-intercept: 0
y-intercept: 0

3.

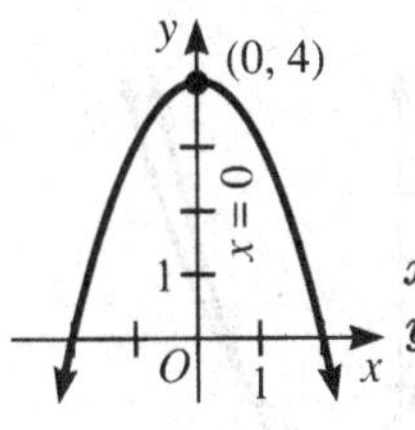

x-intercepts: ± 2
y-intercept: 4

4.

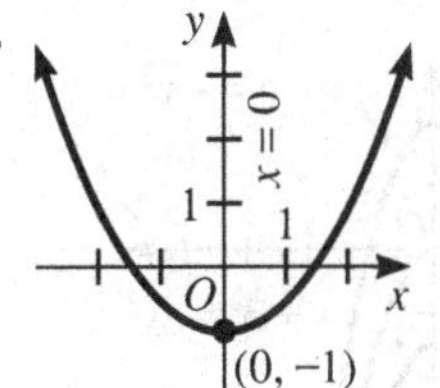

x-intercepts: $\pm\sqrt{2}$
y-intercept: -1

5.

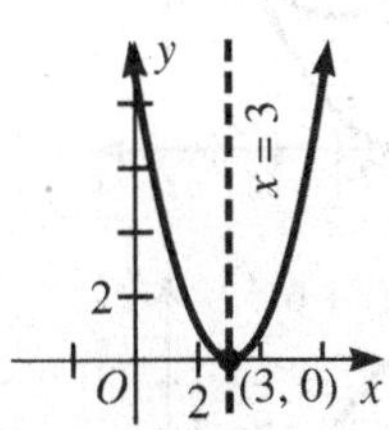

x-intercept: 3
y-intercept: 9

6.

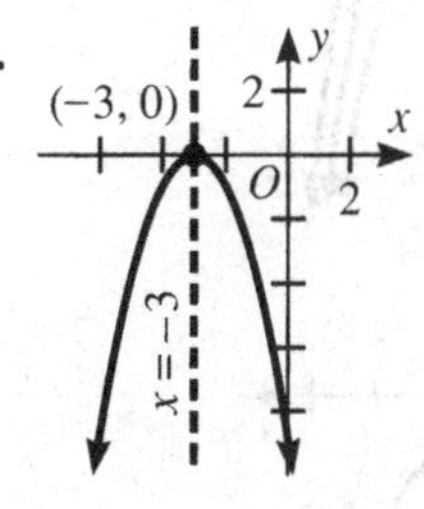

x-intercept: -3
y-intercept: -9

7.

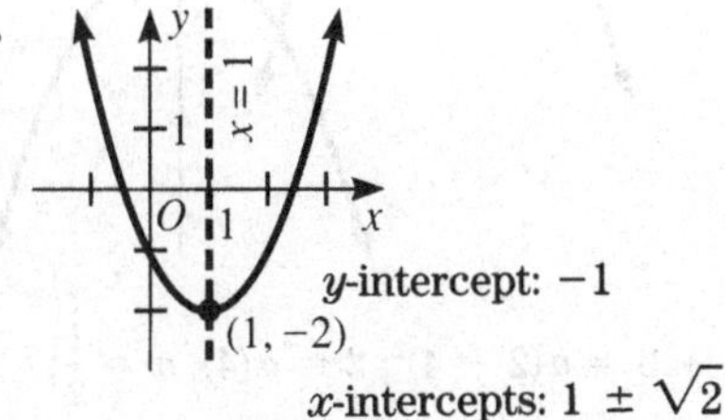

y-intercept: -1
x-intercepts: $1 \pm \sqrt{2}$

8.

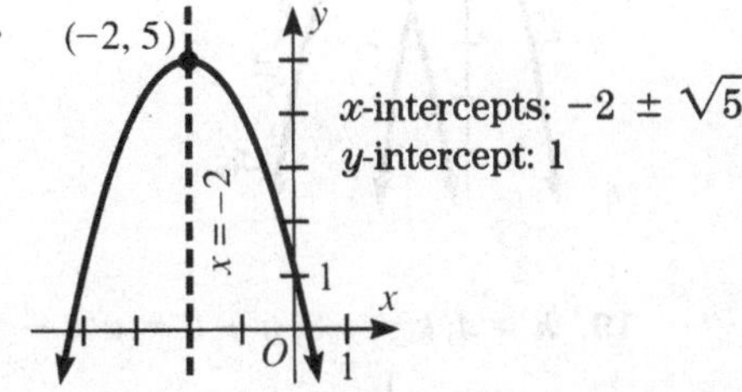

x-intercepts: $-2 \pm \sqrt{5}$
y-intercept: 1

9.

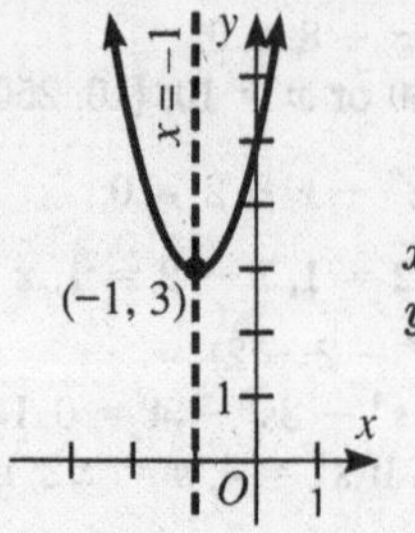

x-intercept: none
y-intercept: 5

10.

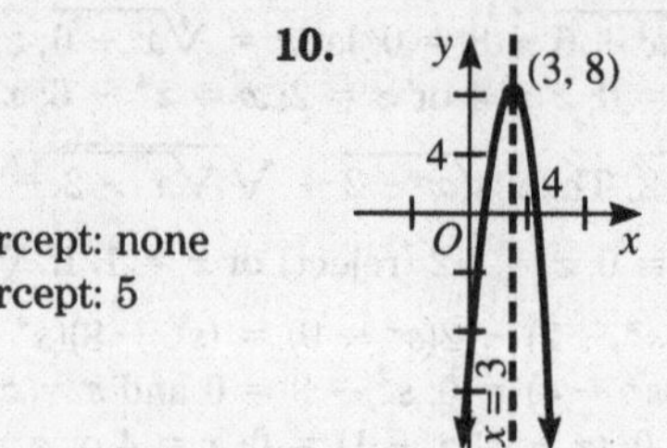

x-intercepts: 1, 5
y-intercept: −10

11.

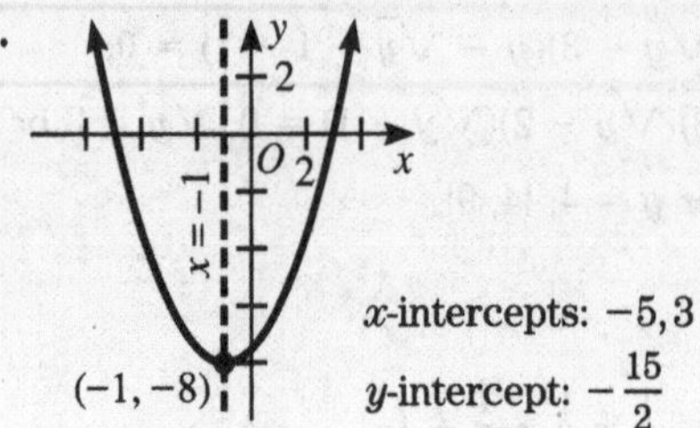

x-intercepts: −5, 3
y-intercept: $-\frac{15}{2}$

12.

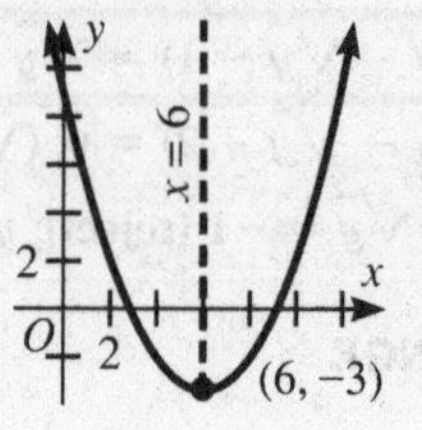

x-intercepts: 3, 9
y-intercept: 9

13.

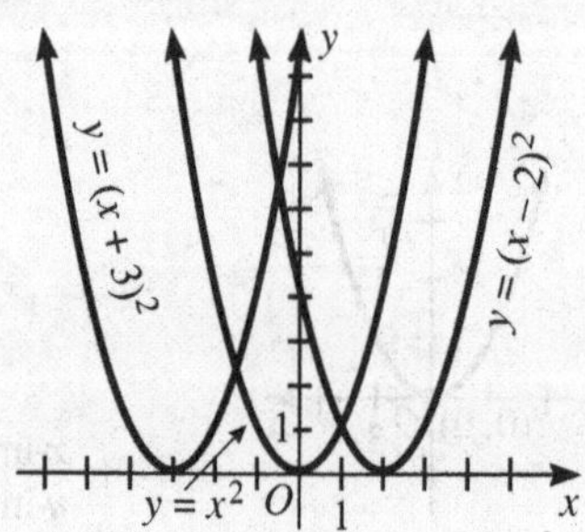

14.

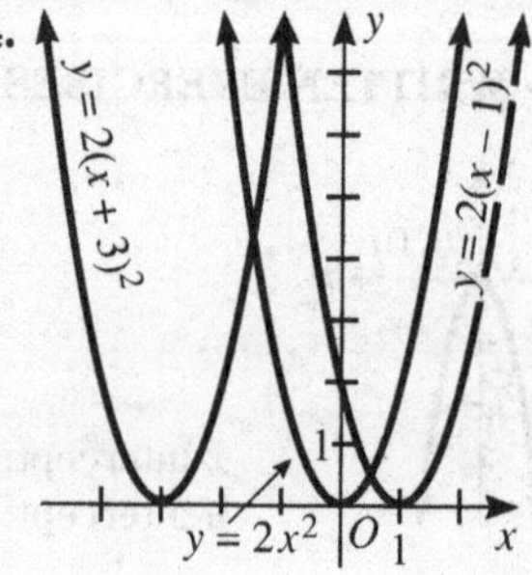

15.

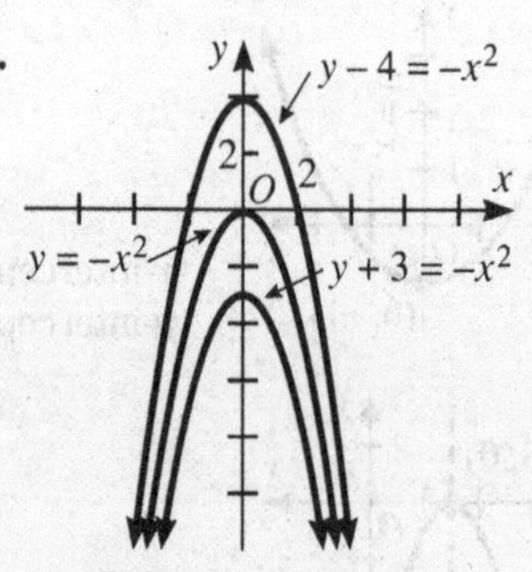

16.

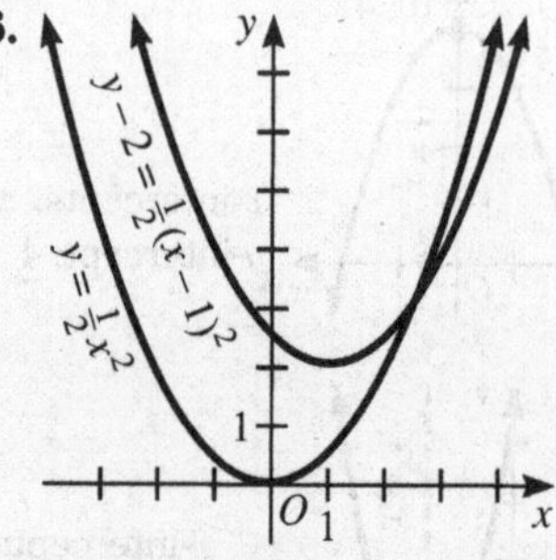

17.

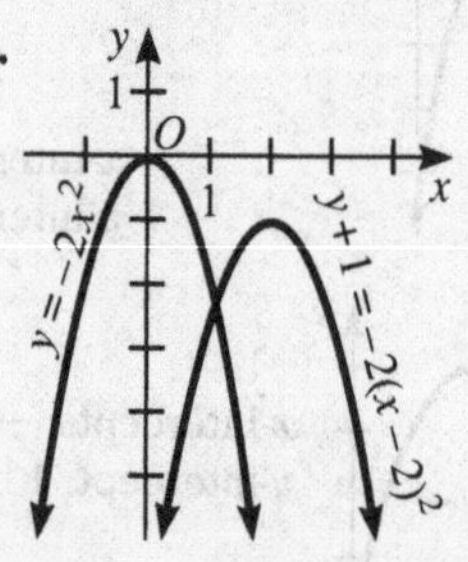

18.

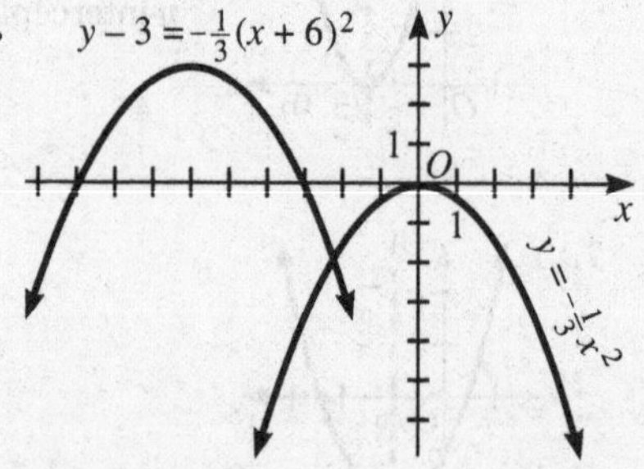

19. $h = 4$; $k = -3$; $y + 3 = a(x - 4)^2$; $-1 + 3 = a(2 - 4)^2$; $2 = a(4)$; $a = \frac{1}{2}$;
$y + 3 = \frac{1}{2}(x - 4)^2$

20. $h = 4$; $k = 5$; $y - 5 = a(x - 4)^2$; $3 - 5 = a(5 - 4)^2$; $-2 = a$; $y - 5 = -2(x - 4)^2$

21. $h = k = 0$; $y = ax^2$; $3 = a(-3)^2$; $a = \frac{3}{9} = \frac{1}{3}$; $y = \frac{1}{3}x^2$

22. $h = -3$; $k = 6$; $y - 6 = a(x + 3)^2$; $0 - 6 = a(0 + 3)^2$; $a = -\frac{6}{9} = -\frac{2}{3}$; $y - 6 = -\frac{2}{3}(x + 3)^2$

B

23. $h = 3$; $k = 5$; $y - 5 = a(x - 3)^2$; $2 - 5 = a(0 - 3)^2$; $-3 = 9a$; $a = -\frac{1}{3}$; $y - 5 = -\frac{1}{3}(x - 3)^2$

24. $h = -2$; $k = 6$; $y - 6 = a(x + 2)^2$; $-2 - 6 = a(0 + 2)^2$; $-8 = 4a$; $a = -2$; $y - 6 = -2(x + 2)^2$

25. $h = 4$; $k = 2$; $y - 2 = a(x - 4)^2$; $0 - 2 = a(3 - 4)^2$; $-2 = a$; $y - 2 = -2(x - 4)^2$

26. $h = -3$; $k = 4$; $y - 4 = a(x + 3)^2$; $0 - 4 = a(-1 + 3)^2$; $-4 = 4a$; $a = -1$; $y - 4 = -1(x + 3)^2$

27. $h = 5$ **28.** $0 - k = -3(0 - 1)^2$; $-k = -3$; $k = 3$ **29.** $5 - 3 = a(2 - 1)^2$; $2 = a$

30. $4 + 5 = a(0 + 2)^2$; $9 = 4a$; $a = \frac{9}{4}$

31. $\begin{array}{l} 11 - k = a(3 - 1)^2 \\ 3 - k = a(1 - 1)^2 \end{array}$; $\begin{array}{l} 11 - k = 4a \\ 3 - k = 0 \end{array}$; $k = 3$; $11 - 3 = 4a$; $a = 2$; $a = 2$ and $k = 3$

32. $\begin{array}{l} 1 - k = a(-5 + 3)^2 \\ 7 - k = a(1 + 3)^2 \end{array}$; $\begin{array}{l} 1 - k = 4a \\ 7 - k = 16a \end{array}$; $k = 1 - 4a$; $7 - (1 - 4a) = 16a$; $6 = 12a$; $a = \frac{1}{2}$; $k = 1 - 4\left(\frac{1}{2}\right) = -1$; $a = \frac{1}{2}$ and $k = -1$

C

33.

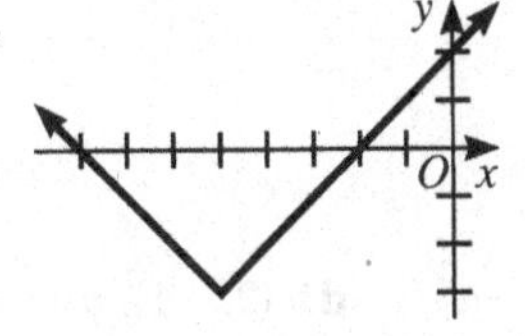

34.

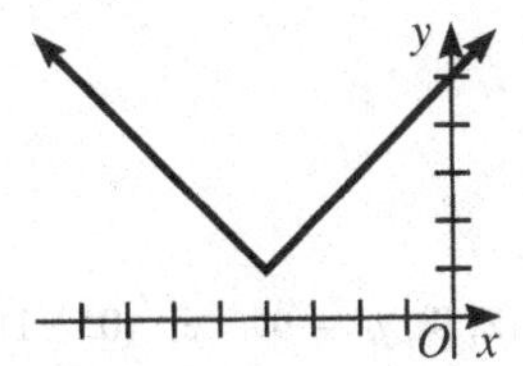

35. Let $x = h + r$ and $y = s$; since (x, y) is on the parabola, $s - k = a(h + r - h)^2$; $s - k = ar^2$; $s - k = a(-r)^2$; $s - k = a(h - r - h)^2$; since $(h - r, s)$ satisfies the equation of the parabola, it is also on the graph. This proves that the parabola is symmetric about the line $x = h$.

36. a.

y	x
−3	9
−2	4
−1	1
0	0
1	1
2	4
3	9

b.

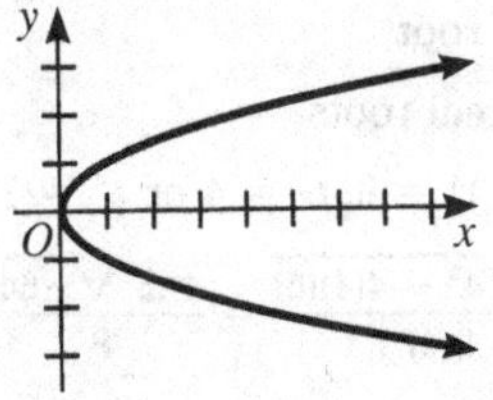

c. No; two values of y correspond to every positive value of x.

37. a.

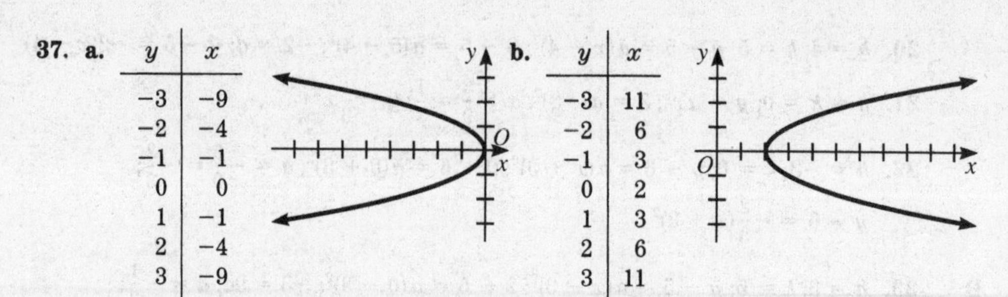

y	x
−3	−9
−2	−4
−1	−1
0	0
1	−1
2	−4
3	−9

b.

y	x
−3	11
−2	6
−1	3
0	2
1	3
2	6
3	11

c.

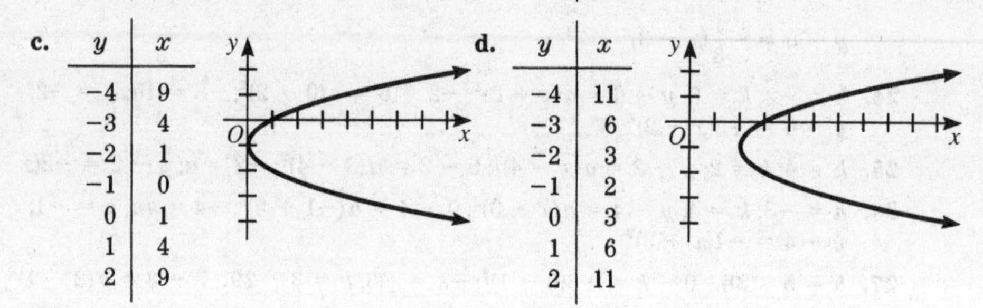

y	x
−4	9
−3	4
−2	1
−1	0
0	1
1	4
2	9

d.

y	x
−4	11
−3	6
−2	3
−1	2
0	3
1	6
2	11

e.

y	x
−1	$-\frac{3}{2}$
0	1
1	$\frac{5}{2}$
2	3
3	$\frac{5}{2}$
4	1
5	$-\frac{3}{2}$

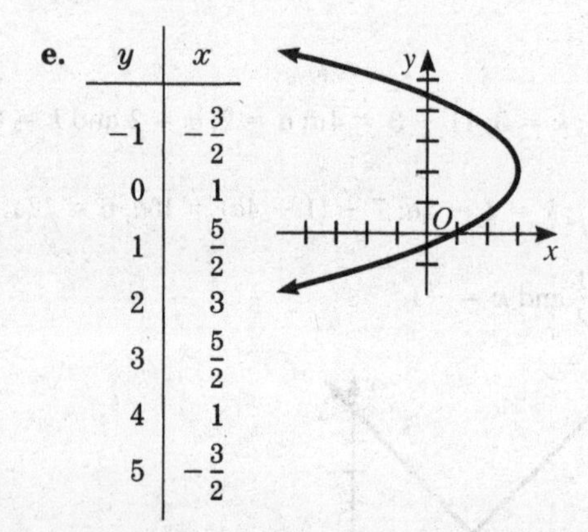

38. a. $(0, 0)$; $y = 0$ **b.** $(2, 0)$; $y = 0$ **c.** $(0, -1)$; $y = -1$ **d.** $(2, -1)$; $y = -1$
e. $(3, 2)$; $y = 2$

39. a. $x - h = a(y - k)^2$ **b.** 1 x-intercept; 0, 1, or 2 y-intercepts

Page 332 • MIXED REVIEW EXERCISES

1. $D = -31$; two imaginary conjugate roots.
2. $D = 0$; one real double rational root
3. $D = 5$; two different irrational real roots
4. $t^4 - 5t^2 + 4 = 0$; $(t^2 - 4)(t^2 - 1) = 0$; $t^2 = 4$ or $t^2 = 1$; $t = \pm 2$ or $t = \pm 1$; $\{\pm 1, \pm 2\}$
5. $4w^2 - 4w + 5 = 0$; $w = \frac{4 \pm \sqrt{4^2 - 4(4)(5)}}{2(4)} = \frac{4 \pm \sqrt{-64}}{8} = \frac{4 \pm 8i}{8} = \frac{1}{2} \pm i$; $\left\{\frac{1}{2} \pm i\right\}$
6. $x + \sqrt{x} - 6 = 0$; let $z = \sqrt{x}$; $z^2 + z - 6 = 0$; $(z + 3)(z - 2) = 0$; $z = -3$ (reject) or $z = 2$; $x = z^2$; $x = 4$; $\{4\}$

Pages 336–337 • WRITTEN EXERCISES

A **1.** 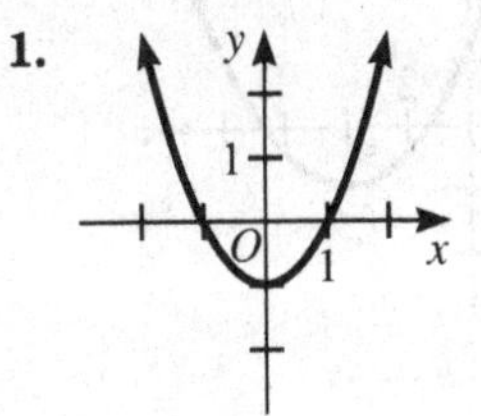

2. 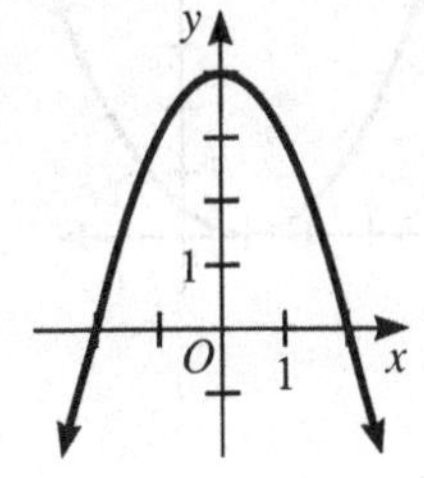

3. 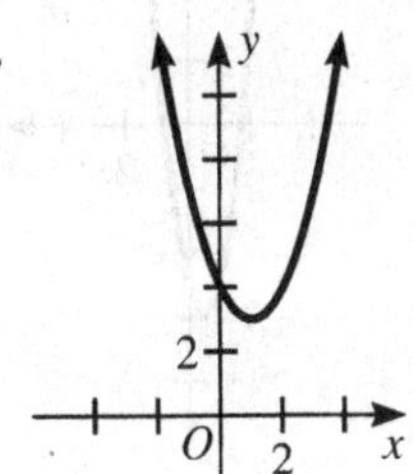

4. 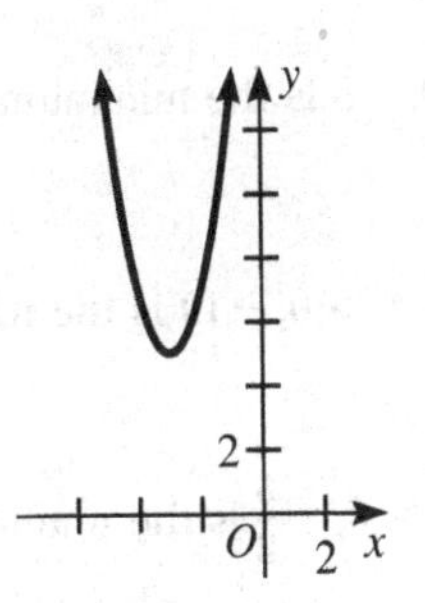

5. 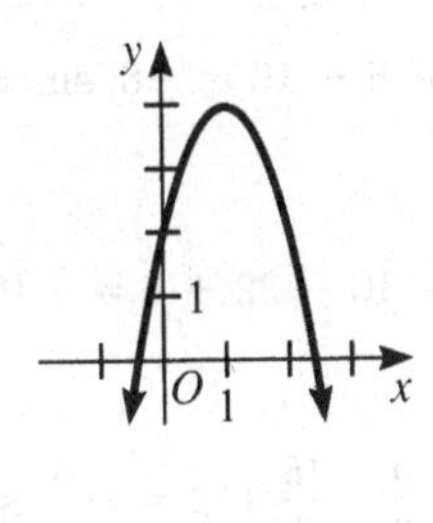

6. 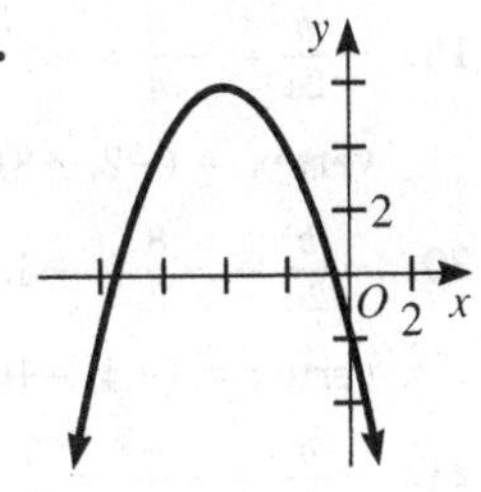

7. 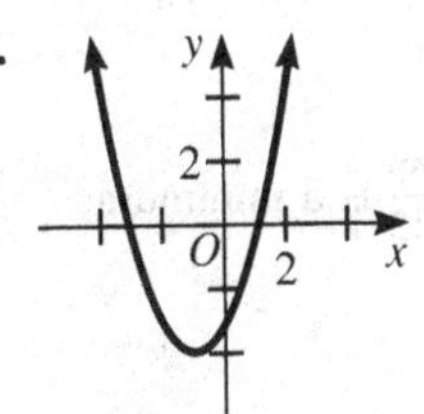

8. 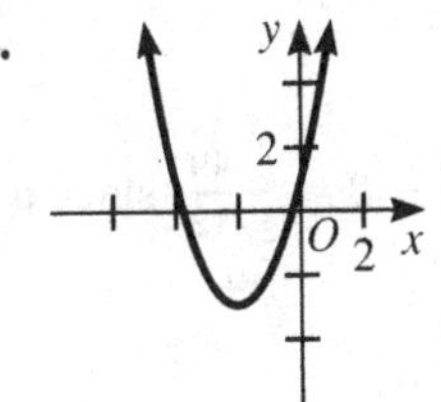

9. 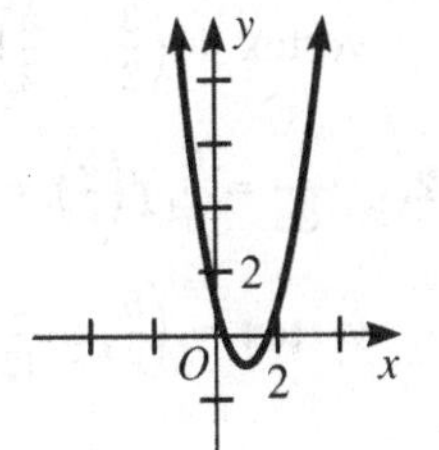

10. 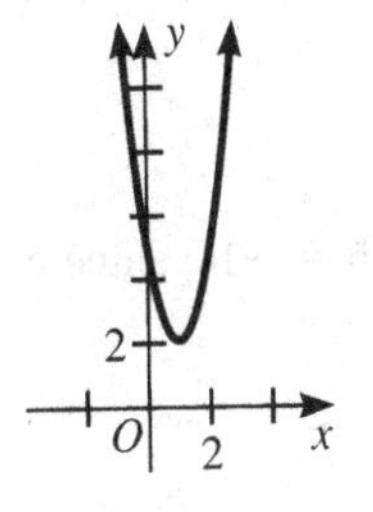

11. 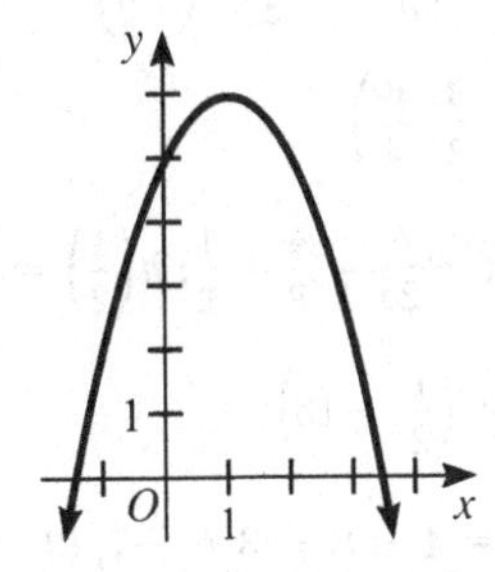

12. 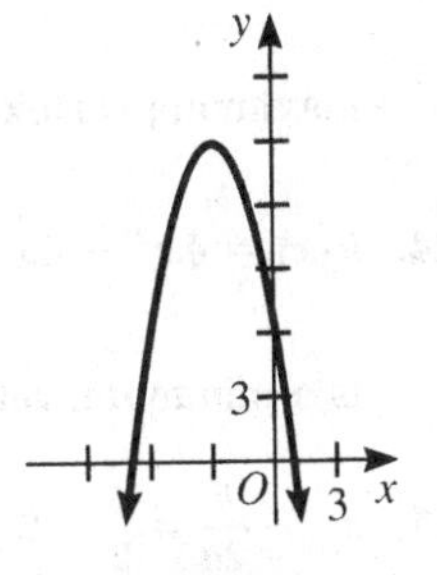

13. 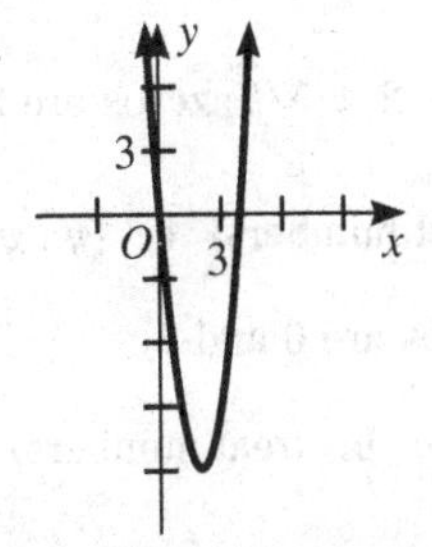

14. 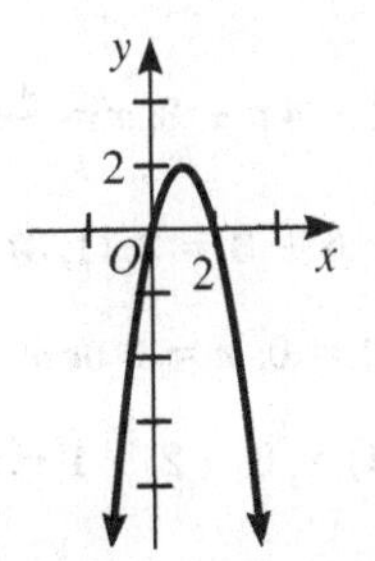

15. 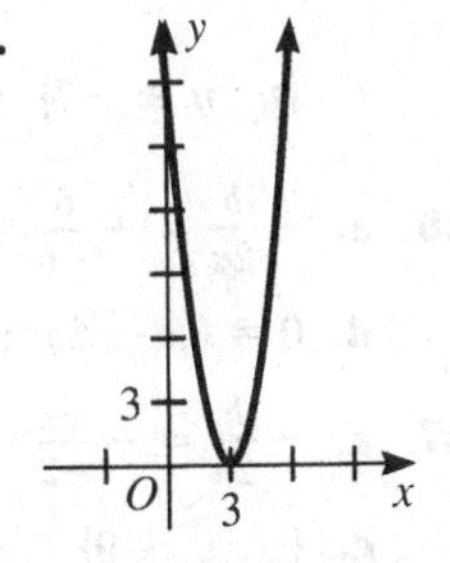

16.

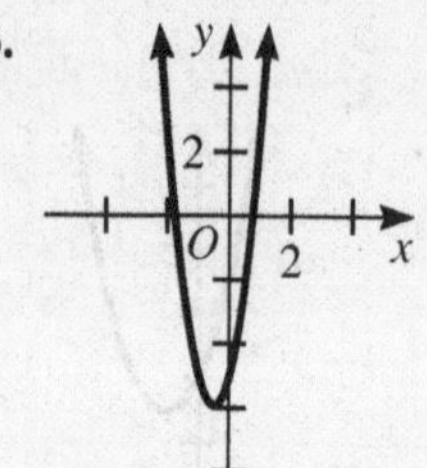

17.

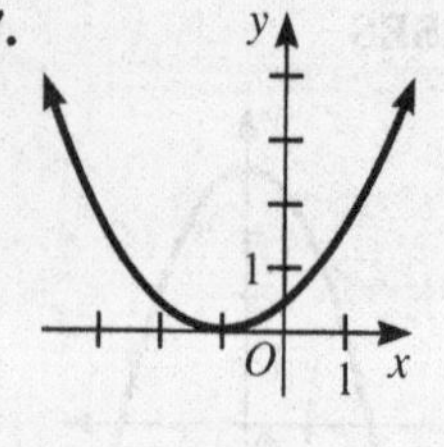

18.

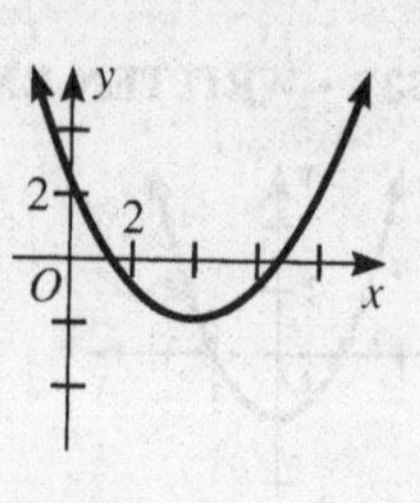

19. $-\frac{b}{2a} = -\frac{8}{4} = -2$; $g(-2) = 8 - 16 = -8$; since $a > 0$, -8 is the minimum; vertex $= (-2, -8)$

20. $-\frac{b}{2a} = -\frac{8}{2} = -4$; $f(-4) = 16 - 32 + 6 = -10$; since $a > 0$, -10 is the minimum; vertex $= (-4, -10)$

21. $-\frac{b}{2a} = -\frac{-6}{4} = \frac{3}{2}$; $g\left(\frac{3}{2}\right) = \frac{9}{2} - \frac{18}{2} + 2 = -\frac{5}{2}$; since $a > 0$, $-\frac{5}{2}$ is the minimum; vertex $= \left(\frac{3}{2}, -\frac{5}{2}\right)$

22. $-\frac{b}{2a} = \frac{5}{6}$; $f\left(\frac{5}{6}\right) = \frac{25}{12} - \frac{25}{6} - 2 = -\frac{49}{12}$; since $a > 0$, $-\frac{49}{12}$ is a minimum; vertex $= \left(\frac{5}{6}, -\frac{49}{12}\right)$

23. $h(x) = 10 - 3x - x^2$; $-\frac{b}{2a} = -\frac{3}{2}$; $h\left(-\frac{3}{2}\right) = 10 + \frac{9}{2} - \frac{9}{4} = \frac{49}{4}$; since $a < 0$, $\frac{49}{4}$ is a maximum; vertex $= \left(-\frac{3}{2}, \frac{49}{4}\right)$

24. $h(x) = 4x^2 - 4x - 15$; $-\frac{b}{2a} = \frac{4}{8} = \frac{1}{2}$; $h\left(\frac{1}{2}\right) = 1 - 2 - 15 = -16$; since $a > 0$, -16 is a minimum; vertex $= \left(\frac{1}{2}, -16\right)$

25. **a.** $-\frac{b}{2a} = \frac{4}{2} = 2$; $f(2) = 4 - 8 - 3 = -7$; $(2, -7)$ **b.** {real numbers}
c. $\{y : y \geq -7\}$ **d.** $0 = x^2 - 4x - 3$; $x = \frac{4 \pm \sqrt{28}}{2} = 2 \pm \sqrt{7}$; zeros are $2 \pm \sqrt{7}$

26. **a.** $-\frac{b}{2a} = -\frac{6}{-6} = 1$; $g(1) = 6 - 3 = 3$; $(1, 3)$ **b.** {real numbers} **c.** $\{y : y \leq 3\}$
d. $0 = 6x - 3x^2$; $3x(2 - x) = 0$; $x = 0$ or $x = 2$; zeros are 0 and 2

27. **a.** $-\frac{b}{2a} = -\frac{-2}{-2} = -1$; $f(-1) = 8 + 2 - 1 = 9$; $(-1, 9)$ **b.** {real numbers}
c. $\{y : y \leq 9\}$
d. $0 = 8 - 2x - x^2$; $(4 + x)(2 - x) = 0$; $x = -4$ or $x = 2$; zeros are -4 and 2

28. a. $-\frac{b}{2a} = -\frac{-8}{-2} = -4; f(-4) = 9 + 32 - 16 = 25; (-4, 25)$ **b.** {real numbers}

c. $\{y : y \leq 25\}$

d. $0 = 9 - 8x - x^2; (1 - x)(9 + x) = 0; x = 1$ or $x = -9$; zeros are -9 and 1

29. a. $-\frac{b}{2a} = -\frac{-2}{2} = 1; f(1) = 1 - 2 - 5 = -6; (1, -6)$ **b.** {real numbers}

c. $\{y : y \geq -6\}$ **d.** $0 = x^2 - 2x - 5; x = \frac{2 \pm \sqrt{24}}{2} = 1 \pm \sqrt{6}$; zeros are $1 \pm \sqrt{6}$

30. a. $-\frac{b}{2a} = -\frac{8}{4} = -2; G(-2) = 8 - 16 + 5 = -3; (-2, -3)$ **b.** {real numbers}

c. $\{y : y \geq -3\}$

d. $0 = 2x^2 + 8x + 5; x = \frac{-8 \pm \sqrt{24}}{4} = \frac{-4 \pm \sqrt{6}}{2}$; zeros are $\frac{-4 \pm \sqrt{6}}{2}$

B **31. a.** $h(x) = 2(x^2 - 2x - 35) = 2x^2 - 4x - 70; -\frac{b}{2a} = -\frac{-4}{4} = 1; h(1) =$

$2 - 4 - 70 = -72; (1, -72)$

b. {real numbers} **c.** $\{y : y \geq -72\}$

d. $0 = 2(x - 7)(x + 5); x = 7$ or $x = -5$; zeros are -5 and 7

32. a. $g(x) = \frac{1}{2}(24 + 10x + x^2) = \frac{1}{2}x^2 + 5x + 12; -\frac{b}{2a} = -\frac{5}{1} = -5;$

$g(-5) = \frac{25}{2} - 25 + 12 = -\frac{1}{2}; \left(-5, -\frac{1}{2}\right)$

b. {real numbers} **c.** $\left\{y : y \geq -\frac{1}{2}\right\}$

d. $0 = \frac{1}{2}(6 + x)(4 + x); x = -6$ or $x = -4$; zeros are -6 and -4

33. a. $y - 9 = -(x + 6)^2; (-6, 9)$ **b.** {real numbers} **c.** $\{y : y \leq 9\}$

d. $0 = 9 - (x + 6)^2; (x + 6)^2 = 9; x + 6 = \pm 3; x = -6 \pm 3$; zeros are -9 and -3

34. a. $y + 8 = 2(x - 5)^2; (5, -8)$ **b.** {real numbers} **c.** $\{y : y \geq -8\}$

d. $0 = 2(x - 5)^2 - 8; 4 = (x - 5)^2; \pm 2 = x - 5; x = 5 \pm 2$; zeros are 3 and 7

35. a. $y - 2 = -\frac{1}{2}(x + 1)^2; (-1, 2)$ **b.** {real numbers} **c.** $\{y : y \leq 2\}$

d. $0 = -\frac{1}{2}(x + 1)^2 + 2; 4 = (x + 1)^2; \pm 2 = x + 1; x = -1 \pm 2$; zeros are -3 and 1

36. a. $H(x) = \frac{1}{2}(9x^2 - 18x + 8) = \frac{9}{2}x^2 - 9x + 4; -\frac{b}{2a} = -\frac{-9}{9} = 1;$

$H(1) = \frac{9}{2} - 9 + 4 = -\frac{1}{2}; \left(1, -\frac{1}{2}\right)$

b. {real numbers} **c.** $\left\{y : y \geq -\frac{1}{2}\right\}$

d. $0 = \frac{1}{2}(3x - 2)(3x - 4); x = \frac{2}{3}$ or $x = \frac{4}{3}$; zeros are $\frac{2}{3}$ and $\frac{4}{3}$

37. a. No zeros, so $b^2 - 4ac < 0$. **b.** $c =$ y-intercept > 0 **c.** Opens upward, $a > 0$

d. Since $-\frac{b}{2a} = 0$, $b = 0$.

38. a. 2 zeros, $b^2 - 4ac > 0$. **b.** $c =$ y-intercept $= 0$. **c.** Opens downward, $a < 0$

d. $-\frac{b}{2a} > 0$ and $a < 0$, so $-b < 0$ and $b > 0$

39. a. Double root, $b^2 - 4ac = 0$ **b.** $c =$ y-intercept > 0 **c.** Opens upward, $a > 0$

d. $-\frac{b}{2a} < 0$ and $a > 0$, so $-b < 0$ and $b > 0$

40. $y = (x^2 - 6x + 9) + 1$; $y - 1 = (x - 3)^2$

a. Since it opens upward and the vertex is (3, 1), the parabola does not intersect the x-axis

b. If $y = 1$, $1 - 1 = (x - 3)^2$; $0 = (x - 3)^2$; $x = 3$; once

c. If $y = 2$, $2 - 1 = (x - 3)^2$; $1 = (x - 3)^2$; $\pm 1 = x - 3$; $x = 4$ or $x = 2$; twice

41. $y = x^2 + bx + c$; $y = x^2 + bx + \frac{b^2}{4} - \frac{b^2}{4} + c$; $y = \left(x + \frac{b}{2}\right)^2 + \frac{4c - b^2}{4}$;

$y - \frac{4c - b^2}{4} = \left(x - \frac{-b}{2}\right)^2$

42. $y = ax^2 + bx + c$; $y - c = a\left(x^2 + \frac{b}{a}x\right)$; $y - c + \frac{b^2}{4a} = a\left(x^2 + \frac{b}{a}x + \frac{b^2}{4a^2}\right)$;

$y - \frac{4ac - b^2}{4a} = a\left(x - \frac{-b}{2a}\right)^2$

C **43.** If $b = 0$, then $f(-x) = a(-x)^2 + c = ax^2 + c = f(x)$. Conversely, if $f(-x) = f(x)$, then $a(-x)^2 + b(-x) + c = ax^2 + bx + c$; $ax^2 - bx + c = ax^2 + bx + c$; $-bx = bx$; $b = 0$.

44. Suppose that for all x, f is an odd function, that is, $f(-x) = -f(x)$ where $f(x) = ax^2 + bx + c$ $(a \neq 0)$. Then $a(-x)^2 + b(-x) + c = -(ax^2 + bx + c)$; $ax^2 - bx + c = -ax^2 - bx - c$; $2ax^2 = -2c$; $x^2 = -\frac{c}{a}$ for all x. But this is impossible since $-\frac{c}{a}$ is constant and x^2 varies over all nonnegative real numbers. Therefore f is not an odd function.

Pages 342–343 • WRITTEN EXERCISES

A **1.** $x^2 - 3x + 6 = 0$; $x = \frac{3 \pm \sqrt{9 - 24}}{2} = \frac{3 \pm i\sqrt{15}}{2}$; $\left\{\frac{3}{2} \pm \frac{\sqrt{15}}{2}i\right\}$; sum $= 3$;

product $= \frac{9 + 15}{4} = 6$

2. $x^2 - 6x + 8 = 0$; $(x - 4)(x - 2) = 0$; $x = 4$ or $x = 2$; $\{2, 4\}$; sum $= 6$; product $= 8$

3. $2y^2 - y - 6 = 0$; $(2y + 3)(y - 2) = 0$; $y = -\frac{3}{2}$ or $y = 2$; $\left\{-\frac{3}{2}, 2\right\}$; sum $= \frac{1}{2}$;

product $= -3$

4. $2t^2 - 6t + 1 = 0$; $t = \frac{6 \pm \sqrt{36 - 8}}{4} = \frac{6 \pm 2\sqrt{7}}{4} = \frac{3 \pm \sqrt{7}}{2}$; $\left\{\frac{3 \pm \sqrt{7}}{2}\right\}$; sum $= 3$;

product $= \frac{9 - 7}{4} = \frac{1}{2}$

5. $2x^2 + 2 = 3x$; $2x^2 - 3x + 2 = 0$; $x = \frac{3 \pm \sqrt{9 - 16}}{4} = \frac{3 \pm i\sqrt{7}}{4}$; $\left\{\frac{3}{4} \pm \frac{\sqrt{7}}{4}i\right\}$;

sum $= \frac{3}{2}$; product $= \frac{9 + 7}{16} = 1$

6. $3u^2 - 4 = 0$; $u^2 = \frac{4}{3}$; $u = \pm\frac{2}{\sqrt{3}} = \pm\frac{2\sqrt{3}}{3}$; $\left\{\pm\frac{2\sqrt{3}}{3}\right\}$; sum $= 0$; product $= -\frac{4}{3}$

Exercises 7–24. Answers may vary by an integral factor. Answers with relatively prime coefficients are given.

7. $2 + 5 = 7$; $2 \cdot 5 = 10$; $x^2 - 7x + 10 = 0$

8. $-3 + 1 = -2$; $-3 \cdot 1 = -3$; $x^2 + 2x - 3 = 0$

9. $-2 + \frac{5}{2} = \frac{1}{2}$; $-2 \cdot \frac{5}{2} = -5$; $x^2 - \frac{1}{2}x - 5 = 0$; $2x^2 - x - 10 = 0$

10. $\frac{3}{2} - \frac{1}{2} = 1$; $\frac{3}{2}\left(-\frac{1}{2}\right) = -\frac{3}{4}$; $x^2 - x - \frac{3}{4} = 0$; $4x^2 - 4x - 3 = 0$

11. $\sqrt{3} - \sqrt{3} = 0$; $(\sqrt{3})(-\sqrt{3}) = -3$; $x^2 - 3 = 0$

12. $-\frac{\sqrt{5}}{2} + \frac{\sqrt{5}}{2} = 0$; $-\frac{\sqrt{5}}{2} \cdot \frac{\sqrt{5}}{2} = -\frac{5}{4}$; $x^2 - \frac{5}{4} = 0$; $4x^2 - 5 = 0$

13. $(1 + \sqrt{3}) + (1 - \sqrt{3}) = 2$; $(1 + \sqrt{3})(1 - \sqrt{3}) = 1 - 3 = -2$; $x^2 - 2x - 2 = 0$

14. $(2 + \sqrt{7}) + (2 - \sqrt{7}) = 4$; $(2 + \sqrt{7})(2 - \sqrt{7}) = 4 - 7 = -3$; $x^2 - 4x - 3 = 0$

15. $\frac{1 + \sqrt{2}}{3} + \frac{1 - \sqrt{2}}{3} = \frac{2}{3}$; $\left(\frac{1 + \sqrt{2}}{3}\right)\left(\frac{1 - \sqrt{2}}{3}\right) = \frac{1 - 2}{9} = -\frac{1}{9}$; $x^2 - \frac{2}{3}x - \frac{1}{9} = 0$;

$9x^2 - 6x - 1 = 0$

16. $\frac{-2 + \sqrt{5}}{4} + \frac{-2 - \sqrt{5}}{4} = -1$; $\left(\frac{-2 + \sqrt{5}}{4}\right)\left(\frac{-2 - \sqrt{5}}{4}\right) = \frac{4 - 5}{16} = -\frac{1}{16}$;

$x^2 + x - \frac{1}{16} = 0$; $16x^2 + 16x - 1 = 0$

17. $i\sqrt{5} - i\sqrt{5} = 0$; $(i\sqrt{5})(-i\sqrt{5}) = 5$; $x^2 + 5 = 0$

18. $2i\sqrt{2} - 2i\sqrt{2} = 0$; $(2i\sqrt{2})(-2i\sqrt{2}) = 8$; $x^2 + 8 = 0$

19. $(3 + i) + (3 - i) = 6$; $(3 + i)(3 - i) = 9 + 1 = 10$; $x^2 - 6x + 10 = 0$

20. $(4 + 2i) + (4 - 2i) = 8$; $(4 + 2i)(4 - 2i) = 16 + 4 = 20$; $x^2 - 8x + 20 = 0$

21. $(5 + i\sqrt{2}) + (5 - i\sqrt{2}) = 10$; $(5 + i\sqrt{2})(5 - i\sqrt{2}) = 25 + 2 = 27$;
$x^2 - 10x + 27 = 0$

22. $(-2 + i\sqrt{7}) + (-2 - i\sqrt{7}) = -4$; $(-2 + i\sqrt{7})(-2 - i\sqrt{7}) = 4 + 7 = 11$;
$x^2 + 4x + 11 = 0$

23. $\frac{1 - i\sqrt{5}}{4} + \frac{1 + i\sqrt{5}}{4} = \frac{1}{2}$; $\left(\frac{1 - i\sqrt{5}}{4}\right)\left(\frac{1 + i\sqrt{5}}{4}\right) = \frac{1 + 5}{16} = \frac{3}{8}$; $x^2 - \frac{1}{2}x + \frac{3}{8} = 0$;

$8x^2 - 4x + 3 = 0$

24. $\frac{2 + i\sqrt{3}}{2} + \frac{2 - i\sqrt{3}}{2} = 2; \left(\frac{2 + i\sqrt{3}}{2}\right)\left(\frac{2 - i\sqrt{3}}{2}\right) = \frac{4 + 3}{4} = \frac{7}{4}; x^2 - 2x + \frac{7}{4} = 0;$
$4x^2 - 8x + 7 = 0$

25. $f(x) = a(x - 1)(x - 3)$; the vertex is $\left(\frac{1 + 3}{2}, 10\right) = (2, 10); 10 = a(2 - 1)(2 - 3);$
$10 = -a; a = -10; f(x) = -10(x - 1)(x - 3) = -10(x^2 - 4x + 3);$
$f(x) = -10x^2 + 40x - 30$

26. $f(x) = a(x + 2)(x - 4)$; vertex is $\left(\frac{-2 + 4}{2}, 6\right) = (1, 6); 6 = a(1 + 2)(1 - 4);$
$6 = -9a; a = -\frac{2}{3}; f(x) = -\frac{2}{3}(x + 2)(x - 4) = -\frac{2}{3}(x^2 - 2x - 8);$
$f(x) = -\frac{2}{3}x^2 + \frac{4}{3}x + \frac{16}{3}$

27. $f(x) = ax(x - 8)$; vertex is $\left(\frac{0 + 8}{2}, -8\right) = (4, -8); -8 = a(4)(4 - 8) = -16a;$
$a = \frac{1}{2}; f(x) = \frac{1}{2}x(x - 8) = \frac{1}{2}(x^2 - 8x); f(x) = \frac{1}{2}x^2 - 4x$

28. $f(x) = a(x + 2)(x - 3)$; vertex is $\left(\frac{-2 + 3}{2}, -5\right) = \left(\frac{1}{2}, -5\right); -5 = a\left(\frac{1}{2} + 2\right)\left(\frac{1}{2} - 3\right);$
$-5 = -\frac{25}{4}a; a = \frac{4}{5}; f(x) = \frac{4}{5}(x + 2)(x - 3) = \frac{4}{5}(x^2 - x - 6);$
$f(x) = \frac{4}{5}x^2 - \frac{4}{5}x - \frac{24}{5}$

B **29.** $f(x) = a(x + 4)(x - 8); 12 = a(2 + 4)(2 - 8) = -36a; a = -\frac{1}{3};$
$f(x) = -\frac{1}{3}(x + 4)(x - 8) = -\frac{1}{3}(x^2 - 4x - 32); f(x) = -\frac{1}{3}x^2 + \frac{4}{3}x + \frac{32}{3}$

30. $f(x) = a(x + 6)(x - 4); -10 = a(-1 + 6)(-1 - 4) = -25a; a = \frac{2}{5};$
$f(x) = \frac{2}{5}(x + 6)(x - 4) = \frac{2}{5}(x^2 + 2x - 24); f(x) = \frac{2}{5}x^2 + \frac{4}{5}x - \frac{48}{5}$

31. $f(x) = a(x + 1)(x - 5)$; vertex is $\left(\frac{-1 + 5}{2}, -6\right) = (2, -6);$
$-6 = a(2 + 1)(2 - 5) = -9a; \frac{2}{3} = a; f(x) = \frac{2}{3}(x + 1)(x - 5) = \frac{2}{3}(x^2 - 4x - 5);$
$f(x) = \frac{2}{3}x^2 - \frac{8}{3}x - \frac{10}{3}$

32. $f(x) = a(x + 6)(x)$; vertex is $\left(\frac{-6 + 0}{2}, 9\right) = (-3, 9); 9 = a(-3 + 6)(-3) = -9a;$
$a = -1; f(x) = -1(x + 6)(x); f(x) = -x^2 - 6x$

33. Let r_2 be the other zero; $\frac{1 + r_2}{2} = -2; 1 + r_2 = -4; r_2 = -5; f(x) = a(x - 1)(x + 5);$
$6 = a(-2 - 1)(-2 + 5) = -9a; a = -\frac{2}{3}; f(x) = -\frac{2}{3}(x - 1)(x + 5) =$
$-\frac{2}{3}(x^2 + 4x - 5); f(x) = -\frac{2}{3}x^2 - \frac{8}{3}x + \frac{10}{3}$

34. Let r_2 be the other zero; $\frac{6 + r_2}{2} = 3$; $6 + r_2 = 6$; $r_2 = 0$; $f(x) = a(x - 6)(x)$;

$-4 = a(3 - 6)(3) = -9a$; $a = \frac{4}{9}$; $f(x) = \frac{4}{9}(x - 6)(x)$; $f(x) = \frac{4}{9}x^2 - \frac{8}{3}x$

35. $f(x) = a(x - 1)(x - 5)$; $2 = a(0 - 1)(0 - 5)$; $2 = 5a$; $a = \frac{2}{5}$;

$f(x) = \frac{2}{5}(x - 1)(x - 5) = \frac{2}{5}(x^2 - 6x + 5)$; $f(x) = \frac{2}{5}x^2 - \frac{12}{5}x + 2$

36. Vertex is $\left(\frac{-2 + 4}{2}, 9\right) = (1, 9)$; $f(x) = a(x + 2)(x - 4)$; $9 = a(1 + 2)(1 - 4) = -9a$;

$a = -1$; $f(x) = -1(x + 2)(x - 4) = -(x^2 - 2x - 8)$; $f(x) = -x^2 + 2x + 8$

37. a. $(3 + i\sqrt{2})^2 - 6(3 + i\sqrt{2}) + 11 = 7 + 6i\sqrt{2} - 18 - 6i\sqrt{2} + 11 = 0$

b. Since the sum of the roots is 6, the other root is $6 - (3 + i\sqrt{2}) = 3 - i\sqrt{2}$

38. a. $16\left(\frac{5 - i\sqrt{2}}{4}\right)^2 - 40\left(\frac{5 - i\sqrt{2}}{4}\right) + 27 = 23 - 10i\sqrt{2} - 50 + 10i\sqrt{2} + 27 = 0$

b. Since the sum of the roots is $\frac{40}{16} = \frac{5}{2}$, the other root is $\frac{5}{2} - \left(\frac{5 - i\sqrt{2}}{4}\right) =$

$\frac{5 + i\sqrt{2}}{4}$

C **39.** The roots are reciprocals if and only if the product of the roots is 1; that is, $\frac{c}{a} = 1$,

or $a = c$.

40. Let the roots be r_1 and r_2. Then $\frac{1}{r_1} + \frac{1}{r_2} = \frac{r_2 + r_1}{r_1 r_2} = \frac{-\frac{b}{a}}{\frac{c}{a}} = -\frac{b}{c}$.

Pages 343–345 • PROBLEMS

A **1.** $20 - x$; $p(x) = x(20 - x) = -x^2 + 20x$; maximum value of p occurs when

$x = -\frac{20}{-2} = 10$; $p(10) = -100 + 200 = 100$; the maximum product is 100

2. $x + 8$; $x(x + 8) = x^2 + 8x$; the minimum value of p occurs when $x = \frac{-8}{2} = -4$;

$p(-4) = 16 - 32 = -16$; the minimum product is -16

3. Let the numbers be x and $40 - x$, and let their product be
$p(x) = x(40 - x) = -x^2 + 40x$; the maximum value of p occurs when

$x = -\frac{40}{-2} = 20$; $p(20) = -400 + 800 = 400$; the maximum product is 400

4. Let the numbers be x and $20 - x$, and let the sum of their squares be
$s(x) = x^2 + (20 - x)^2 = 2x^2 - 40x + 400$; the minimum value of s occurs when

$x = \frac{40}{4} = 10$; $20 - x = 10$; the numbers are 10 and 10

5. Let the width and length (in cm) be x and $50 - x$, and let $A(x) = x(50 - x) = -x^2 + 50x$ be the area in cm²; the maximum value of A occurs when $x = -\frac{50}{-2} = 25$; $A(25) = 625$; the maximum area is 625 cm²

6. Let the width (in cm) be x, and let the area be $A(x) = x(100 - 2x) = -2x^2 + 100x$; the maximum value of A occurs when $x = -\frac{100}{-4} = 25$; $A(25) = 25(50) = 1250$; the greatest possible area is 1250 m²

7. a. $(20 + 10)(8 - 0.10(10)) = (30)(7) = 210$; \$210; $(20 + 15)(8 - 0.10(15)) = (35)(6.50) = 227.5$; \$227.50; $(20 + n)(8 - 0.10n)$

b. Let the dues money be $D(n) = (20 + n)(8 - 0.10n) = -0.10n^2 + 6n + 160$; maximum value of D occurs when $n = -\frac{6}{-0.2} = 30$; the maximum amount of money will be collected if 30 new members are recruited

8. Let n be the number of new members, and let the dues money be $D(n) = (24 + n)(8 - 0.10n) = -0.10n^2 + 5.6n + 192$; the maximum value of D occurs when $n = -\frac{5.6}{-0.2} = 28$; $D(28) = (52)(5.2) = 270.4$; with 28 new members the maximum amount of money, \$270.40, will be collected

9. Let the number of passengers in excess of 20 be n, and let the fare revenue be $f(x) = (20 + n)(60 - 2n) = -2n^2 + 20n + 1200$; the maximum value of f occurs when $n = -\frac{20}{-4} = 5$; the maximum revenue occurs when there are 20 + 5 or 25 passengers

B

10. Let x = number of dollars of increase; then $10 + x$ = new fare and $300 - 15x$ = number of passengers per day; income $= (10 + x)(300 - 15x) = 3000 + 150x - 15x^2$; maximum income occurs when $x = -\frac{150}{-30} = 5$; the fare yielding the greatest income is \$15

11. Maximum power occurs at $I = -\frac{120}{-32} = \frac{15}{4} = 3.75$; maximum power is $P\left(\frac{15}{4}\right) = 450 - 225 = 225$; a current of 3.75 amps produces the maximum power of 225 watts

12. a. Maximum height occurs when $t = -\frac{80}{-32} = \frac{5}{2}$; $h = 80\left(\frac{5}{2}\right) - 16\left(\frac{25}{4}\right) = 200 - 100 = 100$; 100 ft

b. The ball hits the ground when $h = 0$, so $0 = 80t - 16t^2 = 16t(5 - t)$; $t = 0$ or $t = 5$; the ball will hit the ground 5 s after it is thrown

13. x = length of 2 sides parallel to the partitioning side, so the length of each long side is $\frac{800 - 3x}{2}$; $A(x) = x\left(\frac{800 - 3x}{2}\right) = \frac{800}{2}x - \frac{3}{2}x^2 = 400x - \frac{3}{2}x^2$; the maximum area occurs when $x = -\frac{400}{-3} = \frac{400}{3}$; $A\left(\frac{400}{3}\right) = \frac{160{,}000}{3} - \frac{80{,}000}{3} = \frac{80{,}000}{3}$; $26{,}666\frac{2}{3}$ m²

14. If there is 300 m of fencing and a 12 m opening, the lot perimeter will be 312 m with width $= x$ and length $= \frac{312}{2} - x$ or $156 - x$; $A(x) = x(156 - x) = 156x - x^2$; the maximum area occurs when $x = -\frac{156}{-2} = 78$; 78 m by 78 m

15. a. Maximum height occurs when $x = -\dfrac{\frac{4}{3}}{-\frac{2}{90}} = 60$; $y = \frac{4}{3}(60) - \frac{(60)^2}{90} = 40$; maximum height is 40 ft

b. When $x = 105$, $y = \frac{4}{3}(105) - \frac{(105)^2}{90} = 140 - 122\frac{1}{2} = 17\frac{1}{2}$ ft; the ball will clear the crossbar

C **16.** If the height of the triangle is 8, the height of $\triangle APQ$ is $8 - y$; $\triangle APQ$ is similar to $\triangle ABC$, so $\frac{x}{10} = \frac{8 - y}{8}$; $8x = 80 - 10y$; $8x - 80 = -10y$; $y = 8 - \frac{4}{5}x$;
$A = xy = x\left(8 - \frac{4}{5}x\right) = 8x - \frac{4}{5}x^2$; maximum area occurs when $x = -\dfrac{8}{-\frac{8}{5}} = 5$;
$A = 8(5) - \frac{4}{5} \cdot 25 = 20$; maximum area of the rectangle is 20

Page 345 • MIXED REVIEW EXERCISES

1.

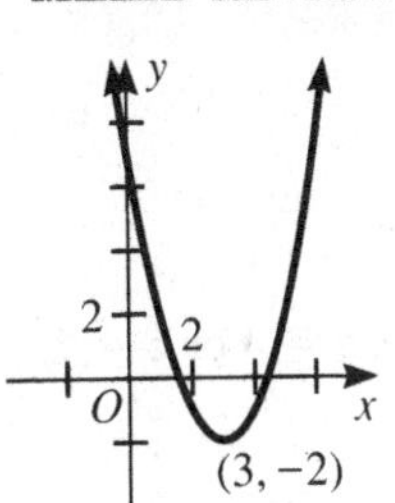

2.

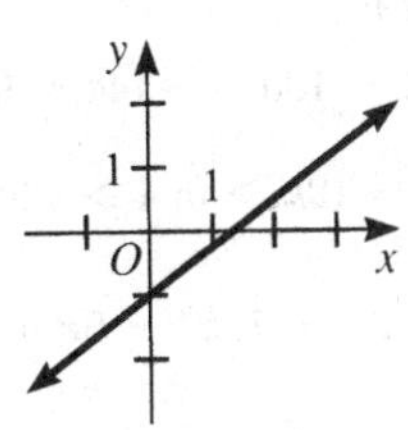

3.

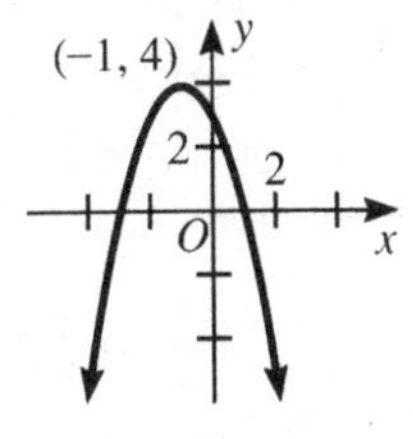

4.

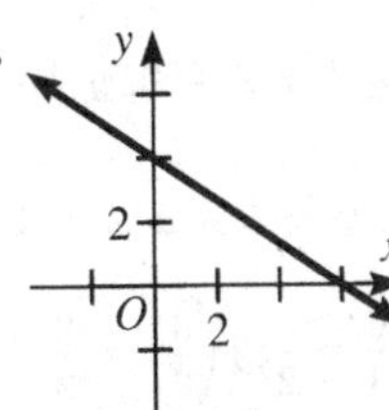

5.

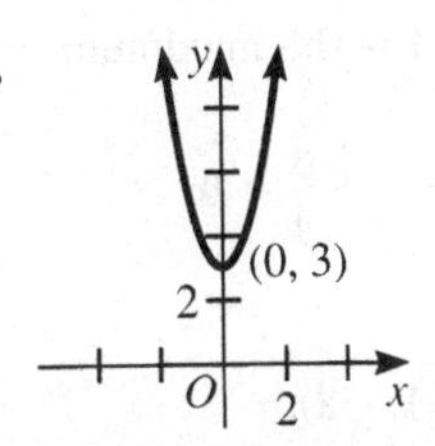

6.

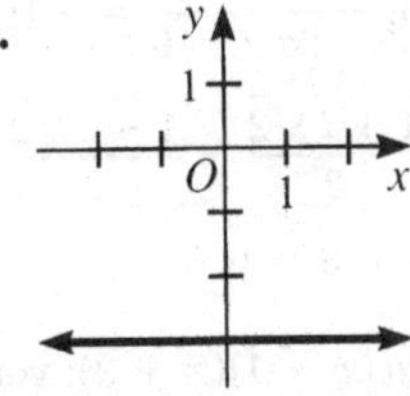

7. $D = \{\text{real numbers}\}$; $0 = 9 - x^2$; $x^2 = 9$; $x = \pm 3$; zeros are ± 3

8. $D = \{\text{real numbers}\}$; $0 = 3x - 8$; $x = \frac{8}{3}$; zero is $\frac{8}{3}$

9. $D = \{\text{real numbers}\}$; $0 = x^2 + 6x - 2$; $x = \frac{-6 \pm \sqrt{36 + 8}}{2} = -3 \pm \sqrt{11}$; zeros are $-3 \pm \sqrt{11}$

10. $D = \{\text{real numbers}\}$; the graph is horizontal, so there are no zeros

11. $D = \{\text{real numbers}\}$; $0 = 2x^2 - 3x + 4$; $x = \frac{3 \pm \sqrt{9 - 32}}{4} = \frac{3 \pm i\sqrt{23}}{4}$; there are no real zeros

12. $D = \left\{x: x \neq \frac{5}{2}\right\}$; $\frac{4x + 1}{2x - 5} = 0$; $4x + 1 = 0$; $x = -\frac{1}{4}$; zero is $-\frac{1}{4}$

Pages 346–347 • CHAPTER REVIEW

1. c; $2(x - 1)^2 = -16$; $(x - 1)^2 = -8$; $x - 1 = \pm\sqrt{-8}$; $x - 1 = \pm 2i\sqrt{2}$; $x = 1 \pm 2i\sqrt{2}$

2. b; $3y^2 - 18y + d = (\sqrt{3}\,y - \sqrt{d})(\sqrt{3}\,y - \sqrt{d})$; $-2\sqrt{3d} = -18$; $\sqrt{3d} = 9$; $3d = 81$; $d = 27$

3. a; $2x^2 = 3x - 1$; $2x^2 - 3x + 1 = 0$; $(2x - 1)(x - 1) = 0$; $x = \frac{1}{2}$ or $x = 1$

4. b; let $x =$ the amount of increase on each dimension; $(8 + x)(12 + x) = 2(8)(12)$; $x^2 + 20x + 96 = 192$; $x^2 + 20x - 96 = 0$; $(x - 4)(x + 24) = 0$; $x = 4$ or $x = -24$ (reject); 4 ft

5. a; $D = 36 - 180 = -144 < 0$

6. d; $D = 4 - 12k > 0$; $4 > 12k$; $k < \frac{1}{3}$

7. a; let $z = 2x + 1$; $z^2 - 5z + 6 = 0$; $(z - 3)(z - 2) = 0$; $z = 3$ or $z = 2$; $x = \frac{z - 1}{2}$; $x = 1$ or $x = \frac{1}{2}$

8. a; $y^{-2} - 2y^{-1} + 2 = 0$; $y^{-1} = \frac{2 \pm \sqrt{-4}}{2} = 1 \pm i$; $y = \frac{1}{1 \pm i} = \frac{1 \pm i}{2}$

9. c **10.** d; $y - 4 = a(x + 1)^2$; $2 - 4 = a(1 + 1)^2$; $-2 = 4a$; $a = -\frac{1}{2}$

11. b; $-\frac{b}{2a} = \frac{6}{4} = \frac{3}{2}$; $f\left(\frac{3}{2}\right) = \frac{9}{2} - 9 + 5 = \frac{1}{2}$

12. c **13.** a; $-\frac{b}{2a} = \frac{6}{-6} = -1$; $f(-1) = 4$; since $a < 0$, 4 is the maximum

14. c; $-\frac{b}{a} = \frac{1 + i\sqrt{2}}{2} + \frac{1 - i\sqrt{2}}{2} = 1$; $\frac{c}{a} = \frac{1 + 2}{2 \cdot 2} = \frac{3}{4}$; $x^2 - x + \frac{3}{4} = 0$; $4x^2 - 4x + 3 = 0$

15. d; $f(x) = a(x - 1)(x + 3)$; vertex $= \left(\frac{1 - 3}{2}, -2\right) = (-1, -2)$; $f(-1) = a(-2)(2) = -4a = -2$; $a = \frac{1}{2}$; $f(x) = \frac{1}{2}(x^2 + 2x - 3) = \frac{1}{2}x^2 + x - \frac{3}{2}$

Page 348 • CHAPTER TEST

1. $(3x + 1)^2 = 8; 3x + 1 = \pm\sqrt{8}; 3x = -1 \pm 2\sqrt{2}; x = \frac{-1 \pm 2\sqrt{2}}{3}; \left\{\frac{-1 \pm 2\sqrt{2}}{3}\right\}$

2. $2x^2 + 6x + 3 = 0; 2x^2 + 6x = -3; x^2 + 3x = -\frac{3}{2}; x^2 + 3x + \frac{9}{4} = \frac{9}{4} - \frac{3}{2};$

   $\left(x + \frac{3}{2}\right)^2 = \frac{3}{4}; x + \frac{3}{2} = \pm\frac{\sqrt{3}}{2}; x = \frac{-3 \pm \sqrt{3}}{2}; \left\{\frac{-3 \pm \sqrt{3}}{2}\right\}$

3. $4x^2 - 3x + 2 = 0; x = \frac{3 \pm \sqrt{9 - 32}}{8} = \frac{3 \pm i\sqrt{23}}{8}; \left\{\frac{3}{8} \pm \frac{\sqrt{23}}{8}i\right\}$

4. Let x and $7 - x$ be the numbers; then $x(7 - x) = 11; -x^2 + 7x - 11 = 0;$

   $x = \frac{-7 \pm \sqrt{49 - 44}}{-2} = \frac{7 \pm \sqrt{5}}{2}; \frac{7 + \sqrt{5}}{2}$ and $\frac{7 - \sqrt{5}}{2}$

5. a. $D = 49 - 40 = 9$; two different rational real roots

   b. $D = 16 - 24 = -8$; two conjugate imaginary roots

6. $D = k^2 - 24; k^2 - 24 = 0; k^2 = 24; k = \pm 2\sqrt{6}$

7. a. $x^4 + x^2 - 12 = 0; (x^2 + 4)(x^2 - 3) = 0; x^2 = -4$ or $x^2 = 3; x = \pm 2i$ or $x = \pm\sqrt{3}; \{\pm 2i, \pm\sqrt{3}\}$

   b. $x^{-2} - 2x^{-1} - 1 = 0$; let $z = x^{-1}; z^2 - 2z - 1 = 0; z = \frac{2 \pm \sqrt{4 + 4}}{2} = 1 \pm \sqrt{2};$

   $x = \frac{1}{z}; x = \frac{1}{1 + \sqrt{2}}$ or $x = \frac{1}{1 - \sqrt{2}}; x = \frac{1 - \sqrt{2}}{1 - 2}$ or $x = \frac{1 + \sqrt{2}}{1 - 2}; \{-1 \pm \sqrt{2}\}$

8.

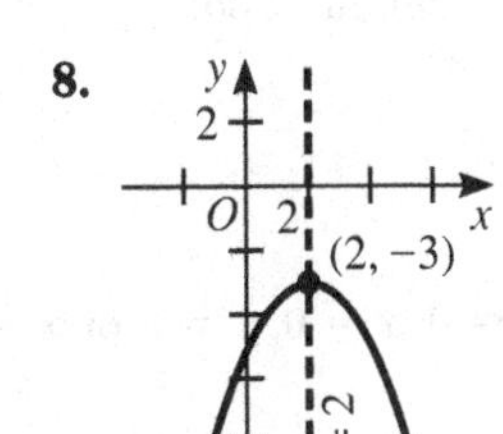

9. $y - 5 = a(x + 2)^2; 9 - 5 = a(2 + 2)^2; 4 = 16a; a = \frac{1}{4};$

   $y - 5 = \frac{1}{4}(x + 2)^2$

10. $y - 1 = 2(x^2 - 2x); y - 1 + 2 = 2(x^2 - 2x + 1); y + 1 = 2(x - 1)^2$

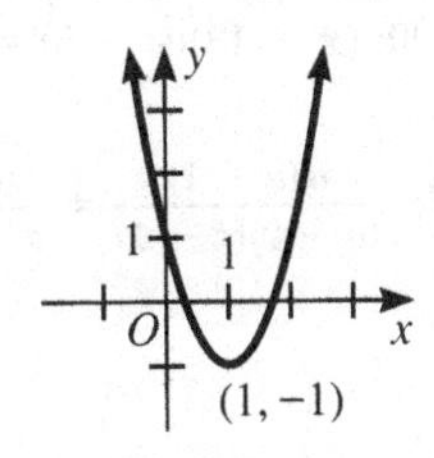

11. $D = \{\text{real numbers}\}$; $-\frac{b}{2a} = \frac{6}{2} = 3$; $g(3) = 9 - 18 + 4 = -5$; since $a > 0$, -5 is a minimum; $R = \{y: y \geq -5\}$; $0 = x^2 - 6x + 4$; $x = \frac{6 \pm \sqrt{36 - 16}}{2} = 3 \pm \sqrt{5}$; zeros $3 + \sqrt{5}$ and $3 - \sqrt{5}$

12. $r_1 + r_2 = \frac{1}{2}$; $r_1 r_2 = -\frac{1}{8}$; $x^2 - \frac{1}{2}x - \frac{1}{8} = 0$; $8x^2 - 4x - 1 = 0$

13. $f(x) = a\left(x - \frac{1}{2}\right)\left(x + \frac{5}{2}\right)$; vertex $= \left(\frac{\frac{1}{2} - \frac{5}{2}}{2}, -9\right) = (-1, -9)$;
$-9 = a\left(-1 - \frac{1}{2}\right)\left(-1 + \frac{5}{2}\right)$; $-9 = a\left(-\frac{3}{2}\right)\left(\frac{3}{2}\right)$; $-9 = -\frac{9}{4}a$; $a = 4$;
$f(x) = 4\left(x - \frac{1}{2}\right)\left(x + \frac{5}{2}\right) = 4\left(x^2 + 2x - \frac{5}{4}\right)$; $f(x) = 4x^2 + 8x - 5$

14. Let w = width in cm; then $\frac{20 - 2w}{2} = 10 - w$ = length; area $= A(w) = w(10 - w) = -w^2 + 10w$; maximum value of A occurs when $w = -\frac{10}{-2} = 5$; the rectangle of maximum area is 5 cm by 5 cm

Pages 348–349 • CUMULATIVE REVIEW

1. $6x^2 - 8x + 2 - 5x^2 - x + 6 = x^2 - 9x + 8$ **2.** $-12a^5b^3$ **3.** $x^8y^4z^{12}$
4. $8y^2 + 20y - 6y - 15 = 8y^2 + 14y - 15$ **5.** $(2x - 3)(x - 4)$
6. $x(3x - 2) + 2y(3x - 2) = (x + 2y)(3x - 2)$ **7.** $(4a - 3b)(4a + 3b)$
8. $3y^2(y^2 - 2y - 3) = 3y^2(y - 3)(y + 1)$
9. $(x - 4)(x + 1) = 0$; $x = 4$ or $x = -1$; $\{-1, 4\}$
10. $x^2 - 10x + 25 = 0$; $(x - 5)^2 = 0$; $x = 5$; $\{5\}$
11. $x^3 = 9x$; $x^3 - 9x = 0$; $x(x^2 - 9) = 0$; $x(x - 3)(x + 3) = 0$; $x = 0$, $x = 3$ or $x = -3$; $\{-3, 0, 3\}$
12. $y^2 + y < 20$; $y^2 + y - 20 < 0$; $(y + 5)(y - 4) < 0$; $\{y: -5 < y < 4\}$
13. Let the integers be n and $n + 2$; $n(n + 2) = 99$; $n^2 + 2n - 99 = 0$; $(n - 9)(n + 11) = 0$; $n = 9$ or $n = -11$; the numbers are 9 and 11 or -11 and -9
14. Let x = the length, in cm, of the hypotenuse; $(x - 8)^2 + (x - 1)^2 = x^2$; $x^2 - 16x + 64 + x^2 - 2x + 1 = x^2$; $x^2 - 18x + 65 = 0$; $(x - 13)(x - 5) = 0$; $x = 5$ (reject since $x > 8$) or $x = 13$; 13 cm
15. $\frac{12x^3y}{16x^2y^4} = \frac{3x}{4y^3}$ **16.** $(x^{-3}y^2)(x^{-4}y^2) = x^{-7}y^4 = \frac{y^4}{x^7}$ **17.** $\frac{a(a - 1)}{(a + 2)(a - 1)} = \frac{a}{a + 2}$
18. $\frac{18x^2}{(x - 4)(x + 2)} \cdot \frac{(x - 3)(x + 2)}{12x} \cdot \frac{x - 4}{3(x - 3)} = \frac{x}{2}$
19. $\frac{1}{2(y + 2)} + \frac{1}{y(y + 2)} = \frac{y + 2}{2y(y + 2)} = \frac{1}{2y}$
20. $\frac{1 - \frac{1}{m^2}}{\frac{1}{m} - 1} = \frac{m^2 - 1}{m - m^2} = \frac{(m - 1)(m + 1)}{-m(m - 1)} = \frac{m + 1}{-m} = -\frac{m + 1}{m}$

21. $\frac{x}{x+2} - \frac{1}{x+1} = \frac{2}{(x+2)(x+1)}$; $x(x+1) - (x+2) = 2$; $x^2 + x - x - 2 = 2$; $x^2 = 4$; $x = -2$ (reject) or $x = 2$; $\{2\}$

22. $y + \sqrt{y-1} = 7$; $\sqrt{y-1} = 7 - y$; $y - 1 = 49 - 14y + y^2$; $y^2 - 15y + 50 = 0$; $(y-5)(y-10) = 0$; $y = 5$ or $y = 10$ (reject); $\{5\}$

23. Let x = dollars invested at 5%; $0.05x + 0.08(4000 - x) = 284$; $-0.03x + 320 = 284$; $-0.03x = -36$; $x = 1200$; he invested \$1200 at 5% and \$2800 at 8%

24. $4\sqrt{5}$ **25.** $2\sqrt{6} - \frac{\sqrt{6}}{2} = \frac{3\sqrt{6}}{2}$ **26.** $21 + 28\sqrt{5} - 3\sqrt{5} - 20 = 1 + 25\sqrt{5}$

27. $\frac{2}{\sqrt{7}-\sqrt{3}} \cdot \frac{\sqrt{7}+\sqrt{3}}{\sqrt{7}+\sqrt{3}} = \frac{2(\sqrt{7}+\sqrt{3})}{7-3} = \frac{\sqrt{7}+\sqrt{3}}{2}$

28. $(2i\sqrt{2})(i\sqrt{6}) = -2\sqrt{12} = -4\sqrt{3}$

29. $\frac{3-2i}{3+2i} \cdot \frac{3-2i}{3-2i} = \frac{9 - 12i - 4}{9+4} = \frac{5-12i}{13} = \frac{5}{13} - \frac{12}{13}i$

30. Let $N = 0.1\overline{54}$; then $100N = 15.4\overline{54}$ and $99N = 15.3$; $N = \frac{15.3}{99} = \frac{17}{110}$

31. $4x^2 - 12x + 7 = 0$; $4(x^2 - 3x) = -7$; $4\left(x^2 - 3x + \frac{9}{4}\right) = -7 + 9$; $4\left(x - \frac{3}{2}\right)^2 = 2$;

$\left(x - \frac{3}{2}\right)^2 = \frac{1}{2}$; $x - \frac{3}{2} = \pm\frac{\sqrt{2}}{2}$; $x = \frac{3}{2} \pm \frac{\sqrt{2}}{2}$; $\left\{\frac{3 \pm \sqrt{2}}{2}\right\}$

32. $9y^2 + 12y + 5 = 0$; $y = \frac{-12 \pm \sqrt{144 - 180}}{18} = \frac{-12 \pm 6i}{18} = \frac{-2 \pm i}{3}$; $\left\{-\frac{2}{3} \pm \frac{1}{3}i\right\}$

33. $D = 36 - 12k$; $36 - 12k < 0$; $36 < 12k$; $k > 3$

34. $(4x - 3)^2 - 6(4x - 3) + 5 = 0$; let $z = 4x - 3$; $z^2 - 6z + 5 = 0$;

$(z - 5)(z - 1) = 0$; $z = 5$ or $z = 1$; $x = \frac{z+3}{4}$; $x = 2$ or $x = 1$; $\{1, 2\}$

35.

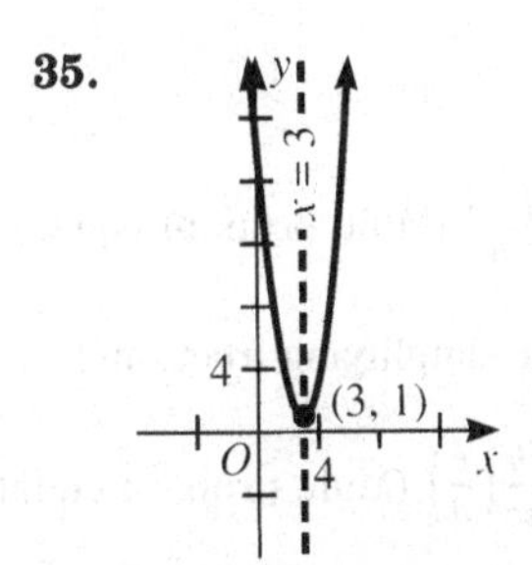

36. D = {real numbers}; $-\frac{b}{2a} = \frac{8}{2} = 4$; $f(4) = 16 - 32 + 9 = -7$; since $a > 0$, -7 is the minimum; $R = \{y: y \geq -7\}$; $0 = x^2 - 8x + 9$; $x = \frac{8 \pm \sqrt{64 - 36}}{2} = 4 \pm \sqrt{7}$; zeros are $4 + \sqrt{7}$ and $4 - \sqrt{7}$

37. Let the numbers be x and $(x + 6)$, and let their product be $p(x) = x(x + 6) = x^2 + 6x$; minimum value of p occurs when $x = -\frac{6}{2} = -3$; $p(-3) = -3(3) = -9$; since $a > 0$, -9 is the minimum product

CHAPTER 8 • Variation and Polynomial Equations

Pages 354–355 • WRITTEN EXERCISES

A **1.** $\frac{y_1}{x_1} = \frac{y_2}{x_2}; \frac{6}{15} = \frac{y_2}{25}, 15y_2 = 150, y_2 = 10$ **2.** $\frac{s_1}{t_1} = \frac{s_2}{t_2}; \frac{40}{15} = \frac{64}{t_2}; 40t_2 = 960, t_2 = 24$

3. $\frac{p_1}{q_1} = \frac{p_2}{q_2}; \frac{9}{7.5} = \frac{24}{q_2}, 9q_2 = 180, q_2 = 20$ **4.** $\frac{a_1}{b_1} = \frac{a_2}{b_2}; \frac{75}{40} = \frac{a_2}{12}, 40a_2 = 900, a_2 = 22.5;$

5. $\frac{s_1}{r_1^2} = \frac{s_2}{r_2^2}; \frac{12}{2^2} = \frac{s_2}{5^2}, 300 = 4s_2, s_2 = 75$

6. $\frac{y_1}{\sqrt{x_1}} = \frac{y_2}{\sqrt{x_2}}; \frac{25}{\sqrt{3}} = \frac{100}{\sqrt{x_2}}, 25\sqrt{x_2} = 100\sqrt{3}, \sqrt{x_2} = 4\sqrt{3}, x_2 = (4\sqrt{3})^2 = 48$

7. $p = m(r - 2); 20 = m(6 - 2), 20 = 4m, m = 5; p = 5(12 - 2) = 50$

8. $w = m(2x - 1); 9 = m(2(2) - 1), 9 = 3m, m = 3; 15 = 3(2x - 1), 5 = 2x - 1,$ $6 = 2x, x = 3$

9. $\frac{a}{b} = \frac{b}{c}; b^2 = ac; a = 2, c = 18; b^2 = 2 \cdot 18 = 36, b = 6$

10. $b^2 = ac; a = 3, c = 27; b^2 = 3(27) = 81, b = 9$

11. $b^2 = ac; a = 8, c = 9; b^2 = 8 \cdot 9 = 72, b = \sqrt{72} = 6\sqrt{2}$

12. $b^2 = ac, a = 5, c = 15; b^2 = 5 \cdot 15 = 75, b = \sqrt{75} = 5\sqrt{3}$

B **13.** 1. $\frac{a}{b} = \frac{c}{d}$; a, b, c, and d nonzero (Given)

2. $\frac{bd}{1}\left(\frac{a}{b}\right) = \frac{bd}{1}\left(\frac{c}{d}\right)$ (Mult. prop. of equal.) 3. $\frac{bda}{b} = \frac{bdc}{d}$ (Mult. rule for fractions)

4. $da = bc$ (Rule for simplifying fractions) 5. $ad = bc$ (Comm. prop. for mult.)

14. 1. $\frac{a}{b} = \frac{c}{d}$; a, b, c, and d nonzero (Given)

2. $\frac{b}{c}\left(\frac{a}{b}\right) = \frac{b}{c}\left(\frac{c}{d}\right)$ (Mult. prop. of equal.) 3. $\frac{ba}{cb} = \frac{bc}{cd}$ (Mult. rule for fractions)

4. $\frac{a}{c} = \frac{b}{d}$ (Rule for simplifying fractions)

15. 1. $\frac{a}{b} = \frac{c}{d}$; a, b, c, and d nonzero (Given) 2. $\frac{d}{a}\left(\frac{a}{b}\right) = \frac{d}{a}\left(\frac{c}{d}\right)$ (Mult. prop. of equal.)

3. $\frac{da}{ab} = \frac{dc}{ad}$ (Mult. rule for fractions) 4. $\frac{d}{b} = \frac{c}{a}$ (Rule for simplifying fractions)

16. 1. $\frac{a}{b} = \frac{c}{d}$; a, b, c, and d nonzero (Given) 2. $\frac{db}{ac}\left(\frac{a}{b}\right) = \frac{db}{ac}\left(\frac{c}{d}\right)$ (Mult. prop. of equal.)

3. $\frac{dba}{acb} = \frac{dbc}{acd}$ (Mult. rule for fractions) 4. $\frac{d}{c} = \frac{b}{a}$ (Rule for simplifying fractions)

17. 1. $\frac{a}{b} = \frac{c}{d}$; a, b, c, and d nonzero (Given) 2. $\frac{a}{b} + 1 = \frac{c}{d} + 1$ (Add. prop. of equal.)

3. $\frac{a}{b} + b \cdot \frac{1}{b} = \frac{c}{d} + d \cdot \frac{1}{d}$ (Prop. of recip.) 4. $\frac{a}{b} + \frac{b}{b} = \frac{c}{d} + \frac{d}{d}$ (Def. of div.)

5. $\frac{a + b}{b} = \frac{c + d}{d}$ (Add. rule for fractions)

18. 1. $\frac{a}{b} = \frac{c}{d}$; a, b, c, and d nonzero (Given)

2. $\frac{a}{b} - 1 = \frac{c}{d} - 1$ (Add. prop. of equal.; def. of subtr.)

3. $\frac{a}{b} - b \cdot \frac{1}{b} = \frac{c}{d} - d \cdot \frac{1}{d}$ (Prop. of recip.) 4. $\frac{a}{b} - \frac{b}{b} = \frac{c}{d} - \frac{d}{d}$ (Def. of div.)

5. $\frac{a - b}{b} = \frac{c - d}{d}$ (Subtr. rule for fractions)

19. 1. $\frac{a}{b} = \frac{c}{d}$; a, b, c, and d nonzero; $c \neq d$ (Given) 2. $\frac{a - b}{b} = \frac{c - d}{d}$ (Ex. 18)

3. $\frac{a - b}{c - d} = \frac{b}{d}$ (Ex. 14) 4. $\frac{a}{c} = \frac{b}{d}$ (Ex. 14) 5. $\frac{a - b}{c - d} = \frac{a}{c}$ (Subst.)

20. 1. $\frac{a}{b} = \frac{c}{d}$; a, b, c, and d nonzero; $a \neq b$ and $c \neq d$ (Given)

2. $\frac{a + b}{b} = \frac{c + d}{d}$ and $\frac{a - b}{b} = \frac{c - d}{d}$ (Ex. 17 and Ex. 18)

3. $\frac{a + b}{c + d} = \frac{b}{d}$ and $\frac{a - b}{c - d} = \frac{b}{d}$ (Ex. 14)

4. $\frac{a + b}{c + d} = \frac{a - b}{c - d}$ (Trans. prop. of equal.) 5. $\frac{a + b}{a - b} = \frac{c + d}{c - d}$ (Ex. 14)

C

21. 1. g is a direct variation over the set of real numbers. (Given)

2. There is a real number m such that for every real number x, $g(x) = mx$. (Def. of direct variation)

3. $g(a + c) = m(a + c)$; $g(a) + g(c) = ma + mc$ (Def. of direct variation; a and c are real numbers)

4. $m(a + c) = ma + mc$ (Dist. prop.) 5. $g(a + c) = g(a) + g(c)$ (Subst.)

22. 1. For every real number $x, f(x) = mx + b$, $m \neq 0$, $b \neq 0$. (Def. of linear function; f is not a direct variation, and f is not the constant function 0.)

2. $f(a + c) - [f(a) + f(c)] = m(a + c) + b - (ma + b + mc + b) = ma + mc + b - ma - mc - 2b = -b$ (Subst.; dist. prop.)

3. $b \neq 0$ and $-b \neq 0$ (Step 1)

4. $f(a + c) \neq f(a) + f(c)$ (For real numbers x and y, $x = y$ if and only if $x - y = 0$.)

23. Given y and z vary directly as x. There exist constants k and c such that $y = kx$ and $z = cx$. $y + z = kx + cx = (k + c)x$. Since $k + c$ is a constant, $y + z$ varies directly as x.

24. Given $y = kx$ and $z = cx$, where k and c are constants. $yz = (kx)(cx) = kcx^2$, $\sqrt{yz} = \sqrt{kcx^2} = x\sqrt{kc}$. Since $\sqrt{kc}$ is a constant, $\sqrt{yz}$ varies directly as x.

25. Given $y = kx$ and $z = cx$ where k and c are constants. $yz = (kx)(cx) = kcx^2$; $y^2 + z^2 = k^2x^2 + c^2x^2 = (k^2 + c^2)x^2$. Since $x^2 = \left(\frac{1}{kc}\right)yz$ and $x^2 = \left(\frac{1}{k^2 + c^2}\right)(y^2 + z^2)$, $\left(\frac{1}{kc}\right)yz = \left(\frac{1}{k^2 + c^2}\right)(y^2 + z^2)$ or $yz = \left(\frac{kc}{k^2 + c^2}\right)(y^2 + z^2)$.

Since $\frac{kc}{k^2 + c^2}$ is a constant, yz varies directly as $y^2 + z^2$.

Pages 356–357 • PROBLEMS

A

1. $y = 9.8x$; $147 = 9.8x$, $x = 15$; 15 m

2. Let t = tax in dollars on a purchase costing p dollars; $\frac{t_1}{p_1} = \frac{t_2}{p_2}$; $\frac{3.90}{60} = \frac{t_2}{280}$, $60t_2 = 1092$, $t_2 = 18.2$; \$18.20

3. Let c = the commission in dollars on a house costing h dollars; $\frac{c_1}{h_1} = \frac{c_2}{h_2}$; $\frac{5400}{120{,}000} = \frac{c_2}{145{,}000}$; $c_2 = \frac{(5400)(145{,}000)}{120{,}000} = 6525$; \$6525

4. Let a = acceleration in m/s² and f = force in newtons; $\frac{a_1}{f_1} = \frac{a_2}{f_2}$; $\frac{150}{240} = \frac{100}{f_2}$; $f_2 = \frac{(240)(100)}{150} = 160$; 160 newtons

5. Let a distance of x feet be represented on the map by a distance of y inches; $\frac{x_1}{y_1} = \frac{x_2}{y_2}$; $\frac{280}{8} = \frac{x_2}{5}$, $x_2 = \frac{5(280)}{8} = 175$; 175 feet.

6. The smaller can costs $\frac{39}{575} \approx 0.0678$ cents/g; the larger costs $\frac{52}{810} \approx 0.0642$ cents/g; the larger can is the better buy.

7. The estimated proportion of banded birds is $\frac{48}{1000} = \frac{6}{125}$; $\frac{6}{125} = \frac{600}{x}$, $6x = 75{,}000$, $x = 12{,}500$; approximately 12,500 birds

8. The estimated proportion of voters favoring the bond measure is $\frac{252}{450} = \frac{14}{25}$; $\frac{14}{25} = \frac{x}{20{,}000}$, $25x = 280{,}000$, $x = 11{,}200$; approximately 11,200

9. Let y be the stretch in cm produced by a x kg load; $\frac{x_1}{y_1} = \frac{x_2}{y_2}$; $\frac{15}{3.6} = \frac{x_2}{6}$; $x_2 = \frac{(15)(6)}{3.6} = 25$; 25 kg

10. Let y = the speed in m/s after falling t seconds; $\frac{t_1}{y_1} = \frac{t_2}{y_2}$; $\frac{1.5}{14.7} = \frac{5}{y_2}$, $y_2 = \frac{5(14.7)}{1.5} = 49$; 49 m/s

B

11. Let y = volume in L occupied by a gas at x degrees C; $y = m(x + 273)$; $100 = m(-13 + 273)$, $100 = 260m$, $m = \frac{100}{260} = \frac{5}{13}$; $y = \frac{5}{13}(26 + 273) = \frac{5}{13}(299) = 115$; 115 L

12. Let r = the rate of cooling in degrees C/min at t degrees C; $r = m(t - 20)$; $50 = m(270 - 20)$, $m = \frac{50}{250} = \frac{1}{5}$; $r = \frac{1}{5}(100 - 20) = 16$; 16°C/min

13. Let y be the unstretched length in cm of the spring; $\frac{12}{15 - y} = \frac{30}{18 - y}$, $12(18 - y) = 30(15 - y)$, $216 - 12y = 450 - 30y$, $18y = 234$, $y = 13$; 13 cm

14. Let y be the force in N when the speed is x m/s; $y = mx^2$; $2240 = m(8^2)$,

$m = \frac{2240}{64} = 35$; $y = 35(12)^2 = 5040$; 5040 N

15. Let y = distance in feet fallen after x seconds; $y = mx^2$; $4 = m\left(\frac{1}{2}\right)^2$, $m = 16$;

$y = 16(2.5)^2 = 100$; $100 - 4 = 96$; 96 feet

16. Let s = speed in ft/sec when the object has fallen x feet; $s = m\sqrt{x}$; $48 = m\sqrt{36}$,

$48 = 6m$, $m = 8$; $80 = 8\sqrt{x}$, $\sqrt{x} = 10$, $x = 100$; $100 - 36 = 64$; 64 feet

17. Let y be the power in watts developed by a current of x amperes; $y = mx^2$;

$100 = m(0.5)^2$, $m = 400$; 1.6 kilowatts = 1600 watts; $1600 = 400x^2$, $x^2 = \frac{1600}{400} = 4$,

$x = 2$; 2 amperes

18. Let x = mL of blood sample in y mL of diluted solution; $\frac{x}{y} = \frac{1}{1 + 199} = \frac{1}{200}$;

$\frac{1}{200} = \frac{x}{6}$, $x = \frac{6}{200} = \frac{3}{100} = 0.03$; in 0.03 mL of blood there are $0.03 \times 5 \times 10^6 =$

$1.5 \times 10^5 = 150{,}000$ cells

19. Let V = volume in cm^3 of a sphere with a diameter of d cm; $V = md^3$;

$288\pi = m(12)^3$, $m = \frac{288\pi}{1728} = \frac{\pi}{6}$; $V = \frac{\pi}{6}d^3$

C **20.** Let E be the kinetic energy of the object at v km/h; let E_0 be the energy at v_0 km/h;

$\frac{E_0}{2E_0} = \frac{v_0^2}{v^2}$; $E_0v^2 = v_0^2(2E_0)$, $v^2 = \frac{2v_0^2E_0}{E_0} = 2v_0^2$, $v = \sqrt{2v_0^2} = v_0\sqrt{2}$; The increase is

$v_0\sqrt{2} - v_0$ km/h

Page 357 • MIXED REVIEW EXERCISES

1. $3x^2 - 5x + 1 = 0$, $x = \frac{5 \pm \sqrt{25 - 12}}{2(3)} = \frac{5 \pm \sqrt{13}}{6}$; $\left\{\frac{5 + \sqrt{13}}{6}, \frac{5 - \sqrt{13}}{6}\right\}$

2. $\frac{y - 1}{y + 2} = 1 - \frac{2}{y}$, $y(y - 1) = 1(y)(y + 2) - 2(y + 2)$, $y^2 - y = y^2 + 2y - 2y - 4$,

$-y = -4$, $y = 4$; $\{4\}$

3. $2m^2 = 5m$, $2m^2 - 5m = 0$, $m(2m - 5) = 0$; $m = 0$ or $2m - 5 = 0$; $m = 0$ or

$m = \frac{5}{2}$; $\left\{0, \frac{5}{2}\right\}$

4. $\left|\frac{a}{2} + 1\right| = 3$; $\frac{a}{2} + 1 = 3$ or $\frac{a}{2} + 1 = -3$; $a + 2 = 6$ or $a + 2 = -6$; $a = 4$ or

$a = -8$; $\{-8, 4\}$

5. $3(2 - c) = c + 4$, $6 - 3c = c + 4$, $2 = 4c$, $c = \frac{1}{2}$; $\left\{\frac{1}{2}\right\}$

6. $\frac{w^2}{2} + \frac{7w}{4} = 1$, $2w^2 + 7w = 4$, $2w^2 + 7w - 4 = 0$, $(2w - 1)(w + 4) = 0$; $2w - 1 = 0$

or $w + 4 = 0$; $w = \frac{1}{2}$ or $w = -4$; $\left\{-4, \frac{1}{2}\right\}$

7. $p^{-2} - 2p^{-1} - 1 = 0, 1 - 2p - p^2 = 0, p = \frac{2 \pm \sqrt{4+4}}{-2} = -1 \pm \sqrt{2};$

$\{-1 + \sqrt{2}, -1 - \sqrt{2}\}$

8. $\sqrt{5n+6} = n, n^2 = 5n + 6, n^2 - 5n - 6 = 0, (n-6)(n+1) = 0; n - 6 = 0$ or $n + 1 = 0; n = 6$ or $n = -1$ (reject); $\{6\}$

9. $(3k-1)^2 = 12, 3k - 1 = \pm\sqrt{12}; 3k - 1 = 2\sqrt{3}$ or $3k - 1 = -2\sqrt{3};$

$3k = 1 + 2\sqrt{3}$ or $3k = 1 - 2\sqrt{3}; k = \frac{1+2\sqrt{3}}{3}$ or $k = \frac{1-2\sqrt{3}}{3};$

$\left\{\frac{1+2\sqrt{3}}{3}, \frac{1-2\sqrt{3}}{3}\right\}$

Pages 360–361 • WRITTEN EXERCISES

A

1. $xy = k; 6(3) = k, k = 18; 18x = 18, x = 1$

2. $zr = k; 32(1.5) = k, k = 48; 8r = 48, r = 6$

3. $wv^2 = k; 3(6)^2 = k, k = 108; w(3)^2 = 108, 9w = 108, w = 12$

4. $p\sqrt{q} = k; 12\sqrt{36} = k, k = 72; p\sqrt{16} = 72, 4p = 72, p = 18$

5. $z = kxy; 18 = k(0.4)(3), k = 15; z = 15(1.2)(2) = 36$

6. $w = kuv; 24 = k(0.8)(5), k = 6; 18 = 6(u)(2), 18 = 12u, u = \frac{18}{12} = 1.5$

B

7. $s = \frac{kr}{t}; 10 = \frac{k(5)}{3}, 30 = 5k, k = 6; 3 = \frac{6(4)}{t}, 3t = 24, t = 8$

8. $r = \frac{kp}{q^2}; 27 = \frac{k(3)}{(2)^2}, 3k = 108, k = 36; r = \frac{36(2)}{3^2} = 8$

9. $z = \frac{kuv}{w}; 0.8 = \frac{k(8)(6)}{5}, 4 = 48k, k = \frac{4}{48} = \frac{1}{12}; z = \frac{\frac{1}{12}(3)(10)}{5} = 0.5$

10. $w = \frac{kz^2}{xy}; 10 = \frac{k(5)^2}{(15)(2)}, 300 = 25k, k = 12; 2 = \frac{12z^2}{(8)(27)}, 432 = 12z^2, z^2 = 36, z = \pm 6$

Pages 361–362 • PROBLEMS

A

1. Let f = frequency in kHz and w = wave length in m; $fw = k; (1200)(250) = k, k = 3 \times 10^5; f(400) = 3 \times 10^5, f = 750$; 750 kHz

2. Let r = resistance in ohms, and c = current in amperes; $cr = k; 5(24) = k, k = 120; 8r = 120, r = 15$; 15 Ω

3. Let h = heat loss in BTU, A = area of window in m², and d = temperature difference in C°; $h = kAd; 720 = k(3)(15), k = \frac{720}{45} = 16; h = 16(4.5)(12) = 864;$

864 BTU

4. Let c = conductance in mho, d = diameter of the wire in mm, and l = length in m;

$c = \frac{kd^2}{l}; 0.12 = \frac{k(2)^2}{50}, 6 = 4k, k = 1.5; c = \frac{1.5(2.5)^2}{75} = 0.125$; 0.125 mho

5. Let I = intensity of light in lux and d = distance in m; $Id^2 = k; 24(7.5)^2 = k, k = 1350; I(15)^2 = 1350, I = 6$; 6 lux

6. Let I = intensity in lux and d = distance in ft; $Id^2 = k$; $25(4.8)^2 = k$, $k = 576$; since the radius of the table is 3.6 ft, a point at the edge of the table is $\sqrt{(4.8)^2 + (3.6)^2} = 6$ ft from the light; $I(6)^2 = 576$, $I = 16$; 16 lux

7. Let s = angular speed in r/min, C = circumference in inches; $sC = k$; $216(8\pi) = k$, $k = 1728\pi$; $s(3\pi) = 1728\pi$, $s = 576$; the smaller gear rotates at 576 r/min; $s(28\pi) = 1728\pi$, $s = \frac{1728\pi}{28\pi} \approx 61.7$ r/min; the wheel is rotating at about 61.7 r/min.

8. Let V = volume in cm^3, h = height in cm, and r = base radius in cm; $V = khr^2$; $54\pi = k(8)(4.5)^2$, $k = \frac{54\pi}{162} = \frac{\pi}{3}$; $V = \frac{\pi}{3}r^2h$

B

9. Let x = length of stretch in mm, d = diameter of wire in mm, and l = length in meters; $x = \frac{kl}{d^2}$; $1.2 = \frac{k(2)}{(1.5)^2}$, $k = \frac{1.2(1.5)^2}{2} = 1.35$; $x = \frac{1.35(3)}{(2.0)^2} = 1.0125$; 1.0125 mm

10. Let V = volume in L, t = absolute temperature, and p = pressure in kPa; $V = \frac{kt}{p}$; 2°C = 275 K and 27°C = 300 K; $23.1 = \frac{k(275)}{99}$, $\frac{(23.1)(99)}{275} = k = 8.316$; $V = \frac{(8.316)(300)}{121} \approx 20.6$; approximately 20.6 L

11. Let w, l, and d be the width, length, and depth in cm, and let L = load in kg; $L = \frac{kwd^2}{l}$; $630 = \frac{k(3)(5)^2}{l}$, $\frac{k}{l} = \frac{630}{75} = 8.4$; when the beam is on its side, the length remains the same, $w = 5$ and $d = 3$, $L = (8.4)(5)(3)^2 = 378$; 378 kg

12. Let w_1, l_1, and d_1 be the width, length and depth of the original beam, and let L_1 = original load; $L_1 = \frac{kw_1d_1^2}{l_1}$; the second beam can bear a load

$$L_2 = \frac{k\left(\frac{1}{2}w_1\right)(3d_1)^2}{2l_1} = \frac{9}{4}\left(\frac{kw_1d_1^2}{l_1}\right) = \frac{9}{4}L_1;\ L_2 : L_1 = \frac{9}{4}L_1 : L_1 = 9 : 4$$

C

13. Let p = period in hours and r = radius of orbit in km; $p^2 = kr^3$; $(5.6)^2 = k(9600 + 6400)^3$, $k = \frac{(5.6)^2}{(1.6 \times 10^4)^3} \approx 7.66 \times 10^{-12}$; $(24)^2 = (7.66 \times 10^{-12})r^3$, $r^3 \approx 7.52 \times 10^{13}$, $r \approx 4.22 \times 10^4$; $42{,}200 - 6400 = 35{,}800$; about 35,800 km

14. Using Newton's law of gravitation, the force F_1 between the two spheres is: $F_1 = \frac{k(3200)(3200)}{3^2} \approx 1.1 \times 10^6k$; using 6.4×10^6 m for the distance from the center of the earth to the monument, and 6×10^{24} kg as the mass of the earth, the force between the earth and a sphere is: $F_2 = k\frac{(3200)(6 \times 10^{24})}{(6.4 \times 10^6)^2} = 4.7 \times 10^{14}k$; $F_2 : F_1 \approx \frac{4.7 \times 10^{14}k}{1.1 \times 10^6k} \approx 4 \times 10^8$; about 4×10^8 times greater.

Page 363 • CHALLENGE

Let x = number in group; $\frac{78}{x-2} - \frac{78}{x} = 1.30$, $78x - 78(x-2) = 1.3x(x-2)$, $156 = 1.3(x^2 - 2x)$, $x^2 - 2x = 120$, $x^2 - 2x - 120 = 0$, $(x-12)(x+10) = 0$, $x = 12$ or $x = -10$ (reject); $x = 12$; 12 people

Pages 366–367 • WRITTEN EXERCISES

A

1.
$$\begin{array}{r} x+1 \\ x+2\,\overline{)\,x^2+3x-4} \\ \underline{x^2+2x} \\ x-4 \\ \underline{x+2} \\ -6 \end{array}$$
$x + 1 + \frac{-6}{x+2}$

2.
$$\begin{array}{r} x-2 \\ x+1\,\overline{)\,x^2-x+3} \\ \underline{x^2+x} \\ -2x+3 \\ \underline{-2x-2} \\ 5 \end{array}$$
$x - 2 + \frac{5}{x+1}$

3.
$$\begin{array}{r} x+4 \\ -x+2\,\overline{)\,-x^2-2x+6} \\ \underline{-x^2+2x} \\ -4x+6 \\ \underline{-4x+8} \\ -2 \end{array}$$
$x + 4 + \frac{-2}{-x+2}$

4.
$$\begin{array}{r} -z+6 \\ z-3\,\overline{)\,-z^2+9z+0} \\ \underline{-z^2+3z} \\ 6z+0 \\ \underline{6z-18} \\ 18 \end{array}$$
$-z + 6 + \frac{18}{z-3}$

5.
$$\begin{array}{r} 2t-3 \\ 2t+1\,\overline{)\,4t^2-4t+1} \\ \underline{4t^2+2t} \\ -6t+1 \\ \underline{-6t-3} \\ 4 \end{array}$$
$2t - 3 + \frac{4}{2t+1}$

6.
$$\begin{array}{r} 2u+3 \\ 3u-1\,\overline{)\,6u^2+7u+5} \\ \underline{6u^2-2u} \\ 9u+5 \\ \underline{9u-3} \\ 8 \end{array}$$
$2u + 3 + \frac{8}{3u-1}$

7.
$$\begin{array}{r} x^2+2x-4 \\ x-3\,\overline{)\,x^3-x^2-10x+10} \\ \underline{x^3-3x^2} \\ 2x^2-10x \\ \underline{2x^2-6x} \\ -4x+10 \\ \underline{-4x+12} \\ -2 \end{array}$$
$x^2 + 2x - 4 + \frac{-2}{x-3}$

8.
$$\begin{array}{r} z^2+5z-3 \\ z-2\,\overline{)\,z^3+3z^2-13z+6} \\ \underline{z^3-2z^2} \\ 5z^2-13z \\ \underline{5z^2-10z} \\ -3z+6 \\ \underline{-3z+6} \\ 0 \end{array}$$
$z^2 + 5z - 3$

9.
$$\begin{array}{r} 2s^2-8s+3 \\ s+4\,\overline{)\,2s^3+0s^2-29s+13} \\ \underline{2s^3+8s^2} \\ -8s^2-29s \\ \underline{-8s^2-32s} \\ 3s+13 \\ \underline{3s+12} \\ 1 \end{array}$$
$2s^2 - 8s + 3 + \frac{1}{s+4}$

10.
$$\begin{array}{r} 3y^2+2y-3 \\ 5y-3\,\overline{)\,15y^3+y^2-21y+0} \\ \underline{15y^3-9y^2} \\ 10y^2-21y \\ \underline{10y^2-6y} \\ -15y+0 \\ \underline{-15y+9} \\ -9 \end{array}$$
$3y^2 + 2y - 3 + \frac{-9}{5y-3}$

11.
$$\begin{array}{r} 2t^2 - t + 3 \\ 3t + 2\overline{)6t^3 + t^2 + 7t + 10} \\ \underline{6t^3 + 4t^2} \\ -3t^2 + 7t \\ \underline{-3t^2 - 2t} \\ 9t + 10 \\ \underline{9t + 6} \\ 4 \end{array}$$

$2t^2 - t + 3 + \dfrac{4}{3t + 2}$

12.
$$\begin{array}{r} 3x - 1 \\ 2x^2 - x + 3\overline{)6x^3 - 5x^2 + 15x - 5} \\ \underline{6x^3 - 3x^2 + 9x} \\ -2x^2 + 6x - 5 \\ \underline{-2x^2 + x - 3} \\ 5x - 2 \end{array}$$

$3x - 1 + \dfrac{5x - 2}{2x^2 - x + 3}$

13.
$$\begin{array}{r} 5z + 3 \\ 3z^2 - 2z - 1\overline{)15z^3 - z^2 - 11z - 3} \\ \underline{15z^3 - 10z^2 - 5z} \\ 9z^2 - 6z - 3 \\ \underline{9z^2 - 6z - 3} \\ 0 \end{array}$$

$5z + 3$

14.
$$\begin{array}{r} 2u^3 - u^2 - 3u - 6 \\ 2u - 1\overline{)4u^4 - 4u^3 - 5u^2 - 9u - 1} \\ \underline{4u^4 - 2u^3} \\ -2u^3 - 5u^2 \\ \underline{-2u^3 + u^2} \\ -6u^2 - 9u \\ \underline{-6u^2 + 3u} \\ -12u - 1 \\ \underline{-12u + 6} \\ -7 \end{array}$$

$2u^3 - u^2 - 3u - 6 + \dfrac{-7}{2u - 1}$

15.
$$\begin{array}{r} 2x^2 - x + 3 \\ 3x^2 - 2\overline{)6x^4 - 3x^3 + 5x^2 + 2x - 6} \\ \underline{6x^4 - 4x^2} \\ -3x^3 + 9x^2 + 2x \\ \underline{-3x^3 + 2x} \\ 9x^2 - 6 \\ \underline{9x^2 - 6} \\ 0 \end{array}$$

$2x^2 - x + 3$

16.
$$\begin{array}{r} 2t^2 + 3 \\ 2t^2 - t - 3\overline{)4t^4 - 2t^3 + 0t^2 - 3t - 9} \\ \underline{4t^4 - 2t^3 - 6t^2} \\ 6t^2 - 3t - 9 \\ \underline{6t^2 - 3t - 9} \\ 0 \end{array}$$

$2t^2 + 3$

17.
$$\begin{array}{r} 3u^2 - 2 \\ 3u^2 + 2u + 2\overline{)9u^4 + 6u^3 + 0u^2 + 4u + 4} \\ \underline{9u^4 + 6u^3 + 6u^2} \\ -6u^2 + 4u + 4 \\ \underline{-6u^2 - 4u - 4} \\ 8u + 8 \end{array}$$

$3u^2 - 2 + \dfrac{8u + 8}{3u^2 + 2u + 2}$

18.
$$\begin{array}{r} 2x^2 - 2x + 5 \\ x^2 + x - 3\overline{)2x^4 + 0x^3 - 3x^2 + 7x - 8} \\ \underline{2x^4 + 2x^3 - 6x^2} \\ -2x^3 + 3x^2 + 7x \\ \underline{-2x^3 - 2x^2 + 6x} \\ 5x^2 + x - 8 \\ \underline{5x^2 + 5x - 15} \\ -4x + 7 \end{array}$$

$2x^2 - 2x + 5 + \dfrac{-4x + 7}{x^2 + x - 3}$

B

19.

$$\begin{array}{r} x^2 + 2ax \\ x + 2a\overline{)x^3 + 4ax^2 + 4a^2x + a^3} \\ \underline{x^3 + 2ax^2 \qquad\qquad\qquad} \\ 2ax^2 + 4a^2x \qquad \\ \underline{2ax^2 + 4a^2x} \qquad \\ 0 + a^3 \end{array}$$

$$x^2 + 2ax + \frac{a^3}{x + 2a}$$

20.

$$\begin{array}{r} p^2 - pq + q^2 \\ 2p + q\overline{)2p^3 - p^2q + pq^2 - 2q^3} \\ \underline{2p^3 + p^2q \qquad\qquad\qquad} \\ -2p^2q + pq^2 \qquad \\ \underline{-2p^2q - pq^2} \qquad \\ 2pq^2 - 2q^3 \\ \underline{2pq^2 + q^3} \\ -3q^3 \end{array}$$

$$p^2 - pq + q^2 + \frac{-3q^3}{2p + q}$$

21.

$$\begin{array}{r} 3t^2 - ct - c^2 \\ 2t^2 + ct + c^2\overline{)6t^4 + ct^3 + 0t^2 - c^3t + c^4} \\ \underline{6t^4 + 3ct^3 + 3c^2t^2 \qquad\qquad\qquad} \\ -2ct^3 - 3c^2t^2 - c^3t \qquad \\ \underline{-2ct^3 - c^2t^2 - c^3t} \qquad \\ -2c^2t^2 + 0 + c^4 \\ \underline{-2c^2t^2 - c^3t - c^4} \\ c^3t + 2c^4 \end{array}$$

$$3t^2 - ct - c^2 + \frac{c^3t + 2c^4}{2t^2 + ct + c^2}$$

22.

$$\begin{array}{r} x^2 - xy + 2y^2 \\ 2x^2 + xy - 2y^2\overline{)2x^4 - x^3y + x^2y^2 + 4xy^3 - 4y^4} \\ \underline{2x^4 + x^3y - 2x^2y^2 \qquad\qquad\qquad} \\ -2x^3y + 3x^2y^2 + 4xy^3 \qquad \\ \underline{-2x^3y - x^2y^2 + 2xy^3} \qquad \\ 4x^2y^2 + 2xy^3 - 4y^4 \\ \underline{4x^2y^2 + 2xy^3 - 4y^4} \\ 0 \end{array}$$

$$x^2 - xy + 2y^2$$

23.

$$\begin{array}{r} x^2 + x + 1 \\ x^4 - x^2 + 1\overline{)x^6 + x^5 + 0x^4 + x^3 + 0x^2 + x + 1} \\ \underline{x^6 \qquad - x^4 \qquad + x^2 \qquad\qquad} \\ x^5 + x^4 + x^3 - x^2 + x \qquad \\ \underline{x^5 \qquad - x^3 \qquad + x} \qquad \\ x^4 + 2x^3 - x^2 \qquad + 1 \\ \underline{x^4 \qquad - x^2 \qquad + 1} \\ 2x^3 \qquad\qquad\qquad \end{array}$$

$$x^2 + x + 1 + \frac{2x^3}{x^4 - x^2 + 1}$$

24.

$$\begin{array}{r} x^3 \qquad\qquad - 1 \\ x^2 - x + 1\overline{)x^5 - x^4 + x^3 - x^2 + x - 1} \\ \underline{x^5 - x^4 + x^3} \qquad\qquad\qquad \\ -x^2 + x - 1 \\ \underline{-x^2 + x - 1} \\ 0 \end{array}$$

$$x^3 - 1$$

25.
$$
\begin{array}{r}
x^2 \qquad\qquad - a^2 \\
x^2 + a^2 \overline{) x^4 + 0x^3 + 0x^2 + 0x + a^4} \\
\underline{x^4 \qquad + a^2x^2 \qquad\qquad} \\
-a^2x^2 + 0x + a^4 \\
\underline{-a^2x^2 \qquad - a^4} \\
2a^4
\end{array}
$$

$x^2 - a^2 + \dfrac{2a^4}{x^2 + a^2}$

26.
$$
\begin{array}{r}
x^4 + ax^3 + a^2x^2 + a^3x + a^4 \\
x - a \overline{) x^5 + 0x^4 + 0x^3 + 0x^2 + 0x - a^5} \\
\underline{x^5 - ax^4} \qquad\qquad\qquad\qquad \\
ax^4 + 0x^3 \qquad\qquad\qquad \\
\underline{ax^4 - a^2x^3} \qquad\qquad\qquad \\
a^2x^3 + 0x^2 \qquad\qquad \\
\underline{a^2x^3 - a^3x^2} \qquad\qquad \\
a^3x^2 + 0x \qquad \\
\underline{a^3x^2 - a^4x} \qquad \\
a^4x - a^5 \\
\underline{a^4x - a^5} \\
0
\end{array}
$$

$x^4 + ax^3 + a^2x^2 + a^3x + a^4$

27.
$$
\begin{array}{r}
x^4 - ax^3 \qquad + a^3x - a^4 \\
x^2 + ax + a^2 \overline{) x^6 + 0x^5 + 0x^4 + 0x^3 + 0x^2 + 0x - a^6} \\
\underline{x^6 + ax^5 + a^2x^4} \qquad\qquad\qquad\qquad \\
-ax^5 - a^2x^4 + 0x^3 \qquad\qquad\qquad \\
\underline{-ax^5 - a^2x^4 - a^3x^3} \qquad\qquad\qquad \\
a^3x^3 + 0x^2 \qquad\qquad \\
\underline{a^3x^3 + a^4x^2 + a^5x} \qquad \\
-a^4x^2 - a^5x - a^6 \\
\underline{-a^4x^2 - a^5x - a^6} \\
0
\end{array}
$$

$x^4 - ax^3 + a^3x - a^4$

28.
$$
\begin{array}{r}
x^5 + ax^4 \qquad\qquad + a^4x + a^5 \\
x^3 - ax^2 + a^2x - a^3 \overline{) x^8 + 0x^7 + 0x^6 + 0x^5 + 0x^4 + 0x^3 + 0x^2 + 0x - a^8} \\
\underline{x^8 - ax^7 + a^2x^6 - a^3x^5} \qquad\qquad\qquad\qquad\qquad \\
ax^7 - a^2x^6 + a^3x^5 + 0x^4 \qquad\qquad\qquad\qquad \\
\underline{ax^7 - a^2x^6 + a^3x^5 - a^4x^4} \qquad\qquad\qquad\qquad \\
a^4x^4 + 0x^3 + 0x^2 + 0x \qquad \\
\underline{a^4x^4 - a^5x^3 + a^6x^2 - a^7x} \qquad \\
a^5x^3 - a^6x^2 + a^7x - a^8 \\
\underline{a^5x^3 - a^6x^2 + a^7x - a^8} \\
0
\end{array}
$$

$x^5 + ax^4 + a^4x + a^5$

29. $\dfrac{P(x)}{x - 3} = x^2 + 2x + 6 + \dfrac{8}{x - 3}$; $P(x) = (x - 3)(x^2 + 2x + 6) + 8$;
$P(x) = x^3 + 2x^2 + 6x - 3x^2 - 6x - 18 + 8$; $P(x) = x^3 - x^2 - 10$

C

30. $\frac{x^3 - 7x + 4}{D(x)} = x^2 - 3x + 2 - \frac{2}{D(x)}$; $x^3 - 7x + 4 = (D(x))(x^2 - 3x + 2) - 2$;

$x^3 - 7x + 6 = (D(x))(x^2 - 3x + 2)$; $D(x) = \frac{x^3 - 7x + 6}{x^2 - 3x + 2}$;

$$\begin{array}{r|l} & x + 3 \\ \hline x^2 - 3x + 2 & x^3 + 0x^2 - 7x + 6 \\ & \underline{x^3 - 3x^2 + 2x} \\ & 3x^2 - 9x + 6 \\ & \underline{3x^2 - 9x + 6} \\ & 0 \end{array}$$

$; D(x) = x + 3$

31.

$$\begin{array}{r|l} & x^2 + (k + 2)x + (k + 4) \\ \hline x - 2 & x^3 + kx^2 \quad - kx \quad + 1 \\ & \underline{x^3 - 2x^2} \\ & (k + 2)x^2 - kx \\ & \underline{(k + 2)x^2 - 2(k + 2)x} \\ & (k + 4)x + 1 \\ & \underline{(k + 4)x - 2(k + 4)} \\ & 2k + 9 \end{array}$$

$2k + 9 = 0, k = -\frac{9}{2}$

32.

$$\begin{array}{r|l} & x^2 + (k - 2)x + (k^2 - 2k + 4) \\ \hline x + 2 & x^3 + kx^2 + k^2x \quad + 14 \\ & \underline{x^3 + 2x^2} \\ & (k - 2)x^2 + k^2x \\ & \underline{(k - 2)x^2 + 2(k - 2)x} \\ & (k^2 - 2k + 4)x + 14 \\ & \underline{(k^2 - 2k + 4)x + (2k^2 - 4k + 8)} \\ & 6 - 2k^2 + 4k \end{array}$$

$6 - 2k^2 + 4k = 0$, $k^2 - 2k - 3 = 0$, $(k - 3)(k + 1) = 0$, $k - 3 = 0$ or $k + 1 = 0$, $k = 3$ or $k = -1$

33. $\frac{3x^2 - 5x + c}{x + k} = 3x + 1 + \frac{3}{x + k}$, $3x^2 - 5x + c = (3x + 1)(x + k) + 3$,
$3x^2 - 5x + c = 3x^2 + 3kx + x + k + 3$, $3x^2 - 5x + c =$
$3x^2 + (3k + 1)x + (k + 3)$; $-5 = 3k + 1$ and $c = k + 3$; $k = -2$ and
$c = -2 + 3 = 1$

34. $\frac{P(x)}{D(x)} = Q(x) + \frac{R(x)}{D(x)}$ if and only if $D(x) \neq 0$ and $P(x) = Q(x)D(x) + R(x)$;
$(x^2 + 4x + 3)(x - 2) + 5 = x^3 + 2x^2 - 5x - 1$; $(x^2 + 4x + 2)(x - 2) + x + 3 = x^3 + 2x^2 - 5x - 1$; in the second of the given equations, the degree of R is not less than the degree of D. Rewriting the right side of the equation to produce a remainder with degree less than that of D produces the following: $x^2 + 4x + 2 + \frac{x + 3}{x - 2} = x^2 + 4x + 2 + 1 + \frac{5}{x - 2} = x^2 + 4x + 3 + \frac{5}{x - 2}$

Page 367 • MIXED REVIEW EXERCISES

1. $\frac{6}{8} = \frac{9}{y}, 6y = 72, y = 12$ **2.** $\frac{\frac{1}{2}}{4} = \frac{2}{y}, \frac{1}{2}y = 8, y = 16$

3. $\frac{\sqrt{2}}{3} = \frac{\sqrt{6}}{y}, y\sqrt{2} = 3\sqrt{6}, y = \frac{3\sqrt{6}}{\sqrt{2}} = 3\sqrt{3}$ **4.** $\frac{0.2}{3.2} = \frac{1.6}{y}, 0.2y = 5.12, y = 25.6$

5. $6(8) = 9y, y = \frac{48}{9} = \frac{16}{3}$ **6.** $\frac{1}{2}(4) = 2y, 2 = 2y, y = 1$

7. $(\sqrt{2})(3) = (\sqrt{6})y, y = \frac{3\sqrt{2}}{\sqrt{6}} = \frac{3}{\sqrt{3}} = \frac{3\sqrt{3}}{3} = \sqrt{3}$

8. $(0.2)(3.2) = (1.6)y, y = \frac{(0.2)(3.2)}{1.6} = 0.4$

Page 370 • WRITTEN EXERCISES

A

1.
$$\begin{array}{r|rrr:r} 2 & 3 & -5 & 1 & -2 \\ & & 6 & 2 & 6 \\ \hline & 3 & 1 & 3 & 4 \end{array}$$
$3x^2 + x + 3 + \frac{4}{x - 2}$

2.
$$\begin{array}{r|rrr:r} 3 & 2 & -4 & -7 & 5 \\ & & 6 & 6 & -3 \\ \hline & 2 & 2 & -1 & 2 \end{array}$$
$2x^2 + 2x - 1 + \frac{2}{x - 3}$

3.
$$\begin{array}{r|rrr:r} -3 & 1 & 3 & -2 & -6 \\ & & -3 & 0 & 6 \\ \hline & 1 & 0 & -2 & 0 \end{array}$$
$x^2 - 2$

4.
$$\begin{array}{r|rrr:r} -1 & 3 & -2 & 1 & 4 \\ & & -3 & 5 & -6 \\ \hline & 3 & -5 & 6 & -2 \end{array}$$
$3x^2 - 5x + 6 + \frac{-2}{x + 1}$

5.
$$\begin{array}{r|rrrr:r} -5 & 1 & 5 & 0 & -2 & -7 \\ & & -5 & 0 & 0 & 10 \\ \hline & 1 & 0 & 0 & -2 & 3 \end{array}$$
$t^3 - 2 + \frac{3}{t + 5}$

6.
$$\begin{array}{r|rrrr:r} 4 & 2 & -5 & -12 & 2 & -8 \\ & & 8 & 12 & 0 & 8 \\ \hline & 2 & 3 & 0 & 2 & 0 \end{array}$$
$2u^3 + 3u^2 + 2$

7.
$$\begin{array}{r|rrrr:r} 3 & 2 & -7 & 0 & 7 & 6 \\ & & 6 & -3 & -9 & -6 \\ \hline & 2 & -1 & -3 & -2 & 0 \end{array}$$
$2s^3 - s^2 - 3s - 2$

8.
$$\begin{array}{r|rrrr:r} -2 & 1 & 0 & -4 & 1 & 4 \\ & & -2 & 4 & 0 & -2 \\ \hline & 1 & -2 & 0 & 1 & 2 \end{array}$$
$y^3 - 2y^2 + 1 + \frac{2}{y + 2}$

9.
$$\begin{array}{r|rrrrr:r} 1 & 1 & 0 & 0 & 0 & 0 & -1 \\ & & 1 & 1 & 1 & 1 & 1 \\ \hline & 1 & 1 & 1 & 1 & 1 & 0 \end{array}$$
$x^4 + x^3 + x^2 + x + 1$

10.
$$\begin{array}{r|rrrrrr:r} -1 & 1 & 0 & 0 & 0 & 0 & 0 & -1 \\ & & -1 & 1 & -1 & 1 & -1 & 1 \\ \hline & 1 & -1 & 1 & -1 & 1 & -1 & 0 \end{array}$$
$x^5 - x^4 + x^3 - x^2 + x - 1$

11.
$$\begin{array}{r|rrrr:r} -1 & 2 & 1 & 0 & -1 & -2 \\ & & -2 & 1 & -1 & 2 \\ \hline & 2 & -1 & 1 & -2 & 0 \end{array}$$
$2x^3 - x^2 + x - 2$

12.
$$\begin{array}{r|rrrrrr:r} 1 & 3 & -2 & -1 & 0 & -1 & -2 & 3 \\ & & 3 & 1 & 0 & 0 & -1 & -3 \\ \hline & 3 & 1 & 0 & 0 & -1 & -3 & 0 \end{array}$$
$3x^5 + x^4 - x - 3$

B

13. $$\begin{array}{r|rrrr} -\frac{1}{2} & 2 & -3 & 4 & -2 \\ & & -1 & 2 & -3 \\ \hline & 2 & -4 & 6 & \vdots\, -5 \end{array}$$ $$\frac{1}{2}\left(2x^2 - 4x + 6 + \frac{-5}{x + \frac{1}{2}}\right) = x^2 - 2x + 3 + \frac{-5}{2x + 1}$$

14. $$\begin{array}{r|rrrr} -\frac{3}{2} & 4 & 2 & -4 & 3 \\ & & -6 & 6 & -3 \\ \hline & 4 & -4 & 2 & \vdots\, 0 \end{array}$$ $$\frac{1}{2}(4x^2 - 4x + 2) = 2x^2 - 2x + 1$$

15. $$\begin{array}{r|rrrrr} \frac{2}{3} & 6 & 5 & 0 & -10 & 4 \\ & & 4 & 6 & 4 & -4 \\ \hline & 6 & 9 & 6 & -6 & \vdots\, 0 \end{array}$$ $$\frac{1}{3}(6t^3 + 9t^2 + 6t - 6) = 2t^3 + 3t^2 + 2t - 2$$

16. $$\begin{array}{r|rrrrr} \frac{3}{5} & 5 & -3 & 0 & 10 & 2 \\ & & 3 & 0 & 0 & 6 \\ \hline & 5 & 0 & 0 & 10 & \vdots\, 8 \end{array}$$ $$\frac{1}{5}\left(5s^3 + 10 + \frac{8}{s - \frac{3}{5}}\right) = s^3 + 2 + \frac{8}{5s - 3}$$

17. $$\begin{array}{r|rrrr} 2i & 1 & -2 & 4 & -5 \\ & & 2i & -4 - 4i & 8 \\ \hline & 1 & -2 + 2i & -4i & \vdots\, 3 \end{array}$$ $$z^2 + (-2 + 2i)z - 4i + \frac{3}{z - 2i}$$

18. $$\begin{array}{r|rrrr} i & 1 & 3 & -2 & 3 \\ & & i & -1 + 3i & -3 - 3i \\ \hline & 1 & 3 + i & -3 + 3i & \vdots\, -3i \end{array}$$ $$z^2 + (3 + i)z + (-3 + 3i) + \frac{-3i}{z - i}$$

19. $$\begin{array}{r|rrrr} -3 & 2 & 5 & 0 & 4 \\ & & -6 & 3 & -9 \\ \hline & 2 & -1 & 3 & \vdots\, -5 \end{array}$$ $Q(x) = 2x^2 - x + 3;\ R = -5$

20. $$\begin{array}{r|rrrrr} 5 & 1 & -5 & 0 & 2 & -5 \\ & & 5 & 0 & 0 & 10 \\ \hline & 1 & 0 & 0 & 2 & \vdots\, 5 \end{array}$$ $Q(x) = x^3 + 2;\ R = 5$

21. $$\begin{array}{r|rrrr} -2i & 2 & -3 & 8 & -10 \\ & & -4i & -8 + 6i & 12 \\ \hline & 2 & -3 - 4i & 6i & \vdots\, 2 \end{array}$$ $Q(z) = 2z^2 - (3 + 4i)z + 6i;\ R = 2$

22. $$\begin{array}{r|rrrr} 2 - i & 1 & -2 & -3 & 10 \\ & & 2 - i & -1 - 2i & -10 \\ \hline & 1 & -i & -4 - 2i & \vdots\, 0 \end{array}$$ $Q(z) = z^2 - iz - (4 + 2i);\ R = 0$

C

23. $$\begin{array}{r|rrrr} -2 & 2 & 3 & 0 & k \\ & & -4 & 2 & -4 \\ \hline & 2 & -1 & 2 & \vdots\, k - 4 \end{array}$$ $R = k - 4 = 0,\ k = 4$

24. $$\begin{array}{r|rrrrr} 2 & 1 & -2 & 0 & k & 6 \\ & & 2 & 0 & 0 & 2k \\ \hline & 1 & 0 & 0 & k & \vdots\, 6 + 2k \end{array}$$ $R = 6 + 2k = 0;\ -2k = 6,\ k = -3$

Page 371 • READING ALGEBRA

1. An equation of the form $ax^2 + bx + c = 0$ may be solved by (a) factoring and setting each factor equal to 0 or (b) by the quadratic formula. The first method is not always possible but is faster and easier if the correct factorization is found. The second method always works but can be more difficult since it may involve fractions and radicals.

2. If $\frac{I}{(6.0)^2} = \frac{25}{(4.8)^2}$, then $I = \frac{(6.0)^2(25)}{(4.8)^2} = 39.0625$; $I > 25$; this is not reasonable; the intensity at the center of the table should be greater; the equation is incorrect; it should be $\frac{I}{(4.8)^2} = \frac{25}{(6.0)^2}$.

3. If an equal amount of money (\$1100) was invested at each rate, the total annual yield would be $0.045(1100) + 0.07(1100) = 49.50 + 77 = 126.50$; since the actual yield of \$144 is more than \$126.50, there must be more money in the account with the higher rate, that is, the 7% account.

4. Less than 2 km/h; if it were greater than 2 km/h, the log would have reached the starting point before the canoeist returned.

5. a. Let x = the rate of Susan and of Tom; $\frac{3}{x} + \frac{3}{x} = 1$, $\frac{6}{x} = 1$, $x = 6$; 6 h

b. less than; Tom's time alone must be greater than Sue's

c. Let t = Tom's time working alone; $3 \cdot \frac{1}{t} + 3 \cdot \frac{1}{5} = 1$, $\frac{3}{t} + \frac{3}{5} = 1$, $15 + 3t = 5t$, $2t = 15$, $t = 7.5$, 7.5 h

Pages 375–376 • WRITTEN EXERCISES

A

1. $\begin{array}{r|rrrr} 4 & 1 & -2 & -5 & -7 \\ & & 4 & 8 & 12 \\ \hline & 1 & 2 & 3 & 5 \end{array}$; $P(4) = 5$

2. $\begin{array}{r|rrrr} -5 & 1 & 4 & -8 & -6 \\ & & -5 & 5 & 15 \\ \hline & 1 & -1 & -3 & 9 \end{array}$; $P(-5) = 9$

3. $\begin{array}{r|rrrr} -3 & 2 & 3 & -5 & 2 \\ & & -6 & 9 & -12 \\ \hline & 2 & -3 & 4 & -10 \end{array}$; $P(-3) = -10$

4. $\begin{array}{r|rrrr} 6 & 1 & -4 & -7 & 1 \\ & & 6 & 12 & 30 \\ \hline & 1 & 2 & 5 & 31 \end{array}$; $P(6) = 31$

5. $\begin{array}{r|rrrr} \frac{3}{2} & 4 & -4 & 5 & 1 \\ & & 6 & 3 & 12 \\ \hline & 4 & 2 & 8 & 13 \end{array}$; $P\left(\frac{3}{2}\right) = 13$

6. $\begin{array}{r|rrrr} -\frac{1}{3} & 6 & -1 & 4 & 3 \\ & & -2 & 1 & -\frac{5}{3} \\ \hline & 6 & -3 & 5 & \frac{4}{3} \end{array}$; $P\left(-\frac{1}{3}\right) = \frac{4}{3}$

7. $\begin{array}{r|rrrrr} -\frac{3}{2} & 2 & -1 & 0 & 1 & -2 \\ & & -3 & 6 & -9 & 12 \\ \hline & 2 & -4 & 6 & -8 & 10 \end{array}$; $P\left(-\frac{3}{2}\right) = 10$

8. $\begin{array}{r|rrrrr} -\frac{1}{2} & 2 & -3 & 3 & 0 & 1 \\ & & -1 & 2 & -\frac{5}{2} & \frac{5}{4} \\ \hline & 2 & -4 & 5 & -\frac{5}{2} & \frac{9}{4} \end{array}$; $P\left(-\frac{1}{2}\right) = \frac{9}{4}$

9. $P(-1) = (-1)^7 - (-1)^5 + (-1)^3 - (-1) = 0$; yes

10. $P(-1) = (-1)^5 + (-1)^4 + (-1)^3 + (-1)^2 + (-1) + 1 = 0$; yes

11. $P(-1) = (-1)^6 - (-1)^5 - (-1) + 1 = 4$; no

12. $P(-2) = (-2)^5 + 2(-2)^4 + (-2)^3 + 2(-2)^2 + (-2) + 2 = 0$; yes

13. $P(\sqrt{3}) = (\sqrt{3})^3 - 2(\sqrt{3})^2 - 3\sqrt{3} + 6 = 3\sqrt{3} - 6 - 3\sqrt{3} + 6 = 0$; yes

14. $P(-\sqrt{2}) = (-\sqrt{2})^5 + (-\sqrt{2})^4 + 4(-\sqrt{2}) + 4 = -4\sqrt{2} + 4 - 4\sqrt{2} + 4 = -8\sqrt{2} + 8$; no

15. $P(i) = (i)^7 + (i)^6 + (i)^5 + (i)^4 + (i)^3 + (i)^2 + i + 1 =$
$-i - 1 + i + 1 - i - 1 + i + 1 = 0$; yes

16. $P(-2i) = (-2i)^3 + (-2i)^2 + 4(-2i) + 4 = 8i - 4 - 8i + 4 = 0$; yes

17. $\begin{array}{r|rrrr} -3 & 1 & 3 & -3 & -9 \\ & & -3 & 0 & 9 \\ \hline & 1 & 0 & -3 & 0 \end{array}$; $x^2 - 3 = 0, x^2 = 3, x = \pm\sqrt{3}$; $\{-3, \sqrt{3}, -\sqrt{3}\}$

18. $\begin{array}{r|rrrr} -2 & 2 & 9 & 7 & -6 \\ & & -4 & -10 & 6 \\ \hline & 2 & 5 & -3 & 0 \end{array}$; $2x^2 + 5x - 3 = 0, (2x - 1)(x + 3) = 0, x = \frac{1}{2}$ or $x = -3$;

$\left\{-3, -2, \frac{1}{2}\right\}$

19. $\begin{array}{r|rrrr} -4 & 1 & 0 & -11 & 20 \\ & & -4 & 16 & -20 \\ \hline & 1 & -4 & 5 & 0 \end{array}$; $t^2 - 4t + 5 = 0, t = \frac{4 \pm \sqrt{16 - 20}}{2} = \frac{4 \pm \sqrt{-4}}{2} = 2 \pm i$;

$\{-4, 2 + i, 2 - i\}$

20. $\begin{array}{r|rrrr} \frac{3}{2} & 2 & 1 & -8 & 3 \\ & & 3 & 6 & -3 \\ \hline & 2 & 4 & -2 & 0 \end{array}$; $2z^2 + 4z - 2 = 0, z^2 + 2z - 1 = 0,$

$z = \frac{-2 \pm \sqrt{4 + 4}}{2} = \frac{-2 \pm 2\sqrt{2}}{2} = -1 \pm \sqrt{2}$; $\left\{\frac{3}{2}, -1 + \sqrt{2}, -1 - \sqrt{2}\right\}$

21. $P(x) = (x - 1)(x - 2)(x + 3)$; $x^3 - 7x + 6 = 0$

22. $P(x) = (x + 2)(x - 2)(x + 3)$; $x^3 + 3x^2 - 4x - 12 = 0$

23. $P(x) = (x - 0)(x + 1)(x - 2)(x + 3)$; $x^4 + 2x^3 - 5x^2 - 6x = 0$

24. $P(x) = (x + 2)(x + i)(x - i)$; $x^3 + 2x^2 + x + 2 = 0$

B **25.** $P(x) = (2x - 1)(x + 2)(x - 3)$; $2x^3 - 3x^2 - 11x + 6 = 0$

26. $P(x) = (x - 1)(2x + 3)(x - 2)$; $2x^3 - 3x^2 - 5x + 6 = 0$

27. $P(x) = (x + 2)^2(x - 1)(x - 4)$; $x^4 - x^3 - 12x^2 - 4x + 16 = 0$

28. $P(x) = (x - 3)(x - 1 - 2i)(x - 1 + 2i)$; $x^3 - 5x^2 + 11x - 15 = 0$

29. $\begin{array}{r|rrrrr} -1 & 1 & -3 & -8 & 12 & 16 \\ & & -1 & 4 & 4 & -16 \\ \hline 4 & 1 & -4 & -4 & 16 & 0 \\ & & 4 & 0 & -16 & \\ \hline & 1 & 0 & -4 & 0 & \end{array}$

$x^2 - 4 = 0, x^2 = 4, x = \pm 2$; $\{-1, 4, 2, -2\}$

30. $\begin{array}{r|rrrrr} -2 & 2 & -5 & -11 & 20 & 12 \\ & & -4 & 18 & -14 & -12 \\ \hline 3 & 2 & -9 & 7 & 6 & 0 \\ & & 6 & -9 & -6 & \\ \hline & 2 & -3 & -2 & 0 & \end{array}$

$2x^2 - 3x - 2 = 0, (2x + 1)(x - 2) = 0, x = -\frac{1}{2}$ or $x = 2$; $\left\{-2, 3, -\frac{1}{2}, 2\right\}$

31.
$$\begin{array}{r|rrrrr}
1 & 3 & 5 & -7 & -3 & 2 \\
 & & 3 & 8 & 1 & -2 \\ \hline
-\frac{2}{3} & 3 & 8 & 1 & -2 & \vdots\ 0 \\
 & & -2 & -4 & 2 & \\ \hline
 & 3 & 6 & -3 & \vdots\ 0 &
\end{array}$$

$3x^2 + 6x - 3 = 0,\ x^2 + 2x - 1 = 0,\ x = \dfrac{-2 \pm \sqrt{4 + 4}}{2} = -1 \pm \sqrt{2};$

$\left\{1, -\dfrac{2}{3}, -1 + \sqrt{2}, -1 - \sqrt{2}\right\}$

32.
$$\begin{array}{r|rrrrr}
2 & 2 & -3 & 0 & -3 & -2 \\
 & & 4 & 2 & 4 & 2 \\ \hline
-\frac{1}{2} & 2 & 1 & 2 & 1 & \vdots\ 0 \\
 & & -1 & 0 & -1 & \\ \hline
 & 2 & 0 & 2 & \vdots\ 0 &
\end{array}$$

$2x^2 + 2 = 0,\ x^2 = -1,\ x = \pm i,\ \left\{2, -\dfrac{1}{2}, i, -i\right\}$

33.
$$\begin{array}{r|rrrrr}
-1 & 1 & 0 & 2 & 8 & 5 \\
 & & -1 & 1 & -3 & -5 \\ \hline
-1 & 1 & -1 & 3 & 5 & \vdots\ 0 \\
 & & -1 & 2 & -5 & \\ \hline
 & 1 & -2 & 5 & \vdots\ 0 &
\end{array}$$

$\therefore P(-1) = 0$

$\therefore Q(-1) = 0$, where $Q(x) = P(x) \div (x + 1)$

34.
$$\begin{array}{r|rrrrr}
\frac{3}{2} & 4 & -12 & 13 & -12 & 9 \\
 & & 6 & -9 & 6 & -9 \\ \hline
\frac{3}{2} & 4 & -6 & 4 & -6 & \vdots\ 0 \\
 & & 6 & 0 & 6 & \\ \hline
 & 4 & 0 & 4 & \vdots\ 0 &
\end{array}$$

$P\left(\dfrac{3}{2}\right) = 0$

$\therefore Q\left(\dfrac{3}{2}\right) = 0$, where $Q(x) = P(x) \div \left(x - \dfrac{3}{2}\right)$

35.
$$\begin{array}{r|rrrrr}
-2 & 1 & 4 & 0 & -16 & -16 \\
 & & -2 & -4 & 8 & 16 \\ \hline
-2 & 1 & 2 & -4 & -8 & \vdots\ 0 \\
 & & -2 & 0 & 8 & \\ \hline
-2 & 1 & 0 & -4 & \vdots\ 0 & \\
 & & -2 & 4 & & \\ \hline
-2 & 1 & -2 & \vdots\ 0 & & \\
 & & -2 & & & \\ \hline
 & 1 & \vdots\ -4 & & &
\end{array}$$

three times

36.
$$\begin{array}{r|rrrrrr}
-1 & 1 & 3 & 2 & -2 & -3 & -1 \\
 & & -1 & -2 & 0 & 2 & 1 \\ \hline
-1 & 1 & 2 & 0 & -2 & -1 & \vdots\ 0 \\
 & & -1 & -1 & 1 & 1 & \\ \hline
-1 & 1 & 1 & -1 & -1 & \vdots\ 0 & \\
 & & -1 & 0 & 1 & & \\ \hline
-1 & 1 & 0 & -1 & \vdots\ 0 & & \\
 & & -1 & 1 & & & \\ \hline
-1 & 1 & -1 & \vdots\ 0 & & & \\
 & & -1 & & & & \\ \hline
 & 1 & \vdots\ -2 & & & &
\end{array}$$

four times

37. $$\begin{array}{r|rrrr} c & 1 & -5 & 4 & 5 \\ & & c & c^2 - 5c & c^3 - 5c^2 + 4c \\ \hline & 1 & c - 5 & c^2 - 5c + 4 & c^3 - 5c^2 + 4c + 5 \end{array}$$

$x^2 - 3x - 2 = x^2 + (c - 5)x + (c^2 - 5c + 4)$; $c - 5 = -3$, $c = 2$

C **38.** $x - a - b = x - (a + b)$ is a factor of $x^3 - a^3 - b^3 - 3ab(a + b)$ if $a + b$ is a root of $x^3 - a^3 - b^3 - 3ab(a + b) = 0$; $(a + b)^3 - a^3 - b^3 - 3ab(a + b) = a^3 + 3a^2b + 3ab^2 + b^3 - a^3 - b^3 - 3a^2b - 3ab^2 = 0$

39. $x(x - a)$ is a factor of $ax^n - a^nx$ if 0 and a are roots of $ax^n - a^nx = 0$; $a(0^n) - a^n(0) = 0 - 0 = 0$; for every positive integer n and every nonzero number a, $a(a^n) - a^n(a) = a^{n+1} - a^{n+1} = 0$.

Page 376 • MIXED REVIEW EXERCISES

1. $$\begin{array}{r|rrr} -2 & 1 & 3 & -1 \\ & & -2 & -2 \\ \hline & 1 & 1 & -3 \end{array}$$ $x + 1 + \dfrac{-3}{x + 2}$

2. $$\begin{array}{r} y - 1 \\ y^2 + y + 1 \overline{)\, y^3 + 0y^2 + 0y - 1} \\ y^3 + y^2 + y \\ \hline -y^2 - y - 1 \\ -y^2 - y - 1 \\ \hline 0 \end{array}$$ $y - 1$

3. $$\begin{array}{r|rrr} \frac{1}{2} & 4 & -8 & 3 \\ & & 2 & -3 \\ \hline & 4 & -6 & 0 \end{array}$$ $\frac{1}{2}(4u - 6) = 2u - 3$

4. $$\begin{array}{r} 3w^2 + 2 \\ w^2 - 2 \overline{)\, 3w^4 - 4w^2 - 5} \\ 3w^4 - 6w^2 \\ \hline 2w^2 - 5 \\ 2w^2 - 4 \\ \hline -1 \end{array}$$ $3w^2 + 2 + \dfrac{-1}{w^2 - 2}$

5. $$\begin{array}{r|rrrrrr} -1 & 1 & 0 & -4 & 0 & 3 & 0 \\ & & -1 & 1 & 3 & -3 & 0 \\ \hline & 1 & -1 & -3 & 3 & 0 & 0 \end{array}$$

$a^4 - a^3 - 3a^2 + 3a$

6. $$\begin{array}{r} c + 2 \\ 3c^2 + 2c - 4 \overline{)\, 3c^3 + 8c^2 + 0c - 8} \\ 3c^3 + 2c^2 - 4c \\ \hline 6c^2 + 4c - 8 \\ 6c^2 + 4c - 8 \\ \hline 0 \end{array}$$ $c + 2$

7. $D = 9 - 4(4) = -7$; imaginary **8.** $D = 9 - 4(2) = 1$; rational

9. $D = 9 + 4(2) = 17$; irrational

Pages 380–381 • WRITTEN EXERCISES

A **1.** $-5i$ is also a root; $P(x) = (x + 1)(x - 5i)(x + 5i)$; $x^3 + x^2 + 25x + 25 = 0$

2. $-i\sqrt{2}$ is also a root; $P(x) = (x - 3)(x - i\sqrt{2})(x + i\sqrt{2})$; $x^3 - 3x^2 + 2x - 6 = 0$

3. $-1 - i$ is also a root; $P(x) = (x + 2)(x + 1 - i)(x + 1 + i) = (x + 2)(x^2 + 2x + 2)$; $x^3 + 4x^2 + 6x + 4 = 0$

4. $2 + 3i$ is also a root; $P(x) = (x - 1)(x - 2 + 3i)(x - 2 - 3i) = (x - 1)(x^2 - 4x + 13)$; $x^3 - 5x^2 + 17x - 13 = 0$

5. Since $2i$ is a root, $-2i$ is a root; $(-2i)^3 - 3(-2i)^2 + 4(-2i) - 12 = -8i^3 - 12i^2 - 8i - 12 = 8i + 12 - 8i - 12 = 0$; $-2i$

6. Since $1 - i$ is a root, $1 + i$ is a root; $(1 + i)^3 - 2(1 + i) + 4 = 1 + 3i + 3i^2 + i^3 - 2 - 2i + 4 = 1 + 3i - 3 - i - 2 - 2i + 4 = 0$; $1 + i$

7. Since $1 - 2i$ is a root, $1 + 2i$ is also a root; $(1 + 2i)^4 - 2(1 + 2i)^3 + 4(1 + 2i)^2 + 2(1 + 2i) - 5 = 1 + 8i + 24i^2 + 32i^3 + 16i^4 - 2(1 + 6i + 12i^2 + 8i^3) + 4(1 + 4i + 4i^2) + 2 + 4i - 5 = 1 + 8i - 24 - 32i + 16 - 2 - 12i + 24 + 16i + 4 + 16i - 16 + 2 + 4i - 5 = 0$; $1 + 2i$

8. Since $i\sqrt{2}$ is a root, $-i\sqrt{2}$ is also a root; $(i\sqrt{2})^4 - 3(i\sqrt{2})^3 + 4(i\sqrt{2})^2 - 6(i\sqrt{2}) - 4 = 4i^4 - 6i^3\sqrt{2} + 8i^2 - 6i\sqrt{2} + 4 = 4 + 6i\sqrt{2} - 8 - 6i\sqrt{2} + 4 = 0$; $-i\sqrt{2}$

9. Since $-1 + 2i$ is a root, $-1 - 2i$ is also a root;

$$\begin{array}{r|rrrr}
-1+2i & 1 & 0 & 1 & -10 \\
 & & -1+2i & -3-4i & 10 \\ \hline
-1-2i & 1 & -1+2i & -2-4i & 0 \\
 & & -1-2i & 2+4i & \\ \hline
 & 1 & -2 & 0 &
\end{array}$$

The depressed equation is $x - 2 = 0$; $x = 2$; $\{-1 + 2i, -1 - 2i, 2\}$

10. Since $i\sqrt{5}$ is a root, $-i\sqrt{5}$ is also a root;

$$\begin{array}{r|rrrr}
i\sqrt{5} & 2 & -1 & 10 & -5 \\
 & & 2i\sqrt{5} & -10 - i\sqrt{5} & 5 \\ \hline
-i\sqrt{5} & 2 & -1 + 2i\sqrt{5} & -i\sqrt{5} & 0 \\
 & & -2i\sqrt{5} & +i\sqrt{5} & \\ \hline
 & 2 & -1 & 0 &
\end{array}$$

The depressed equation is $2x - 1 = 0$, $x = \frac{1}{2}$; $\left\{\frac{1}{2}, i\sqrt{5}, -i\sqrt{5}\right\}$

11. Since $3 + i$ is a root, $3 - i$ is also a root;

$$\begin{array}{r|rrrrr}
3+i & 1 & -6 & 0 & 60 & -100 \\
 & & 3+i & -10 & -30-10i & 100 \\ \hline
3-i & 1 & -3+i & -10 & 30-10i & 0 \\
 & & 3-i & 0 & -30+10i & \\ \hline
 & 1 & 0 & -10 & 0 &
\end{array}$$

The depressed equation is $x^2 - 10 = 0$, $x^2 = 10$, $x = \pm\sqrt{10}$; $\{\sqrt{10}, -\sqrt{10}, 3 + i, 3 - i\}$

12. Since $-1 + i$ is a root, $-1 - i$ is also a root;

$$\begin{array}{r|rrrrr}
-1+i & 1 & 0 & -5 & -10 & -6 \\
 & & -1+i & -2i & 7-3i & 6 \\ \hline
-1-i & 1 & -1+i & -5-2i & -3-3i & 0 \\
 & & -1-i & 2+2i & 3+3i & \\ \hline
 & 1 & -2 & -3 & 0 &
\end{array}$$

The depressed equation is $x^2 - 2x - 3 = 0$, $(x - 3)(x + 1) = 0$, $x = 3$ or $x = -1$; $\{-1, 3, -1 + i, -1 - i\}$

B

13. $P(x) = x^4 + 3x^2 - 4$ has 1 sign change, so $P(x) = 0$ has one positive root; $P(-x) = x^4 + 3x^2 - 4$ has one sign change, so $P(x) = 0$ has 1 negative root; 1 positive, 1 negative, and 2 imaginary conjugate roots

14. $P(x) = x^4 - x + 3$ has two sign changes, so $P(x) = 0$ has 2 or 0 positive roots; $P(-x) = x^4 + x + 3$ has no sign changes, so $P(x) = 0$ has no negative roots; 2 positive and 2 imaginary or 4 imaginary roots

15. $P(x) = x^4 + 2x^3 + x^2 + 1$ has no sign changes, so $P(x) = 0$ has no positive roots; $P(-x) = x^4 - 2x^3 + x^2 + 1$ has two sign changes, so $P(x) = 0$ has 2 or 0 negative roots; 2 negative and two imaginary or four imaginary roots

16. $P(x) = x^4 - 3x^3 + 5x^2 - 2x + 5$ has 4 sign changes, so $P(x) = 0$ has 4, 2, or 0 positive roots; $P(-x) = x^4 + 3x^3 + 5x^2 + 2x + 5$ has no sign changes, so $P(x) = 0$ has no negative roots; four imaginary roots, two positive and two imaginary, or four positive roots

17. $P(x) = x^5 - x^3 - x - 2 = 0$ has one sign change, so $P(x) = 0$ has one positive root; $P(-x) = -x^5 + x^3 + x - 2$ has two changes, so $P(x) = 0$ has two or zero negative roots; one positive root and either two negative and two imaginary or four imaginary roots

18. $P(x) = x^5 - x^4 + 2x - 3$ has three sign changes so $P(x) = 0$ has 3 or 1 positive roots; $P(-x) = -x^5 - x^4 - 2x - 3$ has no sign changes, so $P(x) = 0$ has no negative roots; three positive and two imaginary or one positive and four imaginary roots

19. $P(x) = x^5 - x^3 - x^2 + x - 2$ has three sign changes, so $P(x) = 0$ has 3 or 1 positive roots; $P(-x) = -x^5 + x^3 - x^2 - x - 2$ has 2 sign changes, so $P(x) = 0$ has 2 or 0 negative roots. The possibilities are:

No. of pos. roots	No. of neg. roots	No. of imaginary roots
3	2	0
3	0	2
1	2	2
1	0	4

20. $P(x) = x^6 + x^5 + x^4 + 3x - 2$ has one sign change so $P(x) = 0$ has one positive root; $P(-x) = x^6 - x^5 + x^4 - 3x - 2$ has 3 sign changes so $P(x) = 0$ has 3 or 1 negative roots; one positive root and either 3 negative and 2 imaginary, or 1 negative and 4 imaginary roots.

21. The other two roots are $-2i$ and $1 + i$; $P(x) =$ $(x - 2i)(x + 2i)(x - 1 + i)(x - 1 - i) = (x^2 + 4)(x^2 - 2x + 2)$; $x^4 - 2x^3 + 6x^2 - 8x + 8 = 0$

22. The other two roots are $1 - i$ and $2 - i$; $P(x) =$ $(x - 1 + i)(x - 1 - i)(x - 2 - i)(x - 2 + i) = (x^2 - 2x + 2)(x^2 - 4x + 5)$; $x^4 - 6x^3 + 15x^2 - 18x + 10 = 0$

23. a. $(-1 + i)^3 + 2(-1 + i)^2 + (-1 + i) - 1 + i =$ $2 + 2i - 4i - 1 + i - 1 + i = 0$; $-1 + i$ is a root

b. $(-1 - i)^3 + 2(-1 - i)^2 + (-1 - i) - 1 + i = 2 - 2i + 4i - 1 - i - 1 + i =$ $2i$; $(-1 - i)$ is *not* a root

24. a. $(2 - i)^3 - 2(2 - i)^2 + 2(2 - i) + 5i = 2 - 11i - 2(3 - 4i) + 4 - 2i + 5i =$ $2 - 11i - 6 + 8i + 4 - 2i + 5i = 0$; $2 - i$ is a root

b. $(2 + i)^3 - 2(2 + i)^2 + 2(2 + i) + 5i = 2 + 11i - 2(3 + 4i) + 4 + 2i + 5i =$ $2 + 11i - 6 - 8i + 4 + 2i + 5i = 10i$; $2 + i$ is *not* a root

25. The theorem applies to polynomials with real coefficients

26.

No. of pos. roots	No. of neg. roots	No. of imaginary roots
3	0	0
2	1	0
1	0	2
1	2	0
0	1	2
0	3	0

27. $\underline{1}|$ 1 −1 2 −2 3 −3

1	1	−1	2	−2	3	−3
		1	0	2	0	3
	1	0	2	0	3	0

1 is a root; The depressed equation is $Q(x) = 0$, where $Q(x) = x^4 + 2x^2 + 3$; $Q(x)$ has no sign changes and $Q(-x) = x^4 + 2x^2 + 3$ has no sign changes; $\therefore$ there are no further positive or negative roots

28.

−1	1	1	1	1	2	2
		−1	0	−1	0	−2
	1	0	1	0	2	0

-1 is a root; the depressed equation is $Q(x) = 0$, where $Q(x) = x^4 + x^2 + 2$; both $Q(x)$ and $Q(-x) = x^4 + x^2 + 2$ have no sign changes; $\therefore$ there are no further positive or negative roots

29. 1. $S(a + bi) = [(a + bi) - (a + bi)][(a + bi) - (a - bi)] = 0(2bi) = 0$;
$S(a - bi) = [(a - bi) - (a + bi)][(a - bi) - (a - bi)] = (-2bi)0 = 0$

2. Division algorithm; since the divisor $S(x)$ is quadratic, the remainder has the form $cx + d$, which is linear if $c \neq 0$ or constant if $c = 0$.

3. Since $a + bi$ is a root of $P(x) = 0$, $P(a + bi) = 0$; also, part (1) showed that $S(a + bi) = 0$.

4. From part (3), $0 = 0 + c(a + bi) + d$; so $c(a + bi) + d = 0$, $ac + bci + d = 0$, and $(ac + d) + bci = 0$.

5. If $(ac + d) + bci = 0 + 0i$, the imaginary parts must be equal; so $bc = 0$, since $b \neq 0$ is given, $c = 0$ by the zero-product property.

6. If $(ac + d) + bci = 0 + 0i$, the real parts must be equal; so $ac + d = 0$; since $c = 0$ by part (5), $a \cdot 0 + d = 0$; so $d = 0$.

7. From part (2), $P(x) = Q(x)S(x) + cx + d$; since $c = d = 0$ by parts (5) and (6), $P(x) = Q(x)S(x)$.

8. Setting $x = a - bi$ in part (7), you obtain $P(a - bi) = Q(a - bi)S(a - bi)$; since $S(a - bi) = 0$ by part (1), $P(a - bi) = Q(a - bi) \cdot 0 = 0$

Pages 384–385 • WRITTEN EXERCISES

A **1.** $P(x) = x^3 - 7x + 6 = 0$; possible rational roots are $\pm1, \pm2, \pm3, \pm6$; $P(1) = 0$, so 1 is a root; $\frac{P(x)}{x - 1} = x^2 + x - 6$; $(x + 3)(x - 2) = 0$, $x = 2, -3$; $\{-3, 1, 2\}$

2. $P(x) = x^3 + x^2 - 4x + 4 = 0$; possible rational roots are $\pm1, \pm2, \pm4$; none of these satisfy the equation; $P(x) = 0$ has no rational root

3. $P(x) = x^3 - 3x^2 + 2x - 8 = 0$; possible rational roots are $\pm1, \pm2, \pm4, \pm8$, the equation has no negative roots; $P(1) = -8$, $P(2) = -8$, $P(4) = 16$, $P(8) = 328$; there are no rational roots

4. $P(x) = x^4 + 3x^3 - x^2 - 9x - 6 = 0$; possible rational roots are $\pm1, \pm2, \pm3, \pm6$; $P(-1) = 0$, $P(-2) = 0$; $\frac{P(x)}{x + 1} = x^3 + 2x^2 - 3x - 6 = Q(x)$; $\frac{Q(x)}{x + 2} = x^2 - 3$; $x^2 - 3 = 0$, $x^2 = 3$, $x = \pm\sqrt{3}$; $\{-1, -2, -\sqrt{3}, \sqrt{3}\}$

5. $P(x) = x^4 - 2x^2 - 16x - 15 = 0$; possible rational roots are $\pm 1, \pm 3, \pm 5, \pm 15$;

$P(-1) = 0, P(3) = 0; \dfrac{P(x)}{(x+1)(x-3)} = x^2 + 2x + 5; x^2 + 2x + 5 = 0,$

$x = \dfrac{-2 \pm \sqrt{4 - 20}}{2} = \dfrac{-2 \pm 4i}{2} = -1 \pm 2i; \{-1, 3, -1 + 2i, -1 - 2i\}$

6. $P(x) = x^4 + 3x^2 - 8x + 10 = 0$; possible rational roots are $\pm 1, \pm 2, \pm 5, \pm 10$; there are no negative roots; $P(1) = 6, P(2) = 22, P(5) = 670, P(10) = 10{,}230$; there are no rational roots

7. $P(x) = 2x^3 + 7x^2 + 6x - 5 = 0$; possible rational roots are $\pm 1, \pm 5, \pm \frac{1}{2}, \pm \frac{5}{2}$;

$P\left(\frac{1}{2}\right) = 0; \dfrac{P(x)}{x - \frac{1}{2}} = 2x^2 + 8x + 10; 2(x^2 + 4x + 5) = 0, x = \dfrac{-4 \pm \sqrt{16 - 20}}{2} =$

$\dfrac{-4 \pm 2i}{2} = -2 \pm i; \left\{\frac{1}{2}, -2 + i, -2 - i\right\}$

8. $P(x) = 2x^3 - 5x^2 - 11x - 4 = 0$; possible rational roots are $\pm 1, \pm 2, \pm 4, \pm \frac{1}{2}$;

$P(-1) = 0; \dfrac{P(x)}{x+1} = 2x^2 - 7x - 4; 2x^2 - 7x - 4 = 0, (2x + 1)(x - 4) = 0, x = -\frac{1}{2}$

or $x = 4; \left\{-1, 4, -\frac{1}{2}\right\}$

9. $P(x) = 2x^3 - 11x^2 + 16x - 6 = 0$; possible rational roots are $\pm 1, \pm 2, \pm 3, \pm 6,$

$\pm \frac{1}{2}, \pm \frac{3}{2}$; there are no negative roots; $P\left(\frac{3}{2}\right) = 0; \dfrac{P(x)}{x - \frac{3}{2}} = 2x^2 - 8x + 4;$

$2(x^2 - 4x + 2) = 0, x = \dfrac{4 \pm \sqrt{16 - 8}}{2} = \dfrac{4 \pm 2\sqrt{2}}{2} = 2 \pm \sqrt{2}; \left\{\frac{3}{2}, 2 + \sqrt{2}, 2 - \sqrt{2}\right\}$

10. $P(x) = 4x^4 + 4x^3 + 17x^2 + 16x + 4 = 0$; possible rational roots are $\pm 1, \pm 2, \pm 4,$

$\pm \frac{1}{2}, \pm \frac{1}{4}$; there are no positive roots; $P\left(-\frac{1}{2}\right) = 0; \dfrac{P(x)}{x + \frac{1}{2}} = 4x^3 + 2x^2 + 16x + 8;$

$2x^2(2x + 1) + 8(2x + 1) = 0, (2x + 1)(2x^2 + 8) = 0, x = -\frac{1}{2}$ (so $-\frac{1}{2}$ is a double

root of $P(x) = 0$) or $x^2 = -4, x = \pm 2i; \left\{-\frac{1}{2}, 2i, -2i\right\}$

11. $P(x) = 3x^4 + 4x^3 - x^2 + 4x - 4 = 0$; possible rational roots are $\pm 1, \pm 2, \pm 4, \pm \frac{1}{3},$

$\pm \frac{2}{3}, \pm \frac{4}{3}; P(-2) = 0, P\left(\frac{2}{3}\right) = 0; \dfrac{P(x)}{(x+2)\left(x - \frac{2}{3}\right)} = 3x^2 + 3; 3x^2 + 3 = 0, x^2 = -1,$

$x = \pm i; \left\{-2, \frac{2}{3}, i, -i\right\}$

12. $P(x) = 6x^4 - 7x^3 + 8x^2 - 7x + 2 = 0$; possible rational roots are $\pm 1, \pm 2, \pm\frac{1}{2}$, $\pm\frac{1}{3}, \pm\frac{1}{6}, \pm\frac{2}{3}$; there are no negative roots; $P\left(\frac{1}{2}\right) = 0$, $P\left(\frac{2}{3}\right) = 0$;
$\dfrac{P(x)}{\left(x - \frac{1}{2}\right)\left(x - \frac{2}{3}\right)} = 6x^2 + 6$; $6x^2 + 6 = 0$, $x^2 = -1$, $x = \pm i$; $\left\{\frac{1}{2}, \frac{2}{3}, i, -i\right\}$

13. $\sqrt{3}$ is a root of the equation $x^2 - 3 = 0$; the only possible rational roots are ± 1 and ± 3, none of which satisfy the equation. Since $x^2 - 3 = 0$ has no rational roots, $\sqrt{3}$ is irrational.

14. $\sqrt{6}$ is a root of the equation $x^2 - 6 = 0$; the only possible rational roots are ± 1, ± 2, ± 3, and ± 6, none of which satisfy the equation. Since $x^2 - 6 = 0$ has no rational roots, $\sqrt{6}$ is irrational.

15. $\sqrt[3]{-4}$ is a root of the equation $x^3 + 4 = 0$; the only possible rational roots are ± 1, ± 2, and ± 4, none of which satisfy the equation. Since $x^3 + 4 = 0$ has no rational roots, $\sqrt[3]{-4}$ is irrational.

16. $\sqrt[3]{2}$ is a root of the equation $x^3 - 2 = 0$; the only possible rational roots are ± 1, and ± 2, none of which satisfy the equation. Since $x^3 - 2 = 0$ has no rational roots, $\sqrt[3]{2}$ is irrational.

17. $\sqrt[4]{8}$ is a root of the equation $x^4 - 8 = 0$; the only possible rational roots are ± 1, ± 2, ± 4, and ± 8, none of which satisfy the equation. Since $x^4 - 8 = 0$ has no rational roots $\sqrt[4]{8}$ is irrational.

18. $\sqrt[5]{-9}$ is a root of the equation $x^5 + 9 = 0$; the only possible rational roots are ± 1, ± 3, and ± 9, none of which satisfy the equation. Since $x^5 + 9 = 0$ has no rational roots, $\sqrt[5]{-9}$ is irrational.

19. $(\sqrt{3} + \sqrt{2})^4 - 10(\sqrt{3} + \sqrt{2})^2 + 1 = 49 + 20\sqrt{6} - 10(5 + 2\sqrt{6}) + 1 =$ $49 + 20\sqrt{6} - 50 - 20\sqrt{6} + 1 = 0$; The only possible rational roots of $x^4 - 10x^2 + 1 = 0$ are 1 and -1, neither of which satisfy the equation; $\sqrt{3} + \sqrt{2}$ is irrational.

20. $(\sqrt{5} - \sqrt{3})^4 - 16(\sqrt{5} - \sqrt{3})^2 + 4 = 124 - 32\sqrt{15} - 16(8 - 2\sqrt{15}) + 4 =$ $124 - 32\sqrt{15} - 128 + 32\sqrt{15} + 4 = 0$; the only possible rational roots of $x^4 - 16x^2 + 4 = 0$ are ± 1, ± 2, and ± 4, none of which satisfy the equation; $\sqrt{5} - \sqrt{3}$ is irrational.

B

21. Multiply both sides by the LCD of the coefficients to produce an equivalent equation with integral coefficients. Then use the Rational Root theorem.

22. $\frac{1}{3}x^3 - \frac{1}{2}x^2 + \frac{1}{3}x + \frac{1}{3} = 0$; $P(x) = 2x^3 - 3x^2 + 2x + 2 = 0$; possible rational roots are $\pm 1, \pm 2, \pm\frac{1}{2}$; $P\left(-\frac{1}{2}\right) = 0$; $\dfrac{P(x)}{x + \frac{1}{2}} = 2x^2 - 4x + 4$; $2(x^2 - 2x + 2) = 0$,
$x = \dfrac{2 \pm \sqrt{4 - 8}}{2} = \dfrac{2 \pm 2i}{2} = 1 \pm i$; $\left\{-\frac{1}{2}, 1 + i, 1 - i\right\}$

23. $\frac{1}{3}x^3 + \frac{1}{2}x^2 + \frac{2}{3}x + 1 = 0$; $P(x) = 2x^3 + 3x^2 + 4x + 6 = 0$; possible rational roots are $\pm1, \pm2, \pm3, \pm6, \pm\frac{1}{2}, \pm\frac{3}{2}$; there are no positive roots; $P\left(-\frac{3}{2}\right) = 0$; $\frac{P(x)}{x + \frac{3}{2}} = 2x^2 + 4$; $2(x^2 + 2) = 0$; $x^2 = -2$; $x = \pm i\sqrt{2}$; $\left\{-\frac{3}{2}, i\sqrt{2}, -i\sqrt{2}\right\}$

24. $2.0x^3 - 0.8x^2 + 0.5x - 0.2 = 0$; $P(x) = 20x^3 - 8x^2 + 5x - 2 = 0$; possible rational roots are $\pm1, \pm2, \pm\frac{1}{2}, \pm\frac{1}{4}, \pm\frac{1}{5}, \pm\frac{1}{10}, \pm\frac{1}{20}, \pm\frac{2}{5}$; there are no negative roots; $P\left(\frac{2}{5}\right) = 0$; $\frac{P(x)}{x - \frac{2}{5}} = 20x^2 + 5$; $5(4x^2 + 1) = 0$; $x^2 = -\frac{1}{4}$, $x = \pm\frac{i}{2}$; $\left\{\frac{2}{5}, \frac{i}{2}, -\frac{i}{2}\right\}$

25. $0.2x^3 - 0.5x^2 + 0.8x - 2.0 = 0$; $2x^3 - 5x^2 + 8x - 20 = 0$; possible rational roots are $\pm1, \pm2, \pm4, \pm5, \pm10, \pm20, \pm\frac{1}{2}, \pm\frac{5}{2}$; there are no negative roots; $P\left(\frac{5}{2}\right) = 0$; $\frac{P(x)}{\left(x - \frac{5}{2}\right)} = 2x^2 + 8$; $2(x^2 + 4) = 0$; $x^2 = -4$, $x = \pm 2i$; $\left\{\frac{5}{2}, 2i, -2i\right\}$

C **26.** The possible rational roots of $x^n - k = 0$ are the integral factors of k. Since $\sqrt[n]{k}$ is rational and $\sqrt[n]{k}$ is a root of $x^n - k = 0$, then $\sqrt[n]{k}$ is an integral factor of k and there is an integer z such that $\sqrt[n]{k} \cdot z = k$; $\sqrt[n]{k} = \frac{k}{z}$ (an integer); $k = \left(\frac{k}{z}\right)^n$.

27. 1. $\frac{h}{k}$ is a root of the equation; 2. Mult. prop. of equality; 3. Add. prop. of equality; 4. Div. prop. of equality; 5. Closure props. for the integers

28. 1. $a\left(\frac{h}{k}\right)^3 + b\left(\frac{h}{k}\right)^2 + c\left(\frac{h}{k}\right) + d = 0$ $\left(\frac{h}{k}\right.$ is a root of the equation$\left.\right)$

2. $ah^3 + bh^2k + chk^2 + dk^3 = 0$ (Mult. prop. of equality)
3. $ah^3 = -bh^2k - chk^2 - dk^3$ (Add. prop. of equality)
4. $\frac{ah^3}{k} = -bh^2 - chk - dk^2$ (Div. prop. of equality)
5. $\frac{ah^3}{k}$ is an integer. (Closure props. for integers)
6. k is a factor of a. (All prime factors of k divide out with prime factors of ah^3 and h and k are relatively prime.)

Page 385 • MIXED REVIEW EXERCISES

1. $4(2 - m) + 5 = 3m - 8$, $8 - 4m + 5 = 3m - 8$, $7m = 21$, $m = 3$; $\{3\}$

2. $3u^2 - 4u + 2 = 0$, $u = \frac{4 \pm \sqrt{16 - 24}}{6} = \frac{4 \pm 2i\sqrt{2}}{6} = \frac{2 \pm i\sqrt{2}}{3}$; $\left\{\frac{2}{3} + \frac{\sqrt{2}}{3}i, \frac{2}{3} - \frac{\sqrt{2}}{3}i\right\}$

3. $\sqrt{2r+1} = r - 1, 2r + 1 = r^2 - 2r + 1, r^2 - 4r = 0, r(r-4) = 0, r = 0$ (reject) or $r = 4$; $\{4\}$

4. $\frac{1}{w} + \frac{w}{w-1} = \frac{1}{w - w^2}; w(w-1)\left(\frac{1}{w} + \frac{w}{w-1}\right) = w(w-1)\left(\frac{-1}{w(w-1)}\right);$
$w - 1 + w^2 = -1, w^2 + w = 0, w(w+1) = 0, w = 0$ (reject) or $w = -1, \{-1\}$

5. $2v^{-2} - 5v^{-1} - 12 = 0, (v^{-1} - 4)(2v^{-1} + 3) = 0, v^{-1} = 4$ or $v^{-1} = -\frac{3}{2}; v = \frac{1}{4}$ or
$v = -\frac{2}{3}; \left\{-\frac{2}{3}, \frac{1}{4}\right\}$

6. $n^4 - 2n^2 - 8 = 0, (n^2 + 2)(n^2 - 4) = 0, n^2 = -2$ or $n^2 = 4, n = \pm i\sqrt{2}$ or $n = \pm 2; \{\pm i\sqrt{2}, \pm 2\}$

7. $x^2(x-2) + 1(x-2) = 0, (x-2)(x^2+1) = 0; x - 2 = 0$ or $x^2 + 1 = 0; x = 2$ or $x^2 = -1, x = 2$ or $x = \pm i; \{2, \pm i\}$

8.
```
-3| 1   1  -7  -3
       -3   6   3
    1  -2  -1 | 0
```
$c^2 - 2c - 1 = 0, c = \frac{2 \pm \sqrt{4+4}}{2} = \frac{2 \pm 2\sqrt{2}}{2} = 1 \pm \sqrt{2};$
$\{-3, 1 \pm \sqrt{2}\}$

9. Since $2 - i$ is a root, $2 + i$ is a root;
```
2 - i| 1     -3       1      5
            2 - i  -3 - i   -5
2 + i| 1  -1 - i   -2 - i | 0
            2 + i   2 + i
       1      1    |  0
```
$a + 1 = 0, a = -1;$
$\{-1, 2 \pm i\}$

10. Since $1 + i$ is a root, $1 - i$ is a root;
```
1 + i| 1    -3        -2        10     -12
           1 + i   -3 - i   -4 - 6i    12
1 - i| 1  -2 + i   -5 - i    6 - 6i |  0
           1 - i   -1 + i   -6 + 6i
       1    -1       -6    |  0
```
$y^2 - y - 6 = 0,$
$(y-3)(y+2) = 0, y = 3$ or
$y = -2; \{-2, 3, 1 + i, 1 - i\}$

Pages 388–389 • WRITTEN EXERCISES

A **1.** $x \approx 2.5$ **2.** $x \approx -2$ **3.** $x \approx -1.5$

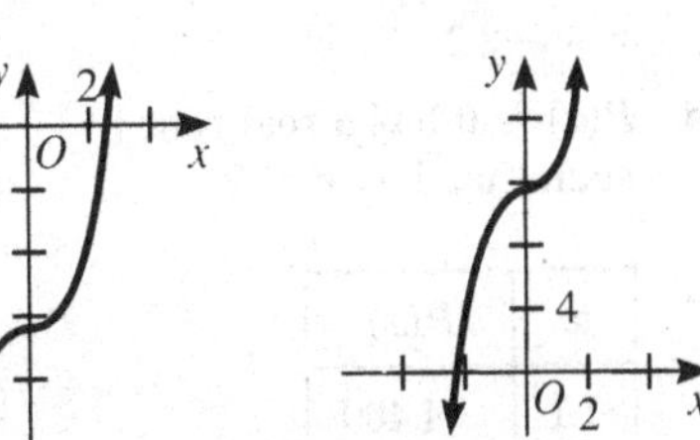
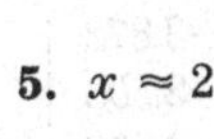
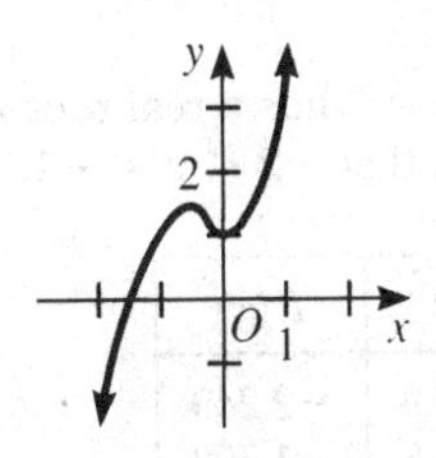

4. $x \approx 1.5$ **5.** $x \approx 2$ **6.** $x \approx -0.5$

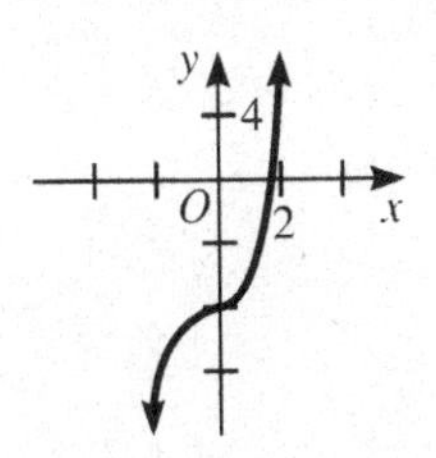
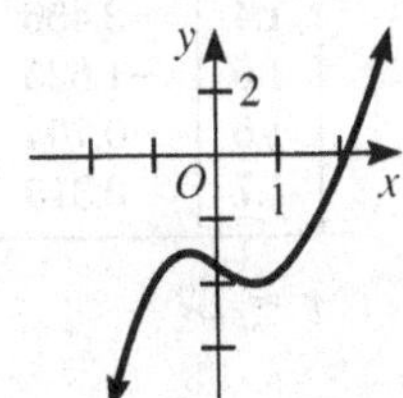
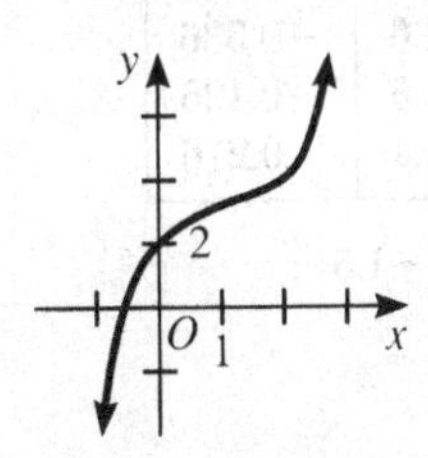

7. $x \approx -1.5, -0.5, 2$

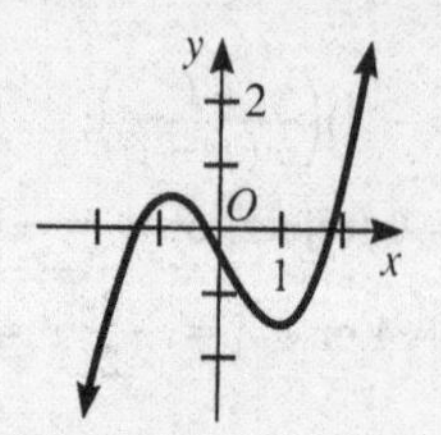

8. $x \approx -2, 0.5, 2$

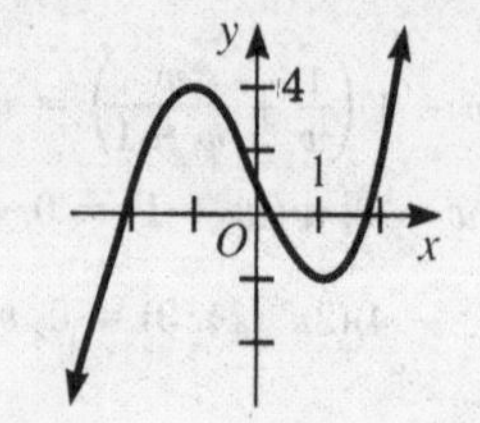

9. $x \approx 1.5, 2.5$

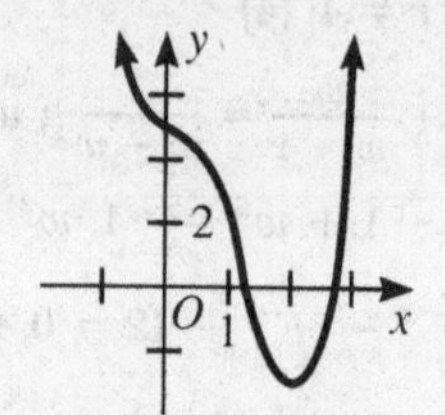

10. $x \approx -3.5, -1, 1, 2.5$

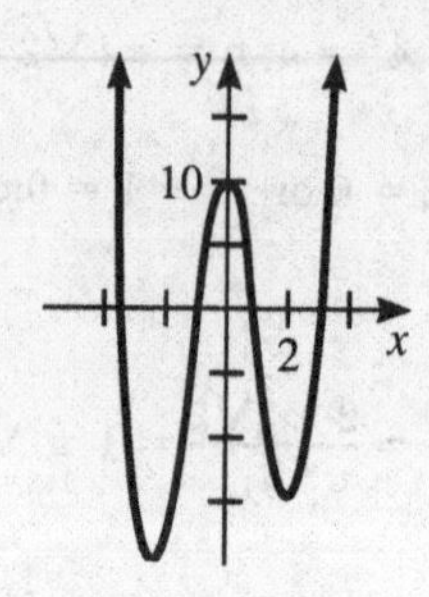

11. $P(x) = 0$ has a real root r such that $2 < r < 3$.

x	$P(x)$
2.1	−6.739
2.2	−5.352
2.3	−3.833
2.4	−2.176
2.5	−0.375
2.6	1.576

$r \approx 2.5$

12. $P(x) = 0$ has a real root r such that $-3 < r < -2$.

x	$P(x)$
−2.9	−13.389
−2.8	−10.952
−2.6	−6.576
−2.5	−4.625
−2.4	−2.824
−2.3	−1.167
−2.2	0.352

$r \approx -2.2$

13. $P(x) = 0$ has a real root r such that $-2 < r < -1$.

x	$P(x)$
−1.9	−2.249
−1.8	−1.592
−1.7	−1.023
−1.6	−0.536
−1.5	−0.125
−1.4	0.216

$r \approx -1.5$

14. $P(x) = 0$ has a real root r such that $1 < r < 2$.

x	$P(x)$
1.1	−4.469
1.2	−3.872
1.3	−3.203
1.4	−2.456
1.5	−1.625
1.6	−0.704
1.7	0.313

$r \approx 1.7$

15. $P(x) = 0$ has a real root r such that $2 < r < 3$.

x	$P(x)$
2.1	−0.249
2.2	0.608

$r \approx 2.1$

16. $P(x) = 0$ has a real root r such that $-1 < r < 0$.

x	$P(x)$
−0.9	−3.859
−0.8	−2.832
−0.7	−1.913
−0.6	−1.096
−0.5	−0.375
−0.4	0.256

$r \approx -0.4$

B

17. $P(x) = 0$ has real roots r_1, r_2, and r_3 such that $-2 < r_1 < -1$, $-1 < r_2 < 0$, and $1 < r_3 < 2$.

x	$P(x)$
−1.9	−2.159
−1.8	−1.432
−1.7	−0.813
−1.6	−0.296
−1.5	0.125

$r_1 \approx -1.5$

x	$P(x)$
−0.9	0.971
−0.8	0.888
−0.7	0.757
−0.6	0.584
−0.5	0.375
−0.4	0.136
−0.3	−0.127

$r_2 \approx -0.3$

x	$P(x)$
1.1	−2.969
1.2	−2.872
1.3	−2.703
1.4	−2.456
1.5	−2.125
1.6	−1.704
1.7	−1.187
1.8	−0.568
1.9	0.159

$r_3 \approx 1.9$

18. $P(x) = 0$ has real roots r_1, r_2, and r_3 such that $-3 < r_1 < -2$, $0 < r_2 < 1$, and $1 < r_3 < 2$.

x	$P(x)$
−2.9	−11.789
−2.8	−9.752
−2.7	−7.883
−2.6	−6.176
−2.5	−4.625
−2.4	−3.224
−2.3	−1.967
−2.2	−0.848
−2.1	0.139

$r_1 \approx -2.1$

x	$P(x)$
0.1	0.601
0.2	0.208
0.3	−0.173

$r_2 \approx 0.3$

x	$P(x)$
1.1	−2.069
1.2	−2.072
1.3	−2.003
1.4	−1.856
1.5	−1.625
1.6	−1.304
1.7	−0.887
1.8	−0.368
1.9	0.259

$r_3 \approx 1.9$

19. $P(x) = 0$ has real roots r_1 and r_2 such that $1 < r_1 < 2$ and $2 < r_2 < 3$.

x	$P(x)$
1.1	2.471
1.2	1.890
1.3	1.265
1.4	0.610
1.5	−0.062

$r_1 \approx 1.5$

x	$P(x)$
2.1	−3.335
2.2	−3.518
2.3	−3.517
2.4	−3.294
2.5	−2.813
2.6	−2.030
2.7	−0.905
2.8	0.610

$r_2 \approx 2.8$

20. $P(x) = 0$ has real roots r_1, r_2, r_3, and r_4 such that $-4 < r_1 < -3$, $-2 < r_2 < -1$, $0 < r_3 < 1$, and $2 < r_4 < 3$.

x	$P(x)$
−3.9	45.525
−3.8	34.442
−3.7	24.663
−3.6	15.106
−3.5	8.688
−3.4	2.330
−3.3	−3.045

$r_1 \approx -3.4$

x	$P(x)$
−1.9	−12.327
−1.8	−10.534
−1.7	−8.661
−1.5	−4.812
−1.4	−2.902
−1.3	−1.041
−1.2	0.746

$r_2 \approx -1.2$

x	$P(x)$
0.1	9.501
0.2	8.810
0.3	7.935
0.4	6.890
0.5	5.688
0.6	4.346
0.7	2.883
0.8	1.322
0.9	−0.315

$r_3 \approx 0.9$

x	$P(x)$
2.1	−13.791
2.2	−13.126
2.3	−11.949
2.4	−10.198
2.5	−7.813
2.6	−4.726
2.7	−0.873
2.8	3.818

$r_4 \approx 2.7$

21. $P(1) = 2, P(4) = 11; P(1) < 6 < P(4); c^2 - 2c + 3 = 6, c^2 - 2c - 3 = 0,$ $(c - 3)(c + 1) = 0, c = 3$ or $c = -1$ (reject); $c = 3$

22. $P(-5) = 15; P(-1) = -5; P(-1) < 7 < P(-5); c^2 + c - 5 = 7, c^2 + c - 12 = 0,$ $(c + 4)(c - 3) = 0, c = -4$ or $c = 3$ (reject); $c = -4$

23. $P(-2) = -6; P(2) = 14; P(-2) < -1 < P(2); 2c^2 + 5c - 4 = -1,$ $2c^2 + 5c - 3 = 0, (2c - 1)(c + 3) = 0, c = \frac{1}{2}$ or $c = -3$ (reject); $c = \frac{1}{2}$

24. $P(-3) = -17; P(2) = 3; P(-3) < -5 < P(2); c^3 + c^2 - 2c - 5 = -5,$ $c^3 + c^2 - 2c = 0, c(c^2 + c - 2) = 0, c(c + 2)(c - 1) = 0; c = 0, -2,$ or 1

C **25.** Since $P(1.5) = -0.125 < 0$ and $P(1.6) = 0.296 > 0$, $P(x)$ has a zero r such that $1.5 < r < 1.6$.

x	$P(x)$
1.51	−0.087
1.52	−0.048
1.53	−0.008
1.54	0.032

$r \approx 1.53$

26. Since $P(-2.6) = -1.016 < 0$ and $P(-2.5) = 0.125 > 0$, $P(x)$ has a zero r such that $-2.6 < r < -2.5$.

x	$P(x)$
−2.59	−0.896
−2.58	−0.777
−2.57	−0.660
−2.56	−0.544
−2.55	−0.429
−2.54	−0.315
−2.53	−0.203
−2.52	−0.093
−2.51	0.017

$r \approx -2.51$

27. For all $x > m$, $x - m > 0$ and, since $x > 0$ and the coefficients of $Q(x)$ are nonnegative, $Q(x) > 0$. Then, since $P(m)$ is nonnegative, $P(x) = (x - m)Q(x) + P(m) > 0$ for all $x > m$. Therefore $P(x) = 0$ has no roots greater than m.

28. Apply the method of Exercise 27 to $P(-x) = 0$ or $-P(-x) = 0$, whichever polynomial has a positive leading coefficient. The opposite of the least upper bound that you find is the greatest lower bound of $P(x) = 0$.

29. $P(x) = 2x^3 - 5x^2 - 8x - 9$; for $m = 1$, 2, and 3, the coefficients of the quotient $Q(x)$ when $P(x)$ is divided by $x - m$ are not all positive; for $m = 4$, $P(x) = (x - 4)(2x^2 + 3x + 4) + 7$; the least integral upper bound is 4; $-P(-x) = 2x^3 + 5x^2 - 8x + 9$; for $m = 1$, the coefficients of the quotient $Q(x)$ when $-P(-x)$ is divided by $x - m$ are not all positive; for $m = 2$, $-P(-x) = (x - 2)(2x^3 + 4x^2 + 2x + 7)$; the greatest integral lower bound is -2; 4 and -2.

30. $P(x) = 2x^4 - 6x^2 - 3x - 9$; for $m = 1$ and 2, the coefficients of the quotient $Q(x)$ when $P(x)$ is divided by $x - m$ are not all positive; for $m = 3$, $P(x) = (x - 3) \times (2x^3 + 6x^2 + 12x + 33) + 90$; the least integral upper bound is 3; $P(-x) = 2x^4 - 6x^2 + 3x - 9$; for $m = 1$, the coefficients of $Q(x)$ when $P(-x)$ is divided by $x - m$ are not all positive; for $m = 2$, $P(-x) = (x - 2)(2x^3 + 4x^2 + 2x + 7) + 5$; the greatest integral lower bound is -2; 3 and -2.

Page 390 • COMPUTER KEY-IN

1. a. $x \approx -0.7, 2.0, 2.7$ **b.** $x \approx 2.73$ **2. a.** $x \approx -1.6, -0.2, 2.2$ **b.** $x \approx 3.6, 10.0$

3. $\sqrt[5]{2} \approx 1.149$

4. No zeros are found. The zeros are $\frac{1}{7}$ and $\frac{1}{6}$, both of which are between 0.1 and 0.2.

Pages 394–395 • WRITTEN EXERCISES

A 1.

		Year	Population		
10	5	1910	92	d	14
		1915	p		
		1920	106		

$\frac{d}{14} = \frac{5}{10} = \frac{1}{2}$, $2d = 14$, $d = 7$;

$p \approx 92 + 7 = 99$; 99 million

2.

		Year	Population		
10	3	1960	179	d	24
		1963	p		
		1970	203		

$\frac{3}{10} = \frac{d}{24}$, $10d = 72$, $d \approx 7$;

$p \approx 179 + 7 = 186$; 186 million

3.

$$\begin{array}{c|c} \text{Year} & \text{Population} \\ \hline 10\left[8\left[\begin{array}{c} 1960 \\ 1968 \end{array} \right. \begin{array}{c} \\ \\ \end{array} \right. \begin{array}{c} 1960 \\ 1968 \\ 1970 \end{array} & \left. \begin{array}{c} 179 \\ p \\ 203 \end{array} \left. \right] d \right] 24 \end{array}$$

$\frac{d}{24} = \frac{8}{10} = \frac{4}{5}$; $5d = 96$, $d \approx 19$;

$p \approx 179 + 19 = 198$; 198 million

4.

$$\begin{array}{c|c} \text{Year} & \text{Population} \\ \hline 10\left[6\left[\right. \right. \begin{array}{c} 1970 \\ 1976 \\ 1980 \end{array} & \left. \begin{array}{c} 203 \\ p \\ 227 \end{array} \left. \right] d \right] 24 \end{array}$$

$\frac{d}{24} = \frac{6}{10} = \frac{3}{5}$; $5d = 72$, $d \approx 14$;

$p \approx 203 + 14 = 217$; 217 million

5.

$$\begin{array}{c|c} \text{Year} & \text{Population} \\ \hline 10\left[c\left[\right. \right. \begin{array}{c} 1910 \\ y \\ 1920 \end{array} & \left. \begin{array}{c} 92 \\ 100 \\ 106 \end{array} \left. \right] 8 \right] 14 \end{array}$$

$\frac{c}{10} = \frac{8}{14} = \frac{4}{7}$; $7c = 40$, $c \approx 6$;

$y \approx 1910 + 6 = 1916$

6.

$$\begin{array}{c|c} \text{Year} & \text{Population} \\ \hline 10\left[c\left[\right. \right. \begin{array}{c} 1920 \\ y \\ 1930 \end{array} & \left. \begin{array}{c} 106 \\ 115 \\ 123 \end{array} \left. \right] 9 \right] 17 \end{array}$$

$\frac{c}{10} = \frac{9}{17}$; $17c = 90$, $c \approx 5$;

$y \approx 1920 + 5 = 1925$

7.

$$\begin{array}{c|c} \text{Year} & \text{Population} \\ \hline 10\left[c\left[\right. \right. \begin{array}{c} 1950 \\ y \\ 1960 \end{array} & \left. \begin{array}{c} 151 \\ 170 \\ 179 \end{array} \left. \right] 19 \right] 28 \end{array}$$

$\frac{c}{10} = \frac{19}{28}$, $28c = 190$, $c \approx 7$;

$y \approx 1950 + 7 = 1957$

8.

$$\begin{array}{c|c} \text{Year} & \text{Population} \\ \hline 10\left[c\left[\right. \right. \begin{array}{c} 1970 \\ y \\ 1980 \end{array} & \left. \begin{array}{c} 203 \\ 220 \\ 227 \end{array} \left. \right] 17 \right] 24 \end{array}$$

$\frac{c}{10} = \frac{17}{24}$; $24c = 170$, $c \approx 7$;

$y \approx 1970 + 7 = 1977$

9.

$$\begin{array}{c|c} \text{Altitude} & \text{Density} \\ \hline 500\left[200\left[\right. \right. \begin{array}{c} 1000 \\ 1200 \\ 1500 \end{array} & \left. \begin{array}{c} 1.112 \\ y \\ 1.058 \end{array} \left. \right] d \right] 0.054 \end{array}$$

$\frac{d}{0.054} = \frac{200}{500} = \frac{2}{5}$; $5d = 0.108$,

$d = 0.0216$; $y \approx 1.112 - 0.022 = 1.090$; 1.090 kg/m^3

10.

$$\begin{array}{c|c} \text{Altitude} & \text{Density} \\ \hline 500\left[200\left[\right. \right. \begin{array}{c} 3000 \\ 3200 \\ 3500 \end{array} & \left. \begin{array}{c} 0.909 \\ y \\ 0.863 \end{array} \left. \right] d \right] 0.046 \end{array}$$

$\frac{d}{0.046} = \frac{200}{500} = \frac{2}{5}$; $5d = 0.092$,

$d = 0.0184$; $y \approx 0.909 - 0.018 = 0.891$; 0.891 kg/m^3

11.

$$\begin{array}{c|c} \text{Altitude} & \text{Density} \\ \hline 500\left[400\left[\right. \right. \begin{array}{c} 0 \\ 400 \\ 500 \end{array} & \left. \begin{array}{c} 1.225 \\ y \\ 1.167 \end{array} \left. \right] d \right] 0.058 \end{array}$$

$\frac{d}{0.058} = \frac{400}{500} = \frac{4}{5}$; $5d = 0.232$,

$d \approx 0.046$; $y \approx 1.225 - 0.046 = 1.179$; 1.179 kg/m^3

12.

$$\begin{array}{c|c} \text{Altitude} & \text{Density} \\ \hline 500\left[320\left[\right. \right. \begin{array}{c} 0 \\ 320 \\ 500 \end{array} & \left. \begin{array}{c} 1.225 \\ y \\ 1.167 \end{array} \left. \right] d \right] 0.058 \end{array}$$

$\frac{d}{0.058} = \frac{320}{500} = \frac{16}{25}$; $25d = 0.928$,

$d \approx 0.037$; $y \approx 1.225 - 0.037 = 1.188$; 1.188 kg/m^3

13.

		Altitude	Density		
	c	0	1.225	0.025	
500		x	1.200		0.058
		500	1.167		

$\frac{0.025}{0.058} = \frac{c}{500}$, $c \approx 216$;

$x \approx 0 + 216 = 216$; 216 m

14.

		Altitude	Density		
	c	1500	1.058	0.028	
500		x	1.030		0.051
		2000	1.007		

$\frac{c}{500} = \frac{0.028}{0.051}$; $c \approx 275$;

$x \approx 1500 + 275 = 1775$; 1775 m

15.

		Altitude	Density		
	c	2000	1.007	0.007	
500		x	1.000		0.050
		2500	0.957		

$\frac{c}{500} = \frac{0.007}{0.050}$, $c = 70$;

$x \approx 2000 + 70 = 2070$; 2070 m

16.

		Altitude	Density		
	c	2500	0.957	0.027	
500		x	0.930		0.048
		3000	0.909		

$\frac{0.027}{0.048} = \frac{c}{500}$; $c \approx 281$;

$x \approx 2500 + 281 = 2781$; 2781 m

B

17.

		N	$\sqrt{N}$		
	0.03	7.6	2.757	d	
0.1		7.63	y		0.018
		7.7	2.775		

$\frac{d}{0.018} = \frac{0.03}{0.1} = \frac{3}{10}$; $d \approx 0.005$

$y \approx 2.757 + 0.005 = 2.762$

18.

		N	$\sqrt{N}$		
	0.07	4.8	2.191	d	
0.1		4.87	y		0.023
		4.9	2.214		

$\frac{d}{0.023} = \frac{0.07}{0.1} = \frac{7}{10}$, $d \approx 0.016$;

$y \approx 2.191 + 0.016 = 2.207$

19.

		N	$\sqrt{N}$		
	0.8	67	8.185	d	
1		67.8	y		0.061
		68	8.246		

$\frac{d}{0.061} = \frac{0.8}{1}$, $d \approx 0.049$;

$y \approx 8.185 + 0.049 = 8.234$

20.

		N	$\sqrt{N}$		
	0.2	24	4.899	d	
1		24.2	y		0.101
		25	5.000		

$\frac{0.2}{1} = \frac{d}{0.101}$, $d \approx 0.020$;

$y \approx 4.899 + 0.020 = 4.919$

21.

		N	$\sqrt[3]{N}$		
	0.06	5.2	1.732	d	
1		5.26	y		0.012
		5.3	1.744		

$\frac{d}{0.012} = \frac{0.06}{0.1} = \frac{3}{5}$; $d \approx 0.007$;

$y \approx 1.732 + 0.007 = 1.739$

22.

		N	$\sqrt[3]{N}$		
	6	520	8.041	d	
10		526	y		0.052
		530	8.093		

$\frac{d}{0.052} = \frac{6}{10} = \frac{3}{5}$, $d \approx 0.031$;

$y \approx 8.041 + 0.031 = 8.072$

23.

$$\begin{array}{c|c} N & \sqrt[3]{N} \\ \hline \end{array}$$
$$1\left[\begin{array}{l} 0.8\left[\begin{array}{c|c} 26 & 2.962 \\ 26.8 & y \end{array}\right]d \\ \begin{array}{c|c} 27 & 3.000 \end{array} \end{array}\right]0.038$$

$\frac{d}{0.038} = \frac{0.8}{1}$; $d \approx 0.030$;

$y \approx 2.962 + 0.030 = 2.992$

24.

$$\begin{array}{c|c} N & \sqrt[3]{N} \\ \hline \end{array}$$
$$1\left[\begin{array}{l} 0.3\left[\begin{array}{c|c} 84 & 4.380 \\ 84.3 & y \end{array}\right]d \\ \begin{array}{c|c} 85 & 4.397 \end{array} \end{array}\right]0.017$$

$\frac{d}{0.017} = \frac{0.3}{1}$, $d \approx 0.005$;

$y \approx 4.380 + 0.005 = 4.385$

25.

$$\begin{array}{c|c} N & \sqrt{N} \\ \hline \end{array}$$
$$1\left[\begin{array}{l} 0.8\left[\begin{array}{c|c} 52 & 7.211 \\ 52.8 & y \end{array}\right]d \\ \begin{array}{c|c} 53 & 7.280 \end{array} \end{array}\right]0.069$$

$\frac{d}{0.069} = \frac{0.8}{1}$; $d \approx 0.055$;

$y \approx 7.211 + 0.055 = 7.266$;

$\therefore \sqrt{5280} = 10\sqrt{52.8} \approx 72.66$

26.

$$\begin{array}{c|c} N & \sqrt[3]{N} \\ \hline \end{array}$$
$$1\left[\begin{array}{l} 0.3\left[\begin{array}{c|c} 62 & 3.958 \\ 62.3 & y \end{array}\right]d \\ \begin{array}{c|c} 63 & 3.979 \end{array} \end{array}\right]0.021$$

$\frac{d}{0.021} = \frac{0.3}{1}$, $d \approx 0.006$;

$y \approx 3.958 + 0.006 = 3.964$

$\therefore \sqrt[3]{62300} = 10\sqrt[3]{62.3} \approx 39.64$

27.

$$\begin{array}{c|c} x & P(x) \\ \hline \end{array}$$
$$0.1\left[\begin{array}{l} c\left[\begin{array}{c|c} 1.3 & -0.203 \\ x & 0 \end{array}\right]0.203 \\ \begin{array}{c|c} 1.4 & 0.544 \end{array} \end{array}\right]0.747$$

$\frac{c}{0.1} = \frac{0.203}{0.747}$; $c \approx 0.03$;

$x \approx 1.3 + 0.03 = 1.33$; 1.33

28.

$$\begin{array}{c|c} x & P(x) \\ \hline \end{array}$$
$$0.1\left[\begin{array}{l} c\left[\begin{array}{c|c} 2.4 & -0.696 \\ x & 0 \end{array}\right]0.696 \\ \begin{array}{c|c} 2.5 & 0.125 \end{array} \end{array}\right]0.821$$

$\frac{c}{0.1} = \frac{0.696}{0.821}$, $c \approx 0.08$; $x \approx 2.4 + 0.08 = 2.48$; 2.48

29.

$$\begin{array}{c|c} x & P(x) \\ \hline \end{array}$$
$$0.1\left[\begin{array}{l} c\left[\begin{array}{c|c} -2.4 & 0.936 \\ x & 0 \end{array}\right]0.936 \\ \begin{array}{c|c} -2.5 & -0.375 \end{array} \end{array}\right]1.311$$

$\frac{c}{0.1} = \frac{0.936}{1.311}$, $c \approx 0.07$;

$x \approx -2.4 - 0.07 = -2.47$; -2.47

30.

$$\begin{array}{c|c} x & P(x) \\ \hline \end{array}$$
$$0.1\left[\begin{array}{l} c\left[\begin{array}{c|c} -1.6 & 0.704 \\ x & 0 \end{array}\right]0.704 \\ \begin{array}{c|c} -1.7 & -0.313 \end{array} \end{array}\right]1.017$$

$\frac{c}{0.1} = \frac{0.704}{1.017}$; $c \approx 0.07$;

$x \approx -1.6 - 0.07 = -1.67$; -1.67

Page 395 • COMPUTER EXERCISES

1.
```
10 INPUT "ENTER X1, F(X1), X2, F(X2):"; X1, F1, X2, F2
20 INPUT "ENTER VALUE OF X TO BE INTERPOLATED:"; X
30 LET F = F1 + (X - X1)/(X2 - X1) * (F2 - F1)
40 PRINT "F("; X; ") = "; F
50 END
```

2. a. F(1916) = 100.4
F(1949) = 149.1
F(1972) = 207.8

b. F(1920) = 107.5 The program estimate is greater than the table value by 1.5 million

3. F(1890) = 60
F(1895) = 68
F(1995) = 251
F(2000) = 259

4. To estimate the function for Exercise 5(a), use the following program

```
10 INPUT "ENTER X1, X2:"; X1, X2
15 DEF FN Y(X) = X ↑ 3
16 LET F1 = FN Y(X1)
17 LET F2 = FN Y(X2)
20 INPUT "ENTER VALUE OF X TO BE INTERPOLATED:"; X
30 LET F = F1 + (X - X1)/(X2 - X1) * (F2 - F1)
40 PRINT "F("; X;") = "; F
45 LET FF = FN Y(X)
46 PRINT "EXACT VALUE IS"; FF
50 END
```

5. a. F(2.8) = 23.2
`EXACT VALUE IS 21.952`

b. Change line 15 to: `15 DEF FN Y(X) = 3 * X - 7`
F(7) = 14
`EXACT VALUE IS 14`

c. Change line 15 to: `15 DEF FN Y(X) = 1/X`
F(13.71) = .08145
`EXACT VALUE IS .0729394603`

d. Change line 15 to:
`15 DEF FN Y(X) = X ↑ 5 + .75 * X ↑ 3 - X ↑ 2 + 8`
F(14.3) = 606292.576
`EXACT VALUE IS 599967.756`

Pages 397–398 • CHAPTER REVIEW

1. c; $\frac{21}{12} = \frac{t}{28}, \frac{7}{4} = \frac{t}{28}, t = 49$ **2.** b; Let x = Harrison's votes; $\frac{260}{480} = \frac{x}{12{,}000}, x = 6500$

3. d; $z = \frac{kx^2}{y}; 8 = \frac{k(4)^2}{6}, k = 3; z = \frac{3(6)^2}{12} = 9$

4. c; $E = kmv^2; 24 = k(3)(4)^2, k = \frac{1}{2}; E = \frac{1}{2}(4)(3)^2 = 18$

5. b;
$$\begin{array}{r} 3x - 1 \\ x^2 - 2\,\overline{)\,3x^3 - x^2 - 4x + 1} \\ \underline{3x^3 \qquad\; - 6x \qquad} \\ -x^2 + 2x + 1 \\ \underline{-x^2 \qquad\;\; + 2} \\ 2x - 1 \end{array}$$

6. c;
$$\begin{array}{r|rrrrr} \underline{-2} & 1 & 4 & 0 & -5 & 3 \\ & & -2 & -4 & 8 & -6 \\ \hline & 1 & 2 & -4 & 3 & -3 \end{array}$$

7. c; $P(x) = x^{13} - 2x^7 + 3x + k; P(-1) = -1 + 2 - 3 + k = k - 2; k - 2 = 0, k = 2$

8. a; $P(2) = 32 - 32 + 12 - 1 = 11$

9. c;
$$\begin{array}{r|rrrrr} 1+i\sqrt{2} & 1 & -4 & 4 & 0 & -9 \\ & & 1+i\sqrt{2} & -5-2i\sqrt{2} & 3-3i\sqrt{2} & 9 \\ \hline 1-i\sqrt{2} & 1 & -3+i\sqrt{2} & -1-2i\sqrt{2} & 3-3i\sqrt{2} & 0 \\ & & 1-i\sqrt{2} & -2+2i\sqrt{2} & -3+3i\sqrt{2} & \\ \hline & 1 & -2 & -3 & 0 & \end{array}$$

$x^2 - 2x - 3 = 0$, $(x - 3)(x + 1) = 0$, $x = 3$ or $x = -1$;

$\{1 + i\sqrt{2}, 1 - i\sqrt{2}, 3, -1\}$

10. d; $P(x) = (x + 2)(x - 3 + i)(x - 3 - i) = (x + 2)(x^2 - 6x + 10) = x^3 - 4x^2 - 2x + 20$; $x^3 - 4x^2 - 2x + 20 = 0$

11. c; Only possible rational roots are $\pm 1, \pm 2, \pm 4, \pm 8, \pm\frac{1}{2}, \pm\frac{1}{3}, \pm\frac{1}{6}, \pm\frac{2}{3}, \pm\frac{4}{3}, \pm\frac{8}{3}$

12. b; $P(1.5) = -0.625$, $P(1.6) = 0.096$

13. c; $\frac{2.64 - 2.6}{2.7 - 2.6} = \frac{d}{5.12 - 4.97}$, $\frac{0.04}{0.1} = \frac{d}{0.15}$, $d = 0.06$; $P(2.64) \approx 4.97 + 0.06 = 5.03$

Page 398 • CHAPTER TEST

1. Let d = distance in ft an object falls in t seconds; $d = kt^2$; $64 = k(2)^2$, $k = 16$; $d = 16(3)^2$, $d = 144$; 144 ft

2. Let V = volume in cm^3 of a cone with height h cm and base radius r cm; $V = khr^2$;

$32\pi = k(6)(4)^2$, $k = \frac{1}{3}\pi$; $V = \frac{1}{3}\pi(4)(6)^2 = 48\pi$; 48π cm^3

3.
$$\begin{array}{r} x^2 - x - 4 \\ x^2 - 2x + 2\overline{\smash{)}x^4 - 3x^3 + 0x^2 + 6x - 5} \\ \underline{x^4 - 2x^3 + 2x^2} \qquad\qquad \\ -x^3 - 2x^2 + 6x \qquad \\ \underline{-x^3 + 2x^2 - 2x} \qquad \\ -4x^2 + 8x - 5 \\ \underline{-4x^2 + 8x - 8} \\ 3 \end{array}$$

$x^2 - x - 4 + \frac{3}{x^2 - 2x + 2}$

4.
$$\begin{array}{r|rrrrr} -2 & 1 & 2 & 0 & 4 & 5 \\ & & -2 & 0 & 0 & -8 \\ \hline & 1 & 0 & 0 & 4 & -3 \end{array}$$

$x^3 + 4 + \frac{-3}{x + 2}$

5.
$$\begin{array}{r|rrrr} \frac{1}{2} & 6 & -1 & 3 & 5 \\ & & 3 & 1 & 2 \\ \hline & 6 & 2 & 4 & 7 \end{array}$$

$P\left(\frac{1}{2}\right) = 7$

6. Since $1 - i\sqrt{2}$ is a root, $1 + i\sqrt{2}$ is also a root and

$(x - 1 + i\sqrt{2})(x - 1 - i\sqrt{2}) = x^2 - 2x + 3$ is a factor;

$$\begin{array}{r} x^2 \qquad - 3 \qquad\qquad\qquad \\ x^2 - 2x + 3\overline{\smash{)}x^4 - 2x^3 + 0x^2 + 6x - 9} \\ \underline{x^4 - 2x^3 + 3x^2} \qquad\qquad \\ -3x^2 + 6x - 9 \\ \underline{-3x^2 + 6x - 9} \\ 0 \end{array}$$

$x^2 - 3 = 0$, $x^2 = 3$, $x = \pm\sqrt{3}$,
$\{1 \pm i\sqrt{2}, \pm\sqrt{3}\}$

7. Possible rational roots are $\pm 1, \pm 2, \pm 4, \pm\frac{1}{2}$; 1 and $-\frac{1}{2}$ are roots;

$$\begin{array}{r|rrrrr} 1 & 2 & 3 & -11 & 2 & 4 \\ & & 2 & 5 & -6 & -4 \\ \hline -\frac{1}{2} & 2 & 5 & -6 & -4 & 0 \\ & & -1 & -2 & 4 & \\ \hline & 2 & 4 & -8 & 0 & \end{array}$$

$2x^2 + 4x - 8 = 0, x^2 + 2x - 4 = 0, x = \frac{-2 \pm \sqrt{4 + 16}}{2} = \frac{-2 \pm 2\sqrt{5}}{2} =$

$-1 \pm \sqrt{5}; \left\{1, -\frac{1}{2}, -1 \pm \sqrt{5}\right\}$

8. $x \approx 1.5$

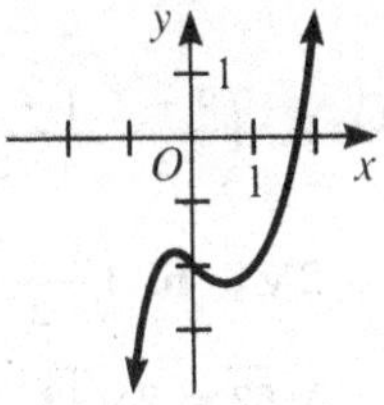

9.

x	$f(x)$
-1.7	4.63
-1.76	y
-1.8	4.45

(0.1 spans -1.7 to -1.8; 0.06 spans -1.7 to -1.76; d spans 4.63 to y; 0.18 spans 4.63 to 4.45)

$\frac{0.06}{0.1} = \frac{d}{0.18}, d \approx 0.11, y \approx 4.63 - 0.11 = 4.52$

Page 399 • PREPARING FOR COLLEGE ENTRANCE EXAMS

1. B; Let $y = x^2 + 1$; $2y^2 + y - 3 = 0, (2y + 3)(y - 1) = 0, y = -\frac{3}{2}$ or $y = 1$;

$x^2 + 1 = -\frac{3}{2}$ (reject) or $x^2 + 1 = 1, x^2 = 0, x = 0$

2. C; $1.5y^2 - 5y + 2 = 0, 3y^2 - 10y + 4 = 0, D = 100 - 48 = 52$; roots are irrational

3. E;
$$\begin{array}{r|rrrr} 1 - i & 2 & -1 & 3 & 1 \\ & & 2 - 2i & -1 - 3i & -1 - 5i \\ \hline & 2 & 1 - 2i & 2 - 3i & -5i \end{array}$$

4. D; $\frac{0.2}{1} = \frac{d}{0.075}, d = 0.015; \sqrt{44.2} \approx 6.633 + 0.015 = 6.648$

5. B; $z = \frac{kx}{y}$; $12 = \frac{k(4)}{5}, k = 15; z = \frac{15(6)}{45} = 2$

6. E; 3 is not a factor of 10

7. C; $x^2 - (-2)x + \left(-\frac{3}{2}\right) = 0, 2x^2 + 4x - 3 = 0$

8. C; $g(x) = -2x^2 - 8x + 7; -\frac{b}{2a} = -2; g(-2) = 15$

9. E; $V_1 = kh_1r_1^2; V_2 = k(2h_1)\left(\frac{r_1}{2}\right)^2 = \frac{kh_1r_1^2}{2} = \frac{1}{2}V_1$

CHAPTER 9 • Analytic Geometry

Pages 404–405 • WRITTEN EXERCISES

A

1. a. $|13 - 0| = 13$ **b.** $\left(\frac{13 + 0}{2}, \frac{6 + 6}{2}\right) = \left(\frac{13}{2}, 6\right)$

2. a. $\sqrt{(-6 - 0)^2 + (0 - 8)^2} = \sqrt{36 + 64} = \sqrt{100} = 10$

b. $\left(\frac{0 + (-6)}{2}, \frac{8 + 0}{2}\right) = (-3, 4)$

3. a. $\sqrt{(-5 - 0)^2 + (-1 - 6)^2} = \sqrt{25 + 49} = \sqrt{74}$

b. $\left(\frac{0 + (-5)}{2}, \frac{6 + (-1)}{2}\right) = \left(-\frac{5}{2}, \frac{5}{2}\right)$

4. a. $\sqrt{(2 - 9)^2 + (-1 - 1)^2} = \sqrt{49 + 4} = \sqrt{53}$ **b.** $\left(\frac{9 + 2}{2}, \frac{1 + (-1)}{2}\right) = \left(\frac{11}{2}, 0\right)$

5. a. $\sqrt{(5 - 3)^2 + (6 - 2)^2} = \sqrt{4 + 16} = \sqrt{20} = 2\sqrt{5}$ **b.** $\left(\frac{3 + 5}{2}, \frac{2 + 6}{2}\right) = (4, 4)$

6. a. $\sqrt{[2 - (-4)]^2 + [1 - (-3)]^2} = \sqrt{36 + 16} = \sqrt{52} = 2\sqrt{13}$

b. $\left(\frac{-4 + 2}{2}, \frac{-3 + 1}{2}\right) = (-1, -1)$

7. a. $\sqrt{\left(\frac{1}{3} - 2\right)^2 + (-2 - 2)^2} = \sqrt{\left(-\frac{5}{3}\right)^2 + (-4)^2} = \sqrt{\frac{25}{9} + 16} = \sqrt{\frac{169}{9}} = \frac{13}{3}$

b. $\left(\frac{2 + \frac{1}{3}}{2}, \frac{2 + (-2)}{2}\right) = \left(\frac{\frac{7}{3}}{2}, 0\right) = \left(\frac{7}{6}, 0\right)$

8. a. $\sqrt{\left(-1 - \frac{1}{2}\right)^2 + [1 - (-1)]^2} = \sqrt{\left(\frac{3}{2}\right)^2 + (2)^2} = \sqrt{\frac{9}{4} + 4} = \sqrt{\frac{25}{4}} = \frac{5}{2}$

b. $\left(\frac{\frac{1}{2} + (-1)}{2}, \frac{-1 + 1}{2}\right) = \left(\frac{-\frac{1}{2}}{2}, 0\right) = \left(-\frac{1}{4}, 0\right)$

9. a. $\sqrt{(11 - 0)^2 + (11 - 0)^2} = \sqrt{121 + 121} = \sqrt{242} = 11\sqrt{2}$

b. $\left(\frac{0 + 11}{2}, \frac{0 + 11}{2}\right) = \left(\frac{11}{2}, \frac{11}{2}\right)$

10. a. $\sqrt{(5 - 0)^2 + (5 - 0)^2} = \sqrt{25 + 25} = \sqrt{50} = 5\sqrt{2}$ **b.** $\left(\frac{0 + 5}{2}, \frac{0 + 5}{2}\right) = \left(\frac{5}{2}, \frac{5}{2}\right)$

11. a. $\sqrt{(-\sqrt{2} - \sqrt{2})^2 + (0 - 1)^2} = \sqrt{(-2\sqrt{2})^2 + 1} = \sqrt{8 + 1} = \sqrt{9} = 3$

b. $\left(\frac{\sqrt{2} + (-\sqrt{2})}{2}, \frac{1 + 0}{2}\right) = \left(0, \frac{1}{2}\right)$

12. a. $\sqrt{(3 - 5)^2 + (-\sqrt{5} - \sqrt{5})^2} = \sqrt{4 + (-2\sqrt{5})^2} = \sqrt{4 + 20} = \sqrt{24} = 2\sqrt{6}$

b. $\left(\frac{5 + 3}{2}, \frac{\sqrt{5} + (-\sqrt{5})}{2}\right) = (4, 0)$

13. a. $\sqrt{[(1-\sqrt{5})-(1+\sqrt{5})]^2+[(-2+\sqrt{3})-(2+\sqrt{3})]^2}=$
$\sqrt{(-2\sqrt{5})^2+(-4)^2}=\sqrt{20+16}=\sqrt{36}=6$

b. $\left(\frac{1+\sqrt{5}+1-\sqrt{5}}{2},\frac{2+\sqrt{3}+(-2)+\sqrt{3}}{2}\right)=\left(\frac{2}{2},\frac{2\sqrt{3}}{2}\right)=(1,\sqrt{3})$

14. a. $\sqrt{[(\sqrt{6}-1)-(\sqrt{6}+1)]^2+[(\sqrt{3}+\sqrt{2})-(\sqrt{3}-\sqrt{2})]^2}=$
$\sqrt{(-2)^2+2(\sqrt{2})^2}=\sqrt{4+8}=\sqrt{12}=2\sqrt{3}$

b. $\left(\frac{\sqrt{6}+1+\sqrt{6}-1}{2},\frac{\sqrt{3}-\sqrt{2}+\sqrt{3}+\sqrt{2}}{2}\right)=\left(\frac{2\sqrt{6}}{2},\frac{2\sqrt{3}}{2}\right)=(\sqrt{6},\sqrt{3})$

15. a. $|a-0|=|a|$ **b.** $\left(\frac{a+0}{2},\frac{b+b}{2}\right)=\left(\frac{a}{2},b\right)$

16. a. $\sqrt{[2a-(-a)]^2+(4b-b)^2}=\sqrt{(3a)^2+(3b)^2}=\sqrt{9a^2+9b^2}=\sqrt{9(a^2+b^2)}=$
$3\sqrt{a^2+b^2}$ **b.** $\left(\frac{-a+2a}{2},\frac{b+4b}{2}\right)=\left(\frac{a}{2},\frac{5b}{2}\right)$

17. a. $\sqrt{[b-a-(a+b)]^2+[b+a-(a-b)]^2}=\sqrt{(-2a)^2+(2b)^2}=$
$\sqrt{4a^2+4b^2}=\sqrt{4(a^2+b^2)}=2\sqrt{a^2+b^2}$

b. $\left(\frac{a+b+b-a}{2},\frac{a-b+b+a}{2}\right)=\left(\frac{2b}{2},\frac{2a}{2}\right)=(b,a)$

18. a. $\sqrt{(b-a)^2+(-\sqrt{ab}-\sqrt{ab})^2}=\sqrt{(b-a)^2+(-2\sqrt{ab})^2}=$
$\sqrt{b^2-2ab+a^2+4ab}=\sqrt{b^2+2ab+a^2}=\sqrt{(b+a)^2}=|b+a|=|a+b|$

b. $\left(\frac{a+b}{2},\frac{\sqrt{ab}-\sqrt{ab}}{2}\right)=\left(\frac{a+b}{2},0\right)$

B **19–24.** Let $Q=(x,y)$.

19. $\left(\frac{x+0}{2},\frac{y+0}{2}\right)=(3,5)$; $\frac{x}{2}=3$ and $\frac{y}{2}=5$; $x=6$ and $y=10$; $Q(6,10)$

20. $\left(\frac{-4+x}{2},\frac{3+y}{2}\right)=(0,0)$; $\frac{-4+x}{2}=0$ and $\frac{3+y}{2}=0$; $-4+x=0$ and $3+y=0$;
$x=4$ and $y=-3$; $Q(4,-3)$

21. $\left(\frac{-4+x}{2},\frac{0+y}{2}\right)=(3,3)$; $\frac{-4+x}{2}=3$ and $\frac{0+y}{2}=3$; $-4+x=6$ and $y=6$; $x=10$
and $y=6$; $Q(10,6)$

22. $\left(\frac{6+x}{2},\frac{-2+y}{2}\right)=(0,5)$; $\frac{6+x}{2}=0$ and $\frac{-2+y}{2}=5$; $6+x=0$ and $-2+y=10$;
$x=-6$ and $y=12$; $Q(-6,12)$

23. $\left(\frac{h+x}{2},\frac{k+y}{2}\right)=(0,0)$; $\frac{h+x}{2}=0$ and $\frac{k+y}{2}=0$; $x=-h$ and $y=-k$; $Q(-h,-k)$

24. $\left(\frac{0+x}{2},\frac{0+y}{2}\right)=(h,k)$; $\frac{x}{2}=h$ and $\frac{y}{2}=k$; $x=2h$ and $y=2k$; $Q(2h,2k)$

25. $AB=\sqrt{17}$; $BC=\sqrt{17}$; $AC=\sqrt{34}$ **a.** Since $AB=BC$, $\triangle ABC$ is isosceles
b. $(AB)^2+(BC)^2=17+17=34=(AC)^2$; $\triangle ABC$ is right;

$$\text{Area}=\frac{1}{2}\cdot AB\cdot BC=\frac{1}{2}(\sqrt{17})(\sqrt{17})=\frac{17}{2}$$

26. $AB = \sqrt{45} = 3\sqrt{5}$; $BC = \sqrt{180} = 6\sqrt{5}$; $AC = \sqrt{225} = 15$ **a.** not isosceles

b. Since $(AB)^2 + (BC)^2 = 45 + 180 = 225 = (AC)^2$, $\triangle ABC$ is right;

Area $= \frac{1}{2} \cdot AB \cdot BC = \frac{1}{2}(3\sqrt{5})(6\sqrt{5}) = 45$

27. $AB = \sqrt{128} = 8\sqrt{2}$; $BC = \sqrt{50} = 5\sqrt{2}$; $AC = \sqrt{50} = 5\sqrt{2}$

a. Since $AC = BC$, $\triangle ABC$ is isosceles

b. $\triangle ABC$ is not right, since $(BC)^2 + (AC)^2 \neq (AB)^2$

28. $AB = 6$; $BC = \sqrt{18} = 3\sqrt{2}$; $AC = \sqrt{18} = 3\sqrt{2}$

a. Since $BC = AC$, $\triangle ABC$ is isosceles.

b. Since $(AC)^2 + (BC)^2 = 18 + 18 = 36 = (AB)^2$, $\triangle ABC$ is right;

area $= \frac{1}{2} \cdot AC \cdot BC = \frac{1}{2}(\sqrt{18})(\sqrt{18}) = \frac{18}{2} = 9$

29. Dist. from (1, 2) to (7, 4) $= \sqrt{(7-1)^2 + (4-2)^2} = \sqrt{40} = 2\sqrt{10}$; dist. from (7, 4) to (−2, 1) $= \sqrt{(7+2)^2 + (4-1)^2} = \sqrt{90} = 3\sqrt{10}$; dist. from (1, 2) to (−2, 1) $= \sqrt{(-2-1)^2 + (1-2)^2} = \sqrt{10}$; since $\sqrt{10} + 2\sqrt{10} = 3\sqrt{10}$, the points are collinear

30. Dist. from (5, 0) to (−7, 3) $= \sqrt{(-7-5)^2 + (3-0)^2} = \sqrt{12^2 + 3^2} = \sqrt{153} = 3\sqrt{17}$; dist. from (−7, 3) to (1, 1) $= \sqrt{(1+7)^2 + (1-3)^2} = \sqrt{68} = 2\sqrt{17}$; dist. from (5, 0) to (1, 1) $= \sqrt{(5-1)^2 + (1-0)^2} = \sqrt{17}$; since $\sqrt{17} + 2\sqrt{17} = 3\sqrt{17}$, the points are collinear

31. Dist. from (−5, −2) to (−2, 1) $= \sqrt{(-2+5)^2 + (1+2)^2} = \sqrt{3^2 + 3^2} = 3\sqrt{2}$; dist. from (−2, 1) to (1, 3) $= \sqrt{(1+2)^2 + (3-1)^2} = \sqrt{3^2 + 2^2} = \sqrt{13}$; dist. from (−5, −2) to (1, 3) $= \sqrt{(1+5)^2 + (3+2)^2} = \sqrt{36 + 25} = \sqrt{61}$; since $3\sqrt{2} + \sqrt{13} \neq \sqrt{61}$, not collinear

32. Dist. from (1, 5) to (2, 0) $= \sqrt{(2-1)^2 + (0-5)^2} = \sqrt{26}$; dist. from (2, 0) to (4, −10) $= \sqrt{(4-2)^2 + (-10-0)^2} = \sqrt{104} = 2\sqrt{26}$; dist. from (1, 5) to (4, −10) $= \sqrt{(4-1)^2 + (-10-5)^2} = \sqrt{234} = 3\sqrt{26}$; since $\sqrt{26} + 2\sqrt{26} = 3\sqrt{26}$, the points are collinear.

Pages 405–406 • PROBLEMS

A **1–4.** Let j be the perpendicular bisector.

1. Slope of $\overline{AB} = \frac{5-0}{0-(-3)} = \frac{5}{3}$; slope of $j = -\frac{3}{5}$; j passes through $\left(\frac{-3+0}{2}, \frac{0+5}{2}\right) = \left(-\frac{3}{2}, \frac{5}{2}\right)$; $\frac{y - \frac{5}{2}}{x - \left(-\frac{3}{2}\right)} = -\frac{3}{5}$; $y - \frac{5}{2} = -\frac{3}{5}\left(x + \frac{3}{2}\right)$, or $3x + 5y - 8 = 0$

2. Slope of $\overline{AB} = \frac{3-1}{-2-2} = -\frac{1}{2}$; slope of $j = 2$; j passes through $\left(\frac{2+(-2)}{2}, \frac{1+3}{2}\right) = (0, 2)$; $\frac{y-2}{x-0} = 2$, $y - 2 = 2x$, or $2x - y + 2 = 0$

3. Slope of $\overline{AB} = \frac{5-(-3)}{-2-8} = -\frac{4}{5}$; slope of $j = \frac{5}{4}$; j passes through $\left(\frac{8+(-2)}{2}, \frac{-3+5}{2}\right) = (3, 1)$; $\frac{y-1}{x-3} = \frac{5}{4}$; $4y - 4 = 5x - 15$, or $5x - 4y - 11 = 0$

4. Slope of $\overline{AB} = \frac{-7-(-3)}{1-(-9)} = -\frac{2}{5}$; slope of $j = \frac{5}{2}$; j passes through $\left(\frac{-9+1}{2}, \frac{-3+(-7)}{2}\right) = (-4, -5)$; $\frac{y+5}{x+4} = \frac{5}{2}$; $2y + 10 = 5x + 20$, or $5x - 2y + 10 = 0$

5. The perpendicular bisector of $\overline{AB}$, $3x + 5y - 8 = 0$, contains all points equidistant from A and B; the x-intercept of $3x + 5y - 8 = 0$ is $x = \frac{8}{3}$; the y-intercept of $3x + 5y - 8 = 0$ is $y = \frac{8}{5}$; $\left(\frac{8}{3}, 0\right)$ and $\left(0, \frac{8}{5}\right)$

6. a; $\sqrt{(x-0)^2 + (y-0)^2} = \sqrt{x^2 + y^2}$

7. $CD = |5 - 0| = 5$; $DE = \sqrt{(8-5)^2 + (5-0)^2} = \sqrt{34}$; $EF = |8 - 3| = 5$; $CF = \sqrt{(3-0)^2 + (5-0)^2} = \sqrt{34}$; $CE = \sqrt{(8-0)^2 + (5-0)^2} = \sqrt{89}$; $DF = \sqrt{(3-5)^2 + (5-0)^2} = \sqrt{29}$; $(CD)^2 + (DE)^2 + (EF)^2 + (CF)^2 = 5^2 + (\sqrt{34})^2 + 5^2 + (\sqrt{34})^2 = 118$; $(CE)^2 + (DF)^2 = (\sqrt{89})^2 + (\sqrt{29})^2 = 118$; $118 = 118$

8. Let E, F, G, and H be the midpoints of $\overline{AB}$, $\overline{BC}$, $\overline{CD}$, and $\overline{DA}$, respectively. $E = \left(\frac{-2+2}{2}, \frac{3+7}{2}\right) = (0, 5)$; $F = \left(\frac{2+6}{2}, \frac{7+1}{2}\right) = (4, 4)$; $G = \left(\frac{6+0}{2}, \frac{1+(-3)}{2}\right) = (3, -1)$; $H = \left(\frac{-2+0}{2}, \frac{3+(-3)}{2}\right) = (-1, 0)$; $EF = \sqrt{(4-0)^2 + (4-5)^2} = \sqrt{17}$; $FG = \sqrt{(3-4)^2 + (-1-4)^2} = \sqrt{26}$; $GH = \sqrt{(-1-3)^2 + (0+1)^2} = \sqrt{17}$; $EH = \sqrt{(0+1)^2 + (5-0)^2} = \sqrt{26}$; since $EF = GH$ and $FG = EH$, $EFGH$ is a parallelogram.

B

9. Let $A(0, 0)$, $B(a, 0)$, and $C(b, c)$ be the vertices of a triangle. Let E and F be the midpoints of $\overline{AB}$ and $\overline{BC}$ respectively. $E = \left(\frac{0+a}{2}, \frac{0+0}{2}\right) = \left(\frac{a}{2}, 0\right)$; $F = \left(\frac{a+b}{2}, \frac{0+c}{2}\right) = \left(\frac{a+b}{2}, \frac{c}{2}\right)$; Slope of $\overline{EF} = \frac{\frac{c}{2} - 0}{\frac{a+b}{2} - \frac{a}{2}} = \frac{c}{a+b-a} = \frac{c}{b}$; slope of $\overline{AC} = \frac{c-0}{b-0} = \frac{c}{b}$; $\therefore \overline{AC} \parallel \overline{EF}$. $EF = \sqrt{\left(\frac{a+b}{2} - \frac{a}{2}\right)^2 + \left(\frac{c}{2} - 0\right)^2} = \sqrt{\left(\frac{b}{2}\right)^2 + \left(\frac{c}{2}\right)^2} = \sqrt{\frac{b^2 + c^2}{4}} = \frac{1}{2}\sqrt{b^2 + c^2}$; $AC = \sqrt{(b-0)^2 + (c-0)^2} = \sqrt{b^2 + c^2}$; $\therefore EF = \frac{1}{2}AC$

10. Methods may vary; example: let M, N, and P be the given points. Draw $\overline{NP}$ and construct j through M parallel to $\overline{NP}$. Draw $\overline{MP}$ and construct k through N parallel to $\overline{MP}$, intersecting j at A. Extend $\overrightarrow{AN}$ through N to B so that $NB = AN$; extend $\overrightarrow{AM}$ through M to C so that $MC = AM$. Draw $\overline{BC}$. $\triangle ABC$ is the desired triangle.

11. Let $P_1(x_1, y_1)$ and $P_2(x_2, y_2)$ be any two points. Their midpoint $M = \left(\frac{x_1 + x_2}{2}, \frac{y_1 + y_2}{2}\right)$.

$P_1P_2 = \sqrt{(x_2 - x_1)^2 + (y_2 - y_1)^2}$; $MP_1 = \sqrt{\left(\frac{x_1 + x_2}{2} - x_1\right)^2 + \left(\frac{y_1 + y_2}{2} - y_1\right)^2} =$

$\sqrt{\left(\frac{x_2 - x_1}{2}\right)^2 + \left(\frac{y_2 - y_1}{2}\right)^2} = \frac{1}{2}\sqrt{(x_2 - x_1)^2 + (y_2 - y_1)^2} = \frac{1}{2}P_1P_2$;

$MP_2 = \sqrt{\left(\frac{x_1 + x_2}{2} - x_2\right)^2 + \left(\frac{y_1 + y_2}{2} - y_2\right)^2} = \sqrt{\left(\frac{x_1 - x_2}{2}\right)^2 + \left(\frac{y_1 - y_2}{2}\right)^2} =$

$\frac{1}{2}\sqrt{(x_2 - x_1)^2 + (y_2 - y_1)^2} = \frac{1}{2}P_1P_2 \therefore MP_1 = MP_2 = \frac{1}{2}P_1P_2$

C

12. Let $A(0, 0)$, $B(a, 0)$, $C(a + b, c)$, and $D(b, c)$ be the vertices of a parallelogram. $AB = |a - 0| = |a|$; $BC = \sqrt{(a + b - a)^2 + (c - 0)^2} = \sqrt{b^2 + c^2}$; $CD = |a + b - b| = |a|$; $AD = \sqrt{b^2 + c^2}$; $AC = \sqrt{(a + b)^2 + c^2}$; $BD = \sqrt{(a - b)^2 + c^2}$. $(AB)^2 + (BC)^2 + (CD)^2 + (AD)^2 = a^2 + (b^2 + c^2) + a^2 + (b^2 + c^2) = 2a^2 + 2b^2 + 2c^2$; $(AC)^2 + (BD)^2 = ((a + b)^2 + c^2) + ((a - b)^2 + c^2) = a^2 + 2ab + b^2 + c^2 + a^2 - 2ab + b^2 + c^2 = 2a^2 + 2b^2 + 2c^2$. $\therefore (AB)^2 + (BC)^2 + (CD)^2 + (AD)^2 = (AC)^2 + (BD)^2$

13. Let $A(0, 0)$, $B(2a, 0)$, $C(2b, 2c)$, and $D(2d, 2e)$ be the vertices of a quadrilateral. Let E, F, G, and H be the midpoints of $\overline{AB}$, $\overline{BC}$, $\overline{CD}$, and $\overline{AD}$, respectively. $E = (a, 0)$; $F = (a + b, c)$; $G = (b + d, c + e)$; $H = (d, e)$. Slope of $\overline{EF} = \frac{c - 0}{a + b - a} = \frac{c}{b}$; slope of $\overline{FG} = \left(\frac{c + e - c}{b + d - (a + b)}\right) = \frac{e}{d - a}$; slope of $\overline{GH} = \frac{e - (c + e)}{d - (b + d)} = \frac{-c}{-b} = \frac{c}{b}$; slope of $\overline{EH} = \frac{e - 0}{d - a} = \frac{e}{d - a}$. Since $\overline{EF} \parallel \overline{GH}$ and $\overline{FG} \parallel \overline{EH}$, $EFGH$ is a parallelogram.

14. a. Since L_1 and L_2 intersect at (r, s), $s = m_1r + b_1$ and $s = m_2r + b_2$; let $T_1 = (x_1, y_1)$ and $T_2 = (x_2, y_2)$; since T_1 and T_2 are on $x = r + 1$, $x_1 = r + 1$ and $x_2 = r + 1$; $y_1 = m_1x_1 + b_1 = m_1(r + 1) + b_1 = m_1r + m_1 + b_1 = s + m_1$ and $y_2 = m_2x_2 + b_2 = m_2(r + 1) + b_2 = m_2r + m_2 + b_2 = s + m_2$; $T_1 = (r + 1, s + m_1)$ and $T_2 = (r + 1, s + m_2)$.

b. $T_1T_2 = \sqrt{[r + 1 - (r + 1)]^2 + [s + m_1 - (s + m_2)]^2} = \sqrt{(m_1 - m_2)^2} = |m_1 - m_2|$; $PT_1 = \sqrt{[r - (r + 1)]^2 + [s - (s + m_1)]^2} = \sqrt{1 + m_1^2}$; $PT_2 = \sqrt{[r - (r + 1)]^2 + [s - (s + m_2)]^2} = \sqrt{1 + m_2^2}$

c. $(T_1T_2)^2 = (m_1 - m_2)^2 = m_1^2 - 2m_1m_2 + m_2^2 = m_1^2 - 2(-1) + m_2^2 = m_1^2 + 2 + m_2^2 = m_1^2 + 1 + m_2^2 + 1 = (PT_1)^2 + (PT_2)^2$

d. Since $\triangle T_1PT_2$ has a right angle at P, $(T_1T_2)^2 = (PT_1)^2 + (PT_2)^2$; $(m_1 - m_2)^2 = 1 + m_1^2 + 1 + m_2^2$; $m_1^2 - 2m_1m_2 + m_2^2 = 2 + m_1^2 + m_2^2$; $-2m_1m_2 = 2$; $m_1m_2 = -1$.

Page 406 • MIXED REVIEW EXERCISES

1.
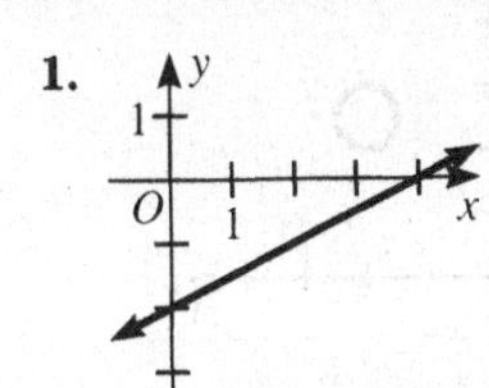

2.
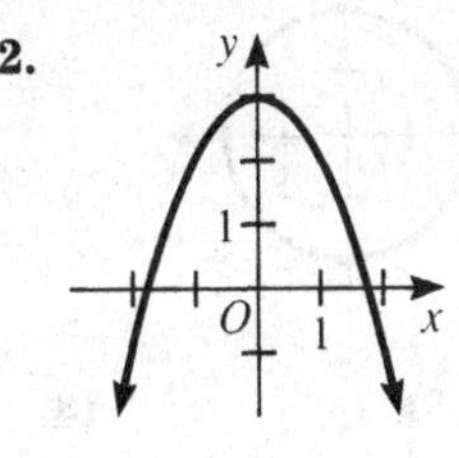

3.
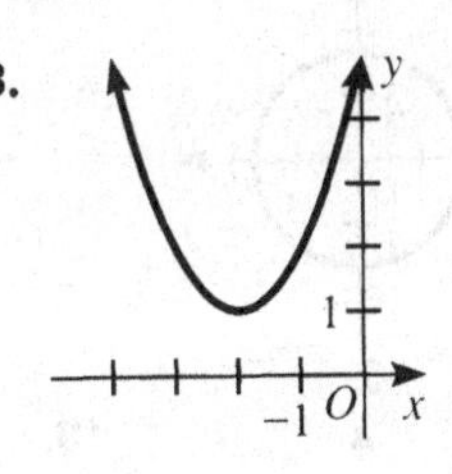

4. $f(-3) = -(-3) + 5 = 8$

5. $g(-3) = \dfrac{(-3) - 2}{3(-3) - 1} = \dfrac{-5}{-10} = \dfrac{1}{2}$

6. $h(-3) = (-3)^5 - 7(-3)^3 - 13(-3) + 11 = -243 + 189 + 39 + 11 = -4$

Page 406 • COMPUTER EXERCISES

1.
```
10 INPUT "ENTER X1, Y1: "; X1, Y1
20 INPUT "ENTER X2, Y2: "; X2, Y2
30 LET D = SQR((Y2 - Y1) ↑ 2 + (X2 - X1) ↑ 2)
40 PRINT "DISTANCE = "; D
50 END
```

2. **a.** 7.07106782 **b.** 18.4390889 **c.** 294.49618

3.
```
10 INPUT "ENTER XA, YA: "; XA, YA
20 INPUT "ENTER XB, YB: "; XB, YB
30 INPUT "ENTER XC, YC: "; XC, YC
40 LET AB = SQR((XB - XA) ↑ 2 + (YB - YA) ↑ 2)
50 LET BC = SQR((XC - XB) ↑ 2 + (YC - YB) ↑ 2)
60 LET AC = SQR((XC - XA) ↑ 2 + (YC - YA) ↑ 2)
70 LET FLAG = 0
80 IF ABS(AB - BC - AC) < .00001 THEN LET FLAG = 1
90 IF ABS(AC - BC - AB) < .00001 THEN LET FLAG = 1
100 IF ABS(BC - AC - AB) < .00001 THEN LET FLAG = 1
110 IF FLAG = 0 THEN PRINT "PERIMETER = "; AB + BC + AC
120 IF FLAG = 1 THEN PRINT "A, B, AND C ARE COLLINEAR."
130 END
```

4. **a.** PERIMETER = 22.471793 **b.** PERIMETER = 150.512173

Pages 410–411 • WRITTEN EXERCISES

A

1. $(x - 3)^2 + y^2 = 9$ 2. $x^2 + (y + 1)^2 = 1$ 3. $(x - 2)^2 + (y + 5)^2 = 64$

4. $(x + 3)^2 + (y - 1)^2 = 25$ 5. $x^2 + y^2 = 144$ 6. $(x + 4)^2 + (y + 2)^2 = 100$

7. $(x - 6)^2 + (y - 1)^2 = 2$ 8. $(x + 5)^2 + (y - 3)^2 = \dfrac{1}{36}$

9. 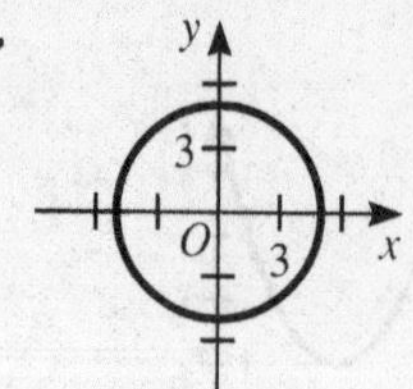

10. 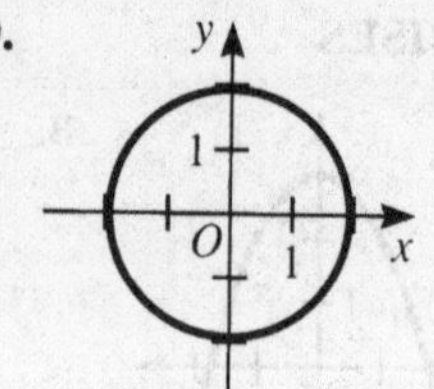

11. 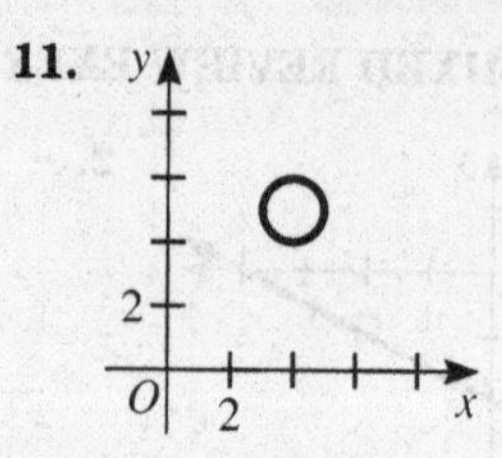

12. 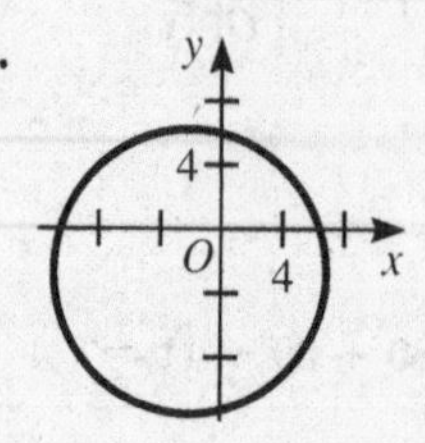

13. 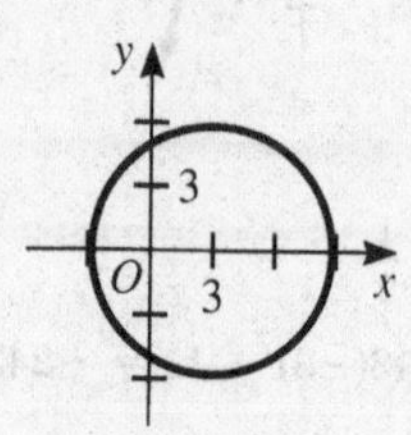

14. 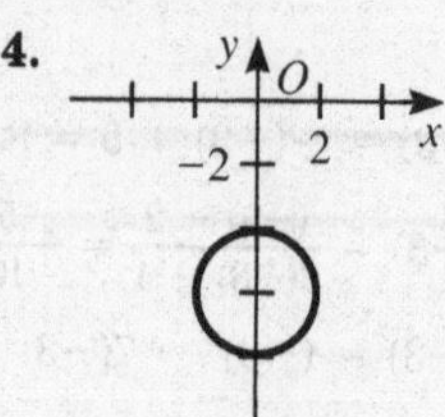

15. $x^2 + y^2 - 16 = 0$; $x^2 + y^2 = 16$; center $= (0, 0)$; radius $= \sqrt{16} = 4$

16. $x^2 + y^2 - 81 = 0$; $x^2 + y^2 = 81$; center $= (0, 0)$; radius $= \sqrt{81} = 9$

17. $x^2 + y^2 = -8y$; $x^2 + y^2 + 8y = 0$; $x^2 + (y^2 + 8y + 16) = 16$; $x^2 + (y + 4)^2 = 16$; center $= (0, -4)$; radius $= \sqrt{16} = 4$

18. $x^2 + y^2 - 6x = 0$; $x^2 - 6x + 9 + y^2 = 9$; $(x - 3)^2 + y^2 = 9$; center $= (3, 0)$; radius $= 3$

19. $x^2 + y^2 - 4x + 2y - 4 = 0$; $x^2 - 4x + 4 + y^2 + 2y + 1 = 4 + 4 + 1$; $(x - 2)^2 + (y + 1)^2 = 9$; center $= (2, -1)$; radius $= \sqrt{9} = 3$

20. $x^2 + y^2 + 10x - 4y + 20 = 0$; $x^2 + 10x + 25 + y^2 - 4y + 4 = -20 + 25 + 4$; $(x + 5)^2 + (y - 2)^2 = 9$; center $= (-5, 2)$; radius $= \sqrt{9} = 3$.

21. $x^2 + y^2 + 8x + 2y + 18 = 0$; $x^2 + 8x + 16 + y^2 + 2y + 1 = -18 + 16 + 1$; $(x + 4)^2 + (y + 1)^2 = -1$; no graph

22. $x^2 + y^2 + 12x - 6y = 0$; $x^2 + 12x + 36 + y^2 - 6y + 9 = 36 + 9$; $(x + 6)^2 + (y - 3)^2 = 45$; center $= (-6, 3)$; radius $= \sqrt{45} = 3\sqrt{5}$

23. $x^2 + y^2 + 3x - 4y = 0$; $x^2 + 3x + \frac{9}{4} + y^2 - 4y + 4 = \frac{9}{4} + 4$; $\left(x + \frac{3}{2}\right)^2 + (y - 2)^2 = \frac{25}{4}$; center $= \left(-\frac{3}{2}, 2\right)$; radius $= \sqrt{\frac{25}{4}} = \frac{5}{2}$

24. $x^2 + y^2 - 5y + 4 = 0$; $x^2 + y^2 - 5y + \frac{25}{4} = -4 + \frac{25}{4}$; $x^2 + \left(y - \frac{5}{2}\right)^2 = \frac{9}{4}$; center $= \left(0, \frac{5}{2}\right)$; radius $= \sqrt{\frac{9}{4}} = \frac{3}{2}$

B **25.** 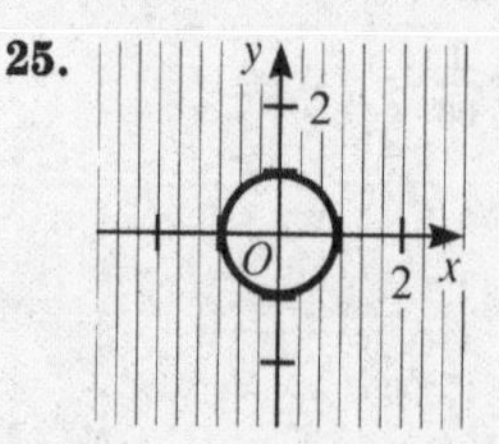

26. 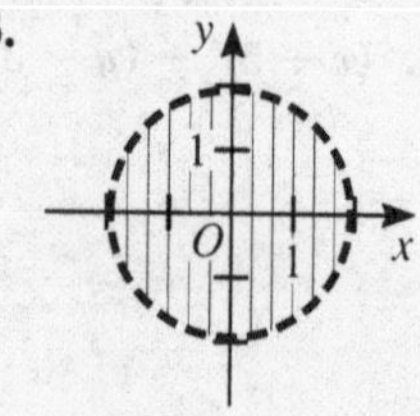

27. $x^2 + y^2 - 4y > 0;$
$x^2 + y^2 - 4y + 4 > 4;$
$x^2 + (y - 2)^2 > 4;$

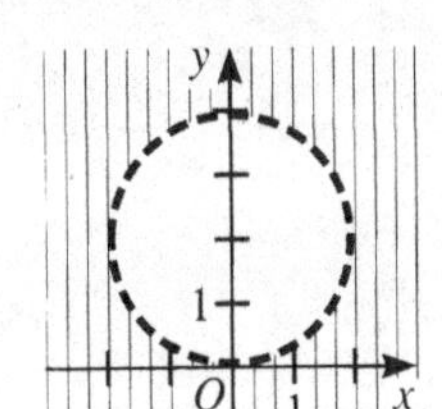

28. $x^2 + y^2 \geq 2y;$
$x^2 + y^2 - 2y + 1 \geq 1;$
$x^2 + (y - 1)^2 \geq 1;$

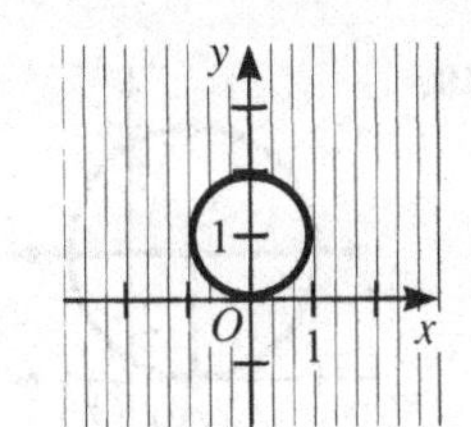

29. $x^2 + y^2 + 6x - 6y + 9 \leq 0; x^2 + 6x + 9 + y^2 - 6y + 9 \leq -9 + 9 + 9;$
$(x + 3)^2 + (y - 3)^2 \leq 9;$

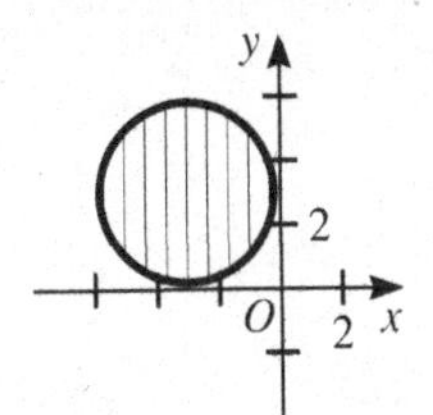

30. $x^2 + y^2 + 4x - 10y < 7; x^2 + 4x + 4 + y^2 - 10y + 25 < 7 + 4 + 25;$
$(x + 2)^2 + (y - 5)^2 < 36;$

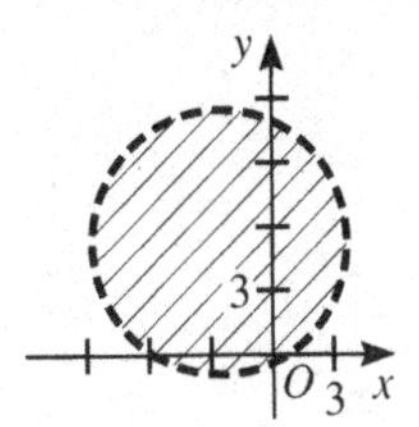

31. $4x^2 + 4y^2 - 16x - 24y + 36 = 0; x^2 + y^2 - 4x - 6y + 9 = 0;$
$x^2 - 4x + 4 + y^2 - 6y + 9 = -9 + 4 + 9; (x - 2)^2 + (y - 3)^2 = 4;$
center = (2, 3); radius = 2

32. $9x^2 + 9y^2 + 6x + 18y + 9 = 0; x^2 + y^2 + \frac{2}{3}x + 2y + 1 = 0; x^2 + \frac{2}{3}x + \frac{1}{9} +$

$y^2 + 2y + 1 = -1 + \frac{1}{9} + 1; \left(x + \frac{1}{3}\right)^2 + (y + 1)^2 = \frac{1}{9}$; center = $\left(-\frac{1}{3}, -1\right)$;

radius = $\frac{1}{3}$

33. $16x^2 + 16y^2 - 32x + 8y = 0; x^2 + y^2 - 2x + \frac{1}{2}y = 0; x^2 - 2x + 1 + y^2 +$

$\frac{1}{2}y + \frac{1}{16} = 1 + \frac{1}{16}; (x - 1)^2 + \left(y + \frac{1}{4}\right)^2 = \frac{17}{16}$; center = $\left(1, -\frac{1}{4}\right)$; radius = $\frac{\sqrt{17}}{4}$

34. $3x^2 + 3y^2 - 6x + 24y + 24 = 0; x^2 + y^2 - 2x + 8y + 8 = 0; x^2 - 2x + 1 +$
$y^2 + 8y + 16 = -8 + 1 + 16; (x - 1)^2 + (y + 4)^2 = 9$; center = (1, −4); radius = 3

35. $(x - 0)^2 + (y - 5)^2 = r^2; (0 - 0)^2 + (0 - 5)^2 = r^2; 25 = r^2; x^2 + (y - 5)^2 = 25$

36. $(x + 2)^2 + y^2 = r^2; (2 + 2)^2 + 0^2 = r^2; 16 = r^2; (x + 2)^2 + y^2 = 16$

37. center $= \left(\frac{2+0}{2}, \frac{5+3}{2}\right) = (1, 4)$; $r = \frac{1}{2}\sqrt{(0-2)^2 + (3-5)^2} = \frac{1}{2}\sqrt{8} = \sqrt{2}$;
$(x-1)^2 + (y-4)^2 = 2$

38.

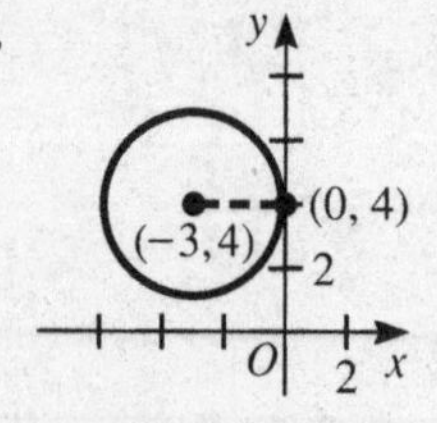

$(x+3)^2 + (y-4)^2 = 9$

39.

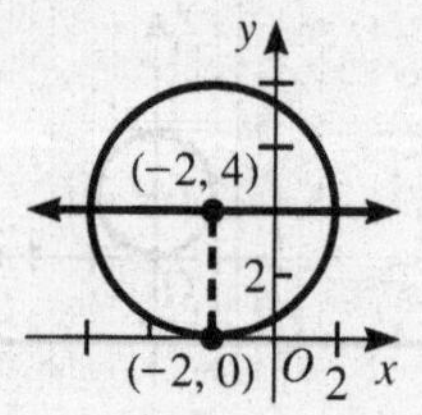

$(x+2)^2 + (y-4)^2 = 16$

40.

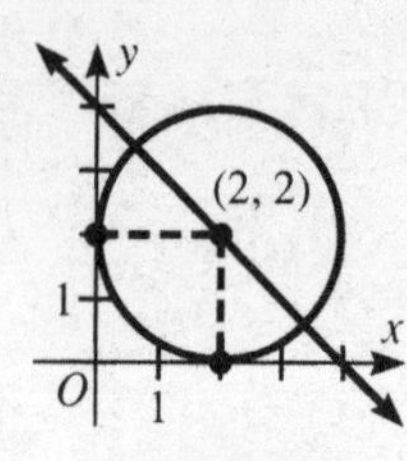

$(x-2)^2 + (y-2)^2 = 4$

41.

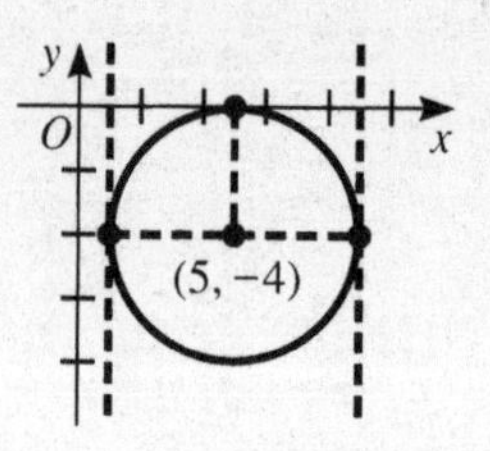

$(x-5)^2 + (y+4)^2 = 16$

42.

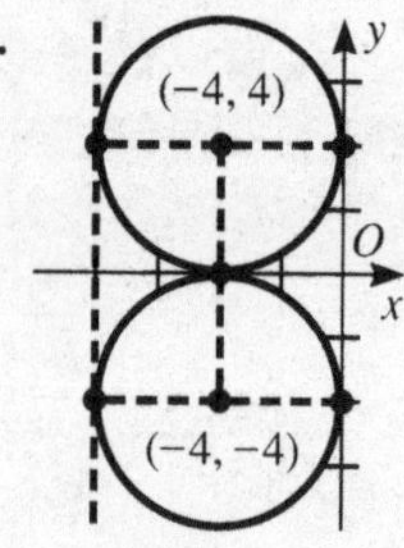

$(x+4)^2 + (y-4)^2 = 16$ or $(x+4)^2 + (y+4)^2 = 16$

43.

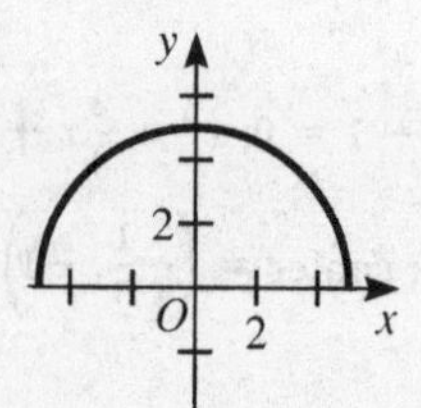

44.

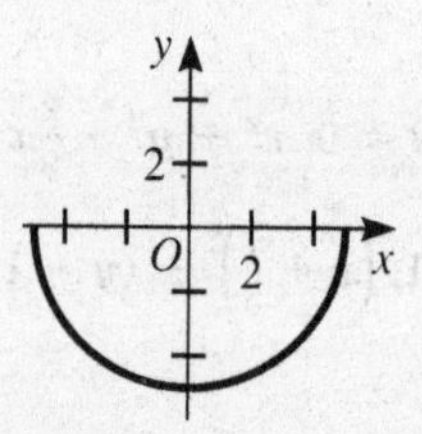

45. $y = \sqrt{4x - x^2}$; $y^2 = 4x - x^2$; $x^2 - 4x + 4 + y^2 = 4$; $(x - 2)^2 + y^2 = 4$ and $y \geq 0$;

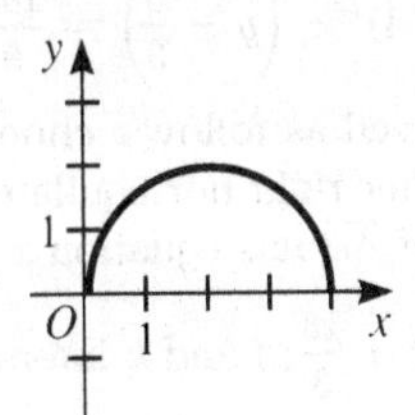

46. $x = \sqrt{2y - y^2}$; $x^2 = 2y - y^2$; $y^2 - 2y + 1 + x^2 = 1$; $x^2 + (y - 1)^2 = 1$ and $x \geq 0$;

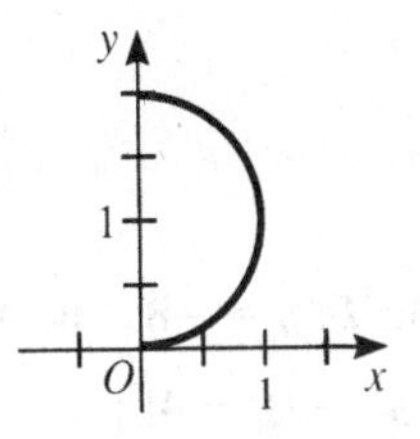

47. Let the buoys be positioned at $O(0, 0)$ and $B(3, 0)$. A point $P(x, y)$ is on the path of the boat if $PO = 2(PB)$; $\sqrt{x^2 + y^2} = 2\sqrt{(x - 3)^2 + y^2}$; $x^2 + y^2 = 4[(x^2 - 6x + 9) + y^2]$; $x^2 + y^2 = 4x^2 - 24x + 36 + 4y^2$; $3x^2 - 24x + 3y^2 = -36$; $x^2 - 8x + y^2 = -12$; $x^2 - 8x + 16 + y^2 = -12 + 16$; $(x - 4)^2 + y^2 = 4$; the path is a circle centered at (4, 0) with radius 2 mi.

48. $P(x, y)$ is the midpoint of the ladder and the endpoints of the ladder are $(2x, 0)$ and $(0, 2y)$. Since the ladder is 6 m long, $6 = \sqrt{(2x - 0)^2 + (2y - 0)^2}$; $36 = 4x^2 + 4y^2$; $x^2 + y^2 = 9$; the path is an arc of the circle centered where the wall meets the ground and with radius 3 m.

49. CT_1OT_2 is a square with sides of length 4; $\therefore OC = 4\sqrt{2}$ and the coordinates of C are $(0, 4\sqrt{2})$;

$x^2 + (y - 4\sqrt{2})^2 = 16$

50. Let $P(x, y)$ be any point on the semicircle; slope of $\overline{PA} = \frac{y - 0}{x - (-r)} = \frac{y}{x + r}$; slope of $\overline{PB} = \frac{y - 0}{x - r} = \frac{y}{x - r}$; $\frac{y}{x + r} \cdot \frac{y}{x - r} = \frac{y^2}{x^2 - r^2} = \frac{y^2}{-(r^2 - x^2)} = \frac{y^2}{-y^2} = -1$; since the product of the slopes of $\overline{PA}$ and $\overline{PB}$ is -1, $\overline{PA} \perp \overline{PB}$ and $\angle P$ is a right angle.

Page 411 • CHALLENGE

Answers may vary. Example: the circle with equation $(x - 4)^2 + \left(y - \frac{5}{3}\right)^2 = \frac{169}{9}$ has lattice points (0, 0), (8, 0), and (4, 6). The equation was derived as follows: choose points A, B, and C with integer coordinates so that $\triangle ABC$ is neither right nor equilateral. For $A(0, 0)$, $B(8, 0)$, and $C(4, 6)$, the perpendicular bisector, j, of $\overline{AB}$ has equation $x = 4$ and the perpendicular bisector, k, of $\overline{AC}$ has equation $y = -\frac{2}{3}x + \frac{13}{3}$; j and k intersect at $P\left(4, \frac{5}{3}\right)$ and $PC = \frac{13}{3}$. By substituting integral values for x, it can be easily shown that $(x - 4)^2 + \left(y - \frac{5}{3}\right)^2 = \frac{169}{9}$ has only 3 lattice points.

Pages 415–416 • WRITTEN EXERCISES

A 1. $F(4, 7)$ 2. $F(2, 6)$ 3. $D: y = 4$ 4. $D: x = 5$ 5. $D: y = -8$ 6. $V(0, 0)$

7. $\sqrt{(x - 0)^2 + (y - 0)^2} = \sqrt{(x - x)^2 + (y - 4)^2}$; $x^2 + y^2 = (y - 4)^2$; $x^2 = -8y + 16$

8. $\sqrt{(x - 0)^2 + (y - 0)^2} = \sqrt{(x - 4)^2 + (y - y)^2}$; $x^2 + y^2 = (x - 4)^2$; $y^2 = -8x + 16$

9. $D: y = 4$; $\sqrt{(x - 0)^2 + (y + 4)^2} = \sqrt{(x - x)^2 + (y - 4)^2}$; $x^2 + (y + 4)^2 = (y - 4)^2$; $x^2 = -16y$

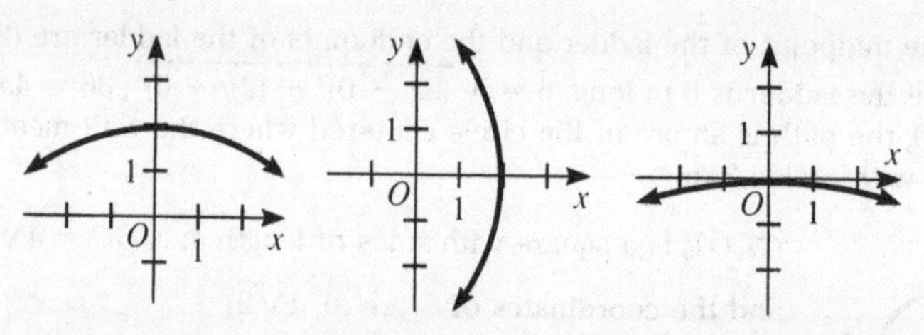

Ex. 7 Ex. 8 Ex. 9

10. $D: x = -3$; $\sqrt{(x + 3)^2 + (y - y)^2} = \sqrt{(x - 3)^2 + (y - 0)^2}$; $(x + 3)^2 = (x - 3)^2 + y^2$; $12x = y^2$

11. $F(1, 0)$; $\sqrt{(x - 1)^2 + (y - 0)^2} = \sqrt{(x + 1)^2 + (y - y)^2}$; $(x - 1)^2 + y^2 = (x + 1)^2$; $y^2 = 4x$

12. $F(0, 4)$; $\sqrt{(x - 0)^2 + (y - 4)^2} = \sqrt{(x - x)^2 + (y + 4)^2}$; $x^2 + (y - 4)^2 = (y + 4)^2$; $x^2 = 16y$

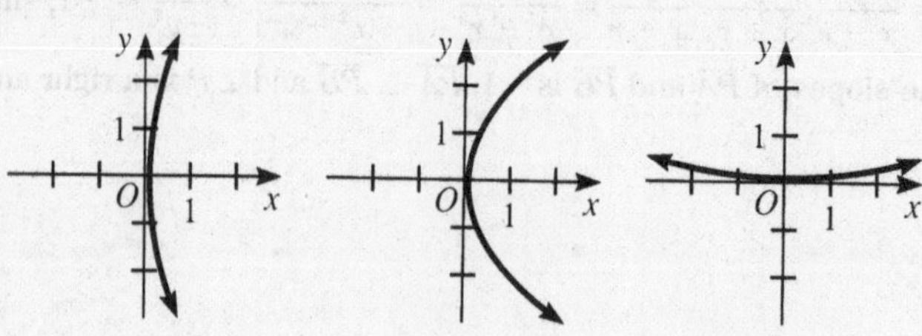

Ex. 10 Ex. 11 Ex. 12

13. $\sqrt{(x-0)^2+(y-2)^2}=\sqrt{(x-2)^2+(y-y)^2}$; $x^2+(y-2)^2=(x-2)^2$;

$x-1=-\frac{1}{4}(y-2)^2$

14. $\sqrt{(x+2)^2+(y-0)^2}=\sqrt{(x-x)^2+(y-3)^2}$; $(x+2)^2+y^2=(y-3)^2$;

$(x+2)^2=-6y+9$; $y-\frac{3}{2}=-\frac{1}{6}(x+2)^2$

15. D: $y=0$; $\sqrt{(x-3)^2+(y-4)^2}=\sqrt{(x-x)^2+(y-0)^2}$; $(x-3)^2+(y-4)^2=y^2$;

$(x-3)^2=8y-16$; $y-2=\frac{1}{8}(x-3)^2$

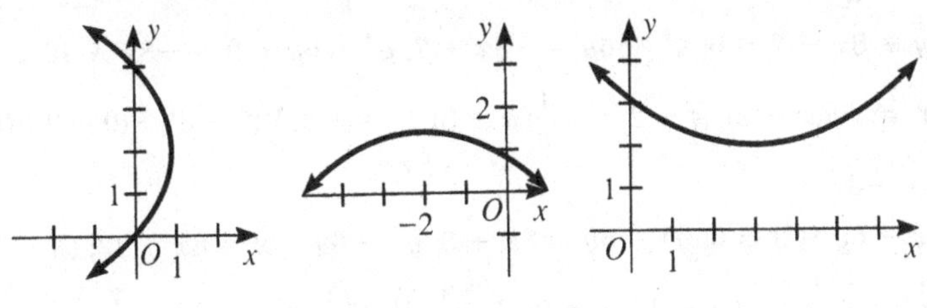

Ex. 13 **Ex. 14** **Ex. 15**

16. D: $x=-4$; $\sqrt{(x+2)^2+(y-1)^2}=\sqrt{(x+4)^2+(y-y)^2}$; $(x+2)^2+(y-1)^2=$

$(x+4)^2$; $(y-1)^2=4x+12$; $x+3=\frac{1}{4}(y-1)^2$

17. $y=\frac{1}{6}x^2$; $c=\frac{6}{4}=\frac{3}{2}$; $V(0,0)$; $F\left(0,\frac{3}{2}\right)$; D: $y=-\frac{3}{2}$; axis: $x=0$

18. $6x+y^2=0$; $x=-\frac{1}{6}y^2$; $c=-\frac{3}{2}$; $V(0,0)$; $F\left(-\frac{3}{2},0\right)$; D: $x=\frac{3}{2}$; axis: $y=0$

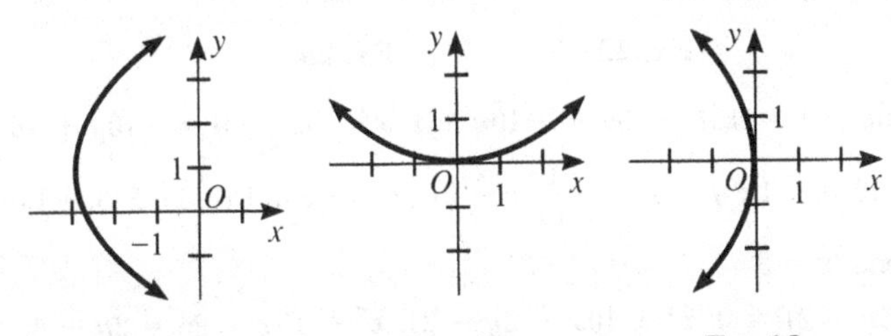

Ex. 16 **Ex. 17** **Ex. 18**

19. $4x=y^2-4y$; $4x+4=y^2-4y+4$; $4(x+1)=(y-2)^2$; $(x+1)=\frac{1}{4}(y-2)^2$;

$c=1$; $V(-1,2)$; $F(0,2)$; D: $x=-2$; axis: $y=2$

20. $x^2=y+2x$; $x^2-2x+1=y+1$; $y+1=(x-1)^2$; $c=\frac{1}{4}$; $V(1,-1)$; $F\left(1,-\frac{3}{4}\right)$;

D: $y=-\frac{5}{4}$; axis: $x=1$

(Continued)

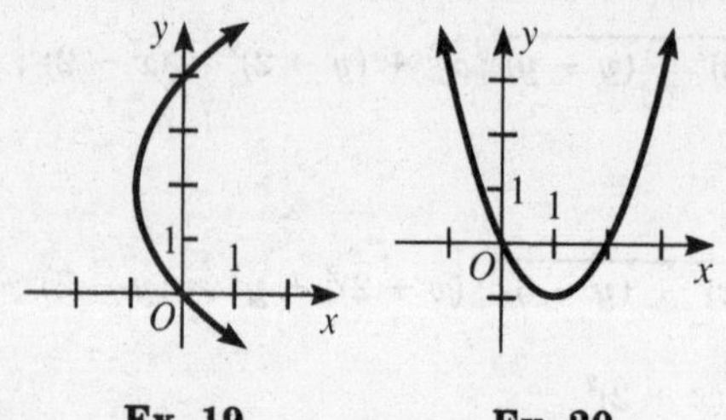

Ex. 19 **Ex. 20**

B **21.** $x^2 + 8y + 4x - 4 = 0$; $x^2 + 4x = -8y + 4$; $x^2 + 4x + 4 = -8y + 8$; $(x + 2)^2 = -8(y - 1)$; $y - 1 = -\frac{1}{8}(x + 2)^2$; $c = -2$; $V(-2, -1)$; $F(-2, 1)$; D: $y = 3$; axis: $x = -2$

22. $y^2 + 6y + 8x - 7 = 0$; $y^2 + 6y = -8x + 7$; $y^2 + 6y + 9 = -8x + 16$; $(y + 3)^2 = -8(x - 2)$; $x - 2 = -\frac{1}{8}(y + 3)^2$; $c = -2$; $V(2, -3)$; $F(0, -3)$; D: $x = 4$; axis: $y = -3$

23. $y^2 - 8x - 6y - 3 = 0$; $y^2 - 6y = 8x + 3$; $y^2 - 6y + 9 = 8x + 12$; $(y - 3)^2 = 8\left(x + \frac{3}{2}\right)$; $x + \frac{3}{2} = \frac{1}{8}(y - 3)^2$; $c = 2$; $V\left(-\frac{3}{2}, 3\right)$; $F\left(\frac{1}{2}, 3\right)$; D: $x = -\frac{7}{2}$; axis: $y = 3$

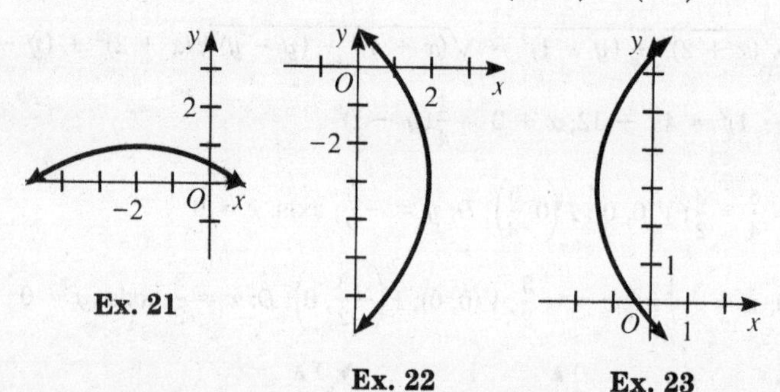

Ex. 21 **Ex. 22** **Ex. 23**

24. $x^2 - 6x + 10y - 1 = 0$; $x^2 - 6x = -10y + 1$; $x^2 - 6x + 9 = -10y + 10$; $(x - 3)^2 = -10(y - 1)$; $y - 1 = -\frac{1}{10}(x - 3)^2$; $c = -2.5$; $V(3, 1)$; $F(3, -1.5)$; D: $y = 3.5$; axis: $x = 3$

25. $x^2 + 10x - 2y + 21 = 0$; $x^2 + 10x = 2y - 21$; $x^2 + 10x + 25 = 2y + 4$; $(x + 5)^2 = 2(y + 2)$; $y + 2 = \frac{1}{2}(x + 5)^2$; $c = \frac{1}{2}$; $V(-5, -2)$; $F(-5, -1.5)$; D: $y = -2.5$; axis: $x = -5$

26. $y^2 + 3x - 2y - 11 = 0$; $y^2 - 2y = -3x + 11$; $y^2 - 2y + 1 = -3x + 12$; $(y - 1)^2 = -3(x - 4)$; $-\frac{1}{3}(y - 1)^2 = x - 4$; $c = -0.75$; $V(4, 1)$; $F(3.25, 1)$; D: $x = 4.75$; axis: $y = 1$

(Continued)

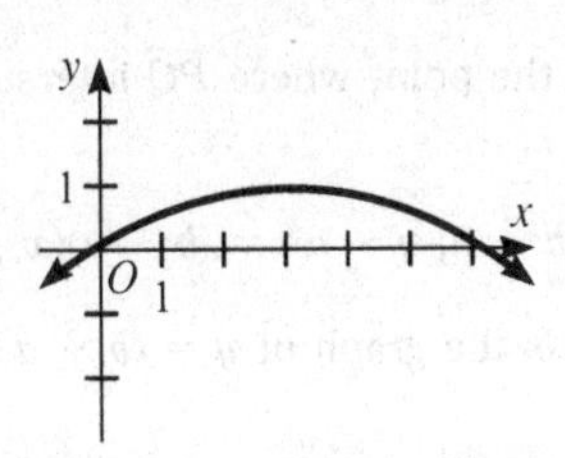

Ex. 24

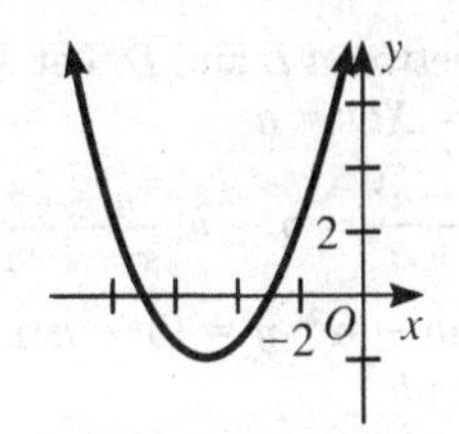

Ex. 25

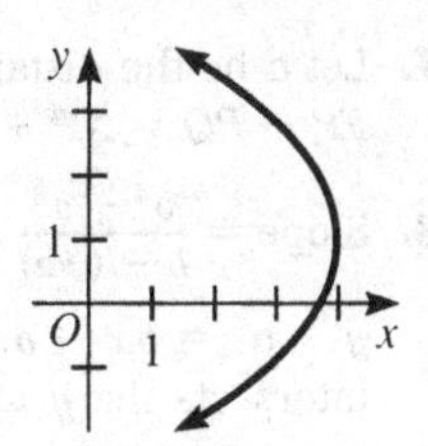

Ex. 26

27.

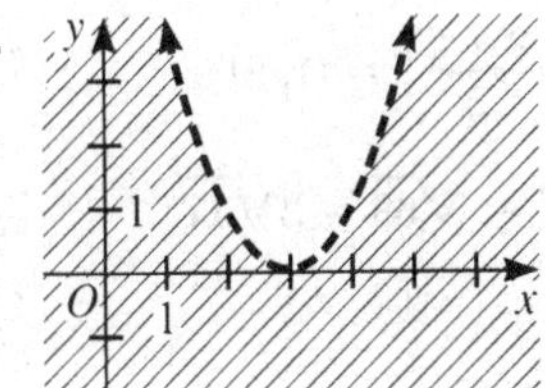

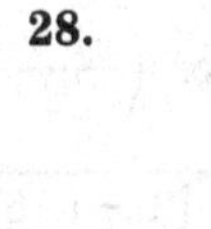
28.

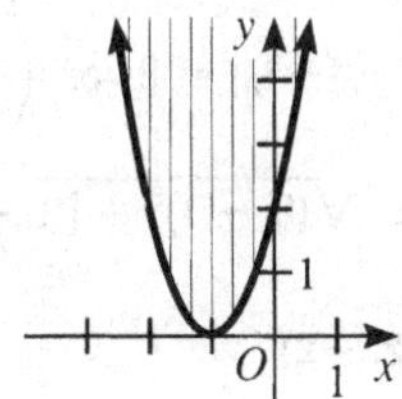

29.

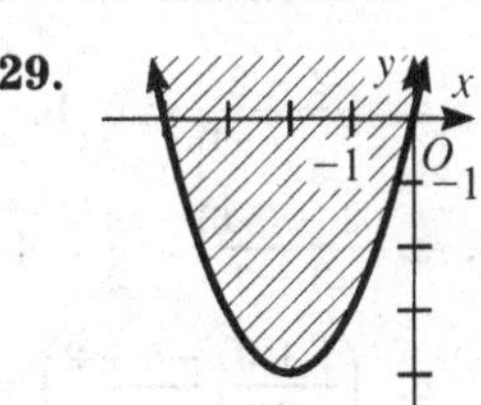

30. $x - 11 < y^2 + 6y$; $x - 11 + 9 < y^2 + 6y + 9$; $x - 2 < (y + 3)^2$

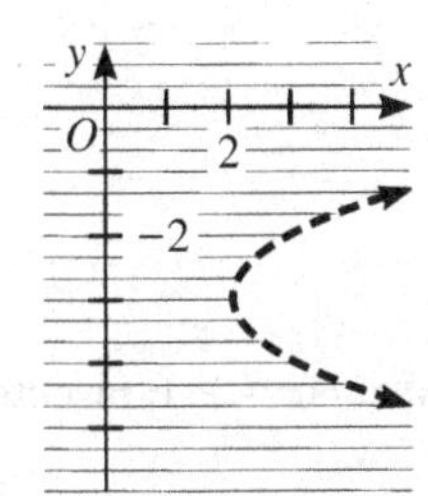

31.

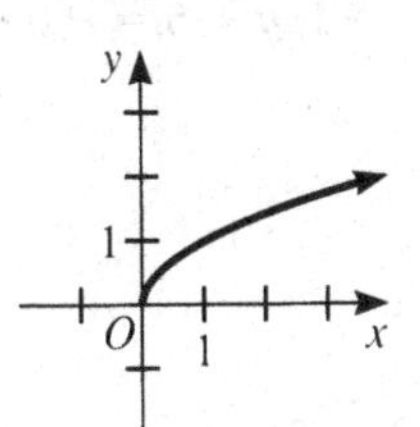

32.

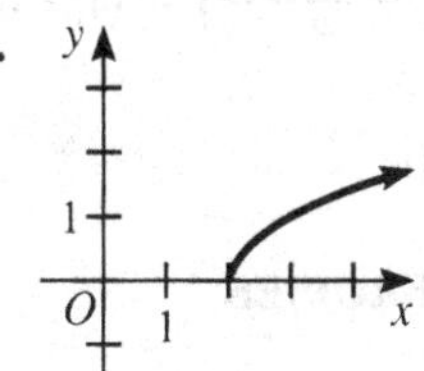

33.

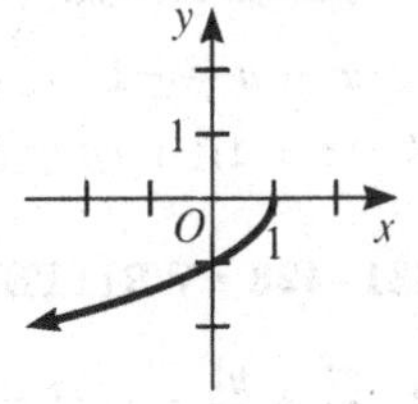

34.

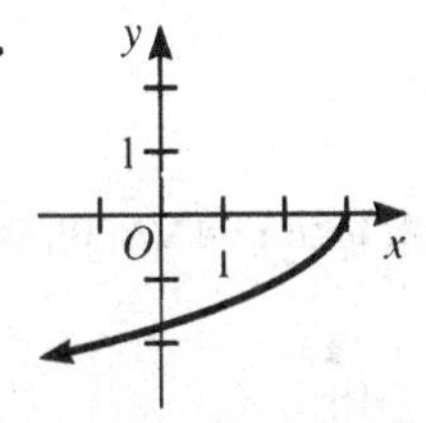

C **35.** Let F and j be the focus and directrix of the parabola and A, B, and C the points where perpendiculars from P, F, and Q intersect j. Since $\overleftrightarrow{PQ} \parallel j$, $PA = FB$ and $QC = FB$; by the definition of a parabola, $PF = PA$ and $FQ = QC$; then $PQ = PF + FQ = PA + QC = FB + FB = 2 \cdot FB$.

36. Let $P(x, y)$ be any point on the parabola; $PF = \sqrt{(x - h)^2 + (y - (k + c))^2}$ and $PD = |y - (k - c)|$. Since $PF = PD$, $(x - h)^2 + (y - k - c)^2 = (y - k + c)^2$;
$(x - h)^2 = (y - k + c)^2 - (y - k - c)^2$;
$(x - h)^2 = [(y - k + c) - (y - k - c)][(y - k + c) + (y - k - c)]$;
$(x - h)^2 = (2c)(2y - 2k)$; $(x - h)^2 = 4c(y - k)$; $y - k = \frac{1}{4c}(x - h)^2$

37. Let a be the distance between L and D. Let X be the point where $\overleftrightarrow{PQ}$ intersects D; $FP + PQ = XP + PQ = XQ = a$.

38. Slope $= \dfrac{b^2 - a^2}{b - (-a)} = \dfrac{b^2 - a^2}{b + a} = b - a; \dfrac{y - a^2}{x - (-a)} = b - a; y - a^2 = (b - a)(x + a);$
$y - a^2 = bx - ax + ab - a^2; y = (b - a)x + ab;$ the graph of $y = (b - a)x + ab$ intersects the y-axis at ab.

Page 417 • MIXED REVIEW EXERCISES

1. a. $\dfrac{2 - 2}{5 - (-3)} = 0$ **b.** $|5 - (-3)| = 8$ **c.** $\left(\dfrac{-3 + 5}{2}, \dfrac{2 + 2}{2}\right) = (1, 2)$

2. a. $\dfrac{2 - (-6)}{3 - 1} = \dfrac{8}{2} = 4$ **b.** $\sqrt{(3 - 1)^2 + [2 - (-6)]^2} = \sqrt{68} = 2\sqrt{17}$

c. $\left(\dfrac{1 + 3}{2}, \dfrac{-6 + 2}{2}\right) = (2, -2)$

3. a. $\dfrac{4 - 3}{-3 - 4} = -\dfrac{1}{7}$ **b.** $\sqrt{[4 - (-3)]^2 + (3 - 4)^2} = \sqrt{50} = 5\sqrt{2}$

c. $\left(\dfrac{4 + (-3)}{2}, \dfrac{3 + 4}{2}\right) = \left(\dfrac{1}{2}, \dfrac{7}{2}\right)$

4. $\dfrac{y - (-3)}{x - (-2)} = \dfrac{2}{3}; y + 3 = \dfrac{2}{3}(x + 2)$, or $2x - 3y = 5$

5. Slope of segment $= \dfrac{-2 - (-8)}{7 - 1} = \dfrac{6}{6} = 1$; slope of perpendicular $= -1$; bisector passes through $\left(\dfrac{7 + 1}{2}, \dfrac{-2 + (-8)}{2}\right) = (4, -5); \dfrac{y - (-5)}{x - 4} = -1; y + 5 = -1(x - 4)$ or $x + y = -1$

6. $(x + 1)^2 + (y - 3)^2 = 16$

Pages 421–423 • WRITTEN EXERCISES

A

1. $\dfrac{x^2}{9} + \dfrac{y^2}{4} = 1; c^2 = 9 - 4 = 5; c = \sqrt{5}$; foci: $(-\sqrt{5}, 0), (\sqrt{5}, 0)$

2. $\dfrac{x^2}{16} + \dfrac{y^2}{25} = 1; c^2 = 25 - 16 = 9; c = 3$; foci: $(0, -3), (0, 3)$

3. $x^2 + 9y^2 = 36; \dfrac{x^2}{36} + \dfrac{y^2}{4} = 1; c^2 = 36 - 4 = 32; c = 4\sqrt{2}$; foci: $(-4\sqrt{2}, 0), (4\sqrt{2}, 0)$

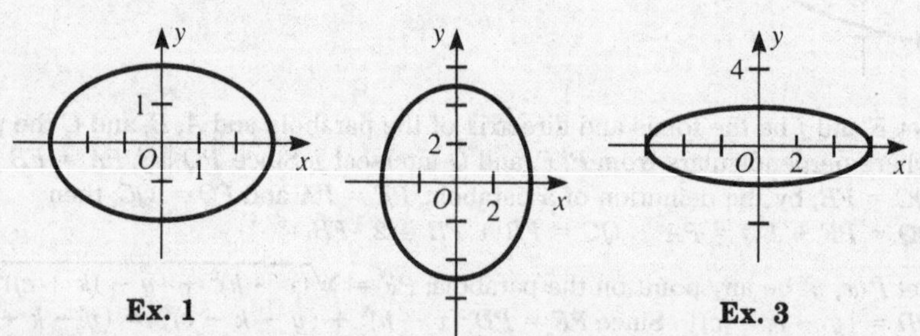

Ex. 1 Ex. 2 Ex. 3

4. $x^2 + 4y^2 = 16; \frac{x^2}{16} + \frac{y^2}{4} = 1; c^2 = 16 - 4 = 12; c = 2\sqrt{3}$; foci: $(-2\sqrt{3}, 0), (2\sqrt{3}, 0)$

5. $3x^2 + y^2 = 9; \frac{x^2}{3} + \frac{y^2}{9} = 1; c^2 = 9 - 3 = 6; c = \sqrt{6}$; foci: $(0, -\sqrt{6}), (0, \sqrt{6})$

6. $2x^2 + 3y^2 = 6; \frac{x^2}{3} + \frac{y^2}{2} = 1; c^2 = 3 - 2 = 1; c = 1$; foci: $(-1, 0), (1, 0)$

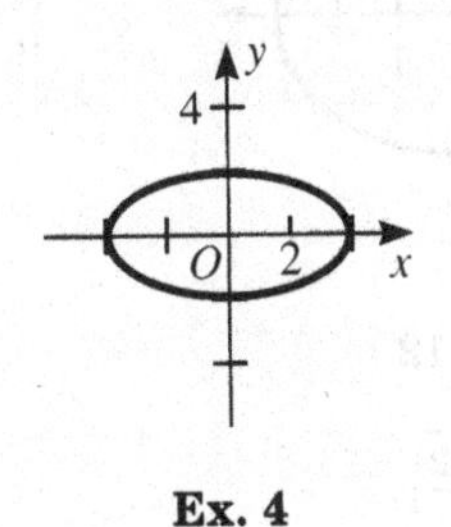

Ex. 4

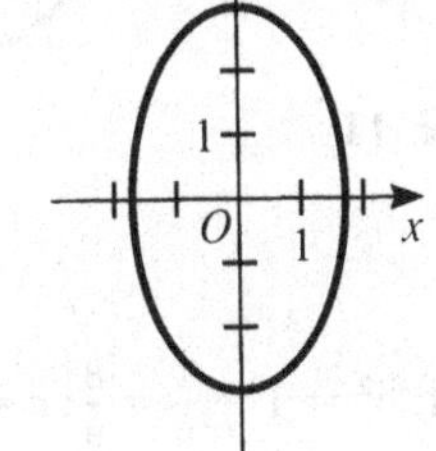

Ex. 5

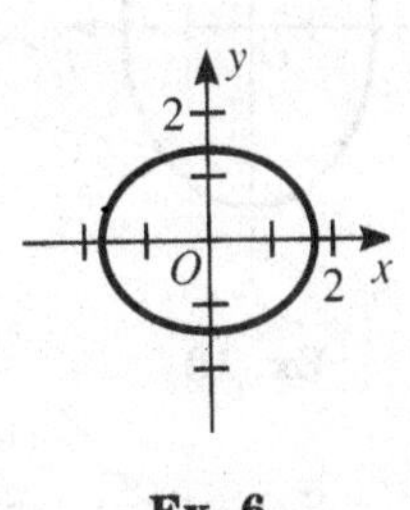

Ex. 6

7. $5x^2 + y^2 = 25; \frac{x^2}{5} + \frac{y^2}{25} = 1; c^2 = 25 - 5 = 20; c = 2\sqrt{5}$; foci: $(0, -2\sqrt{5}), (0, 2\sqrt{5})$

8. $x^2 + 25y^2 = 100; \frac{x^2}{100} + \frac{y^2}{4} = 1; c^2 = 100 - 4 = 96; c = 4\sqrt{6}$; foci: $(-4\sqrt{6}, 0)$, $(4\sqrt{6}, 0)$

9. $3x^2 + y^2 = 12; \frac{x^2}{4} + \frac{y^2}{12} = 1; c^2 = 12 - 4 = 8; c = 2\sqrt{2}$; foci: $(0, -2\sqrt{2}), (0, 2\sqrt{2})$

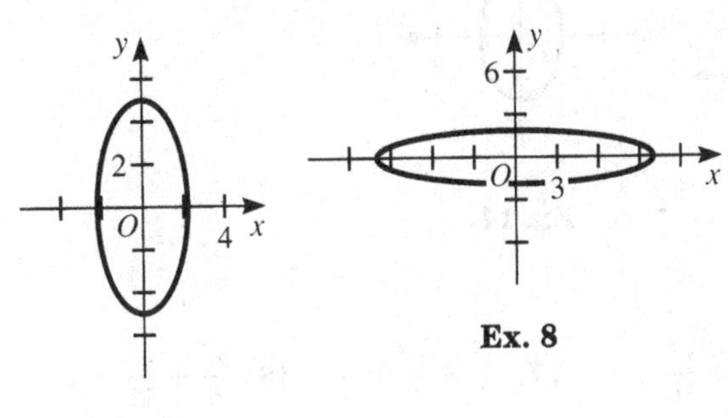

Ex. 7

Ex. 8

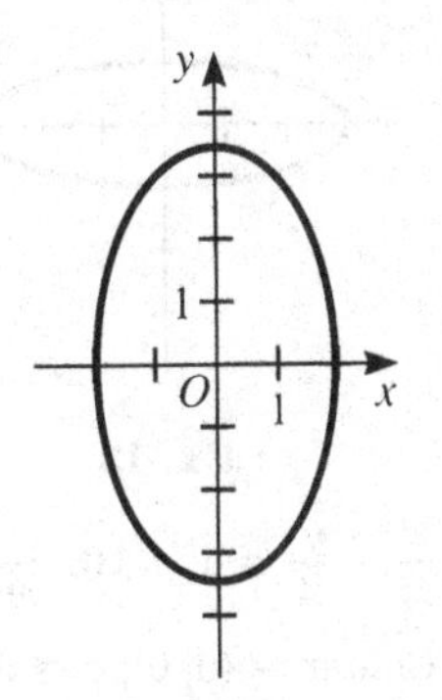

Ex. 9

10. $2x^2 + y^2 = 8; \frac{x^2}{4} + \frac{y^2}{8} = 1; c^2 = 8 - 4 = 4; c = 2$; foci: $(0, -2), (0, 2)$

11. $4x^2 + 3y^2 = 48; \frac{x^2}{12} + \frac{y^2}{16} = 1; c^2 = 16 - 12 = 4; c = 2$; foci: $(0, -2), (0, 2)$

(*Continued*)

12. $5x^2 + 9y^2 = 45; \frac{x^2}{9} + \frac{y^2}{5} = 1; c^2 = 9 - 5 = 4; c = 2$; foci: $(-2, 0), (2, 0)$

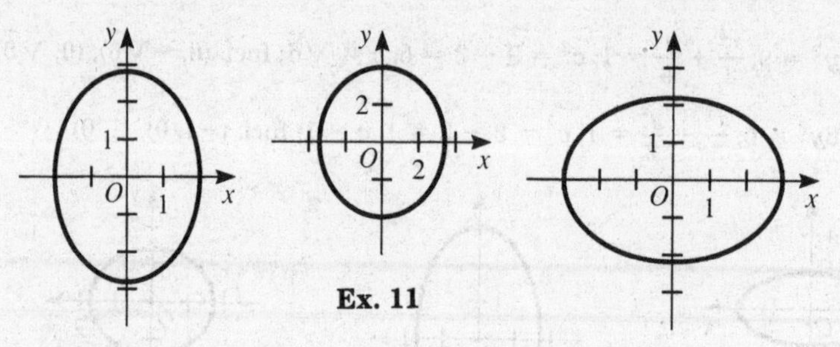

Ex. 11

Ex. 10

Ex. 12

13. $x^2 + 9y^2 = 1; \frac{x^2}{1} + \frac{y^2}{\frac{1}{9}} = 1; c^2 = 1 - \frac{1}{9} = \frac{8}{9}; c = \frac{2\sqrt{2}}{3}$;

foci: $\left(-\frac{2\sqrt{2}}{3}, 0\right), \left(\frac{2\sqrt{2}}{3}, 0\right)$

14. $9x^2 + 4y^2 = 9; \frac{x^2}{1} + \frac{y^2}{\frac{9}{4}} = 1; c^2 = \frac{9}{4} - 1 = \frac{5}{4}; c = \frac{\sqrt{5}}{2}$; foci: $\left(0, -\frac{\sqrt{5}}{2}\right), \left(0, \frac{\sqrt{5}}{2}\right)$

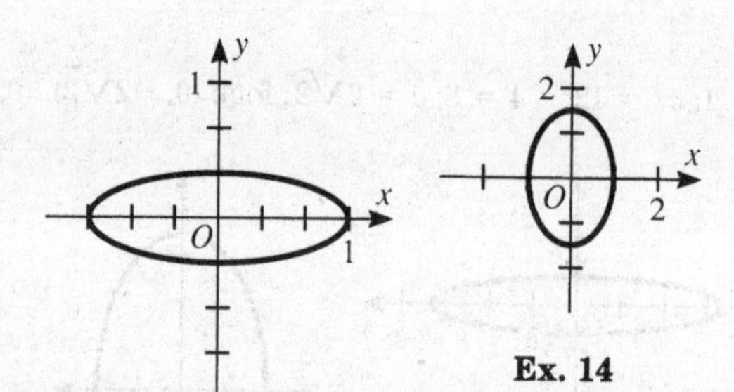

Ex. 14

Ex. 13

15. $\frac{x^2}{25} + \frac{y^2}{4} = 1$ **16.** $\frac{x^2}{9} + \frac{y^2}{16} = 1$ **17.** $\frac{x^2}{4} + \frac{y^2}{2} = 1$ **18.** $\frac{x^2}{6} + \frac{y^2}{12} = 1$

B

19. Center = $(0, 0)$; $c = 6$; $2a = 18$, $a = 9$; $a^2 = b^2 + c^2$; $81 = b^2 + 36$; $b^2 = 45$; foci are on x-axis so major axis is horizontal; $\frac{x^2}{81} + \frac{y^2}{45} = 1$

20. Center = $(0, 0)$; $c = 5$; $2a = 20$, $a = 10$; $100 = b^2 + 25$, $b^2 = 75$; foci are on y-axis so major axis is vertical; $\frac{x^2}{75} + \frac{y^2}{100} = 1$

21. Center = $(0, 0)$; $c = 4$; $2a = 24$; $a = 12$; $12^2 = b^2 + 4^2$; $b^2 = 144 - 16 = 128$; foci are on y-axis so major axis is vertical; $\frac{x^2}{128} + \frac{y^2}{144} = 1$

22. Center = $(0, 0)$; $c = 9$; $2a = 30$, $a = 15$; $(15)^2 = b^2 + (9)^2$; $b^2 = 225 - 81 = 144$; foci are on x-axis so major axis is horizontal; $\frac{x^2}{225} + \frac{y^2}{144} = 1$

23. Let $B = (0, b)$; draw the circle with center B and radius a, intersecting the major axis at F_1 and F_2; $F_1B + F_2B = a + a = 2a$, and F_1 and F_2 are the foci of the ellipse.

24. **a.** c is the distance from center to focus; since $0 \le c < a$, $0 \le \frac{c}{a} < 1$. **b.** A

25. **a.** $c = \sqrt{a^2 - b^2} = \sqrt{a^2 - a^2} = 0$ **b.** $e = \frac{c}{a} = \frac{0}{a} = 0$ **c.** At the center

d. circle

26. The origin, (0, 0)

27. Choose a coordinate system centered directly under the highest point of the arch. Equation of the arch: $\frac{x^2}{(6)^2} + \frac{y^2}{(4)^2} = 1$, with $y \ge 0$. The desired point corresponds to $x = 4$; $\frac{(4)^2}{36} + \frac{y^2}{16} = 1$; $\frac{y^2}{16} = \frac{5}{9}$, $y^2 = \frac{80}{9}$, $y = \frac{4\sqrt{5}}{3} \approx 3$ m.

28.

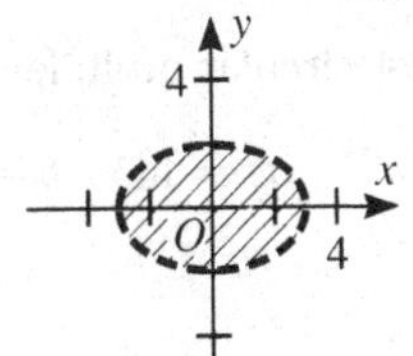

29.

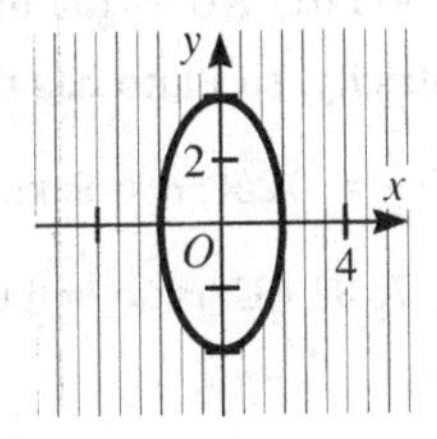

30.

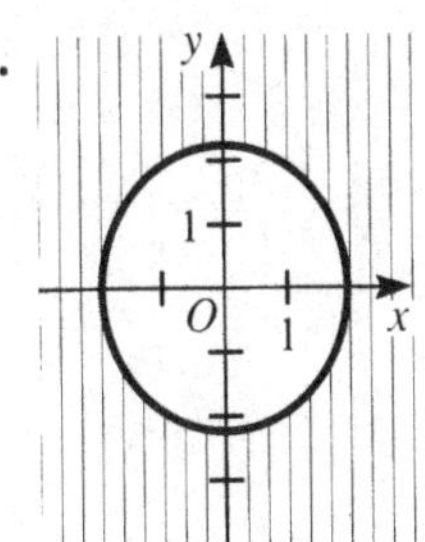

31.

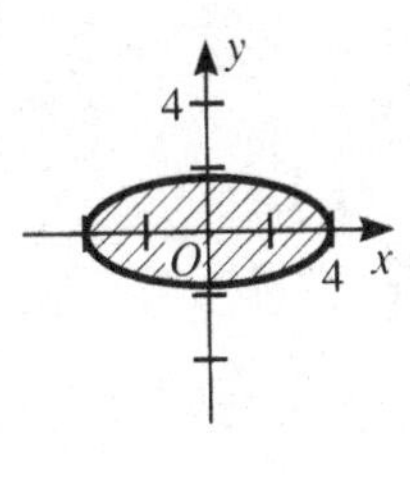

32.

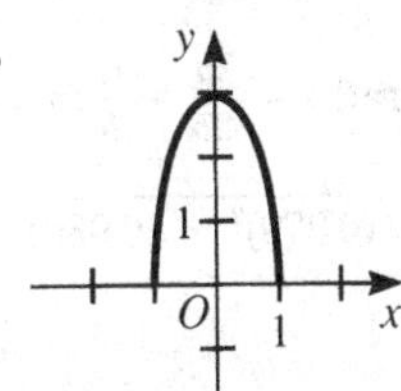

33.

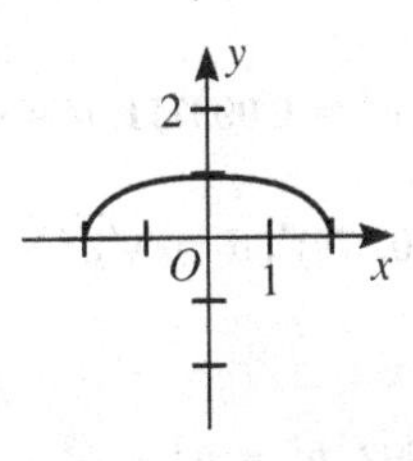

C **34.**

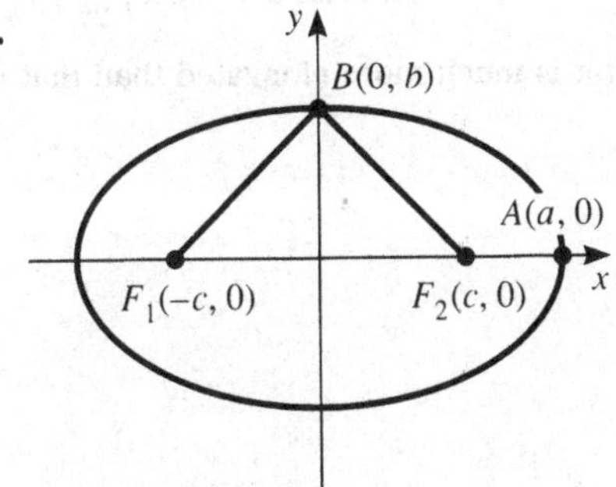

Since $F_1B = F_2B$, and $F_1B + F_2B = 2a$, $\sqrt{(-c-0)^2 + (0-b)^2} + \sqrt{(c-0)^2 + (0-b)^2} = 2a$; $2\sqrt{c^2 + b^2} = 2a$; $c^2 + b^2 = a^2$; $b^2 = a^2 - c^2$

35. Let $P(x, y)$ be any point on the ellipse. Since $PF_1 + PF_2 = 2a$, $\sqrt{[x - (-c)]^2 + (y - 0)^2} + \sqrt{(x - c)^2 + (y - 0)^2} = 2a$; $\sqrt{(x + c)^2 + y^2} = 2a - \sqrt{(x - c)^2 + y^2}$; $(x + c)^2 + y^2 = 4a^2 - 4a\sqrt{(x - c)^2 + y^2} + (x - c)^2 + y^2$; $x^2 + 2cx + c^2 + y^2 = 4a^2 - 4a\sqrt{(x - c)^2 + y^2} + x^2 - 2cx + c^2 + y^2$; $4a\sqrt{(x - c)^2 + y^2} = 4a^2 - 4cx$; $a\sqrt{(x - c)^2 + y^2} = a^2 - cx$; $a^2(x^2 - 2cx + c^2 + y^2) = a^4 - 2a^2cx + c^2x^2$; $a^2x^2 - 2a^2cx + a^2c^2 + a^2y^2 = a^4 - 2a^2cx + c^2x^2$; $(a^2 - c^2)x^2 + a^2y^2 = a^4 - a^2c^2$; $(a^2 - c^2)x^2 + a^2y^2 = a^2(a^2 - c^2)$; let $b^2 = a^2 - c^2$; $b^2x^2 + a^2y^2 = a^2b^2$; $\frac{x^2}{a^2} + \frac{y^2}{b^2} = 1$

Page 425 • APPLICATION

1. $a = 1$; $c = 0.017$; minimum distance $= a - c = 0.983$ AU ≈ 147 million km; maximum distance $= a + c = 1.017$ AU ≈ 153 million km
2. Pluto has the greatest eccentricity, so Pluto has the least circular orbit; length of major axis $= 2a = 78.88$ AU; $\frac{c}{a} = 0.250$; $c = 9.86$; $b^2 = a^2 - c^2 = 1458$; $b = 38.19$; length of minor axis $= 2b = 76.38$ AU; ratio $\approx 1.03:1$.

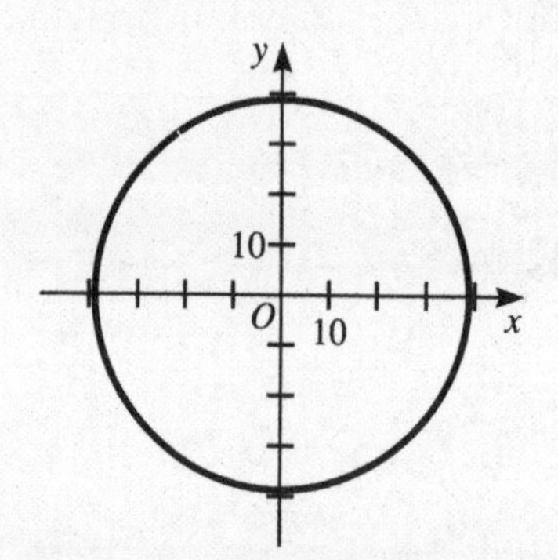

3. $a = 1$; $c = 0.017$; $b^2 = a^2 - c^2 = 0.999711$; $b = 0.9986$; ratio $= \frac{2a}{2b} = \frac{a}{b} \approx 1.0001:1$
4. $\frac{0}{(0.387)^2} + \frac{y^2}{(0.379)^2} = 1$; $y^2 = (0.379)^2$; $d = \sqrt{y^2 + c^2} = \sqrt{(0.379)^2 + (0.080)^2} \approx$ 0.387 AU
5. $a = 1.078$; $\frac{c}{a} = 0.827$; $c = 0.892$; $b^2 = a^2 - c^2 = 0.36642$; $b = 0.605$; $\frac{2a}{2b} = \frac{a}{b} \approx 1.78:1$; since the ratio is much larger, the orbit is much more elongated than that of Earth.

Pages 430–431 • WRITTEN EXERCISES

A

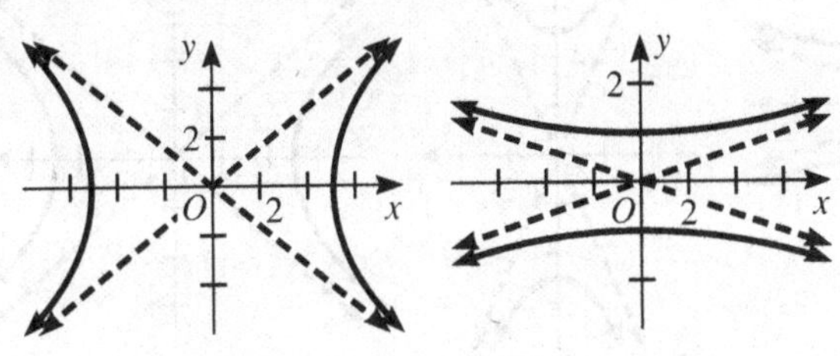

Ex. 1. a **Ex. 2. a**

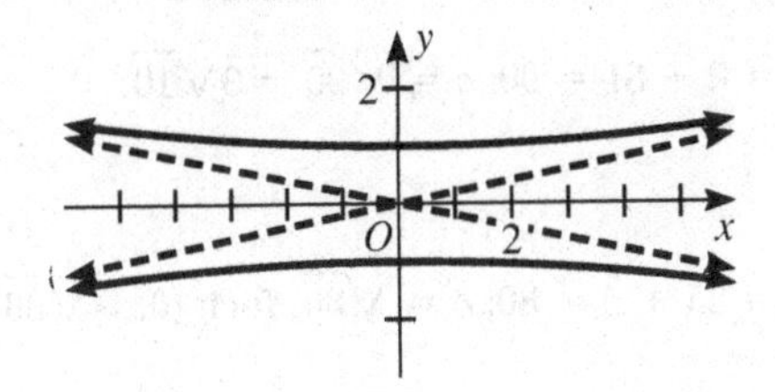

Ex. 3. a

1. **b.** $\frac{x^2}{25} - \frac{y^2}{16} = 1$; $c^2 = 25 + 16 = 41$; $c = \sqrt{41}$; foci: $(-\sqrt{41}, 0)$, $(\sqrt{41}, 0)$

2. **b.** $\frac{y^2}{1} - \frac{x^2}{9} = 1$; $c^2 = 1 + 9 = 10$; $c = \sqrt{10}$; foci: $(0, -\sqrt{10})$, $(0, \sqrt{10})$

3. **b.** $x^2 - 25y^2 + 25 = 0$; $\frac{y^2}{1} - \frac{x^2}{25} = 1$; $c^2 = 1 + 25 = 26$; $c = \sqrt{26}$;

   foci: $(0, -\sqrt{26})$, $(0, \sqrt{26})$

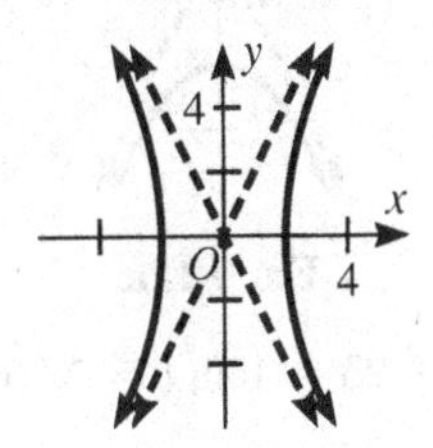

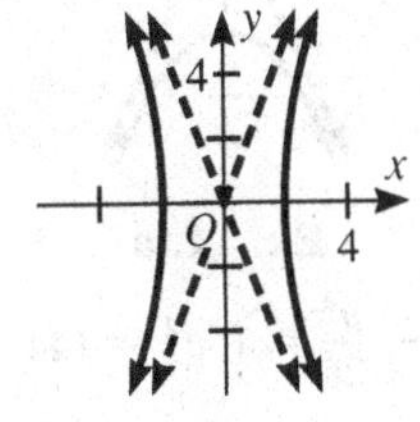

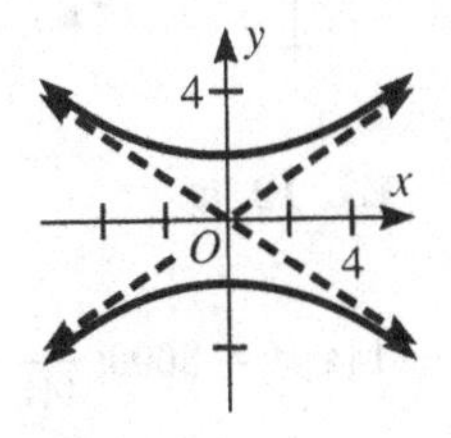

Ex. 4. a **Ex. 5. a** **Ex. 6. a**

4. **b.** $4x^2 - y^2 = 16$; $\frac{x^2}{4} - \frac{y^2}{16} = 1$; $c^2 = 4 + 16 = 20$; $c = \sqrt{20} = 2\sqrt{5}$;

   foci: $(-2\sqrt{5}, 0)$, $(2\sqrt{5}, 0)$

5. **b.** $25x^2 - 4y^2 = 100$; $\frac{x^2}{4} - \frac{y^2}{25} = 1$; $c^2 = 4 + 25 = 29$; $c = \sqrt{29}$; foci: $(-\sqrt{29}, 0)$, $(\sqrt{29}, 0)$

6. **b.** $4x^2 - 9y^2 + 36 = 0$; $\frac{y^2}{4} - \frac{x^2}{9} = 1$; $c^2 = 4 + 9 = 13$; $c = \sqrt{13}$; foci: $(0, -\sqrt{13})$, $(0, \sqrt{13})$

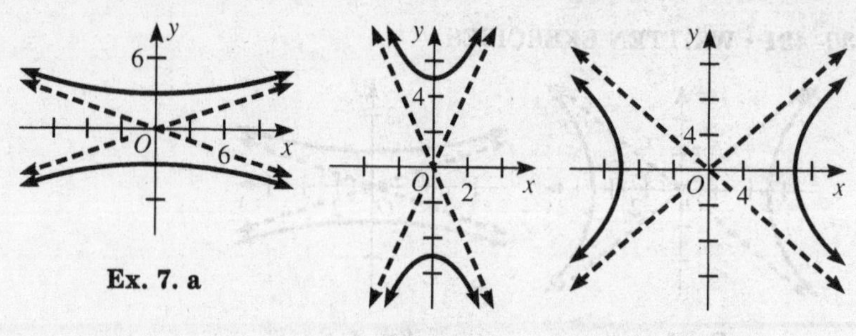

Ex. 7. a

Ex. 8. a

Ex. 9. a

7. b. $x^2 = 9y^2 - 81; \frac{y^2}{9} - \frac{x^2}{81} = 1; c^2 = 9 + 81 = 90; c = \sqrt{90} = 3\sqrt{10};$

foci: $(0, -3\sqrt{10})$, $(0, 3\sqrt{10})$

8. b. $y^2 = 5x^2 + 25; \frac{y^2}{25} - \frac{x^2}{5} = 1; c^2 = 25 + 5 = 30; c = \sqrt{30}$; foci: $(0, -\sqrt{30})$, $(0, \sqrt{30})$

9. b. $75x^2 - 100y^2 = 7500; \frac{x^2}{100} - \frac{y^2}{75} = 1; c^2 = 100 + 75 = 175; c = \sqrt{175} = 5\sqrt{7};$
foci: $(-5\sqrt{7}, 0)$, $(5\sqrt{7}, 0)$

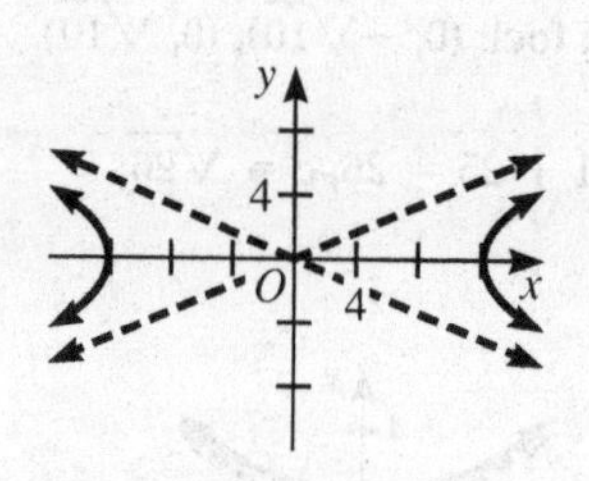

Ex. 10. a

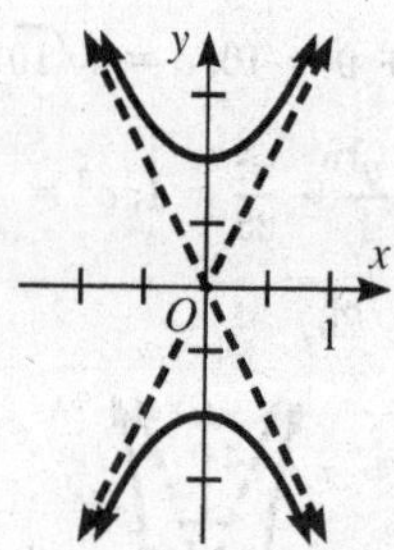

Ex. 11. a

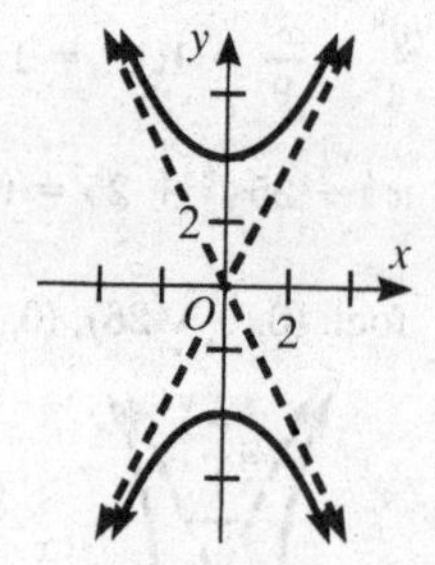

Ex. 12. a

10. b. $25x^2 - 144y^2 = 3600; \frac{x^2}{144} - \frac{y^2}{25} = 1; c^2 = 144 + 25 = 169; c = \sqrt{169} = 13;$

foci: $(-13, 0)$, $(13, 0)$

11. b. $4x^2 - y^2 + 1 = 0; \frac{y^2}{1} - \frac{x^2}{\frac{1}{4}} = 1; c^2 = 1 + \frac{1}{4} = \frac{5}{4}; c = \frac{\sqrt{5}}{2}$; foci: $\left(0, -\frac{\sqrt{5}}{2}\right)$, $\left(0, \frac{\sqrt{5}}{2}\right)$

12. b. $16x^2 - 4y^2 + 64 = 0; \frac{y^2}{16} - \frac{x^2}{4} = 1; c^2 = 16 + 4 = 20; c = 2\sqrt{5}$; foci: $(0, -2\sqrt{5})$, $(0, 2\sqrt{5})$

13. Center: $(0, 0)$; $c = 8$; $2a = 10$; $a = 5$; $b^2 = c^2 - a^2 = 8^2 - 5^2 = 39$; since foci are on y-axis, the y^2 term is positive; $\frac{y^2}{25} - \frac{x^2}{39} = 1$

14. Center: $(0, 0)$; $c = 4$; $2a = 4$, $a = 2$; $b^2 = c^2 - a^2 = 4^2 - 2^2 = 12$; since foci are on the x-axis, the x^2 term is positive; $\frac{x^2}{4} - \frac{y^2}{12} = 1$

15. Since the foci are on the y-axis, the equation has the form $\frac{y^2}{a^2} - \frac{x^2}{b^2} = 1$; the asymptotes are $y = \pm\frac{a}{b}x$, so $\frac{3}{2} = \frac{a}{b}$, and $a = \frac{3}{2}b$; $c = \sqrt{13}$; $c^2 = a^2 + b^2$; $13 = \frac{9}{4}b^2 + b^2$; $13 = \frac{13}{4}b^2$; $b^2 = 4$; $a^2 = \left(\frac{3}{2}b\right)^2 = \frac{9}{4}b^2 = \frac{9}{4}(4) = 9$; $\frac{y^2}{9} - \frac{x^2}{4} = 1$

16. Since the foci are on the y-axis, the equation has the form $\frac{y^2}{a^2} - \frac{x^2}{b^2} = 1$; $c = \sqrt{6}$; asymptotes are $y = \pm\frac{a}{b}x$, so $\frac{a}{b} = \frac{\sqrt{2}}{2}$ and $a = \frac{\sqrt{2}}{2}b$; $c^2 = a^2 + b^2$; $6 = \frac{1}{2}b^2 + b^2$; $6 = \frac{3}{2}b^2$; $b^2 = 4$; $a^2 = \left(\frac{\sqrt{2}}{2}b\right)^2 = \frac{1}{2}b^2 = \frac{1}{2}(4) = 2$; $\frac{y^2}{2} - \frac{x^2}{4} = 1$

B **17.** Since the graph has y-intercepts, the equation has the form $\frac{y^2}{a^2} - \frac{x^2}{b^2} = 1$; $a = 3$; asymptotes are $y = \pm\frac{a}{b}x$, so $\frac{a}{b} = 3$, $\frac{3}{b} = 3$, and $b = 1$; $\frac{y^2}{9} - \frac{x^2}{1} = 1$

18. Since the foci are on the x-axis, the equation has the form $\frac{x^2}{a^2} - \frac{y^2}{b^2} = 1$; $c = 4$; asymptotes are $y = \pm\frac{b}{a}x$, so $\frac{b}{a} = 1$ and $a = b$; $c^2 = a^2 + b^2$; $16 = a^2 + a^2 = 2a^2$; $a^2 = 8$; $b^2 = 8$; $\frac{x^2}{8} - \frac{y^2}{8} = 1$

19.

20.

21.

22.

23.

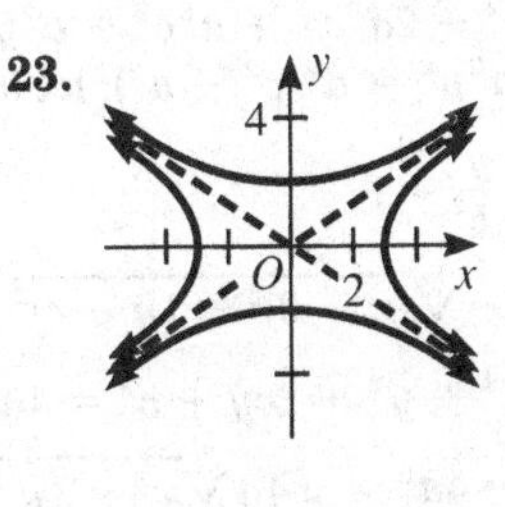

24.

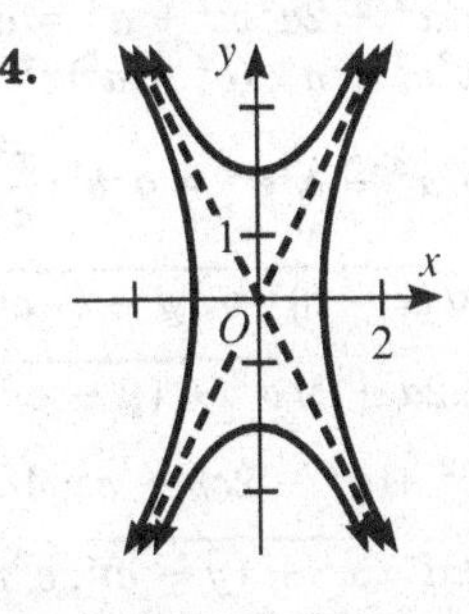

25.

26.

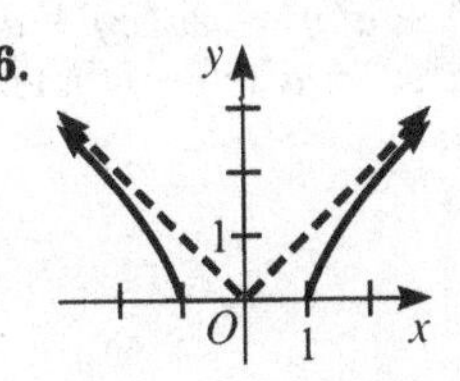

27.

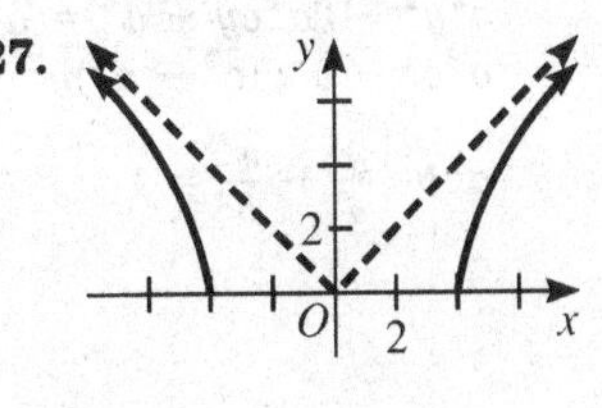

28.

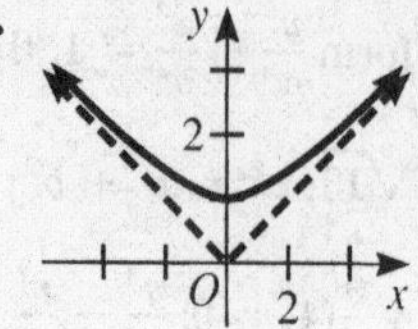

29. $x > 0, y > 0$; x varies inversely as y.

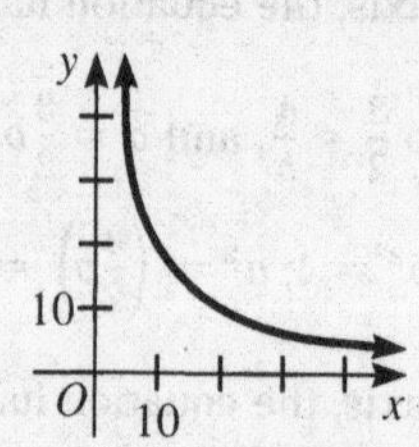

30. Let $P(x, y)$ be any point on the hyperbola. Since $|PF_1 - PF_2| = 4$, $(PF_1 - PF_2) = \pm 4$, and $\sqrt{x^2 + (y + 5)^2} - \sqrt{x^2 + (y - 5)^2} = \pm 4$; $\sqrt{x^2 + (y + 5)^2} = \pm 4 + \sqrt{x^2 + (y - 5)^2}$; $x^2 + (y + 5)^2 = 16 \pm 8\sqrt{x^2 + (y - 5)^2} + x^2 + (y - 5)^2$; $20y = 16 \pm 8\sqrt{x^2 + (y - 5)^2}$; $5y - 4 = \pm 2\sqrt{x^2 + (y - 5)^2}$; $25y^2 - 40y + 16 = 4(x^2 + (y - 5)^2)$; $25y^2 - 40y + 16 = 4x^2 + 4y^2 - 40y + 100$; $21y^2 - 4x^2 = 84$; $\frac{y^2}{4} - \frac{x^2}{21} = 1$

31. Let $P(x, y)$ be any point on the hyperbola. Since $|PF_1 - PF_2| = 2$, $(PF_1 - PF_2) = \pm 2$, and $\sqrt{(x + 3)^2 + y^2} - \sqrt{(x - 3)^2 + y^2} = \pm 2$; $\sqrt{(x + 3)^2 + y^2} = \pm 2 + \sqrt{(x - 3)^2 + y^2}$; $(x + 3)^2 + y^2 = 4 \pm 4\sqrt{(x - 3)^2 + y^2} + (x - 3)^2 + y^2$; $12x - 4 = \pm 4\sqrt{(x - 3)^2 + y^2}$; $3x - 1 = \pm\sqrt{(x - 3)^2 + y^2}$; $9x^2 - 6x + 1 = (x - 3)^2 + y^2$; $9x^2 - 6x + 1 = x^2 - 6x + 9 + y^2$; $8x^2 - y^2 = 8$; $\frac{x^2}{1} - \frac{y^2}{8} = 1$

C **32.** $\sqrt{[x - (-c)]^2 + (y - 0)^2} - \sqrt{(x - c)^2 + (y - 0)^2} = \pm 2a$; $\sqrt{(x + c)^2 + y^2} = \pm 2a + \sqrt{(x - c)^2 + y^2}$; $x^2 + 2cx + c^2 + y^2 = 4a^2 \pm 4a\sqrt{(x - c)^2 + y^2} + x^2 - 2cx + c^2 + y^2$; $4cx - 4a^2 = \pm 4a\sqrt{(x - c)^2 + y^2}$; $cx - a^2 = \pm a\sqrt{(x - c)^2 + y^2}$; $c^2x^2 - 2a^2cx + a^4 = a^2(x^2 - 2cx + c^2 + y^2)$; $c^2x^2 - 2a^2cx + a^4 = a^2x^2 - 2a^2cx + a^2c^2 + a^2y^2$; $(c^2 - a^2)x^2 - a^2y^2 = a^2c^2 - a^4$; $(c^2 - a^2)x^2 - a^2y^2 = a^2(c^2 - a^2)$; let $b^2 = c^2 - a^2$; $b^2x^2 - a^2y^2 = a^2b^2$; $\frac{x^2}{a^2} - \frac{y^2}{b^2} = 1$

33. $\sqrt{(x - 0)^2 + [y - (-c)]^2} - \sqrt{(x - 0)^2 + (y - c)^2} = \pm 2a$; $\sqrt{x^2 + (y + c)^2} = \pm 2a + \sqrt{x^2 + (y - c)^2}$; $x^2 + y^2 + 2cy + c^2 = 4a^2 \pm 4a\sqrt{x^2 + (y - c)^2} + x^2 + y^2 - 2cy + c^2$; $4cy - 4a^2 = \pm 4a\sqrt{x^2 + (y - c)^2}$; $cy - a^2 = \pm a\sqrt{x^2 + (y - c)^2}$; $c^2y^2 - 2a^2cy + a^4 = a^2(x^2 + y^2 - 2cy + c^2)$; $c^2y^2 - 2a^2cy + a^4 = a^2x^2 + a^2y^2 - 2a^2cy + a^2c^2$; $(c^2 - a^2)y^2 - a^2x^2 = a^2c^2 - a^4$; $(c^2 - a^2)y^2 - a^2x^2 = a^2(c^2 - a^2)$; let $b^2 = c^2 - a^2$; $b^2y^2 - a^2x^2 = a^2b^2$; $\frac{y^2}{a^2} - \frac{x^2}{b^2} = 1$

34. $\sqrt{(x-a)^2+(y-a)^2} - \sqrt{[x-(-a)]^2+[y-(-a)]^2} = \pm 2a;$
$\sqrt{(x-a)^2+(y-a)^2} = \pm 2a + \sqrt{(x+a)^2+(y+a)^2};$
$x^2 - 2ax + a^2 + y^2 - 2ay + a^2 = 4a^2 \pm 4a\sqrt{(x+a)^2+(y+a)^2} +$
$x^2 + 2ax + a^2 + y^2 + 2ay + a^2;\ -4ax - 4ay - 4a^2 =$
$\pm 4a\sqrt{(x+a)^2+(y+a)^2};\ x + y + a = \pm\sqrt{(x+a)^2+(y+a)^2},\ (a \neq 0);$
$x^2 + y^2 + a^2 + 2xy + 2ax + 2ay = x^2 + 2ax + a^2 + y^2 + 2ay + a^2;\ 2xy = a^2;$
$xy = \frac{a^2}{2}$

35. $\sqrt{[x-(-a)]^2+(y-a)^2} - \sqrt{(x-a)^2+[y-(-a)]^2} = \pm 2a;$
$\sqrt{(x+a)^2+(y-a)^2} = \pm 2a + \sqrt{(x-a)^2+(y+a)^2};$
$x^2 + 2ax + a^2 + y^2 - 2ay + a^2 = 4a^2 \pm 4a\sqrt{(x-a)^2+(y+a)^2} + x^2 - 2ax +$
$a^2 + y^2 + 2ay + a^2;\ 4ax - 4ay - 4a^2 = \pm 4a\sqrt{(x-a)^2+(y+a)^2};$
$x - y - a = \pm\sqrt{(x-a)^2+(y+a)^2},\ (a \neq 0);\ x^2 + y^2 + a^2 - 2xy -$
$2ax + 2ay = x^2 - 2ax + a^2 + y^2 + 2ay + a^2;\ -2xy = a^2;\ xy = -\frac{a^2}{2}$

Page 431 • MIXED REVIEW EXERCISES

1.
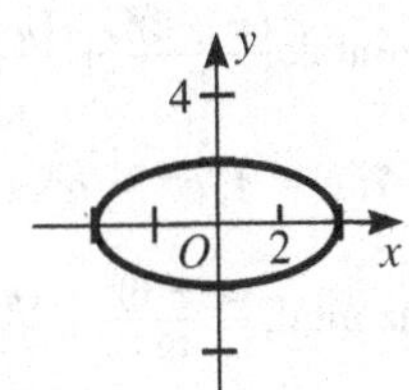

2.
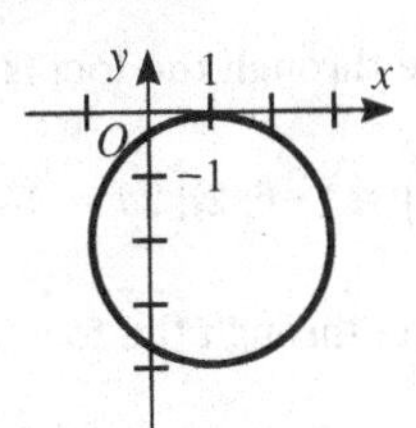

3.
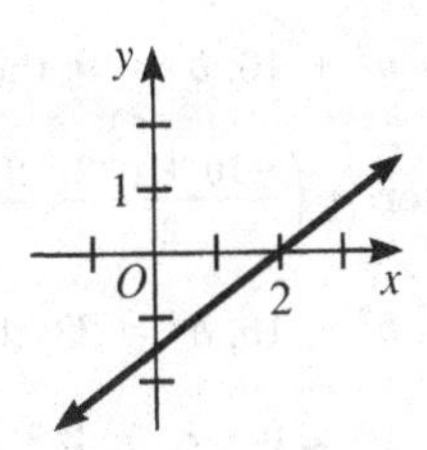

4.
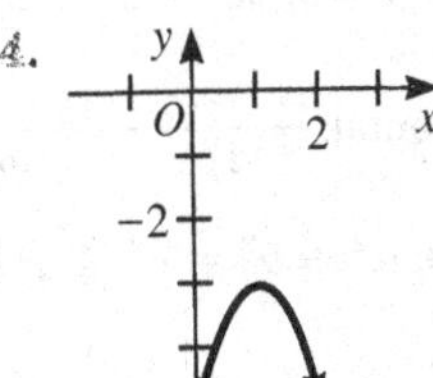

5.
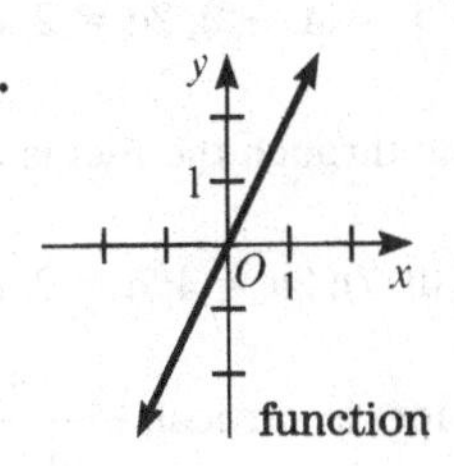

6.
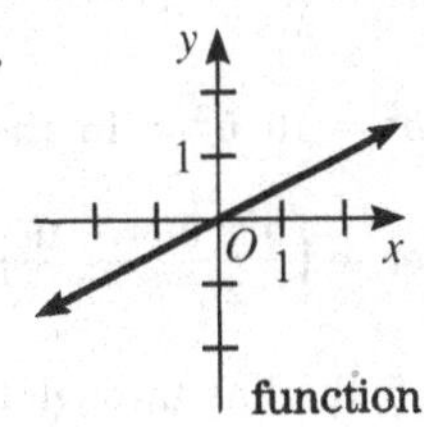

7.
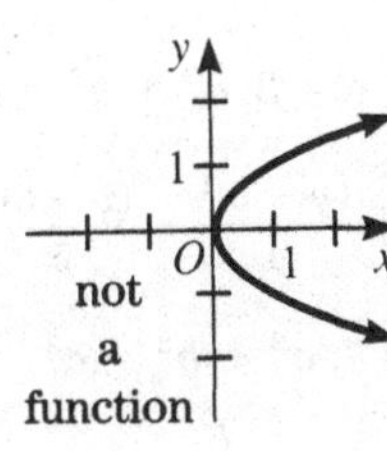

8.
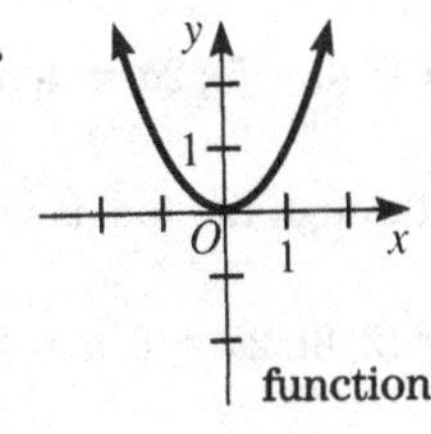

9.
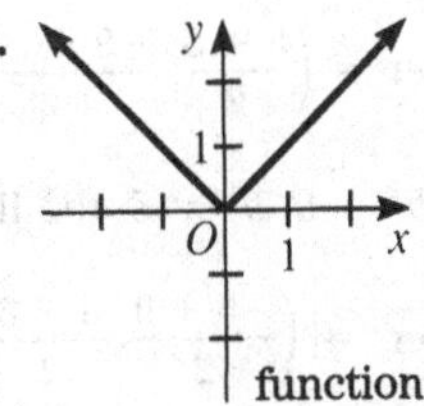

10.
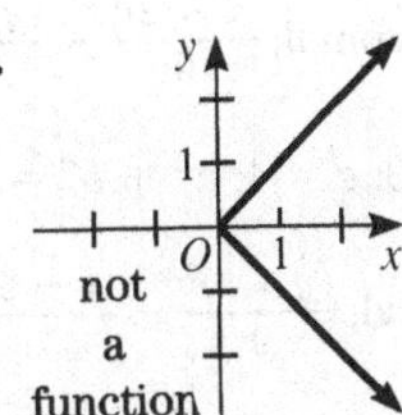

Pages 434–435 • WRITTEN EXERCISES

A **1.** Center $= \left(\frac{6+6}{2}, \frac{0+6}{2}\right) = (6, 3)$; $2a = 10$, $a = 5$; $c = 3$; $a^2 = b^2 + c^2$, $25 = b^2 + 9$, $b^2 = 16$; line containing the foci is vertical; $\frac{(x-6)^2}{16} + \frac{(y-3)^2}{25} = 1$

2. Center $= \left(\frac{0+0}{2}, \frac{0+8}{2}\right) = (0, 4)$; $2a = 12$, $a = 6$; $c = 4$; $a^2 = b^2 + c^2$, $36 = b^2 + 16$, $b^2 = 20$; line containing foci is vertical; $\frac{x^2}{20} + \frac{(y-4)^2}{36} = 1$

3. Center $= \left(\frac{-3+(-3)}{2}, \frac{-3+3}{2}\right) = (-3, 0)$; $c = 3$; $2a = 8$, $a = 4$; $a^2 = b^2 + c^2$, $16 = b^2 + 9$, $b^2 = 7$; the line through the foci is vertical; $\frac{(x+3)^2}{7} + \frac{y^2}{16} = 1$

4. Center $= \left(\frac{-5+3}{2}, \frac{1+1}{2}\right) = (-1, 1)$; $2a = 16$, $a = 8$; $c = 4$; $a^2 = b^2 + c^2$, $64 = b^2 + 16$, $b^2 = 48$; the line through the foci is horizontal; $\frac{(x+1)^2}{64} + \frac{(y-1)^2}{48} = 1$

5. Center $= \left(\frac{-2+6}{2}, \frac{-3+(-3)}{2}\right) = (2, -3)$; $2a = 10$; $a = 5$; $c = 4$; $a^2 = b^2 + c^2$, $25 = b^2 + 16$, $b^2 = 9$; the line through the foci is horizontal; $\frac{(x-2)^2}{25} + \frac{(y+3)^2}{9} = 1$

6. Center $= \left(\frac{-10+(-2)}{2}, \frac{2+2}{2}\right) = (-6, 2)$; $2a = 14$, $a = 7$; $c = 4$; $a^2 = b^2 + c^2$, $49 = b^2 + 16$, $b^2 = 33$; the line through the foci is horizontal; $\frac{(x+6)^2}{49} + \frac{(y-2)^2}{33} = 1$

7. Center $= \left(\frac{0+8}{2}, \frac{-2+(-2)}{2}\right) = (4, -2)$; $2a = 2$, $a = 1$; $c = 4$; $a^2 + b^2 = c^2$, $1 + b^2 = 16$, $b^2 = 15$; the line through the foci is horizontal; $\frac{(x-4)^2}{1} - \frac{(y+2)^2}{15} = 1$

8. Center $= \left(\frac{0+0}{2}, \frac{4+10}{2}\right) = (0, 7)$; $2a = 4$; $a = 2$; $c = 3$; $a^2 + b^2 = c^2$, $4 + b^2 = 9$, $b^2 = 5$; the line through the foci is vertical; $\frac{(y-7)^2}{4} - \frac{x^2}{5} = 1$

9. Center $= \left(\frac{3+3}{2}, \frac{-8+(-2)}{2}\right) = (3, -5)$; $2a = 4$, $a = 2$; $c = 3$; $a^2 + b^2 = c^2$, $4 + b^2 = 9$, $b^2 = 5$; the line through the foci is vertical; $\frac{(y+5)^2}{4} - \frac{(x-3)^2}{5} = 1$

10. Center $= \left(\frac{-5+9}{2}, \frac{3+3}{2}\right) = (2, 3)$; $2a = 6$, $a = 3$; $c = 7$; $a^2 + b^2 = c^2$, $9 + b^2 = 49$, $b^2 = 40$; the line through the foci is horizontal; $\frac{(x-2)^2}{9} - \frac{(y-3)^2}{40} = 1$

11. Center $= \left(\frac{5+5}{2}, \frac{-9+(-1)}{2}\right) = (5, -5)$; $2a = 6$, $a = 3$; $c = 4$; $a^2 + b^2 = c^2$, $9 + b^2 = 16$, $b^2 = 7$; the line through the foci is vertical; $\frac{(y+5)^2}{9} - \frac{(x-5)^2}{7} = 1$

12. Center $= \left(\frac{-4+4}{2}, \frac{-4+(-4)}{2}\right) = (0, -4)$; $2a = 6$, $a = 3$; $c = 4$; $a^2 + b^2 = c^2$,

$9 + b^2 = 16$, $b^2 = 7$; the line through the foci is horizontal; $\frac{x^2}{9} - \frac{(y+4)^2}{7} = 1$

13. $x^2 - 4y^2 - 2x - 24y - 39 = 0$; $x^2 - 2x - 4(y^2 + 6y) = 39$;
$x^2 - 2x + 1 - 4(y^2 + 6y + 9) = 39 + 1 - 36$; $(x-1)^2 - 4(y+3)^2 = 4$;

$\frac{(x-1)^2}{4} - \frac{(y+3)^2}{1} = 1$; hyperbola with center $(1, -3)$; line through foci is horizontal;

$c^2 = a^2 + b^2 = 4 + 1 = 5$, $c = \sqrt{5}$; foci: $(1 + \sqrt{5}, -3)$, $(1 - \sqrt{5}, -3)$

14. $x^2 + 9y^2 + 2x - 18y + 1 = 0$; $x^2 + 2x + 9(y^2 - 2y) = -1$; $(x^2 + 2x + 1) +$

$9(y^2 - 2y + 1) = -1 + 1 + 9$; $(x+1)^2 + 9(y-1)^2 = 9$; $\frac{(x+1)^2}{9} + \frac{(y-1)^2}{1} = 1$;

ellipse with center $(-1, 1)$; major axis is horizontal; $a^2 = b^2 + c^2$, $9 = 1 + c^2$,

$c^2 = 8$, $c = \sqrt{8} = 2\sqrt{2}$; foci: $(-1 + 2\sqrt{2}, 1)$, $(-1 - 2\sqrt{2}, 1)$

15. $x^2 + y^2 - 6x - 16y + 57 = 0$; $x^2 - 6x + y^2 - 16y = -57$;
$(x^2 - 6x + 9) + (y^2 - 16y + 64) = -57 + 9 + 64$; $(x-3)^2 + (y-8)^2 = 16$;
circle of radius 4 and center $(3, 8)$

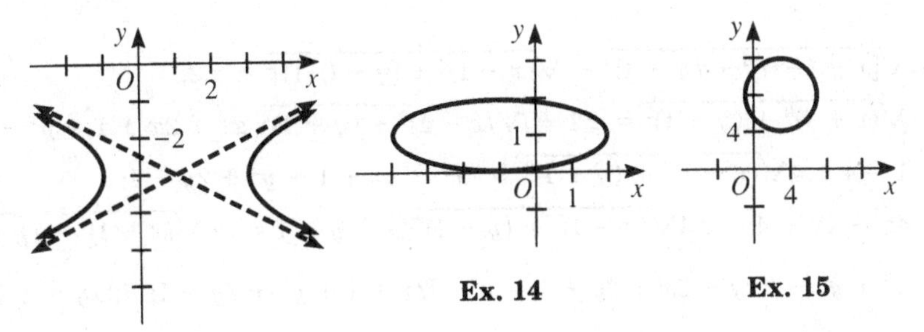

Ex. 14

Ex. 15

Ex. 13

16. $9x^2 - y^2 - 18x - 6y - 9 = 0$; $9x^2 - 18x - (y^2 + 6y) = 9$;
$9(x^2 - 2x + 1) - (y^2 + 6y + 9) = 9 + 9 - 9$; $9(x-1)^2 - (y+3)^2 = 9$;

$\frac{(x-1)^2}{1} - \frac{(y+3)^2}{9} = 1$; hyperbola with center $(1, -3)$; line through foci is horizontal;

$c^2 = a^2 + b^2 = 10$; $c = \pm\sqrt{10}$; foci: $(1 + \sqrt{10}, -3)$ and $(1 - \sqrt{10}, -3)$

17. $9x^2 + 25y^2 + 36x - 150y + 36 = 0$; $9(x^2 + 4x) + 25(y^2 - 6y) = -36$;
$9(x^2 + 4x + 4) + 25(y^2 - 6y + 9) = -36 + 36 + 225$; $9(x+2)^2 + 25(y-3)^2 = 225$;

$\frac{(x+2)^2}{25} + \frac{(y-3)^2}{9} = 1$; ellipse with center $(-2, 3)$; major axis is horizontal;

$c^2 = a^2 - b^2 = 25 - 9 = 16$; $c = \pm 4$; foci: $(2, 3)$ and $(-6, 3)$

18. $16x^2 - 9y^2 + 64x + 18y + 199 = 0$; $16(x^2 + 4x) - 9(y^2 - 2y) = -199$;
$16(x^2 + 4x + 4) - 9(y^2 - 2y + 1) = -199 + 64 - 9$; $16(x+2)^2 - 9(y-1)^2 =$

-144; $\frac{(y-1)^2}{16} - \frac{(x+2)^2}{9} = 1$; hyperbola with center $(-2, 1)$; line containing foci is

vertical; $a^2 + b^2 = c^2$, $16 + 9 = c^2$, $c^2 = 25$; $c = 5$; foci: $(-2, -4)$ and $(-2, 6)$

(Continued)

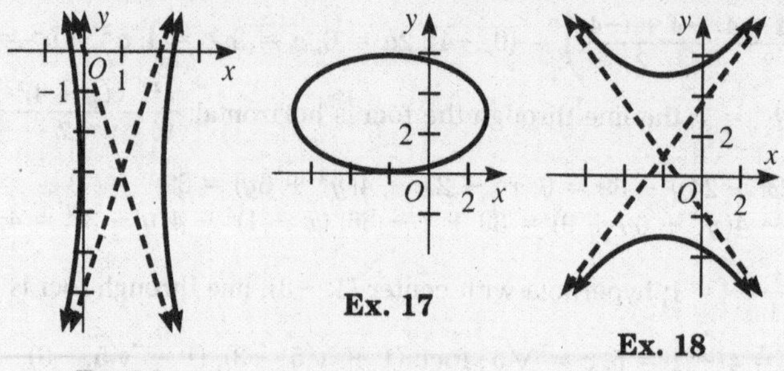

B **19.** $\sqrt{(x-1)^2+(y-1)^2}+\sqrt{[x-(-1)]^2+[y-(-1)]^2}=3$; $\sqrt{(x-1)^2+(y-1)^2}=3-\sqrt{(x+1)^2+(y+1)^2}$; $x^2-2x+1+y^2-2y+1=9-6\sqrt{(x+1)^2+(y+1)^2}+x^2+2x+1+y^2+2y+1$; $-4x-4y-9=-6\sqrt{(x+1)^2+(y+1)^2}$; $16x^2+16y^2+32xy+72x+72y+81=36(x^2+2x+1+y^2+2y+1)$; $16x^2+16y^2+32xy+72x+72y+81=36x^2+72x+36y^2+72y+72$; $20x^2+20y^2-32xy-9=0$

20. $\sqrt{[x-(-1)]^2+(y-1)^2}-\sqrt{(x-1)^2+[y-(-1)]^2}=\pm 2$; $\sqrt{(x+1)^2+(y-1)^2}=\pm 2+\sqrt{(x-1)^2+(y+1)^2}$; $x^2+2x+1+y^2-2y+1=4\pm 4\sqrt{(x-1)^2+(y+1)^2}+x^2-2x+1+y^2+2y+1$; $4x-4y-4=\pm 4\sqrt{(x-1)^2+(y+1)^2}$; $x-y-1=\pm\sqrt{(x-1)^2+(y+1)^2}$; $x^2+y^2-2xy-2x+2y+1=x^2-2x+1+y^2+2y+1$; $-2xy=1$; $xy=-\frac{1}{2}$

C **21. a.** $1x^2+0y^2+2x-8y+1=0$; $8y=x^2+2x+1$; $y=\frac{1}{8}(x+1)^2$; parabola

b. $1x^2+1y^2+2x-8y+1=0$; $x^2+2x+1+y^2-8y+16=-1+1+16$; $(x+1)^2+(y-4)^2=16$; circle

c. $1x^2+4y^2+2x-8y+1=0$; $x^2+2x+4(y^2-2y)=-1$; $x^2+2x+1+4(y^2-2y+1)=-1+1+4$; $(x+1)^2+4(y-1)^2=4$; $\frac{(x+1)^2}{4}+\frac{(y-1)^2}{1}=1$; ellipse

d. $1x^2-4y^2+2x-8y+1=0$; $x^2+2x-4(y^2+2y)=-1$; $x^2+2x+1-4(y^2+2y+1)=-1+1-4$; $(x+1)^2-4(y+1)^2=-4$; $\frac{(y+1)^2}{1}-\frac{(x+1)^2}{4}=1$; hyperbola

e. circle: $A=B$; parabola: $AB=0$; ellipse: $AB>0$ and $A\neq B$; hyperbola: $AB<0$

(Continued)

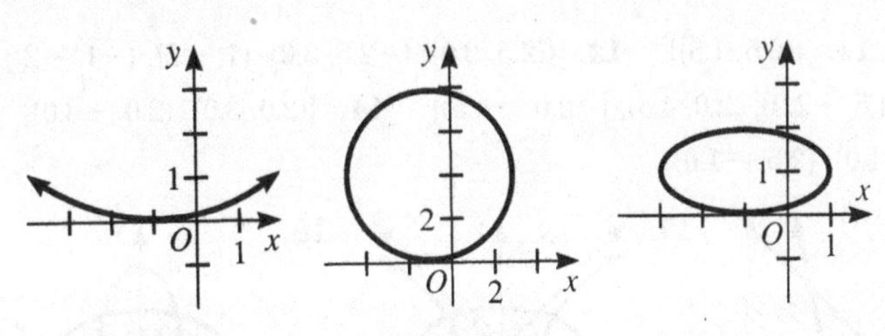

Ex. 21. a **Ex. 21. b** **Ex. 21. c**

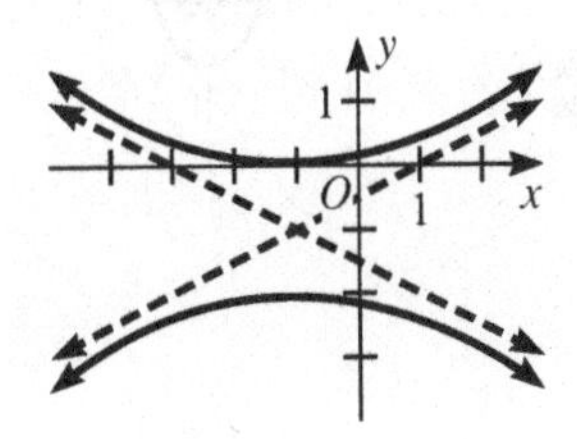

Ex. 21. d

Page 438 • WRITTEN EXERCISES

A **1.**

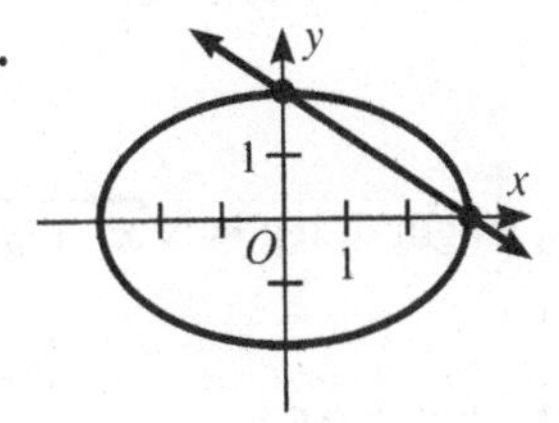

two

2.

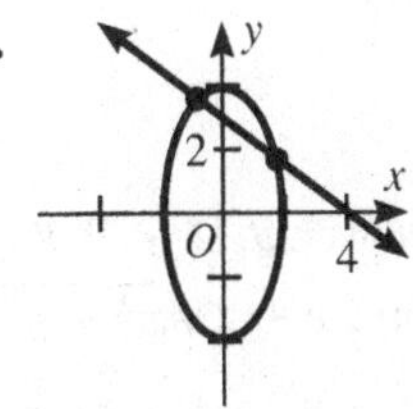

two

3.

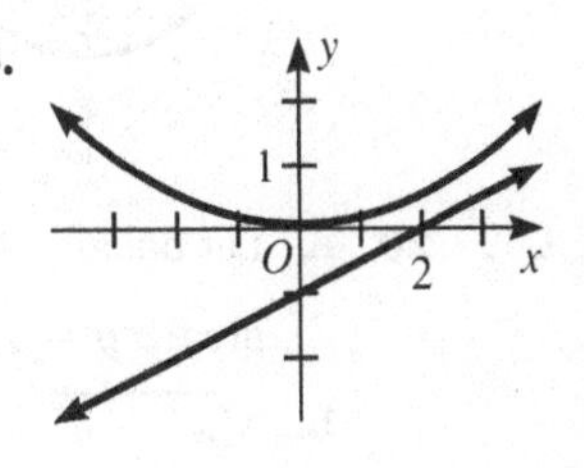

zero

4.

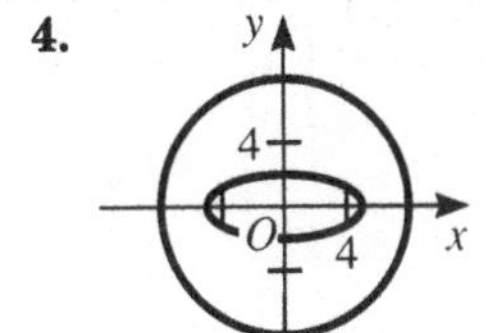

zero

5.

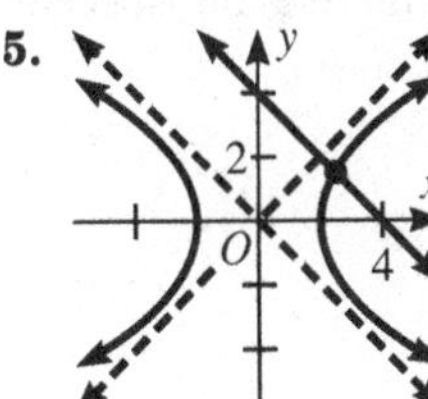

one

6.

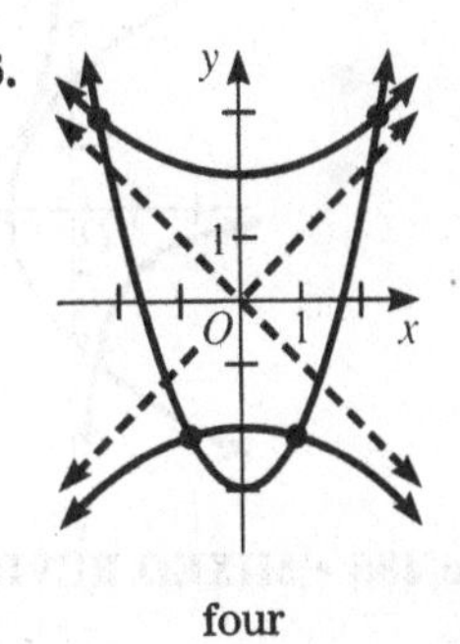

four

7.

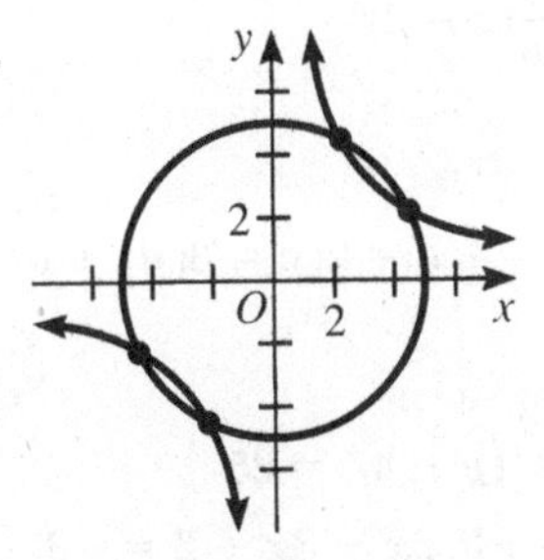

four

8.

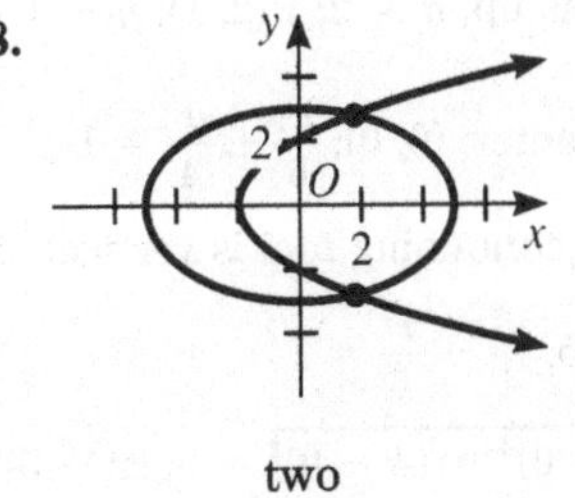

two

9.

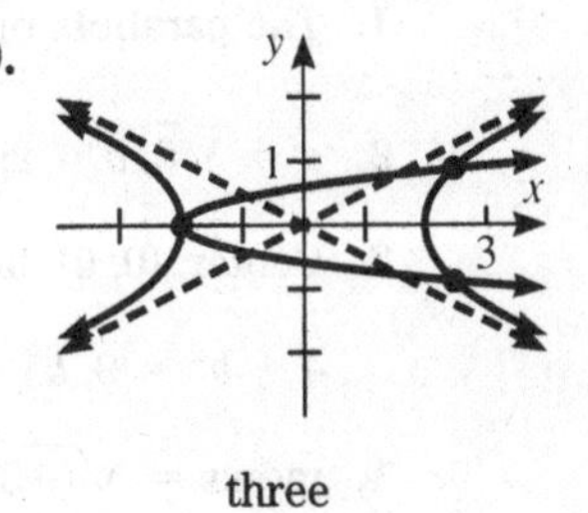

three

10. no solution **11.** {(2.5, 1.5)} **12.** {(2.5, 3.0), (−2.5, 3.0), (1, −2), (−1, −2)}

13. {(4.5, 2.0), (−4.5, −2.0), (2.0, 4.5), (−2.0, −4.5)} **14.** {(2.0, 3.0), (2.0, −3.0)}

15. {(−2, 0), (2.5, 1.0), (2.5, −1.0)}

B **16.**

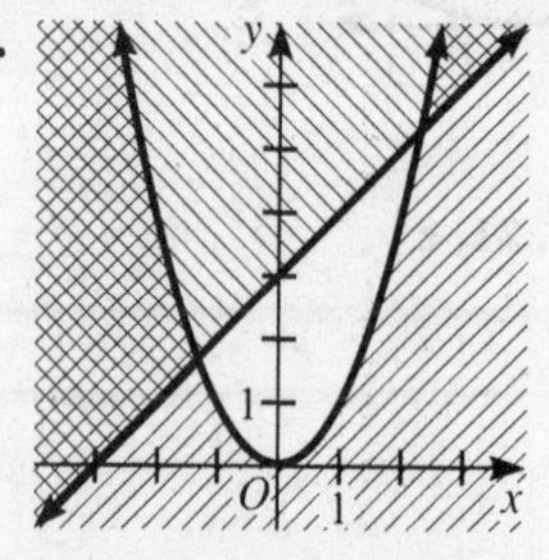

17.

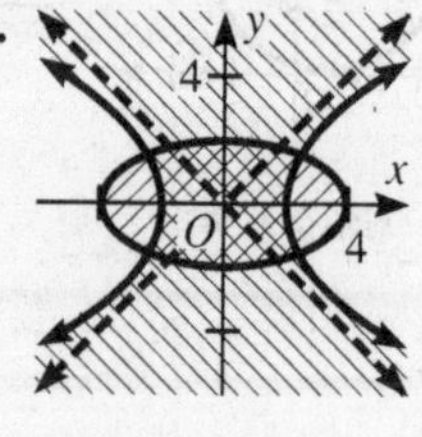

18.

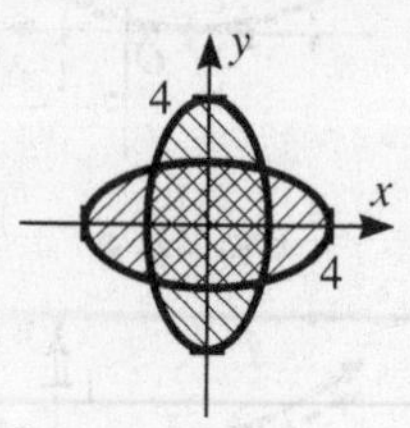

19.

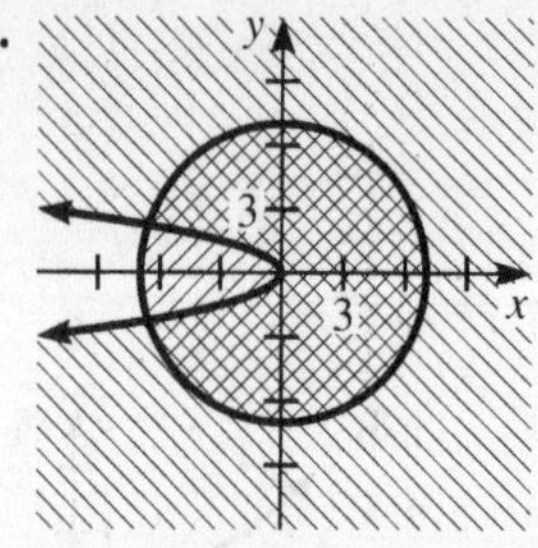

C **20.** **a.** Let base = $2x$ and height = y, $(x > 0, y > 0)$; length of leg = $\sqrt{x^2 + y^2}$;

area: $xy = 1$; perimeter: $2x + 2\sqrt{x^2 + y^2} = 4$

b. $\sqrt{x^2 + y^2} = 2 - x$; $x^2 + y^2 = 4 - 4x + x^2$; $y^2 = 4 - 4x$

c.

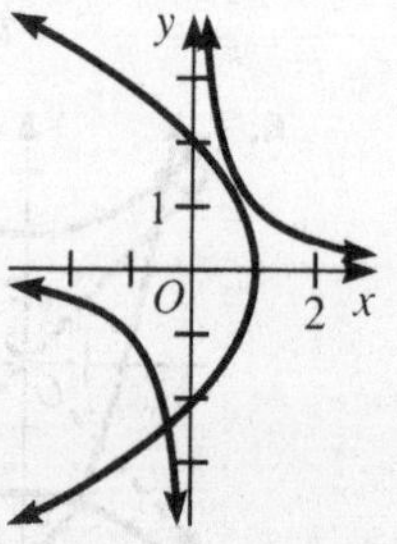

Since the graphs intersect only for negative values of x and y, there is no isosceles triangle with perimeter 4 and area 1.

Page 438 • MIXED REVIEW EXERCISES

1. The parabola opens up; $a = 2$; $V(2, 1)$; $y - 1 = \frac{1}{8}(x - 2)^2$

2. $a = \sqrt{6}$, $b = 2$; Center: (0, 0); $\frac{x^2}{6} + \frac{y^2}{4} = 1$

3. Center: (0, 0); line containing foci is vertical; $2a = 4$, $a = 2$; $c = 3$; $a^2 + b^2 = c^2$,

$4 + b^2 = 9$, $b^2 = 5$; $\frac{y^2}{4} - \frac{x^2}{5} = 1$

4. radius = $\sqrt{(-3 - 0)^2 + (4 - 0)^2} = 5$; $(x + 3)^2 + (y - 4)^2 = 25$

5. $y = 3x + 2$ and $2x - y = -3$; $2x - (3x + 2) = -3$, $2x - 3x - 2 = -3$, $-x = -1$, $x = 1$; $y = 3(1) + 2 = 5$; {(1, 5)}

6. $\begin{matrix} x - 3y = 5 \\ 4x + y = 7 \end{matrix}$; $\begin{matrix} 4x - 12y = 20 \\ 4x + y = 7 \end{matrix}$; $-13y = 13$, $y = -1$; $4x + (-1) = 7$, $4x = 8$, $x = 2$; $\{(2, -1)\}$

7. $\begin{matrix} 5x + 2y = 9 \\ 4x - 3y = 21 \end{matrix}$; $\begin{matrix} 15x + 6y = 27 \\ 8x - 6y = 42 \end{matrix}$; $23x = 69$, $x = 3$; $5(3) + 2y = 9$, $2y = -6$, $y = -3$; $\{(3, -3)\}$

Pages 441–442 • WRITTEN EXERCISES

A 1. $x^2 - y = 5$, $2x + y = 3$; $y = 3 - 2x$; $x^2 - (3 - 2x) = 5$; $x^2 + 2x - 8 = 0$; $(x + 4)(x - 2) = 0$; $x = -4$ or $x = 2$; if $x = -4$, $y = 3 - 2(-4) = 11$; if $x = 2$, $y = 3 - 2(2) = -1$; $\{(-4, 11), (2, -1)\}$

2. $x = y^2 - 9$, $x - 4y - 12 = 0$; $x = 4y + 12$; $4y + 12 = y^2 - 9$; $y^2 - 4y - 21 = 0$; $(y - 7)(y + 3) = 0$; $y = 7$ or $y = -3$; if $y = 7$, $x = 4(7) + 12 = 40$; if $y = -3$, $x = 4(-3) + 12 = 0$; $\{(40, 7), (0, -3)\}$

3. $y = x^2$, $x^2 + y^2 = 12$; $y + y^2 = 12$; $y^2 + y - 12 = 0$; $(y + 4)(y - 3) = 0$; $y = -4$ or $y = 3$; if $y = -4$, $x^2 + (-4)^2 = 12$, $x^2 = -4$, no real solution; if $y = 3$, $x^2 + 3^2 = 12$, $x^2 = 3$, $x = \sqrt{3}$ or $x = -\sqrt{3}$; $\{(\sqrt{3}, 3), (-\sqrt{3}, 3)\}$

4. $y^2 = 2x$, $x^2 + y^2 = 8$; $x^2 + 2x = 8$; $x^2 + 2x - 8 = 0$; $(x + 4)(x - 2) = 0$; $x = -4$ or $x = 2$; if $x = -4$, $y^2 = 2(-4) = -8$, no real solution; if $x = 2$, $y^2 = 2(2) = 4$, $y = 2$ or -2; $\{(2, 2), (2, -2)\}$

5. $x^2 - y^2 = 15$, $x + y = 1$; $y = 1 - x$; $x^2 - (1 - x)^2 = 15$; $-1 + 2x = 15$; $2x = 16$, $x = 8$; if $x = 8$, $y = 1 - 8 = -7$; $\{(8, -7)\}$

6. $x^2 + y^2 = 61$, $x - 2y + 7 = 0$; $x = 2y - 7$; $(2y - 7)^2 + y^2 = 61$;

$5y^2 - 28y - 12 = 0$; $(5y + 2)(y - 6) = 0$; $y = -\frac{2}{5}$ or $y = 6$; if $y = -\frac{2}{5}$,

$x = 2\left(-\frac{2}{5}\right) - 7 = -\frac{39}{5}$; if $y = 6$, $x = 2(6) - 7 = 5$; $\left\{\left(-\frac{39}{5}, -\frac{2}{5}\right), (5, 6)\right\}$

7. $xy = 8$, $x + y = 6$; $y = 6 - x$; $x(6 - x) = 8$; $x^2 - 6x + 8 = 0$; $(x - 2)(x - 4) = 0$; $x = 2$ or $x = 4$; if $x = 2$, $y = 6 - 2 = 4$; if $x = 4$, $y = 6 - 4 = 2$; $\{(2, 4), (4, 2)\}$

8. $xy + 6 = 0$, $x - y = 5$; $x = y + 5$; $(y + 5)y + 6 = 0$; $y^2 + 5y + 6 = 0$; $(y + 2)(y + 3) = 0$; $y = -2$ or $y = -3$; if $y = -2$, $x = -2 + 5 = 3$; if $y = -3$, $x = -3 + 5 = 2$; $\{(3, -2), (2, -3)\}$

9. $2y^2 + 3x = 33$, $x + 4y + 7 = 0$; $x = -4y - 7$; $2y^2 + 3(-4y - 7) = 33$; $2y^2 - 12y - 54 = 0$; $y^2 - 6y - 27 = 0$; $(y - 9)(y + 3) = 0$; $y = 9$ or $y = -3$; if $y = 9$, $x = -4(9) - 7 = -43$; if $y = -3$, $x = -4(-3) - 7 = 5$; $\{(-43, 9), (5, -3)\}$

10. $4x^2 - y^2 + 12 = 0$, $x + y = 3$; $y = 3 - x$; $4x^2 - (3 - x)^2 + 12 = 0$; $3x^2 + 6x + 3 = 0$; $x^2 + 2x + 1 = 0$; $(x + 1)^2 = 0$; $x = -1$; if $x = -1$, $y = 3 - (-1) = 4$; $\{(-1, 4)\}$

11. $\begin{matrix} x^2 + y^2 = 25 \\ x^2 - y^2 = 7 \end{matrix}$; $2x^2 = 32$; $x^2 = 16$; $x = 4$ or $x = -4$; if $x = 4$, $4^2 + y^2 = 25$, $y^2 = 9$,

$y = 3$ or $y = -3$; if $x = -4$, $(-4)^2 + y^2 = 25$, $y^2 = 9$, $y = 3$ or $y = -3$; $\{(4, 3), (4, -3), (-4, 3), (-4, -3)\}$

12. $\begin{matrix} 8x^2 + y^2 = 25 \\ 8x^2 - y^2 = 39 \end{matrix}$; $16x^2 = 64$; $x^2 = 4$; $x = 2$ or $x = -2$; if $x = 2$, $8(2)^2 + y^2 = 25$,

$32 + y^2 = 25$, $y^2 = -7$, no real solution; if $x = -2$, $8(-2)^2 + y^2 = 25$, $32 + y^2 = 25$, $y^2 = -7$, no real solution; no real solution

B **13.** $\begin{matrix} 2x^2 - 3y^2 = 30 \\ x^2 + y^2 = 25 \end{matrix}; \begin{matrix} 2x^2 - 3y^2 = 30 \\ 3x^2 + 3y^2 = 75 \end{matrix}; 5x^2 = 105; x^2 = 21; x = \sqrt{21}$ or $x = -\sqrt{21}$; if $x = \sqrt{21}$, $(\sqrt{21})^2 + y^2 = 25$; $y^2 = 4$, $y = 2$ or $y = -2$; if $x = -\sqrt{21}$, $(-\sqrt{21})^2 + y^2 = 25$; $y^2 = 4$, $y = 2$ or $y = -2$; $\{(\sqrt{21}, 2), (\sqrt{21}, -2), (-\sqrt{21}, 2), (-\sqrt{21}, -2)\}$

14. $\begin{matrix} x^2 + 2y^2 = 12 \\ 3x^2 - y^2 = 8 \end{matrix}; \begin{matrix} x^2 + 2y^2 = 12 \\ 6x^2 - 2y^2 = 16 \end{matrix}; 7x^2 = 28; x^2 = 4; x = 2$ or $x = -2$; if $x = 2$, $3(2)^2 - y^2 = 8$; $y^2 = 4$, $y = 2$ or $y = -2$; if $x = -2$, $3(-2)^2 - y^2 = 8$; $y^2 = 4$, $y = 2$ or $y = -2$; $\{(2, 2), (2, -2), (-2, 2), (-2, -2)\}$

15. $\begin{matrix} 5x^2 + 3y^2 = 7 \\ 3x^2 - 7y^2 = 13 \end{matrix}; \begin{matrix} 35x^2 + 21y^2 = 49 \\ 9x^2 - 21y^2 = 39 \end{matrix}; 44x^2 = 88; x^2 = 2; x = \sqrt{2}$ or $x = -\sqrt{2}$; if $x = \sqrt{2}$, $5(\sqrt{2})^2 + 3y^2 = 7$; $3y^2 = -3$; $y^2 = -1$, no real solution; if $x = -\sqrt{2}$, $5(-\sqrt{2})^2 + 3y^2 = 7$; $3y^2 = -3$; $y^2 = -1$, no real solution; no real solution

16. $9x^2 + 9y^2 = 1$; $x = y^2 + 1$; $y^2 = x - 1$; $9x^2 + 9(x - 1) = 1$; $9x^2 + 9x - 10 = 0$; $(3x - 2)(3x + 5) = 0$; $x = \frac{2}{3}$ or $x = -\frac{5}{3}$; if $x = \frac{2}{3}$, $y^2 = -\frac{1}{3}$, no real solution; if $x = -\frac{5}{3}$, $y^2 = -\frac{8}{3}$, no real solution; no real solution

17. $x^2 + y^2 = 13$; $xy + 6 = 0$; $y = -\frac{6}{x}$; $x^2 + \left(-\frac{6}{x}\right)^2 = 13$; $x^2 + \frac{36}{x^2} = 13$; $x^4 - 13x^2 + 36 = 0$; $(x^2 - 9)(x^2 - 4) = 0$; $x^2 = 9$ or $x^2 = 4$; $x = 3$ or $x = -3$ or $x = 2$ or $x = -2$; if $x = 3$, $y = -\frac{6}{3} = -2$; if $x = -3$, $y = -\frac{6}{-3} = 2$; if $x = 2$, $y = -\frac{6}{2} = -3$; if $x = -2$, $y = -\frac{6}{-2} = 3$; $\{(3, -2), (-3, 2), (2, -3), (-2, 3)\}$

18. $2x^2 - y^2 = 7$; $xy = 3$; $y = \frac{3}{x}$; $2x^2 - \left(\frac{3}{x}\right)^2 = 7$; $2x^2 - \frac{9}{x^2} = 7$; $2x^4 - 7x^2 - 9 = 0$; $(2x^2 - 9)(x^2 + 1) = 0$; $x^2 = \frac{9}{2}$ or $x^2 = -1$ (no real solution); $x = \frac{3\sqrt{2}}{2}$ or $-\frac{3\sqrt{2}}{2}$; if $x = \frac{3\sqrt{2}}{2}$, $y = \frac{3}{\frac{3\sqrt{2}}{2}} = \sqrt{2}$; if $x = -\frac{3\sqrt{2}}{2}$, $y = \frac{3}{-\frac{3\sqrt{2}}{2}} = -\sqrt{2}$;

$\left\{\left(\frac{3\sqrt{2}}{2}, \sqrt{2}\right), \left(-\frac{3\sqrt{2}}{2}, -\sqrt{2}\right)\right\}$

19. $\begin{matrix} y^2 = x + 7 \\ xy = 6 \end{matrix}; y = \frac{6}{x}; \left(\frac{6}{x}\right)^2 = x + 7; \frac{36}{x^2} = x + 7; 36 = x^3 + 7x^2; x^3 + 7x^2 - 36 = 0$; testing possible rational roots yields solutions $x = 2, -3$, and -6; if $x = 2$, $y = \frac{6}{2} = 3$; if $x = -3$, $y = \frac{6}{-3} = -2$; if $x = -6$, $y = \frac{6}{-6} = -1$; $\{(2, 3), (-3, -2), (-6, -1)\}$

20. $\begin{array}{l} y = x^2 - 1 \\ xy + 6 = 0 \end{array}$; $xy = -6$; $y = -\frac{6}{x}$; $-\frac{6}{x} = x^2 - 1$; $-6 = x^3 - x$; $x^3 - x + 6 = 0$;

testing possible rational roots yields the solution $x = -2$; if $x = -2$, $y = \frac{-6}{-2} = 3$; $(-2, 3)$; the depressed equation $x^2 - 2x + 3$ has discriminant -8 and therefore has no real roots.

Exercises 21–26. Let a square root be $x + yi$, where x and y are real. $(x + yi)^2 = x^2 - y^2 + 2xyi$.

C **21.** $x^2 - y^2 + 2xyi = 3 + 4i$, $\begin{array}{l} x^2 - y^2 = 3 \\ 2xy = 4 \end{array}$; $y = \frac{2}{x}$; $x^2 - \left(\frac{2}{x}\right)^2 = 3$, $x^2 - \frac{4}{x^2} = 3$, $x^4 - 4 = 3x^2$, $x^4 - 3x^2 - 4 = 0$, $(x^2 - 4)(x^2 + 1) = 0$, $x^2 = 4$, $x^2 = -1$ (reject); $x = 2$ or $x = -2$; if $x = 2$, $y = 1$; if $x = -2$, $y = -1$; $\{2 + i, -2 - i\}$

22. $x^2 - y^2 + 2xyi = 7 - 24i$; $\begin{array}{l} x^2 - y^2 = 7 \\ 2xy = -24 \end{array}$; $y = -\frac{12}{x}$; $x^2 - \left(-\frac{12}{x}\right)^2 = 7$;

$x^2 - \frac{144}{x^2} = 7$, $x^4 - 144 = 7x^2$, $x^4 - 7x^2 - 144 = 0$, $(x^2 - 16)(x^2 + 9) = 0$, $x^2 = 16$ or $x^2 = -9$ (reject); $x = 4$ or $x = -4$; if $x = 4$, $y = -3$; if $x = -4$, $y = 3$; $\{4 - 3i, -4 + 3i\}$

23. $x^2 - y^2 + 2xyi = 5 + 12i$; $\begin{array}{l} x^2 - y^2 = 5 \\ 2xy = 12 \end{array}$; $y = \frac{6}{x}$; $x^2 - \left(\frac{6}{x}\right)^2 = 5$, $x^2 - \frac{36}{x^2} = 5$, $x^4 - 36 = 5x^2$, $x^4 - 5x^2 - 36 = 0$, $(x^2 - 9)(x^2 + 4) = 0$, $x^2 = 9$ or $x^2 = -4$ (reject); $x = 3$ or $x = -3$; if $x = 3$, $y = 2$; if $x = -3$, $y = -2$; $\{3 + 2i, -3 - 2i\}$

24. $x^2 - y^2 + 2xyi = -5 - 12i$; $\begin{array}{l} x^2 - y^2 = -5 \\ 2xy = -12 \end{array}$; $x = -\frac{6}{y}$; $\left(-\frac{6}{y}\right)^2 - y^2 = -5$,

$\frac{36}{y^2} - y^2 = -5$, $36 - y^4 = -5y^2$, $y^4 - 5y^2 - 36 = 0$, $(y^2 - 9)(y^2 + 4) = 0$, $y^2 = 9$ or $y^2 = -4$ (reject); $y = 3$ or $y = -3$; if $y = 3$, $x = -2$; if $y = -3$, $x = 2$; $\{-2 + 3i, 2 - 3i\}$

25. $x^2 - y^2 + 2xyi = -7 + 24i$; $\begin{array}{l} x^2 - y^2 = -7 \\ 2xy = 24 \end{array}$; $x = \frac{12}{y}$; $\left(\frac{12}{y}\right)^2 - y^2 = -7$,

$\frac{144}{y^2} - y^2 = -7$, $144 - y^4 = -7y^2$, $y^4 - 7y^2 - 144 = 0$, $(y^2 - 16)(y^2 + 9) = 0$; $y^2 = 16$ or $y^2 = -9$ (reject); $y = 4$ or $y = -4$; if $y = 4$, $x = 3$; if $y = -4$, $x = -3$; $\{3 + 4i, -3 - 4i\}$

26. $x^2 - y^2 + 2xyi = 12 - 16i$; $\begin{array}{l} x^2 - y^2 = 12 \\ 2xy = -16 \end{array}$; $x = -\frac{8}{y}$; $\left(-\frac{8}{y}\right)^2 - y^2 = 12$,

$\frac{64}{y^2} - y^2 = 12$, $64 - y^4 = 12y^2$, $y^4 + 12y^2 - 64 = 0$, $(y^2 + 16)(y^2 - 4) = 0$, $y^2 = -16$ (reject) or $y^2 = 4$; $y = 2$ or $y = -2$; if $y = 2$, $x = -4$; if $y = -2$, $x = 4$; $\{4 - 2i, -4 + 2i\}$

Pages 442–443 • PROBLEMS

A **1.** Let x and y be the two numbers; $\begin{array}{l} x + y = 16 \\ x^2 + y^2 = 146 \end{array}$; $y = 16 - x$; $x^2 + (16 - x)^2 = 146$,

$x^2 + 256 - 32x + x^2 = 146$, $2x^2 - 32x + 110 = 0$, $x^2 - 16x + 55 = 0$, $(x - 5)(x - 11) = 0$, $x = 5$ or $x = 11$; if $x = 5$, $y = 11$; if $x = 11$, $y = 5$; 5 and 11

2. Let x and y be the two numbers; $\begin{matrix} xy = 1 \\ x^2 - y^2 = \frac{15}{4} \end{matrix}$; $y = \frac{1}{x}$, $x^2 - \frac{1}{x^2} = \frac{15}{4}$, $4x^4 - 4 = 15x^2$; $4x^4 - 15x^2 - 4 = 0$, $(4x^2 + 1)(x^2 - 4) = 0$, $x^2 = -\frac{1}{4}$ (reject) or $x^2 = 4$; $x = 2$ or $x = -2$; if $x = 2$, $y = \frac{1}{2}$; if $x = -2$, $y = -\frac{1}{2}$; 2 and $\frac{1}{2}$ or -2 and $-\frac{1}{2}$

3. Let x and y be the length and width respectively, in meters; $\begin{matrix} 2x + 2y = 156 \\ xy = 1505 \end{matrix}$; $y = 78 - x$; $x(78 - x) = 1505$, $78x - x^2 = 1505$, $x^2 - 78x + 1505 = 0$; $(x - 43)(x - 35) = 0$; $x = 43$ or $x = 35$; if $x = 43$, $y = 35$; if $x = 35$; $y = 43$; 35 m by 43 m

4. Let x and y be the length and width of the rectangle; $\begin{matrix} xy = 12 \\ 2x + 2y = 14 \end{matrix}$; $y = 7 - x$; $x(7 - x) = 12$, $7x - x^2 = 12$; $x^2 - 7x + 12 = 0$, $(x - 4)(x - 3) = 0$, $x = 3$ or $x = 4$; if $x = 3$, $y = 4$; if $x = 4$, $y = 3$; the rectangle is 3 units by 4 units; $2a = 4$, $a = 2$; $2b = 3$, $b = \frac{3}{2}$; $\frac{x^2}{2^2} + \frac{y^2}{\left(\frac{3}{2}\right)^2} = 1$; $\frac{x^2}{4} + \frac{4y^2}{9} = 1$

5. Let x and y be the length and width in feet of the rectangle; $\begin{matrix} 2x + 2y = 34 \\ x^2 + y^2 = 13^2 \end{matrix}$; $y = 17 - x$; $x^2 + (17 - x)^2 = 169$, $x^2 + 289 - 34x + x^2 = 169$, $2x^2 - 34x + 120 = 0$, $x^2 - 17x + 60 = 0$, $(x - 12)(x - 5) = 0$, $x = 12$ or $x = 5$; if $x = 12$, $y = 5$; if $x = 5$, $y = 12$; 5 ft by 12 ft

6. Let x and y be the lengths, in meters, of the legs of the triangle; $\begin{matrix} x + y + 25 = 56 \\ x^2 + y^2 = 25^2 \end{matrix}$; $y = 31 - x$; $x^2 + (31 - x)^2 = 625$, $x^2 + 961 - 62x + x^2 = 625$, $2x^2 - 62x + 336 = 0$, $x^2 - 31x + 168 = 0$, $(x - 24)(x - 7) = 0$, $x = 7$ or $x = 24$; if $x = 7$, $y = 24$; if $x = 24$, $y = 7$; 7 m and 24 m

7. Let t and u be the tens and units digits respectively; the number is $10t + u$; $\begin{matrix} (10t + u)t = 285 \\ u = 2 + t \end{matrix}$; $\begin{matrix} 10t^2 + ut = 285 \\ u = 2 + t \end{matrix}$; $10t^2 + (2 + t)t = 285$, $10t^2 + 2t + t^2 = 285$, $11t^2 + 2t - 285 = 0$, $(t - 5)(11t + 57) = 0$, $t = 5$ or $t = -\frac{57}{11}$ (reject); $u = 7$; 57

8. Let x and y be the dimensions; $xy = 10$; $x^2 + y^2 = 25$; $y = \frac{10}{x}$; $x^2 + \left(\frac{10}{x}\right)^2 = 25$; $x^2 + \frac{100}{x^2} = 25$; $x^4 + 100 = 25x^2$; $x^4 - 25x^2 + 100 = 0$; $(x^2 - 20)(x^2 - 5) = 0$; $x^2 = 20$ or $x^2 = 5$; $x = 2\sqrt{5}$ or $-2\sqrt{5}$ (reject), or $x = \sqrt{5}$ or $-\sqrt{5}$ (reject); if $x = 2\sqrt{5}$, $y = \sqrt{5}$; if $x = \sqrt{5}$, $y = 2\sqrt{5}$; $\sqrt{5}$ by $2\sqrt{5}$

B

9. $\begin{aligned} 3x + 2y &= 180 \\ xy &= 1350 \end{aligned}$; $y = 90 - \frac{3}{2}x$; $x\left(90 - \frac{3}{2}x\right) = 1350$, $90x - \frac{3}{2}x^2 = 1350$,

$\frac{3}{2}x^2 - 90x + 1350 = 0$, $x^2 - 60x + 900 = 0$, $(x - 30)^2 = 0$, $x = 30$; $y = 45$;

30 m by 45 m

10. Let x and y be the original length and width, respectively, in cm; $xy = 560$; $4(x - 8)(y - 8) = 960$; $(x - 8)(y - 8) = 240$, $xy - 8x - 8y + 64 = 240$, $560 - 8(x + y) + 64 = 240$, $-8(x + y) = -384$, $x + y = 48$; $y = 48 - x$; $x(48 - x) = 560$, $48x - x^2 = 560$, $x^2 - 48x + 560 = 0$, $(x - 28)(x - 20) = 0$, $x = 28$ or $x = 20$; if $x = 28$, $y = 20$; if $x = 20$, $y = 28$; 20 cm by 28 cm

11. Let x and y be the rates, in km/h, of the slower and faster walkers, respectively. $y = x + 1$; $x^2 + y^2 = 6^2$; $x^2 + (x + 1)^2 = 36$, $x^2 + x^2 + 2x + 1 = 36$,

$2x^2 + 2x - 35 = 0$, $x = \frac{-2 \pm \sqrt{4 - 4(-35)(2)}}{2(2)} = \frac{-2 \pm \sqrt{284}}{4} = \frac{-1 \pm \sqrt{71}}{2}$;

$x \approx 3.7$ or $x \approx -4.7$ (reject); $y = 3.7 + 1 = 4.7$; 3.7 km/h and 4.7 km/h

12. Let x be the distance in m of the bottom of the shorter ladder from the bottom of the building; let y = distance up the building in m of the tops of the ladders.

$\begin{aligned} x^2 + y^2 &= 15^2 \\ (x + 7)^2 + y^2 &= 20^2 \end{aligned}$; $x^2 - (x + 7)^2 = 225 - 400$, $x^2 - (x^2 + 14x + 49) = -175$,

$-14x = -126$, $x = 9$; $81 + y^2 = 225$, $y^2 = 144$, $y = -12$ (reject) or $y = 12$; 12 m

C

13. Let $P(x, y)$ be the point on the circle closest to $A(4, 3)$. Then the shortest path from A to $O(0, 0)$ is $AP + PO$. Since the shortest path from A to O is $\overline{AO}$, P is the point where $\overline{AO}$ intersects the circle. Using similar triangles, $\frac{y}{3} = \frac{x}{4}$; $y = \frac{3x}{4}$; $x^2 + y^2 = 1$;

$x^2 + \left(\frac{3x}{4}\right)^2 = 1$; $x^2 + \frac{9x^2}{16} = 1$; $25x^2 = 16$; $x^2 = \frac{16}{25}$; $x = \frac{4}{5}$ or $x = -\frac{4}{5}$ (reject),

[(x, y) is in the first quadrant]; $y = \frac{3x}{4} = \frac{3}{4}\left(\frac{4}{5}\right) = \frac{3}{5}$; $\left(\frac{4}{5}, \frac{3}{5}\right)$

14. With the coordinate system described, the sloping side passes through (10, 0) and

(510, 300); $m = \frac{300 - 0}{510 - 10} = \frac{300}{500} = \frac{3}{5}$; $y = \frac{3}{5}x + b$; $0 = \frac{3}{5}(10) + b$; $0 = 6 + b$; $b = -6$;

equation for sloping wall: $y = \frac{3}{5}x - 6$; $\frac{3}{5}x - 6 = 300 - \frac{x^2}{80}$; $48x - 480 =$

$24{,}000 - x^2$; $x^2 + 48x - 24{,}480 = 0$; $x = -24 + 12\sqrt{174} \approx 134.3$;

$y = \frac{3}{5}(-24 + 12\sqrt{174}) - 6 = \frac{-102 + 36\sqrt{174}}{5} \approx 74.6$;

distance $= \sqrt{(-24 + 12\sqrt{174} - 0)^2 + \left(\frac{-102 + 36\sqrt{174}}{5} - 300\right)^2} \approx 262.4$ m

Pages 447–448 • WRITTEN EXERCISES

A

1. $\begin{aligned} x + y - 3z &= 10 \\ y + z &= 12 \\ z &= -2 \end{aligned}$; $y + (-2) = 12$, $y = 14$; $x + 14 - 3(-2) = 10$, $x = -10$;

$\{(-10, 14, -2)\}$

2. $$\begin{array}{rl} x + 2y + 3z = -1 & \\ 3y + 2z = -1 & ;\ 3y + 2(-2) = -1, 3y = 3, y = 1; x + 2(1) + 3(-2) = -1, \\ z = -2 & \ x + 2 - 6 = -1, x = 3; \{(3, 1, -2)\} \end{array}$$

3. $$\begin{array}{rl} x + 2y - z = 3 & \\ 3y + z = -10 & ;\ z = -4; 3y + (-4) = -10, 3y = -6, y = -2; \\ -2z = 8 & \ x + 2(-2) - (-4) = 3, x = 3; \{(3, -2, -4)\} \end{array}$$

4. $$\begin{array}{rl} 5x - 3y + 4z = 4 & \\ 4y - 3z = 10 & ;\ z = -2; 4y - 3(-2) = 10, 4y = 4, y = 1; \\ 3z = -6 & \ 5x - 3(1) + 4(-2) = 4, 5x = 15, x = 3; \{(3, 1, -2)\} \end{array}$$

5. $$\begin{array}{rl} 2z + 3y - x = 0 & \\ 4y - x = -4 & ;\ x = -4, 4y - (-4) = -4, 4y = -8, y = -2; \\ -2x = 8 & \ 2z + 3(-2) - (-4) = 0, 2z = 2, z = 1; \{(-4, -2, 1)\} \end{array}$$

6. $$\begin{array}{rl} z + 3x + y = 3 & \\ 2x + 3y = 10 & ;\ y = 4; 2x + 3(4) = 10, 2x = -2, x = -1; z + 3(-1) + 4 = 3, \\ 2y = 8 & \ z = 2; \{(-1, 4, 2)\} \end{array}$$

7. $$\begin{array}{rcrl} 2x - y - z = 2 & & 2x - y - z = 2 & \\ x - 5y + 3z = -13 & ; & -12y + 7z = -28 & ;\ y = 0; 7z = -28, z = -4; \\ -2x - 2y + z = -2 & & -3y = 0 & \end{array}$$

$2x - 0 - (-4) = 2, 2x = -2, x = -1; \{(-1, 0, -4)\}$

8. $$\begin{array}{rcrcrl} x + 3y + 2z = -1 & & x + 3y + 2z = -1 & & x + 3y + 2z = -1 & \\ -3x - 2y + z = 3 & ; & 7y + 7z = 0 & ; & 7y + 7z = 0 & ;\ z = -1; \\ 2x - y + 3z = -8 & & -7y - z = -6 & & 6z = -6 & \end{array}$$

$7y + 7(-1) = 0, y = 1; x + 3 - 2 = -1, x = -2; \{(-2, 1, -1)\}$

9. $$\begin{array}{rcrcrl} 2x + y + 3z = 10 & & x - 2y + z = 10 & & x - 2y + z = 10 & \\ x - 2y + z = 10 & ; & 5y + z = -10 & ; & 5y + z = -10 & ;\ z = 5; \\ -4x + 3y + 2z = 5 & & -5y + 6z = 45 & & 7z = 35 & \end{array}$$

$5y + 5 = -10, 5y = -15, y = -3; x - 2(-3) + 5 = 10, x = -1; \{(-1, -3, 5)\}$

10. $$\begin{array}{rcrcrl} 2x + 5y + 2z = -5 & & x + 4y - z = 3 & & x + 4y - z = 3 & \\ -3x + 3y + 5z = 2 & ; & -3y + 4z = -11 & ; & -3y + 4z = -11 & ;\ z = -2; \\ x + 4y - z = 3 & & 15y + 2z = 11 & & 22z = -44 & \end{array}$$

$-3y + 4(-2) = -11, -3y = -3, y = 1; x + 4(1) - (-2) = 3, x + 6 = 3, x = -3;$
$\{(-3, 1, -2)\}$

11. $$\begin{array}{rcrcrl} 2x + 3y = 6 + z & & x - 2y + z = -1 & & x - 2y + z = -1 & \\ x - 2y = -1 - z & ; & 2x + 3y - z = 6 & ; & 7y - 3z = 8 & ; \\ 3x + y = -1 + 3z & & 3x + y - 3z = -1 & & 7y - 6z = 2 & \end{array}$$

$$\begin{array}{rl} x - 2y + z = -1 & \\ 7y - 3z = 8 & ;\ z = 2; 7y - 3(2) = 8, 7y = 14, y = 2; \\ -3z = 6 & \end{array}$$

$x - 2(2) + 2 = -1, x = 1; \{(1, 2, 2)\}$

12. $\begin{array}{l} 2x - y = 3z - 3 \\ 3x + 2y = z - 1 \\ x + 3y = z - 10 \end{array}$; $\begin{array}{l} x + 3y - z = -10 \\ 2x - y - 3z = -3 \\ 3x + 2y - z = -1 \end{array}$; $\begin{array}{l} x + 3y - z = -10 \\ -7y - z = 17 \\ -7y + 2z = 29 \end{array}$;

$\begin{array}{l} x + 3y - z = -10 \\ -7y - z = 17 \\ 3z = 12 \end{array}$; $z = 4$; $-7y - 4 = 17$, $-7y = 21$, $y = -3$; $x + 3(-3) - 4 = -10$, $x = 3$; $\{(3, -3, 4)\}$

B **13.** $\begin{array}{l} 3a - 2b + 2c = 1 \\ 2a + 5b - 5c = 7 \\ 4a - 3b + c = -3 \end{array}$; $\begin{array}{l} -5a + 4b = 7 \\ 22a - 10b = -8 \\ 4a - 3b + c = -3 \end{array}$; $\begin{array}{l} -25a + 20b = 35 \\ 44a - 20b = -16 \\ 4a - 3b + c = -3 \end{array}$;

$\begin{array}{l} 19a = 19 \\ 11a - 5b = -4 \\ 4a - 3b + c = -3 \end{array}$; $a = 1$; $11 - 5b = -4$, $b = 3$; $4(1) - 3(3) + c = -3$, $c = 2$; $\{(1, 3, 2)\}$

14. $\begin{array}{l} 2x + 2y + z = 3 \\ 3x + 2y - 2z = -1 \\ 5x - 2y - 6z = 17 \end{array}$; $\begin{array}{l} 2x + 2y + z = 3 \\ 7x + 6y = 5 \\ 17x + 10y = 35 \end{array}$; $\begin{array}{l} 2x + 2y + z = 3 \\ 35x + 30y = 25 \\ 51x + 30y = 105 \end{array}$;

$\begin{array}{l} 2x + 2y + z = 3 \\ 7x + 6y = 5 \\ 16x = 80 \end{array}$; $x = 5$; $7(5) + 6y = 5$, $y = -5$; $2(5) + 2(-5) + z = 3$; $z = 3$; $\{(5, -5, 3)\}$

15. $\begin{array}{l} 3u + 2v + w = 4 \\ 5u + 3v - w = -2 \\ 2u + w = 1 \end{array}$; $\begin{array}{l} u + 2v = 3 \\ 7u + 3v = -1 \\ 2u + w = 1 \end{array}$; $\begin{array}{l} u + 2v = 3 \\ -11v = -22 \\ 2u + w = 1 \end{array}$;

$v = 2$; $u + 2(2) = 3$, $u = -1$; $2(-1) + w = 1$, $w = 3$; $\{(-1, 2, 3)\}$

16. $\begin{array}{l} a + 3b + 4c = 6 \\ a - 2b + c = 10 \\ 2a + 3b - c = 0 \end{array}$; $\begin{array}{l} a + 3b + 4c = 6 \\ -5b - 3c = 4 \\ -3b - 9c = -12 \end{array}$; $\begin{array}{l} a + 3b + 4c = 6 \\ -5b - 3c = 4 \\ 12b = -24 \end{array}$; $b = -2$;

$-5(-2) - 3c = 4$; $-3c = -6$, $c = 2$; $a + 3(-2) + 4(2) = 6$, $a = 4$; $\{(4, -2, 2)\}$

17. $\begin{array}{l} \frac{1}{x} - \frac{2}{y} + \frac{3}{z} = -3 \\ \frac{2}{x} - \frac{3}{y} - \frac{1}{z} = 7 \\ \frac{3}{x} + \frac{1}{y} - \frac{2}{z} = 6 \end{array}$; let $a = \frac{1}{x}$, $b = \frac{1}{y}$, and $c = \frac{1}{z}$; $\begin{array}{l} a - 2b + 3c = -3 \\ 2a - 3b - c = 7 \\ 3a + b - 2c = 6 \end{array}$;

$\begin{array}{l} a - 2b + 3c = -3 \\ b - 7c = 13 \\ 7b - 11c = 15 \end{array}$; $\begin{array}{l} a - 2b + 3c = -3 \\ b - 7c = 13 \\ 38c = -76 \end{array}$; $c = -2$; $b - 7(-2) = 13$,

$b = -1$; $a - 2(-1) + 3(-2) = -3$, $a = 1$; $x = \frac{1}{1} = 1$, $y = \frac{1}{-1} = -1$, $z = \frac{1}{-2}$;

$\left\{\left(1, -1, -\frac{1}{2}\right)\right\}$

18. $\frac{1}{r} + \frac{3}{s} - \frac{2}{t} = 1$

$\frac{2}{r} + \frac{3}{s} - \frac{4}{t} = 1$; let $x = \frac{1}{r}$, $y = \frac{1}{s}$, and $z = \frac{1}{t}$; $\begin{array}{r} x + 3y - 2z = 1 \\ 2x + 3y - 4z = 1 \\ x - 6y - 6z = 0 \end{array}$;

$\frac{1}{r} - \frac{6}{s} - \frac{6}{t} = 0$

$\begin{array}{r} x + 3y - 2z = 1 \\ -3y \quad = -1 \\ -9y - 4z = -1 \end{array}$; $y = \frac{1}{3}$; $-9\left(\frac{1}{3}\right) - 4z = -1, -4z = 2, z = -\frac{1}{2}$;

$x + 3\left(\frac{1}{3}\right) - 2\left(-\frac{1}{2}\right) = 1, x = -1; r = -1, s = 3, t = -2; \{(-1, 3, -2)\}$

19. a. $\begin{array}{r} x - 2y + 3z = 1 \\ x + y - 3z = 7 \\ 3x - 4y + 5z = 7 \end{array}$; $\begin{array}{r} x - 2y + 3z = 1 \\ 3y - 6z = 6 \\ 2y - 4z = 4 \end{array}$; $\begin{array}{r} x - 2y + 3z = 1 \\ y - 2z = 2 \\ y - 2z = 2 \end{array}$;

$\begin{array}{r} x - 2y + 3z = 1 \\ y - 2z = 2 \\ 0 = 0 \end{array}$; $y = 2z + 2; x - 2(2z + 2) + 3z = 1, x - 4z - 4 + 3z = 1,$

$x = z + 5; \{(z + 5, 2z + 2, z): z \text{ is a real number}\}$

b. Examples: (5, 2, 0), (8, 8, 3), (3, −2, −2)

20. a. $\begin{array}{r} x + 2y - 2z = 3 \\ x + 3y - 4z = 6 \\ 4x + 5y - 2z = 3 \end{array}$; $\begin{array}{r} x + 2y - 2z = 3 \\ y - 2z = 3 \\ -3y + 6z = -9 \end{array}$; $\begin{array}{r} x + 2y - 2z = 3 \\ y - 2z = 3 \\ 0 = 0 \end{array}$; $y = 2z + 3$;

$x + 2(2z + 3) - 2z = 3, x + 4z + 6 - 2z = 3, x = -2z - 3;$
$\{(-2z - 3, 2z + 3, z): z \text{ is a real number}\}$

b. Examples: (−3, 3, 0), (−5, 5, 1), (−9, 9, 3)}

C

21. $\begin{array}{r} x - 2y - z = -1 \\ 2x - y + z = 3 \\ x + 4y + 5z = 5 \end{array}$; $\begin{array}{r} x - 2y - z = -1 \\ 3y + 3z = 5 \\ 6y + 6z = 6 \end{array}$; $\begin{array}{r} x - 2y - z = -1 \\ 3y + 3z = 5 \\ 0 = -4 \end{array}$; $0 \neq -4$;

the system is inconsistent

22. $\begin{array}{r} x + 2y - 2z = 3 \\ x + 3y - 4z = 6 \\ 4x + 5y - 2z = 6 \end{array}$; $\begin{array}{r} x + 2y - 2z = 3 \\ y - 2z = 3 \\ -3y + 6z = -6 \end{array}$; $\begin{array}{r} x + 2y - 2z = 3 \\ y - 2z = 3 \\ 0 = 3 \end{array}$; $0 \neq 3$;

the system is inconsistent

23. $\begin{array}{r} x \quad - 2z = 0 \\ 2x - y + z = 0 \\ x - y + 3z = 0 \end{array}$; $\begin{array}{r} x \quad - 2z = 0 \\ -y + 5z = 0 \\ -y + 5z = 0 \end{array}$; $\begin{array}{r} x \quad - 2z = 0 \\ -y + 5z = 0 \\ 0 = 0 \end{array}$; $y = 5z; x = 2z;$

$\{(2z, 5z, z): z \text{ is a real number}\}$

24. $\begin{array}{r} x + 2y - 2z = 0 \\ 2x + 5y + 2z = 0 \\ 3x + 4y - 2z = 0 \end{array}$; $\begin{array}{r} x + 2y - 2z = 0 \\ y + 6z = 0 \\ -2y + 4z = 0 \end{array}$; $\begin{array}{r} x + 2y - 2z = 0 \\ y + 6z = 0 \\ 16z = 0 \end{array}$;

(0, 0, 0) is the only solution

25. $\begin{array}{r} x - 2y + 4z = 0 \\ 3x - y + 2z = 0 \\ x + 3y - 6z = 0 \end{array}$; $\begin{array}{r} x - 2y + 4z = 0 \\ 5y - 10z = 0 \\ 5y - 10z = 0 \end{array}$; $\begin{array}{r} x - 2y + 4z = 0 \\ 5y - 10z = 0 \\ 0 = 0 \end{array}$; $y = 2z$;

$x - 2(2z) + 4z = 0, x = 0; \{(0, 2z, z): z \text{ is a real number}\}$

Pages 448–449 • PROBLEMS

A

1. Let n, d, and q be the numbers of nickels, dimes, and quarters respectively;

$$\begin{aligned} 5n + 10d + 25q &= 235 \\ d &= (n + q) - 3 \\ n + d + q &= 19 \end{aligned} \; ; \quad \begin{aligned} n + 2d + 5q &= 47 \\ -n + d - q &= -3 \\ n + d + q &= 19 \end{aligned} \; ; \quad \begin{aligned} n + 2d + 5q &= 47 \\ 3d + 4q &= 44 \\ -d - 4q &= -28 \end{aligned} \; ;$$

$$\begin{aligned} n + 2d + 5q &= 47 \\ -d - 4q &= -28 \\ -8q &= -40 \end{aligned} \; ; \quad q = 5, -d - 4(5) = -28, -d = -8, d = 8;$$

$n + 2(8) + 5(5) = 47, n = 6$; 6 nickels, 8 dimes, 5 quarters

2. Let x, y, and z be the numbers of 15¢, 25¢ and 45¢ stamps respectively;

$$\begin{aligned} 15x + 25y + 45z &= 950 \\ x + y + z &= 38 \\ y &= 8 + 2z \end{aligned} \; ; \quad \begin{aligned} 3x + 5y + 9z &= 190 \\ x + y + z &= 38 \\ y - 2z &= 8 \end{aligned} \; ; \quad \begin{aligned} x + y + z &= 38 \\ 2y + 6z &= 76 \\ y - 2z &= 8 \end{aligned} \; ;$$

$$\begin{aligned} x + y + z &= 38 \\ y - 2z &= 8 \\ 10z &= 60 \end{aligned} \; ; \quad z = 6; y - 2(6) = 8, y = 20; x + 20 + 6 = 38, x = 12;$$

twelve 15¢ stamps, twenty 25¢ stamps, six 45¢ stamps

3. Let x, y, and z be the masses of the diamonds, in carats;

$$\begin{aligned} x + y &= 6 \\ y + z &= 10 \\ x + z &= 12 \end{aligned} \; ; \quad \begin{aligned} x + y &= 6 \\ y + z &= 10 \\ -y + z &= 6 \end{aligned} \; ; \quad \begin{aligned} x + y &= 6 \\ y + z &= 10 \\ 2z &= 16 \end{aligned} \; ; \quad z = 8, y = 2,$$

$x = 4$; 2 carats, 4 carats, 8 carats

4. Let x, y, and z be the masses in grams;

$$\begin{aligned} x + y &= z + 9 \\ y + z &= x + 27 \\ x + z &= y + 15 \end{aligned} \; ; \quad \begin{aligned} x + y - z &= 9 \\ -x + y + z &= 27 \\ x - y + z &= 15 \end{aligned} \; ; \quad 2x = 24; x = 12; 2y = 36; y = 18;$$

$2z = 42; z = 21$; 12 g, 18 g, 21 g

5. Let x, y, and z be the degree measures of the angles of the triangle, from smallest to largest;

$$\begin{aligned} x + y + z &= 180 \\ z &= 20 + 2x \\ 5x &= y + z \end{aligned} \; ; \quad \begin{aligned} x + y + z &= 180 \\ -2x + z &= 20 \\ 5x - y - z &= 0 \end{aligned} \; ; \quad \begin{aligned} x + y + z &= 180 \\ 2y + 3z &= 380 \\ -6y - 6z &= -900 \end{aligned} \; ;$$

$$\begin{aligned} x + y + z &= 180 \\ 2y + 3z &= 380 \\ 3z &= 240 \end{aligned} \; ; \quad z = 80, 2y + 3(80) = 380, 2y = 140, y = 70;$$

$x + 70 + 80 = 180, x = 30$; 30°, 70°, 80°

6. Let l, w, and h be the length, width, and height of the box in cm respectively;

$$\begin{aligned} l + w + h &= 75 \\ l &= 2(w + h) \\ 2w &= 5 + h \end{aligned} \; ; \quad \begin{aligned} l + w + h &= 75 \\ l - 2w - 2h &= 0 \\ 2w - h &= 5 \end{aligned} \; ; \quad \begin{aligned} l + w + h &= 75 \\ -3w - 3h &= -75 \\ 2w - h &= 5 \end{aligned} \; ; \quad \begin{aligned} l + w + h &= 75 \\ w + h &= 25 \\ 3w &= 30 \end{aligned} \; ;$$

$w = 10; h = 25 - 10 = 15; l + 10 + 15 = 75, l = 50$; 50 cm by 10 cm by 15 cm.

B

7. Let p, s, and d be the numbers of patron, sponsor, and donor tickets respectively;

$$\begin{cases} 10p + 5s + 2.5d = 1432.5 \\ d = 24 + s + p \\ p + s + d = 326 \end{cases} ; \quad \begin{cases} p + s + d = 326 \\ -p - s + d = 24 \\ 4p + 2s + d = 573 \end{cases} ; \quad \begin{cases} p + s + d = 326 \\ 2d = 350 \\ -2s - 3d = -731 \end{cases} ; \; d = 175,$$

$-2s - 3(175) = -731$, $-2s = -206$, $s = 103$; $p + 103 + 175 = 326$, $p = 48$; 48 patron, 103 sponsor, 175 donor

8. Let h, t, and u be the hundreds, tens, and units digits respectively; the number is $100h + 10t + u$.

$$\begin{cases} h + t + u = 21 \\ t + h = 2u - 3 \\ 100u + 10t + h = 198 + 100h + 10t + u \end{cases} ;$$

$$\begin{cases} h + t + u = 21 \\ h + t - 2u = -3 \\ -99h + 99u = 198 \end{cases} ; \quad \begin{cases} h + t + u = 21 \\ -3u = -24 \\ t + 2u = 23 \end{cases} ; \; u = 8; t + 2(8) = 23, t = 7;$$

$h + 7 + 8 = 21$, $h = 6$; 678

9. $y = ax^2 + bx + c$; $4 = a(-1)^2 + b(-1) + c$; $7 = a(2)^2 + b(2) + c$;

$$0 = a(1)^2 + b(1) + c; \quad \begin{cases} a - b + c = 4 \\ 4a + 2b + c = 7 \\ a + b + c = 0 \end{cases} ; \quad \begin{cases} a - b + c = 4 \\ 6b - 3c = -9 \\ 2b = -4 \end{cases} ; \; b = -2;$$

$6(-2) - 3c = -9$; $-3c = 3$, $c = -1$; $a - (-2) + (-1) = 4$, $a = 3$; $y = 3x^2 - 2x - 1$

10. $y = ax^2 + bx + c$; $3 = a(1)^2 + b(1) + c$; $10 = a(2)^2 + b(2) + c$;

$$-6 = a(-2)^2 + b(-2) + c; \quad \begin{cases} a + b + c = 3 \\ 4a + 2b + c = 10 \\ 4a - 2b + c = -6 \end{cases} ; \quad \begin{cases} a + b + c = 3 \\ -2b - 3c = -2 \\ -6b - 3c = -18 \end{cases} ;$$

$$\begin{cases} a + b + c = 3 \\ -2b - 3c = -2 \\ 6c = -12 \end{cases} ; \; c = -2; -2b - 3(-2) = -2, -2b = -8, b = 4;$$

$a + 4 + (-2) = 3$, $a = 1$; $y = x^2 + 4x - 2$

11. $x^2 + y^2 + Cx + Dy + E = 0$; $(2)^2 + (-1)^2 + C(2) + D(-1) + E = 0$; $(4)^2 + (-3)^2 + C(4) + D(-3) + E = 0$; $(0)^2 + (-3)^2 + C(0) + D(-3) + E = 0$;

$$\begin{cases} 4 + 1 + 2C - D + E = 0 \\ 16 + 9 + 4C - 3D + E = 0 \\ 9 - 3D + E = 0 \end{cases} ; \quad \begin{cases} 2C - D + E = -5 \\ 4C - 3D + E = -25 \\ -3D + E = -9 \end{cases} ; \quad \begin{cases} 2C - D + E = -5 \\ 4C = -16 \\ -3D + E = -9 \end{cases} ;$$

$$C = -4; \quad \begin{cases} -8 - D + E = -5 \\ -3D + E = -9 \end{cases} ; \quad \begin{cases} -D + E = 3 \\ -3D + E = -9 \end{cases} ; \; 2D = 12, D = 6; -6 + E = 3,$$

$E = 9$; $x^2 + y^2 - 4x + 6y + 9 = 0$

12. $x^2 + y^2 + Cx + Dy + E = 0$; $(-6)^2 + (-3)^2 + C(-6) + D(-3) + E = 0$; $(1)^2 + (4)^2 + C(1) + D(4) + E = 0$; $(2)^2 + (3)^2 + C(2) + D(3) + E = 0$;

$$\begin{cases} 36 + 9 - 6C - 3D + E = 0 \\ 1 + 16 + C + 4D + E = 0 \\ 4 + 9 + 2C + 3D + E = 0 \end{cases} ; \quad \begin{cases} -6C - 3D + E = -45 \\ C + 4D + E = -17 \\ 2C + 3D + E = -13 \end{cases} ;$$

$$\begin{cases} C + 4D + E = -17 \\ 21D + 7E = -147 \\ -5D - E = 21 \end{cases} ; \quad \begin{cases} C + 4D + E = -17 \\ -5D - E = 21 \\ -14D = 0 \end{cases} ; \; D = 0; E = -21;$$

$C + 4(0) - 21 = -17$, $C = 4$; $x^2 + y^2 + 4x - 21 = 0$

Page 449 • MIXED REVIEW EXERCISES

1. $x^2 - y^2 = 1$; $2x^2 = 4, x^2 = 2, x = -\sqrt{2}$ or $x = \sqrt{2}$; if $x = \sqrt{2}, (\sqrt{2})^2 + y^2 = 3,$
   $x^2 + y^2 = 3$
   $y^2 = 1, y = -1$ or $y = 1$; if $x = -\sqrt{2}, (-\sqrt{2})^2 + y^2 = 3, y^2 = 1, y = -1$ or $y = 1$;
   $\{(\sqrt{2}, 1), (-\sqrt{2}, 1), (\sqrt{2}, -1), (-\sqrt{2}, -1)\}$
2. $4x - y = 3$; $y = 4x - 3; x + 3(4x - 3) = 17, x + 12x - 9 = 17, 13x = 26,$
   $x + 3y = 17$ $\qquad x = 2; y = 4(2) - 3 = 5; \{(2, 5)\}$
3. $y^2 = x + 1$; $x = y^2 - 1; 2(y^2 - 1) + y = 4, 2y^2 - 2 + y = 4, 2y^2 + y - 6 = 0,$
   $2x + y = 4$
   $(2y - 3)(y + 2) = 0, y = \frac{3}{2}$ and $x = \left(\frac{3}{2}\right)^2 - 1 = \frac{5}{4}$, or $y = -2$ and
   $x = (-2)^2 - 1 = 3; \left\{(3, -2), \left(\frac{5}{4}, \frac{3}{2}\right)\right\}$
4. $(3x^{-1}y^2)^{-2} = 3^{-2}x^2y^{-4} = \frac{x^2}{9y^4}$ 5. $3\sqrt{16x^3} = 3\sqrt{(16x^2)x} = 12x\sqrt{x}$
6. $(4x^3y)(-3x^2y^4) = (4)(-3)x^{3+2}y^{1+4} = -12x^5y^5$
7. $(2x\sqrt{3})^2 = (2x)^2(\sqrt{3})^2 = 4x^2 \cdot 3 = 12x^2$
8. $\frac{10xy^{-2}}{6x^{-1}y^3} = \frac{10}{6} \cdot x^{1-(-1)} \cdot y^{-2-3} = \frac{5}{3}x^2y^{-5} = \frac{5x^2}{3y^5}$
9. $\frac{18x^3y}{30x^2y^4} = \frac{18}{30}x^{3-2} \cdot y^{1-4} = \frac{3}{5}xy^{-3} = \frac{3x}{5y^3}$ 10. $\sqrt{\frac{27x^4}{4}} = \frac{\sqrt{9x^4 \cdot 3}}{\sqrt{4}} = \frac{3x^2\sqrt{3}}{2}$
11. $\left(\frac{x}{y^2}\right)^{-1} \cdot \left(\frac{y}{x^2}\right)^2 = \frac{y^2}{x} \cdot \frac{y^2}{x^4} = \frac{y^4}{x^5}$

Pages 451–453 • CHAPTER REVIEW

1. d; $\sqrt{(-6 - (-4))^2 + (-1 - 3)^2} = \sqrt{4 + 16} = \sqrt{20} = 2\sqrt{5}$
2. b; $\left(\frac{-4 + (-6)}{2}, \frac{3 + (-1)}{2}\right) = (-5, 1)$
3. c; $-6 = \frac{-4 + x}{2}, -12 = -4 + x, x = -8; -1 = \frac{3 + y}{2}, -2 = 3 + y, y = -5;$
   $(-8, -5)$
4. b; $(x - 4)^2 + (y + 3)^2 = 25, x^2 - 8x + 16 + y^2 + 6y + 9 = 25,$
   $x^2 + y^2 - 8x + 6y = 0$
5. a; $x^2 + y^2 - 8x + 4y + 12 = 0, x^2 - 8x + y^2 + 4y = -12; (x^2 - 8x + 16) +$
   $(y^2 + 4y + 4) = -12 + 16 + 4, (x - 4)^2 + (y + 2)^2 = 8$
6. d; Center $= (-4, 4)$; radius $= 5$; $(x + 4)^2 + (y - 4)^2 = 25, x^2 + 8x + 16 + y^2 -$
   $8y + 16 = 25, x^2 + y^2 + 8x - 8y + 7 = 0$
7. c; $a = 2; y - 0 = -\frac{1}{4(2)}(x - 0)^2; y = -\frac{1}{8}x^2, x^2 = -8y$
8. b; $4x + 4 = y^2 - 4y + 4; 4(x + 1) = (y - 2)^2; x + 1 = \frac{1}{4}(y - 2)^2$
9. c; $V(3, 0)$; since it opens to the left, the equation has the form $x - 3 = -\frac{1}{4a}(y - 0)^2$;
   $x - 3 = -\frac{1}{4a}y^2; y^2 = -4ax + 12a$; the only suitable choice is c.

10. c; Center is (0, 0); $c = 2$; $2a = 8$, $a = 4$; $a^2 = b^2 + c^2$, $16 = b^2 + 4$, $b^2 = 12$; $\frac{x^2}{12} + \frac{y^2}{16} = 1$

11. a; $a^2 = 20$, $b^2 = 4$, foci are on the y-axis; $20 = 4 + c^2$, $c^2 = 16$, $c = 4$; foci are $(0, -4)$, $(0, 4)$

12. b; $8x^2 - 3y^2 = 48$, $\frac{x^2}{6} - \frac{y^2}{16} = 1$, $a^2 = 6$, $b^2 = 16$, $c^2 = 6 + 16 = 22$; $c = \sqrt{22}$; foci are on the x-axis; foci are $(\sqrt{22}, 0)$ and $(-\sqrt{22}, 0)$

13. c; $a = 2$, $b = 2$; $\frac{x^2}{4} - \frac{y^2}{4} = 1$, $x^2 - y^2 = 4$

14. a; $9x^2 - y^2 - 18x + 4y - 31 = 0$; $9(x^2 - 2x) - (y^2 - 4y) = 31$; $9(x^2 - 2x + 1) - (y^2 - 4y + 4) = 31 + 9 - 4$; $9(x - 1)^2 - (y - 2)^2 = 36$; Center $= (1, 2)$

15. d; Center $= \left(\frac{1 + 3}{2}, \frac{0 + 0}{2}\right) = (2, 0)$; $c = 1$; $2a = 4$, $a = 2$; major axis is horizontal; $(2)^2 = b^2 + 1^2$, $b^2 = 3$; $\frac{(x - 2)^2}{4} + \frac{y^2}{3} = 1$; $3(x - 2)^2 + 4y^2 = 12$, $3(x^2 - 4x + 4) + 4y^2 = 12$, $3x^2 - 12x + 12 + 4y^2 = 12$; $3x^2 + 4y^2 = 12x$

16. c; $x^2 - 4y^2 = 4$ and $x + y^2 = 1$; $\frac{x^2}{4} - \frac{y^2}{1} = 1$ and $x - 1 = -y^2$; two solutions

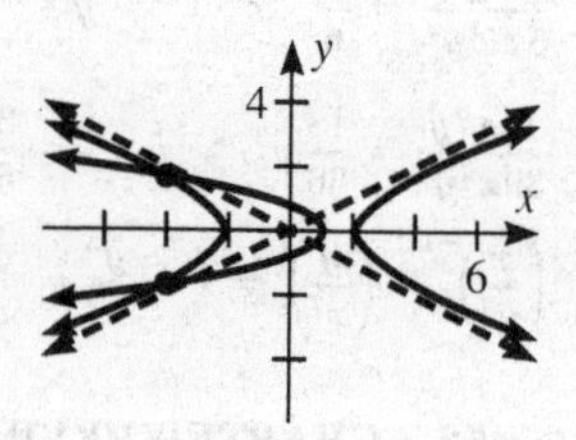

17. d; $x^2 + y^2 = 17$ and $x^2 - 2y = 9$; $x^2 = 9 + 2y$; $(9 + 2y) + y^2 = 17$; $y^2 + 2y - 8 = 0$; $(y - 2)(y + 4) = 0$; $y = 2$ or $y = -4$; if $y = 2$, $x^2 = 9 + 2(2)$, $x^2 = 13$, $x = -\sqrt{13}$ or $x = \sqrt{13}$; if $y = -4$, $x^2 = 9 + 2(-4)$, $x^2 = 1$, $x = -1$ or $x = 1$; $\{(\sqrt{13}, 2), (-\sqrt{13}, 2), (1, -4), (-1, -4)\}$

18. c; Let l and w be the length and width in meters; $\begin{matrix} 2(l + w) = 14 \\ l^2 + w^2 = 5^2 \end{matrix}$; $l = 7 - w$; $(7 - w)^2 + w^2 = 25$, $49 - 14w + w^2 + w^2 = 25$, $2w^2 - 14w + 24 = 0$, $w^2 - 7w + 12 = 0$, $(w - 3)(w - 4) = 0$; $w = 3$ or $w = 4$; if $w = 3$, $l = 7 - 3 = 4$; if $w = 4$, $l = 7 - 4 = 3$; 3 m by 4 m

19. c; $\begin{matrix} x + y + z = 2 \\ x - 2y - z = 2 \\ 3x + 2y + z = 2 \end{matrix}$; $\begin{matrix} x + y + z = 2 \\ 3y + 2z = 0 \\ -y - 2z = -4 \end{matrix}$; $\begin{matrix} x + y + z = 2 \\ 3y + 2z = 0 \\ 2y = -4 \end{matrix}$; $y = -2$; $3(-2) + 2z = 0$; $-6 + 2z = 0$; $2z = 6$; $z = 3$; $x + (-2) + 3 = 2$; $x + 1 = 2$; $x = 1$; $\{(1, -2, 3)\}$

20. b; Let x, y, and z be the number of \$1, \$5, and \$10 bills respectively.
$\begin{matrix} x + y + z = 10 \\ x + 5y + 10z = 36 \\ y - z = 0 \end{matrix}$; $\begin{matrix} x + y + z = 10 \\ 4y + 9z = 26 \\ y - z = 0 \end{matrix}$; $\begin{matrix} x + y + z = 10 \\ 4y + 9z = 26 \\ 13z = 26 \end{matrix}$; $z = 2$; $y = 2$; $x + 2 + 2 = 10$; $x = 6$; 6 \$1 bills, 2 \$5 bills, 2 \$10 bills

Page 453 • CHAPTER TEST

1. a. $PQ = \sqrt{(-5 - 3)^2 + [6 - (-4)]^2} = \sqrt{164} = 2\sqrt{41}$

   b. $\left(\frac{3 + (-5)}{2}, \frac{-4 + 6}{2}\right) = (-1, 1)$

   c. Let (x, y) be the coordinates of X. $3 = \frac{-5 + x}{2}$, $6 = -5 + x$, $x = 11$; $-4 = \frac{6 + y}{2}$,

   $-8 = 6 + y$, $y = -14$; $(11, -14)$

2. $(x - 6)^2 + (y + 3)^2 = r^2$; $(-4 - 6)^2 + (1 + 3)^2 = r^2$; $r^2 = 100 + 16 = 116$; $(x - 6)^2 + (y + 3)^2 = 116$

3. $x^2 + y^2 - 8x + 2y + 11 = 0$; $x^2 - 8x + y^2 + 2y = -11$; $(x^2 - 8x + 16) + (y^2 + 2y + 1) = -11 + 16 + 1$; $(x - 4)^2 + (y + 1)^2 = 6$; $C(4, -1)$; $r = \sqrt{6}$

4. Let $P(x, y)$ be any such point. $\sqrt{(x - 2)^2 + (y - 0)^2} = |y - (-4)|$; $(x - 2)^2 + y^2 = (y + 4)^2$; $(x - 2)^2 + y^2 = y^2 + 8y + 16$; $(x - 2)^2 = 8(y + 2)$;

   $y + 2 = \frac{1}{8}(x - 2)^2$

5. $V(1, -3)$; $\frac{1}{4a} = \frac{1}{8}$, $a = 2$; the parabola opens to the right; $F(3, -3)$; directrix: $x = -1$

6. Center: $(0, 0)$; major axis is horizontal; $2a = 6$, $a = 3$; $c = \sqrt{5}$; $(3)^2 = b^2 + (\sqrt{5})^2$,

   $b^2 = 4$; $\frac{x^2}{9} + \frac{y^2}{4} = 1$

7. $x^2 + 4y^2 = 16$; $\frac{x^2}{16} + \frac{y^2}{4} = 1$

8. $x^2 - y^2 + 4 = 0$; $\frac{y^2}{4} - \frac{x^2}{4} = 1$

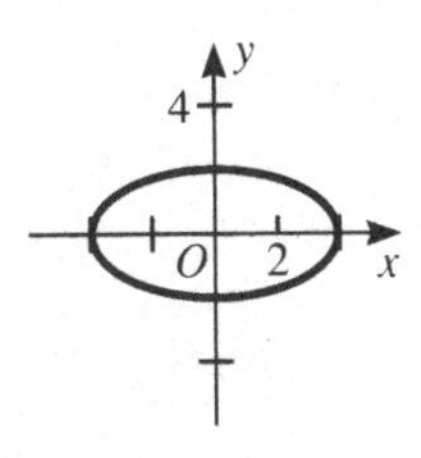

Ex. 7

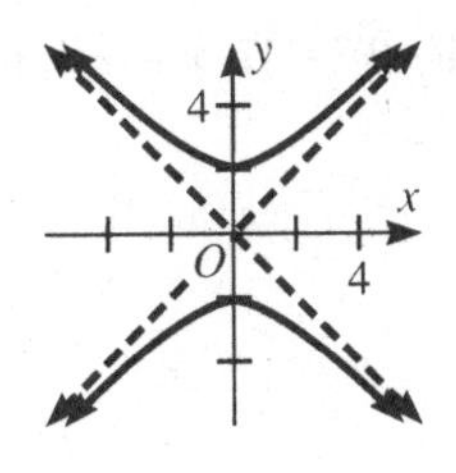

Ex. 8

9. Center: $(2, 0)$; $c = 2$; major axis is horizontal; $2a = 8$, $a = 4$; $(4)^2 = b^2 + (2)^2$,

   $b^2 = 12$; $\frac{(x - 2)^2}{16} + \frac{y^2}{12} = 1$

10. $x^2 - 4y^2 - 4x - 8y - 4 = 0$; $x^2 - 4x - 4(y^2 + 2y) = 4$; $(x^2 - 4x + 4) - 4(y^2 + 2y + 1) = 4 + 4 - 4$; $(x - 2)^2 - 4(y + 1)^2 = 4$; $\frac{(x - 2)^2}{4} - \frac{(y + 1)^2}{1} = 1$;

    a hyperbola centered at $(2, -1)$; $(2)^2 + (1)^2 = c^2$, $c^2 = 5$, $c = \sqrt{5}$; foci $(2 + \sqrt{5}, -1)$ and $(2 - \sqrt{5}, -1)$

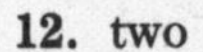

11. three

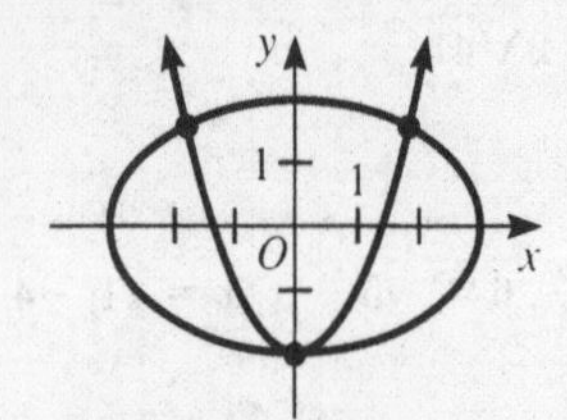

12. two

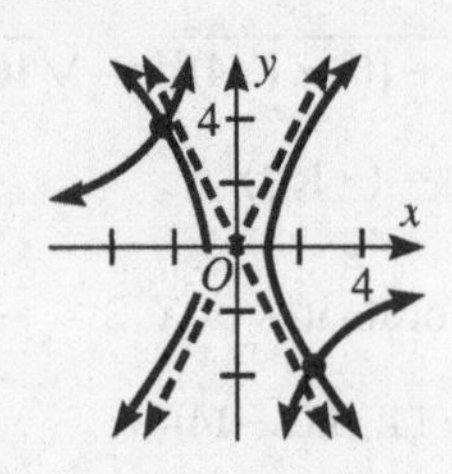

13. $x^2 - 4y^2 = 4$, $y^2 = x + 2$; $x^2 - 4(x + 2) = 4$, $x^2 - 4x - 8 = 4$, $x^2 - 4x - 12 = 0$,
$(x - 6)(x + 2) = 0$, $x = 6$ or $x = -2$; if $x = 6$, $y^2 = 8$, and $y = -2\sqrt{2}$ or $2\sqrt{2}$; if $x = -2$, $y^2 = 0$, and $y = 0$; $\{(-2, 0), (6, 2\sqrt{2}), (6, -2\sqrt{2})\}$

14. Let x and y be the length and width, in meters, of the rectangle; $\begin{matrix} xy = 36 \\ x^2 + y^2 = (5\sqrt{3})^2 \end{matrix}$;

$y = \frac{36}{x}$; $x^2 + \left(\frac{36}{x}\right)^2 = 75$, $x^4 + 1296 = 75x^2$, $x^4 - 75x^2 + 1296 = 0$,
$(x^2 - 48)(x^2 - 27) = 0$; $x^2 = 48$ or $x^2 = 27$; since $x > 0$, $x = \sqrt{48} = 4\sqrt{3}$ or
$x = \sqrt{27} = 3\sqrt{3}$; if $x = 4\sqrt{3}$, $y = \frac{36}{4\sqrt{3}} = \frac{9}{\sqrt{3}} = 3\sqrt{3}$; if $x = 3\sqrt{3}$, $y = 4\sqrt{3}$;
$3\sqrt{3}$ m by $4\sqrt{3}$ m.

15. $\begin{matrix} 2x - y - 3z = -1 \\ 2x - y + z = -9 \\ x + 2y - 4z = 17 \end{matrix}$; $\begin{matrix} x + 2y - 4z = 17 \\ -y + z = -7 \\ 4z = -8 \end{matrix}$; $4z = -8$; $z = -2$; $-y - 2 = -7$,
$y = 5$; $x + 2(5) - 4(-2) = 17$, $x = -1$; $\{(-1, 5, -2)\}$

CHAPTER 10 • Exponential and Logarithmic Functions

Page 458 • WRITTEN EXERCISES

A

1. $\sqrt{81} = 9$ **2.** $\sqrt[3]{27} = 3$ **3.** $\frac{1}{49^{1/2}} = \frac{1}{\sqrt{49}} = \frac{1}{7}$ **4.** $\frac{1}{32^{1/5}} = \frac{1}{\sqrt[5]{32}} = \frac{1}{2}$

5. $(4^{1/2})^3 = (\sqrt{4})^3 = 2^3 = 8$ **6.** $(27^{1/3})^2 = (\sqrt[3]{27})^2 = 3^2 = 9$

7. $(16^{1/4})^3 = (\sqrt[4]{16})^3 = 2^3 = 8$ **8.** $\frac{1}{(25^{1/2})^3} = \frac{1}{(\sqrt{25})^3} = \frac{1}{5^3} = \frac{1}{125}$

9. $\frac{1}{\sqrt[3]{-125}} = -\frac{1}{5}$ **10.** $\frac{1}{(\sqrt[5]{-32})^3} = \frac{1}{(-2)^3} = -\frac{1}{8}$ **11.** $4^{-1/2} = \frac{1}{\sqrt{4}} = \frac{1}{2}$

12. $\left(\frac{9}{4}\right)^{3/2} = \left(\sqrt{\frac{9}{4}}\right)^3 = \left(\frac{3}{2}\right)^3 = \frac{27}{8}$ **13.** $-(\sqrt[3]{8})^2 = -2^2 = -4$ **14.** $-(\sqrt{9})^3 = -27$

15. $\frac{1}{(\sqrt[3]{5})^3} = \frac{1}{5}$ **16.** $\frac{1}{(\sqrt[3]{7^2})^3} = \frac{1}{7^2} = \frac{1}{49}$ **17.** $16^{-1/4} = \frac{1}{\sqrt[4]{16}} = \frac{1}{2}$

18. $27^{-1/3} = \frac{1}{\sqrt[3]{27}} = \frac{1}{3}$ **19.** $(\sqrt{9} + \sqrt{16})^2 = (3 + 4)^2 = 7^2 = 49$

20. $[(\sqrt[3]{8})^2 - \sqrt[3]{8}]^3 = (4 - 2)^3 = 8$ **21.** $(x^3y^5)^{1/2} = x^{3/2}y^{5/2}$

22. $(p^4q)^{1/3} = p^{4/3}q^{1/3}$ **23.** $(a^{-2}b^3)^{1/2} = a^{-1}b^{3/2}$ **24.** $(x^6y^{-4})^{1/3} = x^2y^{-4/3}$

25. $[(a^{-2}b)^{1/2}]^5 = (a^{-1}b^{1/2})^5 = a^{-5}b^{5/2}$ **26.** $(8b^6c^{-4})^{1/3} = 2b^2c^{-4/3}$

27. $\frac{16^{3/4} \cdot a^{-2/4}}{b^{6/4}} = \frac{2^3 \cdot a^{-1/2}}{b^{3/2}} = 8a^{-1/2}b^{-3/2}$ **28.** $(p^4q^{-8})^{-1/4} = p^{-1}q^2$

29. $\sqrt[3]{4 \cdot 4} = \sqrt[3]{16} = 2\sqrt[3]{2}$ **30.** $8^{1/2} \cdot 8^{1/6} = 8^{4/6} = 8^{2/3} = 2^2 = 4$

31. $(2^2)^{1/3} \cdot 2^{-1/6} = 2^{2/3} \cdot 2^{-1/6} = 2^{3/6} = 2^{1/2} = \sqrt{2}$

32. $[(3^3)^3]^{1/5} \cdot [(3^2)^2]^{-1/5} = 3^{9/5} \cdot 3^{-4/5} = 3^{5/5} = 3$

33. $(2^5)^{1/10} \div (2^2)^{1/8} = 2^{1/2} \div 2^{1/4} = 2^{1/4} = \sqrt[4]{2}$

34. $((2^3)^3)^{1/6} \div ((2^2)^2)^{1/6} = 2^{9/6} \div 2^{4/6} = 2^{5/6} = \sqrt[6]{2^5} = \sqrt[6]{32}$

35. $\sqrt[4]{3^3} \cdot \sqrt[8]{3^2} = 3^{3/4} \cdot 3^{2/8} = 3^{3/4+1/4} = 3$

36. $\sqrt[4]{2^7} \cdot \sqrt[8]{2^8} = (2\sqrt[4]{2^3}) \cdot 2 = 4\sqrt[4]{2^3} = 4\sqrt[4]{8}$

B

37. $x^{1/2} \cdot x^{1/3} \cdot x^{1/6} = x^{6/6} = x$ **38.** $a^{2/3} \cdot a^{4/3} = a^{6/3} = a^2$

39. $x^{1/4} \cdot x^{1/6} \div x^{1/3} = x^{1/4+1/6-1/3} = x^{1/12}$ **40.** $(b^{-1/3})^{3/4} = b^{-1/4}$

41. $a^{1/2} \cdot a^{3/2} - 2a^{1/2}a^{1/2} = a^2 - 2a$ **42.** $\frac{x^{3/2}}{x^{1/2}} - \frac{2x^{5/2}}{x^{1/2}} = x^{2/2} - 2x^{4/2} = x - 2x^2$

43. **a.** $a^{3/4} = 8, (a^{3/4})^{4/3} = 8^{4/3}, a = 8^{4/3} = 2^4 = 16; \{16\}$

b. $(3x + 1)^{3/4} = 8, [(3x + 1)^{3/4}]^{4/3} = 8^{4/3}, 3x + 1 = 2^4 = 16, 3x = 15, x = 5; \{5\}$

44. **a.** $y^{-1/2} = 6, (y^{-1/2})^{-2} = 6^{-2}, y = \frac{1}{36}; \left\{\frac{1}{36}\right\}$

b. $(3y)^{-1/2} = 6, [(3y)^{-1/2}]^{-2} = 6^{-2}, 3y = \frac{1}{36}, y = \frac{1}{108}; \left\{\frac{1}{108}\right\}$

45. **a.** $2y^{-1/2} = 10, y^{-1/2} = 5, (y^{-1/2})^{-2} = 5^{-2}, y = \frac{1}{25}; \left\{\frac{1}{25}\right\}$

b. $(2y)^{-1/2} = 10, [(2y)^{-1/2}]^{-2} = 10^{-2}, 2y = \frac{1}{100}, y = \frac{1}{200}; \left\{\frac{1}{200}\right\}$

46. **a.** $[(9t)^{-2/3}]^{-3/2} = 4^{-3/2}, 9t = 2^{-3}, 9t = \frac{1}{8}, t = \frac{1}{72}; \left\{\frac{1}{72}\right\}$

b. $9t^{-2/3} = 4, t^{-2/3} = \frac{4}{9}, (t^{-2/3})^{-3/2} = \left(\frac{4}{9}\right)^{-3/2}, t = \left(\frac{2}{3}\right)^{-3}, t = \frac{27}{8}; \left\{\frac{27}{8}\right\}$

47. $(8 - y)^{1/3} = 4, [(8 - y)^{1/3}]^3 = 4^3, 8 - y = 64, -y = 56, y = -56; \{-56\}$

48. $(3n - 1)^{-2/3} = \frac{1}{4}, [(3n - 1)^{-2/3}]^{-3/2} = \left(\frac{1}{4}\right)^{-3/2}, 3n - 1 = 8, 3n = 9, n = 3; \{3\}$

49. $(x^2 + 4)^{2/3} = 25, [(x^2 + 4)^{2/3}]^{3/2} = 25^{3/2}, x^2 + 4 = 125, x^2 = 125 - 4 = 121,$
$x = \pm\sqrt{121} = \pm 11; \{-11, 11\}$

50. $(x^2 + 9)^{1/2} = 5, [(x^2 + 9)^{1/2}]^2 = 5^2, x^2 + 9 = 25, x^2 = 16, x = \pm 4; \{4, -4\}$

Page 458 • MIXED REVIEW EXERCISES

1. $\frac{x}{x-1} - \frac{2}{x^2-1} = \frac{x(x+1)}{(x-1)(x+1)} - \frac{2}{(x-1)(x+1)} = \frac{x^2 + x - 2}{(x+1)(x-1)} =$
$\frac{(x+2)(x-1)}{(x+1)(x-1)} = \frac{x+2}{x+1}$

2. $\sqrt{\frac{8x}{y^3}} = \sqrt{\frac{2^3xy}{y^4}} = \frac{2\sqrt{2xy}}{y^2}$ **3.** $a^2 + 5 - 4 - a + a^2 = 2a^2 - a + 1$

4. $(-2c^2)(4c^2) = -8c^4$ **5.** $(ab^{-2})^{-2} \cdot (a^{-3}b)^{-1} = (a^{-2}b^4)(a^3b^{-1}) = ab^3$

6. $2n^2 - 8n + 3n - 12 = 2n^2 - 5n - 12$

Pages 461–462 • WRITTEN EXERCISES

A **1.** **a.** $3^{\sqrt{2}+\sqrt{2}} = 3^{2\sqrt{2}} = 9^{\sqrt{2}}$ **b.** $3^{2\sqrt{2}} = 9^{\sqrt{2}}$ **c.** $3^2 = 9$

d. $3^{(\sqrt{2}+2)-(\sqrt{2}-2)} = 3^4 = 81$

2. **a.** $7^{\sqrt{3}+\sqrt{2}}$ **b.** $7^{2\sqrt{3}} = 49^{\sqrt{3}}$ **c.** $7^{\sqrt{2}\sqrt{3}} = 7^{\sqrt{6}}$

d. $7^{\sqrt{3}+2} \div 7^2 = 7^{(\sqrt{3}+2)-2} = 7^{\sqrt{3}}$

3. $10^{2\pi} = 100^{\pi}$ **4.** 5^{π} **5.** $(6^{2\pi})^{1/2} = 6^{\pi}$ **6.** $(4^{6\pi})^{1/3} = 4^{2\pi} = 16^{\pi}$

7. $10^{(\sqrt{3}-2)-(\sqrt{3}+2)} = 10^{-4} = \frac{1}{10{,}000}$ **8.** $6^{\sqrt{2}+2\sqrt{2}-3\sqrt{2}} = 6^0 = 1$ **9.** 1

10. $(\sqrt{3})^{\sqrt{2}-\sqrt{2}} = (\sqrt{3})^0 = 1$ **11.** $2^{-1} = \frac{1}{2}$ **12.** $(\sqrt{2})^2 = 2$

13. $(2^3)^{1.2} \cdot 2^{-3.6} = 2^{3.6} \cdot 2^{-3.6} = 2^0 = 1$ **14.** $(5^2)^{2.4} \div 5^{5.8} = 5^{4.8} \div 5^{5.8} = 5^{-1} = \frac{1}{5}$

15. $(1 + \sqrt{3})^{\pi-1-(\pi+1)} = (1 + \sqrt{3})^{-2} = \frac{1}{(1 + \sqrt{3})^2} = \frac{1}{4 + 2\sqrt{3}} = \frac{4 - 2\sqrt{3}}{4} = \frac{2 - \sqrt{3}}{2}$

16. $(\sqrt{2} - 1)^{2+\pi-\pi} = (\sqrt{2} - 1)^2 = 3 - 2\sqrt{2}$

17. $(9^{(1-\pi)-(1+\pi)})^{1/4} = (9^{-2\pi})^{1/4} = (3^{-4\pi})^{1/4} = 3^{-\pi} = \frac{1}{3^{\pi}}$

18. $(2^{\sqrt{3}+3} \div 2^3)^{1/2} = (2^{\sqrt{3}})^{1/2} = 2^{\sqrt{3}/2}$ **19.** $3^x = \frac{1}{27}, 3^x = 3^{-3}; x = -3; \{-3\}$

20. $5^x = \sqrt{125}, 5^x = (5^3)^{1/2}, 5^x = 5^{3/2}, x = \frac{3}{2}; \left\{\frac{3}{2}\right\}$

21. $8^{2+x} = 2, (2^3)^{2+x} = 2, 2^{6+3x} = 2^1, 6 + 3x = 1, 3x = -5, x = -\frac{5}{3}; \left\{-\frac{5}{3}\right\}$

22. $4^{1-x} = 8, (2^2)^{1-x} = 2^3, 2^{2-2x} = 2^3, 2 - 2x = 3, -2x = 1, x = -\frac{1}{2}; \left\{-\frac{1}{2}\right\}$

23. $27^{2x-1} = 3, (3^3)^{2x-1} = 3, 3^{6x-3} = 3^1, 6x - 3 = 1, 6x = 4, x = \frac{2}{3}; \left\{\frac{2}{3}\right\}$

24. $49^{x-2} = 7\sqrt{7}, (7^2)^{x-2} = 7^{3/2}, 2x - 4 = \frac{3}{2}, 2x = \frac{11}{2}, x = \frac{11}{4}; \left\{\frac{11}{4}\right\}$

25. $4^{2x+5} = 16^{x+1}, (2^2)^{2x+5} = (2^4)^{x+1}, 2^{4x+10} = 2^{4x+4}, 4x + 10 = 4x + 4, 10 = 4$; no solution

26. $3^{-(x+5)} = 9^{4x}, 3^{-x-5} = (3^2)^{4x}, -x-5 = 8x, 9x = -5, x = -\frac{5}{9}; \left\{-\frac{5}{9}\right\}$

27. $25^{2x} = 5^{x+6}, (5^2)^{2x} = 5^{x+6}, 4x = x + 6, 3x = 6, x = 2; \{2\}$

28. $6^{x+1} = 36^{x-1}, 6^{x+1} = (6^2)^{x-1}, x + 1 = 2x - 2, x = 3; \{3\}$

29. $10^{x-1} = 100^{4-x}, 10^{x-1} = (10^2)^{4-x}, x - 1 = 8 - 2x, 3x = 9, x = 3; \{3\}$

B **30.** $3^{2x} - 6 \cdot 3^x + 9 = 0, (3^x - 3)^2 = 0, 3^x - 3 = 0, 3^x = 3, x = 1; \{1\}$

31. $4^{2x} - 63 \cdot 4^x - 64 = 0, (4^x - 64)(4^x + 1) = 0, 4^x = 64$ or $4^x = -1$ (reject); $4^x = 64, 4^x = 4^3, x = 3; \{3\}$

32. $3^{2x} - 10 \cdot 3^x + 9 = 0, (3^x - 9)(3^x - 1) = 0, 3^x = 9$ or $3^x = 1, 3^x = 3^2$ or $3^x = 3^0$; $x = 2$ or $x = 0$; $\{0, 2\}$

33.

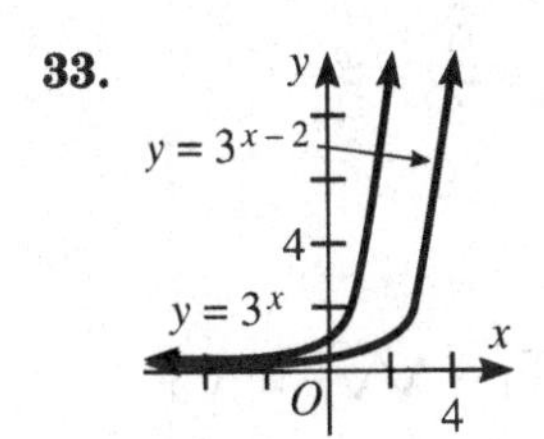

34.

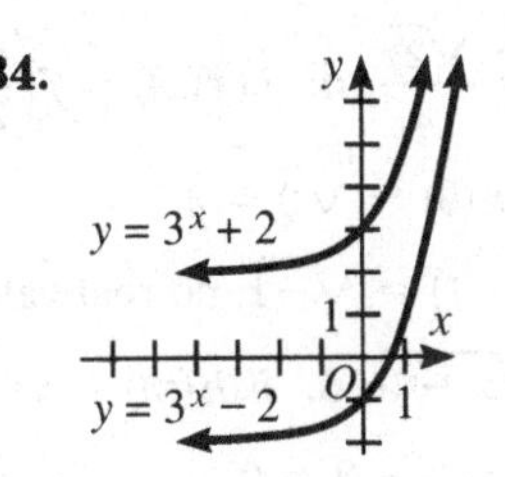

35.

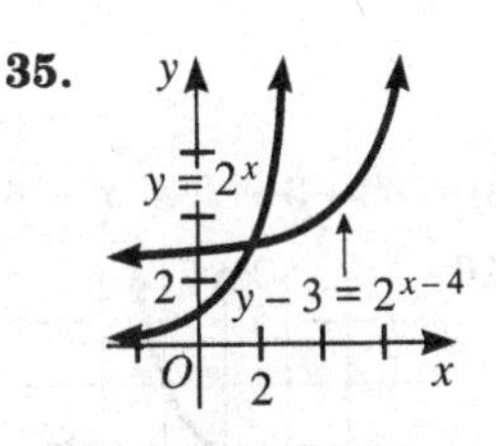

36.

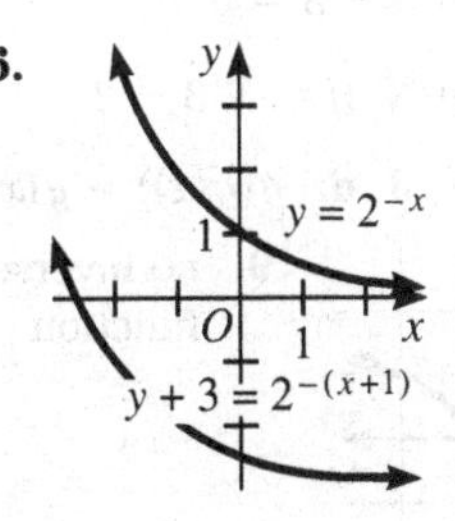

C **37.** $2^{(2/3)x+1} - 3 \cdot 2^{(1/3)x} - 20 = 0$; let $y = 2^{(1/3)x}$; $2y^2 - 3y - 20 = 0$,

$(2y + 5)(y - 4) = 0; y = -\frac{5}{2}$ or $y = 4$; $2^{(1/3)x} = -\frac{5}{2}$ (reject), or $2^{(1/3)x} = 4 = 2^2$;

$\frac{1}{3}x = 2, x = 6; \{6\}$

38. $2^{2x-1} - 3 \cdot 2^{x-1} + 1 = 0$, $2^{2x} - 3 \cdot 2^x + 2 = 0$, $(2^x - 2)(2^x - 1) = 0$, $2^x = 2$ or $2^x = 1$; $x = 1$ or $x = 0$; $\{0, 1\}$

39. $2^x - 3^x = 0$, $2^x = 3^x$, $\frac{2^x}{3^x} = 1$, $\left(\frac{2}{3}\right)^x = 1$, $x = 0$; $\{0\}$

Pages 466–467 • WRITTEN EXERCISES

A

1. a. $f(g(8)) = f(8 - 3) = f(5) = \frac{5}{2}$ **b.** $f(g(-5)) = f(-5 - 3) = f(-8) = -\frac{8}{2} = -4$

c. $f(g(0)) = f(0 - 3) = f(-3) = -\frac{3}{2}$ **d.** $f(g(x)) = f(x - 3) = \frac{x - 3}{2}$

2. a. $g(f(8)) = g\left(\frac{8}{2}\right) = g(4) = 4 - 3 = 1$

b. $g(f(-5)) = g\left(-\frac{5}{2}\right) = -\frac{5}{2} - 3 = -\frac{5}{2} - \frac{6}{2} = -\frac{11}{2}$

c. $g(f(0)) = g\left(\frac{0}{2}\right) = g(0) = 0 - 3 = -3$ **d.** $g(f(x)) = g\left(\frac{x}{2}\right) = \frac{x}{2} - 3$

3. a. $f(h(9)) = f(\sqrt{9}) = f(3) = \frac{3}{2}$ **b.** $f(h(4)) = f(\sqrt{4}) = f(2) = \frac{2}{2} = 1$

c. $f(h(-4)) = f(\sqrt{-2})$; no real value **d.** $f(h(x)) = f(\sqrt{x}) = \frac{\sqrt{x}}{2}$

4. a. $h(f(32)) = h\left(\frac{32}{2}\right) = h(16) = \sqrt{16} = 4$

b. $h(f(16)) = h\left(\frac{16}{2}\right) = h(8) = \sqrt{8} = 2\sqrt{2}$

c. $h(f(x)) = h\left(\frac{x}{2}\right) = \sqrt{\frac{x}{2}} = \frac{\sqrt{2x}}{2}$ **d.** $f(f(x)) = f\left(\frac{x}{2}\right) = \frac{\frac{x}{2}}{2} = \frac{x}{4}$

5. a. $h(g(12)) = h(12 - 3) = h(9) = \sqrt{9} = 3$

b. $h(g(2)) = h(2 - 3) = h(-1) = \sqrt{-1}$; no real value

c. $h(g(x)) = h(x - 3) = \sqrt{x - 3}$ **d.** $h(h(x)) = h(\sqrt{x}) = \sqrt{\sqrt{x}} = \sqrt[4]{x}$

6. a. $g(h(9)) = g(\sqrt{9}) = g(3) = 3 - 3 = 0$

b. $g(h(\sqrt{3})) = g(\sqrt{\sqrt{3}}) = g(\sqrt[4]{3}) = \sqrt[4]{3} - 3$

c. $g(h(x)) = g(\sqrt{x}) = \sqrt{x} - 3$ **d.** $g(g(x)) = g(x - 3) = x - 3 - 3 = x - 6$

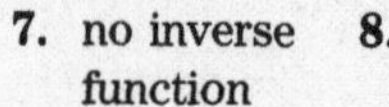

7. no inverse function

8.

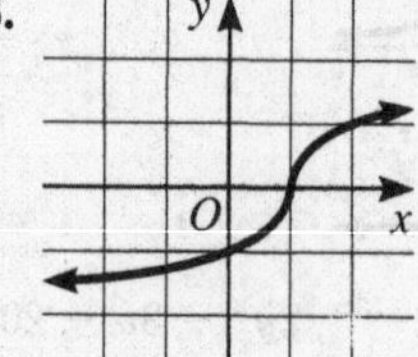

9. no inverse function

10.

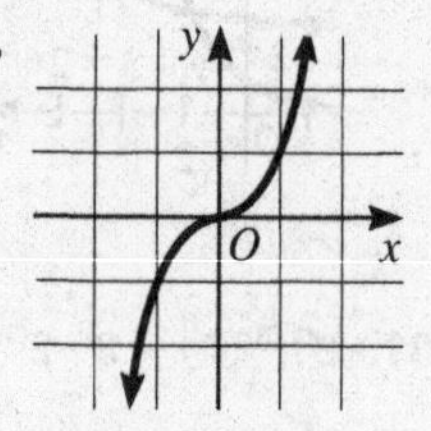

11. $x = 2y - 3, x + 3 = 2y, y = \frac{x+3}{2}; f^{-1}(x) = \frac{x+3}{2};$

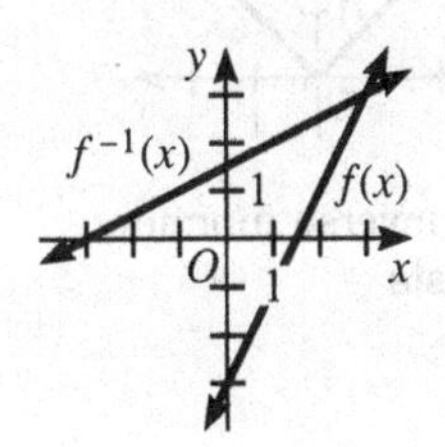

12. $x = \frac{y+6}{3}, 3x = y + 6, 3x - 6 = y; f^{-1}(x) = 3x - 6;$

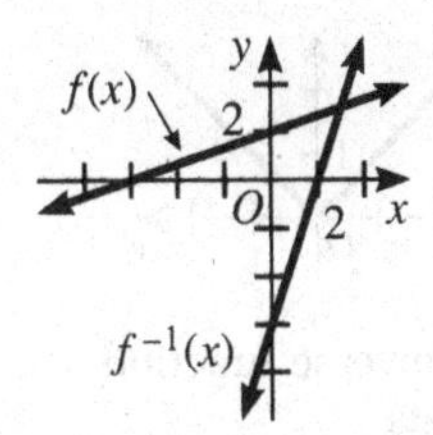

13. $x = y^3, y = x^{1/3}; f^{-1}(x) = x^{1/3} = \sqrt[3]{x}$

14. $x = \frac{12}{y}, y = \frac{12}{x}; f^{-1}(x) = \frac{12}{x}$

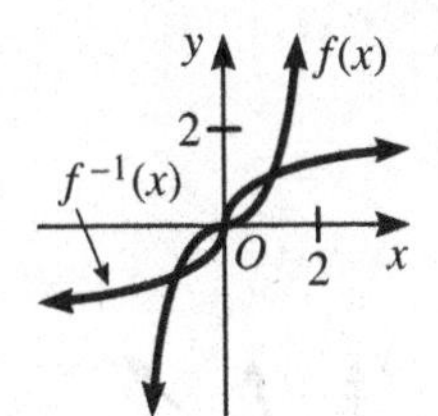

Ex. 13

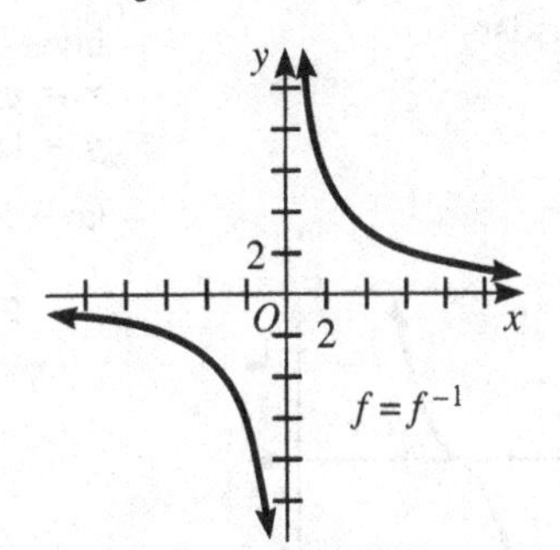

Ex. 14

15. inverse function, g^{-1} exists; $x = \left(\frac{8}{y}\right)^3, x^{1/3} = \frac{8}{y}, y = \frac{8}{x^{1/3}};$

$g^{-1}(x) = 8x^{-1/3} = \frac{8}{\sqrt[3]{x}}$

16.

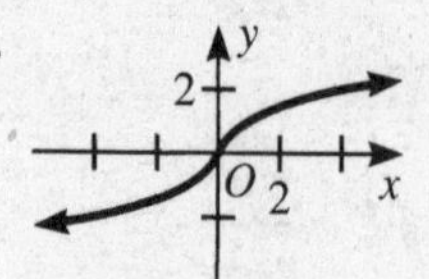

inverse function exists; $x = \sqrt[3]{2y}$, $x^3 = 2y$, $y = \frac{1}{2}x^3$; $g^{-1}(x) = \frac{x^3}{2}$

17.

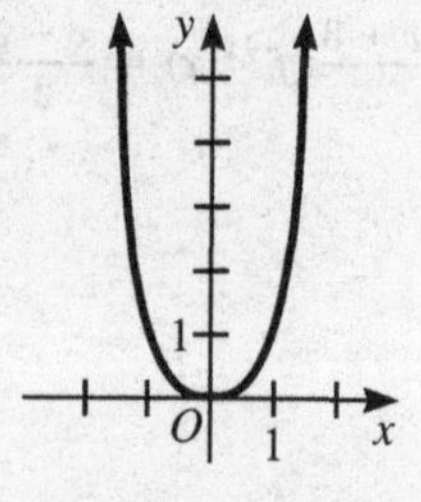

no inverse function exists

18.

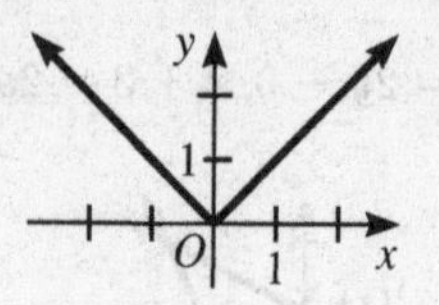

no inverse function exists

B **19.**

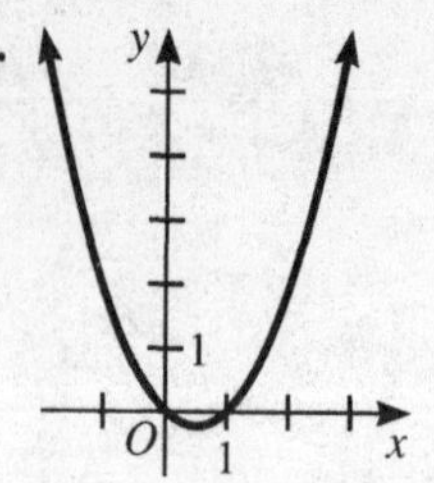

no inverse function exists

20.

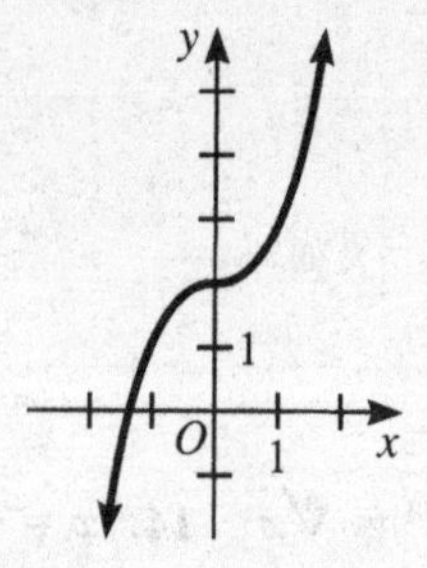

inverse function, g^{-1} exists; $x = y^3 + 2$, $x - 2 = y^3$, $y = (x - 2)^{1/3}$; $g^{-1}(x) = (x - 2)^{1/3} = \sqrt[3]{x - 2}$

21.

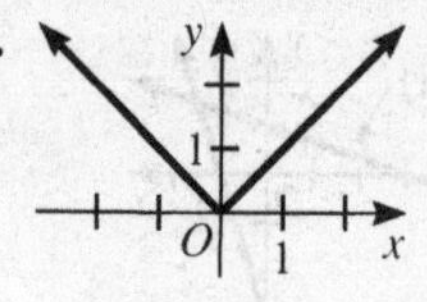

no inverse function exists

22.

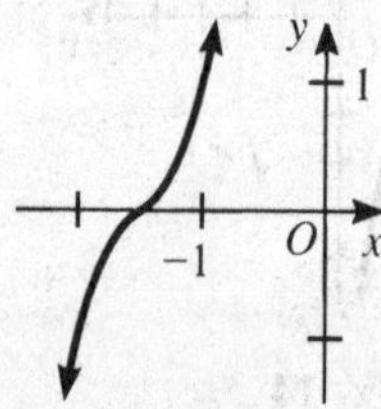

inverse function exists; $x = (2y + 3)^5$, $x^{1/5} = 2y + 3$, $\frac{x^{1/5} - 3}{2} = y$; $g^{-1}(x) = \frac{x^{1/5} - 3}{2} = \frac{\sqrt[5]{x} - 3}{2}$

23.

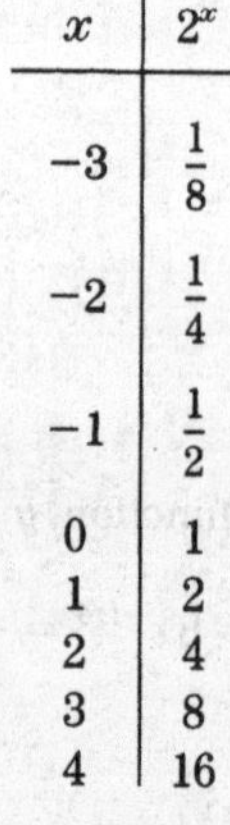

x	2^x
−3	$\frac{1}{8}$
−2	$\frac{1}{4}$
−1	$\frac{1}{2}$
0	1
1	2
2	4
3	8
4	16

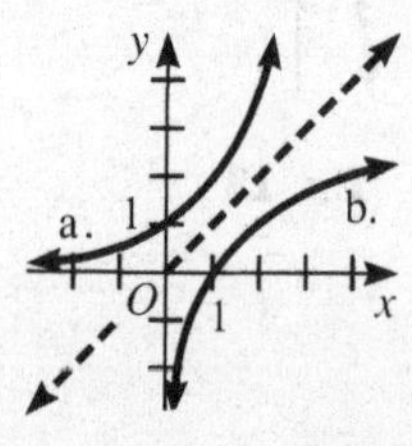

c. $f^{-1}(2) = 1, f^{-1}(4) = 2,$ $f^{-1}(8) = 3, f^{-1}\left(\frac{1}{2}\right) = -1$

d. f: domain is {real numbers}, range is $\{y : y > 0\}$; f^{-1}: domain is $\{x : x > 0\}$, range is {real numbers}

24. $x = \sqrt{y}$, $y = x^2$, $g^{-1}(x) = x^2$; Since the range of g is the set of nonnegative numbers, the domain of g^{-1} is the set of nonnegative numbers. But domain of f is the set of all reals. Thus $f \neq g^{-1}$

C **25.** $f(x) = mx + b, m \neq 0$; $x = my + b$, $\frac{x - b}{m} = y$, $f^{-1}(x) = \frac{1}{m}x - \frac{b}{m}$. If $f = f^{-1}$, $\frac{1}{m} = m$ and $b = -\frac{b}{m}$; $m^2 = 1$ and $m = \pm 1$; if $m = 1$, $b = -b$ and $b = 0$; if $m = -1$ $b = b$, and b is any real number.

26. Let $f(x) = mx + b, m \neq 0$. Then, as in exercise 25, $f^{-1}(x) = \frac{1}{m}x - \frac{b}{m}$. If the graphs are perpendicular, $m\left(\frac{1}{m}\right) = -1$; but $m\left(\frac{1}{m}\right) = 1$; Therefore, the graphs are not perpendicular.

Page 467 • MIXED REVIEW EXERCISES

1. $25^{-3/2} = 5^{-3} = \frac{1}{125}$ **2.** $\sqrt{18} + \sqrt{32} = 3\sqrt{2} + 4\sqrt{2} = 7\sqrt{2}$

3. $(2 - 3i)^2 = 4 - 12i + 9i^2 = -5 - 12i$ **4.** $(3^{\sqrt{2}})^{2\sqrt{2}} = 3^4 = 81$

5. $\sqrt{-48} \cdot \sqrt{-12} = (4i\sqrt{3})(2i\sqrt{3}) = (8i^2)(3) = -24$ **6.** $2^{\pi-2-(\pi+2)} = 2^{-4} = \frac{1}{16}$

7. $(-27)^{2/3} = (-3)^2 = 9$ **8.** $\frac{(\sqrt{2} - 3)(1 - \sqrt{2})}{(1 + \sqrt{2})(1 - \sqrt{2})} = \frac{-5 + 4\sqrt{2}}{1 - 2} = 5 - 4\sqrt{2}$

9. $\frac{5^2 - 1}{1 - 3^2} = \frac{25 - 1}{1 - 9} = \frac{24}{-8} = -3$ **10.** $16^{1.75} = 16^{7/4} = 2^7 = 128$

11. $\frac{(4 + 3i)(2 + i)}{(2 - i)(2 + i)} = \frac{5 + 10i}{4 - i^2} = \frac{5(1 + 2i)}{5} = 1 + 2i$

12. $4^{1.5} \cdot 2^{-2} = 4^{3/2} \cdot 2^{-2} = 2^3 \cdot 2^{-2} = 2^1 = 2$

Pages 470–472 • WRITTEN EXERCISES

A

1. $\log_5 125 = \log_5 5^3 = 3$ **2.** $\log_4 16 = \log_4 4^2 = 2$ **3.** $\log_3 81 = \log_3 3^4 = 4$

4. $\log_6 6 = \log_6 6^1 = 1$ **5.** $\log_3 1 = \log_3 3^0 = 0$ **6.** $\log_8 4 = \log_8 8^{2/3} = \frac{2}{3}$

7. $\log_5 \frac{1}{25} = \log_5 5^{-2} = -2$ **8.** $\log_2 \frac{1}{8} = \log_2 2^{-3} = -3$ **9.** $\log_6 6\sqrt{6} = \log_6 6^{3/2} = \frac{3}{2}$

10. $\log_5 25\sqrt{5} = \log_5 5^{5/2} = \frac{5}{2}$ **11.** $\log_4 \sqrt{2} = \log_4 4^{1/4} = \frac{1}{4}$

12. $\log_{27} \sqrt{3} = \log_{27} 27^{1/6} = \frac{1}{6}$ **13.** $\log_7 \sqrt[3]{49} = \log_7 7^{2/3} = \frac{2}{3}$

14. $\log_3 \sqrt[5]{9} = \log_3 3^{2/5} = \frac{2}{5}$ **15.** $\log_{1/2} 8 = \log_{1/2}\left(\frac{1}{2}\right)^{-3} = -3$

16. $\log_{1/3} 27 = \log_{1/3}\left(\frac{1}{3}\right)^{-3} = -3$ **17.** $\log_2 \sqrt[3]{\frac{1}{4}} = \log_2 2^{-2/3} = -\frac{2}{3}$

18. $\log_{10} \frac{1}{\sqrt{1000}} = \log_{10} 10^{-3/2} = -\frac{3}{2}$ **19.** $\log_7 x = 2; 7^2 = x, x = 49; \{49\}$

20. $\log_6 x = 3; 6^3 = x, x = 216; \{216\}$ **21.** $\log_9 x = -\frac{1}{2}; 9^{-1/2} = x, x = \frac{1}{3}; \left\{\frac{1}{3}\right\}$

22. $\log_6 x = 2.5; 6^{2.5} = x, x = 36\sqrt{6}; \{36\sqrt{6}\}$ **23.** $\log_4 x = -\frac{3}{2}; 4^{-3/2} = x, x = \frac{1}{8}; \left\{\frac{1}{8}\right\}$

24. $\log_{1/9} x = -\frac{1}{2}; \left(\frac{1}{9}\right)^{-1/2} = x, x = 3; \{3\}$

B

25. $\log_x 27 = \frac{3}{2}; x^{3/2} = 27, x = 27^{2/3}, x = 3^2 = 9; \{9\}$

26. $\log_x 64 = 6; x^6 = 64, x = 64^{1/6} = 2; \{2\}$

27. $\log_x 7 = -\frac{1}{2}$; $x^{-1/2} = 7$, $x = 7^{-2} = \frac{1}{49}$; $\left\{\frac{1}{49}\right\}$ **28.** $\log_x 7 = 1$; $x^1 = 7$, $x = 7$; $\{7\}$

29. $\log_x 1 = 0$, $x^0 = 1$; true for all positive x; $\{x : x > 0 \text{ and } x \neq 1\}$

30. $\log_x 2 = 0$, $x^0 = 2$; no solution

31. **a.** $\log_2 8 = \log_2 2^3 = 3$; $\log_2 4 = \log_2 2^2 = 2$; $\log_2 32 = \log_2 2^5 = 5$; $3 + 2 = 5$

b. $\log_9 3 = \log_9 9^{1/2} = \frac{1}{2}$; $\log_9 27 = \log_9 9^{3/2} = \frac{3}{2}$; $\log_9 81 = \log_9 9^2 = 2$; $\frac{1}{2} + \frac{3}{2} = 2$

c. For all positive numbers a, b, and c, $a \neq 1$, $\log_a b + \log_a c = \log_a bc$

32. **a.** $\log_2 8 = \log_2 2^3 = 3$; $\log_8 2 = \log_8 8^{1/3} = \frac{1}{3}$

b. $\log_3 \sqrt{3} = \log_3 3^{1/2} = \frac{1}{2}$; $\log_{\sqrt{3}} 3 = \log_{\sqrt{3}}(\sqrt{3})^2 = 2$

c. For all positive numbers a and b, $a \neq 1$ and $b \neq 1$, $\log_a b = \frac{1}{\log_b a}$

33. **a.** $\log_6 x$ **b.** $f^{-1}(36) = \log_6 36 = 2$; $f^{-1}\left(\frac{1}{\sqrt{6}}\right) = \log_6 \frac{1}{\sqrt{6}} = -\frac{1}{2}$

c. f: domain is {all real nos.}, range is $\{y : y > 0\}$; f^{-1}: domain is $\{x : x > 0\}$, range is {all real nos.}

34. **a.** 4^x **b.** $g^{-1}(2) = 4^2 = 16$; $g^{-1}\left(-\frac{3}{2}\right) = 4^{-3/2} = \frac{1}{8}$

c. g: domain is $\{x : x > 0\}$; range is {all real nos.} g^{-1}: domain is {all real nos.}, range is $\{y : y > 0\}$

35.

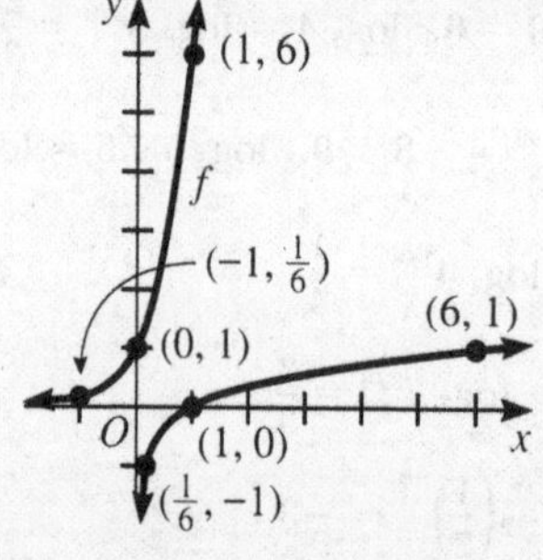

36.

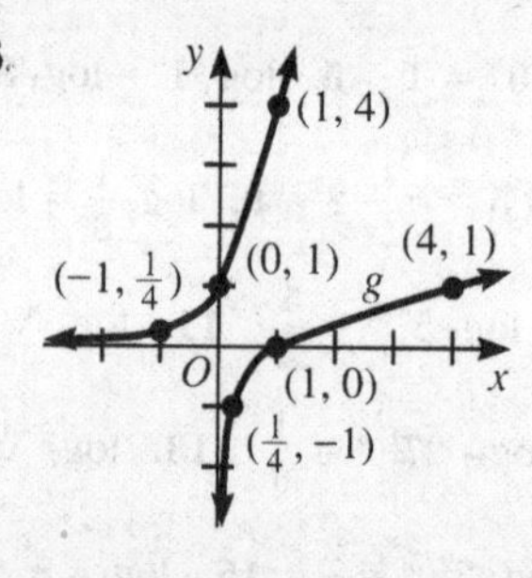

37.

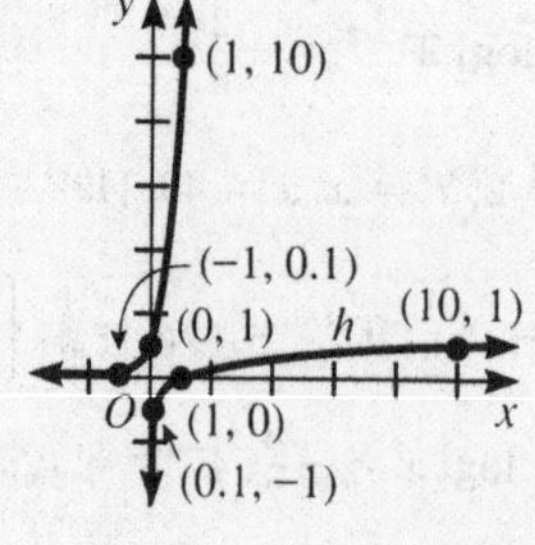

38.

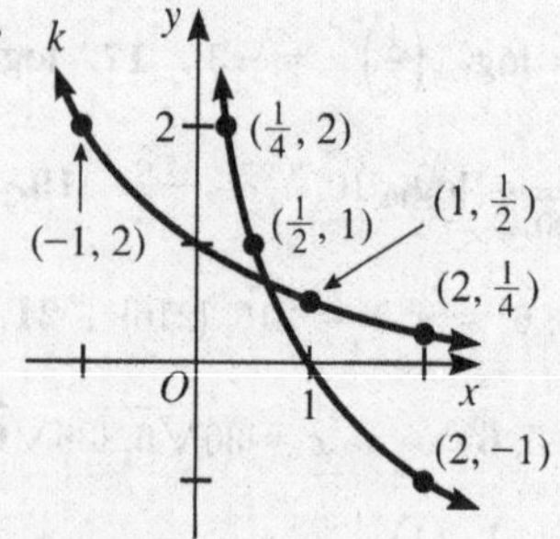

C **39.** $\log_5(\log_3 x) = 0$; $\log_3 x = 5^0 = 1$; $3^1 = x$; $x = 3$; $\{3\}$

40. $\log_4(\log_3(\log_2 x)) = 0$; $\log_3(\log_2 x) = 4^0 = 1$; $3^1 = \log_2 x$; $\log_2 x = 3$; $2^3 = x$; $8 = x$; $\{8\}$

41. positive; for example, $\log_{1/3} \frac{1}{9} = \log_{1/3}\left(\frac{1}{3}\right)^2 = 2$

42. negative; for example, $\log_4(\log_4 2) = \log_4(\log_4 4^{1/2}) = \log_4 \frac{1}{2} = \log_4 4^{-1/2} = -\frac{1}{2}$

43. **a.** $D = 10 \log_{10}(10^{12}) = 10(12) = 120$; 120dB

b. Let I_1 = intensity of the subway and I_2 = intensity of conversation;

$100 = 10 \log_{10}\left(\frac{I_1}{I_0}\right)$, $10 = \log_{10} \frac{I_1}{I_0}$, $10^{10} = \frac{I_1}{I_0}$, $I_1 = 10^{10} I_0$; $60 = 10 \log_{10}\left(\frac{I_2}{I_0}\right)$,

$6 = \log_{10} \frac{I_2}{I_0}$, $\frac{I_2}{I_0} = 10^6$, $I_2 = 10^6 I_0$; $\frac{I_1}{I_2} = \frac{10^{10} I_0}{10^6 I_0} = \frac{10^{10}}{10^6} = 10^4$; $I_1 = 10^4 I_2$; 10,000 times as intense

Pages 476–477 • WRITTEN EXERCISES

A

1. $\log_2 M^6 + \log_2 N^3 = 6 \log_2 M + 3 \log_2 N$

2. $\log_2 (MN)^4 = 4 \log_2 (MN) = 4[\log_2 M + \log_2 N] = 4 \log_2 M + 4 \log_2 N$

3. $\log_2 M + \log_2 \sqrt{N} = \log_2 M + \frac{1}{2} \log_2 N$

4. $\frac{1}{3} \log_2 M^2 N = \frac{1}{3}[\log_2 M^2 + \log_2 N] = \frac{1}{3}[2 \log_2 M + \log_2 N] = \frac{2}{3} \log_2 M + \frac{1}{3} \log_2 N$

5. $\log_2 M^4 - \log_2 N^3 = 4 \log_2 M - 3 \log_2 N$

6. $7 \log_2 \frac{M}{N} = 7[\log_2 M - \log_2 N] = 7 \log_2 M - 7 \log_2 N$

7. $\frac{1}{2} \log_2 \frac{M}{N^3} = \frac{1}{2}[\log_2 M - \log_2 N^3] = \frac{1}{2}[\log_2 M - 3 \log_2 N] = \frac{1}{2} \log_2 M - \frac{3}{2} \log_2 N$

8. $-\log_2 MN = -[\log_2 M + \log_2 N] = -\log_2 M - \log_2 N$

9. $\log_{10} 81 = \log_{10} 9^2 = 2 \log_{10} 9 = 2(0.95) = 1.90$

10. $\log_{10} 9 - \log_{10} 2 = 0.95 - 0.30 = 0.65$ **11.** $\log_{10} 2^{1/2} = \frac{1}{2} \log_{10} 2 = \frac{1}{2}(0.30) = 0.15$

12. $\log_{10} 3 = \log_{10} 9^{1/2} = \frac{1}{2} \log_{10} 9 = \frac{1}{2}(0.95) = 0.48$

13. $\log_{10} 2^3 = 3 \log_{10} 2 = 3(0.30) = 0.90$

14. $\log_{10}(9 \cdot 2^2) = \log_{10} 9 + 2 \log_{10} 2 = (0.95) + 2(0.30) = 1.55$

15. $\log_{10} 20 - \log_{10} 9 = \log_{10} 2 \cdot 10 - \log_{10} 9 = \log_{10} 2 + \log_{10} 10 - \log_{10} 9 = 0.30 + 1 - 0.95 = 0.35$

16. $\log_{10}(9 \cdot 10^2) = \log_{10} 9 + \log_{10} 10^2 = 0.95 + 2 = 2.95$ **17.** $-\log_{10} 9 = -0.95$

18. $-\log_{10}(2 \cdot 10^3) = -[\log_{10} 2 + \log_{10} 10^3] = -[0.30 + 3] = -3.30$

19. $\frac{1}{3} \log_{10} \frac{2}{9} = \frac{1}{3}[\log_{10} 2 - \log_{10} 9] = \frac{1}{3}[0.30 - 0.95] = -0.22$

20. $\log_{10} 2 \cdot 9^2 = \log_{10} 2 + 2 \log_{10} 9 = 0.30 + 2(0.95) = 2.20$

21. $\log_4 p^5 + \log_4 q = \log_4 p^5 q$ **22.** $\log_{10} x - \log_{10} y^4 = \log_{10} \frac{x}{y^4}$

23. $\log_3 A^4 - \log_3 B^{1/2} = \log_3\left(\frac{A^4}{B^{1/2}}\right) = \log_3 \frac{A^4}{\sqrt{B}}$

24. $\log_5 M + \log_5 N^{1/4} = \log_5 MN^{1/4} = \log_5(M\sqrt[4]{N})$

B **25.** $\log_2 MN + \log_2 2^3 = \log_2(8MN)$ **26.** $\log_5\left(\frac{x}{y}\right) + \log_5 5^2 = \log_5\left(\frac{x}{y}\right)(5^2) = \log_5\left(\frac{25x}{y}\right)$

27. $\log_5 5 - \log_5 x^3 = \log_5 \frac{5}{x^3}$

28. $\frac{1}{2}(\log_9 9 + \log_9 x) = \frac{1}{2}(\log_9 9x) = \log_9 \sqrt{9x} = \log_9(3\sqrt{x})$

29. $\log_{10} 5^2 + \log_{10} 4 = \log_{10} 100 = 2$ **30.** $\log_3 6^2 - \log_3 4 = \log_3 \frac{36}{4} = \log_3 9 = 2$

31. $\log_4 \frac{40}{5} = \log_4 8 = \log_4 4^{3/2} = \frac{3}{2}$ **32.** $\log_4 \frac{3}{48} = \log_4 \frac{1}{16} = \log_4 4^{-2} = -2$

33. $\log_a x = 2 \log_a 3 + \log_a 5, \log_a x = \log_a(3^2 \cdot 5), x = 3^2 \cdot 5, x = 45; \{45\}$

34. $\log_a x = \frac{3}{2} \log_a 9 + \log_a 2, \log_a x = \log_a 9^{3/2} \cdot 2, \log_a x = \log_a 54, x = 54; \{54\}$

35. $\log_b(x + 3) = \log_b 8 - \log_b 2, \log_b(x + 3) = \log_b \frac{8}{2}, (x + 3) = 4, x = 1; \{1\}$

36. $\log_b(x^2 + 7) = \frac{2}{3} \log_b 64, \log_b(x^2 + 7) = \log_b 64^{2/3}, x^2 + 7 = 64^{2/3}, x^2 + 7 = 16,$
$x^2 = 9, x = \pm 3; \{\pm 3\}$

37. $\log_a x - \log_a(x - 5) = \log_a 6, \log_a \frac{x}{x - 5} = \log_a 6, \frac{x}{x - 5} = 6, x = 6x - 30, 5x = 30,$
$x = 6; \{6\}$

38. $\log_a(3x + 5) - \log_a(x - 5) = \log_a 8, \log_a(3x + 5) = \log_a 8 + \log_a(x - 5),$
$\log_a(3x + 5) = \log_a 8(x - 5), 3x + 5 = 8x - 40, 5x = 45, x = 9; \{9\}$

39. $\log_2(x^2 - 9) = 4, x^2 - 9 = 2^4, x^2 = 16 + 9 = 25, x = \pm 5; \{\pm 5\}$

40. $\log_3(x + 2) + \log_3 6 = 3, \log_3[(x + 2)(6)] = 3, 6(x + 2) = 3^3, 6x + 12 = 27,$
$6x = 15, x = \frac{5}{2}; \left\{\frac{5}{2}\right\}$

41. **a.** $f(g(3)) = f(4^3) = f(64) = \log_2 64 = 6$

b. $g\left(f\left(\frac{1}{2}\right)\right) = g\left(\log_2 \frac{1}{2}\right) = g(-1) = 4^{-1} = \frac{1}{4}$

c. $f(g^{-1}(16)) = f(\log_4 16) = f(2) = \log_2(2) = 1$

42. **a.** $f(f(-1)) = f(3^{-1}) = f\left(\frac{1}{3}\right) = 3^{1/3} = \sqrt[3]{3}$

b. $g\left(g\left(\frac{1}{81}\right)\right) = g\left(\log_9 \frac{1}{81}\right) = g(-2) = \log_9(-2)$; undefined

c. $f^{-1}(g(9)) = f^{-1}(\log_9 9) = f^{-1}(1) = \log_3 1 = 0$

43. Let $\log_b M = x$ and $\log_b N = y$; $b^x = M$ and $b^y = N$; $\log_b \frac{M}{N} = \log_b \frac{b^x}{b^y} = \log_b b^{x-y} =$
$x - y = \log_b M - \log_b N$

44. $4^{\log_2(2^{\log_2 5})} = 4^{\log_2 5} = (2^2)^{\log_2 5} = 2^{2 \log_2 5} = 2^{\log_2 25} = 25$

C **45.** $\log_5(\log_3 x) = 0, 5^0 = \log_3 x, \log_3 x = 1, 3^1 = x, x = 3; \{3\}$

46. $\log_2(\log_4 x) = 1, 2^1 = \log_4 x, \log_4 x = 2, 4^2 = x, x = 16; \{16\}$

47. $\log_6(x + 1) + \log_6 x = 1; \log_6 x(x + 1) = \log_6 6; x(x + 1) = 6; x^2 + x = 6;$
$x^2 + x - 6 = 0; (x + 3)(x - 2) = 0; x = -3$ (reject) or $x = 2$; $\{2\}$

48. $\log_{10}(x + 6) + \log_{10}(x - 6) = 2; \log_{10}(x + 6)(x - 6) = \log_{10} 100; x^2 - 36 = 100;$
$x^2 = 136; x = -\sqrt{136}$ (reject) or $x = \sqrt{136}; \{2\sqrt{34}\}$

49. $\frac{1}{2}\log_a(x + 2) + \frac{1}{2}\log_a(x - 2) = \frac{2}{3}\log_a 27; \log_a(x + 2)^{1/2} + \log_a(x - 2)^{1/2} =$
$\log_a 27^{2/3}; \log_a(\sqrt{x + 2}\cdot\sqrt{x - 2}) = \log_a 9; \sqrt{x + 2}\cdot\sqrt{x - 2} = 9; x^2 - 4 = 81;$
$x^2 = 85; x = -\sqrt{85}$ (reject) or $x = \sqrt{85}; \{\sqrt{85}\}$

50. $2\log_3 x - \log_3(x - 2) = 2; \log_3 x^2 - \log_3(x - 2) = \log_3 9; \log_3 \frac{x^2}{x - 2} = \log_3 9;$
$\frac{x^2}{x - 2} = 9; x^2 = 9x - 18; x^2 - 9x + 18 = 0; (x - 6)(x - 3) = 0; x = 6$ or $x = 3;$
$\{3, 6\}$

51. $\log_b(x - 1) + \log_b(x + 2) = \log_b(8 - 2x); \log_b(x - 1)(x + 2) = \log_b(8 - 2x);$
$(x - 1)(x + 2) = 8 - 2x; x^2 + x - 2 = 8 - 2x; x^2 + 3x - 10 = 0;$
$(x + 5)(x - 2) = 0; x = -5$ (reject) or $x = 2; \{2\}$

Page 477 • MIXED REVIEW EXERCISES

1. $\log_2 x = -\frac{1}{2}, 2^{-1/2} = x, x = \frac{1}{\sqrt{2}} = \frac{\sqrt{2}}{2}; \left\{\frac{\sqrt{2}}{2}\right\}$

2. $x^3 - 7x + 6 = 0; x = 1$ is a root; $\frac{x^3 - 7x + 6}{x - 1} = x^2 + x - 6$; the depressed equation is $x^2 + x - 6 = 0, (x - 2)(x + 3) = 0, x = 2$ or $x = -3; \{1, 2, -3\}$

3. $2^{x+3} = 4^{x-1}, 2^{x+3} = (2^2)^{x-1}, x + 3 = 2x - 2, x = 5; \{5\}$

4. $\sqrt{x} + 2 = x, x - \sqrt{x} - 2 = 0, (\sqrt{x} - 2)(\sqrt{x} + 1) = 0, \sqrt{x} = 2$ or $\sqrt{x} = -1$ (reject), $x = 4; \{4\}$

5. $3^x = \frac{\sqrt{3}}{9}, 3^x = \frac{3^{1/2}}{3^2} = 3^{-3/2}, x = -\frac{3}{2}; \left\{-\frac{3}{2}\right\}$

6. $3(2x - 1) = 5x + 4, 6x - 3 = 5x + 4, x = 7; \{7\}$

7. $\frac{x}{x + 1} - 1 = \frac{1}{x}, x^2 - x(x + 1) = x + 1, x^2 - x^2 - x = x + 1, 2x = -1, x = -\frac{1}{2};$
$\left\{-\frac{1}{2}\right\}$

8. $\log_x 8 = \frac{3}{2}, x^{3/2} = 8, x = 8^{2/3}, x = 4; \{4\}$

9. $(x - 2)^2 = 5, x - 2 = \pm\sqrt{5}, x = 2 \pm \sqrt{5}; \{2 + \sqrt{5}, 2 - \sqrt{5}\}$

10. $f(-2) = (-2)^2 - 1 = 3$ **11.** $g(3) = \sqrt{3 + 1} = 2$

12. $f(g(1)) = f(\sqrt{2}) = 2 - 1 = 1$ **13.** $g(f(-1)) = g(0) = \sqrt{1} = 1$

Pages 481–482 • WRITTEN EXERCISES

A

1. Let $x = (1.06)^{10}; \log x = 10\log 1.06 = 10(0.0253) = 0.253; x \approx 1.79$

2. Let $x = (10.6)^{10}; \log x = 10\log 10.6 = 10(1.0253) = 10.253; x \approx 1.79 \times 10^{10}$

3. Let $x = (0.38)^5; \log x = 5\log 0.38 = 5(0.5798 - 1) = (2.8990 - 5);$
$x \approx 7.93 \times 10^{-3} = 0.00793$

4. Let $x = (347)^{1.5}; \log x = 1.5\log 347 = 1.5(2.5403) = 3.8105; x \approx 6.460 \times 10^3 = 6460$

5. Let $x = (12.7)^{5/2}$; $\log x = 2.5 \log 12.7 = 2.5(1.1038) = 2.7595$; $x \approx 5.75 \times 10^2 = 575$

6. Let $x = \sqrt[6]{786}$; $\log x = \frac{1}{6} \log 786 = \frac{1}{6}(2.8954) = 0.4826$; $x \approx 3.04$

7. Let $x = \sqrt[5]{(81.2)^4}$; $\log x = \frac{4}{5} \log 81.2 = \frac{4}{5}(1.9096) = 1.5277$; $x \approx 3.37 \times 10^1 = 33.7$

8. Let $x = \sqrt[3]{(412)^2}$; $\log x = \frac{2}{3} \log 412 = \frac{2}{3}(2.6149) = 1.7433$; $x \approx 5.54 \times 10^1 = 55.4$

9. $x = 7.13$ **10.** $x = 2.55$ **11.** $x = 6.92 \times 10^2 = 692$ **12.** $x = 4.03 \times 10^1 = 40.3$

13. $\log x = 0.2000 - 2$; $x = 1.58 \times 10^{-2} = 0.0158$

14. $\log x = 0.0900 - 3$; $x = 1.23 \times 10^{-3} = 0.00123$

15. **a.** $3^x = 30$, $\log 3^x = \log 30$, $x \log 3 = \log 30$, $x = \frac{\log 30}{\log 3}$ **b.** $x \approx \frac{1.4771}{0.4771} \approx 3.10$

16. **a.** $5^t = 10$, $t \log 5 = \log 10$, $t = \frac{\log 10}{\log 5} = \frac{1}{\log 5}$ **b.** $t \approx \frac{1}{0.6990} \approx 1.43$

17. **a.** $(5.6)^x = 56$, $x \log 5.6 = \log 56$, $x = \frac{\log 56}{\log 5.6}$ **b.** $x \approx \frac{1.7482}{0.7482} \approx 2.34$

18. **a.** $(1.02)^x = 2$, $x \log 1.02 = \log 2$, $x = \frac{\log 2}{\log 1.02}$ **b.** $x \approx \frac{0.3010}{0.0086} \approx 35.0$

19. **a.** $30^{-x} = 5$, $-x \log 30 = \log 5$, $x = -\frac{\log 5}{\log 30}$ **b.** $x \approx -\frac{0.6990}{1.4771} \approx -0.473$

20. **a.** $12^{2x} = 1000$, $2x \log 12 = \log 1000$, $x = \frac{\log 1000}{2 \log 12} = \frac{3}{2 \log 12}$

b. $x \approx \frac{3}{2(1.0792)} \approx 1.39$

21. **a.** $(3.5)^{2t} = 60$, $2t \log 3.5 = \log 60$, $t = \frac{\log 60}{2 \log 3.5}$ **b.** $t \approx \frac{1.7782}{2(0.5441)} \approx 1.63$

22. **a.** $\frac{4^{2-t}}{3} = 7$, $4^{2-t} = 21$, $\log 4^{2-t} = \log 21$, $(2 - t) \log 4 = \log 21$, $2 - t = \frac{\log 21}{\log 4}$,

$t = 2 - \frac{\log 21}{\log 4}$

b. $t \approx 2 - \frac{1.3222}{0.6021} \approx -0.196$

23. $4^x = 8\sqrt{2}$, $(2^2)^x = 2^3 \cdot 2^{1/2}$, $2^{2x} = 2^{7/2}$, $2x = \frac{7}{2}$, $x = \frac{7}{4}$; $\left\{\frac{7}{4}\right\}$

24. $3^x = \sqrt[5]{9}$, $3^x = (3^2)^{1/5}$, $x = \frac{2}{5}$; $\left\{\frac{2}{5}\right\}$

25. $125^x = 25\sqrt{5}$, $(5^3)^x = 5^2 \cdot 5^{1/2}$, $5^{3x} = 5^{5/2}$, $3x = \frac{5}{2}$, $x = \frac{5}{6}$; $\left\{\frac{5}{6}\right\}$

26. $8^x = 16\sqrt[3]{2}$, $(2^3)^x = 2^4 \cdot 2^{1/3}$, $2^{3x} = 2^{13/3}$, $3x = \frac{13}{3}$, $x = \frac{13}{9}$; $\left\{\frac{13}{9}\right\}$

27. $x^{2/5} = 34$, $x = 34^{5/2}$, $\log x = \frac{5}{2} \log 34$, $\log x \approx \frac{5}{2}(1.5315) = 3.8288$;

$x \approx 6.740 \times 10^3 = 6740$; $\{6740\}$

28. $x^{2/3} = 50$, $x = 50^{3/2}$, $\log x = \frac{3}{2} \log 50 \approx 1.5(1.6990) = 2.5485$; $x \approx 3.54 \times 10^2 = 354$;

$\{354\}$

29. $\sqrt[3]{x^4} = 60, x^{4/3} = 60, x = 60^{3/4}, \log x = \frac{3}{4} \log 60 \approx 0.75(1.7782) = 1.3337;$
$x \approx 2.16 \times 10^1 = 21.6; \{21.6\}$

30. $\sqrt[5]{x^3} = 900, x^{3/5} = 900, x = 900^{5/3}, \log x = \frac{5}{3} \log 900 \approx \frac{5}{3}(2.9542) = 4.9237;$
$x \approx 8.39 \times 10^4 = 83{,}900; \{83{,}900\}$

B **31.** $2x^5 = 100; x^5 = 50; x = 50^{1/5}; \log x = \frac{1}{5} \log 50 \approx \frac{1}{5}(1.6990) = 0.3398; x = 2.19;$
$\{2.19\}$

32. $\frac{\sqrt[5]{x}}{9} = 7; \sqrt[5]{x} = 63; x = 63^5; \log x = 5 \log 63 \approx 5(1.7993) = 8.9965; x = 992{,}000{,}000;$
$\{992{,}000{,}000\}$

33. $(3y - 1)^6 = 80; 3y - 1 = 80^{1/6}; \log(3y - 1) = \frac{1}{6} \log 80 \approx \frac{1}{6}(1.9031) = 0.3172;$
$3y - 1 = 2.08; 3y = 3.08; y = 1.03; \{1.03\}$

34. $\sqrt[3]{4t + 3} = 8.15; 4t + 3 = 8.15^3; \log(4t + 3) = 3 \log 8.15 \approx 3(0.9112) = 2.7336;$
$4t + 3 = 542; 4t = 539; t = 135; \{135\}$

35. $\log_2 9 = \frac{\log 9}{\log 2} \approx \frac{0.9542}{0.3010} \approx 3.17$ **36.** $\log_6 8 = \frac{\log 8}{\log 6} \approx \frac{0.9031}{0.7782} \approx 1.16$

37. $\log_3 40 = \frac{\log 40}{\log 3} \approx \frac{1.6021}{0.4771} \approx 3.36$ **38.** $\log_7 \frac{1}{2} = \frac{\log \frac{1}{2}}{\log 7} \approx \frac{-0.3010}{0.8451} \approx -0.356$

39. Let $y = 3^x; y^2 - 7y + 10 = 0; (y - 5)(y - 2) = 0; y = 5$ or $y = 2$; if $y = 5, 3^x = 5;$
$\log 3^x = \log 5; x \log 3 = \log 5; x = \frac{\log 5}{\log 3} = \frac{0.6990}{0.4771} = 1.47;$ if $y = 2, 3^x = 2;$
$x = \frac{\log 2}{\log 3} = \frac{0.3010}{0.4771} = 0.631; \{1.47, 0.631\}$

40. Let $y = 3^x; y^2 - 7y + 12 = 0; (y - 4)(y - 3) = 0; y = 4$ or $y = 3$; if $y = 4, 3^x = 4;$
$\log 3^x = \log 4; x \log 3 = \log 4; x = \frac{\log 4}{\log 3} = \frac{0.6021}{0.4771} = 1.26;$ if $y = 3, 3^x = 3; x = 1;$
$\{1.26, 1\}$

41. a. $\log_7 49 = \log_7 7^2 = 2; \log_{49} 7 = \log_{49} 49^{1/2} = \frac{1}{2}$

b. $\log_2 8 = \log_2 2^3 = 3; \log_8 2 = \log_8 8^{1/3} = \frac{1}{3}$

c. If a and b are positive numbers not equal to 1, $\log_a b = \frac{1}{\log_b a}$. By the change-of-base formula, $\log_a b = \frac{\log_b b}{\log_b a} = \frac{1}{\log_b a}$

C **42.** Let $\log_a x = y$. Then $x = a^y$ and $\log_b x = \log_b a^y, \log_b x = y \log_b a, y = \frac{\log_b x}{\log_b a}$.
Since $y = \log_a x, \log_a x = \frac{\log_b x}{\log_b a}$.

Pages 486–488 • PROBLEMS

A **1. a.** $A = 1000(1.12)^1 = 1120$; \$1120.00 **b.** $A = 1000(1.12)^2 = 1254.40$; \$1254.40

c. $A = 1000(1.12)^3 = 1404.93$; \$1404.93 **d.** $A = 1000(1.12)^{10} = 3105.85$; \$3105.85

2. a. $A = 100(1.072)^1 = 107.20$; \$107.20 **b.** $A = 100(1.072)^5 = 141.57$; \$141.57

c. $A = 100(1.072)^{10} = 200.42$; \$200.42 **d.** $A = 100(1.072)^{20} = 401.69$; \$401.69

e. approximately 10 years

3. a. $A = 1000\left(1 + \frac{0.12}{4}\right)^{4(1)} = 1000(1.03)^4 = 1125.51$; \$1125.51

b. $A = 1000\left(1 + \frac{0.12}{4}\right)^{4(2)} = 1000(1.03)^8 = 1266.77$; \$1266.77

c. $A = 1000\left(1 + \frac{0.12}{4}\right)^{4(3)} = 1000(1.03)^{12} = 1425.76$; \$1425.76

d. $A = 1000\left(1 + \frac{0.12}{4}\right)^{4(10)} = 1000(1.03)^{40} = 3262.04$; \$3262.04

4. a. $A = 1000\left(1 + \frac{0.12}{12}\right)^{12(1)} = 1000(1.01)^{12} = 1126.83$; \$1126.83

b. $A = 1000\left(1 + \frac{0.12}{12}\right)^{12(2)} = 1000(1.01)^{24} = 1269.73$; \$1269.73

c. $A = 1000\left(1 + \frac{0.12}{12}\right)^{12(3)} = 1000(1.01)^{36} = 1430.77$; \$1430.77

d. $A = 1000\left(1 + \frac{0.12}{12}\right)^{12(10)} = 1000(1.01)^{120} = 3300.39$; \$3300.39

5. Let A = amount of money the car is worth after t years; $A = 12{,}500(0.80)^t$

a. $A = 12{,}500(0.8)^1 = 10{,}000$; \$10,000 **b.** $A = 12{,}500(0.8)^2 = 8000.00$; \$8000

c. $A = 12{,}500(0.8)^3 = 6400$; \$6400 **d.** $A = 12{,}500(0.8)^{10} = 1342.18$; \$1342.18

6. Let A be the dollar value of the boat after t years; $A = 3500(0.90)^t$;

a. $A = 3500(0.9)^1 = 3150$; \$3150 **b.** $3500(0.9)^5 = 2066.72$; \$2066.72

c. $A = 3500(0.9)^{10} = 1220.37$; \$1220.37 **d.** $A = 3500(0.9)^{20} = 425.52$; \$425.52

7. Let N = number of bacteria after t weeks; $N = N_0 2^{t/3}$; **a.** $N = N_0 2^{6/3} = 4N_0$

b. $N = N_0 2^{15/3} = 2^5 N_0 = 32N_0$ **c.** $N = N_0 2^{w/3}$

8. Let N = size of culture in t hours; $N = N_0 2^{t/(1/3)} = N_0 2^{3t}$ **a.** $N = N_0 2^3 = 8N_0$

b. $N = N_0 2^{3(12)} = (6.87 \times 10^{10})N_0$ **c.** $N = N_0 2^{3(24)} = N_0 \cdot 2^{72} = (4.72 \times 10^{21})N_0$

9. Let N = kg of carbon-14 left after t years; $N = 100\left(\frac{1}{2}\right)^{t/6000}$

a. $N = 100 \cdot \left(\frac{1}{2}\right)^{12{,}000/6000} = 100 \cdot \left(\frac{1}{2}\right)^2 = 25$; 25 kg

b. $N = 100 \cdot \left(\frac{1}{2}\right)^{24{,}000/6000} = 100 \cdot \left(\frac{1}{2}\right)^4 = 6.25$; 6.25 kg

c. $N = 100 \cdot \left(\frac{1}{2}\right)^{y/6000}$ kg

10. Let N = amount of radon left after t days; $N = 100\left(\frac{1}{2}\right)^{t/3.5}$; $t = 7$;

$N = 100\left(\frac{1}{2}\right)^{7/3.5} = 100\left(\frac{1}{2}\right)^2 = 25$; 25 g

B **11.** $A = P(1.08)^t$; Let $A = 2P$; $2P = P(1.08)^t$, $2 = (1.08)^t$, $\log 2 = t \log 1.08$, $\frac{\log 2}{\log 1.08} = t$,

$t \approx \frac{0.3010}{0.0334} \approx 9.01$; approximately 9 years

12. $A = P(1.06)^t$; let $A = 3P$; $3P = P(1.06)^t$, $3 = (1.06)^t$, $\log 3 = t \log 1.06$,

$t = \frac{\log 3}{\log 1.06} \approx \frac{0.4771}{0.0253} = 18.9$; approximately 19 years

13. $A = 1\left(1 + \frac{0.12}{4}\right)^4 = (1.03)^4 = 1.1255$; $1.1255 - 1 = 0.1255$; 12.55%

14. Compare effective yields (problem 13); Bank A: $1\left(1 + \frac{0.06}{12}\right)^{12} = (1.005)^{12} = 1.0617$; 6.17%; Bank B: $1\left(1 + \frac{0.061}{4}\right)^4 = (1.01525)^4 = 1.0624$; 6.24%; Bank B pays more interest.

15. Let N = amount of plutonium left after t years; let N_0 be the initial amount; $N = N_0\left(\frac{1}{2}\right)^{t/25,000}$; $N = N_0\left(\frac{1}{2}\right)^{100/25,000} = N_0\left(\frac{1}{2}\right)^{1/250} = 0.997N_0$; after 100 years, 0.997 of the original amount remains; $N = N_0\left(\frac{1}{2}\right)^{10^6/25,000} = N_0\left(\frac{1}{2}\right)^{40} = (9.09 \times 10^{-13})N_0$; after 1 million years, 9.09×10^{-13} of the original amount remains.

16. Let N = the amount of sugar left after t minutes; $N = N_0\left(\frac{1}{2}\right)^{t/2}$; $0.01N_0 = N_0\left(\frac{1}{2}\right)^{t/2}$, $0.1 = \left(\frac{1}{2}\right)^{t/2}$, $\log 0.1 = \frac{t}{2} \log\left(\frac{1}{2}\right)$, $-1 = \frac{t}{2}(-0.300)$, $t = \frac{-2}{-0.3010} \approx 6.64$; 90% is dissolved 6.64 min after the sugar is put in the water; $6.64 - 2 = 4.64$ min

17. Let r = average annual rate of appreciation; $100(1 + r)^8 = 238$, $(1 + r)^8 = 2.38$, $(1 + r) = \sqrt[8]{2.38} \approx 1.114$, $r \approx 0.114$; 11.4%

18. Let r = average annual rate of appreciation; $250(1 + r)^{10} = 1000$, $(1 + r)^{10} = 4$, $1 + r = \sqrt[10]{4} \approx 1.149$, $r \approx 0.149$; 14.9%

19. Let r = average annual rate of depreciation; $12,000(1 - r)^5 = 4000$, $(1 - r)^5 = \frac{1}{3}$, $1 - r = \sqrt[5]{\frac{1}{3}} \approx 0.803$, $r = 0.197$; 19.7%

20. Let r = average annual rate of depreciation; $8000(1 - r)^4 = 3200$, $(1 - r)^4 = 0.4$, $(1 - r) = \sqrt[4]{0.4} \approx 0.795$, $r \approx 0.205$; 20.5%

C **21.** **a.** $A = 10^6\left(1 + \frac{0.064}{4}\right)^4 = 10^6(1.016)^4 \approx 1,065,552.45$; \$1,065,552.45

b. $A = 10^6\left(1 + \frac{0.064}{365}\right)^{365} = 10^6(1.000175)^{365} \approx 1,066,086$; \$1,066,086

c. There are 8760 h in a year; $A = 10^6\left(1 + \frac{0.064}{8760}\right)^{8760} \approx (1.0000073)^{8760} \approx$ 1,066,092; \$1,066,092

d. Compounding produces interest on the interest the investment earns. The more frequently interest is compounded, the more additional interest is earned. However, the additional interest is small compared to the amount invested.

22. Let N = number of bacteria t hours after 8:00 A.M.; $N = (6.5 \times 10^6)2^{t/d}$;

$9.75 \times 10^6 = (6.5 \times 10^6)2^{2.5/d}$; $1.5 = 2^{2.5/d}$; $\log 1.5 = \frac{2.5}{d} \log 2$, $\frac{\log 1.5}{2.5 \log 2} = \frac{1}{d}$,

$\frac{1}{d} \approx 0.2340$; $N = (6.5 \times 10^6)2^{(0.234)(4)}$, $N \approx 1.24 \times 10^7$; approximately

1.24×10^7 members

Page 488 • MIXED REVIEW EXERCISES

1. $\log_4 1 = 0$; $\log_4 2 = \log_4 4^{1/2} = \frac{1}{2}$; $\log_4 4 = 1$; $\left\{0, \frac{1}{2}, 1\right\}$

2. $g(1) = |1 - 3| = 2$; $g(2) = |2 - 3| = 1$; $g(4) = |4 - 3| = 1$; $\{1, 2\}$

3. $h(1) = (\sqrt{2})^1 = \sqrt{2}$; $h(2) = (\sqrt{2})^2 = 2$; $h(4) = (\sqrt{2})^4 = (2^{1/2})^4 = 4$; $\{\sqrt{2}, 2, 4\}$

4. $F(1) = 1 - 3 + 2 = 0$; $F(2) = 4 - 6 + 2 = 0$; $F(4) = 16 - 12 + 2 = 6$; $\{0, 6\}$

5. $G(1) = \frac{1}{3}$; $G(2) = \frac{2}{4} = \frac{1}{2}$; $G(4) = \frac{4}{6} = \frac{2}{3}$; $\left\{\frac{1}{3}, \frac{1}{2}, \frac{2}{3}\right\}$

6. $H(1) = 1^{1/2} = 1$; $H(2) = 2^{1/2} = \sqrt{2}$; $H(4) = 4^{1/2} = 2$; $\{1, \sqrt{2}, 2\}$

7. $\log_3 12 - 2 \log_3 2 = \log_3 12 - \log_3 2^2 = \log_3 \frac{12}{4} = \log_3 3 = 1$

8. $(4^{1/3})^{3/2} = 4^{1/3 \cdot 3/2} = 4^{1/2} = 2$ **9.** $\dfrac{\frac{1}{2} - \frac{1}{4}}{1 + \frac{1}{2}} = \dfrac{2 - 1}{4 + 2} = \dfrac{1}{6}$

10. $\frac{8^{1/2}}{2^{3/2}} = \frac{(2^3)^{1/2}}{2^{3/2}} = \frac{2^{3/2}}{2^{3/2}} = 1$ **11.** $\sqrt{\frac{1}{9} + \frac{1}{16}} = \sqrt{\frac{16 + 9}{16(9)}} = \sqrt{\frac{25}{144}} = \frac{5}{12}$

12. $\log_6 24 + 2 \log_6 3 = \log_6 24 + \log_6 3^2 = \log_6 (24 \cdot 3^2) = \log_6 216 = \log_6 6^3 = 3$

Pages 490–491 • WRITTEN EXERCISES

A **1.** $e^{2.08} = 8$ **2.** $e^{4.61} = 100$ **3.** $e^{-1.10} = \frac{1}{3}$ **4.** $e^{-2} = \frac{1}{e^2}$ **5.** $\ln 20.1 = 3$

6. $\ln 1097 = 7$ **7.** $\ln 1.65 = \frac{1}{2}$ **8.** $\ln 1.40 = \frac{1}{3}$ **9.** $\ln e^2 = 2$ **10.** $\ln e^{10} = 10$

11. $\ln \frac{1}{e^3} = \ln e^{-3} = -3$ **12.** $\ln \frac{1}{\sqrt{e}} = \ln e^{-1/2} = -\frac{1}{2}$ **13.** $\ln 1 = \ln e^0 = 0$

14. $\ln 0$ is undefined **15.** $e^{\ln 5} = 5$ **16.** $e^{\ln 0.5} = 0.5$

17. $\ln 3 + \ln 4 = \ln(3 \cdot 4) = \ln 12$ **18.** $\ln 8 - \ln 2 = \ln \frac{8}{2} = \ln 4$

19. $2 \ln 3 - \ln 5 = \ln 3^2 - \ln 5 = \ln \frac{3^2}{5} = \ln \frac{9}{5}$

20. $\ln 7 + \frac{1}{2} \ln 9 = \ln 7 + \ln 9^{1/2} = \ln 7 \cdot 9^{1/2} = \ln 21$

21. $\frac{1}{3} \ln 8 + \ln 5 + 3 = \ln 8^{1/3} + \ln 5 + \ln e^3 = \ln(2 \cdot 5 \cdot e^3) = \ln 10e^3$

22. $4 \ln 2 - \ln 3 - 1 = \ln 2^4 - \ln 3 - \ln e = \ln \frac{2^4}{3e} = \ln \frac{16}{3e}$ **23.** $\ln x = 3$; $e^3 = x$; $\{e^3\}$

24. $\ln \frac{1}{x} = 2$, $-\ln x = 2$, $\ln x = -2$, $x = e^{-2}$; $\{e^{-2}\}$

25. $\ln(x - 4) = -1$, $e^{-1} = x - 4$, $x = e^{-1} + 4$; $\{e^{-1} + 4\}$

26. $\ln |x| = 1$, $e^1 = |x|$, $x = e$ or $x = -e$; $\{e, -e\}$

27. $\ln x^2 = 9$, $x^2 = e^9$, $x = \pm\sqrt{e^9} = \pm e^{9/2}$; $\{\pm e^{9/2}\}$

28. $\ln \sqrt{x} = 3$, $\frac{1}{2} \ln x = 3$, $\ln x = 6$, $x = e^6$; $\{e^6\}$ **29.** $e^x = 2$, $\ln 2 = x$; $\{\ln 2\}$

30. $e^{-x} = 3$, $\ln 3 = -x$, $x = -\ln 3 = \ln \frac{1}{3}$; $\left\{\ln \frac{1}{3}\right\}$

31. $e^{2x} = 25$, $\ln 25 = 2x$, $x = \frac{1}{2} \ln 25 = \ln 25^{1/2} = \ln 5$; $\{\ln 5\}$

32. $e^{3x} = 8$, $3x = \ln 8$, $3x = \ln 2^3$, $3x = 3 \ln 2$, $x = \ln 2$; $\{\ln 2\}$

33. $e^{x-2} = 2$, $\ln 2 = x - 2$, $x = 2 + \ln 2$; $\{2 + \ln 2\}$

34. $\frac{1}{e^x} = 7$, $e^x = \frac{1}{7}$, $x = \ln \frac{1}{7}$; $\left\{\ln \frac{1}{7}\right\}$

35. $\sqrt{e^x} = 3$, $e^x = 9$, $x = \ln 9$; $\{\ln 9\}$

36. $e^{-2x} = 0.2$, $-2x = \ln \frac{1}{5}$, $-2x = -\ln 5$, $x = \frac{1}{2} \ln 5$; $\left\{\frac{1}{2} \ln 5\right\}$

37. $(e^x)^5 = 1000$, $e^x = 10^{3/5}$, $x = \ln 10^{3/5} = \frac{3}{5} \ln 10$; $\left\{\frac{3}{5} \ln 10\right\}$

38. $3e^{2x} + 2 = 50$, $3e^{2x} = 48$, $e^{2x} = 16$, $2x = \ln 16$, $2x = \ln 4^2 = 2 \ln 4$, $x = \ln 4$; $\{\ln 4\}$

39. $\ln(\ln x) = 0$, $e^{\ln(\ln x)} = e^0$, $\ln x = 1$, $e^{\ln x} = e^1$, $x = e$; $\{e\}$

40. $|\ln x| = 1$, $\ln x = 1$ or $\ln x = -1$, $x = e$ or $x = e^{-1}$; $\{e, e^{-1}\}$

41. $\ln x + \ln(x + 3) = \ln 10$, $\ln x(x + 3) = \ln 10$, $x(x + 3) = 10$, $x^2 + 3x = 10$, $x^2 + 3x - 10 = 0$, $(x + 5)(x - 2) = 0$, $x = -5$ (reject) or $x = 2$; $\{2\}$

42. $2 \ln x = \ln(x + 1)$, $\ln x^2 = \ln(x + 1)$, $x^2 = x + 1$, $x^2 - x - 1 = 0$,
$x = \frac{1 \pm \sqrt{1 + 4}}{2} = \frac{1 \pm \sqrt{5}}{2}$, $x = \frac{1 - \sqrt{5}}{2}$ (reject) or $x = \frac{1 + \sqrt{5}}{2}$; $\left\{\frac{1 + \sqrt{5}}{2}\right\}$

43. $e^{2x} - 7e^x + 12 = 0$; let $y = e^x$; $y^2 - 7y + 12 = 0$, $(y - 4)(y - 3) = 0$, $y = 4$ or $y = 3$; $e^x = 4$ or $e^x = 3$; $x = \ln 4$ or $x = \ln 3$; $\{\ln 3, \ln 4\}$

B **44.** domain: $\{x: x > 0\}$; range: {all real numbers}

45. domain: $\{x: x \neq 0\}$; range: {all real numbers}

46. domain: $\{x: x \neq 0\}$; range: {all real numbers}

47. domain: $\{x: x > 5\}$; range: {all real numbers}

48.

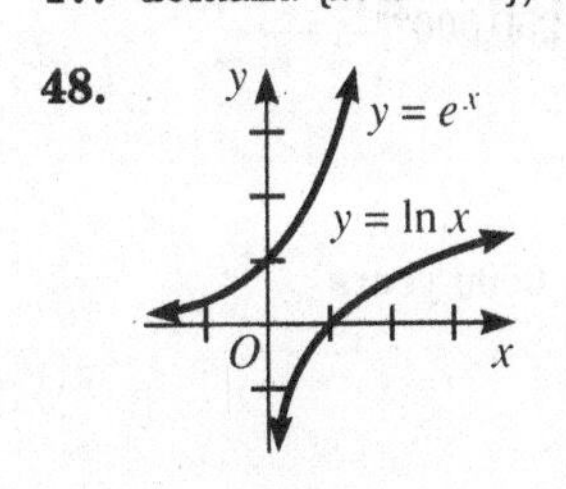

49.

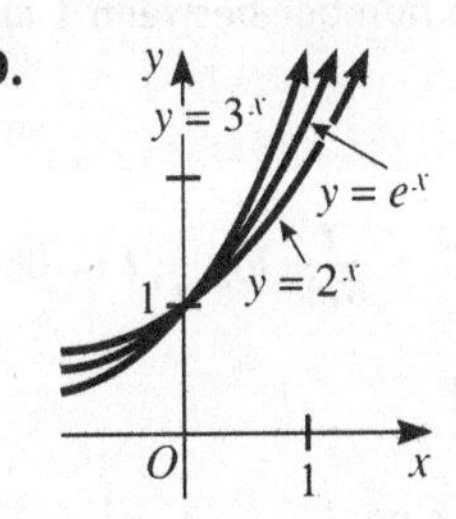

C **50. a.** For n very large, $\left(1+\frac{1}{n}\right)^{5n} = \left[\left(1+\frac{1}{n}\right)^n\right]^5 \approx e^5$

b. For n very large, $\left(1+\frac{2}{n}\right)^n \approx \left(1+\frac{2}{n}+\frac{1}{n^2}\right)^n = \left[\left(1+\frac{1}{n}\right)^2\right]^n = \left[\left(1+\frac{1}{n}\right)^n\right]^2 = e^2$

c. For n very large, $\left(\frac{n}{n+1}\right)^{2n} = \left(\frac{n+1}{n}\right)^{-2n} = \left(1+\frac{1}{n}\right)^{-2n} = \left[\left(1+\frac{1}{n}\right)^n\right]^{-2} \approx e^{-2}$

51. a. $A = P\left(1+\frac{r}{n}\right)^{nt} = P\left(1+\frac{1}{\frac{n}{r}}\right)^{r(n/r)t} = P\left[\left(1+\frac{1}{\frac{n}{r}}\right)^{n/r}\right]^{rt} \approx Pe^{rt}$, because

$\left(1+\frac{1}{\frac{n}{r}}\right)^{n/r}$ is approximately equal to e for large n (and constant r) just as

$\left(1+\frac{1}{n}\right)^n$ is. **b.** $A \approx 1000e^{0.06(1)}$; $A \approx 1061.84$; \$1061.84

Page 492 • CALCULATOR KEY-IN

1. a. $1000e^{0.06} = 1061.84$; \$1061.84 **b.** $1000e^{0.06 \cdot 2} = 1000e^{0.12} = 1127.50$; \$1127.50

c. $1000e^{0.06 \cdot 10} = 1000e^{0.6} = 1822.12$; \$1822.12

2. Investment A: $P = 1000e^{0.08 \cdot 10} = 1000e^{0.8} = 2225.54$
Investment B: $2000e^{(0.08)5} = 2983.65$; Investment B

3. a.

x	0	0.1	0.2	0.3	0.4	0.5	0.6	0.7	0.8	0.9	1.0
y	1	0.99	0.96	0.91	0.85	0.78	0.70	0.61	0.53	0.44	0.37

b.

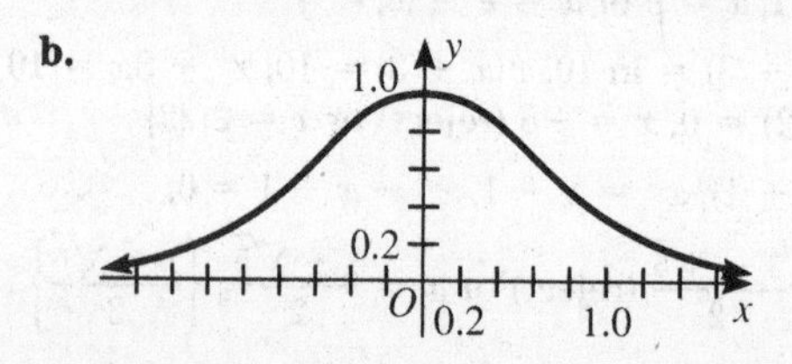

4. a. 2.718280469

b. They are equal to 5 decimal places.

5. $1 + 1 + \frac{1}{2} + \frac{1}{6} + \frac{1}{24} + \frac{1}{120} + \frac{1}{720} \approx 2.718056 \approx e$

Page 492 • CHALLENGE

20; first ask "Is the number between 1 and 500,000, inclusive?" thus eliminating 500,000 numbers. Continue asking such questions. For example, if the answer to the above question is yes, the next question should be "Is the number between 1 and 250,000?"

Pages 493–494 • APPLICATION

1. $\frac{N}{N_0} = 0.45 = \left(\frac{1}{2}\right)^{t/5730}$; $\log 0.45 = \frac{t}{5730}\log\frac{1}{2}$; $t \approx 6600$; 6600 years

2. a. $\frac{0.08}{10^{12}} \div \frac{1}{10^{12}} = 0.08$; 0.08 : 1

b. $\frac{N}{N_0} = 0.08 = \left(\frac{1}{2}\right)^{t/5730}$; $\log 0.08 = \frac{t}{5730}\log\frac{1}{2}$; $t = \frac{5730 \log 0.08}{\log 0.5} \approx 21{,}000$;
21,000 years

3. a. $\frac{N}{N_0} = \left(\frac{1}{2}\right)^{400/5730} \approx 0.953$; 95.3% **b.** $\frac{N}{N_0} = \left(\frac{1}{2}\right)^{600/5730} \approx 0.930$; 93.0%

Pages 496–497 • CHAPTER REVIEW

1. c; $(x^{1/2} - y^{1/2})^2 = (x^{1/2})^2 - 2(x^{1/2})(y^{1/2}) + (y^{1/2})^2 = x - 2\sqrt{x}\sqrt{y} + y = x - 2\sqrt{xy} + y$

2. c; $\frac{2}{\sqrt[6]{8}} = \frac{2}{2^{3/6}} = 2^{1-1/2} = 2^{1/2} = \sqrt{2}$ **3.** d; $(5^2)^{x+2} = 5^{3x-3}$; $2x + 4 = 3x - 3, x = 7$

4. d; $(2^{1+\sqrt{2}-(1-\sqrt{2})})^{\sqrt{2}} = (2^{2\sqrt{2}})^{\sqrt{2}} = 2^4 = 16$ **5.** b

6. b; $g(f(x)) = g(3x - 2) = 2(3x - 2) - 1 = 6x - 4 - 1 = 6x - 5$

7. a; $g(f(x)) = \dfrac{3\left(\frac{5}{3}x + 1 - 1\right)}{5} = x; f(g(x)) = \frac{5}{3}\left(\frac{3(x-1)}{5}\right) + 1 = x$

8. c; $x = 9y - 7, x + 7 = 9y, y = \frac{x+7}{9}$ **9.** b; $\log_4 64 = \log_4 4^3 = 3$

10. d; $5^3 < 150 < 5^4$ **11.** a; $\log_6 \frac{36}{6^{-10}} = \log_6 \frac{6^2}{6^{-10}} = \log_6 6^{12} = 12$

12. a; $\log_b z = \log_b x^{1/3} + \log_b y = \log_b x^{1/3}y; z = x^{1/3}y = y\sqrt[3]{x}$

13. d; $10^{5t} = 2, 5t \log_{10} 10 = \log_{10} 2, t = \frac{\log_{10} 2}{5 \log_{10} 10} = \frac{\log_{10} 2}{5}$

14. b; $5 = 40\left(\frac{1}{2}\right)^{12/h}, \frac{1}{8} = \left(\frac{1}{2}\right)^{12/h}, \left(\frac{1}{2}\right)^3 = \left(\frac{1}{2}\right)^{12/h}, \frac{12}{h} = 3, h = 4$

15. b; $\ln \frac{1}{e^3} = \ln e^{-3} = -3$ **16.** c; $2x - 1 = \ln 3, 2x = 1 + \ln 3, x = \frac{1 + \ln 3}{2}$

Page 497 • CHAPTER TEST

1. a. $\left(\frac{1}{16}\right)^{-3/4} = x, (2^{-4})^{-3/4} = x, x = 2^3 = 8$ **b.** $27^x = 81, 3^{3x} = 3^4, 3x = 4, x = \frac{4}{3}$

2. a. $\sqrt[3]{\sqrt{125y^6}}$; $((5^3y^6)^{1/2})^{1/3} = (5^3y^6)^{1/2 \cdot 1/3} = (5^3y^6)^{1/6} = 5^{3 \cdot 1/6}y^{6 \cdot 1/6} = 5^{1/2}y = y\sqrt{5}$

b. $(64^{2/3} + 27^{2/3})^{3/2} = [(\sqrt[3]{64})^2 + (\sqrt[3]{27})^2]^{3/2} = (4^2 + 3^2)^{3/2} = 25^{3/2} = (\sqrt{25})^3 = 5^3 = 125$

3. $4^{x-2} = 8^{\pi+1} \div 8^{\pi-1}; 4^{x-2} = 8^{\pi+1-(\pi-1)}; 4^{x-2} = 8^2; (2^2)^{x-2} = (2^3)^2, 2x - 4 = 6, 2x = 10, x = 5; \{5\}$

4. a. $f(g(-2)) = f(8) = 15$

b. $g(f(x)) = g(2x - 1) = (2x - 1)^2 + 4 = 4x^2 - 4x + 1 + 4 = 4x^2 - 4x + 5$

5. $f(g(x)) = \sqrt[3]{x^3 + 1 - 1} = \sqrt[3]{x^3} = x; g(f(x)) = (\sqrt[3]{x - 1})^3 + 1 = x - 1 + 1 = x$

6. a. $(2^5)^{3/5} = 2^3 = 8; \log_2 8 = 3$ **b.** $16^{-3/2} = \frac{1}{64}$

7. a. 3 **b.** $\log_3 (3^3)^{\sqrt{2}} = \log_3 3^{3\sqrt{2}} = 3\sqrt{2}$

8. a. $\log_3 x = \log_3 12 + \log_3 2 - \log_3 6, \log_3 x = \log_3 \frac{12(2)}{6} = \log_3 4; x = 4; \{4\}$

b. $\log_4(x - 6) + \log_4 x = 2, \log_4 x(x - 6) = 2, x(x - 6) = 4^2, x(x - 6) = 16, x^2 - 6x - 16 = 0, (x - 8)(x + 2) = 0, x = 8$ or $x = -2$ (reject); $\{8\}$

9. a. $\log_{10} 8 = \log_{10} 2^3 = 3 \log_{10} 2 = 3(0.301) = 0.903$

b. $\log_{10} 12 = \log_{10}(2^2 \cdot 3) = 2 \log_{10} 2 + \log_{10} 3 = 2(0.301) + 0.477 = 1.079$

c. $\log_{10} 15 = \log_{10} \frac{10 \cdot 3}{2} = \log_{10} 10 + \log_{10} 3 - \log_{10} 2 = 1 + 0.477 - 0.301 = 1.176$

10. $5^{3t} = 2, 3t \log 5 = \log 2, t = \frac{\log 2}{3 \log 5}$

11. $N = N_0 2^{t/5}; \frac{N}{N_0} = 3 = 2^{t/5}, \log 3 = \frac{t}{5} \log 2, t = \frac{5 \log 3}{\log 2} \approx 7.9$; 7.9 hours

12. $\ln x^2 = 8, e^{\ln x^2} = e^8, x^2 = e^8, x = \pm\sqrt{e^8} = \pm e^4$

13. $\frac{1}{2} - \ln 7 = \ln e^{1/2} - \ln 7 = \ln \frac{e^{1/2}}{7} = \ln \frac{\sqrt{e}}{7}$

Page 498 • MIXED PROBLEM SOLVING

A

1. Let x = mL of iodine to be added;

	% iodine	mL of solution	mL iodine
before	0.10	50	5
after	0.25	$50 + x$	$5 + x$

$5 + x = 0.25(50 + x)$,
$5 + x = 12.5 + 0.25x$, $0.75x = 7.5$,
$x = 10$; 10 mL

2. Let n = the number; $1 - \frac{1}{n} = n, n - 1 = n^2, n^2 - n + 1 = 0, n = \frac{1 \pm \sqrt{1-4}}{2} = \frac{1 \pm \sqrt{-3}}{2} = \frac{1 \pm i\sqrt{3}}{2}$; there is no real solution

3. Let x, y, and z be the numbers of representatives from CA, NY, and NC, respectively;
$\begin{matrix} x + y + z = 90 \\ y = 23 + z \\ x = y + z \end{matrix}$; $\begin{matrix} x + y + z = 90 \\ y - z = 23 \\ x - y - z = 0 \end{matrix}$; $\begin{matrix} x + y + z = 90 \\ y - z = 23 \\ 2x = 90 \end{matrix}$; $x = 45$; $\begin{matrix} y + z = 45 \\ y - z = 23 \end{matrix}$;
$2y = 68, y = 34; 34 + z = 45, z = 11$; CA: 45, NY: 34, NC: 11

4. Let t = number of teeth and s = speed in r/min; $st = k$; $(200)(36) = k$; $k = 7200$; $s(60) = 7200, s = 120$; 120 r/min

5. Let x and $6 + x$ be the two numbers; let $P(x)$ be their product; $P(x) = x(6 + x) = x^2 + 6x; -\frac{b}{2a} = -\frac{6}{2} = -3; P(-3) = (-3)(3) = -9$; the minimum product is -9.

6. Let l and w be the length and width, in m, of the garden; $2(l + w) = 44, l + w = 22, l = 22 - w; (l + 4)(w + 4) = 224, (22 - w + 4)(w + 4) = 224, (-w + 26)(w + 4) = 224, -w^2 + 22w + 104 = 224, w^2 - 22w + 120 = 0, (w - 12)(w - 10) = 0, w = 12$ or $w = 10$; if $w = 10, l + 10 = 22, l = 12$; if $w = 12, l + 12 = 22, l = 10$; 12 m by 10 m

7. Let $f(x)$ be the amount saved from earnings of x dollars; $f(x) = mx + b$;
$\begin{matrix} 600 = m(15{,}000) + b \\ 900 = m(18{,}000) + b \end{matrix}$; $300 = 3{,}000m, m = 0.1; 600 = 0.1(15{,}000) + b$,
$600 = (1500) + b, b = -900; f(x) = 0.1x - 900; f(24{,}000) = 0.1(24{,}000) - 900 = 1500$; \$1500

8. Let e = number of eagles, and q = number of quarter-eagles worth \$2.50; $10e + 2.50q = 25$, $2.50q = 25 - 10e$, $q = 10 - 4e$;

e	0	1	2
q	10	6	2

; 0 eagles and 10 quarter-eagles; 1 eagle and 6 quarter-eagles; or 2 eagles and 2 quarter-eagles

B

9. Let A = area and C = circumference; $A = kC^2$; $49\pi = k(14\pi)^2$, $k = \frac{49\pi}{196\pi^2}$, $k = \frac{1}{4\pi}$; $A = \frac{C^2}{4\pi}$

10. Let n, $n + 1$, and $n + 2$ be consecutive integers; $(n + n + 1)^2 = 80 + (n + 1)^2 + (n + 2)^2$, $4n^2 + 4n + 1 = 80 + n^2 + 2n + 1 + n^2 + 4n + 4$, $2n^2 - 2n - 84 = 0$, $n^2 - n - 42 = 0$, $(n - 7)(n + 6) = 0$, $n = 7$ or $n = -6$; 7, 8, 9 or $-6, -5, -4$

11. Let t = time in hours, the larger plant would take; $\frac{5}{t} + \frac{5}{t + 4} = 1$; $5(t + 4) + 5t = t(t + 4)$, $5t + 20 + 5t = t^2 + 4t$, $t^2 - 6t - 20 = 0$; $t = \frac{6 \pm \sqrt{116}}{2}$, $t \approx -2.39$ (reject) or $t \approx 8.38$; larger plant, 8.4 h; smaller plant, 12.4 h

12. Let A = value of the car in t years; $A = A_0(1 - 0.12)^t$; $\frac{A}{A_0} = (0.88)^t = \frac{1}{2}$; $t \log 0.88 = \log \frac{1}{2}$, $t = \frac{-\log 2}{\log 0.88} \approx 5.4$; about 5.4 years

13. Let x and y be the time in hours she spent jogging and walking respectively;
$\begin{aligned} 8x + 5y &= 23 \\ 5x + 8y &= 29 \end{aligned}$; $\begin{aligned} -40x - 25y &= -115 \\ 40x + 64y &= 232 \end{aligned}$; $39y = 117$; $y = 3$; $8x + 5(3) = 23$, $8x = 8$, $x = 1$; $3 + 1 = 4$; 4 h

Page 499 • PREPARING FOR COLLEGE ENTRANCE EXAMS

1. C; slope of segment from $(-7, 4)$ to $(3, 6)$ $= \frac{6 - 4}{3 - (-7)} = \frac{1}{5}$; slope of $\perp$ bisector $= -5$; midpt $= \left(\frac{-7 + 3}{2}, \frac{4 + 6}{2}\right) = (-2, 5)$; equation of $\perp$ bisector: $y - 5 = -5(x + 2)$, $5x + y = -5$

2. D; $9x^2 - y^2 = 18$, $\frac{x^2}{2} - \frac{y^2}{18} = 1$

3. E; $-3 \log_8 4 = -3 \log_8 8^{2/3} = (-3)\left(\frac{2}{3}\right) = -2$; $\ln \frac{1}{e^2} = \ln e^{-2} = -2$

4. B; $a^2 = b^2 + c^2$; $36 = 16 + c^2$, $c^2 = 20$, $c = 2\sqrt{5}$; foci are on the y-axis

5. A; $x = \frac{4}{y} - 1$, $x + 1 = \frac{4}{y}$, $\frac{1}{x + 1} = \frac{y}{4}$, $y = \frac{4}{x + 1}$; $f^{-1}(x) = \frac{4}{x + 1}$, $f^{-1}(7) = \frac{4}{8} = \frac{1}{2}$

6. E; $(3^3)^{2t-1} = (3^4)^{t+2}$; $6t - 3 = 4t + 8$, $2t = 11$, $t = \frac{11}{2}$

7. E; $y = \frac{3}{x}$; $x^2 + 16\left(\frac{3}{x}\right)^2 = 25$, $x^4 + 144 = 25x^2$, $x^4 - 25x^2 + 144 = 0$,

$(x^2 - 16)(x^2 - 9) = 0$, $x^2 = 16$ or $x^2 = 9$, $x = \pm 4$ or $x = \pm 3$; $(x, y) = \left(4, \frac{3}{4}\right)$, $\left(-4, -\frac{3}{4}\right)$, (3, 1), or $(-3, -1)$

8. C; $\begin{aligned} 5x - 3y + z &= 5 \\ 4x + 3y - 2z &= -4 \\ 2x - 3y - 7z &= 13 \end{aligned}$; $\begin{aligned} x - \frac{3}{2}y - \frac{7}{2}z &= \frac{13}{2} \\ \frac{9}{2}y + \frac{37}{2}z &= -\frac{55}{2} \\ 9y + 12z &= -30 \end{aligned}$; $\begin{aligned} x - \frac{3}{2}y - \frac{7}{2}z &= \frac{13}{2} \\ 9y + 37z &= -55 \\ -25z &= 25 \end{aligned}$; $z = -1$

CHAPTER 11 • Sequences and Series

Pages 504–506 • WRITTEN EXERCISES

A **1.** arithmetic; 8, 5 **2.** arithmetic; 21, 25 **3.** geometric; 625, 3125

4. geometric; 1, $\frac{1}{4}$ **5.** arithmetic; 30, 38 **6.** arithmetic; 0, -16 **7.** neither; $\frac{1}{25}, \frac{1}{36}$

8. geometric; 2, -1 **9.** geometric; $4^{9/2}, 4^{11/2}$ **10.** neither; $\frac{5}{16}, \frac{6}{17}$

11. 7, 11, 15, 19; arithmetic **12.** 3, 5, 7, 9; arithmetic **13.** 1, 3, 9, 27; geometric

14. 6, 18, 54, 162; geometric **15.** $-\frac{1}{4}, \frac{1}{2}, -1, 2$; geometric

16. 9, 5, 1, -3; arithmetic **17.** log 2, log 3, log 4, log 5; neither

18. $t_n = n \log 10 = n$; 1, 2, 3, 4; arithmetic

19. a. arithmetic **b.** geometric

20. a. geometric **b.** the sequence is 0, 2, 4, 6; arithmetic

B **21.** The sequence of differences is: 2, 4, 6, 8, 10, 12, . . . ; 32, 44

22. The sequence of differences is: 4, 8, 12, 16, 20, 24, . . . ; 57, 81

23. The sequence of differences is: $-12, -10, -8, -6, -4, -2, \ldots$; 20, 18

24. The sequence of differences is: $-1, -2, -4, -8, -16, -32, \ldots$; $-7, -39$

25. The sequence of differences is: 2, 4, 8, 16, 32, 64, . . . ; 63, 127

26. The sequence of differences is: 1, 3, 9, 27, 81, 243, . . . ; 121, 364

27. The sequence of differences is: 0, 1, 1, 2, 3, 5, 8, 13, . . . (each term is the sum of the two preceding terms); 21, 34

28. The sequence of differences is: 1, 4, 9, 16, 25, 36, . . . ; 56, 92

29. The sequence of the differences is 2, 3, 5, 8, 12, . . . ; the differences of the differences form the sequence 1, 2, 3, 4, . . . ; the next two terms in the sequence of differences are $12 + 5 = 17$ and $17 + 6 = 23$; thus, the next two terms of the sequence are $31 + 17 = 48$ and $48 + 23 = 71$.

30. The sequence of the differences is 2, 3, 6, 11, 18, . . . ; the differences of the differences form the sequence 1, 3, 5, 7, . . . ; the next two terms in the sequence of differences are $18 + 9 = 27$ and $27 + 11 = 38$; thus, the next two terms are $45 + 27 = 72$ and $72 + 38 = 110$.

31. a. $t_5 = 15$; $t_6 = 21$ **b.** $t_{10} = 1 + 2 + 3 + 4 + 5 + 6 + \cdots + 10 = 55$

32. a. $t_5 = 35$; $t_6 = 51$

b. The sequence of differences is 4, 7, 10, . . . ; the first ten terms of the pentagonal number sequence are 1, 5, 12, 22, 35, 51, 70, 92, 117, 145. The tenth pentagonal number is 145.

33. a. $t_6 = 9$ **b.** 0, 2, 5, 9, 14, 20, 27, 35; $t_{10} = 35$

34. a. $t_4 = 11$ regions; $t_5 = 16$ regions **b.** $16 + 6 = 22$ regions

C **35. a.** $t_5 = 16$; $t_6 = 31$; no

b. The sequence: 1, 2, 4, 8, 16, 31, . . .

1st differences: 1, 2, 4, 8, 15, . . .

2nd differences: 1, 2, 4, 7, . . .

3rd differences: 1, 2, 3, . . .

The next 3rd difference is 4, the next 2nd difference is $7 + 4 = 11$, and the next first difference is $15 + 11 = 26$. Therefore, the next term of the sequence is $31 + 26 = 57$; $t_7 = 57$.

Page 506 • MIXED REVIEW EXERCISES

1.

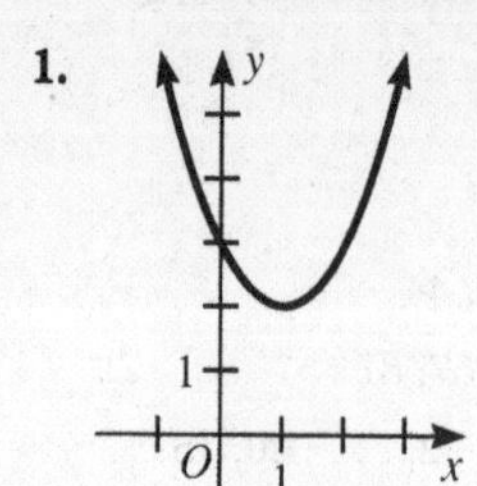

2.

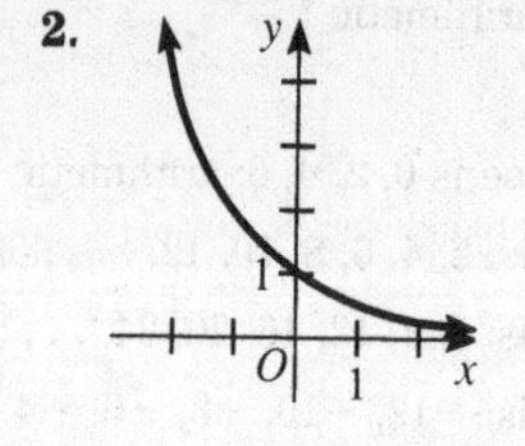

3.

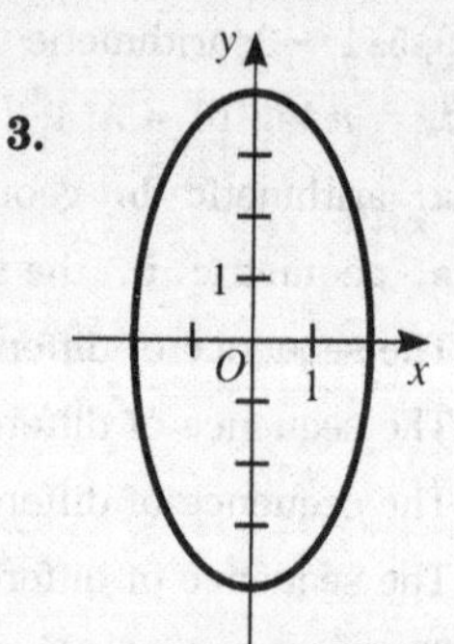

4.

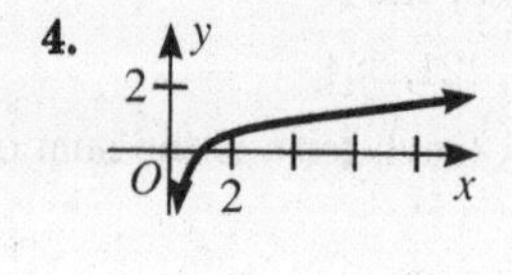

5.

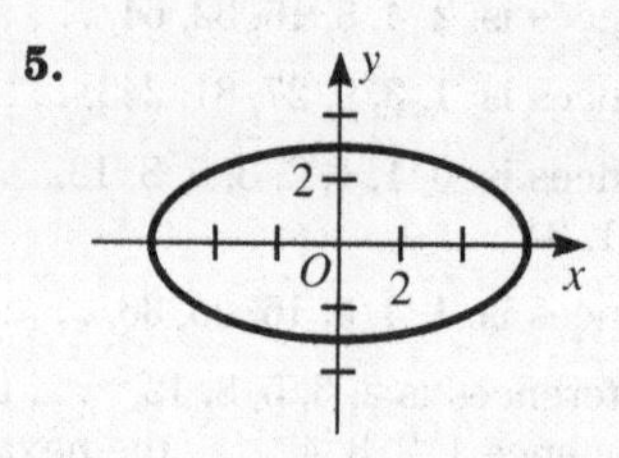

6.

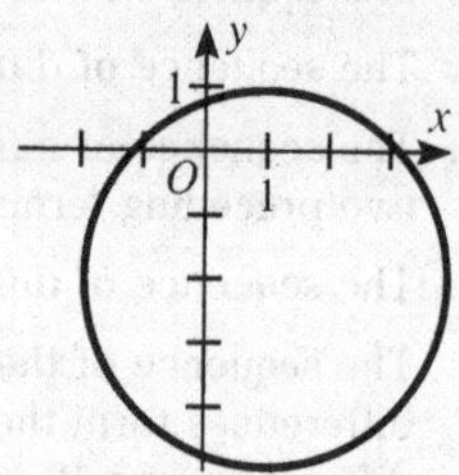

7. $\begin{aligned} 2x + y &= 1 \\ x - y &= 5 \end{aligned}$; $3x = 6, x = 2; 2 - y = 5, y = -3; (2, -3)$

8. $\begin{aligned} y &= 2x^2 - 1 \\ x + y &= 2 \end{aligned}$; $y = 2 - x; 2 - x = 2x^2 - 1, 2x^2 + x - 3 = 0, (2x + 3)(x - 1) = 0, x = -\frac{3}{2}$ and $y = 2 - \left(-\frac{3}{2}\right) = \frac{7}{2}$ or $x = 1$ and $y = 1$; $(1, 1)$ or $\left(-\frac{3}{2}, \frac{7}{2}\right)$

9. $\begin{aligned} x^2 + y^2 &= 5 \\ x^2 - y^2 &= 3 \end{aligned}$; $2x^2 = 8, x^2 = 4; 4 + y^2 = 5, y^2 = 1; x = \pm 2, y = \pm 1; (2, 1), (-2, 1), (2, -1), (-2, -1)$

Page 509 • WRITTEN EXERCISES

A **1.** $t_1 = 24, d = 8; t_n = 24 + (n - 1)8 = 24 + 8n - 8; t_n = 16 + 8n$

2. $t_n = 30 + (n - 1)(-10) = 30 - 10n + 10; t_n = 40 - 10n$

3. $t_n = -3 + (n - 1)(-7) = -3 - 7n + 7; t_n = 4 - 7n$

4. $t_n = -6 + (n - 1)(5) = -6 + 5n - 5; t_n = -11 + 5n$

5. $t_n = 7 + (n - 1)(4) = 7 + 4n - 4; t_n = 3 + 4n$

6. $t_n = 13 + (n - 1)(-9) = 13 - 9n + 9; t_n = 22 - 9n$

7. $t_{21} = 4 + (21 - 1)(5) = 104$ **8.** $t_{31} = 3 + (31 - 1)8 = 243$

9. $t_{25} = 100 + (25 - 1)(-2) = 52$ **10.** $t_{101} = 3 + (101 - 1)(0.5) = 53$

11. $t_{101} = -2 + (101 - 1)(-9) = -902$

12. $t_{1000} = 17 + (1000 - 1)(-10) = -9973$

13. $t_3 = 5 + (3 - 1)d = 20,\ 5 + 2d = 20,\ 2d = 15,\ d = 7.5;$
$t_{12} = 5 + (12 - 1)(7.5) = 87.5$

14. $\begin{matrix} 7 = t_1 + (2 - 1)d \\ 8 = t_1 + (4 - 1)d \end{matrix};\ \begin{matrix} 7 = t_1 + d \\ 8 = t_1 + 3d \end{matrix};\ 2d = 1,\ d = 0.5;\ 7 = t_1 + 0.5,\ t_1 = 6.5$

15. $\begin{matrix} 24 = t_1 + (5 - 1)d \\ 40 = t_1 + (9 - 1)d \end{matrix};\ \begin{matrix} 24 = t_1 + 4d \\ 40 = t_1 + 8d \end{matrix};\ 4d = 16,\ d = 4;\ 24 = t_1 + 4(4),\ t_1 = 8$

16. $\begin{matrix} 60 = t_1 + (8 - 1)d \\ 48 = t_1 + (12 - 1)d \end{matrix};\ \begin{matrix} 60 = t_1 + 7d \\ 48 = t_1 + 11d \end{matrix};\ 4d = -12,\ d = -3;\ 60 = t_1 + 7(-3),$
$t_1 = 81;\ t_{40} = 81 + (40 - 1)(-3) = -36$

17. $\begin{matrix} -19 = t_1 + (7 - 1)d \\ -28 = t_1 + (10 - 1)d \end{matrix};\ \begin{matrix} -19 = t_1 + 6d \\ -28 = t_1 + 9d \end{matrix};\ 3d = -9,\ d = -3;\ -19 = t_1 + 6(-3),$
$t_1 = -1;\ t_{21} = -1 + (21 - 1)(-3) = -61$

18. $\begin{matrix} 41 = t_1 + (10 - 1)d \\ 61 = t_1 + (15 - 1)d \end{matrix};\ \begin{matrix} 41 = t_1 + 9d \\ 61 = t_1 + 14d \end{matrix};\ 5d = 20,\ d = 4;\ 41 = t_1 + 9(4),$
$t_1 = 5;\ t_3 = 5 + (3 - 1)4 = 13$

19. $\frac{-3 + 7}{2} = 2$ **20.** $\frac{2.3 + 9.1}{2} = 5.7$ **21.** $\frac{1}{2}\left(\frac{4}{5} + \frac{11}{5}\right) = \frac{3}{2}$

22. $\frac{1}{2}(-\sqrt{2} + 3\sqrt{2}) = \frac{1}{2}(2\sqrt{2}) = \sqrt{2}$

B

23. a. $33 = -27 + (4 - 1)d,\ 33 = -27 + 3d,\ d = 20;\ -27, -7, 13, 33$

b. $33 = -27 + (5 - 1)d,\ 33 = -27 + 4d,\ d = 15;\ -27, -12, 3, 18, 33$

c. $33 = -27 + (6 - 1)d,\ 33 = -27 + 5d,\ d = 12;\ -27, -15, -3, 9, 21, 33$

24. a. $45 = 15 + (4 - 1)d,\ 45 = 15 + 3d,\ d = 10;\ 15, 25, 35, 45$

b. $45 = 15 + (5 - 1)d,\ 45 = 15 + 4d,\ d = 7.5;\ 15, 22.5, 30, 37.5, 45$

c. $45 = 15 + (6 - 1)d,\ 45 = 15 + 5d,\ d = 6;\ 15, 21, 27, 33, 39, 45$

25. a. $35 = 11 + (4 - 1)d,\ 35 = 11 + 3d,\ d = 8;\ 11, 19, 27, 35$

b. $35 = 11 + (5 - 1)d,\ 35 = 11 + 4d,\ d = 6;\ 11, 17, 23, 29, 35$

c. $35 = 11 + (6 - 1)d,\ 35 = 11 + 5d,\ d = 4.8;\ 11, 15.8, 20.6, 25.4, 30.2, 35$

26. a. $20 = 0 + (4 - 1)d,\ 20 = 0 + 3d,\ d = \frac{20}{3};\ 0, \frac{20}{3}, \frac{40}{3}, 20$

b. $20 = 0 + (5 - 1)d,\ 20 = 0 + 4d,\ d = 5;\ 0, 5, 10, 15, 20$

c. $20 = 0 + (6 - 1)d,\ 20 = 0 + 5d,\ d = 4;\ 0, 4, 8, 12, 16, 20$

27. $t_1 = 18,\ d = 6;\ 618 = 18 + (n - 1)6,\ 600 = 6(n - 1),\ 100 = n - 1,\ n = 101$

28. $t_1 = 44,\ d = -8;\ -380 = 44 + (n - 1)(-8),\ -424 = -8(n - 1),\ n - 1 = 53,\ n = 54$

29. The multiples of 3 between 100 and 1000 form an arithmetic sequence with $t_1 = 102$ and $d = 3$; let t_n be the last term; $t_n = 999 = 102 + (n - 1)3;\ 999 = 102 + 3n - 3;$ $3n = 900;\ n = 300.$

30. The multiples of 7 between 50 and 500 form an arithmetic sequence with $t_1 = 56$ and $d = 7$; let t_n be the last term; $t_n = 497 = 56 + (n - 1)(7)$; $497 = 56 + 7n - 7$; $7n = 448$; $n = 64$

31. $t_1 = 25, d = 8; 145 = 25 + (n - 1)(8), 8(n - 1) = 120, n - 1 = 15, n = 16$

32. $t_1 = 40, d = -3; -29 = 40 + (n - 1)(-3), -69 = -3(n - 1), 23 = n-1, n = 24$

C **33.** The difference between t_1 and t_2 is $\frac{a + b}{2} - a = \frac{a + b - 2a}{2} = \frac{b - a}{2}$; The difference between t_3 and t_2 is $b - \frac{a + b}{2} = \frac{2b - a - b}{2} = \frac{b - a}{2}$; since the difference between both pairs of successive terms is constant, the sequence is arithmetic.

Pages 513–514 • WRITTEN EXERCISES

A **1.** $t_n = 2(3)^{n-1}$ **2.** $t_n = 500\left(\frac{1}{5}\right)^{n-1}$ **3.** $t_n = (\sqrt{2})^{n-1}$ **4.** $t_n = 8\left(\frac{3}{2}\right)^{n-1}$

5. $t_n = 64\left(-\frac{3}{4}\right)^{n-1}$ **6.** $t_n = -(-0.1)^{n-1}$ **7.** $t_{10} = 2(3)^{10-1} = 2 \cdot 3^9 = 39{,}366$

8. $t_{12} = 5(2)^{12-1} = 5 \cdot 2^{11} = 10{,}240$ **9.** $t_8 = 320\left(\frac{1}{4}\right)^{8-1} = \frac{320}{4^7} = \frac{5}{256}$

10. $t_8 = 1(-3)^{8-1} = (-3)^7 = -2187$

11. $t_{11} = 40\left(-\frac{1}{2}\right)^{11-1} = \frac{40}{2^{10}} = \frac{5}{2^7} = \frac{5}{128}$ **12.** $t_9 = -10(-5)^{9-1} = -10(5)^8 = -3{,}906{,}250$

13. $\begin{matrix} 18 = t_1 \cdot r^{2-1} \\ 12 = t_1 \cdot r^{3-1} \end{matrix}$; $\begin{matrix} 18 = t_1 r \\ 12 = t_1 r^2 \end{matrix}$; $t_1 = \frac{18}{r}$; $12 = \frac{18}{r} \cdot r^2$, $12 = 18r$, $r = \frac{2}{3}$; $t_1 = \frac{18}{\frac{2}{3}} = 27$; $t_5 = 27\left(\frac{2}{3}\right)^{5-1} = \frac{16}{3}$

14. $\begin{matrix} -12 = t_1 \cdot r^{3-1} \\ 96 = t_1 \cdot r^{6-1} \end{matrix}$; $\begin{matrix} -12 = t_1 r^2 \\ 96 = t_1 r^5 \end{matrix}$; $\frac{96}{-12} = \frac{t_1 r^5}{t_1 r^2}$, $-8 = r^3$, $r = -2$; $-12 = t_1(-2)^2$, $t_1 = -3$; $t_9 = -3(-2)^{9-1} = -768$

15. $80 = 5 \cdot r^{3-1}$, $16 = r^2$, $r = 4$ or -4; if $r = 4$, $t_6 = 5(4)^{6-1} = 5120$; if $r = -4$, $t_6 = 5(-4)^{6-1} = -5120$

16. $\begin{matrix} 8 = t_1 \cdot r^{2-1} \\ 72 = t_1 \cdot r^{4-1} \end{matrix}$; $\begin{matrix} 8 = t_1 r \\ 72 = t_1 r^3 \end{matrix}$; $t_1 = \frac{8}{r}$; $72 = \frac{8}{r} \cdot r^3$, $72 = 8r^2$, $r^2 = 9$, $r = 3$ or $r = -3$; if $r = 3$, $t_1 = \frac{8}{3}$; if $r = -3$, $t_1 = \frac{8}{-3} = -\frac{8}{3}$

17. $t_{20} = y \cdot (y^2)^{20-1}$, $t_{20} = y \cdot y^{2(19)} = y^{39}$

18. $t_{25} = ab^2 \cdot (ab^3)^{25-1}$, $t_{25} = ab^2 \cdot a^{24}b^{3(24)} = a^{25}b^{74}$ **19.** $\sqrt{2 \cdot 8} = \sqrt{16} = 4$

20. $\sqrt{\frac{1}{12}\left(\frac{1}{18}\right)} = \sqrt{\frac{1}{216}} = \frac{1}{6\sqrt{6}} = \frac{\sqrt{6}}{36}$ **21.** $\sqrt{(\sqrt{3})(3\sqrt{3})} = \sqrt{9} = 3$

22. $-\sqrt{(-18)(-36)} = -\sqrt{648} = -18\sqrt{2}$

23. $80 = 5r^{5-1}$, $r^4 = 16$, $r = \pm 2$; 5, 10, 20, 40, 80 or 5, −10, 20, −40, 80

24. $108 = -4r^3$, $r^3 = -27$, $r = -3$; −4, 12, −36, 108

25. $2 = 1 \cdot r^5$, $r = \sqrt[5]{2}$; 1, $\sqrt[5]{2}$, $\sqrt[5]{4}$, $\sqrt[5]{8}$, $\sqrt[5]{16}$, 2

26. $\frac{5}{4} = \frac{1}{5}r^4$, $r^4 = \frac{25}{4}$, $r = \pm\sqrt{\frac{5}{2}} = \pm\frac{\sqrt{10}}{2}$; $\frac{1}{5}, \frac{\sqrt{10}}{10}, \frac{1}{2}, \frac{\sqrt{10}}{4}, \frac{5}{4}$ or $\frac{1}{5}, -\frac{\sqrt{10}}{10}, \frac{1}{2}, -\frac{\sqrt{10}}{4}, \frac{5}{4}$

B **27.** arithmetic; $t_n = 2 + 2(n - 1) = 2 + 2n - 2, t_n = 2n$

28. arithmetic; $t_n = 3 + (n - 1)2 = 3 + 2n - 2, t_n = 2n + 1$

29. arithmetic; $t_n = 25 + (n - 1)8 = 25 + 8n - 8, t_n = 17 + 8n$

30. arithmetic; $t_n = -17 + (n - 1)6 = -17 + 6n - 6, t_n = -23 + 6n$

31. geometric; $t_n = 200\left(-\frac{1}{2}\right)^{n-1}$ **32.** geometric; $t_n = e^{nx}$

33. arithmetic; $t_n = (2a + 1) + (n - 1)(a + 2) = 2a + 1 + n(a + 2) - a - 2 = a - 1 + n(a + 2) = na + a + 2n - 1 = (n + 1)a + (2n - 1)$

34. geometric; $t_n = \frac{a^2}{2}\left(\frac{a^2}{2}\right)^{n-1} = \frac{a^2}{2}\left(\frac{a^2}{2}\right)^{-1}\left(\frac{a^2}{2}\right)^n = \left(\frac{a^2}{2}\right)^n$

35. $-10, -20, -30, -40 \ldots$ is arithmetic; $t_n = -10 + (n - 1)(-10) = -10n$

36. $1, 5, 9, 13, 17, \ldots$ is arithmetic; $t_n = 1 + (n - 1)(4) = -3 + 4n$

37. $t_n = \frac{n + 1}{n^2}$ **38.** $t_n = \frac{n}{2 + (n - 1)3} = \frac{n}{3n - 1}$

C **39.** $\frac{t_2}{t_1} = \frac{\sqrt{ab}}{a}$; $\frac{t_3}{t_2} = \frac{b}{\sqrt{ab}} = \frac{b\sqrt{ab}}{ab} = \frac{\sqrt{ab}}{a}$; since $\frac{t_2}{t_1} = \frac{t_3}{t_2}$, the sequence is geometric

40. Since $8, x, y$ is arithmetic, let $x = 8 + d$ and $y = 8 + 2d$; since $x, y, 36$ is geometric, $\frac{y}{x} = \frac{36}{y}$, $y^2 = 36x$, $(8 + 2d)^2 = 36(8 + d)$, $64 + 32d + 4d^2 = 288 + 36d$, $4d^2 - 4d - 224 = 0$, $d^2 - d - 56 = 0$, $(d - 8)(d + 7) = 0$, $d = 8$ or $d = -7$; if $d = 8$, $x = 16$ and $y = 24$; if $d = -7$, $x = 1$ and $y = -6$

Pages 514–515 • PROBLEMS

A **1.** $t_5 = 17{,}600 + (5 - 1)(850) = 21{,}000$; \$21,000

2. The yearly salaries form a geometric sequence with $t_1 = 15{,}000$ and $r = 1.04$; $t_3 = (15{,}000)(1.04)^2 = 16{,}224$; \$16,224

3. The costs form a geometric sequence with $t_1 = 20$, $r = 1.1$; $t_7 = 20(1.1)^6 \approx 35.43$; \$35.43

4. The prices form a geometric sequence with $t_1 = 70$ and $r = 1.08$; $t_5 = 70(1.08)^4 \approx 95.23$; \$95.23

5. The last "step" is the upper floor, so let $t_n = 330$ and $n - 1 =$ number of steps; $t_n = t_1 + (n - 1)d$; $t_n = 330$, $t_1 = 22$ and $d = 22$; $330 = 22 + (n - 1)22$; $22n = 330$; $n = 15$; $n - 1 = 14$; 14 steps.

6. The widths at each meter of height form an arithmetic sequence with $t_1 = 229.22$ and $d = -1.57$; $t_{86} = 229.22 + (85)(-1.57) = 95.77$; 95.77 m

7. The populations at each 4-hour mark form a geometric sequence with $t_1 = 3 \times 10^6$ and $r = 2$; $t_7 = (3 \times 10^6) \cdot 2^6 = 192 \times 10^6$; 192 million

8. The values of the investment at each 5-year mark form a geometric sequence with $t_1 = 2000$, and $r = 2$; $t_9 = (2000)(2)^8 = 512{,}000$; \$512,000

B **9. a.** The rows are arranged so that the numbers of bricks in the rows form an arithmetic sequence with $t_1 = 85$ and $d = -6$; $t_{12} = 85 + (11)(-6) = 19$; 19 bricks.

b. $t_n = 1$, so $1 = 85 + (n - 1)(-6)$; $1 = 85 - 6n + 6$; $-6n = -90$; $n = 15$; 15

10. a. The numbers of ft/sec form an arithmetic sequence with $t_1 = 15{,}840$ and $d = -32$; $t_{45} = 15{,}840 + (44)(-32) = 14{,}432$; 14,432 ft.

b. The first second of the tenth minute is the $9(60) + 1$ or 541st second; $t_{541} = 15{,}840 + (540)(-32) = -1440$; 1440 ft downward.

11. The values form a geometric sequence with $t_1 = 12{,}000$ and $r = 0.75$; $t_8 = (12{,}000)(0.75)^7 \approx 1601.81$; \$1601.81

12. The values form a geometric sequence with $t_1 = 80{,}000$ and $r = \frac{96{,}000}{80{,}000} = 1.2$; $t_4 = (80{,}000)(1.2)^3 = 138{,}240$; \$138,240

13. The salaries for Job A form an arithmetic sequence with $t_1 = 12{,}000$ and $d = 800$; the salaries for Job B form a geometric sequence with $t_1 = 11{,}000$ and $r = 1.1$. After three years, the salary for Job A $= 12{,}000 + (3)(800) = 14{,}400$, and the salary for Job B $= 11{,}000 \cdot (1.1)^3 = 14{,}641$. After 5 years the salary for Job A $= 12{,}000 + 5(800) = 16{,}000$ and the salary for Job B $= 11{,}000(1.1)^5 = 17{,}715.61$. Job B pays more after 3 years and more after 5 years.

C **14.** For the given sequence $t_1 = 220$ and $t_{13} = 440$; $440 = (220)r^{12}$, $r^{12} = 2$, $r = 2^{1/12}$; frequency of middle C $= t_4 = 220(2^{1/12})^3 = 220(2^{1/4}) \approx 261.6$; 261.6 Hz

Page 515 • MIXED REVIEW EXERCISES

1. $|2x - 5| > 9$; $2x - 5 > 9$ or $2x - 5 < -9$; $2x > 14$ or $2x < -4$; $x > 7$ or $x < -2$; $\{x: x < -2 \text{ or } x > 7\}$;

−8 −4 0 4 8 10

2. $x^2 + x \le 6$, $x^2 + x - 6 \le 0$, $(x + 3)(x - 2) \le 0$; $-3 \le x \le 2$; $\{x: -3 \le x \le 2\}$;

−4 −2 0 2 4

3. $2 \le \frac{x}{2} + 4 < 5$, $-2 \le \frac{x}{2} < 1$, $-4 \le x < 2$; $\{x: -4 \le x < 2\}$;

−6 −4 −2 0 2 4

4. $x^3 > 4x$, $x^3 - 4x > 0$, $x(x^2 - 4) > 0$, $x(x - 2)(x + 2) > 0$; $x(x - 2)(x + 2)$; $\{x: -2 < x < 0 \text{ or } x > 2\}$;

−4 −2 0 2 4

5. $5 - 3x \ge -1$, $-3x \ge -6$, $x \le 2$; $\{x: x \le 2\}$;

−2 −1 0 1 2 3 4

6. $|x + 3| < 2$; $-2 < x + 3 < 2$, $-5 < x < -1$; $\{x: -5 < x < -1\}$;

−6 −5 −4 −3 −2 −1 0

7. $m = \frac{3 - 0}{-2 - 1} = -1$; $y - 0 = -1(x - 1)$, $y = -x + 1$, $x + y = 1$

8. $V(0, 0)$; parabola opens downward; $a = 1$; $y = -\frac{1}{4}x^2$

9. Center at $(0, 0)$; $\frac{x^2}{2^2} + \frac{y^2}{(\sqrt{3})^2} = 1$, $\frac{x^2}{4} + \frac{y^2}{3} = 1$

Page 516 • CHALLENGE

The first sequence is $t_n = 2 + (n - 1)12 = 12n - 10$. The second sequence is $t_m = 1 + (m - 1)7 = 7m - 6$. A common term is $12n - 10 = 7m - 6$; $12n - 7m = 4$; three solutions are $(m, n) = (8, 5), (20, 12)$, and $(32, 19)$; three common terms are 50, 134, and 218

Page 517 • EXTRA

1. $m = d = 6$ 2. $m = d = -4$ 3. $m = -2$ 4. $m = d = 5$

5–8. {real numbers}; {positive integers}

5.

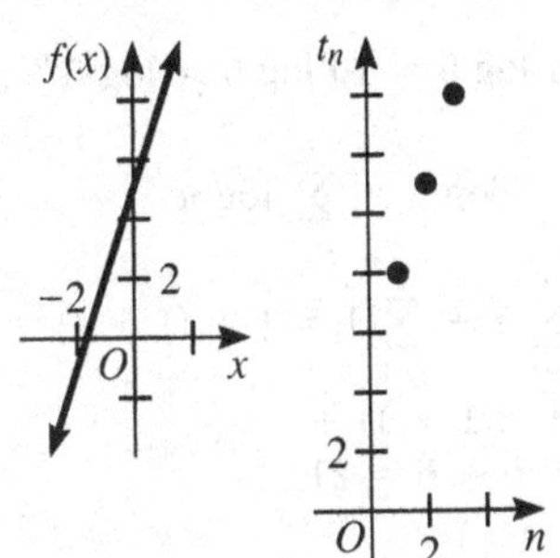

6.

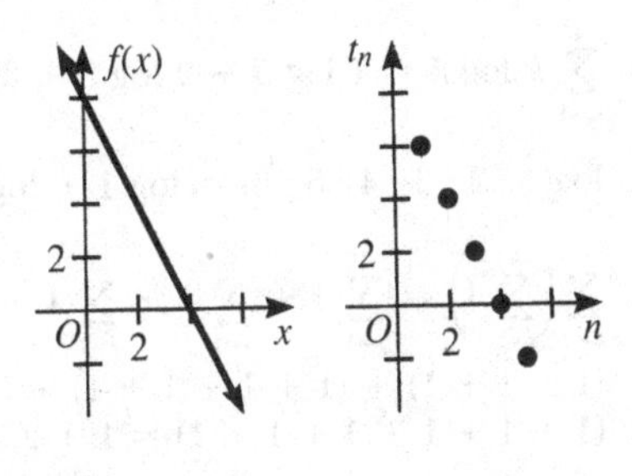

7.

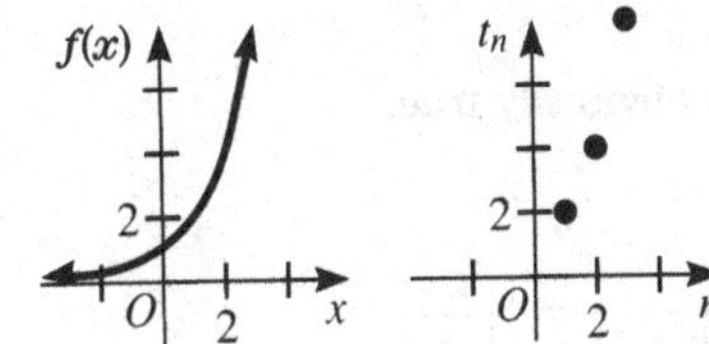

8.

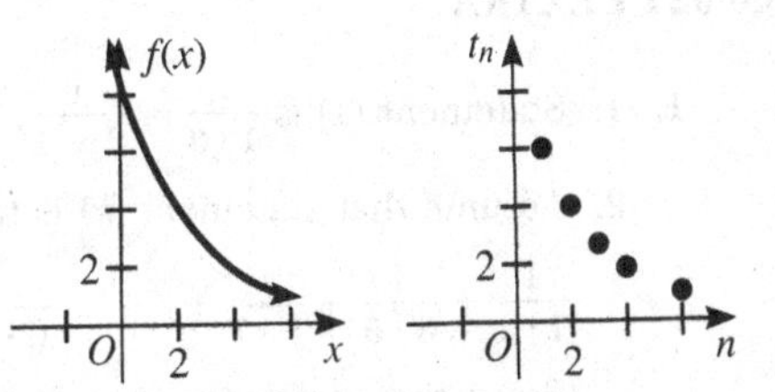

Pages 521–522 • WRITTEN EXERCISES

A

1. $11 + 12 + 13 + 14 + 15 + 16$ 2. $3 + 6 + 9 + 12 + 15 + 18 + 21 + 24$

3. $2 + 4 + 8 + 16 + 32 + 64$ 4. $10 + 13 + 16 + 19 + 22 + 25 + 28$

5. $1 - \frac{1}{2} + \frac{1}{3} - \frac{1}{4} + \frac{1}{5} - \frac{1}{6}$ 6. $1 + \frac{1}{4} + \frac{1}{16} + \frac{1}{64}$ 7. $2 + 1 + 0 + 1 + 2 + 3$

8. $1 + (-2)^3 + (-3)^4 + (-4)^5 = 1 - 8 + 81 - 1024$

9.–30. Answers may vary. Examples are given.

9. $\sum_{n=1}^{500} 2n$ 10. $\sum_{n=1}^{50} 5n$ 11. $\sum_{n=1}^{20} n^3$ 12. $\sum_{n=1}^{24} 3(4)^n$ 13. $\sum_{n=1}^{99} \frac{n}{n+1}$ 14. $\sum_{n=1}^{13} 5^{-(n+2)}$

15. $\sum_{n=1}^{100} (2n - 1)$ 16. $\sum_{n=1}^{100} (4n - 1)$ 17. $\sum_{n=0}^{6} 2^n$ 18. $\sum_{n=1}^{11} \sqrt{7n}$ 19. $\sum_{n=1}^{\infty} \frac{1}{n}$

20. $\sum_{n=0}^{\infty} \frac{1}{3^n}$

B **21.** $\sum_{n=1}^{\infty} 27\left(-\frac{1}{3}\right)^n$ **22.** $\sum_{n=0}^{\infty}(8)\left(-\frac{1}{2}\right)^n$ **23.** $\sum_{n=0}^{3}(6)(-2)^n$ **24.** $\sum_{n=1}^{6}(n^2+1)$ **25.** $\sum_{n=1}^{\infty}\frac{1}{n^2}$

26. $\sum_{n=0}^{\infty}\frac{(-1)^n}{2n+1}$ **27.** $\sum_{n=20}^{199} 5n$ **28.** $\sum_{n=1}^{9}(10n+2)$ **29.** $\sum_{n=0}^{\infty}\left(\frac{1}{4}\right)^n$

30. $508 = 8 + (11-1)d$, $508 = 8 + 10d$, $10d = 500$, $d = 50$; $\sum_{n=1}^{11}[8 + (n-1)50] = \sum_{n=1}^{11}(50n - 42)$

31. $\sum_{k=5}^{8}\frac{k}{k+4} = \frac{5}{9} + \frac{6}{10} + \frac{7}{11} + \frac{8}{12} = \sum_{j=1}^{4}\frac{j+4}{j+8}$

32. $\sum_{k=6}^{9}\frac{k+1}{k-1} = \frac{7}{5} + \frac{8}{6} + \frac{9}{7} + \frac{10}{8} = \sum_{j=7}^{10}\frac{j}{j-2}$

C **33.** $\sum_{k=1}^{4} k\log 5 = 1\log 5 + 2\log 5 + 3\log 5 + 4\log 5 = 10\log 5 = \log 5^{10}$

34. $\log(1\cdot 2\cdot 3\cdot 4\cdot 5\cdot 6) = \log 1 + \log 2 + \cdots + \log 6 = \sum_{n=1}^{6}\log n$

35. $\sum_{k=1}^{6}\left(\sum_{j=1}^{k} 1\right) = \sum_{j=1}^{1} 1 + \sum_{j=1}^{2} 1 + \sum_{j=1}^{3} 1 + \sum_{j=1}^{4} 1 + \sum_{j=1}^{5} 1 + \sum_{j=1}^{6} 1 = 1 + (1+1) + (1+1+1) + (1+1+1+1) + (1+1+1+1+1) + (1+1+1+1+1+1) = 1 + 2 + 3 + 4 + 5 + 6 = 21$

Page 524 • EXTRA

1. 1. Statement (1) is $\frac{1}{1\cdot 3} = \frac{1}{2+1}$. This is obviously true.

2. Assume that statement (k) is true:

$$\frac{1}{1\cdot 3} + \frac{1}{3\cdot 5} + \frac{1}{5\cdot 7} + \cdots + \frac{1}{(2k-1)(2k+1)} = \frac{k}{2k+1}$$

Prove that statement ($k+1$) is true:

$$\frac{1}{1\cdot 3} + \frac{1}{3\cdot 5} + \frac{1}{5\cdot 7} + \cdots + \frac{1}{(2k-1)(2k+1)} + \frac{1}{(2k+1)(2k+3)} = \frac{k+1}{2k+3}$$

Proof:

$$\frac{1}{1\cdot 3} + \frac{1}{3\cdot 5} + \frac{1}{5\cdot 7} + \cdots + \frac{1}{(2k-1)(2k+1)} + \frac{1}{(2k+1)(2k+3)} = \frac{k}{2k+1} + \frac{1}{(2k+1)(2k+3)} = \frac{k(2k+3)}{(2k+1)(2k+3)} + \frac{1}{(2k+1)(2k+3)} = \frac{2k^2+3k+1}{(2k+1)(2k+3)} = \frac{(2k+1)(k+1)}{(2k+1)(2k+3)} = \frac{k+1}{2k+3}\ \checkmark$$

2. 1. Statement (1) is $\frac{1}{1\cdot 4} = \frac{1}{3+1}$. This is obviously true.

2. Assume that statement (k) is true:

$$\frac{1}{1\cdot 4} + \frac{1}{4\cdot 7} + \frac{1}{7\cdot 10} + \cdots + \frac{1}{(3k-2)(3k+1)} = \frac{k}{3k+1}$$

(Continued)

Prove that statement $(k + 1)$ is true:

$$\frac{1}{1 \cdot 4} + \frac{1}{4 \cdot 7} + \frac{1}{7 \cdot 10} + \cdots + \frac{1}{(3k-2)(3k+1)} + \frac{1}{(3k+1)(3k+4)} = \frac{k+1}{3k+4}$$

Proof:

$$\frac{1}{1 \cdot 4} + \frac{1}{4 \cdot 7} + \frac{1}{7 \cdot 10} + \cdots + \frac{1}{(3k-2)(3k+1)} + \frac{1}{(3k+1)(3k+4)} = \frac{k}{3k+1} +$$

$$\frac{1}{(3k+1)(3k+4)} = \frac{k(3k+4)}{(3k+1)(3k+4)} + \frac{1}{(3k+1)(3k+4)} = \frac{3k^2+4k+1}{(3k+1)(3k+4)} =$$

$$\frac{(3k+1)(k+1)}{(3k+1)(3k+4)} = \frac{k+1}{3k+4} \checkmark$$

3. 1. Statement (1) is $1^2 = \frac{1 \cdot 2 \cdot 3}{6}$. This is true.

2. Assume that statement (k) is true:

$$1^2 + 2^2 + 3^2 + \cdots + k^2 = \frac{k(k+1)(2k+1)}{6}$$

Prove that statement $(k + 1)$ is true:

$$1^2 + 2^2 + 3^2 + \cdots + k^2 + (k+1)^2 = \frac{(k+1)(k+2)(2k+3)}{6}$$

Proof:

$$1^2 + 2^2 + 3^2 + \cdots + k^2 + (k+1)^2 = \frac{k(k+1)(2k+1)}{6} + (k+1)^2 =$$

$$\frac{k(k+1)(2k+1)}{6} + \frac{6(k+1)^2}{6} = \frac{(k+1)[k(2k+1) + 6(k+1)]}{6} =$$

$$\frac{(k+1)(2k^2+7k+6)}{6} = \frac{(k+1)(k+2)(2k+3)}{6} \checkmark$$

4. 1. Statement (1) is $1 \cdot 2 = \frac{1 \cdot 2 \cdot 3}{3}$. This is true.

2. Assume that statement (k) is true:

$$1 \cdot 2 + 2 \cdot 3 + 3 \cdot 4 + \cdots + k(k+1) = \frac{k(k+1)(k+2)}{3}$$

Prove that statement $(k + 1)$ is true:

$$1 \cdot 2 + 2 \cdot 3 + 3 \cdot 4 + \cdots + k(k+1) + (k+1)(k+2) = \frac{(k+1)(k+2)(k+3)}{3}$$

Proof:

$$1 \cdot 2 + 2 \cdot 3 + 3 \cdot 4 + \cdots + k(k+1) + (k+1)(k+2) = \frac{k(k+1)(k+2)}{3} +$$

$$(k+1)(k+2) = \frac{k(k+1)(k+2)}{3} + \frac{3(k+1)(k+2)}{3} = \frac{(k+1)(k+2)(k+3)}{3} \checkmark$$

5. 1. Statement (1) is: If, in a room of 1 person, every person shakes hands once with every other person, there will be $\frac{1^2 - 1}{2} = 0$ handshakes. This is true.

2. Assume that statement (k) is true:

If, in a room of k persons, every person shakes hands once with every other person, there will be $\frac{k^2 - k}{2}$ handshakes.

Prove that statement ($k + 1$) is true:

If, in a room of $k + 1$ persons, every person shakes hands once with every other person, there will be $\frac{(k + 1)^2 - (k + 1)}{2} = \frac{k^2 + k}{2}$ handshakes.

Proof:

Begin with k persons. Adding one more person to the room adds k handshakes, since the extra person shakes hands with each of the k persons. The total number of handshakes is thus $\frac{k^2 - k}{2} + k = \frac{k^2 - k}{2} + \frac{2k}{2} = \frac{k^2 + k}{2}$. ✓

6. 1. Statement (3) is: A convex polygon with 3 sides (a triangle) has $\frac{3^2 - 3 \cdot 3}{2} = 0$ diagonals. Since any triangle has no diagonals, this is true.

2. Assume that statement (k) is true:

A convex polygon with k sides has $\frac{k^2 - 3k}{2}$ diagonals.

Prove that statement ($k + 1$) is true:

A convex polygon with $k + 1$ sides has $\frac{(k + 1)^2 - 3(k + 1)}{2} = \frac{k^2 - k - 2}{2} = \frac{(k - 2)(k + 1)}{2}$ diagonals.

Proof:

Begin with a convex polygon with k sides. Now "add" a vertex, so that the convex polygon has $k + 1$ sides. Adding this extra vertex adds $k - 1$ diagonals to the polygon. Thus the total number of diagonals is $\frac{k^2 - 3k}{2} + k - 1 = \frac{k^2 - 3k}{2} + \frac{2k - 2}{2} = \frac{k^2 - k - 2}{2} = \frac{(k - 2)(k + 1)}{2}$. ✓

7. 1. Statement (1) is $1^3 + 2 \cdot 1$ is a multiple of 3. Since $1^3 + 2 \cdot 1 = 3 = 3 \cdot 1$, the statement is true.

2. Assume that statement (k) is true: $k^3 + 2k$ is a multiple of 3.

Prove that statement ($k + 1$) is true:

$(k + 1)^3 + 2(k + 1) = k^3 + 3k^2 + 5k + 3$ is a multiple of 3.

Proof:

$k^3 + 3k^2 + 5k + 3 = (k^3 + 2k) + 3(k^2 + k + 1)$. Since $k^3 + 2k$ is a multiple of 3 and $3(k^2 + k + 1)$ is a multiple of 3, $(k + 1)^3 + 2(k + 1)$ is a multiple of 3 ✓

8. 1. Statement (1) is $1^3 = (1)^2$, which is obviously true.

2. Assume that statement (k) is true:

$1^3 + 2^3 + 3^3 + \cdots + k^3 = (1 + 2 + 3 + \cdots + k)^2.$

Prove that statement ($k + 1$) is true:

$1^3 + 2^3 + 3^3 + \cdots + k^3 + (k + 1)^3 = (1 + 2 + 3 + \cdots + k + k + 1)^2.$

Proof:

$[(1 + 2 + 3 + \cdots + k) + (k + 1)]^2 = (1 + 2 + 3 + \cdots + k)^2 +$
$2(k + 1)(1 + 2 + 3 + \cdots + k) + (k + 1)^2 = (1^3 + 2^3 + 3^3 + \cdots + k^3) +$
$2(k + 1)\left[\frac{k(k + 1)}{2}\right] + (k + 1)^2 = 1^3 + 2^3 + 3^3 + \cdots + k^3 + [k(k + 1)^2 +$
$(k + 1)^2] = 1^3 + 2^3 + 3^3 + \cdots + k^3 + [(k + 1)^2(k + 1)] =$
$1^3 + 2^3 + 3^3 + \cdots + k^3 + (k + 1)^3$ ✓

Pages 527–528 • WRITTEN EXERCISES

A

1. $S_{20} = \frac{20(5 + 62)}{2} = 670$ **2.** $S_{100} = \frac{100(17 + 215)}{2} = 11{,}600$

3. $S_{40} = \frac{40(-12 + 183)}{2} = 3420$ **4.** $S_{50} = \frac{50(187 + 40)}{2} = 5675$

5. $n = 100, t_1 = 5, t_{100} = 500; S_{100} = \frac{100(5 + 500)}{2} = 25{,}250$

6. $n = 24, t_1 = 1, t_{24} = 47; S_{24} = \frac{24(1 + 47)}{2} = 576$

7. $n = 50, t_1 = 5, t_{50} = 152; S_{50} = \frac{50(5 + 152)}{2} = 3925$

8. $n = 11, t_1 = 20, t_{11} = 10; S_{11} = \frac{11(20 + 10)}{2} = 165$

9. $n = 100, t_1 = 4, t_{100} = 4 + 99(3) = 301; S_{100} = \frac{100(4 + 301)}{2} = 15{,}250$

10. $n = 100, t_1 = 100, t_{100} = 100 + (99)(-2) = -98; S_{100} = \frac{100(100 - 98)}{2} = 100$

11. $t_1 = 11, d = 4; t_n = 83 = 11 + (n - 1)4, 83 = 4n + 7, 76 = 4n, n = 19;$

$S_{19} = \frac{19(11 + 83)}{2} = 893$

12. $t_1 = 50, d = -2, t_n = 10 = 50 + (n - 1)(-2), 10 = 52 - 2n, 2n = 42, n = 21;$

$S_{21} = \frac{21(50 + 10)}{2} = 630$

13. $S_8 = \frac{1(1 - 2^8)}{1 - 2} = \frac{-255}{-1} = 255$ **14.** $S_{10} = \frac{1(1 - (-2)^{10})}{1 - (-2)} = \frac{-1023}{3} = -341$

15. $S_{10} = \frac{2(1 - (-3)^{10})}{1 - (-3)} = \frac{2(-59{,}048)}{4} = -29{,}524$

16. $S_{12} = \frac{\frac{1}{9}(1 - 3^{12})}{1 - 3} = \frac{\frac{1}{9}(-531{,}440)}{-2} = \frac{265{,}720}{9} = 29{,}524\frac{4}{9}$

17. $n = 12, r = \frac{1}{2}, t_1 = \frac{1}{2}; S_{12} = \dfrac{\frac{1}{2}\left(1 - \left(\frac{1}{2}\right)^{12}\right)}{1 - \frac{1}{2}} = 1 - \left(\frac{1}{2}\right)^{12} = \frac{4095}{4096}$

18. $n = 10, t_1 = -\frac{1}{2}, r = \left(-\frac{1}{2}\right); S_{10} = \dfrac{\left(-\frac{1}{2}\right)\left(1 - \left(-\frac{1}{2}\right)^{10}\right)}{1 - \left(-\frac{1}{2}\right)} = \dfrac{\left(-\frac{1}{2}\right)\left(1 - \frac{1}{2^{10}}\right)}{\frac{3}{2}} =$

$\dfrac{-\frac{1023}{1024}}{3} = -\frac{341}{1024}$

19. a. $t_1 = 24; d = -12; t_{10} = 24 + 9(-12) = -84; S_{10} = \frac{10(24 - 84)}{2} = -300$

b. $t_1 = 24, r = \frac{1}{2}; S_{10} = \dfrac{24\left(1 - \left(\frac{1}{2}\right)^{10}\right)}{1 - \frac{1}{2}} = \dfrac{24\left(\frac{1023}{1024}\right)}{\frac{1}{2}} = \frac{3069}{64}$

20. a. $t_1 = 1, d = 0.1, t_{20} = 1 + 19(0.1) = 2.9; S_{20} = \frac{20(1 + 2.9)}{2} = 39$

b. $t_1 = 1, r = 1.1; S_{20} = \frac{1(1 - (1.1)^{20})}{1 - 1.1} \approx \frac{-5.7275}{-0.1} = 57.275$

B **21.** $3 + 13 + 23 + \cdots + 193 = \frac{(20)(3 + 193)}{2} = 1960$

22. $14 + 24 + \cdots + 94 = \frac{9(14 + 94)}{2} = 486$

23. $101 + 103 + 105 + \cdots + 995 + 997 + 999 = S_n; t_1 = 101, d = 2,$
$t_n = 999 = 101 + (n - 1)(2), 999 = 99 + 2n, n = 450;$

$S_{450} = \frac{450(101 + 999)}{2} = 247{,}500$

24. $102 + 108 + \cdots + 996 = S_n; t_1 = 102, d = 6, t_n = 996 = 102 + (n - 1)6,$
$996 = 96 + 6n, n = 150; S_{150} = \frac{150(102 + 996)}{2} = 82{,}350$

25. a. $t_1 = 2, d = 2, t_{20} = 2 + 19(2) = 40; S_{20} = \frac{20(2 + 40)}{2} = 420$

b. $t_1 = 2, r = 2, S_{20} = \frac{2(1 - 2^{20})}{1 - 2} = \frac{2(-1{,}048{,}575)}{-1} = 2{,}097{,}150$

26. a. $5^1 + 5^2 + \cdots + 5^{10} = \frac{5(1 - 5^{10})}{1 - 5} = \frac{5(-9{,}765{,}624)}{-4} = 12{,}207{,}030$

b. $5^2 + 5^4 + \cdots + 5^{20} = \frac{5^2[1 - (5^2)^{10}]}{1 - 5^2} \approx 9.93 \times 10^{13}$

27. $10 + 11 + 13 + 14 + \cdots + 97 + 98 = (10 + 13 + 16 + \cdots + 97) +$
$(11 + 14 + \cdots + 98) = \frac{30(10 + 97)}{2} + \frac{30(11 + 98)}{2} = 1605 + 1635 = 3240$

28. The sum of all the two-digit integers is $10 + 11 + \cdots + 99 = \frac{90(10 + 99)}{2} = 4905$;

the sum of the two-digit integers divisible by 5 is $10 + 15 + \cdots + 95 =$

$\frac{18(10 + 95)}{2} = 945$; $4905 - 945 = 3960$

29. a. $\sum_{k=1}^{n} 2^{k-1}$ is a geometric series with $t_1 = 1$ and $r = 2$, so

$$\sum_{k=1}^{n} 2^{k-1} = \frac{1(1 - 2^n)}{1 - 2} = \frac{1 - 2^n}{-1} = 2^n - 1.$$

b. $2^n - 1 > 1{,}000{,}000$; $2^n > 1{,}000{,}001$; $n \log 2 > \log 1{,}000{,}001$;

$n > \frac{\log 1{,}000{,}001}{\log 2} = 19.93$; $n = 20$

30. (A) is a geometric series with $t_1 = 1$ and $r = \frac{1}{2}$; (B) is a geometric series with $t_1 = 1$ and $r = -\frac{1}{2}$; for n even, the sum of series A is $\frac{1\left(1 - \left(\frac{1}{2}\right)^n\right)}{1 - \frac{1}{2}} = \frac{1 - \left(\frac{1}{2}\right)^n}{\frac{1}{2}} =$

$2\left(1 - \left(\frac{1}{2}\right)^n\right)$ and the sum of series B is $\frac{1\left(1 - \left(-\frac{1}{2}\right)^n\right)}{1 + \frac{1}{2}} = \frac{1 - \left(\frac{1}{2}\right)^n}{\frac{3}{2}} =$

$\frac{2\left(1 - \left(\frac{1}{2}\right)^n\right)}{3}$; thus, the sum of (A) is 3 times the sum of (B).

31. $S_1 = 8(3 - 1) = 16 = t_1$; $S_2 = 8(3^2 - 1) = 64$; $64 - 16 = 48 = t_2$; $S_3 = 8(3^3 - 1) = 208$; $208 - 64 = 144 = t_3$; the first three terms are 16, 48, 144; the series is geometric.

32. $S_1 = t_1 = 2 + 5 = 7$; $S_2 = 8 + 10 = 18$; $t_2 = 18 - 7 = 11$; $S_3 = 18 + 15 = 33$; $t_3 = 33 - 18 = 15$; the series is arithmetic with $t_1 = 7$ and $d = 4$;

$2n^2 + 5n = \frac{n(7 + t_n)}{2}$; $7n + nt_n = 4n^2 + 10n$; $t_n = 4n + 3$

33. Answers will vary. **a.** 0.00000095 **b.** 0.00002656 **c.** 0.00001427

C **34. a.** 0 **b.** $\frac{t_1}{1 - r}$

35. The series consists of 50 terms, 25 pairs (2 − 4, 6 − 8, 10 − 12, and so on) which each produce a sum of −2; the sum is 25(−2) or −50. The sums may also be found as follows:

$(2 + 6 + 10 + \cdots + 98) - (4 + 8 + 12 + \cdots + 100) = \frac{25(2 + 98)}{2} - \frac{25(4 + 100)}{2} =$

$25(50) - 25(52) = -50.$

36. $(1 + 4 + 7 + 10 + \cdots + 97) + (2 + 5 + 8 + 11 + \cdots + 98) =$

$\frac{33(1 + 97)}{2} + \frac{33(2 + 98)}{2} = 33[49 + 50] = 3267$

37. $\sum_{k=1}^{20} 2^k + \sum_{k=1}^{20} k = \frac{2(1-2^{20})}{1-2} + \frac{20(1+20)}{2} = \frac{2(-1{,}048{,}575)}{-1} = 2{,}097{,}150 + 210 = 2{,}097{,}360$

38. $\sum_{n=1}^{12} (2^n - 1) = \sum_{n=1}^{12} 2^n - \sum_{n=1}^{12} 1 = \frac{2(1-2^{12})}{1-2} - 12 = 8190 - 12 = 8178$

Pages 528–530 • PROBLEMS

A

1. The numbers of seats in the rows form an arithmetic sequence, $n = 20$, $d = 2$, $t_1 = 25$, $t_{20} = 25 + 19(2) = 63$; $S_{20} = \frac{20(25+63)}{2} = 880$; 880 seats

2. The point values of the questions form an arithmetic sequence; $d = 3$, $t_1 = 5$, $t_{15} = 5 + (14)(3) = 47$; $S_{15} = \frac{15(5+47)}{2} = 390$; 390 points

3. The numbers of times it chimes from 1 A.M. to noon form an arithmetic sequence with $d = 1$, $t_1 = 1$, $t_{12} = 12$; $S_{12} = \frac{12(1+12)}{2} = 78$; since the pattern is the same from 1 P.M. to midnight, the total number of chimes is $2 \times 78 = 156$.

4. During one four-hour period, the numbers of times it chimes form an arithmetic sequence with $d = 1$, $t_1 = 1$, $n = 8$, $t_8 = 8$; $S_8 = \frac{8(1+8)}{2} = 36$; in one day it strikes $6 \times 36 = 216$ times.

5. The numbers of ancestors in each generation form a geometric sequence with $t_1 = 2$ and $r = 2$; $S_{10} = \frac{2(1-2^{10})}{1-2} = 2046$; 2046 ancestors

6. Their yearly rents form a geometric sequence with $t_1 = 12 \times 600 = 7200$ and $r = 1.05$; $S_6 = \frac{7200(1-1.05^6)}{1-1.05} \approx 48{,}973.77$; \$48,973.77

B

7. Plan A is an arithmetic sequence with $n = 14$, $t_1 = 1$ and $t_{14} = 14$; $S_{14} = \frac{14(1+14)}{2} = 105$; \$105 on plan A; plan B is a geometric sequence with $n = 14$, $t_1 = 0.01$, and $r = 2$; $S_{14} = \frac{0.01(1-2^{14})}{1-2} = 163.83$; \$163.83 on plan B; plan B pays \$163.83 − \$105 = \$58.83 more.

8. Plan A: $t_1 = 1$, $d = 1$, $n = 21$, $t_{21} = 21$; $S_{21} = \frac{21(1+21)}{2} = 231$; \$231 on plan A; plan B: $t_1 = 0.01$, $n = 21$, $r = 2$; $S_{21} = \frac{0.01(1-2^{21})}{1-2} \approx 20{,}971$; \$20,971 on plan B

9. Job A: salaries are an arithmetic sequence with $t_1 = 20{,}000$, $d = 1500$; $t_5 = 20{,}000 + 4(1500) = 26{,}000$; $S_5 = \frac{5(20{,}000 + 26{,}000)}{2} = \$115{,}000$. Job A pays \$26,000 in the fifth year and \$115,000 in all; Job B: salaries are a geometric sequence with $t_1 = 18{,}000$ and $r = 1.10$; $t_5 = 18{,}000(1.10)^4 = 26{,}353.80$;

$S_5 = \frac{(18{,}000)(1 - (1.10)^5)}{1 - 1.10} = 109{,}891.80$; Job B pays \$26,353.80 in the fifth year and \$109,891.80 in all; Job B has the higher fifth-year salary; Job A pays the greater total amount.

10. Job A: $t_{10} = 20{,}000 + 9(1500) = 33{,}500$; $S_{10} = \frac{10(20{,}000 + 33{,}500)}{2} = 267{,}500$; Job B:

$S_{10} = \frac{(18{,}000)(1 - (1.1)^{10})}{1 - 1.1} \approx 286{,}873.64$; $286{,}873.64 - 267{,}500 = 19{,}373.64$; Job B pays \$19,373.64 more in the ten-year period.

11. The values of the investments form a geometric sequence with $t_1 = 1000(1.06) = 1060$ and $r = 1.06$; $S_{10} = \frac{1060(1 - 1.06^{10})}{1 - 1.06} \approx 13{,}971.64$; \$13,971.64

12. The numbers of calls in each round form a geometric sequence with $t_1 = 6$ and $r = 3$; $S_n = \frac{6(1 - 3^n)}{1 - 3} \ge 1560$, $1 - 3^n \le -520$, $3^n \ge 521$, $n \log 3 \ge \log 521$,

$n \ge \frac{\log 521}{\log 3} \approx 5.7$; 6 rounds are necessary

13. a. $T_n = 1 + 2 + \cdots + n = \frac{n(n + 1)}{2}$ **b.** $\sum_{k=1}^{n} k = \frac{n(n + 1)}{2}$

C **14.** $T_3 + T_4 = 6 + 10 = 16$; 16 is a perfect square. Conjecture: The sum of any two consecutive triangular numbers is a perfect square. Proof: Let T_n and T_{n+1} be two consecutive triangular numbers; $T_n + T_{n+1} = \frac{n(n + 1)}{2} + \frac{(n + 1)(n + 1 + 1)}{2} =$

$\frac{n(n + 1)}{2} + \frac{(n + 1)(n + 2)}{2} = \frac{n^2 + n + n^2 + 3n + 2}{2} = \frac{2n^2 + 4n + 2}{2} =$

$n^2 + 2n + 1 = (n + 1)^2$. The sum of 2 consecutive triangular numbers is the square of the index of the second number.

15. Example: $8(T_3) + 1 = 8 \cdot 6 + 1 = 49$; 49 is a perfect square. Conjecture: One more than eight times a triangular number is a perfect square. Proof: Let T_n be a triangular number; $8(T_n) + 1 = 8\left(\frac{n(n + 1)}{2}\right) + 1 = 4(n^2 + n) + 1 =$

$4n^2 + 4n + 1 = (2n + 1)^2$, a perfect square.

Page 530 • MIXED REVIEW EXERCISES

1. $8^{-1/2} = \frac{1}{\sqrt{8}} = \frac{1}{2\sqrt{2}} = \frac{\sqrt{2}}{4}$ **2.** $2(-2)^2 - 8 = 2(4) - 8 = 8 - 8 = 0$

3. $(-2)^{-1} \cdot (8)^{2/3} = \frac{1}{-2} \cdot 4 = -2$ **4.** $\sqrt{-(-2)(8)} = \sqrt{16} = 4$

5. $\frac{8}{(-2)^3} = \frac{8}{-8} = -1$ **6.** $\sqrt{(-2)^2 + (8)^2} = \sqrt{4 + 64} = \sqrt{68} = 2\sqrt{17}$

7. $|(-2)(8)| = |-16| = 16$ **8.** $\log_4\left(-\frac{-2}{8}\right) = \log_4\left(\frac{1}{4}\right) = -1$

9. $\frac{8 - (-2)^2}{-2} = \frac{4}{-2} = -2$ **10.** $m = -\frac{A}{B} = -\frac{3}{-2} = \frac{3}{2}$

11. $x^2 - 4x + y^2 + 6y = 3, (x^2 - 4x + 4) + (y^2 + 6y + 9) = 3 + 4 + 9,$
$(x - 2)^2 + (y + 3)^2 = 16; r = \sqrt{16} = 4$

12. $\frac{4x^2}{36} - \frac{9y^2}{36} = 1, \frac{x^2}{9} - \frac{y^2}{4} = 1$; x-intercepts are (3, 0) and (−3, 0)

Page 530 • COMPUTER EXERCISES

1. This program uses the series for exercise 2(a):

```
10 DEF FN Y(N) = 3 * N + 1
20 PRINT "ENTER LOWER AND UPPER SUMMATION LIMITS"
30 INPUT K1, K2
40 LET S = 0
50 FOR K = K1 TO K2
60 LET S = S + FN Y(K)
70 NEXT K
80 PRINT "SUM FROM "; K1; " TO "; K2; "="; S
90 END
```

2. a. Use program listed for problem (1.), above.

```
SUM FROM 10 TO 20 = 506
```

b. Change line 10 to: `10 DEF FN Y(N) = (2/3) ↑ N`

```
SUM FROM 1 TO 30 = 1.99998957
```

c. Change line 10 to: `10 DEF FN Y(N) = 1/(N * N - 1)`

```
SUM FROM 2 TO 100 = .740049503
```

Pages 533–534 • WRITTEN EXERCISES

A **1.** $S = \frac{24}{1 - \frac{1}{2}} = 48$ **2.** $S = \frac{24}{1 - \left(-\frac{1}{2}\right)} = \frac{24}{\frac{3}{2}} = 16$

3. $S = \frac{27}{1 - \left(-\frac{2}{3}\right)} = \frac{27}{\frac{5}{3}} = \frac{81}{5} = 16.2$ **4.** $S = \frac{27}{1 - \frac{2}{3}} = \frac{27}{\frac{1}{3}} = 81$

5. $r = \frac{5}{4}$; no sum **6.** $S = \frac{500}{1 - \frac{4}{5}} = \frac{500}{\frac{1}{5}} = 2500$ **7.** $r = \frac{4}{3}$; no sum

8. $S = \frac{\frac{1}{2}}{1 - \left(-\frac{2}{3}\right)} = \frac{\frac{1}{2}}{\frac{5}{3}} = \frac{3}{10}$

9. $S = \dfrac{3\sqrt{3}}{1 - \left(-\dfrac{1}{\sqrt{3}}\right)} = \dfrac{9}{\sqrt{3}+1} \cdot \dfrac{(\sqrt{3}-1)}{(\sqrt{3}-1)} = \dfrac{9(\sqrt{3}-1)}{2} = \dfrac{9}{2}(\sqrt{3}-1)$

10. $S = \dfrac{4^{-1/2}}{1 - 4^{-1}} = \dfrac{\frac{1}{2}}{1 - \frac{1}{4}} = \dfrac{2}{4-1} = \dfrac{2}{3}$ **11.** $S = \dfrac{3}{1 - \frac{1}{4}} = \dfrac{3}{\frac{3}{4}} = 4$

12. $S = \dfrac{\frac{2}{5}}{1 - \frac{2}{5}} = \dfrac{\frac{2}{5}}{\frac{3}{5}} = \dfrac{2}{3}$

13. $S_1 = 8, S_2 = 8 + 2 = 10, S_3 = 10 + \frac{1}{2} = 10.5, S_4 = 10.5 + \frac{1}{8} = 10.625,$

$S_5 = 10.625 + \left(\frac{1}{8}\right)\left(\frac{1}{4}\right) = 10.65625; S = \dfrac{8}{1 - \frac{1}{4}} = \dfrac{8}{\frac{3}{4}} = \dfrac{32}{3} = 10.6\overline{6}$

14. $S_1 = 9, S_2 = 9.9, S_3 = 9.99, S_4 = 9.999, S_5 = 9.9999; S = \dfrac{9}{1 - \frac{1}{10}} = \dfrac{9}{0.9} = 10$

15. $S_1 = \frac{3}{4}, S_2 = \frac{3}{4} - \frac{3}{8} = \frac{3}{8}, S_3 = \frac{3}{8} + \frac{3}{16} = \frac{9}{16}, S_4 = \frac{9}{16} - \frac{3}{32} = \frac{15}{32}, S_5 = \frac{15}{32} + \frac{3}{64} = \frac{33}{64};$

$S = \dfrac{\frac{3}{4}}{1 - \left(-\frac{1}{2}\right)} = \dfrac{\frac{3}{4}}{\frac{3}{2}} = \dfrac{1}{2}$

16. $S_1 = \frac{1}{3}, S_2 = \frac{1}{3} + \frac{1}{9} = \frac{4}{9}, S_3 = \frac{4}{9} + \frac{1}{27} = \frac{13}{27}, S_4 = \frac{13}{27} + \frac{1}{81} = \frac{40}{81}, S_5 = \frac{40}{81} + \frac{1}{243} = \frac{121}{243};$

$S = \dfrac{\frac{1}{3}}{1 - \frac{1}{3}} = \dfrac{\frac{1}{3}}{\frac{2}{3}} = \dfrac{1}{2}$

17. $0.3333 \cdots = 0.3 + 0.03 + 0.003 + \cdots = \dfrac{0.3}{1 - 0.1} = \dfrac{0.3}{0.9} = \dfrac{1}{3}$

18. $0.444 \cdots = 0.4 + 0.04 + 0.004 + \cdots = \dfrac{0.4}{1 - 0.1} = \dfrac{0.4}{0.9} = \dfrac{4}{9}$

19. $3.123123123 \cdots = 3 + 0.123 + 0.000123 + 0.000000123 \cdots = 3 + \dfrac{0.123}{1 - 0.001} =$

$3 + \dfrac{0.123}{0.999} = 3\dfrac{41}{333} = \dfrac{1040}{333}$

20. $0.363636 \cdots = 0.36 + 0.0036 + 0.000036 + \cdots = \dfrac{0.36}{1 - 0.01} = \dfrac{0.36}{0.99} = \dfrac{4}{11}$

21. $0.4999 \cdots = 0.4 + 0.09 + 0.009 + \cdots = 0.4 + \dfrac{0.9}{1 - 0.1} = 0.4 + \dfrac{0.09}{0.9} = 0.4 + 0.1 =$

$0.5 = \dfrac{1}{2}$

22. $1.045045045 \cdots = 1 + 0.045 + 0.000045 + 0.000000045 + \cdots = 1 + \dfrac{0.045}{1 - 0.001} =$

$1 + \dfrac{0.045}{0.999} = 1 + \dfrac{5}{111} = 1\dfrac{5}{111} = \dfrac{116}{111}$

B 23. $12 = \frac{8}{1-r}, 1 - r = \frac{8}{12}, 1 - \frac{8}{12} = r, r = \frac{1}{3}; 8, \frac{8}{3}, \frac{8}{9}$

24. $200 = \frac{40}{1-r}, 1 - r = \frac{40}{200} = \frac{1}{5}, r = 1 - \frac{1}{5} = \frac{4}{5}$; 40, 32, 25.6

25. $30 = \frac{t_1}{1 - \left(-\frac{1}{3}\right)} = \frac{t_1}{\frac{4}{3}}, 40 = t_1; 40, -\frac{40}{3}, \frac{40}{9}$

26. $125 = \frac{t_1}{1 - \frac{2}{5}} = \frac{t_1}{\frac{3}{5}}, t_1 = 75$; 75, 30, 12

27. If there were such a series, $4 = \frac{10}{1-r}, 1 - r = 2.5, r = -1.5$; but for a geometric series to have a sum, $|r| < 1$.

28. $1 = 100r^{3-1}, r^2 = \frac{1}{100}, r = \frac{1}{10}$ or $-\frac{1}{10}$; if $r = \frac{1}{10}, S = \frac{100}{1 - \frac{1}{10}} = \frac{1000}{9} = 111.\overline{1}$;

if $r = -\frac{1}{10}, S = \frac{100}{1 - \left(-\frac{1}{10}\right)} = \frac{1000}{11} = 90.\overline{90}$

C 29. a. $S = \frac{1}{1 - \frac{2}{3}} = \frac{1}{\frac{1}{3}} = 3$

b. $S_n = \frac{1\left(1 - \left(\frac{2}{3}\right)^n\right)}{1 - \frac{2}{3}} = 3\left(1 - \left(\frac{2}{3}\right)^n\right) = 3 - 3\left(\frac{2}{3}\right)^n; S - S_n = 3 - \left[3 - 3\left(\frac{2}{3}\right)^n\right] =$

$3 - 3 + 3\left(\frac{2}{3}\right)^n = 3\left(\frac{2}{3}\right)^n$; if $S - S_n < 0.00001$, then $3\left(\frac{2}{3}\right)^n < 0.00001$;

$\log 3 + n \log \frac{2}{3} < \log 0.00001; 0.4771 + n(-0.1761) < -5$;

$n(-0.1761) < -5.4771; n > \frac{-5.4771}{-0.1761} = 31.1; n = 32$

30. $S - xS = (1 + 2x + 3x^2 + \cdots) - (x + 2x^2 + 3x^3 + \cdots) =$
$1 + x + x^2 + x^3 + \cdots$; $S - xS$ is a geometric series with $t_1 = 1$ and $r = x$;

$S - xS = \frac{1}{1-x}; S(1-x) = \frac{1}{1-x}, S = \frac{1}{(1-x)^2}$

Pages 534–536 • PROBLEMS

A 1. $12 + 12\left(\frac{5}{6}\right) + 12\left(\frac{5}{6}\right)^2 + \cdots = \frac{12}{1 - \frac{5}{6}} = 72$; 72 ft

2. $1 - \frac{1}{2} + \frac{1}{4} - \frac{1}{8} + \cdots = \frac{1}{1 - \left(-\frac{1}{2}\right)} = \frac{2}{3}$; $\frac{2}{3}$ mi east

3. The lengths of the sides of the squares are 12, $6\sqrt{2}$, 6, $3\sqrt{2}$, 3, . . . ; $t_1 = 12$ and $r = \frac{1}{\sqrt{2}} = \frac{\sqrt{2}}{2}$; $S = \frac{12}{1 - \frac{\sqrt{2}}{2}} = \frac{24}{2 - \sqrt{2}} \cdot \frac{2 + \sqrt{2}}{2 + \sqrt{2}} = \frac{48 + 24\sqrt{2}}{2} = 24 + 12\sqrt{2}$;

$4S = 96 + 48\sqrt{2}$; $96 + 48\sqrt{2}$ cm.

4.

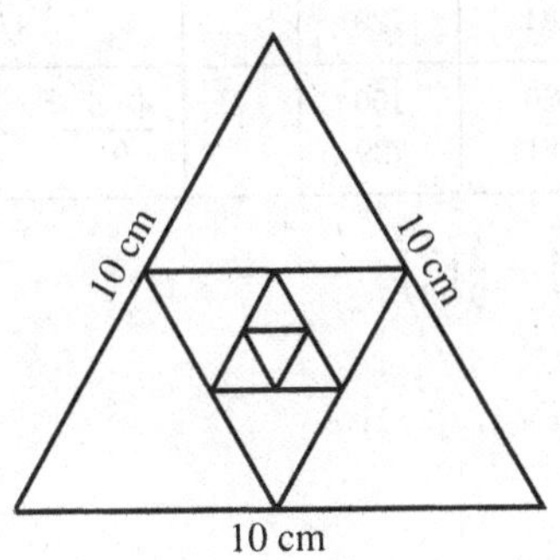

The lengths of the sides of the triangles are 10, 5, 2.5, 1.25, . . . ; $t_1 = 10$ and $r = \frac{1}{2}$;

$S = \frac{10}{1 - \frac{1}{2}} = 20$; $3S = 60$; 60 cm.

5. The areas of the squares are 144, 72, 36, 18, 9, . . . ; $t_1 = 144$ and $r = \frac{1}{2}$;

$S = \frac{144}{1 - \frac{1}{2}} = 288$; 288 cm^2.

6. The areas of the triangles are $25\sqrt{3}$, $\frac{25\sqrt{3}}{4}$, $\frac{25\sqrt{3}}{16}$, . . . ; $t_1 = 25\sqrt{3}$, $r = \frac{1}{4}$;

$S = \frac{25\sqrt{3}}{1 - \frac{1}{4}} = \frac{100\sqrt{3}}{3}$; $\frac{100\sqrt{3}}{3}$ cm^2.

B

7. $24 + 24(0.95) + 24(0.95)^2 + \cdots = \frac{24}{1 - 0.95} = \frac{24}{0.05} = 480$; 480 m

8. 10 m

$10 + 2 \cdot 10(0.95) + 2 \cdot 10(0.95)^2 + 2 \cdot 10(0.95)^3 + \cdots =$

$10 + \frac{20(0.95)}{1 - 0.95} = 10 + \frac{19}{0.05} = 10 + 380 = 390$; 390 m

9. a. $t_{26} = 50\left(\frac{4}{5}\right)^{25} \approx 0.18889$; 0.1889 in.

b. $S_{26} = \frac{50\left(1 - \left(\frac{4}{5}\right)^{26}\right)}{1 - \frac{4}{5}} \approx 249.24$; approx. 249.24 in.

c. $S = \frac{50}{1 - \frac{4}{5}} = 250$; 250 in.

10. a. $t_{60} = 1.5(0.92)^{59} \approx 0.01095$; 0.01095 m

b. $S_{60} \approx S = \frac{1.5}{1 - 0.92} = \frac{1.5}{0.08} = 18.75$; 18.75 m

C **11. a.**

	Fig. 1	Fig. 2	Fig. 3	Fig. 4	$\cdots$	Fig. n
No. of new squares	1	4	20	100	$\cdots$	$4(5)^{n-2}$
Area of each new square	1	$\frac{1}{9}$	$\frac{1}{81}$	$\frac{1}{729}$	$\cdots$	$\left(\frac{1}{9}\right)^{n-1}$
Total new area	1	$\frac{4}{9}$	$\frac{20}{81}$	$\frac{100}{729}$	$\cdots$	$\frac{4 \cdot 5^{n-2}}{9^{n-1}} = \frac{4}{9}\left(\frac{5}{9}\right)^{n-2}$

b. $1 + \frac{4}{9} + \frac{20}{81} + \frac{100}{729} + \cdots = 1 + \frac{4}{9} + \frac{4}{9}\left(\frac{5}{9}\right) + \frac{4}{9}\left(\frac{5}{9}\right)^2 + \cdots =$

$$1 + \frac{\frac{4}{9}}{1 - \frac{5}{9}} = 1 + \frac{\frac{4}{9}}{\frac{4}{9}} = 1 + 1 = 2; 2$$

12. The perimeters at each step are $4, \frac{20}{3}, \frac{100}{9}, \frac{500}{27}, \ldots$; The sum of these perimeters form an infinite geometric series with $r = \frac{5}{3}$, which increases without bound. Therefore this curve has no perimeter.

13. An equilateral triangle with sides of length s has area $\frac{s^2\sqrt{3}}{4}$; $A_1 = \frac{1^2\sqrt{3}}{4} = \frac{\sqrt{3}}{4}$;

$$A_2 = 3\left[\frac{\left(\frac{1}{3}\right)^2\sqrt{3}}{4}\right] = \frac{\sqrt{3}}{12}; A_3 = 12\left[\frac{\left(\frac{1}{9}\right)^2\sqrt{3}}{4}\right] = \frac{\sqrt{3}}{27};$$

$$A_4 = 48\left[\frac{\left(\frac{1}{27}\right)^2\sqrt{3}}{4}\right] = \frac{4\sqrt{3}}{243}; \text{ thus, } S = \frac{\sqrt{3}}{4} + \frac{\sqrt{3}}{12} + \frac{\sqrt{3}}{27} + \frac{4\sqrt{3}}{243} =$$

$$\frac{\sqrt{3}}{4} + \frac{\sqrt{3}}{12}\left(1 + \frac{4}{9} + \left(\frac{4}{9}\right)^2 + \cdots\right) = \frac{\sqrt{3}}{4} + \frac{\sqrt{3}}{12}\left(\frac{1}{1 - \frac{4}{9}}\right) = \frac{\sqrt{3}}{4} + \frac{\sqrt{3}}{12} \cdot \frac{9}{5} =$$

$\frac{8\sqrt{3}}{20} = \frac{2\sqrt{3}}{5}$ (square units).

14. Each repetition of the construction multiplies the perimeter by $\frac{4}{3}$. (If s is the length of a side, building a triangle on the middle third of s adds $2 \cdot \frac{s}{3}$ to the perimeter, and deleting the base subtracts $\frac{s}{3}$. Thus s becomes $\frac{4}{3}$ s.) The starting perimeter is 3, so after n repetitions the perimeter is $3\left(\frac{4}{3}\right)^n$, which grows without bound as n increases.

Page 539 • WRITTEN EXERCISES

A **1.** $x^3 + 3x^2y + 3xy^2 + y^3$ **2.** $x^4 + 4x^3y + 6x^2y^2 + 4xy^3 + y^4$
3. $c^5 - 5c^4d + 10c^3d^2 - 10c^2d^3 + 5cd^4 - d^5$

4. $p^6 - 6p^5q + 15p^4q^2 - 20p^3q^3 + 15p^2q^4 - 6pq^5 + q^6$

5. $a^8 + 8a^7 + 28a^6 + 56a^5 + 70a^4 + 56a^3 + 28a^2 + 8a + 1$

6. $x^3 + 3x^2(-2) + 3x(-2)^2 + (-2)^3 = x^3 - 6x^2 + 12x - 8$

7. $(3t)^5 + 5(3t)^4(4) + 10(3t)^3(4)^2 + 10(3t)^2(4)^3 + 5(3t)(4)^4 + (4)^5 =$
$243t^5 + 1620t^4 + 4320t^3 + 5760t^2 + 3840t + 1024$

8. $(2y)^4 + 4(2y)^3(-3) + 6(2y)^2(-3)^2 + 4(2y)(-3)^3 + (-3)^4 =$
$16y^4 - 96y^3 + 216y^2 - 216y + 81$

9. $(x^2)^6 - 6(x^2)^5 + 15(x^2)^4 - 20(x^2)^3 + 15(x^2)^2 - 6(x^2) + 1 =$
$x^{12} - 6x^{10} + 15x^8 - 20x^6 + 15x^4 - 6x^2 + 1$

10. $(\sqrt{x})^4 + 4(\sqrt{x})^3(3) + 6(\sqrt{x})^2(3)^2 + 4(\sqrt{x})(3)^3 + 3^4 =$
$x^2 + 12x\sqrt{x} + 54x + 108\sqrt{x} + 81$

11. $(p^2)^3 + 3(p^2)^2(q^3) + 3(p^2)(q^3)^2 + (q^3)^3 = p^6 + 3p^4q^3 + 3p^2q^6 + q^9$

12. $a^5 + 5a^4\left(\frac{1}{a}\right) + 10a^3\left(\frac{1}{a}\right)^2 + 10a^2\left(\frac{1}{a}\right)^3 + 5a\left(\frac{1}{a}\right)^4 + \left(\frac{1}{a}\right)^5 =$

$a^5 + 5a^3 + 10a + \frac{10}{a} + \frac{5}{a^3} + \frac{1}{a^5}$

13. The last three coefficients must be 136, 17, 1; $136x^2y^{15} + 17xy^{16} + y^{17}$

14. The last three coefficients must be 231, −22, and 1; $231p^2q^{20} - 22pq^{21} + q^{22}$

15. The twelfth coefficient must be 167,960; $167{,}960x^9$

16. The ninth coefficient must be 6435; $6435p^7q^8$

B

17. $(a^7 + 7a^6b + 21a^5b^2 + 35a^4b^3 + 35a^3b^4 + 21a^2b^5 + 7ab^6 + b^7) +$
$(a^7 - 7a^6b + 21a^5b^2 - 35a^4b^3 + 35a^3b^4 - 21a^2b^5 + 7ab^6 - b^7) =$
$2a^7 + 42a^5b^2 + 70a^3b^4 + 14ab^6$

18. $(a^8 + 8a^7b + 28a^6b^2 + 56a^5b^3 + 70a^4b^4 + 56a^3b^5 + 28a^2b^6 + 8ab^7 + b^8) -$
$(a^8 - 8a^7b + 28a^6b^2 - 56a^5b^3 + 70a^4b^4 - 56a^3b^5 + 28a^2b^6 - 8ab^7 + b^8) =$
$16a^7b + 112a^5b^3 + 112a^3b^5 + 16ab^7$

19. $(a^2 + 2ab + b^2)^3 = ((a + b)^2)^3 = (a + b)^6 =$
$a^6 + 6a^5b + 15a^4b^2 + 20a^3b^3 + 15a^2b^4 + 6ab^5 + b^6$

20. $[(x - 1)(x + 1)]^4 = (x^2 - 1)^4 = (x^2)^4 + 4(x^2)^3(-1) + 6(x^2)^2(-1)^2 +$
$4(x^2)(-1)^3 + (-1)^4 = x^8 - 4x^6 + 6x^4 - 4x^2 + 1$

21. $(2.1)^7 = (2 + 0.1)^7 \approx (2)^7 + 7(2)^6(0.1) + 21(2)^5(0.1)^2 = 128 + 44.8 + 6.72 = 179.52$

22. $(9.8)^4 = (10 - 0.2)^4 \approx 10^4 - 4(10)^3(0.2) + 6(10)^2(0.2)^2 - 4(10)(0.2)^3 =$
$10{,}000 - 800 + 24 - 0.32 = 9223.68$

C

23. **a.** 1, 2, 4, 8, 16, 32, 64

b. Sum of entries in the nth row is 2^n
Proof: Let $p_1, p_2, \ldots p_{n+1}$ be the entries in the nth row of the triangle. Then
$(a + b)^n = p_1a^n + p_2a^{n-1}b^1 + p_3a^{n-2}b^2 + \cdots + p_{n+1}b^n$.
If $a = b = 1$, then $2^n = (1 + 1)^n = p_1 + p_2 + p_3 + \cdots + p_{n+1}$.

24. Using Exercise 23, the sum of all entries in rows 0 through n is

$$2^0 + 2^1 + 2^2 + \cdots + 2^n = \frac{2^0(1 - 2^{n+1})}{1 - 2} = 2^{n+1} - 1$$

Page 539 • MIXED REVIEW EXERCISES

1. neither; $t_n = \frac{2n}{2n+1}$ **2.** geometric; $t_n = \frac{9}{16}\left(\frac{4}{3}\right)^{n-1}$

3. arithmetic; $t_n = 7 + (n-1)(-4) = 11 - 4n$ **4.** geometric; $t_n = -24\left(-\frac{1}{2}\right)^{n-1}$

5. $t_1 = 5, d = 4, t_n = 45 = 5 + (n-1)4, 45 = 1 + 4n, n = 11; S_{11} = \frac{11(5+45)}{2} = 275$

6. $S = \frac{6}{1 - \frac{3}{4}} = \frac{6}{\frac{1}{4}} = 24$ **7.** $S_6 = \frac{6(1-2^6)}{1-2} = 378$

Pages 542–543 • WRITTEN EXERCISES

A **1.** 720 **2.** 5040 **3.** $\frac{5 \cdot 4 \cdot 3!}{3!} = 20$ **4.** $\frac{8 \cdot 7!}{7!} = 8$ **5.** $\frac{100 \cdot 99!}{99!} = 100$

6. $\frac{20 \cdot 19 \cdot 18!}{18!} = 380$ **7.** $\frac{10 \cdot 9 \cdot 8 \cdot 7!}{7!\,(3 \cdot 2 \cdot 1)} = 120$ **8.** $\frac{10 \cdot 9 \cdot 8 \cdot 7 \cdot 6!}{(4 \cdot 3 \cdot 2 \cdot 1) \cdot 6!} = 210$

9. $\frac{(n+1)(n!)}{n!} = n + 1$ **10.** $\frac{n(n-1)(n-2)!}{(n-2)!} = n(n-1)$

11. $\frac{(n+1)(n)(n-1)!}{(n-1)!\,(2 \cdot 1)} = \frac{n^2+n}{2}$ **12.** $\frac{n(n-1)(n-2)(n-3)!}{(3 \cdot 2 \cdot 1)(n-3)!} = \frac{n(n-1)(n-2)}{6}$

13. a. $a^{14} + \frac{14!}{13!\,1!}a^{13}b + \frac{14!}{12!\,2!}a^{12}b^2 + \frac{14!}{11!\,3!}a^{11}b^3 =$

$a^{14} + 14a^{13}b + 91a^{12}b^2 + 364a^{11}b^3$

b. $a^{14} - 14a^{13}b + 91a^{12}b^2 - 364a^{11}b^3$

14. a. $a^{12} + \frac{12!}{11!\,1!}a^{11}b + \frac{12!}{10!\,2!}a^{10}b^2 + \frac{12!}{9!\,3!}a^9b^3 = a^{12} + 12a^{11}b + 66a^{10}b^2 + 220a^9b^3$

b. $a^{12} - 12a^{11}b + 66a^{10}b^2 - 220a^9b^3$

15. a. $a^{19} + \frac{19!}{18!\,1!}a^{18}b + \frac{19!}{17!\,2!}a^{17}b^2 + \frac{19!}{16!\,3!}a^{16}b^3 =$

$a^{19} + 19a^{18}b + 171a^{17}b^2 + 969a^{16}b^3$

b. $x^{19} + 19x^{18}(-2y) + 171x^{17}(-2y)^2 + 969x^{16}(-2y)^3 =$

$x^{19} - 38x^{18}y + 684x^{17}y^2 - 7752x^{16}y^3$

16. a. $a^{21} + 21a^{20}b + \frac{21 \cdot 20}{1 \cdot 2}a^{19}b^2 + \frac{21 \cdot 20 \cdot 19}{1 \cdot 2 \cdot 3}a^{18}b^3 =$

$a^{21} + 21a^{20}b + 210a^{19}b^2 + 1330a^{18}b^3$

b. $c^{21} + 21c^{20}(-d^2) + 210c^{19}(-d^2)^2 + 1330c^{18}(-d^2)^3 =$

$c^{21} - 21c^{20}d^2 + 210c^{19}d^4 - 1330c^{18}d^6$

17. $\frac{20!}{15!\,5!}a^{15}b^5 = 15{,}504a^{15}b^5$ **18.** $-\frac{15!}{2!\,13!}a^2b^{13} = -105a^2b^{13}$

19. $\frac{14!}{4!\,10!}s^4t^{10} = 1001s^4t^{10}$ **20.** $\frac{18!}{1!\,17!}s^1t^{17} = 18st^{17}$

B **21.** $\frac{9!}{4!\,5!}a^4(2b)^5 = (126a^4)(32b^5) = 4032a^4b^5$

22. $\frac{7!}{2!\,5!}(2x)^2(-y)^5 = 21(4x^2)(-y^5) = -84x^2y^5$

23. $\frac{8!}{4!\,4!}(c^2)^4(-2d)^4 = (70c^8)(16d^4) = 1120c^8d^4$

24. $\frac{5!}{2!\,3!}a^2(3b^3)^3 = (10a^2)(27b^9) = 270a^2b^9$

25. False; for example, let $a = 2$ and $b = 3$; $(2 \cdot 3)! = 6! = 720$, but $2!\,3! = 12$

26. False; for example, let $n = 2$; $(2^2)! = 4! = 24$, but $(2!)^2 = 4$

27. False; for example, let $n = 3$; $(2n)! = (6!) = 720$, but $2^3(3!) = 48$

C **28.** The term which does not contain y is $\frac{12!}{m!\,(12-m)!}y^m(y^{-2})^{12-m} =$

$\frac{12!}{m!\,(12-m)!}y^{-24+3m}$, where $-24 + 3m = 0$; $m = 8$; $\frac{12!}{8!\,4!}y^8(y^{-2})^4 = 495y^0 = 495$

29. a. $1^{1/2} + \frac{1}{2}(1^{-1/2})x + \frac{\left(\frac{1}{2}\right)\left(-\frac{1}{2}\right)}{1 \cdot 2}(1^{-3/2})x^2 + \frac{\left(\frac{1}{2}\right)\left(-\frac{1}{2}\right)\left(-\frac{3}{2}\right)}{1 \cdot 2 \cdot 3}(1^{-5/2})x^3 =$

$1 + \frac{x}{2} - \frac{1}{8}x^2 + \frac{x^3}{16}$

b. $\sqrt{2} = (1 + 1)^{1/2} = 1 + \frac{1}{2} - \frac{1}{8} + \frac{1}{16} \approx 1.4375$

Page 543 • CALCULATOR KEY-IN

1. 3,628,800 **2.** Answers will vary. **3. a.** 2.433×10^{18} **b.** $\frac{36!}{18!\,18!} = 9.075 \times 10^9$

4. Answers will vary

Pages 545–546 • CHAPTER REVIEW

1. b **2.** c; $-1 - 3 = -4$ **3.** b; $d = 2.5$, $t_{21} = -4 + 20(2.5) = 46$

4. c; $13 = -2 + 3d$, $d = 5$; $-2, 3, 8, 13$ **5.** c; $r = \frac{2}{3}$; $t_9 = \frac{81}{8}\left(\frac{2}{3}\right)^8 = \frac{32}{81}$

6. b; $\sqrt{10 \cdot 40} = \sqrt{400} = 20$ **7.** a; $2^{-1} + 2^0 + 2^1 + 2^2 = \frac{1}{2} + 1 + 2 + 4$

8. b; $d = -6$; $t_n = 47 + (n - 1)(-6) = 53 - 6n$; $53 - 6n = 5$, $n = 8$

9. c; $t_1 = 5$, $t_{25} = 77$; $S_{25} = \frac{25(5 + 77)}{2} = 1025$ **10.** b; $S_7 = \frac{5(1 - (-2)^7)}{1 - (-2)} = 215$

11. c; $r = \frac{3}{4}$; $S = \frac{64}{1 - \frac{3}{4}} = 256$

12. c; $(x^2)^4 + 4(x^2)^3(-2) + 6(x^2)^2(-2)^2 + 4(x^2)(-2)^3 + (-2)^4 =$
$x^8 - 8x^6 + 24x^4 - 32x^2 + 16$

13. a; $\frac{6!}{3!\,3!}(3x)^3(-y^2)^3 = -540x^3y^6$

Page 546 • CHAPTER TEST

1. neither; $t_n = \frac{n+1}{2n+1}$; $t_5 = \frac{6}{11}$ **2.** $d = 4$; $t_n = -7 + (n - 1)(4) = 4n - 11$

3. $47 = 1 + 4d$, $46 = 4d$, $d = 11.5$; $1, 12.5, 24, 35.5, 47$

4. $r = -2;\ t_8 = 11(-2)^7 = -1408$ **5.** $\sqrt{\left(\frac{3}{2}\right)\left(\frac{8}{3}\right)} = \sqrt{4} = 2$ **6.** $\sum_{n=1}^{\infty} \frac{(-1)^{n-1}}{2n}$

7. $d = -7;\ t_{20} = 53 + 19(-7) = -80;\ S_{20} = \frac{20[53 + (-80)]}{2} = -270$

8. $S_5 = \frac{2(1 - 3^5)}{1 - 3} = 242$ **9.** $r = \frac{3}{5};\ S = \frac{250}{1 - \frac{3}{5}} = \frac{250}{\frac{2}{5}} = 625$

10. $(a^2)^8 + 8(a^2)^7b + 28(a^2)^6b^2 + 56(a^2)^5b^3 + 70(a^2)^4b^4 + 56(a^2)^3b^5 + 28(a^2)^2b^6 + 8(a^2)b^7 + b^8 = a^{16} + 8a^{14}b + 28a^{12}b^2 + 56a^{10}b^3 + 70a^8b^4 + 56a^6b^5 + 28a^4b^6 + 8a^2b^7 + b^8$

11. $\frac{13!}{2!\,11!}(2x)^2(-y)^{11} = 78(4x^2)(-y^{11}) = -312x^2y^{11}$

Page 547 • CUMULATIVE REVIEW

1. $z = \frac{kx}{y^2};\ 2 = \frac{k(36)}{3^2},\ k = \frac{1}{2};\ z = \frac{\frac{1}{2}(24)}{2^2} = 3$

2.

$$\begin{array}{r|l} & 4x^2 - 6x + 3 \\ \hline 2x + 3 & 8x^3 + 0x^2 - 12x + 11 \\ & \underline{8x^3 + 12x^2} \\ & -12x^2 - 12x \\ & \underline{-12x^2 - 18x} \\ & 6x + 11 \\ & \underline{6x + 9} \\ & 2 \end{array}$$

$4x^2 - 6x + 3 + \frac{2}{2x + 3}$

3. $2 - 3i$ must also be a root;

$$\begin{array}{r|rrrrr} 2 + 3i & 1 & -2 & 4 & 30 & -13 \\ & & 2 + 3i & -9 + 6i & -28 - 3i & 13 \\ \hline 2 - 3i & 1 & 3i & -5 + 6i & 2 - 3i & 0 \\ & & 2 - 3i & 4 - 6i & -2 + 3i & \\ \hline & 1 & 2 & -1 & 0 & \end{array}$$

The depressed equation is $x^2 + 2x - 1 = 0;\ x = \frac{-2 \pm \sqrt{4 + 4}}{2} = -1 \pm \sqrt{2};$

$\{2 \pm 3i, -1 \pm \sqrt{2}\}$

4. $x^2 - 6x + y^2 + 8y = -21;\ (x^2 - 6x + 9) + (y^2 + 8y + 16) = -21 + 9 + 16;$

$(x - 3)^2 + (y + 4)^2 = 4;\ C(3, -4),\ r = \sqrt{4} = 2$

5. opens to right; $a = 4;\ x - 4 = \frac{1}{4 \cdot 4}(y - 0)^2;\ x = \frac{1}{16}y^2 + 4$

6. $c^2 = 16 + 4 = 20,\ c = \pm\sqrt{20} = \pm 2\sqrt{5}$; major axis horizontal; foci are $(2\sqrt{5}, 0)$ and $(-2\sqrt{5}, 0)$

(Continued)

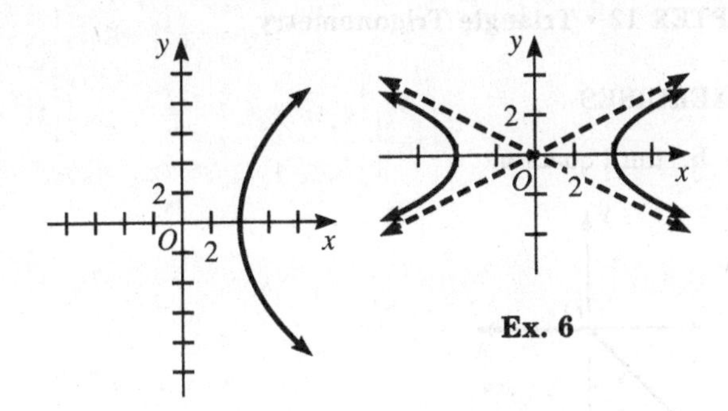

Ex. 6

Ex. 5

7. $\begin{aligned} 2x^2 + y^2 &= 6 \\ x - y &= 3 \end{aligned}$; $x = y + 3$; $2(y + 3)^2 + y^2 = 6$, $2(y^2 + 6y + 9) + y^2 = 6$,

$3y^2 + 12y + 12 = 0$, $y^2 + 4y + 4 = 0$, $(y + 2)^2 = 0$, $y = -2$; $x = 1$; $(1, -2)$

8. $\begin{aligned} y &= x^2 - 1 \\ y^2 - x^2 &= 5 \end{aligned}$; $x^2 = y + 1$; $y^2 - (y + 1) = 5$, $y^2 - y - 6 = 0$, $(y - 3)(y + 2) = 0$,

$y = 3$ and $x = \pm 2$, or $y = -2$ (reject); $(2, 3)$, $(-2, 3)$

9. $\begin{aligned} x - y - z &= 5 \\ 2x - y + z &= 3 \\ x + 2y - 2z &= 4 \end{aligned}$; $\begin{aligned} x - y - z &= 5 \\ y + 3z &= -7 \\ 3y - z &= -1 \end{aligned}$; $\begin{aligned} x - y - z &= 5 \\ y + 3z &= -7 \\ -10z &= 20 \end{aligned}$; $z = -2$;

$y + 3(-2) = -7$; $y = -1$; $x - (-1) - (-2) = 5$, $x = 2$; $(2, -1, -2)$

10. $\begin{aligned} 5x - 3y + z &= -6 \\ x + 3y - z &= 0 \\ 4x + y + z &= 7 \end{aligned}$; $\begin{aligned} x + 3y - z &= 0 \\ -18y + 6z &= -6 \\ -11y + 5z &= 7 \end{aligned}$; $\begin{aligned} x + 3y - z &= 0 \\ -3y + z &= -1 \\ -11y + 5z &= 7 \end{aligned}$;

$\begin{aligned} x &= -1 \\ -3y + z &= -1 \\ 4y &= 12 \end{aligned}$; $x = -1$; $y = 3$; $-3(3) + z = -1$, $z = 8$; $(-1, 3, 8)$

11. $64^{2/3-(-1/2)} = 64^{7/6} = 2^7 = 128$

12. **a.** $f(g(1)) = f(-1) = 3$ **b.** $g(f(1)) = g(3) = 3$

13. $9^{x+2} = 27$; $3^{2(x+2)} = 3^3$, $2(x + 2) = 3$, $x + 2 = \frac{3}{2}$, $x = -\frac{1}{2}$; $\left\{-\frac{1}{2}\right\}$

14. $4^{x-2} = \frac{1}{8}$; $2^{2(x-2)} = 2^{-3}$; $2(x - 2) = -3$, $x - 2 = -\frac{3}{2}$, $x = \frac{1}{2}$; $\left\{\frac{1}{2}\right\}$

15. $\log_9 x = 1.5$, $9^{1.5} = x$, $x = 9^{3/2} = 27$; $\{27\}$

16. $\log_x 16 = -2$, $x^{-2} = 16$, $x = 16^{-1/2} = \frac{1}{4}$; $\left\{\frac{1}{4}\right\}$

17. $5^x = 40$, $x \log 5 = \log 40$, $x = \frac{\log 40}{\log 5} \approx \frac{1.6021}{0.6990} \approx 2.29$ **18.** $e^{2\ln 3} = e^{\ln 3^2} = e^{\ln 9} = 9$

19. geometric; $t_n = 108\left(-\frac{2}{3}\right)^{n-1}$ **20.** arithmetic; $t_1 = 32$, $t_{11} = 2$; $S_{11} = \frac{11(32 + 2)}{2} = 187$

21. $x^4 + 4x^3(-y^2) + 6x^2(-y^2)^2 + 4x(-y^2)^3 + (-y^2)^4 =$
$x^4 - 4x^3y^2 + 6x^2y^4 - 4xy^6 + y^8$

22. $\frac{13!}{2!\,11!}(2x)^2(y^{11}) = 312x^2y^{11}$

CHAPTER 12 • Triangle Trigonometry

Pages 552–554 • WRITTEN EXERCISES

A **1.** **a.** second quadrant **b.** third quadrant

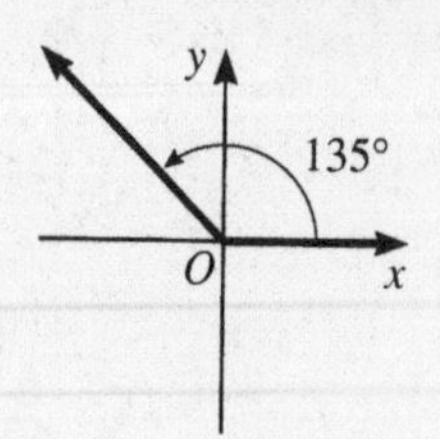

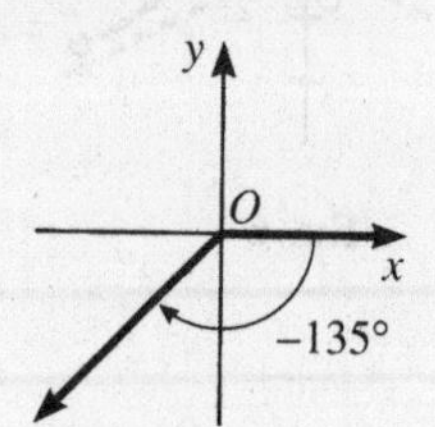

2. **a.** first quadrant **b.** fourth quadrant

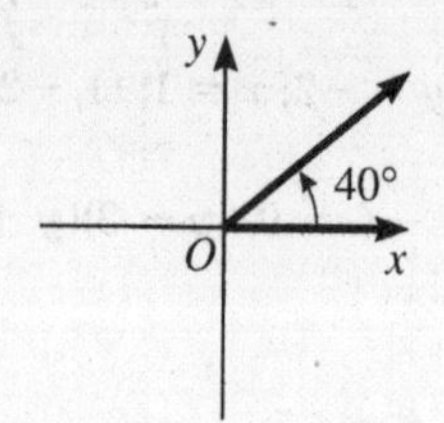

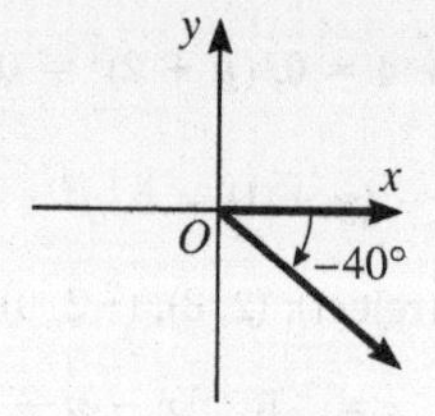

3. **a.** fourth quadrant **b.** first quadrant

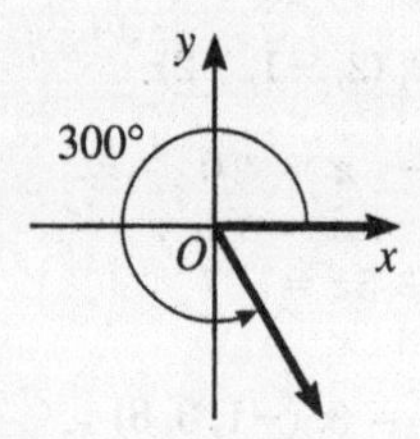

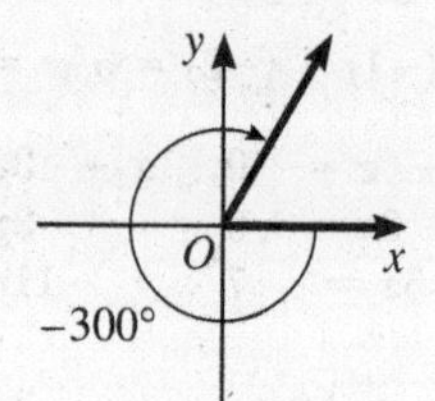

4. **a.** third quadrant **b.** second quadrant

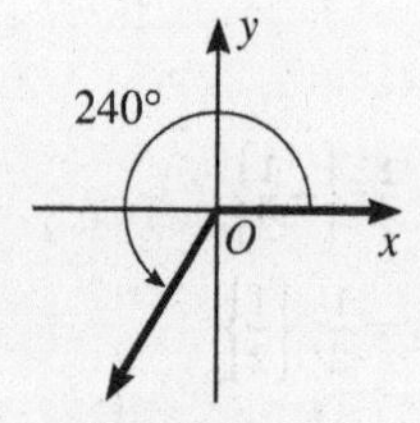

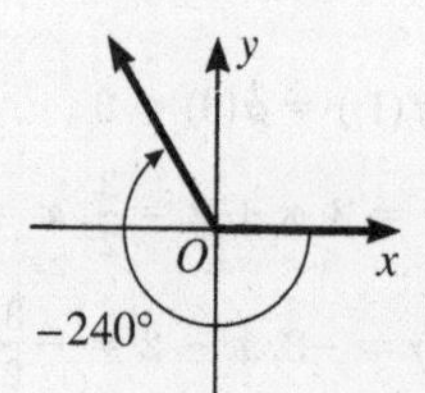

5. quadrantal **6.** fourth quadrant

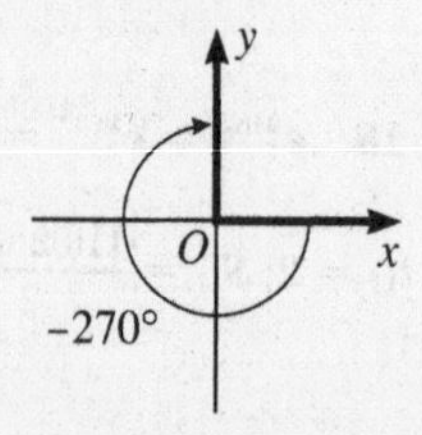

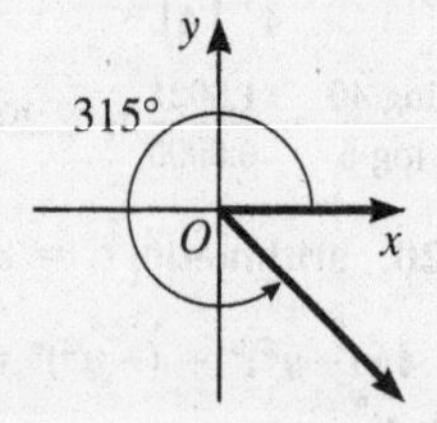

7. fourth quadrant

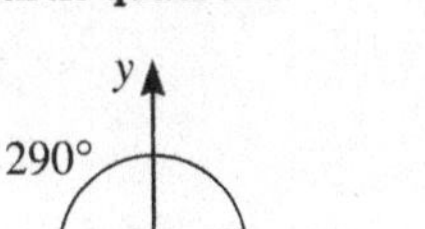

8. quadrantal

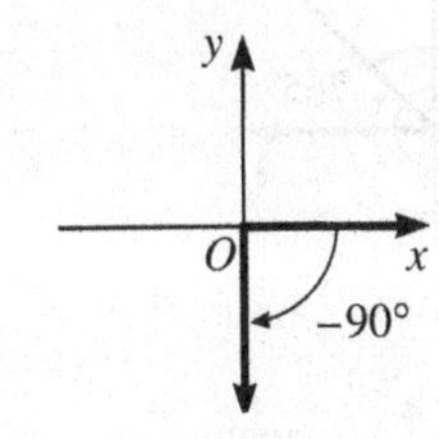

9. second quadrant

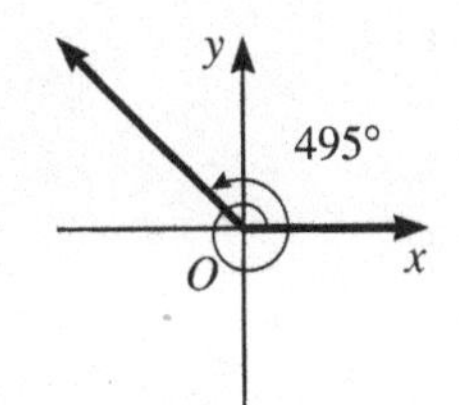

10. quadrantal

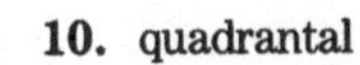

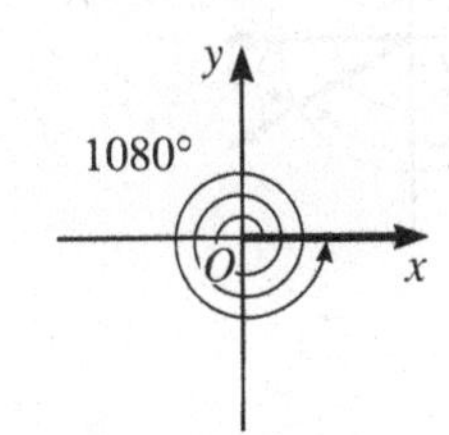

11. quadrantal

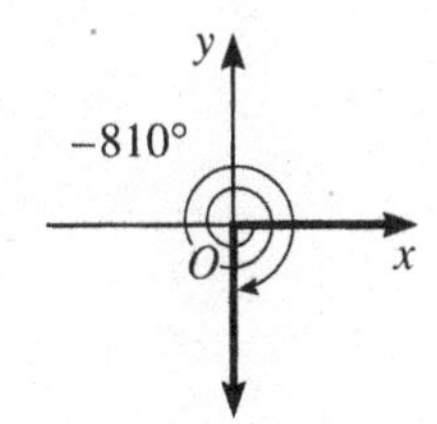

12. first quadrant

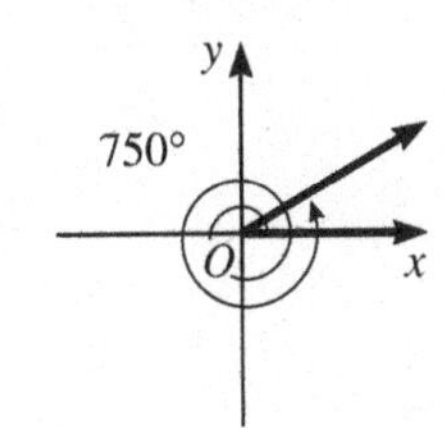

13. $\frac{2}{3} \times 360 = 240$; $240°$

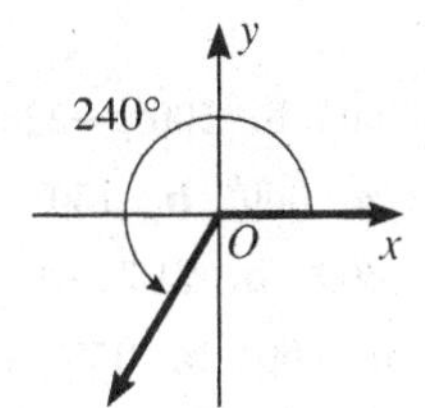

14. $\frac{3}{8} \times 360 = 135$; $135°$

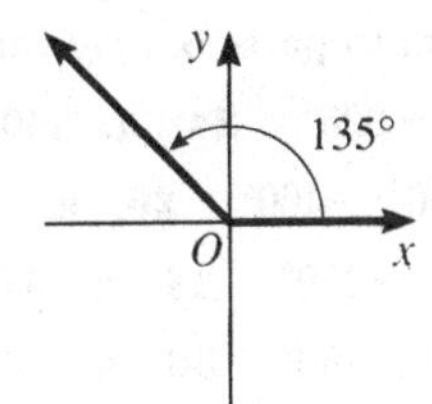

15. $\frac{3}{4} \times (-360) = -270$; $-270°$

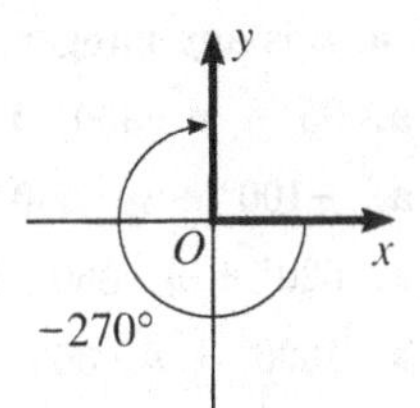

16. $\frac{1}{6} \times (-360) = -60$; $-60°$

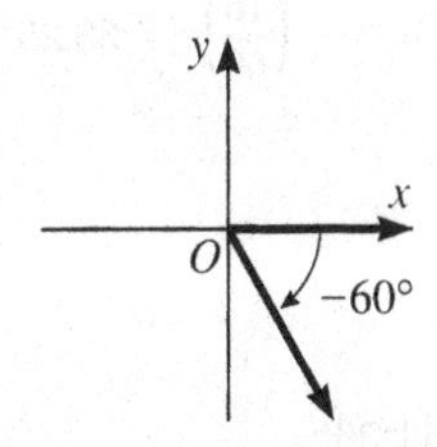

17. $\frac{8}{5} \times 360 = 576$; $576°$

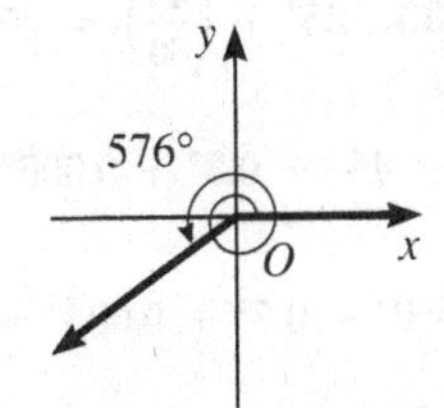

18. $\frac{7}{3} \times 360 = 840$; $840°$

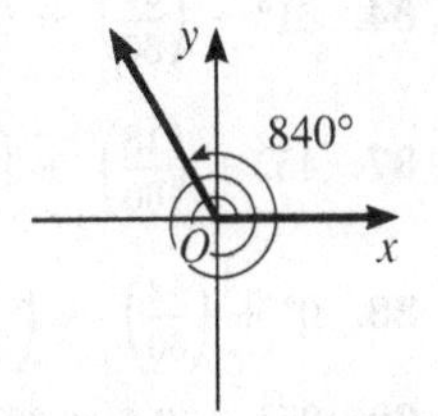

19.

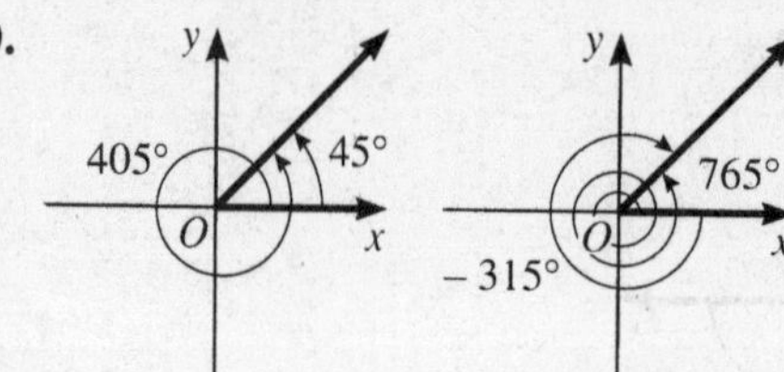

20.

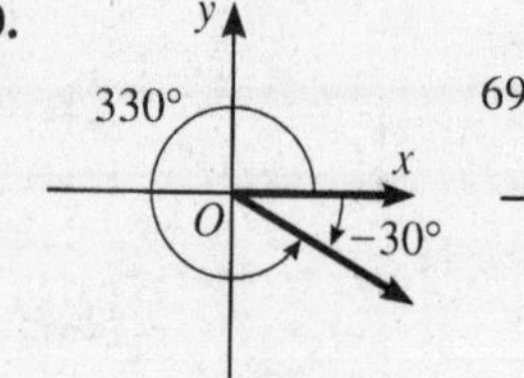

21.

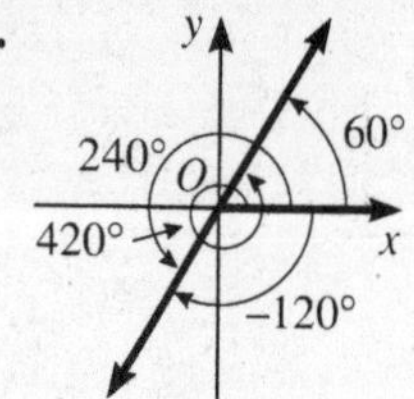

22.

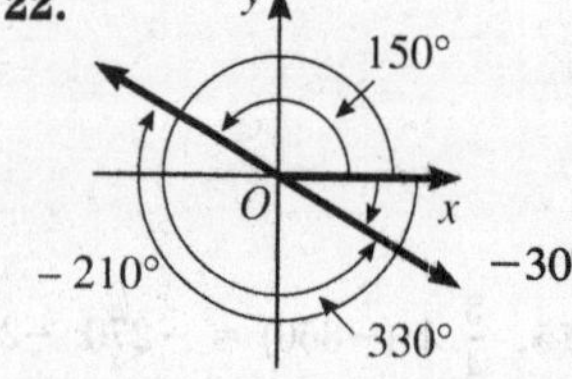

Ex. **23–30.** **a.** n is any integer. Answers to parts **b.** may vary.

23. a. $35° + n \cdot 360°$ **b.** $395°, -325°$ **24. a.** $140° + n \cdot 360°$ **b.** $500°, -220°$

25. a. $-100° + n \cdot 360°$ **b.** $260°, -460°$ **26. a.** $-210° + n \cdot 360°$ **b.** $150°, -570°$

27. a. $520° + n \cdot 360°$ **b.** $160°, -200°$ **28. a.** $355° + n \cdot 360°$ **b.** $715°, -5°$

29. a. $1000° + n \cdot 360°$ **b.** $280°, -80°$ **30. a.** $-3605° + n \cdot 360°$ **b.** $355°, -5°$

31. $15° + \left(\frac{30}{60}\right)^{\circ} = 15.5°$ **32.** $47° + \left(\frac{36}{60}\right)^{\circ} = 47.6°$ **33.** $72° + \left(\frac{50}{60}\right)^{\circ} \approx 72.8°$

34. $51° + \left(\frac{20}{60}\right)^{\circ} \approx 51.3°$ **35.** $25° + \left(\frac{45}{60}\right)^{\circ} = 25.75°$ **36.** $33° + \left(\frac{15}{60}\right)^{\circ} = 33.25°$

37. $45° + \left(\frac{18}{60}\right)^{\circ} + \left(\frac{20}{3600}\right)^{\circ} = 45° + 0.3° + 0.00\overline{5}° \approx 45.31°$

38. $0° + \left(\frac{42}{60}\right)^{\circ} + \left(\frac{30}{3600}\right)^{\circ} = 0° + 0.7° + 0.08\overline{3}° \approx 0.71°$

39. $25° + (0.4 \times 60)' = 25°24'$ **40.** $63° + (0.6 \times 60)' = 63°36'$

41. $44° + (0.9 \times 60)' = 44°54'$ **42.** $27° + (0.1 \times 60)' = 27°6'$

43. $34° + (0.41 \times 60)' = 34° + 24.6' = 34°24' + (0.6 \times 60)'' = 34°24'36''$

44. $18° + (0.27 \times 60)' = 18° + 16.2' = 18°16' + (0.2 \times 60)'' = 18°16'12''$

45. $23° + (0.67 \times 60)' = 23° + 40.2' = 23°40' + (0.2 \times 60)'' = 23°40'12''$

46. $58° + (0.83 \times 60)' = 58° + 49.8' = 58°49' + (0.8 \times 60)'' = 58°49'48''$

47. 315°

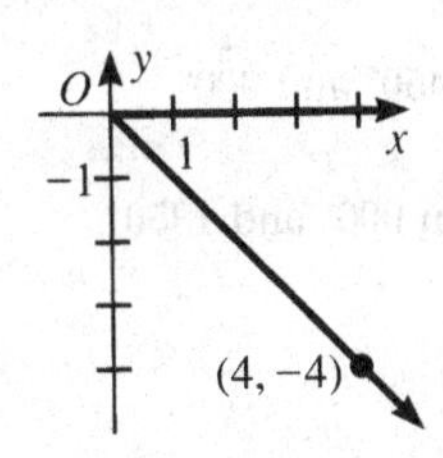

48. 53°

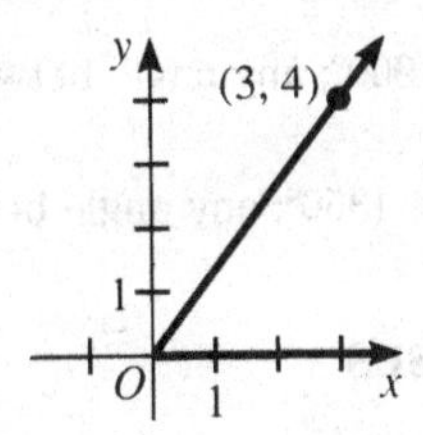

49. 37°

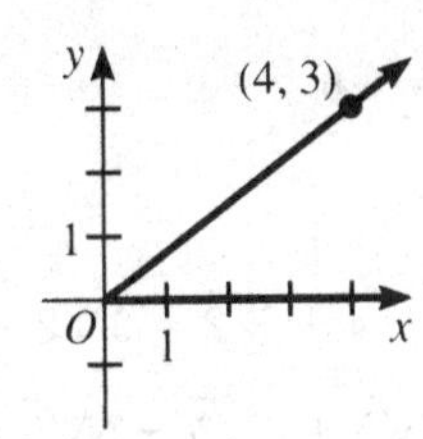

50. 135°

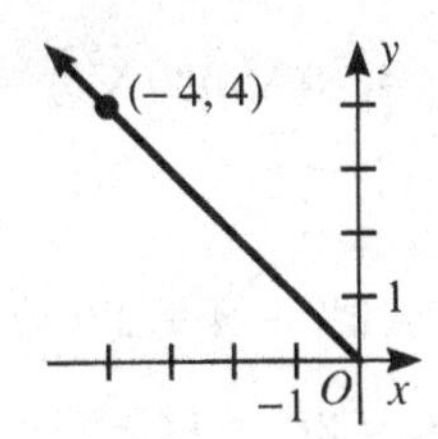

51. 30°

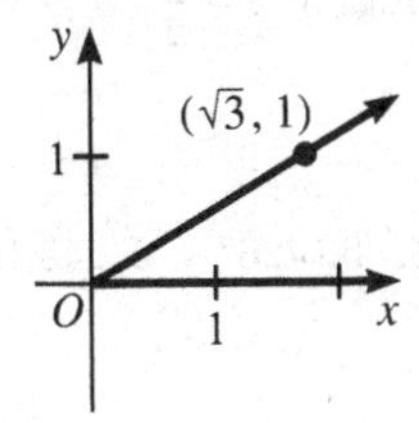

52. 120°

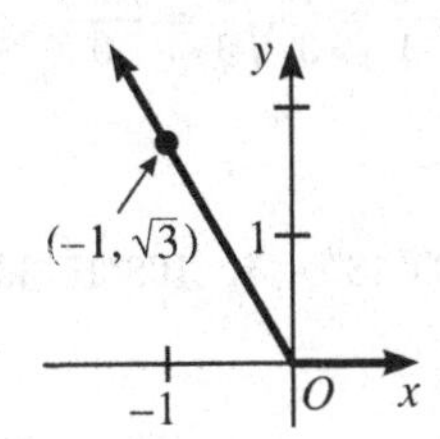

53. 240°

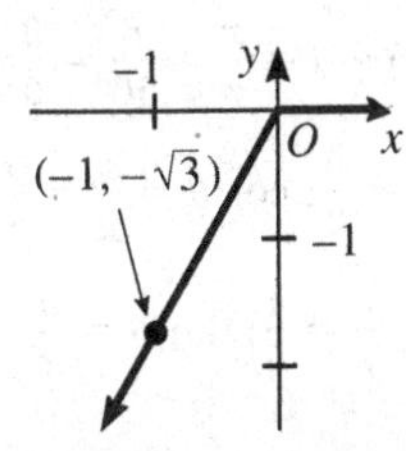

54. 330°

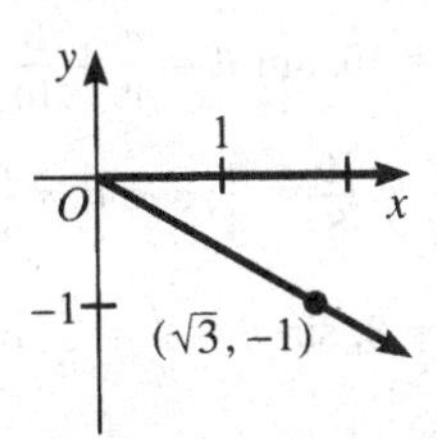

B **55.** $0° < 4\theta < 90°$; $0° < \theta < 22.5°$; any angle between 0° and 22.5°

56. $180° < 4\theta < 270°$; $45° < \theta < 67.5°$; any angle between 45° and 67.5°

57. $270° < 4\theta < 360°$; $67.5° < \theta < 90°$; any angle between 67.5° and 90°

58. $90° < 6\theta < 180°$; $15° < \theta < 30°$; any angle between 15° and 30°

59. $180° < 6\theta < 270°$; $30° < \theta < 45°$; any angle between 30° and 45°

60. $270° < 6\theta < 360°$; $45° < \theta < 60°$; any angle between 45° and 60°

61. $0° < \frac{1}{2}\theta < 90°$; $0° < \theta < 180°$; any angle between 0° and 180°

62. $90° < \frac{1}{2}\theta < 180°$; $180° < \theta < 360°$; any angle between 180° and 360°

63. $180° < \frac{1}{2}\theta < 270°$; $360° < \theta < 540°$; any angle between 360° and 540°

64. $0° < \frac{1}{5}\theta < 90°$; $0° < \theta < 450°$; any angle between 0° and 450°

65. $90° < \frac{1}{5}\theta < 180°$; $450° < \theta < 900°$; any angle between 450° and 900°

66. $180° < \frac{1}{5}\theta < 270°$; $900° < \theta < 1350°$; any angle between 900° and 1350°

Page 554 • MIXED REVIEW EXERCISES

1. $\left(\frac{5!}{3!\,2!}\right)(x)^3(2y)^2 = 40x^3y^2$ **2.** $\frac{8!}{6!\,2!}a^6(-3b)^2 = 252a^6b^2$

3. $\frac{13!}{11!\,2!}(m^2)^{11}(n^3)^2 = 78m^{22}n^6$ **4.** $(i\sqrt{3})(2i\sqrt{3}) = 6i^2 = -6$

5. $\log_2 \frac{14}{7} = \log_2 2 = 1$

6. $(2^{3/4})^2 - 2(2^{3/4})(2^{1/4}) + (2^{1/4})^2 = 2^{3/2} - 4 + 2^{1/2} = 2\sqrt{2} - 4 + \sqrt{2} = 3\sqrt{2} - 4$

7. $\ln(e^{2/3}) = \frac{2}{3}$ **8.** $12 + 3i - 8i - 2i^2 = 14 - 5i$ **9.** $2\sqrt{5} + 3\sqrt{5} - 5\sqrt{5} = 0$

10. $\frac{-6(-2)}{(2)^2} = \frac{12}{4} = 3$ **11.** $\sqrt{\frac{49 \cdot 2}{9 \cdot 3}} = \frac{7}{3}\sqrt{\frac{2}{3}} = \frac{7\sqrt{6}}{9}$ **12.** $\log_3 3^{3/2} = \frac{3}{2}$

Page 554 • CALCULATOR KEY-IN

1. 58°36′ **2.** 29°42′ **3.** 86°25′48″ **4.** 108°15′36″ **5.** $36.42\overline{6}°$ **6.** $45.1886\overline{1}°$
7. $73.8736\overline{1}°$ **8.** $115.7141\overline{6}°$

Pages 559–560 • WRITTEN EXERCISES

A

1. $y = 8, x = 6; r = \sqrt{6^2 + 8^2} = 10; \sin\theta = \frac{y}{r} = \frac{8}{10} = \frac{4}{5}, \cos\theta = \frac{x}{r} = \frac{6}{10} = \frac{3}{5};$
$\tan\theta = \frac{y}{x} = \frac{8}{6} = \frac{4}{3}; \csc\theta = \frac{r}{y} = \frac{10}{8} = \frac{5}{4}; \sec\theta = \frac{r}{x} = \frac{10}{6} = \frac{5}{3}; \cot\theta = \frac{x}{y} = \frac{6}{8} = \frac{3}{4}$

2. $x = 4, r = 5; y = \sqrt{5^2 - 4^2} = 3; \sin\theta = \frac{y}{r} = \frac{3}{5}; \cos\theta = \frac{x}{r} = \frac{4}{5}; \tan\theta = \frac{y}{x} = \frac{3}{4};$
$\csc\theta = \frac{r}{y} = \frac{5}{3}; \sec\theta = \frac{r}{x} = \frac{5}{4}; \cot\theta = \frac{x}{y} = \frac{4}{3}$

3. $x = y = 2; r = \sqrt{2^2 + 2^2} = 2\sqrt{2}; \sin\theta = \frac{y}{r} = \frac{2}{2\sqrt{2}} = \frac{1}{\sqrt{2}} = \frac{\sqrt{2}}{2}; \cos\theta = \frac{x}{r} =$
$\frac{2}{2\sqrt{2}} = \frac{\sqrt{2}}{2}; \tan\theta = \frac{y}{x} = \frac{2}{2} = 1; \csc\theta = \frac{r}{y} = \frac{2\sqrt{2}}{2} = \sqrt{2}; \sec\theta = \frac{r}{x} = \frac{2\sqrt{2}}{2} = \sqrt{2};$
$\cot\theta = \frac{x}{y} = \frac{2}{2} = 1$

4. $x = 2, y = 1; r = \sqrt{2^2 + 1^2} = \sqrt{5}; \sin\theta = \frac{y}{r} = \frac{1}{\sqrt{5}} = \frac{\sqrt{5}}{5}; \cos\theta = \frac{x}{r} = \frac{2}{\sqrt{5}} =$
$\frac{2\sqrt{5}}{5}; \tan\theta = \frac{y}{x} = \frac{1}{2}; \csc\theta = \frac{r}{y} = \frac{\sqrt{5}}{1} = \sqrt{5}; \sec\theta = \frac{r}{x} = \frac{\sqrt{5}}{2}; \cot\theta = \frac{x}{y} = \frac{2}{1} = 2$

5. $x = 8, y = 15; r = \sqrt{8^2 + 15^2} = 17; \sin\theta = \frac{15}{17}; \cos\theta = \frac{8}{17}; \tan\theta = \frac{15}{8}; \csc\theta = \frac{17}{15};$

$\sec\theta = \frac{17}{8}; \cot\theta = \frac{8}{15}$

6. $x = 3, y = 4; r = \sqrt{3^2 + 4^2} = 5; \sin\theta = \frac{4}{5}; \cos\theta = \frac{3}{5}; \tan\theta = \frac{4}{3}; \csc\theta = \frac{5}{4};$

$\sec\theta = \frac{5}{3}; \cot\theta = \frac{3}{4}$

7. $x = 3, y = 1; r = \sqrt{3^2 + 1^2} = \sqrt{10}; \sin\theta = \frac{1}{\sqrt{10}} = \frac{\sqrt{10}}{10}; \cos\theta = \frac{3}{\sqrt{10}} = \frac{3\sqrt{10}}{10};$

$\tan\theta = \frac{1}{3}; \csc\theta = \frac{\sqrt{10}}{1} = \sqrt{10}; \sec\theta = \frac{\sqrt{10}}{3}; \cot\theta = \frac{3}{1} = 3$

8. $x = y = 5; r = \sqrt{5^2 + 5^2} = 5\sqrt{2}; \sin\theta = \frac{5}{5\sqrt{2}} = \frac{\sqrt{2}}{2}; \cos\theta = \frac{5}{5\sqrt{2}} = \frac{\sqrt{2}}{2};$

$\tan\theta = \frac{5}{5} = 1; \csc\theta = \frac{5\sqrt{2}}{5} = \sqrt{2}; \sec\theta = \frac{5\sqrt{2}}{5} = \sqrt{2}; \cot\theta = \frac{5}{5} = 1$

	9.	**10.**	**11.**	**12.**	**13.**	**14.**	**15.**
$\sin\theta$	$\frac{3}{5}$	$\frac{\sqrt{3}}{2}$	$\frac{1}{2}$	$\frac{\sqrt{2}}{3}$	$\frac{\sqrt{161}}{15}$	$\frac{12}{13}$	$\frac{\sqrt{15}}{4}$
$\cos\theta$	$\frac{4}{5}$	$\frac{1}{2}$	$\frac{\sqrt{3}}{2}$	$\frac{\sqrt{7}}{3}$	$\frac{8}{15}$	$\frac{5}{13}$	$\frac{1}{4}$
$\tan\theta$	$\frac{3}{4}$	$\sqrt{3}$	$\frac{\sqrt{3}}{3}$	$\frac{\sqrt{14}}{7}$	$\frac{\sqrt{161}}{8}$	$\frac{12}{5}$	$\sqrt{15}$

16. $\phi = 90° - 50° = 40°$ **17.** $\phi = 90° - 40° = 50°$ **18.** $\phi = 90° - 17° = 73°$

19. $\phi = 90° - 80° = 10°$

20. $\angle B = 90° - 30° = 60°; \csc 30° = \frac{c}{a} = \frac{c}{6} = 2, c = 12; \sin 60° = \frac{b}{c} = \frac{b}{12} = \frac{\sqrt{3}}{2},$

$b = 6\sqrt{3}$

21. $\angle B = 90° - 45° = 45°; \tan 45° = \frac{a}{b} = \frac{a}{2} = 1; a = 2; \csc 45° = \frac{c}{a} = \frac{c}{2} = \sqrt{2},$

$c = 2\sqrt{2}$

22. $\angle B = 90° - 45° = 45°; \sin 45° = \frac{a}{c} = \frac{a}{10} = \frac{\sqrt{2}}{2}, a = 5\sqrt{2}; \tan 45° = \frac{b}{a} =$

$\frac{b}{5\sqrt{2}} = 1, b = 5\sqrt{2}$

23. $\angle B = 90° - 60° = 30°; \sin 60° = \frac{a}{20} = \frac{\sqrt{3}}{2}, a = 10\sqrt{3}; \cos 60° = \frac{b}{c} = \frac{b}{20} = \frac{1}{2},$

$b = 10$

24. $b = \sqrt{c^2 - a^2} = \sqrt{6^2 - 3^2} = \sqrt{27} = 3\sqrt{3}; \sin A = \frac{a}{c} = \frac{3}{6} = \frac{1}{2}; \angle A = 30°;$

$\angle B = 90° - 30° = 60°$

25. $c = \sqrt{4^2 + 4^2} = 4\sqrt{2}; \tan A = \frac{a}{b} = \frac{4}{4} = 1; \angle A = 45°; \angle B = 90° - 45° = 45°$

B **26.** Let x_1, x_2, and y be as shown; $\cos 45° = \frac{x_1}{15}$; $x_1 = \frac{\sqrt{2}}{2} \cdot 15 = \frac{15\sqrt{2}}{2}$;

$y = x_1 = \frac{15\sqrt{2}}{2}$; $\tan 60° = \frac{y}{x_2}$; $\sqrt{3}x_2 = \frac{15\sqrt{2}}{2}$; $x_2 = \frac{15\sqrt{2}}{2\sqrt{3}} = \frac{5\sqrt{6}}{2}$;

$x = x_1 + x_2 = \frac{15\sqrt{2}}{2} + \frac{5\sqrt{6}}{2} = \frac{15\sqrt{2} + 5\sqrt{6}}{2}$

27. Let x_1, x_2, and y be as shown; $\cos 30° = \frac{x_1}{12}$;

$x_1 = 12\left(\frac{\sqrt{3}}{2}\right) = 6\sqrt{3}$; $\sin 30° = \frac{y}{12}$; $y = 12\left(\frac{1}{2}\right) = 6$;

$x_2 = y = 6$; $x = x_1 + x_2 = 6\sqrt{3} + 6$

28. Let y be as shown; $\tan 45° = \frac{x + y}{24}$; $1 = \frac{x + y}{24}$; $x + y = 24$;

$x = 24 - y$; $\tan 30° = \frac{y}{24}$; $y = 24\left(\frac{\sqrt{3}}{3}\right) = 8\sqrt{3}$; $x = 24 - 8\sqrt{3}$

29. Let y be as shown; $\cot 30° = \frac{y}{18}$; $y = 18\sqrt{3}$; $\tan 60° = \frac{18 + x}{y}$;

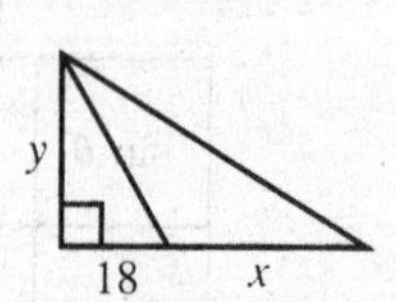

$\sqrt{3} = \frac{18 + x}{18\sqrt{3}}$; $54 = 18 + x$; $x = 36$

30. $\frac{\cos \theta}{\sin \theta} = \frac{\frac{x}{r}}{\frac{y}{r}} = \frac{x}{r} \cdot \frac{r}{y} = \frac{x}{y} = \cot \theta$

31. $\frac{1}{\cos^2 \theta}(\sin^2 \theta + \cos^2 \theta) = \frac{1}{\cos^2 \theta}(1)$; $\frac{\sin^2 \theta}{\cos^2 \theta} + \frac{\cos^2 \theta}{\cos^2 \theta} = \frac{1}{\cos^2 \theta}$; $\left(\frac{\sin \theta}{\cos \theta}\right)^2 + 1 = \left(\frac{1}{\cos \theta}\right)^2$;

therefore, $\tan^2 \theta + 1 = \sec^2 \theta$; $\frac{1}{\sin^2 \theta}(\sin^2 \theta + \cos^2 \theta) = \frac{1}{\sin^2 \theta}(1)$; $\frac{\sin^2 \theta}{\sin^2 \theta} + \frac{\cos^2 \theta}{\sin^2 \theta} =$

$\frac{1}{\sin^2 \theta}$; $1 + \left(\frac{\cos \theta}{\sin \theta}\right)^2 = \left(\frac{1}{\sin \theta}\right)^2$; therefore, $1 + \cot^2 \theta = \csc^2 \theta$

32. Let $R_1 = (x, 0)$ and $R_2 = (x', 0)$. $\triangle OPR_1$ and $\triangle OQR_2$ are right triangles, and $\triangle OPR_1 \sim \triangle OQR_2$ by the AA Similarity Theorem. Then $\frac{y}{y'} = \frac{r}{s}$ and $\frac{y}{r} = \frac{y'}{s}$. Similarly, $\frac{x}{r} = \frac{x'}{s}$, and $\frac{y}{x} = \frac{y'}{x'}$.

C **33.** $\cos^2 \theta = 1 - \sin^2 \theta$; $\cos \theta = \sqrt{1 - \sin^2 \theta} = \sqrt{1 - u^2}$; $\tan \theta = \frac{\sin \theta}{\cos \theta} = \frac{u}{\sqrt{1 - u^2}} =$

$\frac{u\sqrt{1 - u^2}}{1 - u^2}$; $\csc \theta = \frac{1}{\sin \theta} = \frac{1}{u}$; $\sec \theta = \frac{1}{\cos \theta} = \frac{1}{\sqrt{1 - u^2}} = \frac{\sqrt{1 - u^2}}{1 - u^2}$;

$\cot \theta = \frac{1}{\tan \theta} = \frac{\sqrt{1 - u^2}}{u}$

34. $\sin^2 \phi = 1 - \cos^2 \phi$; $\sin \phi = \sqrt{1 - \cos^2 \phi} = \sqrt{1 - v^2}$; $\tan \phi = \frac{\sin \phi}{\cos \phi} = \frac{\sqrt{1 - v^2}}{v}$;

$\csc \phi = \frac{1}{\sin \phi} = \frac{1}{\sqrt{1 - v^2}} = \frac{\sqrt{1 - v^2}}{1 - v^2}$; $\sec \phi = \frac{1}{\cos \phi} = \frac{1}{v}$; $\cot \phi = \frac{1}{\tan \phi} =$

$\frac{v}{\sqrt{1 - v^2}} = \frac{v\sqrt{1 - v^2}}{1 - v^2}$

Pages 566–567 • WRITTEN EXERCISES

A 1. $x = 3, y = -4; r = \sqrt{(3)^2 + (-4)^2} = 5; \sin\theta = -\frac{4}{5}; \cos\theta = \frac{3}{5}; \tan\theta = -\frac{4}{3};$

$\csc\theta = -\frac{5}{4}; \sec\theta = \frac{5}{3}; \cot\theta = -\frac{3}{4}$

2. $x = -5, y = 12; r = \sqrt{(-5)^2 + (12)^2} = 13; \sin\theta = \frac{12}{13}; \cos\theta = -\frac{5}{13}; \tan\theta = -\frac{12}{5};$

$\csc\theta = \frac{13}{12}; \sec\theta = -\frac{13}{5}; \cot\theta = -\frac{5}{12}$

3. $x = -7, y = 24; r = \sqrt{(-7)^2 + 24^2} = 25; \sin\theta = \frac{24}{25}; \cos\theta = -\frac{7}{25}; \tan\theta = -\frac{24}{7};$

$\csc\theta = \frac{25}{24}; \sec\theta = -\frac{25}{7}; \cot\theta = -\frac{7}{24}$

4. $x = -8, y = -15; r = \sqrt{(-8)^2 + (-15)^2} = 17; \sin\theta = -\frac{15}{17}; \cos\theta = -\frac{8}{17};$

$\tan\theta = \frac{15}{8}; \csc\theta = -\frac{17}{15}; \sec\theta = -\frac{17}{8}; \cot\theta = \frac{8}{15}$

	θ	$\sin\theta$	$\cos\theta$	$\tan\theta$	$\sec\theta$	$\csc\theta$	$\cot\theta$
5.	0°	0	1	0	1	undef.	undef.
6.	90°	1	0	undef.	undef.	1	0
7.	180°	0	−1	0	−1	undef.	undef.
8.	270°	−1	0	undef.	undef.	−1	0

9. $\alpha = 233° - 180° = 53°$ 10. $\alpha = 180° - 126° = 54°$

11. $360° + (-205°) = 155°; 180° - 155° = 25°; \alpha = 25°$

12. $360° + (-112°) = 248°; 248° - 180° = 68°; \alpha = 68°$

13. $512° - 360° = 152°; 180° - 152° = 28°; \alpha = 28°$ 14. $\alpha = 720° - 659° = 61°$

15. $1080° + (-725°) = 355°; 360° - 355° = 5°; \alpha = 5°$

16. $-611° + 720° = 109°; 180° - 109° = 71°; \alpha = 71°$ 17. $\alpha = 180° - 96.4° = 83.6°$

18. $\alpha = 180° - 134.7° = 45.3°$

19. $360° - 184.1° = 175.9°; 180° - 175.9° = 4.1°; \alpha = 4.1°$

20. $\alpha = 360° - 344.2° = 15.8°$ 21. $\alpha = 180° - 156°20' = 23°40'$

22. $\alpha = 213°40' - 180° = 33°40'$

23. $-152°30' + 360° = 207°30'; 207°30' - 180° = 27°30'; \alpha = 27°30'$

24. $\alpha = 360° - 312°50' = 47°10'$ 25. $\alpha = 36°; \cos 216° = -\cos 36°$

26. $\alpha = 26°; \tan 334° = -\tan 26°$ 27. $\alpha = 17°; \sin(-17°) = -\sin 17°$

28. $\alpha = 74°; \sec(-106°) = -\sec 74°$ 29. $\alpha = 72.9°; \cot 287.1° = -\cot 72.9°$

30. $\alpha = 62.2°; \csc 117.8° = \csc 62.2°$ 31. $\alpha = 41.9°; \cos(-221.9°) = -\cos 41.9°$

32. $\alpha = 46.6°; \sin(-46.6°) = -\sin 46.6°$ 33. $\alpha = 85°20'; \tan 265°20' = \tan 85°20'$

34. $\alpha = 42°50'; \cot 137°10' = -\cot 42°50'$

35. $\alpha = 32°40'; \sin 212°40' = -\sin 32°40'$

36. $\alpha = 35°30'$; $\sin 324°30' = -\sin 35°30'$

37. $\alpha = 30°$; $\sin 330° = -\sin 30° = -\frac{1}{2}$; $\cos 330° = \cos 30° = \frac{\sqrt{3}}{2}$; $\tan 330° = -\tan 30° = -\frac{\sqrt{3}}{3}$; $\csc 330° = -\csc 30° = -2$; $\sec 330° = \sec 30° = \frac{2\sqrt{3}}{3}$; $\cot 330° = -\cot 30° = -\sqrt{3}$

38. $\alpha = 60°$; $\sin 240° = -\sin 60° = -\frac{\sqrt{3}}{2}$; $\cos 240° = -\cos 60° = -\frac{1}{2}$; $\tan 240° = \tan 60° = \sqrt{3}$; $\csc 240° = -\csc 60° = -\frac{2\sqrt{3}}{3}$; $\sec 60° = -\sec 60° = -2$; $\cot 240° = \cot 60° = \frac{\sqrt{3}}{3}$

39. $\alpha = 45°$; $\sin 135° = \frac{\sqrt{2}}{2}$; $\cos 135° = -\frac{\sqrt{2}}{2}$; $\tan 135° = -1$; $\csc 135° = \sqrt{2}$; $\sec 135° = -\sqrt{2}$; $\cot 135° = -1$

40. $\alpha = 60°$; $\sin(-60°) = -\frac{\sqrt{3}}{2}$; $\cos(-60°) = \frac{1}{2}$; $\tan(-60°) = -\sqrt{3}$; $\csc(-60°) = -\frac{2\sqrt{3}}{3}$; $\sec(-60°) = 2$; $\cot(-60°) = -\frac{\sqrt{3}}{3}$

41. $\alpha = 45°$; $\sin 315° = -\frac{\sqrt{2}}{2}$; $\cos 315° = \frac{\sqrt{2}}{2}$; $\tan 315° = -1$; $\csc 315° = -\sqrt{2}$; $\sec 315° = \sqrt{2}$; $\cot 315° = -1$

42. $\alpha = 60°$; $\sin 300° = -\frac{\sqrt{3}}{2}$; $\cos 300° = \frac{1}{2}$; $\tan 300° = -\sqrt{3}$; $\csc 300° = -\frac{2\sqrt{3}}{3}$; $\sec 300° = 2$; $\cot 300° = -\frac{\sqrt{3}}{3}$

43. $\alpha = 30°$; $\sin(-150°) = -\frac{1}{2}$; $\cos(-150°) = -\frac{\sqrt{3}}{2}$; $\tan(-150°) = \frac{\sqrt{3}}{3}$; $\csc(-150°) = -2$; $\sec(-150°) = -\frac{2\sqrt{3}}{3}$; $\cot(-150°) = \sqrt{3}$

44. $\alpha = 60°$; $\sin 480° = \frac{\sqrt{3}}{2}$; $\cos 480° = -\frac{1}{2}$; $\tan 480° = -\sqrt{3}$; $\csc 480° = \frac{2\sqrt{3}}{3}$; $\sec 480° = -2$; $\cot 480° = -\frac{\sqrt{3}}{3}$

B **45.** quadrant II; Let $x = -8$, $r = 17$; then $y = \sqrt{17^2 - (-8)^2} = 15$; $\sin \theta = \frac{15}{17}$; $\tan \theta = -\frac{15}{8}$; $\csc \theta = \frac{17}{15}$; $\sec \theta = -\frac{17}{8}$; $\cot \theta = -\frac{8}{15}$

46. quadrant III; Let $y = -4$, $r = 5$; then $x = -\sqrt{5^2 - (-4)^2} = -3$; $\cos \theta = -\frac{3}{5}$; $\tan \theta = \frac{4}{3}$; $\csc \theta = -\frac{5}{4}$; $\sec \theta = -\frac{5}{3}$; $\cot \theta = \frac{3}{4}$

47. quadrant IV; Let $y = -5$, $r = 13$; $x = \sqrt{13^2 - 5^2} = 12$; $\cos \theta = \frac{12}{13}$; $\tan \theta = -\frac{5}{12}$; $\csc \theta = -\frac{13}{5}$; $\sec \theta = \frac{13}{12}$; $\cot \theta = -\frac{12}{5}$

48. quadrant II; Let $x = -3$, $r = 5$; $y = \sqrt{5^2 - (-3)^2} = 4$; $\sin\theta = \frac{4}{5}$; $\tan\theta = -\frac{4}{3}$; $\csc\theta = \frac{5}{4}$; $\sec\theta = -\frac{5}{3}$; $\cot\theta = -\frac{3}{4}$

49. quadrant I; Let $x = 2$, $r = 3$; $y = \sqrt{3^2 - 2^2} = \sqrt{5}$; $\sin\theta = \frac{\sqrt{5}}{3}$; $\tan\theta = \frac{\sqrt{5}}{2}$; $\csc\theta = \frac{3}{\sqrt{5}} = \frac{3\sqrt{5}}{5}$; $\sec\theta = \frac{3}{2}$; $\cot\theta = \frac{2}{\sqrt{5}} = \frac{2\sqrt{5}}{5}$

50. quadrant IV; Let $y = -2$, $r = 5$; $x = \sqrt{5^2 - (-2)^2} = \sqrt{21}$; $\cos\theta = \frac{\sqrt{21}}{5}$; $\tan\theta = -\frac{2}{\sqrt{21}} = -\frac{2\sqrt{21}}{21}$; $\csc\theta = -\frac{5}{2}$; $\sec\theta = \frac{5}{\sqrt{21}} = \frac{5\sqrt{21}}{21}$; $\cot\theta = -\frac{\sqrt{21}}{2}$

51. quadrant II; Let $y = 3$, $x = -4$; then $r = \sqrt{(-4)^2 + (3)^2} = 5$; $\sin\theta = \frac{3}{5}$; $\cos\theta = -\frac{4}{5}$; $\csc\theta = \frac{5}{3}$; $\sec\theta = -\frac{5}{4}$; $\cot\theta = \frac{1}{\tan\theta} = -\frac{4}{3}$

52. quadrant IV; Let $x = 5$, $r = 13$; $y = -\sqrt{13^2 - 5^2} = -12$; $\sin\theta = -\frac{12}{13}$; $\cos\theta = \frac{5}{13}$; $\tan\theta = -\frac{12}{5}$; $\csc\theta = -\frac{13}{12}$, $\cot\theta = -\frac{5}{12}$

53. 0°, 180° **54.** 90°, 270° **55.** 0°, 180° **56.** 90° **57.** 45°, 225° **58.** 180° **59.** 270° **60.** 30°, 150° **61.** 150°, 210° **62.** 240°, 300° **63.** 15°, 195° **64.** 40°, 140° **65.** 70°, 290° **66.** 100°, 260° **67.** 20°, 200°

C

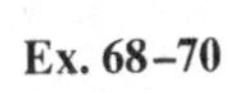

Ex. 68–70

68. If $\sin\theta = \frac{y}{r}$, then $\sin(-\theta) = -\frac{y}{r} = -\sin\theta$

69. If $\cos\theta = \frac{x}{r}$, then $\cos(-\theta) = \frac{x}{r} = \cos\theta$

70. If $\tan\theta = \frac{y}{x}$, then $\tan(-\theta) = -\frac{y}{x} = -\tan\theta = -\frac{\sin\theta}{\cos\theta}$

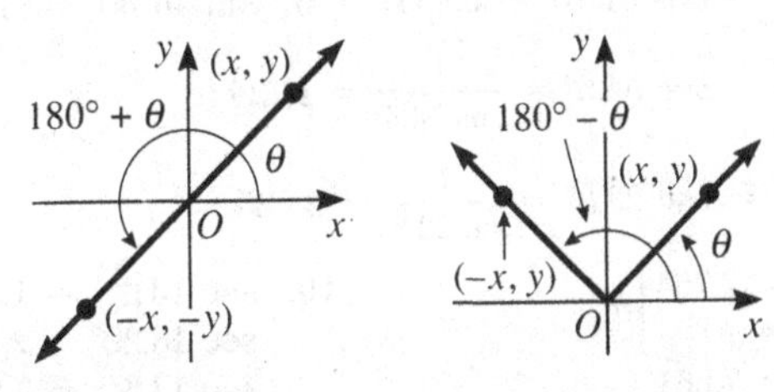

Ex. 71, 73, 75 Ex. 72, 74, 76

71. If $\sin\theta = \frac{y}{r}$, then $\sin(180° + \theta) = -\frac{y}{r} = -\sin\theta$

72. If $\sin\theta = \frac{y}{r}$, then $\sin(180° - \theta) = \frac{y}{r} = \sin\theta$

73. If $\cos\theta = \frac{x}{r}$, then $\cos(180° + \theta) = -\frac{x}{r} = -\cos\theta$

74. If $\cos\theta = \frac{x}{r}$, then $\cos(180° - \theta) = -\frac{x}{r} = -\cos\theta$

75. If $\tan\theta = \frac{y}{x}$, then $\tan(180° + \theta) = \frac{-y}{-x} = \frac{y}{x} = \tan\theta = \frac{\sin\theta}{\cos\theta}$

76. If $\tan\theta = \frac{y}{x}$, then $\tan(180° - \theta) = \frac{y}{-x} = -\tan\theta = -\frac{\sin\theta}{\cos\theta}$

Page 567 • MIXED REVIEW EXERCISES

1. $S_8 = \frac{5(1 - 2^8)}{1 - 2} = 1275$ **2.** $t_{20} = 3(20) + 1 = 61$; $S_{20} = \frac{20(4 + 61)}{2} = 650$

3. $S = \frac{10}{1 - \frac{3}{5}} = \frac{10}{\frac{2}{5}} = 25$ **4.** $3x + 5 = 0$, $x = -\frac{5}{3}$; $-\frac{5}{3}$

5. $\log(x - 1) = 0$, $10^0 = x - 1$, $1 = x - 1$, $x = 2$; 2

6. $2x^2 + x - 3 = 0$, $(2x + 3)(x - 1) = 0$, $x = -\frac{3}{2}$ or $x = 1$; 1, $-\frac{3}{2}$

7. $\frac{x^3 - 4x}{x^2 + 1} = 0$, $\frac{x(x - 2)(x + 2)}{x^2 + 1} = 0$, $x = 0$, $x = 2$, or $x = -2$; 0, 2, -2

8. $x^2 - 4x + 5 = 0$, $x = \frac{4 \pm \sqrt{16 - 4(5)}}{2} = \frac{4 \pm \sqrt{-4}}{2} = 2 \pm i$; no real zeros

9. $\left(\frac{1}{2}\right)^x = 0$; no real zeros

Page 572 • WRITTEN EXERCISES

A **1.** $\tan 15.2° = 0.2717$ **2.** $\cos 38.7° = 0.7804$

3. $\sin 65.2° = 0.9078$ **4.** $\cot 81.1° = \frac{1}{\tan 81.1°} = 0.1566$

5. $\cos 31°10' = \cos 31.1\overline{6}° = 0.8557$ **6.** $\sin 46°30' = \sin 46.5° = 0.7254$

7. $\sec 54°40' = \sec 54.\overline{6}° = \frac{1}{\cos 54.\overline{6}°} = 1.729$

8. $\csc 23°20' = \csc 23.\overline{3}° = \frac{1}{\sin 23.\overline{3}°} = 2.525$

9. $\left.\begin{array}{l}\csc 7.4° = 7.764 \\ \csc 7.44° = x\end{array}\right\} d;$
$\csc 7.5° = 7.661$

$\frac{4}{10} = \frac{d}{-0.103}$; $d = -0.041$,

$x \approx 7.764 - 0.041 = 7.723$

10. $\left.\begin{array}{l}\sec 13.2° = 1.027 \\ \sec 13.22° = x\end{array}\right\} d;$
$\sec 13.3° = 1.028$

$\frac{2}{10} = \frac{d}{0.001}$, $d = 0.0002$;

$x \approx 1.027$

11. $\left.\begin{array}{l}\cos 32.4° = 0.8443 \\ \cos 32.43° = x\end{array}\right\} d;$
$\cos 32.5° = 0.8434$

$\frac{3}{10} = \frac{d}{0.0009}$, $d = 0.0003$;

$x = 0.8443 - 0.0003 = 0.8440$

12. $\left.\begin{array}{l}\sin 26.5° = 0.4462 \\ \sin 26.57° = x\end{array}\right\} d;$
$\sin 26.6° = 0.4478$

$\frac{7}{10} = \frac{d}{0.0016}$, $d = 0.0011$;

$x = 0.4462 + 0.0011 = 0.4473$

13. $\left.\begin{array}{l}\cos 52°40' = 0.6065\\ \cos 52°43' = x\end{array}\right\}d$
$\cos 52°50' = 0.6041$

$\frac{3}{10} = \frac{d}{0.0024}$, $d = 0.0007$;

$x = 0.6065 - 0.0007 = 0.6058$

14. $\left.\begin{array}{l}\tan 29°30' = 0.5658\\ \tan 29°36' = x\end{array}\right\}d$
$\tan 29°40' = 0.5696$

$\frac{6}{10} = \frac{d}{0.0038}$, $d = 0.0023$;

$x = 0.5658 + 0.0023 = 0.5681$

15. $\left.\begin{array}{l}\cot 78°10' = 0.2095\\ \cot 78°15' = x\end{array}\right\}d;$
$\cot 78°20' = 0.2065$

$\frac{5}{10} = \frac{d}{0.0030}$, $d = 0.0015$;

$x = 0.2095 - 0.0015 = 0.2080$

16. $\left.\begin{array}{l}\sin 87°50' = 0.9993\\ \sin 87°53' = x\end{array}\right\}d;$
$\sin 88°00' = 0.9994$

$\frac{3}{10} = \frac{d}{0.0001}$, $d = 0.00003$;

$x = 0.9993$

17. $\sec 111.3° = -\sec 68.7° = -2.753$

18. $\csc 163.4° = \csc 16.6° = 3.500$

19. $\sin 268.5° = -\sin 88.5° = -0.9997$

20. $\cos 328.1° = \cos 31.9° = 0.8490$

21. $\cot 143°30' = -\cot 36°30' = -1.351$

22. $\tan 173°20' = -\tan 6°40' = -0.1169$

23. $\cos 231°30' = -\cos 51°30' = -0.6225$

24. $\sin 312°40' = -\sin 47°20' = -0.7353$

25. $\theta = \sin^{-1} 0.3400 = 19.87687°$; $19.9°$

26. $\theta = \cos^{-1} 0.8400 = 32.85988°$; $32.9°$

27. Since $\cot \theta = 1.700$, $\tan \theta = \frac{1}{1.700} = 0.5882$; $\theta = \tan^{-1} 0.5882 = 30.4655°$; $30.5°$

28. $\theta = \tan^{-1} 1.325 = 52.9575°$; $53.0°$

29. Since $\sec \theta = 3.555$, $\cos \theta = \frac{1}{3.555} = 0.2813$; $\theta = \cos^{-1} 0.2813 = 73.66219°$; $73.7°$

30. Since $\csc \theta = 3.000$, $\sin \theta = \frac{1}{3.000} = 0.3333$; $\theta = \sin^{-1} 0.3333 = 19.46919°$; $19.5°$

31. $d\begin{cases}\cos 30°20' = 0.8631\\ \cos \theta = 0.8621\end{cases}$; $\frac{d}{10} = \frac{0.0010}{0.0015}$, $d = 7$; $\theta = 30°20' + 7' = 30°27'$
$\cos 30°30' = 0.8616$

32. $d\begin{cases}\sin 15°20' = 0.2644\\ \sin \theta = 0.2654\end{cases}$; $\frac{d}{10} = \frac{0.0010}{0.0028}$, $d = 4$; $\theta = 15°20' + 4' = 15°24'$
$\sin 15°30' = 0.2672$

33. $d\begin{cases}\tan 8°20' = 0.1465\\ \tan \theta = 0.1482\end{cases}$; $\frac{d}{10} = \frac{0.0017}{0.0030}$, $d = 6$; $\theta = 8°20' + 6' = 8°26'$
$\tan 8°30' = 0.1495$

34. $d\begin{cases}\cos 74°10' = 0.2728\\ \cos \theta = 0.2715\end{cases}$; $\frac{d}{10} = \frac{0.0013}{0.0028}$, $d = 5$; $\theta = 74°10' + 5' = 74°15'$
$\cos 74°20' = 0.2700$

35. $d\begin{cases}\sin 47°00' = 0.7314\\ \sin \theta = 0.7321\end{cases}$; $\frac{d}{10} = \frac{0.0007}{0.0019}$, $d = 4$; $\theta = 47°00' + 4' = 47°4'$
$\sin 47°10' = 0.7333$

36. $d\begin{cases}\tan 68°30' = 2.539 \\ \tan \theta = 2.550\end{cases}$; $\frac{d}{10} = \frac{0.011}{0.022}$, $d = 5$; $\theta = 68°30' + 5' = 68°35'$
$\tan 68°40' = 2.561$

B **37.** $\alpha = 29.2°$; $180° - 29.2° = 150.8°$; $\theta = 29.2°$ or $\theta = 150.8°$

38. $\alpha = 38.3°$; $360° - 38.3° = 321.7°$; $\theta = 321.7°$ or $\theta = 38.3°$

39. $\alpha = 60.3°$; $180° - 60.3° = 119.7°$; $360° - 60.3° = 299.7°$; $\theta = 119.7°$ or $\theta = 299.7°$

40. $\alpha = 56.1°$; $180° + 56.1° = 236.1°$; $360° - 56.1° = 303.9°$; $\theta = 236.1°$ or $\theta = 303.9°$

41. $\alpha = 75.4°$; $360° - 75.4° = 284.6°$; $\theta = 75.4°$ or $\theta = 284.6°$

42. $\alpha = 31.7°$; $180° + 31.7° = 211.7°$; $\theta = 31.7°$ or $\theta = 211.7°$

43. $\alpha = 64.7°$; θ is an quadrant IV; $\theta = 360° - 64.7° = 295.3°$

44. $\alpha = 31.4°$; θ is in quadrant III; $180° + 31.4° = 211.4°$; $\theta = 211.4°$

45. $\alpha = 37.7°$; θ is in quadrant IV; $\theta = 360° - 37.7° = 322.3°$

46. $\alpha = 38.6°$; θ is in quadrant IV; $\theta = 360° - 38.6° = 321.4°$

Pages 577–578 • WRITTEN EXERCISES

A **1.** $\sin 36.2° = \frac{a}{68}$, $a = (0.5906)(68) = 40.2$; $\cos 36.2° = \frac{b}{68}$, $b = (0.8070)(68) = 54.9$;
$\angle B = 90° - 36.2° = 53.8°$

2. $\sin 15.8° = \frac{b}{12.2}$, $b = (12.2)(0.2723) = 3.32$; $\cos 15.8° = \frac{a}{12.2}$, $a = (12.2)(0.9622) =$
11.7; $\angle A = 90° - 15.8° = 74.2°$

3. $\sec 65.4° = \frac{c}{2.35}$, $c = (2.402)(2.35) = 5.65$; $\tan 65.4° = \frac{b}{2.35}$, $b = (2.184)(2.35) = 5.13$;
$\angle A = 90° - 65.4° = 24.6°$

4. $\tan 82.1° = \frac{a}{246}$, $a = (7.207)(246) = 1770$; $\sec 82.1° = \frac{c}{246}$, $c = (7.28)(246) = 1790$;
$\angle B = 90° - 82.1° = 7.9°$

5. $\csc 48.3° = \frac{c}{74.7}$, $c = (74.7)(1.339) = 100$; $\cot 48.3° = \frac{a}{74.7}$, $a = (74.7)(0.8910) = 66.6$;
$\angle A = 90° - 48.3° = 41.7°$

6. $\csc 24.0° = \frac{c}{5.25}$, $c = (5.25)(2.459) = 12.9$; $\cot 24.0° = \frac{b}{5.25}$, $b = (5.25)(2.246) = 11.8$;
$\angle B = 90° - 24.0° = 66.0°$

7. $\sin A = \frac{230}{320} = 0.7188$; $\angle A = 46.0°$; $\cos 46.0° = \frac{b}{320}$, $b = (320)(0.6947) = 222$;
$\angle B = 90° - 46.0° = 44.0°$

8. $\tan A = \frac{52.5}{28.0} = 1.875$; $\angle A = 61.9°$; $\angle B = 90° - 61.9° = 28.1°$; $\csc 61.9° = \frac{c}{52.5}$,
$c = (52.5)(1.134) = 59.5$

9. $\cot A = \frac{0.315}{0.123} = 2.561$; $\angle A = 21.3°$; $\csc 21.3° = \frac{c}{0.123}$, $c = (2.753)(0.123) = 0.339$;
$\angle B = 90° - 21.3° = 68.7°$

10. $\sin B = \frac{3.90}{42.5} = 0.0918$; $\angle B = 5.3°$; $\cot 5.3° = \frac{a}{3.90}$, $a = (10.78)(3.90) = 42.0$;

$\angle A = 90° - 5.3° = 84.7°$

11. $\sin 58°10' = \frac{b}{420}$, $b = (0.8496)(420) = 357$; $\cos 58°10' = \frac{a}{420}$,

$a = (0.5275)(420) = 222$; $\angle A = 90°00' - 58°10' = 31°50'$

12. $\sin 38°40' = \frac{a}{42.5}$, $a = (0.6248)(42.5) = 26.6$; $\cos 38°40' = \frac{b}{42.5}$,

$b = (0.7808)(42.5) = 33.2$; $\angle B = 90°00' - 38°40' = 51°20'$

13. $\csc 15°30' = \frac{c}{4.50}$, $c = (4.50)(3.742) = 16.8$; $\cot 15°30' = \frac{b}{4.50}$,

$b = (4.50)(3.606) = 16.2$; $\angle B = 90° - 15°30' = 74°30'$

14. $\sec 67°20' = \frac{c}{450}$, $c = (450)(2.595) = 1170$; $\tan 67°20' = \frac{b}{450}$,

$b = (450)(2.394) = 1080$; $\angle A = 90° - 67°20' = 22°40'$

15. $\tan 30°50' = \frac{a}{53.5}$, $a = (53.5)(0.5969) = 31.9$; $\sec 30°50' = \frac{c}{53.5}$,

$c = (53.5)(1.165) = 62.3$; $\angle B = 90° - 30°50' = 59°10'$

16. $\cot 85°10' = \frac{a}{0.620}$, $a = (0.620)(0.0846) = 0.052$; $\csc 85°10' = \frac{c}{0.620}$,

$c = (1.004)(0.620) = 0.622$; $\angle A = 90° - 85°10' = 4°50'$

B **17.** Draw $\overline{OP} \perp \overline{AB}$ at P; $AP = 5$ cm; $\sin \angle AOP = \frac{5}{13} = 0.3846$; $\angle AOP = 22.6°$;

$\therefore \angle AOB = 2(22.6°) = 45.2°$

18. Draw $\overline{DP_1} \perp \overline{AB}$ at P_1 and $\overline{CP_2} \perp \overline{AB}$ at P_2; $P_1P_2 = DC = 4$; $AP_1 = P_2B$ and

$AP_1 + P_2B = 20 - 4 = 16$; $AP_1 = P_2B = 8$; $\tan \angle A = \frac{6}{8} = 0.7500$; $\angle A = 36.9°$;

$\angle B = \angle A = 36.9°$; $\angle ADC = \angle DCB = 180° - 36.9° = 143.1°$

19. $\sin \angle A = \frac{4}{5} = 0.8000$; $\angle A = \angle C = 53.1°$; $\angle D = \angle B = 180° - 53.1° = 126.9°$

20–24. Let O be the center of the circle, $\overline{OL}$ and $\overline{OR}$, the radii (left to right), and S the right angle.

20. a. $\angle LOR = \frac{1}{5}(360°) = 72°$; $\angle SOR = \frac{1}{2}\angle LOR = 36°$; $\sin 36° = \frac{SR}{1}$; $SR = 0.588$;

perimeter $= 10 \cdot SR = 5.88$

b. $\angle LOR = \frac{1}{5}(360°) = 72°$; $\angle SOR = \frac{1}{2}\angle LOR = 36°$; $\tan 36° = \frac{SR}{1}$; $SR = 0.727$;

perimeter $= 10 \cdot SR = 7.27$

21. a. $\angle LOR = \frac{1}{10}(360°) = 36°$; $\angle SOR = \frac{1}{2}\angle LOR = 18°$; $\sin 18° = \frac{SR}{1}$; $SR = 0.309$;

perimeter $= 20 \cdot SR = 6.18$

b. $\angle LOR = \frac{1}{10}(360°) = 36°$; $\angle SOR = \frac{1}{2}\angle LOR = 18°$; $\tan 18° = \frac{SR}{1}$; $SR = 0.325$;

perimeter $= 20 \cdot SR = 6.50$

22. a. $\angle LOR = \frac{1}{20}(360°) = 18°$; $\angle SOR = \frac{1}{2}\angle LOR = 9°$; $\sin 9° = \frac{SR}{1}$; $SR = 0.1564$;

perimeter $= 40 \cdot SR = 6.26$

b. $\angle LOR = \frac{1}{20}(360°) = 18°$; $\angle SOR = \frac{1}{2}\angle LOR = 9°$; $\tan 9° = \frac{SR}{1}$; $SR = 0.1584$;

perimeter $= 40 \cdot SR = 6.34$

23. 2π = circumference of a unit circle, which is greater than the perimeter of the inscribed polygon and less than the perimeter of the circumscribed polygon.

C **24. a.** $\angle LOR = \frac{1}{n}(360°) = \left(\frac{360}{n}\right)^\circ$; $\angle SOR = \frac{1}{2}\angle LOR = \left(\frac{180}{n}\right)^\circ$; $\sin\left(\frac{180}{n}\right)^\circ = \frac{SR}{1}$;

$SR = \sin\left(\frac{180}{n}\right)^\circ$; perimeter $= 2n \cdot SR = 2n \sin\left(\frac{180}{n}\right)^\circ$;

$\angle LOR = \frac{1}{n}(360°) = \left(\frac{360}{n}\right)^\circ$; $\angle SOR = \frac{1}{2}\angle LOR = \left(\frac{180}{n}\right)^\circ$; $\tan\left(\frac{180}{n}\right)^\circ = \frac{SR}{1}$;

$SR = \tan\left(\frac{180}{n}\right)^\circ$; perimeter $= 2n \cdot SR = 2n \tan\left(\frac{180}{n}\right)^\circ$; $2n \sin\left(\frac{180}{n}\right)^\circ$, $2n \tan\left(\frac{180}{n}\right)^\circ$

b. As n gets larger and larger, the perimeters of both polygons approach the circumference of the circle; $2n \sin\left(\frac{180}{n}\right)^\circ$ and $2n \tan\left(\frac{180}{n}\right)^\circ$ both approach 2π, that is, $n \sin\left(\frac{180}{n}\right)^\circ$ and $n \tan\left(\frac{180}{n}\right)^\circ$ both approach π.

Pages 578–579 • PROBLEMS

A **1.** Let $x°$ = the angle of elevation of the sun; $\tan x° = \frac{6.25}{10.1} = 0.6188$; $x = 31.7$; 31.7°

2. Let $x°$ = the angle of elevation of the kite; $\cos x° = \frac{30}{50} = 0.6000$; $x = 53.1$; 53.1°

3. Let $x°$ = the angle the cable makes with the ground; $\cos x° = \frac{1.75}{4} = 0.4375$;

$x = 64.1$; 64.1°

4. Let x = the distance in feet between the base of the ladder and the base of the building; $\cos 75° = \frac{x}{30}$, $x = 30(0.2588) = 7.76$; 7.76 ft

5. Let x = the vertical distance in feet; $\sin 33° = \frac{x}{1000}$, $x = 1000(0.5446) = 545$; 545 ft

6. Let x = the distance in meters at which the descent begins; $\cot 11° = \frac{x}{9500}$,

$x = (5.14)(9500) = 48{,}900$; 48,900 m

7. Let x = the height in feet of the balloon; $\tan 48° = \frac{x}{285}$, $x = (285)(1.111) = 317$;

317 ft

8.

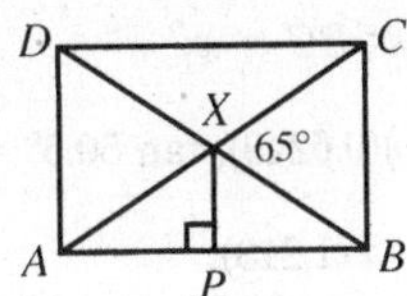

$\angle AXB = 180° - 65° = 115°$; $AX = \frac{1}{2}AC = 180$; $\angle AXP = \frac{1}{2}\angle AXB = 57.5°$;

$\cos 57.5° = \frac{XP}{180}$, $XP = 180(0.5373) = 96.7$; $\sin 57.5° = \frac{AP}{180}$,

$AP = (180)(0.8434) = 152$; $AB = DC = 2(AP) = 2(152) = 304$; $CB = DA = 2(XP) =$ $2(96.7) = 193$; 193 m by 304 m

B

9.

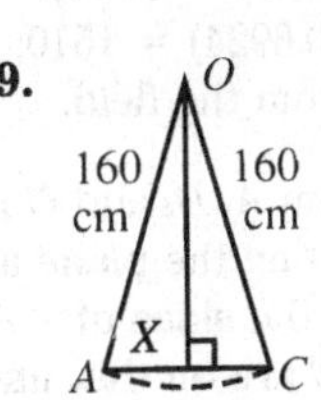

$AC = 65$; $XC = 32.5$; $\sin \angle XOC = \frac{32.5}{160} = 0.2031$; $\angle XOC = 11.7°$;

$\angle AOC = 2(\angle XOC) = 23.4°$; $23.4°$

10. Let x = half the width of the tent in cm; $\cot 55° = \frac{x}{210}$, $x = (210)(0.7002) = 147$; the width is $2(147) = 294$ cm

11. Let y and x = the distances in feet between the bottom of the tower and the farthest and nearest fires respectively; $\cot 42.5° = \frac{x}{135}$, $x = 135(1.091) = 147$;

$\cot 32.6° = \frac{y}{135}$, $y = 135(1.564) = 211$; $x + y = 147 + 211 = 358$; 358 ft

12. Let x = the height in meters of the tower; let y = the height in meters of the cliff;

$\angle ACP = 62.2°$; $\angle BCP = 59.5°$; $\tan 62.2° = \frac{x + y}{250}$, $x + y = 250(1.897) = 474.2$;

$\tan 59.5° = \frac{y}{250}$, $y = 250(1.698) = 424.4$; $x = 474.2 - 424.4 = 49.8$; 49.8 m

13.

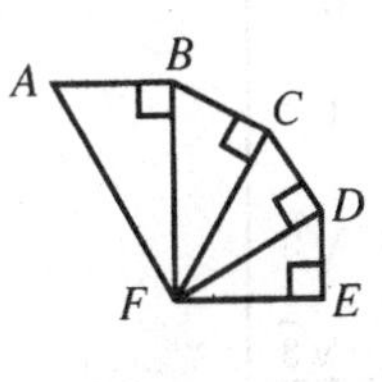

In a 30°-60°-90° $\triangle$ with longer leg y and hypotenuse h,

$\sec 30° = \frac{2\sqrt{3}}{3}$; $h = \frac{2y\sqrt{3}}{3}$; $FD = \frac{2x\sqrt{3}}{3}$; $FC = \frac{2\sqrt{3}}{3}\left(\frac{2x\sqrt{3}}{3}\right) =$

$\frac{4x}{3}$; $FB = \frac{2\sqrt{3}}{3}\left(\frac{4x}{3}\right) = \frac{8x\sqrt{3}}{9}$; $AF = \frac{2\sqrt{3}}{3}\left(\frac{8x\sqrt{3}}{9}\right) = \frac{16x}{9}$;

$\frac{16x}{9} = 2$; $FE = x = 1.13$

14.

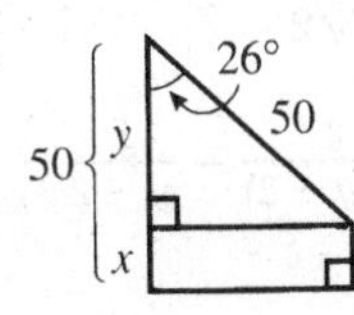

$\cos 26° = \frac{y}{50}$, $y = 50(0.8988) = 44.94$; $x = 50 - y = 5.06$;

5.06 cm

C 15.

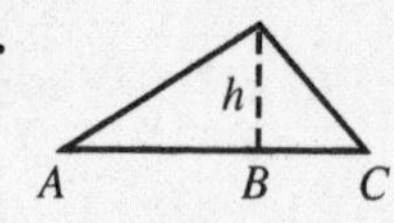

Note: Figure not drawn to scale. Let $BC = x$;

$\tan 32° = \dfrac{h}{1600 - x}$; $h = (1600 - x)(0.6249)$; $\tan 50.5° = \dfrac{h}{x}$;

$h = x(1.213)$; $(1600 - x)(0.6249) = x(1.213)$;
$999.84 - 0.6249x = 1.213x$; $1.8379x = 999.84$; $x = 554$;
$h = 544(1.213) = 660$; 660 m

16.

B, h, P, x Z 1000, Y

$\angle BZP = 34.7°$; $\angle BYP = 25.4°$; $\tan 34.7° = \dfrac{h}{x}$, $h = x(0.6924)$;

$\tan (25.4°) = \dfrac{h}{x + 1000}$, $h = 0.4748(x + 1000)$;

$h = x(0.4748) + 474.8$; $x(0.6924) = x(0.4748) + 474.8$,
$x(0.2176) = 474.8$, $x = 2180$; $h = (2182)(0.6924) = 1510$;
The balloon is 1510 ft high and 2180 ft from the field.

17.

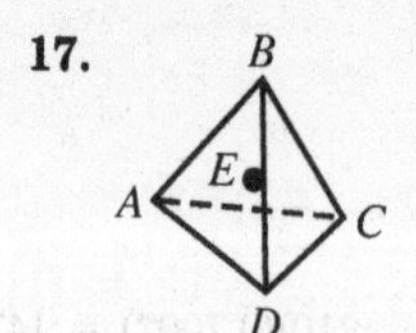

The set of all points in space equidistance from A, D, and C is a line perpendicular to the plane of $\triangle ADC$, intersecting the plane at P, the intersection of the perpendicular bisectors of the sides of $\triangle ADC$, which are also the medians of$\triangle ADC$. B and E are on that line. Draw $\triangle BPD$. Let x be the length of an edge of the tetrahedron. Since P is the point where the medians of equilateral $\triangle ADC$ intersect,

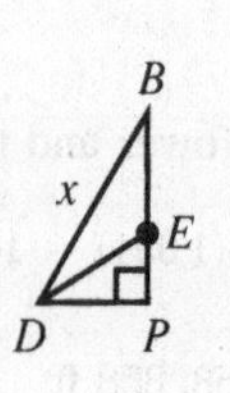

$DP = \dfrac{2}{3}$ (length of median) $= \dfrac{2}{3} \cdot \dfrac{x\sqrt{3}}{2} = \dfrac{x\sqrt{3}}{3}$; $\sin \angle DBP =$

$\dfrac{\frac{x\sqrt{3}}{3}}{x} = \dfrac{\sqrt{3}}{3} = 0.5774$; $\angle DBP = 35.3°$. Since E is the center of the tetrahedron, $DE = BE$ and $\triangle DEB$ is isosceles; $\angle DEB = 180° - 2(\angle DBP) = 180° - 70.6° = 109.4°$.

Page 579 • MIXED REVIEW EXERCISES

	θ	$\sin \theta$	$\cos \theta$	$\tan \theta$	$\csc \theta$	$\sec \theta$	$\cot \theta$
1.	450°	1	0	undef.	1	undef.	0
2.	−135°	$-\frac{\sqrt{2}}{2}$	$-\frac{\sqrt{2}}{2}$	1	$-\sqrt{2}$	$-\sqrt{2}$	1
3.	330°	$-\frac{1}{2}$	$\frac{\sqrt{3}}{2}$	$-\frac{\sqrt{3}}{3}$	−2	$\frac{2\sqrt{3}}{3}$	$-\sqrt{3}$
4.	−240°	$\frac{\sqrt{3}}{2}$	$-\frac{1}{2}$	$-\sqrt{3}$	$\frac{2\sqrt{3}}{3}$	−2	$-\frac{\sqrt{3}}{3}$

5. $\dfrac{(x^{-1} - 1)x}{(x - x^{-1})x} = \dfrac{1 - x}{x^2 - 1} = \dfrac{-(x - 1)}{(x + 1)(x - 1)} = -\dfrac{1}{x + 1}$ **6.** $5m^2\sqrt{2}$

7. $\dfrac{1(y - 2)}{(y + 2)(y - 2)} + \dfrac{4}{(y + 2)(y - 2)} = \dfrac{y - 2 + 4}{(y + 2)(y - 2)} = \dfrac{y + 2}{(y + 2)(y - 2)} = \dfrac{1}{y - 2}$

8. $(25a^6b^2)(8a^6b^3) = 200a^{12}b^5$ **9.** $x^{-2/4} = x^{-1/2} = \dfrac{1}{x^{1/2}}$

10. $2u^3 + 2u^2 - 4u - 3u^2 - 3u + 6 = 2u^3 - u^2 - 7u + 6$

Pages 582–583 • WRITTEN EXERCISES

A

1. $c^2 = 6^2 + 7^2 - 2(6)(7)\cos 20° = 36 + 49 - 84(0.9397) = 6.06$; $c = 2.46$
2. $a^2 = 12^2 + 17^2 - 2(12)(17)\cos 74° = 144 + 289 - 408(0.2756) = 321$; $a = 17.9$
3. $b^2 = 15^2 + 13^2 - 2(15)(13)\cos 83° = 225 + 169 - 390(0.1219) = 346.5$; $b = 18.6$
4. $c^2 = 3^2 + 4^2 - 2(3)(4)\cos 40° = 9 + 16 - 24(0.7660) = 6.615$; $c = 2.57$
5. $a^2 = 15^2 + 30^2 - 2(15)(30)\cos 140° = 225 + 900 - (900)(0.7660) = 1814$; $a = 42.6$
6. $b^2 = 100^2 + 200^2 - 2(100)(200)\cos 150° = 10^4 + 4 \times 10^4 - (4 \times 10^4)(-0.8660) = 8.46 \times 10^4$; $b = 2.91 \times 10^2 = 291$
7. $10^2 = 8^2 + 12^2 - 2(8)(12)\cos B$; $100 = 64 + 144 - 192 \cos B$; $-108 = -192(\cos B)$, $\cos B = \frac{-108}{-192} = 0.5625$; $\angle B = 55.8°$
8. $15^2 = 9^2 + 10^2 - 2(9)(10)(\cos C)$; $225 = 81 + 100 - 180 \cos C$, $44 = -180 \cos C$, $\cos C = -\frac{44}{180} = -0.2444$; $\angle C = 104.1°$
9. smallest angle $= \angle A$; $13^2 = 30^2 + 40^2 - 2(30)(40)\cos A$, $169 = 900 + 1600 - 2400 \cos A$, $-2331 = -2400 \cos A$, $\cos A = \frac{-2331}{-2400} = 0.9713$; $\angle A = 13.8°$
10. largest angle $= \angle C$; $40^2 = 30^2 + 20^2 - 2(30)(20)\cos C$, $1600 = 900 + 400 - 1200 \cos C$, $300 = -1200 \cos C$, $\cos C = \frac{300}{-1200} = -0.2500$; $\angle C = 104.5°$
11. largest angle $= \angle C$; $1.8^2 = 1.6^2 + 0.9^2 - 2(1.6)(0.9)\cos C$, $3.24 = 2.56 + 0.81 - 2.88 \cos C$, $-0.13 = -2.88 \cos C$, $\cos C = \frac{-0.13}{-2.88} = 0.0451$; $\angle C = 87.4°$
12. smallest angle $= \angle A$; $1.2^2 = 2.4^2 + 2.0^2 - 2(2.4)(2.0)\cos A$, $1.44 = 5.76 + 4.0 - 9.6 \cos A$, $-8.32 = -9.6 \cos A$, $\cos A = \frac{-8.32}{-9.6} = 0.8667$; $\angle A = 29.9°$

B

13. $(AC)^2 = 10.1^2 + 15.5^2 - 2(10.1)(15.5)(\cos 26°10') = 102.01 + 240.25 - (313.10)(0.8975) = 61.25$; $AC = 7.83$
14. Let the lengths of the shorter and longer diagonals be x and y respectively; $x^2 = 6^2 + 8^2 - 2(6)(8)\cos 65° = 36 + 64 - 96(0.4226) = 59.43$; $x = 7.71$; $y^2 = 6^2 + 8^2 - 2(6)(8)(\cos 115°) = 36 + 64 - 96(-0.4226) = 140.57$; $y = 11.9$; 7.71 cm and 11.9 cm
15. Let the circle with center A have radius 36 in., the circle with center B have radius 30 in., and the circle with center C have radius 25 in.; $(25 + 30)^2 = (25 + 36)^2 + (36 + 30)^2 - 2(61)(66)\cos A$; $3025 = 3721 + 4356 - 8052 \cos A$, $-5052 = -8052 \cos A$, $\cos A = 0.6274$; $\angle A = 51.1°$; $61^2 = 66^2 + 55^2 - 2(66)(55)\cos B$, $3721 = 4356 + 3025 - 7260 \cos B$, $\cos B = 0.5041$; $\angle B = 59.7°$; $\angle C = 180° - (51.1° + 59.7°) = 69.2°$; 51.1°, 59.7°, 69.2°
16. Let x and y be the lengths of the shorter and longer sides of the parallelogram respectively; $x^2 = 3^2 + 5^2 - 2(3)(5)\cos 35° = 9 + 25 - 30(0.8192) = 9.425$; $x = 3.07$; $y^2 = 3^2 + 5^2 - 2(3)(5)\cos 145° = 9 + 25 - 30(-0.8192) = 58.57$; $y = 7.65$; 3.07, 7.65
17. $d_1^2 = a^2 + b^2 - 2ab \cos \theta$; $d_2^2 = a^2 + b^2 - 2ab \cos(180° - \theta) = a^2 + b^2 + 2ab \cos \theta$; $d_1^2 + d_2^2 = a^2 + b^2 - 2ab \cos \theta + a^2 + b^2 + 2ab \cos \theta = 2a^2 + 2b^2 = 2(a^2 + b^2)$

C **18.** Let M be the midpoint of $\overline{BC}$; $\cos B = \dfrac{2^2 + 3^2 - 4^2}{2(2)(3)} = -\dfrac{3}{12} = -0.25$;
$(AM)^2 = 3^2 + 1^2 - 2(3)(1)(-0.25) = 11.5$; $AM = 3.39$

19. (1) $b^2 = 1^2 + 1^2 - 2(1)(1)\cos 2\theta = 2 - 2\cos 2\theta$; (2) $\sin\theta = \dfrac{\frac{b}{2}}{1} = \dfrac{b}{2}$; $b = 2\sin\theta$;
$b^2 = 4\sin^2\theta$; $2 - 2\cos 2\theta = 4\sin^2\theta$; $-2\cos 2\theta = -2 + 4\sin^2\theta$;
$\cos 2\theta = 1 - 2\sin^2\theta$

Pages 583–584 • PROBLEMS

A **1.** $d^2 = 15^2 + 19^2 - 2(15)(19)\cos 104° = 225 + 361 - 570(-0.2419) = 723.90$; $d = 26.9$; 26.9 km

2. $d^2 = (2 \cdot 500)^2 + (2 \cdot 300)^2 - 2(1000)(600)\cos 135° = 1 \times 10^6 + 3.6 \times 10^5 - 1.2 \times 10^6(-0.7071) = 2.21 \times 10^6$; $d = 1.49 \times 10^3$; 1490 km

3. Let $\angle A$, $\angle B$, and $\angle C$ be the angles in order of increasing size;
$80^2 = 130^2 + 150^2 - 2(130)(150)\cos A$; $6400 = 16{,}900 + 22{,}500 - 39{,}000\cos A$,
$\cos A = \dfrac{-33{,}000}{-39{,}000} = 0.8462$; $\angle A = 32.2°$; $130^2 = 150^2 + 80^2 - 2(150)(80)\cos B$;
$-12{,}000 = -24{,}000\cos B$, $\cos B = \dfrac{1}{2}$, $\angle B = 60.0°$, $\angle C = 180° - (60.0° + 32.2°) =$
$87.8°$; $32.2°$, $60.0°$, and $87.8°$

4. $d^2 = 60^2 + 65^2 - 2(60)(65)\cos 52° = 3600 + 4225 - 7800(0.6157) = 3022.8$;
$d = 55.0$; the third side is 55 m; perimeter $= 60 + 65 + 55 = 180$ m

5. $d^2 = 8^2 + 10^2 - 2(8)(10)\cos 135° = 64 + 100 - 160(-0.7071) = 277.1$; $d = 16.6$; 16.6 mi

6. $40^2 = (2 \cdot 10)^2 + (2 \cdot 25)^2 - 2(20)(50)\cos x$; $1600 = 400 + 2500 - 2000\cos x$,
$\cos x = \dfrac{-1300}{-2000} = 0.6500$; $x = 49.5$; $49.5°$

7. $d^2 = (60.5)^2 + (90)^2 - 2(60.5)(90)\cos 45° = 3660.25 + 8100 - 10{,}890(0.7071) =$
4059.9; $d = 63.7$; 63.7 ft

8. $d^2 = 2(9.58 \times 10^{-9})^2 - 2(9.58 \times 10^{-9})^2\cos 104.8° =$
$2(9.58 \times 10^{-9})^2[1 - \cos 104.8°] = (1.84 \times 10^{-16})[1 - (-0.2554)] = 2.31 \times 10^{-16}$;
$d = 1.52 \times 10^{-8}$; 1.52×10^{-8} cm

B **9.** Let x and y (in km) be the lengths of the shorter and longer sides of the park respectively; $x^2 = 6^2 + 10^2 - 2(6)(10)\cos 60° = 36 + 100 - 120\left(\dfrac{1}{2}\right) = 76$; $x = 8.7$;
$y^2 = 6^2 + 10^2 - 2(6)(10)\cos 120° = 36 + 100 - 120\left(-\dfrac{1}{2}\right) = 196$; $y = 14$;
perimeter $= 2(8.72) + 2(14) = 45.44$; perimeter $= 45.4$ km

$\sin 60° = \dfrac{AP}{6}$, $\dfrac{\sqrt{3}}{2}(6) = AP$, $AP = 3\sqrt{3}$;
area $\triangle ABD = \dfrac{1}{2}(DB)(AP) = \dfrac{1}{2}(20)(3\sqrt{3}) = 30\sqrt{3}$;
area of $ABCD = 2(30\sqrt{3}) = 60\sqrt{3} = 103.9$;
area $= 103.9$ km^2

10. $\cos(90° - \theta) = \sin\theta = \dfrac{4^2 + 6^2 - 5^2}{2(4)(6)} =$

$\dfrac{27}{48} = 0.5625;\ \theta = 34.2°$

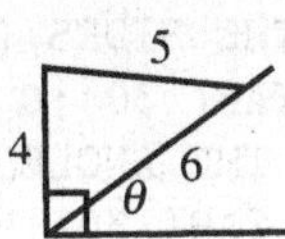

11.

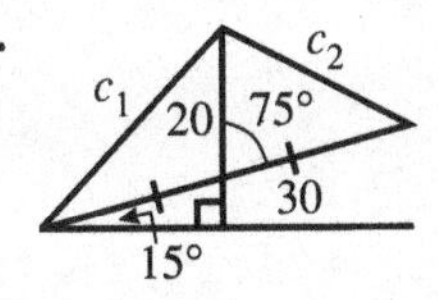

$c_1^2 = 30^2 + 20^2 - 2(30)(20)\cos 105° = 900 + 400 - 1200(-0.2588) = 1610.56;$
$c_1 = 40.1;\ c_2^2 = 30^2 + 20^2 - 2(30)(20)\cos 75° = 900 + 400 - 1200(0.2588) = 989.44;$
$c_2 = 31.5$; 40.1 m and 31.5 m

C **12.** $\cos\theta = \dfrac{50^2 + 80^2 - 90^2}{2(50)(80)} = \dfrac{800}{8000} = 0.1000;\ \theta = 84.3°$; since θ is acute, the given diagonal is the shorter one; let d = length of longer diagonal;
$d^2 = 50^2 + 80^2 - 2(50)(80)(\cos(180° - 84.3°)) = 2500 + 6400 + 8000\cos 84.3° =$
$9694.4;\ d = 98.5$; 98.5 cm

Page 584 • COMPUTER EXERCISES

1.
```
10 PRINT "ENTER THE LENGTHS A, B, C (USING 0 FOR"
20 INPUT "THE UNKNOWN LENGTH): ";A,B,C
30 IF A = 0 THEN LET A = SQR (C ↑ 2 - B ↑ 2)
40 IF B = 0 THEN LET B = SQR (C ↑ 2 - A ↑ 2)
50 IF C = 0 THEN LET C = SQR (A ↑ 2 + B ↑ 2)
60 LET AA = ATN (A / B) * 180 / 3.14159
70 LET AB = 90 - AA
80 PRINT "THE LENGTHS OF THE SIDES (A,B,C) ARE: "
90 PRINT A; TAB( 15);B; TAB( 30);C
100 PRINT "THE MEASURES OF THE ANGLES (A,B,C) ARE: "
110 PRINT AA; TAB( 15);AB; TAB( 30);"90"
120 END
```

2. a. $c = 64.4,\ \angle A = 53.8°,\ \angle B = 36.2°$

b. $b = 37,\ \angle A = 38.6°,\ \angle B = 51.4°$

c. $a = 6.86,\ \angle A = 49.2°,\ \angle B = 40.8°$

3.
```
10 PRINT "ENTER THE LENGTHS A,B,C (USING ZEROS"
20 INPUT "FOR THE UNKNOWN LENGTHS): ";A,B,C
30 PRINT "ENTER THE ANGLES A,B (USING 0 FOR"
40 INPUT "THE UNKNOWN ANGLE): ";AA,AB
50 IF AA = 0 THEN LET AA = 90 - AB
60 IF AB = 0 THEN LET AB = 90 - AA
70 IF A = 0 AND C = 0 THEN LET A = B * TAN (AA * 3.14159/180):
   LET C =  SQR (A ↑ 2 + B ↑ 2)
80 IF B = 0 AND C = 0 THEN LET B = A * TAN (AB * 3.14159/180):
   LET C =  SQR (A ↑ 2 + B ↑ 2)
```

(Continued)

```
90 IF A = 0 AND B = 0 THEN LET A = C * SIN (AA * 3.14159/180):
   LET B =  SQR (C ↑ 2 - A ↑ 2)
100 PRINT "THE LENGTHS OF THE SIDES (A,B,C) ARE: "
110 PRINT A; TAB( 15); B; TAB( 30);C
120 PRINT "THE MEASURES OF THE ANGLES (A,B,C) ARE: "
130 PRINT AA; TAB( 15);AB; TAB( 30);"90"
140 END
```

4. a. $b = 59.2$, $c = 69.8$, $\angle B = 58°$

b. $a = 65.7$, $c = 68$, $\angle A = 75°$

c. $a = 9.31$, $b = 3.35$, $\angle A = 70.2°$

5.

```
10 PRINT "ENTER THE LENGTHS A,B,C (USING 0 FOR "
20 INPUT "THE UNKNOWN LENGTH): ";A,B,C
30 PRINT "ENTER THE ANGLES A,B,C (USING 0 FOR"
40 INPUT "THE UNKNOWN ANGLE): ";AA,AB,AC
50 IF AA = 0 THEN  LET AA = 180 - AB - AC
60 IF AB = 0 THEN  LET AB = 180 - AA - AC
70 IF AC = 0 THEN  LET AC = 180 - AA - AB
80 IF A = 0 THEN  LET A =  SQR (B ↑ 2 + C ↑ 2 -
   2 * B * C * COS (AA * 3.14159 / 180))
90 IF B = 0 THEN  LET B =  SQR (A ↑ 2 + C ↑ 2 -
   2 * A * C * COS (AB * 3.14159 / 180))
100 IF C = 0 THEN  LET C =  SQR (A ↑ 2 + B ↑ 2 -
    2 * A * B * COS (AC * 3.14159 / 180))
110 PRINT "THE LENGTHS OF THE SIDES (A,B,C) ARE: "
120 PRINT A; TAB( 15);B; TAB( 30);C
130 PRINT "THE MEASURES OF THE ANGLES (A,B,C) ARE: "
140 PRINT AA; TAB( 15);AB; TAB( 30);AC
150 END
```

6. a. $b = 20.58$, $\angle C = 40°$

b. $a = 48.33$, $\angle C = 25.9°$

c. $b = 8.45$, $\angle A = 52°$

Page 585 • READING ALGEBRA

1.

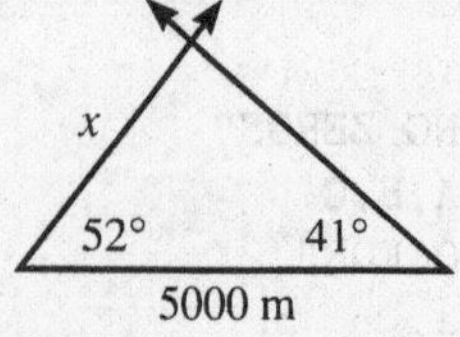

2.

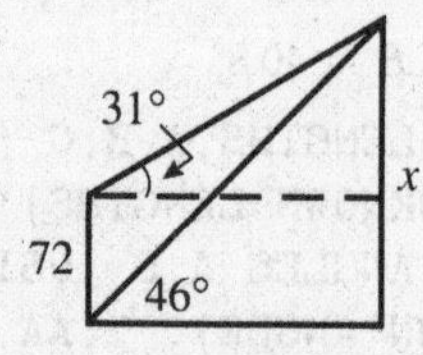

3.

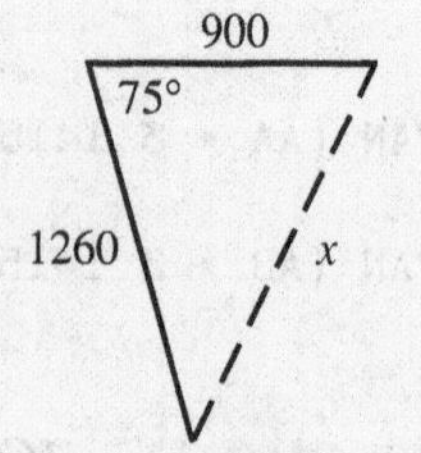

4.

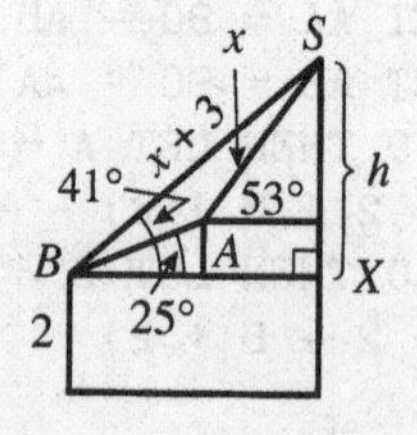

Pages 588–589 • WRITTEN EXERCISES

A

1. $\frac{\sin 25°}{14} = \frac{\sin 75°}{b}$, $b = \frac{14(\sin 75°)}{\sin 25°} = \frac{14(0.9659)}{0.4226} = 32.0$

2. $\frac{\sin 69°}{12} = \frac{\sin 42°}{a}$, $a = \frac{12(\sin 42°)}{\sin 69°} = \frac{12(0.6691)}{0.9336} = 8.60$

3. $\angle B = 180° - (110° + 50°) = 20°$; $\frac{\sin 20°}{3.40} = \frac{\sin 110°}{a}$, $a = \frac{(3.40)(\sin 110°)}{\sin 20°} =$ $\frac{(3.40)(0.9397)}{0.3420} = 9.34$

4. $\angle A = 180° - (100° + 60°) = 20°$; $\frac{\sin 20°}{2.60} = \frac{\sin 100°}{c}$, $c = \frac{2.60(\sin 100°)}{\sin 20°} = \frac{(2.60)(0.9848)}{0.3420} = 7.49$

5. $\angle B = 180° - (102° + 38°) = 40°$; $\frac{\sin 40°}{b} = \frac{\sin 102°}{35}$, $b = \frac{35(\sin 40°)}{\sin 102°} = \frac{35(0.6428)}{0.9781} = 23.0$

6. $\angle A = 180° - (95° + 35°) = 50°$; $\frac{\sin 50°}{a} = \frac{\sin 95°}{130}$, $a = \frac{130(\sin 50°)}{\sin 95°} = \frac{130(0.7660)}{0.9962} = 100$

7. $\frac{\sin 40°}{4} = \frac{\sin B}{3}$, $\sin B = \frac{3(\sin 40°)}{4} = (0.75)(0.6428) = 0.4821$; $\angle B = 28.8°$ or $151.2°$ (reject); $\angle B = 28.8°$

8. $\frac{\sin A}{4.5} = \frac{\sin 35°}{6.0}$, $\sin A = \frac{4.5(0.5736)}{6.0} = 0.4302$; $\angle A = 25.5°$ or $154.5°$ (reject); $\angle A = 25.5°$

9. $\frac{\sin A}{4.0} = \frac{\sin 125°}{6.4}$, $\sin A = \frac{(4.0)(0.8192)}{6.4} = 0.5120$; $\angle A = 30.8°$ or $149.2°$ (reject); $\angle B = 180° - (125° + 30.8°) = 24.2°$

10. $\frac{\sin 110°}{18} = \frac{\sin B}{12}$, $\sin B = \frac{12(0.9397)}{18} = 0.6265$; $\angle B = 38.8°$ or $141.2°$ (reject); $\angle C = 180° - (38.8° + 110°) = 31.2°$

11. $\frac{\sin 42°}{5} = \frac{\sin C}{7}$, $\sin C = \frac{7(0.6691)}{5} = 0.9368$; $\angle C = 69.5°$ or $110.5°$

12. $\frac{\sin B}{15} = \frac{\sin 40°}{11}$, $\sin B = \frac{15(0.6428)}{11} = 0.8765$; $\angle B = 61.2°$ or $118.8°$

13. $\sin^2 B = 1 - \left(\frac{4}{5}\right)^2 = \frac{9}{25}$, $\sin B = \frac{3}{5}$; $\frac{a}{b} = \frac{\frac{2}{3}}{\frac{3}{5}} = \frac{10}{9}$

14. $\sin^2 A = 1 - \cos^2 A = 1 - \left(\frac{3}{5}\right)^2 = \frac{16}{25}$, $\sin A = \frac{4}{5}$; $\frac{a}{b} = \frac{\frac{4}{5}}{\frac{4}{5}} = 1$

15. $\sin^2 A = 1 - \cos^2 A = 1 - \left(\frac{5}{13}\right)^2 = \frac{144}{169}$; $\sin A = \frac{12}{13}$; $\sin^2 B = 1 - \cos^2 B =$ $1 - \left(\frac{3}{5}\right)^2 = \frac{16}{25}$; $\sin B = \frac{4}{5}$; $\frac{a}{b} = \frac{\frac{12}{13}}{\frac{4}{5}} = \frac{15}{13}$

16. $\sin^2 A = 1 - \cos^2 A = 1 - \frac{64}{289} = \frac{225}{289}$; $\sin A = \frac{15}{17}$; $\sin^2 B = 1 - \cos^2 B =$

$1 - \left(\frac{15}{17}\right)^2 = 1 - \frac{225}{289} = \frac{64}{289}$; $\sin B = \frac{8}{17}$; $\frac{a}{b} = \frac{\frac{15}{17}}{\frac{8}{17}} = \frac{15}{8}$

17. $\sin^2 A = 1 - \cos^2 A = 1 - \frac{3}{4} = \frac{1}{4}$, $\sin A = \frac{1}{2}$; $\sin^2 B = 1 - \cos^2 B = 1 - \frac{1}{2} = \frac{1}{2}$;

$\sin B = \frac{\sqrt{2}}{2}$; $\frac{a}{b} = \frac{\frac{1}{2}}{\frac{\sqrt{2}}{2}} = \frac{1}{\sqrt{2}} = \frac{\sqrt{2}}{2}$

18. $\sin^2 A = 1 - \cos^2 A = 1 - \frac{1}{4} = \frac{3}{4}$; $\sin A = \frac{\sqrt{3}}{2}$; $\angle B = 45°$, $\sin B = \frac{\sqrt{2}}{2}$;

$\frac{a}{b} = \frac{\frac{\sqrt{3}}{2}}{\frac{\sqrt{2}}{2}} = \frac{\sqrt{3}}{\sqrt{2}} = \frac{\sqrt{6}}{2}$

19–20. Note: $0° < \theta < 180°$ so $\sin \theta \neq 0$; also $b \neq 0$.

B **19.** $\frac{\sin A}{a} = \frac{\sin B}{b}$; $\frac{\sin A}{\sin B} = \frac{a}{b}$; $\frac{\sin A}{\sin B} + 1 = \frac{a}{b} + 1$; $\frac{\sin A}{\sin B} + \frac{\sin B}{\sin B} = \frac{a}{b} + \frac{b}{b}$; $\frac{\sin A + \sin B}{\sin B} =$

$\frac{a + b}{b}$

20. $\frac{\sin A}{a} = \frac{\sin B}{b}$; $\frac{\sin A}{\sin B} = \frac{a}{b}$; $\frac{\sin A}{\sin B} - 1 = \frac{a}{b} - 1$; $\frac{\sin A}{\sin B} - \frac{\sin B}{\sin B} = \frac{a}{b} - \frac{b}{b}$; $\frac{\sin A - \sin B}{\sin B} =$

$\frac{a - b}{b}$

C **21.** Using the given right triangles, $\sin \theta = \frac{\frac{b}{2}}{1} = \frac{b}{2}$; $b = 2 \sin \theta$; by the law of sines,

$\frac{\sin 2\theta}{b} = \frac{\sin(90° - \theta)}{1}$; $\sin 2\theta = b \cos \theta$; $b = \frac{\sin 2\theta}{\cos \theta}$; $\frac{\sin 2\theta}{\cos \theta} = 2 \sin \theta$;

$\sin 2\theta = 2 \sin \theta \cos \theta$

22. $\frac{\sin \theta}{x} = \frac{\sin \alpha}{a}$; $\frac{\sin \theta}{\sin \alpha} = \frac{x}{a}$; $\frac{\sin \theta}{y} = \frac{\sin \beta}{b}$; since $\beta = 180 - \alpha$, $\sin \beta = \sin \alpha$;

$\frac{\sin \theta}{y} = \frac{\sin \alpha}{b}$; $\frac{\sin \theta}{\sin \alpha} = \frac{y}{b}$; $\therefore \frac{x}{a} = \frac{y}{b}$, and $\frac{x}{y} = \frac{a}{b}$.

Pages 589–590 • PROBLEMS

A **1.** The largest angle is $180° - (32° + 53°) = 95°$; let x = length of shortest side;

$\frac{\sin 32°}{x} = \frac{\sin 95°}{55}$, $x = \frac{55(\sin 32°)}{\sin 95°} = \frac{55(0.5299)}{0.9962} = 29.3$; 29.3 cm

2. The third angle is $180° - (75° + 51°) = 54°$, so the side opposite 51° is the shortest;

$\frac{\sin 75°}{25} = \frac{\sin 51°}{x}$, $x = \frac{25(0.7771)}{0.9659} = 20.1$; 20.1 in.

3. Let x = the length in cm of half the base; $\cos 23° = \frac{x}{27}$, $x = 27(0.9205) = 24.85$;
$2x = 49.7$; 49.7 cm

4. Let x = the length in inches of one of the equal sides of the pennant; $\csc\left(\frac{35}{2}\right)^\circ = \frac{x}{8}$, $x = 8 \csc 17.5^\circ = 8(3.326) = 26.6$; 26.6 in.

5. Case 1: Fire is in-between the 2 stations:

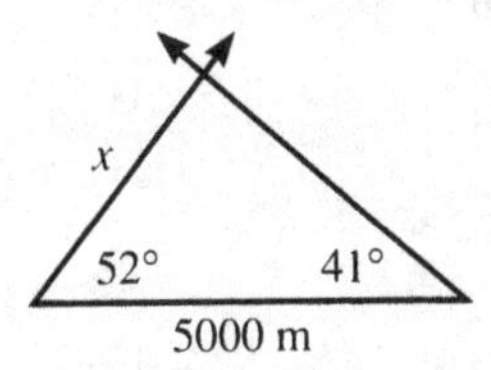

$\frac{\sin 41^\circ}{x} = \frac{\sin 87^\circ}{5000}$, $x = \frac{5000(\sin 41^\circ)}{\sin 87^\circ} = \frac{5000(0.6561)}{0.9986} = 3285$; 3280 m;

Case 2: Both stations are on the same side of the fire:

$\frac{\sin 11}{5000} = \frac{\sin 41}{a}$, $a = \frac{5000(0.6561)}{0.1908} = 17{,}193$; 17,200 m

6. $\angle PRT = 180^\circ - (72^\circ + 63^\circ) = 45^\circ$; $\frac{\sin 45^\circ}{180} = \frac{\sin 63^\circ}{RP}$, $RP = \frac{180(\sin 63^\circ)}{\sin 45^\circ} = \frac{180(0.8910)}{0.7071} =$ 227; 227 m

7. $\angle ABC = 180^\circ - (85^\circ + 66^\circ) = 29^\circ$; $\frac{\sin 29^\circ}{25} = \frac{\sin 66^\circ}{AB}$; $AB = \frac{25 \sin 66^\circ}{\sin 29^\circ} = \frac{25(0.9135)}{0.4848} =$ 47.1; 47.1 m

8. Let y = the distance in feet between the hang glider and the nearer end of the field;

$\frac{\sin 6^\circ}{5000} = \frac{\sin 24^\circ}{y}$; $y = \frac{5000(\sin 24^\circ)}{\sin 6^\circ} = \frac{5000(0.4067)}{0.1045} = 19{,}500$; 19,500 ft

B

9. Let x = height of ramp in meters and θ = new angle made with the ground;

$\sin 25^\circ = \frac{x}{5}$, $x = 5 \sin 25^\circ = 5(0.4226) = 2.11$; $\sin \theta = \frac{2.11}{15} = 0.1407$; $\theta = 8.1^\circ$ or 171.9° (reject); 8.1°

10. $\frac{\sin(90^\circ + 31^\circ)}{y} = \frac{\sin 15^\circ}{72}$,

$y = \frac{72 \sin 121^\circ}{\sin 15^\circ} = \frac{72(0.8572)}{(0.2588)} =$ 238.5; $\sin 46^\circ = \frac{x}{238.5}$, $x = (238.5)(0.7193) = 172$; 172 ft

11. $\frac{\sin 35°}{10} = \frac{\sin F}{6}$; $\sin F = \frac{6 \sin 35°}{10} = \frac{3(0.5736)}{5} = 0.3442$; $\angle F = 20.1°$ or $159.9°$; $159.9°$ is not a solution since $159.9° + 35° > 180°$; $\angle F = 20.1°$; $\angle N = 180° - (35° + 20.1°) = 124.9°$; $\frac{\sin 35°}{10} = \frac{\sin 124.9°}{n}$; $n = \frac{10 \sin 124.9°}{\sin 35°} = \frac{10(0.8202)}{0.5736} \approx 14.3$; 14.3 km

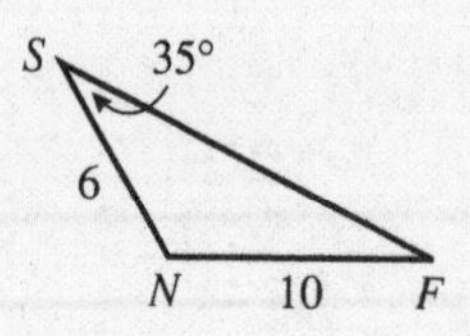

12. $\frac{\sin 143°}{30} = \frac{\sin \theta}{10}$, $\sin \theta = \frac{10 \sin 143°}{30} = \frac{10(0.6018)}{30} = 0.2006$;

$\theta = 11.6°$; $11.6° + 53° = 64.6°$; $64.6°$

10 m
143°
30 m
θ
37°
53°

C 13. Let C be the base of the tree and let h be the height of the tree;

$\angle BCA = 180° - (82° + 51°) = 47°$; $\frac{\sin 47°}{70} = \frac{\sin 51°}{AC}$, $AC = \frac{70(0.7771)}{(0.7314)} = 74.38$;

$\tan 10° = \frac{h}{74.38}$, $h = (0.1763)(74.38) = 13.1$; 13.1 m

Page 590 • MIXED REVIEW EXERCISES

1. $\cos 78.2° = 0.2045$ 2. $\tan(-43°10') = -\tan(43°10') = -0.9380$

3. $\sin 213.7° = -\sin 33.7° = -0.5548$

4. $\csc 305°45' = -\csc 54°15'$; $\left.\begin{array}{l}\csc 54°10' = 1.234\\ \csc 54°15' = x\\ \csc 54°20' = 1.231\end{array}\right\}d$; $\frac{5}{10} = \frac{d}{0.003}$; $d = 0.0015$; $x = 1.2325$; $\csc 305°45' = -1.232$

5. $\cot(-101.9°) = \cot(78.1°) = 0.2107$

6. $\sec 488°34' = \sec 128°34' = -\sec 51°26'$;

$\left.\begin{array}{l}\sec 51°20' = 1.601\\ \sec 51°26' = x\\ \sec 51°30' = 1.606\end{array}\right\}d$; $\frac{6}{10} = \frac{d}{0.005}$, $d = 0.003$; $x = 1.601 + 0.003 = 1.604$; $\sec 488°34' = -1.604$

7. $(x + 1)^2 + (y - 4)^2 = 9$

8. $m = \frac{5 - 0}{-3 - 2} = -1$; $y - 0 = -1(x - 2)$, $x + y = 2$

9. $V = (0, 0)$; opens downward; $a = 2$; $y - 0 = -\frac{1}{4(2)}(x - 0)^2$, $y = -\frac{1}{8}x^2$

Pages 594–595 • WRITTEN EXERCISES

A 1. $\angle A = 180° - (20° + 60°) = 100°$; $\frac{\sin 100°}{17} = \frac{\sin 20°}{b}$, $b = \frac{17(\sin 20°)}{\sin 100°} = \frac{17(0.3420)}{(0.9848)} = 5.90$; $\frac{\sin 100°}{17} = \frac{\sin 60°}{c}$, $c = \frac{17(\sin 60°)}{\sin 100°} = \frac{17(0.8660)}{(0.9848)} = 14.9$

2. $b^2 = 8^2 + 13^2 - 2(8)(13)\cos 150° = 64 + 169 - (208)(-0.8660) = 413.13, b = 20.3;$

$\frac{\sin A}{8} = \frac{\sin 150°}{20.3}, \sin A = \frac{8 \sin 150°}{20.3} = 0.1970; \angle A = 11.4°;$

$\angle C = 180° - (150° + 11.4°) = 18.6°$

3. $5^2 = 7^2 + 11^2 - 2(7)(11)\cos A, 25 = 49 + 121 - 154 \cos A, -145 = -154 \cos A,$

$\cos A = 0.9416; A = 19.7°; \frac{\sin 19.7°}{5} = \frac{\sin B}{7}, \sin B = \frac{7(0.3371)}{5} = 0.4719; \angle B$ is acute;

$\angle B = 28.2°; \angle C = 180° - (19.7° + 28.2°) = 132.1°$

4. $\frac{\sin 100°}{15} = \frac{\sin 25°}{c}, c = \frac{15(0.4226)}{(0.9848)} = 6.44; \angle A = 180° - (100° + 25°) = 55°;$

$\frac{\sin 100°}{15} = \frac{\sin 55°}{a}, a = \frac{15(0.8192)}{(0.9848)} = 12.5$

5. $a^2 = 10^2 + 13^2 - 2(10)(13)\cos 120° = 100 + 169 - 260(-0.5) = 399; a = 20.0;$

$\frac{\sin 120°}{20.0} = \frac{\sin B}{10}, \sin B = \frac{10(0.8660)}{20} = 0.4330; \angle B$ is acute; $\angle B = 25.7°;$

$\angle C = 180° - (120° + 25.7°) = 34.3°$

6. $30^2 = 25^2 + 10^2 - 2(25)(10)\cos C, 900 = 625 + 100 - 500 \cos C, 175 = -500 \cos C,$

$\cos C = -\frac{175}{500} = -0.3500; \angle C = 110.5°; \frac{\sin 110.5°}{30} = \frac{\sin A}{10},$

$\sin A = \frac{10(0.9367)}{30} = 0.3122; \angle A$ is acute; $\angle A = 18.2°;$

$\angle B = 180° - (110.5° + 18.2°) = 51.3°$

7. $\frac{\sin 130°}{30} = \frac{\sin \angle B}{20}, \sin \angle B = \frac{20(0.7660)}{30} = 0.5107; \angle B$ is acute; $\angle B = 30.7°;$

$\angle C = 180° - (130° + 30.7°) = 19.3°; \frac{\sin 130°}{30} = \frac{\sin 19.3°}{c}, c = \frac{30(0.3305)}{0.7660} = 12.9$

8. $\frac{\sin C}{18} = \frac{\sin 120°}{20}, \sin C = \frac{18(0.8660)}{20} = 0.7794; \angle C$ is acute; $\angle C = 51.2°;$

$\angle A = 180° - (120° + 51.2°) = 8.8°; \frac{\sin 8.8°}{a} = \frac{\sin 120°}{20}, a = \frac{20(0.1530)}{0.8660} = 3.53$

9. $\frac{\sin A}{9} = \frac{\sin 40°}{10}, \sin A = \frac{9(0.6428)}{10} = 0.5785; \angle A$ is acute; $\angle A = 35.3°;$

$\angle C = 180° - (40° + 35.3°) = 104.7°; \frac{\sin 104.7°}{c} = \frac{\sin 40°}{10}, c = \frac{10(0.9673)}{0.6428} = 15.0$

10. $\frac{\sin B}{11} = \frac{\sin 35°}{12}, \sin B = \frac{11(0.5736)}{12} = 0.5258; \angle B$ is acute; $\angle B = 31.7°;$

$\angle C = 180° - (35° + 31.7°) = 113.3°; \frac{\sin 113.3°}{c} = \frac{\sin 35°}{12}, c = \frac{12(0.9184)}{0.5736} = 19.2$

11. $\frac{\sin 50°}{14} = \frac{\sin C}{18}, \sin C = \frac{18(0.7660)}{14} = 0.9849; \angle C = 80.0°$ or $\angle C = 100°$; Case I: if

$\angle C = 80.0°, \angle A = 180° - (50° + 80°) = 50°$, and $a = b = 14$; Case II: if $\angle C = 100°,$

$\angle A = 180° - (100° + 50°) = 30°; \frac{\sin 30°}{a} = \frac{\sin 50°}{14}, a = \frac{14(0.5)}{0.7660} = 9.14$

12. $\frac{\sin 70°}{14.5} = \frac{\sin B}{15}$, $\sin B = \frac{15(0.9397)}{14.5} = 0.9721$; $\angle B = 76.4°$ or $\angle B = 103.6°$; Case I: if $\angle B = 76.4°$, $\angle A = 180° - (70° + 76.4°) = 33.6°$; $\frac{\sin 33.6°}{a} = \frac{\sin 70°}{14.5}$, $a = \frac{(14.5)(0.5534)}{0.9397} = 8.54$; Case II: if $\angle B = 103.6°$, $\angle A = 180° - (103.6° + 70°) = 6.4°$; $\frac{\sin 6.4°}{a} = \frac{\sin 70°}{14.5}$, $a = \frac{14.5(0.1115)}{0.9397} = 1.72$

B

13. Let M = the midpoint of $\overline{AB}$; $c^2 = 4^2 + 5^2 - 2(4)(5)\cos 110° = 16 + 25 - 40(-0.3420) = 54.68$; $c = 7.395$; $BM = \frac{1}{2}c = 3.698$; $\frac{\sin 110°}{7.395} = \frac{\sin B}{5}$, $\sin B = \frac{5(0.9397)}{7.395} = 0.6354$, $\angle B$ is acute; $\angle B = 39.4°$; $(CM)^2 = 4^2 + (3.698)^2 - 2(4)(3.698)\cos 39.4° = 6.82$, $CM = 2.61$

14. Let M = the midpoint of $\overline{AC}$; $\frac{\sin 40°}{AC} = \frac{\sin 100°}{10}$, $AC = \frac{10(0.6428)}{0.9848} = 6.527$; $AM = \frac{1}{2}AC = 3.264$; $(MB)^2 = (3.264)^2 + 10^2 - 2(3.264)(10)(\cos 40°) = 10.65 + 100 - 65.28(0.7660) = 60.65$; $MB = 7.79$

15. $\angle ACB = 180° - (80° + 30°) = 70°$; $\frac{\sin 70°}{10} = \frac{\sin 80°}{AC}$, $AC = \frac{10(0.9848)}{0.9397} = 10.48$; $(CD)^2 = (10.48)^2 + 8^2 - 2(10.48)(8)\cos 80° = 109.83 + 64 - (167.68)(0.1736) = 144.71$; $CD = 12.0$

16. $(AC)^2 = 5^2 + 6^2 - 2(5)(6)\cos 110° = 25 + 36 - 60(-0.3420) = 81.52$; $AC = 9.03$; $\angle 2 = 180° - (75° + 35°) = 70°$; $\frac{\sin 75°}{9.03} = \frac{\sin 70°}{CD}$, $CD = \frac{(9.03)(\sin 70°)}{\sin 75°} = \frac{(9.03)(0.9397)}{0.9659} = 8.78$

17.

Draw $\overline{BE} \parallel \overline{CD}$; $ED = BC = 2$; $AE = 3$; $\angle BEA = 60°$ and $\angle ABE = 180° - (50° + 60°) = 70°$; $\frac{\sin 60°}{BA} = \frac{\sin 70°}{3}$; $BA = \frac{3 \sin 60°}{\sin 70°} = \frac{3(0.8660)}{0.9397} = 2.76$; $(BD)^2 = (2.76)^2 + 5^2 - 2(2.76)(5)\cos 50° = 7.6176 + 25 - 27.6(0.6428) = 14.8767$; $BD = 3.86$; $\frac{\sin 50°}{BE} = \frac{\sin 70°}{3}$; $BE = \frac{3 \sin 50°}{\sin 70°} = \frac{3(0.7660)}{0.9397} = 2.45$; $CD = BE = 2.45$; $(AC)^2 = (2.45)^2 + 5^2 - 2(2.45)(5)\cos 60° = 6.0025 + 25 - 24.5(0.5) = 18.7525$; $AC = 4.33$

18. 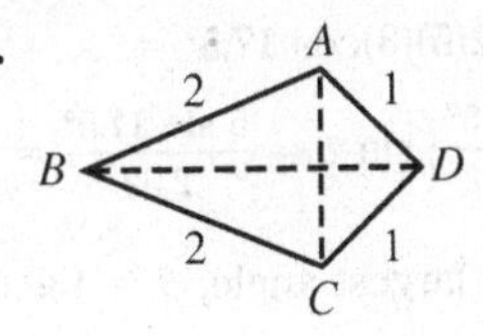

$(BD)^2 = 1^2 + 2^2 - 2(1)(2)\cos 118° = 1 + 4 - 4(-0.4695) = 6.878$; $BD = 2.62$;

$\frac{\sin \angle ABD}{1} = \frac{\sin 118°}{2.62}$; $\sin \angle ABD = \frac{0.8829}{2.62} = 0.3370$; since $\angle BAD$ is obtuse, $\angle ABD$ is acute; $\angle ABD = 19.7°$; $\angle DBC = \angle ABD$; $\angle ABC = 2 \cdot \angle ABD = 39.4°$;
$(AC)^2 = 2^2 + 2^2 - 2(2)(2)\cos 39.4° = 4 + 4 - 8(0.7727) = 1.82$; $AC = 1.35$

C **19.** Let $\angle A = 57°$, $\angle B = 60°$, and $\angle C = 63°$; the shortest side has length a, the longest has length $c = a + 5$. $\frac{\sin 57°}{a} = \frac{\sin 63°}{a + 5}$; $a \sin 63° = a \sin 57° + 5 \sin 57°$;

$a(\sin 63° - \sin 57°) = 5 \sin 57°$; $a = \frac{5 \sin 57°}{\sin 63° - \sin 57°} = \frac{5(0.8387)}{0.8910 - 0.8387} = \frac{4.1935}{0.0523} =$ 80.2; $c = a + 5 = 85.2$; $\frac{\sin 60°}{b} = \frac{\sin 57°}{80.2}$; $b = \frac{80.2 \sin 60°}{\sin 57°} = \frac{80.2(0.8660)}{0.8387} = 82.8$. (If a calculator is used and only the final result is rounded, then the answers will be $a = 80.1$, $b = 82.7$, and $c = 85.1$.)

20. 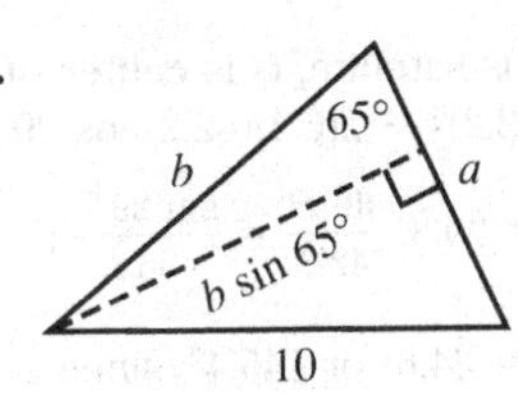

Area $= 20 = \frac{1}{2}a(b \sin 65°)$; $ab = \frac{40}{\sin 65°} = \frac{40}{0.9063} = 44.14$; $10^2 = a^2 + b^2 - 2ab \cos 65°$, $100 = a^2 + b^2 - 2(44.14)(0.4226)$, $a^2 + b^2 = 100 + 37.30 = 137.30$; $(a + b)^2 = a^2 + 2ab + b^2 = 137.30 + 2(44.14) = 225.58$; $a + b = 15.0$; $a + b + 10 = 25.0$; perimeter $= 25.0$

Pages 595–596 • PROBLEMS

A **1.** $d^2 = (3 \cdot 300)^2 + (3 \cdot 420)^2 - 2(3 \cdot 300)(3 \cdot 420)(\cos 75°) = 1{,}810{,}598$; $d = 1346$; 1350 km

2. Let d = the distance in miles of her second leg; $\frac{\sin 20°}{640} = \frac{\sin 45°}{d}$, $d = \frac{640(\sin 45°)}{\sin 20°} = \frac{640(0.7071)}{(0.3420)} = 1323$; $\frac{1323}{320} = 4.13$; 4.13 h

3. Let θ = the acute angle the shorter cable makes with the ground; let x = the distance between the cables along the ground; $\frac{\sin 48°}{270} = \frac{\sin \theta}{300}$, $\sin \theta = \frac{300(0.7431)}{270} =$ 0.8257; $\theta = 55.7°$; $180° - (48° + 55.7°) = 76.3°$; $\frac{\sin 76.3°}{x} = \frac{\sin 48°}{270}$, $x = \frac{(270)(0.9715)}{(0.7431)} =$ 353; 353 m

4. Let x = the height in ft of the mast; let y = the height in ft of the building; $\tan 34° = \frac{y}{750}$, $y = 750(0.6745) = 505.9$; $\tan 50° = \frac{x + y}{750}$, $x + y = (750)(1.192) =$ 893.8; $x = 893.8 - 505.9 = 387.9$; 388 ft

5. Let 100 km be the unit of measure; $d = 5^2 + 3^2 - 2(5)(3)\cos 17.5° =$ $25 + 9 - 30(0.9537) = 5.39$; $d = 2.32$; $\frac{\sin \theta}{5} = \frac{\sin 17.5°}{2.32}$; $\sin \theta = \frac{5 \sin 17.5°}{2.32} = \frac{5(0.3007)}{2.32} = 0.6481$; $\theta = 40.4°$ or $139.6°$; since θ is the largest angle, $\theta = 139.6°$; Jim is 232 km from Vista and should turn through an angle of $180° - \theta = 40.4°$

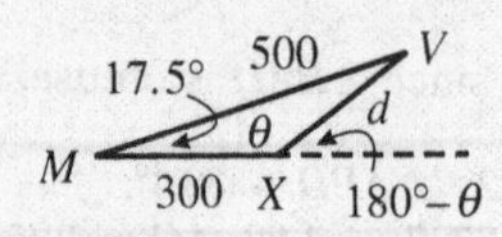

6.

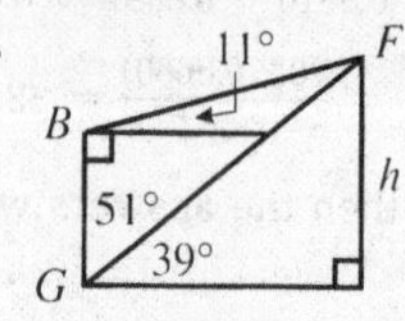

$\theta = 90° - 62° = 28°$; $\phi = 62° - \left(90° - \frac{1}{2}(140°)\right) = 42°$; $\frac{\sin 42°}{15} = \frac{\sin 28°}{d}$, $d = \frac{15(0.4695)}{0.6691} = 10.5$; 10.5 m

B **7.** $\angle FBG = 11° + 90° = 101°$; $\angle GFB = 180° - (101° + 51°) = 28°$; $\frac{\sin 28°}{10} = \frac{\sin 101°}{FG}$, $FG = \frac{10(0.9816)}{(0.4695)} = 20.9$; $\sin 39° = \frac{h}{20.9}$, $h = 20.9(0.6293) = 13.2$; 13.2 m

8. Note: Figure not drawn to scale. H is Houston, S is satellite, C is center of Earth; let 1000 km be the unit measure; $(SH)^2 = (6.4)^2 + (42.2)^2 - 2(6.4)(42.2)\cos 29.7° =$ $40.96 + 1780.84 - 540.16(0.8686) = 1352.60$; $SH = 36.8$; $\frac{\sin H}{42.2} = \frac{\sin 29.7°}{36.8}$; $\sin H = \frac{42.2 \sin 29.7°}{36.8} = \frac{42.2(0.4955)}{36.8} = 0.5682$; $\angle H = 34.6°$ or $145.4°$; since $\angle H$ is the largest angle, $\angle H = 145.4°$; $\theta = 145.4° - 90° = 55.4°$

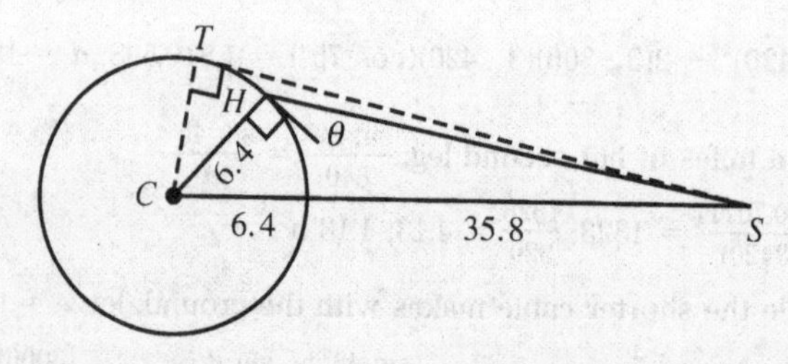

9. Draw a tangent from S intersecting the circle in the figure at T; the latitude of T is the greatest latitude from which a signal can travel in a straight line; latitude of $T = \angle TCS$; $\cos \angle TCS = \frac{6.4}{42.2} = 0.1517$; $\angle TCS = 81.3°$; 81.3°N or 81.3°S.

10. Let x_1 = air distance of the first site from top of post, x_2 = air distance of second site from top of post, d = distance between sites; $\csc 10° = \frac{x_1}{90}$, $x_1 = 90(5.759) =$ 518.3; $\csc 13° = \frac{x_2}{90}$, $x_2 = 90(4.445) = 400.1$; $d^2 = (518.3)^2 + (400.1)^2 -$ $2(518.3)(400.1)\cos 35° = 88{,}977$; $d = 298$; 298 m

C **11.** $\cos \angle ABD = \dfrac{6^2 - 3^2 - 7^2}{-(2)(3)(7)} = 0.5238$; $\angle ABD = 58.4°$; $\cos \angle CBD = \dfrac{5^2 - 4^2 - 7^2}{-(2)(4)(7)} = 0.7143$; $\angle CBD = 44.4°$; $\angle ABC = 58.4° + 44.4° = 102.8°$; $(AC)^2 = 3^2 + 4^2 - 2(3)(4)\cos 102.8° = 30.32$; $AC = 5.51$

12. Let $AS = x$; then $BS = x + 3$; $\angle SBA = 41° - 25° = 16°$; $\angle ASX = 90° - 53° = 37°$; $\angle BSX = 90° - 41° = 49°$; $\angle BSA = 49° - 37° = 12°$; $\angle BAS = 180° - (16° + 12°) = 152°$; $\dfrac{\sin 152°}{x + 3} = \dfrac{\sin 16°}{x}$, $(x + 3)(0.2756) = x(0.4695)$, $x(0.1938) = 0.8269$, $x = 4.27$; $x + 3 = 7.27$; $\sin 41° = \dfrac{h}{7.27}$, $h = 7.27(0.6561) = 4.77$; $4.77 + 2 = 6.77$; 6.77 km above sea level

13. $\angle ADB = 85°$; $\angle ACB = 71°$; $\dfrac{\sin 24°}{CB} = \dfrac{\sin 71°}{100}$, $CB = \dfrac{100 \sin 24°}{\sin 71°} = \dfrac{100(0.4067)}{0.9455} = 43.0$; $\dfrac{\sin 85°}{100} = \dfrac{\sin 55°}{DB}$, $DB = \dfrac{100 \sin 55°}{\sin 85°} = \dfrac{100(0.8192)}{0.9962} = 82.2$; $(CD)^2 = (43.0)^2 + (82.2)^2 - 2(43.0)(82.2)\cos 45°$, $(CD)^2 = 3607$; $CD = 60.1$; 60.1 in.

14. Note: Figure not drawn to scale. Consider $\triangle AXY$; $\angle XAY = 180° - (25° + 96° + 19°) = 40°$; $\dfrac{\sin 25°}{AX} = \dfrac{\sin 40°}{1}$; $AX = \dfrac{\sin 25°}{\sin 40°} = \dfrac{0.4226}{0.6428} = 0.657$.

Consider $\triangle BYX$; $\angle XBY = 180° - (25° + 113° + 19°) = 23°$; $\dfrac{\sin 19°}{BY} = \dfrac{\sin 23°}{1}$; $BY = \dfrac{0.3256}{0.3907} = 0.833$. Now consider $\triangle AXW$ and $\triangle BYZ$; $\sin 65° = \dfrac{AW}{0.657}$ and $\sin 42° = \dfrac{BZ}{0.833}$; $AW = 0.657 \sin 65° = 0.657(0.9063) = 0.595$ km; $BZ = 0.833 \sin 42° = 0.833(0.6691) = 0.557$ km. The balloon at A is 595 m high; the balloon at B is 557 m high; A is thus 38 m higher than B. Likewise, $\cos 65° = \dfrac{WX}{0.657}$ and $\cos 42° = \dfrac{YZ}{0.833}$; $WX = 0.657 \cos 65° = 0.657(0.4226) = 0.278$ km; $YZ = 0.833 \cos 42° = 0.833(0.7431) = 0.619$ km. $AC = WZ = WX + XY + YZ = 0.278 + 1 + 0.619 = 1.897$ km; $BC = 38$ m; $AB = \sqrt{1897^2 + 38^2} = \sqrt{3{,}600{,}053} = 1897$ m; the distance between the balloons is 1900 m, or 1.9 km.

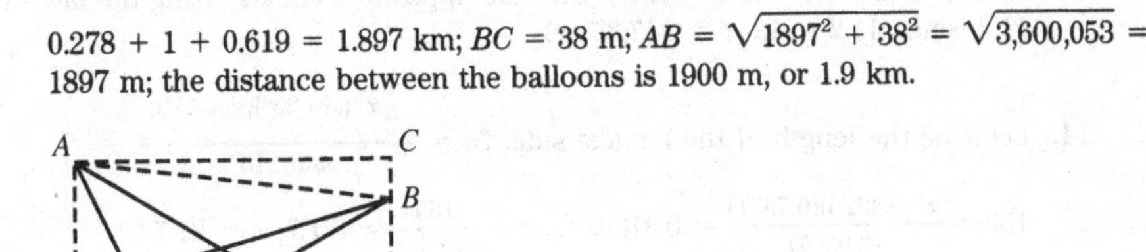

Pages 599–600 • WRITTEN EXERCISES

A **1.** $\angle C = 105°$; $K = \frac{1}{2}\left(\frac{30^2(\sin 25°)(\sin 105°)}{\sin 50°}\right) = \frac{\frac{1}{2}(900)(0.4226)(0.9659)}{0.7660} = 239.8$; 240 sq units

2. $K = \frac{1}{2}(18)(10)(\sin 45°) = 90(0.7071) = 63.64$; 63.6 sq units

3. $K = \frac{1}{2}(6)(14)\sin 62° = (42)(0.8829) = 37.1$; 37.1 sq units

4. $K = \frac{1}{2}(15)(36)\sin 70° = 270(0.9397) = 254$; 254 sq units

5. $s = \frac{1}{2}(12 + 8 + 12) = 16$; $K = \sqrt{(16)(16 - 12)(16 - 8)(16 - 12)} = \sqrt{(16)(4)(8)(4)} = 32\sqrt{2} = 45.3$; 45.3 sq units

6. $\angle A = 45°$; $K = \frac{\frac{1}{2}(16)^2(\sin 20°)(\sin 45°)}{\sin 115°} = \frac{128(0.3420)(0.7071)}{(0.9063)} = 34.2$; 34.2 sq units

7. $K = \frac{1}{2}(15)(22)(\sin 150°) = 165(0.5) = 82.5$; 82.5 sq units

8. $s = \frac{1}{2}(7 + 12 + 8) = 13.5$; $K = \sqrt{(13.5)(13.5 - 7)(13.5 - 12)(13.5 - 8)} = \sqrt{(13.5)(6.5)(1.5)(5.5)} = \sqrt{723.938} = 26.9$; 26.9 sq units

9. $K = 2\left[\frac{1}{2}(10)(18)\sin 45°\right] = 180(0.7071) = 127$

10. Each side has length $\frac{48}{4} = 12$; $K = 2\left[\frac{1}{2}(12)(12)\sin 55°\right] = 144(0.8192) = 118$

B **11.** $36 = \frac{1}{2}a(8)\sin 30° = 4a\left(\frac{1}{2}\right) = 2a$, $a = 18$

12. $20 = \frac{1}{2}(6)(c)\sin 130° = 3c(0.7660) = 2.298c$, $c = \frac{20}{2.298} = 8.70$

13. Let θ be the largest angle; $48 = \frac{1}{2}(9)(12)\sin\theta = 54\sin\theta$, $\sin\theta = \frac{48}{54} = 0.8889$; $\theta = 62.7°$ or $117.3°$; if $\theta = 62.7°$, the side opposite θ equals, using the law of cosines, 11.2; since $11.2 < 12$, $\theta = 117.3°$ only.

14. Let x be the length of the longest side; $75 = \frac{\frac{1}{2}x^2(\sin 25°)(\sin 45°)}{\sin 110°}$, $150 = \frac{x^2(0.4226)(0.7071)}{(0.9397)} = 0.3180x^2$, $x^2 = \frac{150}{0.3180} = 471.7$; $x = 21.7$

15. (figure: regular octagon with side 10, central angle θ, base angles α, α)

$\theta = \frac{360}{8} = 45°$; $\alpha = \frac{1}{2}(180° - 45°) = 67.5°$;

$K = 8\left(\frac{1}{2}\right)(10)^2 \frac{(\sin 67.5°)^2}{\sin 45°} = 400\frac{(0.9239)^2}{(0.7071)} = 483$; 483 cm^2

16. (figure: regular octagon inscribed in a circle, triangle with sides 1, 1 and central angle θ)

$\theta = \frac{360°}{8} = 45°$; $K = 8\left[\frac{1}{2}(1)^2 \sin 45°\right] = 4(0.7071) = 2.83$; 2.83 cm^2

17. $K^2 = \left(\frac{1}{2}ab \sin C\right)^2 = \frac{1}{4}a^2b^2\sin^2 C$

18. $2(s - b) = 2s - 2b = a + b + c - 2b = a - b + c$; $2(s - c) = 2s - 2c = a + b + c - 2c = a + b - c$

C **19.** **a.** Law of cosines **b.** square both sides of **a**; substitute $\cos^2 C = 1 - \sin^2 C$

c. distributive law; exercise 17 **d.** Addition property of equality

e. factoring the difference of two squares

f. associative property of addition; $(a + b)^2 = a^2 + 2ab + b^2$; $-(a - b)^2 = -a^2 + 2ab - c^2$

g. factoring the difference of two squares **h.** exercise 18

i. Division property of equality; property of square roots

Page 600 • MIXED REVIEW EXERCISES

1. $c^2 = 8^2 + 5^2 - 2(8)(5)\cos 62° = 64 + 25 - 80(0.4695) = 51.44$; $c = 7.17$

2. $\frac{\sin 100°}{a} = \frac{\sin 30°}{15}$, $a = \frac{15 \sin 100°}{\sin 30°} = \frac{15(0.9848)}{0.5} = 29.5$

3. $9^2 = 6^2 + 4^2 - 2(6)(4)\cos C$, $\cos C = \frac{9^2 - 6^2 - 4^2}{-2(6)(4)} = \frac{29}{-48} = -0.6042$; $\angle C = 127.2°$

4. $\angle A = 180° - (76° + 48°) = 56°$; $\frac{\sin 56°}{20} = \frac{\sin 76°}{b}$, $b = \frac{20(\sin 76°)}{\sin 56°} = \frac{20(0.9703)}{(0.8290)} = 23.4$

5. $\alpha = 30°$; $\theta = 180° - 30° = 150°$; $\cos \theta = -\cos 30° = -\frac{\sqrt{3}}{2}$; $\tan \theta = -\tan 30° = -\frac{\sqrt{3}}{3}$; $\csc \theta = \frac{1}{\sin \theta} = 2$, $\sec \theta = \frac{1}{\cos \theta} = -\frac{2\sqrt{3}}{3}$, $\cot \theta = \frac{1}{\tan \theta} = -\sqrt{3}$

6. $\sin \theta = -\sqrt{1 - \cos^2 \theta} = -\sqrt{1 - \left(-\frac{3}{4}\right)^2} = -\frac{\sqrt{7}}{4}$; $\tan \theta = \frac{\sin \theta}{\cos \theta} = \frac{-\frac{\sqrt{7}}{4}}{-\frac{3}{4}} = \frac{\sqrt{7}}{3}$;

$\csc \theta = \frac{1}{\sin \theta} = -\frac{4}{\sqrt{7}} = -\frac{4\sqrt{7}}{7}$; $\sec \theta = \frac{1}{\cos \theta} = -\frac{4}{3}$; $\cot \theta = \frac{1}{\tan \theta} = \frac{3}{\sqrt{7}} = \frac{3\sqrt{7}}{7}$

7. $\alpha = 45°$, $\theta = 360° - 45° = 315°$; $\sin \theta = -\sin 45° = -\frac{\sqrt{2}}{2}$; $\cos \theta = \cos 45° = \frac{\sqrt{2}}{2}$;

$\csc \theta = \frac{1}{\sin \theta} = -\sqrt{2}$; $\sec \theta = \frac{1}{\cos \theta} = \sqrt{2}$; $\cot \theta = \frac{1}{\tan \theta} = -1$

8. $\cos\theta = \sqrt{1-\sin^2\theta} = \sqrt{1-\left(\frac{5}{13}\right)^2} = \frac{12}{13}$; $\tan\theta = \frac{\sin\theta}{\cos\theta} = \frac{\frac{5}{13}}{\frac{12}{13}} = \frac{5}{12}$;

$\csc\theta = \frac{1}{\sin\theta} = \frac{13}{5}$; $\sec\theta = \frac{1}{\cos\theta} = \frac{13}{12}$; $\cot\theta = \frac{1}{\tan\theta} = \frac{12}{5}$

Page 601 • CHALLENGE

The visitor could ask "In which direction do you live?". The local person would point to the truth-telling village.

Pages 602–604 • CHAPTER REVIEW

1. b **2.** c; $45^\circ + \left(\frac{14}{60}\right)^\circ + \left(\frac{42}{3600}\right)^\circ = 45^\circ + 0.2\overline{3}^\circ + 0.011\overline{6}^\circ = 45.245^\circ$

3. b; $(\sin\theta\csc\theta)(\cos\theta\sec\theta)(\tan\theta\cot\theta) = 1\cdot 1\cdot 1 = 1$

4. b; $\cos 60^\circ = \frac{c}{10}$, $c = 10\left(\frac{1}{2}\right) = 5$

5. b; the short leg of the 30°-60°-90° triangle is $\frac{12}{2} = 6$; x = the hypotenuse of the 45°-45°-90° triangle $= 6\sqrt{2}$

6. c; $230^\circ - 180^\circ = 50^\circ$; $\cos 230^\circ = -\cos 50^\circ$

7. a; $\sin\theta = \sqrt{1-\left(\frac{8}{17}\right)^2} = \frac{15}{17}$; $\tan\theta = \frac{\frac{15}{17}}{\frac{8}{17}} = \frac{15}{8}$

8. c; $\sin 300^\circ = -\sin 60^\circ = -\frac{\sqrt{3}}{2}$ **9.** d **10.** b; $\alpha = 54^\circ 50'$; $\theta = 180^\circ - \alpha = 125^\circ 10'$

11. a; $\cos F = \frac{8}{10} = 0.8000$; $\angle F = 36.9^\circ$ **12.** a; $\csc 55^\circ = \frac{b}{12}$, $b = 12(1.221) = 14.6$

13. a; $x = \frac{1}{2}(25 - 15) = 5$; $h = x = 5$

14. b; $\cos B = \frac{b^2 - a^2 - c^2}{-2ac} = \frac{10^2 - 6^2 - 7^2}{-2(6)(7)} = -\frac{15}{84} = -0.1786$; $\angle B = 100.3^\circ$

15. c; $d^2 = (2\cdot 300)^2 + (2\cdot 450)^2 - 2(2\cdot 300)(2\cdot 450)\cos 135^\circ = 1{,}933{,}675$; $d = 1390$

16. c; $\frac{\sin A}{8} = \frac{\sin 95^\circ}{15.4}$; $\sin A = \frac{8\sin 95^\circ}{15.4} = \frac{8(0.9962)}{15.4} = .5175$; $\angle A = 31.2^\circ$

17. a; $\frac{\sin 138^\circ}{30} = \frac{\sin\theta}{20}$, $\sin\theta = \frac{20\sin 138^\circ}{30} = \frac{20(0.6691)}{30} = 0.4461$,

$\theta = 26.5^\circ$; $\phi = 180^\circ - (138^\circ + 26.5^\circ) = 15.5^\circ$

18. b; there will be two solutions if $c\sin B < b < c$; $20\sin 30^\circ < b < 20$, $10 < b < 20$

19. d; Let y = the length of the diagonal; $\frac{\sin 100°}{y} = \frac{\sin 30°}{8}$, $y = \frac{8(0.9848)}{0.5} = 15.77$;

$x^2 = (15.77)^2 + 9^2 - 2(15.77)(9)(\cos 110°) = 426.79$; $x = 20.7$

20. d; $K = \frac{1}{2}(8)(15)\sin 40° = (60)(0.6428) = 38.6$

Page 604 • CHAPTER TEST

1. $13.24° = 13° + (0.24)(60') = 13° + 14.4' = 13° + 14' + (0.4)(60)'' = 13°14'24''$

2. Answers may vary. $285° + 360° = 645°$; $285° - 360° = -75°$; $645°, -75°$

3. Let y = the length of the diagonal; let z = the length of the side opposite the 30° angle; $y = 12\sqrt{2}$; $z = \frac{y}{2} = 6\sqrt{2}$; $x = z\sqrt{3} = 6\sqrt{6}$

4. $\sin\theta = -\sqrt{1 - \cos^2\theta} = -\sqrt{1 - \left(-\frac{3}{4}\right)^2} = -\frac{\sqrt{7}}{4}$; $\tan\theta = \frac{\sin\theta}{\cos\theta} = \frac{-\frac{\sqrt{7}}{4}}{-\frac{3}{4}} = \frac{\sqrt{7}}{3}$

5. $\alpha = 240° - 180° = 60°$; $\sin 240° = -\sin 60° = -\frac{\sqrt{3}}{2}$; $\cos 240° = -\cos 60° = -\frac{1}{2}$;

$\tan 240° = \tan 60° = \sqrt{3}$; $\csc 240° = -\csc 60° = -\frac{2\sqrt{3}}{3}$;

$\sec 240° = -\sec 60° = -2$; $\cot 240° = \cot 60° = \frac{\sqrt{3}}{3}$

6. **a.** $\sec 145.8° = -\sec 34.2° = -1.209$

b. $\alpha = 55.9°$; θ is in quadrant IV; $\theta = 360° - 55.9° = 304.1°$

7. $\tan 55.6° = \frac{h}{150}$, $h = 150(1.460) = 219$; 219 ft

8. $5^2 = 3^2 + 3^2 - 2(3)(3)\cos\theta$, $\cos\theta = \frac{5^2 - 2(3^2)}{-2 \cdot 3^2} = -\frac{7}{18} = -0.3889$; $\theta = 112.9°$

9. $\angle F = 180° - (32° + 108°) = 40°$; $\frac{\sin 40°}{12} = \frac{\sin 108°}{e}$, $e = \frac{12(0.9511)}{0.6428} = 17.8$;

$\frac{\sin 40°}{12} = \frac{\sin 32°}{d}$, $d = \frac{12(0.5299)}{0.6428} = 9.89$

10. $\frac{\sin 40°}{6} = \frac{\sin B}{8}$, $\sin B = \frac{8(0.6428)}{6} = 0.8571$; $\angle B = 59.0°$ or $\angle B = 121.0°$;

Case I: if $\angle B = 59.0°$, then $\angle C = 180° - (59.0° + 40°) = 81°$; $\frac{\sin 81°}{c} = \frac{\sin 40°}{6}$,

$c = \frac{6(0.9877)}{0.6428} = 9.22$; Case II: if $\angle B = 121°$, then $\angle C = 180° - (121° + 40°) = 19°$;

$\frac{\sin 19°}{c} = \frac{\sin 40°}{6}$, $c = \frac{6(0.3256)}{0.6428} = 3.04$

11. $s = \frac{1}{2}(200 + 150 + 100) = 225$; $K = \sqrt{(225)(225 - 200)(225 - 150)(225 - 100)} =$

$\sqrt{(225)(25)(75)(125)} = (15)(5)(5\sqrt{3})(5\sqrt{5}) = 1875\sqrt{15} = 7261.8$; 7260 m^2

Page 605 • PREPARING FOR COLLEGE ENTRANCE EXAMS

1. C; $21 + 10 = 31$ **2.** C; $S_6 = \dfrac{\frac{1}{2}\left(1 - \left(\frac{1}{2}\right)^6\right)}{1 - \frac{1}{2}} = 1 - \dfrac{1}{64} = \dfrac{63}{64}$; $64S_6 = 63$

3. C; the series is geometric with $r = -\dfrac{5}{4}$; $|r| > 1$ **4.** C

5. A; $\csc^2 \theta = 1 + \cot^2 \theta$, θ is in quadrant II; $\cot \theta = -\sqrt{\csc^2 \theta - 1} = -\sqrt{3^2 - 1} = -\sqrt{8} = -2\sqrt{2}$

6. B; $\dfrac{\sin 45°}{x} = \dfrac{\sin 30°}{8}$, $x = \dfrac{8\left(\frac{\sqrt{2}}{2}\right)}{\frac{1}{2}} = 8\sqrt{2}$

7. D; $s = \dfrac{1}{2}(5 + 6 + 7) = 9$, $K = \sqrt{9(9 - 5)(9 - 6)(9 - 7)} = \sqrt{9(4)(3)(2)} = 6\sqrt{6}$

8. E; $r^2 = (15)^2 + (12)^2 - 2(15)(12)\cos 137.4° = 225 + 144 - 360(-0.7361) = 634.00$; $r = 25$

CHAPTER 13 • Trigonometric Graphs and Identities

Pages 610–611 • WRITTEN EXERCISES

A **1.** $45 \cdot \frac{\pi}{180} = \frac{\pi}{4}$ **2.** $30 \cdot \frac{\pi}{180} = \frac{\pi}{6}$ **3.** $60 \cdot \frac{\pi}{180} = \frac{\pi}{3}$ **4.** $270 \cdot \frac{\pi}{180} = \frac{3\pi}{2}$

5. $-120 \cdot \frac{\pi}{180} = -\frac{2\pi}{3}$ **6.** $135 \cdot \frac{\pi}{180} = \frac{3\pi}{4}$ **7.** $150 \cdot \frac{\pi}{180} = \frac{5\pi}{6}$ **8.** $-180 \cdot \frac{\pi}{180} = -\pi$

9. $-330 \cdot \frac{\pi}{180} = -\frac{11\pi}{6}$ **10.** $240 \cdot \frac{\pi}{180} = \frac{4\pi}{3}$ **11.** $-315 \cdot \frac{\pi}{180} = -\frac{7\pi}{4}$

12. $495 \cdot \frac{\pi}{180} = \frac{11\pi}{4}$ **13.** $\frac{\pi}{6} \cdot \frac{180°}{\pi} = 30°$ **14.** $-\frac{\pi}{4} \cdot \frac{180°}{\pi} = -45°$ **15.** $\frac{\pi}{3} \cdot \frac{180°}{\pi} = 60°$

16. $-\frac{\pi}{2} \cdot \frac{180°}{\pi} = -90°$ **17.** $\frac{4\pi}{3} \cdot \frac{180°}{\pi} = 240°$ **18.** $\frac{5\pi}{6} \cdot \frac{180°}{\pi} = 150°$

19. $-\frac{7\pi}{6} \cdot \frac{180°}{\pi} = -210°$ **20.** $\frac{3\pi}{4} \cdot \frac{180°}{\pi} = 135°$

21. $3\pi \cdot \frac{180°}{\pi} = 540°$ **22.** $-\frac{7\pi}{4} \cdot \frac{180°}{\pi} = -315°$ **23.** $-\frac{7\pi}{2} \cdot \frac{180°}{\pi} = -630°$

24. $\frac{9\pi}{4} \cdot \frac{180°}{\pi} = 405°$ **25.** $4 \cdot \frac{180°}{\pi} = \frac{720°}{\pi}$ **26.** $3 \cdot \frac{180°}{\pi} = \frac{540°}{\pi}$ **27.** $-2 \cdot \frac{180°}{\pi} = -\frac{360°}{\pi}$

28. $-\frac{1}{2} \cdot \frac{180°}{\pi} = -\frac{90°}{\pi}$ **29.** $10 \cdot \frac{\pi}{180} = \frac{\pi}{18} \approx \frac{3.1416}{18} \approx 0.17$

30. $-50 \cdot \frac{\pi}{180} = -\frac{5\pi}{18} \approx -\frac{5(3.1416)}{18} \approx -0.87$ **31.** $80 \cdot \frac{\pi}{180} = \frac{4\pi}{9} \approx \frac{4(3.1416)}{9} \approx 1.40$

32. $300 \cdot \frac{\pi}{180} = \frac{5\pi}{3} \approx \frac{5(3.1416)}{3} \approx 5.24$ **33.** $48 \cdot \frac{\pi}{180} = \frac{4\pi}{15} \approx \frac{4(3.1416)}{15} \approx 0.84$

34. $265 \cdot \frac{\pi}{180} = \frac{53\pi}{36} \approx \frac{53(3.1416)}{36} \approx 4.63$

35. $-174 \cdot \frac{\pi}{180} = -\frac{29\pi}{30} \approx -\frac{29(3.1416)}{30} \approx -3.04$ **36.** $255 \cdot \frac{\pi}{180} = \frac{17\pi}{12} \approx \frac{17(3.1416)}{12} \approx 4.45$

37. $3 \cdot \frac{180°}{\pi} = \frac{540°}{\pi} \approx \frac{540°}{3.1416} \approx 171.9°$ **38.** $-2.5 \cdot \frac{180°}{\pi} = -\frac{450°}{\pi} \approx -\frac{450°}{3.1416} \approx -143.2°$

39. $0.4 \cdot \frac{180°}{\pi} = \frac{72°}{\pi} \approx \frac{72°}{3.1416} \approx 22.9°$ **40.** $-1.6 \cdot \frac{180°}{\pi} = -\frac{288°}{\pi} \approx -\frac{288°}{3.1416} \approx -91.7°$

41. $-1.5 \cdot \frac{180°}{\pi} = -\frac{270°}{\pi} \approx -\frac{270°}{3.1416} \approx -85.9°$ **42.** $5.5 \cdot \frac{180°}{\pi} = \frac{990°}{\pi} \approx \frac{990°}{3.1416} \approx 315.1°$

43. $15 \cdot \frac{180°}{\pi} = \frac{2700°}{\pi} \approx \frac{2700°}{3.1416} \approx 859.4°$ **44.** $8 \cdot \frac{180°}{\pi} = \frac{1440°}{\pi} \approx \frac{1440°}{3.1416} \approx 458.4°$

45. $s = r\theta = 4 \cdot 1 = 4; A = \frac{1}{2}(4^2)(1) = 8$

46. $s = (5)(2.5) = 12.5; A = \frac{1}{2}(5^2)(2.5) = 31.25$ **47.** $\theta = \frac{s}{r} = \frac{12}{4} = 3; A = \frac{1}{2}(4^2)(3) = 24$

48. $\theta = \frac{s}{r} = \frac{30}{5} = 6; A = \frac{1}{2}(5^2)(6) = 75$

B **49.** $15 = \frac{1}{2}(5^2)\theta$, $\theta = \frac{30}{25} = \frac{6}{5} = 1.2$; $s = (5)\left(\frac{6}{5}\right) = 6$

50. $6 = \frac{1}{2}(2^2)\theta$, $\theta = \frac{6}{2} = 3$; $s = 2(3) = 6$ **51.** $r = \frac{s}{\theta} = \frac{10}{2.5} = 4$; $A = \frac{1}{2}(4^2)(2.5) = 20$

52. $r = \frac{s}{\theta} = \frac{1.2}{0.5} = 2.4$; $A = \frac{1}{2}(2.4^2)(0.5) = 1.44$ **53.** $3 = \frac{1}{2}(2)s$, $s = 3$, $\theta = \frac{s}{r} = \frac{3}{2}$

54. $6 = \frac{1}{2}(8)s$, $s = \frac{6}{4} = \frac{3}{2} = 1.5$; $\theta = \frac{s}{r} = \frac{\frac{3}{2}}{8} = \frac{3}{16} = 0.1875$

55. $8 = \frac{1}{2}r^2(4)$, $r^2 = \frac{8}{2} = 4$, $r = 2$; $s = (2)(4) = 8$

56. $6 = \frac{1}{2}r^2(3)$, $r^2 = 4$, $r = 2$; $s = (2)(3) = 6$ **57.** $8.12 - 2\pi \approx 8.12 - 6.28 = 1.84$

58. $6.55 - 2\pi \approx 6.55 - 6.28 = 0.27$ **59.** $-3 + 2\pi \approx -3 + 6.28 = 3.28$

60. $-20 + 8\pi \approx -20 + 25.13 = 5.13$

Pages 611–612 • PROBLEMS

A **1.** $\theta = 29.8 \cdot \frac{\pi}{180} \approx 0.52$; $s = 4000(0.52) = 2080$; 2100 mi

2. $\theta = 90° - 40.7° = 49.3°$; $49.3 \cdot \frac{\pi}{180} = 0.86$; $s = (0.86)(4000) = 3442$; 3400 mi

3. $\omega = 45 \cdot 2\pi = 90\pi$ rad/min; $r = \frac{12}{2} = 6$ in; $v = \omega r = 90\pi(6) = 540\pi$ in./min; $540\pi \approx 1700$; 1700 in.

4. $\omega = 10 \cdot 2\pi = 20\pi$ rad/sec $= 1200\pi$ rad/min; $r = \frac{2}{2} = 1$ ft; $v = \omega r = (1200\pi)(1) = 1200\pi$ ft/min; $1200\pi \approx 3800$; 3800 ft

5. $\omega = \frac{1}{2} \cdot 2\pi = \pi$ rad/min; $r = \frac{50}{2} = 25$ ft, $v = \omega r = \pi(25) = 25\pi$ ft/min; $25\pi \approx 79$; 79 ft/min

6. $\omega = 4 \cdot 2\pi = 8\pi$ rad/min; $r = \frac{40}{2} = 20$ ft; $v = \omega r = (8\pi)(20) = 160\pi$ ft/min ≈ 500 ft/min

7. $s = r\theta = (1.5 \times 10^8)(9.3 \times 10^{-3}) = 13.95 \times 10^5 \approx 1.4 \times 10^6$; 1.4×10^6 km

8. $\theta = 0.518 \times \frac{\pi}{180} = 0.0090$; $r = \frac{s}{\theta} = \frac{2200}{0.0090} = 243{,}341$; 240,000 mi

B **9.** rim speed of smaller wheel = rim speed of larger wheel $= \omega r = 50 \cdot 2\pi \cdot 15 = 1500\pi$ cm/min ≈ 4700 cm/min; angular speed of smaller wheel $= \frac{v}{r} = \frac{1500\pi}{6} = 250\pi$ radians/min

10. $\theta = 24° = 24 \cdot \frac{\pi}{180} \approx 0.42$; distance traveled in one roundtrip $= 2s = 2r\theta \approx 2(1)(0.42) = 0.84$ m; number of trips in one day $= \frac{24 \cdot 60 \cdot 60}{2} = 43{,}200$; total distance traveled in one day $= 43{,}200(0.84) = 36{,}288$ m ≈ 36 km

11. $\omega = \dfrac{\dfrac{2\pi}{12}\text{ rad/h}}{3600\text{ s/h}} = \dfrac{2\pi}{12 \cdot 3600}\text{ rad/s} = 0.000145\text{ rad/s}; 0.00015\text{ rad/s};$
$v = (50)(0.000145) = 0.00725; 0.0073\text{ mm/s}$

12. $\omega = 1\text{ rev/day} = \dfrac{1}{24 \cdot 60 \cdot 60} \cdot 2\pi\text{ rad/s} \approx 7.3 \times 10^{-5}\text{rad/s}$

C **13.** $\overline{OA}$, $\overline{OB}$ and $\overline{OC}$ are radii, each with length 2;
$\angle ODC = 90°$; $OD = OB - DB = 2 - 1 = 1$.
Therefore $\angle DOC = 60° = \angle DOA$ and $DC = \sqrt{3} = DA$;
area of $\triangle AOC = \frac{1}{2} \cdot 2\sqrt{3} \cdot 1 = \sqrt{3}$; area of the sector determined by $\angle AOC = \pi \cdot 2^2 \cdot \frac{120}{360} = \frac{4\pi}{3}$.

Area of the shaded region $= \frac{4\pi}{3} - \sqrt{3} = \frac{4\pi - 3\sqrt{3}}{3}$; volume of water $= \frac{4\pi - 3\sqrt{3}}{3}h$, where h is the height of the cylinder. Area of circle $O = 4\pi$; capacity volume $=$ $4\pi h$. Ratio of water to capacity $= \dfrac{\dfrac{4\pi h - 3\sqrt{3}h}{3}}{4\pi h} = \dfrac{1}{3} - \dfrac{\sqrt{3}}{4\pi} \approx$
$0.333 - \dfrac{1.73}{4 \cdot 3.14} = 0.333 - 0.138 = 0.195$; about 20%

Page 612 • MIXED REVIEW EXERCISES

1. $c^2 = 8^2 + 5^2 - 2(8)(5)\cos 42° = 64 + 25 - 80(0.7431) = 29.55$; $c = 5.44$;
$\dfrac{\sin B}{5} = \dfrac{\sin 42°}{5.44}$, $\sin B = \dfrac{(0.6691)(5)}{5.44} = 0.6150$; $\angle B = 38.0°$
$\angle A = 180° - (42° + 38.0°) = 100.0°$

2. $\dfrac{\sin 75°}{a} = \dfrac{\sin 30°}{12}$, $a = \dfrac{12(0.9659)}{0.5} = 23.2$; $\angle C = 180° - (75° + 30°) = 75°$; $c = a = 23.2$

3. $\dfrac{\sin C}{7} = \dfrac{\sin 104°}{10}$, $\sin C = \dfrac{7(0.9703)}{10} = 0.6792$; $\angle C$ is acute; $\angle C = 42.8°$;
$\angle A = 180° - (104° + 42.8°) = 33.2°$; $a^2 = 10^2 + 7^2 - 2(10)(7)\cos 33.2° =$
$100 + 49 - 140(0.8368) = 31.85$; $a = 5.64$

4. $9^2 = 5^2 + 6^2 - 2(5)(6)\cos C$, $\cos C = \dfrac{81 - 25 - 36}{-60} = -0.3333$; $\angle C = 109.5°$;
$\cos A = \dfrac{5^2 - 6^2 - 9^2}{-2(6)(9)} = 0.8519$; $\angle A = 31.6°$; $\angle B = 180° - (109.5° + 31.6°) = 38.9°$

5. $K = \frac{1}{2}(8)(5)\sin 42° = 20(0.6691) = 13.4$

6. $\angle C = 75°$; $K = \left(\dfrac{1}{2}\right)\dfrac{(12)^2(\sin 75°)(\sin 75°)}{\sin 30°} = \left(\dfrac{1}{2}\right)\dfrac{(144)(0.9659)^2}{0.5} = 134$

7. $\angle A = 33.2°$; $K = \frac{1}{2}(10)(7)\sin 33.2° = 35(0.5476) = 19.2$

8. $s = \frac{1}{2}(5 + 6 + 9) = 10$; $K = \sqrt{10(10 - 5)(10 - 6)(10 - 9)} = \sqrt{10(5)(4)(1)} = \sqrt{200} = 10\sqrt{2} = 14.1$

Page 617 • WRITTEN EXERCISES

A

1. $\sin s = -\frac{4}{5}$; $\cos s = \frac{3}{5}$; $\tan s = \frac{-\frac{4}{5}}{\frac{3}{5}} = -\frac{4}{3}$; $\csc s = -\frac{5}{4}$; $\sec s = \frac{5}{3}$; $\cot s = -\frac{3}{4}$

2. $\sin s = \frac{12}{13}$; $\cos s = -\frac{5}{13}$; $\tan s = \frac{\frac{12}{13}}{-\frac{5}{13}} = -\frac{12}{5}$; $\csc s = \frac{13}{12}$; $\sec s = -\frac{13}{5}$; $\cot s = -\frac{5}{12}$

3. $\sin s = \frac{3}{4}$; $\cos s = \frac{\sqrt{7}}{4}$; $\tan s = \frac{\frac{3}{4}}{\frac{\sqrt{7}}{4}} = \frac{3}{\sqrt{7}} = \frac{3\sqrt{7}}{7}$; $\csc s = \frac{4}{3}$; $\sec s = \frac{4}{\sqrt{7}} = \frac{4\sqrt{7}}{7}$; $\cot s = \frac{\sqrt{7}}{3}$

4. $\sin s = -\frac{\sqrt{21}}{5}$; $\cos s = -\frac{2}{5}$; $\tan s = \frac{-\frac{\sqrt{21}}{5}}{-\frac{2}{5}} = \frac{\sqrt{21}}{2}$; $\csc s = -\frac{5}{\sqrt{21}} = -\frac{5\sqrt{21}}{21}$; $\sec s = -\frac{5}{2}$; $\cot s = \frac{2}{\sqrt{21}} = \frac{2\sqrt{21}}{21}$

5. $\sin 1.25 = 0.9490$; $\cos 1.25 = 0.3153$; $\tan 1.25 = 3.0096$

6. $\sin 1.4 = 0.9854$; $\cos 1.4 = 0.1700$; $\tan 1.4 = 5.7979$

7. $\sin 0.25 = 0.2474$; $\cos 0.25 = 0.9689$; $\tan 0.25 = 0.2553$

8. $\sin 0.7 = 0.6442$; $\cos 0.7 = 0.7648$; $\tan 0.7 = 0.8423$

Ex.	s	$\sin s$	$\cos s$	$\tan s$	$\csc s$	$\sec s$	$\cot s$
9.	$\frac{\pi}{3}$	$\frac{\sqrt{3}}{2}$	$\frac{1}{2}$	$\sqrt{3}$	$\frac{2\sqrt{3}}{3}$	2	$\frac{\sqrt{3}}{3}$
10.	$\frac{\pi}{4}$	$\frac{\sqrt{2}}{2}$	$\frac{\sqrt{2}}{2}$	1	$\sqrt{2}$	$\sqrt{2}$	1
11.	$\frac{3\pi}{2}$	-1	0	undef.	-1	undef.	0
12.	$\frac{3\pi}{4}$	$\frac{\sqrt{2}}{2}$	$-\frac{\sqrt{2}}{2}$	-1	$\sqrt{2}$	$-\sqrt{2}$	-1
13.	$\frac{11\pi}{6}$	$-\frac{1}{2}$	$\frac{\sqrt{3}}{2}$	$-\frac{\sqrt{3}}{3}$	-2	$\frac{2\sqrt{3}}{3}$	$-\sqrt{3}$
14.	π	0	-1	0	undef.	-1	undef.
15.	$\frac{8\pi}{3}$	$\frac{\sqrt{3}}{2}$	$-\frac{1}{2}$	$-\sqrt{3}$	$\frac{2\sqrt{3}}{3}$	-2	$-\frac{\sqrt{3}}{3}$
16.	$\frac{15\pi}{4}$	$-\frac{\sqrt{2}}{2}$	$\frac{\sqrt{2}}{2}$	-1	$-\sqrt{2}$	$\sqrt{2}$	-1
17.	$-\frac{5\pi}{6}$	$-\frac{1}{2}$	$-\frac{\sqrt{3}}{2}$	$\frac{\sqrt{3}}{3}$	-2	$-\frac{2\sqrt{3}}{3}$	$\sqrt{3}$
18.	$-\frac{3\pi}{4}$	$-\frac{\sqrt{2}}{2}$	$-\frac{\sqrt{2}}{2}$	1	$-\sqrt{2}$	$-\sqrt{2}$	1

B **19.** $x = 0.76$ **20.** $\sin x = 0.982318$; $x = 1.38$ **21.** $x = \frac{\pi}{3}$ **22.** $x = \frac{\pi}{4}$

23. $\left(\cos \frac{3\pi}{4}\right)^2 + \left(\sin \frac{3\pi}{4}\right)^2 = \left(-\frac{\sqrt{2}}{2}\right)^2 + \left(\frac{\sqrt{2}}{2}\right)^2 = \frac{1}{2} + \frac{1}{2} = 1$

24. $\left(\cos \frac{7\pi}{6}\right)^2 + \left(\sin \frac{7\pi}{6}\right)^2 = \left(-\frac{\sqrt{3}}{2}\right)^2 + \left(-\frac{1}{2}\right)^2 = \frac{3}{4} + \frac{1}{4} = 1$

25. $(\cos 0.7)^2 + (\sin 0.7)^2 = (0.7648)^2 + (0.6442)^2 = 0.5850 + 0.4150 = 1.0000$

26. $(\cos 1)^2 + (\sin 1)^2 = (0.5403)^2 + (0.8415)^2 = 0.2919 + 0.7081 = 1.0000$

27. $\sin 7 = \sin(7 + 2\pi n)$ for every integer n; let $n = -1$; $\sin 7 = \sin(7 - 2\pi) \approx \sin 0.72 = 0.6594$

28. Since $0 < s < \frac{\pi}{2}$, $\sin s$, $\cos s$, and $\tan s$ are all positive; $\triangle OAQ \sim \triangle OMP$ so $\frac{OA}{\cos s} = \frac{AQ}{\sin s}$; $\frac{1}{\cos s} = \frac{AQ}{\sin s}$; $\frac{\sin s}{\cos s} = AQ$; $\tan s = AQ$.

29. Since $0 < s < \frac{\pi}{2}$, $\sin s$, $\cos s$ and $\tan s$ are all positive; $\triangle OAQ \sim \triangle OMP$ so $\frac{OA}{\cos s} = \frac{OQ}{OP}$; $\frac{1}{\cos s} = \frac{OQ}{1}$; $\frac{1}{\cos s} = OQ$; $\sec s = OQ$.

C **30.** The shortest distance from P to $\overleftrightarrow{OA}$ is the perpendicular. $\overline{PM} = \sin s$; therefore, $\sin s < s$.

31. Area of sector $OAP <$ area of $\triangle OAQ$; $\frac{1}{2}(1)^2(s) < \frac{1}{2}(OA)(AQ)$; $\frac{1}{2}s < \frac{1}{2}(1)(\tan s)$ (by exercise 28); therefore, $s < \tan s$

32. By exercises 30 and 31, $0 < \sin s < s < \tan s$; dividing by $\sin s$ yields

$$\frac{\sin s}{\sin s} < \frac{s}{\sin s} < \frac{\tan s}{\sin s};\ 1 < \frac{s}{\sin s} < \frac{\frac{\sin s}{\cos s}}{\sin s};\ 1 < \frac{s}{\sin s} < \frac{1}{\cos s}$$

Pages 621–623 • WRITTEN EXERCISES

A **1.** odd

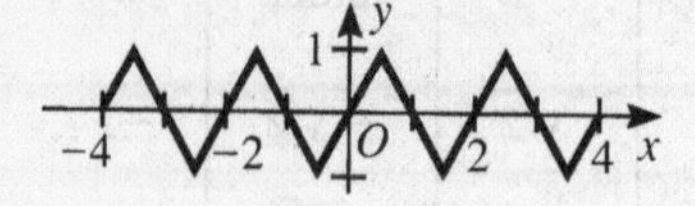

2. even

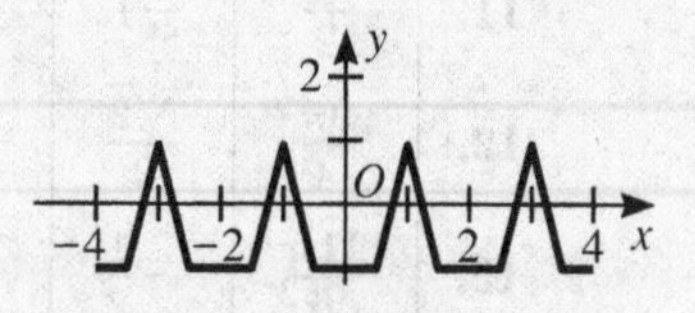

3. neither

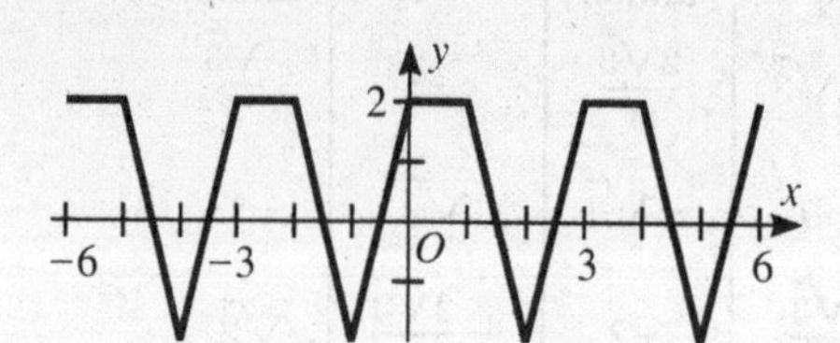

4. even

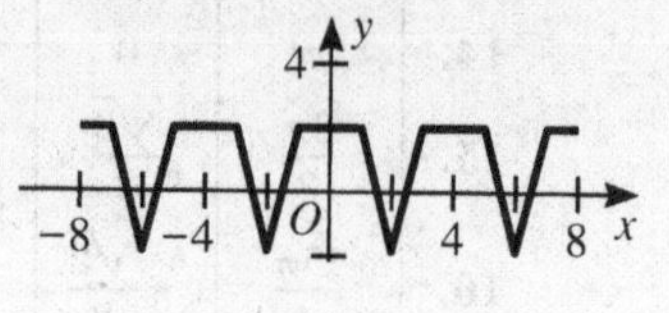

5. odd

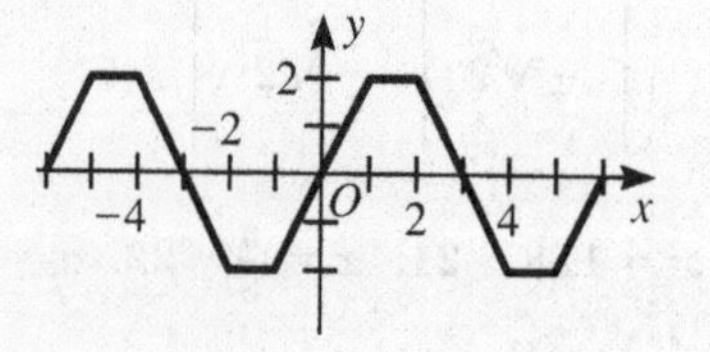

6. neither

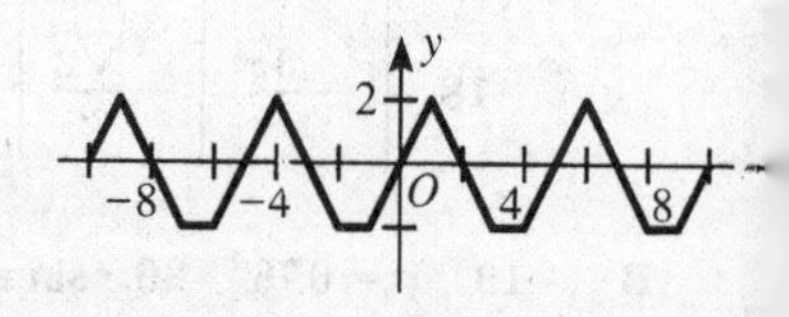

7. a.

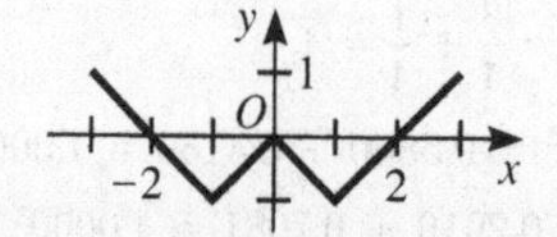

b.

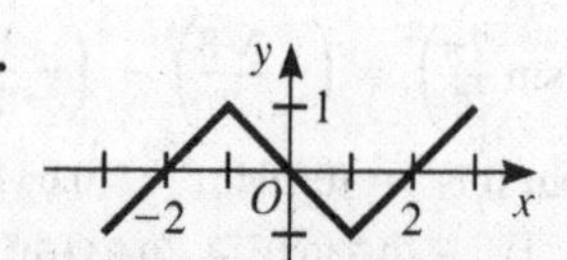

8. a.

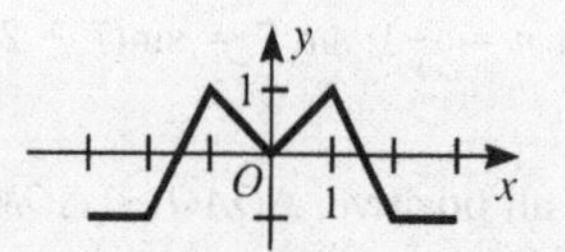

b.

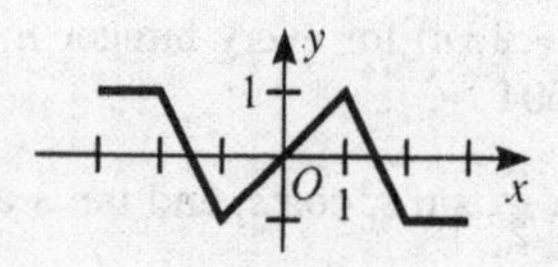

9. a.

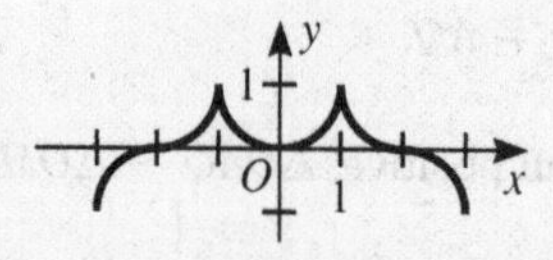

b.

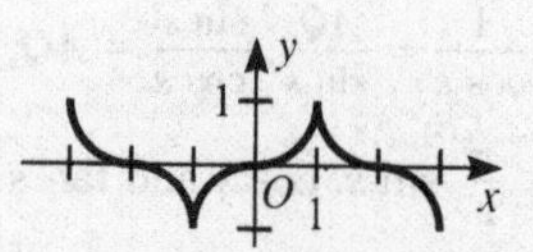

10. a.

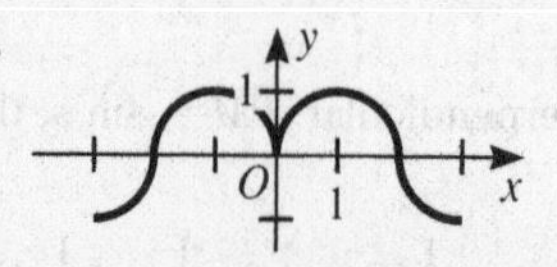

b.

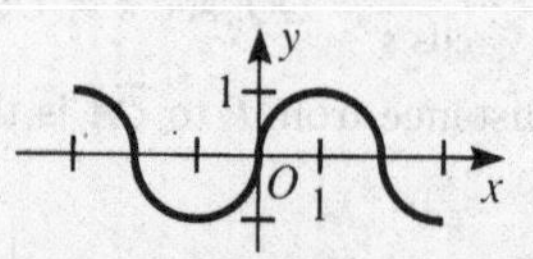

11. $f(-x) = (-x)^3 + (-x) = -x^3 - x = -(x^3 + x) = -f(x)$; odd

12. $f(-x) = (-x^3) + 5(-x) + 3 = -x^3 - 5x + 3$; neither

13. $f(-x) = (-x)^4 + (-x)^3 = x^4 - x^3$; neither

14. $f(-x) = (-x)^4 + 2(-x)^2 + 1 = x^4 + 2x^2 + 1 = f(x)$; even

15. $f(-x) = \dfrac{(-x)^2}{(-x)^2 + 4} = \dfrac{x^2}{x^2 + 4} = f(x)$; even

16. $f(-x) = (-x)\sqrt{(-x)^2 + 1} = -x\sqrt{x^2 + 1} = -f(x)$; odd

B **17.** $f(-x) = -x \sin(-x) = (-x)(-\sin x) = x \sin x = f(x)$; even

18. $f(-x) = (-x)(\cos(-x)) = (-x)(\cos x) = -x \cos x = -f(x)$; odd

19. $f(-x) = \sin(-x)\cos(-x) = -\sin x \cos x = -f(x)$; odd

20. $f(x) = \sin(-x) + \cos(-x) = -\sin x + \cos x$; neither

21. Let f and g be odd functions with the same domain; that is, for every x in the common domain, $f(-x) = -f(x)$ and $g(-x) = -g(x)$; then $f(-x) \cdot g(-x) = -f(x)[-g(x)] = f(x) \cdot g(x)$ and the product of the two functions is even.

22. Let f and g be functions with the same domain, f even and g odd; that is, for every x in the common domain, $f(-x) = f(x)$ and $g(-x) = -g(x)$; then $f(-x) \cdot g(-x) = f(x)[-g(x)] = -f(x) \cdot g(x)$ and the product of the two functions is odd.

23. Since $f(x)$ and $g(x)$ have period p, $f(x + p) = f(x)$ and $g(x + p) = g(x)$. If $h(x) = f(x) + g(x)$ then $h(x + p) = f(x + p) + g(x + p)$. By substitution then $h(x + p)$ must equal $h(x)$ and therefore $h(x)$ has period p.

24. Let $f(x)$ be an even function and $g(x)$ be an odd function with the same domain, where neither function is the constant function valued at 0. Let $h(x) = f(x) + g(x)$; $h(-x) = f(-x) + g(-x) = f(x) - g(x)$. Suppose $h(x)$ is even, then $h(-x) = h(x)$ and $f(x) + g(x) = f(x) - g(x)$, $2g(x) = 0$, and $g(x) = 0$ for all x. (unallowed). Suppose $h(x)$ is odd, then $h(-x) = -h(x)$ and $-(f(x) + g(x)) = f(x) - g(x)$, $2f(x) = 0$, $f(x) = 0$ for all x (unallowed). Hence $h(x)$ is neither even or odd.

25. If $\sin 2(x + p) = \sin 2x$ for all x, then $2(x + p) = 2x + n \cdot 2\pi$, where n is an integer; $2p = 2n\pi$, $p = n \cdot \pi$; the smallest positive such p is $p = \pi$; therefore the period of $\sin 2x$ is π.

26. If $\cos 2(x + p) = \cos 2x$ for all x, then $2(x + p) = 2x + n \cdot 2\pi$ where n is an integer; $2p = 2n\pi$, $p = n \cdot \pi$; the smallest positive such p is $p = \pi$; therefore the period of $\cos 2x$ is π.

27. If $\cos \frac{1}{2}(x + p) = \cos \frac{1}{2}x$ for all x, then $\frac{1}{2}(x + p) = \frac{1}{2}x + n \cdot 2\pi$, where n is an integer; $\frac{1}{2}p = n \cdot 2\pi$; $p = n \cdot 4\pi$; the smallest positive such p is $p = 4\pi$; therefore the period of $\cos \frac{1}{2}x$ is 4π.

28. If $\sin \frac{1}{2}(x + p) = \sin \frac{1}{2}x$ for all x, then $\frac{1}{2}(x + p) = \frac{1}{2}x + n \cdot 2\pi$, where n is an integer; $\frac{1}{2}p = n \cdot 2\pi$, $p = n \cdot 4\pi$; the smallest positive such p is $p = 4\pi$; therefore the period of $\sin \frac{1}{2}x$ is 4π.

C **29.** Since $f(x)$ is periodic with period p, $f(x) = f(x + p)$ and $f(kx) = f(kx + p) = f\left[k\left(x + \frac{p}{k}\right)\right]$; therefore $f(kx)$ is periodic with period $\leq \frac{p}{k}$. Assume $f(kx)$ has period p_1, $0 < p_1 \leq \frac{p}{k}$; $0 < p_1k \leq p$ and $f[k(x + p_1)] = f(kx + kp_1) = f(kx)$ for all x. But this indicates that $f(x)$ has period $\leq kp_1$ and we know $f(x)$ has period equal to p. So $kp_1 = p$ and $p_1 = \frac{p}{k}$.

30. a. $O(-x) = \frac{f(-x) - f[-(-x)]}{2} = \frac{f(-x) - f(x)}{2} = -\frac{f(x) - f(-x)}{2} = -O(x)$;

$E(-x) = \frac{f(-x) + f[-(-x)]}{2} = \frac{f(-x) + f(x)}{2} = \frac{f(x) + f(-x)}{2} = E(x)$

b. $O(x) + E(x) = \frac{f(x) - f(-x)}{2} + \frac{f(x) + f(-x)}{2} = \frac{f(x) - f(-x) + f(x) + f(-x)}{2} = \frac{2f(x)}{2} = f(x)$

c. $O(x) = \frac{x^3 - 3x^2 + 2x + 1 - (-x^3 - 3x^2 - 2x + 1)}{2} = \frac{2x^3 + 4x}{2} = x^3 + 2x$;

$E(x) = \frac{x^3 - 3x^2 + 2x + 1 + (-x^3) - 3x^2 - 2x + 1}{2} = \frac{-6x^2 + 2}{2} = -3x^2 + 1$

d. $O(x) = \frac{e^x - e^{-x}}{2}$; $E(x) = \frac{e^x + e^{-x}}{2}$

Page 623 • MIXED REVIEW EXERCISES

1.

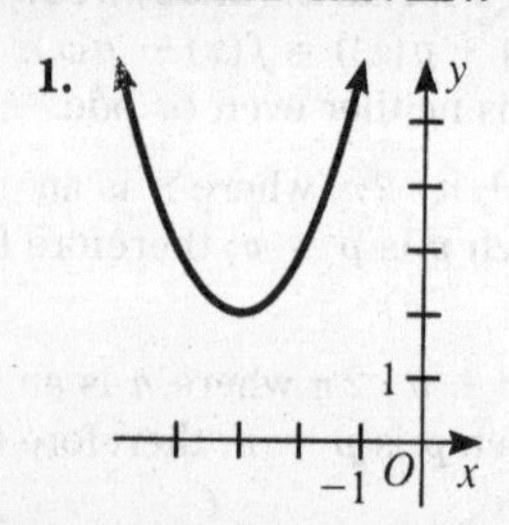

2.

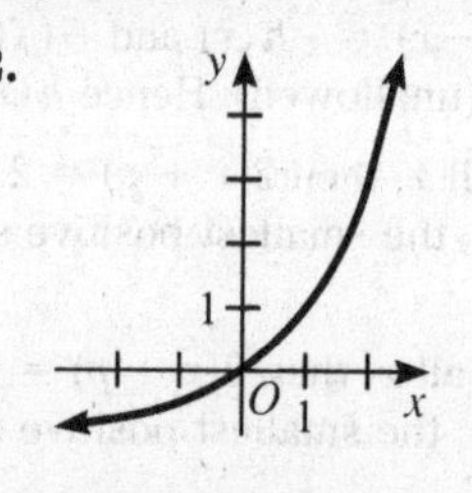

3.

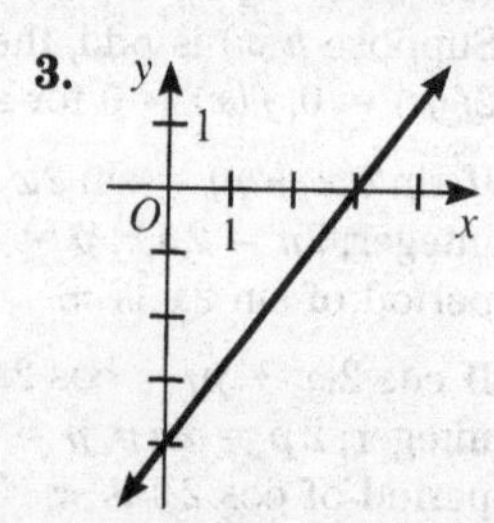

4.

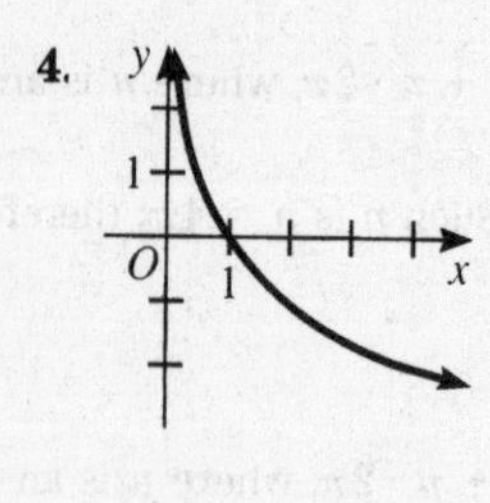

5.

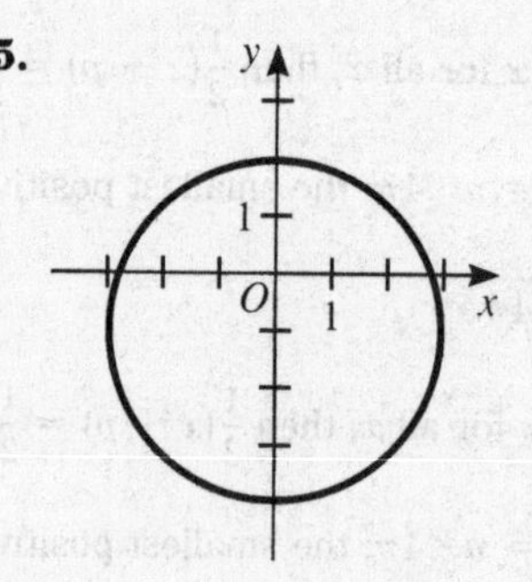

6.

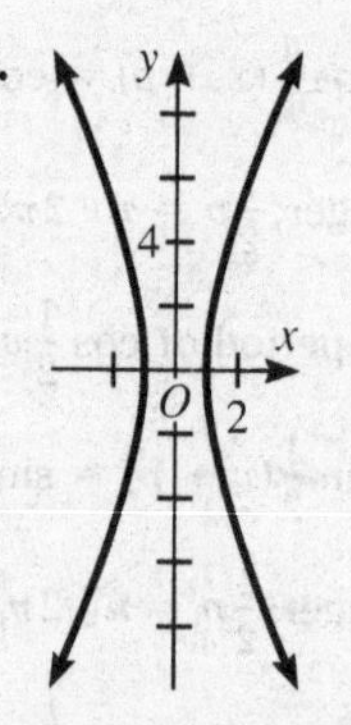

7. $\sqrt{7x + 4} = x + 2$, $7x + 4 = x^2 + 4x + 4$, $x^2 - 3x = 0$, $x(x - 3) = 0$, $x = 0$ or $x = 3$; $\{0, 3\}$

8. $2x + 7 = 1 - x$, $3x = -6$, $x = -2$; $\{-2\}$

9. $x^3 - 2x^2 + 2x - 4 = 0; x^2(x - 2) + 2(x - 2) = 0; (x^2 + 2)(x - 2) = 0; x^2 + 2 = 0$ or $x - 2 = 0; x^2 = -2$ or $x = 2; x = \pm i\sqrt{2}$ or $x = 2$; $\{2, \pm i\sqrt{2}\}$

10. $\frac{x^2}{12} + 1 = \frac{2x}{3}, x^2 + 12 = 8x, x^2 - 8x + 12 = 0, (x - 6)(x - 2) = 0, x = 6$ or $x = 2$; $\{2, 6\}$

11. $2x^2 + x - 10 = 0, (2x + 5)(x - 2) = 0, x = -\frac{5}{2}$ or $x = 2$; $\left\{-\frac{5}{2}, 2\right\}$

12. $\frac{1}{x - 1} + \frac{1}{x} = \frac{3}{x^2 - x}; x + 1(x - 1) = 3, x + x - 1 = 3, 2x - 1 = 3, 2x = 4, x = 2$; $\{2\}$

Page 623 • CHALLENGE

yes; $h(x)$ has period 12 since 12 is the LCM of 4 and 6.

Pages 628–629 • WRITTEN EXERCISES

A **1. a.** 2 **b.** $M = 2; m = -2$ **c.** 2π **2. a.** $\frac{1}{2}$ **b.** $M = \frac{1}{2}; m = -\frac{1}{2}$ **c.** 2π

3. a. 1 **b.** $M = 1; m = -1$ **c.** $\frac{2\pi}{4} = \frac{\pi}{2}$ **4. a.** 1 **b.** $M = 1; m = -1$ **c.** $\frac{2\pi}{2} = \pi$

5. a. 3 **b.** $M = 3; m = -3$ **c.** $\frac{2\pi}{3}$ **6. a.** $\frac{1}{2}$ **b.** $M = \frac{1}{2}; m = -\frac{1}{2}$ **c.** $\frac{2\pi}{2} = \pi$

7. a. $\frac{1}{2}$ **b.** $M = \frac{1}{2}; m = -\frac{1}{2}$ **c.** $\frac{2\pi}{2\pi} = 1$ **8. a.** 2 **b.** $M = 2; m = -2$ **c.** $\frac{2\pi}{\pi} = 2$

9. a. 2 **b.** $M = 2; m = -2$ **c.** $\frac{2\pi}{\frac{\pi}{2}} = 4$

10. a. 3 **b.** $M = 3; m = -3$ **c.** $\frac{2\pi}{\frac{\pi}{4}} = 8$

11. a. 1 **b.** $M = 0; m = -2$ **c.** $\frac{2\pi}{2\pi} = 1$ **12. a.** 2 **b.** $M = 5, m = 1$ **c.** $\frac{2\pi}{\pi} = 2$

13. sine graph; $M = 2, m = -2, a = 2$; period $= 2\pi$; $y = 2 \sin x$

14. sine graph; $M = 1, m = -1, a = 1$; period $= \pi$; $b = \frac{2\pi}{\pi} = 2$; $y = \sin 2x$

15. cosine graph; $M = 0.5, m = -0.5, a = 0.5$; period $= 4\pi$; $b = \frac{2\pi}{4\pi} = \frac{1}{2}$; $y = \frac{1}{2} \cos \frac{1}{2}x$

16. cosine graph; $M = 2, m = -2, a = 2$; period $= \pi$; $b = \frac{2\pi}{\pi} = 2$; $y = 2 \cos 2x$

17. sine graph; $M = 1, m = -1, a = 1$; period $= 2$; $b = \frac{2\pi}{2} = \pi$; $y = \sin \pi x$

18. cosine graph; $M = 3, m = -3, a = 3$; period $= 8$; $b = \frac{2\pi}{8} = \frac{\pi}{4}$; $y = 3 \cos \frac{\pi}{4}x$

19. cosine graph; $M = 6, m = 0, a = \frac{6 - 0}{2} = 3$; period $= 8$; $b = \frac{2\pi}{8} = \frac{\pi}{4}$;

$y = 3 + 3 \cos \frac{\pi}{4}x$

20. cosine graph; $M = 0$, $m = -2$, $a = \dfrac{0 - (-2)}{2} = 1$; period $= 5$; $b = \dfrac{2\pi}{5}$;

$y = -1 + \cos \dfrac{2\pi}{5}x$

21. $a = \dfrac{3 - (-3)}{2} = 3$; $c = \dfrac{3 + (-3)}{2} = 0$; $b = \dfrac{2\pi}{2\pi} = 1$; $y = 3 \sin x$

22. $a = \dfrac{1 - (-1)}{2} = 1$; $c = \dfrac{1 + (-1)}{2} = 0$; $b = \dfrac{2\pi}{8\pi} = \dfrac{1}{4}$; $y = \sin \dfrac{1}{4}x$

23. $a = \dfrac{2 - (-2)}{2} = 2$; $c = \dfrac{2 + (-2)}{2} = 0$; $b = \dfrac{2\pi}{2} = \pi$; $y = 2 \sin \pi x$

24. $a = \dfrac{2 - (-2)}{2} = 2$; $c = \dfrac{2 + (-2)}{2} = 0$; $b = \dfrac{2\pi}{3}$; $y = 2 \sin \dfrac{2\pi}{3}x$

25. $a = \dfrac{7 - 1}{2} = 3$; $c = \dfrac{7 + 1}{2} = 4$; $b = \dfrac{2\pi}{\pi} = 2$; $y = 4 + 3 \sin 2x$

26. $a = \dfrac{0 - (-6)}{2} = 3$; $c = \dfrac{0 + (-6)}{2} = -3$; $b = \dfrac{2\pi}{4} = \dfrac{\pi}{2}$; $y = -3 + 3 \sin \dfrac{\pi}{2}x$

27.

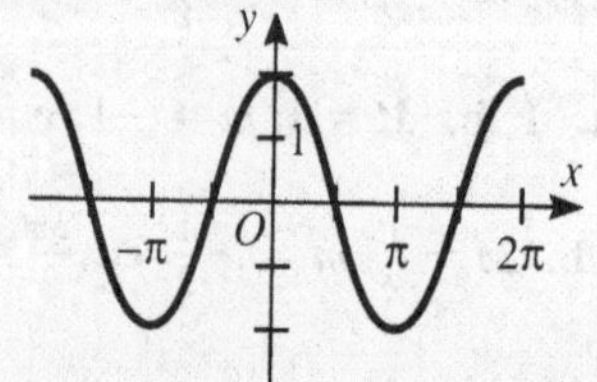

28.

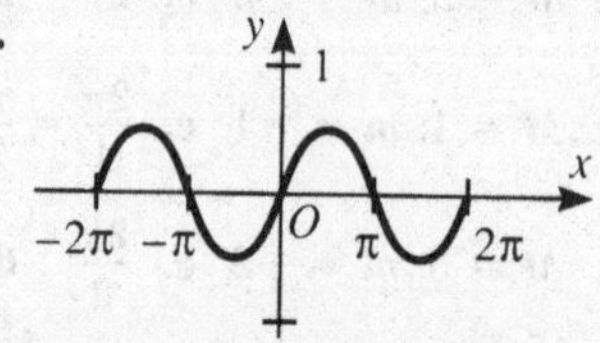

29.

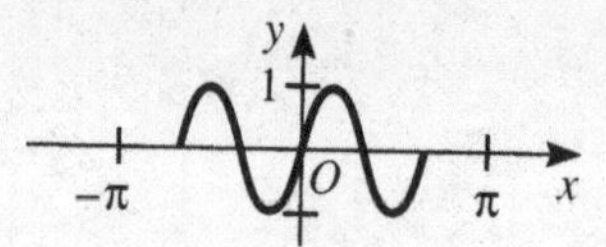

30.

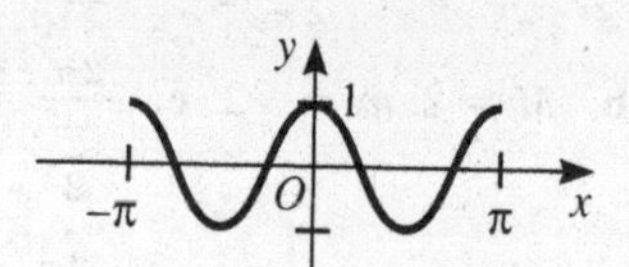

31.

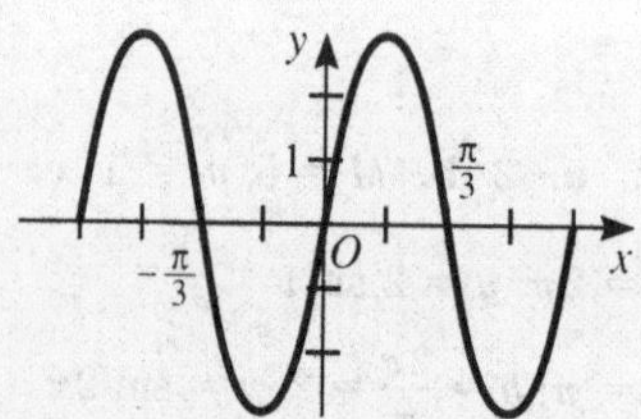

32.

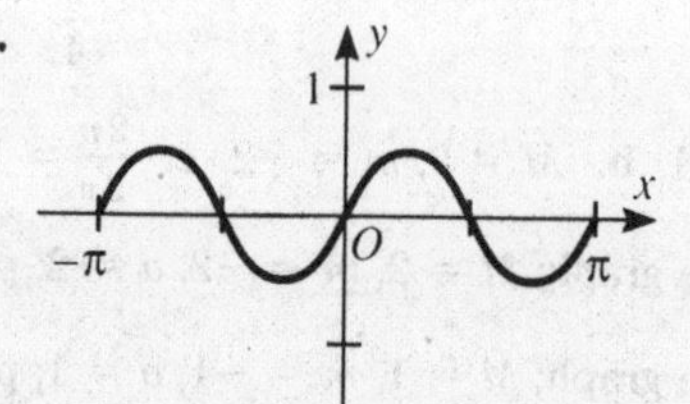

B **33.**

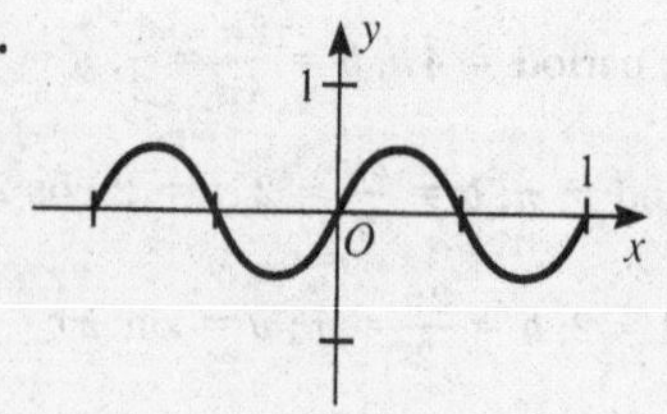

34.

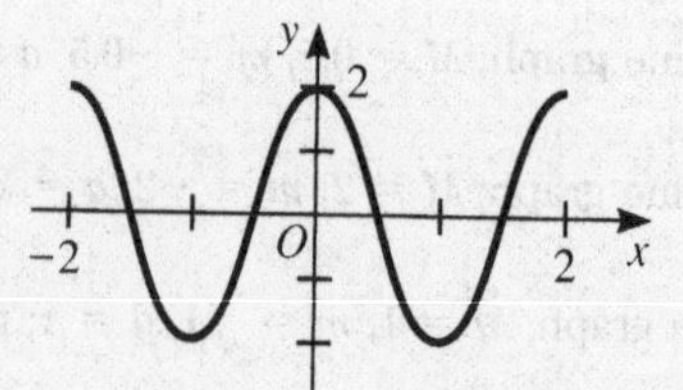

35.

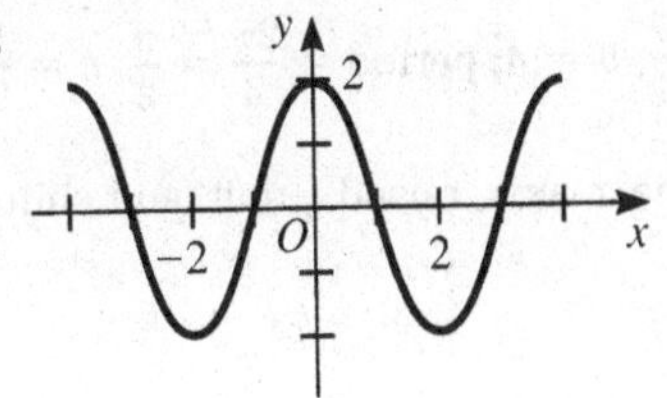

36.

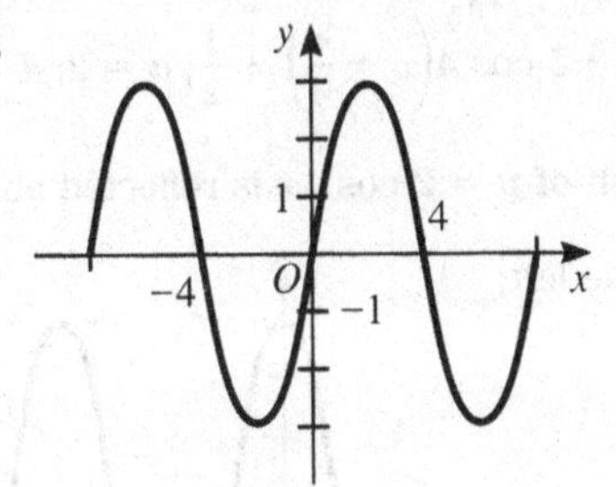

37.

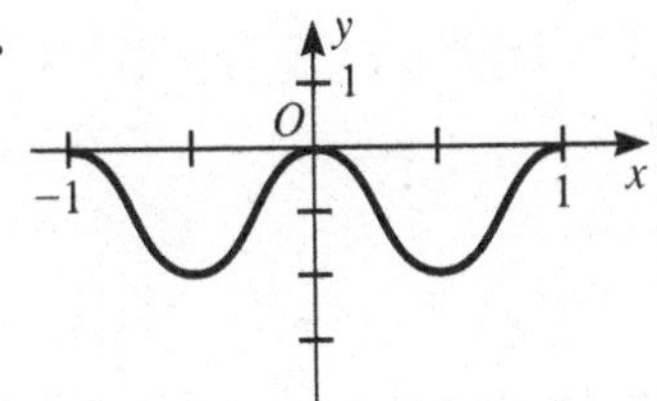

38.

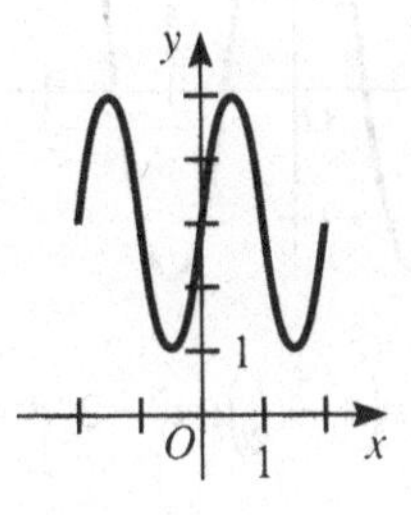

39. $d = \frac{\pi}{4}$; shift graph of $y = \cos x - 1$ to the right $\frac{\pi}{4}$ units; $c = -1$, $a = 1$,

period $= 2\pi$

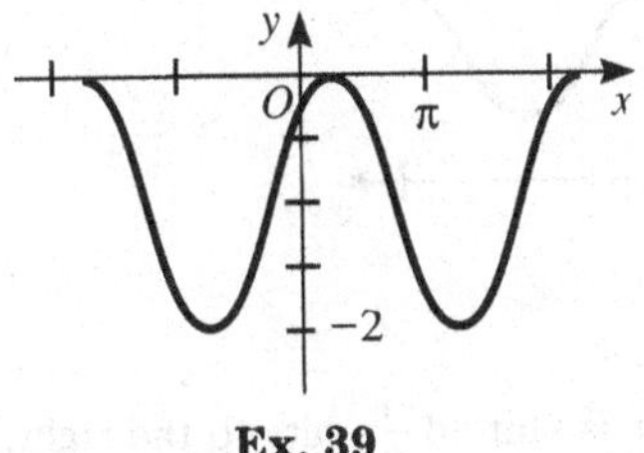

Ex. 39

Ex. 40

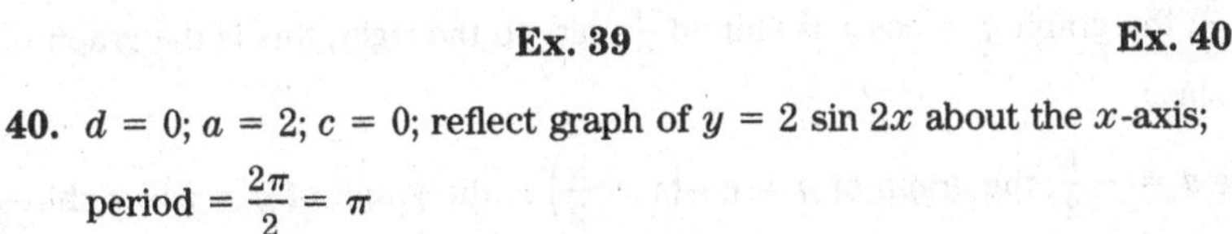

40. $d = 0$; $a = 2$; $c = 0$; reflect graph of $y = 2 \sin 2x$ about the x-axis;

period $= \frac{2\pi}{2} = \pi$

41. $d = -\frac{\pi}{3}$; $a = 1$; period $= \frac{2\pi}{2} = \pi$; $c = 0$; the graph of $y = \cos 2x$ is reflected about the x-axis and shifted $\frac{\pi}{3}$ units to the left

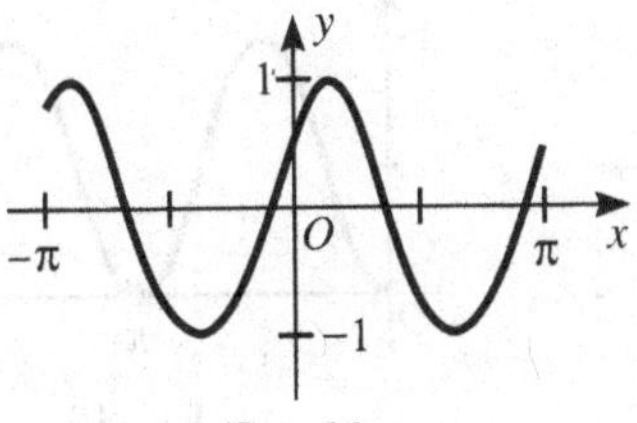

Ex. 41

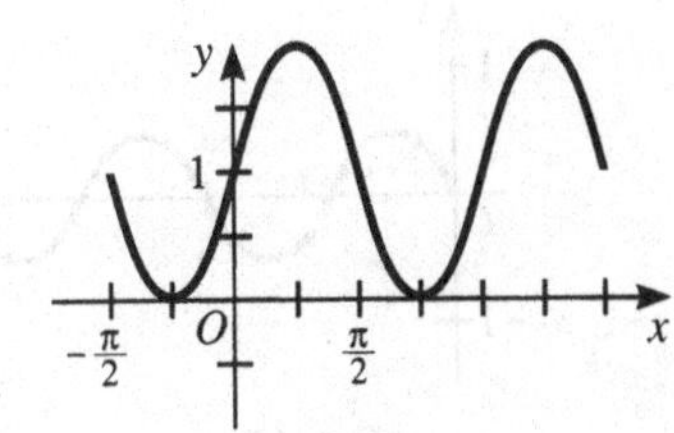

Ex. 42

C **42.** $y = -\sin 2\left(x - \frac{\pi}{2}\right) + 1$; $a = 1$; $d = \frac{\pi}{2}$; period $= \frac{2\pi}{2} = \pi$, $c = 1$; graph of $y = \sin 2x$ is reflected about the x-axis, raised 1 unit, and shifted $\frac{\pi}{2}$ units to the right

43. $y = -2 \cos 4\left(x + \frac{\pi}{4}\right) + \frac{1}{2}$; $a = 2$; $d = -\frac{\pi}{4}$; $b = 4$; period $= \frac{2\pi}{4} = \frac{\pi}{2}$; $c = \frac{1}{2}$; the graph of $y = 2 \cos 4x$ is reflected about the x-axis, raised $\frac{1}{2}$ unit, and shifted $\frac{\pi}{4}$ units to the left;

44. $y = 4 - 2 \cos 2\pi\left(x - \frac{1}{2}\right)$; $a = 2$; $d = \frac{1}{2}$; $b = 2\pi$; period $= \frac{2\pi}{2\pi} = 1$, $c = 4$; the graph of $y = 2 \cos 2\pi x$ is reflected about the x-axis, raised 4 units, and shifted $\frac{1}{2}$ unit to the right;

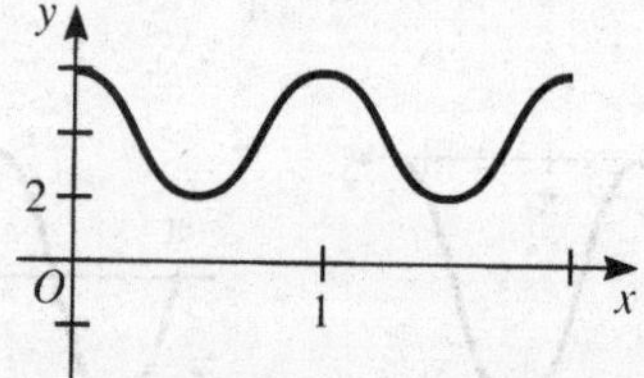

45. $d = \frac{\pi}{2}$; the graph $y = \cos x$ is shifted $\frac{\pi}{2}$ units to the right; this is the graph of $y = \sin x$

46. Since $d = -\frac{\pi}{2}$, the graph of $y = \cos\left(x + \frac{\pi}{2}\right)$ is the graph of $y = \cos x$ shifted $\frac{\pi}{2}$ units to the left. The resulting graph is the reflection of $y = \sin x$ in the x-axis.

47. $y = \sin x \cos x = \frac{1}{2}(2 \sin x \cos x) = \frac{1}{2} \sin 2x$; $a = \frac{1}{2}$; period $= \frac{2\pi}{2} = \pi$; $c = 0$.

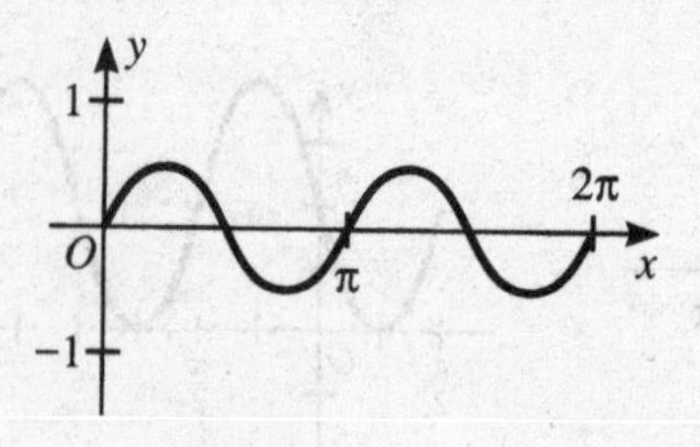

Ex. 47

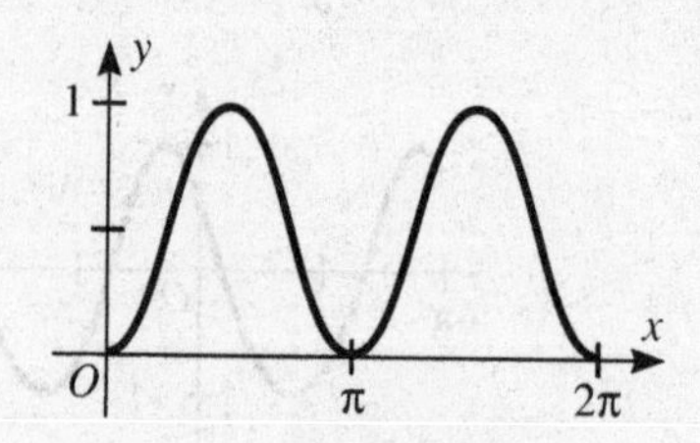

Ex. 48

48. $y = \sin^2 x = \frac{1}{2} - \frac{1}{2}[1 - 2 \sin^2 x] = \frac{1}{2} - \frac{1}{2} \cos 2x = -\left[\frac{1}{2} \cos 2x - \frac{1}{2}\right]$; reflect graph of $y = \frac{1}{2} \cos 2x - \frac{1}{2}$ in the x-axis; $a = \frac{1}{2}$; period $= \frac{2\pi}{2} = \pi$; $c = -\frac{1}{2}$

Page 633 • WRITTEN EXERCISES

A **1.** $\cot(-x) = \dfrac{\cos(-x)}{\sin(-x)} = \dfrac{\cos x}{-\sin x} = -\cot x$; odd

2. $\sec(-x) = \dfrac{1}{\cos(-x)} = \dfrac{1}{\cos x} = \sec x$; even

3. $\csc(-x) = \dfrac{1}{\sin(-x)} = \dfrac{1}{-\sin x} = -\csc x$; odd

4. $\tan(-x) + \sec(-x) = \dfrac{\sin(-x)}{\cos(-x)} + \dfrac{1}{\cos(-x)} = -\tan x + \sec x$; neither

5. $\sec(-x) - \csc(-x) = \dfrac{1}{\cos(-x)} - \dfrac{1}{\sin(-x)} = \dfrac{1}{\cos x} - \dfrac{1}{-\sin x} = \dfrac{1}{\cos x} + \dfrac{1}{\sin x} =$

$\sec x + \csc x$; neither

6. $(-x)\csc(-x) = (-x) \cdot \dfrac{1}{\sin(-x)} = -x \cdot \dfrac{1}{-\sin x} = x \cdot \dfrac{1}{\sin x} = x \csc x$; even

7. $(-x)^2\cot(-x) = x^2 \cdot \dfrac{\cos(-x)}{\sin(-x)} = x^2 \cdot \dfrac{\cos x}{-\sin x} = -x^2 \cdot \dfrac{\cos x}{\sin x} = -x^2 \cot x$; odd

8. $\sec(-x)\tan(-x) = \dfrac{1}{\cos(-x)} \cdot \dfrac{\sin(-x)}{\cos(-x)} = \dfrac{1}{\cos x} \cdot \dfrac{-\sin x}{\cos x} = -\dfrac{1}{\cos x} \cdot \dfrac{\sin x}{\cos x} =$

$-\sec x \tan x$; odd

9.

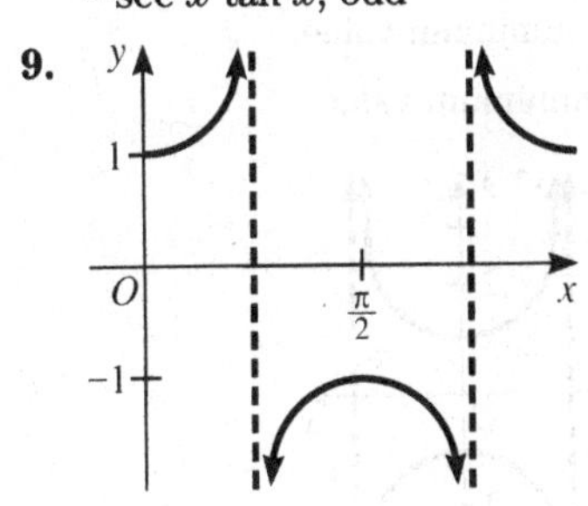

10.

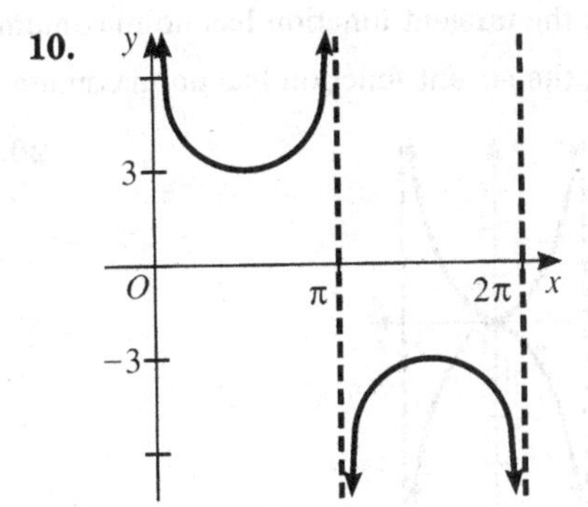

11.

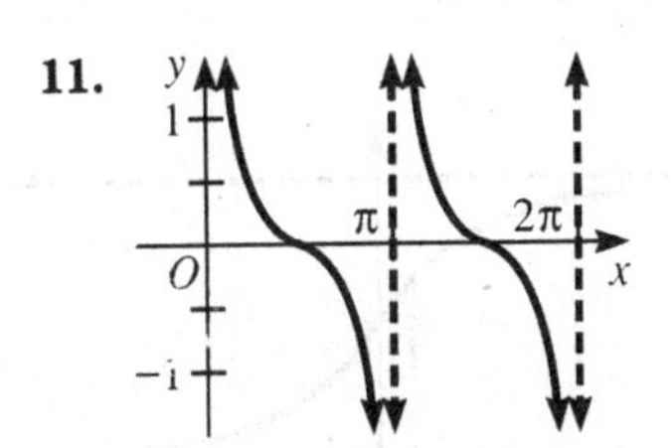

12.

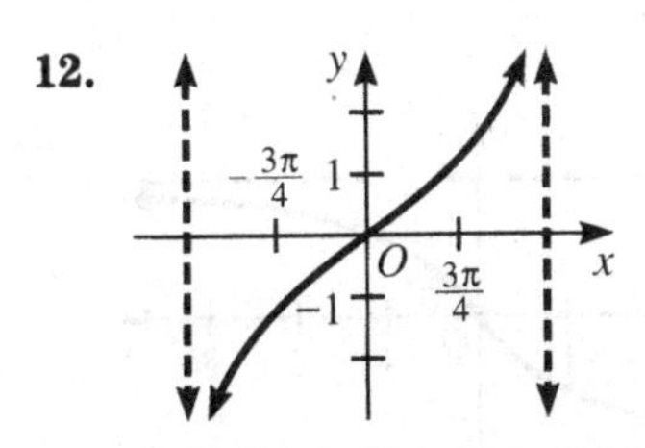

13. 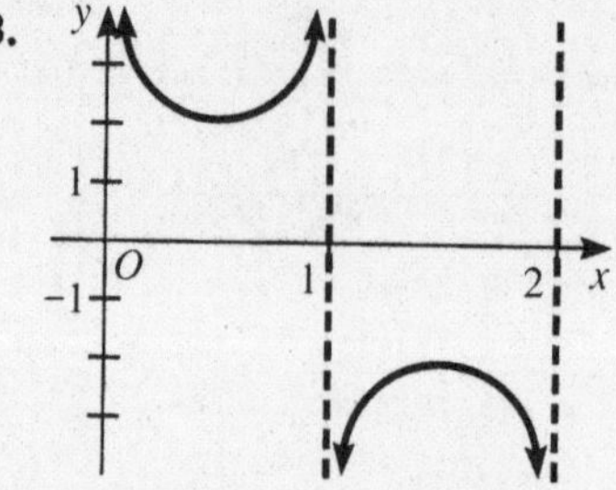

14. 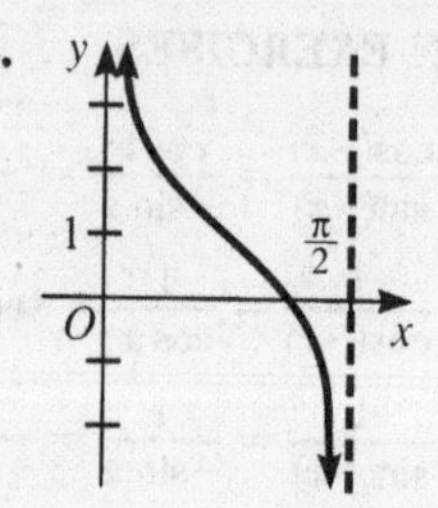

15. 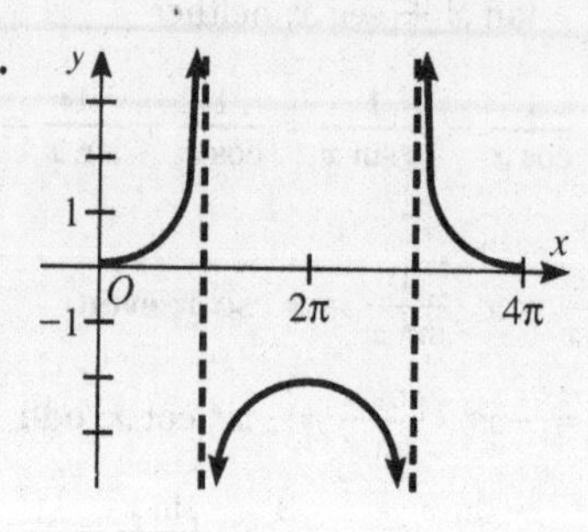

16. 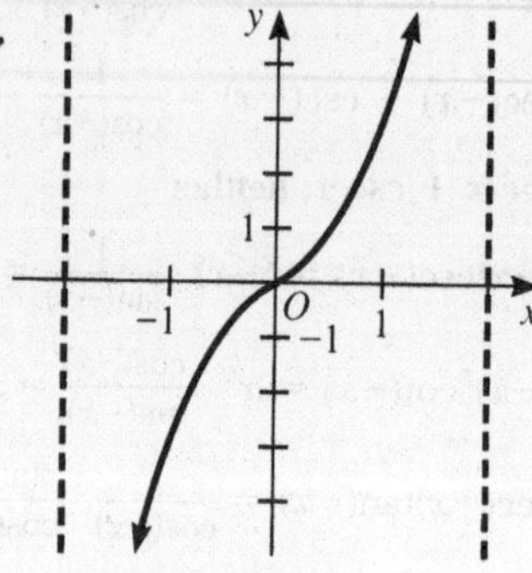

17. No; the tangent function has no maximum or minimum value.

18. No; the secant function has no maximum or minimum value.

B

19. 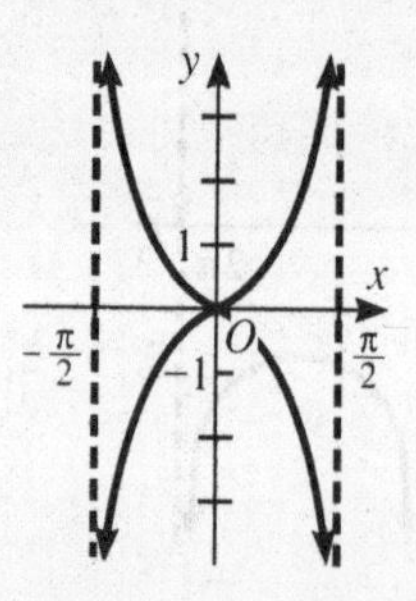

20. 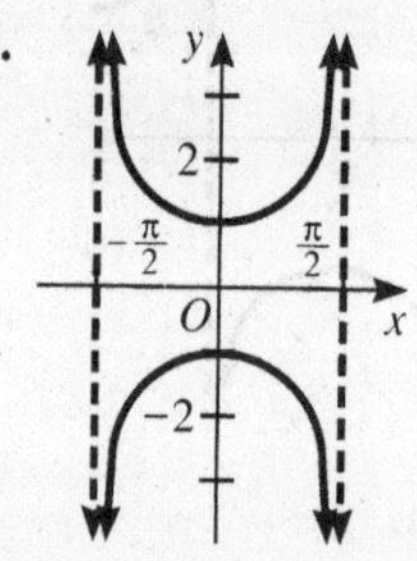

21. 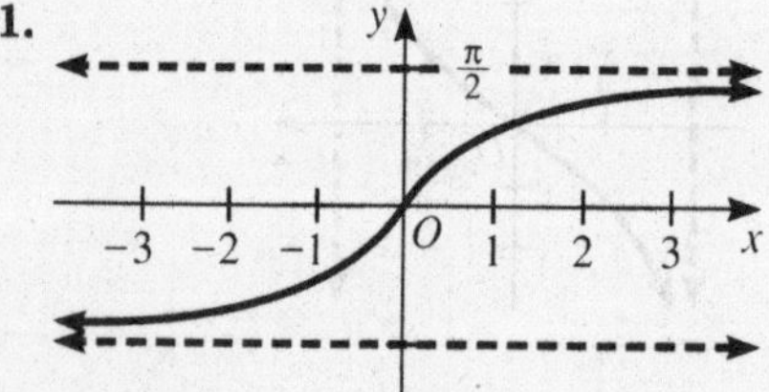

22. 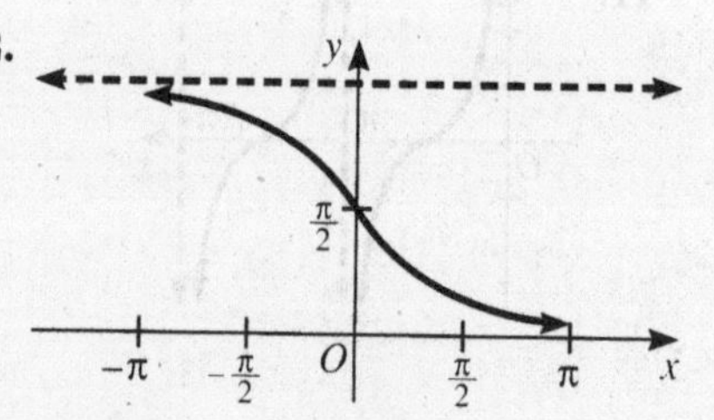

23. 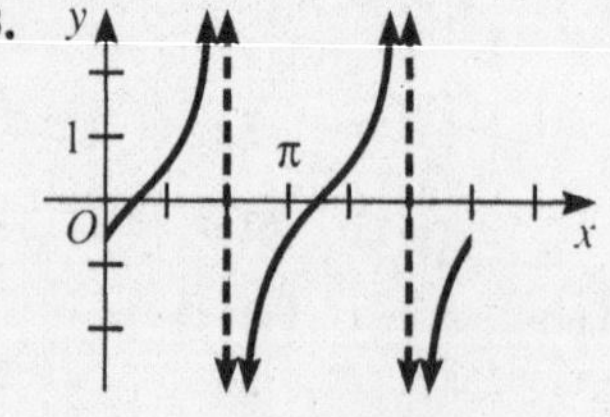

24. 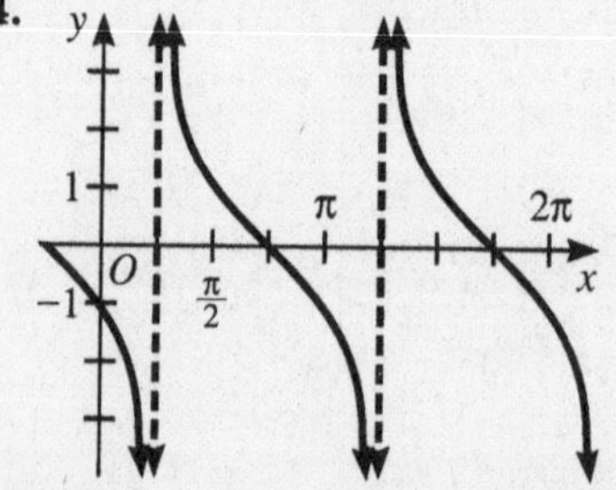

25.

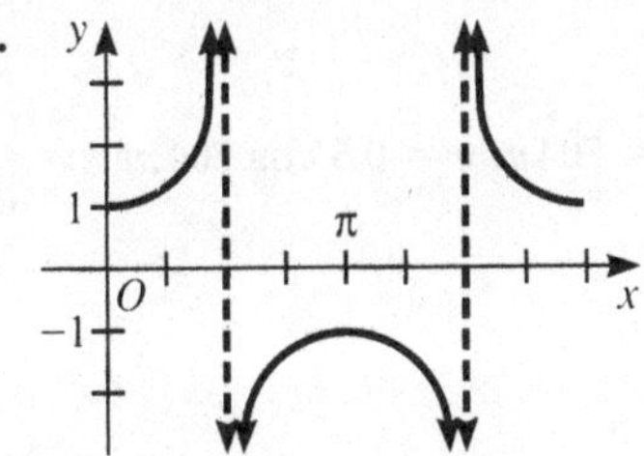

26.

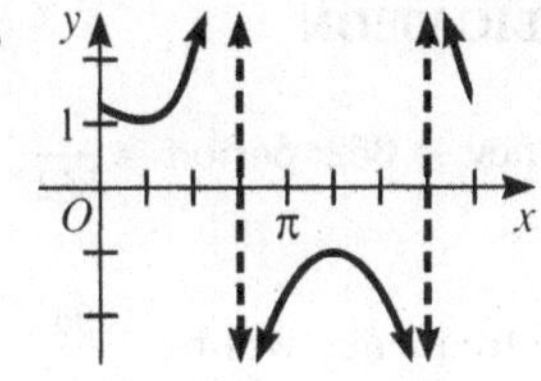

27.

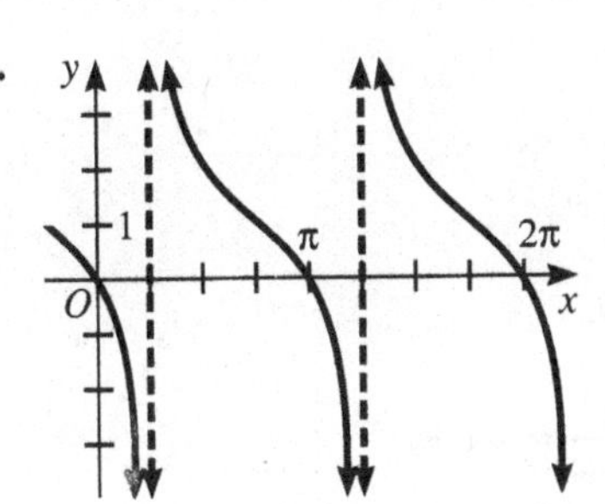

28.

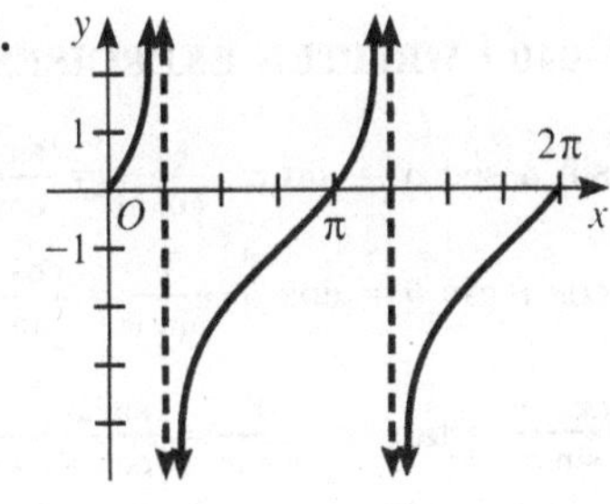

C **29.**

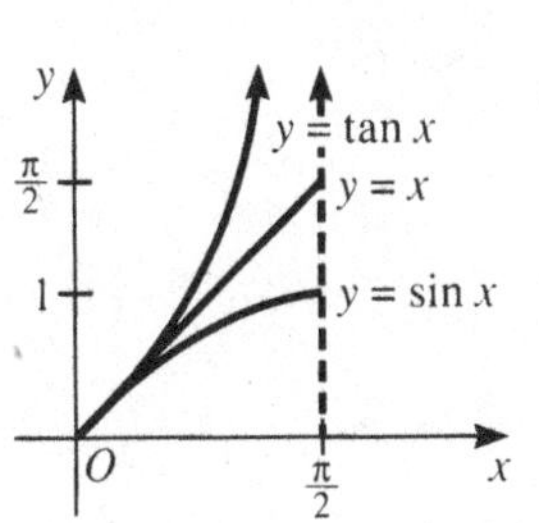

For $0 < x < \frac{\pi}{2}$, the graph of $y = x$ lies between the graphs of $y = \sin x$ and $y = \tan x$; therefore, for $0 < x < \frac{\pi}{2}$, $\sin x < x < \tan x$.

Page 633 • MIXED REVIEW EXERCISES

Ex.	x	$\sin x$	$\cos x$	$\tan x$	$\csc x$	$\sec x$	$\cot x$
1.	$\frac{5\pi}{2}$	1	0	undef.	1	undef.	0
2.	$-\frac{4\pi}{3}$	$\frac{\sqrt{3}}{2}$	$-\frac{1}{2}$	$-\sqrt{3}$	$\frac{2\sqrt{3}}{3}$	−2	$-\frac{\sqrt{3}}{3}$
3.	$\frac{19\pi}{6}$	$-\frac{1}{2}$	$-\frac{\sqrt{3}}{2}$	$\frac{\sqrt{3}}{3}$	−2	$-\frac{2\sqrt{3}}{3}$	$\sqrt{3}$
4.	$-\frac{5\pi}{4}$	$\frac{\sqrt{2}}{2}$	$-\frac{\sqrt{2}}{2}$	−1	$\sqrt{2}$	$-\sqrt{2}$	−1

5. $\frac{-2-4}{-2+4} = \frac{-6}{2} = -3$ **6.** $\log_4(-(-2)) = \log_4 2 = \log_4 4^{1/2} = \frac{1}{2}$

7. $\sum_{n=1}^{5} 4 \cdot (-2)^{n-1} = \frac{4(1-(-2)^5)}{1-(-2)} = \frac{4(1-(-32))}{3} = 44$ **8.** $4^{-1/2} = \frac{1}{\sqrt{4}} = \frac{1}{2}$

Page 635 • APPLICATION

1. frequency = 352; period = $\frac{1}{352}$; $b = \frac{2\pi}{\frac{1}{352}} = 704\pi$; $y = 0.5 \cos 704\pi t$

2. **a.** the frequency will be $\frac{396}{\frac{3}{4}} = 528$ Hz; C′

   b. Let x = the length of the vibrating string; $30(330) = 396x$, $x = 25$; 25 cm

Pages 639–640 • WRITTEN EXERCISES

A

1. $\sin\alpha \sec\alpha = \sin\alpha \cdot \frac{1}{\cos\alpha} = \frac{\sin\alpha}{\cos\alpha} = \tan\alpha$

2. $\cos\theta \csc\theta = \cos\theta \cdot \frac{1}{\sin\theta} = \frac{\cos\theta}{\sin\theta} = \cot\theta$

3. $\frac{\tan x}{\sin x} = \tan x \cdot \frac{1}{\sin x} = \frac{\sin x}{\cos x} \cdot \frac{1}{\sin x} = \frac{1}{\cos x} = \sec x$

4. $\frac{\cos t}{\cot t} = \cos t \cdot \frac{1}{\cot t} = \cos t \cdot \tan t = \cos t \cdot \frac{\sin t}{\cos t} = \sin t$

5. $(1 - \sin\theta)(1 + \sin\theta) = 1 - \sin^2\theta = \cos^2\theta$

6. $(\sec\phi - 1)(\sec\phi + 1) = \sec^2\phi - 1 = \tan^2\phi$

7. $\cos\alpha \csc\alpha \tan\alpha = \cos\alpha \cdot \frac{1}{\sin\alpha} \cdot \frac{\sin\alpha}{\cos\alpha} = 1$

8. $\cot t \sec t \sin t = \frac{\cos t}{\sin t} \cdot \frac{1}{\cos t} \cdot \sin t = 1$

9. $\frac{\sin x}{\csc x} + \frac{\cos x}{\sec x} = \frac{\sin x}{\frac{1}{\sin x}} + \frac{\cos x}{\frac{1}{\cos x}} = \sin^2 x + \cos^2 x = 1$

10. $\frac{\csc x}{\sin x} - \frac{\cot x}{\tan x} = \frac{\csc x}{\frac{1}{\csc x}} - \frac{\cot x}{\frac{1}{\cot x}} = \csc^2 x - \cot^2 x = 1$

11. $\frac{\sec\theta}{\cos\theta} - 1 = \frac{\sec\theta}{\frac{1}{\sec\theta}} - 1 = \sec^2\theta - 1 = \tan^2\theta$

12. $\frac{\sec t}{\cos t} - \sec t \cos t = \frac{\sec t}{\frac{1}{\sec t}} - \sec t \cdot \frac{1}{\sec t} = \sec^2 t - 1 = \tan^2 t$

13. $\frac{1 + \tan^2\alpha}{\tan^2\alpha} = \frac{1}{\tan^2\alpha} + 1 = \cot^2\alpha + 1 = \csc^2\alpha$

14. $\frac{1 + \tan^2\theta}{1 + \cot^2\theta} = \frac{\sec^2\theta}{\csc^2\theta} = \frac{\frac{1}{\cos^2\theta}}{\frac{1}{\sin^2\theta}} = \frac{\sin^2\theta}{\cos^2\theta} = \tan^2\theta$

15. $\cos^2 50° + \sin^2 50° = 1$ **16.** $1 + \tan^2 50° = \sec^2 50°$

17. $\csc^2 t - \cot^2 t = 1$ **18.** $\sec^2 350° - \tan^2 350° = 1$

19. $\frac{\sin\alpha\cos\alpha}{1 - \sin^2\alpha} = \frac{\sin\alpha\cos\alpha}{\cos^2\alpha} = \frac{\sin\alpha}{\cos\alpha} = \tan\alpha$

20. $\frac{1-\cos^2\theta}{\sin\theta\cos\theta} = \frac{\sin^2\theta}{\sin\theta\cos\theta} = \frac{\sin\theta}{\cos\theta} = \tan\theta$

21. $\sec x - \sin x\tan x = \frac{1}{\cos x} - \sin x\cdot\frac{\sin x}{\cos x} = \frac{1}{\cos x}(1-\sin^2 x) = \frac{\cos^2 x}{\cos x} = \cos x$

22. $\cos^2 t(\cot^2 t + 1) = \cos^2 t(\csc^2 t) = \frac{\cos^2 t}{\sin^2 t} = \cot^2 t$

23. $\frac{1-\sin^2\phi}{1-\sin\phi} - 1 = \frac{(1-\sin\phi)(1+\sin\phi)}{(1-\sin\phi)} - 1 = 1 + \sin\phi - 1 = \sin\phi$

24. $\frac{\sec^2\alpha - 1}{\sec\alpha + 1} + 1 = \frac{(\sec\alpha - 1)(\sec\alpha + 1)}{(\sec\alpha + 1)} + 1 = \sec\alpha - 1 + 1 = \sec\alpha$

25. $\sec x = \frac{1}{\cos x} = \pm\frac{1}{\sqrt{1-\sin^2 x}}$ **26.** $\csc x = \frac{1}{\sin x} = \pm\frac{1}{\sqrt{1-\cos^2 x}}$

27. $\tan t = \frac{\sin t}{\cos t} = \pm\frac{\sin t}{\sqrt{1-\sin^2 t}}$ **28.** $\tan t = \frac{\sin t}{\cos t} = \pm\frac{\sqrt{1-\cos^2 t}}{\cos t}$

29. $\tan\alpha\sec\alpha = \frac{\sin\alpha}{\cos\alpha}\cdot\frac{1}{\cos\alpha} = \frac{\sin\alpha}{\cos^2\alpha} = \frac{\sin\alpha}{1-\sin^2\alpha}$

30. $\tan\alpha\sec\alpha = \frac{\sin\alpha}{\cos\alpha}\cdot\frac{1}{\cos\alpha} = \frac{\sin\alpha}{\cos^2\alpha} = \pm\frac{\sqrt{1-\cos^2\alpha}}{\cos^2\alpha}$

31. $\sin^2 x(1+\cot^2 x) = \sin^2 x(\csc^2 x) = \sin^2 x\cdot\frac{1}{\sin^2 x} = 1$

32. $\sin^2\alpha(\csc^2\alpha + \sec^2\alpha) = \sin^2\alpha\csc^2\alpha + \sin^2\alpha\sec^2\alpha = \sin^2\alpha\cdot\frac{1}{\sin^2\alpha} +$

$\sin^2\alpha\cdot\frac{1}{\cos^2\alpha} = 1 + \frac{\sin^2\alpha}{\cos^2\alpha} = 1 + \tan^2\alpha = \sec^2\alpha$

33. $\cos^2\theta - \sin^2\theta = (1-\sin^2\theta) - \sin^2\theta = 1 - 2\sin^2\theta$

34. $\cos^2 t - \sin^2 t = \cos^2 t - (1-\cos^2 t) = 2\cos^2 t - 1$

35. $\cot\phi + \tan\phi = \frac{\cos\phi}{\sin\phi} + \frac{\sin\phi}{\cos\phi} = \frac{\cos^2\phi + \sin^2\phi}{\sin\phi\cos\phi} = \frac{1}{\sin\phi\cos\phi} = \csc\phi\sec\phi$

36. $\sec^2\alpha + \csc^2\alpha = \frac{1}{\cos^2\alpha} + \frac{1}{\sin^2\alpha} = \frac{\sin^2\alpha + \cos^2\alpha}{\cos^2\alpha\sin^2\alpha} = \frac{1}{\cos^2\alpha\sin^2\alpha} = \sec^2\alpha\csc^2\alpha$

37. $\cos^4 x - \sin^4 x = (\cos^2 x + \sin^2 x)(\cos^2 x - \sin^2 x) = 1(\cos^2 x - \sin^2 x) =$
$\cos^2 x - \sin^2 x$

38. $\cos^2\theta\tan^2\theta + \sin^2\theta\tan^2\theta + 1 = \tan^2\theta(\cos^2\theta + \sin^2\theta) + 1 = \tan^2\theta(1) + 1 =$
$\tan^2\theta + 1 = \sec^2\theta$

B **39.** $\frac{\tan t + \cot t}{\sec^2 t} = \cos^2 t\left(\tan t + \frac{1}{\tan t}\right) = \cos^2 t\left(\frac{\tan^2 t + 1}{\tan t}\right) = \cos^2 t\left(\frac{\sec^2 t}{\tan t}\right) =$

$\cos^2 t\left(\frac{1}{\cos^2 t}\cdot\frac{1}{\tan t}\right) = \frac{1}{\tan t} = \cot t$

40. $\frac{\sec\alpha - \cos\alpha}{\tan^2\alpha} = \cot^2\alpha\left(\frac{1}{\cos\alpha} - \cos\alpha\right) = \frac{\cos^2\alpha}{\sin^2\alpha}\left(\frac{1-\cos^2\alpha}{\cos\alpha}\right) = \frac{\cos\alpha(\sin^2\alpha)}{\sin^2\alpha} = \cos\alpha$

41. $\cot\theta(\cos\theta\tan\theta + \sin\theta) = \cos\theta\tan\theta\cot\theta + \sin\theta\cot\theta = \cos\theta +$

$\sin\theta\cdot\frac{\cos\theta}{\sin\theta} = \cos\theta + \cos\theta = 2\cos\theta$

42. $\sin\phi + \cos\phi\cot\phi = \sin\phi + \frac{\cos^2\phi}{\sin\phi} = \frac{\sin^2\phi + \cos^2\phi}{\sin\phi} = \frac{1}{\sin\phi} = \csc\phi$

43. $\dfrac{\tan^2 x}{\sec x + 1} + 1 = \dfrac{\sec^2 x - 1}{\sec x + 1} + 1 = \dfrac{(\sec x - 1)(\sec x + 1)}{(\sec x + 1)} + 1 = \sec x - 1 + 1 = \sec x$

44. $\dfrac{\sec t + \csc t}{1 + \tan t} = \dfrac{\dfrac{1}{\cos t} + \dfrac{1}{\sin t}}{1 + \dfrac{\sin t}{\cos t}} = \dfrac{\sin t + \cos t}{\sin t \cos t + \sin^2 t} = \dfrac{\sin t + \cos t}{\sin t(\cos t + \sin t)} = \dfrac{1}{\sin t} = \csc t$

45. $\dfrac{\tan\theta}{1 + \sec\theta} + \dfrac{1 + \sec\theta}{\tan\theta} = \dfrac{\tan^2\theta + (1 + \sec\theta)^2}{(1 + \sec\theta)\tan\theta} = \dfrac{\tan^2\theta + 1 + 2\sec\theta + \sec^2\theta}{\tan\theta(1 + \sec\theta)} =$

$\dfrac{2\sec^2\theta + 2\sec\theta}{\tan\theta(1 + \sec\theta)} = \dfrac{2\sec\theta(\sec\theta + 1)}{\tan\theta(1 + \sec\theta)} = \dfrac{\dfrac{2}{\cos\theta}}{\dfrac{\sin\theta}{\cos\theta}} = \dfrac{2}{\sin\theta} = 2\csc\theta$

46. $\dfrac{\sin\alpha}{1 + \cos\alpha} + \dfrac{1 + \cos\alpha}{\sin\alpha} = \dfrac{\sin^2\alpha + (1 + \cos\alpha)^2}{\sin\alpha(1 + \cos\alpha)} = \dfrac{\sin^2\alpha + 1 + 2\cos\alpha + \cos^2\alpha}{\sin\alpha(1 + \cos\alpha)} =$

$\dfrac{2 + 2\cos\alpha}{\sin\alpha(1 + \cos\alpha)} = \dfrac{2(1 + \cos\alpha)}{\sin\alpha(1 + \cos\alpha)} = \dfrac{2}{\sin\alpha} = 2\csc\alpha$

47. $(\cos t + \sin t)^2 + (\cos t - \sin t)^2 = \cos^2 t + 2\cos t\sin t + \sin^2 t + \cos^2 t - 2\cos t\sin t + \sin^2 t = 2(\cos^2 t + \sin^2 t) = 2$

48. $(1 + \tan x)^2 + (1 - \tan x)^2 = 1 + 2\tan x + \tan^2 x + 1 - 2\tan x + \tan^2 x = 2(1 + \tan^2 x) = 2\sec^2 x$

49. $\dfrac{\sec x + 1}{\sec x - 1} = \dfrac{\dfrac{1}{\cos x} + 1}{\dfrac{1}{\cos x} - 1} = \dfrac{1 + \cos x}{1 - \cos x}$

50. $\dfrac{\csc\phi}{\csc\phi - 1} + \dfrac{\csc\phi}{\csc\phi + 1} = \dfrac{\csc\phi(\csc\phi + 1) + \csc\phi(\csc\phi - 1)}{(\csc\phi - 1)(\csc\phi + 1)} = \dfrac{2\csc^2\phi}{\csc^2\phi - 1} =$

$\dfrac{2\csc^2\phi}{\cot^2\phi} = \dfrac{2 \cdot \dfrac{1}{\sin^2\phi}}{\dfrac{\cos^2\phi}{\sin^2\phi}} = \dfrac{2}{\cos^2\phi} = 2\sec^2\phi$

51. $(\cot\alpha + \tan\alpha)^2 = \left(\dfrac{\cos\alpha}{\sin\alpha} + \dfrac{\sin\alpha}{\cos\alpha}\right)^2 = \left(\dfrac{\cos^2\alpha + \sin^2\alpha}{\sin\alpha\cos\alpha}\right)^2 = \left(\dfrac{1}{\sin\alpha\cos\alpha}\right)^2 = (\csc\alpha\sec\alpha)^2 = \csc^2\alpha\sec^2\alpha$

52. $(\tan t + \cot t)(\cos t + \sin t) = \left(\dfrac{\sin t}{\cos t} + \dfrac{\cos t}{\sin t}\right)(\cos t + \sin t) = \left(\dfrac{\sin^2 t + \cos^2 t}{\cos t\sin t}\right)(\cos t + \sin t) = \dfrac{\cos t + \sin t}{\cos t\sin t} = \dfrac{\cos t}{\cos t\sin t} + \dfrac{\sin t}{\cos t\sin t} = \dfrac{1}{\sin t} + \dfrac{1}{\cos t} = \sec t + \csc t$

53. $\csc x - \cot x = \dfrac{1}{\sin x} - \dfrac{\cos x}{\sin x} = \dfrac{1 - \cos x}{\sin x} = \dfrac{(1 - \cos x)(1 + \cos x)}{\sin x(1 + \cos x)} =$

$\dfrac{1 - \cos^2 x}{\sin x(1 + \cos x)} = \dfrac{\sin^2 x}{\sin x(1 + \cos x)} = \dfrac{\sin x}{1 + \cos x}$

54. $\dfrac{\sec y - \tan y}{1 - \sin y} = \dfrac{\dfrac{1}{\cos y} - \dfrac{\sin y}{\cos y}}{1 - \sin y} = \dfrac{\dfrac{1 - \sin y}{\cos y}}{1 - \sin y} = \dfrac{1}{\cos y} = \sec y$

55. $\dfrac{1}{\sec t - \tan t} = \dfrac{1}{\dfrac{1}{\cos t} - \dfrac{\sin t}{\cos t}} = \dfrac{1}{\dfrac{1 - \sin t}{\cos t}} = \dfrac{\cos t}{1 - \sin t}$

56. $\dfrac{\sec \theta - 1}{\tan \theta} = \dfrac{(\sec \theta - 1)(\sec \theta + 1)}{\tan \theta(\sec \theta + 1)} = \dfrac{\sec^2 \theta - 1}{\tan \theta(\sec \theta + 1)} = \dfrac{\tan^2 \theta}{\tan \theta(\sec \theta + 1)} = \dfrac{\tan \theta}{\sec \theta + 1}$

C 57. $\dfrac{\sin^2 \phi + 2 \cos \phi - 1}{\sin^2 \phi + 3 \cos \phi - 3} = \dfrac{1 - \cos^2 \phi + 2 \cos \phi - 1}{1 - \cos^2 \phi + 3 \cos \phi - 3} = \dfrac{-\cos^2 \phi + 2 \cos \phi}{-\cos^2 \phi + 3 \cos \phi - 2} =$
$\dfrac{-\cos \phi(\cos \phi - 2)}{-(\cos \phi - 2)(\cos \phi - 1)} = \dfrac{\cos \phi}{\cos \phi - 1} = \dfrac{1}{1 - \dfrac{1}{\cos \phi}} = \dfrac{1}{1 - \sec \phi}$

58. $\sqrt{\dfrac{1 - \cos x}{1 + \cos x}} = \sqrt{\dfrac{1 - \cos x}{1 + \cos x} \cdot \dfrac{1 - \cos x}{1 - \cos x}} = \sqrt{\dfrac{1 - 2 \cos x + \cos^2 x}{1 - \cos^2 x}} =$
$\sqrt{\dfrac{1 - 2 \cos x + \cos^2 x}{\sin^2 x}} = \sqrt{\dfrac{1}{\sin^2 x} - \dfrac{2 \cos x}{\sin x \cdot \sin x} + \dfrac{\cos^2 x}{\sin^2 x}} =$
$\sqrt{\csc^2 x - 2 \csc x \cot x + \cot^2 x} = \sqrt{(\csc x - \cot x)^2} = |\csc x - \cot x|$

Pages 643–644 • WRITTEN EXERCISES

A 1. $\cos 105° = \cos(60° + 45°) = \cos 60° \cos 45° - \sin 60° \sin 45° =$
$\dfrac{1}{2} \cdot \dfrac{\sqrt{2}}{2} - \dfrac{\sqrt{3}}{2} \cdot \dfrac{\sqrt{2}}{2} = \dfrac{\sqrt{2} - \sqrt{6}}{4}$

2. $\sin 15° = \sin(45° - 30°) = \sin 45° \cos 30° - \cos 45° \sin 30° = \dfrac{\sqrt{2}}{2} \cdot \dfrac{\sqrt{3}}{2} - \dfrac{\sqrt{2}}{2} \cdot \dfrac{1}{2} =$
$\dfrac{\sqrt{6} - \sqrt{2}}{4}$

3. $\sin 165° = \sin(135° + 30°) = \sin 135° \cos 30° + \cos 135° \sin 30° =$
$\dfrac{\sqrt{2}}{2} \cdot \dfrac{\sqrt{3}}{2} + \left(-\dfrac{\sqrt{2}}{2}\right) \cdot \left(\dfrac{1}{2}\right) = \dfrac{\sqrt{6} - \sqrt{2}}{4}$

4. $\cos 285° = \cos(240° + 45°) = \cos 240° \cos 45° - \sin 240° \sin 45° =$
$-\dfrac{1}{2} \cdot \dfrac{\sqrt{2}}{2} - \left(-\dfrac{\sqrt{3}}{2} \cdot \dfrac{\sqrt{2}}{2}\right) = \dfrac{-\sqrt{2} + \sqrt{6}}{4} = \dfrac{\sqrt{6} - \sqrt{2}}{4}$

5. $\cos 195° = \cos(150° + 45°) = \cos 150° \cos 45° - \sin 150° \sin 45° =$
$-\dfrac{\sqrt{3}}{2} \cdot \dfrac{\sqrt{2}}{2} - \dfrac{1}{2} \cdot \dfrac{\sqrt{2}}{2} = \dfrac{-\sqrt{6} - \sqrt{2}}{4}$

6. $\sin 255° = \sin(300° - 45°) = \sin 300° \cos 45° - \cos 300° \sin 45° =$
$-\dfrac{\sqrt{3}}{2} \cdot \dfrac{\sqrt{2}}{2} - \dfrac{1}{2} \cdot \dfrac{\sqrt{2}}{2} = \dfrac{-\sqrt{6} - \sqrt{2}}{4}$

7. $\cos 20° \cos 40° - \sin 20° \sin 40° = \cos(20° + 40°) = \cos 60°; \dfrac{1}{2}$

8. $\sin 50° \cos 5° - \cos 50° \sin 5° = \sin(50° - 5°) = \sin 45°; \dfrac{\sqrt{2}}{2}$

9. $\sin 130° \cos 80° + \cos 130° \sin 80° = \sin(130° + 80°) = \sin 210°; -\dfrac{1}{2}$

10. $\cos 50° \cos 140° + \sin 50° \sin 140° = \cos(50° - 140°) = \cos(-90°); 0$

11. $\cos \dfrac{\pi}{4} \cos \dfrac{\pi}{12} + \sin \dfrac{\pi}{4} \sin \dfrac{\pi}{12} = \cos\left(\dfrac{\pi}{4} - \dfrac{\pi}{12}\right) = \cos\left(\dfrac{\pi}{6}\right); \dfrac{\sqrt{3}}{2}$

12. $\sin \frac{\pi}{3} \cos \frac{\pi}{12} - \cos \frac{\pi}{3} \sin \frac{\pi}{12} = \sin\left(\frac{\pi}{3} - \frac{\pi}{12}\right) = \sin \frac{\pi}{4}; \frac{\sqrt{2}}{2}$

13. $\sin 3\theta \cos \theta - \cos 3\theta \sin \theta = \sin(3\theta - \theta) = \sin 2\theta$

14. $\cos 2\phi \cos \phi - \sin 2\phi \sin \phi = \cos(2\phi + \phi) = \cos 3\phi$

15. $\sin\left(\frac{\pi}{2} + \theta\right) = \sin \frac{\pi}{2} \cos \theta + \cos \frac{\pi}{2} \sin \theta = 1 \cdot \cos \theta + 0 \cdot \sin \theta = \cos \theta$

16. $\cos\left(\frac{\pi}{2} - \theta\right) = \cos \frac{\pi}{2} \cos \theta + \sin \frac{\pi}{2} \sin \theta = 0 \cdot \cos \theta + 1 \cdot \sin \theta = \sin \theta$

17. $\cos(\pi - x) = \cos \pi \cos x + \sin \pi \sin x = -1 \cdot \cos x + 0 \cdot \sin x = -\cos x$

18. $\sin(\pi + x) = \sin \pi \cos x + \cos \pi \sin x = 0 \cdot \cos x + (-1)\sin x = -\sin x$

19. $\sin\left(\frac{3\pi}{2} - x\right) = \sin \frac{3\pi}{2} \cos x - \cos \frac{3\pi}{2} \sin x = -1 \cdot \cos x - 0 \cdot \sin x = -\cos x$

20. $\cos\left(\frac{3\pi}{2} + x\right) = \cos \frac{3\pi}{2} \cos x - \sin \frac{3\pi}{2} \sin x = 0 \cdot \cos x - (-1)\sin x = \sin x$

B **21.** $\sin\left(\frac{\pi}{6} + \theta\right) + \sin\left(\frac{\pi}{6} - \theta\right) = \sin \frac{\pi}{6} \cos \theta + \cos \frac{\pi}{6} \sin \theta + \sin \frac{\pi}{6} \cos \theta -$

$\cos \frac{\pi}{6} \sin \theta = 2 \sin \frac{\pi}{6} \cos \theta = 2 \cdot \frac{1}{2} \cdot \cos \theta = \cos \theta$

22. $\cos\left(\frac{\pi}{3} + \theta\right) + \cos\left(\frac{\pi}{3} - \theta\right) = \cos \frac{\pi}{3} \cos \theta - \sin \frac{\pi}{3} \sin \theta + \cos \frac{\pi}{3} \cos \theta +$

$\sin \frac{\pi}{3} \sin \theta = 2 \cos \frac{\pi}{3} \cos \theta = 2 \cdot \frac{1}{2} \cdot \cos \theta = \cos \theta$

23. $\cos(x - y)\cos y - \sin(x - y)\sin y = \cos[(x - y) + y] = \cos x$

24. $\sin(x + y)\cos y - \cos(x + y)\sin y = \sin[(x + y) - y] = \sin x$

25. $\frac{\sin(\alpha + \beta)}{\cos \alpha \cos \beta} = \frac{\sin \alpha \cos \beta + \cos \alpha \sin \beta}{\cos \alpha \cos \beta} = \frac{\sin \alpha \cos \beta}{\cos \alpha \cos \beta} + \frac{\cos \alpha \sin \beta}{\cos \alpha \cos \beta} =$

$\frac{\sin \alpha}{\cos \alpha} + \frac{\sin \beta}{\cos \beta} = \tan \alpha + \tan \beta$

26. $\frac{\sin(\alpha + \beta)}{\sin \alpha \sin \beta} = \frac{\sin \alpha \cos \beta + \cos \alpha \sin \beta}{\sin \alpha \sin \beta} = \frac{\sin \alpha \cos \beta}{\sin \alpha \sin \beta} + \frac{\cos \alpha \sin \beta}{\sin \alpha \sin \beta} = \frac{\cos \beta}{\sin \beta} + \frac{\cos \alpha}{\sin \alpha} =$

$\cot \beta + \cot \alpha = \cot \alpha + \cot \beta$

27. $\cos \theta \cos \phi(\tan \theta + \tan \phi) = \cos \theta \cos \phi \frac{\sin \theta}{\cos \theta} + \cos \theta \cos \phi \frac{\sin \phi}{\cos \phi} =$

$\cos \phi \sin \theta + \cos \theta \sin \phi = \sin(\theta + \phi)$

28. $\sin \theta \sin \phi(\cot \theta \cot \phi - 1) = \sin \theta \sin \phi \cdot \frac{\cos \theta}{\sin \theta} \cdot \frac{\cos \phi}{\sin \phi} - \sin \theta \sin \phi =$

$\cos \theta \cos \phi - \sin \theta \sin \phi = \cos(\theta + \phi)$

29. $\sin(\alpha - \beta) + \sin(\alpha + \beta) = \sin \alpha \cos \beta - \cos \alpha \sin \beta + \sin \alpha \cos \beta +$
$\cos \alpha \sin \beta = 2 \sin \alpha \cos \beta$

30. $\cos(\alpha - \beta) + \cos(\alpha + \beta) = \cos \alpha \cos \beta + \sin \alpha \sin \beta + \cos \alpha \cos \beta -$
$\sin \alpha \sin \beta = 2 \cos \alpha \cos \beta$

Ex. 31. and 32.: $\cos \alpha = -\sqrt{1 - \left(-\frac{3}{5}\right)^2} = -\frac{4}{5}$; $\sin \beta = -\sqrt{1 - \left(\frac{8}{17}\right)^2} = -\frac{15}{17}$

31. a. $\sin(\alpha + \beta) = \sin \alpha \cos \beta + \cos \alpha \sin \beta = \left(-\frac{3}{5}\right)\left(\frac{8}{17}\right) + \left(-\frac{4}{5}\right)\left(-\frac{15}{17}\right) =$

$\frac{-24 + 60}{85} = \frac{36}{85}$

b. $\cos(\alpha + \beta) = \cos \alpha \cos \beta - \sin \alpha \sin \beta = \left(-\frac{4}{5}\right)\left(\frac{8}{17}\right) - \left(-\frac{3}{5}\right)\left(-\frac{15}{17}\right) =$

$\frac{-32 - 45}{85} = -\frac{77}{85}$

c. Since $\sin(\alpha + \beta)$ is positive and $\cos(\alpha + \beta)$ is negative, $\alpha + \beta$ is in quadrant II

32. a. $\sin(\alpha - \beta) = \sin \alpha \cos \beta - \cos \alpha \sin \beta = \left(-\frac{3}{5}\right)\left(\frac{8}{17}\right) - \left(-\frac{4}{5}\right)\left(-\frac{15}{17}\right) =$

$\frac{-24 - 60}{85} = -\frac{84}{85}$

b. $\cos(\alpha - \beta) = \cos \alpha \cos \beta + \sin \alpha \sin \beta = \left(-\frac{4}{5}\right)\left(\frac{8}{17}\right) + \left(-\frac{3}{5}\right)\left(-\frac{15}{17}\right) =$

$\frac{-32 + 45}{85} = \frac{13}{85}$

c. Since $\sin(\alpha - \beta)$ is negative and $\cos(\alpha - \beta)$ is positive, $\alpha - \beta$ is in quadrant IV

33. $\sin(\alpha - \beta) = \sin(\alpha + (-\beta)) = \sin \alpha \cos(-\beta) + \cos \alpha \sin(-\beta) =$
$\sin \alpha \cos \beta + \cos \alpha(-\sin \beta) = \sin \alpha \cos \beta - \cos \alpha \sin \beta$

34. $\sin 2\theta = \sin(\theta + \theta) = \sin \theta \cos \theta + \cos \theta \sin \theta = 2 \sin \theta \cos \theta$

35. $\tan(\pi - \alpha) = \frac{\sin(\pi - \alpha)}{\cos(\pi - \alpha)} = \frac{\sin \pi \cos \alpha - \cos \pi \sin \alpha}{\cos \pi \cos \alpha + \sin \pi \sin \alpha} = \frac{0 \cdot \cos \alpha - (-1)\sin \alpha}{(-1)\cos \alpha + (0) \cdot \sin \alpha} =$

$\frac{\sin \alpha}{-\cos \alpha} = -\tan \alpha$

C **36.** Using the Law of Sines, $\frac{\sin \alpha}{h} = \frac{\sin(90 - \alpha)}{x}$, or $\frac{\sin \alpha}{h} = \frac{\cos \alpha}{x}$; $x = \frac{h \cos \alpha}{\sin \alpha}$;

$\frac{\sin \beta}{h} = \frac{\sin(90 - \beta)}{d - x}$; $d - x = \frac{h \cos \beta}{\sin \beta}$; $d = d - x + x = \frac{h \cos \beta}{\sin \beta} + \frac{h \cos \alpha}{\sin \alpha} =$

$\frac{h \cos \beta \sin \alpha + h \cos \alpha \sin \beta}{\sin \beta \sin \alpha} = \frac{h \sin(\alpha + \beta)}{\sin \alpha \sin \beta}$; $h = \frac{d \sin \alpha \sin \beta}{\sin(\alpha + \beta)}$. h can also be found

using area formulas: $\frac{1}{2}dh = \frac{1}{2}d^2 \frac{\sin \alpha \sin \beta}{\sin[180° - (\alpha + \beta)]} = \frac{1}{2}d^2 \frac{\sin \alpha \sin \beta}{\sin(\alpha + \beta)}$; $h = \frac{d \sin \alpha \sin \beta}{\sin(\alpha + \beta)}$

37. Using the Law of Sines, $\frac{\sin(180° - \alpha)}{h} = \frac{\sin[90° - (180° - \alpha)]}{x}$; $\frac{\sin \alpha}{h} = \frac{-\cos \alpha}{x}$;

$x = \frac{-h \cos \alpha}{\sin \alpha}$; $\frac{\sin \beta}{h} = \frac{\sin(90° - \beta)}{d + x}$; $\frac{\sin \beta}{h} = \frac{\cos \beta}{d + x}$; $d + x = \frac{h \cos \beta}{\sin \beta}$; $d = d + x - x =$

$\frac{h \cos \beta}{\sin \beta} + \frac{h \cos \alpha}{\sin \alpha} = \frac{h \cos \beta \sin \alpha + h \cos \alpha \sin \beta}{\sin \beta \sin \alpha} = \frac{h \sin(\alpha + \beta)}{\sin \alpha \sin \beta}$; $h = \frac{d \sin \alpha \sin \beta}{\sin(\alpha + \beta)}$.

h can also be found using area formulas; see Ex. 36.

Page 645 • MIXED REVIEW EXERCISES

1.

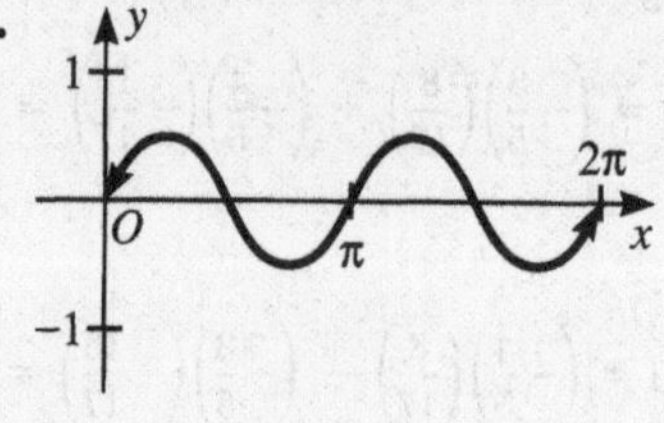

2.

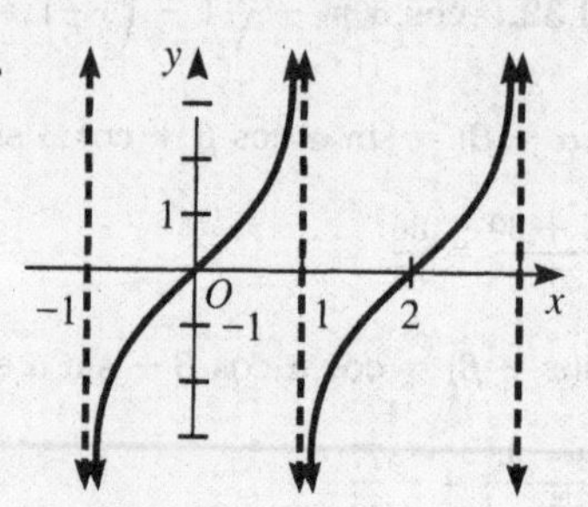

3.

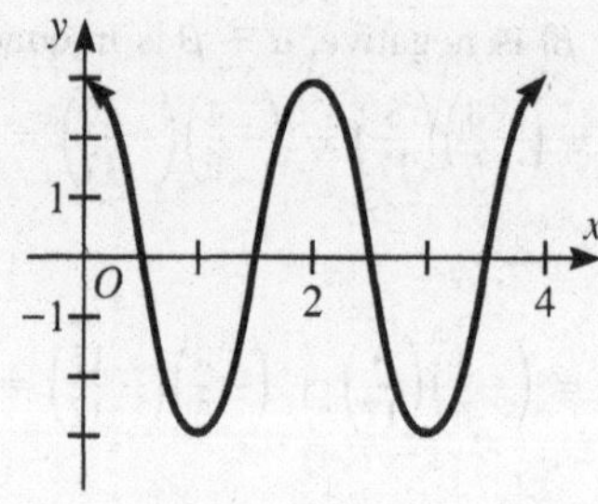

4. $\sin^2 x(1 + \cot^2 x) = \sin^2 x(\csc^2 x) =$

$\sin^2 x \cdot \frac{1}{\sin^2 x} = 1$

5. $x^6(x^{n-2})^3 = x^6 x^{3n-6} = x^{3n}$

6. $\sqrt[3]{16x^6} = 2x^2\sqrt[3]{2}$

7. $\frac{\log_2 x}{\log_2 \frac{1}{x}} = \frac{\log_2 x}{-\log_2 x} = -1$

8. $\frac{(1 + \sqrt{3})}{(1 - \sqrt{3})} \cdot \frac{(1 + \sqrt{3})}{(1 + \sqrt{3})} = \frac{4 + 2\sqrt{3}}{1 - 3} = \frac{2(2 + \sqrt{3})}{-2} = -2 - \sqrt{3}$

9. $\sqrt{\frac{1 - \left(-\frac{5}{13}\right)}{2}} = \sqrt{\frac{\frac{18}{13}}{2}} = \sqrt{\frac{9}{13}} = \frac{3}{\sqrt{13}} = \frac{3\sqrt{13}}{13}$

10. $\frac{(x^{2/3})^6}{(x^{1/2})^6} = \frac{x^4}{x^3} = x^{4-3} = x$ **11.** $\frac{1}{x} + \frac{1}{x(x-1)} = \frac{(x-1)+1}{x(x-1)} = \frac{x}{x(x-1)} = \frac{1}{x-1}$

12. $\csc x - \cos x \cot x = \frac{1}{\sin x} - \cos x \cdot \frac{\cos x}{\sin x} = \frac{1 - \cos^2 x}{\sin x} = \frac{\sin^2 x}{\sin x} = \sin x$

Page 645 • COMPUTER EXERCISES

1.

```
10 LET S5 = 0.087155743
20 LET C5 =  SQR (1 - S5 ↑ 2)
30 LET A = 5
40 LET S54 =  INT (10000 * S5 + 0.5) / 10000
45 PRINT "X"; TAB( 12);"SIN X"
50 PRINT A; TAB (11);S54
60 LET S0 = S5
70 LET C0 = C5
80 FOR A = 10 TO 90 STEP 5
90 LET SN = S0 * C5 + S5 * C0
100 LET CN = SQR (1 - SN ↑ 2)
110 LET SN4 = INT (10000 * SN + 0.5) / 10000
120 PRINT A; TAB( 10); SN4
130 LET S0 = SN
140 LET C0 = CN
150 NEXT A
160 END
```

2.
```
10 LET S5 = 0.087155743
20 LET C5 =  SQR (1 - S5 ↑ 2)
21 LET C54 = INT (10000 * C5 + 0.5) / 10000
25 LET T5 = S5 / C5
26 LET T54 = INT (10000 * T5 + 0.5) / 10000
30 LET A = 5
40 LET S54 = INT (10000 * S5 + 0.5) / 10000
45 PRINT "X"; TAB( 10);"SIN X"; TAB( 20);"COS X"; TAB( 30);
   "TAN X"
50 PRINT A; TAB( 10);S54; TAB( 20);C54; TAB( 30 );T54
60 LET S0 = S5
70 LET C0 = C5
80 FOR A = 10 TO 85 STEP 5
90 LET SN = S0 * C5 + S5 * C0
100 LET CN = SQR (1 - SN ↑ 2)
101 LET TN = SN / CN
102 LET TN4 = INT (10000 * TN + 0.5) / 10000
110 LET SN4 = INT (10000 * SN + 0.5) / 10000
120 LET CN4 = INT (10000 * CN + 0.5) / 10000
130 PRINT A; TAB( 10);SN4; TAB( 20);CN4; TAB( 30 );TN4
140 LET S0 = SN
150 LET C0 = CN
160 NEXT A
170 END
```

X	SIN X	COS X	TAN X
5	.0872	.9962	.0875
10	.1737	.9848	.1764
15	.2589	.9659	.2681
20	.3421	.9396	.3641
25	.4227	.9063	.4665
30	.5001	.866	.5775
35	.5737	.8191	.7005
40	.6429	.7659	.8395
45	.7072	.707	1.0004
50	.7662	.6426	1.1922
55	.8193	.5733	1.4291
60	.8662	.4997	1.7333
65	.9065	.4222	2.1468
70	.9399	.3415	2.7519
75	.9661	.2581	3.7426
80	.9849	.1729	5.6958
85	.9962	.0867	11.4903

3.
```
5 PRINT "ENTER N, SIN(X)"
10 INPUT N, SX
20 LET CX = SQR(1 - SX ↑ 2)
50 LET S0 = SX
```

(Continued)

```
60 LET CO = CX
70 FOR A = 2 TO N
80 LET SN = SO * CX + SX * CO
90 LET CN = SQR(1 - SN ↑ 2)
110 LET SO = SN
120 LET CO = CN
130 NEXT A
140 PRINT "SIN("; N; "X) = "; SN
150 END
```

4. a. SIN(7X) = 0.890966414 **b.** SIN(15X) = 1

Page 649 • WRITTEN EXERCISES

A

1. $\cos^2 10° - \sin^2 10° = \cos(2 \cdot 10°) = \cos 20°$

2. $2 \sin 105° \cos 105° = \sin(2 \cdot 105°) = \sin 210°$

3. $1 - 2\sin^2 4° = \cos(2 \cdot 4°) = \cos 8°$ **4.** $2\cos^2 \pi - 1 = \cos 2\pi$ **5.** $\sin \frac{\alpha}{2}$

6. $\cos \frac{\alpha}{2}$ **7.** $1 - 2\sin^2 \frac{\theta}{2} = \cos\left(2 \cdot \frac{\theta}{2}\right) = \cos \theta$ **8.** $2 \cos 2\alpha \sin 2\alpha = \sin(2 \cdot 2\alpha) = \sin 4\alpha$

9. $\cos^2 2t - \sin^2 2t = \cos(2 \cdot 2t) = \cos 4t$ **10.** $2\cos^2 \frac{x}{2} - 1 = \cos\left(2 \cdot \frac{x}{2}\right) = \cos x$

11. $\sqrt{\frac{1 - \cos 2\alpha}{2}} = \sin \alpha$ **12.** $\sqrt{\frac{1 + \cos 2\alpha}{2}} = \cos \alpha$

13. $2 \sin 15° \cos 15° = \sin(2 \cdot 15°) = \sin 30° = \frac{1}{2}$

14. $2\cos^2 22.5° - 1 = \cos(2 \cdot 22.5°) = \cos 45° = \frac{\sqrt{2}}{2}$

15. $\cos^2 \frac{\pi}{12} - \sin^2 \frac{\pi}{12} = \cos\left(2 \cdot \frac{\pi}{12}\right) = \cos \frac{\pi}{6} = \frac{\sqrt{3}}{2}$ **16.** $\cos^2 \frac{\pi}{8} + \sin^2 \frac{\pi}{8} = 1$

17. $1 - 2\sin^2 105° = \cos(2 \cdot 105°) = \cos 210° = -\frac{\sqrt{3}}{2}$

18. $2 \sin 165° \cos 165° = \sin(2 \cdot 165°) = \sin 330° = -\frac{1}{2}$

19. $\cos 22.5° = \cos \frac{45°}{2} = +\sqrt{\frac{1 + \cos 45°}{2}} = \sqrt{\frac{1 + \frac{\sqrt{2}}{2}}{2}} = \sqrt{\frac{2 + \sqrt{2}}{4}} = \frac{1}{2}\sqrt{2 + \sqrt{2}}$

20. $\sin 75° = \sin \frac{150°}{2} = +\sqrt{\frac{1 - \cos 150°}{2}} = \sqrt{\frac{1 - \left(-\frac{\sqrt{3}}{2}\right)}{2}} = \sqrt{\frac{2 + \sqrt{3}}{4}} = \frac{1}{2}\sqrt{2 + \sqrt{3}}$

21. $\sin \frac{7\pi}{12} = \sin \frac{\frac{7\pi}{6}}{2} = +\sqrt{\frac{1 - \cos \frac{7\pi}{6}}{2}} = \sqrt{\frac{1 - \left(\frac{\sqrt{3}}{2}\right)}{2}} = \sqrt{\frac{2 + \sqrt{3}}{4}} = \frac{1}{2}\sqrt{2 + \sqrt{3}}$

22. $\cos \frac{5\pi}{8} = \cos \frac{\frac{5\pi}{4}}{2} = -\sqrt{\frac{1 + \cos \frac{5\pi}{4}}{2}} = -\sqrt{\frac{1 + \left(-\frac{\sqrt{2}}{2}\right)}{2}} = -\sqrt{\frac{2 - \sqrt{2}}{4}} =$
$-\frac{1}{2}\sqrt{2 - \sqrt{2}}$

23. $\sin 112.5° = \sin \frac{225°}{2} = +\sqrt{\frac{1 - \cos 225°}{2}} = \sqrt{\frac{1 - \left(-\frac{\sqrt{2}}{2}\right)}{2}} = \sqrt{\frac{2 + \sqrt{2}}{4}} =$
$\frac{1}{2}\sqrt{2 + \sqrt{2}}$

24. $\cos 202.5° = \cos \frac{405°}{2} = -\sqrt{\frac{1 + \cos 405°}{2}} = -\sqrt{\frac{1 + \frac{\sqrt{2}}{2}}{2}} = -\sqrt{\frac{2 + \sqrt{2}}{4}} =$
$-\frac{1}{2}\sqrt{2 + \sqrt{2}}$

Ex. 25–28.: $\sin \alpha = \sqrt{1 - \left(-\frac{4}{5}\right)^2} = \frac{3}{5}$

25. $\cos 2\alpha = 2 \cos^2 \alpha - 1 = 2\left(-\frac{4}{5}\right)^2 - 1 = \frac{32}{25} - 1 = \frac{7}{25}$

26. $\sin 2\alpha = 2 \sin \alpha \cos \alpha = 2\left(\frac{3}{5}\right)\left(-\frac{4}{5}\right) = -\frac{24}{25}$

27. $\sin \frac{\alpha}{2} = +\sqrt{\frac{1 - \cos \alpha}{2}} = \sqrt{\frac{1 - \left(-\frac{4}{5}\right)}{2}} = \sqrt{\frac{9}{10}} = \frac{3}{\sqrt{10}} = \frac{3\sqrt{10}}{10}$

28. $\cos \frac{\alpha}{2} = +\sqrt{\frac{1 + \cos \alpha}{2}} = \sqrt{\frac{1 + \left(-\frac{4}{5}\right)}{2}} = \sqrt{\frac{1}{10}} = \frac{\sqrt{10}}{10}$

Ex. 29–32.: α is in Quadrant IV since $\cos \alpha$ is positive; $\sin \alpha = -\sqrt{1 - \left(\frac{8}{17}\right)^2} = -\frac{15}{17}$;

$\frac{\alpha}{2}$ is in Quadrant II

29. $\sin 2\alpha = 2 \sin \alpha \cos \alpha = 2\left(-\frac{15}{17}\right)\left(\frac{8}{17}\right) = -\frac{240}{289}$

30. $\cos 2\alpha = 2 \cos^2 \alpha - 1 = 2\left(\frac{8}{17}\right)^2 - 1 = \frac{128}{289} - 1 = -\frac{161}{289}$

31. $\cos \frac{\alpha}{2} = -\sqrt{\frac{1 + \cos \alpha}{2}} = -\sqrt{\frac{1 + \frac{8}{17}}{2}} = -\sqrt{\frac{25}{34}} = -\frac{5}{\sqrt{34}} = -\frac{5\sqrt{34}}{34}$

32. $\sin \frac{\alpha}{2} = +\sqrt{\frac{1 - \cos \alpha}{2}} = \sqrt{\frac{1 - \frac{8}{17}}{2}} = \sqrt{\frac{9}{34}} = \frac{3}{\sqrt{34}} = \frac{3\sqrt{34}}{34}$

B **33.** $\cos^4 \theta - \sin^4 \theta = (\cos^2 \theta + \sin^2 \theta)(\cos^2 \theta - \sin^2 \theta) = 1 \cdot (\cos^2 \theta - \sin^2 \theta) = \cos 2\theta$

34. $(\sin \theta + \cos \theta)^2 = \sin^2 \theta + 2 \cos \theta \sin \theta + \cos^2 \theta = 1 + \sin 2\theta$

35. $\sin 4x = \sin(2 \cdot 2x) = 2 \sin 2x \cos 2x = 2(2 \sin x \cos x)(\cos 2x) =$
$4 \sin x \cos x \cos 2x$

36. $\sin x + \sin x \cos 2x = \sin x(1 + \cos 2x) = \sin x(1 + 2\cos^2 x - 1) = \sin x(2\cos^2 x) = (2 \sin x \cos x)(\cos x) = \sin 2x \cos x$

37. $\frac{\sin 2x}{1 + \cos 2x} = \frac{2 \sin x \cos x}{1 + 2\cos^2 x - 1} = \frac{2 \sin x \cos x}{2\cos^2 x} = \frac{\sin x}{\cos x} = \tan x$

38. $\frac{\sin 2x}{1 - \cos 2x} = \frac{2 \sin x \cos x}{1 - (1 - 2\sin^2 x)} = \frac{2 \sin x \cos x}{2 \sin^2 x} = \frac{\cos x}{\sin x} = \cot x$

39. $\cot \alpha + \tan \alpha = \frac{\cos \alpha}{\sin \alpha} + \frac{\sin \alpha}{\cos \alpha} = \frac{\cos^2 \alpha + \sin^2 \alpha}{\sin \alpha \cos \alpha} = \frac{1}{\sin \alpha \cos \alpha} = \frac{1}{\frac{1}{2}(2 \sin \alpha \cos \alpha)} = \frac{2}{\sin 2\alpha} = 2 \csc 2\alpha$

40. $\csc 2\alpha + \cot 2\alpha = \frac{1}{\sin 2\alpha} + \frac{\cos 2\alpha}{\sin 2\alpha} = \frac{1 + (2\cos^2 \alpha - 1)}{\sin 2\alpha} = \frac{2\cos^2 \alpha}{2 \sin \alpha \cos \alpha} = \frac{\cos \alpha}{\sin \alpha} = \cot \alpha$

41. $y = \cos^2 x - \sin^2 x = \cos 2x$; $a = 1$, period $= \pi$

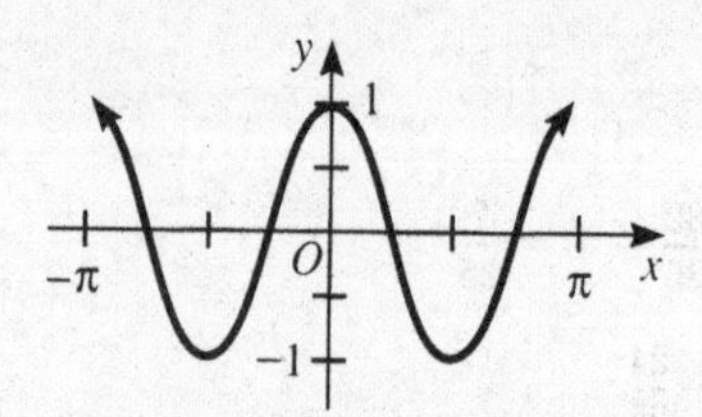

42. $y = \sin x \cos x = \frac{1}{2} \sin 2x$; $a = \frac{1}{2}$, period $= \pi$

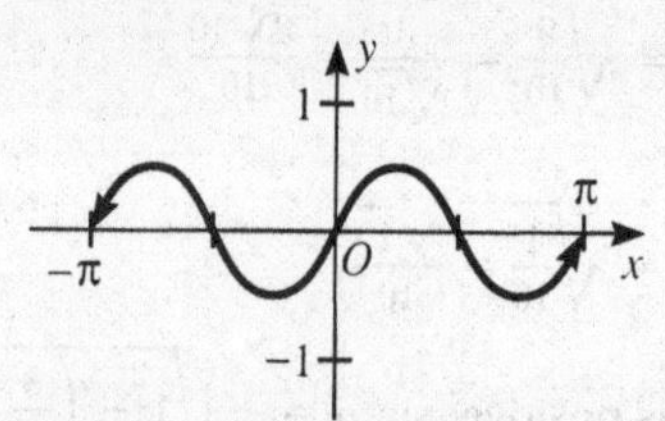

C **43.** $\cos 4\theta = \cos 2(2\theta) = 2\cos^2(2\theta) - 1 = 2(2\cos^2 \theta - 1)^2 - 1 = 2(4\cos^4 \theta - 4\cos^2 \theta + 1) - 1 = 8\cos^4 \theta - 8\cos^2 \theta + 1$

Pages 652–653 • WRITTEN EXERCISES

A **1.** $\tan(80° - 20°) = \tan 60°$ **2.** $\tan(15° + 30°) = \tan 45°$

3. $\tan(140° + 40°) = \tan 180°$ **4.** $\tan(250° - 25°) = \tan 225°$

5. $\tan\left(\frac{7\pi}{12} + \frac{\pi}{4}\right) = \tan \frac{5\pi}{6}$ **6.** $\tan\left(\frac{7\pi}{6} - \frac{\pi}{3}\right) = \tan \frac{5\pi}{6}$ **7.** $\tan[2(22.5°)] = \tan 45°$

8. $\tan[2(67.5°)] = \tan 135°$

9. $\tan 75° = \tan(45° + 30°) = \frac{\tan 45° + \tan 30°}{1 - \tan 45° \tan 30°} = \frac{1 + \frac{\sqrt{3}}{3}}{1 - 1 \cdot \frac{\sqrt{3}}{3}} = \frac{3 + \sqrt{3}}{3 - \sqrt{3}} = \frac{(3 + \sqrt{3})(3 + \sqrt{3})}{(3 - \sqrt{3})(3 + \sqrt{3})} = \frac{12 + 6\sqrt{3}}{6} = 2 + \sqrt{3}$

10. $\tan 15^\circ = \tan(45^\circ - 30^\circ) = \dfrac{\tan 45^\circ - \tan 30^\circ}{1 + \tan 45^\circ \tan 30^\circ} = \dfrac{1 - \frac{\sqrt{3}}{3}}{1 + 1 \cdot \frac{\sqrt{3}}{3}} = \dfrac{3 - \sqrt{3}}{3 + \sqrt{3}} =$

$\dfrac{(3 - \sqrt{3})(3 - \sqrt{3})}{(3 + \sqrt{3})(3 - \sqrt{3})} = \dfrac{12 - 6\sqrt{3}}{6} = 2 - \sqrt{3}$

11. $\tan 165^\circ = \tan(120^\circ + 45^\circ) = \dfrac{\tan 120^\circ + \tan 45^\circ}{1 - \tan 120^\circ \tan 45^\circ} = \dfrac{-\sqrt{3} + 1}{1 - (-\sqrt{3})(1)} = \dfrac{1 - \sqrt{3}}{1 + \sqrt{3}} =$

$\dfrac{(1 - \sqrt{3})(1 - \sqrt{3})}{(1 + \sqrt{3})(1 - \sqrt{3})} = \dfrac{4 - 2\sqrt{3}}{-2} = -2 + \sqrt{3}$

12. $\tan 105^\circ = \tan(60^\circ + 45^\circ) = \dfrac{\tan 60^\circ + \tan 45^\circ}{1 - \tan 60^\circ \tan 45^\circ} = \dfrac{\sqrt{3} + 1}{1 - (\sqrt{3})(1)} = \dfrac{1 + \sqrt{3}}{1 - \sqrt{3}} =$

$\dfrac{(1 + \sqrt{3})(1 + \sqrt{3})}{(1 - \sqrt{3})(1 + \sqrt{3})} = \dfrac{4 + 2\sqrt{3}}{-2} = -2 - \sqrt{3}$

13. $\tan \dfrac{11\pi}{12} = \tan\left(\dfrac{2\pi}{3} + \dfrac{\pi}{4}\right) = \dfrac{\tan \frac{2\pi}{3} + \tan \frac{\pi}{4}}{1 - \tan \frac{2\pi}{3} \tan \frac{\pi}{4}} = \dfrac{-\sqrt{3} + 1}{1 - (-\sqrt{3})(1)} = \dfrac{1 - \sqrt{3}}{1 + \sqrt{3}} =$

$\dfrac{(1 - \sqrt{3})(1 - \sqrt{3})}{(1 + \sqrt{3})(1 - \sqrt{3})} = \dfrac{4 - 2\sqrt{3}}{-2} = -2 + \sqrt{3}$

14. $\tan \dfrac{3\pi}{8} = \tan \dfrac{\frac{3\pi}{4}}{2} = \dfrac{\sin \frac{3\pi}{4}}{1 + \cos \frac{3\pi}{4}} = \dfrac{\frac{\sqrt{2}}{2}}{1 + \left(-\frac{\sqrt{2}}{2}\right)} = \dfrac{\sqrt{2}}{2 - \sqrt{2}} =$

$\dfrac{\sqrt{2}(2 + \sqrt{2})}{(2 - \sqrt{2})(2 + \sqrt{2})} = \dfrac{2\sqrt{2} + 2}{2} = \sqrt{2} + 1$

15. $\tan 22.5^\circ = \tan \dfrac{45^\circ}{2} = \dfrac{\sin 45^\circ}{1 + \cos 45^\circ} = \dfrac{\frac{\sqrt{2}}{2}}{1 + \frac{\sqrt{2}}{2}} = \dfrac{\sqrt{2}}{2 + \sqrt{2}} = \dfrac{\sqrt{2}(2 - \sqrt{2})}{(2 + \sqrt{2})(2 - \sqrt{2})} =$

$\dfrac{2\sqrt{2} - 2}{2} = \sqrt{2} - 1$

16. $\tan 112.5^\circ = \tan \dfrac{225^\circ}{2} = \dfrac{\sin 225^\circ}{1 + \cos 225^\circ} = \dfrac{-\frac{\sqrt{2}}{2}}{1 + \left(-\frac{\sqrt{2}}{2}\right)} = \dfrac{-\sqrt{2}}{2 - \sqrt{2}} =$

$\dfrac{-\sqrt{2}(2 + \sqrt{2})}{(2 - \sqrt{2})(2 + \sqrt{2})} = \dfrac{-2\sqrt{2} - 2}{2} = -\sqrt{2} - 1$

17. $\tan \dfrac{11\pi}{8} = \tan \dfrac{\frac{11\pi}{4}}{2} = \dfrac{\sin \frac{11\pi}{4}}{1 + \cos \frac{11\pi}{4}} = \dfrac{\sin \frac{3\pi}{4}}{1 + \cos \frac{3\pi}{4}} = \dfrac{\frac{\sqrt{2}}{2}}{1 - \frac{\sqrt{2}}{2}} = \dfrac{\sqrt{2}}{2 - \sqrt{2}} =$

$\dfrac{\sqrt{2}(2 + \sqrt{2})}{(2 - \sqrt{2})(2 + \sqrt{2})} = \dfrac{2\sqrt{2} + 2}{2} = \sqrt{2} + 1$

18. $\tan\frac{5\pi}{8} = \tan\frac{\frac{5\pi}{4}}{2} = \frac{1-\cos\frac{5\pi}{4}}{\sin\frac{5\pi}{4}} = \frac{1-\left(-\frac{\sqrt{2}}{2}\right)}{-\frac{\sqrt{2}}{2}} = \frac{2+\sqrt{2}}{-\sqrt{2}} = -\frac{2}{\sqrt{2}} - 1 =$

$-\sqrt{2} - 1$

19. $\cot 195° = \frac{1}{\tan 195°} = \frac{1}{\tan(150° + 45°)} = \frac{1}{\frac{\tan 150° + \tan 45°}{1 - \tan 150° \tan 45°}} =$

$\frac{1}{\frac{-\frac{\sqrt{3}}{3}+1}{1-\left(-\frac{\sqrt{3}}{3}\right)(1)}} = \frac{1}{\frac{-\sqrt{3}+3}{3+\sqrt{3}}} = \frac{3+\sqrt{3}}{3-\sqrt{3}} = \frac{(3+\sqrt{3})(3+\sqrt{3})}{(3-\sqrt{3})(3+\sqrt{3})} =$

$\frac{12+6\sqrt{3}}{6} = 2 + \sqrt{3}$

20. $\cot 255° = \frac{1}{\tan 255°} = \frac{1}{\tan(210° + 45°)} = \frac{1}{\frac{\tan 210° + \tan 45°}{1 - \tan 210° \tan 45°}} =$

$\frac{1}{\frac{\frac{\sqrt{3}}{3}+1}{1-\frac{\sqrt{3}}{3}\cdot 1}} = \frac{1}{\frac{\sqrt{3}+3}{3-\sqrt{3}}} = \frac{3-\sqrt{3}}{3+\sqrt{3}} = \frac{(3-\sqrt{3})(3-\sqrt{3})}{(3+\sqrt{3})(3-\sqrt{3})} = \frac{12-6\sqrt{3}}{6} = 2 - \sqrt{3}$

21. $\tan(\alpha + \beta) = \frac{\tan\alpha + \tan\beta}{1 - \tan\alpha\tan\beta} = \frac{-\frac{8}{15}+\frac{3}{4}}{1-\left(-\frac{8}{15}\right)\left(\frac{3}{4}\right)} = \frac{-32+45}{60+24} = \frac{13}{84}$

22. $\tan(\alpha - \beta) = \frac{\tan\alpha - \tan\beta}{1 + \tan\alpha\tan\beta} = \frac{-\frac{8}{15}-\frac{3}{4}}{1+\left(-\frac{8}{15}\right)\left(\frac{3}{4}\right)} = \frac{-32-45}{60-24} = -\frac{77}{36}$

23. $\tan 2\alpha = \frac{2\tan\alpha}{1-\tan^2\alpha} = \frac{2\left(-\frac{8}{15}\right)}{1-\left(-\frac{8}{15}\right)^2} = \frac{-\frac{16}{15}}{\frac{161}{225}} = -\frac{240}{161}$

24. Since α is in Quadrant II, $\frac{\alpha}{2}$ is in Quadrant I; $\sec\alpha = +\sqrt{1+\left(-\frac{8}{15}\right)^2} = \frac{17}{15}$;

$\cos\alpha = -\frac{15}{17}$; $\sin\alpha = \sqrt{1-\left(-\frac{15}{17}\right)^2} = \frac{8}{17}$; $\tan\frac{\alpha}{2} = \frac{1-\cos\alpha}{\sin\alpha} = \frac{1-\left(-\frac{15}{17}\right)}{\frac{8}{17}} =$

$\frac{32}{8} = 4$

B

25. $\tan(\alpha + \pi) = \frac{\tan\alpha + \tan\pi}{1 - \tan\alpha\tan\pi} = \frac{\tan\alpha + 0}{1 - \tan\alpha(0)} = \tan\alpha$

26. $\tan(\alpha - \pi) = \frac{\tan\alpha - \tan\pi}{1 + \tan\alpha\tan\pi} = \frac{\tan\alpha - 0}{1 + \tan\alpha(0)} = \tan\alpha$

27. $\tan\left(\frac{\pi}{4} - \alpha\right) = \dfrac{\tan\frac{\pi}{4} - \tan\alpha}{1 + \tan\frac{\pi}{4}\tan\alpha} = \dfrac{1 - \tan\alpha}{1 + 1 \cdot \tan\alpha} = \dfrac{1 - \tan\alpha}{1 + \tan\alpha}$

28. $\tan\left(\frac{\pi}{4} + \alpha\right) = \dfrac{\tan\frac{\pi}{4} + \tan\alpha}{1 - \tan\frac{\pi}{4}\tan\alpha} = \dfrac{1 + \tan\alpha}{1 - 1 \cdot \tan\alpha} = \dfrac{1 + \tan\alpha}{1 - \tan\alpha}$

29. $\cot(\alpha + \beta) = \dfrac{1}{\tan(\alpha + \beta)} = \dfrac{1 - \tan\alpha\tan\beta}{\tan\alpha + \tan\beta} = \dfrac{1 - \frac{1}{\cot\alpha}\cdot\frac{1}{\cot\beta}}{\frac{1}{\cot\alpha} + \frac{1}{\cot\beta}} =$

$\dfrac{\frac{\cot\alpha\cot\beta - 1}{\cot\alpha\cot\beta}}{\frac{\cot\beta + \cot\alpha}{\cot\alpha\cot\beta}} = \dfrac{\cot\alpha\cot\beta - 1}{\cot\alpha + \cot\beta}$

30. $\cot(\alpha - \beta) = \dfrac{1}{\tan(\alpha - \beta)} = \dfrac{1 + \tan\alpha\tan\beta}{\tan\alpha - \tan\beta} = \dfrac{1 + \frac{1}{\cot\alpha}\cdot\frac{1}{\cot\beta}}{\frac{1}{\cot\alpha} - \frac{1}{\cot\beta}} =$

$\dfrac{\frac{\cot\alpha\cot\beta + 1}{\cot\alpha\cot\beta}}{\frac{\cot\beta - \cot\alpha}{\cot\alpha\cot\beta}} = \dfrac{\cot\alpha\cot\beta + 1}{\cot\beta - \cot\alpha}$

31. $\cot 2\alpha = \cot(\alpha + \alpha) = \dfrac{\cot\alpha\cot\alpha - 1}{\cot\alpha + \cot\alpha} = \dfrac{\cot^2\alpha - 1}{2\cot\alpha}$

32. $\tan\frac{\theta}{2} = \dfrac{\sin\frac{\theta}{2}}{\cos\frac{\theta}{2}} = \dfrac{2\sin^2\frac{\theta}{2}}{2\sin\frac{\theta}{2}\cos\frac{\theta}{2}} = \dfrac{1 - \cos\theta}{\sin\theta}$

C **33. a.** $\sin\frac{7\pi}{8} = \sin\left[\frac{1}{2}\left(\frac{7\pi}{4}\right)\right] = +\sqrt{\dfrac{1 - \cos\frac{7\pi}{4}}{2}} = \sqrt{\dfrac{1 - \frac{\sqrt{2}}{2}}{2}} = \sqrt{\dfrac{2 - \sqrt{2}}{4}} =$

$\dfrac{\sqrt{2 - \sqrt{2}}}{2}$; $\cos\frac{7\pi}{8} = \cos\left[\frac{1}{2}\left(\frac{7\pi}{4}\right)\right] = -\sqrt{\dfrac{1 + \cos\frac{7\pi}{4}}{2}} = -\sqrt{\dfrac{1 + \frac{\sqrt{2}}{2}}{2}} =$

$-\sqrt{\dfrac{2 + \sqrt{2}}{4}} = \dfrac{-\sqrt{2 + \sqrt{2}}}{2}$

b. $\tan\frac{7\pi}{8} = \dfrac{\sin\frac{7\pi}{8}}{\cos\frac{7\pi}{8}} = \dfrac{\frac{\sqrt{2 - \sqrt{2}}}{2}}{\frac{-\sqrt{2 + \sqrt{2}}}{2}} = \dfrac{\sqrt{2 - \sqrt{2}}}{-\sqrt{2 + \sqrt{2}}} = -\sqrt{\dfrac{2 - \sqrt{2}}{2 + \sqrt{2}}} =$

$-\sqrt{\dfrac{(2 - \sqrt{2})(2 - \sqrt{2})}{(2 + \sqrt{2})(2 - \sqrt{2})}} = -\sqrt{\dfrac{6 - 4\sqrt{2}}{2}} = -\sqrt{3 - 2\sqrt{2}}$

(Continued)

c. $\tan\frac{7\pi}{8} = \tan\left[\frac{1}{2}\left(\frac{7\pi}{4}\right)\right] = \dfrac{1 - \cos\frac{7\pi}{4}}{\sin\frac{7\pi}{4}} = \dfrac{1 - \frac{\sqrt{2}}{2}}{-\frac{\sqrt{2}}{2}} = \dfrac{2 - \sqrt{2}}{-\sqrt{2}} = -\dfrac{2}{\sqrt{2}} + 1 =$

$-\sqrt{2} + 1 = 1 - \sqrt{2}$

d. $-\sqrt{3 - 2\sqrt{2}} = -\sqrt{1 - 2\sqrt{2} + 2} = -\sqrt{(1 - \sqrt{2})^2} = -|1 - \sqrt{2}| =$

$-(\sqrt{2} - 1) = -\sqrt{2} + 1 = 1 - \sqrt{2}$

34. $\dfrac{2\tan\frac{x}{2}}{1 + \tan^2\frac{x}{2}} = \dfrac{2\left(\frac{\sin x}{1 + \cos x}\right)}{1 + \left(\frac{\sin x}{1 + \cos x}\right)^2} = \dfrac{\frac{2\sin x}{1 + \cos x}}{\frac{(1 + \cos x)^2 + \sin^2 x}{(1 + \cos x)^2}} =$

$\dfrac{2\sin x}{1 + \cos x} \cdot \dfrac{(1 + \cos x)^2}{1 + 2\cos x + \cos^2 x + \sin^2 x} = \dfrac{(2\sin x)(1 + \cos x)}{2 + 2\cos x} = \dfrac{2\sin x(1 + \cos x)}{2(1 + \cos x)} =$

$\sin x$

35. $\tan 3\theta = \tan(\theta + 2\theta) = \dfrac{\tan\theta + \tan 2\theta}{1 - \tan\theta\tan 2\theta} = \dfrac{\tan\theta + \frac{2\tan\theta}{1 - \tan^2\theta}}{1 - \tan\theta\left(\frac{2\tan\theta}{1 - \tan^2\theta}\right)} =$

$\dfrac{(1 - \tan^2\theta)\tan\theta + 2\tan\theta}{1 - \tan^2\theta - 2\tan^2\theta} = \dfrac{3\tan\theta - \tan^3\theta}{1 - 3\tan^2\theta}$

Page 653 · MIXED REVIEW EXERCISES

1. $(\sin x - \cos x)^2 = \sin^2 x - 2\sin x\cos x + \cos^2 x = 1 - 2\sin x\cos x = 1 - \sin 2x$

2. $\cos\left(\frac{3\pi}{2} - x\right) = \cos\frac{3\pi}{2}\cos x + \sin\frac{3\pi}{2}\sin x = 0 \cdot \cos x + (-1)\sin x = -\sin x$

3. $\sec x - \sin x\tan x = \dfrac{1}{\cos x} - \sin x \cdot \dfrac{\sin x}{\cos x} = \dfrac{1 - \sin^2 x}{\cos x} = \dfrac{\cos^2 x}{\cos x} = \cos x$

4. $1 - \sin 2x\tan x = 1 - (2\sin x\cos x)\left(\dfrac{\sin x}{\cos x}\right) = 1 - 2\sin^2 x = \cos 2x$

5. $|x - 3| < 2$; $-2 < x - 3 < 2$; $1 < x < 5$; $\{x: 1 < x < 5\}$;

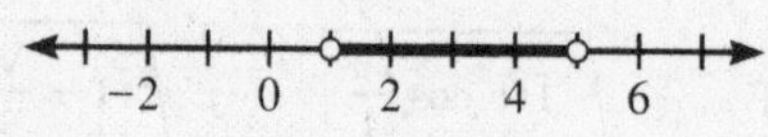

6. $x^2 > 2x + 3$; $x^2 - 2x - 3 > 0$, $(x - 3)(x + 1) > 0$, $x > 3$ or $x < -1$; $\{x: x < -1$ or $x > 3\}$;

-2 0 2 4

7. $2 \le 3x + 5 \le 14$; $-3 \le 3x \le 9$; $-1 \le x \le 3$; $\{x: -1 \le x \le 3\}$;

-2 0 2 4 6

8. $x^3 < 3x^2$; $x^3 - 3x^2 < 0$; $x^2(x - 3) < 0$; since $x^2 \ge 0$ for all x, $x - 3 < 0$ and $x \ne 0$; $x < 3$ and $x \ne 0$; $\{x: x < 3$ and $x \ne 0\}$

-2 0 2 4

9. $|2x + 1| \geq 3$; $2x + 1 \leq -3$ or $2x + 1 \geq 3$; $2x \leq -4$ or $2x \geq 2$; $x \leq -2$ or $x \geq 1$; $\{x: x \leq -2 \text{ or } x \geq 1\}$;

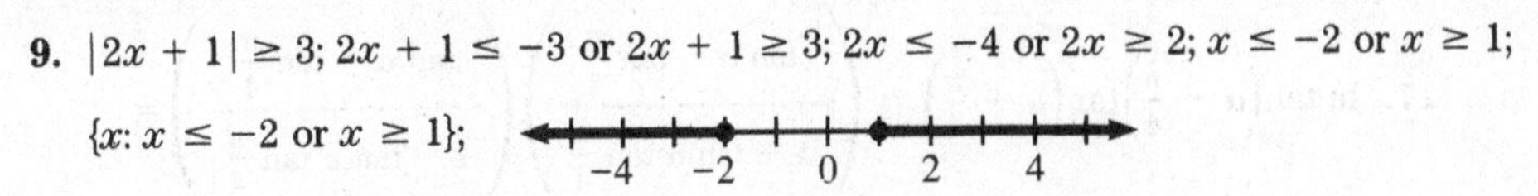

10. $7 - 4x > -1$; $-4x > -8$, $x < 2$; $\{x: x < 2\}$;

11. $3x - 5 > 13$; $3x > 18$; $x > 6$; $\{x: x > 6\}$;

12. $x^2 - 2x \leq 3$; $x^2 - 2x - 3 \leq 0$; $(x - 3)(x + 1) \leq 0$; $-1 \leq x \leq 3$; $\{x: -1 \leq x \leq 3\}$;

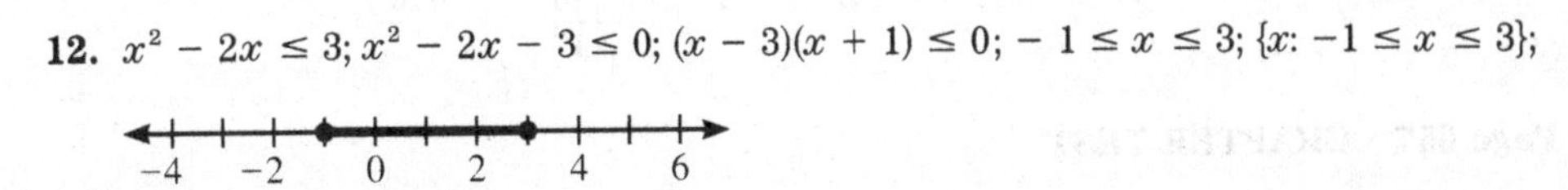

13. $|2x| \geq -1$; true for all x; {real numbers};

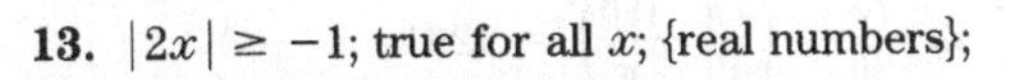

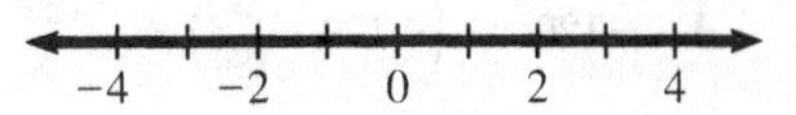

Pages 655–656 • CHAPTER REVIEW

1. c; $\frac{13\pi}{4} \cdot \frac{180}{\pi} = 585$; $585°$ **2.** b; $150 \cdot \frac{\pi}{180} = \frac{5\pi}{6}$

3. d; $\csc\left(-\frac{7\pi}{6}\right) = \csc \frac{5\pi}{6} = \frac{1}{\sin \frac{5\pi}{6}} = \frac{1}{\frac{1}{2}} = 2$ **4.** c

5. a; $f(-x) = \frac{-x}{(-x)^2 - 9} = -\frac{x}{x^2 - 9} = -f(x)$; odd **6.** c; $\frac{8}{2} = 4$

7. c; $a = 2$; period $= 3$; $b = \frac{2\pi}{3}$; $y = 2 \cos \frac{2\pi}{3}x$

8. a; $a = \frac{3 - (-1)}{2} = 2$; $c = \frac{3 + (-1)}{2} = 1$; $b = \frac{2\pi}{\frac{\pi}{3}} = 6$; $y = 2 \sin 6x + 1$

9. d; period $= \frac{2\pi}{\pi} = 2$ **10.** c

11. d; $\sec \theta - \tan \theta \sin \theta = \frac{1}{\cos \theta} - \frac{\sin \theta}{\cos \theta} \cdot \sin \theta = \frac{1 - \sin^2 \theta}{\cos \theta} = \frac{\cos^2 \theta}{\cos \theta} = \cos \theta$

12. a; $\cos t = \pm\sqrt{1 - u^2}$; $\tan t = \frac{\sin t}{\cos t} = \pm\frac{u}{\sqrt{1 - u^2}}$

13. d; $\sin\left(2\pi - \frac{\pi}{6}\right) = \sin \frac{11\pi}{6} = -\frac{1}{2}$

14. b; $\sin 165° = \sin(120° + 45°) = \sin 120° \cos 45° + \cos 120° \sin 45° = \frac{\sqrt{3}}{2} \cdot \frac{\sqrt{2}}{2} + \left(-\frac{1}{2}\right)\left(\frac{\sqrt{2}}{2}\right) = \frac{\sqrt{6} - \sqrt{2}}{4}$

15. d; $\cos 2\theta = 1 - 2 \sin^2 \theta = 1 - 2\left(\frac{2}{3}\right)^2 = 1 - \frac{8}{9} = \frac{1}{9}$

16. d; $\cos \frac{7\pi}{8} = \cos \frac{1}{2}\left(\frac{7\pi}{4}\right) = -\sqrt{\frac{1 + \cos \frac{7\pi}{4}}{2}} = -\sqrt{\frac{1 + \frac{\sqrt{2}}{2}}{2}} = -\sqrt{\frac{2 + \sqrt{2}}{4}} = -\frac{\sqrt{2 + \sqrt{2}}}{2}$

17. b; $\tan\left(\alpha - \frac{\pi}{4}\right)\tan\left(\alpha + \frac{\pi}{4}\right) = \left(\frac{\tan\alpha - \tan\frac{\pi}{4}}{1 + \tan\alpha\tan\frac{\pi}{4}}\right)\left(\frac{\tan\alpha + \tan\frac{\pi}{4}}{1 - \tan\alpha\tan\frac{\pi}{4}}\right) =$

$\left(\frac{\tan\alpha - 1}{1 + \tan\alpha}\right)\left(\frac{\tan\alpha + 1}{1 - \tan\alpha}\right) = -1$

18. a; $\sin\theta = -\sqrt{1 - \left(\frac{8}{17}\right)^2} = -\frac{15}{17}$; $\tan\frac{\theta}{2} = \frac{1 - \frac{8}{17}}{-\frac{15}{17}} = \frac{9}{-15} = -\frac{3}{5}$

Page 657 • CHAPTER TEST

1. $-120° = \left(-120 \cdot \frac{\pi}{180}\right) = -\frac{2\pi}{3}$ **2.** $\frac{7\pi}{10} = \left(\frac{7\pi}{10} \cdot \frac{180}{\pi}\right)^{\circ} = 126°$

3. a. $65° \cdot \frac{\pi}{180°} = \frac{13\pi}{36}$; $\theta = \frac{13\pi}{36}$, $r = \frac{8}{2} = 4$; $s = r\theta = 4 \cdot \frac{13\pi}{36} = \frac{13\pi}{9}$; $\frac{13\pi}{9} \approx 4.5$; 4.5 in.

b. $A = \frac{1}{2}r^2\theta = \frac{1}{2}(4)^2\left(\frac{13\pi}{36}\right) = \frac{26\pi}{9}$; $\frac{26\pi}{9} \approx 9$; 9 in^2

4. $\sin\frac{4\pi}{3} = -\frac{\sqrt{3}}{2}$; $\cos\frac{4\pi}{3} = -\frac{1}{2}$; $\tan\frac{4\pi}{3} = \sqrt{3}$; $\csc\frac{4\pi}{3} = -\frac{2\sqrt{3}}{3}$; $\sec\frac{4\pi}{3} = -2$;
$\cot\frac{4\pi}{3} = \frac{\sqrt{3}}{3}$

5. $f(-x) = -x\sin(-x) - \tan(-x) = (-x)(-\sin x) - (-\tan x) = x\sin x + \tan x$; neither

6. $a = 3$; $M = 3$, $m = -3$; period $= \frac{2\pi}{4} = \frac{\pi}{2}$

7. $a = 3$; period $= 8$; $b = \frac{2\pi}{8} = \frac{\pi}{4}$; $y = 3\sin\frac{\pi}{4}x$

8. period $= \frac{\pi}{\pi} = 1$;

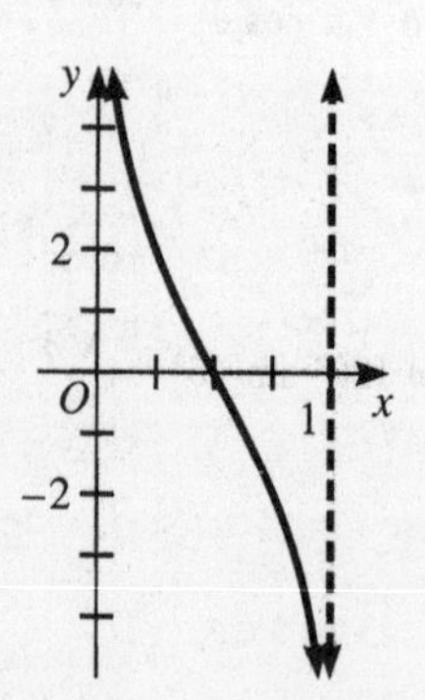

9. $\csc\theta - \cot\theta\cos\theta = \frac{1}{\sin\theta} - \frac{\cos\theta}{\sin\theta} \cdot \cos\theta = \frac{1 - \cos^2\theta}{\sin\theta} = \frac{\sin^2\theta}{\sin\theta} = \sin\theta$

10. $\tan x + \cot x = \frac{\sin x}{\cos x} + \frac{\cos x}{\sin x} = \frac{\sin^2 x + \cos^2 x}{\sin x\cos x} = \frac{1}{\sin x\cos x} = \sec x\csc x$

11. $\cos(\alpha + 45°) + \sin(\alpha - 45°) = \cos\alpha\cos 45° - \sin\alpha\sin 45° + \sin\alpha\cos 45° - \cos\alpha\sin 45° = \cos\alpha\cdot\frac{\sqrt{2}}{2} - \sin\alpha\cdot\frac{\sqrt{2}}{2} + \sin\alpha\cdot\frac{\sqrt{2}}{2} - \cos\alpha\cdot\frac{\sqrt{2}}{2} = 0$

12. $\cos\alpha = -\sqrt{1 - \left(\frac{8}{17}\right)^2} = -\frac{15}{17}$

a. $\sin 2\alpha = 2\sin\alpha\cos\alpha = 2\left(-\frac{15}{17}\right)\left(\frac{8}{17}\right) = -\frac{240}{289}$

b. $\cos 2\alpha = 1 - 2\left(\frac{8}{17}\right)^2 = 1 - \frac{128}{289} = \frac{161}{289}$

c. α is in quadrant II, $\frac{\alpha}{2}$ is in quadrant I; $\sin\frac{\alpha}{2} = +\sqrt{\frac{1-\cos\alpha}{2}} = \sqrt{\frac{1-\left(-\frac{15}{17}\right)}{2}} = \sqrt{\frac{16}{17}} = \frac{4}{\sqrt{17}} = \frac{4\sqrt{17}}{17}$

13. $\cos\theta = \sqrt{1 - \left(-\frac{5}{13}\right)^2} = \frac{12}{13}$; $\tan\theta = \frac{\sin\theta}{\cos\theta} = \frac{-\frac{5}{13}}{\frac{12}{13}} = -\frac{5}{12}$

a. $\tan 2\theta = \frac{2\tan\theta}{1-\tan^2\theta} = \frac{2\left(-\frac{5}{12}\right)}{1-\left(-\frac{5}{12}\right)^2} = \frac{-\frac{5}{6}}{\frac{119}{144}} = -\frac{120}{119}$

b. $\tan\frac{\theta}{2} = \frac{1-\cos\theta}{\sin\theta} = \frac{1-\frac{12}{13}}{-\frac{5}{13}} = \frac{\frac{1}{13}}{-\frac{5}{13}} = -\frac{1}{5}$

Page 664 • WRITTEN EXERCISES

A **1.**

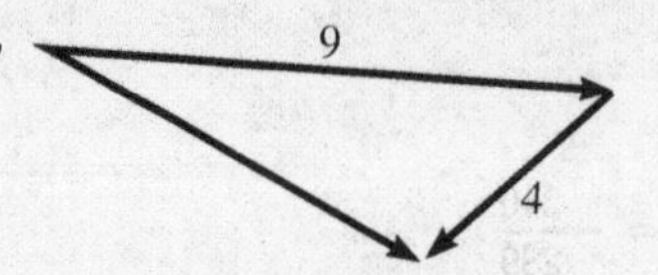

2.

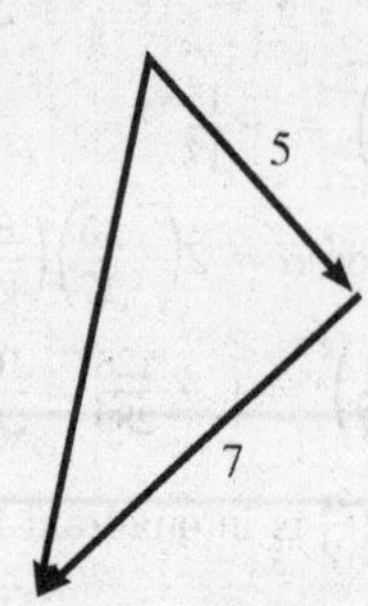

3.

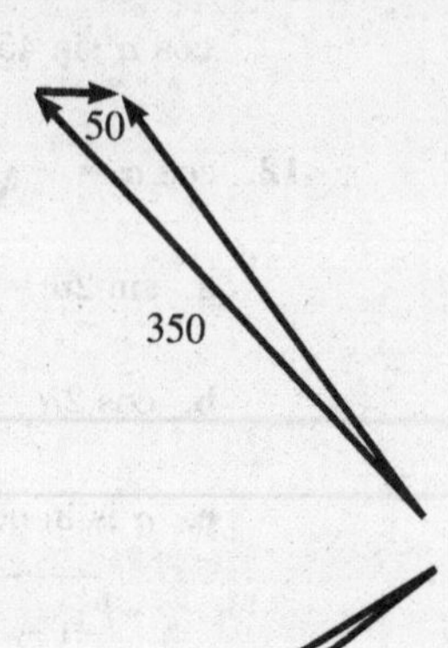

4.

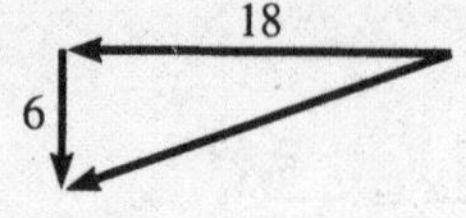

5.

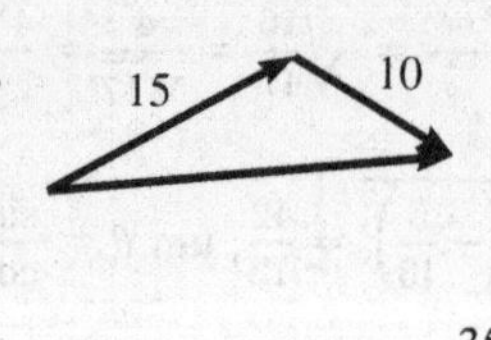

6.

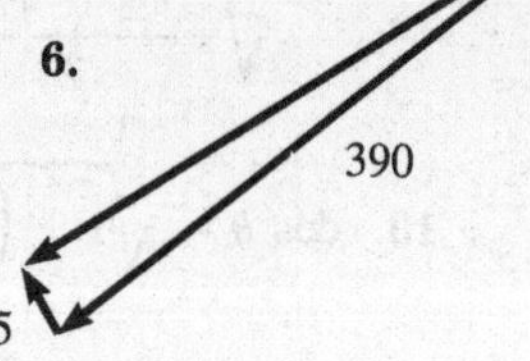

7.

w
u
u + w

8.

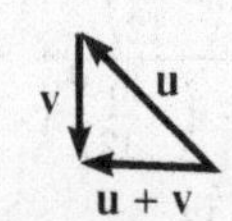

9.

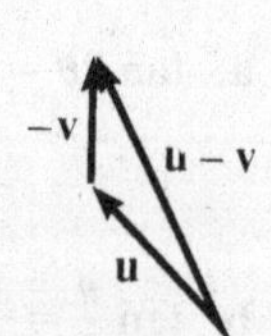

10.

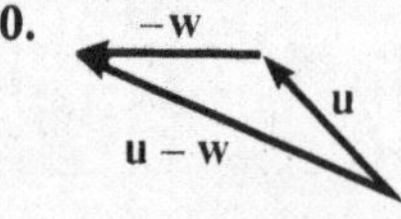

11.

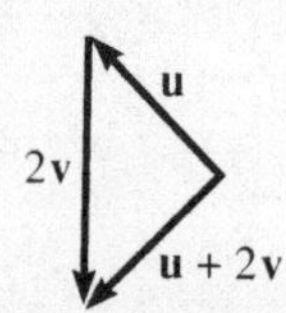

12.

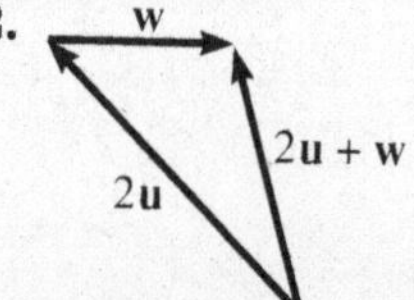

13.

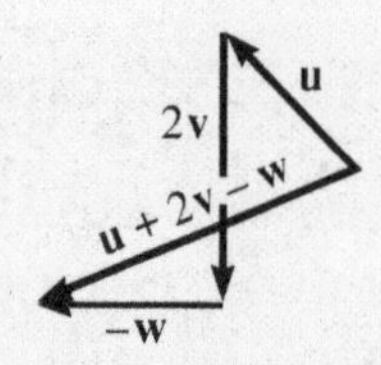

14.

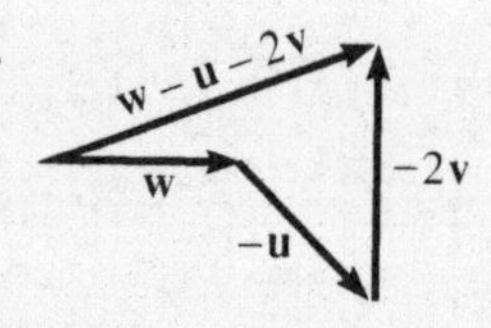

15. $\|\mathbf{w}\|^2 = 117^2 + 102^2 = 24{,}093$; $\|\mathbf{w}\| = 155$; $\tan\theta = \frac{102}{117} = 0.8718$; $\theta = 41.1°$;

bearing $= 130° + 41.1° = 171.1°$

16. $\|\mathbf{w}\|^2 = 218^2 + 170^2 = 76{,}424$; $\|\mathbf{w}\| = 276$; $\tan\theta = \frac{218}{170} = 1.282$; $\theta = 52.1°$;

bearing $= 112° + 180° + 52.1° = 344.1°$

B **17.** $\|\mathbf{w}\|^2 = 272^2 + 197^2 - 2(272)(197)(\cos 80°) = 94{,}183$; $\|\mathbf{w}\| = 307$; $\frac{307}{\sin 80°} = \frac{197}{\sin \theta}$,

$\sin \theta = \frac{(197)(0.9848)}{307} = 0.6319$; $\theta = 39.2°$; bearing $= 360° - (140° + 39.2°) = 180.8°$

18. $\|\mathbf{w}\|^2 = 1850^2 + 5920^2 - 2(1850)(5920)(\cos 80°) = 34{,}665{,}000$; $\|\mathbf{w}\| = 5890$. Let

$\beta =$ the angle between $2\mathbf{v}$ and $\mathbf{u} + 2\mathbf{v}$; $\frac{5890}{\sin 80°} = \frac{1850}{\sin \beta}$; $\sin \beta = \frac{(0.9848)(1850)}{5890} =$

0.3093; $\beta = 18.0°$; $\theta = 180° - (18° + 80°) = 82.0°$; bearing $= 125° - 82° = 43°$

19. $\|\mathbf{w}\|^2 = 460^2 + 712^2 - 2(460)(712)(\cos 50°) = 29{,}749$; $\|\mathbf{w}\| = 545$; $\frac{545}{\sin 50°} = \frac{460}{\sin \theta}$;

$\sin \theta = \frac{460(0.7660)}{545} = 0.6465$; $\theta = 40.3°$; bearing $= 130° - 40.3° = 89.7°$

20. $\|\mathbf{w}\|^2 = 23^2 + 14.5^2 - 2(23)(14.5)(\cos 70°) = 511.12$; $\|\mathbf{w}\| = 22.6$; $\frac{14.5}{\sin \theta} = \frac{22.6}{\sin 70°}$;

$\sin \theta = \frac{(14.5)(0.9397)}{22.6} = 0.6029$; $\theta = 37.1°$; bearing $= 215° - 37.1° = 177.9°$

21. $\|\mathbf{w}\|^2 = (3.62)^2 + (14.5)^2 - 2 \cdot (3.62)(14.5)(\cos 100°) = 241.58$; $\|\mathbf{w}\| = 15.5$; $\frac{15.5}{\sin 100°} =$

$\frac{14.5}{\sin \theta}$; $\sin \theta = \frac{(0.9848)(14.5)}{(15.5)} = 0.9213$; $\theta = 67.1°$; bearing $= 25° + 67.1° = 92.1°$

22. $3(\mathbf{w} + \mathbf{u}) = 2(\mathbf{w} - \mathbf{v})$; $3\mathbf{w} + 3\mathbf{u} = 2\mathbf{w} - 2\mathbf{v}$; $\mathbf{w} = -2\mathbf{v} - 3\mathbf{u}$; $\|\mathbf{w}\|^2 = 672^2 + 1863^2 -$

$2(672)(1863)(\cos 110°) = 4778727.66$; $\|\mathbf{w}\| = 2190$; $\frac{\sin \theta}{672} = \frac{\sin 110°}{2190}$; $\sin \theta =$

$\frac{672(0.9397)}{2190} = 0.2883$; $\theta = 16.8°$; bearing $= 125° + 16.8° = 141.8°$

Page 665 • PROBLEMS

A **1.** $\|\mathbf{d}\| = \sqrt{320^2 + 285^2} = 429$; 429 km; let θ be the angle between the horizontal and

$\mathbf{d}$, $\tan \theta = \frac{320}{285} = 1.123$; $\theta = 48.3°$; bearing $= 270° + 48.3° = 318.3°$

2.

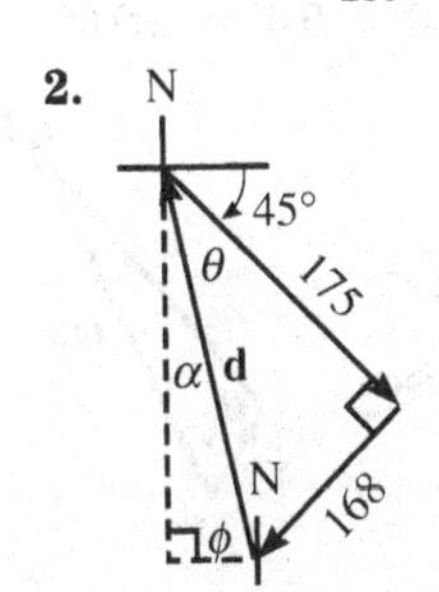

$\|\mathbf{d}\| = \sqrt{175^2 + 168^2} = 243$; 243 km; the bearing of the port from the ship $= 270° + \phi$; $\phi = 90° - \alpha$;

$\alpha = 45° - \theta$; $\tan \theta = \frac{168}{175}$, $\theta = 43.8°$;

$\alpha = 45° - 43.8° = 1.2°$; $\phi = 90° - 1.2° = 88.8°$; the bearing $= 270° + 88.8° = 358.8°$

3. $\|\mathbf{v}\| = \sqrt{580^2 + 45^2} = 582$; 582 km/h; let θ be the angle between $\mathbf{v}$ and the north

direction, $\tan \theta = \frac{45}{580} = 0.776$; $\theta = 4.4°$; heading $= 4.4°$

4.

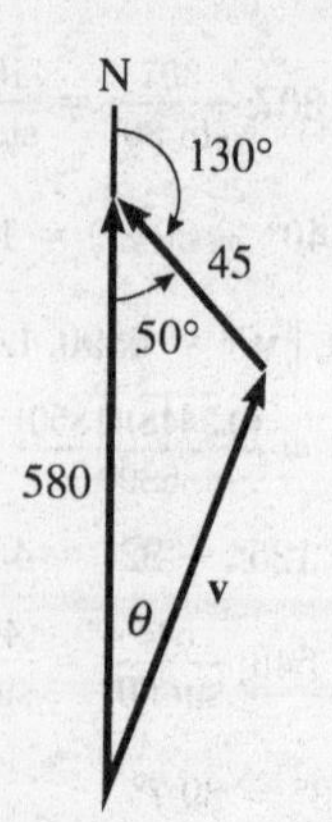

Note: Figure not drawn to scale; $\|\mathbf{v}\|^2 = 580^2 + 45^2 - 2(580)(45)\cos 50° = 304{,}870$; $\|\mathbf{v}\| = 552$; 552 km/h; $\frac{45}{\sin\theta} = \frac{552}{\sin 50°}$; $\sin\theta = \frac{(0.7760)(45)}{552} = 0.0624$; $\theta = 3.6°$; heading $= 3.6°$

5.

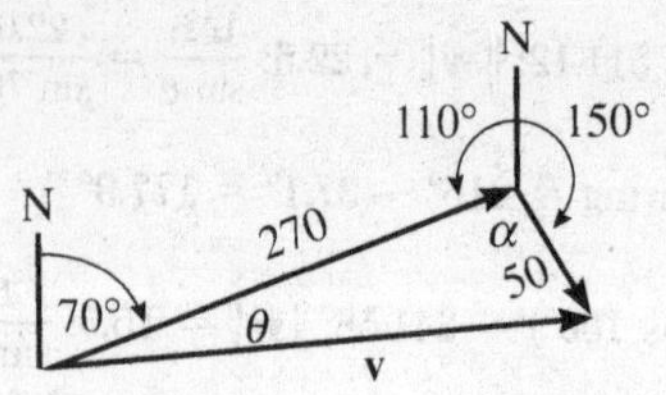

Note: Figure not drawn to scale; $\alpha = 360° - (110° + 150°) = 100°$; $\|\mathbf{v}\|^2 = 270^2 + 50^2 - 2(270)(50)\cos 100° = 80{,}090$; $\|\mathbf{v}\| = 283$; 283 km/h; $\frac{50}{\sin\theta} = \frac{283}{\sin 100°}$; $\sin\theta = \frac{50(0.9848)}{283} = 0.1740$; $\theta = 10°$; bearing $= 70° + 10° = 80°$

6.

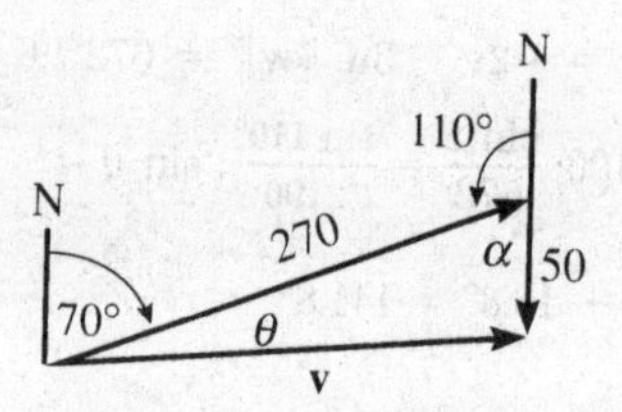

$\alpha = 180° - 110° = 70°$; $\|\mathbf{v}\|^2 = 270^2 + 50^2 - 2(270)(50)(\cos 70°) = 66{,}165$; $\|\mathbf{v}\| = 257$; 257 km/h; $\frac{50}{\sin\theta} = \frac{257}{\sin 70°}$; $\sin\theta = \frac{(0.9397)(50)}{257} = 0.1828$; $\theta = 10.5°$; bearing $= 70° + 10.5° = 80.5°$

7. $\|\mathbf{d}\|^2 = 72^2 + 45^2 - 2(72)(45)\cos 80°$; $\|\mathbf{d}\|^2 = 6084$; $\|\mathbf{d}\| = 78.0$; 78.0 km; $\frac{\sin\theta}{45} = \frac{\sin 80°}{78.0}$; $\sin\theta = \frac{45(0.9848)}{78.0} = 0.5682$; $\theta = 34.6°$; bearing of first ship to second is $34.6° - 25° = 9.6°$; bearing of second ship to first ship is $180° + 9.6° = 189.6°$

B **8.** $\alpha = 180° - (55° + 65°) = 60°$; $\|\mathbf{v}\|^2 = 600^2 + 140^2 - 2(600)(140)\cos 60° = 295{,}600$; $\|\mathbf{v}\| = 544$; $\frac{\sin\theta}{600} = \frac{\sin\alpha}{544}$; $\sin\theta = \frac{600(0.8660)}{544} = 0.9551$; $\theta = 72.8°$; bearing $= 180° - (\theta + 35°) = 145° - 72.8° = 72.2°$; the plane should use a heading of 72.2°; it will have to fly 544 km.

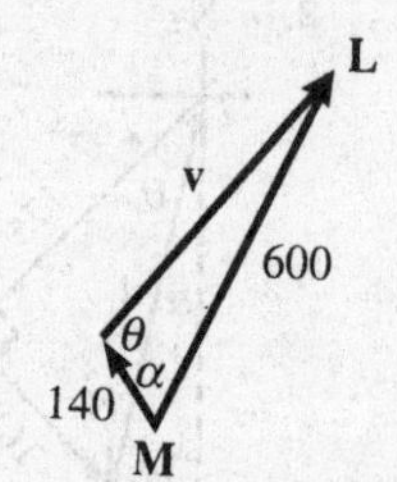

9. Note: Figure not drawn to scale; $\phi = 50° - 20° = 30°$;

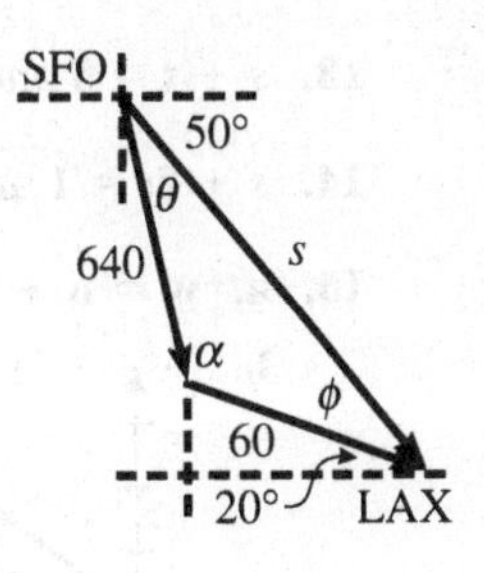

$\frac{\sin\theta}{60} = \frac{\sin\phi}{640}$; $\sin\theta = \frac{60(0.5)}{640} = 0.0469$; $\theta = 2.7°$;

$\alpha = 180° - (2.7° + 30°) = 147.3°$; $\frac{\sin\alpha}{s} = \frac{\sin\phi}{640}$;

$s = \frac{(0.5402)(640)}{0.5} = 691$; since the plane's ground speed

will be 691 km/h, the trip will take $\frac{540}{691} \approx 0.78$ h ≈ 47 min

and the ETA is 2:47 P.M. The compass heading will be $140° + \theta = 142.7°$.

Page 665 • MIXED REVIEW EXERCISES

1. $f(-x) = \frac{-x+2}{-x-3} \neq f(x)$ and $f(-x) \neq -f(x)$; neither

2. $f(-x) = \cos(-x) - \sin(-x) = \cos x + \sin x \neq y$ and $f(-x) \neq -y$; neither

3. $f(-x) = \frac{6(-x)^3 - (-x)}{(-x)^2 + 1} = \frac{-6x^3 + x}{x^2 + 1} = -f(x)$; odd

4. $x^2 + 6x = 8$, $x^2 + 6x + 9 = 8 + 9 = 17$; $(x + 3)^2 = 17$; $x + 3 = \pm\sqrt{17}$;
$x = -3 \pm \sqrt{17}$; $\{-3 \pm \sqrt{17}\}$

5. $|3z - 7| = 5$; $3z - 7 = 5$ or $3z - 7 = -5$; $3z = 12$ or $3z = 2$; $z = 4$ or $z = \frac{2}{3}$;
$\left\{\frac{2}{3}, 4\right\}$

6. $(3x - 2)^2 = 36$, $3x - 2 = \pm 6$, $3x = 2 \pm 6$, $x = \frac{2 \pm 6}{3}$; $x = \frac{8}{3}$ or $x = -\frac{4}{3}$;
$\left\{-\frac{4}{3}, \frac{8}{3}\right\}$

7. $\log_9 x = \frac{3}{2}$, $x = 9^{3/2} = 3^3 = 27$; $\{27\}$

8. $\sqrt{4t + 9} = t - 3$, $4t + 9 = t^2 - 6t + 9$, $t^2 - 10t = 0$, $t(t - 10) = 0$; $t = 0$ (reject), or $t = 10$; $\{10\}$

9. $p^2 + \frac{11p}{2} = 3$; $2p^2 + 11p = 6$, $2p^2 + 11p - 6 = 0$; $(2p - 1)(p + 6) = 0$, $p = \frac{1}{2}$ or
$p = -6$; $\left\{\frac{1}{2}, -6\right\}$

Pages 669–670 • WRITTEN EXERCISES

A **1.** $5\mathbf{i} - 2\mathbf{j}$ **2.** $-\mathbf{i} + 4\mathbf{j}$ **3.** $-5\mathbf{i}$ **4.** $6\mathbf{j}$ **5.** $5\mathbf{i} - \mathbf{j}$ **6.** $3\mathbf{i} + 2\mathbf{j}$

7. $(4 + 2, -3 - 4) = (6, -7)$ **8.** $(-5 + 2, 1 + 1) = (-3, 2)$

9. $4 - x = 2$, $5 - y = -1$; $x = 2$, $y = 6$; $(2, 6)$

10. $0 - x = 6$, $-4 - y = -1$; $x = -6$, $y = -3$; $(-6, -3)$

11. $s + 1 = 2$, $5 = t - 2$; $s = 1$, $t = 7$

12. $3s - 2 = s$, $t = 2t - 3$; $2s = 2$, $t = 3$; $s = 1$, $t = 3$

13. $s + t = 5$ and $s - t = -1$; solving simultaneously, $2s = 4$; $s = 2$; $2 + t = 5$; $t = 3$

14. $s + 2t = 1$ and $s - t = 0$; $t = s$; $s + 2s = 1$; $3s = 1$; $s = t = \frac{1}{3}$

15. a. $\mathbf{w} = \mathbf{u} + \mathbf{v} = (4 + 2)\mathbf{i} + (3 - 1)\mathbf{j} = 6\mathbf{i} + 2\mathbf{j}$

b.

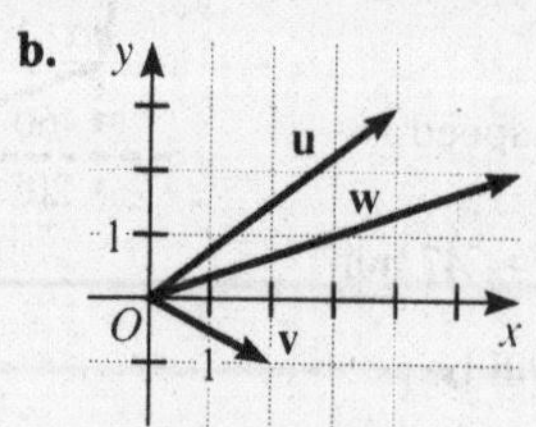

c. $\|\mathbf{w}\| = \sqrt{6^2 + 2^2} = \sqrt{40} = 2\sqrt{10}$

d. $\tan \gamma = \frac{2}{6} = \frac{1}{3}$; $\gamma = 18.4°$

16. a. $\mathbf{w} = \mathbf{u} - \mathbf{v} = (1 - 5)\mathbf{i} + (-1 - 2)\mathbf{j} = -4\mathbf{i} - 3\mathbf{j}$

b.

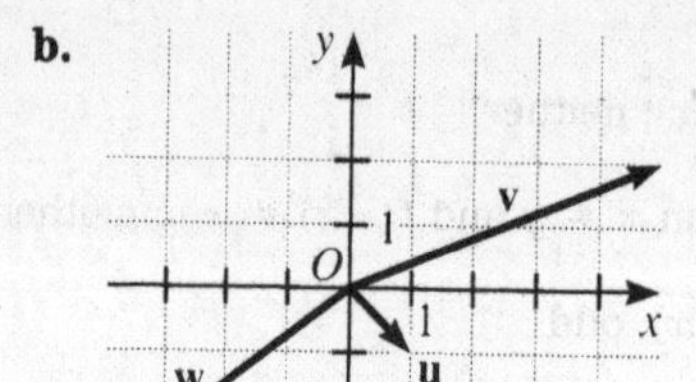

c. $\|\mathbf{w}\| = \sqrt{(-4)^2 + (-3)^2} = 5$

d. $\tan \gamma = \frac{-3}{-4} = 0.75$; $\gamma = 180° + 36.9° = 216.9°$

17. a. $\mathbf{w} = 2\mathbf{u} - \mathbf{v} = (2 \cdot 4 - 2)\mathbf{i} + (2 \cdot 3 + 1)\mathbf{j} = 6\mathbf{i} + 7\mathbf{j}$

b.

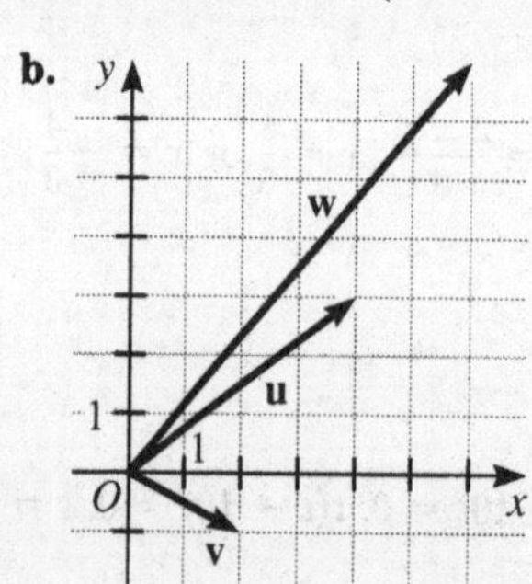

c. $\|\mathbf{w}\| = \sqrt{6^2 + 7^2} = \sqrt{85}$

d. $\tan \gamma = \frac{7}{6} = 1.167$; $\gamma = 49.4°$

18. a. $\mathbf{w} = 2\mathbf{u} + 3\mathbf{v} = [2 \cdot (-4) + 3 \cdot 1]\mathbf{i} + (2 \cdot 3 + 3 \cdot 2)\mathbf{j} = -5\mathbf{i} + 12\mathbf{j}$

b.

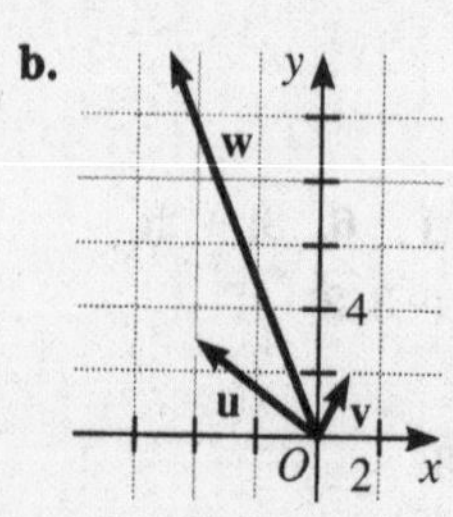

c. $\|\mathbf{w}\| = \sqrt{(-5)^2 + 12^2} = 13$

d. $\tan \gamma = \frac{12}{-5} = -2.4$; $\gamma = 112.6°$

19. $\cos\theta = \dfrac{\mathbf{u}\cdot\mathbf{v}}{\|\mathbf{u}\|\|\mathbf{v}\|} = \dfrac{4\cdot 2 + 3\cdot(-1)}{(\sqrt{4^2+3^2})(\sqrt{2^2+(-1)^2}} = \dfrac{5}{(5)(\sqrt{5})} = \dfrac{1}{\sqrt{5}} = \dfrac{\sqrt{5}}{5} = 0.4472;$

$\theta = 63.4°$

20. $\cos\theta = \dfrac{\mathbf{u}\cdot\mathbf{v}}{\|\mathbf{u}\|\|\mathbf{v}\|} = \dfrac{(5)(2) + (-3)(4)}{(\sqrt{5^2+(-3)^2})(\sqrt{(2)^2+(4)^2})} = \dfrac{-2}{(\sqrt{34})(\sqrt{20})} = \dfrac{-1}{\sqrt{170}} = -0.0767;$

$\theta = 94.4°$

21. $\cos\theta = \dfrac{\mathbf{u}\cdot\mathbf{v}}{\|\mathbf{u}\|\|\mathbf{v}\|} = \dfrac{2(1) + (-1)(3)}{(\sqrt{2^2+(-1)^2})(\sqrt{1^2+(3)^2})} = \dfrac{-1}{(\sqrt{5})(\sqrt{10})} = \dfrac{-1}{5\sqrt{2}} = -0.1414$

$\theta = 98.1°$

22. $\cos\theta = \dfrac{\mathbf{u}\cdot\mathbf{v}}{\|\mathbf{u}\|\|\mathbf{v}\|} = \dfrac{2(6) + (3)(-4)}{(\sqrt{2^2+3^2})(\sqrt{6^2+(-4)^2})} = 0;\ \theta = 90°$

23. Let $\mathbf{u} = x\mathbf{i} + y\mathbf{j}$; $\mathbf{u}\cdot\mathbf{v} = 0$; $1x + 1y = 0$; let $x = 1$ and $y = -1$; $\dfrac{\mathbf{u}}{\|\mathbf{u}\|} =$

$\dfrac{\mathbf{i}-\mathbf{j}}{\sqrt{1^2+(-1)^2}} = \dfrac{1}{\sqrt{2}}\mathbf{i} - \dfrac{1}{\sqrt{2}}\mathbf{j} = \dfrac{\sqrt{2}}{2}\mathbf{i} - \dfrac{\sqrt{2}}{2}\mathbf{j}$

24. Let $\mathbf{u} = x\mathbf{i} + y\mathbf{j}$; $\mathbf{u}\cdot\mathbf{v} = 0$; $5x - 12y = 0$; let $x = 12$ and $y = 5$; $\|\mathbf{u}\| =$

$\sqrt{12^2+5^2} = 13$; $\dfrac{\mathbf{u}}{\|\mathbf{u}\|} = \dfrac{12}{13}\mathbf{i} + \dfrac{5}{13}\mathbf{j}$

25. Let $\mathbf{u} = x\mathbf{i} + y\mathbf{j}$; $\mathbf{u}\cdot\mathbf{v} = 0$; $3x - 4y = 0$; let $x = 4$ and $y = 3$; $\|\mathbf{u}\| =$

$\sqrt{4^2+3^2} = 5$; $\dfrac{\mathbf{u}}{\|\mathbf{u}\|} = \dfrac{4}{5}\mathbf{i} + \dfrac{3}{5}\mathbf{j}$

26. Let $\mathbf{u} = x\mathbf{i} + y\mathbf{j}$; $\mathbf{u}\cdot\mathbf{v} = 0$; $2x + 4y = 0$; let $x = 2$ and $y = -1$; $\|\mathbf{u}\| =$

$\sqrt{2^2+(-1)^2} = \sqrt{5}$; $\dfrac{\mathbf{u}}{\|\mathbf{u}\|} = \dfrac{2}{\sqrt{5}}\mathbf{i} - \dfrac{1}{\sqrt{5}}\mathbf{j} = \dfrac{2\sqrt{5}}{5}\mathbf{i} - \dfrac{\sqrt{5}}{5}\mathbf{j}$

B

27. a. Let $\mathbf{u} = a\mathbf{i} + b\mathbf{j}$ and $\mathbf{v} = c\mathbf{i} + d\mathbf{j}$; $a = \|\mathbf{u}\|\cos 20° = 8(0.9397) = 7.52$; $b = \|\mathbf{u}\|\sin 20° = 8(0.3420) = 2.74$; $c = \|\mathbf{v}\|\cos 80° = 17(0.1736) = 2.95$; $d = \|\mathbf{v}\|\sin 80° = 17(0.9848) = 16.7$; $\mathbf{u} = 7.52\mathbf{i} + 2.74\mathbf{j}$; $\mathbf{v} = 2.95\mathbf{i} + 16.7\mathbf{j}$

b. let θ = the angle between $\mathbf{u}$ and $\mathbf{v}$; $\theta = 80° - 20° = 60°$; $\mathbf{u}\cdot\mathbf{v} = \|\mathbf{u}\|\|\mathbf{v}\|\cos 60° = 8(17)(0.5) = 68.0$

c. $\mathbf{u}\cdot\mathbf{v} = (7.52)(2.95) + (2.74)(16.7) = 22.184 + 45.758 = 67.9$

28. a. Let $\mathbf{u} = a\mathbf{i} + b\mathbf{j}$ and $\mathbf{v} = c\mathbf{i} + d\mathbf{j}$; $a = \|\mathbf{u}\|\cos 15° = 6(0.9659) = 5.80$; $b = \|\mathbf{u}\|\sin 15° = 6(0.2588) = 1.55$; $c = \|\mathbf{v}\|\cos 65° = 10(0.4226) = 4.23$; $d = \|\mathbf{v}\|\sin 65° = 10(0.9063) = 9.06$; $\mathbf{u} = 5.80\mathbf{i} + 1.55\mathbf{j}$; $\mathbf{v} = 4.23\mathbf{i} + 9.06\mathbf{j}$

b. Let θ be the angle between $\mathbf{u}$ and $\mathbf{v}$; $\theta = 65° - 15° = 50°$; $\mathbf{u}\cdot\mathbf{v} = \|\mathbf{u}\|\|\mathbf{v}\|\cos 50° = (6)(10)(0.6428) = 38.6$

c. $\mathbf{u}\cdot\mathbf{v} = (5.80)(4.23) + (1.55)(9.06) = 24.53 + 14.04 = 38.6$

29. a. Let $\mathbf{u} = a\mathbf{i} + b\mathbf{j}$ and $\mathbf{v} = c\mathbf{i} + d\mathbf{j}$; $a = \|\mathbf{u}\|\cos 68° = 12.5(0.3746) = 4.68$; $b = \|\mathbf{u}\|\sin 68° = 12.5(0.9272) = 11.6$; $c = \|\mathbf{v}\|\cos 116° = 18.0(-0.4384) = -7.89$; $d = \|\mathbf{v}\|\sin 116° = 18.0(0.8988) = 16.2$; $\mathbf{u} = 4.68\mathbf{i} + 11.6\mathbf{j}$ and $\mathbf{v} = -7.89\mathbf{i} + 16.2\mathbf{j}$

b. Let θ = angle between $\mathbf{u}$ and $\mathbf{v}$; $\theta = 116° - 68° = 48°$; $\mathbf{u}\cdot\mathbf{v} = \|\mathbf{u}\|\,\|\mathbf{v}\|\cos\theta = 12.5(18.0)(0.6691) = 151$

c. $\mathbf{u}\cdot\mathbf{v} = ac + bd = 4.68(-7.89) + 11.6(16.2) = 151$

30. a. Let $u = a\mathbf{i} + b\mathbf{j}$ and $\mathbf{v} = c\mathbf{i} + d\mathbf{j}$; $a = \|\mathbf{u}\| \cos 57° = 8.70(0.5446) = 4.74$; $b = \|\mathbf{u}\| \cdot \sin 57° = 8.70(0.8387) = 7.30$; $c = \|\mathbf{v}\| \cdot \cos(-28°) = 6.60(0.8829) = 5.83$; $d = \|\mathbf{v}\| \cdot \sin(-28°) = 6.60(-0.4695) = -3.10$; $\mathbf{u} = 4.74\mathbf{i} + 7.30\mathbf{j}$ and $\mathbf{v} = 5.83\mathbf{i} - 3.10\mathbf{j}$

b. Let θ = angle between **u** and **v**; $\theta = 57° - (-28°) = 85°$; $\mathbf{u} \cdot \mathbf{v} = \|\mathbf{u}\|\|\mathbf{v}\| \cos 85° = (8.70)(6.60)(0.0872) = 5.00$

c. $\mathbf{u} \cdot \mathbf{v} = ac + bd = 4.74(5.83) + 7.30(-3.10) = 5.00$

C **31.** By the law of cosines, $\|\mathbf{u} - \mathbf{v}\|^2 = \|\mathbf{u}\|^2 + \|\mathbf{v}\|^2 - 2\|\mathbf{u}\|\|\mathbf{v}\| \cos \theta =$

$\|\mathbf{u}\|^2 + \|\mathbf{v}\|^2 - 2\mathbf{u} \cdot \mathbf{v}$; $\mathbf{u} \cdot \mathbf{v} = \frac{1}{2}[\|\mathbf{u}\|^2 + \|\mathbf{v}\|^2 - \|\mathbf{u} - \mathbf{v}\|^2] =$

$\frac{1}{2}[a^2 + b^2 + c^2 + d^2 - (a - c)^2 - (b - d)^2] =$

$\frac{1}{2}[a^2 + b^2 + c^2 + d^2 - a^2 + 2ac - c^2 - b^2 + 2bd - d^2] = \frac{1}{2}(2ac + 2bd) =$

$ac + bd$

32. Let $\mathbf{u} = a\mathbf{i} + b\mathbf{j}$; $\mathbf{u} \cdot \mathbf{i} = a \cdot 1 + b \cdot 0 = a$ and $\mathbf{u} \cdot \mathbf{j} = a \cdot 0 + b \cdot 1 = b$; $(\mathbf{u} \cdot \mathbf{i})\mathbf{i} + (\mathbf{u} \cdot \mathbf{j})\mathbf{j} = a\mathbf{i} + b\mathbf{j} = \mathbf{u}$.

Pages 670–671 • COMPUTER EXERCISES

1.

```
10 PRINT "ENTER X AND Y COMPONENTS"
20 INPUT X, Y
30 LET M = SQR(X ↑ 2 + Y ↑ 2)
40 LET A = ATN(Y/X) * 180/3.14159265
50 IF X < 0 THEN LET A = A + 180
60 IF A < 0 THEN LET A = A + 360
70 PRINT "MAGNITUDE = "; M
80 PRINT "ANGLE = "; A
90 END
```

2. a.

```
MAGNITUDE = 9.21954447
ANGLE = 319.398705
```

b.

```
MAGNITUDE = 17
ANGLE = 151.927513
```

c.

```
MAGNITUDE = 64.1755406
ANGLE = 206.764687
```

3.

```
10 PRINT "ENTER MAGNITUDE 1, ANGLE 1"
20 INPUT M1, A1
30 PRINT "ENTER MAGNITUDE 2, ANGLE 2"
40 INPUT M2, A2
50 LET Y1 = M1 * SIN(A1 * 3.14159265/180)
60 LET X1 = M1 * COS(A1 * 3.14159265/180)
70 LET Y2 = M2 * SIN(A2 * 3.14159265/180)
80 LET X2 = M2 * COS(A2 * 3.14159265/180)
90 LET X = X1 + X2
100 LET Y = Y1 + Y2
110 LET M = SQR(X ↑ 2 + Y ↑ 2)
120 LET A = ATN(Y/X) * 180/3.14159265
```

(Continued)

```
130 IF X < 0 THEN LET A = A + 180
140 IF A < 0 THEN LET A = A + 360
150 PRINT "MAGNITUDE ="; M
160 PRINT "ANGLE ="; A
170 END
```

4. a. MAGNITUDE = 21.6009675
ANGLE = 79.6485928

b. MAGNITUDE = 11.2980008
ANGLE = 39.5829305

c. MAGNITUDE = 70.0145352
ANGLE = 167.140754

d. MAGNITUDE = 353.163902
ANGLE = 101.425964

e. MAGNITUDE = 50.0000001
ANGLE = 263.130102

Page 674 • APPLICATION

A

1. $\mathbf{F}_3 = -(\mathbf{F}_1 + \mathbf{F}_2) = -[(3 - 1)\mathbf{i} + (-2 + 3)\mathbf{j}] = -2\mathbf{i} - \mathbf{j}$

2. $\mathbf{F}_3 = -(\mathbf{F}_1 + \mathbf{F}_2) = -[(5 - 2)\mathbf{i} + (-1 + 1)\mathbf{j}] = -3\mathbf{i}$

3. $\mathbf{d} = \overrightarrow{AB} = (2 + 2)\mathbf{i} + (3 - 0)\mathbf{j} = 4\mathbf{i} + 3\mathbf{j}$; $W = \mathbf{F} \cdot \mathbf{d} = (3\mathbf{i} - \mathbf{j}) \cdot (4\mathbf{i} + 3\mathbf{j}) = 12 - 3 = 9$; 9 J

4. $\mathbf{d} = \overrightarrow{AB} = (5 + 3)\mathbf{i} + (-1 - 2)\mathbf{j} = 8\mathbf{i} - 3\mathbf{j}$; $W = \mathbf{F} \cdot \mathbf{d} = 5\mathbf{i} \cdot (8\mathbf{i} - 3\mathbf{j}) = 5 \cdot 8 + 0(-3) = 40$; 40 J

5. a. $\mathbf{d}_1 = \overrightarrow{AB} = (3 + 2)\mathbf{i} + (3 - 1)\mathbf{j} = 5\mathbf{i} + 2\mathbf{j}$; $\mathbf{d}_2 = \overrightarrow{BC} = (5 - 3)\mathbf{i} + (0 - 3)\mathbf{j} = 2\mathbf{i} - 3\mathbf{j}$; $W = \mathbf{F} \cdot \mathbf{d}_1 + \mathbf{F} \cdot \mathbf{d}_2 = (3\mathbf{i} - \mathbf{j}) \cdot (5\mathbf{i} + 2\mathbf{j}) + (3\mathbf{i} - \mathbf{j}) \cdot (2\mathbf{i} - 3\mathbf{j}) = 3 \cdot 5 + (-1)2 + 3 \cdot 2 + (-1)(-3) = 22$; 22 J

b. $\mathbf{d} = \overrightarrow{AC} = (5 + 2)\mathbf{i} + (0 - 1)\mathbf{j} = 7\mathbf{i} - \mathbf{j}$; $W = \mathbf{F} \cdot \mathbf{d} = (3\mathbf{i} - \mathbf{j}) \cdot (7\mathbf{i} - \mathbf{j}) = 3 \cdot 7 + (-1)(-1) = 22$; 22 J

6. $\mathbf{d} = \overrightarrow{AB} = (4 + 1)\mathbf{i} + (1 - 0)\mathbf{j} = 5\mathbf{i} + \mathbf{j}$; $W = \mathbf{F} \cdot \mathbf{d} + \mathbf{G} \cdot \mathbf{d} = (2\mathbf{i} + 5\mathbf{j}) \cdot (5\mathbf{i} + \mathbf{j}) + (4\mathbf{i} - 2\mathbf{j}) \cdot (5\mathbf{i} + \mathbf{j}) = 2 \cdot 5 + 5 \cdot 1 + 4 \cdot 5 + (-2)(1) = 33$; 33 J; $\mathbf{F} + \mathbf{G} = (2\mathbf{i} + 5\mathbf{j}) + (4\mathbf{i} - 2\mathbf{j}) = (2 + 4)\mathbf{i} + (5 - 2)\mathbf{j} = 6\mathbf{i} + 3\mathbf{j}$; $W = (\mathbf{F} + \mathbf{G}) \cdot \mathbf{d} = (6\mathbf{i} + 3\mathbf{j}) \cdot (5\mathbf{i} + \mathbf{j}) = 6 \cdot 5 + 3 \cdot 1 = 33$; 33 J

7. $\mathbf{F} = -(\mathbf{F}_1 + \mathbf{F}_2)$; $\alpha = 180° - 60° = 120°$; $\|\mathbf{F}\|^2 = 10^2 + 5^2 - 2(10)(5) \cos 120° = 175$; $\|\mathbf{F}\| = 13.2$; $\frac{\sin \theta}{10} = \frac{\sin 120°}{13.2}$;

$\sin \theta = \frac{10(0.8660)}{13.2} = 0.6561$; $\theta = 41°$; bearing $= 360° - 41° = 319°$;

F:13.2 N, bearing 319°

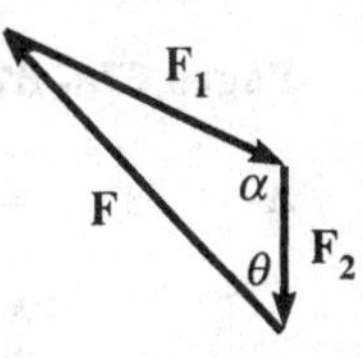

8. $\mathbf{F} = -(\mathbf{F}_1 + \mathbf{F}_2)$; $\alpha = 180° - (60° + 30°) = 90°$; $\|\mathbf{F}\| = \sqrt{15^2 + 6^2} = 16.2$;

$\tan \theta = \frac{6}{15} = 0.4$; $\theta = 21.8°$; bearing $= 270° - (\theta + 60°) = 210° - 21.8° = 188.2°$;

F:16.2 N, bearing 188.2°

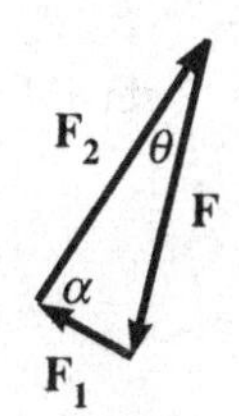

9. The engine must overcome the force of gravity by exerting an upward force of $1500(9.8) = 1.47 \times 10^4$ N; the displacement **d** is also upward and $\|\mathbf{d}\| = 100$; $W = \|\mathbf{F}\|\|\mathbf{d}\| = 1.47 \times 10^4 \times 100 = 1.47 \times 10^6$ J

10. See the figure for Example 1, page 672 in the text with α = angle between **H** and **G**;

$\|\mathbf{G}\| = 50 \times 9.8 = 490$ N; $\alpha = 20°$; $\sin \alpha = \frac{\|\mathbf{F}\|}{\|\mathbf{G}\|}$; $\|\mathbf{F}\| = 490(0.3420) = 168$; 168 N

11. The man must overcome the force of gravity by exerting an upward force of $9.8 \times 75 = 735$ N; the displacement **d** has norm 12; the angle between **F** and **d** is $90° - 78° = 12°$; $W = \mathbf{F} \cdot \mathbf{d} = \|\mathbf{F}\|\|\mathbf{d}\| \cos 12° = 735 \cdot 12(0.9781) = 8627$; 8.63×10^3 J

B **12.** The force **F** needed to overcome the force of gravity is $120{,}000 \times 9.8 = 1.18 \times 10^6$ N; the displacement **d** has norm 5000 and the angle between **F** and **d** is $90° - 22° = 68°$; $\mathbf{W} = \mathbf{F} \cdot \mathbf{d} = \|\mathbf{F}\|\,\|\mathbf{d}\| \cos 68° = (1.18 \times 10^6)(5000)(0.3746) = 2.21 \times 10^9$ J; $(2.21 \times 10^9) \div (3.6 \times 10^6) = 614$; 614 kW · h.

13. Let **F** = the force of 120 N at an angle of 40° with the horizontal and **d** = displacement; $\|\mathbf{d}\| = 200$; angle between **F** and **d** $= 40° - 23° = 17°$; $W = \mathbf{F} \cdot \mathbf{d} = \|\mathbf{F}\|\|\mathbf{d}\| \cos 17° = 120(200)(0.9563) = 2.30 \times 10^4$ J.

14. The force exerted by gravity $= 20 \times 9.8 = 196$ N; $\beta = 60°$; $\alpha = 180° - 120° = 60°$; $\|\mathbf{t}\| = 196$; tension in wire = 196 N.

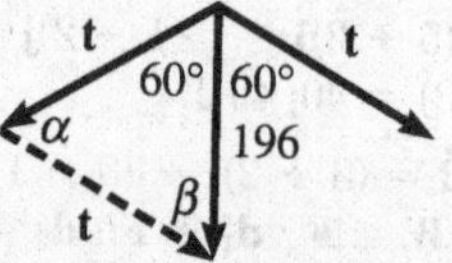

15. $200(9.8) = 1960$; angle between $\mathbf{F}_1$ and $\mathbf{F}_2 = 40° + 60° = 100°$; $\beta = 90° - 40° = 50°$;

$\alpha = 90° - 60° = 30°$; $\frac{\sin \alpha}{\|\mathbf{F}_1\|} = \frac{\sin 100°}{1960}$; $\|\mathbf{F}_1\| = \frac{1960(0.5)}{0.9848} = 995$;

$\frac{\sin \beta}{\|\mathbf{F}_2\|} = \frac{\sin 100°}{1960}$; $\|\mathbf{F}_2\| = 1525$; 995 N and 1525 N

Pages 678–679 • WRITTEN EXERCISES

A **1.** $x = 4 \cos 30° = 4\left(\frac{\sqrt{3}}{2}\right) = 2\sqrt{3}$; $y = 4 \sin 30° = 4\left(\frac{1}{2}\right) = 2$; $(2\sqrt{3}, 2)$

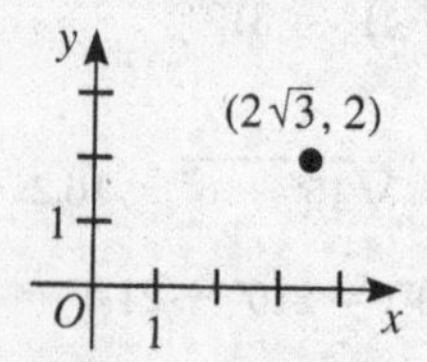

2. $x = 2 \cos 45° = 2\left(\frac{\sqrt{2}}{2}\right) = \sqrt{2}$; $y = 2 \sin 45° = 2\left(\frac{\sqrt{2}}{2}\right) = \sqrt{2}$; $(\sqrt{2}, \sqrt{2})$

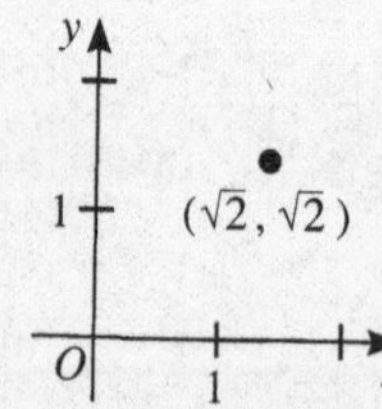

3. $x = -3\cos 120° = -3\left(-\frac{1}{2}\right) = \frac{3}{2}$; $y = -3\sin 120° = -3\left(\frac{\sqrt{3}}{2}\right) = \frac{-3\sqrt{3}}{2}$;

$\left(\frac{3}{2}, -\frac{3\sqrt{3}}{2}\right)$

4. $x = -5\cos 135° = -5\left(-\frac{\sqrt{2}}{2}\right) = \frac{5\sqrt{2}}{2}$; $y = -5\sin 135° = -5\left(\frac{\sqrt{2}}{2}\right) = -\frac{5\sqrt{2}}{2}$;

$\left(\frac{5\sqrt{2}}{2}, -\frac{5\sqrt{2}}{2}\right)$

5. $x = 7\cos(-60°) = 7\left(\frac{1}{2}\right) = \frac{7}{2}$; $y = 7\sin(-60°) = 7\left(-\frac{\sqrt{3}}{2}\right) = -\frac{7\sqrt{3}}{2}$; $\left(\frac{7}{2}, -\frac{7\sqrt{3}}{2}\right)$

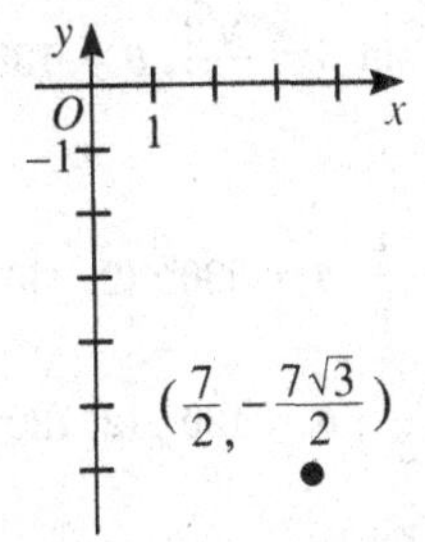

6. $x = 6\cos(-45°) = 6\left(\frac{\sqrt{2}}{2}\right) = 3\sqrt{2}$; $y = 6\sin(-45°) = 6\left(-\frac{\sqrt{2}}{2}\right) = -3\sqrt{2}$;

$(3\sqrt{2}, -3\sqrt{2})$

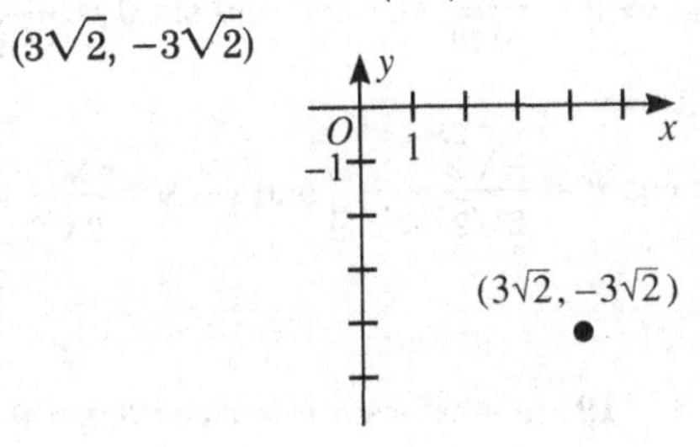

7. $x = -6\cos(-150°) = -6\left(-\frac{\sqrt{3}}{2}\right) = 3\sqrt{3}$; $y = -6\sin(-150°) = -6\left(-\frac{1}{2}\right) = 3$;

$(3\sqrt{3}, 3)$

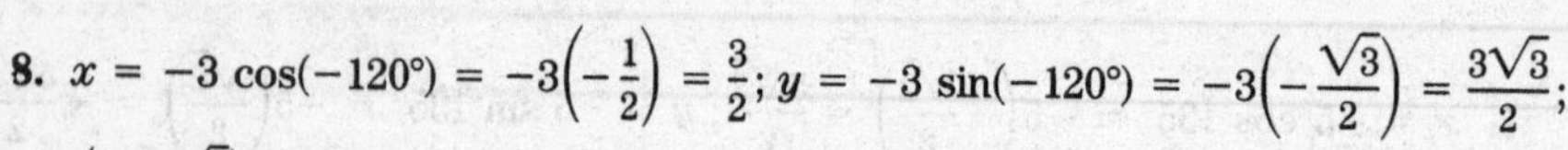

8. $x = -3\cos(-120°) = -3\left(-\frac{1}{2}\right) = \frac{3}{2}$; $y = -3\sin(-120°) = -3\left(-\frac{\sqrt{3}}{2}\right) = \frac{3\sqrt{3}}{2}$;

$\left(\frac{3}{2}, \frac{3\sqrt{3}}{2}\right)$

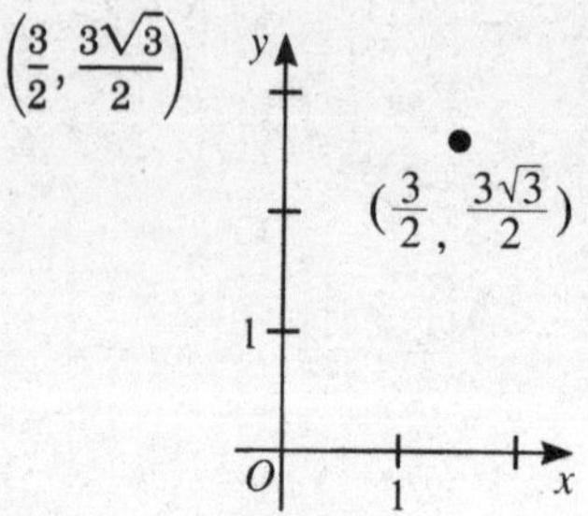

9–16. Answers may vary.

9. $(4, 0°)$ **10.** $(3, 270°)$

11. $r = \sqrt{(-2)^2 + 2^2} = 2\sqrt{2}$; $\cos\theta = \frac{-2}{2\sqrt{2}} = -\frac{\sqrt{2}}{2}$ and $\sin\theta = \frac{\sqrt{2}}{2}$; $\theta = 135°$;

$(2\sqrt{2}, 135°)$

12. $r = \sqrt{(\sqrt{3})^2 + (-1)^2} = 2$; $\cos\theta = \frac{\sqrt{3}}{2}$ and $\sin\theta = -\frac{1}{2}$; $\theta = 330°$; $(2, 330°)$

13. $r = \sqrt{(-1)^2 + (\sqrt{3})^2} = 2$; $\cos\theta = -\frac{1}{2}$ and $\sin\theta = \frac{\sqrt{3}}{2}$; $\theta = 120°$; $(2, 120°)$

14. $r = \sqrt{(-\sqrt{2})^2 + (-\sqrt{2})^2} = 2$; $\cos\theta = \sin\theta = -\frac{\sqrt{2}}{2}$; $\theta = 225°$; $(2, 225°)$

15. $r = \sqrt{(-\sqrt{5})^2 + (\sqrt{5})^2} = \sqrt{10}$, $\cos\theta = \frac{-\sqrt{5}}{\sqrt{10}} = -\frac{\sqrt{2}}{2}$ and $\sin\theta = \frac{\sqrt{5}}{\sqrt{10}} = \frac{\sqrt{2}}{2}$;

$\theta = 135°$; $(\sqrt{10}, 135°)$

16. $r = \sqrt{(-\sqrt{2})^2 + (\sqrt{6})^2} = 2\sqrt{2}$; $\cos\theta = \frac{-\sqrt{2}}{2\sqrt{2}} = -\frac{1}{2}$ and $\sin\theta = \frac{\sqrt{6}}{2\sqrt{2}} = \frac{\sqrt{3}}{2}$;

$\theta = 120°$; $(2\sqrt{2}, 120°)$

17. $x = 5$; $x = r\cos\theta$; $r\cos\theta = 5$

18. $y = -3$; $y = r\sin\theta$; $r\sin\theta = -3$ **19.** $y = x$; $r\sin\theta = r\cos\theta$; $\sin\theta = \cos\theta$

20. $x^2 + y^2 = 9$; $r^2 = 9$, $r = \pm 3$

21. $x^2 + y^2 = 6y$; $r^2 = 6r\sin\theta$; $r = 6\sin\theta$

22. $x^2 + y^2 + 8x = 0$; $r^2 + 8r\cos\theta = 0$, $r + 8\cos\theta = 0$

23. $r = 2$; $r^2 = 4$; $x^2 + y^2 = 4$

24. $\theta = 120°$; $\tan\theta = -\sqrt{3}$; $\dfrac{r\sin\theta}{r\cos\theta} = -\sqrt{3}$, $\dfrac{y}{x} = -\sqrt{3}$; $y = -x\sqrt{3}$

25. $r\sin\theta = 2$; $y = 2$ **26.** $r\cos\theta = -1$; $x = -1$

B **27.** $r = 2\sin\theta$; $r = 2\dfrac{y}{r}$; $r^2 = 2y$; $x^2 + y^2 = 2y$

28. $r + 2\cos\theta = 0$; $r^2 + 2r\cos\theta = 0$; $x^2 + y^2 + 2x = 0$

29. $r(1 - \cos\theta) = 2$; $r - r\cos\theta = 2$; $r = r\cos\theta + 2$; $r^2 = (r\cos\theta)^2 + 4r\cos\theta + 4$; $x^2 + y^2 = x^2 + 4x + 4$; $y^2 = 4x + 4$

30. $r(1 - \sin\theta) = 1$; $r - r\sin\theta = 1$; $r = r\sin\theta + 1$; $r^2 = (r\sin\theta)^2 + 2r\sin\theta + 1$; $x^2 + y^2 = y^2 + 2y + 1$; $x^2 = 2y + 1$

31.

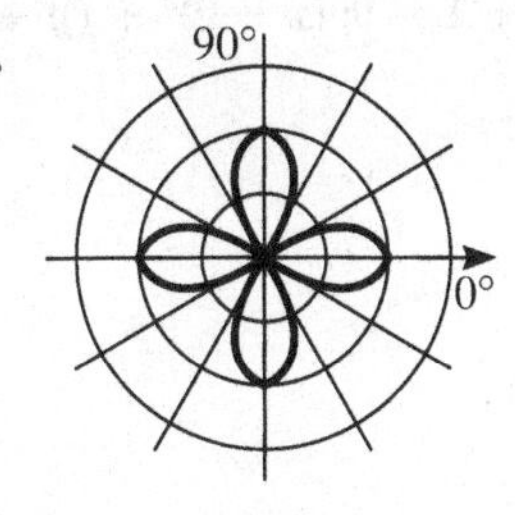

32.

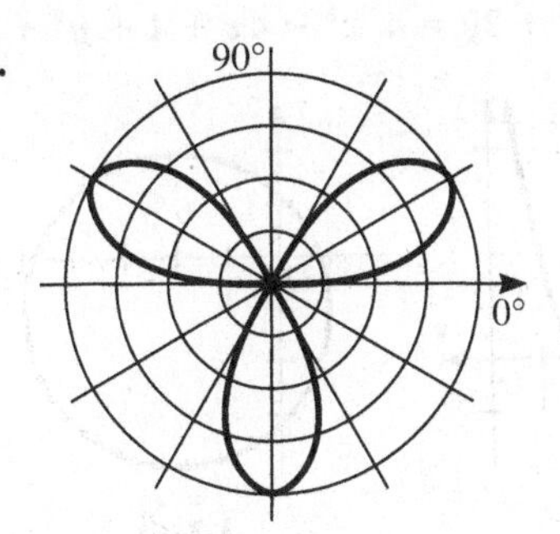

33.

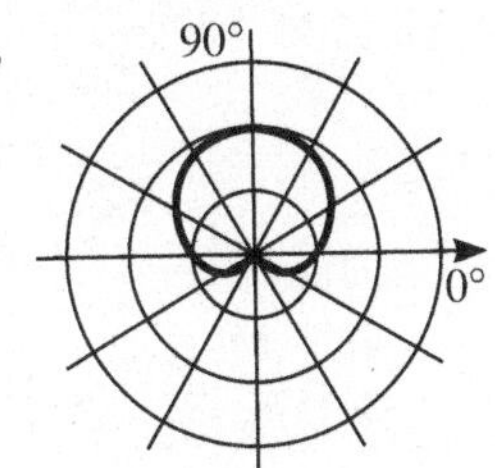

34.

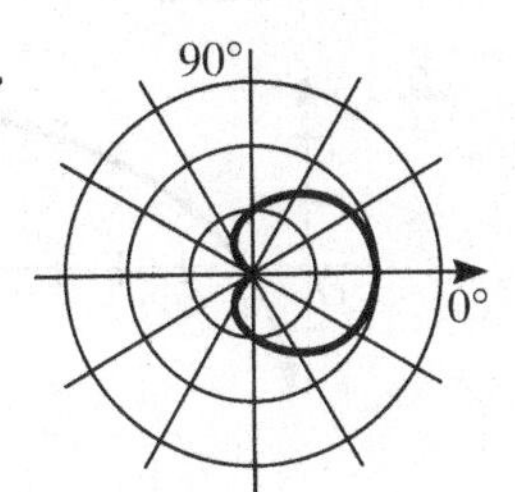

C **35.**

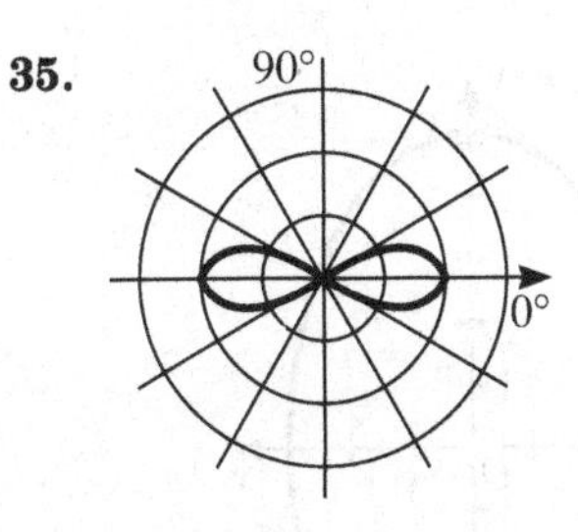

36.

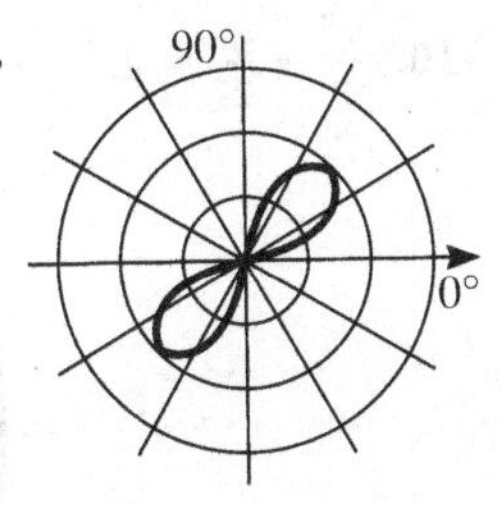

Page 679 • MIXED REVIEW EXERCISES

1. $$\begin{array}{r|rrrrr} -2 & 1 & 0 & -2 & 0 & 3 \\ & & -2 & 4 & -4 & 8 \\ \hline & 1 & -2 & 2 & -4 & 11 \end{array}$$; $\dfrac{x^4 - 2x^2 + 3}{x + 2} = x^3 - 2x^2 + 2x - 4 + \dfrac{11}{x + 2}$

2. $\dfrac{3x^3 + x^2 - 3x - 1}{3x + 1} = \dfrac{x^2(3x + 1) - (3x + 1)}{3x + 1} = \dfrac{(x^2 - 1)(3x + 1)}{3x + 1} = x^2 - 1$

3.

$$\begin{array}{r} 3x - 5 \\ 2x + 2\overline{)6x^2 - 4x + 7} \\ \underline{6x^2 + 6x} \\ -10x + 7 \\ \underline{-10x - 10} \\ 17 \end{array}$$

$\dfrac{6x^2 - 4x + 7}{2x + 2} = 3x - 5 + \dfrac{17}{2x + 2}$

4.

$$\begin{array}{r|rrrr} 2 & -4 & 3 & -2 & 1 \\ & & -8 & -10 & -24 \\ \hline & -4 & -5 & -12 & -23 \end{array}$$

$\dfrac{1 - 2x + 3x^2 - 4x^3}{x - 2} = -4x^2 - 5x - 12 + \dfrac{-23}{x - 2}$

5. $x^2 + 6x + 7 = y$; $y = (x + 3)^2 - 2$

6. $x^2 - 4x + y^2 + 2y = 4$; $x^2 - 4x + 4 + y^2 + 2y + 1 = 9$; $(x - 2)^2 + (y + 1)^2 = 9$

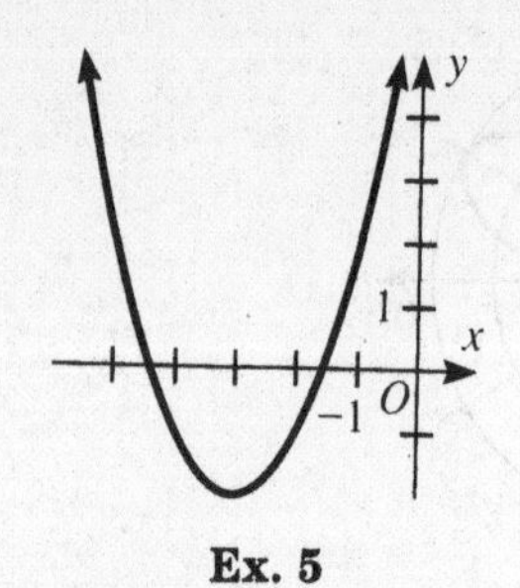

Ex. 5

Ex. 6

7.

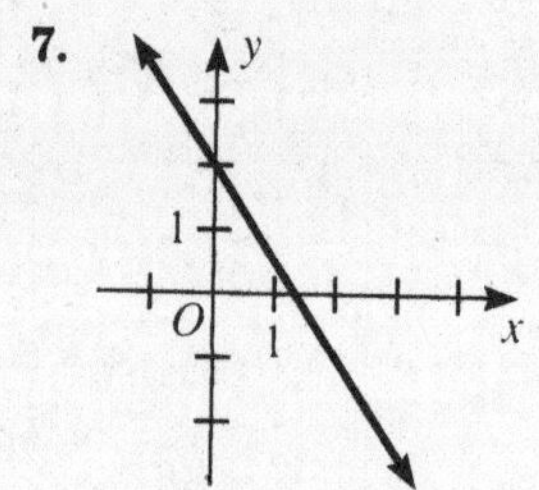

8.

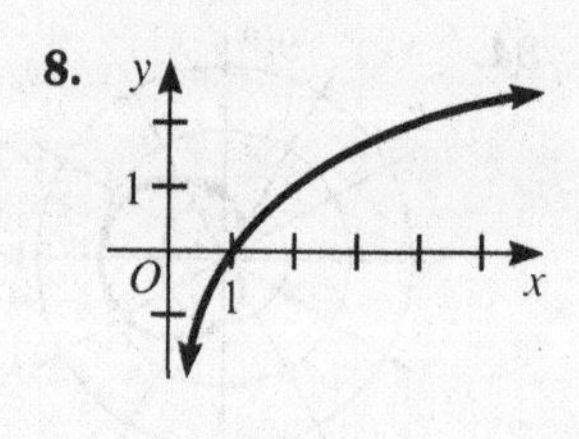

9.

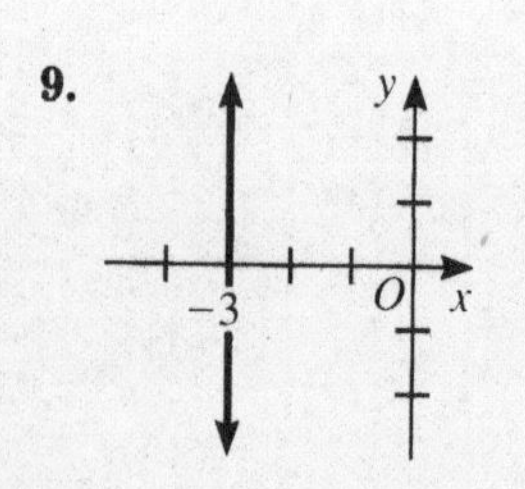

10. $\dfrac{x^2}{9} + \dfrac{y^2}{27} = 1$

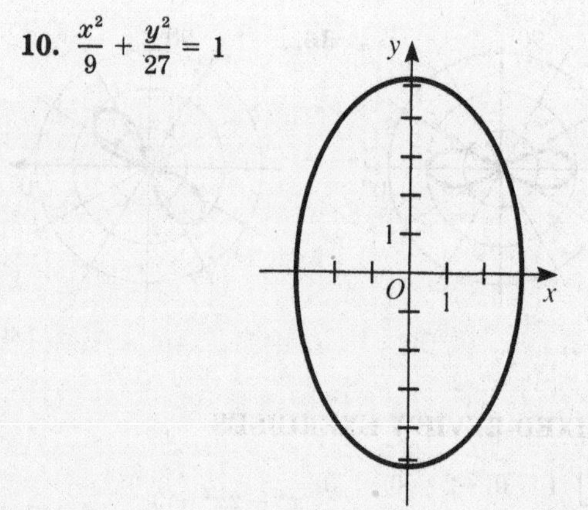

Page 679 • EXTRA

1.

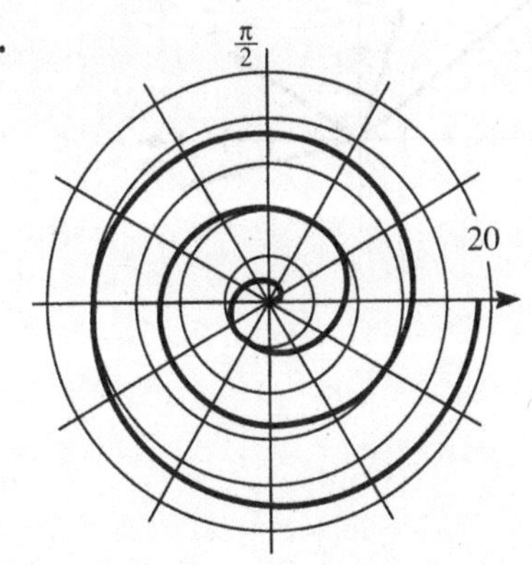

2.

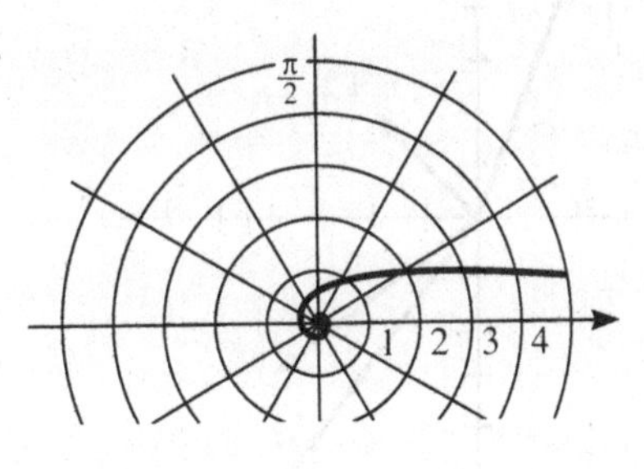

3.

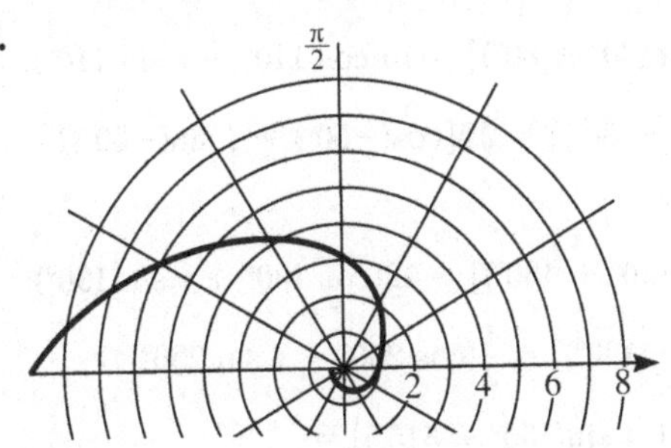

Pages 683–684 • WRITTEN EXERCISES

A 1.

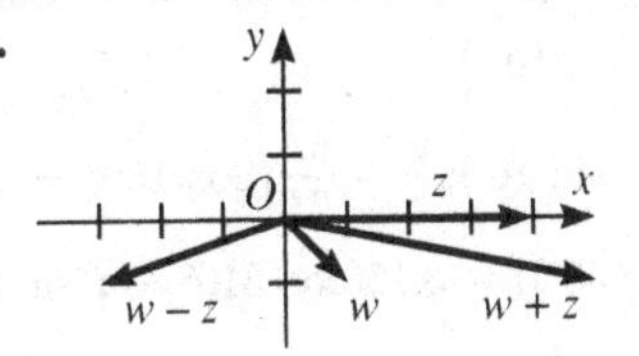

2.

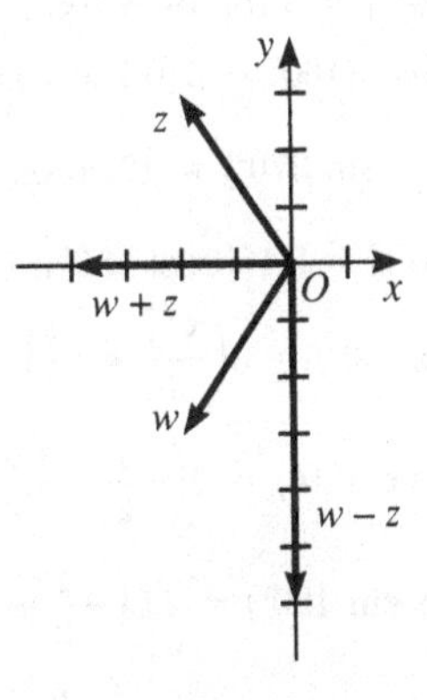

3.

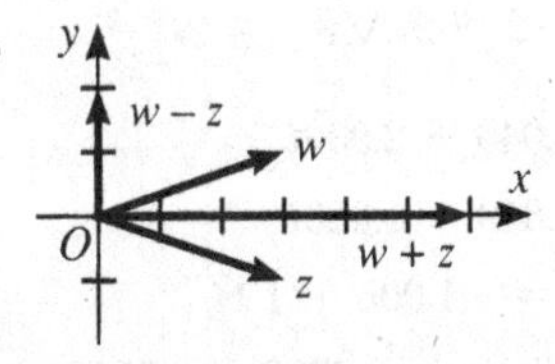

4.

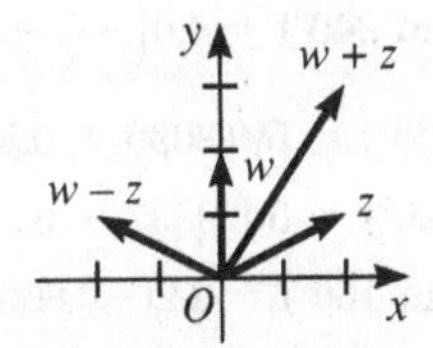

5.

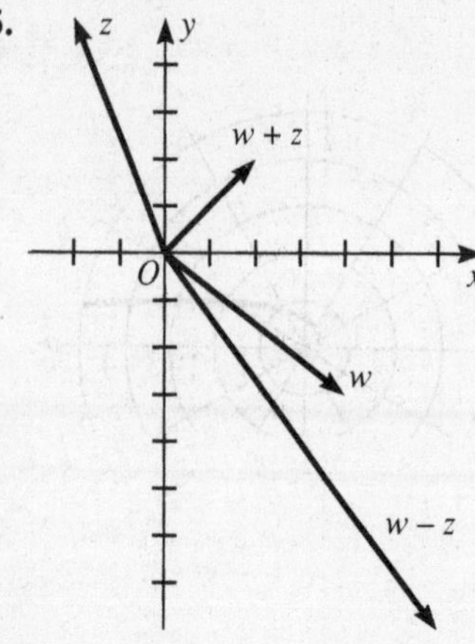

6.

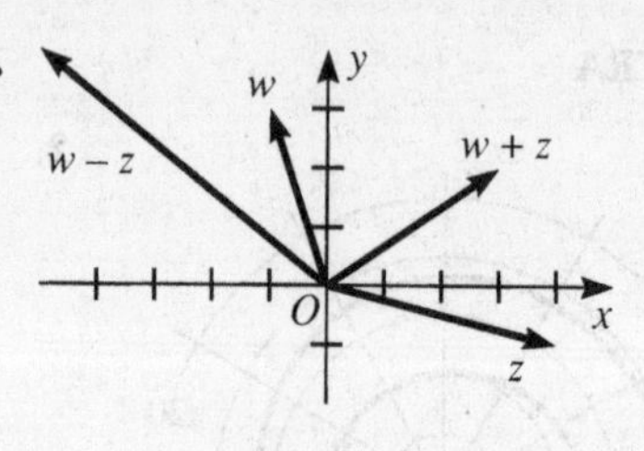

7. $wz = (5)(2)[\cos(30° + 80°) + i \sin(30° + 80°)] = 10(\cos 110° + i \sin 110°)$;

$\frac{w}{z} = \frac{5}{2}[\cos(30° - 80°) + i \sin(30° - 80°)] = 2.5[\cos(-50°) + i \sin(-50°)] =$

$2.5(\cos 310° + i \sin 310°)$

8. $wz = (4)(3)[\cos(0° + 130°) + i \sin(0° + 130°)] = 12(\cos 130° + i \sin 130°)$;

$\frac{w}{z} = \frac{4}{3}[\cos(0° - 130°) + i \sin(0° - 130°)] = \frac{4}{3}(\cos 230° + i \sin 230°)$

9. $wz = (4.5)(1.2)[\cos(150° + 315°) + i \sin(150° + 315°)] =$

$5.4(\cos 465° + i \sin 465°) = 5.4(\cos 105° + i \sin 105°)$; $\frac{w}{z} = \frac{4.5}{1.2}[\cos(150° - 315°) +$

$i \sin(150° - 315°)] = 3.75[\cos(-165°) + i \sin(-165°)] = 3.75(\cos 195° + i \sin 195°)$

10. $wz = (6.3)(2.0)[\cos(160° + 210°) + i \sin(160° + 210°)] =$

$12.6(\cos 370° + i \sin 370°) = 12.6(\cos 10° + i \sin 10°)$; $\frac{w}{z} = \frac{6.3}{2.0}[\cos(160° - 210°) +$

$i \sin(160° - 210°)] = 3.15[\cos(-50°) + i \sin(-50°)] = 3.15(\cos 310° + i \sin 310°)$

11. $3(\cos 30° + i \sin 30°) = 3\left(\frac{\sqrt{3}}{2} + i\frac{1}{2}\right) = \frac{3\sqrt{3}}{2} + \frac{3}{2}i$

12. $2(\cos 120° + i \sin 120°) = 2\left(-\frac{1}{2} + \frac{i\sqrt{3}}{2}\right) = -1 + i\sqrt{3}$

13. $4.5(\cos 120° + i \sin 120°) = 4.5\left(-\frac{1}{2} + i\frac{\sqrt{3}}{2}\right) = -\frac{9}{4} + \frac{9i\sqrt{3}}{4}$

14. $4.0(\cos 240° + i \sin 240°) = 4.0\left(-\frac{1}{2} - \frac{i\sqrt{3}}{2}\right) = -2 - 2i\sqrt{3}$

15. $5(\cos 36° + i \sin 36°) = 5(0.8090 + 0.5878i) = 4.045 + 2.939i$

16. $3(\cos 20° + i \sin 20°) = 3(0.9397 + 0.3420i) = 2.819 + 1.026i$

17. $2.2(\cos 150° + i \sin 150°) = 2.2(-0.8660 + 0.5i) = -1.905 + 1.1i$

18. $0.8(\cos 250° + i \sin 250°) = 0.8(-0.3420 - 0.9397i) = -0.2736 - 0.7518i$

19. $r = \sqrt{1^2 + (-\sqrt{3})^2} = 2$; $\cos\theta = \frac{1}{2}$, $\sin\theta = -\frac{\sqrt{3}}{2}$; $\theta = 300°$; $2(\cos 300° + i \sin 300°)$

20. $2\sqrt{2}(1 - i) = 2\sqrt{2} - 2i\sqrt{2}$; $r = \sqrt{(2\sqrt{2})^2 + (-2\sqrt{2})^2} = 4$; $\cos\theta = \frac{\sqrt{2}}{2}$,

$\sin\theta = -\frac{\sqrt{2}}{2}$; $\theta = 315°$; $4(\cos 315° + i\sin 315°)$

21. $2\sqrt{3}(-1 + i) = -2\sqrt{3} + 2i\sqrt{3}$; $r = \sqrt{(-2\sqrt{3})^2 + (2\sqrt{3})^2} = \sqrt{24} = 2\sqrt{6}$;

$\cos\theta = \frac{-2\sqrt{3}}{2\sqrt{6}} = -\frac{\sqrt{2}}{2}$, $\sin\theta = \frac{2\sqrt{3}}{2\sqrt{6}} = \frac{\sqrt{2}}{2}$; $\theta = 135°$; $2\sqrt{6}(\cos 135° + i\sin 135°)$

22. $r = \sqrt{12^2 + 5^2} = 13$; $\cos\theta = \frac{12}{13} = 0.9231$; θ is in quadrant I; $\theta = 22.6°$;

$13(\cos 22.6° + i\sin 22.6°)$

23. $r = \sqrt{(-3)^2 + (-4)^2} = 5$; $\cos\theta = -\frac{3}{5} = -0.6$; θ is in quadrant III;

$\theta = 180° + 53.1° = 233.1°$; $5(\cos 233.1° + i\sin 233.1°)$

24. $r = \sqrt{5^2 + (-1)^2} = \sqrt{26}$; $\cos\theta = \frac{5}{\sqrt{26}} = 0.9806$; θ is in quadrant IV;

$\theta = 360° - 11.3° = 348.7°$; $\sqrt{26}(\cos 348.7° + i\sin 348.7°)$

25. $r = \sqrt{3^2 + (-2)^2} = \sqrt{13}$; $\cos\theta = \frac{3}{\sqrt{13}} = 0.8321$; θ is in quadrant IV;

$\theta = 360° - 33.7° = 326.3°$; $\sqrt{13}(\cos 326.3° + i\sin 326.3°)$

26. $r = \sqrt{(-\sqrt{5})^2 + 1^2} = \sqrt{6}$; $\cos\theta = -\frac{\sqrt{5}}{\sqrt{6}} = -0.9129$; θ is in quadrant II;

$\theta = 180° - 24.1° = 155.9°$; $\sqrt{6}(\cos 155.9° + i\sin 155.9°)$

B **27. a.** $wz = 3 \cdot 6[\cos(120° + 150°) + i\sin(120° + 150°)] = 18(\cos 270° + i\sin 270°)$

b. $18(0 + i(-1)) = -18i$

c. $w = 3\left(-\frac{1}{2} + i\frac{\sqrt{3}}{2}\right) = -\frac{3}{2} + \frac{3i\sqrt{3}}{2}$; $z = 6\left(-\frac{\sqrt{3}}{2} + \frac{i}{2}\right) = -3\sqrt{3} + 3i$

d. $wz = \left(-\frac{3}{2} + \frac{3i\sqrt{3}}{2}\right)(-3\sqrt{3} + 3i) = \frac{9\sqrt{3}}{2} - \frac{9}{2}i - \frac{27i}{2} - \frac{9\sqrt{3}}{2} = -\frac{36i}{2} = -18i$

28. a. $wz = 2 \cdot 7[\cos(60° + 30°) + i\sin(60° + 30°)] = 14(\cos 90° + i\sin 90°)$

b. $14(0 + i(1)) = 14i$

c. $w = 2\left(\frac{1}{2} + \frac{i\sqrt{3}}{2}\right) = 1 + i\sqrt{3}$; $z = 7\left(\frac{\sqrt{3}}{2} + \frac{i}{2}\right) = \frac{7\sqrt{3}}{2} + \frac{7i}{2}$

d. $wz = (1 + i\sqrt{3})\left(\frac{7\sqrt{3}}{2} + \frac{7i}{2}\right) = \frac{7\sqrt{3}}{2} + \frac{7i}{2} + \frac{21i}{2} - \frac{7\sqrt{3}}{2} = \frac{28i}{2} = 14i$

29. a. $wz = 2 \cdot 4[\cos(30° + 120°) + i\sin(30° + 120°)] = 8(\cos 150° + i\sin 150°)$

b. $8\left(-\frac{\sqrt{3}}{2} + \frac{i}{2}\right) = -4\sqrt{3} + 4i$

c. $w = 2\left(\frac{\sqrt{3}}{2} + \frac{i}{2}\right) = \sqrt{3} + i$; $z = 4\left(-\frac{1}{2} + \frac{i\sqrt{3}}{2}\right) = -2 + 2i\sqrt{3}$

d. $wz = (\sqrt{3} + i)(-2 + 2i\sqrt{3}) = -2\sqrt{3} + 6i - 2i - 2\sqrt{3} = -4\sqrt{3} + 4i$

30. **a.** $wz = 8 \cdot 4[(\cos(150° + 60°) + i \sin(150° + 60°)] = 32(\cos 210° + i \sin 210°)$

b. $32\left(-\frac{\sqrt{3}}{2} - \frac{i}{2}\right) = -16\sqrt{3} - 16i$

c. $w = 8\left(-\frac{\sqrt{3}}{2} + \frac{i}{2}\right) = -4\sqrt{3} + 4i;\ z = 4\left(\frac{1}{2} + \frac{i\sqrt{3}}{2}\right) = 2 + 2i\sqrt{3}$

d. $(-4\sqrt{3} + 4i)(2 + 2i\sqrt{3}) = -8\sqrt{3} - 24i + 8i - 8\sqrt{3} = -16\sqrt{3} - 16i$

31. Let $w = r_1(\cos\theta + i\sin\theta)$ and $z = r_2(\cos\varphi + i\sin\varphi)$;
$|wz| = |r_1r_2[\cos(\theta + \varphi) + i\sin(\theta + \varphi)]| = r_1r_2 = |w||z|$

32. If $w \neq z$ and $w \neq -z$, $|w + z|$ is the length of the diagonal of a parallelogram with sides of length $|w|$ and $|z|$; the sum of the lengths of any two sides of a triangle is greater than the length of the third side; that is, the shortest distance between two points is the length of the segment between them. If $w = z$, then $|w + z| = 2|w| = |w| + |z|$; if $w = -z$, $|w + z| = 0 < |w| + |z|$; in any case, $|w + z| \leq |w| + |z|$.

33. Let z be a complex number, $z = x + yi$; $z\bar{z} = (x + yi)(x - yi) =$
$x^2 + xyi - xyi - y^2i^2 = x^2 + y^2 = (\sqrt{x^2 + y^2})^2 = |z|^2$

34. Let z be a complex number; $\frac{1}{z} = \frac{1 \cdot \bar{z}}{z \cdot \bar{z}} = \frac{\bar{z}}{|z|^2}$

C **35.** Let z be a complex number, $z = b(\cos\beta + i\sin\beta) = b\cos\beta + bi\sin\beta$;
$\frac{1}{z} = \frac{\bar{z}}{|z|^2} = \frac{b\cos\beta - bi\sin\beta}{b^2} = \frac{1}{b}(\cos\beta - i\sin\beta)$

36. Let $w = a(\cos\alpha + i\sin\alpha)$ and $z = b(\cos\beta + i\sin\beta)$;
$\frac{w}{z} = w \cdot \frac{1}{z} = a(\cos\alpha + i\sin\alpha)\left[\frac{1}{b}(\cos\beta - i\sin\beta)\right] =$
$\frac{a}{b}[\cos\alpha\cos\beta + i\sin\alpha\cos\beta - i\sin\beta\cos\alpha + \sin\alpha\sin\beta] =$
$\frac{a}{b}[\cos\alpha\cos\beta + \sin\alpha\sin\beta + i(\sin\alpha\cos\beta - \sin\beta\cos\alpha)] =$
$\frac{a}{b}[\cos(\alpha - \beta) + i\sin(\alpha - \beta)]$

37. Let $w = r_1(\cos\theta + i\sin\theta)$ and $z = r_2(\cos\varphi + i\sin\varphi)$;
$wz = r_1r_2[\cos(\theta + \varphi) + i\sin(\theta + \varphi)]$; the angle between $\overrightarrow{Oz}$ and $\overrightarrow{Owz} = (\theta + \varphi) - \varphi = \theta$; also, $\frac{|w|}{|wz|} = \frac{|w|}{|w||z|}$ (from Ex. 31) $= \frac{1}{|z|}$; by the Side-Angle-Side Similarity Theorem, the two triangles are similar.

Pages 687–688 • WRITTEN EXERCISES

A **1.** $(\sqrt{3} + i)^4 = [2(\cos 30° + i\sin 30°)]^4 = 2^4(\cos 120° + i\sin 120°) =$
$16\left(-\frac{1}{2} + \frac{i\sqrt{3}}{2}\right) = -8 + 8i\sqrt{3}$

2. $(-1 - i)^6 = [\sqrt{2}(\cos 225° + i\sin 225°)]^6 = (\sqrt{2})^6(\cos 1350° + i\sin 1350°) =$
$8(\cos 270° + i\sin 270°) = 8(0 + i(-1)) = -8i$

3. $(-1 + i)^9 = [\sqrt{2}(\cos 135° + i\sin 135°)]^9 = (\sqrt{2})^9(\cos 1215° + i\sin 1215°) =$
$16\sqrt{2}(\cos 135° + i\sin 135°) = 16\sqrt{2}\left(-\frac{\sqrt{2}}{2} + \frac{i\sqrt{2}}{2}\right) = -16 + 16i$

4. $(1 - i)^7 = [\sqrt{2}(\cos 315° + i \sin 315°)]^7 = (\sqrt{2})^7(\cos 2205° + i \sin 2205°) =$
$8\sqrt{2}(\cos 45° + i \sin 45°) = 8\sqrt{2}\left(\frac{\sqrt{2}}{2} + \frac{i\sqrt{2}}{2}\right) = 8 + 8i$

5. $(1 - i\sqrt{3})^7 = [2(\cos 300° + i \sin 300°)]^7 = 2^7(\cos 2100° + i \sin 2100°) =$
$128(\cos 300° + i \sin 300°) = 128\left(\frac{1}{2} - \frac{i\sqrt{3}}{2}\right) = 64 - 64i\sqrt{3}$

6. $(1 + i\sqrt{3})^{10} = [2(\cos 60° + i \sin 60°)]^{10} = 2^{10}(\cos 600° + i \sin 600°) =$
$1024(\cos 240° + i \sin 240°) = 1024\left(-\frac{1}{2} - \frac{i\sqrt{3}}{2}\right) = -512 - 512i\sqrt{3}$

7. $(-\sqrt{3} - i)^8 = [2(\cos 210° + i \sin 210°)]^8 = 2^8(\cos 1680° + i \sin 1680°) =$
$256(\cos 240° + i \sin 240°) = 256\left(-\frac{1}{2} - \frac{i\sqrt{3}}{2}\right) = -128 - 128i\sqrt{3}$

8. $(-\sqrt{3} + i)^9 = [2(\cos 150° + i \sin 150°)]^9 = 2^9(\cos 1350° + i \sin 1350°) =$
$512(\cos 270° + i \sin 270°) = 512(0 + i(-1)) = -512i$

9. $\cos\left(\frac{k \cdot 360°}{9}\right) + i \sin\left(\frac{k \cdot 360°}{9}\right)$, for $k = 0, 1, 2, \ldots, 8$; roots are $\cos 0° + i \sin 0°$, $\cos 40° + i \sin 40°$, $\cos 80° + i \sin 80°$, $\cos 120° + i \sin 120°$, $\cos 160° + i \sin 160°$, $\cos 200° + i \sin 200°$, $\cos 240° + i \sin 240°$, $\cos 280° + i \sin 280°$, $\cos 320° + i \sin 320°$

10. $\cos\left(\frac{k \cdot 360°}{10}\right) + i \sin\left(\frac{k \cdot 360°}{10}\right)$, for $k = 0, 1, 2, \ldots, 9$; roots are $\cos 0° + i \sin 0°$, $\cos 36° + i \sin 36°$, $\cos 72° + i \sin 72°$, $\cos 108° + i \sin 108°$, $\cos 144° + i \sin 144°$; $\cos 180° + i \sin 180°$; $\cos 216° + i \sin 216°$, $\cos 252° + i \sin 252°$, $\cos 288° + i \sin 288°$, $\cos 324° + i \sin 324°$

11. $4\sqrt{3} - 4i = 8(\cos 330° + i \sin 330°)$; cube roots are
$8^{1/3}\left[\cos\left(\frac{330° + k \cdot 360°}{3}\right) + i \sin\left(\frac{330° + k \cdot 360°}{3}\right)\right]$, for $k = 0, 1, 2$; cube roots are
$2(\cos 110° + i \sin 110°)$, $2(\cos 230° + i \sin 230°)$, and $2(\cos 350° + i \sin 350°)$

12. $-4 + 4i\sqrt{3} = 8(\cos 120° + i \sin 120°)$; cube roots are
$8^{1/3}\left[\cos\left(\frac{120° + k \cdot 360°}{3}\right) + i \sin\left(\frac{120° + k \cdot 360°}{3}\right)\right]$ for $k = 0, 1, 2$; cube roots are
$2(\cos 40° + i \sin 40°)$, $2(\cos 160° + i \sin 160°)$, and $2(\cos 280° + i \sin 280°)$

B **13.** $\cos\left(\frac{k \cdot 360°}{3}\right) + i \sin\left(\frac{k \cdot 360°}{3}\right) = \cos(k \cdot 120°) + i \sin(k \cdot 120°)$for $k = 0, 1, 2$; roots are $\cos 0° + i \sin 0° = 1 + 0 = 1$; $\cos 120° + i \sin 120° = -\frac{1}{2} + \frac{i\sqrt{3}}{2}$;
$\cos 240° + i \sin 240° = -\frac{1}{2} - \frac{i\sqrt{3}}{2}$

14. $\cos\left(\frac{k \cdot 360°}{4}\right) + i \sin\left(\frac{k \cdot 360°}{4}\right) = \cos(k \cdot 90°) + i \sin(k \cdot 90°)$, $k = 0, 1, 2, 3$; roots are
$\cos 0° + i \sin 0° = 1 + 0 = 1$; $\cos 90° + i \sin 90° = 0 + i = i$;
$\cos 180° + i \sin 180° = -1 + 0 = -1$; $\cos 270° + i \sin 270° = 0 - i = -i$

15. $\cos\left(\frac{k \cdot 360°}{6}\right) + i \sin\left(\frac{k \cdot 360°}{6}\right) = \cos(k \cdot 60°) + i \sin(k \cdot 60°)$; $k = 0, 1, 2, 3, 4, 5$; roots are $\cos 0° + i \sin 0° = 1 + 0 = 1$; $\cos 60° + i \sin 60° = \frac{1}{2} + \frac{i\sqrt{3}}{2}$;

$\cos 120° + i \sin 120° = -\frac{1}{2} + \frac{i\sqrt{3}}{2}$; $\cos 180° + i \sin 180° = -1 + 0 = -1$;

$\cos 240° + i \sin 240° = -\frac{1}{2} - \frac{i\sqrt{3}}{2}$; $\cos 300° + i \sin 300° = \frac{1}{2} - \frac{i\sqrt{3}}{2}$

16. $\cos\left(\frac{k \cdot 360°}{8}\right) + i \sin\left(\frac{k \cdot 360°}{8}\right) = \cos(k \cdot 45°) + i \sin(k \cdot 45°)$, $k = 0, 1, 2, 3, 4, 5, 6, 7$; roots are $\cos 0° + i \sin 0° = 1 + 0 = 1$; $\cos 45° + i \sin 45° = \frac{\sqrt{2}}{2} + \frac{i\sqrt{2}}{2}$;

$\cos 90° + i \sin 90° = 0 + i = i$; $\cos 135° + i \sin 135° = -\frac{\sqrt{2}}{2} + \frac{i\sqrt{2}}{2}$;

$\cos 180° + i \sin 180° = -1 + 0 = -1$; $\cos 225° + i \sin 225° = -\frac{\sqrt{2}}{2} - \frac{i\sqrt{2}}{2}$;

$\cos 270° + i \sin 270° = 0 - i = -i$; $\cos 315° + i \sin 315° = \frac{\sqrt{2}}{2} - \frac{i\sqrt{2}}{2}$

17. $-1 = \cos 180° + i \sin 180°$; $\cos\left(\frac{180° + k \cdot 360°}{3}\right) + i \sin\left(\frac{180° + k \cdot 360°}{3}\right) =$ $\cos(60° + k \cdot 120°) + i \sin(60° + k \cdot 120°)$ for $k = 0, 1, 2$; cube roots are $\cos 60° + i \sin 60° = \frac{1}{2} + \frac{i\sqrt{3}}{2}$; $\cos 180° + i \sin 180° = -1$; $\cos 300° + i \sin 300° = \frac{1}{2} - \frac{i\sqrt{3}}{2}$

18. $i = \cos 90° + i \sin 90°$; $\cos\left(\frac{90° + k \cdot 360°}{3}\right) + i \sin\left(\frac{90° + k \cdot 360°}{3}\right) =$ $\cos(30° + k \cdot 120°) + i \sin(30° + k \cdot 120°)$ for $k = 0, 1, 2$; cube roots are

$\cos 30° + i \sin 30° = \frac{\sqrt{3}}{2} + \frac{i}{2}$; $\cos 150° + i \sin 150° = -\frac{\sqrt{3}}{2} + \frac{i}{2}$;
$\cos 270° + i \sin 270° = -i$

19. $-6 + 6i\sqrt{3} = 12(\cos 120° + i \sin 120°)$;

$\sqrt[4]{12}\left[\cos\left(\frac{120° + k \cdot 360°}{4}\right) + i \sin\left(\frac{120° + k \cdot 360°}{4}\right)\right] =$

$\sqrt[4]{12}[\cos(30° + k \cdot 90°) + i \sin(30° + k \cdot 90°)]$ for $k = 0, 1, 2, 3$; roots are

$\sqrt[4]{12}(\cos 30° + i \sin 30°) = \sqrt[4]{12}\left(\frac{\sqrt{3}}{2} + \frac{i}{2}\right) = \frac{\sqrt[4]{108}}{2} + \frac{i\sqrt[4]{12}}{2}$;

$\sqrt[4]{12}(\cos 120° + i \sin 120°) = \sqrt[4]{12}\left(-\frac{1}{2} + \frac{i\sqrt{3}}{2}\right) = -\frac{\sqrt[4]{12}}{2} + \frac{i\sqrt[4]{108}}{2}$;

$\sqrt[4]{12}(\cos 210° + i \sin 210°) = \sqrt[4]{12}\left(-\frac{\sqrt{3}}{2} - \frac{i}{2}\right) = -\frac{\sqrt[4]{108}}{2} - \frac{i\sqrt[4]{12}}{2}$;

$\sqrt[4]{12}(\cos 300° + i \sin 300°) = \sqrt[4]{12}\left(\frac{1}{2} - \frac{i\sqrt{3}}{2}\right) = \frac{\sqrt[4]{12}}{2} - \frac{i\sqrt[4]{108}}{2}$

20. $-6 - 6i\sqrt{3} = 12(\cos 240° + i \sin 240°)$;

$12^{1/4}\left[\cos\left(\frac{240° + k \cdot 360°}{4}\right) + i \sin\left(\frac{240° + k \cdot 360°}{4}\right)\right] =$

$\sqrt[4]{12}[\cos(60° + k \cdot 90°) + i \sin(60° + k \cdot 90°)]$ for $k = 0, 1, 2, 3$; roots are

$\sqrt[4]{12}(\cos 60° + i \sin 60°) = \sqrt[4]{12}\left(\frac{1}{2} + \frac{i\sqrt{3}}{2}\right) = \frac{\sqrt[4]{12}}{2} + \frac{i\sqrt[4]{108}}{2}$;

$\sqrt[4]{12}(\cos 150° + i \sin 150°) = \sqrt[4]{12}\left(-\frac{\sqrt{3}}{2} + \frac{i}{2}\right) = -\frac{\sqrt[4]{108}}{2} + \frac{i\sqrt[4]{12}}{2}$;

$\sqrt[4]{12}(\cos 240° + i \sin 240°) = \sqrt[4]{12}\left(-\frac{1}{2} - \frac{i\sqrt{3}}{2}\right) = -\frac{\sqrt[4]{12}}{2} - \frac{i\sqrt[4]{108}}{2}$;

$\sqrt[4]{12}(\cos 330° + i \sin 330°) = \sqrt[4]{12}\left(\frac{\sqrt{3}}{2} - \frac{i}{2}\right) = \frac{\sqrt[4]{108}}{2} - \frac{i\sqrt[4]{12}}{2}$

21. $z = \sqrt{2}(\cos 45° + i \sin 45°)$ **a.** $z^2 = 2(\cos 90° + i \sin 90°) = 2i$

b. $z^3 = 2\sqrt{2}(\cos 135° + i \sin 135°) = -2 + 2i$

c. $z^4 = 4(\cos 180° + i \sin 180°) = -4$

d. $z^5 = 4\sqrt{2}(\cos 225° + i \sin 225°) = -4 - 4i$

e. $z^6 = 8(\cos 270° + i \sin 270°) = -8i$

f. $z^7 = 8\sqrt{2}(\cos 315° + i \sin 315°) = 8 - 8i$

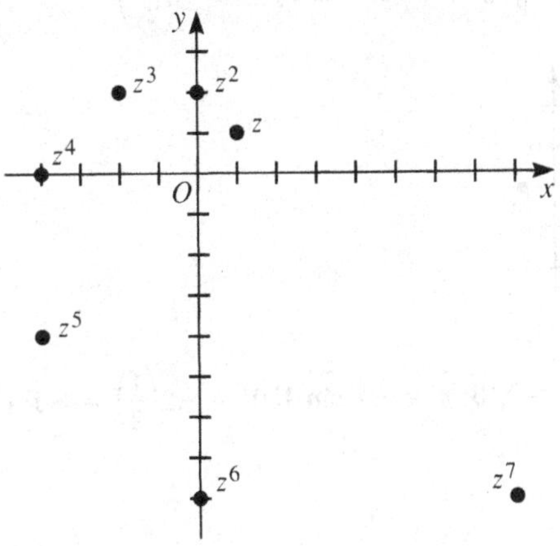

C **22.** **a.** $w^6 = \cos(6 \cdot 60°) + i \sin(6 \cdot 60°) = \cos 360° + i \sin 360° = 1 + 0 = 1$

b. From Ex. 15, the 6th roots of unity are $r_1 = \cos 0° + i \sin 0°$, $r_2 = w$, $r_3 = \cos 120° + i \sin 120°$, $r_4 = \cos 180° + i \sin 180°$, $r_5 = \cos 240° + i \sin 240°$, and $r_6 = \cos 300° + i \sin 300°$;
$w^2 = \cos(2 \cdot 60°) + i \sin(2 \cdot 60°) = \cos 120° + i \sin 120° = r_3$;
$w^3 = \cos(3 \cdot 60°) + i \sin(3 \cdot 60°) = \cos 180° + i \sin 180° = r_4$;
$w^4 = \cos(4 \cdot 60°) + i \sin(4 \cdot 60°) = \cos 240° + i \sin 240° = r_5$;
$w^5 = \cos(5 \cdot 60°) + i \sin(5 \cdot 60°) = \cos 300° + i \sin 300° = r_6$;
$w^6 = \cos(6 \cdot 60°) + i \sin(6 \cdot 60°) = \cos 360° + i \sin 360° =$
$\cos 0° + i \sin 0° = r_1$

23. $(w^5)^1 = w^5 = r_6$; $(w^5)^2 = w^{10} = w^6 \cdot w^4 = (\cos 0° + i \sin 0°)w^4 = (1 + 0)w^4 =$ $w^4 = r_5$; $(w^5)^3 = w^{15} = w^6 \cdot w^6 \cdot w^3 = 1 \cdot 1 \cdot w^3 = w^3 = r_4$; $(w^5)^4 = w^{20} =$ $(w^6)^3 \cdot w^2 = 1^3 \cdot w^2 = w^2 = r_3$; $(w^5)^5 = w^{25} = (w^6)^4 w = 1^4 \cdot w = w = r_2$; $(w^5)^6 =$ $w^{30} = (w^6)^5 = 1^5 = 1 = w^6 = r_1$

Page 688 • MIXED REVIEW EXERCISES

1. $\mathbf{w} = (3 + 2)\mathbf{i} + (1 - 4)\mathbf{j} = 5\mathbf{i} - 3\mathbf{j}$

2. 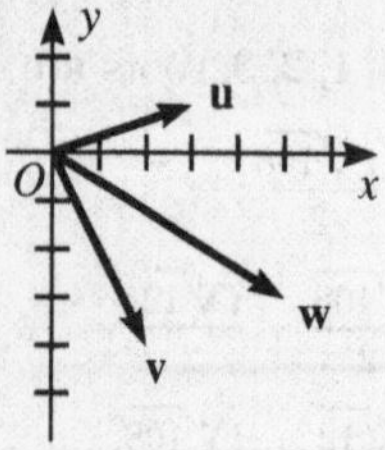

3. $\|\mathbf{w}\| = \sqrt{5^2 + (-3)^2} = \sqrt{34}$

4. $\tan \gamma = \frac{-3}{5} = -0.6$; $\gamma = 360° - 31.0° = 329.0°$

5. $x = 4 \cos 30° = 4\left(\frac{\sqrt{3}}{2}\right) = 2\sqrt{3}$; $y = 4 \sin 30° = 4\left(\frac{1}{2}\right) = 2$; $(2\sqrt{3}, 2)$

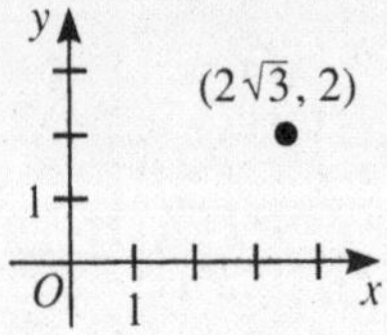

6. $x = 3 \cos(-120°) = 3\left(-\frac{1}{2}\right) = -\frac{3}{2}$; $y = 3 \sin(-120°) = 3\left(-\frac{\sqrt{3}}{2}\right) = -\frac{3\sqrt{3}}{2}$; $\left(-\frac{3}{2}, -\frac{3\sqrt{3}}{2}\right)$

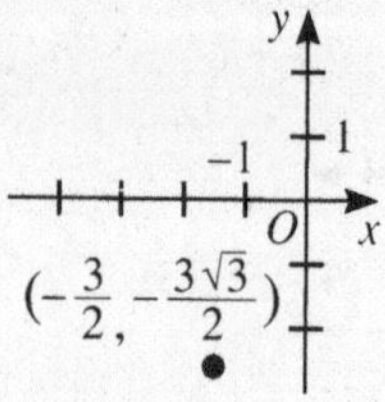

7. $x = -2 \cos 150° = -2\left(-\frac{\sqrt{3}}{2}\right) = \sqrt{3}$; $y = -2 \sin 150° = -2\left(\frac{1}{2}\right) = -1$; $(\sqrt{3}, -1)$

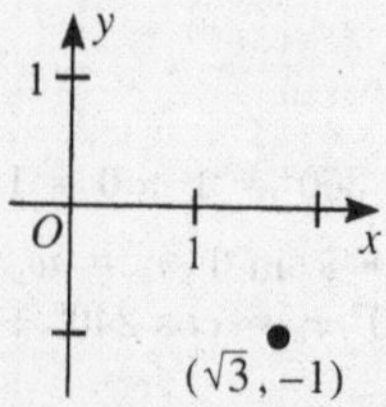

Page 692 • WRITTEN EXERCISES

A 1. $\frac{\pi}{3}$ 2. $\frac{3\pi}{4}$ 3. $\frac{5\pi}{6}$ 4. $\text{Sin}^{-1}\left(\frac{1}{2}\right) = \frac{\pi}{6}$ 5. $\text{Cos}^{-1}\left(-\frac{1}{2}\right) = \frac{2\pi}{3}$

6. $\text{Sin}^{-1}(-1) = -\frac{\pi}{2}$ 7. $\text{Cos}^{-1}\left(\frac{1}{2}\right) = \frac{\pi}{3}$ 8. $\text{Sin}^{-1}\left(-\frac{\sqrt{2}}{2}\right) = -\frac{\pi}{4}$

9. $\text{Cos}^{-1}\left(-\frac{\sqrt{3}}{2}\right) = \frac{5\pi}{6}$ 10. $\cos\left(-\frac{\pi}{3}\right) = \frac{1}{2}$ 11. $\sin\left(\frac{5\pi}{6}\right) = \frac{1}{2}$

12. Let $y = \text{Cos}^{-1}\left(-\frac{4}{5}\right)$; $\cos y = -\frac{4}{5}$ and $\frac{\pi}{2} \le y \le \pi$; $\sin y = \sqrt{1 - \cos^2 y} =$
$\sqrt{1 - \left(-\frac{4}{5}\right)^2} = \frac{3}{5}$

13. Let $y = \text{Sin}^{-1}\left(-\frac{5}{13}\right)$; $\sin y = -\frac{5}{13}$ and $-\frac{\pi}{2} \le y \le 0$; $\cos y = \sqrt{1 - \sin^2 y} =$
$\sqrt{1 - \left(-\frac{5}{13}\right)^2} = \frac{12}{13}$

14. Let $y = \text{Sin}^{-1}\left(\frac{3}{4}\right)$; $\sin y = \frac{3}{4}$ and $0 \le y \le \frac{\pi}{2}$; $\cos y = \sqrt{1 - \sin^2 y} =$
$\sqrt{1 - \left(\frac{3}{4}\right)^2} = \frac{\sqrt{7}}{4}$

15. Let $y = \text{Cos}^{-1}\left(-\frac{2}{5}\right)$; $\cos y = -\frac{2}{5}$ and $\frac{\pi}{2} \le y \le \pi$; $\sin y = \sqrt{1 - \left(-\frac{2}{5}\right)^2} = \frac{\sqrt{21}}{5}$

B **16.** $\cos\left(\frac{\pi}{6} + \frac{\pi}{3}\right) = \cos\left(\frac{\pi}{2}\right) = 0$ **17.** $\sin\left(\frac{2\pi}{3} - \frac{\pi}{6}\right) = \sin\left(\frac{\pi}{2}\right) = 1$

18. Let $y = \text{Cos}^{-1}x$; then $\cos y = x$ and $0 \le y \le \pi$ so $\sin y \ge 0$; $\sin y =$
$\sqrt{1 - \cos^2 y} = \sqrt{1 - x^2}$

19. Let $y = \text{Sin}^{-1}x$; then $\sin y = x$ and $-\frac{\pi}{2} \le y \le \frac{\pi}{2}$ so $\cos y \ge 0$;
$\cos y = \sqrt{1 - \sin^2 y} = \sqrt{1 - x^2}$; $\cos(\text{Sin}^{-1}x) = \cos y = \sqrt{1 - x^2}$

20. Let $y = \text{Cos}^{-1}x$; then $\cos y = x$ and $0 \le y \le \pi$ so $\sin y \ge 0$; $\sin y =$
$\sqrt{1 - \cos^2 y} = \sqrt{1 - x^2}$; $\cos(2\,\text{Cos}^{-1}x) = \cos 2y = 1 - 2\sin^2 y =$
$1 - 2(\sqrt{1 - x^2})^2 = 1 - 2(1 - x^2) = 1 - 2 + 2x^2 = 2x^2 - 1$

21. Let $y = \text{Sin}^{-1}x$; then $\sin y = x$ and $-\frac{\pi}{2} \le y \le \frac{\pi}{2}$ so $\cos y \ge 0$; $\cos y =$
$\sqrt{1 - \sin^2 y} = \sqrt{1 - x^2}$; $\sin(2\,\text{Sin}^{-1}x) = \sin 2y = 2\sin y\cos y = 2x\sqrt{1 - x^2}$

22. Let $a = \text{Sin}^{-1}u$ and $b = \text{Sin}^{-1}v$; then $\sin a = u$, $\sin b = v$, and $-\frac{\pi}{2} \le a \le \frac{\pi}{2}$ and
$-\frac{\pi}{2} \le b \le \frac{\pi}{2}$, so $\cos a$ and $\cos b$ are each ≥ 0; $\cos a = \sqrt{1 - \sin^2 a} = \sqrt{1 - u^2}$;
similarly, $\cos b = \sqrt{1 - v^2}$; $\sin(\text{Sin}^{-1}u + \text{Sin}^{-1}v) = \sin(a + b) = \sin a\cos b +$
$\cos a\sin b = u\sqrt{1 - v^2} + v\sqrt{1 - u^2}$

23. Let $a = \text{Sin}^{-1}1$ and $b = \text{Sin}^{-1}v$; then $\sin a = 1$, $\sin b = v$, $a = \frac{\pi}{2}$ and $-\frac{\pi}{2} \le b \le \frac{\pi}{2}$,
so $\cos a = 0$ and $\cos b \ge 0$; $\cos b = \sqrt{1 - \sin^2 b} = \sqrt{1 - v^2}$;
$\cos(\text{Sin}^{-1}1 - \text{Sin}^{-1}v) = \cos(a - b) = \cos a\cos b + \sin a\sin b = 0 \cdot \sqrt{1 - v^2} +$
$1 \cdot v = v$

C **24.** Let $a = \text{Cos}^{-1}\frac{3}{5}$ and $b = \text{Cos}^{-1}\frac{4}{5}$; $0 \le a \le \frac{\pi}{2}$ and $0 \le b \le \frac{\pi}{2}$ so $-\frac{\pi}{2} \le a - b \le \frac{\pi}{2}$; $0 \le \text{Sin}^{-1}\frac{7}{25} \le \frac{\pi}{2}$; $\sin a = \sqrt{1 - \cos^2 a} = \sqrt{1 - \left(\frac{3}{5}\right)^2} = \frac{4}{5}$; similarly, $\sin b = \frac{3}{5}$; $\sin\left(\text{Cos}^{-1}\frac{3}{5} - \text{Cos}^{-1}\frac{4}{5}\right) = \sin(a - b) = \sin a \cos b - \cos a \sin b = \frac{4}{5} \cdot \frac{4}{5} - \frac{3}{5} \cdot \frac{3}{5} = \frac{7}{25}$; since $\sin(a - b) > 0$, $0 \le a - b \le \frac{\pi}{2}$; thus $\text{Sin}^{-1}\frac{7}{25} = \text{Cos}^{-1}\frac{3}{5} - \text{Cos}^{-1}\frac{4}{5}$

25. Let $a = \text{Cos}^{-1}\frac{5}{13}$ and $b = \text{Sin}^{-1}\frac{4}{5}$; $0 \le a \le \frac{\pi}{2}$ and $0 \le b \le \frac{\pi}{2}$ so $-\frac{\pi}{2} \le a - b \le \frac{\pi}{2}$; $\sin\left(\text{Cos}^{-1}\frac{5}{13}\right) = \frac{12}{13}$; since $\frac{12}{13} > \frac{4}{5}$, $a > b$ and $a - b > 0$; thus $0 \le a - b \le \frac{\pi}{2}$; $0 \le \text{Cos}^{-1}\frac{63}{65} \le \frac{\pi}{2}$; $\sin a = \sqrt{1 - \cos^2 a} = \sqrt{1 - \left(\frac{5}{13}\right)^2} = \frac{12}{13}$; similarly, $\cos b = \frac{3}{5}$; $\cos\left(\text{Cos}^{-1}\frac{5}{13} - \text{Sin}^{-1}\frac{4}{5}\right) = \cos(a - b) = \cos a \cos b + \sin a \sin b = \frac{5}{13} \cdot \frac{3}{5} + \frac{12}{13} \cdot \frac{4}{5} = \frac{63}{65}$; $\text{Cos}^{-1}\frac{63}{65} = \text{Cos}^{-1}\frac{5}{13} - \text{Sin}^{-1}\frac{4}{5}$.

Pages 695–696 • WRITTEN EXERCISES

A **1.** $\frac{\pi}{6}$ **2.** π **3.** $\text{Cot}^{-1}(-\sqrt{3}) = \frac{5\pi}{6}$ **4.** $\text{Sec}^{-1}(\sqrt{2}) = \frac{\pi}{4}$ **5.** $\text{Cot}^{-1}0 = \frac{\pi}{2}$

6. $\text{Tan}^{-1}\left(-\frac{\sqrt{3}}{3}\right) = -\frac{\pi}{6}$ **7.** $\text{Cot}^{-1}(-1) = \frac{3\pi}{4}$ **8.** $\text{Tan}^{-1}(\sqrt{3}) = \frac{\pi}{3}$

9. Let $y = \text{Cot}^{-1}2$; $\cot y = 2$; $\tan y = \frac{1}{\cot y} = \frac{1}{2}$

10. Let $y = \text{Csc}^{-1}3$; $\csc y = 3$; $\sin y = \frac{1}{\csc y} = \frac{1}{3}$

11. Let $y = \text{Sin}^{-1}\left(-\frac{3}{5}\right)$; $\sin y = -\frac{3}{5}$; $-\frac{\pi}{2} \le y \le 0$; $\cos y = \sqrt{1 - \left(-\frac{3}{5}\right)^2} = \frac{4}{5}$;

$\tan y = \frac{\sin y}{\cos y} = \frac{-\frac{3}{5}}{\frac{4}{5}} = -\frac{3}{4}$

12. Let $y = \text{Sin}^{-1}\frac{12}{13}$; $\sin y = \frac{12}{13}$; $0 \le y \le \frac{\pi}{2}$; $\cos y = \sqrt{1 - \left(\frac{12}{13}\right)^2} = \frac{5}{13}$;

$\cot y = \frac{\cos y}{\sin y} = \frac{\frac{5}{13}}{\frac{12}{13}} = \frac{5}{12}$

13. Let $y = \text{Tan}^{-1}2$; $\tan y = 2$; $0 \le y < \frac{\pi}{2}$; $\sec y = \sqrt{1 + 2^2} = \sqrt{5}$; $\cos y = \frac{1}{\sec y} = \frac{1}{\sqrt{5}}$; $\sin y = \sqrt{1 - \cos^2 y} = \sqrt{1 - \frac{1}{5}} = \sqrt{\frac{4}{5}} = \frac{2\sqrt{5}}{5}$

14. Let $y = \text{Cot}^{-1}\frac{1}{2}$; $\cot y = \frac{1}{2}$; $0 < y \le \frac{\pi}{2}$; $\csc y = \sqrt{1 + \left(\frac{1}{2}\right)^2} = \frac{\sqrt{5}}{2}$;

$\sin y = \frac{1}{\csc y} = \frac{2}{\sqrt{5}}$; $\cos y = \sqrt{1 - \sin^2 y} = \sqrt{1 - \frac{4}{5}} = \sqrt{\frac{1}{5}} = \frac{\sqrt{5}}{5}$

B **15.** Let $a = \text{Sin}^{-1}\frac{5}{13}$; $\sin a = \frac{5}{13}$; $0 \le a \le \frac{\pi}{2}$; $\cos a = \sqrt{1 - \left(\frac{5}{13}\right)^2} = \frac{12}{13}$;

$\tan a = \frac{\sin a}{\cos a} = \frac{5}{12}$; Let $b = \text{Tan}^{-1}\frac{8}{15}$; $\tan b = \frac{8}{15}$; $\tan(a + b) = \frac{\tan a + \tan b}{1 - \tan a \tan b} =$

$$\frac{\frac{5}{12} + \frac{8}{15}}{1 - \frac{5}{12} \cdot \frac{8}{15}} = \frac{75 + 96}{180 - 40} = \frac{171}{140}$$

16. Let $a = \text{Tan}^{-1}\frac{4}{3}$; $\tan a = \frac{4}{3}$; $0 \le a < \frac{\pi}{2}$; $\sec a = \sqrt{1 + \left(\frac{4}{3}\right)^2} = \frac{5}{3}$;

$\cos a = \frac{1}{\sec a} = \frac{3}{5}$; $\sin a = \sqrt{1 - \cos^2 a} = \sqrt{1 - \frac{9}{25}} = \sqrt{\frac{16}{25}} = \frac{4}{5}$; Let $b = \text{Sin}^{-1}\frac{5}{13}$;

$0 \le b \le \frac{\pi}{2}$; $\sin b = \frac{5}{13}$; $\cos b = \sqrt{1 - \left(\frac{5}{13}\right)^2} = \frac{12}{13}$; $\cos(a - b) = \cos a \cos b +$

$\sin a \sin b = \left(\frac{3}{5}\right)\left(\frac{12}{13}\right) + \left(\frac{4}{5}\right)\left(\frac{5}{13}\right) = \frac{56}{65}$

17. Let $y = \text{Cot}^{-1}2$; $\cot y = 2$; $0 < y \le \frac{\pi}{2}$; $\csc y = \sqrt{1 + 2^2} = \sqrt{5}$;

$\sin y = \frac{1}{\csc y} = \frac{1}{\sqrt{5}}$; $\cos y = \sqrt{1 - \left(\frac{1}{\sqrt{5}}\right)^2} = \frac{2}{\sqrt{5}}$; $\sin 2y = 2 \sin y \cos y =$

$2\left(\frac{1}{\sqrt{5}}\right)\left(\frac{2}{\sqrt{5}}\right) = \frac{4}{5}$

18. Let $y = \text{Cos}^{-1}\left(-\frac{3}{5}\right)$; $\cos y = -\frac{3}{5}$; $\frac{\pi}{2} \le y \le \pi$; $\sin y = \sqrt{1 - \left(-\frac{3}{5}\right)^2} = \frac{4}{5}$;

$$\tan y = \frac{\frac{4}{5}}{-\frac{3}{5}} = -\frac{4}{3};\ \tan 2y = \frac{2 \tan y}{1 - \tan^2 y} = \frac{2\left(-\frac{4}{3}\right)}{1 - \left(-\frac{4}{3}\right)^2} = \frac{\frac{-8}{3}}{\frac{-7}{9}} = \frac{24}{7}$$

19. Let $y = \text{Sin}^{-1}x$; $\sin y = x$; $\csc y = \frac{1}{\sin y} = \frac{1}{x}$

20. Let $y = \text{Tan}^{-1}x$; $\tan y = x$; $\cot y = \frac{1}{x}$

21. Let $y = \text{Tan}^{-1}x$; $\tan y = x$; $-\frac{\pi}{2} < y < \frac{\pi}{2}$; $\sec y = \sqrt{1 + x^2}$,

$\cos y = \frac{1}{\sec y} = \frac{1}{\sqrt{1 + x^2}} = \frac{\sqrt{1 + x^2}}{1 + x^2}$

22. Let $y = \text{Cot}^{-1}x$; $\cot y = x$; $0 < y < \pi$; $\csc y = \sqrt{1 + x^2}$;

$\sin y = \frac{1}{\csc y} = \frac{1}{\sqrt{1 + x^2}} = \frac{\sqrt{1 + x^2}}{1 + x^2}$

23. Let $y = \text{Tan}^{-1}x$; from Ex. 21, $\cos y = \frac{1}{\sqrt{1+x^2}}$; $\sin y = \tan y \cos y =$

$x \cdot \frac{1}{\sqrt{1+x^2}} = \frac{x}{\sqrt{1+x^2}}$; $\sin 2y = 2 \sin y \cos y = 2 \cdot \frac{x}{\sqrt{1+x^2}} \cdot \frac{1}{\sqrt{1+x^2}} = \frac{2x}{1+x^2}$

24. Let $y = \text{Cot}^{-1}x$; from Ex. 22, $\sin y = \frac{1}{\sqrt{1+x^2}}$; $\cos 2y = 1 - 2\sin^2 y =$

$1 - 2\left(\frac{1}{\sqrt{1+x^2}}\right)^2 = 1 - \frac{2}{1+x^2} = \frac{x^2-1}{1+x^2}$

25. Let $a = \text{Cot}^{-1}x$ and $b = \text{Cot}^{-1}y$; $\tan a = \frac{1}{\cot a}$ $(\cot a \neq 0) = \frac{1}{x}$ and

$\tan b = \frac{1}{\cot b}$ $(\cot b \neq 0) = \frac{1}{y}$; for $xy \neq 1$, $\tan(\text{Cot}^{-1}x + \text{Cot}^{-1}y) = \tan(a+b) =$

$$\frac{\tan a + \tan b}{1 - \tan a \tan b} = \frac{\frac{1}{x} + \frac{1}{y}}{1 - \frac{1}{x} \cdot \frac{1}{y}} = \frac{x+y}{xy-1}.$$

26. Let $a = \text{Tan}^{-1}x$ and $b = \text{Tan}^{-1}y$; $-\frac{\pi}{2} < a < \frac{\pi}{2}$ and $-\frac{\pi}{2} < b < \frac{\pi}{2}$;

$\cot[\text{Tan}^{-1}x - \text{Tan}^{-1}y] = \cot(a-b) = \frac{1}{\tan(a-b)}$ $(\tan(a-b) \neq 0) =$

$\frac{1 + \tan a \tan b}{\tan a - \tan b} = \frac{1+xy}{x-y}$; since $-\pi < a - b < \pi$, $\tan(a-b) \neq 0$ if $a \neq b$;

for $-\frac{\pi}{2} < a < \frac{\pi}{2}$ and $-\frac{\pi}{2} < b < \frac{\pi}{2}$, $a \neq b$ if $\tan a \neq \tan b$, that is, if $x \neq y$; for

$x \neq y$, $\cot[\text{Tan}^{-1}x - \text{Tan}^{-1}y] = \frac{1+xy}{x-y}$.

C **27.**

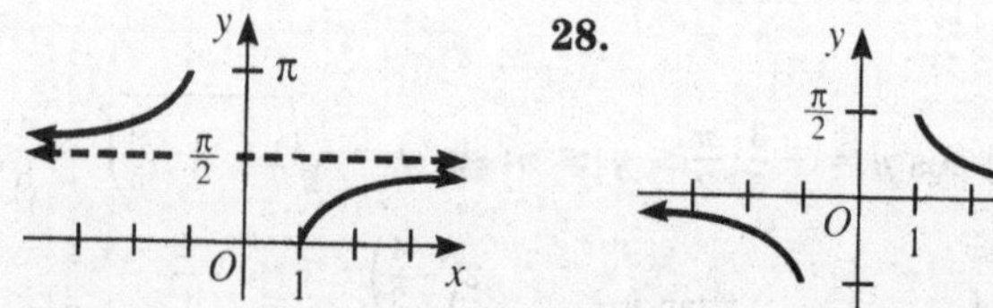

28.

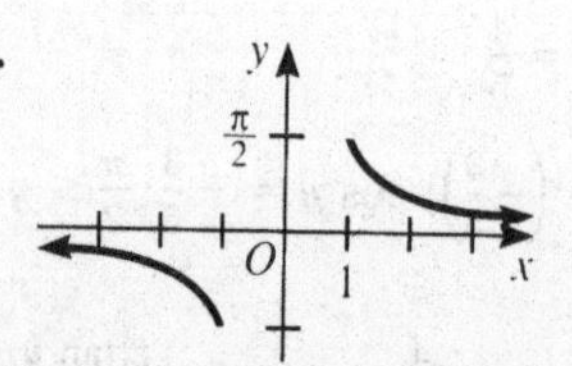

29. Since $\cot(z + \pi) = \cot z$, $\cot z = x$; $x < 0$, so $\tan z = \frac{1}{\cot z} = \frac{1}{x}$ and $-\frac{\pi}{2} < z < 0$,

so $z = \text{Tan}^{-1}\frac{1}{x}$; $\pi + \text{Tan}^{-1}\frac{1}{x} = \pi + z = y = \text{Cot}^{-1}x$.

Page 696 • MIXED REVIEW EXERCISES

1. arithmetic; $t_{21} = 7 + 20(5) = 107$ **2.** geometric; $t_8 = -3(2)^7 = -384$

3. geometric; $t_{11} = 9(2)^{10} = 9216$ **4.** arithmetic; $t_{15} = 5 + 14(-6) = -79$

5. $\sum_{n=1}^{6} 3 \cdot 4^{n-1} = \frac{3(1-4^6)}{1-4} = 4095$ **6.** $\sum_{n=1}^{100} (3n+2) = \frac{100(5+302)}{2} = 15{,}350$

7. $\sum_{n=1}^{20} (4n-9) = \frac{20(-5+71)}{2} = 660$ **8.** $\sum_{n=1}^{\infty} 100\left(\frac{1}{5}\right)^{n-1} = \frac{100}{1-\frac{1}{5}} = 125$

Pages 699–700 • WRITTEN EXERCISES

1.–12. k is an integer.

A **1.** $4 \sin \theta = 3, \sin \theta = \frac{3}{4} = 0.75; \theta = 48.6°$ or $\theta = 131.4°; \{\theta : \theta = 48.6° + k \cdot 360°$ or $\theta = 131.4° + k \cdot 360°\}$

2. $7 \cos \theta = 2, \cos \theta = \frac{2}{7} = 0.2857; \theta = 73.4°$ or $\theta = 286.6°; \{\theta : \theta = 73.4° + k \cdot 360°$ or $\theta = 286.6° + k \cdot 360°\}$

3. $2 \cos^2 x = 1, \cos^2 x = \frac{1}{2}, \cos x = \pm\frac{1}{\sqrt{2}} = \pm\frac{\sqrt{2}}{2}; x = \frac{\pi}{4}, \frac{3\pi}{4}, \frac{5\pi}{4}$, or $\frac{7\pi}{4}$; $\left\{x : x = \frac{\pi}{4} + \frac{k\pi}{2}\right\}$

4. $4 \sin^2 x = 3, \sin^2 x = \frac{3}{4}, \sin x = \pm\frac{\sqrt{3}}{2}; x = \frac{\pi}{3}, \frac{2\pi}{3}, \frac{4\pi}{3}$, or $\frac{5\pi}{3}$; $\left\{x : x = \frac{\pi}{3} + k \cdot \pi \text{ or } x = \frac{2\pi}{3} + k \cdot \pi\right\}$

5. $\sin \theta + \cos \theta = 0, \sin \theta = -\cos \theta, \frac{\sin \theta}{\cos \theta} = -1, \tan \theta = -1; \theta = 135°$ or $\theta = 315°$; $\{\theta : \theta = 135° + k \cdot 180°\}$

6. $\csc \theta = \sec \theta, \frac{\csc \theta}{\sec \theta} = 1, \cot \theta = 1; \theta = 45°$ or $\theta = 225°; \{\theta : \theta = 45° + k \cdot 180°\}$

7. $\csc \theta = 16 \sin \theta; 1 = 16 \sin^2 \theta, \sin^2 \theta = \frac{1}{16}, \sin \theta = \pm\frac{1}{4} = \pm 0.25; \theta = 14.5°, 165.5°, 194.5°, 345.5°; \{\theta : \theta = 14.5° + k \cdot 180°$ or $\theta = 165.5° + k \cdot 180°\}$

8. $5 \sin x + 2 \cos x = 0, 5 \sin x = -2 \cos x, \frac{\sin x}{\cos x} = -\frac{2}{5}, \tan x = -0.4; x = \pi - 0.38 = 2.76$ or $x = 2\pi - 0.38 = 5.90; \{x : x = 2.76 + k \cdot \pi\}$

9. $\cot\left(x - \frac{\pi}{8}\right) = 1, x - \frac{\pi}{8} = \frac{\pi}{4}$ or $x - \frac{\pi}{8} = \frac{5\pi}{4}; x = \frac{3\pi}{8}$ or $x = \frac{11\pi}{8}; \left\{x : x = \frac{3\pi}{8} + k \cdot \pi\right\}$

10. $2 \sin\left(x + \frac{\pi}{4}\right) = 1, \sin\left(x + \frac{\pi}{4}\right) = \frac{1}{2}, x + \frac{\pi}{4} = \frac{\pi}{6} + k \cdot 2\pi$ or $x + \frac{\pi}{4} = \frac{5\pi}{6} + k \cdot 2\pi$; $x = -\frac{\pi}{12} + k \cdot 2\pi$ or $x = \frac{7\pi}{12} + k \cdot 2\pi$; primary solutions are $x = \frac{23\pi}{12}$ and $x = \frac{7\pi}{12}$; $\left\{x : x = \frac{7\pi}{12} + k \cdot 2\pi \text{ or } x = \frac{23\pi}{12} + k \cdot 2\pi\right\}$

11. $\sin(\theta + 25°) = 0, \theta + 25° = 0° + k \cdot 180°; \theta = -25° + k \cdot 180°$; primary solutions are $\theta = 155°$ and $335°; \{\theta : \theta = 155° + k \cdot 180°\}$

12. $\tan(\theta - 20°) = \sqrt{3}, \theta - 20° = 60° + k \cdot 180°, \theta = 80° + k \cdot 180°$; primary solutions are $\theta = 80°$ and $\theta = 260°; \{\theta : \theta = 80° + k \cdot 180°\}$

13. $4 \cos \theta = 3 \sec \theta; \cos^2 \theta = \frac{3}{4}, \cos \theta = \pm\frac{\sqrt{3}}{2}; \{30°, 150°, 210°, 330°\}$

14. $3 \tan \theta = \cot \theta, \tan^2 \theta = \frac{1}{3}, \tan \theta = \pm\frac{1}{\sqrt{3}} = \pm\frac{\sqrt{3}}{3}; \{30°, 150°, 210°, 330°\}$

15. $3 \sec x = \csc x$, $3 = \frac{\csc x}{\sec x} = \cot x$, $x = 0.32$ or $x = \pi + 0.32 = 3.46$; $\{0.32, 3.46\}$

16. $2 \cos 2\theta = 1$, $\cos 2\theta = \frac{1}{2}$; $2\theta = 60° + k \cdot 360°$ or $2\theta = 300° + k \cdot 360°$; $\theta = 30° + k \cdot 180°$ or $\theta = 150° + k \cdot 180°$; $\{30°, 150°, 210°, 330°\}$

17. $\sec^2 \theta = 2$, $\sec \theta = \pm\sqrt{2}$; $\{45°, 135°, 225°, 315°\}$

18. $2 \cot^2 \theta = 1$, $\cot^2 \theta = \frac{1}{2}$, $\cot \theta = \pm\frac{1}{\sqrt{2}} = \pm 0.7071$; $\{54.7°, 125.3°, 234.7°, 305.3°\}$

19. $\sin 2x - \cos x = 0$, $2 \sin x \cos x - \cos x = 0$, $\cos x(2 \sin x - 1) = 0$; $\cos x = 0$ or $\sin x = \frac{1}{2}$; $x = \frac{\pi}{2}, \frac{3\pi}{2}$ or $x = \frac{\pi}{6}, \frac{5\pi}{6}$; $\left\{\frac{\pi}{6}, \frac{\pi}{2}, \frac{5\pi}{6}, \frac{3\pi}{2}\right\}$

20. $\sin 2\theta = 2 \sin \theta$, $2 \sin \theta \cos \theta - 2 \sin \theta = 0$, $2 \sin \theta(\cos \theta - 1) = 0$; $\sin \theta = 0$ or $\cos \theta = 1$; $\theta = 0°, 180°$ or $\theta = 0°$; $\{0°, 180°\}$

21. $\cos 2\theta = \cos \theta$; $2 \cos^2 \theta - 1 = \cos \theta$, $2 \cos^2 \theta - \cos \theta - 1 = 0$, $(2 \cos \theta + 1)(\cos \theta - 1) = 0$; $\cos \theta = -\frac{1}{2}$ or $\cos \theta = 1$; $\theta = 120°, 240°$ or $\theta = 0°$; $\{0°, 120°, 240°\}$

22. $\cos 2x = \sin x$, $1 - 2 \sin^2 x = \sin x$, $2 \sin^2 x + \sin x - 1 = 0$, $(2 \sin x - 1)(\sin x + 1) = 0$; $\sin x = \frac{1}{2}$ or $\sin x = -1$; $x = \frac{\pi}{6}, \frac{5\pi}{6}$ or $x = \frac{3\pi}{2}$; $\left\{\frac{\pi}{6}, \frac{5\pi}{6}, \frac{3\pi}{2}\right\}$

23. $2 \sin 2\theta = \sqrt{3}$, $\sin 2\theta = \frac{\sqrt{3}}{2}$, $2\theta = 60° + k \cdot 360°$ or $2\theta = 120° + k \cdot 360°$; $\theta = 30° + k \cdot 180°$ or $\theta = 60° + k \cdot 180°$; $\{30°, 60°, 210°, 240°\}$

24. $2 \cos x = \csc x$, $2 \cos x \sin x = 1$, $\sin 2x = 1$, $2x = \frac{\pi}{2} + k \cdot 2\pi$, $x = \frac{\pi}{4} + k \cdot \pi$; $\left\{\frac{\pi}{4}, \frac{5\pi}{4}\right\}$

25. $2 \tan^2 \theta + \tan \theta - 3 = 0$, $(2 \tan \theta + 3)(\tan \theta - 1) = 0$; $\tan \theta = -\frac{3}{2} = -1.5$ or $\tan \theta = 1$; $\theta = 123.7°, 303.7°$ or $\theta = 45°, 225°$; $\{45°, 123.7°, 225°, 303.7°\}$

26. $6 \sin^2 \theta = \sin \theta + 1$, $6 \sin^2 \theta - \sin \theta - 1 = 0$, $(2 \sin \theta - 1)(3 \sin \theta + 1) = 0$; $\sin \theta = \frac{1}{2}$ or $\sin \theta = -\frac{1}{3}$; $\theta = 30°, 150°$ or $\theta = 199.5°, 340.5°$; $\{30°, 150°, 199.5°, 340.5°\}$

27. $\cos 2x = 11 \sin x + 6$, $1 - 2 \sin^2 x = 11 \sin x + 6$, $2 \sin^2 x + 11 \sin x + 5 = 0$, $(2 \sin x + 1)(\sin x + 5) = 0$, $\sin x = -\frac{1}{2}$ or $\sin x = -5$ (no soln.); $\left\{\frac{7\pi}{6}, \frac{11\pi}{6}\right\}$

28. $\cos 2x + 7 \sin x + 3 = 0$, $1 - 2 \sin^2 x + 7 \sin x + 3 = 0$, $2 \sin^2 x - 7 \sin x - 4 = 0$, $(2 \sin x + 1)(\sin x - 4) = 0$; $\sin x = -\frac{1}{2}$ or $\sin x = 4$ (no soln.); $\left\{\frac{7\pi}{6}, \frac{11\pi}{6}\right\}$

B **29.** $\tan^2\left(x - \frac{\pi}{3}\right) = 1$, $\tan\left(x - \frac{\pi}{3}\right) = \pm 1$, $x - \frac{\pi}{3} = \frac{\pi}{4} + k \cdot \frac{\pi}{2}$; $x = \frac{7\pi}{12} + k \cdot \frac{\pi}{2}$; $\left\{\frac{\pi}{12}, \frac{7\pi}{12}, \frac{13\pi}{12}, \frac{19\pi}{12}\right\}$

30. $2\cos^2\left(x+\frac{\pi}{6}\right)=1$, $\cos^2\left(x+\frac{\pi}{6}\right)=\frac{1}{2}$, $\cos\left(x+\frac{\pi}{6}\right)=\pm\frac{\sqrt{2}}{2}$; $x+\frac{\pi}{6}=\frac{\pi}{4}+k\cdot\frac{\pi}{2}$,

$x=\frac{\pi}{12}+k\cdot\frac{\pi}{2}$; $\left\{\frac{\pi}{12},\frac{7\pi}{12},\frac{13\pi}{12},\frac{19\pi}{12}\right\}$

31. $\sin 3x+\cos 3x=0$; $\sin 3x=-\cos 3x$; $\tan 3x=-1$; $3x=\frac{3\pi}{4}+k\cdot\pi$;

$x=\frac{\pi}{4}+k\cdot\frac{\pi}{3}$; $\left\{\frac{\pi}{4},\frac{7\pi}{12},\frac{11\pi}{12},\frac{5\pi}{4},\frac{19\pi}{12},\frac{23\pi}{12}\right\}$

32. $\tan^2 3x=3$; $\tan 3x=\pm\sqrt{3}$; $3x=\frac{\pi}{3}+k\cdot\pi$ or $3x=\frac{2\pi}{3}+k\cdot\pi$; $x=\frac{\pi}{9}+k\cdot\frac{\pi}{3}$ or

$x=\frac{2\pi}{9}+k\cdot\frac{\pi}{3}$; $\left\{\frac{\pi}{9},\frac{2\pi}{9},\frac{4\pi}{9},\frac{5\pi}{9},\frac{7\pi}{9},\frac{8\pi}{9},\frac{10\pi}{9},\frac{11\pi}{9},\frac{13\pi}{9},\frac{14\pi}{9},\frac{16\pi}{9},\frac{17\pi}{9}\right\}$

33. $\sin 4\theta=\cos 2\theta$, $2\sin 2\theta\cos 2\theta-\cos 2\theta=0$, $\cos 2\theta(2\sin 2\theta-1)=0$, $\cos 2\theta=0$ or $\sin 2\theta=\frac{1}{2}$; $2\theta=90°+k\cdot180°$ or $2\theta=30°+k\cdot360°$ or $2\theta=150°+k\cdot360°$;

$\theta=45°+k\cdot90°$, $\theta=15°+k\cdot180°$ or $\theta=75°+k\cdot180°$; {15°, 45°, 75°, 135°, 195°, 225°, 255°, 315°}

34. $\cos 3x+\cos x=0$; by Exercise 30, page 644, $\cos(2x-1x)+\cos(2x+1x)=$

$2\cos 2x\cos 1x$; $2\cos 2x\cos 1x=0$; $\cos 2x=0$ or $\cos 1x=0$; $2x=\frac{\pi}{2}+k\cdot\pi$ or

$x=\frac{\pi}{2}+k\cdot\pi$; $x=\frac{\pi}{4}+k\cdot\frac{\pi}{2}$ or $x=\frac{\pi}{2}+k\cdot\pi$; $\left\{\frac{\pi}{4},\frac{\pi}{2},\frac{3\pi}{4},\frac{5\pi}{4},\frac{3\pi}{2},\frac{7\pi}{4}\right\}$

35. $\sin 2x=\cot x$; $2\sin x\cos x=\frac{\cos x}{\sin x}$; $2\sin^2 x\cos x-\cos x=0$;

$\cos x(2\sin^2 x-1)=0$; $\cos x=0$ or $\sin x=\pm\frac{\sqrt{2}}{2}$; $\left\{\frac{\pi}{4},\frac{\pi}{2},\frac{3\pi}{4},\frac{5\pi}{4},\frac{3\pi}{2},\frac{7\pi}{4}\right\}$

36. $2\sin 2\theta=\tan\theta$; $4\sin\theta\cos\theta=\frac{\sin\theta}{\cos\theta}$; $4\sin\theta\cos^2\theta-\sin\theta=0$;

$\sin\theta(4\cos^2\theta-1)=0$; $\sin\theta=0$ or $\cos\theta=\pm\frac{1}{2}$; {0°, 60°, 120°, 180°, 240°, 300°}

37. $\cos 2\theta=2\sin^2\theta$; $1-2\sin^2\theta=2\sin^2\theta$; $\sin^2\theta=\frac{1}{4}$; $\sin\theta=\pm\frac{1}{2}$;

{30°, 150°, 210°, 330°}

38. $\cos 2\theta+2\cos^2\theta=0$; $2\cos^2\theta-1+2\cos^2\theta=0$; $4\cos^2\theta=1$; $\cos^2\theta=\frac{1}{4}$;

$\cos\theta=\pm\frac{1}{2}$; {60°, 120°, 240°, 300°}

39. $\cos(2\theta+10°)=-\frac{1}{2}$, $2\theta+10°=120°+k\cdot360°$ or $2\theta+10°=240°+k\cdot360°$;

$2\theta=110°+k\cdot360°$ or $2\theta=230°+k\cdot360°$; $\theta=55°+k\cdot180°$ or $\theta=115°+k\cdot180°$; {55°, 115°, 235°, 295°}

40. $\sin(3\theta-25°)=\frac{\sqrt{3}}{2}$; $3\theta-25°=60°+k\cdot360°$ or $3\theta-25°=120°+k\cdot360°$;

$3\theta=85°+k\cdot360°$ or $3\theta=145°+k\cdot360°$; $\theta=28.3°+k\cdot120°$ or $\theta=48.3°+k\cdot120°$; {28.3°, 48.3°, 148.3°, 168.3°, 268.3°, 288.3°}

41. $\sin(3x + \pi) = -\frac{\sqrt{2}}{2}$, $-\sin 3x = -\frac{\sqrt{2}}{2}$, $\sin 3x = \frac{\sqrt{2}}{2}$; $3x = \frac{\pi}{4} + k \cdot 2\pi$ or $3x = \frac{3\pi}{4} + k \cdot 2\pi$; $x = \frac{\pi}{12} + k \cdot \frac{2\pi}{3}$ or $x = \frac{\pi}{4} + k \cdot \frac{2\pi}{3}$; $\left\{\frac{\pi}{12}, \frac{\pi}{4}, \frac{3\pi}{4}, \frac{11\pi}{12}, \frac{17\pi}{12}, \frac{19\pi}{12}\right\}$

42. $\tan\left(2x - \frac{\pi}{3}\right) = 1$; $2x - \frac{\pi}{3} = \frac{\pi}{4} + k \cdot \pi$; $2x = \frac{7\pi}{12} + k \cdot \pi$, $x = \frac{7\pi}{24} + k \cdot \frac{\pi}{2}$; $\left\{\frac{7\pi}{24}, \frac{19\pi}{24}, \frac{31\pi}{24}, \frac{43\pi}{24}\right\}$

C **43.** $\tan(\theta + 32°) = \cot(\theta - 20°)$; $\frac{\sin(\theta + 32°)}{\cos(\theta + 32°)} = \frac{\cos(\theta - 20°)}{\sin(\theta - 20°)}$; $\sin(\theta + 32°)\sin(\theta - 20°) = \cos(\theta + 32°)\cos(\theta - 20°)$; $\cos(\theta + 32°)\cos(\theta - 20°) - \sin(\theta + 32°)\sin(\theta - 20°) = 0$; $\cos[(\theta + 32°) + (\theta - 20°)] = \cos(2\theta + 12°) = 0$; $2\theta + 12° = 90° + k \cdot 180°$
$2\theta = 78° + k \cdot 180°$; $\theta = 39° + k \cdot 90°$; $\{39°, 129°, 219°, 309°\}$

44. $\sin(\theta - 10°) = \cos\theta$; $\sin\theta\cos 10° - \cos\theta\sin 10° = \cos\theta$, $\sin\theta\cos 10° = \cos\theta(1 + \sin 10°)$; $\frac{\sin\theta}{\cos\theta} = \frac{1 + \sin 10°}{\cos 10°} = \frac{1 + 0.1736}{0.9848}$; $\tan\theta = 1.192$; $\{50°, 230°\}$

45. $\cos 2\theta = \sin\theta - 1$, $1 - 2\sin^2\theta = \sin\theta - 1$, $2\sin^2\theta + \sin\theta - 2 = 0$;
$\sin\theta = \frac{-1 \pm \sqrt{1 - 4(2)(-2)}}{2(2)} = \frac{-1 \pm \sqrt{17}}{4}$; $\sin\theta = \frac{-1 - \sqrt{17}}{4}$ (reject, since $\sin\theta$ cannot be < -1), $\sin\theta = \frac{-1 + \sqrt{17}}{4} = 0.7808$; $\{51.3°, 128.7°\}$

46. $\cot^2 x - \cos^2 x = \frac{\cos^2 x}{\sin^2 x} - \cos^2 x = \cos^2 x\left(\frac{1}{\sin^2 x} - 1\right) = \cos^2 x\left(\frac{1 - \sin^2 x}{\sin^2 x}\right) = \cos^2 x\left(\frac{\cos^2 x}{\sin^2 x}\right) = \cos^2 x \cot^2 x$ for all x such that $\sin x \neq 0$; the statement is true for $\{x : 0 < x < \pi \text{ or } \pi < x < 2\pi\}$

Page 702 • COMPUTER KEY-IN

1. Answers may vary. Sample results are given.
a. 3.14260537, 3.14158951, 3.14159267 **b.** 3.14196328, 3.14159257, 3.14159302
c. 3.17253103, 3.13905576, 3.14186692 **d.** 3.14163420, 3.14159255, 3.14159256
e. $N = 5$, d; $N = 10$, b; $N = 15$, a

2. a. Answers may vary. For example, $a = \frac{1}{5}$, $b = \frac{2}{3}$
b. Answers may vary. Example: 3.14159298

3. Let $x = \text{Tan}^{-1}a$ and $y = \text{Tan}^{-1}b$, so that $\tan x = a$ and $\tan y = b$. Then $\tan(x + y) = \frac{\tan x + \tan y}{1 - \tan x \tan y} = \frac{a + b}{1 - ab}$ (page 650). If $-\frac{\pi}{2} < x + y < \frac{\pi}{2}$, then $\text{Tan}^{-1}(\tan(x + y)) = x + y = \text{Tan}^{-1}a + \text{Tan}^{-1}b = \text{Tan}^{-1}\left(\frac{a + b}{1 - ab}\right)$.

Pages 703–704 • CHAPTER REVIEW

1. c; Let θ = the angle formed by the heading and the resultant vectors; let α be the angle formed by the heading and current vectors; $\alpha = 360° - (8° + 200°) = 152°$; the length of the heading vector is $\sqrt{25^2 + 6^2 - 2(25)(6)\cos 152°} = 30.43$; $\frac{30.43}{\sin 152°} = \frac{6}{\sin \theta}$; $\sin \theta = \frac{6(0.4695)}{30.43} = 0.0926$; $\theta = 5.3$; heading $= 172° + 5.3° = 177.3°$
2. c; $\|\mathbf{v} - \mathbf{u}\|^2 = 10^2 + 6^2 - 2(10)(6)\cos(160° - 40°) = 196$; $\|\mathbf{v} - \mathbf{u}\| = 14$
3. a; $(4 - (-5), 3 - 4) = (9, -1)$
4. d; $\mathbf{u} = 9\mathbf{i} - 12\mathbf{j}$; $\mathbf{v} = x\mathbf{i} + y\mathbf{j}$; $\mathbf{u} \cdot \mathbf{v} = 9x - 12y$; Let $x = -4$ and $y = -3$; $\frac{\mathbf{v}}{\|\mathbf{v}\|} = -\frac{4}{5}\mathbf{i} - \frac{3}{5}\mathbf{j}$
5. c; $r \cos \theta + r \sin \theta - 2 = 0$; $r(\cos \theta + \sin \theta) = 2$; $r = \frac{2}{\cos \theta + \sin \theta}$
6. a; $x = 5 \cos(-60°) = 5 \cdot \frac{1}{2} = \frac{5}{2}$; $y = 5 \sin(-60°) = 5 \cdot \left(-\frac{\sqrt{3}}{2}\right) = -\frac{5\sqrt{3}}{2}$
7. d; $r = \sqrt{2^2 + (-2\sqrt{3})^2} = 4$; $\cos \theta = \frac{2}{4} = \frac{1}{2}$, $\sin \theta = \frac{-2\sqrt{3}}{4} = -\frac{\sqrt{3}}{2}$; $\theta = 300°$
8. b; $\frac{w}{z} = \frac{10}{5}[\cos(83° - 113°) + i \sin(83° - 113°)] = 2[\cos(-30°) + i \sin(-30°)] = 2\left[\frac{\sqrt{3}}{2} + i\left(-\frac{1}{2}\right)\right] = \sqrt{3} - i$
9. d; $\left(-\frac{\sqrt{2}}{2} + \frac{\sqrt{2}}{2}i\right)^{10} = [1(\cos 135° + i \sin 135°)]^{10} = 1^{10}(\cos 1350° + i \sin 1350°) = (0 + i(-1)) = -i$
10. b; $(-i)^3 = -i^3 = i \neq -i$ **11.** a; $\text{Sin}^{-1}\left(\frac{\sqrt{3}}{2}\right) = \frac{\pi}{3}$
12. b; $\cos(2 \text{ Sin}^{-1}x) = 1 - 2[\sin(\text{Sin}^{-1}x)]^2 = 1 - 2x^2$ **13.** c
14. b; Let $y = \text{Tan}^{-1}(-2)$; $\tan y = -2$ and $-\frac{\pi}{2} < y < 0$; $\sec y = \sqrt{1 + (-2)^2} = \sqrt{5}$; $\cos y = \frac{1}{\sqrt{5}}$; $\sin y = (\tan y)(\cos y) = -\frac{2}{\sqrt{5}}$; $\sin 2y = 2 \sin y \cos y = 2\left(-\frac{2}{\sqrt{5}}\right)\left(\frac{1}{\sqrt{5}}\right) = -\frac{4}{5}$
15. d; $\sin 2\theta = \frac{1}{2}$; $2\theta = 30° + k \cdot 360°$ or $2\theta = 150° + k \cdot 360°$; $\theta = 15° + k \cdot 180°$ or $\theta = 75° + k \cdot 180°$
16. c; $\cos^2(2x + \pi) = \frac{3}{4}$; $\cos(2x + \pi) = \pm\frac{\sqrt{3}}{2}$; $2x + \pi = \frac{\pi}{6} + k \cdot \pi$ or $2x + \pi = \frac{5\pi}{6} + k \cdot \pi$; $x = -\frac{5\pi}{12} + k \cdot \frac{\pi}{2}$ or $-\frac{\pi}{12} + k \cdot \frac{\pi}{2}$; $\left\{\frac{\pi}{12}, \frac{5\pi}{12}, \frac{7\pi}{12}, \frac{11\pi}{12}, \frac{13\pi}{12}, \frac{17\pi}{12}, \frac{19\pi}{12}, \frac{23\pi}{12}\right\}$

Pages 704–705 • CHAPTER TEST

1\.

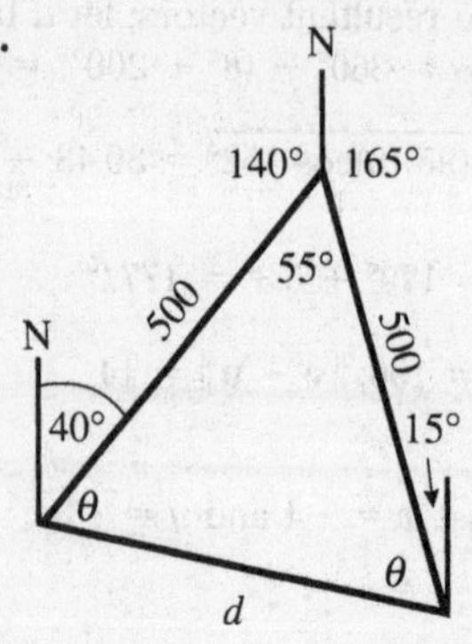

$\theta = \frac{180° - 55°}{2} = 62.5°$; $\frac{\sin 62.5°}{500} = \frac{\sin 55°}{d}$;

$d = \frac{500(0.8192)}{0.8870} \approx 462$; the planes are 462 km apart; their bearings each from the other are $360° - (15° + 62.5°) = 282.5°$ and $40° + 62.5° = 102.5°$

2\. a. $3\mathbf{u} + \mathbf{v} = (3 \cdot 4 - 12)\mathbf{i} + (3 \cdot 3 + 5)\mathbf{j} = 14\mathbf{j}$; $\|3\mathbf{u} + \mathbf{v}\| = 14$

b. Let θ be the angle between $\mathbf{u}$ and $\mathbf{v}$; $\cos\theta = \frac{\mathbf{u} \cdot \mathbf{v}}{\|\mathbf{u}\|\|\mathbf{v}\|} =$

$\frac{4(-12) + 3(5)}{(\sqrt{4^2 + 3^2})(\sqrt{(-12)^2 + 5^2})} = \frac{-48 + 15}{5 \cdot 13} = -\frac{33}{65} = -0.5077$; $\theta = 120.5°$

3\. Polar coordinates may vary. For example:

Polar	(3, 120°)	(4, 270°)	(−6, 135°)	($\sqrt{10}$, 135°)
Rectangular	$\left(-\frac{3}{2}, \frac{3\sqrt{3}}{2}\right)$	(0, −4)	($3\sqrt{2}, -3\sqrt{2}$)	($-\sqrt{5}, \sqrt{5}$)

4\.

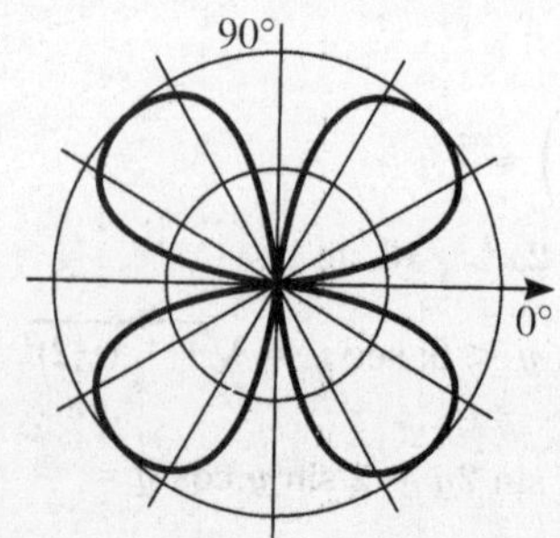

5\. $wz = (9 \cdot 3)[\cos(125° + 230°) + i\sin(125° + 230°)] = 27[\cos 355° + i\sin 355°]$;

$\frac{w}{z} = \frac{9}{3}[\cos(125° - 230°) + i\sin(125° - 230°)] = 3[\cos(-105°) + i\sin(-105°)] =$

$3[\cos 255° + i\sin 255°]$

6\. $-i = (\cos 270° + i\sin 270°)$; $(-i)^{1/5} = \cos\left(\frac{270° + k \cdot 360°}{5}\right) + i\sin\left(\frac{270° + k \cdot 360°}{5}\right)$

for $k = 0, 1, 2, 3, 4$; $r_1 = \cos 54° + i\sin 54°$; $r_2 = \cos 126° + i\sin 126°$; $r_3 = \cos 198° + i\sin 198°$; $r_4 = \cos 270° + i\sin 270°$; $r_5 = \cos 342° + i\sin 342°$

7\. $\cos\left[2\,\mathrm{Sin}^{-1}\left(-\frac{24}{25}\right)\right] = 1 - 2\left[\sin\left(\mathrm{Sin}^{-1}\left(-\frac{24}{25}\right)\right)\right]^2 = 1 - 2\left(-\frac{24}{25}\right)^2 = -\frac{527}{625}$

8. Let $y = \text{Cot}^{-1}(-6)$; $\cot y = -6$ and $\frac{\pi}{2} < y < \pi$; $\tan y = -\frac{1}{6}$;

$\sec y = -\sqrt{1 + \left(-\frac{1}{6}\right)^2} = -\frac{\sqrt{37}}{6}$

9. $\sin 2x = \tan x$; $2 \sin x \cos x = \frac{\sin x}{\cos x}$; $2 \sin x \cos x - \frac{\sin x}{\cos x} = 0$;

$\sin x\left(2 \cos x - \frac{1}{\cos x}\right) = 0$; $\sin x\left(\frac{2 \cos^2 x - 1}{\cos x}\right) = 0$, $\sin x = 0$ or $\cos^2 x = \frac{1}{2}$;

$x = 0 + k \cdot \pi$ or $\cos x = \pm\frac{\sqrt{2}}{2}$; $\left\{x : x = k \cdot \pi \text{ or } x = \frac{\pi}{4} + k \cdot \frac{\pi}{2}, k \text{ is an integer}\right\}$

10. $\sin 2\theta = 2 \sin^2 \theta$; $2 \sin \theta \cos \theta - 2 \sin^2 \theta = 0$; $2 \sin \theta(\cos \theta - \sin \theta) = 0$; $\sin \theta = 0$ or $\cos \theta = \sin \theta$; $\theta = 0 + k \cdot \pi$ or $\tan \theta = 1$; $\{0°, 45°, 180°, 225°\}$

Page 705 • MIXED PROBLEM SOLVING

1. Let x = the number bought; then $x - 40$ = the number sold; $\frac{6250}{x} + 3 = \frac{7130}{x - 40}$;

$6250(x - 40) + 3x(x - 40) = 7130x$; $6250x - 250{,}000 + 3x^2 - 120x = 7130x$;

$3x^2 - 1000x - 250{,}000 = 0$; $(3x + 500)(x - 500) = 0$; $x = -\frac{500}{3}$ (reject), or

$x = 500$; 460 necklaces

2. $\sum_{n=1}^{52} 5n = \frac{52(5 + 260)}{2} = 6890$; \$6890

3. Let x and y be the number of protons in oxygen and nitrogen, respectively;

$\begin{matrix} 3x + 2y = 38 \\ 5x + 3y = 61 \end{matrix}$; $\begin{matrix} 9x + 6y = 114 \\ 10x + 6y = 122 \end{matrix}$; $x = 8$; $3(8) + 2y = 38$, $2y = 14$, $y = 7$; 7 protons

4. Let w = width in meters of the garden; then $\frac{36}{2} - w = 18 - w$ = length;

Area $= A = w(18 - w) = -w^2 + 18w$; maximum area occurs when

$w = -\frac{b}{2a} = \frac{-18}{-2} = 9$; maximum area is $9 \cdot 9 = 81 \text{ m}^2$

5. The distances traveled in successive minutes form a geometric sequence;

$t_n = 2\left(\frac{1}{2}\right)^{n-1}$

a. $t_8 = 2\left(\frac{1}{2}\right)^7 = \frac{1}{2^6} = \frac{1}{64}$ cm **b.** $S = \sum_{n=1}^{\infty} 2\left(\frac{1}{2}\right)^{n-1} = \frac{2}{1 - \frac{1}{2}} = 4$; 4 cm

6. Let x and y be kg of raisins and peanuts respectively; $3x + 5y = 56$; $y = \frac{56 - 3x}{5}$;

possibilities are shown in this table:

(kg raisins) x	2	7	12	17
(kg peanuts) y	10	7	4	1

7. Let x = number of hours Meg worked; $\frac{x + 2}{7} + \frac{x}{5} = 1$; $5(x + 2) + 7x = 35$;

$12x + 10 = 35$, $12x = 25$, $x = \frac{25}{12} = 2\frac{1}{12}$; Meg worked 2 h 5 min, they finished at

1:05 P.M.

8. Let x = air speed in km/h;

	Rate	Time	Distance
with wind	$x + 30$	$\frac{450}{x + 30}$	450
against wind	$x - 30$	$\frac{450}{x - 30}$	450

$\frac{450}{x + 30} + \frac{450}{x - 30} = 6$; $450(x - 30) + 450(x + 30) = 6(x + 30)(x - 30)$;

$75(x - 30) + 75(x + 30) = x^2 - 900$; $150x = x^2 - 900$; $x^2 - 150x - 900 = 0$;

$x = \frac{150 \pm \sqrt{150^2 - 4(-900)}}{2} = \frac{150 \pm \sqrt{26{,}100}}{2} = 75 \pm 15\sqrt{29} = 75 \pm 80.8$; $x = 155.8$;

156 km/h

9. $\frac{9\sqrt{3}}{18^2} = \frac{3\sqrt{3}}{p^2}$; $(9\sqrt{3})p^2 = (3\sqrt{3})(18^2)$; $p^2 = 108$; $p = 6\sqrt{3}$

10. $5 = 50 \cdot 2^{-t/20}$, $10^{-1} = 2^{-t/20}$, $-1 = -\frac{t}{20} \log 2$, $t = \frac{20}{\log 2} = \frac{20}{0.3010} = 66.4$;

about 66 min

11. Let x = the height remaining and y = the length broken; $\tan 25° = \frac{x}{10}$,

$x = 10(0.4663) = 4.66$; $\sec 25° = \frac{y}{10}$, $y = 10(1.103) = 11.03$;

$x + y = 4.66 + 11.03 = 15.69$; 15.7 ft

Page 706 • PREPARING FOR COLLEGE ENTRANCE EXAMS

1. D; if $x \geq 0$, $x = |x|$; if $x < 0$, $x < |x|$ **2.** C; $|a - b| = |-(b - a)| = |b - a|$

3. A; $\csc \frac{10\pi}{3} = \csc \frac{4\pi}{3} = -\frac{2\sqrt{3}}{3}$; $\sec \frac{10\pi}{3} = \sec \frac{4\pi}{3} = -2$; $-2 < -\frac{2\sqrt{3}}{3}$ **4.** C

5. A; $\sqrt{1 + \tan^2\theta} = \sqrt{\sec^2\theta} = |\sec \theta|$; $\sqrt{1 - \cos^2\theta} = \sqrt{\sin^2\theta} = |\sin \theta|$; $|\sec \theta| \geq 1$ and $|\sin \theta| \leq 1$; if $|\sin \theta| = 1$, $\cos \theta = 0$ and $\sec \theta$ is undefined

6. C; $\sin(180° + \theta) = -\sin \theta$; $\cos(90° + \theta) = -\sin \theta$

7. D; let $\mathbf{v} = 4\mathbf{i} + 3\mathbf{j}$; $\mathbf{u} \cdot \mathbf{v} = 6(4) - 8(3) = 0$; $\|\mathbf{v}\| = \sqrt{4^2 + 3^2} = 5$; $\frac{\mathbf{v}}{\|\mathbf{v}\|} = \frac{4}{5}\mathbf{i} + \frac{3}{5}\mathbf{j}$

8. E; let $y = \text{Tan}^{-1}x$; $\tan y = x$; $-\frac{\pi}{2} < y < \frac{\pi}{2}$; $\sec y = \sqrt{1 + x^2}$, $\cos y = \frac{1}{\sqrt{1 + x^2}}$;

$\sin y = \cos y \tan y = \frac{x}{\sqrt{1 + x^2}}$; $\sin 2y = 2 \sin y \cos y = 2\left(\frac{x}{\sqrt{1 + x^2}}\right)\left(\frac{1}{\sqrt{1 + x^2}}\right) =$

$\frac{2x}{1 + x^2}$

9. C; $\cot x + \tan x = -2$, $\frac{\sin x}{\cos x} + \frac{\cos x}{\sin x} = -2$; $\frac{\sin^2 x + \cos^2 x}{\sin x \cos x} = -2$; $1 = -2 \sin x \cos x$;

$-1 = \sin 2x$; $2x = \frac{3\pi}{2} + k \cdot 2\pi$; $x = \frac{3\pi}{4} + k \cdot \pi$; $\left\{\frac{3\pi}{4}, \frac{7\pi}{4}\right\}$

10. C; $(x - 0)^2 + (y - 1)^2 = 1$, $x^2 + y^2 - 2y + 1 = 1$, $x^2 + y^2 = 2y$, $r^2 = 2r \sin \theta$, $r = 2 \sin \theta$

Page 707 • CUMULATIVE REVIEW

1. Examples: $-255°$, $465°$

2. $\sin \theta = \frac{5}{\sqrt{29}} = \frac{5\sqrt{29}}{29}$; $\cos \theta = -\frac{2\sqrt{29}}{29}$; $\tan \theta = -\frac{5}{2}$; $\csc \theta = \frac{\sqrt{29}}{5}$; $\sec \theta = -\frac{\sqrt{29}}{2}$; $\cot \theta = -\frac{2}{5}$

3. Let d = distance from ground to top of ramp; $\sin 20° = \frac{d}{8}$; $d = 8(0.3420) = 2.74$; 2.74 ft

4. $\cos A = \frac{9^2 + 6^2 - 5^2}{2 \cdot 9 \cdot 6} = \frac{92}{108} = 0.8519$; $\angle A = 31.6°$; $\frac{\sin B}{9} = \frac{\sin 31.6°}{5}$; $\sin B = \frac{9(0.5240)}{5} = 0.9432$; $\angle B = 70.6°$ or $109.4°$; since b is the longest side of $\triangle ABC$, $\angle B = 109.4°$; $\angle C = 180° - (109.4° + 31.6°) = 39.0°$

5. $K = \frac{1}{2} bc \sin A = \frac{1}{2}(9)(6)(0.5240) = 14.1$ 6. $-200° = -200 \cdot \frac{\pi}{180} = -\frac{10\pi}{9}$

7. $\sin\left(-\frac{13\pi}{6}\right) = -\frac{1}{2}$; $\cos\left(-\frac{13\pi}{6}\right) = \frac{\sqrt{3}}{2}$; $\tan\left(-\frac{13\pi}{6}\right) = -\frac{\sqrt{3}}{3}$; $\csc\left(-\frac{13\pi}{6}\right) = -2$; $\sec\left(-\frac{13\pi}{6}\right) = \frac{2\sqrt{3}}{3}$; $\cot\left(-\frac{13\pi}{6}\right) = -\sqrt{3}$

8. amplitude = 5; period $= \frac{2\pi}{\frac{\pi}{3}} = 6$; maximum value = 3; minimum value = -7

9. $\frac{\cos \theta}{\sin^3 \theta} = \frac{\cos \theta}{\sin \theta \sin^2 \theta} = \cot \theta \cdot \frac{1}{\sin^2 \theta} = \cot \theta \csc^2 \theta = \cot \theta(1 + \cot^2 \theta)$

10. a. $\frac{\sec x}{\cot x + \tan x} = \frac{\sec x}{\frac{\cos x}{\sin x} + \frac{\sin x}{\cos x}} = \frac{\sec x}{\frac{\cos^2 x + \sin^2 x}{\sin x \cos x}} = \sec x \cdot \frac{\sin x \cos x}{\cos^2 x + \sin^2 x} = \frac{1}{\cos x} \cdot \frac{\sin x \cos x}{1} = \sin x$

b. $\cot(\alpha + \beta) = \frac{1}{\tan(\alpha + \beta)} = \frac{1 - \tan \alpha \tan \beta}{\tan \alpha + \tan \beta} = \frac{1 - \frac{1}{\cot \alpha} \cdot \frac{1}{\cot \beta}}{\frac{1}{\cot \alpha} + \frac{1}{\cot \beta}} = \frac{\frac{\cot \alpha \cot \beta - 1}{\cot \alpha \cot \beta}}{\frac{\cot \beta + \cot \alpha}{\cot \alpha \cot \beta}} = \frac{\cot \alpha \cot \beta - 1}{\cot \alpha + \cot \beta}$

11. Since $90° < \phi < 270°$ and $\sin \phi < 0$, $180° < \phi < 270°$; $\cos \phi = -\sqrt{1 - \sin^2 \phi} = -\sqrt{1 - \frac{9}{25}} = -\frac{4}{5}$

a. Since $180° < \phi < 270°$, $90° < \frac{\phi}{2} < 135°$, and $\cos \frac{\phi}{2} < 0$; $\cos \frac{\phi}{2} = -\sqrt{\frac{1 - \frac{4}{5}}{2}} = -\sqrt{\frac{1}{10}} = -\frac{\sqrt{10}}{10}$

(Continued)

b. $\cos 2\phi = 1 - 2\sin^2\phi = 1 - 2\left(-\frac{3}{5}\right)^2 = \frac{7}{25}$

c. $\tan(180° - \phi) = \tan(-\phi) = -\tan\phi =$

$$-\frac{\sin\phi}{\cos\phi} = -\left(\frac{-\frac{3}{5}}{-\frac{4}{5}}\right) = -\frac{3}{4}$$

d. $\sin(90° + \phi) = \sin[90° - (-\phi)] =$

$\cos(-\phi) = \cos\phi = -\frac{4}{5}$

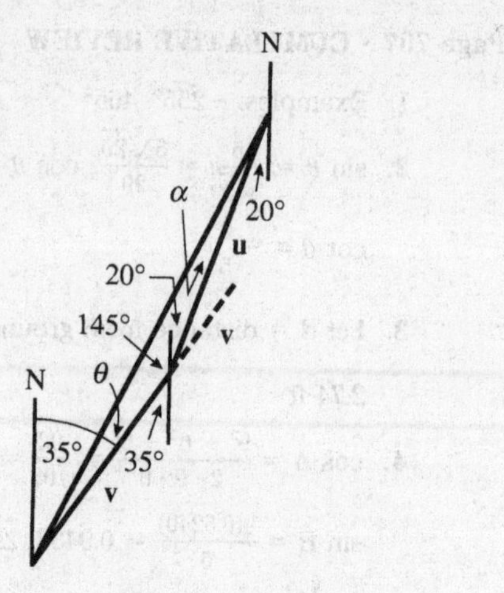

12. $\alpha = 165°$; $\|\mathbf{u} - \mathbf{v}\|^2 = 8^2 + 10^2 - 2(8)(10)\cos 165° = 318.54$; $\|\mathbf{u} - \mathbf{v}\| = 17.8$;
$\frac{\sin\theta}{8} = \frac{\sin 165°}{17.8}$; $\sin\theta = \frac{8(0.2588)}{17.8} = 0.1163$; $\theta = 6.7°$, bearing $= 200° + \theta = 206.7°$

13. Let $\mathbf{u} = a\mathbf{i} + b\mathbf{j}$; $(a\mathbf{i} + b\mathbf{j}) \cdot (2\mathbf{i} - \mathbf{j}) = 0$; $2a - b = 0$; let $a = 1$ and $b = 2$;
$\mathbf{u} = \mathbf{i} + 2\mathbf{j}$; $\frac{\mathbf{u}}{\|\mathbf{u}\|} = \frac{i + 2j}{\sqrt{1^2 + 2^2}} = \frac{\mathbf{i} + 2\mathbf{j}}{\sqrt{5}} = \frac{\sqrt{5}}{5}\mathbf{i} + \frac{2\sqrt{5}}{5}\mathbf{j}$

14. $r = \sqrt{2^2 + (-2\sqrt{3})^2} = 4$; $\cos\theta = \frac{1}{2}$ and $\sin\theta = -\frac{\sqrt{3}}{2}$; let $\theta = 300°$;
$(2 - 2i\sqrt{3})^5 = [4(\cos 300° + i\sin 300°)]^5 = 1024(\cos 1500° + i\sin 1500°) =$
$1024(\cos 60° + i\sin 60°) = 1024\left(\frac{1}{2} + \frac{i\sqrt{3}}{2}\right) = 512 + 512i\sqrt{3}$

15. $-8i = 8(\cos 270° + i\sin 270°)$; $r^3(\cos 3\theta + i\sin 3\theta) = 8(\cos 270° + i\sin 270°)$;
$r^3 = 8$; $r = 2$; $\cos 3\theta = \cos 270°$; $3\theta = 270° + k \cdot 360°$; $\theta = 90° + k \cdot 120°$,
$k = 0, 1, 2$; $r_1 = 2(\cos 90° + i\sin 90°) = 2(0 + i) = 2i$;
$r_2 = 2[\cos(90° + 120°) + i\sin(90° + 120°)] = 2(\cos 210° + i\sin 210°) =$
$2\left(-\frac{\sqrt{3}}{2} - \frac{i}{2}\right) = -\sqrt{3} - i$; $r_3 = 2[\cos(90° + 240°) + i\sin(90° + 240°)] =$
$2(\cos 330° + i\sin 330°) = 2\left(\frac{\sqrt{3}}{2} - \frac{i}{2}\right) = \sqrt{3} - i$

16. π

17. Let y be a first-quadrant angle with $\cot y = \frac{4}{3}$; $\sin y = \frac{3}{5}$ and $\cos y = \frac{4}{5}$;
$\sin\left(\mathrm{Cos}^{-1}\frac{1}{2} - \mathrm{Cot}^{-1}\frac{4}{3}\right) = \sin\left(\frac{\pi}{3} - y\right) = \sin\frac{\pi}{3}\cos y - \cos\frac{\pi}{3}\sin y =$
$\frac{\sqrt{3}}{2}\left(\frac{4}{5}\right) - \frac{1}{2}\left(\frac{3}{5}\right) = \frac{4\sqrt{3} - 3}{10}$

18. Let y be a fourth-quadrant angle with $\sin y = -\frac{5}{13}$; $\tan y = -\frac{5}{12}$;

$$\tan\left[2\ \text{Sin}^{-1}\left(-\frac{5}{13}\right)\right] = \tan 2y = \frac{2\tan y}{1-\tan^2 y} = \frac{2\left(-\frac{5}{12}\right)}{1-\left(-\frac{5}{12}\right)^2} = \frac{-\frac{5}{6}}{\frac{119}{144}} = -\frac{120}{119}$$

19. $2\csc^2 x + 3\csc x - 2 = 0$; $(2\csc x - 1)(\csc x + 2) = 0$; $\csc x = \frac{1}{2}$ (reject) or $\csc x = -2$; $\left\{\frac{7\pi}{6}, \frac{11\pi}{6}\right\}$

20. $x + \frac{\pi}{3} = \frac{7\pi}{6}$ or $x + \frac{\pi}{3} = \frac{11\pi}{6}$; $\left\{\frac{5\pi}{6}, \frac{3\pi}{2}\right\}$

21. $\cos 2\theta - 3\cos\theta - 1 = 0$; $2\cos^2\theta - 1 - 3\cos\theta - 1 = 0$;
$2\cos^2\theta - 3\cos\theta - 2 = 0$; $(\cos\theta - 2)(2\cos\theta + 1) = 0$; $\cos\theta = 2$ (reject) or $\cos\theta = -\frac{1}{2}$; $\{120°, 240°\}$

22. $3\tan^2\theta = 1$; $\tan^2\theta = \frac{1}{3}$; $\tan\theta = \pm\frac{\sqrt{3}}{3}$; $\{30°, 150°, 210°, 330°\}$

CHAPTER 15 • Statistics and Probability

Pages 711–712 • WRITTEN EXERCISES

A

1.

Stem	Leaves
1	6, 9
2	0, 2, 2, 3
3	8
4	0, 6
5	2, 4

2.

Stem	Leaves
3	8, 9
4	2, 8
5	0, 5
6	1, 1, 1, 2, 5, 6

3.

Stem	Leaves
0	2, 5, 7, 9
1	0, 3, 8, 9
2	8, 8, 8
3	4
4	2
5	2
6	1

4.

Stem	Leaves
12	3, 9
13	2, 5
14	0
15	1, 2
16	0, 6, 8, 8, 9

5. **a.** 22 **b.** 23 **c.** $\frac{16 + 19 + 20 + 2(22) + \cdots + 52 + 54}{11} = 32$

6. **a.** 61 **b.** $\frac{55 + 61}{2} = 58$ **c.** $\frac{38 + 39 + \cdots + 65 + 66}{12} = 54$

7. **a.** 28 **b.** 19 **c.** $\frac{2 + 5 + \cdots + 52 + 61}{15} \approx 23.7$

8. **a.** 168 **b.** $\frac{151 + 152}{2} = 151.5$ **c.** $\frac{123 + 129 + \cdots + 2(168) + 169}{12} \approx 149.4$

9. **a.** 184 **b.** 184 **c.** $\frac{175 + 178 + 2(180) + 181 + 3(184) + 2(185) + 188 + 192}{12} = 183$

10. **a.** median $= \frac{12.72 + 15.89}{2} = 14.31$ **b.** $\frac{-0.05 + 2.00 + 6.28 + \cdots + 2.17}{12} \approx 13.89$

11.

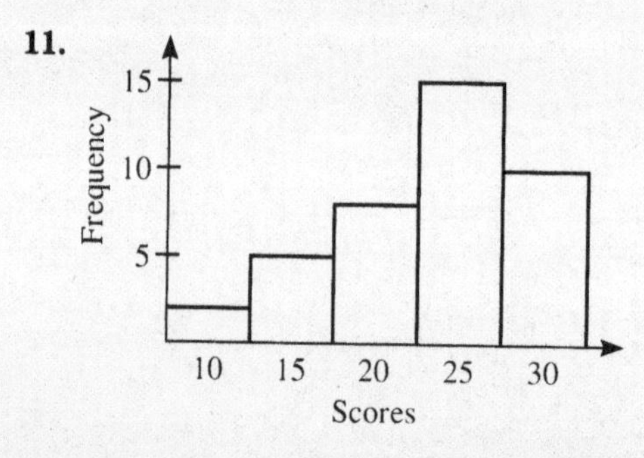

12. **a.** 25 **b.** 25 **c.** $\frac{2(10) + 5(15) + 8(20) + 15(25) + 10(30)}{40} = 23.25$

B

13. Let x = fifth score; $\frac{82 + 73 + 76 + 92 + x}{5} = 82$; $323 + x = 410$, $x = 87$; 87

14. Let s = the sum of the numbers; $\frac{s}{12} = 15$; $s = 15(12) = 180$

15. They would each be 5 points higher **16.** They would each be reduced by 40%

C

17. $\frac{50(75) + 40(80)}{90} \approx 77.2$; 77.2

18. a. $\dfrac{mM_1 + nM_2}{m + n}$

b. if $m = n$, then $\dfrac{mM_1 + nM_2}{m + n} = \dfrac{mM_1 + mM_2}{m + m} = \dfrac{m(M_1 + M_2)}{2m} = \dfrac{M_1 + M_2}{2}$; if $M_1 = M_2$,

then $\dfrac{mM_1 + nM_2}{m + n} = \dfrac{mM_1 + nM_1}{m + n} = \dfrac{M_1(m + n)}{m + n} = M_1 = M_2$, either of which is the mean; $m = n$ or $M_1 = M_2$

Page 712 • MIXED REVIEW EXERCISES

1. $r = \sqrt{(-3)^2 + (3\sqrt{3})^2} = \sqrt{9 + 27} = 6$; $\cos\theta = \dfrac{-3}{6} = -\dfrac{1}{2}$; $\sin\theta = \dfrac{3\sqrt{3}}{6} = \dfrac{\sqrt{3}}{2}$; $\theta = 120°$; $(6, 120°)$

2. $r = \sqrt{(\sqrt{2})^2 + (\sqrt{6})^2} = \sqrt{8} = 2\sqrt{2}$; $\sin\theta = \dfrac{\sqrt{2}}{2\sqrt{2}} = \dfrac{1}{2}$; $\cos\theta = \dfrac{\sqrt{6}}{2\sqrt{2}} = \dfrac{\sqrt{3}}{2}$; $\theta = 30°$; $(2\sqrt{2}, 30°)$

3. $r = 3$, $\theta = 90°$; $(3, 90°)$

4. $\left(\dfrac{m^2n^{-3}}{m^{-4}n}\right)^{-2}\left(\dfrac{mn^{-1}}{m^3n}\right) = (m^6n^{-4})^{-2}(m^{-2}n^{-2}) = (m^{-12}n^8)(m^{-2}n^{-2}) = m^{-14}n^6 = \dfrac{n^6}{m^{14}}$

5. $\dfrac{(w - 4)(w + 1)}{(3w + 2)(w - 4)} = \dfrac{w + 1}{3w + 2}$ **6.** $8^{\sqrt{2}} \cdot 2^{\sqrt{8}} = (2^3)^{\sqrt{2}}(2^{2\sqrt{2}}) = 2^{3\sqrt{2}}2^{2\sqrt{2}} = 2^{5\sqrt{2}}$

Pages 717–718 • WRITTEN EXERCISES

A **1. a.** 25 **b.** 14 **c.** 34 **d.** $47 - 2 = 45$

2. a. $\dfrac{76 + 80}{2} = 78$ **b.** $\dfrac{67 + 71}{2} = 69$ **c.** $\dfrac{84 + 88}{2} = 86$ **d.** $95 - 59 = 36$

3. **4.**

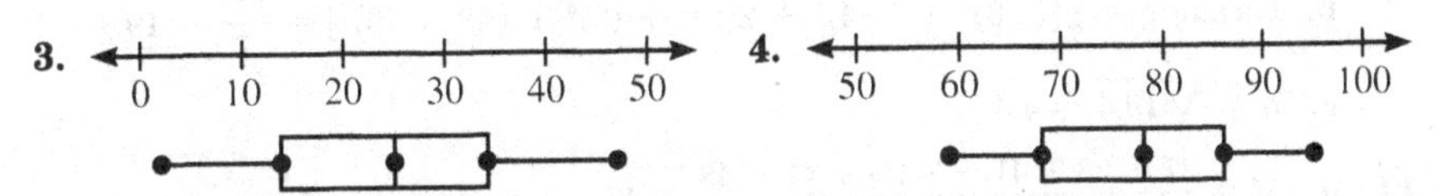

5. Medians are 70, 85, and 80, respectively; Class 2

6. Ranges are $85 - 60 = 25$, $95 - 65 = 30$, and $100 - 60 = 40$, respectively; Class 1

7. Class 2; this has the shortest box

8. Class 2; $\frac{3}{4}$ of its scores are as good as or better than $\frac{1}{4}$ of Class 1 and $\frac{1}{2}$ of Class 3

9.

Item	Frequency	Item × Frequency	Deviation	(Deviation)^2	(Deviation)^2 × Frequency
1	1	1	−5	25	25
4	1	4	−2	4	4
6	2	12	0	0	0
7	1	7	1	1	1
8	3	24	2	4	12
Sums	8	48			42

a. $M = \dfrac{48}{8} = 6$ **b.** $\dfrac{42}{8} = 5.25 \approx 5.3$ **c.** $\sigma = \sqrt{5.25} = 2.3$

10.

Item	Frequency	Item × Frequency	Deviation	(Deviation)^2	(Deviation)^2 × Frequency
3	1	3	−2.25	5.0625	5.0625
4	1	4	−1.25	1.5625	1.5625
5	4	20	−0.25	0.0625	0.25
6	1	6	0.75	0.5625	0.5625
9	1	9	3.75	14.0625	14.0625
Sums	8	42			21.25

a. $M = \frac{42}{8} = 5.25 \approx 5.3$ **b.** $\frac{21.5}{8} = 2.68 \approx 2.7$ **c.** $\sigma = \sqrt{2.68} = 1.6$

11. a. $M = \frac{34 + 42 + 44 + 70 + 73 + 79}{6} = 57$

b. variance $= \frac{(34 - M)^2 + (42 - M)^2 + \cdots + (79 - M)^2}{6} =$

$\frac{(-23)^2 + (-15)^2 + (-13)^2 + (13)^2 + (16)^2 + (22)^2}{6} \approx 305.3$

c. $\sigma = \sqrt{305.33} \approx 17.5$

12. a. $M = \frac{8 + 15 + 38 + 64 + 85 + 102}{6} = 52$

b. variance $= \frac{1}{6}[(-44)^2 + (-37)^2 + (-14)^2 + (12)^2 + (33)^2 + (50)^2] \approx 1205.7$

c. $\sigma = \sqrt{1205.7} = 34.7$

13. a. $M = \frac{42 + 46 + 2(50) + 52 + 54 + 56}{7} = 50$

b. variance $= \frac{1}{7}[(-8)^2 + (-4)^2 + 2(0)^2 + (2)^2 + (4)^2 + (6)^2] = \frac{136}{7} \approx 19.4$

c. $\sigma = \sqrt{19.4} \approx 4.4$

14. a. $M = \frac{37 + 38 + 41 + 2(45) + 47 + 48}{7} = 43$

b. variance $= \frac{1}{7}[(-6)^2 + (-5)^2 + (-2)^2 + 2(2)^2 + 4^2 + 5^2] = \frac{114}{7} \approx 16.3$

c. $\sigma = \sqrt{16.3} \approx 4.0$

15. a. $M = \frac{67 + 69 + 2(70) + 71 + 72 + 2(73) + 74}{9} = 71$

b. variance $= \frac{1}{9}[(-4)^2 + (-2)^2 + 2(-1)^2 + 0^2 + 1^2 + 2(2)^2 + 3^2] = \frac{40}{9} = 4.4$

c. $\sigma = \sqrt{4.4} = 2.1$

16.

Temp.	Frequency	Temp. × Frequency	Deviation	(Deviation)^2	(Deviation)^2 × Frequency
63	1	63	−7	49	49
65	1	65	−5	25	25
66	1	66	−4	16	16
68	2	136	−2	4	8
70	4	280	0	0	0
73	1	73	3	9	9
87	1	87	17	289	289
Sums	11	770			396

a. $M = \frac{770}{11} = 70$ **b.** variance $= \frac{396}{11} = 36$ **c.** $\sigma = \sqrt{36} = 6$

B **17.** Mean increases by 10; standard deviation is unchanged because dispersion is unaffected

18. Since each entry is doubled, the sum of the entries is doubled and hence the mean is doubled; for any entry e, the new entry is $2e$ and the squared deviation from the new mean $= (2e - 2 \cdot (\text{old mean}))^2 = (2 \cdot (\text{original deviation}))^2 =$

$4 \cdot (\text{original deviation})^2$; new $\sigma = \sqrt{\frac{4(\text{sum of original squared deviations})}{n}} =$

2 (original σ); the standard deviation is doubled

19. Answers will vary; Examples are given.

a. 78, 80, 80, 82 **b.** 20, 100, 100, 100 **c.** 70, 70, 90, 90

C **20.** **a.** Group 1, since it has the lowest mean and the greatest dispersion

b. Group 4, since it has the smallest dispersion

c. Group 2 or 3; both have means equal to the overall mean and their standard deviations are "average."

Pages 722–723 • WRITTEN EXERCISES

A **1.** 0.1554 = 15.54% **2.** 2(0.0793) = 0.1586; 15.86%

3. 0.500 − 0.4987 = 0.0013; 0.13% **4.** 2(0.4987) = 0.9974; 99.74%

5. **a.** $\frac{450 - 455}{5} = -1$; the percent of loaves with weights more than 1 standard deviation below the mean is 0.5 − 0.3413 = 0.1587; 15.87%

b. $\frac{445 - 455}{5} = -2$; the percent of loaves with weights greater than or equal to 2 standard deviations below the mean is 0.5 + 0.4772 = 0.9772; 97.72%

c. $\frac{470 - 455}{5} = 3$; the percent of loaves with weights greater than 3 standard deviations above the mean is 0.5 − 0.4987 = 0.0013; 0.13%

d. $\frac{450 - 455}{5} = -1$; $\frac{460 - 455}{5} = 1$; the percent of loaves with weights within one standard deviation of the mean is 2(0.3413) = 0.6826; 68.26%

6. a. $\frac{800 - 500}{100} = 3$; $0.5 - 0.4987 = 0.0013$; 0.13%

b. $\frac{400 - 500}{100} = -1$; $0.5 - 0.3413 = 0.1587$; 15.87%

c. $\frac{700 - 500}{100} = 2$; $\frac{900 - 500}{100} = 4$; $0.500 - 0.4772 = 0.0228$; 2.28%

d. $\frac{800 - 500}{100} = 3$; $\frac{820 - 500}{100} = 3.2$; $0.4993 - 0.4987 = 0.0006$; 0.06%

7. a. 50% **b.** $\frac{984 - 900}{30} = 2.8$; $0.5 - 0.4974 = 0.0026$; 0.26%

8. a. $\frac{0.24 - 0.22}{0.01} = 2$; $0.5 - 0.4772 = 0.0228$; 2.28%

b. $\frac{0.206 - 0.22}{0.01} = -1.4$; $0.5 - 0.4192 = 0.0808$; 8.08%

B **9. a.** 0 **b.** 4.0 **c.** Since $15.87 < 50$, $k < 0$; $0.5 - 0.1587 = 0.3413$; $k = -1$
d. Since $84.13 > 50$, $k > 0$; $0.8413 - 0.5 = 0.3413$; $k = 1$

10. The total area under the standard normal curve is 1.

C **11.** Because the normal curve is symmetric about the y − axis, the fraction of data having absolute value greater than a nonnegative constant k is equal to twice the fraction of data greater than k. By exercise 10, the fraction of data greater than k equals 1 minus the fraction of data less than k.

12. a. $y = \frac{1}{\sqrt{2\pi}}e^{(-1/2)(0)} = \frac{1}{\sqrt{2\pi}}e^{0} = \frac{1}{\sqrt{2\pi}} \approx 0.3989$

b. $y = \frac{1}{\sqrt{2\pi}}e^{(-1/2)(1)} = \frac{1}{\sqrt{2\pi}}e^{-1/2} = \frac{1}{\sqrt{2e\pi}} \approx 0.2420$

c. $y = \frac{1}{\sqrt{2\pi}}e^{(-1/2)(2)2} = \frac{1}{\sqrt{2\pi}}e^{-2} = \frac{1}{e^{2}\sqrt{2\pi}} \approx 0.0540$

Page 723 • MIXED REVIEW EXERCISES

1. a. $m = \frac{5 - (-7)}{0 - 4} = \frac{12}{-4} = -3$ **b.** $b = 5$; $y = -3x + 5$; $3x + y = 5$

2. a. $m = \frac{5 - 2}{7 - 3} = \frac{3}{4}$ **b.** $y - 2 = \frac{3}{4}(x - 3)$; $4y - 8 = 3x - 9$; $3x - 4y = 1$

3. a. $m = \frac{1 - 0}{-2 - 0} = -\frac{1}{2}$ **b.** $b = 0$; $y = -\frac{1}{2}x$; $x + 2y = 0$

4. a. $m = \frac{8 - 6}{1 - (-2)} = \frac{2}{3}$

b. $y - 8 = \frac{2}{3}(x - 1)$; $3y - 24 = 2x - 2$; $2x - 3y = -22$

5. a. $m = \frac{-1 - (-1)}{3 - (-5)} = 0$ **b.** $y = -1$

6. a. $m = \frac{-4 - (-2)}{-1 - (-3)} = \frac{-2}{2} = -1$ **b.** $y + 4 = -1(x + 1)$; $x + y = -5$

Pages 727–729 • WRITTEN EXERCISES

A **1.**

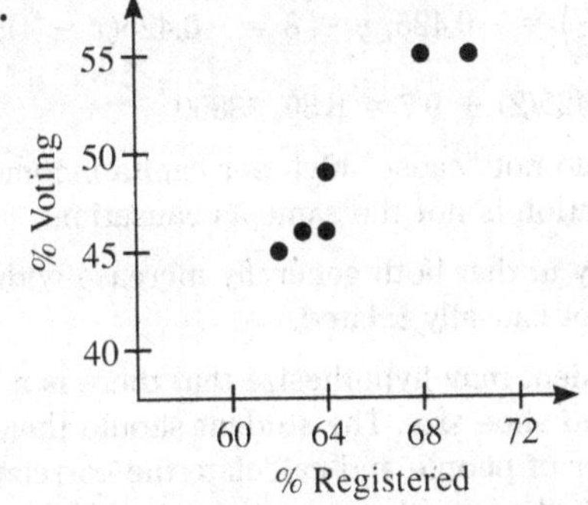

high positive correlation

2.

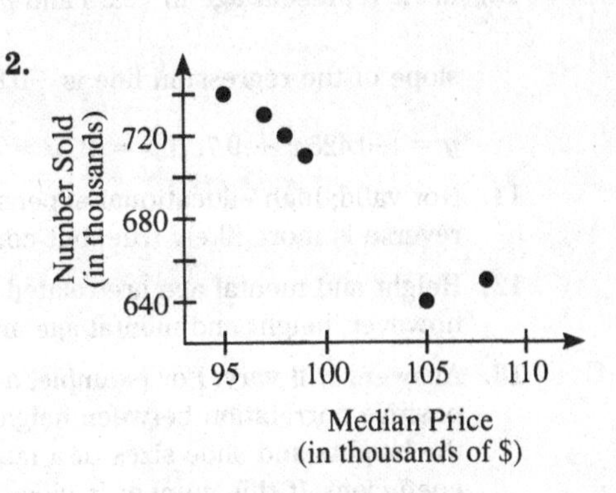

high negative correlation

3.

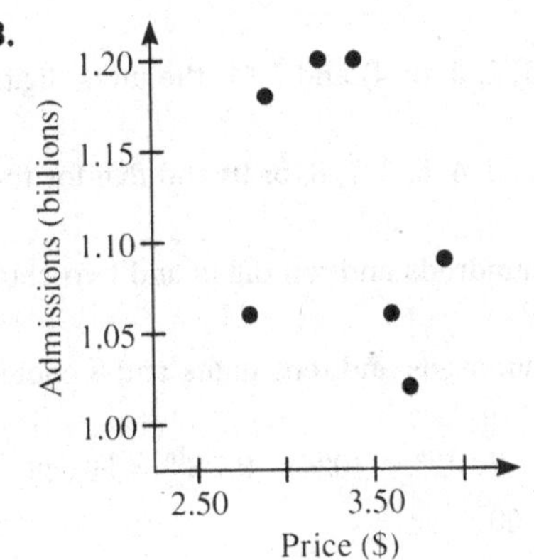

little or no correlation

4.

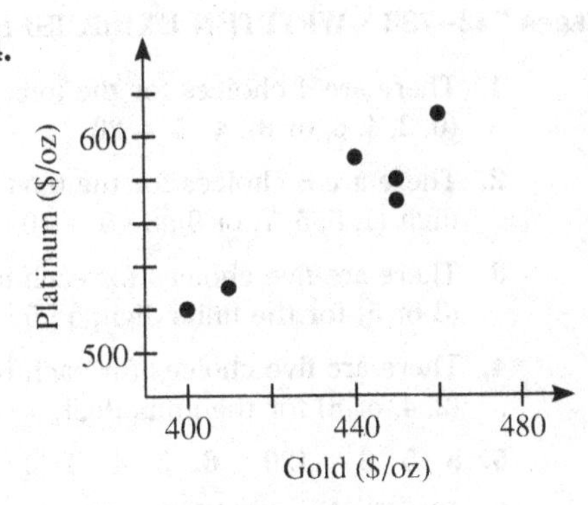

high positive correlation

5. a. $r = \dfrac{3226.33 - (65.17)(49.33)}{(2.85)(4.19)} = 0.96$

b. slope $= (0.96)\left(\dfrac{4.19}{2.85}\right) = 1.41;\ y - 49.33 = 1.41(x - 65.17);\ y = 1.41x - 42.56$

6. a. $r = \dfrac{69{,}893.33 - (100.33)(698.33)}{(4.61)(38.91)} = -0.95$

b. slope $= -0.95\left(\dfrac{38.91}{4.61}\right) = -8.02;\ y - 698.33 = -8.02(x - 100.33);$

$y = -8.02x + 1502.98$

7. $y = 0.7(90) + 15 = 78$; 78

8. $10 = 1.8x + 1.6;\ 8.4 = 1.8x,\ x = 4.67;\ 4\frac{2}{3}$ weeks

B **9.** The slope of regression line is $0.70\left(\dfrac{10}{20}\right) = 0.35$; the regression line is $y - 80 = 0.35(x - 125)$, or $y = 0.35x + 36.25$, where x represents the score on the first test and y on the second. If $x = 100$, $y = 0.35(100) + 36.25 = 71.25$; 71

10. Let x represent age in years and y represent value in thousands of dollars. The slope of the regression line is $-0.85\left(\frac{1}{2}\right) = -0.425$; $y - 8 = -0.425(x - 4)$; $y = -0.425x + 9.7$; If $x = 2$, $y = -0.425(2) + 9.7 = 8.85$; $8850

11. Not valid; high educational expenses do not "cause" high per capita income; the reverse is more likely true, but correlation is not the same as causation.

12. Height and mental age are related only in that both generally increase with age; however, height and mental age are not causally related.

C 13. Answers will vary. For example, a student may hypothesize that there is a high positive correlation between height and shoe size. The student should then gather the heights and shoe sizes of a number of people and calculate the correlation coefficient. If this number is close to 1, the hypothesis is supported. If the number is close to 0 or if it is negative, the hypothesis is *not* supported.

Pages 732–733 • WRITTEN EXERCISES

A 1. There are 4 choices for the tens digit (1, 2, 3, or 4) and 5 for the units digit (0, 2, 4, 6, or 8); $4 \cdot 5 = 20$

2. There are 8 choices for the tens digit (2, 3, 4, 5, 6, 7, 8, or 9) and five for the units digit (1, 3, 5, 7, or 9); $8 \cdot 5 = 40$

3. There are five choices for each of the hundreds and ten digits and two choices (3 or 5) for the units digit; $5 \cdot 5 \cdot 2 = 50$

4. There are five choices for each of the hundreds and tens digits and 3 choices (2, 4, or 8) for the units digit; $5 \cdot 5 \cdot 3 = 75$

5. $8 \cdot 5 \cdot 3 = 120$ **6.** $5 \cdot 4 \cdot 3 \cdot 2 = 120$ **7.** $2^{10} = 1024$ **8.** $3^{10} = 59{,}049$

9. $52 \cdot 51 \cdot 50 = 132{,}600$ **10.** $5 \cdot 4 \cdot 3 = 60$

B 11. $1 \cdot 1 \cdot 2 \cdot 10 \cdot 10 \cdot 10 \cdot 10 = 20{,}000$

12. There are $4 \cdot 5 \cdot 5 \cdot 1$ such four digit numbers, $4 \cdot 5 \cdot 1$ such three digit numbers, $4 \cdot 1$ such two digit numbers, and 1 such 1 digit number. Thus there are a total of $100 + 20 + 4 + 1 = 125$ such numbers.

13. See example 3, page 731; $20{,}280 + 17{,}576 = 37{,}856$.

14. The letters and digits may be arranged in 6 distinct ways: LLDD, LDLD, LDDL, DLLD, DLDL, and DDLL. For each of these arrangements, there are 10 ways to choose each digit and 26 ways to choose each letter. Thus the total number of license plates is $6 \cdot 26 \cdot 26 \cdot 10 \cdot 10 = 405{,}600$

15. 15, 18, 45, 48, 51, 54, 57, 75, 78, 81, 84, 87; 12 multiples

16. 9, 99, 222, 225, 252, 522, 525, 552, 555, and 999; 11 multiples

C 17. There are $36 \times 35 \times 34$ possible combinations. It would take $36 \cdot 35 \cdot 34 \cdot 12$ seconds $= \frac{514,080}{60}$ minutes $= 8568$ minutes $= \frac{8568}{(60)(24)}$ days ≈ 6 days

18. $4^8 = 65{,}536$ **19.** $20^6 = 6.4 \times 10^7$

20. The vowel may be in one of 3 positions. 1 vowel: $3 \cdot 5 \cdot 21 \cdot 21 = 6615$; 2 vowels: $3 \cdot 21 \cdot 5 \cdot 5 = 1575$; 3 vowels: $5^3 = 125$; total $6615 + 1575 + 125 = 8315$

Page 733 • MIXED REVIEW EXERCISES

1. $\frac{8^2}{(-2)^5} = \frac{64}{-32} = -2$ **2.** $|-2 - 8| = |-10| = 10$ **3.** $8^{-2} = \frac{1}{8^2} = \frac{1}{64}$

4. $\sqrt{8(-2)} = \sqrt{-16} = 4i$

5. $x^3 + x^2 - 2x - 2 = 0; x^2(x + 1) - 2(x + 1) = 0; (x + 1)(x^2 - 2) = 0; x + 1 = 0$ or $x^2 - 2 = 0; x = -1$ or $x^2 = 2; x = -1$ or $x = \pm\sqrt{2}; \{\pm\sqrt{2}, -1\}$

6. Since $-i\sqrt{3}$ is a root, $i\sqrt{3}$ is a root;

$$\begin{array}{r|rrrr}
-i\sqrt{3} & 1 & -4 & 3 & -12 \\
 & & -i\sqrt{3} & -3 + 4i\sqrt{3} & 12 \\ \hline
i\sqrt{3} & 1 & -4 - i\sqrt{3} & 4i\sqrt{3} & 0 \\
 & & i\sqrt{3} & -4i\sqrt{3} & \\ \hline
 & 1 & -4 & 0 &
\end{array}$$

the depressed equation is $x - 4 = 0; x = 4; \{-i\sqrt{3}, i\sqrt{3}, 4\}$

7.

$$\begin{array}{r|rrrr}
5 & 2 & -11 & 4 & 5 \\
 & & 10 & -5 & -5 \\ \hline
 & 2 & -1 & -1 & 0
\end{array}$$

the depressed equation is $2x^2 - x - 1 = 0; (2x + 1)(x - 1) = 0; 2x + 1 = 0$ or $x - 1 = 0; x = -\frac{1}{2}$ or $x = 1; \left\{5, -\frac{1}{2}, 1\right\}$

8. Since $4i$ is a root, $-4i$ is a root and $(x - 4i)(x + 4i) = x^2 + 16$ is a factor.

$$\begin{array}{r}
x + 6 \\
x^2 + 16 \overline{)\, x^3 + 6x^2 + 16x + 96} \\
\underline{x^3 + 16x } \\
6x^2 + 96 \\
\underline{6x^2 + 96} \\
0
\end{array}$$

$x + 6 = 0, x = -6; \{4i, -4i, -6\}$

Page 733 • CHALLENGE

All faces same color: 2 ways; 1 face of one color and 5 faces of other color: 2 ways; 2 faces of one color and 4 faces of other color: 4 ways (the 2 faces can either be adjacent or opposite each other); 3 faces of each color: 2 ways; total = 10 ways.

Page 737 • WRITTEN EXERCISES

A **1.** $(6)(120) = 720$ **2.** $3(120) = 360$ **3.** $\frac{8!}{5!} = \frac{8 \cdot 7 \cdot 6 \cdot 5!}{5!} = 8 \cdot 7 \cdot 6 = 336$

4. $\frac{8!}{3!5!} = \frac{8 \cdot 7 \cdot 6 \cdot 5!}{3 \cdot 2 \cdot 1 \cdot 5!} = \frac{8 \cdot 7 \cdot 6}{3 \cdot 2 \cdot 1} = 56$ **5.** ${}_7P_7 = 7! = 5040$

6. ${}_5P_2 = \frac{5!}{(5 - 2)!} = \frac{5 \cdot 4 \cdot 3!}{3!} = 20$ **7.** ${}_6P_1 = \frac{6!}{(6 - 1)!} = \frac{6 \cdot 5!}{5!} = 6$

8. ${}_8P_4 = \frac{8!}{(8 - 4)!} = \frac{8 \cdot 7 \cdot 6 \cdot 5 \cdot 4!}{4!} = 8 \cdot 7 \cdot 6 \cdot 5 = 1680$ **9.** ${}_6P_6 = 6! = 720$

10. ${}_8P_8 = 8! = 40{,}320$ **11.** ${}_{52}P_3 = 52 \cdot 51 \cdot 50 = 132{,}600$ **12.** ${}_7P_4 = 7 \cdot 6 \cdot 5 \cdot 4 = 840$

13. ${}_6P_6 = 6! = 720$ **14.** ${}_5P_3 = 5 \cdot 4 \cdot 3 = 60$

B **15.** $\frac{6!}{3!} = \frac{720}{6} = 120$ **16.** $\frac{9!}{5!} = \frac{9 \cdot 8 \cdot 7 \cdot 6 \cdot 5!}{5!} = 3024$ **17.** $\frac{5!}{2!2!} = \frac{120}{2 \cdot 2} = 30$

18. $\frac{6!}{3!2!} = \frac{720}{6 \cdot 2} = 60$ **19.** $\frac{11!}{4!4!2!} = 34{,}650$ **20.** $\frac{11!}{3!2!2!} = 1{,}663{,}200$ **21.** $\frac{5!}{2!2!} = 30$

22. $\frac{5!}{3!} = 20$ **23.** $\frac{7!}{3!2!} = 420$ **24.** $\frac{9!}{3!4!2!} = 1260$

25. $6({}_5P_3) = 6\left(\frac{5!}{2!}\right) = \frac{6 \cdot 5!}{2!} = \frac{6!}{2!} = {}_6P_4$

26. $5({}_4P_r{-}1) = 5 \cdot \frac{4!}{[4 - (r - 1)]!} = \frac{5 \cdot 4!}{(5 - r)!} = \frac{5!}{(5 - r)!} = {}_5P_r$

27. ${}_nP_5 - {}_nP_4 = \frac{n!}{(n - 5)!} - \frac{n!}{(n - 4)!} = \frac{n!}{(n - 5)!} \cdot \frac{n - 4}{n - 4} - \frac{n!}{(n - 4)!} = \frac{n![(n - 4) - 1]}{(n - 4)!} =$
$\frac{(n - 5)n!}{(n - 4)!} = (n - 5){}_nP_4$

28. ${}_nP_r - {}_nP_{r-1} = \frac{n!}{(n - r)!} - \frac{n!}{[n - (r - 1)]!} = \frac{n!}{(n - r)!}\left[1 - \frac{1}{n - r + 1}\right] =$
$\frac{n!}{(n - r)!}\left[\frac{n - r + 1 - 1}{n - r + 1}\right] = \frac{n!}{(n - r)!}\left(\frac{n - r}{n - (r - 1)}\right) = \frac{n!}{[n - (r - 1)]!} \cdot (n - r) =$
$(n - r){}_nP_{r-1}$

C **29.** ${}_nP_5 = 14({}_nP_4)$; $\frac{n!}{(n - 5)!} = 14\frac{n!}{(n - 4)!}$; $\frac{1}{(n - 5)!} = \frac{14}{(n - 4)(n - 5)!}$; $1 = \frac{14}{n - 4}$; $n - 4 = 14$,
$n = 18$

30. ${}_nP_3 = 17{}_nP_2$; $\frac{n!}{(n - 3)!} = 17\frac{n!}{(n - 2)!}$; $\frac{1}{(n - 3)!} = \frac{17}{(n - 2)(n - 3)!}$; $1 = \frac{17}{n - 2}$, $n - 2 = 17$,
$n = 19$

31. One P: $6! = 720$ permutations; Two P's: there are five ways to drop a letter leaving 6 letters (including two P's); $5 \cdot \frac{6!}{2!} = 1800$; total $= 720 + 1800 = 2520$

Pages 740–741 • WRITTEN EXERCISES

A **1. a.** ∅, {J}, {K}, {J, K} **b.** ∅, {J}, {K}

2. a. {1, 3, 5}, {1, 3, 7}, {1, 5, 7}, {3, 5, 7}

b. {3, 7}, {5, 7}, {1, 3, 5}, {1, 3, 7}, {1, 5, 7}, {3, 5, 7}, {1, 3, 5, 7}

3. ${}_5C_3 = \frac{5!}{3!2!} = \frac{5 \cdot 4}{2 \cdot 1} = 10$ **4.** ${}_6C_1 = \frac{6!}{5!1!} = \frac{6}{1} = 6$ **5.** ${}_8C_6 = \frac{8!}{6!2!} = \frac{8 \cdot 7}{2 \cdot 1} = 28$

6. ${}_7C_4 = \frac{7!}{4!3!} = \frac{7 \cdot 6 \cdot 5}{3 \cdot 2 \cdot 1} = 35$ **7.** ${}_{10}C_8 = \frac{10!}{8!2!} = \frac{10 \cdot 9}{2 \cdot 1} = 45$ **8.** ${}_9C_2 = \frac{9!}{7!2!} = \frac{9 \cdot 8}{2 \cdot 1} = 36$

9. ${}_{12}C_5 = \frac{12!}{5!7!} = \frac{12 \cdot 11 \cdot 10 \cdot 9 \cdot 8}{5 \cdot 4 \cdot 3 \cdot 2 \cdot 1} = 792$ **10.** ${}_{100}C_2 = \frac{100!}{2!98!} = \frac{100 \cdot 99}{2} = 4950$

11. a. ${}_5C_4 = \frac{5!}{4!1!} = 5$ **b.** ${}_5C_3 = \frac{5!}{3!2!} = 10$ **c.** ${}_5C_2 = \frac{5!}{2!3!} = 10$

12. a. ${}_7C_6 = \frac{7!}{6!1!} = 7$ **b.** ${}_7C_4 = \frac{7!}{4!3!} = \frac{7 \cdot 6 \cdot 5}{3 \cdot 2 \cdot 1} = 35$ **c.** ${}_7C_2 = \frac{7!}{2!5!} = \frac{7 \cdot 6}{2 \cdot 1} = 21$

13. ${}_{15}C_7 = \frac{15!}{7!8!} = 6435$ **14.** ${}_{100}C_4 = \frac{100!}{4!96!} = 3{,}921{,}225$ **15.** ${}_{10}C_2 = \frac{10!}{2!8!} = 45$

16. ${}_8C_4 = \frac{8!}{4!4!} = 70$

B **17.** ${}_7C_3 = \frac{7!}{4!3!} = 35$ **18.** ${}_{10}C_4 = \frac{10!}{4!6!} = 210$

19. $({}_{15}C_3)({}_{16}C_3) = \frac{15!}{3!12!} \cdot \frac{16!}{3!13!} = (455)(560) = 254{,}800$

20. $({}_{10}C_3)({}_{10}C_2) = \frac{10!}{3!7!} \cdot \frac{10!}{2!8!} = (120)(45) = 5400$

21. $({}_{13}C_{11})({}_{39}C_2) = \frac{13!}{11!2!} \cdot \frac{39!}{2!37!} = (78)(741) = 57{,}798$

22. $4({}_{13}C_{11})({}_{39}C_2) = 4(78)(741) = 231{,}192$

23. $({}_4C_3)({}_{48}C_2) = \frac{4!}{3!1!} \cdot \frac{48!}{2!46!} = 4 \cdot 1128 = 4512$

24. $({}_{13}C_3)({}_{13}C_3)({}_{13}C_1) = \left(\frac{13!}{3!10!}\right)^2 \cdot 13 = (286)^2(13) = 1{,}063{,}348$

25. 4 students: ${}_8C_4 = \frac{8!}{4!4!} = 70$; 5 students: ${}_8C_5 = \frac{8}{5!3!} = 56$; 6 students: ${}_8C_6 = \frac{8!}{6!2!} = 28$;

7 students: ${}_8C_7 = \frac{8!}{7!1!} = 8$; 8 students: ${}_8C_8 = 1$; total $= 163$

26. 2 students: ${}_6C_1 \cdot {}_5C_1 = 6 \cdot 5 = 30$; 4 students: ${}_6C_2 \cdot {}_5C_2 = 15 \cdot 10 = 150$; $30 + 150 = 180$

C **27.** ${}_nC_{n-r} = \frac{n!}{(n-r)![n-(n-r)]!} = \frac{n!}{(n-r)!r!} = {}_nC_r$

28. ${}_{n-1}C_{r-1} + {}_{n-1}C_r = \frac{(n-1)!}{(r-1)![n-1-(r-1)]!} + \frac{(n-1)!}{r!(n-1-r)!} = \frac{(n-1)!}{(r-1)!(n-r)!} +$

$\frac{(n-1)!}{r!(n-r-1)!} = \frac{(n-1)!}{(r-1)!(n-r)(n-r-1)!} + \frac{(n-1)!}{(r)(r-1)!(n-r-1)!} =$

$\frac{(n-1)!}{(r-1)!(n-r-1)!}\left[\frac{1}{n-r} + \frac{1}{r}\right] = \frac{(n-1)!}{(r-1)!(n-r-1)!}\left(\frac{n}{r(n-r)}\right) = \frac{n!}{r!(n-r)!} = {}_nC_r$

29. **a.** The coefficient of $a^{n-r}b^r$ is ${}_nC_r$ **b.** $(a+b)^n = \sum_{r=0}^{n} {}_nC_r a^{n-r}b^r$

30. For each of the n members of the set, there are two choices: either it is included or it is not included in the subset. ∴ There are 2^n subsets.

Page 741 • MIXED REVIEW EXERCISES

1. $f(4) = \frac{4+6}{2(4)-3} = \frac{10}{5} = 2$ **2.** $g(4) = |1-4| = |-3| = 3$

3. $h(4) = (4+2)^2 = 36$ **4.** $F(4) = -3$ **5.** $G(4) = -2(4) + 1 = -7$

6. $H(4) = 4^4 + 5(4)^3 - 12(4)^2 + 6 = 390$ **7.** $6\sqrt{2} - 3\sqrt{2} + 2\sqrt{2} = 5\sqrt{2}$

8. $\log_6(2 \cdot 3) = \log_6 6 = 1$

9. $\frac{1}{m+2} + \frac{6}{(m-4)(m+2)} = \frac{m-4+6}{(m+2)(m-4)} = \frac{m+2}{(m+2)(m-4)} = \frac{1}{m-4}$

10. $8 + 4i - 6i - 3i^2 = 11 - 2i$ **11.** $\frac{(2t-3)(t+3)}{(t-3)(t+3)} = \frac{2t-3}{t-3}$ **12.** $\frac{13-4}{9} = \frac{9}{9} = 1$

Page 742 • COMPUTER EXERCISES

1.
```
10 PRINT "ENTER N"
20 INPUT N
30 LET F = 1
40 FOR L = 1 TO N
50 LET F = F * L
60 NEXT L
70 PRINT N; "! = "; F
80 END
```

2. a. 3628800 **b.** 6.2270208E + 09 **c.** 2.09227899E + 13 **d.** 2.43290201E + 18

3.
```
10 PRINT "ENTER INTEGERS N, R (N > R > 0)"
20 INPUT N, R
30 IF R < = 0 THEN 10
40 IF N < R THEN 10
50 IF N * R <> INT(N * R) THEN 10
60 LET X = N
70 GOSUB 200
80 LET A = F
90 LET X = R
100 GOSUB 200
110 LET B = F
120 LET X = N - R
130 GOSUB 200
140 LET C = A/(B * F)
150 PRINT N; "C"; R; "="; C
160 GOTO 10
200 LET F = 1
210 FOR L = 1 TO X
220 LET F = F * L
230 NEXT L
240 RETURN
250 END
```

4. a. 220 **b.** 48620

5.
```
10 PRINT "ENTER INTEGERS N, R (N > R > 0)"
20 INPUT N, R
30 IF R < = 0 THEN 10
40 IF N < R THEN 10
50 IF R * N <> INT(R * N) THEN 10
60 LET P = N
70 LET C = N
80 FOR L = 2 TO R
90 LET P = P - 1
100 LET C = C * P
110 NEXT L
120 GOSUB 200
130 LET C = C/F
```

Continued

```
140 PRINT N; "C"; R;"="; C
150 GOTO 10
200 LET F = 1
210 FOR L = 1 TO R
220 LET F = F * L
230 NEXT L
240 RETURN
250 END
```

a. 52 C 5 = 2598960 **b.** 52 C 13 = 6.3501356E + 11 **c.** It is likely.

Page 744 • WRITTEN EXERCISES

A **1.** {(1, 1), (2, 2), (3, 3), (4, 4), (5, 5), (6, 6)} **2.** {(1, 5), (2, 4), (3, 3), (4, 2), (5, 1)}

3. {(2, 6), (3, 4), (4, 3), (6, 2)}

4. {(3, 6), (4, 5), (4, 6), (5, 4), (5, 5), (5, 6), (6, 3), (6, 4), (6, 5), (6, 6)}

5. {(1, 1), (1, 2), (1, 3), (1, 4), (1, 5), (1, 6), (2, 1), (2, 2), (2, 3), (2, 4), (3, 1), (3, 2), (3, 3), (4, 1), (4, 2), (5, 1), (6, 1)}

6. {(2, 1), (3, 1), (3, 2), (4, 1), (4, 2), (4, 3), (5, 1), (5, 2), (5, 3), (5, 4), (6, 1), (6, 2), (6, 3), (6, 4), (6, 5)}

B **7. a.** {(*R*, *R*), (*R*, *B*), (*R*, *Y*), (*R*, *G*), (*B*, *R*), (*B*, *B*), (*B*, *Y*), (*B*, *G*)}

b. {(*R*, *R*), (*R*, *B*), (*R*, *Y*), (*R*, *G*), (*B*, *R*)} **c.** {(*R*, *R*), (*R*, *Y*), (*R*, *G*)}

8. a. $6 \cdot 6 \cdot 6 = 216$ **b.** (1, 1, 1), (2, 2, 2), (3, 3, 3), (4, 4, 4), (5, 5, 5), (6, 6, 6)}

c. {(1, 1, 3), (1, 1, 4), (1, 1, 5), (1, 1, 6), (1, 2, 4), (1, 2, 5), (1, 2, 6), (1, 3, 5), (1, 3, 6), (1, 4, 6), (2, 1, 4), (2, 1, 5), (2, 1, 6), (2, 2, 5), (2, 2, 6), (2, 3, 6), (3, 1, 5), (3, 1, 6), (3, 2, 6), (4, 1, 6)}

9. {(3, 6), (4, 5), (5, 4), (6, 3)}

10. {(1, 2), (1, 3), (1, 4), (1, 5), (1, 6), (2, 3), (2, 4), (2, 5), (2, 6), (3, 4), (3, 5), (3, 6), (4, 5), (4, 6), (5, 6)}

11. {(2, 1), (4, 2), (6, 3)} **12.** {(3, 1), (4, 2), (5, 3), (6, 4)}

C **13.** {(1, 1), (1, 2), (1, 3), (1, 4), (1, 5), (1, 6), (2, 1), (2, 2), (2, 3), (2, 4), (2, 5), (2, 6), (3, 5), (3, 6), (4, 5), (4, 6), (5, 5), (5, 6), (6, 5), (6, 6)}

14. {(1, 1), (1, 3), (2, 2), (3, 1), (3, 3), (4, 4), (5, 5), (6, 6)}

15. {(1, 1), (1, 4), (2, 1), (3, 4), (4, 1), (6, 1)}

16. {(2, 2), (2, 4), (2, 6), (4, 2), (4, 4), (4, 6), (6, 2), (6, 4), (6, 6)}

Pages 748–750 • WRITTEN EXERCISES

A **1. a.** $\frac{1}{10}$ **b.** $\frac{5}{10} = \frac{1}{2}$ **c.** $\frac{3}{10}$ **d.** $\frac{10}{10} = 1$ **e.** $\frac{2}{10} = \frac{1}{5}$ **f.** 0

2. a. $\frac{3}{8}$ **b.** $\frac{5}{8}$ **c.** $\frac{5}{8}$ **d.** $\frac{4}{8} = \frac{1}{2}$ **3. a.** $\frac{4}{16} = \frac{1}{4}$ **b.** $\frac{16}{16} = 1$ **c.** $\frac{12}{16} = \frac{3}{4}$ **d.** $\frac{10}{16} = \frac{5}{8}$

4. a. $\frac{4}{52} = \frac{1}{13}$ **b.** $\frac{13}{52} = \frac{1}{4}$ **c.** $\frac{26}{52} = \frac{1}{2}$ **d.** $\frac{1}{52}$ **e.** $\frac{2}{52} = \frac{1}{26}$ **f.** 0

5. The event space is {(*H*, *H*), (*H*, *T*), (*T*, *H*), (*T*, *T*)}; **a.** $\frac{1}{4}$ **b.** $\frac{3}{4}$ **c.** $\frac{2}{4} = \frac{1}{2}$ **d.** $\frac{2}{4} = \frac{1}{2}$

6. a. $\frac{100}{220} = \frac{5}{11}$ **b.** $\frac{170}{220} = \frac{17}{22}$ **c.** $\frac{10}{220} = \frac{1}{22}$

7. a. 1 **b.** $\frac{9{,}000}{1{,}000{,}000} = \frac{9}{1000}$ **c.** $\frac{991{,}000}{1{,}000{,}000} = \frac{991}{1000}$

8. a. $\frac{3}{36} = \frac{1}{12}$ **b.** $\frac{6}{36} = \frac{1}{6}$ **c.** $\frac{10}{36} = \frac{5}{18}$ **d.** $\frac{11}{36}$

B 9. The event space is $\{(H, H, H), (H, H, T), (H, T, H), (H, T, T), (T, H, H), (T, H, T), (T, T, H), (T, T, T)\}$ **a.** $\frac{1}{8}$ **b.** $\frac{1}{8}$ **c.** $\frac{7}{8}$ **d.** $\frac{3}{8}$

10. Let x = the number of yellow beads; then x = the number of turquoise beads, $2x$ = the number of white beads, and $4x$ = the number of red beads;

a. $\frac{4x}{8x} = \frac{1}{2}$ **b.** $\frac{2x}{8x} = \frac{1}{4}$ **c.** $\frac{x + x}{8x} = \frac{2x}{8x} = \frac{1}{4}$

11. ${}_{12}C_2 = \frac{12 \cdot 11}{2 \cdot 1} = 66$ ways to draw 2 marbles **a.** $\frac{{}_2C_2}{66} = \frac{1}{66}$ **b.** $\frac{{}_4C_2}{66} = \frac{6}{66} = \frac{1}{11}$

c. $\frac{{}_6C_2}{66} = \frac{15}{66} = \frac{5}{22}$ **d.** $\frac{{}_2C_1 \cdot {}_4C_1}{66} = \frac{2 \cdot 4}{66} = \frac{4}{33}$ **e.** $\frac{{}_{10}C_2}{66} = \frac{45}{66} = \frac{15}{22}$ **f.** $\frac{{}_6C_2}{66} = \frac{15}{66} = \frac{5}{22}$

12. There are ${}_{52}C_2 = \frac{52 \cdot 51}{2 \cdot 1} = 1326$ possible two-card combinations;

a. $\frac{{}_{13}C_2}{1326} = \frac{78}{1326} = \frac{1}{17}$ **b.** $\frac{{}_4C_2}{1326} = \frac{6}{1326} = \frac{1}{221}$ **c.** $\frac{{}_{26}C_2}{1326} = \frac{325}{1326} = \frac{25}{102}$

d. $\frac{{}_{39}C_2}{1326} = \frac{741}{1326} = \frac{19}{34}$

13. a. $\frac{20 - 36}{10} = -1.6$; $P(x < -1.6) = 0.5 - 0.4452 = 0.0548$

b. $\frac{60 - 36}{10} = 2.4$; $P(x > 2.4) = 0.5 - 0.4918 = 0.0082$

14. a. $\frac{65 - 74}{5} = -1.8$; $P(x < -1.8) = 0.5 - 0.4641 = 0.0359$

b. $\frac{80 - 74}{5} = 1.2$; $P(x > 1.2) = 0.5 - 0.3849 = 0.1151$

Page 750 • MIXED REVIEW EXERCISES

1. $|t - 2| > 4$; $t - 2 > 4$ or $t - 2 < -4$; $t > 6$ or $t < -2$; $\{t : t > 6 \text{ or } t < -2\}$;

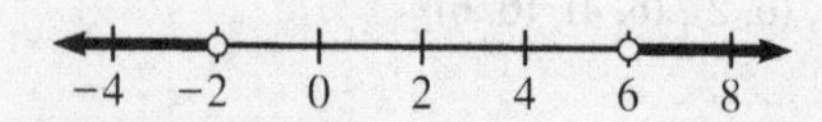

2. $x^2 - x \le 2$; $x^2 - x - 2 \le 0$, $(x - 2)(x + 1) \le 0$; $-1 \le x \le 2$; $\{x : -1 \le x \le 2\}$;

-2 0 2 4

3. $4 - 3n < -2$, $-3n < -6$, $n > 2$; $\{n : n > 2\}$;

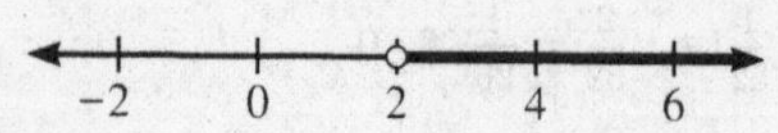

4. $-3 \le 2x - 3 \le 5$; $0 \le 2x \le 8$, $0 \le x \le 4$; $\{x : 0 \le x \le 4\}$;

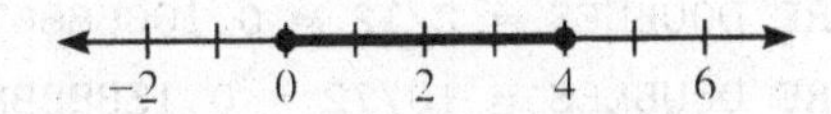

5. $4y^2 > 16$; $y^2 > 4$; $y^2 - 4 > 0$, $(y - 2)(y + 2) > 0$; $y > 2$ or $y < -2$;
$\{y : y < -2 \text{ or } y > 2\}$;

6. $|3k + 1| < 4$; $-4 < 3k + 1 < 4$; $-5 < 3k < 3$; $-\frac{5}{3} < k < 1$; $\left\{k : -\frac{5}{3} < k < 1\right\}$;

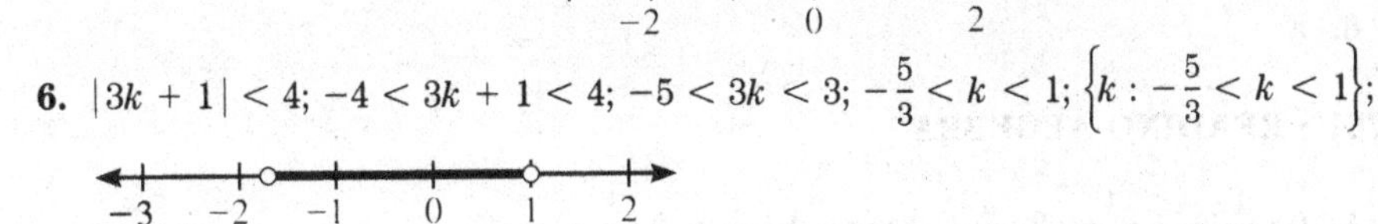

7. $\frac{5!}{2!} = \frac{120}{2} = 60$ **8.** ${}_{24}C_4 = \frac{24!}{4!20!} = 10{,}626$

Page 750 • COMPUTER EXERCISES

1.
```
10 PRINT "ENTER NUMBER OF TOSSES"
20 INPUT NT
30 LET S = 0
40 FOR N = 1 TO NT
50 LET X = INT(RND(1) * 2)
60 IF X = 1 THEN LET S = S + 1
70 NEXT N
80 PRINT "TOTAL NUMBER OF HEADS IN"; NT; "TOSSES = "; S
90 GOTO 10
```

2. Answers will vary. Sample output is given.

a. `TOTAL NUMBER OF HEADS IN 20 TOSSES = 9`

b. `TOTAL NUMBER OF HEADS IN 80 TOSSES = 42`

c. `TOTAL NUMBER OF HEADS IN 200 TOSSES = 88`

d. `TOTAL NUMBER OF HEADS IN 800 TOSSES = 421`

3. b

4.
```
10 PRINT "ENTER NUMBER OF DICE ROLLS"
20 INPUT NR
30 LET S = 0
40 FOR N = 1 to NR
50 LET X = INT(RND(1) * 6) + 1
55 LET Y = INT(RND(1) * 6) + 1
60 IF X = Y THEN LET S = S + 1
70 NEXT N
80 PRINT "FRACTION OF ROLLS THAT WERE DOUBLES ="; S; "/"; NR;
"="; S/NR
90 GOTO 10
```

5. Answers will vary. Sample output is given.

   a. `FRACTION OF ROLLS THAT WERE DOUBLES = 2/12 = 0.16666667`

   b. `FRACTION OF ROLLS THAT WERE DOUBLES = 10/72 = 0.13888889`

   c. `FRACTION OF ROLLS THAT WERE DOUBLES = 19/120 = 0.15833333`

   d. `FRACTION OF ROLLS THAT WERE DOUBLES = 118/720 = 0.16388889`

6. a

Page 751 • READING ALGEBRA

1. $0 \cdot \frac{1}{16} + 1 \cdot \frac{1}{4} + 2 \cdot \frac{3}{8} + 3 \cdot \frac{1}{4} + 4 \cdot \frac{1}{16} = 2$

2. $\frac{{}_4C_2}{2^4} = \frac{6}{16} = \frac{3}{8}$ 3. less than $\frac{1}{2}$

4. $1 \cdot \frac{1}{6} + 2 \cdot \frac{1}{6} + 3 \cdot \frac{1}{6} + 4 \cdot \frac{1}{6} + 5 \cdot \frac{1}{6} + 6 \cdot \frac{1}{6} = 21 \cdot \frac{1}{6} = 3\frac{1}{2}$; no

5. $3\frac{1}{2}$ 6. Expectation is an average score.

Pages 752–753 • APPLICATION

1. a. random b. not random; each bulb is not equally likely to be sampled
2. a. random

   b. not random; the selection of succeeding students is dependent on the selection of the first
3. not random; this is self-selected, not random
4. not random; this is convenience sampling

5–8. Answers may vary

5. An example of the new layout could be shown to a random sample of subscribers; however, not all of those selected will wish to give their opinion.
6. A random telephone poll could be conducted; however, not all selected could be reached by phone or, if reached, would answer.
7. A random sample of a doctor's patients could be taken; there are problems defining "optimist" and "pessimist", and with measuring relative health.
8. A telephone survey of registered voters could be conducted.

Pages 759–761 • WRITTEN EXERCISES

A 1. a. $\frac{5}{10} = \frac{1}{2}$ b. $\frac{5}{10} = \frac{1}{2}$ c. $\frac{3}{10}$ 2. a. $\frac{3+2}{10} = \frac{1}{2}$ b. $\frac{5+2}{10} = \frac{7}{10}$ c. $\frac{10}{10} = 1$

3. a. $\frac{4}{12} \cdot \frac{3}{11} = \frac{1}{11}$ b. $\frac{5}{12} \cdot \frac{4}{11} = \frac{5}{33}$ 4. a. $\frac{2}{8} \cdot \frac{3}{8} = \frac{3}{32}$ b. $\frac{3}{8} \cdot \frac{3}{8} = \frac{9}{64}$

5. a. $P(A) = \frac{1}{6}$; $P(B) = \frac{5}{36}$; $P(A \cup B) = \frac{1}{6} + \frac{5}{36} - \frac{1}{36} = \frac{10}{36} = \frac{5}{18}$; $P(A \cap B) = \frac{1}{36}$

   b. no

6. a. $\{(1, H), (1, T), (2, H), (2, T), (3, H), (3, T), (4, H), (4, T), (5, H), (5, T), (6, H), (6, T)\}$

b. $A = \{(5, H), (5, T), (6, H), (6, T)\}$; $B = \{(1, H), (2, H), (3, H), (4, H), (5, H), (6, H)\}$; $A \cup B = \{(5, T), (6, T), (1, H), (2, H), (3, H), (4, H), (5, H), (6, H)\}$; $A \cap B = \{(5, H), (6, H)\}$

c. $P(A) = \frac{4}{12} = \frac{1}{3}$; $P(B) = \frac{6}{12} = \frac{1}{2}$; $P(A \cup B) = \frac{8}{12} = \frac{2}{3}$; $P(A \cap B) = \frac{2}{12} = \frac{1}{6}$

d. no; yes

7. a. This event is $\{(4, 6), (5, 5), (6, 4)\}$; $\frac{3}{36} = \frac{1}{12}$

b. This event is $\{(1, 3), (2, 2), (3, 1), (4, 4)\}$; $\frac{4}{36} = \frac{1}{9}$

8. a. $\frac{{}_4C_2}{{}_{52}C_2} = \frac{4 \cdot 3}{2 \cdot 1} \div \frac{52 \cdot 51}{2 \cdot 1} = \frac{4 \cdot 3}{52 \cdot 51} = \frac{1}{221}$

b. same as **a**; $\frac{1}{221}$ **c.** the events are mutually exclusive; $\frac{1}{221} + \frac{1}{221} = \frac{2}{221}$

9. There are $2^3 = 8$ possible outcomes

a. this event is {(T, T, H), (T, H, T), (H, T, T), (T, T, T)}; $\frac{4}{8} = \frac{1}{2}$

b. The probability that all three are tails is $\frac{1}{8}$; the probability that not all three are tails is $1 - \frac{1}{8} = \frac{7}{8}$

10. a. $\frac{4}{52} \cdot \frac{4}{52} = \frac{1}{169}$ **b.** $\frac{13}{52} \cdot \frac{13}{52} = \frac{1}{16}$

B

11. $\frac{2}{{}_6P_6} = \frac{2}{6!} = \frac{1}{360}$ **12.** $0.4 + 0.45 - (0.4)(0.45) = 0.67$

13. Let E be the event that the telegram is for an engineer and M the event it is for a man.

a. $P(E) = \frac{5}{10} = \frac{1}{2}$ **b.** $P(M) = \frac{4}{10} = \frac{2}{5}$

c. $P(M \cap E) = \frac{3}{10}$; $P(\overline{M \cap E}) = 1 - \frac{3}{10} = \frac{7}{10}$

14. $P(A) = \frac{1}{2}$; $P(B) = \frac{4}{52} = \frac{1}{13}$; $P(C) = \frac{8}{52} = \frac{2}{13}$

a. $P(A \cap B) = \frac{2}{52} = \frac{1}{26} = P(A) \cdot P(B)$; independent

b. $P(A \cap C) = \frac{4}{52} = \frac{1}{13} = P(A) \cdot P(C)$; independent

c. $P(B \cap C) = 0 \neq P(B) \cdot P(C)$; dependent

15. a. $\frac{1}{4} \cdot \frac{1}{3} = \frac{1}{12}$ **b.** $\frac{1}{3} \cdot \frac{3}{4} \cdot \left(1 - \frac{1}{4}\right) = \frac{3}{16}$

c. $P(K \cap J \cap \overline{R}) + P(K \cap \overline{J} \cap R) + P(\overline{K} \cap J \cap R) + P(K \cap J \cap R) =$

$\frac{1}{4} \cdot \frac{1}{3} \cdot \left(1 - \frac{3}{4}\right) + \frac{1}{4} \cdot \left(1 - \frac{1}{3}\right) \cdot \frac{3}{4} + \left(1 - \frac{1}{4}\right) \cdot \frac{1}{3} \cdot \frac{3}{4} + \frac{1}{4} \cdot \frac{1}{3} \cdot \frac{3}{4} =$

$\frac{1}{48} + \frac{1}{8} + \frac{9}{48} + \frac{1}{16} = \frac{19}{48}$

d. $P(\text{at least one asks}) = 1 - P(\text{no one asks}) = 1 - \left(1 - \frac{1}{4}\right)\left(1 - \frac{1}{3}\right)\left(1 - \frac{3}{4}\right) =$

$1 - \frac{1}{8} = \frac{7}{8}$

16. a. $P(Y \cap \overline{C}) = (0.65)(1 - 0.40) = 0.39$ **b.** $P(Y \cap C) = (0.65)(0.40) = 0.26$

c. $P(\overline{Y} \cap \overline{C}) = (1 - 0.65)(1 - 0.40) = 0.21$

d. $P(Y \cup C) = 1 - P(\overline{Y} \cap \overline{C}) = 1 - 0.21 = 0.79$

C **17. a.** $P(\text{Winning}) = P(\text{Snow}) \cdot P(\text{winning in snow}) + P(\text{no snow})P(\text{winning in no snow}) = \frac{1}{2} \cdot \frac{2}{5} + \frac{1}{2} \cdot \frac{7}{10} = \frac{11}{20}$

b. $\dfrac{P(\text{snowing and winning})}{P(\text{winning})} = \dfrac{\frac{1}{2} \cdot \frac{2}{5}}{\frac{11}{20}} = \dfrac{4}{11}$

Page 762 • COMPUTER KEY-IN

1. Answers will vary.
2. As the probability of a customer arriving increases, more customers are lost.

Pages 764–765 • CHAPTER REVIEW

1. b

2. c; $M = \dfrac{100 + 79 + 86 + 91}{4} = 89;$

$\frac{1}{4}[(100 - 89)^2 + (79 - 89)^2 + (86 - 89)^2 + (91 - 89)^2] =$

$\frac{1}{4}[11^2 + (-10)^2 + (-3)^2 + 2^2] = \frac{234}{4} = 58.5$

3. d; $2(0.4987) = 0.9974$ **4.** b; $13 = 0.45x - 32; 45 = 0.45x, x = 100$

5. c; one-digit: 3; two-digit: $2 \cdot 3 = 6$; total = 9

6. d; ${}_{12}P_3 = 12 \cdot 11 \cdot 10 = 1320$

7. a; $\dfrac{7!}{3!2!} = 420$

8. c; ${}_9C_5 = \dfrac{9 \cdot 8 \cdot 7 \cdot 6 \cdot 5}{5 \cdot 4 \cdot 3 \cdot 2 \cdot 1} = 126$ **9.** c

10. c; $P(3 \text{ heads}) = \frac{1}{8}$; $P(\text{not all 3 heads}) = 1 - \frac{1}{8} = \frac{7}{8}$ **11.** d

12. d; the events are independent; $\frac{1}{2} \cdot \frac{1}{2} = \frac{1}{4}$

Page 765 • CHAPTER TEST

1.

1	3, 6, 7, 7
2	5, 5, 5, 8
3	1, 2, 3

; mode = 25; median = 25; mean =

$$\frac{13 + 16 + \cdots + 32 + 33}{11} = 23.8 \approx 24$$

2.

10 20 30

variance $= \frac{1}{11}[(13 - 24)^2 + (16 - 24)^2 + \cdots + (33 - 24)^2] =$

$\frac{1}{11}[(-11)^2 + (-8)^2 + 2(-7)^2 + 3(1)^2 + (4)^2 + 7^2 + 8^2 + 9^2] = \frac{496}{11} = 45.09 \approx 45;$

$\sigma = \sqrt{45} \approx 7$

3. $\frac{4}{25}$ **4.**

Demand: 300, 240, 180, 120, 60

Price: 6 12 18 24

high negative

5. one-digit: 4; two-digit: $4 \cdot 4 = 16$; three-digit: $3 \cdot 4 \cdot 4 = 48$; total = 68

6. ${}_5P_5 = 5! = 120$ **7.** $\frac{{}_4P_4}{3!} = \frac{4!}{3!} = 4$ **8.** ${}_8C_4 = \frac{8!}{4!4!} = 70$

9. a. {(1, 1), (2, 2), (3, 3), (4, 4), (5, 5), (6, 6)} **b.** {(1, 3), (2, 2), (3, 1)}

10. a. $\frac{13}{52} = \frac{1}{4}$ **b.** $\frac{4}{52} = \frac{1}{13}$ **c.** $\frac{8}{52} = \frac{2}{13}$

11. a. $P(\text{one red and one not-red}) = \frac{3 \cdot 6}{{}_9C_2} = \frac{18}{36} = \frac{1}{2}$; $P(\text{both red}) = \frac{{}_3C_2}{{}_9C_2} = \frac{3}{36} = \frac{1}{12}$;

$P(A) = \frac{1}{2} + \frac{1}{12} = \frac{7}{12}$; $P(B) = \frac{3 \cdot ({}_3C_2)}{{}_9C_2} = \frac{3 \cdot 3}{36} = \frac{1}{4}$; $P(A \cap B) = \frac{{}_3C_2}{{}_9C_2} = \frac{3}{36} =$

$\frac{1}{12}$; $P(A \cup B) = P(A) + P(B) - P(A \cap B) = \frac{7}{12} + \frac{1}{4} - \frac{1}{12} = \frac{9}{12} = \frac{3}{4}$

b. Not mutually exclusive since $P(A \cap B) = \frac{1}{12} \neq 0$; not independent since

$P(A) \cdot P(B) = \frac{7}{12} \cdot \frac{1}{4} = \frac{7}{48} \neq P(A \cap B)$

CHAPTER 16 • Matrices and Determinants

Page 769 • WRITTEN EXERCISES

A **1.** $[0 \quad 0]$ **2.** $\begin{bmatrix} 0 \\ 0 \\ 0 \end{bmatrix}$ **3.** $\begin{bmatrix} 0 & 0 & 0 & 0 & 0 \\ 0 & 0 & 0 & 0 & 0 \end{bmatrix}$ **4.** $\begin{bmatrix} 0 & 0 & 0 \\ 0 & 0 & 0 \\ 0 & 0 & 0 \\ 0 & 0 & 0 \end{bmatrix}$ **5.** $x = y = z = 0$

6. $x = y = z = 0$ **7.** $x + 4 = 0, x = -4; 5y = 0, y = 0; 10 - z = 0; z = 10$

8. $5 - x = 0, x = 5; y + 6 = 0, y = -6; -3z = 0, z = 0$ **9.** $x = -4; y = 1$

10. $x = 4; y = 2$ **11.** $x = 8; y = -5$ **12.** $x = -1; y = 6; z = 4$

B **13.** $x - 3 = 8, x = 11; y = 12; z + 4 = 0, z = -4$

14. $2x = -6, x = -3; y + 2 = 4, y = 2; z = -1$

15. $\begin{matrix} x + y = 2 \\ x - y = 8 \end{matrix}; 2x = 10, x = 5; 5 - y = 8, y = -3$

16. $8 - y = -3y, 2y = -8, y = -4; \begin{matrix} x + 2z = -5 \\ x + z = -1 \end{matrix}; z = -4; x + (-4) = -1, x = 3$

17. $\begin{matrix} 2x + 3y = 3 \\ x - y = 4 \end{matrix}; \begin{matrix} 2x + 3y = 3 \\ 3x - 3y = 12 \end{matrix}; 5x = 15, x = 3; 2(3) + 3y = 3, 3y = -3, y = -1$

18. $\begin{matrix} 2x - y = 6 \\ 3x + 5y = 22 \end{matrix}; \begin{matrix} 10x - 5y = 30 \\ 3x + 5y = 22 \end{matrix}; 13x = 52, x = 4; 2(4) - y = 6, -y = -2, y = 2$

19. $ax = 1, x = \frac{1}{a}; by = 0, y = \frac{0}{b} = 0$

20. $\begin{matrix} ax + y = 1 \\ bx + y = 0 \end{matrix}; ax - bx = 1; x(a - b) = 1; x = \frac{1}{a - b}, a \neq b; y = 1 - ax =$

$1 - a\left(\frac{1}{a - b}\right), y = \frac{a - b}{a - b} - \frac{a}{a - b}, y = -\frac{b}{a - b}, a \neq b$

21. $ax + b = 1, ax = 1 - b, x = \frac{1 - b}{a}, a \neq 0; cy + d = 0, cy = -d, y = -\frac{d}{c}, c \neq 0$

22. $\begin{matrix} ax + by = 1 \\ cx + dy = 1 \end{matrix}; \begin{matrix} adx + bdy = d \\ bcx + bdy = b \end{matrix}; adx - bcx = d - b; x(ad - bc) = d - b;$

$x = \frac{d - b}{ad - bc}, ad \neq bc; \begin{matrix} acx + bcy = c \\ acx + ady = a \end{matrix}; bcy - ady = c - a; y(bc - ad) = c - a;$

$y = \frac{c - a}{bc - ad} = \frac{a - c}{ad - bc}$

Page 769 • MIXED REVIEW EXERCISES

1. $c^2 = 7^2 + 10^2 - 2(7)(10)\cos 49° = 49 + 100 - 140(0.6561) = 57.15; c = 7.56;$

$\frac{\sin 49°}{7.56} = \frac{\sin A}{7}, \sin A = \frac{7(0.7547)}{7.56} = 0.6988; \angle A = 44.3°;$

$\angle B = 180° - (49° + 44.3°) = 86.7°$

2. $\sin 30° = \frac{b}{8}; \frac{1}{2} = \frac{b}{8}, b = 4; \cos 30° = \frac{a}{8}; \frac{\sqrt{3}}{2} = \frac{a}{8}; a = 4\sqrt{3}; \angle A = 90° - 30° = 60°$

3. Since $a = b$, $\angle A = \angle B = \frac{1}{2}(90°) = 45°$; $c = a\sqrt{2} = \frac{3\sqrt{2}}{2} \cdot \sqrt{2} = 3$

4. $\frac{\sin 72°}{24} = \frac{\sin B}{17}$; $\sin B = \frac{17(0.9511)}{24} = 0.6737$; $\angle B = 42.4°$;

$\angle C = 180° - (42.4° + 72°) = 65.6°$; $\frac{\sin 65.6°}{c} = \frac{\sin 72°}{24}$; $c = \frac{24(0.9107)}{0.9511} = 23.0$

5. $K = \frac{1}{2}(7)(10)\sin 49° = 35(0.7547) = 26.4$ **6.** $K = \frac{1}{2}(4)(4\sqrt{3}) = 8\sqrt{3} = 13.9$

7. $K = \frac{1}{2}\left(\frac{3\sqrt{2}}{2}\right)^2 = \frac{18}{8} = \frac{9}{4} = 2.25$ **8.** $K = \frac{1}{2}(24)(17)\sin 65.6° = 204(0.9107) = 186$

Page 773 • WRITTEN EXERCISES

A

1. $\begin{bmatrix} 4+0 & 1+3 \\ -2+2 & 0+3 \end{bmatrix} = \begin{bmatrix} 4 & 4 \\ 0 & 3 \end{bmatrix}$ **2.** $\begin{bmatrix} 2+(-2) & -3+3 \\ -2+2 & 10+(-8) \end{bmatrix} = \begin{bmatrix} 0 & 0 \\ 0 & 2 \end{bmatrix}$

3. $\begin{bmatrix} 8+3 & 0+4 \\ 4+(-1) & 10+6 \end{bmatrix} = \begin{bmatrix} 11 & 4 \\ 3 & 16 \end{bmatrix}$ **4.** $\begin{bmatrix} -8+4 & 5+(-2) \\ 3+(-2) & 0+9 \end{bmatrix} = \begin{bmatrix} -4 & 3 \\ 1 & 9 \end{bmatrix}$

5. $\begin{bmatrix} 4+0 & 7+(-5) \\ 2+(-2) & -1+(-4) \\ 0+(-3) & 5+2 \end{bmatrix} = \begin{bmatrix} 4 & 2 \\ 0 & -5 \\ -3 & 7 \end{bmatrix}$

6. $\begin{bmatrix} 5+(-5) & 8+(-4) \\ -2+(-4) & 14+2 \\ 0+5 & -6+5 \end{bmatrix} = \begin{bmatrix} 0 & 4 \\ -6 & 16 \\ 5 & -1 \end{bmatrix}$

7. $\begin{bmatrix} 0+(-1) & -2+5 & 4+0 \\ 3+(-3) & -2+2 & -6+6 \end{bmatrix} = \begin{bmatrix} -1 & 3 & 4 \\ 0 & 0 & 0 \end{bmatrix}$

8. $\begin{bmatrix} 4+(-18) & 6+(-3) & -8+(-12) \\ -2+(-1) & 5+0 & 0+(-5) \end{bmatrix} = \begin{bmatrix} -14 & 3 & -20 \\ -3 & 5 & -5 \end{bmatrix}$

9. $\begin{bmatrix} 6(7) & 6(8) \\ 6(-4) & 6(0) \end{bmatrix} = \begin{bmatrix} 42 & 48 \\ -24 & 0 \end{bmatrix}$ **10.** $\begin{bmatrix} 12(3) & 12(0) \\ 12(-5) & 12(2) \end{bmatrix} = \begin{bmatrix} 36 & 0 \\ -60 & 24 \end{bmatrix}$

11. $\begin{bmatrix} 0 & 0 & 0 \\ 0 & 0 & 0 \end{bmatrix} + \begin{bmatrix} 3 & 5 & 2 \\ -2 & 8 & 0 \end{bmatrix} = \begin{bmatrix} 3 & 5 & 2 \\ -2 & 8 & 0 \end{bmatrix}$

12. $\begin{bmatrix} 0 & 0 & 0 \\ 0 & 0 & 0 \end{bmatrix} - \begin{bmatrix} 5(3) & 5(0) & 5(-1) \\ 5(6) & 5(2) & 5(4) \end{bmatrix} = \begin{bmatrix} 0+(-15) & 0+0 & 0+5 \\ 0+(-30) & 0+(-10) & 0+(-20) \end{bmatrix} =$

$\begin{bmatrix} -15 & 0 & 5 \\ -30 & -10 & -20 \end{bmatrix}$

13. $\begin{bmatrix} 2(5) & 2(-2) \\ 2(-3) & 2(4) \\ 2(0) & 2(6) \end{bmatrix} + \begin{bmatrix} 1 & 7 \\ 0 & -4 \\ 6 & 5 \end{bmatrix} = \begin{bmatrix} 10+1 & -4+7 \\ -6+0 & 8+(-4) \\ 0+6 & 12+5 \end{bmatrix} = \begin{bmatrix} 11 & 3 \\ -6 & 4 \\ 6 & 17 \end{bmatrix}$

14. $\begin{bmatrix} 4+(-4) & 2+(-2) \\ 1+(-1) & -3+3 \end{bmatrix} = \begin{bmatrix} 0 & 0 \\ 0 & 0 \end{bmatrix}$

B

15. $\begin{bmatrix} 3(2) \\ 3(2) \\ 3(5) \end{bmatrix} + \begin{bmatrix} 5(0) \\ 5(6) \\ 5(3) \end{bmatrix} = \begin{bmatrix} 6+0 \\ 6+30 \\ 15+15 \end{bmatrix} = \begin{bmatrix} 6 \\ 36 \\ 30 \end{bmatrix}$

16. $\begin{bmatrix} 3 & 0 \\ 5 & -4 \\ 0 & -3 \end{bmatrix} - \begin{bmatrix} 4(10) & 4(-2) \\ 4(2) & 4(4) \\ 4(-7) & 4(0) \end{bmatrix} = \begin{bmatrix} 3 + (-40) & 0 + 8 \\ 5 + (-8) & -4 + (-16) \\ 0 + 28 & -3 + 0 \end{bmatrix} = \begin{bmatrix} -37 & 8 \\ -3 & -20 \\ 28 & -3 \end{bmatrix}$

17. $X + \begin{bmatrix} 3 & 2 \\ 1 & 0 \end{bmatrix} = \begin{bmatrix} 6 & 3 \\ 7 & -1 \end{bmatrix}; X = \begin{bmatrix} 6 & 3 \\ 7 & -1 \end{bmatrix} - \begin{bmatrix} 3 & 2 \\ 1 & 0 \end{bmatrix} = \begin{bmatrix} 3 & 1 \\ 6 & -1 \end{bmatrix}$

18. $X + \begin{bmatrix} 0 & 4 \\ 9 & -1 \end{bmatrix} = \begin{bmatrix} 2 & 0 \\ -1 & 2 \end{bmatrix}; X = \begin{bmatrix} 2 & 0 \\ -1 & 2 \end{bmatrix} - \begin{bmatrix} 0 & 4 \\ 9 & -1 \end{bmatrix} = \begin{bmatrix} 2 & -4 \\ -10 & 3 \end{bmatrix}$

19. $X + 3\begin{bmatrix} -3 & 2 \\ 0 & -1 \end{bmatrix} = \begin{bmatrix} -4 & 10 \\ 12 & 0 \end{bmatrix}; X = \begin{bmatrix} -4 & 10 \\ 12 & 0 \end{bmatrix} - 3\begin{bmatrix} -3 & 2 \\ 0 & -1 \end{bmatrix} =$

$\begin{bmatrix} -4 & 10 \\ 12 & 0 \end{bmatrix} - \begin{bmatrix} -9 & 6 \\ 0 & -3 \end{bmatrix} = \begin{bmatrix} 5 & 4 \\ 12 & 3 \end{bmatrix}$

20. $X - \begin{bmatrix} 0 & 5 \\ 1 & -2 \end{bmatrix} = 3\begin{bmatrix} 2 & -3 \\ 3 & 1 \end{bmatrix}; X = 3\begin{bmatrix} 2 & -3 \\ 3 & 1 \end{bmatrix} + \begin{bmatrix} 0 & 5 \\ 1 & -2 \end{bmatrix} = \begin{bmatrix} 6 & -9 \\ 9 & 3 \end{bmatrix} +$

$\begin{bmatrix} 0 & 5 \\ 1 & -2 \end{bmatrix} = \begin{bmatrix} 6 & -4 \\ 10 & 1 \end{bmatrix}$

C **21–28.** Let $A = \begin{bmatrix} a & b \\ c & d \end{bmatrix}$, $B = \begin{bmatrix} e & f \\ g & h \end{bmatrix}$, and $C = \begin{bmatrix} j & k \\ l & m \end{bmatrix}$.

21. $A + B = \begin{bmatrix} a + e & b + f \\ c + g & d + h \end{bmatrix} = \begin{bmatrix} e + a & f + b \\ g + c & h + d \end{bmatrix} = B + A$

22. $(A + B) + C = \begin{bmatrix} a + e & b + f \\ c + g & d + h \end{bmatrix} + \begin{bmatrix} j & k \\ l & m \end{bmatrix} = \begin{bmatrix} (a + e) + j & (b + f) + k \\ (c + g) + l & (d + h) + m \end{bmatrix} =$

$\begin{bmatrix} a + (e + j) & b + (f + k) \\ c + (g + l) & d + (h + m) \end{bmatrix} = \begin{bmatrix} a & b \\ c & d \end{bmatrix} + \begin{bmatrix} e + j & f + k \\ g + l & h + m \end{bmatrix} = A + (B + C)$

23. $(-1)A = (-1)\begin{bmatrix} a & b \\ c & d \end{bmatrix} = \begin{bmatrix} -1(a) & -1(b) \\ -1(c) & -1(d) \end{bmatrix} = \begin{bmatrix} -a & -b \\ -c & -d \end{bmatrix} = -A$

24. $pA = p\begin{bmatrix} a & b \\ c & d \end{bmatrix} = \begin{bmatrix} pa & pb \\ pc & pd \end{bmatrix} = \begin{bmatrix} ap & bp \\ cp & dp \end{bmatrix} = \begin{bmatrix} a & b \\ c & d \end{bmatrix}p = Ap$

25. $pA + qA = \begin{bmatrix} pa & pb \\ pc & pd \end{bmatrix} + \begin{bmatrix} qa & qb \\ qc & qd \end{bmatrix} = \begin{bmatrix} pa + qa & pb + qb \\ pc + qc & pd + qd \end{bmatrix} =$

$\begin{bmatrix} (p + q)a & (p + q)b \\ (p + q)c & (p + q)d \end{bmatrix} = (p + q)A$

26. $(pq)B = (pq)\begin{bmatrix} e & f \\ g & h \end{bmatrix} = \begin{bmatrix} (pq)e & (pq)f \\ (pq)g & (pq)h \end{bmatrix} = \begin{bmatrix} p(qe) & p(qf) \\ p(qg) & p(qh) \end{bmatrix} = p\begin{bmatrix} qe & qf \\ qg & qh \end{bmatrix} = p(qB)$

27. $p \cdot O_{2\times2} = p\begin{bmatrix} 0 & 0 \\ 0 & 0 \end{bmatrix} = \begin{bmatrix} p(0) & p(0) \\ p(0) & p(0) \end{bmatrix} = \begin{bmatrix} 0 & 0 \\ 0 & 0 \end{bmatrix} = O_{2\times2}$

28. $0 \cdot A = 0 \cdot \begin{bmatrix} a & b \\ c & d \end{bmatrix} = \begin{bmatrix} 0(a) & 0(b) \\ 0(c) & 0(d) \end{bmatrix} = \begin{bmatrix} 0 & 0 \\ 0 & 0 \end{bmatrix} = O_{2\times2}$

Pages 777–778 • WRITTEN EXERCISES

A **1.** $\begin{bmatrix} 3 & 1 \end{bmatrix}\begin{bmatrix} 4 \\ 6 \end{bmatrix} = [12 + 6] = [18]$ **2.** $\begin{bmatrix} 0 & -3 & 4 \end{bmatrix}\begin{bmatrix} 1 \\ 0 \\ -4 \end{bmatrix} = [0 + 0 + (-16)] = [-16]$

3. $\begin{bmatrix} 4 \\ -2 \end{bmatrix}\begin{bmatrix} 3 & 0 & -1 & 5 \end{bmatrix} = \begin{bmatrix} 12 & 0 & -4 & 20 \\ -6 & 0 & 2 & -10 \end{bmatrix}$

4. $\begin{bmatrix} 0 & 3 \\ 5 & -1 \end{bmatrix}\begin{bmatrix} -1 \\ 3 \end{bmatrix} = \begin{bmatrix} 0 + 9 \\ -5 + (-3) \end{bmatrix} = \begin{bmatrix} 9 \\ -8 \end{bmatrix}$

5. $\begin{bmatrix} 3 & 0 \\ 1 & 2 \end{bmatrix}\begin{bmatrix} -1 & 8 \\ 0 & 3 \end{bmatrix} = \begin{bmatrix} -3 + 0 & 24 + 0 \\ -1 + 0 & 8 + 6 \end{bmatrix} = \begin{bmatrix} -3 & 24 \\ -1 & 14 \end{bmatrix}$

6. $\begin{bmatrix} 0 & 8 \\ 3 & 1 \\ -1 & 5 \end{bmatrix}\begin{bmatrix} 3 & 1 & -2 \\ 0 & 8 & -5 \end{bmatrix} = \begin{bmatrix} 0 + 0 & 0 + 64 & 0 + (-40) \\ 9 + 0 & 3 + 8 & -6 + (-5) \\ -3 + 0 & -1 + 40 & 2 + (-25) \end{bmatrix} = \begin{bmatrix} 0 & 64 & -40 \\ 9 & 11 & -11 \\ -3 & 39 & -23 \end{bmatrix}$

7. $\begin{bmatrix} 0 & 2 & -1 \\ 4 & 1 & 0 \\ 0 & -1 & 2 \end{bmatrix}\begin{bmatrix} 4 & 3 & 0 \\ -1 & 0 & 2 \\ 1 & 0 & -2 \end{bmatrix} = \begin{bmatrix} 0 - 2 - 1 & 0 + 0 + 0 & 0 + 4 + 2 \\ 16 - 1 + 0 & 12 + 0 + 0 & 0 + 2 + 0 \\ 0 + 1 + 2 & 0 + 0 + 0 & 0 - 2 - 4 \end{bmatrix} =$

$\begin{bmatrix} -3 & 0 & 6 \\ 15 & 12 & 2 \\ 3 & 0 & -6 \end{bmatrix}$

8. $\begin{bmatrix} 1 & 0 & 0 \\ 2 & 0 & -1 \\ 0 & 1 & 0 \end{bmatrix}\begin{bmatrix} 1 & 0 & 2 \\ 0 & -3 & 1 \\ 0 & 1 & 0 \end{bmatrix} = \begin{bmatrix} 1 + 0 + 0 & 0 + 0 + 0 & 2 + 0 + 0 \\ 2 + 0 + 0 & 0 + 0 - 1 & 4 + 0 + 0 \\ 0 + 0 + 0 & 0 - 3 + 0 & 0 + 1 + 0 \end{bmatrix} = \begin{bmatrix} 1 & 0 & 2 \\ 2 & -1 & 4 \\ 0 & -3 & 1 \end{bmatrix}$

9. $\begin{bmatrix} 1 & 2 \\ 3 & -1 \\ 0 & 4 \end{bmatrix}\begin{bmatrix} 1 & 0 & 0 & -1 \\ -1 & 1 & 1 & 0 \end{bmatrix} = \begin{bmatrix} 1 - 2 & 0 + 2 & 0 + 2 & -1 + 0 \\ 3 + 1 & 0 - 1 & 0 - 1 & -3 + 0 \\ 0 - 4 & 0 + 4 & 0 + 4 & 0 + 0 \end{bmatrix} =$

$\begin{bmatrix} -1 & 2 & 2 & -1 \\ 4 & -1 & -1 & -3 \\ -4 & 4 & 4 & 0 \end{bmatrix}$

10. $\begin{bmatrix} 0 & 2 & 0 \\ 0 & 1 & 1 \\ 1 & -1 & 0 \end{bmatrix}\begin{bmatrix} 1 & 1 & 0 \\ 0 & 1 & 0 \\ -1 & 0 & 1 \end{bmatrix} = \begin{bmatrix} 0 + 0 + 0 & 0 + 2 + 0 & 0 + 0 + 0 \\ 0 + 0 - 1 & 0 + 1 + 0 & 0 + 0 + 1 \\ 1 + 0 + 0 & 1 - 1 + 0 & 0 + 0 + 0 \end{bmatrix} = \begin{bmatrix} 0 & 2 & 0 \\ -1 & 1 & 1 \\ 1 & 0 & 0 \end{bmatrix}$

11. $\begin{bmatrix} 1 & 0 & 2 \\ -2 & 1 & 0 \\ 0 & 1 & 0 \end{bmatrix}\begin{bmatrix} a & b & c \\ d & e & f \\ g & h & i \end{bmatrix} = \begin{bmatrix} 1a + 0d + 2g & 1b + 0e + 2h & 1c + 0f + 2i \\ -2a + 1d + 0g & -2b + 1e + 0h & -2c + 1f + 0i \\ 0a + 1d + 0g & 0b + 1e + 0h & 0c + 1f + 0i \end{bmatrix} =$

$\begin{bmatrix} a + 2g & b + 2h & c + 2i \\ -2a + d & -2b + e & -2c + f \\ d & e & f \end{bmatrix}$

12. $\begin{bmatrix} 2 & 0 & 1 \\ 5 & -1 & 0 \\ 0 & -2 & 4 \end{bmatrix}\begin{bmatrix} r & s & t \\ u & v & w \\ x & y & z \end{bmatrix} = \begin{bmatrix} 2r + 0u + 1x & 2s + 0v + 1y & 2t + 0w + 1z \\ 5r - 1u + 0x & 5s - 1v + 0y & 5t - 1w + 0z \\ 0r - 2u + 4x & 0s - 2v + 4y & 0t - 2w + 4z \end{bmatrix} =$

$\begin{bmatrix} 2r + x & 2s + y & 2t + z \\ 5r - u & 5s - v & 5t - w \\ -2u + 4x & -2v + 4y & -2w + 4z \end{bmatrix}$

B

13. $AB = \begin{bmatrix} 1 & 2 \\ 0 & -1 \end{bmatrix}\begin{bmatrix} 0 & -1 \\ 1 & 1 \end{bmatrix} = \begin{bmatrix} 0+2 & -1+2 \\ 0-1 & 0-1 \end{bmatrix} = \begin{bmatrix} 2 & 1 \\ -1 & -1 \end{bmatrix}$;

$BA = \begin{bmatrix} 0 & -1 \\ 1 & 1 \end{bmatrix}\begin{bmatrix} 1 & 2 \\ 0 & -1 \end{bmatrix} = \begin{bmatrix} 0+0 & 0+1 \\ 1+0 & 2-1 \end{bmatrix} = \begin{bmatrix} 0 & 1 \\ 1 & 1 \end{bmatrix}$

14. $BC = \begin{bmatrix} 0 & -1 \\ 1 & 1 \end{bmatrix}\begin{bmatrix} -2 & 0 \\ 0 & 1 \end{bmatrix} = \begin{bmatrix} 0+0 & 0-1 \\ -2+0 & 0+1 \end{bmatrix} = \begin{bmatrix} 0 & -1 \\ -2 & 1 \end{bmatrix}$;

$CB = \begin{bmatrix} -2 & 0 \\ 0 & 1 \end{bmatrix}\begin{bmatrix} 0 & -1 \\ 1 & 1 \end{bmatrix} = \begin{bmatrix} 0+0 & 2+0 \\ 0+1 & 0+1 \end{bmatrix} = \begin{bmatrix} 0 & 2 \\ 1 & 1 \end{bmatrix}$

15. By Exercise 13, $(AB)C = \begin{bmatrix} 2 & 1 \\ -1 & -1 \end{bmatrix}\begin{bmatrix} -2 & 0 \\ 0 & 1 \end{bmatrix} = \begin{bmatrix} -4+0 & 0+1 \\ 2+0 & 0-1 \end{bmatrix} = \begin{bmatrix} -4 & 1 \\ 2 & -1 \end{bmatrix}$; by Exercise 14, $A(BC) = \begin{bmatrix} 1 & 2 \\ 0 & -1 \end{bmatrix}\begin{bmatrix} 0 & -1 \\ -2 & 1 \end{bmatrix} = \begin{bmatrix} 0-4 & -1+2 \\ 0+2 & 0-1 \end{bmatrix} = \begin{bmatrix} -4 & 1 \\ 2 & -1 \end{bmatrix}$

16. $AC + BC = \begin{bmatrix} 1 & 2 \\ 0 & -1 \end{bmatrix}\begin{bmatrix} -2 & 0 \\ 0 & 1 \end{bmatrix} + \begin{bmatrix} 0 & -1 \\ 1 & 1 \end{bmatrix}\begin{bmatrix} -2 & 0 \\ 0 & 1 \end{bmatrix} = \begin{bmatrix} -2 & 2 \\ 0 & -1 \end{bmatrix} + \begin{bmatrix} 0 & -1 \\ -2 & 1 \end{bmatrix} = \begin{bmatrix} -2 & 1 \\ -2 & 0 \end{bmatrix}$; $(A+B)C = \left(\begin{bmatrix} 1 & 2 \\ 0 & -1 \end{bmatrix} + \begin{bmatrix} 0 & -1 \\ 1 & 1 \end{bmatrix}\right)\begin{bmatrix} -2 & 0 \\ 0 & 1 \end{bmatrix} = \begin{bmatrix} 1 & 1 \\ 1 & 0 \end{bmatrix}\begin{bmatrix} -2 & 0 \\ 0 & 1 \end{bmatrix} = \begin{bmatrix} -2 & 1 \\ -2 & 0 \end{bmatrix}$

17. By Exercise 16, $A + B = \begin{bmatrix} 1 & 1 \\ 1 & 0 \end{bmatrix}$; $A - B = \begin{bmatrix} 1 & 2 \\ 0 & -1 \end{bmatrix} - \begin{bmatrix} 0 & -1 \\ 1 & 1 \end{bmatrix} = \begin{bmatrix} 1 & 3 \\ -1 & -2 \end{bmatrix}$;

$(A+B)(A-B) = \begin{bmatrix} 1 & 1 \\ 1 & 0 \end{bmatrix}\begin{bmatrix} 1 & 3 \\ -1 & -2 \end{bmatrix} = \begin{bmatrix} 0 & 1 \\ 1 & 3 \end{bmatrix}$; $A^2 = \begin{bmatrix} 1 & 2 \\ 0 & -1 \end{bmatrix}\begin{bmatrix} 1 & 2 \\ 0 & -1 \end{bmatrix} = \begin{bmatrix} 1 & 0 \\ 0 & 1 \end{bmatrix}$;

$B^2 = \begin{bmatrix} 0 & -1 \\ 1 & 1 \end{bmatrix}\begin{bmatrix} 0 & -1 \\ 1 & 1 \end{bmatrix} = \begin{bmatrix} -1 & -1 \\ 1 & 0 \end{bmatrix}$; $A^2 - B^2 = \begin{bmatrix} 1 & 0 \\ 0 & 1 \end{bmatrix} - \begin{bmatrix} -1 & -1 \\ 1 & 0 \end{bmatrix} = \begin{bmatrix} 2 & 1 \\ -1 & 1 \end{bmatrix}$

18. By Exercises 13, 16 and 17, $A + B = \begin{bmatrix} 1 & 1 \\ 1 & 0 \end{bmatrix}$, $A^2 = \begin{bmatrix} 1 & 0 \\ 0 & 1 \end{bmatrix}$, $B^2 = \begin{bmatrix} -1 & -1 \\ 1 & 0 \end{bmatrix}$, and

$AB = \begin{bmatrix} 2 & 1 \\ -1 & -1 \end{bmatrix}$; $(A+B)^2 = \begin{bmatrix} 1 & 1 \\ 1 & 0 \end{bmatrix}\begin{bmatrix} 1 & 1 \\ 1 & 0 \end{bmatrix} = \begin{bmatrix} 2 & 1 \\ 1 & 1 \end{bmatrix}$; $A^2 + 2AB + B^2 =$

$\begin{bmatrix} 1 & 0 \\ 0 & 1 \end{bmatrix} + 2\begin{bmatrix} 2 & 1 \\ -1 & -1 \end{bmatrix} + \begin{bmatrix} -1 & -1 \\ 1 & 0 \end{bmatrix} = \begin{bmatrix} 1 & 0 \\ 0 & 1 \end{bmatrix} + \begin{bmatrix} 4 & 2 \\ -2 & -2 \end{bmatrix} + \begin{bmatrix} -1 & -1 \\ 1 & 0 \end{bmatrix} = \begin{bmatrix} 4 & 1 \\ -1 & -1 \end{bmatrix}$

19. $O_{2\times 2} \cdot A = \begin{bmatrix} 0 & 0 \\ 0 & 0 \end{bmatrix}\begin{bmatrix} 1 & 2 \\ 0 & -1 \end{bmatrix} = \begin{bmatrix} 0 & 0 \\ 0 & 0 \end{bmatrix}$; $A \cdot O_{2\times 2} = \begin{bmatrix} 1 & 2 \\ 0 & -1 \end{bmatrix}\begin{bmatrix} 0 & 0 \\ 0 & 0 \end{bmatrix} = \begin{bmatrix} 0 & 0 \\ 0 & 0 \end{bmatrix}$

20. $I_{2\times 2} \cdot C = \begin{bmatrix} 1 & 0 \\ 0 & 1 \end{bmatrix}\begin{bmatrix} -2 & 0 \\ 0 & 1 \end{bmatrix} = \begin{bmatrix} -2 & 0 \\ 0 & 1 \end{bmatrix}$; $C \cdot I_{2\times 2} = \begin{bmatrix} -2 & 0 \\ 0 & 1 \end{bmatrix}\begin{bmatrix} 1 & 0 \\ 0 & 1 \end{bmatrix} = \begin{bmatrix} -2 & 0 \\ 0 & 1 \end{bmatrix}$

21. $AB = \begin{bmatrix} 2 & -3 \\ 2 & 1 \end{bmatrix} \begin{matrix} \frac{1}{8} & \frac{3}{8} \\ -\frac{1}{4} & \frac{1}{4} \end{matrix} = \begin{bmatrix} 1 & 0 \\ 0 & 1 \end{bmatrix}$ **22.** $BA = \begin{matrix} \frac{1}{8} & \frac{3}{8} \\ -\frac{1}{4} & \frac{1}{4} \end{matrix} \begin{bmatrix} 2 & -3 \\ 2 & 1 \end{bmatrix} = \begin{bmatrix} 1 & 0 \\ 0 & 1 \end{bmatrix}$

23. $D^2 = \begin{bmatrix} 1 & 0 & -1 \\ 0 & 2 & -1 \\ 1 & 0 & 0 \end{bmatrix}\begin{bmatrix} 1 & 0 & -1 \\ 0 & 2 & -1 \\ 1 & 0 & 0 \end{bmatrix} = \begin{bmatrix} 0 & 0 & -1 \\ -1 & 4 & -2 \\ 1 & 0 & -1 \end{bmatrix}$

24. By Exercise 23, $D^3 = D \cdot D^2 = \begin{bmatrix} 1 & 0 & -1 \\ 0 & 2 & -1 \\ 1 & 0 & 0 \end{bmatrix}\begin{bmatrix} 0 & 0 & -1 \\ -1 & 4 & -2 \\ 1 & 0 & -1 \end{bmatrix} = \begin{bmatrix} -1 & 0 & 0 \\ -3 & 8 & -3 \\ 0 & 0 & -1 \end{bmatrix}$

25. $-D = \begin{bmatrix} -1 & 0 & 1 \\ 0 & -2 & 1 \\ -1 & 0 & 0 \end{bmatrix}$; $(-D)^2 = \begin{bmatrix} -1 & 0 & 1 \\ 0 & -2 & 1 \\ -1 & 0 & 0 \end{bmatrix}\begin{bmatrix} -1 & 0 & 1 \\ 0 & -2 & 1 \\ -1 & 0 & 0 \end{bmatrix} = \begin{bmatrix} 0 & 0 & -1 \\ -1 & 4 & -2 \\ 1 & 0 & -1 \end{bmatrix}$;

26. By Exercise 25, $(-D)^3 = (-D)(-D)^2 = \begin{bmatrix} -1 & 0 & 1 \\ 0 & -2 & 1 \\ -1 & 0 & 0 \end{bmatrix}\begin{bmatrix} 0 & 0 & -1 \\ -1 & 4 & -2 \\ 1 & 0 & -1 \end{bmatrix} = \begin{bmatrix} 1 & 0 & 0 \\ 3 & -8 & 3 \\ 0 & 0 & 1 \end{bmatrix}$

C **27–30.** Let $A = \begin{bmatrix} a & b \\ c & d \end{bmatrix}$, $B = \begin{bmatrix} e & f \\ g & h \end{bmatrix}$, and $C = \begin{bmatrix} i & j \\ k & l \end{bmatrix}$

27. $A \cdot I_{2\times2} = \begin{bmatrix} a & b \\ c & d \end{bmatrix}\begin{bmatrix} 1 & 0 \\ 0 & 1 \end{bmatrix} = \begin{bmatrix} a & b \\ c & d \end{bmatrix} = A$; $I_{2\times2} \cdot A = \begin{bmatrix} 1 & 0 \\ 0 & 1 \end{bmatrix}\begin{bmatrix} a & b \\ c & d \end{bmatrix} = \begin{bmatrix} a & b \\ c & d \end{bmatrix} = A$

28. $A \cdot O_{2\times2} = \begin{bmatrix} a & b \\ c & d \end{bmatrix}\begin{bmatrix} 0 & 0 \\ 0 & 0 \end{bmatrix} = \begin{bmatrix} 0 & 0 \\ 0 & 0 \end{bmatrix} = O_{2\times2}$; $O_{2\times2} \cdot A = \begin{bmatrix} 0 & 0 \\ 0 & 0 \end{bmatrix}\begin{bmatrix} a & b \\ c & d \end{bmatrix} =$

$\begin{bmatrix} 0 & 0 \\ 0 & 0 \end{bmatrix} = O_{2\times2}$

29. $(AB)C = \left(\begin{bmatrix} a & b \\ c & d \end{bmatrix}\begin{bmatrix} e & f \\ g & h \end{bmatrix}\right)\begin{bmatrix} i & j \\ k & l \end{bmatrix} = \begin{bmatrix} ae + bg & af + bh \\ ce + dg & cf + dh \end{bmatrix}\begin{bmatrix} i & j \\ k & l \end{bmatrix} =$

$\begin{bmatrix} aei + bgi + afk + bhk & aej + bgj + afl + bhl \\ cei + dgi + cfk + dhk & cej + dgj + cfl + dhl \end{bmatrix} =$

$\begin{bmatrix} a(ei + fk) + b(gi + hk) & a(ej + fl) + b(gj + hl) \\ c(ei + fk) + d(gi + hk) & c(ej + fl) + d(gj + hl) \end{bmatrix}$;

$A(BC) = \begin{bmatrix} a & b \\ c & d \end{bmatrix}\left(\begin{bmatrix} e & f \\ g & h \end{bmatrix}\begin{bmatrix} i & j \\ k & l \end{bmatrix}\right) = \begin{bmatrix} a & b \\ c & d \end{bmatrix}\begin{bmatrix} ei + fk & ej + fl \\ gi + hk & gj + hl \end{bmatrix} =$

$\begin{bmatrix} a(ei + fk) + b(gi + hk) & a(ej + fl) + b(gj + hl) \\ c(ei + fk) + d(gi + hk) & c(ej + fl) + d(gj + hl) \end{bmatrix} = (AB)C$

30. $A(B + C) = \begin{bmatrix} a & b \\ c & d \end{bmatrix}\left(\begin{bmatrix} e & f \\ g & h \end{bmatrix} + \begin{bmatrix} i & j \\ k & l \end{bmatrix}\right) = \begin{bmatrix} a & b \\ c & d \end{bmatrix}\begin{bmatrix} e + i & f + j \\ g + k & h + l \end{bmatrix} =$

$\begin{bmatrix} a(e + i) + b(g + k) & a(f + j) + b(h + l) \\ c(e + i) + d(g + k) & c(f + j) + d(h + l) \end{bmatrix}$;

$AB + AC = \begin{bmatrix} a & b \\ c & d \end{bmatrix}\begin{bmatrix} e & f \\ g & h \end{bmatrix} + \begin{bmatrix} a & b \\ c & d \end{bmatrix}\begin{bmatrix} i & j \\ k & l \end{bmatrix} =$

$\begin{bmatrix} ae + bg & af + bh \\ ce + dg & cf + dh \end{bmatrix} + \begin{bmatrix} ai + bk & aj + bl \\ ci + dk & cj + dl \end{bmatrix} =$

$\begin{bmatrix} ae + bg + ai + bk & af + bh + aj + bl \\ ce + dg + ci + dk & cf + dh + cj + dl \end{bmatrix} =$

$\begin{bmatrix} a(e + i) + b(g + k) & a(f + j) + b(h + l) \\ c(e + i) + d(g + k) & c(f + j) + d(h + l) \end{bmatrix} = A(B + C)$

Page 778 • MIXED REVIEW EXERCISES

1. $\begin{matrix} 2x^2 + y^2 = 5 \\ x^2 = 1 - y^2 \end{matrix}$; $2(1 - y^2) + y^2 = 5$, $2 - 2y^2 + y^2 = 5$, $y^2 = -3$; no real solutions

2. $\begin{matrix} 3s + 4t = 2 \\ s - 2t = 4 \end{matrix}$; $s = 4 + 2t$; $3(4 + 2t) + 4t = 2$, $12 + 6t + 4t = 2$, $10t = -10$, $t = -1$; $s = 4 + 2(-1) = 2$; $(2, -1)$

3. $\begin{matrix} y^2 - x^2 = 24 \\ 2x - 3 = y \end{matrix}$; $(2x - 3)^2 - x^2 = 24$, $4x^2 - 12x + 9 - x^2 = 24$, $3x^2 - 12x - 15 = 0$, $x^2 - 4x - 5 = 0$, $(x - 5)(x + 1) = 0$, $x = 5$ or $x = -1$; if $x = 5$, $y = 2(5) - 3 = 7$; if $x = -1$, $y = 2(-1) - 3 = -5$; $(-1, -5)$, $(5, 7)$

4. $\begin{matrix} 4m + 2n = -8 \\ 3m - n = -11 \end{matrix}$, $\begin{matrix} 4m + 2n = -8 \\ 6m - 2n = -22 \end{matrix}$; $10m = -30$, $m = -3$; $3(-3) - n = -11$; $-n = -2$, $n = 2$; $(-3, 2)$

5. $\begin{matrix} xy - 15 = 0 \\ y^2 - x^2 = -16 \end{matrix}$; $x = \frac{15}{y}$; $y^2 - \left(\frac{15}{y}\right)^2 = -16$, $y^2 - \frac{225}{y^2} = -16$, $y^4 - 225 = -16y^2$, $y^4 + 16y^2 - 225 = 0$, $(y^2 + 25)(y^2 - 9) = 0$; $y^2 = -25$ (reject), or $y^2 = 9$; $y = 3$ or $y = -3$; if $y = 3$, $x = \frac{15}{3} = 5$; if $y = -3$, $x = \frac{15}{-3} = -5$; $(5, 3)$, $(-5, -3)$

6. $\begin{matrix} a + b - c = -2 \\ 2a - b + c = 5 \\ a + 3b + 2c = 2 \end{matrix}$; $\begin{matrix} a + b - c = -2 \\ 3a = 3 \\ 3a + 5b = -2 \end{matrix}$; $a = 1$; $3 + 5b = -2$, $5b = -5$, $b = -1$; $1 - 1 - c = -2$, $-c = -2$, $c = 2$; $(1, -1, 2)$

7. $\sqrt{2x + 3} = x$, $2x + 3 = x^2$, $x^2 - 2x - 3 = 0$, $(x - 3)(x + 1) = 0$, $x = 3$ or $x = -1$ (reject); $\{3\}$

8. $\frac{m^2 + 2m}{3} = \frac{1 - m}{2}$, $2m^2 + 4m = 3 - 3m$, $2m^2 + 7m - 3 = 0$, $m = \frac{-7 \pm \sqrt{49 + 24}}{2(2)} = \frac{-7 \pm \sqrt{73}}{4}$; $\left\{\frac{-7 \pm \sqrt{73}}{4}\right\}$

9. $3x + 8 = 3 - 2x$, $5x = -5$, $x = -1$; $\{-1\}$

Pages 782–784 • WRITTEN EXERCISES

A 1.

To Station

$$\text{From Station } \begin{matrix} A \\ B \\ C \end{matrix} \overset{\begin{matrix} A & B & C \end{matrix}}{\begin{bmatrix} 0 & 1 & 1 \\ 1 & 0 & 0 \\ 1 & 1 & 0 \end{bmatrix}} = M$$

2. $M^2 = \begin{bmatrix} 0 & 1 & 1 \\ 1 & 0 & 0 \\ 1 & 1 & 0 \end{bmatrix} \begin{bmatrix} 0 & 1 & 1 \\ 1 & 0 & 0 \\ 1 & 1 & 0 \end{bmatrix} = \begin{bmatrix} 2 & 1 & 0 \\ 0 & 1 & 1 \\ 1 & 1 & 1 \end{bmatrix}$

3. $M + M^2 = \begin{bmatrix} 0 & 1 & 1 \\ 1 & 0 & 0 \\ 1 & 1 & 0 \end{bmatrix} + \begin{bmatrix} 2 & 1 & 0 \\ 0 & 1 & 1 \\ 1 & 1 & 1 \end{bmatrix} = \begin{bmatrix} 2 & 2 & 1 \\ 1 & 1 & 1 \\ 2 & 2 & 1 \end{bmatrix}$

4. B A C D E

5.

$$\text{From}\ \begin{matrix} & \text{To} \\ & \begin{matrix} A & B & C & D & E \end{matrix} \\ \begin{matrix} A \\ B \\ C \\ D \\ E \end{matrix} & \begin{bmatrix} 0 & 1 & 0 & 0 & 0 \\ 1 & 0 & 1 & 1 & 0 \\ 0 & 1 & 0 & 0 & 1 \\ 0 & 1 & 0 & 0 & 1 \\ 0 & 0 & 0 & 0 & 0 \end{bmatrix} \end{matrix} = A$$

6. E **7.**

$$A^2 = \begin{bmatrix} 0 & 1 & 0 & 0 & 0 \\ 1 & 0 & 1 & 1 & 0 \\ 0 & 1 & 0 & 0 & 1 \\ 0 & 1 & 0 & 0 & 1 \\ 0 & 0 & 0 & 0 & 0 \end{bmatrix} \begin{bmatrix} 0 & 1 & 0 & 0 & 0 \\ 1 & 0 & 1 & 1 & 0 \\ 0 & 1 & 0 & 0 & 1 \\ 0 & 1 & 0 & 0 & 1 \\ 0 & 0 & 0 & 0 & 0 \end{bmatrix} = \begin{bmatrix} 1 & 0 & 1 & 1 & 0 \\ 0 & 3 & 0 & 0 & 2 \\ 1 & 0 & 1 & 1 & 0 \\ 1 & 0 & 1 & 1 & 0 \\ 0 & 0 & 0 & 0 & 0 \end{bmatrix}$$

8. A, B, C, and D **9.** B **10.** $A + A^2 = \begin{bmatrix} 1 & 1 & 1 & 1 & 0 \\ 1 & 3 & 1 & 1 & 2 \\ 1 & 1 & 1 & 1 & 1 \\ 1 & 1 & 1 & 1 & 1 \\ 0 & 0 & 0 & 0 & 0 \end{bmatrix}$

B **11.**

$$\begin{matrix} & \begin{matrix} \text{Anna} & \text{Cindy} & \text{Jane} & \text{Yoko} \end{matrix} \\ \begin{matrix} \text{Anna} \\ \text{Cindy} \\ \text{Jane} \\ \text{Yoko} \end{matrix} & \begin{bmatrix} 0 & 0 & 1 & 0 \\ 1 & 0 & 0 & 1 \\ 0 & 1 & 0 & 0 \\ 1 & 0 & 1 & 0 \end{bmatrix} \end{matrix} = M;\ M^2 = \begin{bmatrix} 0 & 0 & 1 & 0 \\ 1 & 0 & 0 & 1 \\ 0 & 1 & 0 & 0 \\ 1 & 0 & 1 & 0 \end{bmatrix} \begin{bmatrix} 0 & 0 & 1 & 0 \\ 1 & 0 & 0 & 1 \\ 0 & 1 & 0 & 0 \\ 1 & 0 & 1 & 0 \end{bmatrix} =$$

$$\begin{bmatrix} 0 & 1 & 0 & 0 \\ 1 & 0 & 2 & 0 \\ 1 & 0 & 0 & 1 \\ 0 & 1 & 1 & 0 \end{bmatrix}$$

12. $M + M^2 = \begin{bmatrix} 0 & 1 & 1 & 0 \\ 2 & 0 & 2 & 1 \\ 1 & 1 & 0 & 1 \\ 1 & 1 & 2 & 0 \end{bmatrix}$; Cindy wins

13.

$$\text{From}\ \begin{matrix} & \text{To} \\ & \begin{matrix} A & B & C & D \end{matrix} \\ \begin{matrix} A \\ B \\ C \\ D \end{matrix} & \begin{bmatrix} 0 & 1 & 0 & 1 \\ 1 & 0 & 0 & 0 \\ 0 & 1 & 0 & 1 \\ 1 & 0 & 0 & 0 \end{bmatrix} \end{matrix} = M;\ M^2 = \begin{bmatrix} 2 & 0 & 0 & 0 \\ 0 & 1 & 0 & 1 \\ 2 & 0 & 0 & 0 \\ 0 & 1 & 0 & 1 \end{bmatrix}$$

14. $M + M^2 = \begin{bmatrix} 2 & 1 & 0 & 1 \\ 1 & 1 & 0 & 1 \\ 2 & 1 & 0 & 1 \\ 1 & 1 & 0 & 1 \end{bmatrix}$

15. $M^3 = \begin{bmatrix} 0 & 1 & 0 & 1 \\ 1 & 0 & 0 & 0 \\ 0 & 1 & 0 & 1 \\ 1 & 0 & 0 & 0 \end{bmatrix} \begin{bmatrix} 2 & 0 & 0 & 0 \\ 0 & 1 & 0 & 1 \\ 2 & 0 & 0 & 0 \\ 0 & 1 & 0 & 1 \end{bmatrix} = \begin{bmatrix} 0 & 2 & 0 & 2 \\ 2 & 0 & 0 & 0 \\ 0 & 2 & 0 & 2 \\ 2 & 0 & 0 & 0 \end{bmatrix}$

16. $M + M^2 + M^3 = \begin{bmatrix} 2 & 3 & 0 & 3 \\ 3 & 1 & 0 & 1 \\ 2 & 3 & 0 & 3 \\ 3 & 1 & 0 & 1 \end{bmatrix}$

17.

$$\text{From}\ \begin{array}{c} \\ A\\ B\\ C\\ D\\ E \end{array}\!\!\begin{array}{c} \text{To} \\ \begin{array}{ccccc} A & B & C & D & E \end{array} \\ \begin{bmatrix} 0 & 1 & 0 & 0 & 0\\ 1 & 0 & 1 & 0 & 0\\ 1 & 0 & 0 & 1 & 0\\ 1 & 0 & 0 & 0 & 1\\ 1 & 1 & 1 & 1 & 0 \end{bmatrix}\end{array} = A;\ A + A^2 + A^3 = \begin{bmatrix} 0 & 1 & 0 & 0 & 0\\ 1 & 0 & 1 & 0 & 0\\ 1 & 0 & 0 & 1 & 0\\ 1 & 0 & 0 & 0 & 1\\ 1 & 1 & 1 & 1 & 0 \end{bmatrix} +$$

$$\begin{bmatrix} 1 & 0 & 1 & 0 & 0\\ 1 & 1 & 0 & 1 & 0\\ 1 & 1 & 0 & 0 & 1\\ 1 & 2 & 1 & 1 & 0\\ 3 & 1 & 1 & 1 & 1 \end{bmatrix} + \begin{bmatrix} 1 & 1 & 0 & 1 & 0\\ 2 & 1 & 1 & 0 & 1\\ 2 & 2 & 2 & 1 & 0\\ 4 & 1 & 2 & 1 & 1\\ 4 & 4 & 2 & 2 & 1 \end{bmatrix} = \begin{bmatrix} 2 & 2 & 1 & 1 & 0\\ 4 & 2 & 2 & 1 & 1\\ 4 & 3 & 2 & 2 & 1\\ 6 & 3 & 3 & 2 & 2\\ 8 & 6 & 4 & 4 & 2 \end{bmatrix}$$

Each point can send a message back to itself in two ways (using no more than 2 relays).

18. **a.** A dominates B directly. **b.** B can send data to A.

c. A dominates B, and B dominates C.

d. B can send data directly to more points than any other station.

e. A can send data to B through one relay point.

f. C has the greatest total of first- and second-stage dominances.

Page 786 • EXTRA

1. $\begin{aligned} x + y + z &= 0\\ x - y + z &= 2\\ x - y - z &= 10 \end{aligned}$; $\begin{bmatrix} 1 & 1 & 1 & 0\\ 1 & -1 & 1 & 2\\ 1 & -1 & -1 & 10 \end{bmatrix} \longrightarrow \begin{bmatrix} 1 & 1 & 1 & 0\\ 0 & -2 & 0 & 2\\ 0 & -2 & -2 & 10 \end{bmatrix}$, $-2y = 2$,

$y = -1$; $-2(-1) - 2z = 10$, $2 - 2z = 10$, $-2z = 8$, $z = -4$; $x + (-1) + (-4) = 0$, $x = 5$; $(5, -1, -4)$

2. $\begin{aligned} x + 2y - z &= 0\\ -x + y &= 5\\ x + 2z &= 6 \end{aligned}$; $\begin{bmatrix} 1 & 2 & -1 & 0\\ -1 & 1 & 0 & 5\\ 1 & 0 & 2 & 6 \end{bmatrix} \longrightarrow \begin{bmatrix} 1 & 2 & -1 & 0\\ 0 & 1 & 2 & 11\\ 0 & -2 & 3 & 6 \end{bmatrix} \longrightarrow$

$\begin{bmatrix} 1 & 2 & -1 & 0\\ 0 & 1 & 2 & 11\\ 0 & 0 & 7 & 28 \end{bmatrix}$; $7z = 28$, $z = 4$; $y + 2(4) = 11$, $y = 3$; $x + 2(3) - 1(4) = 0$,

$x = -2$; $(-2, 3, 4)$

3. $\begin{aligned} x - 2y + z &= 9\\ 3x + y &= 1\\ -2x - 3y - z &= 0 \end{aligned}$; $\begin{bmatrix} 1 & -2 & 1 & 9\\ 3 & 1 & 0 & 1\\ -2 & -3 & -1 & 0 \end{bmatrix} \longrightarrow \begin{bmatrix} 1 & -2 & 1 & 9\\ 0 & 7 & -3 & -26\\ 0 & -7 & 1 & 18 \end{bmatrix} \longrightarrow$

$\begin{bmatrix} 1 & -2 & 1 & 9\\ 0 & 7 & -3 & -26\\ 0 & 0 & -2 & -8 \end{bmatrix}$; $-2z = -8$, $z = 4$; $7y - 3(4) = -26$, $7y = -14$, $y = -2$;

$x - 2(-2) + 1(4) = 9$, $x = 1$; $(1, -2, 4)$

4. $\begin{aligned} x + 2y + 3z &= 3 \\ 2x + 3y + 4z &= 2 \\ -3x - 5y + 2z &= 4 \end{aligned}$; $\begin{bmatrix} 1 & 2 & 3 & 3 \\ 2 & 3 & 4 & 2 \\ -3 & -5 & 2 & 4 \end{bmatrix} \longrightarrow \begin{bmatrix} 1 & 2 & 3 & 3 \\ 0 & -1 & -2 & -4 \\ 0 & 1 & 11 & 13 \end{bmatrix} \longrightarrow$

$\begin{bmatrix} 1 & 2 & 3 & 3 \\ 0 & -1 & -2 & -4 \\ 0 & 0 & 9 & 9 \end{bmatrix}$; $9z = 9, z = 1; -y - 2(1) = -4, -y = -2, y = 2;$

$x + 2(2) + 3(1) = 3, x = -4; (-4, 2, 1)$

5. $\begin{aligned} 2x + y + z &= 3 \\ 4x \quad + 3z &= 5 \\ 3x + 2y \quad &= 1 \end{aligned}$; $\begin{bmatrix} 2 & 1 & 1 & 3 \\ 4 & 0 & 3 & 5 \\ 3 & 2 & 0 & 1 \end{bmatrix} \longrightarrow \begin{matrix} 2 & 1 & 1 & 3 \\ 0 & -2 & 1 & -1 \\ 0 & \frac{1}{2} & -\frac{3}{2} & -\frac{7}{2} \end{matrix} \longrightarrow$

$\begin{matrix} 2 & 1 & 1 & 3 \\ 0 & -2 & 1 & -1 \\ 0 & 0 & -\frac{5}{4} & -\frac{15}{4} \end{matrix}$; $-\frac{5}{4}z = -\frac{15}{4}, z = 3; -2y + 3 = -1, y = 2;$

$2x + 2 + 3 = 3, x = -1; (-1, 2, 3)$

6. $\begin{aligned} 2x - y - 2z &= 5 \\ 3x - y \quad &= 1 \\ 5x \quad + 4z &= -2 \end{aligned}$; $\begin{bmatrix} 2 & -1 & -2 & 5 \\ 3 & -1 & 0 & 1 \\ 5 & 0 & 4 & -2 \end{bmatrix} \longrightarrow \begin{bmatrix} 1 & -\frac{1}{2} & -1 & \frac{5}{2} \\ 0 & \frac{1}{2} & 3 & -\frac{13}{2} \\ 0 & \frac{5}{2} & 9 & -\frac{29}{2} \end{bmatrix} \longrightarrow$

$\begin{bmatrix} 1 & -\frac{1}{2} & -1 & \frac{5}{2} \\ 0 & 1 & 6 & -13 \\ 0 & 0 & -6 & 18 \end{bmatrix}$; $-6z = 18, z = -3; y + 6(-3) = -13, y = 5;$

$x - \frac{1}{2}(5) - 1(-3) = \frac{5}{2}, x = 2; (2, 5, -3)$

Page 789 • WRITTEN EXERCISES

A **1.** $\begin{vmatrix} 3 & 1 \\ 4 & 3 \end{vmatrix} = 9 - 4 = 5$ **2.** $\begin{vmatrix} 2 & 10 \\ 0 & 3 \end{vmatrix} = 6 - 0 = 6$ **3.** $\begin{vmatrix} 5 & -3 \\ 3 & 1 \end{vmatrix} = 5 - (-9) = 14$

4. $\begin{vmatrix} 15 & 0 \\ 0 & 4 \end{vmatrix} = 60 - 0 = 60$ **5.** $\begin{vmatrix} 0 & 8 \\ -4 & 0 \end{vmatrix} = 0 - (-32) = 32$

6. $\begin{vmatrix} 3 & 9 \\ 2 & 6 \end{vmatrix} = 18 - 18 = 0$ **7.** $\begin{vmatrix} 2 & -5 & 3 \\ 0 & 8 & 1 \\ -5 & 4 & 0 \end{vmatrix} = 0 + 25 + 0 - (-120 + 8 + 0) = 137$

8. $\begin{vmatrix} 3 & 0 & 1 \\ 5 & 2 & 2 \\ -2 & 0 & 4 \end{vmatrix} = 24 + 0 + 0 - (-4) - 0 - 0 = 28$

9. $\begin{vmatrix} 12 & -9 & 13 \\ 0 & 0 & 8 \\ -9 & 2 & 1 \end{vmatrix} = 0 + 648 + 0 - 0 - 192 - 0 = 456$

10. $\begin{vmatrix} -10 & 0 & 0 \\ 0 & 4 & 0 \\ 0 & 0 & -12 \end{vmatrix} = 480 + 0 + 0 - 0 - 0 - 0 = 480$

11. $\begin{vmatrix} 5 & 0 & 0 \\ 0 & -6 & 0 \\ 0 & 0 & 2 \end{vmatrix} = -60 + 0 + 0 - 0 - 0 - 0 = -60$

12. $\begin{vmatrix} 0 & 2 & -3 \\ 3 & 5 & -3 \\ 1 & 2 & 0 \end{vmatrix} = 0 + (-6) + (-18) - (-15) - 0 - 0 = -9$

B 13. $\begin{vmatrix} 8 & -1 & -5 \\ 0 & 9 & 6 \\ -2 & 0 & 3 \end{vmatrix} = 216 + 12 + 0 - 90 - 0 - 0 = 138$

14. $\begin{vmatrix} 2 & 3 & -1 \\ -3 & 0 & -8 \\ 11 & -4 & 6 \end{vmatrix} = 0 + (-264) + (-12) - 0 - 64 - (-54) = -286$

15. If $A = \begin{bmatrix} a & b \\ 0 & 0 \end{bmatrix}$, $\det A = a \cdot 0 - b \cdot 0 = 0$; if $A = \begin{bmatrix} 0 & 0 \\ a & b \end{bmatrix}$, $\det A = 0 \cdot b - 0 \cdot a = 0$;

if $A = \begin{bmatrix} a & 0 \\ b & 0 \end{bmatrix}$, $\det A = a \cdot 0 - 0 \cdot b = 0$; if $A = \begin{bmatrix} 0 & a \\ 0 & b \end{bmatrix}$, $\det A = 0 \cdot b - a \cdot 0 = 0$.

16. If $B = \begin{bmatrix} 0 & 0 & 0 \\ a & b & c \\ d & e & f \end{bmatrix}$, $\det B = 0 \cdot bf + 0 \cdot cd + 0 \cdot ae - 0 \cdot bd - 0 \cdot ce - 0 \cdot af = 0$;

if $B = \begin{bmatrix} a & b & c \\ 0 & 0 & 0 \\ d & e & f \end{bmatrix}$, $\det B = 0 \cdot af + 0 \cdot bd + 0 \cdot ce - 0 \cdot cd - 0 \cdot ae - 0 \cdot bf = 0$;

if $B = \begin{bmatrix} a & b & c \\ d & e & f \\ 0 & 0 & 0 \end{bmatrix}$, $\det B = 0 \cdot ae + 0 \cdot bf + 0 \cdot cd - 0 \cdot ec - 0 \cdot af - 0 \cdot bd = 0$;

if $B = \begin{bmatrix} 0 & a & d \\ 0 & b & e \\ 0 & c & f \end{bmatrix}$, $\det B = 0 \cdot bf + 0 \cdot ae + 0 \cdot cd - 0 \cdot bd - 0 \cdot ce - 0 \cdot af = 0$;

if $B = \begin{bmatrix} a & 0 & d \\ b & 0 & e \\ c & 0 & f \end{bmatrix}$, $\det B = 0 \cdot af + 0 \cdot ec + 0 \cdot db - 0 \cdot cd - 0 \cdot ae - 0 \cdot bf = 0$;

if $B = \begin{bmatrix} a & d & 0 \\ b & e & 0 \\ c & f & 0 \end{bmatrix}$, $\det B = 0 \cdot ae + 0 \cdot cd + 0 \cdot bf - 0 \cdot ec - 0 \cdot af - 0 \cdot bd = 0$.

17. If $A = \begin{bmatrix} a & b \\ a & b \end{bmatrix}$, then $\det(A) = ab - ab = 0$

18. Let $A = \begin{bmatrix} a & b \\ c & d \end{bmatrix}$; $\begin{vmatrix} a & b \\ c & d \end{vmatrix} = ad - bc$; $\begin{vmatrix} ra & rb \\ c & d \end{vmatrix} = ra \cdot d - rb \cdot c = r(ad - bc)$;

$\begin{vmatrix} a & b \\ rc & rd \end{vmatrix} = a \cdot rd - b \cdot rc = r(ad - bc)$; $\begin{vmatrix} ra & b \\ rc & d \end{vmatrix} = ra \cdot d - b \cdot rc = r(ad - bc)$;

$\begin{vmatrix} a & rb \\ c & rd \end{vmatrix} = a \cdot rd - rb \cdot c = r(ad - bc)$

C **19.** Let $A = \begin{bmatrix} a & b \\ c & d \end{bmatrix}$; $\det A = ad - bc$; $\det(rA) = \begin{vmatrix} ra & rb \\ rc & rd \end{vmatrix} = ra \cdot rd - rb \cdot rc =$
$r^2(ad - bc) = r^2 \det A$

20. Let $A = \begin{bmatrix} a & b \\ c & d \end{bmatrix}$ and $B = \begin{bmatrix} e & f \\ g & h \end{bmatrix}$; $AB = \begin{bmatrix} ae + bg & af + bh \\ ce + dg & cf + dh \end{bmatrix}$; $\det(AB) =$
$(ae + bg)(cf + dh) - (ce + dg)(af + bh) = acef + adeh + bcfg + bdgh -$
$(acef + bceh + adfg + bdgh) = adeh + bcfg - bceh - adfg$;
$(\det A)(\det B) = (ad - bc)(eh - fg) = adeh - adfg - bceh + bcfg = \det(AB)$

Page 789 • MIXED REVIEW EXERCISES

1. $\frac{t^2 - 3t + 2}{t^2 - 5t + 6} = \frac{(t - 2)(t - 1)}{(t - 2)(t - 3)} = \frac{t - 1}{t - 3}$ **2.** $\frac{a^2b^3}{a^3b^7} = \frac{1}{ab^4}$

3. $\frac{3}{s + 1} + \frac{4}{3(s - 1)} = \frac{9(s - 1) + 4(s + 1)}{3(s - 1)(s + 1)} = \frac{13s - 5}{3(s - 1)(s + 1)}$ **4.** $a^{2/3} \cdot a^{4/3} = a^{6/3} = a^2$

5. $\frac{\frac{1}{c} - 1}{c - \frac{1}{c}} = \frac{\frac{1 - c}{c}}{\frac{c^2 - 1}{c}} = \frac{1 - c}{c} \cdot \frac{c}{c^2 - 1} = \frac{-(c - 1)}{(c - 1)(c + 1)} = -\frac{1}{c + 1}$

6. $\frac{y + 5}{y - 4} \div \frac{(y - 5)(y + 5)}{(y - 4)(y - 2)} = \frac{(y + 5)}{(y - 4)} \cdot \frac{(y - 2)(y - 4)}{(y + 5)(y - 5)} = \frac{y - 2}{y - 5}$

7. $(-9pr^4q^3)(4p^2r^{-4}q^3) = -36p^3q^6$ **8.** $\frac{(x - 1)(x^2 + x + 1)}{(x + 4)(x - 1)} = \frac{x^2 + x + 1}{x + 4}$

9. $(2^{\pi})^{-1/\pi} = 2^{-1} = \frac{1}{2}$

Page 792 • WRITTEN EXERCISES

A **1.** $\begin{vmatrix} 2 & 1 \\ -1 & 2 \end{vmatrix} = 4 - (-1) = 5; \frac{1}{5}\begin{bmatrix} 2 & -1 \\ 1 & 2 \end{bmatrix} = \begin{bmatrix} \frac{2}{5} & -\frac{1}{5} \\ \frac{1}{5} & \frac{2}{5} \end{bmatrix}$

2. $\begin{vmatrix} 5 & 3 \\ 2 & 1 \end{vmatrix} = 5 - 6 = -1; \frac{1}{-1}\begin{bmatrix} 1 & -3 \\ -2 & 5 \end{bmatrix} = \begin{bmatrix} -1 & 3 \\ 2 & -5 \end{bmatrix}$

3. $\begin{vmatrix} 4 & 6 \\ 2 & 3 \end{vmatrix} = 12 - 12 = 0$; no inverse

4. $\begin{vmatrix} -3 & 1 \\ 4 & -2 \end{vmatrix} = 6 - 4 = 2; \frac{1}{2}\begin{bmatrix} -2 & -1 \\ -4 & -3 \end{bmatrix} = \begin{bmatrix} -1 & -\frac{1}{2} \\ -2 & -\frac{3}{2} \end{bmatrix}$

5. $\begin{vmatrix} 1 & 0 \\ 0 & 1 \end{vmatrix} = 1; \frac{1}{1}\begin{bmatrix} 1 & 0 \\ 0 & 1 \end{bmatrix} = \begin{bmatrix} 1 & 0 \\ 0 & 1 \end{bmatrix}$

6. $\begin{vmatrix} 0 & 9 \\ -1 & 3 \end{vmatrix} = 0 - (-9) = 9; \frac{1}{9}\begin{bmatrix} 3 & -9 \\ 1 & 0 \end{bmatrix} = \begin{bmatrix} \frac{1}{3} & -1 \\ \frac{1}{9} & 0 \end{bmatrix}$

7. $\begin{vmatrix} 3 & -1 \\ 6 & 2 \end{vmatrix} = 6 - (-6) = 12; \frac{1}{12}\begin{bmatrix} 2 & 1 \\ -6 & 3 \end{bmatrix} = \begin{bmatrix} \frac{1}{6} & \frac{1}{12} \\ -\frac{1}{2} & \frac{1}{4} \end{bmatrix}$

8. $\begin{vmatrix} 0 & 0 \\ 5 & -7 \end{vmatrix} = 0 - 0 = 0$; no inverse

9. $\begin{bmatrix} 2 & -1 \\ 3 & 2 \end{bmatrix}\begin{bmatrix} x \\ y \end{bmatrix} = \begin{bmatrix} 6 \\ -19 \end{bmatrix}; \begin{vmatrix} 2 & -1 \\ 3 & 2 \end{vmatrix} = 4 - (-3) = 7; \begin{bmatrix} x \\ y \end{bmatrix} = \frac{1}{7}\begin{bmatrix} 2 & 1 \\ -3 & 2 \end{bmatrix}\begin{bmatrix} 6 \\ -19 \end{bmatrix} =$
$\frac{1}{7}\begin{bmatrix} -7 \\ -56 \end{bmatrix} = \begin{bmatrix} -1 \\ -8 \end{bmatrix}$; $(-1, -8)$

10. $\begin{bmatrix} 3 & 2 \\ 3 & -1 \end{bmatrix}\begin{bmatrix} x \\ y \end{bmatrix} = \begin{bmatrix} 5 \\ 2 \end{bmatrix}; \begin{vmatrix} 3 & 2 \\ 3 & -1 \end{vmatrix} = -3 - 6 = -9; \begin{bmatrix} x \\ y \end{bmatrix} = -\frac{1}{9}\begin{bmatrix} -1 & -2 \\ -3 & 3 \end{bmatrix}\begin{bmatrix} 5 \\ 2 \end{bmatrix} =$
$\frac{1}{-9}\begin{bmatrix} -9 \\ -9 \end{bmatrix} = \begin{bmatrix} 1 \\ 1 \end{bmatrix}$; $(1, 1)$

11. $\begin{bmatrix} 2 & 2 \\ 1 & -3 \end{bmatrix}\begin{bmatrix} x \\ y \end{bmatrix} = \begin{bmatrix} 16 \\ -4 \end{bmatrix}; \begin{vmatrix} 2 & 2 \\ 1 & -3 \end{vmatrix} = -6 - 2 = -8; \begin{bmatrix} x \\ y \end{bmatrix} = -\frac{1}{8}\begin{bmatrix} -3 & -2 \\ -1 & 2 \end{bmatrix}\begin{bmatrix} 16 \\ -4 \end{bmatrix} =$
$-\frac{1}{8}\begin{bmatrix} -40 \\ -24 \end{bmatrix} = \begin{bmatrix} 5 \\ 3 \end{bmatrix}$; $(5, 3)$

12. $\begin{bmatrix} 4 & -6 \\ -6 & 9 \end{bmatrix}\begin{bmatrix} x \\ y \end{bmatrix} = \begin{bmatrix} 8 \\ -12 \end{bmatrix}; \begin{vmatrix} 4 & -6 \\ -6 & 9 \end{vmatrix} = 36 - 36 = 0$; no unique solution

13. $\begin{bmatrix} 1 & 1 \\ 2 & 0 \end{bmatrix}\begin{bmatrix} x \\ y \end{bmatrix} = \begin{bmatrix} 6 \\ 4 \end{bmatrix}; \begin{vmatrix} 1 & 1 \\ 2 & 0 \end{vmatrix} = 0 - 2 = -2; \begin{bmatrix} x \\ y \end{bmatrix} = -\frac{1}{2}\begin{bmatrix} 0 & -1 \\ -2 & 1 \end{bmatrix}\begin{bmatrix} 6 \\ 4 \end{bmatrix} =$
$-\frac{1}{2}\begin{bmatrix} -4 \\ -8 \end{bmatrix} = \begin{bmatrix} 2 \\ 4 \end{bmatrix}$; $(2, 4)$

14. $\begin{bmatrix} 4 & 3 \\ 4 & 1 \end{bmatrix}\begin{bmatrix} x \\ y \end{bmatrix} = \begin{bmatrix} 1 \\ -5 \end{bmatrix}; \begin{vmatrix} 4 & 3 \\ 4 & 1 \end{vmatrix} = 4 - 12 = -8; \begin{bmatrix} x \\ y \end{bmatrix} = -\frac{1}{8}\begin{bmatrix} 1 & -3 \\ -4 & 4 \end{bmatrix}\begin{bmatrix} 1 \\ -5 \end{bmatrix} =$
$\begin{bmatrix} -\frac{1}{8} & \frac{3}{8} \\ \frac{1}{2} & -\frac{1}{2} \end{bmatrix}\begin{bmatrix} 1 \\ -5 \end{bmatrix} = \begin{bmatrix} -2 \\ 3 \end{bmatrix}$; $(-2, 3)$

15. $\begin{bmatrix} 1 & 1 \\ 2 & 2 \end{bmatrix}\begin{bmatrix} x \\ y \end{bmatrix} = \begin{bmatrix} 1 \\ 5 \end{bmatrix}; \begin{vmatrix} 1 & 1 \\ 2 & 2 \end{vmatrix} = 2 - 2 = 0$; no unique solution

16. $\begin{bmatrix} 1 & 0 \\ -1 & 1 \end{bmatrix}\begin{bmatrix} x \\ y \end{bmatrix} = \begin{bmatrix} 3 \\ 2 \end{bmatrix}; \begin{vmatrix} 1 & 0 \\ -1 & 1 \end{vmatrix} = 1 - 0 = 1; \begin{bmatrix} x \\ y \end{bmatrix} = \begin{bmatrix} 1 & 0 \\ 1 & 1 \end{bmatrix}\begin{bmatrix} 3 \\ 2 \end{bmatrix} = \begin{bmatrix} 3 \\ 5 \end{bmatrix}$; $(3, 5)$

B **17.** $\begin{vmatrix} 1 & 3 \\ 2 & 7 \end{vmatrix} = 7 - 6 = 1; X = \begin{bmatrix} 7 & -3 \\ -2 & 1 \end{bmatrix}\begin{bmatrix} 4 & 1 \\ -2 & 3 \end{bmatrix} = \begin{bmatrix} 34 & -2 \\ -10 & 1 \end{bmatrix}$

18. $\begin{vmatrix} 4 & 4 \\ 3 & 4 \end{vmatrix} = 16 - 12 = 4; X = \frac{1}{4}\begin{bmatrix} 4 & -4 \\ -3 & 4 \end{bmatrix}\begin{bmatrix} 1 & 0 \\ 0 & 1 \end{bmatrix} = \begin{bmatrix} 1 & -1 \\ -\frac{3}{4} & 1 \end{bmatrix}$

19. $\begin{bmatrix} 4 & 2 \\ 1 & 1 \end{bmatrix} X = \begin{bmatrix} 2 & 3 \\ 0 & 1 \end{bmatrix} + \begin{bmatrix} 0 & \frac{1}{2} \\ -1 & \frac{3}{2} \end{bmatrix} = \begin{bmatrix} 2 & \frac{7}{2} \\ -1 & \frac{5}{2} \end{bmatrix}; \begin{vmatrix} 4 & 2 \\ 1 & 1 \end{vmatrix} = 4 - 2 = 2; X = \frac{1}{2}\begin{bmatrix} 1 & -2 \\ -1 & 4 \end{bmatrix}$

$\begin{bmatrix} 2 & \frac{7}{2} \\ -1 & \frac{5}{2} \end{bmatrix} = \frac{1}{2}\begin{bmatrix} 4 & -\frac{3}{2} \\ -6 & \frac{13}{2} \end{bmatrix} = \begin{bmatrix} 2 & -\frac{3}{4} \\ -3 & \frac{13}{4} \end{bmatrix}$

20. $\begin{bmatrix} 5 & 3 \\ 3 & 2 \end{bmatrix} X = \begin{bmatrix} 1 & 2 \\ -1 & 3 \end{bmatrix} + \begin{bmatrix} 1 & 3 \\ 2 & 1 \end{bmatrix} = \begin{bmatrix} 2 & 5 \\ 1 & 4 \end{bmatrix}; \begin{vmatrix} 5 & 3 \\ 3 & 2 \end{vmatrix} = 10 - 9 = 1;$

$X = \begin{bmatrix} 2 & -3 \\ -3 & 5 \end{bmatrix}\begin{bmatrix} 2 & 5 \\ 1 & 4 \end{bmatrix} = \begin{bmatrix} 1 & -2 \\ -1 & 5 \end{bmatrix}$

Pages 796–797 • WRITTEN EXERCISES

A

1. $\begin{vmatrix} 2 & 1 & 3 \\ -2 & 1 & 4 \\ 1 & 2 & 5 \end{vmatrix} = 2\begin{vmatrix} 1 & 4 \\ 2 & 5 \end{vmatrix} - 1\begin{vmatrix} -2 & 4 \\ 1 & 5 \end{vmatrix} + 3\begin{vmatrix} -2 & 1 \\ 1 & 2 \end{vmatrix} = 2(-3) - 1(-14) + 3(-5) = -7$

2. $\begin{vmatrix} 2 & 3 & 1 \\ 0 & -1 & 4 \\ 5 & 0 & 0 \end{vmatrix} = 5\begin{vmatrix} 3 & 1 \\ -1 & -4 \end{vmatrix} - 0 + 0 = 5(-11) = -55$

3. $\begin{vmatrix} -2 & -2 & 0 \\ 0 & 2 & 3 \\ 1 & -1 & 1 \end{vmatrix} = -2\begin{vmatrix} 2 & 3 \\ -1 & 1 \end{vmatrix} - 0 + 1\begin{vmatrix} -2 & 0 \\ 2 & 3 \end{vmatrix} = -2(5) + (-6) = -16$

4. $\begin{vmatrix} 4 & 0 & -5 \\ 9 & 1 & 11 \\ -4 & 0 & 3 \end{vmatrix} = 0 + 1\begin{vmatrix} 4 & -5 \\ -4 & 3 \end{vmatrix} - 0 = 0 - 8 - 0 = -8$

5. $\begin{vmatrix} -1 & 3 & 4 \\ 0 & 1 & 0 \\ 3 & 6 & -2 \end{vmatrix} = 0 + 1\begin{vmatrix} -1 & 4 \\ 3 & -2 \end{vmatrix} + 0 = -10$

6. $\begin{vmatrix} 2 & 0 & 0 \\ 10 & 1 & -1 \\ 3 & 0 & 4 \end{vmatrix} = 2\begin{vmatrix} 1 & -1 \\ 0 & 4 \end{vmatrix} - 0 + 0 = 2(4) = 8$

7. $\begin{vmatrix} 1 & -1 & 0 \\ 2 & 3 & -1 \\ 10 & -4 & 0 \end{vmatrix} = 0 - (-1)\begin{vmatrix} 1 & -1 \\ 10 & -4 \end{vmatrix} + 0 = 6$

8. $\begin{vmatrix} 0 & -2 & 4 \\ 1 & 3 & -1 \\ 0 & 0 & 5 \end{vmatrix} = 0 - 1\begin{vmatrix} -2 & 4 \\ 0 & 5 \end{vmatrix} + 0 = -1(-10) = 10$

9–12. Choice of row or column may vary.

9. $\begin{vmatrix} 1 & 0 & -1 \\ 0 & 1 & 2 \\ -1 & 2 & 1 \end{vmatrix} = 1\begin{vmatrix} 1 & 2 \\ 2 & 1 \end{vmatrix} - 0 + (-1)\begin{vmatrix} 0 & 1 \\ -1 & 2 \end{vmatrix} = -3 - 1 = -4$

10. $\begin{vmatrix} 0 & 2 & 1 \\ 4 & 0 & -2 \\ -1 & 3 & 1 \end{vmatrix} = 0 - 2\begin{vmatrix} 4 & -2 \\ -1 & 1 \end{vmatrix} + 1\begin{vmatrix} 4 & 0 \\ -1 & 3 \end{vmatrix} = 0 - 2(2) + 1(12) = 8$

11. $\begin{vmatrix} 0 & 3 & 1 \\ 4 & -1 & 2 \\ 0 & 2 & 0 \end{vmatrix} = 0 - 2\begin{vmatrix} 0 & 1 \\ 4 & 2 \end{vmatrix} + 0 = -2(-4) = 8$

12. $\begin{vmatrix} 1 & -1 & 2 \\ 3 & 5 & 1 \\ 4 & 2 & -2 \end{vmatrix} = 1\begin{vmatrix} 5 & 1 \\ 2 & -2 \end{vmatrix} - 3\begin{vmatrix} -1 & 2 \\ 2 & -2 \end{vmatrix} + 4\begin{vmatrix} -1 & 2 \\ 5 & 1 \end{vmatrix} =$

$-12 - 3(-2) + 4(-11) = -50$

B 13. $\begin{vmatrix} 2 & 1 & 1 \\ 1 & 2 & 1 \\ x & 1 & 2 \end{vmatrix} = 2\begin{vmatrix} 2 & 1 \\ 1 & 2 \end{vmatrix} - 1\begin{vmatrix} 1 & 1 \\ 1 & 2 \end{vmatrix} + x\begin{vmatrix} 1 & 1 \\ 2 & 1 \end{vmatrix} = 6 - 1 - x; 6 - 1 - x = 4;$

$-x = -1, x = 1; \{1\}$

14. $\begin{vmatrix} 1 & 3 & 4 \\ 5 & 15 & 10 \\ -1 & x & 2 \end{vmatrix} = -1\begin{vmatrix} 3 & 4 \\ 15 & 10 \end{vmatrix} - x\begin{vmatrix} 1 & 4 \\ 5 & 10 \end{vmatrix} + 2\begin{vmatrix} 1 & 3 \\ 5 & 15 \end{vmatrix} = 30 + 10x + 0;$

$30 + 10x = 80, 10x = 50, x = 5; \{5\}$

15. $\begin{vmatrix} 12 & -7 & 19 \\ 0 & x & 5 \\ -9 & 3 & 43 \end{vmatrix} = 0 + x\begin{vmatrix} 12 & 19 \\ -9 & 43 \end{vmatrix} - 5\begin{vmatrix} 12 & -7 \\ -9 & 3 \end{vmatrix} = 0 + 687x + 135;$

$687x + 135 = 135, 687x = 0, x = 0; \{0\}$

16. $\begin{vmatrix} 4 & -3 & 9 \\ 8 & x & -4 \\ 1 & 5 & 3 \end{vmatrix} = -8\begin{vmatrix} -3 & 9 \\ 5 & 3 \end{vmatrix} + x\begin{vmatrix} 4 & 9 \\ 1 & 3 \end{vmatrix} + 4\begin{vmatrix} 4 & -3 \\ 1 & 5 \end{vmatrix} = 432 + 3x + 92;$

$432 + 3x + 92 = 545, 3x = 21, x = 7; \{7\}$

17. $\begin{vmatrix} 5 & 0 & 0 & 0 \\ 3 & -3 & 0 & 0 \\ 8 & 2 & 2 & 0 \\ -4 & 10 & 3 & 2 \end{vmatrix} = 5\begin{vmatrix} -3 & 0 & 0 \\ 2 & 2 & 0 \\ 10 & 3 & 2 \end{vmatrix} - 0 + 0 - 0 = 5\left(-3\begin{vmatrix} 2 & 0 \\ 3 & 2 \end{vmatrix} - 0 + 0\right) =$

$5(-12) = -60$

18. $\begin{vmatrix} 1 & 2 & 3 & 4 \\ 5 & 6 & 7 & 8 \\ 9 & 10 & 11 & 12 \\ 13 & 14 & 15 & 16 \end{vmatrix} = -13\begin{vmatrix} 2 & 3 & 4 \\ 6 & 7 & 8 \\ 10 & 11 & 12 \end{vmatrix} + 14\begin{vmatrix} 1 & 3 & 4 \\ 5 & 7 & 8 \\ 9 & 11 & 12 \end{vmatrix} - 15\begin{vmatrix} 1 & 2 & 4 \\ 5 & 6 & 8 \\ 9 & 10 & 12 \end{vmatrix} +$

$16\begin{vmatrix} 1 & 2 & 3 \\ 5 & 6 & 7 \\ 9 & 10 & 11 \end{vmatrix} = -13(168 + 240 + 264 - 280 - 176 - 216) +$

$14(84 + 216 + 220 - 252 - 88 - 180) - 15(72 + 144 + 200 - 216 - 80 - 120) +$
$16(66 + 126 + 150 - 162 - 70 - 110) = -13(0) + 14(0) - 15(0) + 16(0) = 0$

C 19. $\begin{vmatrix} a & b & c \\ a & b & c \\ d & e & f \end{vmatrix} = a\begin{vmatrix} b & c \\ e & f \end{vmatrix} - a\begin{vmatrix} b & c \\ e & f \end{vmatrix} + d\begin{vmatrix} b & c \\ b & c \end{vmatrix} =$

$a(bf - ec) - a(bf - ec) + d(bc - bc) = 0;$

$\begin{vmatrix} a & b & c \\ d & e & f \\ a & b & c \end{vmatrix} = a\begin{vmatrix} e & f \\ b & c \end{vmatrix} - d\begin{vmatrix} b & c \\ b & c \end{vmatrix} + a\begin{vmatrix} b & c \\ e & f \end{vmatrix} =$

$a(ec - bf) - d(bc - bc) + a(bf - ec) = aec - abf + abf - aec = 0;$

$$\begin{vmatrix} a & b & c \\ d & e & f \\ d & e & f \end{vmatrix} = a\begin{vmatrix} e & f \\ e & f \end{vmatrix} - d\begin{vmatrix} b & c \\ e & f \end{vmatrix} + d\begin{vmatrix} b & c \\ e & f \end{vmatrix} =$$

$$a(ef - ef) - d(bf - ec) + d(bf - ec) = 0$$

Page 797 • MIXED REVIEW EXERCISES

1. $125^{-2/3} = (5^3)^{-2/3} = 5^{-2} = \frac{1}{5^2} = \frac{1}{25}$ **2.** $\cos\frac{3\pi}{4} = -\frac{\sqrt{2}}{2}$

3. $\frac{8!}{3!\,5!} = \frac{8 \cdot 7 \cdot 6 \cdot 5!}{3 \cdot 2 \cdot 1 \cdot 5!} = 56$ **4.** $\sqrt{-2} \cdot \sqrt{-8} = \sqrt{16} = 4$

5. $\log_3 9\sqrt{3} = \log_3(3^2 \cdot 3^{1/2}) = \log_3(3^{5/2}) = \frac{5}{2}$ **6.** $\sec^2 20° - \tan^2 20° = 1$

Page 800 • WRITTEN EXERCISES

A **1.** $\begin{vmatrix} 41 & 13 & -5 \\ 0 & 5 & 9 \\ 41 & 13 & -5 \end{vmatrix} = 0$ (by property 2) **2.** $\begin{vmatrix} -2 & 0 & 12 \\ 4 & 0 & 0 \\ 3 & 0 & 6 \end{vmatrix} = 0$ (by property 1)

3. $\begin{vmatrix} 2 & -1 & 1 \\ 1 & 3 & -3 \\ 7 & -8 & 8 \end{vmatrix} = \begin{vmatrix} 2 & -1 & -1+1 \\ 1 & 3 & 3+(-3) \\ 7 & -8 & -8+8 \end{vmatrix} = \begin{vmatrix} 2 & -1 & 0 \\ 1 & 3 & 0 \\ 7 & -8 & 0 \end{vmatrix} = 0$

4. $\begin{vmatrix} 5 & 0 & 0 \\ 0 & 5 & 0 \\ 0 & 0 & 5 \end{vmatrix} = \begin{vmatrix} 5 \cdot 1 & 0 & 0 \\ 0 & 5 \cdot 1 & 0 \\ 0 & 0 & 5 \cdot 1 \end{vmatrix} = 5^3\begin{vmatrix} 1 & 0 & 0 \\ 0 & 1 & 0 \\ 0 & 0 & 1 \end{vmatrix} = 5^3 \cdot (1) = 125$

5. $\begin{vmatrix} 2 & -4 & 6 \\ 5 & 0 & -8 \\ 3 & -6 & 9 \end{vmatrix} = \frac{2}{3}\begin{vmatrix} \frac{3}{2}(2) & \frac{3}{2}(-4) & \frac{3}{2}(6) \\ 5 & 0 & -8 \\ 3 & -6 & 9 \end{vmatrix} = \frac{2}{3}\begin{vmatrix} 3 & -6 & 9 \\ 5 & 0 & -8 \\ 3 & -6 & 9 \end{vmatrix} = 0$

6. $\begin{vmatrix} -1 & 4 & 12 \\ 1 & -2 & -12 \\ 8 & 16 & 6 \end{vmatrix} = \begin{vmatrix} -1+1 & 4+(-2) & 12+(-12) \\ 1 & -2 & -12 \\ 8 & 16 & 6 \end{vmatrix} = \begin{vmatrix} 0 & 2 & 0 \\ 1 & -2 & -12 \\ 8 & 16 & 6 \end{vmatrix} =$

$2 \cdot 2\begin{vmatrix} 0 & 1 & 0 \\ 1 & -2 & -12 \\ 4 & 8 & 3 \end{vmatrix} = -4\begin{vmatrix} 1 & -12 \\ 4 & 3 \end{vmatrix} = -4(51) = -204$

7. $\begin{vmatrix} 1 & 5 & 10 \\ 0 & -5 & -8 \\ 1 & 5 & -2 \end{vmatrix} = 5 \cdot 2\begin{vmatrix} 1 & 1 & 5 \\ 0 & -1 & -4 \\ 1 & 1 & -1 \end{vmatrix} = 10\begin{vmatrix} 0 & 0 & 6 \\ 0 & -1 & -4 \\ 1 & 1 & -1 \end{vmatrix} = 10 \cdot 6\begin{vmatrix} 0 & 0 & 1 \\ 0 & -1 & -4 \\ 1 & 1 & -1 \end{vmatrix} =$

$60\begin{vmatrix} 0 & -1 \\ 1 & 1 \end{vmatrix} = 60(1) = 60$

8. $\begin{vmatrix} 26 & 29 & 29 \\ 25 & 28 & 26 \\ 25 & 30 & 27 \end{vmatrix} = \begin{vmatrix} 26-25 & 29-28 & 29-26 \\ 25 & 28 & 26 \\ 25-25 & 30-28 & 27-26 \end{vmatrix} = \begin{vmatrix} 1 & 1 & 3 \\ 25 & 28 & 26 \\ 0 & 2 & 1 \end{vmatrix} =$

$\begin{vmatrix} 1 & 1-1 & 3-1 \\ 25 & 28-25 & 26-25 \\ 0 & 2-0 & 1-0 \end{vmatrix} = \begin{vmatrix} 1 & 0 & 2 \\ 25 & 3 & 1 \\ 0 & 2 & 1 \end{vmatrix} = 1\begin{vmatrix} 3 & 1 \\ 2 & 1 \end{vmatrix} - 25\begin{vmatrix} 0 & 2 \\ 2 & 1 \end{vmatrix} + 0 = 1 - 25(-4) =$

101

9. $\begin{vmatrix} 5 & 1 & 1 \\ 1 & 5 & 1 \\ 1 & 1 & 5 \end{vmatrix} = \begin{vmatrix} 5-5\cdot 1 & 1-1 & 1 \\ 1-5\cdot 1 & 5-1 & 1 \\ 1-5\cdot 5 & 1-5 & 5 \end{vmatrix} = \begin{vmatrix} 0 & 0 & 1 \\ -4 & 4 & 1 \\ -24 & -4 & 5 \end{vmatrix} = 1\begin{vmatrix} -4 & 4 \\ -24 & -4 \end{vmatrix} =$

$1(-4)(-4)\begin{vmatrix} 1 & -1 \\ 6 & 1 \end{vmatrix} = 16(7) = 112$

B **10.** $\begin{vmatrix} 4 & 0 & 0 & 0 \\ 0 & 4 & 0 & 0 \\ 0 & 0 & 4 & 0 \\ 0 & 0 & 0 & 4 \end{vmatrix} = 4^4\begin{vmatrix} 1 & 0 & 0 & 0 \\ 0 & 1 & 0 & 0 \\ 0 & 0 & 1 & 0 \\ 0 & 0 & 0 & 1 \end{vmatrix} = 4^4\left(\begin{vmatrix} 1 & 0 & 0 \\ 0 & 1 & 0 \\ 0 & 0 & 1 \end{vmatrix} - 0 + 0 - 0\right) = 4^4(1) = 256$

11. $\begin{vmatrix} 1 & -1 & -1 & 1 \\ 1 & 1 & 1 & -1 \\ -1 & -1 & 1 & 1 \\ -1 & 1 & -1 & -1 \end{vmatrix} = -1\begin{vmatrix} 1 & -1 & -1 & (-1)(1) \\ 1 & 1 & 1 & (-1)(-1) \\ -1 & -1 & 1 & (-1)(1) \\ -1 & 1 & -1 & (-1)(-1) \end{vmatrix} = -1\begin{vmatrix} 1 & -1 & -1 & -1 \\ 1 & 1 & 1 & 1 \\ -1 & -1 & 1 & -1 \\ -1 & 1 & -1 & 1 \end{vmatrix} =$

$-1 \cdot 0 = 0$ (since columns 2 and 4 are the same)

12. $\begin{vmatrix} 1 & 1 & 1 & -1 \\ 2 & 2 & -2 & 2 \\ -3 & -3 & 3 & 3 \\ -4 & 4 & 4 & 4 \end{vmatrix} = \begin{vmatrix} 1+(-1) & 1 & 1 & -1 \\ 2+2 & 2 & -2 & 2 \\ -3+3 & -3 & 3 & 3 \\ -4+4 & 4 & 4 & 4 \end{vmatrix} = \begin{vmatrix} 0 & 1 & 1 & -1 \\ 4 & 2 & -2 & 2 \\ 0 & -3 & 3 & 3 \\ 0 & 4 & 4 & 4 \end{vmatrix} =$

$-4\begin{vmatrix} 1 & 1 & -1 \\ -3 & 3 & 3 \\ 4 & 4 & 4 \end{vmatrix} = -4\cdot 3\cdot 4\begin{vmatrix} 1 & 1 & -1 \\ -1 & 1 & 1 \\ 1 & 1 & 1 \end{vmatrix} = -48\begin{vmatrix} 1 & 1 & -1 \\ 0 & 2 & 0 \\ 0 & 0 & 2 \end{vmatrix} =$

$-48\cdot 2\cdot 2\begin{vmatrix} 1 & 1 & -1 \\ 0 & 1 & 0 \\ 0 & 0 & 1 \end{vmatrix} = -192\cdot 1 = -192$

C **13.** If two rows (or columns) of a determinant are equal, by property 5, one may be subtracted from the other, leaving a row (or column) of zeros. By property 1, the resulting determinant is zero.

14. For a third-order determinant with identical rows, see the solution to Exercise 19, p. 797.

$\begin{vmatrix} a & a & d \\ b & b & e \\ c & c & f \end{vmatrix} = a\begin{vmatrix} b & e \\ c & f \end{vmatrix} - a\begin{vmatrix} b & e \\ c & f \end{vmatrix} + d\begin{vmatrix} b & b \\ c & c \end{vmatrix} = 0;\ \begin{vmatrix} a & d & a \\ b & e & b \\ c & f & c \end{vmatrix} = a\begin{vmatrix} e & b \\ f & c \end{vmatrix} -$

$d\begin{vmatrix} b & b \\ c & c \end{vmatrix} + a\begin{vmatrix} b & e \\ c & f \end{vmatrix} = a(ce - bf) - d(bc - bc) + a(bf - ce) = 0;$

$\begin{vmatrix} a & d & d \\ b & e & e \\ c & f & f \end{vmatrix} = a\begin{vmatrix} e & e \\ f & f \end{vmatrix} - d\begin{vmatrix} b & e \\ c & f \end{vmatrix} + d\begin{vmatrix} b & e \\ c & f \end{vmatrix} = 0$

15. Let $A = \begin{bmatrix} a & b \\ c & d \end{bmatrix}$; $\det A = ad - bc$; $\begin{vmatrix} a & b+ka \\ c & d+kc \end{vmatrix} = a(d+kc) - (b+ka)c =$

$ad + akc - bc - akc = ad - bc = \det A$; $\begin{vmatrix} a+kb & b \\ c+kd & d \end{vmatrix} = (a+kb)d - b(c+kd) =$

$ad + kbd - bc - bkd = ad - bc = \det A$; $\begin{vmatrix} a+kc & b+kd \\ c & d \end{vmatrix} =$

(Continued)

$(a + kc)d - (b + kd)c = ad + kcd - bc - ckd = ad - bc = \det A;$

$$\begin{vmatrix} a & b \\ c + ka & d + kb \end{vmatrix} = a(d + kb) - b(c + ka) = ad + akb - bc - bka =$$

$ad - bc = \det A.$

Pages 804–805 • WRITTEN EXERCISES

A 1. $D = \begin{vmatrix} 1 & -5 \\ 2 & 1 \end{vmatrix} = 11; D_x = \begin{vmatrix} 2 & -5 \\ 4 & 1 \end{vmatrix} = 22; D_y = \begin{vmatrix} 1 & 2 \\ 2 & 4 \end{vmatrix} = 0; x = \frac{22}{11} = 2;$

$y = \frac{0}{11} = 0;$ (2, 0)

2. $D = \begin{vmatrix} 2 & 3 \\ 3 & 4 \end{vmatrix} = -1; D_x = \begin{vmatrix} 7 & 3 \\ 10 & 4 \end{vmatrix} = -2; D_y = \begin{vmatrix} 2 & 7 \\ 3 & 10 \end{vmatrix} = -1; x = \frac{-2}{-1} = 2,$

$y = \frac{-1}{-1} = 1;$ (2, 1)

3. $D = \begin{vmatrix} 2 & 1 & -1 \\ 1 & 1 & 1 \\ 1 & 2 & 1 \end{vmatrix} = 2(-1) - 3 + 2 = -3; D_x = \begin{vmatrix} 2 & 1 & -1 \\ 7 & 1 & 1 \\ 4 & 2 & 1 \end{vmatrix} =$

$2(-1) - 7(3) + 4(2) = -15; D_y = \begin{vmatrix} 2 & 2 & -1 \\ 1 & 7 & 1 \\ 1 & 4 & 1 \end{vmatrix} = 2(3) - 6 + 9 = 9;$

$D_z = \begin{vmatrix} 2 & 1 & 2 \\ 1 & 1 & 7 \\ 1 & 2 & 4 \end{vmatrix} = 2(-10) - 0 + 5 = -15; x = \frac{D_x}{D} = \frac{-15}{-3} = 5; y = \frac{D_y}{D} = \frac{9}{-3} = -3;$

$z = \frac{D_z}{D} = \frac{-15}{-3} = 5;$ (5, −3, 5)

4. $D = \begin{vmatrix} 1 & -3 & -2 \\ 3 & 2 & 6 \\ 4 & -1 & 3 \end{vmatrix} = \begin{vmatrix} 1 & -3 & -2 \\ 3 - 3(1) & 2 - 3(-3) & 6 - 3(2) \\ 4 - 4(1) & -1 - 4(-3) & 3 - 4(2) \end{vmatrix} = \begin{vmatrix} 1 & -3 & -2 \\ 0 & 11 & 12 \\ 0 & 11 & 11 \end{vmatrix} =$

$\begin{vmatrix} 11 & 12 \\ 11 & 11 \end{vmatrix} = 11\begin{vmatrix} 1 & 12 \\ 1 & 11 \end{vmatrix} = 11(-1) = -11; D_x = \begin{vmatrix} 9 & -3 & -2 \\ 20 & 2 & 6 \\ 25 & -1 & 3 \end{vmatrix} = 2\begin{vmatrix} 9 & -3 & -2 \\ 10 & 1 & 3 \\ 25 & -1 & 3 \end{vmatrix} =$

$2\begin{vmatrix} 9 & -3 & -2 \\ -15 & 2 & 0 \\ 25 & -1 & 3 \end{vmatrix} = 2\left(9\begin{vmatrix} 2 & 0 \\ -1 & 3 \end{vmatrix} + 3\begin{vmatrix} -15 & 0 \\ 25 & 3 \end{vmatrix} - 2\begin{vmatrix} -15 & 2 \\ 25 & -1 \end{vmatrix}\right) = 2(54 - 135 + 70) =$

$2(-11) = -22; D_y = \begin{vmatrix} 1 & 9 & -2 \\ 3 & 20 & 6 \\ 4 & 25 & 3 \end{vmatrix} = \begin{vmatrix} 1 & 9 & -2 \\ 3 - 3(1) & 20 - 3(9) & 6 - 3(-2) \\ 4 - 4(1) & 25 - 4(9) & 3 - 4(-2) \end{vmatrix} =$

$\begin{vmatrix} 1 & 9 & -2 \\ 0 & -7 & 12 \\ 0 & -11 & 11 \end{vmatrix} = 1\begin{vmatrix} -7 & 12 \\ -11 & 11 \end{vmatrix} = (1)(11)\begin{vmatrix} -7 & 12 \\ -1 & 1 \end{vmatrix} = 11(5) = 55;$

$D_z = \begin{vmatrix} 1 & -3 & 9 \\ 3 & 2 & 20 \\ 4 & -1 & 25 \end{vmatrix} = \begin{vmatrix} 1 & -3 & 9 \\ 3 - 3(1) & 2 - 3(-3) & 20 - 3(9) \\ 4 - 4(1) & -1 - 4(-3) & 25 - 4(9) \end{vmatrix} = \begin{vmatrix} 1 & -3 & 9 \\ 0 & 11 & -7 \\ 0 & 11 & -11 \end{vmatrix} =$

(Continued)

$\begin{vmatrix} 11 & -7 \\ 11 & -11 \end{vmatrix} = 11\begin{vmatrix} 1 & -7 \\ 1 & -11 \end{vmatrix} = 11(-4) = -44; x = \frac{-22}{-11} = 2, y = \frac{55}{-11} = -5,$

$z = \frac{-44}{-11} = 4$; (2, −5, 4)

5. $D = \begin{vmatrix} 1 & 1 & -1 \\ 2 & 1 & -2 \\ 3 & 0 & -4 \end{vmatrix} = -1\begin{vmatrix} 2 & -2 \\ 3 & -4 \end{vmatrix} + 1\begin{vmatrix} 1 & -1 \\ 3 & -4 \end{vmatrix} = (-1)(-2) + 1(-1) = 1;$

$D_x = \begin{vmatrix} 0 & 1 & -1 \\ 1 & 1 & -2 \\ 1 & 0 & -4 \end{vmatrix} = \begin{vmatrix} 0 & 1 & 0 \\ 1 & 1 & -1 \\ 1 & 0 & -4 \end{vmatrix} = (-1)\begin{vmatrix} 1 & -1 \\ 1 & -4 \end{vmatrix} = (-1)(-3) = 3;$

$D_y = \begin{vmatrix} 1 & 0 & -1 \\ 2 & 1 & -2 \\ 3 & 1 & -4 \end{vmatrix} = \begin{vmatrix} 1 & 0 & -1 \\ 2 & 1 & -2 \\ 1 & 0 & -2 \end{vmatrix} = 1\begin{vmatrix} 1 & -1 \\ 1 & -2 \end{vmatrix} = 1(-1) = -1; D_z = \begin{vmatrix} 1 & 1 & 0 \\ 2 & 1 & 1 \\ 3 & 0 & 1 \end{vmatrix} =$

$(1)\begin{vmatrix} 1 & 1 \\ 0 & 1 \end{vmatrix} - (1)\begin{vmatrix} 2 & 1 \\ 3 & 1 \end{vmatrix} = 2; x = \frac{3}{1} = 3, y = \frac{-1}{1} = -1, z = \frac{2}{1} = 2$; (3, −1, 2)

6. $D = \begin{vmatrix} 1 & 1 & 1 \\ 2 & -1 & -1 \\ 3 & 2 & 4 \end{vmatrix} = \begin{vmatrix} 1 & 1 & 1 \\ 3 & 0 & 0 \\ 3 & 2 & 4 \end{vmatrix} = -3\begin{vmatrix} 1 & 1 \\ 2 & 4 \end{vmatrix} = (-3)(2) = -6;$

$D_x = \begin{vmatrix} -2 & 1 & 1 \\ -1 & -1 & -1 \\ -15 & 2 & 4 \end{vmatrix} = \begin{vmatrix} -3 & 0 & 0 \\ -1 & -1 & -1 \\ -15 & 2 & 4 \end{vmatrix} = -3\begin{vmatrix} -1 & -1 \\ 2 & 4 \end{vmatrix} = (-3)(-2) = 6;$

$D_y = \begin{vmatrix} 1 & -2 & 1 \\ 2 & -1 & -1 \\ 3 & -15 & 4 \end{vmatrix} = \begin{vmatrix} 1 & -2 & 0 \\ 2 & -1 & -3 \\ 3 & -15 & 1 \end{vmatrix} = \begin{vmatrix} -1 & -3 \\ -15 & 1 \end{vmatrix} - (-2)\begin{vmatrix} 2 & -3 \\ 3 & 1 \end{vmatrix} =$

$-46 + 22 = -24; D_z = \begin{vmatrix} 1 & 1 & -2 \\ 2 & -1 & -1 \\ 3 & 2 & -15 \end{vmatrix} = \begin{vmatrix} 1 & 0 & -2 \\ 2 & -3 & -1 \\ 3 & -1 & -15 \end{vmatrix} =$

$\begin{vmatrix} -3 & -1 \\ -1 & -15 \end{vmatrix} + (-2)\begin{vmatrix} 2 & -3 \\ 3 & -1 \end{vmatrix} = 44 - 14 = 30; x = \frac{6}{-6} = -1, y = \frac{-24}{-6} = 4,$

$z = \frac{30}{-6} = -5$; (−1, 4, −5)

7. $D = \begin{vmatrix} 1 & -1 & 1 \\ 0 & 1 & 1 \\ 0 & -1 & 1 \end{vmatrix} = 1\begin{vmatrix} 1 & 1 \\ -1 & 1 \end{vmatrix} = 2; D_x = \begin{vmatrix} 3 & -1 & 1 \\ 3 & 1 & 1 \\ 1 & -1 & 1 \end{vmatrix} = \begin{vmatrix} 2 & 0 & 0 \\ 3 & 1 & 1 \\ 1 & -1 & 1 \end{vmatrix} =$

$2\begin{vmatrix} 1 & 1 \\ -1 & 1 \end{vmatrix} = 4; D_y = \begin{vmatrix} 1 & 3 & 1 \\ 0 & 3 & 1 \\ 0 & 1 & 1 \end{vmatrix} = 1\begin{vmatrix} 3 & 1 \\ 1 & 1 \end{vmatrix} = 2; D_z = \begin{vmatrix} 1 & -1 & 3 \\ 0 & 1 & 3 \\ 0 & -1 & 1 \end{vmatrix} = 1\begin{vmatrix} 1 & 3 \\ -1 & 1 \end{vmatrix} = 4;$

$x = \frac{4}{2} = 2, y = \frac{2}{2} = 1, z = \frac{4}{2} = 2$; (2, 1, 2)

8. $D = \begin{vmatrix} 1 & 3 & 1 \\ 1 & 0 & 4 \\ 0 & -6 & 1 \end{vmatrix} = 1\begin{vmatrix} 0 & 4 \\ -6 & 1 \end{vmatrix} - 1\begin{vmatrix} 3 & 1 \\ -6 & 1 \end{vmatrix} = 24 - 9 = 15; D_x = \begin{vmatrix} 0 & 3 & 1 \\ -2 & 0 & 4 \\ 1 & -6 & 1 \end{vmatrix} =$

$2\begin{vmatrix} 3 & 1 \\ -6 & 1 \end{vmatrix} + 1\begin{vmatrix} 3 & 1 \\ 0 & 4 \end{vmatrix} = 18 + 12 = 30; D_y = \begin{vmatrix} 1 & 0 & 1 \\ 1 & -2 & 4 \\ 0 & 1 & 1 \end{vmatrix} = 1\begin{vmatrix} -2 & 4 \\ 1 & 1 \end{vmatrix} + 1\begin{vmatrix} 1 & -2 \\ 0 & 1 \end{vmatrix} =$

$-6 + 1 = -5; D_z = \begin{vmatrix} 1 & 3 & 0 \\ 1 & 0 & -2 \\ 0 & -6 & 1 \end{vmatrix} = 1\begin{vmatrix} 0 & -2 \\ -6 & 1 \end{vmatrix} - 3\begin{vmatrix} 1 & -2 \\ 0 & 1 \end{vmatrix} = -12 - 3 = -15;$

$x = \frac{30}{15} = 2, y = \frac{-5}{15} = -\frac{1}{3}, z = \frac{-15}{15} = -1; \left(2, -\frac{1}{3}, -1\right)$

9. $D = \begin{vmatrix} 2 & 1 & -1 \\ 4 & -1 & 4 \\ 0 & -3 & 2 \end{vmatrix} = 2\begin{vmatrix} -1 & 4 \\ -3 & 2 \end{vmatrix} - 4\begin{vmatrix} 1 & -1 \\ -3 & 2 \end{vmatrix} = 2(10) - 4(-1) = 24;$

$D_x = \begin{vmatrix} 3 & 1 & -1 \\ 0 & -1 & 4 \\ 6 & -3 & 2 \end{vmatrix} = 3\begin{vmatrix} -1 & 4 \\ -3 & 2 \end{vmatrix} + 6\begin{vmatrix} 1 & -1 \\ -1 & 4 \end{vmatrix} = 3(10) + 6(3) = 48;$

$D_y = \begin{vmatrix} 2 & 3 & -1 \\ 4 & 0 & 4 \\ 0 & 6 & 2 \end{vmatrix} = -3\begin{vmatrix} 4 & 4 \\ 0 & 2 \end{vmatrix} - 6\begin{vmatrix} 2 & -1 \\ 4 & 4 \end{vmatrix} = -3 \cdot 8 - 6 \cdot 12 = -96;$

$D_z = \begin{vmatrix} 2 & 1 & 3 \\ 4 & -1 & 0 \\ 0 & -3 & 6 \end{vmatrix} = 3\begin{vmatrix} 2 & 3 \\ 4 & 0 \end{vmatrix} + 6\begin{vmatrix} 2 & 1 \\ 4 & -1 \end{vmatrix} = 3(-12) + 6(-6) = -72; x = \frac{48}{24} = 2,$

$y = \frac{-96}{24} = -4, z = \frac{-72}{24} = -3; (2, -4, -3)$

10. $D = \begin{vmatrix} 1 & -2 & 0 \\ 1 & 0 & 2 \\ 0 & -1 & -2 \end{vmatrix} = 1\begin{vmatrix} 0 & 2 \\ -1 & -2 \end{vmatrix} - 1\begin{vmatrix} -2 & 0 \\ -1 & -2 \end{vmatrix} = 2 - 4 = -2;$

$D_x = \begin{vmatrix} 8 & -2 & 0 \\ 3 & 0 & 2 \\ 2 & -1 & -2 \end{vmatrix} = -2\begin{vmatrix} 8 & -2 \\ 2 & -1 \end{vmatrix} + (-2)\begin{vmatrix} 8 & -2 \\ 3 & 0 \end{vmatrix} = 8 - 12 = -4;$

$D_y = \begin{vmatrix} 1 & 8 & 0 \\ 1 & 3 & 2 \\ 0 & 2 & -2 \end{vmatrix} = 1\begin{vmatrix} 3 & 2 \\ 2 & -2 \end{vmatrix} - 1\begin{vmatrix} 8 & 0 \\ 2 & -2 \end{vmatrix} = -10 + 16 = 6;$

$D_z = \begin{vmatrix} 1 & -2 & 8 \\ 1 & 0 & 3 \\ 0 & -1 & 2 \end{vmatrix} = 1\begin{vmatrix} 0 & 3 \\ -1 & 2 \end{vmatrix} - 1\begin{vmatrix} -2 & 8 \\ -1 & 2 \end{vmatrix} = 3 - 4 = -1; x = \frac{-4}{-2} = 2,$

$y = \frac{6}{-2} = -3, z = \frac{-1}{-2} = \frac{1}{2}; \left(2, -3, \frac{1}{2}\right)$

11. $D = \begin{vmatrix} 2 & -1 \\ -2 & 1 \end{vmatrix} = 0, D_y = \begin{vmatrix} 2 & 5 \\ -2 & -1 \end{vmatrix} = 8 \neq 0$; no solution

12. $D = \begin{vmatrix} 3 & 9 \\ 6 & 18 \end{vmatrix} = 0; D_y = \begin{vmatrix} 3 & 14 \\ 6 & 28 \end{vmatrix} = 0$; infinite number of solutions

13. $D = \begin{vmatrix} 4 & 3 \\ 8 & 6 \end{vmatrix} = 0; D_y = \begin{vmatrix} 4 & 16 \\ 8 & 10 \end{vmatrix} = -88 \neq 0$; no solution

14. $D = \begin{vmatrix} 5 & -9 \\ -2 & 5 \end{vmatrix} = 7 \neq 0$; one solution

B **15.** $D = \begin{vmatrix} 2 & -3 & 1 & -3 \\ 1 & 2 & 3 & -1 \\ 3 & 5 & 6 & 0 \\ 3 & -1 & 0 & -2 \end{vmatrix} = \begin{vmatrix} -1 & -9 & -8 & 0 \\ 1 & 2 & 3 & -1 \\ 3 & 5 & 6 & 0 \\ 1 & -5 & -6 & 0 \end{vmatrix} = \begin{vmatrix} -1 & -9 & -8 & 0 \\ 1 & 2 & 3 & -1 \\ 3 & 5 & 6 & 0 \\ 4 & 0 & 0 & 0 \end{vmatrix} =$

$-1\begin{vmatrix} -1 & -9 & -8 \\ 3 & 5 & 6 \\ 4 & 0 & 0 \end{vmatrix} = 4\begin{vmatrix} 1 & 9 & 8 \\ 3 & 5 & 6 \\ 1 & 0 & 0 \end{vmatrix} = 4(54 - 40) = 56; D_a = \begin{vmatrix} -1 & -3 & 1 & -3 \\ 1 & 2 & 3 & -1 \\ 4 & 5 & 6 & 0 \\ 6 & -1 & 0 & -2 \end{vmatrix} =$

$\begin{vmatrix} -4 & -9 & -8 & 0 \\ 1 & 2 & 3 & -1 \\ 4 & 5 & 6 & 0 \\ 4 & -5 & -6 & 0 \end{vmatrix} = \begin{vmatrix} -4 & -9 & -8 & 0 \\ 1 & 2 & 3 & -1 \\ 4 & 5 & 6 & 0 \\ 8 & 0 & 0 & 0 \end{vmatrix} = -1\begin{vmatrix} -4 & -9 & -8 \\ 4 & 5 & 6 \\ 8 & 0 & 0 \end{vmatrix} =$

$8\begin{vmatrix} 4 & 9 & 8 \\ 4 & 5 & 6 \\ 1 & 0 & 0 \end{vmatrix} = 8(14) = 112; D_b = \begin{vmatrix} 2 & -1 & 1 & -3 \\ 1 & 1 & 3 & -1 \\ 3 & 4 & 6 & 0 \\ 3 & 6 & 0 & -2 \end{vmatrix} = \begin{vmatrix} -1 & -4 & -8 & 0 \\ 1 & 1 & 3 & -1 \\ 3 & 4 & 6 & 0 \\ 1 & 4 & -6 & 0 \end{vmatrix} =$

$-1\begin{vmatrix} -1 & -4 & -8 \\ 3 & 4 & 6 \\ 1 & 4 & -6 \end{vmatrix} = -1\begin{vmatrix} 0 & 0 & -14 \\ 3 & 4 & 6 \\ 1 & 4 & -6 \end{vmatrix} = 14\begin{vmatrix} 0 & 0 & 1 \\ 3 & 4 & 6 \\ 1 & 4 & -6 \end{vmatrix} = 14(12 - 4) = 112;$

$D_c = \begin{vmatrix} 2 & -3 & -1 & -3 \\ 1 & 2 & 1 & -1 \\ 3 & 5 & 4 & 0 \\ 3 & -1 & 6 & -2 \end{vmatrix} = \begin{vmatrix} -1 & -9 & -4 & 0 \\ 1 & 2 & 1 & -1 \\ 3 & 5 & 4 & 0 \\ 1 & -5 & 4 & 0 \end{vmatrix} = -1\begin{vmatrix} -1 & -9 & -4 \\ 3 & 5 & 4 \\ 1 & -5 & 4 \end{vmatrix} =$

$-1\begin{vmatrix} 0 & -14 & 0 \\ 3 & 5 & 4 \\ 1 & -5 & 4 \end{vmatrix} = 14\begin{vmatrix} 3 & 4 \\ 1 & 4 \end{vmatrix} = -14(12 - 4) = -112; D_d = \begin{vmatrix} 2 & -3 & 1 & -1 \\ 1 & 2 & 3 & 1 \\ 3 & 5 & 6 & 4 \\ 3 & -1 & 0 & 6 \end{vmatrix} =$

$\begin{vmatrix} -7 & -3 & 1 & -19 \\ 7 & 2 & 3 & 13 \\ 18 & 5 & 6 & 34 \\ 0 & -1 & 0 & 0 \end{vmatrix} = -1\begin{vmatrix} -7 & 1 & -19 \\ 7 & 3 & 13 \\ 18 & 6 & 34 \end{vmatrix} = -1\begin{vmatrix} 0 & 1 & 0 \\ 28 & 3 & 70 \\ 60 & 6 & 148 \end{vmatrix} = \begin{vmatrix} 28 & 70 \\ 60 & 148 \end{vmatrix} = -56;$

$a = \frac{112}{56} = 2; b = \frac{112}{56} = 2; c = -\frac{112}{56} = -2; d = -\frac{56}{56} = -1; (2, 2, -2, -1)$

16. $D = \begin{vmatrix} 1 & -2 & 1 & 0 \\ 2 & 0 & -1 & 1 \\ 0 & 1 & 2 & -3 \\ 3 & -3 & 2 & 0 \end{vmatrix} = \begin{vmatrix} 1 & -2 & 1 & 0 \\ 2 & 0 & -1 & 1 \\ 6 & 1 & -1 & 0 \\ 3 & -3 & 2 & 0 \end{vmatrix} = \begin{vmatrix} 1 & -2 & 1 \\ 6 & 1 & -1 \\ 3 & -3 & 2 \end{vmatrix} = \begin{vmatrix} 1 & -2 & 1 \\ 7 & -1 & 0 \\ 1 & 1 & 0 \end{vmatrix} =$

$\begin{vmatrix} 7 & -1 \\ 1 & 1 \end{vmatrix} = 8; D_p = \begin{vmatrix} -4 & -2 & 1 & 0 \\ -3 & 0 & -1 & 1 \\ 14 & 1 & 2 & -3 \\ -13 & -3 & 2 & 0 \end{vmatrix} = \begin{vmatrix} -4 & -2 & 1 & 0 \\ -3 & 0 & -1 & 1 \\ -23 & 1 & -1 & 0 \\ -13 & -3 & 2 & 0 \end{vmatrix} =$

$$\begin{vmatrix} -4 & -2 & 1 \\ -23 & 1 & -1 \\ -13 & -3 & 2 \end{vmatrix} = \begin{vmatrix} -4 & -2 & 1 \\ -27 & -1 & 0 \\ -5 & 1 & 0 \end{vmatrix} = \begin{vmatrix} -27 & -1 \\ -5 & 1 \end{vmatrix} = -32;$$

$$D_q = \begin{vmatrix} 1 & -4 & 1 & 0 \\ 2 & -3 & -1 & 1 \\ 0 & -14 & 2 & -3 \\ 3 & -13 & 2 & 0 \end{vmatrix} = \begin{vmatrix} 1 & -4 & 1 & 0 \\ 2 & -3 & -1 & 1 \\ 6 & -23 & -1 & 0 \\ 3 & -13 & 2 & 0 \end{vmatrix} = \begin{vmatrix} 1 & -4 & 1 \\ 6 & -23 & -1 \\ 3 & -13 & 2 \end{vmatrix} =$$

$$-46 + 12 - 78 + 69 - 13 + 48 = -8; D_r = \begin{vmatrix} 1 & -2 & -4 & 0 \\ 2 & 0 & -3 & 1 \\ 0 & 1 & -14 & -3 \\ 3 & -3 & -13 & 0 \end{vmatrix} =$$

$$\begin{vmatrix} 1 & -2 & -4 & 0 \\ 2 & 0 & -3 & 1 \\ 6 & 1 & -23 & 0 \\ 3 & -3 & -13 & 0 \end{vmatrix} = \begin{vmatrix} 1 & -2 & -4 \\ 6 & 1 & -23 \\ 3 & -3 & -13 \end{vmatrix} = -13 + 138 + 72 + 12 - 69 - 156 = -16;$$

$$D_s = \begin{vmatrix} 1 & -2 & 1 & -4 \\ 2 & 0 & -1 & -3 \\ 0 & 1 & 2 & -14 \\ 3 & -3 & 2 & -13 \end{vmatrix} = \begin{vmatrix} 1 & 0 & 5 & -32 \\ 2 & 0 & -1 & -3 \\ 0 & 1 & 2 & -14 \\ 3 & 0 & 8 & -55 \end{vmatrix} = -\begin{vmatrix} 1 & 5 & -32 \\ 2 & -1 & -3 \\ 3 & 8 & -55 \end{vmatrix} =$$

$$-(55 - 45 - 512 - 96 + 24 + 550) = 24; p = -\frac{32}{8} = -4; q = -\frac{8}{8} = -1,$$

$$r = -\frac{16}{8} = -2, s = \frac{24}{8} = 3; (-4, -1, -2, 3)$$

C **Ex. 17–19:** $\begin{matrix} m_1x - y = -b_1 \\ m_2x - y = -b_2 \end{matrix}; D = \begin{vmatrix} m_1 & -1 \\ m_2 & -1 \end{vmatrix} = -m_1 + m_2; D_y = \begin{vmatrix} m_1 & -b_1 \\ m_2 & -b_2 \end{vmatrix} =$
$-b_2m_1 + b_1m_2$

17. If $D \neq 0$, then $-m_1 + m_2 \neq 0$ and thus $m_1 \neq m_2$; if $m_1 \neq m_2$, then $-m_1 + m_2 \neq 0$ and thus $D \neq 0$; therefore, $D \neq 0$ if and only if $m_1 \neq m_2$

18. If $D = 0$ and $D_y \neq 0$, then $-m_1 + m_2 = 0$ and $-b_2m_1 + b_1m_2 \neq 0$; since $-m_1 + m_2 = 0$, $m_1 = m_2$ and $-b_2m_1 + b_1m_1 \neq 0$; if $m_1 \neq 0$, $-b_2 + b_1 \neq 0$, so $b_1 \neq b_2$; if $m_1 = m_2$ and $b_1 \neq b_2$, then $-m_1 + m_2 = 0$ and $-b_2 + b_1 \neq 0$; $-m_1b_2 + m_1b_1 \neq 0$; $-m_1b_2 + m_2b_1 \neq 0$; therefore, $D = 0$ and $D_y \neq 0$; therefore, $D = 0$ and $D_y \neq 0$ if and only if $m_1 = m_2$ and $b_1 \neq b_2$

19. If $D = 0$ and $D_y = 0$, then $-m_1 + m_2 = 0$ and $-b_2m_1 + b_1m_2 = 0$; $m_1 = m_2$; $-b_2m_1 + b_1m_1 = 0$; if $m_1 \neq 0$, $-b_2 + b_1 = 0$; therefore $b_1 = b_2$; if $m_1 = m_2$ and $b_1 = b_2$, then $-m_1 + m_2 = 0$ and $m_1b_1 = m_1b_2$; $-b_2m_1 + b_1m_1 = 0$; $-b_2m_1 + b_1m_2 = 0$; therefore $D = 0$ and $D_y = 0$; therefore $D = 0$ and $D_y = 0$ if and only if $m_1 = m_2$ and $b_1 = b_2$.

Page 805 • MIXED REVIEW EXERCISES

1. $\begin{bmatrix} 6 & 0 \\ 3 & 4 \end{bmatrix}$ **2.** $\begin{bmatrix} 8 & -4 \\ 12 & 0 \end{bmatrix}$ **3.** $\begin{bmatrix} 0 + 8 & -1 + 2 \\ 0 + 12 & -2 + 3 \end{bmatrix} = \begin{bmatrix} 8 & 1 \\ 12 & 1 \end{bmatrix}$

4.

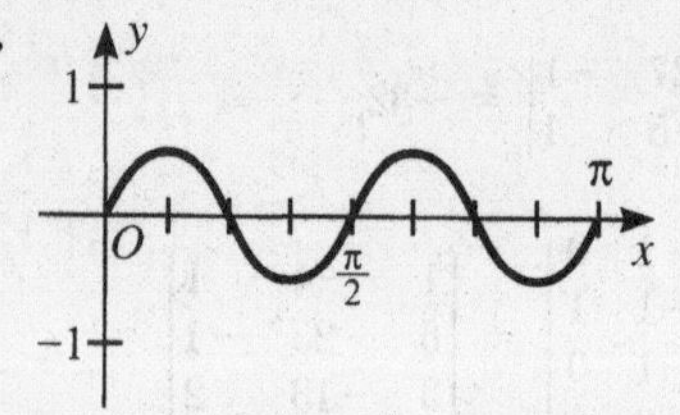

5.

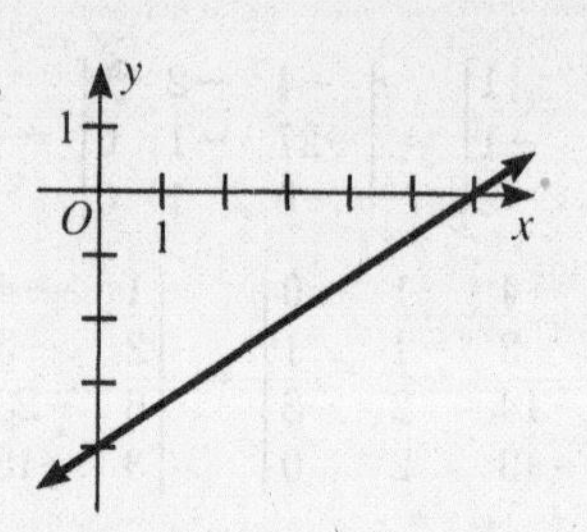

6.

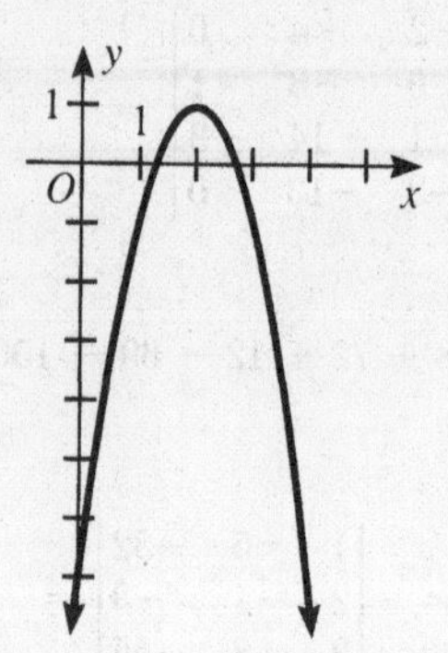

Pages 806–807 • CHAPTER REVIEW

1. d; $4 - x = 0$ and $3y = 0$, $x = 4$ and $y = 0$

2. b; $B - 2A = \begin{bmatrix} 3 & -2 \\ -1 & 4 \end{bmatrix} - \begin{bmatrix} -4 & 6 \\ -2 & 12 \end{bmatrix} = \begin{bmatrix} 7 & -8 \\ 1 & -8 \end{bmatrix}$

3. c; $BA = \begin{bmatrix} 3 & -2 \\ -1 & 4 \end{bmatrix}\begin{bmatrix} -2 & 3 \\ -1 & 6 \end{bmatrix} = \begin{bmatrix} -6 + 2 & 9 - 12 \\ 2 - 4 & -3 + 24 \end{bmatrix} = \begin{bmatrix} -4 & -3 \\ -2 & 21 \end{bmatrix}$

4. a; $\begin{bmatrix} 0 & 1 & 0 \\ 1 & 0 & 1 \\ 1 & 0 & 0 \end{bmatrix}\begin{bmatrix} 0 & 1 & 0 \\ 1 & 0 & 1 \\ 1 & 0 & 0 \end{bmatrix} = \begin{bmatrix} 1 & 0 & 1 \\ 1 & 1 & 0 \\ 0 & 1 & 0 \end{bmatrix}$ **5.** d; $4(3) - (-1)(2) = 12 + 2 = 14$

6. b; $0 + 2 + 0 - 0 - 0 - 0 = 2$

7. a; $\begin{vmatrix} -2 & 1 \\ 0 & 6 \end{vmatrix} = -12$; $-\frac{1}{12}\begin{bmatrix} 6 & -1 \\ 0 & -2 \end{bmatrix} = \begin{bmatrix} -\frac{1}{2} & \frac{1}{12} \\ 0 & \frac{1}{6} \end{bmatrix}$

8. c; $-1\begin{vmatrix} 1 & 0 \\ -1 & 3 \end{vmatrix} - 0\begin{vmatrix} 2 & 0 \\ 1 & 3 \end{vmatrix} + 1\begin{vmatrix} 2 & 1 \\ 1 & -1 \end{vmatrix} = (-1)(3) - 0 + (1)(-3) = -6$

9. d; $\begin{vmatrix} 3 & 2 & -2 \\ 1 & 0 & 2 \\ -12 & 3 & 8 \end{vmatrix} = \begin{vmatrix} 3 & 2 & -2 \\ 1 & 0 & 2 \\ 0 & 11 & 0 \end{vmatrix} = -11\begin{vmatrix} 3 & -2 \\ 1 & 2 \end{vmatrix} = -11 \cdot 8 = -88$

10. a; $D = \begin{vmatrix} 2 & 1 & 3 \\ 5 & 2 & 0 \\ 0 & 2 & 3 \end{vmatrix} = 27$; $D_x = \begin{vmatrix} -2 & 1 & 3 \\ 5 & 2 & 0 \\ -13 & 2 & 3 \end{vmatrix} = 81$; $D_y = \begin{vmatrix} 2 & -2 & 3 \\ 5 & 5 & 0 \\ 0 & -13 & 3 \end{vmatrix} = -135$;

(Continued)

$$D_z = \begin{vmatrix} 2 & 1 & -2 \\ 5 & 2 & 5 \\ 0 & 2 & -13 \end{vmatrix} = -27; x = \frac{81}{27} = 3, y = -\frac{135}{27} = -5, z = -\frac{27}{27} = -1; (3, -5, -1)$$

Page 808 • CHAPTER TEST

1. $2x - 6 = 0, x = 3; y + 4 = 0, y = -4$

2. $A + B = \begin{bmatrix} 2 + (-2) & 1 + 1 & 3 + 5 \\ 0 + 5 & -1 + (-5) & 1 + 1 \\ 4 + 0 & -1 + 3 & 0 + (-1) \end{bmatrix} = \begin{bmatrix} 0 & 2 & 8 \\ 5 & -6 & 2 \\ 4 & 2 & -1 \end{bmatrix}$

3. $B - A = \begin{bmatrix} -2 - 2 & 1 - 1 & 5 - 3 \\ 5 - 0 & -5 - (-1) & 1 - 1 \\ 0 - 4 & 3 - (-1) & -1 - 0 \end{bmatrix} = \begin{bmatrix} -4 & 0 & 2 \\ 5 & -4 & 0 \\ -4 & 4 & -1 \end{bmatrix}$

4. $4A = \begin{bmatrix} 4(2) & 4(\ 1) & 4(3) \\ 4(0) & 4(-1) & 4(1) \\ 4(4) & 4(-1) & 4(0) \end{bmatrix} = \begin{bmatrix} 8 & 4 & 12 \\ 0 & -4 & 4 \\ 16 & -4 & 0 \end{bmatrix}$

5. $A - 2B = \begin{bmatrix} 2 & 1 & 3 \\ 0 & -1 & 1 \\ 4 & -1 & 0 \end{bmatrix} - \begin{bmatrix} -4 & 2 & 10 \\ 10 & -10 & 2 \\ 0 & 6 & -2 \end{bmatrix} = \begin{bmatrix} 6 & -1 & -7 \\ -10 & 9 & -1 \\ 4 & -7 & 2 \end{bmatrix}$

6. $AB = \begin{bmatrix} 2 & 1 & 3 \\ 0 & -1 & 1 \\ 4 & -1 & 0 \end{bmatrix}\begin{bmatrix} -2 & 1 & 5 \\ 5 & -5 & 1 \\ 0 & 3 & -1 \end{bmatrix} = \begin{bmatrix} 1 & 6 & 8 \\ -5 & 8 & -2 \\ -13 & 9 & 19 \end{bmatrix}$

7. $B^2 = \begin{bmatrix} -2 & 1 & 5 \\ 5 & -5 & 1 \\ 0 & 3 & -1 \end{bmatrix}\begin{bmatrix} -2 & 1 & 5 \\ 5 & -5 & 1 \\ 0 & 3 & -1 \end{bmatrix} = \begin{bmatrix} 9 & 8 & -14 \\ -35 & 33 & 19 \\ 15 & -18 & 4 \end{bmatrix}$

8. From/To

$$\begin{array}{c|cccc} & A & B & C & D \\ \hline A & 0 & 1 & 1 & 1 \\ B & 0 & 0 & 1 & 0 \\ C & 0 & 0 & 0 & 1 \\ D & 1 & 1 & 1 & 0 \end{array} = M; M^2 = \begin{bmatrix} 0 & 1 & 1 & 1 \\ 0 & 0 & 1 & 0 \\ 0 & 0 & 0 & 1 \\ 1 & 1 & 1 & 0 \end{bmatrix}\begin{bmatrix} 0 & 1 & 1 & 1 \\ 0 & 0 & 1 & 0 \\ 0 & 0 & 0 & 1 \\ 1 & 1 & 1 & 0 \end{bmatrix} = \begin{bmatrix} 1 & 1 & 2 & 1 \\ 0 & 0 & 0 & 1 \\ 1 & 1 & 1 & 0 \\ 0 & 1 & 2 & 2 \end{bmatrix};$$

The matrix $M + M^2$ has $1 + 1 = 2$ in the first row, second column. Therefore there are 2 routes from A to B using at most one relay.

9. $\begin{vmatrix} 6 & 3 \\ -2 & -2 \end{vmatrix} = -12 - (-6) = -6$

10. $\begin{vmatrix} 1 & 0 & -1 \\ 3 & 1 & 1 \\ 0 & 2 & 2 \end{vmatrix} = 1\begin{vmatrix} 1 & 1 \\ 2 & 2 \end{vmatrix} - 3\begin{vmatrix} 0 & -1 \\ 2 & 2 \end{vmatrix} + 0 = 1(0) - 3(2) = -6$

11. $\begin{bmatrix} 2 & 3 \\ -1 & 0 \end{bmatrix}A = \begin{bmatrix} 7 & 3 \\ 4 & 0 \end{bmatrix}; \begin{vmatrix} 2 & 3 \\ -1 & 0 \end{vmatrix} = 3; A = \frac{1}{3}\begin{bmatrix} 0 & -3 \\ 1 & 2 \end{bmatrix}\begin{bmatrix} 7 & 3 \\ 4 & 0 \end{bmatrix} = \frac{1}{3}\begin{bmatrix} -12 & 0 \\ 15 & 3 \end{bmatrix} =$
$\begin{bmatrix} -4 & 0 \\ 5 & 1 \end{bmatrix}$

12. $1\begin{vmatrix} 0 & -1 \\ -1 & 1 \end{vmatrix} - (-1)\begin{vmatrix} 3 & -1 \\ 2 & 1 \end{vmatrix} + 0 = -1 + 5 = 4$

13. $\begin{vmatrix} 10 & 5 & -5 \\ 16 & 8 & -8 \\ 3 & 0 & -4 \end{vmatrix} = 5 \cdot 8 \begin{vmatrix} 2 & 1 & -1 \\ 2 & 1 & -1 \\ 3 & 0 & -4 \end{vmatrix} = 0$

14. $\begin{vmatrix} 4 & 3 & -1 \\ -3 & -3 & 5 \\ 5 & 5 & 3 \end{vmatrix} = \begin{vmatrix} 4 + 4(-1) & 3 + 3(-1) & -1 \\ -3 + 4(5) & -3 + 3(5) & 5 \\ 5 + 4(3) & 5 + 3(3) & 3 \end{vmatrix} = \begin{vmatrix} 0 & 0 & -1 \\ 17 & 12 & 5 \\ 17 & 14 & 3 \end{vmatrix} =$

$17 \cdot 2 \begin{vmatrix} 0 & 0 & -1 \\ 1 & 6 & 5 \\ 1 & 7 & 3 \end{vmatrix} = 34 \cdot -1 \begin{vmatrix} 1 & 6 \\ 1 & 7 \end{vmatrix} = (-34)(1) = -34$

15. $D = \begin{vmatrix} 4 & -3 & 0 \\ 6 & 0 & -8 \\ 0 & 1 & -2 \end{vmatrix} = 2 \cdot 2 \begin{vmatrix} 2 & -3 & 0 \\ 3 & 0 & -4 \\ 0 & 1 & -1 \end{vmatrix} = 4 \begin{vmatrix} 2 & -3 & -3 \\ 3 & 0 & -4 \\ 0 & 1 & 0 \end{vmatrix} = (4)(-1) \begin{vmatrix} 2 & -3 \\ 3 & -4 \end{vmatrix} =$

$(-4)(1) = -4; D_x = \begin{vmatrix} 1 & -3 & 0 \\ 1 & 0 & -8 \\ 0 & 1 & -2 \end{vmatrix} = \begin{vmatrix} 1 & -3 & 0 \\ 0 & 3 & -8 \\ 0 & 1 & -2 \end{vmatrix} = \begin{vmatrix} 3 & -8 \\ 1 & -2 \end{vmatrix} = 2;$

$D_y = \begin{vmatrix} 4 & 1 & 0 \\ 6 & 1 & -8 \\ 0 & 0 & -2 \end{vmatrix} = 2(-2) \begin{vmatrix} 2 & 1 & 0 \\ 3 & 1 & 4 \\ 0 & 0 & 1 \end{vmatrix} = -4 \begin{vmatrix} 2 & 1 \\ 3 & 1 \end{vmatrix} = 4; D_z = \begin{vmatrix} 4 & -3 & 1 \\ 6 & 0 & 1 \\ 0 & 1 & 0 \end{vmatrix} =$

$-1 \begin{vmatrix} 4 & 1 \\ 6 & 1 \end{vmatrix} = 2; x = \frac{2}{-4} = -\frac{1}{2}, y = \frac{4}{-4} = -1, z = \frac{2}{-4} = -\frac{1}{2}; \left(-\frac{1}{2}, -1, -\frac{1}{2}\right)$

Page 809 • PREPARING FOR COLLEGE ENTRANCE EXAMS

1. D; Choice (A) is the matrix A and can be eliminated; since both the identity (choice B) and the zero matrix (choice C) commute with A, they can be eliminated. Choice D is correct; $\begin{bmatrix} 1 & -1 \\ 2 & 4 \end{bmatrix} \begin{bmatrix} 4 & 2 \\ -1 & 1 \end{bmatrix} = \begin{bmatrix} 5 & 1 \\ 4 & 8 \end{bmatrix}$, while $\begin{bmatrix} 4 & 2 \\ -1 & 1 \end{bmatrix} \begin{bmatrix} 1 & -1 \\ 2 & 4 \end{bmatrix} = \begin{bmatrix} 8 & 4 \\ 1 & 5 \end{bmatrix}$; Choice E is A^{-1} and can thus be eliminated.

2. C; $\begin{vmatrix} 5 & -6 \\ 2 & 4 \end{vmatrix} = 32; \frac{1}{32} \begin{bmatrix} 4 & 6 \\ -2 & 5 \end{bmatrix} = \begin{bmatrix} \frac{1}{8} & \frac{3}{16} \\ -\frac{1}{16} & \frac{5}{32} \end{bmatrix}$ 3. B; $\frac{7!}{3!} = 840$

4. B; this event is {(1, 1), (1, 2), (1, 3), (1, 4), (2, 1), (2, 2), (3, 1), (4, 1)}; $\frac{8}{36} = \frac{2}{9}$ 5. E

EXPLORATIONS

Page 832 • EXPLORING IRRATIONAL NUMBERS

1. a. $\triangle ABC$ is an isosceles right triangle since $AB = BC = 1$ and $\angle B$ is a right angle.

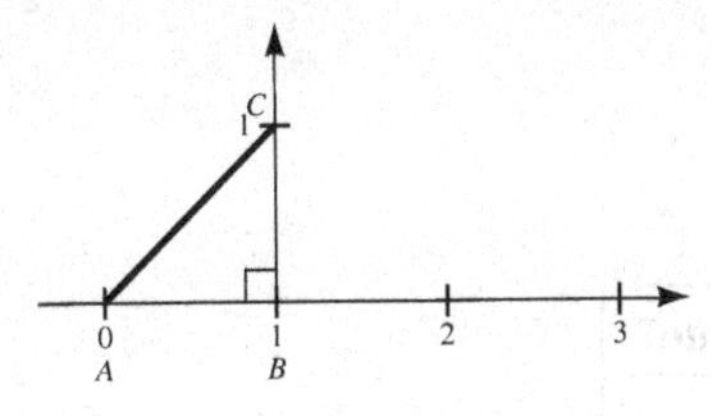

b. $AB = 1$ and $BC = 1$ (legs); $(AC)^2 = (AB)^2 + (BC)^2 = 1^2 + 1^2 = 2$, so $AC = \sqrt{2}$ (hypotenuse)

2. a. $AD = \sqrt{2}$ and $DE = 1$ (legs); $(AE)^2 = (AD)^2 + (DE)^2 = (\sqrt{2})^2 + 1^2 = 3$, so $AE = \sqrt{3}$ (hypotenuse)

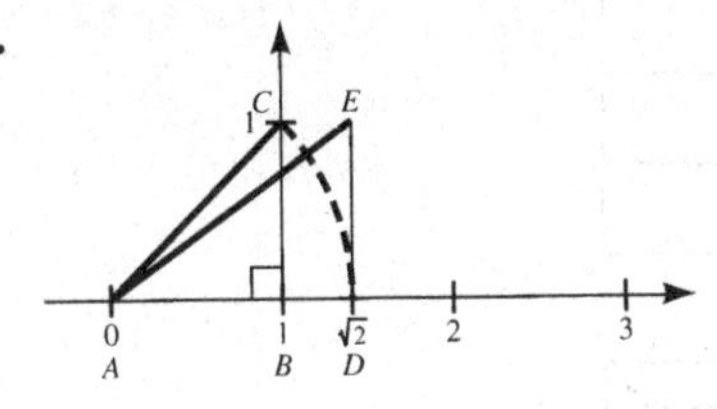

b. $\sqrt{2}$

3. a. $AF = \sqrt{3}$ and $FG = 1$ (legs); $(AG)^2 = (AF)^2 + (FG)^2 = (\sqrt{3})^2 + 1^2 = 4$, so $AG = \sqrt{4} = 2$ (hypotenuse)

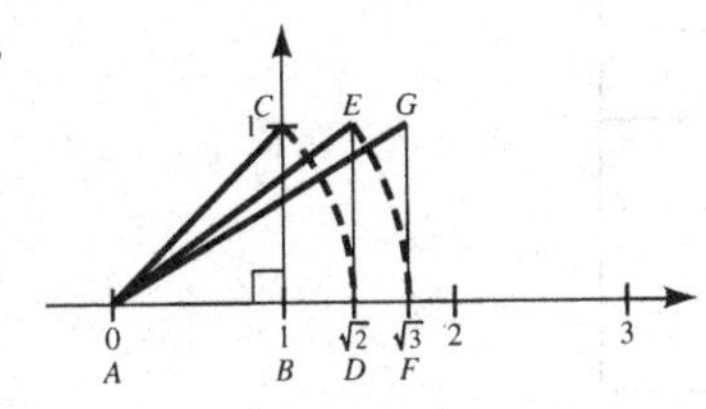

b. $\sqrt{3}$

4.

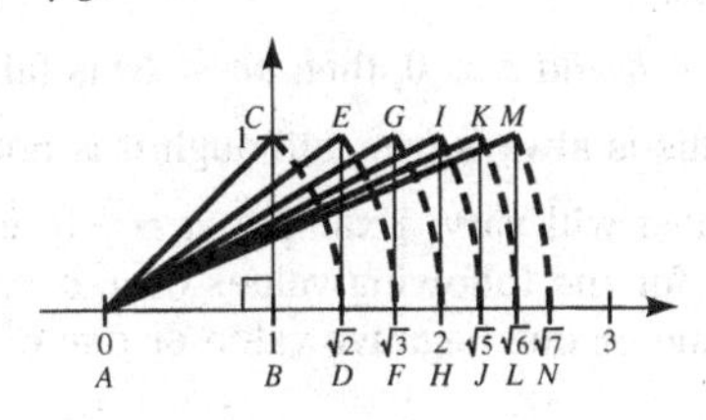

$\triangle AHI$: $AH = 2$ and $HI = 1$ (legs); $(AI)^2 = (AH)^2 + (HI)^2 = 2^2 + 1^2 = 5$,
$AI = \sqrt{5}$ (hypotenuse);
$\triangle AJK$: $AJ = \sqrt{5}$ and $JK = 1$ (legs); $(AK)^2 = (AJ)^2 + (JK)^2 = (\sqrt{5})^2 + 1^2 = 6$,
$AK = \sqrt{6}$ (hypotenuse);
$\triangle ALM$: $AL = \sqrt{6}$ and $LM = 1$ (legs); $(AM)^2 = (AL)^2 + (LM)^2 = (\sqrt{6})^2 + 1^2 = 7$,
$AK = \sqrt{7}$ (hypotenuse).
The irrational numbers located are $\sqrt{2}$, $\sqrt{3}$, $\sqrt{5}$, $\sqrt{6}$, and $\sqrt{7}$.

5. a. $C = \pi d = \pi \cdot 1 = \pi$

b. The circumference of the circle is π, so the length of the string is π. Since one end of the string is at zero, the other end lies at $\pi \approx 3.14$.

6. To locate $\sqrt{8}$, continue the constructions done in Exercise **4** for one more triangle. To locate $-\sqrt{5}$, draw an arc the length of $\sqrt{5}$ that crosses the number line to the left of 0.

7. Start with a circle with diameter 3 units to locate 3π, with diameter $\frac{1}{2}$ unit to locate $\frac{\pi}{2}$. Or, use the string from Exercise **5** three times to locate 3π or folded in half to locate $\frac{\pi}{2}$.

Page 833 • EXPLORING INEQUALITIES

1. a.

a	b	c	ac	bc	$ac < bc$ true?
3	5	4	12	20	Yes
−5	2	4	−20	8	Yes
−7	−4	4	−28	−16	Yes
0	3	4	0	12	Yes
−6	0	4	−24	0	Yes

b.

a	b	c	ac	bc	$ac < bc$ true?
3	5	−3	−9	−15	No
−5	2	−3	15	−6	No
−7	−4	−3	21	12	No
0	3	−3	0	−9	No
−6	0	−3	18	0	No

c. If $c = 0$, then $ac = bc = 0$, and $ac < bc$ is false.

d. If $a < b$ and $c > 0$, then $ac < bc$ is true. If $a < b$ and $c \leq 0$, then $ac < bc$ is false.

2. a. Answers will vary; some students may think this is always true, although it is not.

b. Students' cases for which the statement is false will vary. Example: $a = -3$, $b = -4$, $c = 2$, $d = 1$; $-6 \ngtr -4$. The statement is true for the following values of a, b, c, and d: (1) all positive values; (2) at most one zero value or one negative value or one of each; (3) $b = d = 0$. Otherwise, it is false.

$a > b$		$c > d$		ac	bd	$ac > bd$ true?
5	3	4	2	20	6	Yes
5	3	5	−4	25	−12	Yes
5	3	−6	−7	−30	−21	No
5	3	4	0	20	0	Yes
5	3	0	−3	0	−9	Yes

$a > b$		$c > d$		ac	bd	$ac > bd$ true?
4	−2	4	2	16	−4	Yes
4	−2	5	−19	20	38	No
4	−2	−6	−7	−24	14	No
4	−2	4	0	16	0	Yes
4	−2	0	−3	0	6	No

$a > b$		$c > d$		ac	bd	$ac > bd$ true?
−1	−2	4	2	−4	−4	No
−1	−4	5	−4	−5	16	No
−1	−4	−6	−7	6	28	No
−1	−4	4	0	−4	0	No
−1	−4	0	−3	0	12	No

$a > b$		$c > d$		ac	bd	$ac > bd$ true?
4	0	3	2	12	0	Yes
4	0	5	−4	20	0	Yes
4	0	−6	−7	−24	0	No
4	0	4	0	16	0	Yes
4	0	0	−3	0	0	No

$a > b$		$c > d$		ac	bd	$ac > bd$ true?
0	−3	4	2	0	−6	Yes
0	−3	5	−4	0	12	No
0	−3	−6	−7	0	21	No
0	−3	4	0	0	0	No
0	−3	0	−3	0	9	No

3. **a.** Yes; for example, $4 > 3$, but $\frac{1}{4} < \frac{1}{3}$.

b. Yes; for example, $-3 > -5$, but $-\frac{1}{3} < -\frac{1}{5}$.

c. For example, $3 > -2$, but $\frac{1}{3} \nless -\frac{1}{2}$.

4. False. See Exercise **2,** when all four values were negative, then $-1 > -4$ and $-6 > -7$, but $-1 \cdot -6 < -4 \cdot -7$, as $6 < 28$.

5. From Exercise **3,** since $\frac{1}{2} > 0$, the given inequality and the transformation in step 2 will hold only if $\frac{1}{x + 2} > 0$. This requires that $x + 2 > 0$ and $x > -2$. So the complete solution is $-2 < x < 0$.

Page 834 • EXPLORING FUNCTIONS

1. Divide the weight by 16 to change ounces to pounds, and determine what whole numbers of pounds the given weight is between.

2. a. Each package weighs 1 lb or less, so each delivery charge is \$4.

b. Each package weighs more than 1 lb but not more than 2 lb, so each delivery charge is \$8.

c. Each package weighs more than 2 lb but not more than 3 lb, so each delivery charge is \$12.

3.

Delivery charge ($)
12
8
4
0 1 2 3
Weight (lb)

4. Yes; Yes

5. a. $f(2) = 2$ **b.** $f(3\frac{1}{2}) = 3$ **c.** $f(3.\overline{6}) = 3$ **d.** $f(\sqrt{2}) = 1$

6.

y
4
3
2
1
0 1 2 3 4 x

7. The graphs of these functions look like steps, rather than points, lines, or curves.

8. Given any number x, $f(x) = x$ if x is an integer; $f(x) =$ the next integer greater than x if x is not an integer.

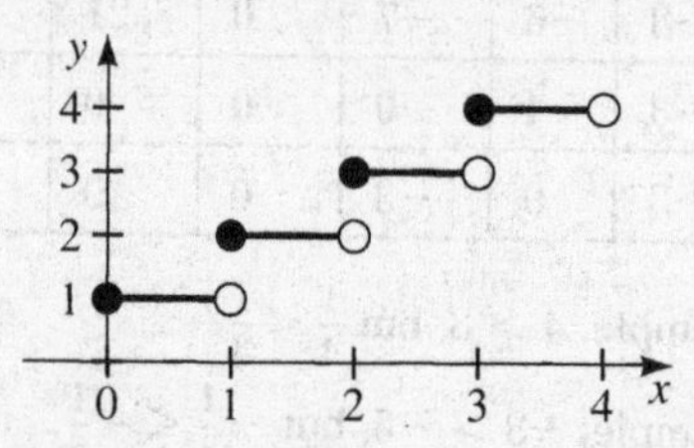

Page 835 • EXPLORING POLYNOMIAL FACTORS

1. a. $3x, x + 2$ **b.** $3x^2 + 6x = 3x(x + 2)$

2. a. 4 blue x-by-x tiles, 8 blue 1-by-x tiles, and 3 blue 1-by-1 tiles

c. $2x + 1, 2x + 3$

d. $4x^2 + 8x + 3 = (2x + 1)(2x + 3)$; factors are $2x + 1$ and $2x + 3$.

3. a. 1 blue x-by-x tile, 1 blue 1-by-x tile, and 12 red 1-by-1 tiles

b. No

c. Because adding $3x$ and $-3x$ to the polynomial is equivalent to adding zero.

d. $x + 4, x - 3$

e. $x^2 + x - 12 = (x + 4)(x - 3)$; factors are $x + 4$ and $x - 3$.

4. Let the shaded tiles represent negative quantities.

a. $5x^2 - 10x = 5x(x - 2)$

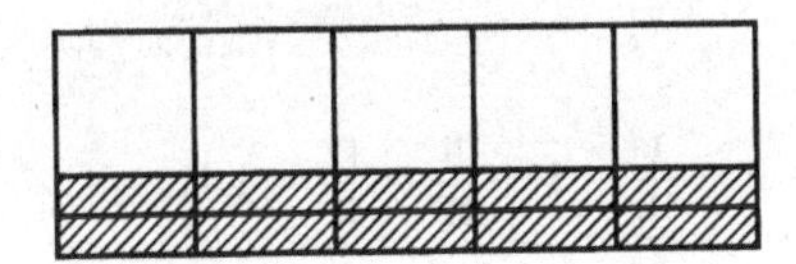

b. $x^2 + 9x + 14 = (x + 7)(x + 2)$

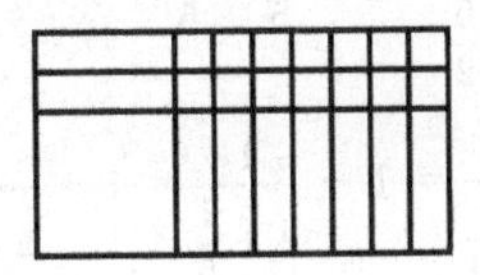

c. $x^2 - 5x + 6 = (x - 3)(x - 2)$

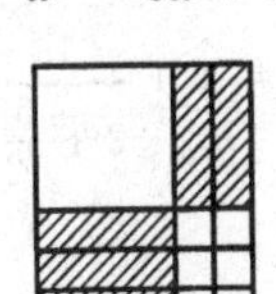

d. $3x^2 + 7x + 2 = (x + 2)(3x + 1)$

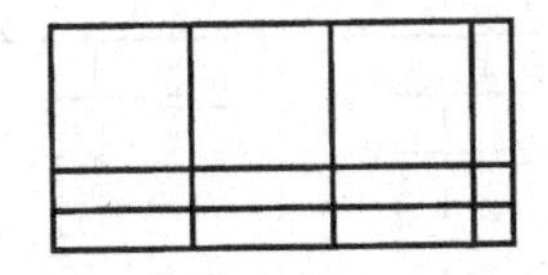

e. $x^2 - 16 = (x + 4)(x - 4)$

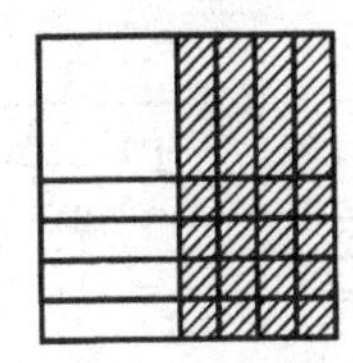

f. $x^2 - 2x + 1 = (x - 1)(x - 1) = (x - 1)^2$

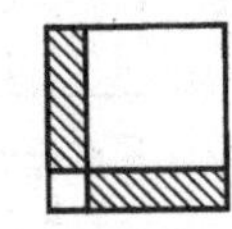

Page 836 • EXPLORING CONTINUED FRACTIONS

1. $2 + \cfrac{1}{3 + \cfrac{1}{4 + \cfrac{1}{2}}} = 2 + \cfrac{1}{3 + \cfrac{1}{\frac{9}{2}}} = 2 + \cfrac{1}{3 + \frac{2}{9}} = 2 + \cfrac{1}{\frac{29}{9}} = 2 + \frac{9}{29} = \frac{67}{29}$

2. a. $2 + \cfrac{1}{3 + \frac{1}{4}} = 2 + \cfrac{1}{\frac{13}{4}} = 2 + \frac{4}{13} = \frac{30}{13}$

b. $3 + \cfrac{1}{2 + \cfrac{1}{1 + \cfrac{1}{6 + \frac{1}{2}}}} = 3 + \cfrac{1}{2 + \cfrac{1}{1 + \cfrac{1}{\frac{13}{2}}}} = 3 + \cfrac{1}{2 + \cfrac{1}{1 + \frac{2}{13}}} = 3 + \cfrac{1}{2 + \cfrac{1}{\frac{15}{13}}} = 3 + \cfrac{1}{2 + \frac{13}{15}} =$

$3 + \cfrac{1}{\frac{43}{15}} = 3 + \frac{15}{43} = \frac{144}{43}$

3. [2, 3, 4]; [3, 2, 1, 6, 2]

4. a. $2 + \cfrac{1}{1 + \cfrac{1}{3 + \cfrac{1}{4}}} = 2 + \cfrac{1}{1 + \cfrac{1}{\frac{13}{4}}} = 2 + \cfrac{1}{1 + \frac{4}{13}} = 2 + \cfrac{1}{\frac{17}{13}} = 2 + \frac{13}{17} = \frac{47}{17}$

b. $4 + \cfrac{1}{2 + \frac{1}{3}} = 4 + \cfrac{1}{\frac{7}{3}} = 4 + \frac{3}{7} = \frac{31}{7}$

5. a. $1 + \frac{1}{2} = \frac{3}{2} = 1.5$

b. $1 + \cfrac{1}{2 + \frac{1}{2}} = \cfrac{1}{\frac{5}{2}} = 1 + \frac{2}{5} = \frac{7}{5} = 1.4$

c. $1 + \cfrac{1}{2 + \cfrac{1}{2 + \frac{1}{2}}} = 1 + \cfrac{1}{2 + \cfrac{1}{\frac{5}{2}}} = 1 + \cfrac{1}{2 + \frac{2}{5}} = 1 + \cfrac{1}{\frac{12}{5}} = 1 + \frac{5}{12} = \frac{17}{12} = 1.41\overline{6}$

d. $1 + \cfrac{1}{2 + \cfrac{1}{2 + \cfrac{1}{2 + \frac{1}{2}}}} = 1 + \cfrac{1}{2 + \cfrac{1}{2 + \cfrac{1}{\frac{5}{2}}}} = 1 + \cfrac{1}{2 + \cfrac{1}{2 + \frac{2}{5}}} = 1 + \cfrac{1}{2 + \cfrac{1}{\frac{12}{5}}} = 1 + \cfrac{1}{2 + \frac{5}{12}} =$

$1 + \cfrac{1}{\frac{29}{12}} = 1 + \frac{12}{29} = \frac{41}{29} \approx 1.4138$

e. $1 + \cfrac{1}{2 + \cfrac{1}{2 + \cfrac{1}{2 + \cfrac{1}{2 + \frac{1}{2}}}}} = 1 + \cfrac{1}{2 + \cfrac{1}{2 + \cfrac{1}{2 + \cfrac{1}{\frac{5}{2}}}}} = 1 + \cfrac{1}{2 + \cfrac{1}{2 + \cfrac{1}{2 + \frac{2}{5}}}} = 1 + \cfrac{1}{2 + \cfrac{1}{2 + \cfrac{1}{\frac{12}{5}}}} =$

$1 + \cfrac{1}{2 + \cfrac{1}{2 + \frac{5}{12}}} = 1 + \cfrac{1}{2 + \cfrac{1}{\frac{29}{12}}} = 1 + \cfrac{1}{2 + \frac{12}{29}} = 1 + \cfrac{1}{\frac{70}{29}} = 1 + \frac{29}{70} = \frac{99}{70} \approx 1.4143$

f. $\sqrt{2}$

6. a. $1 + \cfrac{1}{1 + \cfrac{1}{2 + \cfrac{1}{1 + \cfrac{1}{2 + \cfrac{1}{1 + \cdots}}}}} = 1 + \cfrac{1}{1 + \cfrac{1}{2 + \cfrac{1}{1 + \frac{1}{3}}}} = 1 + \cfrac{1}{1 + \cfrac{1}{2 + \cfrac{1}{\frac{4}{3}}}} = 1 + \cfrac{1}{1 + \cfrac{1}{2 + \frac{3}{4}}} =$

$1 + \cfrac{1}{1 + \cfrac{1}{\frac{11}{4}}} = 1 + \cfrac{1}{1 + \frac{4}{11}} = 1 + \cfrac{1}{\frac{15}{11}} = 1 + \frac{11}{15} = \frac{26}{15} \approx 1.732 \approx \sqrt{3}$

b. $2 + \cfrac{1}{2 + \cfrac{1}{4 + \cfrac{1}{2 + \cfrac{1}{4 + \cdots}}}} = 2 + \cfrac{1}{2 + \cfrac{1}{4 + \cfrac{1}{\frac{9}{4}}}} = 2 + \cfrac{1}{2 + \cfrac{1}{4 + \frac{4}{9}}} = 2 + \cfrac{1}{2 + \cfrac{1}{\frac{40}{9}}} = 2 + \cfrac{1}{2 + \frac{9}{40}} =$

$2 + \cfrac{1}{\frac{89}{40}} = 2 + \frac{40}{89} \approx 2.449 \approx \sqrt{6}$

7. Rational numbers are represented by finite continued fractions. Irrational numbers are represented by infinite continued fractions.

Page 837 • EXPLORING RADICALS

1. a. $\sqrt{64} + \sqrt{36} = 8 + 6 = 14; \sqrt{64 + 36} = \sqrt{100} = 10$

b. $\sqrt{15} - \sqrt{8} = 3.873 - 2.828 = 1.045; \sqrt{15 - 8} = \sqrt{7} = 2.646$

c. $\sqrt[3]{27} + \sqrt[3]{125} = 3 + 5 = 8; \sqrt[3]{27 + 125} = \sqrt[3]{152} = 5.337$

d. $\sqrt[3]{27} - \sqrt[3]{64} = 3 - 4 = -1; \sqrt[3]{27 - 64} = \sqrt[3]{-37} = -3.332$

2. a. No **b.** No

3. a. $\sqrt{64} \cdot \sqrt{9} = 8 \cdot 3 = 24; \sqrt{64 \cdot 9} = \sqrt{576} = 24$

b. $\frac{\sqrt{24}}{\sqrt{2}} = \frac{4.899}{1.414} = 3.464; \sqrt{\frac{24}{2}} = \sqrt{12} = 3.464$

c. $\sqrt[3]{7} \cdot \sqrt[3]{2} = 1.913 \cdot 1.260 = 2.410; \sqrt[3]{7 \cdot 2} = \sqrt[3]{14} = 2.410$

d. $\frac{\sqrt[3]{27}}{\sqrt[3]{8}} = \frac{3}{2} = 1.5; \sqrt[3]{\frac{27}{8}} = \sqrt[3]{3.375} = 1.5$

4. a. Yes **b.** Yes

5. a. $\sqrt[3 \cdot 2]{64} = \sqrt[6]{64} = 2; \sqrt[3]{\sqrt{64}} = \sqrt[3]{8} = 2$

b. $\sqrt[2 \cdot 3]{18} = \sqrt[6]{18} = 1.619; \sqrt{\sqrt[3]{18}} = \sqrt{2.621} = 1.619$

c. $\sqrt[3]{8^2} = \sqrt[3]{64} = 4; (\sqrt[3]{8})^2 = (2)^2 = 4$

d. $\sqrt{2^3} = \sqrt{8} = 2.828; (\sqrt{2})^3 = 2.828$

6. a. Yes **b.** Yes

7. a. $\sqrt{9 + 16} = \sqrt{25} = 5$

b. $\sqrt{100 - 64} = \sqrt{36} = 6$

c. $\sqrt{16 \cdot 36} = \sqrt{16} \cdot \sqrt{36} = 4 \cdot 6 = 24$

d. $\sqrt[3]{\frac{125}{64}} = \frac{\sqrt[3]{125}}{\sqrt[3]{64}} = \frac{5}{4} = 1.25$

Page 838 • EXPLORING QUADRATIC EQUATIONS

1.

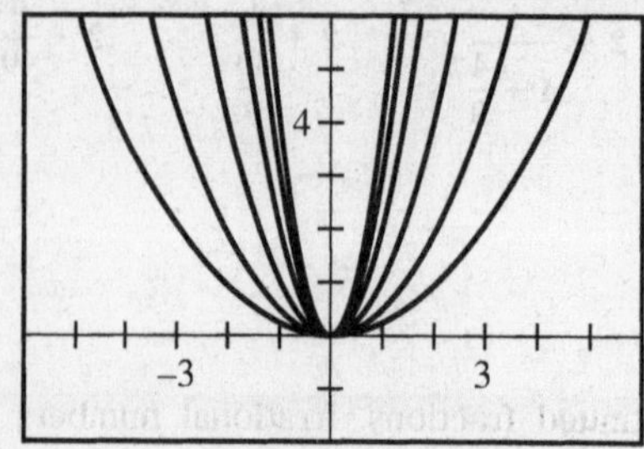

For larger values of a, the graph is narrower.

2.

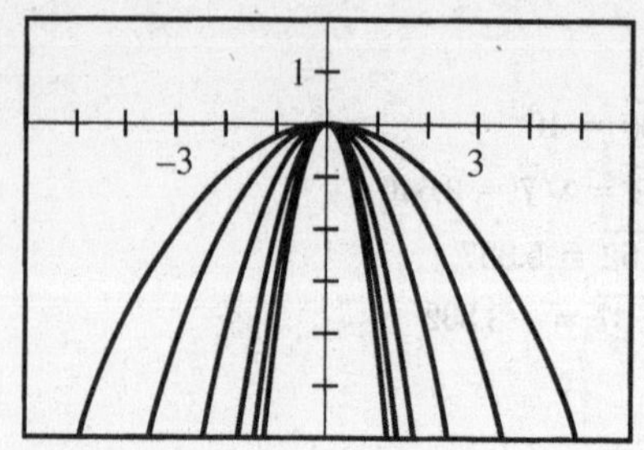

a. The graph opens upward if $a > 0$ and downward if $a < 0$.

b. The shape of all the graphs is in general similar, but for larger values of $|a|$, the graph is narrower.

3. a–b.

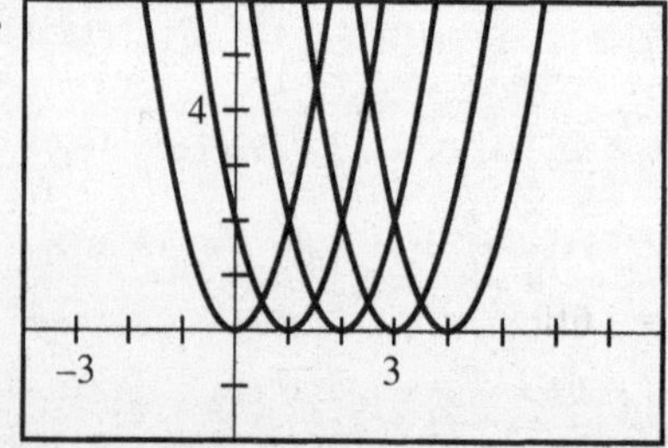

c. The new graph is the previous graph slid 1 unit to the right.

4.

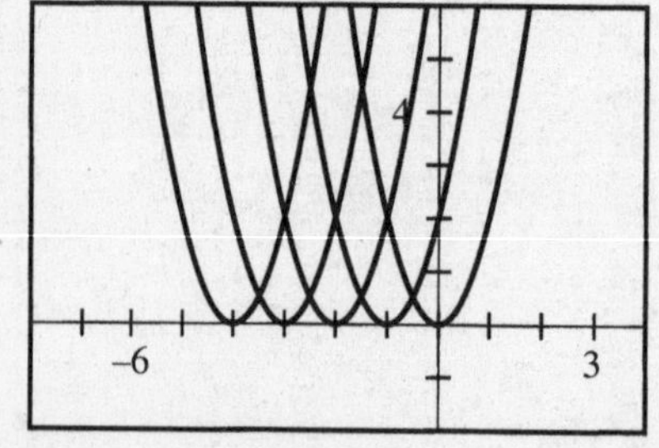

The new graph slides 1 unit to the left.

5. **a–c.**

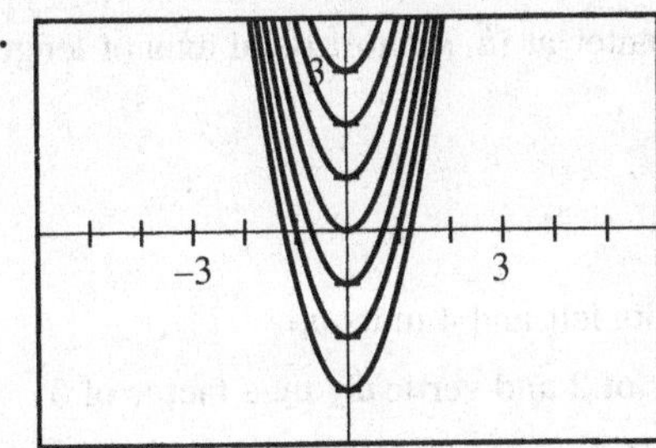

d. Increasing the value of k slides the graph up; decreasing it slides the graph down.

6. **a.** Graph $y = 2x^2$. Then slide the graph 3 units right and 1 unit up.

   b. Graph $y = 2x^2$. Then slide the graph 7 units left and 3 units down.

7. **a.** It would be narrower.

   b. It would be wider and it would open downward instead of upward.

Page 839 • EXPLORING DIRECT VARIATION

1–4. Answers will vary, depending on springs and weights used.

5. It is a constant.

6. No; a different quotient may result but the quotient is still a constant in each case.

7. No; a different quotient may result but the quotient is still a constant in each case.

8. Answers will vary.

9. **a.** first column **b.** fourth column **c.** fifth column

Page 840 • EXPLORING CIRCLES AND ELLIPSES

1.

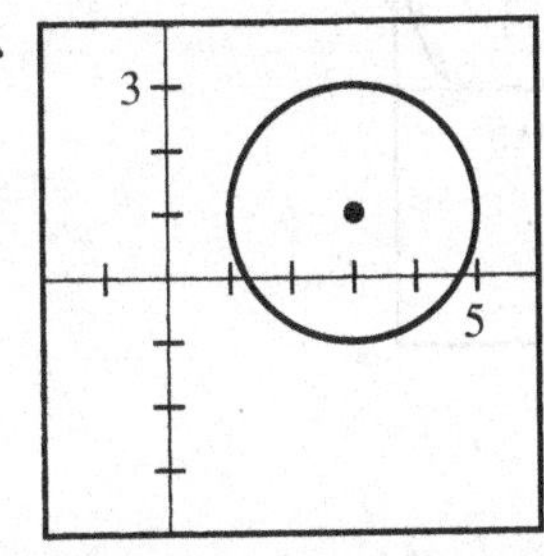

The graph is a circle with center (3, 1) and radius 2.

2. In each case, the graph is a circle with center at (h, k) and radius r.

3.

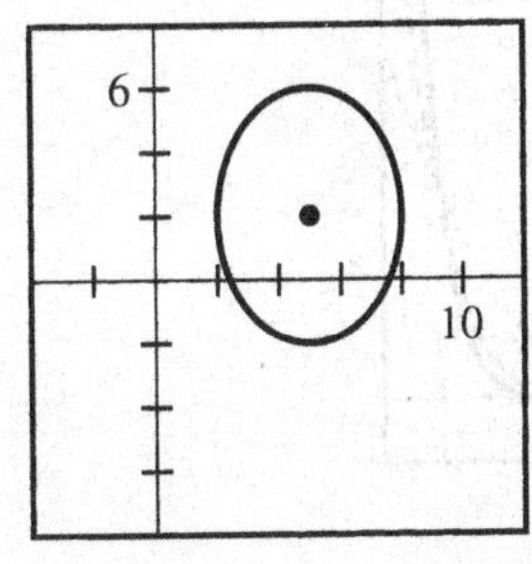

The graph is an ellipse with center (5, 2), horizontal minor axis of length 6, and vertical major axis of length 8.

4. In each case, the graph is an ellipse with center at (h, k), horizontal axis of length $2a$, and vertical axis of length $2b$.

5. a. double the radius

b. divide the radius by 4

c. triple the radius and slide the circle 2 units left and 4 units up

d. Stretch the circle horizontally by a factor of 2 and vertically by a factor of 3.

e. place center at (1, 3) and stretch as in part **d**

f. place center at (2, −3), shrink horizontally by a factor of $\frac{1}{2}$, and stretch vertically by a factor of 4

Page 841 • EXPLORING POWERS AND ROOTS

1. a. first and third quadrants

b. $y = x$

c. $y = x^5$

2. a. first and third quadrants

b. $y = x^{13}$; $y = x^{15}$

c.

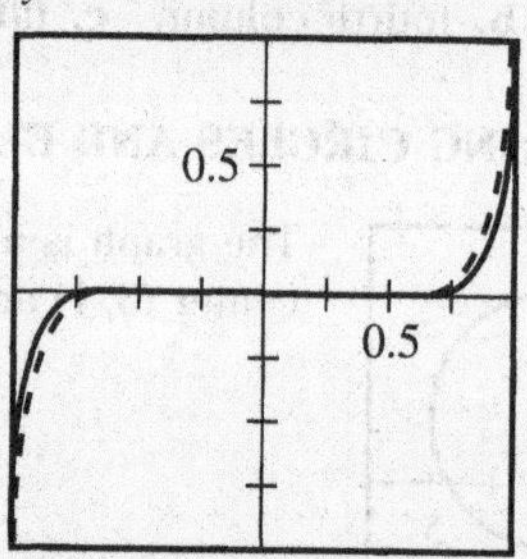

d. Yes

3. a. first and second quadrants

b. $y = x^2$; $y = x^6$

c. Since the graph of $y = x^2$ is above that of $y = x^6$ in the interval $0 < x < 1$, $(0.9)^2$ is larger than $(0.9)^6$. Since the graph of $y = x^6$ is above that of $y = x^2$ when $x > 1$, $(1.01)^6$ is larger than $(1.01)^2$.

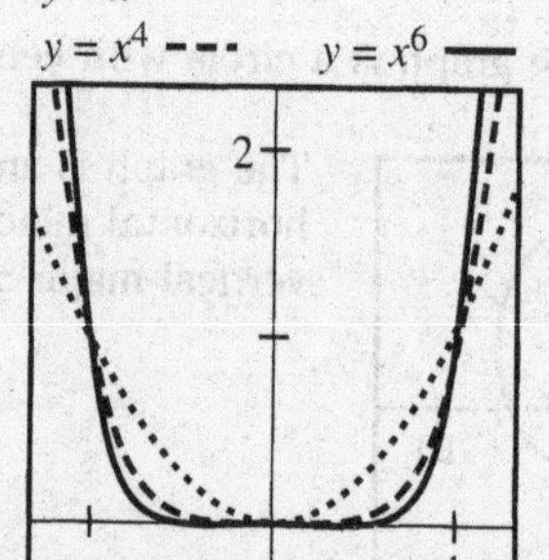

4. a. between 1 and 2 and between −1 and −2

b. 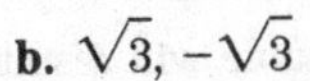 $\sqrt{3}, -\sqrt{3}$

c. Answers may vary. $1.6 < x < 1.8$

d. $\sqrt{3} \approx 1.732$

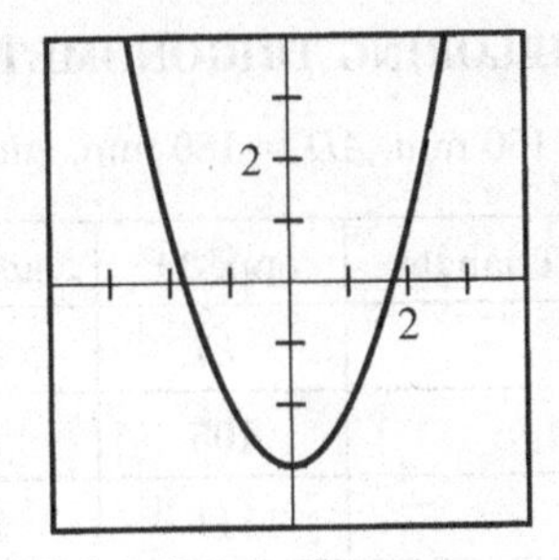

5. As indicated by the explorations in Exercises **1–3,** for a base greater than 1, a greater exponent yields a greater power, but when the base is between 0 and 1, the lesser exponent yields the greater power. That is, for $a^m > a^n$ it is necessary that $a > 1$ and $m > n$ or $0 < a < 1$ and $m < n$.

6. 

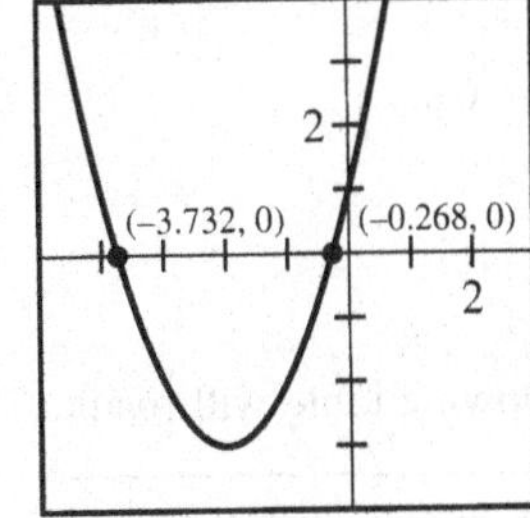

−3.732; −0.268

Page 842 • EXPLORING PASCAL'S TRIANGLE

1. Row 7: 1, 7, 21, 35, 35, 21, 7, 1; Row 8: 1, 8, 28, 56, 70, 56, 28, 8, 1

2. The second diagonal from the left (or right): 1, 2, 3, 4, 5, 6, . . .

3. The third diagonal from the left (or right): 1, 3, 6, 10, 15, . . .

4. Fibonacci sequence: 1, 1, 2, 3, 5, 8, . . .

5. $1 = 2^0, 1 + 1 = 2^1, 1 + 2 + 1 = 4 = 2^2, 1 + 3 + 3 + 1 = 8 = 2^3, \ldots, 2^n$

6. $1 - 1 = 0, 1 - 2 + 1 = 0, 1 - 3 + 3 - 1 = 0, 1 - 4 + 6 - 4 + 1 = 0$; all sums equal zero.

7. Yes; it will always appear as the middle element of a later row.
Samples: row 1, $1^2 + 1^2 = 2$; row 2, $1^2 + 2^2 + 1^2 = 6$; row 3, $1^2 + 3^2 + 3^2 + 1^2 = 20$

8. Answers will vary. Sample: the sum of numbers along any diagonal equals the number one row down and one number to the right of the diagonal. For example, the second diagonal from the left is 1, 2, 3, 4, 5. The sum of these numbers is 15, the number one row down and one number to the right.

Page 843 • EXPLORING TRIGONOMETRIC RATIOS

1–5. If $AB = 150$ mm, $AD = 180$ mm, and $AF = 190$ mm, the following table will result.

Right Triangle	opp. 30°	adj. 30°	hyp.	tan 30°	sin 30°	cos 30°
ABC	87	150	173	0.58	0.5	0.87
ADE	105	180	208	0.58	0.5	0.87
AFG	111	190	219	0.58	0.5	0.87

$\triangle ABC$: $\tan 30° = \frac{\text{opp.}}{\text{adj.}} = \frac{87}{150} = 0.58$, $\sin 30° = \frac{\text{opp.}}{\text{hyp.}} = \frac{87}{173} = 0.5$,

$\cos 30° = \frac{\text{adj.}}{\text{hyp.}} = \frac{150}{173} = 0.87$;

$\triangle ADE$: $\tan 30° = \frac{\text{opp.}}{\text{adj.}} = \frac{105}{180} = 0.58$, $\sin 30° = \frac{\text{opp.}}{\text{hyp.}} = \frac{105}{208} = 0.5$,

$\cos 30° = \frac{\text{adj.}}{\text{hyp.}} = \frac{180}{208} = 0.87$;

$\triangle AFG$: $\tan 30° = \frac{\text{opp.}}{\text{adj.}} = \frac{111}{190} = 0.58$, $\sin 30° = \frac{\text{opp.}}{\text{hyp.}} = \frac{111}{219} = 0.5$,

$\cos 30° = \frac{\text{adj.}}{\text{hyp.}} = \frac{190}{219} = 0.87$

6. $\tan 30° = 0.58$; $\sin 30° = 0.5$; $\cos 30° = 0.866$

7. If $AB = 150$ mm, $AD = 165$ mm, and $AF = 177$ mm, the following table will result.

Right Triangle	opp. 45°	adj. 45°	hyp.	tan 45°	sin 45°	cos 45°
ABC	150	150	212	1	0.71	0.71
ADE	165	165	234	1	0.71	0.71
AFG	177	177	251	1	0.71	0.71

$\triangle ABC$: $\tan 45° = \frac{\text{opp.}}{\text{adj.}} = \frac{150}{150} = 1$, $\sin 45° = \frac{\text{opp.}}{\text{hyp.}} = \frac{150}{212} = 0.71$,

$\cos 45° = \frac{\text{adj.}}{\text{hyp.}} = \frac{150}{212} = 0.71$;

$\triangle ADE$: $\tan 45° = \frac{\text{opp.}}{\text{adj.}} = \frac{165}{165} = 1$, $\sin 45° = \frac{\text{opp.}}{\text{hyp.}} = \frac{165}{234} = 0.71$,

$\cos 45° = \frac{\text{adj.}}{\text{hyp.}} = \frac{165}{234} = 0.71$;

$\triangle AFG$: $\tan 45° = \frac{\text{opp.}}{\text{adj.}} = \frac{177}{177} = 1$, $\sin 45° = \frac{\text{opp.}}{\text{hyp.}} = \frac{177}{251} = 0.71$,

$\cos 45° = \frac{\text{adj.}}{\text{hyp.}} = \frac{177}{251} = 0.71$; so $\tan 45° = 1$, $\sin 45° = 0.71$, and $\cos 45° = 0.71$.

If $AB = 150$ mm, $AD = 165$ mm, and $AF = 174$ mm, the following table will result.

Right Triangle	opp. 60°	adj. 60°	hyp.	tan 60°	sin 60°	cos 60°
ABC	260	150	299	1.73	0.87	0.5
ADE	285	165	328	1.73	0.87	0.5
AFG	301	174	346	1.73	0.87	0.5

$\triangle ABC$: $\tan 60^\circ = \frac{\text{opp.}}{\text{adj.}} = \frac{260}{150} = 1.73$, $\sin 60^\circ = \frac{\text{opp.}}{\text{hyp.}} = \frac{260}{299} = 0.87$,

$\cos 60^\circ = \frac{\text{adj.}}{\text{hyp.}} = \frac{174}{346} = 0.5$;

$\triangle ADE$: $\tan 60^\circ = \frac{\text{opp.}}{\text{adj.}} = \frac{285}{165} = 1.73$, $\sin 60^\circ = \frac{\text{opp.}}{\text{hyp.}} = \frac{285}{328} = 0.87$,

$\cos 60^\circ = \frac{\text{adj.}}{\text{hyp.}} = \frac{174}{346} = 0.5$;

$\triangle AFG$: $\tan 60^\circ = \frac{\text{opp.}}{\text{adj.}} = \frac{301}{174} = 1.73$, $\sin 60^\circ = \frac{\text{opp.}}{\text{hyp.}} = \frac{301}{346} = 0.87$,

$\cos 60^\circ = \frac{\text{adj.}}{\text{hyp.}} = \frac{174}{346} = 0.5$; so $\tan 60^\circ = 1.73$, $\sin 60^\circ = 0.87$, and $\cos 60^\circ = 0.5$.

8. For each table, the ratios should be equal in each column. Since the triangles are similar, the sides are proportional.

Page 844 • EXPLORING SINE CURVES

2. For $x = \frac{\pi}{4}$, $\sin x = \frac{\sqrt{2}}{2}$, $2 \sin x = \sqrt{2}$, so $y = \sin x + 2 \sin x = \frac{3\sqrt{2}}{2} \approx 2.12$.

For $x = \frac{\pi}{2}$, $\sin x = 1$, $2 \sin x = 2$, so $y = \sin x + 2 \sin x = 3$.

For $x = \frac{2\pi}{3}$, $\sin x = \frac{\sqrt{3}}{2}$, $2 \sin x = \sqrt{3}$, so $y = \sin x + 2 \sin x = \frac{3\sqrt{3}}{2} \approx 2.60$.

3. The ruler must be slid downward; a negative y-value is being added.

4. For $x = \frac{\pi}{2}$, $y = \sin (x + \pi) = -1$, $y = 2 \sin x = 2$, so the sum is $y = -1 + 2 = 1$.

For $x = \frac{3\pi}{4}$, $y = \sin (x + \pi) = -\frac{\sqrt{2}}{2}$, $y = 2 \sin x = \sqrt{2}$, so the sum is $y =$
$-\frac{\sqrt{2}}{2} + \sqrt{2} = -\frac{\sqrt{2}}{2} + \frac{2\sqrt{2}}{2} = \frac{-\sqrt{2} + 2\sqrt{2}}{2} = \frac{\sqrt{2}}{2}$, or ≈ 0.71.

For $x = \pi$, $y = \sin (x + \pi) = 0$, $y = 2 \sin x = 0$, so the sum is 0.

For $x = \frac{4\pi}{3}$, $y = \sin (x + \pi) = \frac{\sqrt{3}}{2}$, $y = 2 \sin x = -\sqrt{3}$, so the sum is $\frac{\sqrt{3}}{2} + (-\sqrt{3}) =$
$\frac{\sqrt{3}}{2} - \frac{2\sqrt{3}}{2} = \frac{\sqrt{3} - 2\sqrt{3}}{2} = -\frac{\sqrt{3}}{2}$, or ≈ -0.87

5. a.

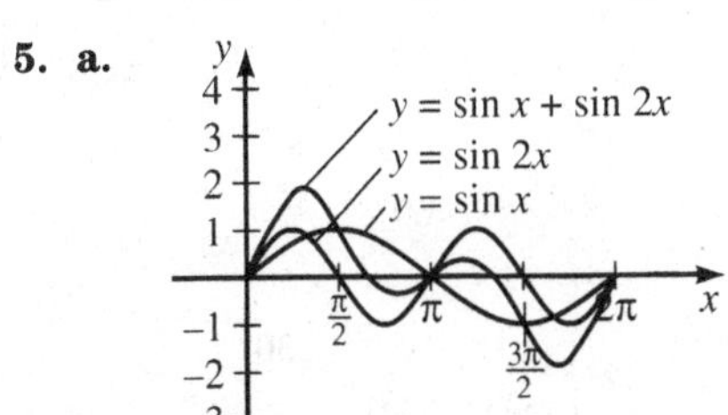

b.

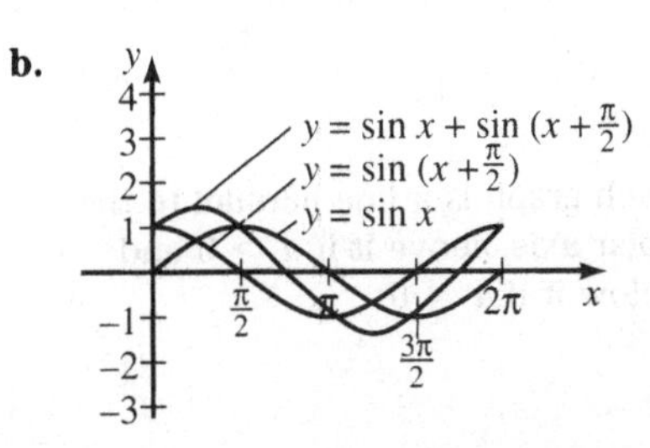

6. Destructive interference, which decreases the volume of sound or the brightness of light.

Page 845 • EXPLORING POLAR COORDINATE EQUATIONS

1. Each graph is a line perpendicular to the polar axis.

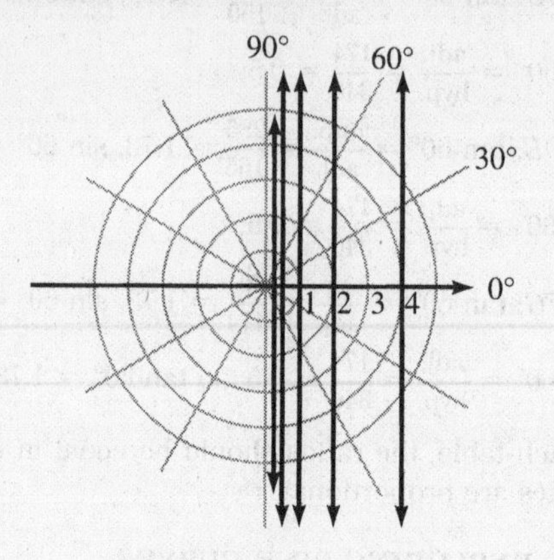

2. Each graph is a line perpendicular to the extension of (the ray opposite to) the polar axis.

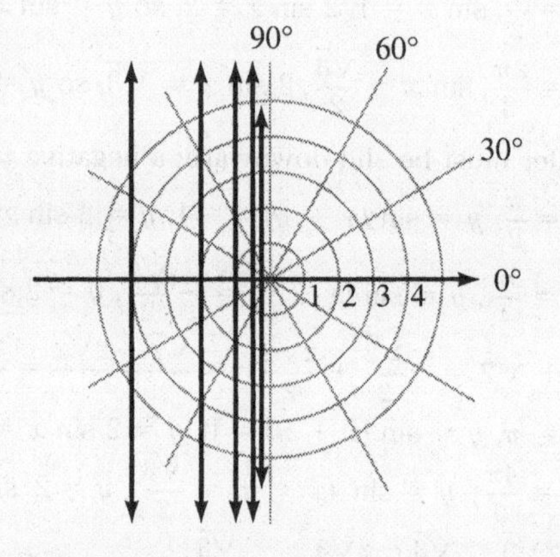

3. Each graph is a line parallel to the polar axis, above it if $a > 0$ and below it if $a < 0$.

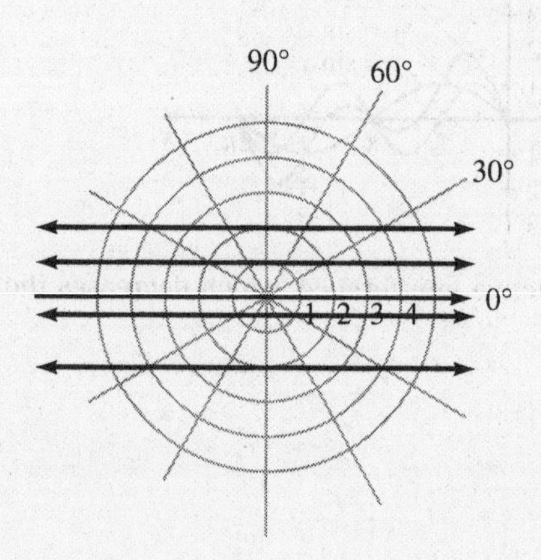

4. a.

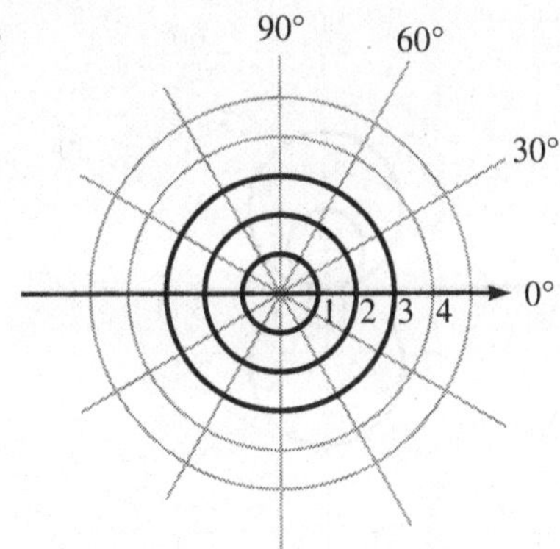

b.

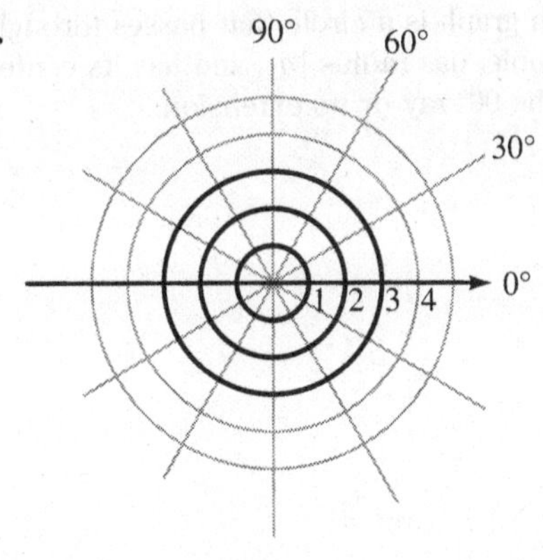

c. They are the same.

5. Each graph is a line that passes through (p, k) but not through the pole.

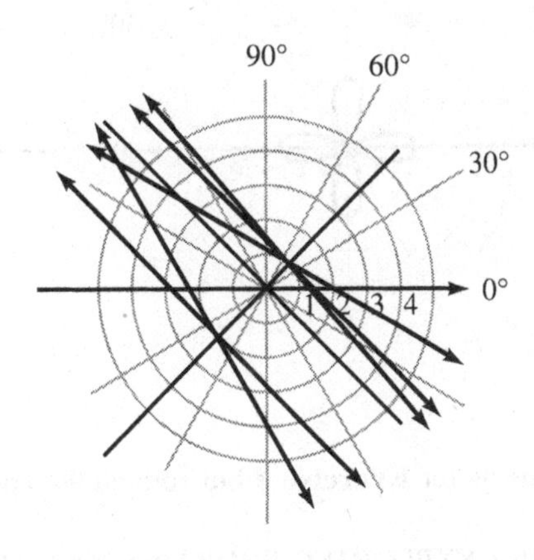

6. Each graph is a circle that passes through the pole, has radius $|a|$, and has its center on the polar axis or its extension.

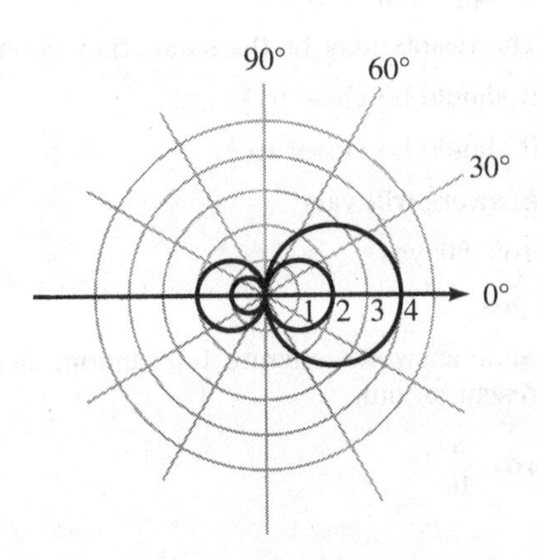

7. Each graph is a circle that passes through the pole, has radius $|a|$, and has its center on the 90° ray or its extension.

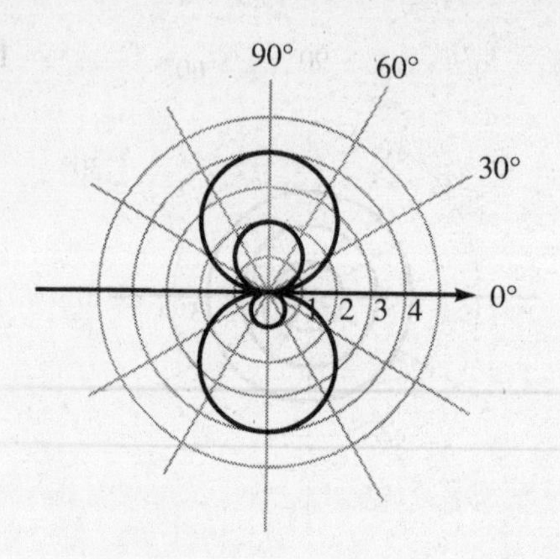

8. The first graph is a four-leafed rose, the second is a three-leafed rose.

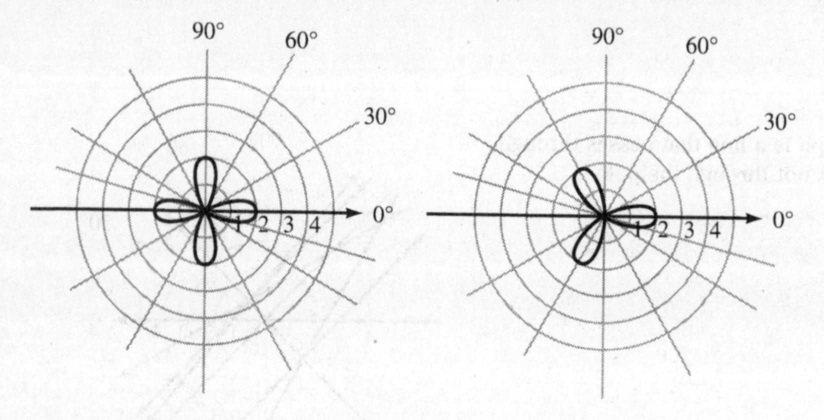

9. Same as for **Exercise 8** but rotated 90° counterclockwise.

Page 846 • EXPLORING PROBABILITY WITH EXPERIMENTS

1. a. The probability of "heads" should be approximately $\frac{1}{2}$; the probability of "tails" should be approximately $\frac{1}{2}$.

b. The results may be the same; they should be approximately the same.

c. It should be close to $\frac{1}{2}$.

d. It should be closer to $\frac{1}{2}$.

e. Answers will vary.

2. approx. 50; yes

3. No; yes

4. Possible answer: Generate 100 random digits 0–9; let 0, 1, and 2 represent a hit and 3–9 represent an out.

5. approx. $\frac{3}{10}$

Page 847 • EXPLORING MATRICES IN GEOMETRY

1.

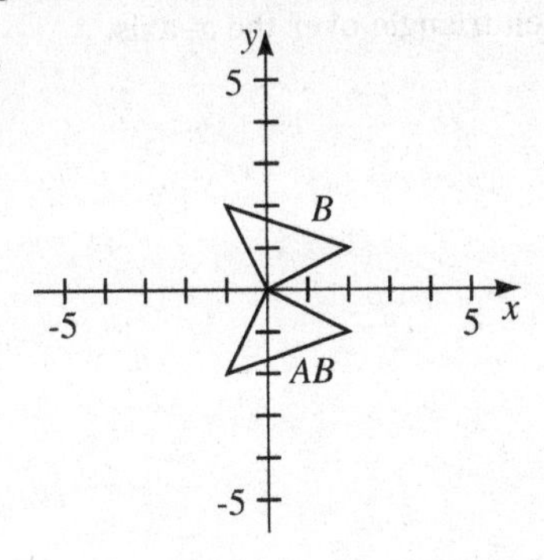

AB is the result of flipping (reflecting) *B* over the x-axis.

2. For $B = \begin{bmatrix} 2 & 3 & 1 \\ 3 & 5 & 2 \end{bmatrix}$, $AB = \begin{bmatrix} 2 & 3 & 1 \\ -3 & -5 & -2 \end{bmatrix}$

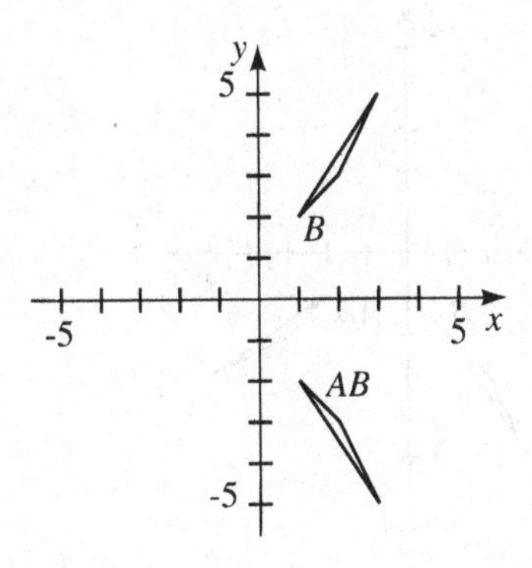

For $B = \begin{bmatrix} -2 & -3 & -1 \\ -3 & -5 & -2 \end{bmatrix}$, $AB = \begin{bmatrix} -2 & -3 & -1 \\ 3 & 5 & 2 \end{bmatrix}$

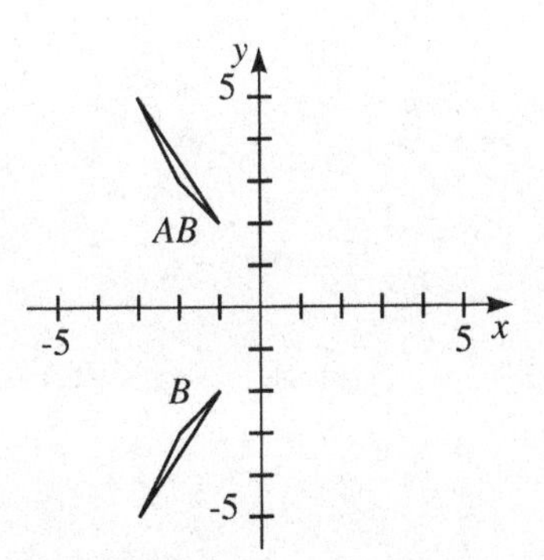

For $B = \begin{bmatrix} 0 & 0 & 3 \\ 2 & -1 & 1 \end{bmatrix}$, $AB = \begin{bmatrix} 0 & 0 & 3 \\ -2 & 1 & -1 \end{bmatrix}$; Yes, multiplying by A flips (reflects) each triangle over the x-axis.

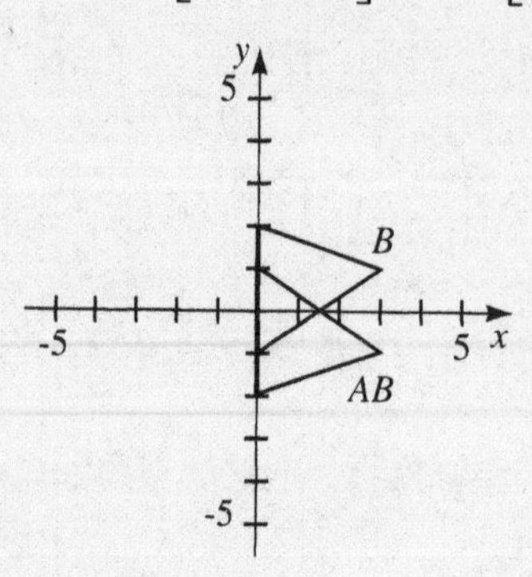

3. For $B = \begin{bmatrix} 2 & 3 & 1 \\ 3 & 5 & 2 \end{bmatrix}$,

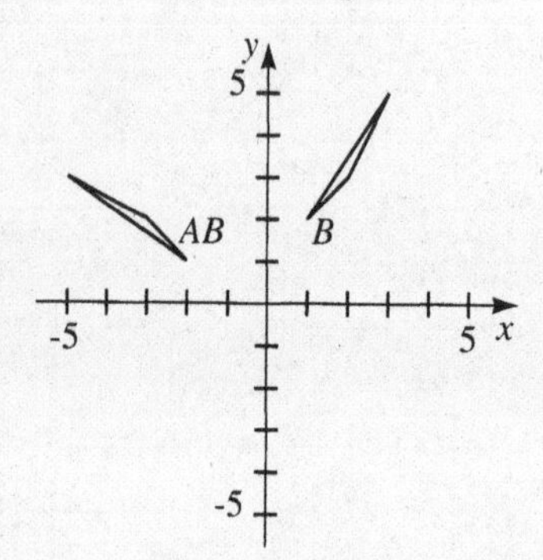

For $B = \begin{bmatrix} -2 & -3 & -1 \\ -3 & -5 & -2 \end{bmatrix}$,

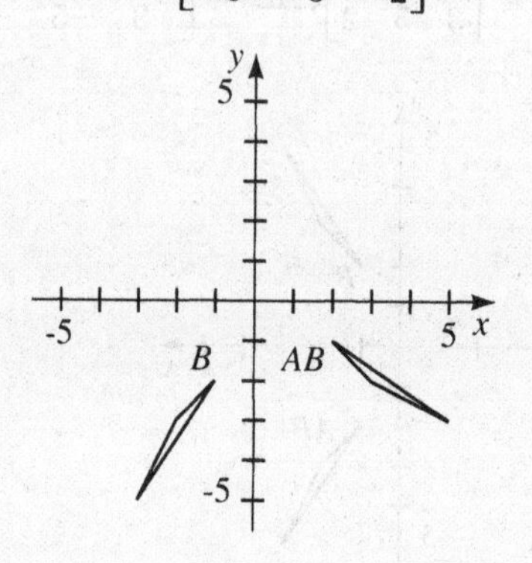

For $B = \begin{bmatrix} 0 & 0 & 3 \\ 2 & -1 & 1 \end{bmatrix}$,

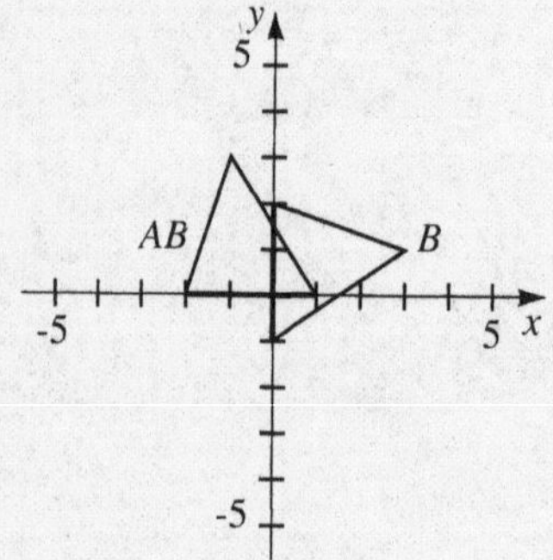

A is a turn (rotation) of 90° counterclockwise.

4. $AB = \begin{bmatrix} 1 & 2 & 4 \\ 1 & -1 & 0 \\ 1 & 1 & 1 \end{bmatrix}$

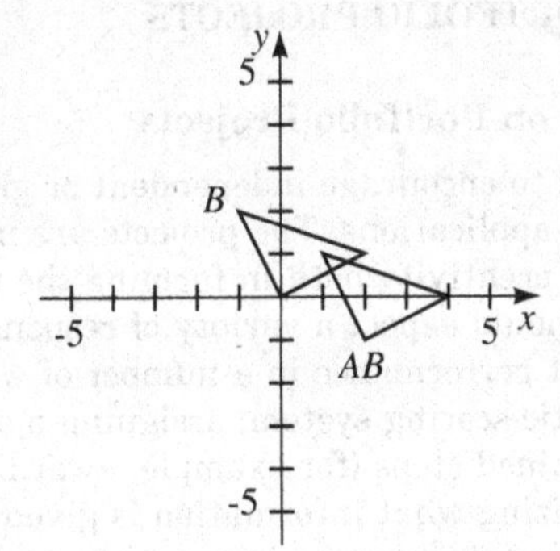

A is a slide (translation) 2 units to the right and 1 unit down.

5. a. Sample: For $B = \begin{bmatrix} 1 & 2 \\ 3 & 4 \end{bmatrix}$, $\begin{bmatrix} 1 & 2 \\ 3 & 4 \end{bmatrix}\begin{bmatrix} -1 & 0 \\ 0 & 1 \end{bmatrix} = \begin{bmatrix} -1 & 2 \\ -3 & 4 \end{bmatrix}$; multiplying by A flips (reflects) B over the y-axis.

b. Sample: For $B = \begin{bmatrix} 1 & 2 \\ 3 & 4 \end{bmatrix}$, $\begin{bmatrix} 1 & 2 \\ 3 & 4 \end{bmatrix}\begin{bmatrix} -1 & 0 \\ 0 & -1 \end{bmatrix} = \begin{bmatrix} -1 & -2 \\ -3 & -4 \end{bmatrix}$; multiplying by A turns (rotates) B 180°.

6. From Exercise **4**, the number in the first row, third column represents a horizontal translation, and the number in the second row, third column represents a vertical translation. Thus, the transformation matrix is $\begin{bmatrix} 1 & 0 & -2 \\ 0 & 1 & 3 \\ 0 & 0 & 1 \end{bmatrix}$.

PORTFOLIO PROJECTS

Assessing Student Performance on Portfolio Projects

The Portfolio Projects are designed to encourage independent or group exploration of mathematical concepts within new applications. The projects are intended to be idea-starters. Students should use their creativity both in forming the problem and in shaping the solution. Because of this, you should expect a variety of responses from students. Similarly, you can evaluate student performance in a number of ways.

Some teachers prefer an analytic scoring system, assigning a specific number of points to each of a list of predetermined steps (for example, awarding 2 points for understanding the problem, recognizing what information is given and what must be found; 2 points for making a plan and choosing an appropriate problem-solving strategy; 2 points for carrying out the plan appropriately; and 2 points for the presentation of results). Other teachers prefer a holistic approach, assessing each student's work in its entirety rather than as a collection of discrete parts.

Holistic Scoring and Scoring Rubrics

Many teachers who use holistic scoring start with written descriptions, or scoring rubrics, that distinguish among different levels of performance. Rather than assigning so many points per part of an answer, scoring rubrics tend to focus on qualitative distinctions. As you read the student responses the first time through, the rubrics should help you sort the works into four categories. The first group includes responses that show complete understanding and in which the ideas are clearly expressed. The second group includes responses that show some understanding of the basic ideas and concepts but which are incomplete or unclear. The third group includes responses that show little or no understanding of the problem or its solution and suggest the need for remediation. The fourth group includes responses that show no effort. After the initial sorting of all student responses, the responses within each category can be arranged into subcategories as necessary in a second reading.

General Rubrics and Specific Rubrics

Scoring rubrics help clarify the key assessment criteria for yourself and for your students. General scoring rubrics serve as a guideline. This broad framework helps establish a dependable system, familiar to students, colleagues, administrators, and parents. One such general rubric follows:

Complete Understanding

4 points Complete responses that demonstrate competence

Some Understanding

3 points Responses show competence, though they may not be complete or entirely accurate

2 points Responses show limited competence and contain significant errors

Little or No Understanding

1 point Responses that show effort but little evidence of competence

No Attempt

0 points Responses that show no effort

This is an example of a 4-point scoring system, with the primary emphasis being the distinction among the strongest responses, the weakest responses, and those in the middle. Which general rubric you use will depend somewhat on your own needs and preferences. Many educators with experience using rubrics, however, recommend using the general rubrics only as a framework from which specific rubrics for each problem or activity are written.

Specific rubrics allow you to highlight the project's distinctive requirements. The process of creating specific scoring rubrics for a project helps define the project's essential elements. Sharing these rubrics with students helps focus their work. Many teachers, in fact, involve the students in writing the project's specific scoring rubrics.

Writing Scoring Rubrics

Scoring rubrics written for a specific project should be general enough to allow for the unexpected (in order to recognize what each student might bring to the problem). At the same time, they need to be specific enough to make qualitative distinctions among the levels of performance. The elements you may want to consider in writing specific rubrics for a project are mathematical content, connections, the problem-solving process, reasoning, and communication.

The project-specific rubrics you develop should reflect your instructional goals and the needs of your students. Consider the elements as you identify the qualities that make up a complete response for a given project, as well as the qualitative differences between top-level and lower-level performance. Each of the Portfolio Projects will call upon students to use their abilities in all five of these areas, but some projects rely more heavily on one of these areas than on another. Your scoring rubrics for a particular project should focus primarily on the key elements for that project.

Suggestions for Specific Scoring Rubrics

45° Paths (Chapter 4)
Complete Understanding
Drawings are clean and accurate and labeled as in the sample diagrams. All lengths of paths are given. Pattern from drawings is used to make correct predictions about lengths of paths and closed paths.
Some Understanding
Drawings are done with some degree of accuracy and some labeling. Pattern from drawing is discovered, but one or both predictions may be incorrect.
Little or No Understanding
Some drawings are done. Pattern not discovered. No predictions are made.

Population Growth (Chapter 7)
Complete Understanding
Students explore a variety of values for r. Accurate tables and graphs given for all r-values. Report is well-written and details what happens as value of r increases.
Some Understanding
Students use only values of r given in the project. Tables and graphs may be less than accurate. Report may give only data and not reach any general conclusions.
Little or No Understanding
Students use only values of r given in the project. Tables and graphs not drawn or inaccurate. Written report is fragmented or nonexistent.

Using Rubrics to Encourage Excellence

Assessment should not be considered the end of the instructional sequence. Many teachers find holistic scoring rubrics useful in encouraging students toward higher levels of performance. Scoring rubrics can be particularly helpful in a "review-and-revise" cycle within the process of working on the projects. The review and preliminary rating can be done by the teacher, or it can be done within a conference among students. In either case, because holistic scoring rubrics focus on qualitative distinctions among varying levels of performance, this preliminary review often helps the student see more clearly how to move his or her work from mid-range to top-level performance.

APPENDIX: Computation with Common Logarithms

Page 857 • WRITTEN EXERCISES

A **1.** $d = \frac{5}{10} \times 0.0013 \approx 0.0007$; $\log 3.475 \approx 0.5403 + 0.0007 = 0.5410$

2. $d = \frac{2}{10} \times 0.0005 = 0.0001$; $\log 8.612 \approx 0.9350 + 0.0001 = 0.9351$

3. $d = \frac{8}{10} \times 0.0005 = 0.0004$; $\log 7.768 \approx 0.8899 + 0.0004 = 0.8903$; $\log 77.68 \approx 1.8903$

4. $d = \frac{6}{10} \times 0.0018 \approx 0.0011$; $\log 2.396 \approx 0.3784 + 0.0011 = 0.3795$; $\log 239.6 \approx 2.3795$

5. $d = \frac{4}{10} \times 0.0008 \approx 0.0003$; $\log 5.624 \approx 0.7497 + 0.0003 = 0.7500$;

$\log 0.5624 \approx 9.7500 - 10$ or -0.2500

6. $d = \frac{7}{10} \times 0.0011 \approx 0.0008$; $\log 3.857 \approx 0.5855 + 0.0008 = 0.5863$;

$\log 0.03857 \approx 8.5863 - 10$ or -1.4137

7. $d = \frac{44}{100} \times 0.0006 \approx 0.0003$; $\log 6.8244 \approx 0.8338 + 0.0003 = 0.8341$;

$\log 68{,}244 \approx 4.8341$

8. $d = \frac{76}{100} \times 0.0031 \approx 0.0024$; $\log 1.38760 \approx 0.1399 + 0.0024 = 0.1423$;

$\log 138{,}760 \approx 5.1423$

9. $d = \frac{2}{10} \times 0.0009 \approx 0.0002$; $\log 4.962 \approx 0.6955 + 0.0002 = 0.6957$;

$\log 0.4962 \approx 9.6957 - 10$ or -0.3043

10. $d = \frac{4}{10} \times 0.0026 \approx 0.0010$; $\log 1.634 \approx 0.2122 + 0.0010 = 0.2132$;

$\log 0.001634 \approx 7.2132 - 10$ or -2.7868

11. $d = \frac{6}{10} \times 0.0009 \approx 0.0005$; $\log 4.856 \approx 0.6857 + 0.0005 = 0.6862$; $\log 48{,}560 \approx 4.6862$

12. $d = \frac{2}{10} \times 0.0005 = 0.0001$; $\log 7.982 \approx 0.9020 + 0.0001 = 0.9021$; $\log 79{,}820 \approx 4.9021$

13. $\frac{c}{0.010} = \frac{0.0004}{0.0008}$; $c \approx 0.005$; antilog $0.6968 \approx 4.97 + 0.005 = 4.975$

14. $\frac{c}{0.010} = \frac{0.0005}{0.0008}$; $c \approx 0.006$; antilog $0.7728 \approx 5.92 + 0.006 = 5.926$

15. $\frac{c}{0.010} = \frac{0.0005}{0.0018}$; $c \approx 0.003$; antilog $0.3843 \approx 2.42 + 0.003 = 2.423$;

antilog $1.3843 \approx 2.423 \times 10^1 = 24.23$

16. $\frac{c}{0.010} = \frac{0.0001}{0.0006}$; $c \approx 0.002$; antilog $0.8402 \approx 6.92 + 0.002 = 6.922$;

antilog $3.8402 \approx 6.922 \times 10^3 = 6922$

17. $\frac{c}{0.010} = \frac{0.003}{0.005}$; $c = 0.006$; antilog $0.9531 \approx 8.97 + 0.006 = 8.976$;

antilog $(8.9531 - 10) \approx 8.976 \times 10^{-2} = 0.08976$

18. $\frac{c}{0.010} = \frac{0.0019}{0.0032}$; $c \approx 0.006$; antilog $0.1322 \approx 1.35 + 0.006 = 1.356$;
antilog $(5.1322 - 10) \approx 1.356 \times 10^{-5} = 0.00001356$

19. $\frac{c}{0.010} = \frac{0.0002}{0.0005}$; $c = 0.004$; antilog $0.9296 \approx 8.50 + 0.004 = 8.504$;
antilog $(9.9296 - 10) \approx 8.504 \times 10^{-1} = 0.8504$

20. $\frac{c}{0.010} = \frac{0.0008}{0.0025}$; $c \approx 0.003$; antilog $0.2388 \approx 1.73 + 0.003 = 1.733$;
antilog $(7.2388 - 10) \approx 1.733 \times 10^{-3} = 0.001733$

21. antilog $0.8041 = 6.370$; antilog $(6.8041 - 10) = 6.370 \times 10^{-4} = 0.0006370$

Page 861 • WRITTEN EXERCISES

A

1. $\log AC = \log A + \log C = 3.6100 + 1.2000 = 4.8100$

2. $\log BC = \log B + \log C = 8.1234 - 10 + 1.2000 = 9.3234 - 10$ or -0.6766

3. $\log \frac{A}{B} = \log A - \log B = 3.6100 - (8.1234 - 10) = (13.6100 - 10) -$
$(8.1234 - 10) = 5.4866$ **4.** $\log \frac{A}{C} = \log A - \log C = 3.6100 - 1.2000 = 2.4100$

5. $\log 100B = \log 100 + \log B = 2 + (8.1234 - 10) = 0.1234$

6. $\log 0.01A = \log 0.01 + \log A = -2 + 3.6100 = 1.6100$

7. $\log \frac{1000}{C} = \log 1000 - \log C = 3 - (1.2000) = 1.8000$

8. $\log \frac{0.001}{B} = \log 0.001 - \log B = -3 - (8.1234 - 10) = (17 - 20) - (8.1234 - 10) =$
$8.8766 - 10$ or -1.1234

9. $\log B^2 = 2 \log B = 2(8.1310 - 10) = 16.2620 - 20 = 6.2620 - 10$ or -3.7380

10. $\log C^{10} = 10 \log C = 10(3.2148) = 32.148$

11. $\log \sqrt{C} = \log C^{1/2} = \frac{1}{2}\log C = \frac{1}{2}(3.2148) = 1.6074$

12. $\log \sqrt[3]{A} = \log A^{1/3} = \frac{1}{3}\log A = \frac{1}{3}(13.600) = 4.5333$

13. $\log C^{3/4} = \frac{3}{4}\log C = \frac{3}{4}(3.2148) = 2.4111$

14. $\log \sqrt[3]{B^2} = \log B^{2/3} = \frac{2}{3}\log B = \frac{2}{3}(8.1310 - 10) = \frac{2}{3}(28.1310 - 30) =$
$18.7540 - 20 = 8.7540 - 10$ or -1.2460

15. $\log \frac{\sqrt{A}}{\sqrt[3]{C}} = \log (A^{1/2} C^{-1/3}) = \frac{1}{2} \log A - \frac{1}{3} \log C = \frac{1}{2}(13.600) - \frac{1}{3}(3.2148) =$
$6.800 - 1.0716 = 5.7284$

16. $\log \frac{B}{\sqrt{A}} = \log B - \frac{1}{2} \log A = (8.1310 - 10) - \frac{1}{2}(13.600) = 8.1310 - 10 - 6.800 =$
$1.331 - 10$ or -8.669

17. $N = 281 \times 0.94$; $\log N = \log 281 + \log 0.94 = 2.4487 + (9.9731 - 10) = 12.4218 - 10 = 2.4218$; $N = 264$

18. $N = 0.749 \times 0.562$; $\log N = \log 0.749 + \log 0.562 = (9.8745 - 10) + (9.7497 - 10) = 19.6242 - 20 = 9.6242 - 10$; $N = 0.421$

19. $N = 943 \times 804$; $\log N = \log 943 + \log 804 = 2.9745 + 2.9053 = 5.8798$; $N = 758{,}000$

20. $N = 0.321 \times 8.35$; $\log N = \log 0.321 + \log 8.35 = (9.5065 - 10) + 0.9217 = 0.4282$; $N = 2.68$

21. $N = \frac{117}{3.26}$; $\log N = \log 117 - \log 3.26 = 2.0682 - 0.5132 = 1.5550$; $N = 35.9$

22. $N = \frac{4960}{54{,}600}$; $\log N = \log 4960 - \log 54{,}600 = 3.6955 - 4.7372 =$

$(13.6955 - 10) - 4.7372 = 8.9583 - 10$; $N = 0.0908$

23. $N = \frac{0.013}{427}$; $\log N = \log 0.013 - \log 427 = (8.1139 - 10) - 2.6304 = 5.4835 - 10$;

$N = 0.0000304$

24. $N = \frac{0.526}{0.049}$; $\log N = \log 0.526 - \log 0.049 = (9.7210 - 10) - (8.6902 - 10) = 1.0308$;

$N = 10.7$

25. $N = (2.81)^{10}$; $\log N = 10 \log 2.81 = 10(0.4487) = 4.4870$; $N = 30{,}700$

26. $N = (90.3)^5$; $\log N = 5 \log 90.3 = 5(1.9557) = 9.7785$; $N = 6{,}000{,}000{,}000$

27. $N = (0.395)^7$; $\log N = 7 \log 0.395 = 7(9.5966 - 10) = 67.1762 - 70 = 7.1762 - 10$; $N = 0.00150$

28. $N = (0.0431)^2$; $\log N = 2 \log 0.0431 = 2(8.6345 - 10) = 17.2690 - 20 = 7.2690 - 10$; $N = 0.00186$

29. $N = (21.4)^{1/3}$; $\log N = \frac{1}{3}\log 21.4 = \frac{1}{3}(1.3304) = 0.4435$; $N = 2.78$

30. $N = (8.26)^{2/3}$; $\log N = \frac{2}{3}\log 8.26 = \frac{2}{3}(0.9170) = 0.6113$; $N = 4.09$

31. $N = \sqrt{12.4}$; $\log N = \frac{1}{2}\log 12.4 = \frac{1}{2}(1.0934) = 0.5467$; $N = 3.52$

32. $N = \sqrt[3]{1.36}$; $\log N = \frac{1}{3}\log 1.36 = \frac{1}{3}(0.1335) = 0.0445$; $N = 1.11$

B

33. $N = 0.572 \times 6370$; $\log N = \log 0.572 + \log 6370 = (9.7574 - 10) + 3.8041 = 13.5615 - 10 = 3.5615$; $N = 3643$

34. $N = 23.64 \times 1.47$; $\log N = \log 23.64 + \log 1.47 = 1.3736 + 0.1673 = 1.5409$; $N = 34.75$

35. $N = 0.8215 \times 0.051$; $\log N = \log 0.8215 + \log 0.051 = (9.9146 - 10) + (8.7076 - 10) = 18.6222 - 20 = 8.6222 - 10$; $N = 0.04190$

36. $N = \frac{0.1496}{0.582}$; $\log N = \log 0.1496 - \log 0.582 = (9.1749 - 10) - (9.7649 - 10) =$

$(19.1749 - 20) - (9.7649 - 10) = 9.4100 - 10$; $N = 0.2570$

37. $N = \frac{137}{5242}$; $\log N = \log 137 - \log 5242 = 2.1367 - 3.7195 =$

$(12.1367 - 10) - 3.7195 = 8.4172 - 10$; $N = 0.02614$

38. $N = \frac{0.05274}{0.9412}$; $\log N = \log 0.05274 - \log 0.9412 = (8.7221 - 10) - (9.9737 - 10) =$
$(18.7221 - 20) - (9.9737 - 10) = 8.7484 - 10; N = 0.05603$

39. $N = 2.16 \times 46.73 \times 134.5$; $\log N = \log 2.16 + \log 46.73 + \log 134.5 =$
$0.3345 + 1.6696 + 2.1287 = 4.1328; N = 13{,}580$

40. $N = 94 \times 0.05 \times 1.728$; $\log N = \log 94 + \log 0.05 + \log 1.728 =$
$1.9731 + (8.6990 - 10) + 0.2375 = 0.9096; N = 8.120$

41. $N = 1.8 \times 32 \times 0.01347$; $\log N = \log 1.8 + \log 32 + \log 0.01347 =$
$0.2553 + 1.5051 + (8.1293 - 10) = 9.8897 - 10; N = 0.7757$

42. $N = (12.4)^3(3.86)^2$; $\log N = 3 \log 12.4 + 2 \log 3.86 = 3(1.0934) + 2(0.5866) =$
$3.2802 + 1.1732 = 4.4534; N = 28{,}410$

43. $N = (37.4)^5(812)^2$; $\log N = 5 \log 37.4 + 2 \log 812 = 5(1.5729) + 2(2.9096) =$
$7.8645 + 5.8192 = 13.6837; N = 48{,}270{,}000{,}000{,}000$

44. $N = (42.3)^4(0.0016)^2$; $\log N = 4 \log 42.3 + 2 \log 0.0016 =$
$4(1.6263) + 2(7.2041 - 10) = 6.5052 + (14.4082 - 20) = 0.9134; N = 8.192$

45. $N = \sqrt{\frac{427}{0.592}}$; $\log N = \frac{1}{2}(\log 427 - \log 0.592) = \frac{1}{2}(2.6304 - (9.7723 - 10)) =$
$\frac{1}{2}((12.6304 - 10) - (9.7723 - 10)) = \frac{1}{2}(2.8581) = 1.4291; N = 26.86$

46. $N = \sqrt[3]{\frac{(2.37)^2}{1.15}}$; $\log N = \frac{1}{3}(2 \log 2.37 - \log 1.15) = \frac{1}{3}(2(0.3747) - 0.0607) =$
$\frac{1}{3}(0.7494 - 0.0607) = \frac{1}{3}(0.6887) = 0.2296; N = 1.697$

47. $N = \sqrt{\frac{(2.03)^3}{97.5 \times 1.98}}$; $\log N = \frac{1}{2}(3 \log 2.03 - (\log 97.5 + \log 1.98)) = \frac{1}{2}(3(0.3075) -$
$(1.9890 + 0.2967)) = \frac{1}{2}(0.9225 - 2.2857) = \frac{1}{2}((10.9225 - 10) - 2.2857) =$
$\frac{1}{2}(8.6368 - 10) = 4.3184 - 5 = 9.3184 - 10; N = 0.2082$

C **48.** $N = \sqrt[5]{\frac{(527.4)^2}{1542 \times (0.2592)^2}}$; $\log N = \frac{1}{5}(2 \log 527.4 - (\log 1542 + 2 \log 0.2592)) =$
$\frac{1}{5}(2(2.7221) - (3.1881 + 2(9.4136 - 10))) = \frac{1}{5}(5.4442 - (3.1881 + (18.8272 - 20))) =$
$\frac{1}{5}(5.4442 - (3.1881 + (8.8272 - 10))) = \frac{1}{5}(5.4442 - 2.0153) = \frac{1}{5}(3.4289) = 0.6858;$
$N = 4.851$

49. $N = \sqrt{\frac{12{,}560^3}{79.21 \times 8004}}$; $\log N = \frac{1}{2}(3 \log 12{,}560 - (\log 79.21 + \log 8004)) =$
$\frac{1}{2}(3(4.0990) - (1.8988 + 3.9033)) = \frac{1}{2}(12.2970 - 5.8021) = \frac{1}{2}(6.4949) = 3.2475;$
$N = 1768$

50. $N = 92.37^{0.562}$; $\log N = 0.562 \log 92.37 = 0.562(1.9656) = 1.1047; N = 12.73$

51. $N = 0.3142^{1.273}$; $\log N = 1.273 \log 0.3142 = 1.273(9.4972 - 10) =$
$12.0899 - 12.7300 = 12.0899 - 2.7300 - 10 = 9.3599 - 10; N = 0.2291$

52. $V = \frac{4}{3}(3.142)(0.1526)^3$; $\log V = \log 1.333 + \log 3.142 + 3 \log 0.1526 =$

$0.1249 + 0.4972 + 3(9.1835 - 10) = 0.6221 + (27.5505 - 30) =$
$0.6221 + (7.5505 - 10) = 8.1726 - 10$; $V = 0.01488$

53. $N = 3^{51}$; $\log N = 51 \log 3 = 51(0.4771) = 24.3321$; since the characteristic of $\log 3^{51}$ is 24, 3^{51} has 25 digits.